WITHDRAWN

Consumers' Guide to PRODUCT GRADES and TERMS

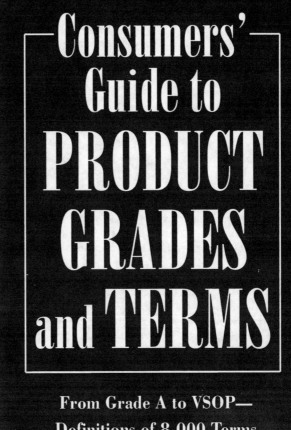

Consumers' Guide to PRODUCT GRADES and TERMS

From Grade A to VSOP—
Definitions of 8,000 Terms
Describing Food, Housewares,
and Other Everyday Items

Timothy L. Gall
and Susan B. Gall

 Gale Research Inc.

DETROIT • WASHINGTON DC • LONDON

The *Consumers' Guide to Product Grades and Terms* was produced by:
Eastword Publications Development, Cleveland, Ohio

Gale Research Inc. Staff

Lawrence W. Baker, *Senior Developmental Editor*
Carol DeKane Nagel, *Developmental Editor*

Mary Beth Trimper, *Production Director*
Evi Seoud, *Assistant Production Manager*
Shanna P. Heilveil, *Production Assistant*

Cynthia Baldwin, *Art Director*
Arthur Chartow, *Technical Design Services Manager*
Mary Krzewinski, *Cover Designer*

This book is printed on acid-free paper that meets the minimum requirements of American National Standard for Information Sciences--Permanence Paper for Printed Library Materials, ANSI Z39.48-1984. ∞™

ISBN 0-8103-8898-7
Printed in the United States of America

Published simultaneously in the United Kingdom
by Gale Research International Limited
(An affiliated company of Gale Research Inc.)

Preface

The *Consumers' Guide to Product Grades and Terms* provides definitions and explanations for 8000 terms, symbols, and phrases that appear on 630 consumer products. Terms may relate to the product itself or to some feature of its packaging. Included are words describing product characteristics, intended uses, or recommended methods of product disposal, as well as reproductions of 110 grading symbols and trademarks and 125 explanatory charts and diagrams. Up-to-date information on nutrition and environmental labeling regulations are included too. Consumers, advertising agencies, do-it-yourselfers, students, and others with questions about product labeling terms, grade stamps, and grade marks will find the *Consumers' Guide to Product Grades and Terms* a valuable tool.

ARRANGEMENT

The terms included in this book are arranged according to broad product categories. In each section, entries describing specific products are arranged alphabetically. The terms, phrases, and symbols which apply to that product are arranged in a clear sequence, making it easy to find definitions quickly. An expanded table of contents for quick access to product categories is included, as well as a comprehensive line item index. The appendix lists organizations that set standards or guidelines for product labeling.

PRODUCTS COVERED

Section 1—*Advertising & Standards* covers terms that may be used on food and non-food products, and discusses words, phrases, and symbols that describe product features for advertising purposes. Section 2 deals with labeling related to environmental issues. Sections 3 through 12 cover non-food products, and Sections 13 through 21 focus on foods. The information represents the latest information available on labeling regulations, guidelines, and industry practices.

Following is an overview of the products covered in each section:

Section 1—Advertising & Standards
Includes general advertising terms, such as "Introductory Offer" and "New, Improved." Also covers product labeling symbols used on a wide variety of products, such as the Universal Product Code mark and the Underwriters Laboratories Mark.

Section 2—Environmental Concerns
Includes descriptions of government and independent agency efforts to provide consumers with information on a product's impact on the environment. In addition, industry-wide symbols used to indicate appropriate recycling options for products, guidelines for labeling hazardous substances, and information on carcinogens are included.

Section 3—Automotive
Includes definitions of auto and tire terminology, as well as labeling terms used on fuels and lubricants. Also features information on buying a used car.

Section 4—Consumer Electronics
Includes all types of consumer electronic products, such as audio, video, and computer equipment and peripherals.

Section 5—Health & Beauty
Includes terminology used on such personal care products cosmetics, fragrances, contact lenses, and nonprescription medications.

Section 6—Housewares & Appliances

Includes products such as bedding, major and small appliances, energy efficiency labeling for appliances, and cookware.

Section 7—Jewelry

Defines terminology for clocks, watches, gemstones, gold jewelry, and pearls.

Section 8—Materials

Defines building materials (except wood, see *Section 11—Wood*), including brick, roofing materials, and steels.

Section 9—Sports & Hobbies

Includes definitions for terms used to grade and qualify sporting goods, collectibles, and equipment for other leisure pursuits.

Section 10—Textiles & Apparel

Explains guidelines for textile and wearing apparel related to fiber content, country of origin, and fabric care methods. Also provides tables for estimating useful life of wearing apparel and for calculating value of used clothing.

Section 11—Wood

Lists grading rules set by numerous wood inspection agencies. Defines quality grades of wood and characteristics of wood that affect its serviceability for interior and exterior applications. Includes treated wood, plywood, hardboard, softwood, hardwood, and architectural millwork.

Section 12—Yard & Garden

Includes grades for all types of lawn and landscape maintenance products including bark and mulch products, grass seed, fertilizer, and sod.

Section 13—Food Overview

Defines general food labeling guidelines, including terms that describe additives, processing, or packaging that apply to more than one food category. Includes information on nutrition labeling terms such as "lite," "low fat," and "reduced salt." Also describes government grading procedures.

Sections 14 through 20—Beverages, Dairy Products, Fruits, Meat and Poultry, Nuts, Seafood, Vegetables

Each of these sections covers labeling of products in the specific category and includes information on government grading regulations and industry standards.

Section 21—Miscellaneous Foods

This section covers spices, ingredients (such as sugar), and processed foods that are not readily included in another category. Covered are labeling terms and government standards.

SOURCES CONSULTED

More than two hundred standards-setting organizations, industry groups, and government agencies were consulted in the compilation of this book. Each entry is accompanied by a detailed source citation, which users are encouraged to consult for more complete and detailed information on restrictions and applications of the labeling terminology. Users may also wish to consult the many consumer-oriented periodical publications available that often feature articles on product labeling. Of special note are *Consumer Reports, Consumer Research Magazine,* and *FDA Consumer,* a publication of the U.S. Food and Drug Administration. In addition, many general interest magazines, like *Golf* and *Backpacker,* feature annual buyers guide issues that are valuable sources of information on consumer products.

Acknowledgments

The editors gratefully acknowledge the following people whose thoughtful consideration of the concept for this book helped to shape and direct our research efforts: Catherine Alloway, Director, East Shore Area Library, Dauphin County (PA) Library System; Donna Foust, Department Head and Librarian, Library for the Blind, Public Library of Cincinnati and Hamilton County; Diane Strauss, Associate University Librarian for Public Services, Davis Library, University of North Carolina at Chapel Hill.

The editors also wish to thank the many individuals employed by trade groups, consumer products companies, standards-setting organizations, and government agencies who helped us find and define the 8000 terms appearing in this book. Those listed below deserve special recognition:

Adolph Coors Company
Agricultural Marketing Service
American Association of Textile Chemists and Colorists
American Beekeeping Federation, Inc.
American Cancer Society
American Petroleum Institute
American Spice Trade Association
Lisa Baldino, Sony Corporation of America
Steve Bobbitt, American Numismatic Association
Brick Institute of America
Linda Brown, Scientific Certification Systems
California Raisin Advisory Board
Carpet Cushion Council
Champagne News and Information Bureau
Jeanne Chircop, Electronic Industries Association
Chocolate Manufacturers Association
Andrew Christie, Gemological Institute of America
Coffee Development Group
Emilio G. Collado, American Watch Association
Cognac Information Bureau
Consumer Product Safety Commission
Council on Plastics and Packaging in the Environment
Debra Lynn Dadd, author
William G. Daddi, Cotton Incorporated
Department of Energy
Department of the Interior
John Eckert, Wool Bureau
Lynn Elsasser, Green Seal
Environmental Protection Agency
Malcolm Epley, Western Wood Products Association
Marjorie Exton, Lenox China
Federal Trade Commission
Duane J. Fike, National Lubricating Grease Institute
Food and Drug Administration
Food Safety and Inspection Service
Foundation of the Wall and Ceiling Industry
Glass Tempering Association
Walter H. Hoffman, Underwriters Laboratories
International Bottled Water Association
International Silk Association
Jewelers of American, Inc.
Julia King, Clock Manufacturers and Marketing Association

Robert LaGasse, National Soil and Bark Producers
Alane Mackay, Information Center, Association of Home Appliance Manufacturers
Marble Institute of America
Richard Margosian, National Particleboard Association
National Decorating Products Association
National Roofing Contractors Association
Ann Noll, Battery Council International
Chandra C. Nutt, Nonprescription Drug Manufacturers Association
Oneida Ltd. Silversmiths
Owens-Corning Fiberglas
Joel M. Padmore, North Carolina Department of Agriculture
Paint Quality Institute
Dr. Arthur Pober, Children's Advertising Review Unit, Better Business Bureau
Porcelain Enamel Institute
Primary Glass Manufacturers Council
Doug Raha, Manufacturing Jewelers and Silversmiths of America, Inc.
Recreation Vehicle Institute of America
Resilient Floor Covering Institute
Robert Saigh, American Dental Association
Lynn Schweizer, International Fabricare Institute
Tom Searles, American Lumber Standards Committee
Rob Seitz, Ford Motor Company
Holly Schubert, Underwriters Laboratories
Lucinda Sikes, U.S. Public Interest Research Group
Sid Smith, National Association of Hosiery Manufacturers
Society of the Plastics Industry
The Specialty Coffee Association of America
Specialty Vehicle Institute of American
Steel Door Institute
Milton Stevens, American Watchmakers Institute
The Sugar Association
Robert E. Swift, Crafted With Pride In U.S.A. Council, Inc.
Tea Association of the U.S.A. Inc.
Tiffany and Company
Tire Industry Safety Council
Michael M. Westfall, Cedar Shake & Shingle Bureau
David F. Wilkins, The Goodyear Tire and Rubber Company
Woodwork Institute of California

We also express our gratitude to Barbara Beach and Carol Nagel at Gale Research for their considerable contributions of guidance and inspiration. Special thanks to our staff members Brian Rajewski and Judith Arth. Personal thanks to the following friends and colleagues, without whose support this book would never have been completed: Arthur and Alice Gall, Joan Bevan, Linda Wolff, Susan Stern, Nancy Benacci, Ruta Marino, and Deb Nelson. And thanks to Elizabeth and Adam Gall for their enthusiastic interest at all stages of the project.

EDITORS' NOTE

This book is intended as a general guide to help consumers understand the terms, phrases, and symbols associated with food and other products. It is not intended as a grading or standards manual, and it must be emphasized that the information in this book cannot be substituted for any standards or grading regulations. Users are referred to the original source of the regulation or standard for more information; in most cases, the standards are the province of the promulgating organization. Symbols that appear in this book are registered trademarks and are reprinted with permission of the trademark holder.

COMMENTS WELCOME

Every effort was made to compile a comprehensive list of labeling terms for consumer products and to provide the most accurate and up-to-date information available to define those terms. Comments and suggestions are welcome, as are suggestions for terms, phrases, or symbols that should be included in the next edition.

The Editors
Consumers' Guide to Product Grades and Terms
Gale Research Inc.
835 Penobscot Building
Detroit, MI 48226-4094
Phone: (313) 961-2242
Fax: (313) 961-6815
Toll-free: (800) 347-GALE

Contents

Contents

(Expanded)

3—Automotive

4—Consumer Electronics

5—Health & Beauty

6—Housewares & Appliances

7—Jewelry

8—Materials

9—Sports & Hobbies

10—Textiles & Apparel

11—Wood

12—Yard & Garden

13—Food Overview

14—Beverages

15—Dairy Products

16—Fruits

19—Seafood

20—Vegetables

Consumers' Guide to PRODUCT GRADES and TERMS

Advertising
& Standards

Bait Advertising

Bait advertising is an alluring but insincere offer to sell a product or service which the advertiser in truth does not intend or want to sell. Its purpose is to switch consumers from buying the advertised merchandise in order to sell something else, usually at a higher price or on a basis more advantageous to the advertiser. The primary aim of a bait advertisement is to obtain leads on persons interested in buying merchandise of the type so advertised.

Source:
Federal Trade Commission, "Guides Against Bait Advertising," 16 CFR sections 238.0 to 238.4 (1992), Washington: Government Printing Office.

Cents Off Sales

The Federal Trade Commission requires that *Cents Off Sales* meet certain requirements including:
- The commodity must have been previously sold in the area at an ordinary and customary price.
- The packager sells the product to either the distributor or public at a reduction equal to the "cents off" representation.
- The original price is listed for comparison.
- The packager or labeler does not initiate more than three "cents off" promotions in the same trade area within a 12 month period and waits 30 days between promotions.
- Maintains the promotion for no more than 6 months within any 12 month period.

Source:
Federal Trade Commission, "Regulations Under Section 5(C) of the Fair Packaging and Labeling Act," 16 CFR sections 502.1 to 502.100 (1992), Washington: Government Printing Office.

Children's Advertising

The Children's Advertising Review Unit (CARU) of the Council of Better Business Bureaus (BBB) was established in 1974 by the advertising industry to promote responsible national advertising to children and to respond to public concerns. The central mission of CARU is the review and evaluation of child-directed advertising in all media. When children's advertising is found to be misleading, inaccurate or inconsistent with its Guidelines, CARU seeks changes through the voluntary cooperation of advertisers.

CARU provides a general advisory service for advertisers and agencies. It also is a clearinghouse source of information for children, parents, and educators. CARU actively encourages advertisers to develop and promote the dissemination of educational messages to children consistent with the Children's Television Advertising Act of 1990. CARU maintains an extensive collection of research on children's advertising and has published an annotated bibliography of the same.

The CARU *Self-Regulatory Guidelines for Children's Advertising* provide a basis for evaluating child-directed advertising. A copy of the complete guidelines can be obtained by contacting CARU directly at 845 Third Avenue, New York, NY 10022.

If an ad in your local area runs afoul of the self-regulatory standards of the CARU, the Better Business Bureau (BBB) suggests contacting the local BBB. The BBB will intervene directly with the advertiser in seeking to resolve the complaint. National advertising comes under the scope of the CARU directly. National ads promote goods or services on a national or broad regional basis. For example, a difference here in terms of children's advertising might be a department store on the local level and a specific toy on the national level. Complaints regarding national advertisements should be addressed to the CARU at the address above.

Source:
Children's Advertising Review Unit, *Self-Regulatory Guidelines for Children's Advertising,* fourth edition, New York: Council of Better Business Bureaus, Inc., 1991.

Free

The offer of "Free" merchandise is often used as a promotional device to attract customers. The Federal Trade Commission has issued guidelines to help advertisers use the word in a way that will not confuse consumers. The following terms have been considered:

Free. When a purchaser is told that an article is "free" if another article is purchased, the word "free" indicates that he is paying nothing for that article and no more than the regular price for the other. Thus, he has a right to believe that the merchant will not recover the cost of the free merchandise or service by such tactics as marking up the price of the article which must be purchased or substituting inferior merchandise or service.

Regular Price. The price, in the same quantity, quality, and with the same service, at which the seller or advertiser of the product or service has openly and actively sold the product or service in the geographic market or trade market in which he is making a "free" or similar offer in the most recent and regular course of business, and for a reasonably substantial period of time, i.e., a 30-day period. For consumer products or services which fluctuate in price, the regular price is the lowest price at which any substantial sales were made during the aforesaid 30-day period. Except in the case of introductory offers, if no substantial sales were made, in fact, at the "regular" price, a "free" or similar offer would not be proper.

Free in Introductory Offers. No "free" offer should be made in connection with the introduction of a new product or service offered for sale at a specified price unless the offeror expects to discontinue the offer after a limited time and to commence selling the product or service promoted separately and at the same price at which it was promoted with the "free" offer. If free is used in connection with an introductory offer, it should not be used in a trade area for more than 6 months in any 12-month period. At least 30 days should elapse before another offer is promoted in the same area. No more than three such offers should be made in the same area in any 12 month period.

Bonus, Gift, or Given Without Charge. These terms are bound by the same guidelines as the word "free."

Source:
Federal Trade Commission, "Guide Concerning use of the word "Free" and Similar Representations," 16 CFR sections 251.1 (1992), Washington: Government Printing Office.

Good Housekeeping Seal

The Good Housekeeping Institute was established in 1900, fifteen years after *Good Housekeeping* magazine started publishing. Its purpose was to offer American woman a modern approach to housekeeping. Headquartered in Springfield, Massachusetts, it was originally called the Good Housekeeping Experiment Station, and was known as "a central headquarters to which all may apply for help toward the higher life of the household."

The staff at the Experiment Station periodically printed articles of their own research and soon realized that good methods and practices were of little value without reliable products. Accordingly, in 1902 the publisher of Good Housekeeping announced a guarantee for every item advertised in it pages. Called the "ironclad contract," it was the predecessor of the Good Housekeeping Seal. William Randolph Hearst purchased Good Housekeeping in 1912. In 1928 it was moved to Hearst corporate headquarters in New York city. Today, Good Housekeeping replaces or refunds, at its own expense, products which are advertised in the magazine or which bear the Good Housekeeping Seal if they are defective within one year from the date they were first sold to the consumer. The Policy does not extend to products such as insurance, cars, and prescription drugs, among others, as set forth in the Good Housekeeping Consumers' Policy, detailed on page six of every issue of the magazine.

Source:
Good Housekeeping, Public Relations Department, Press Release, New York: Hearst Magazines, 1992.

Introductory Offers

In the case of an introductory offer, the Federal Trade Commission requires that the product being offered on sale is either new or has been changed in a functionally significant and substantial respect, or is being introduced into the trade area for the first time. The offer should be qualified by the phrase "Introductory Offer" and the sale should not exceed 6 months. Also, the price must in fact be lower than the anticipated ordinary and customary price.

Source:
Federal Trade Commission, "Regulations Under Section 5(C) of the Fair Packaging and labeling Act," 16 CFR sections 502.1 to 502.100 (1992), Washington: Government Printing Office.

Labels on Consumer Commodities

In general, consumer commodities (books, brooms, gloves, safety pins, toys, etc.) must be labeled with the name and place of business of the manufacturer, packer, or distributor; net quantity of contents; and net quantity of servings, uses, or applications represented to be present.

SIZE

The size abbreviations below have been approved by the Federal Trade Commission. Supplemental statements of net quantity of contents should not include any term qualifying a unit of weight, measure, or count that tend to exaggerate the amount of commodity contained in the package, e.g. *Giant Quart, Full Gallon,* etc.

Unit	Abbreviation
Inch	in.
Feet or foot	ft.
Fluid	fl.
Liquid	liq.
Ounce	oz.
Gallon	gal.
Pint	pt.
Pound	lb.
Quart	qt.
Square	sq.
Weight	wt.
Yard	yd.
Avoirdupois	avp.
Cubic	cu.

Serving Size. The serving size or applications size must conform to any voluntary product standard that is in effect.

Economy Size. Products can be labeled *Economy Size, Economy Pack, Budget Pack, Bargain Size, Value Size,* etc. if there is at least one other size in the product line and if no other package in the line is similarly labeled. The price of the *Economy Size* package should be at least 5 percent reduced from the actual price.

Source:
Federal Trade Commission, "Regulations Under Section 4 of the Fair Packaging and Labeling Act," 16 CFR part 500 (1992), Washington: Government Printing Office.

Meets ASTM or ANSI Standards

ASTM (formerly the American Society for Testing and Materials) and ANSI (American National Standards Institute) are voluntary organizations that work to standardize products used in industry and commerce. Many standards set minimum requirements for safety and performance and manufacturers often represent their products as meeting established ASTM or ANSI standards. These organizations are only two of many similar groups existing in the United States. A listing of organizations developing standards of interest to consumers appears in the appendix to this volume.

ANSI

ANSI coordinates and harmonizes private sector standards activity in the United States. The Institute does not develop standards. They are developed by qualified technical and professional societies, trade associations, and other groups which voluntarily submit them to ANSI for approval. It assists participants in the voluntary standards system reach agreement on needs for standards, encourages qualified organizations to develop them, and follows up on progress. It provides standards developers with procedures and services to use their resources effectively, avoid duplication of effort, and resolve conflicts. Standards are approved by ANSI as American National Standards when it finds that its criteria for due process have been met and that a consensus for approval exists among those directly and materially affected. 9,500 standards approved by ANSI are designated American National Standards and are widely adopted and referenced by government at the federal, state, and local levels.

ANSI was formerly the American Engineering Standards Committee (1918), American Standards Association (1928), and United States of America Standards Institute (1968).

ASTM

ASTM is a nonprofit organization formed to develop standards on characteristics and performance of materials, products, systems, and services, and to promote related knowledge. Standards include classifications, guides, practices, specifications, terminology, and test methods.

Standards cover iron and steel products; nonferrous metal products; metal test methods and analytical procedures; construction; petroleum products; lubricants and fossil fuels; paints; related coatings and aromatics; textiles; plastics; rubber; electrical, insulation, and electronics; water and environmental technology; nuclear, solar, and geothermal energy; medical devices; general methods and instrumentation general products, chemical specialties, and end use products. Standards developed by the Society's committees are published in the 68 volume Annual Book of ASTM Standards.

ASTM standards are developed by those having expertise in the specific areas who choose, voluntarily, to work with the ASTM system-producers, users, ultimate consumers, and representatives of government and academia. ASTM provides a forum within which these people can meet on a common ground to write standards that will best meet the needs of all the interested parties. The ASTM system adheres to the principles of due process, assuring equal access to and equal voice in the standards forum.

Source:
Toth, Robert B., editor, National Institute of Standards and Technology, United States Department of Commerce, *NIST Special Publication 806: Standards Activities of Organizations in the United States,* Washington: Government Printing Office, 1991.

Pricing

The Federal Trade Commission has issued guidelines designed to help advertisers from employing pricing techniques in their advertising that may mislead the consumer. Some general guidelines follow:

Bargain. A price advertised as a *bargain price* or *reduced price* should be one that is in fact significantly lower than the sellers *regular* or *usual* price. The seller should not artificially inflate the price and then mark it down and advertise the new price as *reduced* or *bargain*. The *regular* price should be one at which the product was openly and actively offered for sale, for a reasonably substantial period of time, in the recent regular course of his business, honestly and in good faith. It doesn't matter if the seller made no sales at the advertised price.

Manufacturers Suggested Retail or List Price. Often times manufacturers suggest prices at which their product should be sold. These are called the *Suggested Retail* or *List Price*. It may be, however, that few if any resellers ever sell the product at the manufacturer's list price. To the extent that list or suggested retail prices do not in fact correspond to prices at which a substantial number of sales of the article are made, an advertisement offering a reduction off the manufacturers list price may mislead the consumer.

Bargain Offers (Free, Buy One-Get One Free, 2 For 1 Sale, Half Price Sales, 1 Cent Sale, 50% Off, etc.) When products are so advertised, the seller should not increase his regular price, decrease the quantity and quality of the article, or otherwise attach strings to the offer.

Price Comparisons. Retailers should not advertise a retail price as a wholesale price. They should not represent that they are selling at factory prices when they are not selling at the prices paid by those purchasing directly from the manufacturer. They should not offer seconds, imperfect, or irregular merchandise at a reduce price without disclosing the higher comparative price refers to the price of the merchandise if perfect. They should not offer an advance sale under circumstances where they do not in good faith expect to increase the price at a later date, or make a limited offer which, in fact, is not limited. In all of these situations, as well as in others too numerous to mention. advertisers should make certain that the bargain offer is genuine and truthful.

Source:
Federal Trade Commission, "Guides Against Deceptive Pricing," 16 CFR part 233 (1992), Washington: Government Printing Office.

Testimonials and Endorsements

Testimonials and endorsements are advertising messages which consumers are likely to believe reflect the opinions, beliefs, findings, or experience of a party other than the sponsoring advertiser. An endorsement may be made by a individual, group, or institution. However, not everything said by characters on TV commercials are considered endorsements. For example, a TV commercial depicts two women in a supermarket buying a laundry detergent. The women are not identified outside the context of the advertisement. One comments to the other how clean her brand makes her family's clothes, and the other then comments that she will try it because she has not been fully satisfied with her own brand. The obvious fictional dramatization of a real life situation would not be an endorsement. However, if Barbara Bush was the

one to comment on how clean the product makes her cloths, it would be an endorsement.

Source:
Federal Trade Commission, "Guides Concerning Use of Endorsements and Testimonials in Advertising," 16 CFR sections 255.0 to 255.5 (1992), Washington: Government Printing Office.

UL Mark

The UL Mark stands for Underwriters Laboratories Inc., a not-for-profit, independent organization formed in 1894 to help reduce bodily injury, loss of life, and property damage. They do this by investigating thousands of types of products, materials, constructions, and systems to evaluate their electric, fire, and casualty hazards, their burglary resistance, or their ability to detect, control, or limit fires. Products that bear the UL Mark have been tested to recognized safety standards and found to be reasonably free from foreseeable risk of fire, electric shock, and related hazards. Some typical examples of the UL Mark appear below:

SERVICES OF INTEREST TO CONSUMERS

Listing Service. Samples of products bearing the UL Mark have been tested and evaluated, and they comply with UL requirements.

Classification Service. UL will classify industrial or commercial products with respect to certain properties of the product, a limited spectrum of hazards to life and property, suitability for certain uses, and other special conditions. Products covered under this service are identified by a Classification Marking which includes UL's name and a statement to indicate the extent of UL's evaluation of the product, such as "Classified by Underwriters Laboratories Inc. with respect to (nature of hazard) only." An example of a "Classified" marking appears below:

Component Recognition Service. This service covers the evaluation of component parts that will later be used in a complete product or system. These parts are intended solely for use as factory-installed components in equipment where the complete product is covered by UL's Listing, Classification, or Certificate service. An example of the Recognized Component Mark follows:

Certificate Service. When it is impractical to apply the UL listing Mark or Classification Marking to individual products or systems, e.g., a field installed system burglary alarm. In a case like this, a Certificate is provided to the alarm service company to use for identification purposes. The extent of protection and type of system are indicated on the Certificate. The UL Certificate is released to the authorized installer for issuance to property owners or ultimate users. UL conducts countercheck field examinations of representative installations.

Source:
Show the UL Mark, promotional material supplied by Underwriters Laboratories, Inc., Milville, New York.

Universal Product Code (UPC)

This Universal Product Code (UPC) system was developed by the food industry to give every product a unique code number. This number allows simpler and more accurate product identification. The symbol makes possible the use of scanner-equipped checkstands which speed customer checkout operation, reduce item price-marking requirements, and enables the retailer to collect complete and accurate information on all aspects of sales transactions. The symbol is a 12-digit, all numeric code that will identify the consumer package. The code consists of a number system character, a 5-digit manufacturer identification number, a 5-digit item code number, and a check digit.

Number System Character. The first position in the 12 digit UPC code. The number system character serves to "key" the other numbers as to meaning and category. There are currently seven categories of the number system character:

O -assigned to all items except those following below.
2 -assigned to random-weight items like meat and produce.
3 -assigned to companies which have been delegated their NDC number as their UPC.
4 -assigned for retailer use only.
5 -assigned to coupons.
6 and 7-assigned to industrial applications as well as retail applications, where they serve the same function as O.

Manufacturer Identification Number. The manufacturer identification number is a 5-digit number assigned by the Uniform Code Council, Inc.

Item Code Number. The item code is a 5-digit number assigned and controlled by the member company. The item code should be unique for each consumer package and/or shipping container.

Check Digit. Enables the scanner system to immediately verify the accurate data translation of the Universal Product Code as the symbol is scanned.

The 12-digit Universal Product Code plus the scanner-readable check digit are represented in the bars and spaces that make up the complete scanner-readable symbol.

Source:
Uniform Code Council, Inc., *About the Universal Product Code,* Dayton, OH, 1986.

Warranties and Guarantees

If an advertisement mentions a warranty or guarantee that is offered on the advertised product, the advertisement should disclose that prior to the sale, at the place where the product is sold, prospective purchasers can see the written warranty or guarantee for complete details of the warranty coverage. If made on television, the message indicating where to obtain the details must remain on the screen for at least five seconds. If made in a catalog, the advertisement should instruct the consumer on where to write for details.

Satisfaction Guaranteed. If a seller advertises a product with satisfaction guaranteed, he should refund the full purchase price of the advertised product at the purchaser's request.

Lifetime Warranty. If a product is labeled as having a lifetime warranty the advertisement should disclose the life to which the representation refers. E.g., a muffler may offer a lifetime warranty—good for as long as your car runs.

Source:
Federal Trade Commission, "Guides for the Advertising of Warranties and Guarantees," 16 CFR sections part 239 (1992), Washington: Government Printing Office.

Environmental Concerns

Asbestos

Some products are labeled *Asbestos Free*. Asbestos is a mineral fiber that can be positively identified only with a special type of microscope. In the past, asbestos was added to a variety of products to strengthen them and to provide heat insulation and fire resistance. Breathing high levels of asbestos fibers can lead to an increased risk of lung cancer.

Mesothelioma. A cancer of the lining of the chest and the abdominal cavity.

Asbestosis. In which the lungs become scarred with fibrous tissue.

The risk of lung cancer and mesothelioma increases with the number of fibers inhaled. The risk of lung cancer from inhaling asbestos fibers is also greater for smokers. People who get asbestosis usually have been exposed to high levels of asbestos for a long time. The symptoms of these diseases do not usually appear until about 20 to 30 years after the first exposure to asbestos.

Most people exposed to small amounts of asbestos do not develop these health problems. However, if disturbed, asbestos material may release asbestos fibers, which can be inhaled into the lungs. The fibers can remain there for a long time, increasing the risk of disease. Asbestos material that would crumble easily if handled, or that has been sawed, scraped, or sanded into a powder, is more likely to create a health hazard.

Most products made today do not contain asbestos. Those few products made which still contain asbestos that could be inhaled are required to be labeled as such. However, until the 1970s, many types of building products and insulation materials used in homes contained asbestos. Common products manufactured in the 1970s or earlier that might have contained asbestos and conditions which may release fibers, include:

Steam Pipes, Boilers, and Furnace Ducts. Often insulated with an asbestos blanket or asbestos paper tape. These materials may release asbestos fibers if damaged, repaired, or removed improperly.

Resilient Floor Tiles. (Vinyl asbestos, asphalt, and rubber.) Asbestos may be present in the backing on vinyl sheet flooring and in adhesives used for installing floor tile. Sanding tiles or scraping or sanding the backing of sheet flooring during removal can release fibers.

Cement Sheet, Millboard, and Paper. Often used as insulation around furnaces and wood-burning stoves. Repairing or removing appliances may release asbestos fibers. So may cutting, tearing, sanding, drilling, or sawing insulation.

Door Gaskets. In furnaces, wood stoves, and coal stoves. Worn seals can release asbestos fibers during use.

Soundproofing or Decorative Material. When sprayed on walls and ceilings, loose, crumbly, or water-damaged material may release fibers. So will sanding, drilling, or scraping the material.

Patching and Joint Compounds. Used for walls, ceilings, and textured paints. Sanding, scraping, or drilling these surfaces may release asbestos.

Asbestos Cement Roofing, Shingles, and Siding. These products are not likely to release asbestos fibers unless sawed, drilled, or cut.

Artificial Ashes and Embers. Sold for use in gas-fired fireplaces. Also, other older household products such as fireproof gloves, stove-top pads, ironing board covers, and certain hairdryers.

Automobile Brake Pads. Also linings, clutch facings, and gaskets.

The presence of asbestos in a residence or public building is not hazardous. The danger is that asbestos materials may become damaged over time. Damaged asbestos may release asbestos fibers and become a health hazard. The best thing to do with asbestos material in good condition is to leave it alone. Disturbing it may create a health hazard where none existed.

Source:
American Lung Association, Consumer Product Safety Commission, and
the Environmental Protection Agency, *Asbestos in Your Home* (pamphlet), Washington: Government Printing Office. Copies are available
from each organization.

Biological Pollutants

Pollutants that are or were living organisms fall into this category.
Types include animal dander (minute scales from hair, feathers, or
skin), dust mites and cockroach parts, fungi (molds), infectious
agents (bacteria or viruses), and pollen. Some of these substances
are in the home and it is impossible to eliminate them all. Two
conditions are essential to support growth of biological pollutants:
nutrients and moisture.

Source:
U.S. Consumer Product Safety Commission (CPSC), *Biological Pollutants
in Your Home,* Washington: Government Printing Office, 1990.

Carcinogens

Some consumer products are known to cause cancer in humans. A
substance capable of causing cancer is called a carcinogen. The
U.S. Environmental Protection Agency (EPA) has developed a
system for classifying chemicals on the basis of their cancer-
causing potential.

Group A. *Human Carcinogen.* There is sufficient evidence from
epidemiological studies to support a cause-effect relationship
between the substance and cancer.

Group B. *Probable Human Carcinogen. B1*: Substances are classified as B1 carcinogens on the basis of sufficient evidence
from animal studies and limited evidence from epidemiological studies. *B2*: Substances are classified as B2 carcinogens on
the basis of sufficient evidence from animal studies but the
epidemiological data are inadequate or nonexistent.

Group C. *Possible Human Carcinogen.* For this classification,
there is limited evidence of carcinogenicity from animal
studies and no epidemiological data.

Group D. *Not Classifiable as to Human Carcinogenicity.* The data
from human epidemiological and animal studies are inadequate or completely lacking, so no assessment as to the
substance's cancer-causing hazard is possible.

Group E. *Evidence of Noncarcinogenicity for Humans.* Substances have tested negative in at least two adequate animal
cancer tests in different species and in adequate epidemiological and animal studies. Classification in Group E is based on
available evidence; substances may prove to be carcinogenic
under certain conditions.

KNOWN CARCINOGENS

The American Cancer Society has determined that the following
industrial processes, occupational exposures, and chemicals are

associated with cancer in humans:

4-Aminobiphenyl

Analgesic mixtures containing phenacetin (used as anti-fever
agents)

Arsenic and arsenic compounds

Asbestos

Auramine manufacture

Benzene (used in nail polish remover, varnishes, airplane dopes,
lacquers, and as a solvent)

Benzidine

N,N-Bis (2-Chloroethyl)-2-Naphthylamine (Chlomaphazine)

Bis (chloromethyl) ether and technical-grade chloromethyl methyl
ether

Boot and shoe manufacture and repair

1, 4-Butanediol dimethanesulphonate (Myleran)

Certain combined chemotherapy for lymphomas (including MOPP)

Chlorambucil

Chromium and certain chromium compounds

Coal gasification

Coal tar

Coal tar pitch

Coke production

Conjugated estrogens

Cyclophosphamide

Diethylstilbestrol (DES)

Furniture manufacture

Isopropyl alcohol manufacture

Melphalan

Methoxsalen with ultra-violet A therapy

Mineral oils

Mustard gas

2-Naphthylamine

Nickel refining

Rubber industry (certain occupations)

Soots, tars, and oils

Soot

Tobacco

Treosulphan

Ultraviolet radiation

Underground hematite mining (with exposure to radon)

Vinyl chloride

Source:
Amercian Cancer Society, *Cancer Response System,* June 18, 1992.
Harte, John, Cheryl Holdren, Richard Schneider, and Christine Shirley,
Toxics A to Z: A Guide to Everyday Pollution Hazards, Berkeley:
University of California Press, 1991.

Decibel Level

Decibel. In sound work, decibel is the unit used to express sound
pressure level and sound power level. (Mathematically, the
decibel is a dimensionless quantity which expresses the ratio
of two numbers on a logarithmic scale.)

Frequency. Frequency is the number of pulsations per second
produced by a sound source. Frequency is expressed in cycles

per second (cps) or in Hertz.

Pitch. Expresses, in a general way, if a sound is a "high" note or a "low" note. The pitch of a sound goes up as the frequency increases.

Sound. A pulsation of air pressure capable of being heard.

Sound Level. The reading in decibels taken with a sound level meter. Decibel is abbreviated *db*, and the abbreviation *dba* refers to decibels measured using the *A* scale on a meter.

Sound Pressure. The magnitude of the pressure pulse or sound wave. (A sound level meter registers the root mean square value of the wave.) Sound pressure is measured in microbars. One microbar is approximately one-millionth of a standard atmosphere, or one sixty-eight-thousandth of a pound per square inch.

SOUND PRESSURE LEVEL RELATED TO NOISE

Level, db	Example
Above 120	Deafening
100 - 120	Very Loud: thunder, jet airplane, boiler factory
80 - 100	Loud: noisy factory, cocktail party, loud stereo
60- 80	Moderate: noisy office, average TV, loud conversation
40 - 60	Noticeable: noisy home, average conversation
20 - 40	Faint: quiet home, quiet conversation
0 - 20	Very Faint: whisper, rustle of leaves

HAZARDOUS LEVELS OF NOISE

Symptom	Lowest Decibel Level That Can Cause Symptom
Difficulty falling asleep	35
Increased heart rate and blood pressure; awakening from sleep	70
Discomfort, stress, annoyance	80
Temporary hearing loss from prolonged exposure	85
Pain threshold	110
Extreme pain; permanent deafness if prolonged	135

Source:

Harte, John, Cheryl Holdren, Richard Schneider, and Christine Shirley, *Toxics A to Z: A Guide to Everyday Pollution Hazards,* Berkeley: University of California Press, 1991.
"Noise in the Neighborhood," *Technical Topics,* Air Conditioning Contractors of America, 1982.

Environman

The name "Environman" and the environman symbol are service marks belonging to the U.S. National Park Service. These service marks identify man in his environment. Man's environment is composed of conflicting and harmonizing elements which affect and are affected by man. The purpose of the service mark is to identify the role of the U.S. Government in promoting high-quality environmental education, and to represent and symbolize such activities. The "Environman" symbol is the official sign to identify a National Environmental Study Area (NESA). In addition, the symbol is used in connection with National Environmental Education Development (NEED) and National Environmental Education Landmarks (NEEL). The symbol and term are available for licensing. Inquiries and requests should be addressed to the Director, National Park Service.

Source:

National Park Service, Department of the Interior, "Use of Environman and Human Figure and Design Symbol," 30 CFR part 15 (1991), Washington: Government Printing Office.

Environmental Labeling

The area of environmental labeling is gaining interest as consumers increasingly look for products that do the least amount of harm to the environment. The definitions in this entry are generic in that they define the term. However, they are not *official.* In fact, some terms, like *recycled* (when applied to paper products), are defined differently by different organizations. Government groups have issued guidelines for using these terms in advertising (see *Environmental Labeling, Green Report* and *Environmental Labeling, FTC Guides*). Other groups concerned with awarding environmental seals of approval to products that meet their *green* criteria have their own definitions for these terms (see *Environmental Seals, Green Seal; Environmental Seals, Green Cross*; and *Environmental Seals, Environmental Choice*).

TERMINOLOGY

Biodegradable. The ability to break down or decompose rapidly under natural conditions and processes.

Biodynamically Grown. See *Organically Grown.*

Bottle Bill. Proposed or enacted legislation which requires a returnable deposit on beer or soda containers and provides for retail store or other redemption centers. Such legislation is designed to discourage use of throwaway containers.

Clean Food. Food certified to contain no detected pesticide residues.

Compost. A mixture of garbage and degradable trash with soil in which certain bacteria in the soil break down the garbage and trash into organic fertilizer.

Compostable. A material that will decompose into organic fertilizer in a compost.

Composting. The natural biological decomposition of organic material in the presence of air to form a humus-like material. Controlled methods of composting include mechanical mixing and aerating, ventilating the materials by dropping them through a vertical series of aerated chambers, or placing the compost in piles out in the open air and mixing it or turning it periodically.

Cruelty-Free. The product has not been tested on animals.

Degradability. Ability of materials to break down, by bacterial (biodegradable) or ultraviolet (photodegradable) action.

Energy-Efficient. A term that lacks definition. Typically used to describe a product that uses less energy than the majority of similar products in the marketplace.

Environmentally Friendly. A blanket term that lacks clear definition.

Green. A term, primarily used in advertising to identify programs, ideas, or products associated with the environmental movement.

Incineration. 1. Burning of certain types of solid, liquid, or gaseous materials. 2. A treatment technology involving destruction of waste by controlled burning at high temperatures; e.g., burning sludge to remove the water and reduce the remaining residues to a safe, nonburnable ash which can be disposed of safely on land, in some waters, or in underground locations.

Mandatory Recycling. Programs which by law require consumers to separate trash so that some or all recyclable materials are not burned or dumped in landfills.

Natural. When applied to nonfood consumer products this term lacks clear definition, since every consumer product is made from the natural resources of the earth. Also understood to mean the opposite of man-made, where the substance or material is found in Nature.

Organically Grown. Describes a method of growing plant crops without the use of petrochemical pesticides or fertilizers and using methods that build and maintain soil fertility. *Biodynamically grown* indicates a specialized form of organic agriculture that is especially harmonious with the natural world.

Photodegradable. Refers to a degradability process caused by exposure of materials to the ultraviolet rays from the sun. As an example, plastic ring connectors for beverage "six-packs" sometimes are made photodegradable to help alleviate environmental and wildlife safety issues from careless littering.

Post-Consumer Waste. Waste generated from homes and apartments as differentiated from commercial, office, or industrial waste.

Reclaimed Products. Products made from still-serviceable materials previously used in another product. For example, bricks reclaimed from a demolished building.

Recyclable. Materials that can be separated from waste and made into new products.

Recycle/Reuse. The process of minimizing the generation of waste by recovering usable products that might otherwise become waste. Examples are the recycling of aluminum cans, wastepaper, and bottles.

Restored Products. Products which have been damaged in some way during use and are renewed to a usable condition.

Reused Products. Products that are used again without alteration in any way.

Solid Waste. Nonliquid, nonsoluble materials ranging from municipal garbage to industrial wastes that contain complex, and sometimes hazardous, substances. Solid wastes also include sewage sludge, agricultural refuse, demolition wastes, and mining residues. Technically, *solid waste* also refers to liquids and gases in containers.

Sustainable Products. Products made from materials grown and harvested in a way that allows a renewable resource to be renewed. For example, this term is used to describe practices such as sustainable forestry, where wood is taken for consumer use, while the forest itself still endures.

Wildcrafted Plants. Gathered from their natural, wild habitat, often from remote, pristine areas. When wildcrafting is done sustainably with proper respect, generally only the branches or flowers from plants are taken and the living plant is left, or if it is necessary to take the whole plant, seeds of the plant are placed in the empty hole from which the plant was taken.

Sources:

Dodd, Debra Lynn, *Nontoxic, Natural, and Earthwise,* Los Angeles: Jeremy P. Tarcher, 1990.

Office of Communications and Public Affairs, *Glossary of Environmental Terms and Acronym List,* Washington: U.S. Environmental Protection Agency, 1989.

Environmental Labeling, Green Report

There are few state regulatory guidelines governing the use of many environmental terms and phrases, like *safe for the environment, biodegradable,* or *recyclable* when these terms are used in advertising. However, a task force of the attorneys general of 11 states—California, Florida, Massachusetts, Minnesota, Missouri, New York, Tennessee, Texas, Utah, Washington, and Wisconsin—have issued recommendations for responsible environmental advertising. It is important to note that the recommendations are not laws and do not have the force and effect of law. They are intended simply to provide some guidance to industry so that companies can avoid making environmental advertising claims that violate the current deceptive advertising laws of the various states.

The recommendations of the attorneys general were published in a document entitled *The Green Report II.* The recommendations are summarized as follows:

SPECIFIC CLAIMS

Environmental claims should be as specific as possible, and not general, vague, incomplete, or overly broad.

Terms like *environmentally friendly* or *safe for the envi-

ronment are too vague to be meaningful and may be inaccurate.

ENVIRONMENTALLY FRIENDLY

Generalized environmental claims which imply that a product has no negative or adverse impact on the environment should be avoided. Instead, claims should be specific and state the precise environmental benefit that the product provides.

The attorneys general believe that generalized environmental benefit claims may create an unwarranted impression that a product is good for the environment in all respects. However, the production and use of products necessarily have adverse environmental consequences. For these reasons, such claims should be avoided altogether. Instead, companies should make truthful, narrowly drawn claims that specify the precise environmental attribute of a product.

PRE-EXISTING ENVIRONMENTAL ATTRIBUTES

The promotion of a previously existing but previously unadvertised positive environmental attribute should not create, either explicitly or implicitly, the perception that the product has been recently modified or improved.

For example, some companies have used recycled paper in their packaging materials for years. Consumers are now sensitive to the environmental benefits of recycling and base their purchasing decisions, in part, on whether product packaging is made from recycled materials. The company that has been doing the responsible thing for years may promote that fact, provided that such promotion does not mislead. Clearly, it would be deceptive to promote a product that had been packaged in recycled paper for ten years by saying "Now! Recycled package!" It would not be deceptive, on the other hand, to say "We have used 100 percent recycled paper for years," as long as that claim is true and does not otherwise deceive.

REMOVAL OF HARMFUL INGREDIENT

In promoting the removal of a single harmful ingredient or a few harmful ingredients from a product or package, care should be taken to avoid the impression that the product is good for the environment in all respects.

For example, some aerosol spray products made without CFCs are advertised as *safe for the environment* or *ozone-friendly,* but they may contain other ingredients, such as 1,1,1,-trichloroethane, that contribute to destruction of the stratospheric ozone layer. Promoting a product which contains ozone-depleting ingredients as *ozone-friendly* is clearly misleading. Also, stating that such a product *contains no CFCs* may also mislead because the phrase *no CFCs* may mean *safe for the ozone* to many consumers. Labeling an aerosol spray product that does not contain any ozone-depleting chemicals as *safe for the environment* may also be misleading because many of these products contain volatile organic compounds that are linked to the creation of ground level ozone, a component of smog. A more appropriate, less confusing claim for such a product would be one which states *contains no ozone-depleting ingredients* or *does not contribute to ozone depletion.*

PRODUCTS VERSUS PACKAGING

A clear distinction should be made between the environmental attributes of a product and the environmental attributes of its packaging.

For example, a manufacturer of disposable diapers placed a sticker on the plastic wrapper containing its diapers which states *RECYCLABLE* in large capital letters. Below the word *recyclable,* in smaller print, were the words "This softpac is recyclable where plastic bag recycling facilities exist."

RECYCLED

Recycled content claims should be specific, and separate percentages should be disclosed for post-consumer and pre-consumer materials. To avoid the potential for deception, the task force recommends that only post-consumer materials be referred to as recycled material. Recaptured factory material should be referred to by some other term, such as reprocessed [or recovered] industrial material.

Realistically, when consumers think about recycling, they are thinking only about post-consumer waste—the trash they leave at the curb. The attorneys general contend that consumers commonly believe that products labeled *recycled* contain material that consumers have recycled, e.g., household waste, that has been separated out by the consumer for separate collection by a recycler and reused in creating new products. Because solid waste managers are often unable to locate markets for materials that consumers discard, state policy makers have sought to stimulate these markets by requiring that specific amounts of post-consumer material be incorporated into products before they can be labeled as *recycled.* California, New York, and New Hampshire all require that a product include some percentage of post-consumer waste before it can be labeled *recycled.* Rhode Island requires separate disclosure of pre-consumer and post-consumer waste content for materials labeled *recycled.*

COMPARATIVE CLAIMS

Only complete and full comparisons should be made; the basis for the comparison should be stated.

Any specific claim that includes a comparative statement such as *better for the environment* should only be used if a complete and full comparison is made and the basis for the comparison is stated. Such a comparison might be "This product is better than [our former product or our competitor's product] because..."

PRODUCT LIFE ASSESSMENT

The results of product life assessments should not be used to advertise or promote specific products until uniform methods for conducting such assessments are developed and a general consen-

sus is reached among government, business, environmental and consumer groups on how this type of environmental comparison can be advertised non-deceptively.

Although product life assessments or cradle-to-grave product analyses are expected to be extremely useful for evaluating the overall environmental effects of various manufacturing processes and products, the methodology for this type of assessment has not yet been fully developed. Experts in many fields are now working together to develop a consensus on how to conduct these complex and costly comparisons.

SEALS OF APPROVAL (SEE *GREEN CROSS* AND *GREEN SEAL*)

Environmental certifications and seals of approval must be designed and promoted with great care, to avoid misleading the public.

The task force is concerned about the criteria the grantors of *seals* will use to select product categories and to determine whether a product qualifies for a *seal of approval*. The criteria used are critical in determining whether the *seal* is meaningful or, on the other hand, potentially confusing and deceptive. Another concern is the danger that financial considerations may lead programs to choose product categories and evaluation criteria that are actually at odds with environmental goals because those manufacturers most willing to pay for a *seal* may have products that are environmentally suspect or environmentally inferior to alternatives not included in the seal program.

The task force is equally concerned that certification programs may award seals on the basis of a single criterion that may be arbitrary, trivial, or even intrinsically deceptive. For example, a program might award a seal to an environmentally harmful product simply on the basis of the recycled content of the outer package. Even if a program uses appropriate criteria in granting its certification, problems may still arise when the certification logo is used as a sales tool. No matter how laudable a *seal* program's purposes may be, if the manufacturers who pay for the use of the *seal* advertise it in a confusing and deceptive manner, its implementation may present more problems for consumers than solutions.

The task force believes that the *seal* grantors have an independent duty to effectively monitor the use of their *seals* in order to prevent deception, and may themselves be subject to legal action if they permit their *seals* to be used deceptively. This duty extends not only to the manner in which logos are displayed on packages, but to all advertising by licensees. It also includes an affirmative duty to communicate to the public the true significance of each *seal,* whether through in-store information, separate advertising by the grantor, or information on the logo.

SOURCE REDUCTION CLAIMS

Source reduction claims should be specific, and where possible include percentages. Comparisons should be clear and complete.

To avoid the possibility of deception, such claims should be specific and, where possible, include exact percentages for the reduction in weight or volume (e.g., "Now 10 percent less packaging than before"). Source reduction claims should only be made for a relatively short period of time—six months to one year—immediately following the implementation of the change in size. Comparisons should always be complete (e.g., "10 percent less volume than our previous package"). Size reduction comparisons should be made only to the previous version of the manufacturer's product on the market unless there is a clear disclosure that a comparison is being made to a different product (e.g., "10 percent less packaging than the leading brand").

CLAIMS SHOULD REFLECT CURRENT WASTE MANAGEMENT OPTIONS

Environmental claims relating to the disposability or potential for recovery of a particular product (e.g., compostable or recyclable) should be made in a manner that clearly discloses the general availability of the advertised option where the product is sold.

At the current time, composting is not an available option for the vast majority of consumers in the United States. The advertising today of an environmental attributer that cannot be realized until some uncertain time in the future is confusing and misleads the consumer. Consumers are purchasing products and packaging that must be disposed of in short order. To avoid potential deception, companies that elect to make claims such as "compostable" or "degradable if deposited in a composting facility" must also clearly disclose the current limited availability of this disposal option and the fact that the product is not designed to degrade in a landfill. Recyclability claims present similar problems. Those nationally sold products that are generally recyclable in some communities, but not in others, should only make qualified recyclability claims that inform the public that the product is potentially recyclable without misleading consumers to believe that the product is recyclable everywhere it is sold.

DEGRADABLE

Products that are currently disposed of primarily in landfills or through incineration—whether paper or plastic—should not be promoted as degradable, biodegradable, *or* photodegradable.

Degradability claims should not be made for products likely to be disposed of in landfills. However, it may be appropriate to made claims about the *biodegradability* of a product when that product is disposed of in a waste management facility that is designed to take advantage of biodegradability (such as a municipal solid waste composting facility). In this case, the *biodegradable* product should safely break down at a sufficiently rapid rate and with enough completeness to meet the standards set by any existing state or federal regulations.

COMPOSTABLE

Unqualified compostability claims should not be made for products sold nationally unless a significant amount of the product is currently being composted everywhere the product is sold. In all other cases, compostability claims should be accompanied by a clear disclosure about the limited availability of this disposal option. If a claim of degradability is made in the context of a product's compostability, a disclosure should be made that the product is not designed to degrade in a landfill.

There are currently very few locations in the United States where anything other than yard trimmings is composted. Thus, at the present time, promoting most nationally sold products as *compostable* is meaningless at best and potentially deceptive. Because of the extremely limited availability of municipal solid waste composting facilities, the task force believes that compostability claims for most products sold nationally are premature.

RECYCLABLE

Unqualified recyclability claims should not be made for products sold nationally unless a significant amount of the product is being recycled everywhere the product is sold. Where a product is being recycled in many areas of the country, a qualified recyclability claim can be made. If consumers have little or no opportunity to recycle a product, recyclability claims should not be made.

For example, if a company marketing such a product wants to promote the fact that the product has the potential to be recycled, or that is is technologically possible to recycle it, then that company should clearly disclose all of the material facts, including at least (1) the fact that the technology is in the early stages, or that there are only "pilot" recycling programs if that is the case; (2) the number of locations where the product is being recycled; (3) the types of collection sites if there is no curbside pick-up available (e.g., "at school cafeterias"); and (4) the number of states in which the collection and recycling facilities are located. Finally, a product should not be promoted as *recyclable* if it contains additives or other materials that make the product problematic or unsuitable for recycling.

SAFE FOR DISPOSAL

Vague safety claims concerning disposability should be avoided. Instead, products should specifically disclose those environmentally dangerous materials or additives that have been eliminated.

Simply because a product meets a federal safety standard does not mean that its disposal in a landfill or incinerator is risk-free or has no adverse impact on the environment. To prevent confusion, manufacturers should not promote products as *safe for incineration* or *landfill safe*. If a product does not contain materials or additives that are known to be problematic for environmentally benign disposal, the manufacturer should simply state that the product does not contain them (e.g., "Our packaging material contains no cadmium").

CLAIMS SHOULD BE SUBSTANTIVE

Environmental claims should be substantive.

Nonsubstantive claims are widespread and create a false impression of a product's overall environmental soundness. They also contribute to consumer confusion.

TRIVIAL AND IRRELEVANT CLAIMS

Trivial and irrelevant claims should be avoided.

For example, products promoted as *degradable* that will be disposed of in landfills or incinerators, and trash bags, which are highly unlikely to be used again for any purpose, advertised as *recyclable*.

SINGLE-USE PRODUCTS

Single-use disposable products promoted on the basis of environmental attributes should be promoted carefully to avoid the implication that they do not impose a burden on the environment. Many products that are designed to be thrown away after a single use, such as disposable diapers, paper plates, or shopping bags, sport claims that imply environmental soundness. Such claims convey an implicit message that disposal of a single-use item—perhaps the most environmentally distressing aspect of the product—does not contribute to the overall solid waste problem. Advertisements for single-use products should not convey the message that they impose no burden on the environment.

CLAIMS SHOULD BE SUPPORTED

Environmental claims should be supported by competent and reliable scientific evidence.

Advertising claims must be supported by tests, analysis, research, or studies conducted or evaluated in an objective manner by persons qualified to do so using procedures generally accepted by others in the profession to yield accurate and reliable results.

Source:
The Green Report II: Recommendations for Responsible Environmental Advertising, issued May, 1991 by the Attorneys General of California, Florida, Massachusetts, Minnesota, Missouri, New York, Tennessee, Texas, Utah, Washington, and Wisconsin. Copies available from each office.

Environmental Labeling, FTC Guidelines

BACKGROUND

The Federal Trade Commission's Guides for the Use of Environmental Marketing Claims, issued in August 1992, are based on a review of data obtained during U.S. Federal Trade Commission (FTC) law-enforcement investigations, from two days of hearings the FTC held in July 1991, and from more than 100 written comments received from the public. Like all FTC guides, they are administrative interpretations of laws administered by the FTC. Thus, while they are not themselves legally enforceable, they provide guidance to marketers in conforming with legal requirements. The guides apply to advertising, labeling, and other forms of marketing to consumers. They do not preempt state or local laws or regulations.

Basically, the guides describe various claims, note those that should be avoided because they are likely to be misleading, and illustrate the kinds of qualifying statements that may have to be added to other claims to avoid consumer deception. The claims are followed by examples that illustrate the points. The guides outline principles that apply to all environmental claims, and address the use of eight commonly used environmental marketing claims.

QUALIFICATIONS AND DISCLOSURES

The FTC traditionally has held that in order to be effective, any qualifications or disclosures such as those described in these guides should be sufficiently clear and prominent to prevent deception. Clarity of language, relative type size and proximity to the claim being qualified, and an absence of contrary claims that could undercut effectiveness, will maximize the likelihood that the qualifications and disclosures are appropriately clear and prominent.

DISTINCTION BETWEEN BENEFITS OF PRODUCT AND PACKAGE

An environmental marketing claim should be presented in a way that makes clear whether the environmental attribute or benefit being asserted refers to the product, the product's packaging, or to a portion or component of the product or packaging. In general, if the environmental attribute or benefit applies to all but minor, incidental components of a product or package, the claim need not be qualified to identify that fact. There may be exceptions to this general principle. For example, if an unqualified *recyclable* claim is made and the presence of the incidental component significantly limits the ability to recycle the product, then the claim would be deceptive.

Example 1. A box of aluminum foil is labeled with the claim *recyclable,* without further elaboration. Unless the type of product, surrounding language, or other context of the phrase establishes whether the claim refers to the foil or the box, the claim is deceptive if any part of either the box or the foil, other than minor, incidental components, cannot be recycled.

Example 2. A soft drink bottle is labeled *recycled.* The bottle is made entirely from recycled materials, but the bottle cap is not. Because reasonable consumers are likely to consider the bottle cap to be a minor, incidental component of the package, the claim is not deceptive. Similarly, it would not be deceptive to label a shopping bag *recycled* where the bag is made entirely of recycled material but the easily detachable handle, an incidental component, is not.

OVERSTATEMENT OF ENVIRONMENTAL ATTRIBUTE

An environmental marketing claim should not be presented in a manner that overstates the environmental attribute or benefit, expressly or by implication. Marketers should avoid implications of significant environmental benefits if the benefit is in fact negligible.

Example 1. A package is labeled, "50 percent more recycled content than before." The manufacturer increased the recycled content of its package from 2 percent recycled material to 3 percent recycled material. Although the claim is technically

true, it is likely to convey the false impression that the advertiser has increased significantly the use of recycled material.

Example 2. A trash bag is labeled *recyclable* without qualifications. Because trash bags will ordinarily not be separated out from other trash at the landfill or incinerator for recycling, they are highly unlikely to be used again for any purpose. Even if the bag is technically capable of being recycled, the claim is deceptive since it asserts an environmental benefit where no significant or meaningful benefit exists.

Example 3. A paper grocery sack is labeled *reusable.* The sack can be brought back to the store and reused for carrying groceries but will fall apart after two or three reuses, on average. Because reasonable consumers are unlikely to assume that a paper grocery sack is durable, the unqualified claim does not overstate the environmental benefit conveyed to consumers. The claim is not deceptive and does not need to be qualified to indicate the limited reuse of the sack.

COMPARATIVE CLAIMS

Environmental marketing claims that include a comparative statement should be presented in a manner that makes the basis for the comparison sufficiently clear to avoid consumer deception. In addition, the advertiser should be able to substantiate the comparison.

Example 1. An advertiser notes that its shampoo bottle contains "20 percent more recycled content." The claim in its context is ambiguous. Depending on contextual factors, it could be a comparison either to the advertiser's immediately preceding product or to a competitor's product. The advertiser should clarify the claim to make the basis for comparison clear, for example, by saying "20 percent more recycled content that our previous package." Otherwise, the advertiser should be prepared to substantiate whatever comparison is conveyed to reasonable consumers.

Example 2. An advertiser claims that "our plastic diaper liner has the most recycled content." The advertised diaper does have more recycled content, calculated as a percentage of weight, than any other on the market, although it is still well under 100 percent recycled. Provided the recycled content and the comparative difference between the product and those of competitors are significant and provided the specific comparison can be substantiated, the claim is not deceptive.

Example 3. An ad claims that the advertiser's packaging creates "less waste than the leading national brand." The advertiser's source reduction was implemented sometime ago and is supported by a calculation comparing the relative solid waste contributions of the two packages. The advertiser should be able to substantiate that the comparison remains accurate.

ENVIRONMENTAL MARKETING CLAIMS

Guidance about the use of environmental marketing claims is set forth below. Each guide is followed by several examples that illustrate, but do not provide an exhaustive list of, claims that do and do not comport with the guides. In each case, the general principles set forth above should also be followed. These guides do not address claims based on a *life cycle* theory of environmental benefit. Such analyses are still in their infancy and thus the Federal Trade Commission lacks sufficient information on which to base guidance at this time.

GENERAL ENVIRONMENTAL BENEFIT CLAIMS

In general, unqualified general environmental claims are difficult to interpret and may have a wide range of meanings to consumers. Every express- and material-implied claim conveyed to consumers about an objective quality should be substantiated. Unless they can be substantiated, broad environmental claims should be avoided or qualified.

Example 1. A brand name like *Eco-Safe* would be deceptive if, in the context of the product so named, it leads consumers to believe that the product has environmental benefits which cannot be substantiated by the manufacturer. The claim would not be deceptive if *Eco-Safe* used clear and prominent qualifying language limiting the safety representation to a particular product attribute which could be substantiated, and provided that no other deceptive implications were created by the context.

Example 2. A product wrapper is printed with the claim *environmentally friendly.* Textual comments on the wrapper explain that the wrapper is "environmentally friendly because it was not chlorine bleached, a process that has been shown to create harmful substances." The wrapper was, in fact, not bleached with chlorine. However, the production of the wrapper now creates and releases to the environment significant quantities of other harmful substances. Since consumers are likely to interpret the *environmentally friendly* claim, in combination with the textual explanation, to mean that no significant harmful substances are currently released to the environment, the *environmentally friendly* claim would be deceptive.

Example 3. A pump spray product is labeled *environmentally safe.* Most of the product's active ingredients consist of volatile organic compounds (VOCs) that may cause smog by contributing to ground-level ozone formation. The claim is deceptive because, further qualification absent, it is likely to convey to consumers that use of the product will not result in air pollution or other harm to the environment.

DEGRADABLE/BIODEGRADABLE/PHOTO-DEGRADABLE

In general, unqualified degradability claims should be substantiated by evidence that the product will completely break down and return to nature, that is, decompose into elements found in nature within a reasonably short period of time after consumers dispose of it in the customary way. Such claims should be qualified to the extent necessary to avoid consumer deception about (a) the product or package's ability to degrade in the environment where it is customarily disposed, and (b) the extent and rate of degradation.

Example 1. A trash bag is marketed as *degradable,* with no qualification or other disclosure. The marketer relies on soil burial tests to show that the product will decompose in the presence of water and oxygen. The trash bags are customarily disposed of in incineration facilities or at sanitary landfills that are managed in a way that inhibits degradation by minimizing moisture and oxygen. Degradation will be irrelevant for those trash bags that are incinerated and, for those disposed of in landfills, the marketer does not possess adequate substantiation that the bags will degrade in a reasonably short period of time in a landfill. The claim is therefore deceptive.

Example 2. A commercial agricultural plastic mulch film is advertised as *Photodegradable* and qualified with the phrase, "will break down into small pieces if left uncovered in sunlight." The claim is supported by competent and reliable scientific evidence that the product will break down in a reasonably short period of time after being exposed to sunlight and into sufficiently small pieces to become part of the soil. The qualified claim is not deceptive. Because the claim is qualified to indicate the limited extent of breakdown, the advertiser need not meet the elements for an unqualified photodegradable claim, i.e., that the product will not only break down, but also will decompose into elements found in nature.

Example 3. A soap or shampoo product is advertised as *biodegradable,* with no qualification or other disclosure. The manufacturer has competent and reliable scientific evidence demonstrating that the product, which is customarily disposed of in sewage systems, will break down and decompose into elements found in nature in a short period of time. The claim is not deceptive.

COMPOSTABLE

In general, unqualified compostable claims should be substantiated by evidence that all the materials in the product or package will break down into, or otherwise become part of, usable compost (e.g., soil-conditioning material, mulch) in a safe and timely manner in an appropriate composting program or facility, or in a home compost pile or device. Compostable claims should be qualified to the extent necessary to avoid consumer deception (1) if municipal composting facilities are not available to a substantial majority of consumers or communities where the product is sold, (2) if the claim misleads consumers about the environmental benefit provided when the product is disposed of in a landfill, or (3) if consumers misunderstand the claim to mean that the package can be safely composted in their home compost pile or device, when in fact it cannot.

Example 1. A manufacturer indicates that its unbleached coffee filter is *compostable.* The unqualified claim is not deceptive provided the manufacturer can substantiate that the filter can be converted safely to usable compost in a timely manner in a home compost pile or device, as well as in an appropriate composting program or facility.

Example 2. A lawn and leaf bag is labeled as "compostable in California Municipal Yard Waste Composting Facilities." The bag contains toxic ingredients that are released into the compost material as the bag breaks down. The claim is deceptive if the presence of these toxic ingredients prevents the compost from being usable.

Example 3. A manufacturer indicates that its paper plate is suitable for home composting. If the manufacturer possesses substantiation for claiming that the paper plate can be converted safely to usable compost in a home compost pile or device, this claim is not deceptive even if no municipal composting facilities exist.

Example 4. A manufacturer makes an unqualified claim that its package is *compostable*. Although municipal composting facilities exist where the product is sold, the package will not break down into usable compost in a home compost pile or device. To avoid deception, the manufacturer should disclose that the package is not suitable for home composting.

Example 5. A nationally marketed lawn and leaf bag is labeled *compostable*. Also printed on the bag is a disclosure that the bag is not designed for use in home compost piles. The bags are in fact composted in municipal yard waste composting programs in many communities around the country, but such programs are not available to a substantial majority of consumers where the bag is sold. The claim is deceptive since reasonable consumers living in areas not served by municipal yard waste programs may understand the reference to mean that composting facilities accepting the bags are available in their area. To avoid deception, the claim should be qualified to indicate the limited availability of such programs, for example, by stating, "Appropriate facilities may not exist in your area." Other examples of adequate qualification of the claim include providing the approximate percentage of communities or the population for which such programs are available.

Example 6. A manufacturer sells a disposable diaper that bears the legend, "This diaper can be composted where municipal solid waste composting facilities exist. There are currently (*x* number of) municipal solid waste composting facilities across the country." The claim is not deceptive assuming that composting facilities are available as claimed and the manufacturer can substantiate that the diaper can be converted safely to usable compost in municipal solid waste composting facilities.

Example 7. A manufacturer markets yard waste bags only to consumers residing in particular geographic areas served by county yard waste composting programs. The bags meet specifications for these programs and are labeled, "Compostable Yard Waste Bag for County Composting Programs." The claim is not deceptive. Because the bags are compostable where they are sold, no qualification is required to indicate the limited availability of composting facilities.

RECYCLABLE

In general, a product or package should not be marketed as recyclable unless it can be collected, separated, or otherwise recovered from the solid waste stream for use in the form of raw materials in the manufacture or assembly of a new product or package. Unqualified recyclable claims may be made if the entire product or package, excluding incidental components, is recyclable.

Claims about products with both recyclable and nonrecyclable components should be adequately qualified. If incidental compo-

nents significantly limit the ability to recycle a product, the claim would be deceptive. If, because of its size or shape, a product is not accepted in recycling programs, it should not be marketed *recyclable*. Qualification may be necessary to avoid consumer deception about the limited availability of recycling programs and collection sites if recycling collection sites are not available to a substantial majority of consumers or communities.

Example 1. A packaged product is labeled with an unqualified claim, *recyclable*. It is unclear from the type of product and other context whether the claim refers to the product or its package. The unqualified claim is likely to convey to reasonable consumers that all of both the product and its packaging that remain after normal use of the product, except for minor, incidental components, can be recycled. Unless each such message can be substantiated, the claim should be qualified to indicate what portions are recyclable.

Example 2. A plastic package is labeled on the bottom with the Society of the Plastics Industry (SPI) code, consisting of a design of arrows in a triangular shape containing a number and abbreviation identifying the component plastic resin. Without more, the use of the SPI symbol (or similar industry codes) on the bottom of the package, or in a similarly inconspicuous location, does not constitute a claim of recyclability.

Example 3. A container can be burned in incinerator facilities to produce heat and power. It cannot, however, be recycled into new products or packaging. Any claim that the container is *recyclable* would be deceptive.

Example 4. A nationally marketed bottle bears the unqualified statement that it is *recyclable*. Collection sites for recycling the material in question are not available to a substantial majority of consumers or communities, although collection sites are established in a significant percentage of communities or available to a significant percentage of the population. The unqualified claim is deceptive since, unless evidence shows otherwise, reasonable consumers living in communities not served by programs may conclude that recycling programs for the material are available in their area. To avoid deception, the claim should be qualified to indicate the limited availability of programs, for example, by stating, "Check to see if recycling facilities exist in your area." Other examples of adequate qualifications of the claim include providing the approximate percentage of communities or the population to whom programs are available.

Example 5. A soda bottle is marketed nationally and labeled, *Recyclable where facilities exist*. Recycling programs for material of this type and size are available in a significant percentage of communities or to a significant percentage of the population, but are not available to a substantial majority of consumers. The claim is deceptive since, unless evidence shows otherwise, reasonable consumers living in communities not served by programs may understand this phrase to mean that programs are available in their area. To avoid deception, the claim should be further qualified to indicate the limited availability of programs, for example, by using any of the approaches set forth in Example 4 above.

Example 6. A plastic detergent bottle is marketed as follows: *Recyclable in the few communities with facilities for colored*

HDPE bottles. Collection sites for recycling the container have been established in a half dozen major metropolitan areas. This disclosure illustrates one approach to qualifying a claim adequately to prevent deception about the limited availability of recycling programs where collection facilities are not established in a significant percentage of communities or available to a significant percentage of the population. Other examples of adequate qualification of the claim include providing the number of communities with programs, or the percentage of communities, or the population to which programs are available.

Example 7. A label claims that the package "includes some recyclable material." The package is composed of four layers of different materials, bonded together. One of the layers is made from the recyclable material, but the others are not. While programs for recycling this type of material are available to a substantial majority of consumers, only a few of those programs have the capability to separate out the recyclable layer. Even though it is technologically possible to separate the layers, the claim in not adequately qualified to avoid consumer deception. An appropriately qualified claim would be "includes material recyclable in the few communities that collect multi-layer products." Other examples of adequate qualification of the claim include providing the number of communities with programs, or the percentage of communities or the population to which programs are available.

Example 8. A product is marketed as having a *recyclable* container. The product is distributed and advertised only in Missouri. Collection sites for recycling the container are available to a substantial majority of Missouri residents, but are not yet available nationally. Because programs are generally available where the product is marketed, the unqualified claim does not deceive consumers about the limited availability of recycling programs.

RECYCLED CONTENT

In general, claims of recycled content should only be made for materials that have been recovered or diverted from the solid waste stream, either during the manufacturing process (pre-consumer) or after consumer waste (post-consumer). An advertiser should be able to substantiate that pre-consumer content would otherwise have entered the solid waste stream. Distinctions made between pre- and post-consumer content should be substantiated. Unqualified claims may be made if the entire product or package, excluding minor, incidental components, is made from recycled material. Products or packages only partially made of recycled material should be qualified to indicate the amount, by weight, in the finished product or package.

Example 1. A manufacturer routinely collects spilled raw material and scraps from trimming finished products. After a minimal amount of reprocessing, the manufacturer combines the spills and scraps with virgin material for use in further production of the same product. A claim that the product contains recycled material is deceptive since the spills and scraps to which the claim refers are normally reused by industry within the original manufacturing process, and would not normally have entered the waste stream.

Example 2. A manufacturer purchases material from a firm that collects discarded material from other manufacturers and resells it. All of the material was diverted from the solid waste stream and is not normally reused by industry within the original manufacturing process. The manufacturer includes the weight of this material in its calculations of the recycled content of its products. A claim of recycled content based on this calculation is not deceptive because, except for the purchase and reuse of this material, it would have entered the waste stream.

Example 3. A greeting card is composed 30 percent by weight of paper collected from consumers after use of a paper product, and 20 percent by weight of paper that was generated after completion of the paper-making process, diverted from the solid waste stream, and otherwise would not normally have been reused in the original manufacturing process. The marketer of the card may claim either that the product "contains 50 percent recycled material," or may identify the specific pre-consumer and/or post-consumer content by stating, for example, that the product "contains 50 percent total recycled material, 30 percent of which is post-consumer material."

Example 4. A package with 20 percent recycled content by weight is labeled as containing "20 percent recycled paper." Some of the recycled content was composed of material collected from consumers after use of the original product. The rest was composed of overrun newspaper stock never sold to customers. The claim is not deceptive.

Example 5. A product in a multi-component package, such as a paperboard box in a shrink-wrapped plastic cover, indicates that it has recycled packaging. The paperboard box is made entirely of recycled material, but the plastic cover is not. The claim is deceptive since, without qualification, it suggests that both components are recycled. A claim limited to the paperboard box would not be deceptive.

Example 6. A package is made from layers of foil, plastic, and paper laminated together, although the layers are indistinguishable to consumers. The label claims that "one of the three layers of this package is made of recycled plastic." The plastic layer is made entirely of recycled plastic. The claim is not deceptive provided that recycled plastic layer constitutes a significant component of the entire package.

Example 7. A paper product is labeled as containing "100 percent recycled fiber." The claim is not deceptive if the advertiser can substantiate the conclusion that 100 percent by weight of the fiber in the finished product is recycled.

Example 8. A frozen dinner is marketed in a package composed of a cardboard box over a plastic tray. The package bears the legend, "package made from 30 percent recycled material." Each packaging component amounts to one-half the weight of the total package. The box is 20 percent recycled content by weight, while the plastic tray is 40 percent recycled content by weight. The claim is not deceptive, since the average amount of recycled material is 30 percent.

Example 9. A paper greeting card is labeled as containing 50 percent by weight recycled content. The seller purchases paper stock from several sources and the amount of recycled material in the stock provided by each source varies. Because the 50 percent figure is based on the annual weighted average of recycled material purchases from the sources after accounting for fiber loss during the production process, the claim is permissible.

SOURCE REDUCTION

In general, claims that a product or package has been reduced or is lower in weight, volume, or toxicity should be qualified to the extent necessary to avoid consumer deception about the amount of reduction and the basis for any comparison asserted.

Example 1. An ad claims that solid waste created by disposal of the advertiser's packaging is "now 10 percent less that our previous package." The claim is not deceptive if the advertiser has substantiation that shows that disposal of the current package contributes 10 percent less waste by weight or volume to the solid waste stream when compared with the immediately preceding version of the package.

Example 2. An advertiser notes that disposal of its product generates "10 percent less waste." The claim is ambiguous. Depending on contextual factors, it would be a comparison either to the immediately preceding product or to a competitor's product. The "10 percent less waste" reference is deceptive unless the seller clarifies which comparison is intended and substantiates that comparison, or substantiates both possible interpretations of the claim.

REFILLABLE

In general, an unqualified refillable claim should not be asserted unless a system is provided for (1) the collection and return of the package for refill, or (2) the later refill of the package by consumers with product subsequently sold in another package. The claim should not be made if it is up to consumers to find ways to refill the package.

Example 1. A container is labeled "refillable *x* times." The manufacturer has the capability to refill returned containers and can show that the container will withstand being refilled at least *x* times. The unqualified claim is deceptive because there is not means for collection and return of the container to the manufacturer for refill.

Example 2. A bottle of fabric softener states that it is in a "handy refillable container." The manufacturer also sells a large-sized container that indicates that the consumer is expected to use it to refill the smaller container. The manufacturer sells the large-sized container in the same market areas where it sells the small container. The claim is not deceptive because there is a means for consumers to refill the smaller container from larger containers of the same product.

OZONE-SAFE AND OZONE-FRIENDLY

In general, a product should not be advertised as *ozone-safe, ozone-friendly,* or as not containing CFCs if the product contains any ozone-depleting chemical. Claims about the reduction of a product's ozone-depletion potential may be made if adequately substantiated.

Example 1. A product is labeled *ozone-friendly.* The claim is deceptive if the product contains any ozone-depleting substance, including those substances listed as Class I or Class II chemicals in Title VI of the Clean Air Act Amendments of 1990, Pub. L. No. 101-549, or others subsequently deigned by EPA as ozone-depleting substances. Class I chemicals currently listed in Title VI are chlorofluorocarbons (CFCs), halons, carbon tetrachloride, and 1,1,1-trichloroethane. Class II chemicals currently listed in Title VI are hydrochlorofluorocarbons (HCFCs).

Example 2. The seller of an aerosol product makes an unqualified claim that its product *Contains no CFCs.* Although the product does not contain CFCs, it does contain HCFC-22, another ozone depleting ingredient. Because the claim *Contains no CFCs* may imply to reasonable consumers that the product does not harm the ozone layer, the claim is deceptive.

Example 3. A product is labeled "This product is 95 percent less damaging to the ozone layer than past formulations that contained CFCs." The manufacturer has substituted HCFCs for CFC-12, and can substantiate that this substitution will result in 95 percent less ozone-depletion. The qualified comparative claim is not likely to be deceptive.

Source:
Office of Public Affairs, *Press Release: Guides for the Use of Environmental Marketing Claims,* Washington: Federal Trade Commission, July 1992.

Environmental Seals, Environmental Choice

Environmental Choice is a voluntary Canadian program created to help consumers find products which ease the burden on the environment. The *EcoLogo* is the symbol of certification which appears on goods and services that meet the Environmental Choice product specific criteria.

These criteria are set by the Environmental Choice Board, a body appointed by the Canadian Federal Minister of the Environment, operating at arm's length from the Canadian Government.

For each set of criteria developed, a study of the product's life-cycle is conducted. The purpose of the study is to identify which aspects of the product's life-cycle—manufacture, transport, use or disposal—offer opportunities to significantly reduce its negative impacts on the environment.

Each set of criteria is made available for a public review period of 60 days, during which time manufacturers, environmentalists, consumers and any member of the general public may submit suggestions for the improvement of the criteria.

Suppliers may submit their goods and services for assessment. Those products that meet the criteria set out in the relevant Environmental Choice guideline are eligible for the EcoLogo. The program does not use the words *environmentally friendly* to describe products or services which carry the EcoLogo because they do not want to suggest that these products or services are perfectly harmless to the environment. Very few consumer products or services have no negative environmental impact. However, products or services certified by Environmental Choice help reduce the burden on the environment in specific ways. By reading the brief explanation on the label underneath the EcoLogo, consumers can see how the product or service helps in this reduction.

The EcoLogo and the words *EcoLogo* and *Environmental Choice* are official marks of Environmental Canada.

The following product categories are included in the Canadian Environmental Choice Program:

BATTERIES

The principal risk that batteries pose is the exposure of people and the environment to mercury, during its extraction and processing, and in the manufacture and disposal of the batteries. Mercury, one of the most toxic heavy metals, can cause brain damage and other biological disorders.

Safely disposing of these batteries is a challenge. In landfill sites, mercury and other heavy metals can seep out of battery casings. Batteries in the municipal waste stream account for approximately 35 percent of the total mercury released into the Canadian environment. Even the incineration of batteries releases mercury into the environment.

Hearing Aid Batteries. Of the two types of hearing aid batteries available in Canada (zinc-air and zinc-mercuric oxide), zinc-air batteries contain the least mercury. Using zinc-air batteries will, therefore, decrease the demand for mercury and thereby reduce the amount of mercury released into the environment during its extraction, manufacture, and disposal. To qualify for the EcoLogo, zinc-air batteries must have a mercury content which does not exceed the limit of 40 milligrams per ampere hour.

Alkaline Batteries. Alkaline batteries come in two shapes: cylindrical and button (also known as coin). These are the most commonly used household batteries, representing about 75 percent of the Canadian market. To qualify for the EcoLogo, the two subcategories of alkaline batteries must meet the following requirements: *Alkaline cylindrical batteries* must not contain mercury in excess of 0.025 percent by weight. This limit will be reduced to 0.020 percent by July 1, 1993. *Alkaline manganese button (coin) batteries* must not contain mercury which exceeds the limit of 25 mg per cell.

COMPOSTERS

Composting is the decomposition of organic material by microorganisms found in soil. The product is a humus-like material which improves the texture of soil and enhances its ability to retain nutrients and moisture. Composting kitchen and yard wastes can significantly reduce the volume of residential waste in landfill sites by putting to good use material that would otherwise be thrown away. Compostable household waste such as leaves, grass clippings, and food scraps make up nearly 50 percent of all residential solid waste in landfill sites.

EcoLogo Qualifications. A composting container for residential waste is any container which allows for the controlled breakdown of organic yard and kitchen waste. In order to qualify for the EcoLogo, a composting container must be made for residential use and be designed to provide sufficient air circulation to keep the composting material in an aerobic state. The composting container must be accompanied by a user manual listing waste products that must not be put into the composter, uses for the compost produced, conditions under which the composting process will not work, and ways to avoid potential problems with wild animals, rodents, and pathogens. It must also have a five-year warranty.

DIAPERS

Two hundred fifty thousand tons of disposable diapers and their contents go into Canadian landfill sites each year. They are the third largest single item (after newspapers and beverage and food containers) in the municipal waste stream.

Disposable diapers make up approximately 85 percent of the diaper market. In Canada, the manufacture of disposable diapers consumes approximately 65,500 tons of pulp, 8,800 tons of plastic, and 9,800 tons of packing material a year.

Reusable cloth diapers spare dump sites, and they take a fraction of the material resources to produce. Less than 10 kg of cotton is enough to supply all of the reusable cotton diapers required by a baby during the two and a half years it spends in diapers. It takes about 200 kg of fluff pulp and 130 kg of other materials (mostly plastic) to supply a baby with disposable diapers over the same time period.

Some concern has been raised that a shift towards the use of cloth diapers would increase the production of cotton and, therefore, the use of pesticides. However, even if all disposable diapers were replaced with 100 percent cotton diapers, the impact on the cotton industry would be minimal as the cotton required for the manufacture of cloth diapers would still represent only a small fraction of total cotton production.

EcoLogo Qualifications. All cloth diapers are eligible for the EcoLogo, provided they are home washable and 100 percent reusable (they must be able to endure a minimum of 75 uses).

DIAPER SERVICES

Because cloth diapers are reusable, they place a smaller burden on resources, but they do have to be washed and dried. Through a less efficient use of water, electricity, and detergents, washing and drying cloth diapers at home can place a larger burden on the environment than using a diaper service.

Of all the diaper options available, using cloth diapers and having them washed by a diaper service can be the least harmful to the environment. Providing they use equipment that meets specific commercial standards, operated as required by Environmental Choice, diaper services are estimated to save at least half the water, energy, and detergent that would be used to wash diapers at home. Any additional energy consumed in the transportation of diapers to and from diaper services is outweighed by these savings in water, energy and detergent.

EcoLogo Qualifications. To be eligible for the EcoLogo, diaper services must use commercial washing and drying equipment and antiseptic infection control practices. After laundering, the diapers must have an aerobic bacterial colony count of less than 50 per 100cm^2 of diaper material. An aqueous extract from the diapers must have a pH range of 5.5 to 6.5. The waste water treatment used by the diaper services has to be approved by local authorities if municipal water treatment does not exist. The diapers used by the diaper service must meet the Environmental Choice guideline for diapers. Detergents and other cleaning agents used will have to conform to the Environmental Choice guidelines for these products when they become available.

ETHANOL-BLENDED GASOLINE

Most conventional automobiles and light trucks can use gasoline blended with up to 10 percent ethanol, without any modification to their fuel systems or engines, and still be covered by warranty.

Burning ethanol-blended gasoline produces lower emissions of toxic air pollutants, such as carbon monoxide and benzene, than burning regular gasoline. Mixing ethanol with gasoline increases the fuel's octane rating and helps reduce engine knocking. Ethanol can, therefore, partially replace benzene and other toxic chemicals normally added to gasoline to make engines run more efficiently. (See also *Gasoline* and *Ethanol*.)

Ethanol is a fuel that can be produced in a variety of ways including the fermentation of biomass products such as cereal crops, sugar beets, waste agricultural products, wood, and wood waste. Though carbon dioxide is produced when ethanol is burned, it is partially offset by the absorption of carbon dioxide during the growth of biomass crops. The result is a net reduction in carbon dioxide emissions when gasoline mixed with biomass-derived ethanol is used in place of regular gasoline.

As a renewable resource, biomass-derived ethanol blended with gasoline eases the demand on our nonrenewable petroleum resources.

EcoLogo Qualifications. In order to qualify for the EcoLogo, ethanol-blended gasoline must contain a minimum of 5 percent by volume of ethanol with the remaining part of the mixture being gasoline. The ethanol must be totally derived from biomass products. The ethanol-blended gasoline must meet Canadian General Standards Board standard CAN/CGSB-3.511-M, Oxygenated Unleaded Automotive Gasoline Containing Ethanol.

INSULATION

Thermal insulation made from recycled waste paper and wood is as functional and reliable as insulation made from virgin paper fiber. Canadians now dump 5 million tons of waste paper into landfills every year, amounting to 35 percent by weight of Canadian municipal waste.

EcoLogo Qualifications. To qualify for the EcoLogo, the fiber content of thermal insulation must consist of 100 percent recycled fiber and must not contain ingredients which would require it to be labeled as poisonous, corrosive, flammable, or explosive under Canadian Consumer Chemical and Container Regulations of the Hazardous Products Act.

LIGHTS

The most common residential light source is the ordinary incandescent light bulb. Because of their relative inefficiency, however, these bulbs consume many times more energy than is needed to produce equivalent amounts of illumination. They also have short life spans, requiring frequent replacements. This results in an unnecessary use of resources in their manufacture and in an excessive number of light bulbs destined for landfill sites.

The most energy-efficient electric light source for residential use is the compact discharge lamp. These small fluorescent lamps are made to fit most of the standard lighting fixtures that use incandescent bulbs. They provide the same light, use 70 to 80 percent less electricity, and last up to 10 times longer than incandescent bulbs.

EcoLogo Qualifications. The energy-efficient lamps guideline has two subcategories: compact discharge lamps (either with the ballast attached or separate) and integral-ballasted adapters. To qualify for the EcoLogo, compact discharge lamps must comply with the applicable requirements of Canadian Standards Association (CSA) Technical Information Letters No. B-36A and B-50. The integral-ballasted adapters must comply with CSA Standard C22.2 No. 74. Products in both subcategories must not be manufactured with introduced radioactive isotopes exceeding 15 nanocuries per glow switch. (This is equal to about one-half of the amount of radiation from an illuminating wrist watch dial.)

MAJOR APPLIANCES

Although some energy is needed to manufacture major appliances (refrigerators, freezers, dishwashers, washers, and dryers), far more is used to operate them during their lifetime. In fact, the energy required to manufacture a typical appliance is less than the amount consumed in the first two months of its operation.

According to a 1981 study by the Canadian Electrical Association, improved appliance efficiency could save more than 300,400 gigawatt hours in Canada during the period 1980 to 2005. These savings are equivalent to approximately one full year's hydroelectric production in Canada. By seeking out energy-efficient appliances, consumers will benefit from lower electricity bill and help protect the environment.

EcoLogo Qualifications. To qualify for the EcoLogo, appliances must meet energy-consumption limits established by the Environmental Choice Program (ECP). Limits are based on an appliance's volume and on its maximum energy consumption measured in kWh per month. For example, the energy consumption of a 595-litre, medium-size refrigerator with two doors must not exceed 82 kWh per month. Energy consumption limits are outlined in subcategories developed for each type of appliance. The Environmental Choice Program's labeling initiative for major household appliances complements Energy, Mines, and Resource Canada's EnerGuide program. The latter establishes minimum performance requirements for appliances, while the former indicates to consumers which appliances are the premium performers within a given category (e.g. refrigerators, freezers, etc.) For further information on appliance categories and their certification criteria, please consult the Environmental Choice Program guideline ECP-18-90. Please note guideline ECP-18-90 will include criteria concerning the use of alternatives to CFCs as refrigerants and blowing agents in insulation, water consumption, the inclusion of recycled material, and the recycling of components.

PAINT

The solvent contained in solvent-based paint is a mixture of volatile organic compounds which help keep the paint in a liquid form and then evaporate on application. The high levels of these volatile organic compounds found in many solvent-based paints can contribute to ozone production and *photo-chemical smog* in the lower atmosphere. This can cause eye, nose, and throat irritation and can also be toxic to plants, including agricultural crops and forests.

Solvent-based paints may also contain formaldehyde, aromatic hydrocarbons, halogenated solvents, and compounds of heavy metals such as mercury, lead, cadmium, and chromium. These substances can be found in the preservative, pigment, and solvent and can be toxic and even carcinogenic to humans.

Most of the solvents in solvent-based paints are petroleum-derived, contributing to the depletion of nonrenewable resources. While volatile organic compounds are needed in solvent-based paints to keep the paint in a liquid form, they can be reduced significantly. Formaldehyde, aromatic hydrocarbons, halogenated solvents, and heavy metals can be replaced with less harmful ingredients that serve the same functions. The use of reduced pollution solvent-based paints rather than regular solvent-based paints decreases the risks to human and environmental health. In addition, in many paints the petroleum-based solvents can be replaced with solvents derived from renewable resources.

EcoLogo Qualifications. To qualify for the EcoLogo, solvent-based paints must not contain volatile organic compounds in excess of 380 g per litre. In addition, they cannot be tinted with pigments of lead, cadmium, chromium VI, or their oxides. They must not be formulated or manufactured with formaldehyde, mercury or mercury compounds, or halogenated solvents. Aromatic hydrocarbons must not be in excess of 10 percent by weight. The paints must have a *flash point* of 37.8 degrees C or greater. This means that their vapors mixed with air must not catch fire when exposed to flame at a temperature lower than 37.8 degrees C.

PAPER

There is more paper in landfill sites than any other kind of garbage. Every year another 5 million tons of paper products are added. Every ton of paper recycled saves approximately three cubic meters of landfill space. As well, using recycled paper saves the 17 trees required to yield a ton of newsprint. The production of pulp from recycled fiber requires less refining and, therefore, uses fewer chemicals and consumes less energy than making pulp from virgin fiber.

Newsprint. To qualify for the EcoLogo, newsprint must contain over 40 percent by weight of recycled paper, including a minimum of 25 percent recycled newspapers. Two subcategories in the guideline cover products made from newsprint. Newspapers must contain 35 percent by weight of the qualifying newsprint as defined above, in order to qualify for the EcoLogo. Miscellaneous published material printed on newsprint must contain 100 percent by weight of the qualifying newsprint as defined above.

Craft Paper. The guideline covers form products that are made in various shapes for use as base figures in handicraft work. To qualify for an EcoLogo, these products must contain 100 percent by weight of recycled paper, with a minimum of 10 percent post-consumer fiber. Post-consumer fiber refers to waste paper products disposed of after use by consumers and businesses.

Fine Paper. To qualify for the EcoLogo, fine paper products must contain over 50 percent by weight of recycled paper, with a minimum of 10 percent post-consumer fiber. The following paper products are covered by this category: printing papers, business papers, exercise and related papers, envelope papers, and covers and bristols. Post-consumer fiber refers to waste paper products that were disposed of and used by consumers and businesses. The percentage of post-consumer fiber required in fine paper to obtain an EcoLogo will be raised with the increased availability of the higher quality recycled papers needed to produce fine paper.

PLASTICS

Every year, the plastic products that Canadians discard contribute some 7 percent by weight and 30 percent by volume to the solid waste in municipal landfills. Plastics also form a major proportion of litter on land, shorelines, and in waterways, posing risks to the environment and to wildlife.

Despite the advent of degradable plastics, recycling is still a preferable method of reducing the volume of waste plastic. Degradable plastics do not reduce the overall volume of plastic waste nor do they break down completely in landfill sites not designed for bio- or photo-degradation.

EcoLogo Qualifications. All plastic products in the following categories will qualify for the EcoLogo, provided they contain the required percentage by weight of recycled plastic: construction materials such as fencing or shingles; horticultural supplies such as flower pots, garden stakes, and berry trays; agricultural produce containers for products such as eggs, fruits, and vegetables; office supplies such as presentation folders, file folders, and binder covers; containers for nonfood products as well as reusable packing containers; and recreational equipment and outdoor furniture. Qualifying construction materials must contain over 60 percent by weight of recycled plastic, while all other categories must contain over 90 percent by weight of recycled plastic.

PLUMBING FIXTURES

Well over half the water used in Canadian homes every day is for showers and flushing toilets. Most shower heads transmit between 15 and 30 litres of water per minute, far more than is needed to get clean. Conventional toilets use between 23 and 32 litres of water per flush, at least four times more water than is needed to operate a water-saving toilet. Water-conserving shower heads replace some of the water with air to produce a forceful spray capable of delivering a good shower. Shower heads carrying the EcoLogo use a maximum of 9.5 litres of water per minute, saving between 37 percent and 68 percent of the water previously used, depending on the shower head being replaced. Trickle valves, devices installed within shower heads, can be used to reduce the water flow, rather than leaving it running at full force throughout the shower. Trickle valves carrying the EcoLogo reduce the water flow to 400 ml per minute or less, helping to conserve water and energy that would otherwise be used if the shower was to run continuously. Water-conserving toilets carrying the EcoLogo use only 6 litres of water or less per flush, saving from 75 to 80 percent of the water used by conventional toilets. Toilet retrofit components, such as toilet dams, can be installed in conventional toilets to reduce the amount of water stored in the toilet tank, and subsequently used for flushing, by at least 20 percent

EcoLogo Qualifications. Each water-conserving product must meet the criteria specific to its subcategory: shower heads, trickle valves, toilets, and toilet retrofit devices. Water conserving shower heads must have a maximum flow rate of less than 9.5 litres per minute at 5.5 kg per cm^2. Trickle valves must have a maximum flow rate of 400 ml per minute when in "trickle" mode operation. Water-conserving toilets must use 6 litres or less water per flushing cycle. Water-conserving toilet retrofit devices must reduce the water consumption by at least 20 percent when tested using CSA Standard CAN/CSA-B45.0. All products in this guideline must have a three-year warranty and meet appropriate CSA standards for plumbing fixtures and fittings as specified in each subcategory in the guideline.

RE-REFINED OIL

Disposal practices for used oil—such as road oiling, burying it in landfill sites, and pouring it down the sewer—contaminate soil, surface water, and ground-water. There are more environmentally acceptable means of disposing of used oil, such as incineration or solidification for placement in authorized hazardous waste landfill sites. Apart from being expensive, however, these practices, like any means of disposal, fail to make use of the lubricating value

of used oil. In re-refined oil, impurities are removed from the oil by the re-refining process, restoring it to a reliable and functional condition. By reusing oil, and thereby reducing the demand for new oil, the risk of environmental damage resulting from the production of new oil will be reduced.

EcoLogo Qualifications. All petroleum-based lubricating oils can qualify for the EcoLogo providing they contain over 50 percent by volume re-refined oil and less than five parts per million (ppm) of chlorinated compounds. Their metal content must be less than 25 ppm, with no single metal exceeding 5 ppm. Their safety and performance specifications must meet or exceed accepted North American standards for lubricating oil, as established by the Canadian General Standards Board, the Society of Automotive Engineers, and the American Petroleum Institute.

SHOPPING BAGS

In 1989, 3.14 billion plastic and 53 million kraft paper shopping bags were produced in Canada. Their production consumed 28.5 million kilograms of plastic and 4.8 million kilograms of paper, respectively. While some of these bags are reused for other purposes, most regular plastic and paper shopping bags do not have the strength to endure many uses. As a result, most are discarded.

EcoLogo Qualifications. To qualify for the EcoLogo, a reusable shopping bag must be made of strong and durable material, either natural or synthetic, and have a minimum capacity of 15,000 cubic centimeters. It must be able to endure at least 300 uses carrying 10 kilograms under wet conditions. It must be made of material that will not release hazardous or toxic substances during the life of the bag. The bag must also be washable at home.

VENTILATORS

Newly constructed or renovated houses, which are generally more airtight than older houses, require mechanical ventilation to remove excess humidity and provide fresh air for the occupants. However, ventilation systems that operate either by exhausting air from a house or forcing fresh air into it cause a substantial amount of heat to escape. This heat loss can cause a noticeable increase in energy consumption and heating costs.

Heat recovery ventilators (HRVs) balance the removal of stale air with a supply of fresh air. In the process they typically recover as much as 50 to 70 percent of the heat that would otherwise be lost through the use of other mechanical ventilation systems. To realize the full potential energy savings, HRVs must be used in airtight houses that require mechanical ventilation systems.

EcoLogo Qualifications. Qualifying ventilators must recover 75 percent of the heat contained in the outgoing air at 9 degrees C. In addition, they must have a maximum exhaust air transfer ratio of 5 percent when tested according to the Canadian Standards Association (CSA) Standard CAN/CSA-C439-88. To qualify for the EcoLogo, an HRV must meet the technical requirements specific to its subcategory: heat pipe, flat pipe, rotary wheel, concentric tube, and capillary blower.

PROPOSED GUIDELINES

Five draft guidelines were released to the public by Environment Canada for a review period of 60 days, which began April 18 and ended June 17, 1992.

Domestic Storage Tank Water Heaters. Heating water accounts for as much as 40 to 60 percent of a home's total energy use. As well, the polyurethane foam used to insulate some water heaters requires a blowing agent, usually ozone-depleting CFCs. The draft guideline proposes that eligible storage tank water heaters, whether run on propane, gas, oil, or electricity, must be energy efficient and manufactured without the use of harmful blowing agents.

Building Materials: Acoustical Products. Acoustical products are increasingly used in buildings to dampen the growing noise levels especially evident in towns and cities. These acoustical products include thermal insulation, ceiling tiles, glass fiber board, and mineral wool board. In addition to meeting technical sound absorption criteria, the draft guideline stipulates that these products must contain 100 percent recycled materials if made from cellulose fiber, and over 50 percent if made from other materials.

Dry Cleaning Services. Most dry cleaning services use either perchloroethylene or hydrocarbon solvents in their operations. These solvents contaminate waste water and can bind to the organic component of soils and sediments. From there the chemicals can leach into the ground water, or they may be absorbed by aquatic organisms. As well, hydrocarbon solvent emissions contribute to low-level ozone (smog). Under the proposed guideline, eligible dry cleaning services must support a means to recirculate used cooling water, a system to contain solvent spills, a set level of solvent used per weight of articles cleaned, a reusable fabric bag packaging system or a program to collect and deliver plastic bags to recycling services, and a program to reuse hangers.

Building Materials: Thermal Insulation. Thermal insulation products (board-type, loose-fill, spray-on, and batt-type) are made from materials such as cellulose, mineral wool, glass fiber, or plastics. Products certified under the program must contain set levels of recycled material, ranging from 100 percent to 25 percent, depending on the type of insulation. However, no matter what the type of insulation, it should not be manufactured using ozone-depleting chemicals.

Toner Cartridges. This draft guideline sets criteria for companies which renew, refurbish, refill, and resell conventional single-use cartridges. To qualify for the EcoLogo, renewed cartridges must carry a warranty on the replacement drum good for at least eight uses. Unusable cartridge parts must be transported to recycling centers and reused in new cartridges.

Source:

Environmental Choice Program, 107 Sparks Street, Suite 200, Ottawa, Ontario KIA 0H3, Tel:(613)952-9440, Fax:(613)952-9465.

Environmental Seals, Green Cross (Scientific Certification Systems)

Scientific Certification Systems (SCS) is a neutral scientific organization established to independently verify environmental claims made by companies about the products they sell in the marketplace. At the request (and expense) of a company, SCS verifies environmental claims. SCS allows the use of its Green Cross emblem on certified products. Examples of specific claims that may be certified by SCS include the following:

Recycled Content. The recycled content in a given product (including both post-consumer and pre-consumer waste material) must be in the top 80th percentile documented for that industry. Additionally, the product must meet performance standards comparable to its virgin material counterpart.

Biodegradability. Soaps, detergents, and cleansers can be certified if they biodegrade under aerobic and anaerobic conditions, with no evidence of toxic buildup in the environment.

Energy Efficiency. Products can be certified if manufactured for maximum energy savings during use.

Sustainable Forestry Management. Products can be certified if derived from materials (e.g., wood) obtained from forests managed under certified sustainable forestry management systems.

An example of a typical Green Cross emblem appears below:

TERMINOLOGY

SCS uses the following definitions for some common environmental terms in its certification program:

Pre-Consumer. A product or package which has been discarded by an individual, commercial enterprise, or other public or private entity after having fulfilled its intended application or use.

Pre-Consumer Waste (Pre-Consumer Recovered Industrial Material). A material which has been generated as a by-product of a given process which has properties significantly different than those of the original material and therefore, in its current form, cannot be recycled back through the same general process.

Industrial Scrap. In contrast to pre-consumer waste, industrial scrap is a material which has been generated as a by-product of a given process which has properties allowing it to be recycled back through the same general process.

ENVIRONMENTAL REPORT CARD

SCS also has a program whereby it will evaluate a company's product and packaging through the use of a life cycle inventory. This process collects information about the environmental burdens associated with each stage of the product's manufacture, distribution, use, and disposal. This data is then compiled into an SCS *Environmental Report Card.* An example of the proposed *Environmental Report Card* appears below:

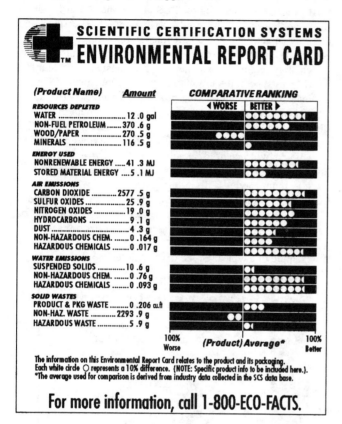

PERSONAL ENVIRONMENTAL REPORT CARD

Under this program consumers fill out a questionnaire about a wide range of daily activities, such as the type of transportation they use, the miles they commute, the products they purchase, and the food they eat. This information is analyzed to calculate the total amount of resources, energy, air pollution, water pollution and solid waste associated with these activities on a weekly basis. *The Personal Environmental Report Card* rates the consumer's environmental profile against that of the average American. Consumers also receive a detailed breakdown of how much each activity contributes to the total environmental load.

Source:

Scientific Certification Systems, 1611 Telegraph Ave., Suite 1111, Oakland, CA 94612-2113, Telephone (510) 832-14115, Fax (510) 832-0359.

Environmental Seals, Green Seal

Green Seal is an independent, nonprofit organization dedicated to reducing the environmental impacts of consumer products. It sets environmental standards and allows the use of its certification mark (see below) on products found to meet them. The goal of Green Seal's standards is to reduce significant environmental impacts of products. Depending on the product, Green Seal's standards seek to reduce or eliminate toxic chemical pollution, improve energy efficiency, protect water resources, minimize impacts on fish and wildlife and their habitat, reduce the destruction of natural areas, cut the waste of natural resources, protect the Earth's atmosphere (including its protective ozone layer), and reduce the risk of global warming.

Green Seal has designated Underwriter's Laboratories (UL) as its primary testing and factory inspection contractor. Where appropriate, UL also offers assistance to Green Seal in the development of its standards. For a majority of Green Seal product categories, UL will conduct the necessary testing and factory inspection to determine whether the product meets Green Seal's environmental standards. For each product tested, UL provides Green Seal with a written report that details the results of the examination. Once a product is found to meet the appropriate standard, the manufacturer signs an agreement before being authorized to use the Green Seal on products, packaging, and in advertising. An example of the Green Seal appears below:

As of June 1992, Green Seal reports progress in the following product categories:

PUBLISHED STANDARDS

Energy-Efficient Lighting (compact fluorescent lamps)-GS-5
Printing and Writing Papers-GS-7
Re-refined Engine Oil-GS-3
Tissue Paper (bathroom and facial tissue)-GS-1
Water-Efficient Fixtures-GS-6

STANDARDS UNDER DEVELOPMENT

Household Cleaners
Laundry Detergents

Newsprint
Paint
Paper Towels and Napkins
Printing Inks
Windows

STANDARDS UNDER CONSIDERATION

Batteries
Composting Systems
Energy-Conserving Appliances
Laundry Detergents
Reusable Shopping Bags

Source:
Green Seal, Suite 275, 1250 23rd Street NW, Washington, DC 20037-1101,
    Telephone (202) 331-7337.

Formaldehyde

Formaldehyde is an important industrial chemical used to make other chemicals, building materials, and household products. It is one of the large family of chemical compounds called volatile organic compounds, or VOCs. The term volatile means that the compound vaporizes becomes a gas at normal room temperature. Formaldehyde serves many purposes in products. It is used as a part of the following:

- the glue or adhesive in pressed wood products (particle board, hardwood plywood, and fiberboard);
- preservatives in some paints, coatings, and cosmetics;
- the coating that provides permanent press quality to fabrics and draperies;
- the finish used to coat paper products; and
- certain insulation materials (urea-formaldehyde foam insulation).

Formaldehyde is released into the air by burning wood, kerosene, or natural gas, by automobiles, and by cigarettes. Formaldehyde can off-gas from materials made with it. It is also a naturally occurring substance.

Formaldehyde is a colorless, strong-smelling gas. When present in the air at levels above 0.1 ppm (parts per million parts of air), it can cause watery eyes; burning sensations in the eyes, nose, and throat; nausea; coughing; chest tightness; wheezing; skin rashes; and allergic reactions. It also causes cancer in humans.

Formaldehyde can affect people differently. Some people are very sensitive to formaldehyde while others may not have any noticeable reaction to the same level.

Persons have developed allergic reactions (allergic skin disease and hives) to formaldehyde through skin contact with solutions of formaldehyde or durable-press clothing containing formaldehyde. Others have developed asthmatic reactions and skin rashes from exposure to formaldehyde.

Formaldehyde is normally present at low levels, usually less than 0.03 ppm , in both outdoor and indoor air. The outdoor air in rural areas has lower concentrations while urban areas have higher concentrations. Residences or offices that contain products that release formaldehyde to the air can have formaldehyde levels of greater than 0.03 ppm. Products that may add formaldehyde to the air include particleboard used as subflooring or shelving, fiberboard in cabinets and furniture, plywood wall panels, and urea-formaldehyde as insulation. As formaldehyde levels increase, illness or discomfort is more likely to occur and may be more serious.

Efforts have been made by both the government and industry to reduce exposure to formaldehyde. The Consumer Product Safety Commission (CPSC) voted to ban urea-formaldehyde foam insulation, but that ban was overturned in the courts. However, these actions greatly reduced the residential use of the product. CPSC, the Department of Housing and Urban Development, and other federal agencies are working with the pressed wood industry to further reduce the release of the chemical from their products. However, it would be unrealistic to expect to completely remove formaldehyde from the air. Some persons who are extremely sensitive to formaldehyde may need to reduce or stop using these products.

Formaldehyde levels in the indoor air depend mainly on what is releasing the formaldehyde (the source), the temperature, the humidity, and the air exchange rate (the amount of outdoor air entering or leaving the indoor area). Increasing the flow of outdoor air to the inside decreases the formaldehyde levels. Decreasing this flow of outdoor air by sealing the residence or office increases the formaldehyde in the indoor air.

As the temperature rises, more formaldehyde comes off from the product. The reverse is also true; less formaldehyde comes off at lower temperature. Humidity also affects the release of formaldehyde from the product. As humidity rises, more formaldehyde is released.

The formaldehyde levels in a residence change with the season and from day to day and day to night. Levels may be high on a hot and humid day and low on a cool, dry day. Understanding these factors is important when you consider measuring the levels of formaldehyde.

Some sources—such as pressed wood products containing urea-formaldehyde glues, urea-formaldehyde foam insulation, durable-press fabrics, and draperies—release more formaldehyde when new. As they age, the formaldehyde release decreases.

SOURCES

Carpets and Gypsum Board. Products such as carpets or gypsum board do not contain formaldehyde when new. They may trap formaldehyde emitted from other sources and later release the formaldehyde into the indoor air when the temperature and humidity change.

Combustion Sources. Burning materials such as wood, kerosene, cigarettes, and natural gas, and operating internal combustion engines (e.g. automobiles), produces small quantities of formaldehyde. Combustion sources add small amounts of formaldehyde to indoor air.

Cosmetics, Paints, Coatings, and Some Wet-Strength Paper Products. The amount of formaldehyde present in these products is small and is of slight concern. However, persons sensitive to formaldehyde may have allergic reactions.

Durable-Press Fabrics, Draperies, and Coated Paper Products. In the early 1960s there were several reports of allergic reactions to formaldehyde from durable-press fabrics and coated paper products. Such reports have declined in recent years as industry has taken steps to reduce formaldehyde levels. Draperies made of formaldehyde-treated durable-press fabrics may add slightly to indoor formaldehyde levels.

Pressed Wood Products. Pressed wood products, especially those containing urea-formaldehyde glues, are a source of formaldehyde. These products include particleboard used in subfloors, shelves, cabinets, and furniture, plywood wall panels, and medium-density fiberboard used in drawers, cabinets, and furniture. Medium-density fiberboard, which contains a higher glue content, has the potential to release the most formaldehyde.

Urea-Formaldehyde Foam Insulation. During the 1970s, many home owners installed this insulation to save energy. Many of these houses had high levels of formaldehyde soon afterwards. Sale of urea-formaldehyde foam insulation has largely stopped. Formaldehyde release from this product decreases rapidly after the first few months and reaches background levels in a few years. Therefore, urea-formaldehyde foam insulation installed 5 to 10 years ago is unlikely to still release formaldehyde.

Source:
Consumer Product Safety Commission, *An Update on Formaldehyde,* Washington: Government Printing Office, 1990.

Hazardous Substances and Articles

Combustible. Any substance having a flash point at or above 100 degrees F to and including 150 degrees F under controlled test conditions.

Corrosive. Any substance which in contact with living tissue will cause destruction of tissue by chemical action, but shall not refer to action on inanimate surfaces.

Extremely Flammable Contents of Self-Pressurized Container. The contents of a self-pressurized container, when tested under controlled conditions, produces a flashback (a flame extending back to the dispenser) at any degree of valve opening and flash point.

Extremely Flammable Solid. A solid substance that ignites and burns at an ambient temperature of 80 degrees F or less when subjected to friction, percussion, or electrical spark under controlled test conditions.

Extremely Flammable. Applies to a substance which has a flash point at or below 20 degrees F under controlled test conditions.

Extremely Hazardous Substance. Any of 406 chemicals identified by Environment Protection Agency on the basis of toxicity and listed under Superfund Amendments and Reauthorization Act of 1986 (SARA) Title III. The list is subject to revision.

Flammable Contents of Self-Pressurized Container. The contents of a self-pressurized container, when tested under controlled conditions, produces a flame projection exceeding 18 inches at full valve opening or produces a flashback at any degree of valve opening.

Flammable Solid. A solid that ignites and burns with a self-sustained flame at a rate greater than $1/10$ inch per second along its major axis under controlled test conditions.

Flammable. Any substance having a flash point above 20 deg. F and below 100 degrees F under controlled test conditions.

Flash Point. The lowest temperature of the sample at which application of a test flame causes the vapor of the sample to ignite under specified conditions of test. The sample is deemed to have flashed when a large flame appears and instantaneously propagates itself over the surface of the sample.

Hazardous Substance. Any substance (or mixture of substances) which is toxic, corrosive, an irritant, a strong sensitizer, flammable or combustible, or generates pressure through decomposition, heat, or other means, which may cause substantial personal injury or substantial illness during or as a proximate result of any customary or reasonably foreseeable handling or use, including reasonably foreseeable ingestion by children. Any radioactive substance sufficiently hazardous to require labeling. Any toy which presents an electrical, mechanical, or thermal hazard. Substances otherwise regulated by the government, such as pesticides and drugs, are excluded from this definition.

Highly Toxic. Any substance which produces death within 14 days in half or more than half of a group of laboratory white rats weighing between 200 and 300 grams, at a single dose of 50 milligrams or less per kilogram of body weight, when orally administered, or produces death within 14 days in half or more than half of a group of rats when inhaled continuously for a period of 1 hour or less, or produces death within 14 days in half or more than half of a group of rabbits tested in a dosage of 200 milligrams or less per kilogram of body weight, when administered by continuous contact with the bare skin for 24 hours or less.

Irritant. Any substance not corrosive which on immediate, prolonged, or repeated contact with normal living tissue will induce a local inflammatory reaction.

Sensitizer. A substance that will induce an immunologically-mediated (allergic) response, including allergic photosensitivity. This allergic reaction will become evident upon reexposure to the same substance. Occasionally, a sensitizer will induce and elicit an allergic response on the first exposure by virtue of active sensitization.

Strong Sensitizer. A substance which will cause on normal living tissue, through an allergic or photodynamic process, a hypersensitivity which becomes evident on reapplication of the same substance and which is designated as such by the Consumer Product Safety Commission.

Toxic. Has the capacity to produce personal injury or illness to man through ingestion, inhalation, or absorption through any body surface.

Source:
Consumer Product Safety Commission, "Hazardous Substances and Articles; Administration and Enforcement Regulations," 16 CFR part 1500 (1992), Washington: Government Printing Office.

Hazardous Substances Labeling Guide

The Consumer Product Safety Commission (CPSC) developed the following labeling guidelines to aid their area offices in answering questions regarding labeling of hazardous substances. They are intended to serve as guides only and are not to be regarded as absolute. They may be revised from time to time so it is important to consult the CPSC on these statements before using them on a product label.

Unless otherwise indicated, the cautionary statements are intended for straight chemicals and cannot necessarily be extrapolated to mixtures.

ACETIC ACID (50 PERCENT+)

Same labeling as HCl (10 percent+).
Concentrations less that 50 percent, or mixtures, require biological testing. 5-10 percent probably not hazardous.

ACETONE

DANGER: EXTREMELY FLAMMABLE.
Contains acetone.
Do not use or store near heat, sparks, or flame.
Use only in a well-ventilated area. Avoid contact with eyes and prolonged contact with skin.
First Aid
Eyes. In case of contact with eyes, flush thoroughly with water. If irritation persists get medical attention.
Keep out of the reach of children.
(Acetone is not toxic by inhalation, ingestion or skin absorption.)

ALCOHOL (DENATURED)

(With less than 5 percent methanol.)
WARNING: FLAMMABLE.
Contains denatured alcohol.
Do not use near heat or flame.
Avoid contact with eyes.
First Aid
Eyes. In case of eye contact, flush thoroughly with water. If irritation persists, get medical attention.
Keep out of the reach of children.

ALUM

(Aluminum Ammonium Sulfate.)
(Aluminum Potassium Sulfate.)
WARNING: HARMFUL IF SWALLOWED.
Contains aluminum potassium sulfate.
First Aid
Internal. If swallowed, give water and call physician.
Keep out of the reach of children.

AMMONIA (3-5 PERCENT)

WARNING: IRRITANT.
HARMFUL IF SWALLOWED.
Contains ammonia.
Do not mix with chlorine type bleaches or other household chemicals.
Avoid contact with eyes and prolonged contact with skin.
First Aid
External. Flood with water, then wash with vinegar. For eyes, flush thoroughly with water and get medical attention.
Internal. Give 1 or 2 glasses of water. Follow with citrus fruit juice, if available. Call physician.
Keep out of the reach of children.
(Less than 3 percent probable eye irritant but need biological test data.)

AMMONIA (5-25 PERCENT)

POISON: MAY CAUSE BURNS.
Contains ammonia.
Do not mix with chlorine type bleaches or other household chemicals.
Avoid contact with eyes and prolonged contact with skin.
First Aid
External. Flood with water, then wash with vinegar. For eyes, flush thoroughly with water, preferably warm, for at least 15 minutes. Then get prompt medical attention.
Internal. Give large quantities of water. Follow with fruit juice and vegetable oil. Get prompt medical attention.
Keep out of the reach of children.

AMMONIA (OVER 25 PERCENT); (CONCENTRATED)

POISON: CAUSES SEVERE BURNS.
MAY BE FATAL IF SWALLOWED.
Contains ammonia.
Avoid contact with skin, eyes, mucous membranes, and clothing.
Avoid breathing vapor.
Do not mix with chlorine type bleaches or other household chemicals.
First Aid
External. Flood with water then wash with vinegar.
Internal. Give several glasses of water. Follow with citrus fruit juice, if available. Follow with vegetable oil.
Eyes. In case of contact with eyes, wash thoroughly with water for 15 minutes. Get prompt medical attention.
Keep out of the reach of children.

AMMONIUM CHLORIDE

Not hazardous.

AMMONIUM NITRATE (REFRIGERATING DEVICE)

WARNING: HARMFUL IF SWALLOWED.

Contains ammonium nitrate.

(*) Use great care to prevent contamination of foods and beverages.

Keep away from fire, open flame, excessive heat, or combustible materials.

First Aid

> *Internal.* If swallowed, give 1 to 2 glasses of water and induce vomiting.
>
> Call physician immediately.

Keep out of the reach of children.

May also be medical device (cold pack).

(*) Use if intended for food cooler.

AMMONIUM SULFATE

CAUTION: HARMFUL IF SWALLOWED.

Contains ammonium sulfate.

Keep out of the reach of children.

AMYL ACETATE

In the absence of date indicating it is not an eye irritant, suggest:

WARNING: IRRITANT, COMBUSTIBLE.

Contains amyl acetate.

Keep away from heat and flame.

Avoid contact with eyes and prolonged contact with skin.

First Aid

> In case of contact flush thoroughly with water.

Keep out of reach of children.

(Not toxic by ingestion, inhalation, or skin absorption.)

AROMATIC HYDROCARBONS

(Other than benzene, toluene, or xylene.)

Same as Petroleum Distillates (aliphatic).

BENZOIC ACID

WARNING: HARMFUL IF SWALLOWED.

Contains benzoic acid.

First Aid

> *Internal.* If swallowed, give 1 or 2 glasses of water.
>
> Induce vomiting and call physician.

Keep out of the reach of children.

BENZENE (BENZOL; 5 PERCENT+)

DANGER: POISON (SKULL & CROSSBONES).

EXTREMELY FLAMMABLE. VAPOR HARMFUL.

Contains benzol.

Keep away from heat, sparks, and flames.

Keep container closed.

(*) Use only in well-ventilated area.

Avoid prolonged or repeated contact with skin and breathing of vapors.

First Aid

> *Internal.* If swallowed, do not induce vomiting.
>
> Call physician immediately.

Keep out of the reach of children.

(*) Consider voluntary supplemental statement "... preferably outdoors." When intended for use in large quantities at a time, may require additional labeling regarding pilot lights, etc.

BENZETHONIUM CHLORIDE

WARNING: HARMFUL IF SWALLOWED. IRRITANT.

Contains benzethonium chloride.

Avoid prolonged contact with skin and contact with eyes.

First Aid

> *Internal.* If swallowed, give 1 or 2 glasses of water, and induce vomiting. Call physician immediately.
>
> *Eyes.* In case of contact with eyes, flush with water for 15 minutes. Get prompt medical attention.

Keep out of the reach of children.

Eye irritant at ½ percent.

BENZOYL PEROXIDE (50 PERCENT IN DIBUTYL PHTHALATE)

WARNING: IRRITANT.

Contains benzoyl peroxide.

Avoid contact with eyes and prolonged contact with skin.

First Aid

> *External.* In case of contact, flush skin thoroughly with water for 15 minutes.
>
> *Internal.* If swallowed, induce vomiting. Call physician immediately.
>
> *Eyes.* For eyes, flush thoroughly with water for 15 minutes; get prompt medical attention.

Keep out of the reach of children.

BICHLORIDE OF MERCURY

DANGER: POISON (Skull and Crossbones)

CAUSES SEVERE BURNS.

MAY BE FATAL IF SWALLOWED.

Contains bichloride of mercury.

Do not breathe dust.

Avoid contact with eyes and mucous membranes and prolonged contact with skin.

Wash hands thoroughly after use.

First Aid

> *External.* For contact with skin, flush thoroughly with water.
>
> *Internal.* If swallowed, give milk or egg whites. Call physician immediately.
>
> *Eyes.* For contact with eyes, flush thoroughly with water. Get prompt medical attention

Keep out of the reach of children.

("POISON" and {Skull and Crossbones symbol} may be on rear panel.)

BLEACH (SODIUM HYPOCHLORITE APPROX. 5 PERCENT)

CAUTION: IRRITANT.

Contains sodium hypochlorite.

Avoid contact with eyes and other mucous membranes.
Do not mix with acids or other household chemicals.
First Aid
> *Internal*. If swallowed, give 1 or 2 glasses of water. Call
>> physician immediately.
> *Eyes*. In case of contact with eyes flush thoroughly with water.
>> If irritation persists get medical attention.

Keep out of the reach of children.
(For over 5 percent, see *Hypochlorite, Ca or Na*)

BORAX

CAUTION: EYE IRRITANT.
Contains borax.
Avoid contact with eyes.
First Aid
> *Eyes*. In case of contact with eyes, flush eyes with water for 15
>> minutes and get medical attention.

Keep out of the reach of children.

BORIC ACID

WARNING: HARMFUL IF SWALLOWED.
Contains boric acid.
First Aid
> *Internal*. If swallowed give 1 or 2 glasses of water, then induce
>> vomiting. Call physician.

Keep out of the reach of children.

BUTANE (LIGHTER FUEL)

DANGER: EXTREMELY FLAMMABLE.
CONTENTS UNDER PRESSURE.
Contains butane.
Do not use near sparks or flame.*
Do not puncture or incinerate container or store at temperatures
> above 120 degrees F.

Keep out of the reach of children.
*Not necessary for disposable insert cartridge containers.

BUTYL ALCOHOL

WARNING: HARMFUL IF SWALLOWED. COMBUSTIBLE.
VAPOR HARMFUL. IRRITANT.
Contains butyl alcohol.
Avoid contact with eyes.
Use in a well-ventilated area. Keep away from heat or flame.
First Aid
> *Internal*. If swallowed, give 1 or 2 glasses of water, then
>> induce vomiting. Call physician.
> *Eyes.* In case of contact with eyes flush with water for 15
>> minutes.

Keep out of the reach of children.
For Butanol: Same as above except "FLAMMABLE" rather than
> "COMBUSTIBLE."

BUTYL CELLOSOLVE (ETHYLENE GLYCOL MONOBUTYL ETHER)

WARNING: HARMFUL IF SWALLOWED OR ABSORBED
> THROUGH SKIN.

VAPOR HARMFUL IRRITANT TO SKIN AND EYES.
Contains butyl cellosolve.
Use only in well-ventilated area. Avoid breathing of vapor and
> prolonged or repeated contact with skin. Keep away from
> eyes.

First Aid
> *External*. Flush with water for 15 minutes. Get prompt medi-
>> cal attention.
> *Internal*. If swallowed, give 1 or 2 glasses of water and call a
>> physician.
> *Eyes*. Flush with water for 15 minutes. Get prompt medical
>> attention.

Keep out of the reach of children.

CADMIUM SILVER SOLDERS

WARNING: POISONOUS FUMES MAY BE FORMED ON
> HEATING.

Contains cadmium.
Do not breathe fumes.
Use only with adequate exhaust ventilation.
First Aid
> If chest pain, cough, or fever develops after use, call physician
>> immediately.

Keep children away when using.

CALCIUM CARBIDE

WARNING: MAY CAUSE SKIN AND EYE IRRITATION.
HARMFUL IF SWALLOWED.
Contains calcium carbide.
First Aid
> *External*. In case of contact, flush skin thoroughly with water.
> *Internal*. If swallowed, give water and call physician immedi-
>> ately.
> *Eyes*. In case of contact, flush eyes thoroughly with water, get
>> prompt medical attention.

Keep out of the reach of children.

CALCIUM CHLORIDE (ANHYDROUS)

CAUTION: HARMFUL IF SWALLOWED.
IRRITANT.
Contains calcium chloride.
Avoid prolonged contact with skin.
First Aid
> *Internal*. If swallowed give 1 or 2 glasses of water and call
>> physician immediately.

Keep out of the reach of children.

CALCIUM HYDROXIDE (HYDRATED LIME) (SLAKED LIME)

CAUTION: INJURIOUS TO EYES.
PROLONGED CONTACT WITH WET SKIN MAY PRODUCE
    BURNS.
Contains hydrated lime.
First Aid
    External. In case of skin contact, flush thoroughly with water.
    Eyes. In case of contact with eyes, flush with water for 15
        minutes. Get prompt medical attention.
Keep out of the reach of children.

CALCIUM HYPOCHLORITE

See *Hypochlorite (Sodium or Calcium).*

CALCIUM OXIDE (QUICKLIME)

DANGER: MAY CAUSE BURNS.
HARMFUL IF SWALLOWED.
Contains quicklime.
Avoid contact with skin and eyes.
First Aid
    External. In case of contact with skin, flush thoroughly with
        water.
    Internal. If swallowed, give large quantities of water. Follow
        with citrus fruit juices, if available. Call physician imme-
        diately.
    Eyes. In case of contact with eyes, flush thoroughly with
        water, get medical attention.
Keep out of the reach of children.

CASTOR BEANS

WARNING:
    MAY BE HARMFUL OR FATAL IF SWALLOWED.
First Aid
    Internal. If swallowed, induce vomiting. Call physician im-
        mediately.
Keep out of the reach of children.

CAUSTIC SODA

(See *Sodium Hydroxide.*)

CARBON BISULFIDE (CARBON DISULFIDE)

DANGER: MAY BE FATAL IF INHALED OR SWALLOWED.
EXTREMELY FLAMMABLE.
Contains carbon bisulfide.
Keep away from heat, sparks, or open flame.
Do not get into eyes, on skin, or on clothing.
Use only in a well-ventilated area.
Store in a cool place and keep container closed.
First Aid

Inhalation. Remove to fresh air and give artificial respiration
    if necessary.
External. Flush skin with plenty of water.
Internal Give several glasses of water and induce vomiting.
    Call physician.
Eyes. Flush eyes with plenty of water, get medical attention.
Keep out of the reach of children.

CELLOSOLVE ACETATE

WARNING: EYE IRRITANT.
Contains cellosolve acetate.
First Aid
    Eyes. In case of contact with eyes, flush with water for 15
        minutes and get medical attention.
Keep out of the reach of children.

CHARCOAL LIGHTER FUEL (PETROLEUM DISTILLATE TYPE, FLASH POINT 80-150 DEGREES F)

DANGER: HARMFUL OR FATAL IF SWALLOWED.
COMBUSTIBLE.
Contains petroleum distillates.
Do not use on burning or glowing coals. Store away from heat or
    flame.
Use in a well-ventilated area.
Avoid prolonged contact with skin.
First Aid
    Internal. If swallowed, do not induce vomiting. Call physician
        immediately.
Keep out of the reach of children.
Note: Requires safety packaging if viscosity is 100 SUS or less.
(16 CFR 1700.14(a)(7))

CHEMISTRY SETS

Suggested warning statements for individual containers of chemi-
    cals in chemistry sets.
**Boric acid, borax, sodium nitrate, potassium chloride, alumi-
num sulfate**
(and other chemicals where the only hazard is oral toxicity).
WARNING:
Read _____ panel before using.
HARMFUL IF SWALLOWED. IRRITANT.
First Aid
    External. In case of contact, flush freely with water.
    Internal. If swallowed, give water. Induce vomiting and call
        physician.
    Eyes. In case of contact, flush freely with water, get medical
        attention.
Keep out of the reach of small children.
Ferric ammonium sulfate, ferrous sulfate
(and other substances which are both toxic orally and irritant).
WARNING:
Read _____ panel before using.
HARMFUL IF SWALLOWED. IRRITANT.
First Aid

External. In case of contact, flush freely with water.

Internal. If swallowed, give water. Induce vomiting and call physician.

Eyes. In case of contact, flush freely with water, get medical attention.

Keep out of the reach of small children.

Cobalt chloride

(and other chemicals which are in the more toxic range but not *highly toxic*).

WARNING:

Read _____ panel before using.

MAY BE FATAL IF SWALLOWED.

First Aid

Internal. If swallowed, give water. Induce vomiting and call physician immediately.

Keep out of the reach of small children.

Copper carbonate

(very toxic as well as irritating).

WARNING:

Read _____ panel before using.

MAY BE FATAL IF SWALLOWED. IRRITANT.

First Aid

External. In case of external contact, flush freely with water.

Internal. If swallowed, give water. Induce vomiting and call physician immediately.

Eyes. For eyes, flush freely with water, get medical attention.

Keep out of the reach of small children.

Calcium oxide

DANGER:

Read _____ panel before using.

MAY CAUSE BURNS.

First Aid

External. In case of external contact, flush freely with water.

Internal. If swallowed, give several glasses of water. Follow with citrus fruit juice, if available. Call physician immediately.

Eyes. In case of contact, flush freely with water, get medical attention.

Keep out of the reach of small children.

Ethyl alcohol

(and other chemicals having as sole hazards flammability with flash point 20 to 80 degrees F., and mild eye irritant).

WARNING:

Read _____ panel before using.

FLAMMABLE.

Keep from heat or flame.

First Aid

Eyes. In case of contact with eyes, flush with water.

Keep out of the reach of small children.

(or its practical equivalent)

Sodium bisulfate, calcium hypochlorite

and other chemicals subject to regulation 1500.129.

POISON:

Read _____ panel before using.

CAUSES BURNS.

First Aid

External. In case of accidental contact, flush freely with water.

Internal. If swallowed, give water and call physician

immediately.

Eyes. In case of contact, flush freely with water, get medical attention.

Keep out of the reach of small children.

In addition, the calcium hypochlorite label should bear a statement such as "Do not mix with acids."

Note: In each case, it is understood that the container is also labeled with the name of the chemical.

Chlorinated Lime

DANGER: MAY CAUSE BURNS.

Contains chlorinated lime.

Avoid contact with eyes and mucous membranes and prolonged contact with skin.

First Aid

Internal. If swallowed, give 1 or 2 glasses of water, follow with raw eggs, and call physician.

Eyes. In case of contact with eyes, flush thoroughly with water. Get prompt medical attention.

Keep out of the reach of children.

(Suspect corrosive. Suggest this labeling in the absence of test data to the contrary.)

Chloroform

WARNING: VAPOR HARMFUL. IRRITANT. HARMFUL IF SWALLOWED.

Contains chloroform.

Avoid contact with eyes and prolonged contact with skin.

Use only in a well-ventilated area.

First Aid

External. In case of contact with skin, flush thoroughly with water.

Internal. If swallowed, induce vomiting, call physician.

Eyes. In case of contact, flush freely with water, get medical attention.

Keep out of the reach of children.

CIGARETTE LIGHTER FUEL

(Petroleum distillate, Flash Point 20 to 80 degrees F.)

DANGER: HARMFUL OR FATAL IF SWALLOWED. FLAMMABLE.

Contains petroleum naphtha.

Use with care to avoid accidental fire.

First Aid

Internal. If swallowed, do not induce vomiting. Call physician immediately.

Keep out of the reach of children.

Note: Requires safety packaging (16 CFR 1700.14 (a)(7)).

See labeling exemption for cigarette lighters (16 CFR 1500.83 (a)(20)).

COBALT CHLORIDE

WARNING: MAY BE FATAL IF SWALLOWED.

Contains cobalt chloride.

First Aid

Internal. If swallowed, give one or two glasses of water, induce vomiting and call physician immediately.

Keep out of the reach of children.

CONTACT BOND CEMENT

(See 16CFR 1500.133.) (Banned 16 CFR 1302.)
DANGER:EXTREMELY FLAMMABLE.
VAPORS MAY CAUSE FLASH FIRE.
Vapors may ignite explosively.
Prevent buildup of vapors—open all windows and doors—use only with cross ventilation.
Keep away from heat, sparks, and open flame. Do not smoke. Extinguish all flames and pilot lights. Turn off stoves, heaters, electric motors, and other sources of ignition during use and until all vapors are gone.
Close container after use.
Keep out of the reach of children.

COPPER CHLORIDE

See *Copper Sulfate.*

COPPER SULFATE (25 PERCENT AND UP)

CAUTION:IRRITANT.
HARMFUL IF SWALLOWED.
Contains copper sulfate.
Avoid contact with eyes and prolonged contact with skin.
First Aid
    External. In case of contact with skin, flush thoroughly with water.
    Internal. If swallowed, give water and call physician.
    Eyes. In case of contact, flush freely with water, get medical attention.
Keep out of the reach of children.
Note: At lower concentrations, animal testing indicated.

CRESYLIC ACID

(Approximately 17.5 percent or more.)
DANGER: CAUSES SEVERE BURNS.
MAY BE FATAL IF SWALLOWED.
Contains cresylic acid.
Avoid contact with eyes and mucous membranes and prolonged contact with skin.
First Aid
    External. Flush with water for 15 minutes.
    Internal. Give large quantities of water. Follow with beaten egg or vegetable oil. Call physician immediately.
    Eyes. In case of contact, flush freely with water, get medical attention.
Keep out of the reach of children.
(If contains 5 percent or more free Phenol, substitute "POISON" for "DANGER".)

CYANOACRYLATE GLUES

WARNING: EYE IRRITANT. INSTANTLY BONDS SKIN.*
Contains cyanoacrylate.
Immediate bonding of eye, skin, or mouth may occur upon contact.*
Avoid contact with eyes.

If bonding occurs to eye lids or lashes, get medical attention immediately.*
First Aid
    External. In case of skin bonding, avoid vigorous efforts to remove by mechanical means.* Quickly flush affected areas under running water.*
    Eyes. In case of contact with eyes, flush thoroughly with plenty of water and get prompt medical attention. Gently pry fingers apart by rolling a paper clip or pencil between the fingers and wedging them apart.*
Keep out of the reach of children.
Note: (See 16 CFR 1500.83 (a) (37)).
* The CPSC suggests that these statements, or their equivalent, be voluntarily included.

CYCLOHEXANONE

WARNING: HARMFUL IF SWALLOWED.
VAPOR HARMFUL. COMBUSTIBLE.
Contains cyclohexanone.
Do not use or store near heat or flame.
Avoid contact with eyes and prolonged contact with skin.
First Aid
    External. Flush skin thoroughly with water. If irritation continues, get medical attention.
    Internal. If swallowed, give 1 or 2 glasses of water and call physician.
    Eyes. Flush with plenty of water for 15 minutes. Get prompt medical attention.
Keep out of the reach of children.

DENATURED ALCOHOL

See *Alcohol (Denatured).*

DETERGENT LABELING

1. Detergents that are toxic and borderline eye irritants
CAUTION: HARMFUL IF SWALLOWED.
Contains _____.*
If swallowed, give water.
In case of eye contact, flush with water.
Call a physician.
Keep out of the reach of children.
2. Detergents that are toxic and are eye irritants
CAUTION: HARMFUL IF SWALLOWED. EYE IRRITANT.
Contains _____.*
If swallowed, give water.
In case of eye contact, flush with water.
Call a physician.
Keep out of the reach of children.
3. Detergents that are moderate eye irritants
CAUTION: EYE IRRITANT.
Contains _____.*
Avoid contact with eyes.
In case of eye contact, flush with water for 15 minutes and get medical attention.
Keep out of the reach of children.
4. Detergents that are toxic and severe eye irritants

WARNING: INJURIOUS TO EYES. HARMFUL IF SWAL-
LOWED.
Contains _____.*
Avoid contact with eyes and mucous membranes and prolonged
skin contact.
For eye contact, flush with water for 15 minutes.
Get prompt medical attention.
If swallowed, give large quantities or water.
Call a physician.
Keep out of the reach of children.

5. Detergents that are toxic and irritant to both eyes and skin
WARNING: INJURIOUS TO SKIN AND EYES. HARMFUL IF
SWALLOWED.
Contains _____*
Avoid contact with eyes and mucous membranes and prolonged
contact with skin.
In case of skin contact, flush with water.
For eye contact, flush with water for 15 minutes.
Get prompt medical attention.
If swallowed, give large quantities of water.
Call a physician.
Keep out of the reach of children.

6. Detergents that are toxic and corrosive to tissue
DANGER: MAY CAUSE BURNS TO SKIN AND EYES.
HARMFUL IF SWALLOWED.
Contains _____.*
Avoid contact with skin, eyes, and mucous membranes.
In case of skin contact, flush with water.
For eyes, flush with water for 15 minutes and get immediate
medical attention.
If swallowed, give large quantities of water.
Call physician immediately.
Keep out of the reach of children.
* Insert name of component or components that contribute sub-
stantially to the hazard. Use specific names, if possible, such
as *Sodium Lauryl Sulfate, Linear Alkyl Sulfonate, Sodium
metasilicate.*

DICHLOROBENZENE (ORTHO)

WARNING: MAY BE FATAL IF SWALLOWED.
IRRITATING TO SKIN AND EYES.
Contains orthodichlorobenzene.
Avoid contact with skin and eyes and prolonged breathing of
vapor.
First Aid
External. In case of contact with skin, flush with water for 15
minutes.
Internal. If swallowed, give 1 or 2 glasses of water and call
physician immediately.
Eyes. In case of contact with eyes, flush with water for 15
minutes. Get prompt medical attention.
Keep out of the reach of children.

DICHLOROBENZENE (PARA)

CAUTION: HARMFUL IF SWALLOWED.
Contains paradichlorobenzene.

First Aid
Internal. If swallowed, induce vomiting and call physician.
Keep out of the reach of children.

DIETHYLENE GLYCOL

WARNING: HARMFUL IF SWALLOWED.
Contains diethylene glycol.
First Aid
Internal. If swallowed, give 1 or 2 glasses of water. Induce
vomiting and call physician.
Keep out of the reach of children.
Note: See labeling exemption under CFR 16 1500.83 (a) (15).
Special labeling required per 16 CFR 1500.14 (b) (1).

DIETHYLENE TRIAMINE

See *Ethylene Diamine.*
Strong sensitizer per 16 CFR 1500.13(c).
Generally corrosive and toxic. Requires a strong labeling.

ETHANOL (ETHYL ALCOHOL)

See *Alcohol, Denatured.*

ETHYLENE DIAMINE

Strong sensitizer per 16 CFR 1500.13 (c).
Generally corrosive, toxic, and requires strong labeling.
Formerly used as epoxy resin hardener but now rarely used in non-
industrial products. If encountered, contact the Consumer
Product Safety Commission.

ETHYLENE DICHLORIDE (1,2 DICHLOROETHANE)

WARNING: MAY BE FATAL IF SWALLOWED.
VAPOR HARMFUL. FLAMMABLE.
Contains ethylene dichloride.
Keep away from heat or flame.
Use only in a well-ventilated area.
Do not breathe vapor or get on skin or in eyes.
First Aid
Internal. If swallowed, induce vomiting. Call physician at
once.
Keep out of the reach of children.

ETHYLENE GLYCOL (10 PERCENT OR MORE BY WEIGHT)

WARNING: HARMFUL OR FATAL IF SWALLOWED.
Contains ethylene glycol.
Do not let stand in open or unlabeled containers.
First Aid
Internal. If swallowed, give 1 or 2 glasses of water and induce
vomiting. Call physician immediately.
Keep out of the reach of children.
Liquid forms containing 10 percent or more by wt. require safety
packaging except those articles exempted from labeling by 16

CFR 1500.83.

Special labeling required per 16 CFR 1500.14 (b) (2). See also 16 CFR 1500.132.

If contains 0.3 percent sodium arsenite, it should be named.

Note: See labeling exemption under 16 CFR 1500.83 (a) (12) & (28).

ETHYLENE GLYCOL MONOMETHYL ETHER

WARNING: HARMFUL IF SWALLOWED OR ABSORBED THROUGH SKIN.

VAPOR HARMFUL.

COMBUSTIBLE.

Contains ethylene glycol monomethyl ether.

Avoid contact with skin and eyes.

Use in well-ventilated area.

Keep away from heat or flame.

First Aid

External. In case of contact with skin, flush thoroughly with water.

Internal. If swallowed, give 1 or 2 glasses of water and induce vomiting. Call physician.

Eyes. In case of contact with eyes, flush thoroughly with water and get medical attention.

Keep out of the reach of children.

ETHYL ETHER (PRESSURIZED CONTAINER*)

DANGER: EXTREMELY FLAMMABLE. CONTENTS UNDER PRESSURE.

Contains ethyl ether.

Keep away from heat, sparks, and open flame.

Use only in well-ventilated area.

Avoid contact with skin and eyes and avoid breathing of vapors.

Do not puncture or incinerate.

Do not store above 120 degrees F.

Keep out of the reach of children.

* Usually sold as automotive starting fluid.

FERRIC CHLORIDE (OVER 40 PERCENT)

DANGER: CAUSES SEVERE BURNS.

HARMFUL IF SWALLOWED.

Contains ferric chloride.

Avoid contact with eyes, skin, and mucous membranes.

First Aid

External. Flush with water for 15 minutes Call physician immediately.

Internal. If swallowed, give 1 or 2 glasses of water, then egg white. Call physician immediately.

Eyes. Flush with water for 15 minutes. Call physician immediately.

Keep out of the reach of children.

FORMALDEHYDE (1-5 PERCENT)

WARNING: HARMFUL IF SWALLOWED. IRRITANT.

Contains formaldehyde.

Keep away from eyes. Contact with skin may cause allergic irritation.

First Aid

External. In case of contact, flush skin or eyes thoroughly with water.

Internal. If swallowed give 1 or 2 glasses of water, induce vomiting. Call physician immediately.

Eyes. Flush eyes thoroughly with water. Get prompt medical attention.

Keep out of the reach of children.

Strong sensitizer at 1 percent or more (16 CFR 1500.13 (d).

FORMALDEHYDE 37-40 PERCENT (USP LEVEL)

DANGER: MAY BE FATAL IF SWALLOWED.

CAUSES SEVERE BURNS.

Contains formaldehyde.

Avoid contact with skin, eyes, and mucous membranes.

Prolonged or repeated contact may cause allergic irritation.

Vapor irritating. Use only in a well-ventilated area.

First Aid

External. In case of contact with skin, flush with water for 15 minutes.

Internal. If swallowed, give 1 or 2 glasses of water. Induce vomiting and call physician immediately.

Eyes. In case of contact with eyes, flush with water for 15 minutes. Get prompt medical attention.

Keep out of the reach of children.

Methanol frequently added to formaldehyde as a stabilizer.

Generally contains 12 percent MeOH. To rear panel warning add "POISON" and Skull and Crossbones; "VAPOR HARMFUL OR CAUSE BLINDNESS"; "Cannot be made non-poisonous"; "Contains Methanol"; and "Use only in well-ventilated area."

Requires safety packaging per 1700.14 (a) (8) if contains over 4 percent methanol.

FORMIC ACID

DANGER: CAN CAUSE BURNS TO SKIN AND EYES.

HARMFUL IF SWALLOWED.

Contains formic acid.

Avoid contact with eyes, skin, and mucous membranes.

Use only in a well-ventilated area.

First Aid

External. In case of contact with skin, flush with water for 15 minutes.

Internal. If swallowed, give 1 or 2 glasses of water. Call physician immediately.

Eyes. In case of contact with eyes, flush with water for 15 minutes. Get prompt medical attention.

Keep out of the reach of children.

FURNITURE POLISH

(Red Oil, Lemon Oil, Seal Oil type.)

DANGER: HARMFUL OR FATAL IF SWALLOWED.

Contains petroleum distillates.

First Aid
> *Internal.* If swallowed, do not induce vomiting. Call physician immediately.

Keep out of reach of children.

(Check flash point. If 80 to 150 degrees F, add statement of hazard "COMBUSTIBLE" and additional statement "Keep from heat or flame".)

(No skin or vapor warnings needed normally.)

(If viscosity is greater than 100 SUS at 100 degrees F., product exempt from petroleum distillate labeling (16 CFR 1500.84 (a) (13)).)

(Safety packaging required (16 CFR 1700.14 (a) (2)).)

GASOLINE

DANGER: EXTREMELY FLAMMABLE.

HARMFUL OR FATAL IF SWALLOWED.

VAPORS MAY CAUSE FLASH FIRE.

*Contains gasoline.

Vapors may ignite explosively.

Prevent buildup of vapors. Do not store indoors.

Keep away from heat, sparks, and flame.

Do not smoke. Do not use or store near flame, pilot lights, stoves, heaters, electric motors, and other sources of ignition.

Close container tightly after each use. Store only in closed container.

Avoid repeated or prolonged contact with skin and breathing of vapor.

First Aid
> *Internal.* If swallowed, do not induce vomiting. Call physician immediately.

Keep out of the reach of children.

* If the name of the hazardous substance appears elsewhere on label, it does not need to be repeated.

Note: See exception to labeling requirements under 16 CFR 1500.83 (a) (14).

Safety packaging required for pre-packaged fuels (16 CFR 1700.14 (a) (7)).

GLYCOLIC ACID

See *Hydroxyacetic Acid.*

GUN POWDER

The Consumer Product Safety Commission has no jurisdiction for gun powder and therefore cannot require any labeling except in firecrackers.

HYDRATED LIME (CALCIUM HYDROXIDE)

WARNING: INJURIOUS TO EYES.

PROLONGED CONTACT WITH WET SKIN MAY PRODUCE BURNS.

Contains hydrated lime.

First Aid
> *External.* In case of skin contact, flush thoroughly with water.
> *Eyes.* In case of contact with eyes, flush with water for 15

minutes. Get prompt medical attention.

Keep out of the reach of children.

HYDROGEN PEROXIDE (5-10 PERCENT)

WARNING: IRRITANT.

Contains hydrogen peroxide.

Avoid contact with eyes or prolonged contact with skin.

Do not add anything to this container, as violent reaction may occur.

Store in original container in cool, dark place.

First Aid
> *Eyes.* In case of contact with eyes, flush with warm water.

Keep out of the reach of children.

HYDROGEN PEROXIDE (10-30 PERCENT)

WARNING: MAY CAUSE BURNS. HARMFUL IF SWALLOWED.

Contains hydrogen peroxide.

(Balance same as Hydrogen Peroxide 30 percent+.)

HYDROGEN PEROXIDE (30 PERCENT+)

DANGER: CAUSES BURNS.

HARMFUL IF SWALLOWED.

Contains hydrogen peroxide.

Avoid contact with skin, eyes, mucous membranes, and combustible materials.

Drying of this material on clothing or combustible materials may cause fire.

Do not mix with anything or explosion may result.

First Aid
> *External.* In case of external contact, flush with water for 15 minutes.
> *Internal.* If swallowed, give 1 or 2 glasses of water and call physician immediately.
> *Eyes.* In case of contact, flush with water for 15 minutes. Get prompt medical attention.

Keep out of the reach of children.

HYDROCHLORIC ACID (2.55 PERCENT AQ.)

WARNING: MAY BE HARMFUL IF SWALLOWED.

Contains dilute hydrochloric acid.

Keep out of the reach of children.

(5 percent not skin or eye irritant but may be irritant to mucous membranes.)

HYDROCHLORIC ACID (5-10 PERCENT)

WARNING: IRRITANT TO EYES AND MUCOUS MEMBRANES.

HARMFUL IF SWALLOWED.

Contains hydrochloric acid.

If swallowed, give 1 or 2 glasses of water and call physician.

In case of contact with eyes, flush thoroughly with water.

If irritation persists, get medical attention.

Do not mix with chlorine-type bleaches or other household chemicals.

Keep out of the reach of children.

HYDROCHLORIC ACID

(Includes muriatic acid (10 percent+).)

POISON: MAY BE FATAL IF SWALLOWED.

CAUSES SEVERE BURNS. VAPOR HARMFUL.

Contains hydrochloric acid.

Keep away from eyes and skin.

Do not inhale or swallow.

Do not mix with chlorine-type bleaches or other household chemicals.

First Aid.

> *External.* Flush with water for 15 minutes.
>
> *Internal.* Drink large quantities of water. Follow with milk of magnesia, beaten eggs, or vegetable oil. Call physician immediately.
>
> *Eyes.* Wash with water for 15 minutes. Get prompt medical attention.

Keep out of the reach of children.

HYDROFLUORIC ACID (1 TO 4 PERCENT)

WARNING: HARMFUL IF SWALLOWED OR INHALED.

MAY CAUSE SEVERE BURNS WHICH MAY NOT BE IMMEDIATELY PAINFUL OR VISIBLE.

Contains hydrofluoric acid.

Avoid contact with eyes or skin.

Use only with rubber gloves.

First Aid

> *Internal.* Call physician immediately. Follow with milk of magnesia, beaten eggs, or vegetable oil.
>
> Call physician immediately.
>
> *Eyes.* Wash with water for 15 minutes Get prompt medical attention.

Keep out of the reach of children.

HYPOCHLORITE (CA OR NA)

(10-30 percent expressed as hypochlorous acid)

POISON: CAUSES BURNS.(*)

Contains calcium hypochlorite.

Avoid contact with eyes, skin, and mucous membranes.

First Aid

> *External.* Wash with water for 15 minutes. For eyes, get prompt medical attention.
>
> *Internal.* Give 1 or 2 glasses of water. Follow with egg white.

Call physician immediately.

Do not breathe dust.

Do not mix with acids or other household chemicals.

Keep out of the reach of children.

(*) at 10-20 percent use MAY CAUSE BURNS.

at 20-30 percent use CAUSES BURNS.

Add "Do not breathe dust" if appropriate.

HYPOCHLORITE (CA OR NA)

(30 percent+ Expressed as Hypochlorous Acid.)

POISON: CAUSES SEVERE BURNS.

MAY BE FATAL IF SWALLOWED.

Contains Hypochlorous Acid.

Avoid contact with skin, eyes, and clothing. Do not take internally. Keep container tightly closed.

Do not mix with other household chemicals.

First Aid

> *External.* Wash with water for 15 minutes. For eyes, get medical attention.
>
> *Internal.* Give 1 or 2 glasses of water. Follow with raw egg white or milk of magnesia. Call Physician immediately.

Keep out of the reach of children.

At 10-20 percent use "MAY CAUSE BURNS" as statement of hazard.

At 20-30 percent use "CAUSES BURNS" as statement of hazard.

Add "Do not breathe dust" if appropriate.

At 70 percent+ add "MAY CAUSE FIRE OR EXPLOSION WHEN MIXED WITH OTHER CHEMICALS."

Check for sanitizer or disinfectant claims.

HYPOCHLORITE (NA OR CA; LESS THAN 10 PERCENT)

CAUTION: IRRITANT.

Contains calcium hypochlorite.

Avoid contact with eyes, skin, and mucous membranes.

Do not mix with acids or other household chemicals.

First Aid

> *Internal.* If swallowed, give 1 or 2 glasses of water. Call physician.
>
> *Eyes.* In case of eye contact, flush thoroughly with water.

Keep out of the reach of children.

ISOPROPYL, ALCOHOL (70 PERCENT)

Less than 70 percent in mixture generally does not require warnings. Flammability principle hazard. Suggest back panel eye irritant precautions (secondary hazard).

See *Alcohol, Denatured.*

JEQUIRITY BEANS

DANGER: POISON (SKULL & CROSSBONES SYMBOL).

MAY BE FATAL IF SWALLOWED.

Contains Jequirity Beans.

First Aid

> *Internal.* If swallowed, call physician, hospital emergency room, or Poison Control Center immediately for instructions to induce vomiting. When medical advice is not available induce vomiting using syrup of ipecac according to directions. If ipecac is unavailable, induce vomiting by placing finger or back of spoon down victims throat. Get prompt medical attention.

Keep out of the reach of children.

Note: Reportedly loses toxicity if heated to 150 degrees F.

KEROSENE

See *Petroleum Distillate.*

LACTIC ACID (OVER 50 PERCENT CONC.)

WARNING: HARMFUL IF SWALLOWED. MAY CAUSE BURNS.

Contains lactic acid.
First Aid.
> *Internal.* If swallowed, give 1 or 2 glasses of water. Follow with milk of magnesia, beaten egg or vegetable oil. Call physician immediately.
> *Eyes and Skin.* Flush with water for 15 minutes. Get prompt medical attention.

Keep out of the reach of children.

LIME

See *Hydrated Lime.*

MEK PEROXIDE

See *Methyl Ethyl Ketone Peroxide.*

METHYL ALCOHOL (4 PERCENT+)

DANGER: POISON (SKULL & CROSSBONES)
FLAMMABLE. VAPOR HARMFUL (if flash point is below 80 degrees F).
MAY BE FATAL OR CAUSE BLINDNESS IF SWALLOWED.
Contains methyl alcohol.
Cannot be made nonpoisonous. Use only in a well-ventilated area.
Keep away from heat and open flame.
(*) Avoid contact with eyes.
First Aid
> *Internal.* If swallowed give 1 or 2 glasses of water. Call physician, hospital emergency room, or Poison Control Center immediately for instructions to induce vomiting. When medical advice is not available induce vomiting using syrup of ipecac according to directions. If ipecac is unavailable induce vomiting with finger or back of spoon. Get prompt medical attention.
> *Eyes.* Flush with water for 15 minutes. Get prompt medical attention.

Keep out of the reach of children.
(*) If over 70 percent.
Note: See labeling exemptions under 1500.83 (a) (10), (19), (26), (34).
Note: Requires safety closures for liquids, other than pressurized spray containers (16 CFR 1700.14 (a) (8)). Spray containers probably need full labeling.
Use "COMBUSTIBLE" if flash point is 80 to 150 degrees F.

METHYL ETHYL KETONE PEROXIDE

(Polyester Resin Hardener)
(60 percent generally in dimethyl or dilutyl phthalate.)

DANGER: CAUSES SEVERE BURNS.
MAY BE FATAL IF SWALLOWED.
Contains methyl ethyl ketone peroxide.
Avoid contact with skin, eyes, or mucous membranes.
First Aid
> *Internal.* If swallowed, give 1 or 2 glasses of water.
> *External.* In case of contact, flush thoroughly with water.
> *Eyes.* For eyes, get prompt medical attention.
> Get medical attention immediately.

Keep out of the reach of children.

METHYL ETHYL KETONE

WARNING: INJURIOUS TO EYES.
HARMFUL IF SWALLOWED. VAPOR HARMFUL.*
FLAMMABLE.
Contains methyl ethyl ketone.
Avoid contact with eyes, mucous membranes, and prolonged skin contact.
Use only in a well-ventilated area.
Do not use near heat or flame.
First Aid.
> *External.* Flush thoroughly with water. If irritation persists, get medical attention.
> *May need testing to support.
> *Internal.* If swallowed, give 1 or 2 glasses of water. Induce vomiting and call physician.
> *Eyes.* Flush with plenty of water for 15 minutes. Get medical attention.

Keep out of the reach of children.
(If used in a mixture with petroleum distillates, aspiration hazard takes precedence over low oral toxicity. Do not induce vomiting.)

METHYL ETHYL KETONE

(Thick Glues.) (Approx. 15-25 percent MEK.)
WARNING: FLAMMABLE. INJURIOUS TO EYES.
Contains methyl ethyl ketone.
Avoid prolonged breathing of vapors.
Do not use near hear or flame.
First Aid
> *Eyes.* In case of eye contact, flush with water for 15 minutes. Get medical attention.

Keep out of the reach of children.

METHENAMINE

CAUTION: HARMFUL IF SWALLOWED.
Contains methenamine.
First Aid
> *Internal.* If swallowed, call a doctor immediately.

Keep out of the reach of children.

METHYL CELLOSOLVE

See *Ethylene Glycol Monomethyl Ether.*

METHYLENE CHLORIDE (DICHLOROMETHANE)

CAUTION: HARMFUL IF SWALLOWED.
Contains methylene chloride.
Use only in a well ventilated area.
Avoid prolonged breathing of vapor or contact with skin or eyes.
First Aid
Internal. If swallowed, induce vomiting. Call physician.
Eyes. In case of contact with eyes, flush with water.
Keep out of the reach of children.
Note: When methylene chloride is used in a pressurized container (usually as a propellant) ingestion warnings are not required.
Note: Be alert for any future regulatory action on methylene chloride.

METHYL CHLOROFORM

See *1,1,1 trichloroethane.*

MINERAL SPIRITS

See *Petroleum Distillates.*

MONOCHLORACETIC ACID

DANGER: MAY BE FATAL IF SWALLOWED.
CAUSES BURNS. VAPOR HARMFUL.
Contains monochloracetic acid.
Avoid contact with eyes, skin, and mucous membranes.
First Aid.
Internal. Give 1 or 2 glasses of water. Follow with beaten egg or vegetable oil. Call physician immediately.
External. Wash thoroughly with soapy water. Follow with vegetable oil.
Eyes. Flush with water for 15 minutes. Get prompt medical attention.
Keep out of the reach of children.

MONCETHANOLAMIDE

CAUTION: EYE IRRITANT.
Contains monoethanolamide.
Avoid contact with eyes.
In case of eye contact, flush with water for 15 minutes and get medical attention.
Keep out of the reach of children.

MURIATIC ACID (TECH. GRADE HCL)

See *Hydrochloric Acid (10 percent+).*

NAPTHALENE

WARNING: MAY BE FATAL IF SWALLOWED.
Contains napthalene.
First Aid

Internal. If swallowed, give 1 or 2 glasses of water. Induce vomiting and call physician immediately.
Keep out of the reach of children.

NICKEL AMMONIUM SULFATE

WARNING: HARMFUL IF SWALLOWED. IRRITANT.
Contains nickel ammonium sulfate.
First Aid
Internal. If swallowed, give water and call physician.
Enternal. In case of contact with skin, flush freely with water.
Eyes. For eyes, flush freely with water and get medical attention.
Keep out of the reach of children.

NITRIC ACID (5 PERCENT+)

POISON: CAUSES SEVERE BURNS. VAPOR HARMFUL.
Contains nitric acid.
Keep away from eyes or skin.
Do not inhale or swallow.
Do not mix with chlorine containing bleaches or other household chemicals.
First Aid
External. Flush with water for 15 minutes.
Internal. Drink large quantities of water. Follow with milk of magnesia, vegetable oil, or beaten eggs. Call physician immediately.
Eyes. Wash with water for 15 minutes. Get medical attention promptly.
Keep out of the reach of children.
Substitute "VAPOR EXTREMELY HAZARDOUS" for "VAPOR HARMFUL" if over 50 percent.
Add "Use only in a well ventilated area" if over 25 percent.

OXALIC ACID (LESS THAN 10 PERCENT)

WARNING: HARMFUL IF SWALLOWED.
Contains oxalic acid.
Avoid contact with eyes.
First Aid
Internal. If swallowed, give large quantities of milk. Call physician immediately.
Keep out of the reach of children.
10 percent not primary skin irritant.
7.5 percent may be eye irritant.

OXALIC ACID (MORE THAN 10 PERCENT)

POISON: EYE IRRITANT.
Contains oxalic acid.
Avoid contact with eyes and prolonged contact with skin.
First Aid
Internal. Give large quantities of milk and induce vomiting. Follow with more milk. Call physician immediately.
Eyes. Flush with water for 15 minutes and get prompt medical attention.
Keep out of the reach of children.

PARA-DICHLOROBENZENE

CAUTION: HARMFUL IF SWALLOWED.

Contains para-dichlorobenzene.

First Aid

  Internal. If swallowed, induce vomiting and call physician.

Keep out of the reach of children.

PARAFORMALDEHYDE (65 PERCENT TO 80 PERCENT)

Will break down into formaldehyde—see 1-5 percent label.

PERCHLOROETHYLENE (TETRACHLOROETHYLENE)

WARNING: VAPOR HARMFUL.

Contains perchloroethylene.

Use only in a well ventilated area.

Avoid prolonged breathing of vapor or contact with skin.

Keep out of the reach of children.

If distributed as an eyelash cleaner, add "Do not apply artificial eyelashes until all odor of chemical is gone."

Note: See labeling exemption under 16 CFR 150.83 (a) (31).

Note: Be alert for future regulatory action.

PETROLEUM DISTILLATES

DANGER: HARMFUL OR FATAL IF SWALLOWED.

*EXTREMELY FLAMMABLE.

Contains Petroleum Distillate(s).

**Avoid frequent or prolonged contact with skin.

**Use only in a well-ventilated area.

Do not use near heat, sparks, or flame.

First Aid

  Internal. If swallowed, do not induce vomiting. Call physician immediately.

Keep out of the reach of children.

Note: See labeling exemptions under 16 CFR 1500.83 (a) (11), (13), (14) and (20).

May require special packaging depending on intended use (see 16 CFR 1700.14).

Normally includes aromatic hydrocarbons, but note that benzene, toluene, or xylene require additional labeling (16 CFR 1500.14 (b) (3) (i) and (III)).

*If Flash Point is 20 to 80 degrees F, substitute "FLAMMABLE" and delete rear panel reference to "sparks."

*If Flash Point is 80 to 150 degrees F, substitute "COMBUSTIBLE."

If product is of a type where more than ½ pt. per application may be used (contact adhesive thinner, etc.) consider use of labeling in 16 CFR 1500.133 (if also extremely flammable).

Note extremely flammable contact adhesives ban at 16 CFR 1302.

**For containers of 1 quart or more.

See special labeling guides for cigarette lighter fluid, charcoal lighter fluid, gasoline, furniture polish, toluene, xylene, benzene, contact bond cement.

POTASSIUM CHLORATE

See *Sodium Chlorate.*

PHENOL (5 PERCENT+; CARBOLIC ACID)

POISON: MAY BE FATAL IF SWALLOWED OR ABSORBED THROUGH SKIN. CAUSES SEVERE BURNS

Contains phenol.

Keep away from eyes, skin, or clothing.

Use only in a well ventilated area.

First Aid

  External. Remove contaminated clothing. Flush with water for 15 minutes. Follow with vegetable oil.

  Internal. Give large quantities of milk. Induce vomiting. Follow with large amounts of vegetable oil. Call physician immediately.

  Eyes. Flush with cool water for at least 15 minutes. Get prompt medical attention.

Keep out of the reach of children.

"POISON" required by 1500.129 (d).

POTASSIUM HYDROXIDE

See *Sodium Hydroxide.*

PHOSPHORIC ACID (LESS THAN 15 PERCENT)

Not Hazardous Substance.

PHOSPHORIC ACID (15-35 PERCENT)

WARNING: IRRITANT TO EYES AND MUCOUS MEMBRANES.

Contains phosphoric acid.

First Aid

  External. In case of external contact, flush with cool water. If irritation persists, get medical attention.

  Internal. If swallowed, give 1 or 2 glasses of water and call physician.

Keep out of the reach of children.

PHOSPHORIC ACID (35-60 PERCENT)

WARNING: MAY BE INJURIOUS TO EYES AND MUCOUS MEMBRANES.

Contains phosphoric acid.

First Aid

  External. In case of external contact, flush with water.

  Internal. If swallowed, give 1 or 2 glasses of water and call physician.

  Eyes. For eyes, get medical attention.

Keep out of the reach of children.

PHOSPHORIC ACID (OVER 60 PERCENT)

DANGER. MAY CAUSE BURNS. HARMFUL IF SWALLOWED.

Contains phosphoric acid.

Avoid contact with skin, eyes and mucous membranes.

First Aid

External. In case of contact, flush with cool water.
Internal. If swallowed, give 1 or 2 glasses of water and call
   physician immediately.
Eyes. For eyes, get prompt medical attention.
Keep out of the reach of children.

PHOSPHOROUS HEXATE

CAUTION: EYE IRRITANT.
Contains phosphorous hexate
Avoid contact with eyes
First Aid
   Eyes. In case of contact, flush with water for 15 minutes.
      Get medical attention.
Keep out of the reach of children.

PORTLAND CEMENT

WARNING: INJURIOUS TO EYES;.
*CAUSES SKIN IRRITATION.
**Contains Portland Cement
Avoid eye contact or prolonged contact with skin.
Wash thoroughly after handling.
First Aid
   Eyes. In case of eye contact, flush with plenty of water for at
      least 15 minutes.
      Consult a physician immediately.
Keep out of the reach of children.
*Where supported by test results
**Unless the words Portland Cement appear elsewhere on the
   label.

POTASSIUM CHLORIDE

WARNING: HARMFUL IF SWALLOWED
Contains potassium chloride.
First Aid
   Internal. If swallowed, give 1 or 2 glasses of water. Induce
      vomiting and call physician.
Keep out of the reach of children.

POTASSIUM NITRATE

Contains potassium nitrate.
Frist Aid
   Internal. If swallowed, give 1 or 2 glasses of water and call
      physician.
Keep out of the reach of children.

POTASSIUM PERMANGANATE

DANGER: CAUSES SEVERE BURNS. HARMFUL IF SWAL-
   LOWED.
Contains potassium permanganate.
Avoid contact with skin, eyes, and mucous membranes.
First Aid
   External. Flood with water.

Internal. Give 1 or 2 glasses of water. Call physician immediately.
Eyes. Flush with plenty of water and get prompt medical
   attention.
Keep out of the reach of children.

PRESSURIZED CONTAINERS

WARNING: CONTENTS UNDER PRESSURE.
Do not puncture or incinerate container.
Do not expose to heat or store at temperatures above 120 degrees
   F.
Keep out of the reach of children.
(See 16 CFR 1500.130.)
Note: Check for future regulatory action on labeling propellant.

PROPANE (TANKS)

DANGER: EXTREMELY FLAMMABLE. CONTENTS UNDER
   PRESSURE.
Use with care to avoid accidental fires.
When tank is exhausted discard in a safe place.
Do not puncture or incinerate
Do not store at temperature above 120 degrees F.
Keep out of the reach of children.
If intended for stoves, lamps, heaters, etc., include a warning such
   as "operate appliances only in a well ventilated area" or some
   similar warning.
See exemption in 16 CFR 1500.83 (a) (1).

PYGROGALLOL

WARNING: MAY BE FATAL IF SWALLOWED OR AB-
   SORBED THROUGH THE SKIN. IRRITATING TO THE
   SKIN.
Contains pygrogallol.
Avoid contact with skin, eyes and mucous membranes.
First Aid.
   External. Flush with water for 15 minutes. Call physician
      immediately.
   Internal. If swallowed give 1 or 2 glasses of water. Induce
      vomiting. Call physician immediately.
   Eyes. Flush with water for 15 minutes. Call physician imme-
      diately.
Keep out of the reach of children.

SHELLAC

(Less than 5 percent Methanol.) (F.P. 20 to 80 degrees F.)
WARNING: FLAMMABLE.
Contains denatured alcohol.
Keep away from heat and open flame.
Avoid contact with eyes.
First Aid
   Eyes. In case of contact with eyes, flush thoroughly with
      water.
Keep out of the reach of children.

SALICYLIC ACID

WARNING: IRRITANT. HARMFUL IF SWALLOWED.

Contains salicylic acid.

Avoid contact with eyes and prolonged contact with skin.

First Aid

    *External.*In case of contact with skin, flush thoroughly with water.

    Internal. If swallowed, give water, induce vomiting and call physician.

    Eyes. In case of contact with eyes, flush thoroughly with water. Get medical attention.

Keep out of the reach of children.

SELENOUS ACID (0.81 PERCENT)

WARNING: MAY BE FATAL IF SWALLOWED.

Contains selenous acid.

Avoid contact with eyes and prolonged contact with skin.

First Aid

    External. In case of contact, flush with water.

    Internal. If swallowed, induce vomiting and call physician immediately.

    *Eyes.*In case of contact, flush with water. Get medical attention.

Keep out of the reach of children.

SILVER NITRATE

WARNING: MAY BE HARMFUL IF SWALLOWED. EYE IRRITANT.

Contains silver nitrate.

First Aid

    Internal. If swallowed, contact physician immediately.

    Eyes. In case of eye contact flush with water for 15 minutes. If irritation continues get medical attention.

Keep out of the reach of children.

SODIUM BISULFATE

DANGER: CAUSES SEVERE BURNS.

Contains sodium bisulfate.

Avoid contact with skin, eyes, or clothing.

Do not mix with other household chemicals.

First Aid

    External. Flush with water for 15 minutes.

    Internal. Drink large quantities of water. Follow with milk of magnesia, vegetable oil, or beaten eggs. Call physician immediately.

    Eyes. Wash with water for 15 minutes. Get medical attention promptly.

Keep out of the reach of children.

SODIUM BROMIDE

WARNING: HARMFUL IF SWALLOWED.

Contains sodium bromide.

First Aid

    Internal. If swallowed, give water, induce vomiting, and call physician.

Keep out of the reach of children.

SODIUM CARBONATE

CAUTION: IRRITANT. HARMFUL IF SWALLOWED.

Contains sodium carbonate.

Avoid contact with eyes and prolonged contact with skin.

First Aid

    Internal. If swallowed, give water, call physician.

    Eyes. In case of eye contact, flush freely with water.

Keep out of the reach of children.

SODIUM CHLORIDE (SALT)

Exempt—16b CFR 1500.83 (a) (16).

SODIUM DITHIONITE

CAUTION: HARMFUL IF SWALLOWED. IRRITANT.

Contains sodium hydrosulfite.

Avoid contact with skin and eyes.

First Aid

    External. In case of contact with skin, flush with water for 15 minutes.

    Internal. If swallowed, give 1 or 2 glasses of water. Call physician immediately.

    Eyes. In case of contact with eyes, flush with water for 15 minutes.

Keep out of the reach of children.

SODIUM HYDROSULFITE

See *Sodium Dithionite.*

SODIUM HYDROXIDE (2-5 PERCENT)

DANGER: MAY CAUSE BURNS. HARMFUL IF SWALLOWED.

Contains sodium hydroxide.

Avoid contact with eyes and mucous membranes or prolonged contact with skin.

First Aid

    External. Flood with water than wash with vinegar.

    Internal. Drink several glasses of water. Follow with citrus fruit juice.

    Eyes. Flush with water for 15 minutes. Get prompt medical attention.

Call physician immediately.

Keep out of the reach of children.

SODIUM HYDROXIDE (5-10 PERCENT)

DANGER: CAUSES SEVERE BURNS. MAY BE FATAL IF SWALLOWED.

Contains sodium hydroxide.

Avoid contact with skin, eyes, and mucous membranes.

First Aid—same as 2-5 percent.

Add "Use rubber gloves" when appropriate (oven cleaners, etc.).

SODIUM HYDROXIDE (CAUSTIC SODA) (10 PERCENT+)

POISON: CAUSES SEVERE BURNS.

Contains sodium hydroxide (caustic soda).

Avoid contact with skin, eyes, mucous membranes, and clothing.

First Aid

    External. Flood with water then wash with vinegar.

    Internal. Drink large quantities of water. Follow with citrus fruit juice, if available.

    Eyes. Flush with water for 15 minutes. Get prompt medical attention.

Call physician immediately.

Keep out of the reach of children.

Add "Use rubber gloves" when appropriate (oven cleaners, etc.).

Liquid drain cleaners banned unless in safety packaging (16 CFR 1500.17 (a)(4)).

SODIUM HYPOCHLORITE

See *Hypochlorite, Calcium or Sodium.*

SODIUM METASILICATE (15 PERCENT+)

DANGER: MAY CAUSE BURNS. HARMFUL IF SWALLOWED.

Contains sodium metasilicate.

Avoid contact with skin, eyes, and mucous membranes.

First Aid

    External. In case of external contact, flush with water.

    Internal. If swallowed, give large quantities of water. Follow with citrus juice if available.

    Eyes. For eyes, flush with water for 15 minutes and get immediate medical attention.

Call physician immediately.

Keep out of the reach of children.

SODIUM SILICATE (10-25 PERCENT) INCLUDES WATERGLASS

CAUTION: IRRITANT.

Contains sodium silicate.

Avoid contact with eyes and prolonged contact with skin.

First Aid

    External. In case of contact, flush with plenty of water.

    Eyes. In case of contact, flush with plenty of water. Get medical attention.

Keep out of the reach of children.

Over 30 percent may be corrosive but biological testing required.

SODIUM BORATE

See *Boric Acid.*

SODIUM PERBORATE

WARNING: HARMFUL IF SWALLOWED.

Contains sodium perborate.

First Aid

    Internal. If swallowed, give 1 or 2 glasses of water, induce vomiting, and call physician.

Keep out of the reach of children.

SULFAMIC ACID*

WARNING: HARMFUL IF SWALLOWED. EYE IRRITANT.

Contains sulfamic acid.

First AId

    Internal. If swallowed, give 1 or 2 glasses of water. Call physician immediately.

    Eyes. In case of contact with eyes, flush thoroughly with water. Get prompt medical attention.

Keep out of the reach of children.

(For powders and granules add to rear panel "Avoid breathing dust".)

*May be corrosive at high concentration (above 50 percent) but requires biological testing.

SULFURIC ACID (10 PERCENT+)

POISON: CAUSES SEVERE BURNS.

Contains sulfuric acid.

Avoid contact with skin, eyes, or clothing.

Do not mix with other household chemicals.

Do not add water to product in container as severe reaction may result. To prevent accidents, rinse empty container before discarding.

First Aid

    External. Flush with water for 15 minutes.

    Internal. Drink large quantities of water. Follow with milk of magnesia, vegetable oil, or beaten eggs.

    Eyes. Wash with water for 15 minutes. Get medical attention promptly.

    Call physician immediately.

Keep out of the reach of children.

Note: Products containing 10 percent or more by weight require safety closure (16 CFR 1700.14 (a) (9)).

SULFURIC ACID (CONCENTRATED; DRAIN OPENER)

POISON: CAUSES SEVERE BURNS.

Contains concentrated sulfuric acid.

Avoid contact with skin, eyes, or clothing.

May cause eruption of hot acid when poured into drain.

Protect face (especially eyes) and other portions of body when using.

After pouring acid into drain, immediately place inverted dish pan, bucket or other deep container over drain opening to protect against possible eruption of drain contents and acid.

Do not mix with other household chemicals.

Never add water to acid while in container because of violent reaction. However, when container is completely empty, rinse with water before discarding to prevent accidental burns.

First Aid
    External. Flush with water for 15 minutes.
    Internal. Drink large quantities of water. Follow with milk of
        magnesia, beaten eggs or vegetable oil.
    Call physician immediately.
    Eyes. Flush with water for 15 minutes and get prompt medical
        attention.
Keep out of the reach of children.
Note:. Requires safety closure (16 CFR 1700.14 (a) (9)).
Note: Be alert for any future regulatory action.

TETRAETHYLENE PENTAMINE

DANGER: CAUSES SEVERE BURNS. COMBUSTIBLE.
HARMFUL IF SWALLOWED OR ABSORBED THROUGH
    SKIN.
Contains tetraethylene pentamine.
Do not get in eyes, on skin, or on clothing.
Avoid prolonged or repeated breathing of vapor.
Keep away from heat or flame.
First Aid
    External. In case of contact with skin, flush freely with water
        for at least 15 minutes.
    Internal. If swallowed, give large amount of water, induce
        vomiting, and call physician.
    Eyes. In case of contact with eyes, flush freely with water for
        at least 15 minutes. Get prompt medical attention.
Keep out of the reach of children.

TETRAHYDROFURAN

DANGER: EXTREMELY FLAMMABLE. HARMFUL IF SWAL-
    LOWED.
Contains tetrahydrofuran.
Use only in a well-ventilated area.
Keep away from heat, sparks, and flame.
First Aid
    Internal. If swallowed, give 1 or 2 glasses of water, induce
        vomiting, and call physician.
Keep out of the reach of children.
May be eye irritant—biological testing required.
Note: If in containers of more than ½ pint, consider additional
    labeling re: pilot lights, etc.

TETRACHLOROETHYLENE

See *Perchloroethylene.*

THIOUREA* (ACIDIFIED)

CAUTION: MAY BE HARMFUL IF SWALLOWED. IRRI-
    TANT.
Contains Thiourea.
Keep away from eyes.

First Aid
    Internal. If swallowed, give water and call physician.
Keep out of the reach of children.
Note: *6 percent thiourea 0.75 percent Hydrochloric Acid.

TOLUENE 10 PERCENT+

See 1500.14 (b) (3) (iii) or (ii).
*DANGER: HARMFUL OR FATAL IF SWALLOWED.
VAPOR HARMFUL. FLAMMABLE.
Contains toluene.
**Use only in a well ventilated area.
Keep away from heat and open flame.
Avoid prolonged contact with skin.
First Aid
    *Internal.**** If swallowed, do not induce vomiting. Call
        physician immediately.
    Keep out of the reach of children.
* If viscosity is greater than 100 SUS may use "WARNING:
    VAPOR HARMFUL. FLAMMABLE" and delete first aid
    instructions.
** If glue or model cement, add "Avoid prolonged or repeated
    breathing of vapors."
*** If used with methyl alcohol, generally declare both, but
    whether or not to induce vomiting must be decided on case by
    case basis.
Note: See labeling exemptions under 16 CFR 1500.83 (a) (11) and
    13.

TRIARYL PHOSPHATE (IF LOW IN ORTHO CRESYL PHOSPHATE)

WARNING: HARMFUL IF SWALLOWED.
Contains triaryl phosphate.
Avoid prolonged contact with skin.
First Aid
    Internal. If swallowed, induce vomiting and call physician
        immediately.
Keep out of the reach of children.

(1,1,1) TRICHLOROETHANE*

Not hazardous under present regulations.
May suggest voluntary use of the following:
WARNING: VAPOR HARMFUL.
Contains 1,1,1-trichloroethane.
Use in a well ventilated area.
Avoid prolonged breathing of vapor.
Keep out of the reach of children."
*Do not confuse with 1,1,2 trichloroethane, which is much more
    hazardous.

TRICHLOROETHYLENE *

WARNING: VAPOR HARMFUL.
MAY BE HARMFUL IF SWALLOWED.
Contains trichloroethylene.
Use only in a well ventilated area.

Avoid prolonged breathing of vapor.
Avoid contact with eyes and prolonged contact with skin.
First Aid
> *Internal.* If swallowed, induce vomiting and call physician. (If near 100 percent.)
> *Eyes.* In case of eye contact, flush thoroughly with water. If irritation persists, get medical attention.

Keep out of the reach of children.

TRICHLOROISOCYANURIC ACID (10 PERCENT+)

DANGER: MAY CAUSE BURNS. HARMFUL IF SWALLOWED.
Contains trichloroisocyanuric acid.
Avoid contact with eyes, skin, or mucous membranes.
Do not breathe dust.
First Aid
> *External.* In case of contact with skin, flush with water for 15 minutes.
> *Internal.* If swallowed, give 1 or 2 glasses of water and call physician.
> *Eyes.* In case of contact with eyes or skin, flush with water for 15 minutes. Get medical attention.

Keep out of the reach of children.

TRIETHYLENETETRAMINE

DANGER: HARMFUL IF SWALLOWED OR ABSORBED THROUGH THE SKIN. MAY CAUSE SKIN AND EYE BURNS.
Contains triethylenetetramine.
Avoid contact with skin and eyes.
Skin contact may cause allergic reaction.
First Aid
> *External.* Flush with water for 15 minutes.
> *Internal.* Do not induce vomiting. Drink large quantities of water. Call physician immediately.
> *Eyes.* Flush with plenty of water for 15 minutes. Get prompt medical attention.

Keep out of the reach of children.

TRISODIUM PHOSPHATE

CAUTION: HARMFUL IF SWALLOWED.
Contains trisodium phosphate.
Avoid contact with eyes and prolonged contact with skin.
First Aid
> *Internal.* If swallowed, give plenty of water.
> *Eyes.* In case of contact with eyes, flush thoroughly with water.

Call physician immediately.
Keep out of the reach of children.

TUNG OIL (100 PERCENT)

This is not a hazardous substance.

TURPENTINE

DANGER: HARMFUL OR FATAL IF SWALLOWED.
COMBUSTIBLE.
IRRITANT TO SKIN AND EYES.
Contains turpentine.*
Do not store or use near heat or flame.
Use in a well-ventilated area. Avoid prolonged breathing of vapor.
Avoid contact with eyes or prolonged contact with skin.
First Aid.
> *External.* Flush thoroughly with water for 15 minutes. Get prompt medical attention.
> *Internal.* If swallowed, give 1 or 2 glasses of water. Call physician immediately.
> *Eyes.* Flush thoroughly with water for 15 minutes. Get prompt medical attention.

Keep out of the reach of children.
* If the word "turpentine" appears on the container as the name of the product, it need not be repeated as part of the warning statement.
Liquid requires safety packaging (16 CFR 1700.14 (a) (16).

XYLENE (10 PERCENT+)[16 CFR 1500.14 (B) (3) (III) OR (II)]

*DANGER: HARMFUL OR FATAL IF SWALLOWED.
VAPOR HARMFUL. COMBUSTIBLE.
Contains xylene.
Use only in a well-ventilated area.
Keep away from heat or flame.
Avoid contact with eyes or prolonged contact with skin.
First Aid
> *Internal.* If swallowed, do not induce vomiting and call physician immediately.

Keep out of the reach of children.
Note: See labeling exemption under 16 CFR 1500.83 (a) (11) and (13).
*If viscosity is greater than 100 SUS, may use "WARNING: VAPOR HARMFUL. COMBUSTIBLE" and delete first aid warnings.

ZINC CHLORIDE

More than 20 percent except petrolatum pastes.
DANGER: MAY BE FATAL IF SWALLOWED. CAUSES SEVERE BURNS.
Contains zinc chloride.
Avoid contact with skin, eyes, and mucous membranes.
First Aid
> *External.* In case of contact with skin, flush with water for at least 15 minutes.
> *Internal.* If swallowed, give plenty of water and take patient to hospital immediately.
> *Eyes.* In case of contact with eyes, flush with water for at least 15 minutes. Get medical attention.

Keep out of the reach of children.
If slightly under 20 percent use "MAY CAUSE SEVERE BURNS."

ZINC CHLORIDE (SOLDERING PASTES) (7 PERCENT+ IN PETROLATUM)

CAUTION: EYE IRRITANT. HARMFUL IF SWALLOWED.
Contains zinc chloride.
First Aid
> *Internal.* If swallowed, give 1 or 2 glasses of water and call physician.
> *Eyes.* In case of eye contact, flush thoroughly with water for 15 minutes. Call physician immediately.

Keep out of the reach of children.

ZINC AND MAGNESIUM SILICO FLUORIDES (CONCRETE HARDENER)

(25 percent Zinc Silico Fluoride; 75 percent Magnesium Silico Fluoride)
WARNING: MAY BE FATAL IF SWALLOWED.
Contains zinc and magnesium silico fluorides.
First Aid
> *Internal.* If swallowed, give 1 or 2 glasses of water. Induce vomiting and call physician immediately.

Keep out of the reach of children.

ZINC SULFATE

WARNING: HARMFUL IF SWALLOWED.
Contains zinc sulfate.
First Aid
> *Internal.* If swallowed, give 1 or 2 glasses of water. Call physician immediately.

Keep out of the reach of children.

WATERGLASS

See *Sodium Silicate.*

Source:
Document 9010.125: Hazardous Substances Labeling Guide, Washington: Consumer Product Safety Commission, 1979.

Inert Ingredient

Components of a chemical product that do not contribute to its efficacy are the inert ingredients. For example, in a pesticide, the active ingredients are those that actually kill the pest. Inert ingredients may be added to help make the pesticide sprayable, sticky, or less concentrated. Although not active in the sense that they do not directly cause the result for which the product was developed (they do not directly kill the pest), they may be chemically or biologically active. Some inert ingredients are toxic or may cause environmental problems. Inert ingredients in consumer products are not regulated by the federal government to the extent of active ingredients and therefore are not required to be listed on product labels. However, efforts are underway by some groups (e.g., the U.S. Public Interest Research Group in Washington D.C.) to require manufacturers to label products with the names of some inert ingedients.

Source:
Harte, John, Cheryl Holdren, Richard Schneider, and Christine Shirley, *Toxics A to Z: A Guide to Everyday Pollution Hazards,* Berkeley: University of California Press, 1991.

Ozone

Ozone (O_3). Ozone is found in two layers of the atmosphere, the stratosphere and the troposphere. In the stratosphere (the atmospheric layer beginning 7 to 10 miles above the earth's surface), ozone is a natural form of oxygen which provides a protective layer, shielding the earth from ultraviolet radiation which can cause harmful health effects on humans and the environment. In the troposphere (the layer extending up 7 to 10 miles from the earth's surface), ozone is a chemical oxidant and major component of photochemical smog.

Ozone can seriously affect the human respiratory system. It is one of the most prevalent and widespread of the pollutants for which the Clean Air Act required the Environmental Protection Agency to set standards. Ozone in the troposphere is produced through complex chemical reactions of nitrogen oxides, which are among the primary pollutants emitted by combustion sources, hydrocarbons, released into the atmosphere through the combustion, handling, and processing of petroleum products, and sunlight.

Ozone-Depletion. This is the destruction of the stratospheric ozone layer which shields the earth from ultraviolet radiation harmful to biological life. This destruction of ozone is caused by the breakdown of certain chlorine- and/or bromine-containing compounds (chlorofluorocarbons or halons) which break down when they reach the stratosphere and catalytically destroy ozone molecules.

Chlorofluorocarbons (CFCs). A family of inert, nontoxic, and easily liquified chemicals used in refrigeration, air conditioning, packaging, insulation, or as solvents and aerosol propellants. Because CFCs are not destroyed in the lower atmosphere they drift into the upper atmosphere where their chlorine components destroy ozone.

CLEAN AIR ACT CATEGORIES

The Clean Air Act Amendments of 1990 specify two classes of ozone-depleting substances. Class I ozone-depleting substances are more harmful to the ozone layer than Class II substances.

Class I Ozone-Depleting Substance. A substance that harms the environment by destroying ozone in the upper atmosphere and is listed as such in Title 6 of the Clean Air Act Amendments of 1990, Pub. L. No. 101-549. (Also included in the definition are any other substance which may in the future be added to the list pursuant to Title 6 of the Act.) Class 1 substances currently include chlorofluorocarbons, halons, carbon tetrachloride and 1,1,1-Trichloroethane.

Class II Ozone-Depleting Substance. A substance that harms the environment by destroying ozone in the upper atmosphere and is listed as such in Title 6 of the Clean Air Act Amendments of 1990, Pub. L. No. 101-549. (Also included in the definition are any other substance which may in the future be added to the list pursuant to Title 6 of the Act.) Class II substances currently include hydrochlorofluorocarbons.

Source:

Office of Communications and Public Affairs, *Glossary of Environmental Terms and Acronym List,* Washington: U.S. Environmental Protection Agency, 1989.

Pesticides

Any substance or mixture of substances intended for preventing, destroying, repelling, or mitigating any pest, or intended for use as a plant regulator, defoliant, or desiccant. Pesticides are categorized into four categories (I - IV) by the Environmental Protection Agency with I being the most toxic.

INGREDIENTS

Active Ingredient. Any substance (or group of structurally similar substances if specified by the EPA) that will prevent, destroy, repel, or mitigate any pest, or that functions as a plant regulator, desiccant, or defoliant.

Inert Ingredient. Any substance (or group of structurally similar substances if designated by the EPA) other than an active ingredient, which is intentionally included in a pesticide product.

TYPES

Aerosols. Contain one or more active ingredients and a solvent, and are ready for immediate use as is.

Baits. Active ingredients mixed with food or other substances to attract the pest.

Dusts. Contain active ingredients plus a very fine dry inert carrier such as clay, talc, or volcanic ash. Dusts are ready for immediate use and are applied dry.

Granulars. Are similar to dusts, but with larger and heavier particles for broadcast applications.

Solutions. Contain the active ingredient and one or more additives, and readily mix with water.

Wettable Powders. Dry, finely ground formulations that generally are mixed with water for spray application. Some also may be used as dusts.

HUMAN HAZARD SIGNAL WORDS

In general the signal word "DANGER" means highly poisonous, "WARNING" means moderately hazardous, and "CAUTION" means least hazardous.

Category I. The front panel has the word "Danger." In addition, if the product was assigned to Toxicity Category I on the basis of its oral, inhalation, or dermal toxicity (as distinct from skin and eye local effects), the word "Poison" shall appear in red on a background of distinctly contrasting color, and the skull and crossbones shall appear in immediate proximity to the word "Poison."

Category II. Bears on the front panel the single word "Warning."

PRECAUTIONARY STATEMENTS BY TOXICITY CATEGORY

Toxicity Category	Oral, inhalation, or dermal toxicity	Skin and eye local effects
I	Fatal (poisonous) if swallowed [inhaled or absorbed through skin]. Do not breathe vapor [dust or spray mist]. Do not get in eyes, on skin, or on clothing [front panel statement of practical treatment required].	Corrosive. Causes eye and skin damage [or skin irritation]. Do not get in eyes, on skin, or on clothing. Wear goggles or face shield and rubber gloves when handling. Harmful or fatal if swallowed. [Appropriate first aid statement required.]
II	May be fatal if swallowed [inhaled or absorbed through the skin]. Do not breathe vapors [dust or spray mist]. Do not get in eyes, on skin, or on clothing. [Appropriate first aid statements required].	Causes eye [and skin] irritation. Do not get in eyes, on skin, or on clothing. Harmful if swallowed. [Appropriate first aid statement required.]
III	Harmful if swallowed [inhaled or absorbed through the skin]. Avoid breathing vapors [dust or spray mist]. Avoid contact with skin [eyes or clothing]. [Appropriate first aid statement required.]	Avoid contact with skin, eyes or clothing. In case of contact immediately flush eyes or skin with plenty of water. Get medical attention if irritation persists.
IV	[No precautionary statements required.]	[No precautionary statements required.]

Category III. Bears on the front panel the single word "Caution."
Category IV. Bears on the front panel the single word "Caution."

ADDITIONAL PESTICIDE LABELING PHRASES

This Pesticide is Toxic to Wildlife (Animals). A pesticide intended for outdoor use containing an active ingredient with a mammalian acute oral LD_{50} of 100 mg/kg (see *Toxicity*) or less.

This Pesticide is Toxic to Fish. A pesticide intended for outdoor use that contains an active ingredient with a fish acute LC_{50} of 1 ppm (see *Toxicity*) or less.

This Pesticide is Toxic to Wildlife (Birds). A pesticide intended for outdoor use that contains an active ingredient with an avian acute oral LD_{50} of 100 mg/kg (see Toxicity) or less, or a subacute dietary LC_{50} of 500 ppm or less.

This Pesticide is Extremely Toxic to Wildlife (Fish). This labeling is used if either accident history or field studies show that use of the pesticide may result in fatality to birds, fish, or mammals.

Source:
Citizen's Guide to Pesticides, Washington: U.S. Environmental Protection Agency, 1991.
Environmental Protection Agency, "Labeling Requirements for Pesticides and Devices," 40 CFR part 156 (1991), Washington: Government Printing Office.

Radiation

Radiation is a form of energy that comes from atoms. Radiation occurs naturally and is not necessarily harmful. For example, a burning log gives off radiant energy (radiation) in the form of both heat and light. However, the hazards most commonly associated with radiation are from *ionizing radiation,* the radiation that results when the structure of an atom's electrons, neutrons, and protons break down. This can happen when some form of ionizing radiation collides with a normal atom, or when an unstable atom (called a radioisotope) decays or breaks down on its on. Radioisotopes release energy in the form of ionizing radiation repeatedly over a specific length of time, until all the atoms become stable.

Humans are exposed to ionizing radiation from soil and rocks, foods, cosmic rays, and many other sources. Natural radiation of this type presents little health hazard. Sources of *man-made radiation* include watching television, smoking, having an X-ray, or wearing certain luminous dial watches. All types of ionizing radiation can be harmful. Long-term exposure to a small source of constant radiation or short-term exposure to a large amount of radiation can cause damage to human cellular structure or tissue.

TYPES OF RADIATION

Background Radiation. Naturally occurring radiation that humans are exposed to continuously in the environment.
Ionizing Radiation. The result of the breakdown, or decay, of an atom's structure.

Man-Made Radiation. The radioactive substances, or sources of radiation, created by man; e.g., a medical X-ray.
Alpha Radiation. Large atomic particles that both natural elements and some man-made substances emit. Alpha radiation has little external penetrating power, but can be harmful if you breathe or swallow radioactive elements.
Beta Radiation. Fast-moving atomic particles with little penetrating power. Beta radiation is frequently found inside a medical or research environment.
Gamma Radiation. Electromagnetic waves resulting from radioactive decay. This type of radiation has greater penetrating power than medical X-rays.
Cosmic Radiation. These are highly energetic atomic particles that originate from the sun and stars and penetrate the earth's atmosphere.
Neutron Radiation. Penetrating atomic particles that result from collisions between cosmic rays and atoms in the atmosphere and from some specialized man-made sources.
X-rays. Machine-generated electromagnetic waves that can penetrate the human body. This type of radiation is primarily in medical and dental settings, and is also found in some industrial environments.

DOSIMETERS

Persons exposed to sources of radiation can keep track of how much radiation they receive by using a measuring device called a dosimeter. The traditional unit for measuring a radiation dose is a rem. One rem equals 0.01 sievert.

Direct Reading Dosimeter (DRD). The DRD allows the user to periodically check the amount of radiation being received at any given moment. A quartz fiber within the dosimeter measures the radiation by moving along a scale and provides an indication of exposure.
Thermoluminescent Dosimeter or Film Badge (TLD). A film badge contains film that darkens; radiation exposure is determined by interpreting how dark the developed film is. TLDs contain small chips of material that absorb radiation in a measurable form.

Source:
U.S. Nuclear Regulatory Commission, *Working Safely with Nuclear Gauges, NUREG/BR-0133,* Washington: Government Printing Office, 1992.

Recycling, Paper

In 1971 the Recycled Paperboard Division of the American Paper Institute adopted the paper recycling symbol as the universal identifying logo for products and packaging made from clean, high quality paper that otherwise might have ended up in landfills. The following two symbols of recycling were designed to identify recycled and recyclable paper and paperboard products. Both of these symbols are expressions of environmental concern, designed to reinforce each other. Together, they create awareness of the recycling process and its contribution to environmental quality.

RECYCLED

This symbol is used to identify the following products:

Packages and other products made entirely or predominantly from recycled paper fibers;

Newspapers or other publications printed on recycled paper;

The concept of recycling in publications, advertisements, or promotional material;

Organizations engaged in paper recycling.

RECYCLABLE

This symbol is used to identify

Paper and paperboard products made from fibers which, after use, are suitable for recycling.

TERMINOLOGY

Definitions of recycled paper vary, largely because of the distinction between post-consumer wastepaper and pre-consumer wastepaper. Both types are used to make recycled paper. The National Recycling Coalition, Inc., has published the following definitions for these terms:

Post-Consumer Wastepaper. Paper that has reached an end user or consumer, such as paper collected through curbside or office recycling programs.

Pre-Consumer Wastepaper. Paper that leaves the mill but is not used by a final consumer. Examples of pre-consumer wastepaper include extra pulp from virgin paper manufacturing and trimmings left after cutting envelopes or other finished products.

Consumer advocates believe that only paper made with post-consumer waste paper should be labeled as recycled. Or, if paper contains both pre-consumer and post-consumer waste the percentages used of each should be listed (see *Environmental Labeling, Green Cross*). Others believe that paper made from pre-consumer waste should be referred to by some name other than recycled. For example, recovered or reprocessed (see *Environmental Labeling*).

GRADES

Waste paper is divided into *grades*. High grade papers include office paper, stationery, and computer printout paper. Lower grade papers include newspaper and telephone book paper. Corrugated boxes, paperboard, and craft papers also are recyclable.

Almost all grades of paper can be recycled, but they can only be recycled into particular products (newspapers, for example, can not be recycled into office paper, but can be recycled into newsprint and telephone directories.)

Source:
Fact Sheet, National Recycling Coalition, Inc., Washington, 1992.
Paper Recycling Committee, Recycled Paperboard Division, American Paper Institute, 260 Madison Avenue, New York, NY 10016.

Recycling, Plastic Containers

The Society of the Plastics Industry, Inc. (SPI) has developed a voluntary coding system for plastic containers which identifies bottles and other containers by material type, thus assisting recyclers in sorting plastic containers by resin composition. Some plastic containers already are being recycled and many more are recyclable. The plastics industry created the container coding system to provide a uniform system for coding that meets the needs of the recycling industry, as defined by the recyclers and collectors themselves.

The plastics recycling systems in place today are predominantly geared toward two resins, polyethylene terephthalate (PET) and high density polyethylene (HDPE)—largely because these resins are used in large volume and because they are used to produce easily identified containers such as the plastic soda bottle (PET) and the plastic milk and juice jug (HDPE). Early plastics recycling technology concentrated on processing these resins to aid in quality control of the end product and to derive the highest possible economic value from the recycled material.

Recycling centers can easily identify PET soda bottles and HDPE milk jugs, but there are other containers made of PET and HDPE. There are also containers made of vinyl, polystyrene, polypropylene, low-density polyethylene, and other resins which are candidates for recycling if they are identified, or "coded," by their resin content.

The SPI symbol code is a three-sided triangular arrow with a number in the center and letters underneath. The number inside and the letters indicate the resin from which the container is made; containers with labels or base cups of a different material may, if appropriate, be coded by their primary, basic material. The code is molded or imprinted on or as near to the bottom of the bottle or container as is feasible.

SYMBOL CODES

1 = PETE (polyethylene terephthalate). A clear, not opaque, plastic that sinks in water. Examples are clear or green-tinted two-liter beverage bottles.

2 = HDPE (high density polyethylene). Containers may be colored (e.g. laundry detergent bottles) or translucent (e.g., dairy bottles), with a dull surface finish. They will float in water. Examples of colored containers include liquid laundry and dishwashing detergent, fabric softener, liquid bleach, skin lotion, baby lotion, and bubble bath bottles. Examples of translucent containers are dairy and water bottles, gallon and half-gallon milk, distilled or spring water, orange juice, and punch drink containers.

3 = V (vinyl). Some shampoo bottles.

4 = LDPE (low density polyethylene). Plastic film and wrap.

5 = PP (polypropylene). Food lids, containers.

6 = PS (polystyrene). Food containers and foam boxes, hot drink cups, plates, occasionally recycled from schools, cafeterias, and restaurants.

7 = Other.

An example of the SPI recycling symbol appears below.

Source:
SPI's Voluntary Plastic Container Coding System, Washington: Society of the Plastics Industry, Inc., 1992.

Toxicity

Toxicity is defined as either the harmful effects produced by a substance or the capacity of a substance to cause any adverse effects, as based on scientifically verifiable data from animal test or epidemiology.

TERMINOLOGY

Acute Dermal LD$_{50}$. A statistically derived estimate of the single dermal dose of a substance that would cause 50 percent mortality to the test population under specified conditions.

Acute Exposure. A single exposure to a toxic substance which results in severe biological harm or death. Acute exposures are usually characterized as lasting no longer than a day.

Acute Inhalation LC$_{50}$. A statistically derived estimate of the concentration of a substance that would cause 50 percent mortality to the test population under specified conditions.

Acute Oral LD$_{50}$. A statistically derived estimate of the single oral dose of a substance that would cause 50 percent mortality to the test population under specified conditions.

Acute Toxicity. The ability of a substance to cause poisonous effects resulting in severe biological harm or death soon after a single exposure or dose. Also, any severe poisonous effect resulting from a single short-term exposure to a toxic substance. Based on the LD$_{50}$.

Chronic Toxicity. The capacity of a substance to cause long-term poisonous human health effects.

Dermal Toxicity. The ability of a pesticide or toxic chemical to poison people or animals by contact with the skin.

Highly Toxic. Any substance which produces death within 14 days in half or more than half of a group of laboratory white rats weighing between 200 and 300 grams, at a single dose of 50 milligrams or less per kilogram of body weight, when orally administered or produces death within 14 days in half or more than half of a group of rats when inhaled continuously for a period of 1 hour or less, or produces death within 14 days in half or more than half of a group of rabbits tested in a dosage of 200 milligrams or less per kilogram of body weight, when administered by continuous contact with the bare skin for 24 hours or less.

Latency Period. The time between exposure to a toxic and the development of discernible effects.

LC$_{50}$/Lethal Concentration. Median level concentration, a standard measure of toxicity. It tells how much of a substance is needed to kill half of a group of experimental organisms. The concentration of a toxic substance that kills 50 percent of the organisms exposed to it; sometimes a time period for exposure to that concentration is specified, as in LC$_{50}$: 7 days.

LD$_{0}$. The highest concentration of a toxic substance at which none of the test organisms die.

LD L$_{0}$. The lowest concentration and dosage of a toxic substance which kills the test organisms.

LD$_{50}$./Lethal Dose. The dose of a substance that kills 50 percent of the organisms in a test. The lower the LD$_{50}$, the more toxic the compound.

Lowest Observed Effect Level (LOEL). The lowest dose of a toxic that causes some effect; most testing of toxins is concerned with whether adverse effects occur, so the term lowest observed adverse effect level (LOAEL) is sometimes used instead.

No Observed Effect Level (NOEL). The highest dose level for which no effects have been observed; most testing of toxins is concerned with determining whether a substance causes no adverse effects, so the term non-observed adverse effect level

(NOAEL) is sometimes used instead.

Permissible Exposure Limit (PEL). An allowable exposure level in workplace air; it generally pertains to the average exposure over an 8-hour shift.

Short-Term Exposure Limit (STEL). The maximum concentration to which workers can be exposed for up to 15 consecutive minutes.

Threshold Limit Value (TLV). Represents the air concentrations of chemical substances to which it is believed workers may be exposed daily without adverse effects.

Time Weighted Average (TWA). An allowable exposure concentration averaged over a normal 8-hour workday or a 40-hour work week.

Toxic Cloud. Airborne mass of gases, vapors, fumes, or aerosols containing toxic materials.

Toxic Substance. A chemical or mixture that may present an unreasonable risk of injury to health or the environment.

Toxic. Has the capacity to produce personal injury or illness to man through ingestion, inhalation, or absorption through any body surface.

Toxicant. A poisonous agent that kills or injures animal or plant life.

Sources:

Environmental Protection Agency, 40 CFR 152.3 (1991), Washington: Government Printing Office.

Harte, John, Cheryl Holdren, Richard Schneider, and Christine Shirley, *Toxics A to Z: A Guide to Everyday Pollution Hazards,* Berkeley: University of California Press, 1991; original source for table: U.S. Forest Service, USDA, 1984. *Agriculture Handbook No. 633, Pesticide Background Statements, Vol. 1, Herbicides,* Washington, D.C.

Office of Communications and Public Affairs, *Glossary of Environmental Terms and Acronym List,* Washington: U.S. Environmental Protection Agency, 1989.

Trace Metals

Metals that are present either in the environment or in the human body in very low concentrations, such as copper, iron, and zinc.

Heavy Metals. Trace metals whose densities are at least five times greater than water, such as cadmium, lead, and mercury.

Source:

Harte, John, Cheryl Holdren, Richard Schneider, and Christine Shirley, *Toxics A to Z: A Guide to Everyday Pollution Hazards,* Berkeley: University of California Press, 1991.

Volatile Organic Compounds (VOCs)

Volatile Organic Compounds (VOCs). Chemical compounds which evaporate under standard conditions. They are found in all hydrocarbon products (which are typically produced from crude oil or natural gas) and in most organic solvents. Gasoline and mineral spirits are common examples. VOCs have been found to contribute to a variety of health and environmental problems. When the emissions from reactive VOCs chemically react with sunlight, they contribute to the buildup of concentrated ozone levels near the ground. Low-level ozone, in combination with an array of other air pollutants, forms smog. (Non-reactive VOCs, which must contain chloride or bromine and have a long atmospheric lifetime, deplete the protective ozone layer in the upper atmosphere.) This destructive cycle is known to contribute to a variety of health problems, such as respiratory disorders and environmental damage to crops and other plant life. In addition, VOCs are associated with water pollution, including water table contamination.

Volatile Organic Substance (VOS). Same as VOC.

Organic Solvent. Any liquid organic compound which has the power to dissolve most organic solids, gases, or liquids. Includes products derived from crude oil, such as mineral spirits. Although technically an organic solvent, water does not contain VOCs.

Hydrocarbon. A large group of chemical compounds composed only of hydrogen and carbon. The largest source is from petroleum crude oil.

Source:

Office of Communications and Public Affairs, *Glossary of Environmental Terms and Acronym List,* Washington: U.S. Environmental Protection Agency, 1989.

Automotive

Aerodynamic Drag

The wind resistance caused by vehicle size, shape, and airflow around the vehicle is referred to as *aerodynamic drag*. It is usually expressed as a *Coefficient of drag* or *Cd number:* the smaller the number, the better the aerodynamics (e.g., 0.32 Cd represents better aerodynamics than 0.46 Cd). Good vehicle aerodynamics should reduce interior wind noise and contribute to better handling, stability, and fuel economy for the vehicle.

Source:
Car and Truck Buying Made Easier, Seventh Edition, Dearborn, MI: Ford Motor Company, 1992.

All-Terrain Vehicles (ATV)

An *all-terrain vehicle* is any motorized off-highway vehicle 50 inches or less in overall width, with an unladen dry weight of 600 pounds or less, designed to travel on four low pressure tires, having a seat designed to be straddled by the operator and handlebars for steering control, and intended for use by a single operator and no passenger. Width and weight do not include accessories and optional equipment. ATVs are subdivided into four categories.

CATEGORIES

Category G (General Use Model). An ATV intended for general recreational and utility use.

Category S (Sport Model). Intended for recreational use by experienced operators only.

Category U (Utility Model). Intended primarily for utility use.

Category Y (Youth Model). Intended for recreational off-road use under adult supervision by operators under age 16.

Category Y-6. A youth model ATV which is intended for use by children age 6 and older.

Category Y-12. A youth model ATV which is intended for use by children age 12 and older.

TERMINOLOGY

Low Pressure Tire. A tire designed for off-road use on all-terrain vehicles; it has a recommended tire pressure of no more than 10 pounds per square inch.

Power Take-off (PTO). An external drive mechanism on an ATV to provide rotational power to drive accessory equipment.

Stopping Distance (S). The straight line distance, measured along the ground, from the point of actuation of the brake to the final stopping point of the vehicle, as measured from the same point on the vehicle.

Vehicle Load Capacity. The highest load, including the operator's weight, recommended by the manufacturer to be carried by a vehicle in its "as manufactured" condition. This does not include the vehicle weight.

Source:
DeLaney, J.C., Letter to editor, March 19, 1992, Irvine, CA: Specialty Vehicle Institute of America, 1992. Original source: *American National Standard for Four-Wheel All-Terrain Vehicles,* ANSI/SVIA 1, New York: American National Standards Institute, 1990.

Batteries

An automotive battery contains six cells, each consisting of metal plates and an electrolyte (sulfuric acid and water). The electrolyte reacts with the plates to deliver electrical current. Over time, the water in the cells breaks down into hydrogen and oxygen that escapes into the atmosphere.

BCI Group Numbers. To assist the North American battery aftermarket in the orderly marketing of batteries, the Battery Council International has a system classifying batteries into numbered size groups according to their voltage, maximum overall dimensions, terminal arrangement, and special features that affect the battery's fit in a specific vehicle.

Cranking Performance. Also know as *cold-cranking amps (CCA)*. The primary function of the battery is to provide power to crank the engine during starting. This requirement involves a large discharge in amperes over a short span of time. Therefore, the cranking performance rating is defined as: The discharge load in amperes that a new fully charged battery at 0 degree F can deliver for 30 seconds and maintain a voltage of 1.2 volts per cell or higher. Values range from 400 to 650.

Dual Battery. Has separate backup cells for emergencies

Freshness Dates. Batteries are dated by the manufacturer with the date the battery was made. However, the date code is not standardized among manufacturers and often does not look like a typical date stamp. Some manufacturers represent the month with a code letter (A for January, B for February, etc.) followed by the date, so that C93 stands for March 1993. Other manufacturers may use a code letter for the year (G for 1990, L for 1991, etc.) and follow with the number for the month (1 for January, 2 for February, etc.), meaning that a battery labeled G-3 would have been made in March 1990.

Low-Maintenance Battery, Dual Alloy or Hybrid Battery. Has removable caps covering the cells. Distilled water can be added to the cells to prolong the life of the battery.

Maintenance-Free Battery. Constructed of materials that prevent water loss. These batteries have no caps over the cells and never need water.

Reserve Capacity. A battery must provide emergency power for ignition, lights, etc., in the event of failure in the vehicle's battery recharging system. This requirement involves a discharge at normal temperature. The *Reserve Capacity* rating is defined as the number of minutes a new fully charged battery at 80 degrees F can be discharged at 25 amperes and maintain a voltage of 1.75 volts per cell or higher.

LABELING

The U.S. Consumer Product Safety Commission believes that certain wet cell batteries—such as automotive, marine, lawn and garden, motorcycle, and golf cart—are products subject to the labeling requirements of the Federal Hazardous Substances Act (FHSA) and its regulations. Acid packs containing sulfuric acid are subject to FHSA labeling requirements; those under five gallons are subject to the packaging requirements of the Poison Prevention Packaging Act and its regulations. As such, batteries and acid packs must bear certain cautionary statements on their labels. These statements include the following:

- Signal words, e.g., DANGER, POISON.
- Affirmative statements of the principal hazards associated with the product, e.g., SULFURIC ACID: CAN CAUSE BLINDNESS OR SEVERE BURNS.

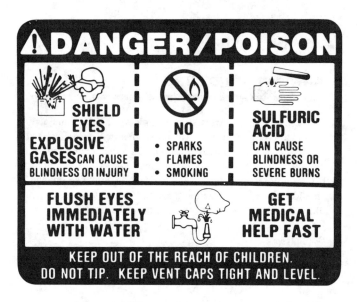

Warning with symbols

POISON | CAUSES SEVERE BURNS

Contains sulfuric acid. Avoid contact with skin, eyes or clothing. In event of accident flush with water and call a physician immediately.

KEEP OUT OF REACH OF CHILDREN

Written warning labels for batteries

BCI Dimensional Group Size	Maximum Overall Dimensions						Assembly Figure No. ♦	PERFORMANCE RANGES	
	Millimeters			Inches				Cranking Performance Amps. @ 0° F (−17.8° C)	Reserve Capacity Minutes @ 80° F (26.7° C)
	L	W	H	L	W	H			
PASSENGER CAR AND LIGHT COMMERCIAL BATTERIES 12-VOLT (6 CELLS)									
21	208	173	222	$8^3/_{16}$	$6^{13}/_{16}$	$8^3/_4$	10	305-370	55-68
21R	208	173	222	$8^3/_{16}$	$6^{13}/_{16}$	$8^3/_4$	11	260-410	68
22F	241	175	211	$9^1/_2$	$6^7/_8$	$8^5/_{16}$	11F	210-370	45-90
22HF	241	175	229	$9^1/_2$	$6^7/_8$	9	11F	280-400	69
22NF	240	140	227	$9^7/_{16}$	$5^1/_2$	$8^{15}/_{16}$	11F	210-240	50-60
22NL	235	133	198	$9^1/_4$	$5^1/_4$	$7^{13}/_{16}$	11(Y)	175	30
22R	229	175	211	9	$6^7/_8$	$8^{15}/_{16}$	11	290-350	45-90
23	273	175	214	$10^3/_4$	$6^7/_8$	$8^7/_{16}$	11L	300-410	70-105
24	260	173	225	$10^1/_4$	$6^{13}/_{16}$	$8^7/_8$	10	165-500	69-140
24F	273	173	229	$10^3/_4$	$6^{13}/_{16}$	9	11F	230-550	69-99
24H	260	173	238	$10^1/_4$	$6^{13}/_{16}$	$9^3/_8$	10	275-375	98
24R	260	173	229	$10^1/_4$	$6^{13}/_{16}$	9	11	440-475	70-100
24T	260	173	248	$10^1/_4$	$6^{13}/_{16}$	$9^3/_4$	10	350-385	110
25	230	175	225	$9^1/_{16}$	$6^7/_8$	$8^7/_8$	10	260-430	62-100
26	208	173	197	$8^3/_{16}$	$6^{13}/_{16}$	$7^3/_4$	10	310-530	60-80
27	306	173	225	$12^1/_{16}$	$6^{13}/_{16}$	$8^7/_8$	10	270-650	102-140
27F	318	173	227	$12^1/_2$	$6^{13}/_{16}$	$8^{15}/_{16}$	11F	360-655	95-140
27H	298	173	235	$11^3/_4$	$6^{13}/_{16}$	$9^1/_4$	10	370-440	125
27HF	318	173	233	$12^1/_2$	$6^{13}/_{16}$	$9^3/_{16}$	11F	435	115-135
29HR	333	173	232	$13^1/_8$	$6^{13}/_{16}$	$9^1/_8$	11	435-480	132-160
29NF	330	140	227	13	$5^1/_2$	$8^{15}/_{16}$	11F	235-350	55-100
33	339	173	240	$13^3/_8$	$6^{13}/_{16}$	$9^1/_2$	11L	1050	170
34	260	173	200	$10^1/_4$	$6^{13}/_{16}$	$7^{13}/_{16}$	10	375-650	100-110
34R	260	173	200	$10^1/_4$	$6^{13}/_{16}$	$7^{13}/_{16}$	11	375-650	100-110
35	230	175	225	$9^1/_{16}$	$6^7/_8$	$8^7/_8$	11	310-405	90-98
41	293	175	175	$11^9/_{16}$	$6^7/_8$	$6^7/_8$	15	435-510	75-95
42	243	173	173	$9^9/_{16}$	$6^{13}/_{16}$	$6^{13}/_{16}$	15	230-495	65-95
43	334	175	205	$13^1/_8$	$6^7/_8$	$8^1/_{16}$	15	375-490	115
44	418	175	205	$16^7/_{16}$	$6^7/_8$	$8^1/_{16}$	15	460-650	136-152
45	240	140	227	$9^7/_{16}$	$5^1/_2$	$8^{15}/_{16}$	10F	300-495	60-80
46	273	173	229	$10^3/_4$	$6^{13}/_{16}$	9	10F	350-450	75-95
47	246	175	190	$9^{11}/_{16}$	$6^7/_8$	$7^1/_2$	24	370-460	85
48	306	175	192	$12^1/_{16}$	$6^7/_8$	$7^9/_{16}$	24	495-560	85-95
49	381	175	192	15	$6^7/_8$	$7^9/_{16}$	24	460-740	140-150
50	343	127	254	$13^1/_2$	5	10	10	600	108
51	238	129	223	$9^3/_8$	$5^1/_{16}$	$8^7/_8$	10	405	70
52	186	147	210	$7^3/_8$	$5^{13}/_{16}$	$8^1/_4$	10	405	70
53	330	119	210	13	$4^{11}/_{16}$	$8^1/_4$	14	210-290	40
54	186	154	212	$7^3/_8$	$6^1/_{16}$	$8^3/_8$	19	305-330	60
55	218	154	212	$8^5/_8$	$6^1/_{16}$	$8^3/_8$	19	370-450	75
56	254	154	212	$10^1/_{16}$	$6^1/_{16}$	$8^3/_8$	19	450	90
57	204	183	177	$8^1/_{16}$	$7^1/_4$	7	22	310	60
58	255	183	177	10	$7^1/_4$	7	21	380-540	75
58R	255	183	177	10	$7^1/_4$	7	23	380-540	75
60	332	160	225	$13^1/_{16}$	$6^5/_{16}$	$8^7/_8$	12	260-385	65-115
61	192	162	225	$7^9/_{16}$	$6^7/_{16}$	$8^7/_8$	20	310	60
62	226	162	225	$8^{15}/_{16}$	$6^7/_{16}$	$8^7/_8$	20	380	75
63	258	162	225	$10^3/_{16}$	$6^7/_{16}$	$8^7/_8$	20	450	90
64	296	162	225	$11^{11}/_{16}$	$6^7/_{16}$	$8^7/_8$	20	435-535	105-120
65	306	190	192	12	$7^1/_2$	$7^9/_{16}$	21	650-850	130-165
70	208	179	196	$8^3/_{16}$	$7^1/_{16}$	$7^3/_4$	17	260-525	60-80
71	208	179	216	$8^3/_{16}$	$7^1/_{16}$	$8^1/_2$	17	275-430	75-90
72	230	179	210	$9^1/_{16}$	$7^1/_{16}$	$8^1/_4$	17	275-350	60-90
73	230	179	216	$9^1/_{16}$	$7^1/_{16}$	$8^1/_2$	17	430-475	80-115
74	260	184	222	$10^1/_4$	$7^1/_4$	$8^3/_4$	17	350-550	75-140
75	230	179	196	$9^1/_8$	$7^1/_{16}$	$7^3/_4$	17	430-630	90
76	333	179	216	$13^1/_8$	$7^1/_{16}$	$8^1/_2$	17	750-1075	150-175

BCI group numbers, dimensional specifications, and ratings

BCI Dimensional Group Size	Maximum Overall Dimensions						Assembly Figure No. ♦	PERFORMANCE RANGES	
	Millimeters			Inches				Cranking Performance Amps. @ 0° F (−17.8° C)	Reserve Capacity Minutes @ 80° F (26.7° C)
	L	W	H	L	W	H			
PASSENGER CAR AND LIGHT COMMERCIAL BATTERIES 12-VOLT (6 CELLS) Cont.									
77	306	184	222	12$^1/_{16}$	7$^1/_4$	8$^3/_4$	17	360-465	125-138
78	260	179	196	10$^1/_4$	7$^1/_{16}$	7$^3/_4$	17	515-770	105-115
85	230	173	203	9$^1/_{16}$	6$^{13}/_{16}$	8	11	515-550	90
86	230	173	203	9$^1/_{16}$	6$^{13}/_{16}$	8	10	550	90
PASSENGER CAR AND LIGHT COMMERCIAL BATTERIES 6-VOLT (3 CELLS)									
1	232	181	238	9$^1/_8$	7$^1/_8$	9$^3/_8$	2	300-520	105-165
2	264	181	238	10$^3/_8$	7$^1/_8$	9$^3/_8$	2	450-545	134-230
2E	492	105	232	19$^3/_8$	4$^1/_8$	9$^1/_8$	5	450	140
2N	254	141	227	10	5$^9/_{16}$	8$^{15}/_{16}$	1	450	135
17HF*	187	175	229	7$^3/_8$	6$^7/_8$	9	2B	270-315	100
HEAVY-DUTY COMMERCIAL BATTERIES 12-VOLT (6 CELLS)									
4D	527	222	250	20$^3/_4$	8$^3/_4$	9$^7/_8$	8	635-750	278-325
6D	527	254	260	20$^3/_4$	10	10$^1/_4$	8	750	310
8D	527	283	250	20$^3/_4$	11$^1/_8$	9$^7/_8$	8	650-1250	235-465
28	261	173	240	10$^5/_{16}$	6$^{13}/_{16}$	9$^7/_{16}$	18	400-500	80-135
29H	333	171	232	13$^1/_8$	6$^3/_4$	9$^3/_{16}$	10	400	147
30H	343	173	235	13$^1/_2$	6$^{13}/_{16}$	9$^1/_4$	10	370-400	120-150
30HR	343	173	235	13$^1/_2$	6$^{13}/_{16}$	9$^1/_4$	11	285-390	90-120
31	330	173	239	13	6$^{13}/_{16}$	9$^7/_{16}$	18	455-950	120-200
32N	362	140	227	14$^1/_4$	5$^1/_2$	8$^{15}/_{16}$	11	315	102
HEAVY-DUTY COMMERCIAL BATTERIES 6-VOLT (3 CELLS)									
3	298	181	238	11$^3/_4$	7$^1/_8$	9$^3/_8$	2	500-660	210-230
4	333	181	238	13$^1/_8$	7$^1/_8$	9$^3/_8$	2	550-975	240-420
5D	349	181	238	13$^3/_4$	7$^1/_8$	9$^3/_8$	2	820	310-380
7D	413	181	238	16$^1/_4$	7$^1/_8$	9$^3/_8$	2	875	370-426
HEAVY-DUTY MOTOR COACH AND BUS BATTERIES 12-VOLT (6 CELLS)**									
4B	540	283	276	21$^1/_4$	11$^1/_8$	10$^7/_8$	8	430	250
SPECIAL TRACTOR BATTERIES 6-VOLT (3-CELLS)									
3EH	491	111	249	19$^5/_{16}$	4$^3/_8$	9$^{13}/_{16}$	5	740-825	220-340
4EH	491	127	249	19$^5/_{16}$	5	9$^{13}/_{16}$	5	850	342-420
SPECIAL TRACTOR BATTERIES 12-VOLT (6-CELLS)									
3EE	491	111	225	19$^5/_{16}$	4$^3/_8$	8$^7/_8$	9	260-360	80-105
3ET	491	111	249	19$^5/_{16}$	4$^3/_8$	9$^{13}/_{16}$	9	355-425	130-135
4DLT	508	208	202	20	8$^3/_{16}$	7$^{15}/_{16}$	16L	625-820	202-290
12T	303	176	278	11$^{15}/_{16}$	6$^{15}/_{16}$	10$^{15}/_{16}$	10	460	160
16TF	421	181	283	16$^9/_{16}$	7$^1/_8$	11$^1/_8$	10F	600	240
17TF	433	176	202	17$^1/_{16}$	6$^{15}/_{16}$	7$^{15}/_{16}$	11L	575	145
20H	198	171	237	7$^{13}/_{16}$	6$^3/_4$	9$^5/_{16}$	10	220	50
GENERAL UTILITY BATTERIES 12-VOLT (6-CELLS)									
U1	197	132	186	7$^3/_4$	5$^3/_{16}$	7$^5/_{16}$	10(X)	120-235	23-40
U1R	197	132	186	7$^3/_4$	5$^3/_{16}$	7$^5/_{16}$	11(X)	200	25-37
U2	160	132	181	6$^5/_{16}$	5$^3/_{16}$	7$^1/_8$	10(X)	120	17
ELECTRIC VEHICLE BATTERIES 6-VOLT (3-CELLS)									
GC2	264	183	270	10$^3/_8$	7$^3/_{16}$	10$^5/_8$	2	②	②
GC2H①	264	183	295	10$^3/_8$	7$^3/_{16}$	11$^5/_8$	2	②	②

NOTES: ♦ See Terminals, Page 7.
   * Rod End Types — Extended Top Ledge with holes for hold-down bolts.
** Ratings for batteries recommended for Motor Coach and Bus service are for double insulation. When double insulation is used in other types, deduct 15% from the rating values for cranking performance.

① Special use battery not shown in application section.
② Capacity test 75 amperes to 5.25 volts at 80° F (26.7° C), cranking performance test not normally required for this battery.

BCI group numbers, dimensional specifications, and ratings (continued)

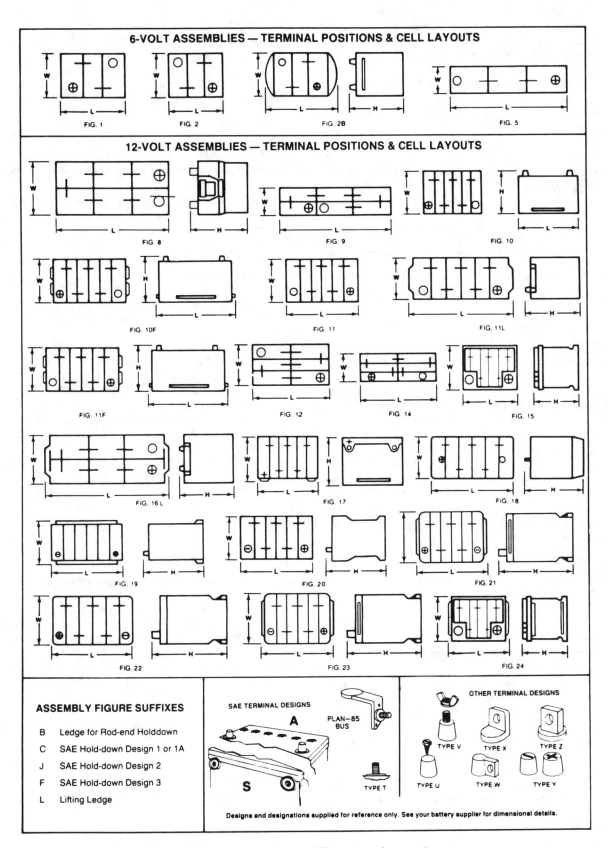

BCI assembly numbers, cell layouts, and terminals

- The common or usual name, or chemical name, of the hazardous substance, e.g., SULFURIC ACID.
- Statements of precautionary measures to follow, e.g., SHIELD EYES.
- Instructions, when appropriate, for special handing and storage, e.g., DO NOT TIP.
- The statement KEEP OUT OF REACH OF CHILDREN or its practical equivalent.
- First aid instructions, e.g., FLUSH EYES IMMEDIATELY WITH WATER.
- The name and place of business of the manufacturer, packer, distributor, or seller.

Sources:
"Auto Batteries," *Consumer Reports,* Vol. 56, no. 10 (October 1991): 683-686.
Battery Replacement Data Book, Chicago: Battery Council International, 1991.
Product Safety Committee, *Recommended Warning Messages for Lead-Acid Batteries, Cartons, and Battery Acid Packs,* Chicago: Battery Council International, 1989.

Brakes

Anti-lock Braking System (ABS). Anti-lock brakes prevent wheel lockup, which could cause loss of steering control. This system allows improved steering control during hard braking and reduced stopping distances—even on slippery roads. The system is available only on selected vehicles.
Disc Brakes. These brakes use pads pressed onto each side of a flat disc to stop the vehicle. Disc brakes are designed to cool quickly and resist fading after repeated stops. Front disc brakes generally are standard on cars. Optional rear disc brakes (if they are available) are normally part of an option package on cars only.

Source:
Car and Truck Buying Made Easier, Seventh Edition, Dearborn, MI: Ford Motor Company, 1991.

Car Alarms

Active System. The alarm gets activated when the car owner pushes a button in the car or on a remote-control device. The owner must also push a button to disarm the system when returning to the car.
Glass Sensor. A tiny microphone placed inside the car trips a siren if it detects the sound of glass breaking.
Motion Sensor. Jacking, swaying, or bouncing the car causes this device to sound the alarm.
Passive System. The alarm is set automatically a few seconds after the driver closes the door.
Shock Sensor. Triggers the siren after detecting vibrations caused by smashing windows or other sharp blows to the vehicle.

Starter Kill. Also called *starter interrupt* and *engine disabler,* it interrupts the starter, fuel-injection, or ignition process to prevent someone from starting the car.

Source:
Therrien, Lois, "To Thwart a Thief: The Latest in Car Protection," *Business Week,* September 7, 1992.

Diesel Fuel

Diesel engines range from small, high-speed engines used in trucks and buses, to large, low-speed stationary engines for power plants, so several grades of diesel fuel are needed. The ASTM grades of fuel are as follows:
Grade 1-D. A volatile distillate fuel for engines in service requiring frequent speed and load changes.
Grade 2-D. A distillate fuel of lower volatility for engines in industrial and heavy mobile service.
Grade 4-D. A fuel for low- and medium-speed engines.

In addition, The Bureau of Mines Petroleum Products Survey 77 groups the fuels according to the following types of service:
Type C-B. Diesel fuel oils for city-bus and similar operations.
Type T-T. Fuels for diesel engines in trucks, tractors, and similar service.
Type R-R. Fuels for railroad diesel engines.
Type S-M. Heavy-distillate and residual fuels for large stationary and marine diesel engines.
The combustion characteristics of diesel fuels are expressed in terms of cetane number, a measure of ignition delay.

Source:
Petroleum Products Survey 77, Washington: Bureau of Mines, 1977.

Dealer Add-ons

Price stickers for new cars at automobile dealers may contain the abbreviations ADM, ADP, or AMV. These abbreviations stand for *Additional Dealer Markup, Additional Dealer Profit,* and *Additional Market Value* respectively. They represent the dealer's demand for profit over and above that built into the manufacturer's price structure.

Source:
"New Car Buying," *Consumer Reports 1992 Buyer's Guide Issue,* Vol. 56, no. 12 (December, 1991): 126.

Drivetrains

The drivetrain consists of the transaxle or transmission, the drive shaft(s), the differential, and the axle shafts. Drivetrain components work together to transmit engine power to the wheels of the vehicle. Drivetrain variations include front-wheel drive, rear-wheel drive, and four-wheel drive.

TYPES

Four-Wheel Drive (4WD) or All-Wheel Drive. This system delivers power to all four wheels. These designations are applied to a wide variety of systems that vary greatly in terms of sophistication. Some deliver the power to all four wheels on a full-time basis while others provide four-wheel drive on a part-time basis only. Some can be used on all road surfaces; some cannot be used on dry paved roads. Therefore it is essential to understand the capabilities and limitations of any system before purchasing and/or operating a vehicle.

Front-Wheel Drive. Engine power acts through the drivetrain (generally a transaxle) to turn the front wheels. The front wheels pull the vehicle. These systems may have less loss of power due to friction during operation, which can contribute to better fuel economy.

Rear-Wheel Drive. Engine power drives the rear wheels. In most applications, the engine is connected to the rear wheels through a transaxle or a transmission, drive shaft, and differential. Rear-wheel drive pushes the vehicle.

TERMINOLOGY

Automatic Transmission. A combination of gears, clutches, and shafts connected to the engine through a torque converter. Once engaged, the transmission automatically selects the proper forward gear and shifts for the driver. Three- and four-speed automatic transmissions are generally available. Some are equipped with overdrive.

Axle Shaft. A rotating rod which transmits power from the differential or the transaxle to the wheel, and upon which the wheel revolves.

Clutch. A friction device used to connect the engine to the gears in a manual transmission. When depressed, the clutch allows the gears in the transmission to be shifted by disconnecting the driveline from the engine.

Continuously Variable Transmission (CVT). Provides a continous range of speed ratios between the engine and drive wheels.

Differential. A gear system that permits wheels connected to the drivetrain to turn at different speeds. This is necessary in a turn when the outside wheels turn faster than the inside wheels.

Drive Shaft. A long tube that carries power from the transmission to the differential. The drive shaft often has flexible couplings called universal joints allowing up and down movement of the rear differential without damaging the drive shaft.

Gears. Wheel-like parts with teeth cut into the rim. Meshing the teeth of two gears enables one to drive the other, thus transmitting power. When gears of different sizes are meshed together, they turn at different speeds multiplying or reducing torque. The transmission takes advantage of this to increase or decrease engine speed and torque relative to drive-wheel speed.

Manual Transmission. A series of gears and a clutch mechanism that allow the driver to control gear selection. The clutch is

normally operated by a foot pedal next to the brake, and gear selection is accomplished by moving a shift lever that is connected to the transmission. Four- and five-speed manual transmissions are generally available. Most are equipped with overdrive.

Overdrive. A gear combination allowing the engine to turn more slowly than when the transmission is in direct drive. By allowing slower engine operation, the overdrive gear contributes to operating economy, reduces noise, and may decrease engine wear over the life of the vehicle.

Torque Converter. A hydraulic link coupling the engine to the gear box, used in an automatic transmission.

Torque. A measure of rotational force measured in "pound-feet." A factor in determining the acceleration potential of the car.

Transaxle. A device that combines the function of the transmission and differential.

Transfer Case. A device that allows power to be delivered to the front and rear axles in a four-wheel drive system.

Transmission. A device that converts the speed and torque of the engine by using gears of different ratios. Manual and automatic transmissions are available.

Source:
Car and Truck Buying Made Easier, Seventh Edition, Dearborn, MI: Ford Motor Company, 1991.
Flammang, James, "A Car Buyer's Glossary," *Consumers Research Magazine,* Vol. 69, no. 4: 36-37

Engine Oil

Engine oils are classified in two general groupings, viscosity (or weight) and performance. An oil of low viscosity will flow more easily than an oil of high viscosity. A low viscosity oil is sometimes referred to as a *light oil* and a high viscosity oil as a *heavy oil.* Oils of different viscosities have been assigned numbers by the Society of Automotive Engineers (SAE). The lower the viscosity, the lower the assigned number. SAE 10 engine oil, for example, may be recommended for cold weather operation because it is a light oil that will flow more easily in cold weather. SAE 30, on the other hand, is a heavier oil that is appropriate for warm weather operation. The added designation of "W" indicates the oil has the added ability to remain fluid or flow at a wider range of temperatures. Viscosity is measured at both 0 degree F and 210 degrees F. SAE 5W, 10W, and 20W viscosity numbers are related to 0 degree (s) F measurements; and SAE 20, 30, 40, and 50 to 210 degrees F measurements. *Multigrade oils,* such as 5W-20 and 10W-30, have viscosity characteristics meeting requirements at both temperatures.

PERFORMANCE LETTER DESIGNATIONS

Performance letter designations are assigned by the American Petroleum Institute (API):

SG. Now recommended for use in all gasoline-powered cars regardless of the year they were built.

SF. Was recommended for gasoline engines in passenger cars and some trucks beginning with 1989 models.

SE. Suitable for most severe service of certain 1971 and all 1972 and later gasoline and other spark ignition engines having emission control devices.

SD. For gasoline engines in 1968 through 1970 cars, certain trucks and some 1971 and/or later models.

SC. For service in gasoline engines in 1964 through 1967 passenger cars and trucks.

SB. Recommended for older cars operating under moderate conditions.

SA. For utility and diesel engines operating under mild conditions.

CE. Meant for heavy-duty turbocharged diesel engines like those found in some European luxury models.

CD. For severe duty diesel engine service.

CC. For moderate to severe duty in diesels and certain heavy-duty gasoline engines.

CB. For mild to moderate diesel service.

CA. For light, normal conditions such as are typical of most farm tractor and trucking conditions.

Energy-Conserving I. Oils with added friction modifiers that are found to provide a 1.5 percent increase in fuel economy.

Energy-Conserving II. Oils with added friction modifiers that are found to provide a 2.7 percent increase in fuel economy.

The SAE vicosity grade number and the API performance numbers can be found on the either the label or the lid of the motor oil container.

Sources:

Goodheart-Willcox Automotive Encyclopedia, South Holland, Ill.: Goodheart-Willcox Company, Inc.

Gorzelany, Jim, "Complete Guide to Motor Oil," *Consumers Digest,* Vol. 30, no. 3 (May/June, 1991): 65-68.

SAE Handbook, "Standard SAE J-300," Warrendale, Pa.: Society of Automotive Engineers, 1990.

Engine Oil, Re-Refined

Previously used automobile motor and transmission oil which has been put through a refining process to remove the physical and chemical contaminants acquired through previous use. It does not mean a virgin oil that has been refined more than once.

Source:

Federal Trade Commission, "Deceptive Use of the Term, Re-refined," 16 CFR Sections 406.1 to 406.5 (1-1-1992), Washington: Government Printing Office.

Engines

There are two basic types of engines: gasoline and diesel. The gasoline engine is far more popular and more available than the diesel version. Diesel engines experienced renewed popularity in the late 1970s due to the higher gasoline fuel prices. At that time, diesel engines were more economical to operate because they were more fuel efficient and because diesel fuel cost less.

TYPES

Diesel Engines. An internal combustion engine that burns diesel oil for fuel. In a diesel engine, the air in the cylinder is highly compressed and becomes very hot. The diesel fuel is injected directly into the cylinder where it is ignited by the hot air. Diesels must be ruggedly constructed to withstand the high compression forces developed in their cylinders.

Eight-Cylinder Engine. Has eight combustion chambers; the most common configuration of an eight-cylinder engine has four combustion chambers on each bank of a *V* configuration. Gasoline power is usual, but some diesel versions are available.

Four-Cylinder Engine. Has four combustion chambers. The most common configurations include *in-line,* with cylinders in a row, and *opposed,* where the engine is flat with two cylinders on each side. Gasoline power is predominant.

Fuel Injection. A precise metering system for delivering fuel to the cylinders of the engine. Throttle body or central fuel injection uses single or dual injectors generally located between the air filter and the engine intake manifold. The injectors atomize a measured amount of gasoline which is mixed with air in the body and delivered to the cylinders through passages in the intake manifold. Multi-port fuel injection uses one injector for each cylinder. Electronic fuel injection (EFI) can be applied to the systems above. It delivers an electronically controlled, precisely metered amount of gasoline into the cylinders. Fuel injection improves fuel economy and engine efficiency.

Gasoline Engines. An internal combustion power source which burns gasoline for fuel. Gasoline is metered by a carburetor or fuel injection system, mixed with air, and ignited within the combustion chamber. The spark plug provides the spark which ignites the air/fuel mixture to create power.

Multi-Valve Engine. Another engine feature is the number of valves per cylinder. The most common configuration has two valves (one intake valve and one exhaust valve) per cylinder. Engines with more than two valves per cylinder are called multi-valve engines. The number of valves per cylinder generally affects how well the engine breathes (how much air or air/fuel mixture can get into the cylinder) and therefore affects the torque and horsepower produced by an engine. Multi-valve engines allow engineering flexibility. By designing different cylinder heads (i.e., a two-valve and a four-valve head) for the same engine, engineers can offer customers a choice of either economy or performance.

Six-Cylinder Engine. Has six combustion chambers, and more moving parts than a four-cylinder engine. *In-line,* with cylinders in a row; *opposed,* where the engine is flat with two cylinders on each side; and *V* configurations are available. Gasoline power is most common.

TERMINOLOGY

Compression Ratio. The compression ratio is a numerical measure of how much the air/fuel mixture is squeezed in the combustion chamber. Generally, the higher the compression ratio, the better the engine efficiency and power.

Combustion Chamber. An area at the top of the cylinder where the air/fuel mixture is burned.

Cylinder. The round enclosed chamber which houses the piston. The number of cylinders and the way they are arranged are often used to describe engines (e.g., in-line four-cylinder, V six-cylinder).

Displacement. The total cylindrical volume through which the pistons of an engine move from one end of the stroke to the other. Generally expressed in liters or cubic inches, the displacement is a good indication of the power of the engine. Large displacement (e.g., 5.0-liter) indicates greater power potential than small displacement (e.g., 1.5 liter).

Horsepower (hp). By definition, a measure of the rate at which work is done. Horsepower is a good indication of the performance or work capabilities of one engine as compared to another. An 150 hp engine is considered as having high power. An 80 hp engine is at the lower end of the scale.

Internal Combustion Engine. A type of engine where air and fuel are mixed and burned inside. In these engines the burned air/fuel mixture expands rapidly and creates power by pushing on a movable part such as a piston, a rotor, or a turbine. The piston-powered internal combustion engine is the most common in automotive use today. Both gasoline and diesel versions are available.

Superchargers. A device that packs extra air and fuel into the cylinder, much like the turbocharger (see *turbocharger*), to increase engine power and torque. The major difference between turbocharger and supercharger is that the supercharger is driven by a belt or chain running from the engine crankshaft to the compressor shaft of the supercharger wheel; a turbocharger is driven by exhaust gases from the engine. Superchargers can significantly increase horsepower and torque, but they add complexity to the engine, which can increase maintenance and repair costs.

Torque. A measure of the amount of twisting effort exerted at the crankshaft of the engine. When comparing engines, the engine with a higher torque rating will generally be better for towing or carrying heavy loads.

Turbo Lag. In a turbocharged (see *Turbocharger*) engine, a delay in the time it takes the engine to respond to an increased demand for power. Turbo lag occurs because the turbocharger does not operate until it is spinning at very high speed (75,000 rpm or more). When there is a power demand, it takes a moment for the exhaust gases to spin the turbocharger up to operating speed.

Turbocharger. Recaptures heat energy from exhaust gas to power a compressor which packs extra air into the cylinder. The fuel system compensates for the increased airflow by delivering more fuel. Because it only operates when the driver requires more power, the system can give a four-cylinder the power of a six- or an eight-cylinder without sacrificing much overall economy. However, the system raises compression in the engine and increases the danger of serious damage if proper operating and maintenance procedures are not observed.

Valve. A trumpet-shaped metal device which slides up and down to open and close a port (hole) in the cylinder head. Valves and their corresponding ports allow air or the fuel/air mixture to enter the cylinder before burning (*intake valves*) and to exit the cylinder head after burning (*exhaust valves*). The valves open and close the ports at precise intervals timed to the position of the piston in each cylinder.

Source:
Car and Truck Buying Made Easier, Seventh Edition, Dearborn, MI: Ford Motor Company, 1991.

Garage Door Openers

A *residential garage door opener* is one which is intended for use on the home garage, is rated 600 volts or less, and is intended to be employed in ordinary locations. The unit is labeled with the ampere rating unless the full-load power factor is 80 percent or more; or, for a cord-connected operator, unless the rating is 50 watts or less. The number of phases shall be indicated if an operator is for use on a polyphase circuit. The date code repetition cycle shall not be less than 20 years.

Source:
Consumer Product Safety Commission, "Safety Standard for Automatic Residential Garage Door Operators," 16 CFR part 1211 (1992), Washington: Government Printing Office.

Gasoline

A complex mixture of relatively volatile hydrocarbons, with or without small quantities of additives, blended to form a fuel suitable for use in spark-ignition engines.

GRADES

Gasoline grades are based on octane levels. In the 1950s, there were basically two grades of gasoline to be purchased: *regular* (85 octane) and *premium* (87 octane). In the 1990s, octane levels range from 82 to 95 with various grades in between. (See *Octane Rating.*)

OCTANE RATING

Smooth engine performance requires that the motor fuel be burned properly in the combustion chamber. Engine knocking, or pinging, occurs when the air/fuel mixture is ignited prematurely as it is compressed by the upward movement of the piston in the combustion chamber. This tendency is especially prevalent in smaller, high-compression engines. Pre-ignition causes the piston to work against the movement of the crankshaft and results in the knocking or pinging sound associated with this problem. Engine knock can lead to a loss of power and, if not rectified, eventually may cause damage to the engine. Eliminating engine knock is often accomplished by burning fuels with a high-octane value.

The octane number for a gasoline is determined by comparing its antiknock performance against a reference fuel with a known octane number. Because of its high antiknock value, iso-octane

(C_8H_{18}) is assigned an octane number of 100. Normal heptane (C_7H_{16}), which has poor antiknock characteristics, is given an octane rating of 0. The octane number of a test gasoline is then the percent of iso-octane in the blend. In a test engine, the antiknock performance of a gasoline component with an unknown octane rating can be compared to the performance of various reference blends of iso-octane and normal heptane. A blending component determined to have an octane rating of 90, for example, will behave similarly to an iso-octane/normal heptane test mixture that has an iso-octane concentration of 90 percent.

The octane rating of gasoline sold to motorists is based on the average of the research octane number (RON) and the motor octane number (MON) and is symbolized as (R+M)/2. The RON is a measure of the performance of a gasoline under laboratory conditions while the MON measures a gasoline's performance under relatively harsh operating conditions, such as when a vehicle is towing a heavy load.

Refiners, importers, producers, distributors, or retailers of gasoline are required to determine the octane rating of their gasoline before they pass it on. Retailers (gas stations) must post the octane rating of all gasoline sold to consumers. The test methods used to determine octane ratings are found in ASTM D 439-78, entitled *Standard Specifications for Automotive Gasoline*. ASTM D 2699-75 is used to determine the research octane number and ASTM D 2700-75 the motor octane number. An example of the label used for the octane rating, which is specified by law, appears below:

```
┌─────────────────────────┐
│  MINIMUM OCTANE RATING   │
│     (R+M)/2 METHOD       │
│                          │
│        89.5              │
│                          │
└─────────────────────────┘
```

TERMINOLOGY

Additives. Chemicals blended in small amounts into gasoline and other petroleum products to improve performance. Some prevent engine knocking (antiknocks); others keep carburetors and valves clean, reduce deposits in combustion chambers, and extend the life of sparkplugs.

Alternative Fuels. The need for alternative fuels to replace gasoline stems from (1) concerns about the environment and (2) the need to reduce U.S. dependence on foreign oil. Air pollutants targeted for control are carbon monoxide (CO), oxides of nitrogen (NO_x), and hydrocarbons (HC). Moreover, there is evidence that carbon dioxide (CO_2) emissions may contribute to global climate change through a phenomenon known as "the greenhouse effect." Increased concentration of CO_2 in the earth's atmosphere from various sources is believed by some in the scientific community to cause an overall warming of the earth's atmosphere. On this basis there has been a push to limit CO_2 emissions from automotive and industrial sources. Alternate fuels include *Methanol, Compressed Natural Gas,* and *Reformulated Gasoline* (see individual entries).

Compressed Natural Gas (CNG). Differs from methanol (see *Methanol*) and ethanol (see *Ethanol*) in that it is a gas at normal temperatures and pressures. Vehicles using CNG fuel greatly reduce CO and HC emissions.

Crude Oil. A mixture of hydrocarbons that exists in liquid state in underground reservoirs and remains liquid at atmospheric pressure after being brought to the surface and processed.

Deposit-Control Additives. Additives that disperse accumulated solids better than detergent compounds (see *Detergent Compound*). These compounds break caked carbon into tiny particles that wash away easily through injectors and intake valves and into the combustion chamber, where they are consumed with the air/fuel mixture.

Detergent Compound. An additive used to prevent the buildup of deposits in carburetors and fuel injectors. The detergents act to break up the deposits, and gasoline washes them away. However, detergents do not always rinse away entirely, and at high temperatures they leave deposits on intake ports and valves. Modern engines require a lower level of deposits. Residues can result in reduced fuel efficiency, increased exhaust emissions, and a loss of power.

Domestic Crude Oil. Crude oil produced in the United States or from its "outer continental shelf."

Ethanol. Ethyl alcohol (grain alcohol) made from a variety of organic materials, such as grain, potatoes, sugar, timber, and wastes. In the United States, most ethanol is made from corn. A mixture of 10 percent ethanol and 90 percent gasoline is called *gasohol* (see *Gasohol*).

Foreign Crude Oil. Crude oil produced outside the United States.

Gasohol. A blend of leaded or unleaded gasoline and alcohol (generally ethanol, but sometimes methanol). The alcohol content of gasohol is limited to 10 percent by volume.

Lead. Tetraethyl lead (TEL). Helps prevent knocking, which is caused by uncontrolled burning of gasoline.

Leaded Gasoline. Contains more than 0.05 gram of lead per gallon or more than 0.005 gram of phosphorus per gallon. Premium and regular grades are included, depending on octane rating. Also included is leaded gasohol.

Methanol. Methyl alcohol made from natural gas, coal, biomass, and many other organic substances. A gasoline octane enhancer accepted by the U.S. Environmental Protection Agency (EPA) for use in gasoline under specified conditions.

Reformulated Gasoline. Gasoline with reduced aromatic content (about 20 percent), reduced olefins (5 percent), lower Reid Vapor Pressure at 9 psi (see *Volatility*), a sulfur content of 250 parts per million or below, and an oxygen content of about 2 percent.

Reid Vapor Pressure (RVP). A measure of volatility (see *Volatility*). The more volatile a gasoline is, the more readily it evaporates and causes vapor lock.

Straight-Run Gasoline. Produced by simple distillation from crude oil. Usually has low octane numbers.

Unleaded Gasoline. Contains not more than 0.05 gram of lead per gallon and not more than 0.005 gram of phosphorus per gallon.

Premium, mid-grade, and regular grades are included, as is unleaded gasohol.

VOLATILITY

Volatility refers to a fuel's tendency to vaporize under prescribed conditions of temperature and pressures. The petroleum industry measures gasoline volatility in pounds per square inch (psi) of *Reid Vapor Pressure (RVP)*. The RVP of a fuel is the surface pressure required to prevent vaporization at 60 degrees under atmospheric pressure. The object for refiners is to produce gasoline that will vaporize readily in the combustion chamber during cold engine starts but will not be so volatile that it will vaporize in the fuel system when the engine is warm. The RVP of motor gasoline ranges from 9 to 15 psi.

At high temperatures and high altitudes, some gasolines can vaporize in the fuel system, leading to a condition known as *vapor lock*. When vapor forms in the fuel line, the gasoline pump is no longer able to draw fuel, and the engine stalls. The engine will not restart until the vaporized gasoline in the fuel line condenses. This condition is particularly prevalent in older cars.

The appropriate RVP for a motor fuel will change with geographic location, altitude, and season. Gasolines sold in the northern regions of the United States tend to have higher RVPs than gasolines sold in the southern portion of the country. In addition, adjustments to volatility are made for altitude. To compensate for the lower air pressures in mountainous regions, refiners will blend gasolines with comparatively low RVPs for these areas. Volatility also varies with the season. During the summer months, when vapor lock is more of a problem, RVPs generally will be lower than during the winter months, when cold starting is more of a consideration.

However, gasolines with a high RVP release more volatile organic compounds (VOCs) to the atmosphere. VOCs react photochemically in the atmosphere and are a major component of smog. Although gasoline fuel systems are designed to capture evaporative emissions, vapors nevertheless escape during operation and refueling. VOCs also are lost to the atmosphere during the transportation and storage of high-RVP gasoline.

To combat these emissions, the U.S. Environmental Protection Agency (EPA) implemented a two-phase program in the spring of 1989 limiting summertime volatility. The regulations limit gasoline RVP to a maximum of 10.5 psi, though certain sections of the country may have RVP standards as low as 9.0 psi.

Sources:
Chamberlain, Irvin, Robert Schmer, Evie Harper, Lynn Greenfield, Li Shyu, *The Motor Gasoline Industry: Past, Present, and Future,* Washington: U.S. Information Administration, U.S. Department of Energy, 1991.
Federal Trade Commission, "Octane Posting and Certification," 16 CFR part 306 (1992), Washington: Government Printing Office.

Gasoline, Fuel Economy

The measure of the amount of fuel used to run a vehicle over a specified distance. Fuel economy is generally expressed in *Miles Per Gallon* (MPG). The "EPA Mileage Rating," affixed to new vehicles, is an estimate of their fuel economy based on testing conducted according to a standard set by the U.S. Environmental Protection Agency (EPA). The rating does not guarantee actual mileage but can be used to compare the fuel economy of different vehicles.

Source:
Car and Truck Buying Made Easier, Seventh Edition, Dearborn, MI: Ford Motor Company, 1991.

Gasoline-Saving Products

The U.S. Federal Trade Commission (FTC) warns consumers to be wary of any gas-saving claims for automotive devices or oil and gas additives. Even for the few gas-saving products that have been found to work, the savings have been small. The U.S. Environmental Protection Agency (EPA) evaluates or tests products to determine whether their use will result in any measurable improvement to fuel economy. However, the EPA cannot say what effect gas-saving products will have on a vehicle over a long period of time because it has not conducted any durability tests. It is possible that some products may harm the car or may otherwise adversely affect its performance. The following list categorizes the various types of "gas-saving" products and explains how those products are used.

Air Bleed Devices. These devices bleed air into the air/fuel mixture after it leaves the carburetor. They usually are installed in the PCV line or as a replacement for idle-mixture screws.

Driving Habit Modifiers. These are lights or sound devices to tell the driver to reduce acceleration or to shift gears.

Fuel Line Devices (Heaters). Devices that heat the fuel before it enters the carburetor, usually by the engine coolant or by the exhaust or electrical system.

Fuel Line Devices (Magnets). These are magnetic devices which are clamped to the outside of the fuel line or installed in the fuel line and claim to change the molecular structure of gasoline.

Fuel Line Devices (Metallic). Typically these contain several dissimilar metals that are installed in the fuel line, claiming to cause ionization of the fuel.

Fuels and Fuel Additives. These materials are added to the gas tank.

Ignition Devices. These devices are attached to the ignition system, or they are used to replace original equipment or parts.

Internal Engine Modifications. Devices which make physical or mechanical function changes to the engine.

Liquid Injection. These products add liquid into the fuel/air intake system and not directly into the combustion chamber.

Mixture Enhancers (Others). Devices which make some general modifications to the vehicle intake system.

Mixture Enhancers (Under the Carburetor). These devices are mounted between the carburetor and intake manifold and claim to enhance the mixing or vaporization of the air/fuel mixture.

Oils and Oil Additives. Usually oils and oil additives are poured into the crankcase of the engine of the car.

Vapor Bleed Devices. Similar to the *air bleed devices*, except that induced air is bubbled through a container of water/antifreeze mixture, which usually is located in the engine compartment.

Source:
Federal Trade Commission, Office of Consumer and Business Education, *Gas-Saving Products: Facts for Consumers*, Washington: Government Printing Office, 1990.

Grease, Lubricating

There are two performance groups of automotive service greases: *chassis lubricants* (letter designation L) and *wheel bearing lubricants* (letter designation G). Performance categories within these groups result in two-letter designations for chassis greases (LA and LB) and three categories for wheel bearing greases (GA, GB, and GC). The automotive industry is in general agreement that the highest performance category in each group (LB and GC) is suitable for service relubrication.

CHASSIS SERVICE (LUBRICANT APPLICATIONS)

LA. Used in service typical of chassis components and universal joints in passenger cars, trucks, and other vehicles under mild duty only. Mild duty will be encountered in vehicles operated with frequent relubrication or in noncritical applications.

LB. Used in service typical of chassis components and universal joints in passenger cars, trucks, and other vehicles under mild to severe duty. Severe duty will be encountered in vehicles operated under conditions which may include prolonged relubrication intervals, or high loads, severe vibration, exposure to water, or other contaminants.

WHEEL BEARING SERVICE (LUBRICANT APPLICATIONS)

GA. Used in service typical of wheel bearings operating in passenger cars, trucks, and other vehicles under mild duty. Mild duty will be encountered in vehicles operated with frequent relubrication in noncritical applications.

GB. Used in service typical of wheel bearings operating in passenger cars, trucks, and other vehicles under mild to moderate duty. Moderate duty will be encountered in most vehicles operated under normal urban, highway, and off-highway service.

GC. This type of grease is used in service typical of wheel bearings operating in passenger cars, trucks, and other vehicles under mild to severe duty. Severe duty will be encountered in certain vehicles operated under conditions resulting in high bearing temperatures. This includes some vehicles equipped with disc brakes, vehicles operated under frequent stop-and-go service (buses, taxis, urban police cars, etc.) and those vehicles that are operating under severe braking service (trailer towing,

heavy loading, mountain driving, etc.).

Source:
Chassis and Wheel Bearing Service Classification System, Kansas City, MO: National Lubricating Grease Institute, 1992.

Handling

A combination of characteristics such as steering, cornering ability, ride characteristics, etc., which determines how a vehicle moves over the road. A vehicle which remains stable in high-speed turns and maintains control in spite of road imperfections is said to have *good handling*.

Source:
Car and Truck Buying Made Easier, Seventh Edition, Dearborn, MI: Ford Motor Company, 1992.

Rebuilt Automobile Parts

Used automobile parts that have been reconditioned for resale are labeled as being:
Repaired
Remanufactured
Reconditioned
Rebuilt or relined
Products so labeled have been cleaned of rust and corrosion; impaired, defective, or worn parts have been restored to a sound condition or replaced with new or rebuilt parts; all missing parts have been replaced; and the product has otherwise been put back into sound working condition.

Source:
Federal Trade Commission, "Guides for the Rebuilt, Reconditioned, and Other Used Automobile Parts Industry," 16 CFR sections 20.0 to 20.3 (1992), Washington: Government Printing Office.

Recreational Vehicle (RV)

Chopped Van (Compact). This unit is built on an automotive manufactured cab and chassis having a Gross Vehicle Weight Requirement (GVWR) under 6,500 pounds. It may provide any or all of the conveniences of the larger unit.

Chopped Van (Low Profile). This unit is built on an automotive manufactured van frame with an attached cab section having a Gross Vehicle Weight Requirement (GVWR) of 6,500 pounds or more with an overall height of less than eight feet. The RV manufacturer completes the body section containing the living area and attaches it to the cab section.

Chopped Van (Mini). This unit is built on an automotive manufactured van frame with an attached cab section having a Gross

Vehicle Weight Requirement (GVWR) of 6,500 pounds or more, with an overall height of more than eight feet. The RV manufacturer completes the body section containing the living area and attaches it to the cab section.

Conventional Motor Home (Type A). The living unit has been entirely constructed on a bare, specially designed motor vehicle chassis.

Conventional Travel Trailer. Ranges typically from 12 feet to 35 feet in length and is towed by means of a bumper or frame hitch attached to the towing vehicle.

Fifth-Wheel Travel Trailer. This unit can be equipped the same as the *conventional travel trailer* but is constructed with a raised forward section that allows a bi-level floor plan. This style is designed to be towed by a vehicle equipped with a device known as a fifth-wheel hitch.

Folding Camping Trailer. A recreational camping unit designed for temporary living quarters which is mounted on wheels and constructed with collapsible sidewalls that fold for towing.

Motor Home. A recreational camping and travel vehicle built on (or as an integral part of) a self-propelled motor vehicle chassis. It provides at least four of the following permanently installed living systems: cooking; refrigeration or ice box; self-contained toilet; heating or air conditioning; a potable water system including water tank, faucet, and sink; separate 110-125 volt electrical system; an LP gas supply; sleeping facilities.

Park Trailer. Designed for seasonal or temporary living. When set up, may be connected to utilities necessary for operation of installed fixtures and appliances. Built on a single chassis mounted on wheels with a gross trailer area not exceeding 400 square feet when in the set-up mode.

Travel Trailer. A trailer designed to be towed by a motorized vehicle (auto, van, or pick-up truck) and of such size and weight as not to require a special highway movement permit. It is designed to provide temporary living quarters for recreational, camping, or travel use and does not require permanent on-site hook-up. A travel trailer can be one of three types: *conventional travel trailer, park trailer, fifth-wheel travel trailer* (see individual entries).

Truck Camper. A recreational camping unit designed to be attached to or mounted on the bed or chassis of a truck constructed to provide temporary living quarters for recreational, camping, or travel use.

Van, Conversion. A completed or incompleted van chassis modified esthetically or decoratively in appearance by the RV manufacturer for transportation and recreational purposes. These changes may include windows, carpeting, paneling, seats, sofas, and accessories.

Van Camper (Type B). A panel-type truck to which the RV manufacturer adds any two of the following conveniences: sleeping, kitchen, and toilet facilities; 110-125 volt hook-up; fresh water storage; city water hook-up; and a top extension to provide more head room.

Source:
Bryan, Robert M., Letter to editor, February 7, 1992, Reston, VA: Recreation Vehicle Industry Association.

Ride Quality

An evaluation of the way a vehicle feels as it moves over the road. Ride quality takes into consideration such factors as smoothness over road imperfections, isolation from road vibration, etc.

Source:
Car and Truck Buying Made Easier, Seventh Edition, Dearborn, MI: Ford Motor Company, 1991.

Suspension Systems

The combination of mechanical components which holds the body above the wheels. The suspension affects quality of ride, cornering ability, and carrying capacity of the vehicle.

Active Suspension. One that adjusts itself automatically to the way a car is driven and to the road conditions. Some current systems actually change the spring rates and add the damping forces provided by the shock absorbers. The advantage is that a suspension calibrated for smooth ride can adjust itself instantly for handling or rough road needs.

Independent Suspension. The left and right wheels are independent of each other and therefore act independently when rolling over a bump. With independent suspension, a bump affecting one wheel is not transmitted to the other, thereby giving the car a smoother ride.

McPherson Strut. A combination of coil spring and shock absorber.

Rack-and-Pinion Steering. A type of steering system that offers more precise control.

Upgraded Suspension System. Suspension upgrading normally includes high-performance springs, shock absorbers, and stabilizer bars and is chosen for improved handling or increased carrying ability. However, this generally results in a firmer ride. Some suspension upgrades require a tire upgrade as well. Also called a *heavy-duty suspension.*

Source:
Car and Truck Buying Made Easier, Seventh Edition, Dearborn, MI: Ford Motor Company, 1991.
Flammang, James, "A Car Buyer's Glossary," *Consumers Research,* Vol. 69, no. 4 (April 1986).

Tires

GRADES

The Uniform Tire Quality Grading System (UTQGS) is a tire information system designed to help buyers make relative comparisons among tires. The UTQGS is not a safety rating and not a guarantee that a tire will last for a prescribed number of miles or perform a certain way. It simply gives tire buyers additional information to combine with other considerations, such as price, brand loyalty, and dealer recommendations. Under UTQGS, tires are graded by the manufacturers in three areas: treadwear, traction, and temperature. The UTQGS grade information can be found on two places on the tire: on a paper label affixed to the tread, and molded into the tire sidewalls. Additionally, brochures which explain the tire grades are available at tire stores.

Traction. Traction grades represent the tire's ability to stop on wet pavement as measured under controlled conditions on asphalt and concrete test surfaces. The traction grades from highest to lowest are *A, B,* and *C.* A tire graded *A* may have relatively better traction performance than a tire graded *B* or *C,* based on straight ahead braking tests. The grades do not reflect the cornering or turning traction performance of the tire.

Temperature. Temperature grades represent the tire's resistance to heat and its ability to dissipate heat when tested under controlled laboratory test conditions. Sustained high temperature can cause the tire to degenerate and reduce tire life, and excessive temperature can lead to sudden tire failure. The temperature grades from highest to lowest are *A, B,* and *C.* The grade *C* corresponds to the minimum performance required by federal safety standard. Grades *B* and *A* represent higher levels of performance than the minimum required by law. The temperature grade is for a tire that is inflated properly and not overloaded. Excessive speed, underinflation, or excessive loading, either separately or in combination, can cause heat build-up and possible tire failure.

Treadwear. The treadwear grade is a comparative rating based on the wear rate of the tire when tested under carefully controlled conditions. For example, a tire graded 200 should have its useful tread last twice as long as a tire graded 100. However, real world tire tread life, in miles, depends on the actual conditions of their use. Tire life is affected by variations in driving habits, service practices, and differences in road characteristics and climate. The numerical range goes from under 100 to over 400.

SPEED RATING

Some tires are now marked with letters to indicate their speed rating, based on laboratory tests which relate to performance on the road. Tires may be marked with one of six speed symbols to identify the particular tire's speed rating. (See also *Sidewall Markings.*) The speed symbols for tires are presented in the table that follows.

Speed Symbol	Maximum Speed
Z	*above 149 mph
V (no service description)	*above 139 mph
V (service description)	149 mph
H	130 mph
U	124 mph
T	118 mph
S	112 mph

*Consult tire manufacturer for maximum speed.

TYPES

There are three types of tire construction:
Radial
Diagonal Bias
Belted Bias

SIDEWALL MARKINGS

Information on a tire's make and performance characteristics is molded into the sidewall of the tire. It shows the name of the tire, its size, whether it is tubeless or tube type, the maximum load and maximum inflation, the safety warning, and other information.

Shown in the figure above is the sidewall of a popular *P-metric* speed-rated auto tire. *P* stands for passenger; *205* represents the width of the tire in millimeters; *60* is the ratio of height to width; *H* is the speed rating; *R* means radial; and *15* is the diameter of the wheel in inches. Some speed-rated tires carry a Service Description instead of showing the speed symbol in the size designation. The Service Description, 90H in this example, consists of the load index and speed symbol. A *B* in place of the *R* means the tire is a belted bias construction. A *D* in place of the *R* means diagonal bias construction. The maximum load is shown in pounds *(lbs.)* and in kilograms *(kg),* maximum pressure in pounds per square inch *(psi)* and in kilopascals *(kPa).* The letters *DOT* certify compliance with all applicable safety standards established by the U.S. Department of Transportation (DOT). Adjacent to this is a tire identification or serial number. This serial number is a code with up to eleven digits that are a combination of numbers and letters. The sidewall also shows the type of cord and number of plies in the sidewall and under the tread.

Shown above is the typical information on the sidewall of a light truck tire. *LT* stands for light truck. *LT235/85R16* is the size designation for a metric light truck tire. *LOAD RANGE D* identifies the load and inflation limits; *RADIAL* identifies that the tire has a radial construction. *MAX LOAD SINGLE 2623 lbs. AT 65 psi COLD* indicates the maximum load rating of the tire and corresponding minimum cold inflation pressure for that load when used as a single. For normal operation, follow pressure recommendations in owner's manual or on vehicle placard; *MAX LOAD DUAL 2381 lbs. AT 65 psi COLD* indicates the maximum load rating of the tire and corresponding minimum cold inflation pressure when used in a dual configuration. The other markings on the sidewall have the same meaning as described for the passenger car tire.

LABELING TERMINOLOGY

A-2. Tire sizes 16.00 and larger in nominal cross-section. Also called *earthmover* or *off-the-road* tires.

A3A. Tires used primarily in off-road applications having cross sections ranging from 12.00 to 14.00 in conventional sizes and 15.5 to 17.5 in wide base sizes.

Aging. Deterioration of physical and chemical properties of rubber by oxidation over a period of time.

Air Pressure. Force exerted by air within tire, expressed in pounds per square inch, kilopascals, or bars.

Air-Water Tire Pressure Gauge. Special watertight gauge used with farm tires that are filled with liquid ballast.

Alignment. Adjustment of steering and suspension components to facilitate the most efficient operation of all tire/wheel assemblies as related to vehicle control and tire wear.

All Season Tire. A highway tire designed to meet the weather conditions in all seasons of the year and which meets the Rubber Manufacturers Association definition of a mud and snow tire.

Ambient Temperature. Temperature of the media surrounding an object such as the air temperature in which a tire may be running.

Anchored Beads. Ply and flipper construction which locks beads in place in the tire. Rubber-coated cord fabric is wrapped around high tensile strength steel wire which has been insulated with rubber. The ends of the fabric, which are several inches in length, are then carried up into the sidewall of the carcass and locked in by the plies when the tire is vulcanized.

Anti-Ozonant. A substance added to rubber to delay aging due to ozone.

Antioxidant. A substance added to rubber to delay aging by oxidation.

Antiskid. The wiping or biting edges of a tread design offering resistance to skidding. A tire's skid efficiency is governed by many factors, including design, location, flexibility, number of blades, and compound.

Antiskid Depth. Thickness of antiskid (tread) design above bottom of tread grooves. Also called *skid depth*.

Aspect Ratio. A numerical term which expresses the relationship between the section height of the tire and the cross section width. (Aspect Ratio of 70 means the tire section is approximately 70 percent as high as it is wide).

Assymetrical. A tire design in which the tread pattern on one side of the tire center line differs from the other side.

Balance. The distribution of weight around a tire or tire/wheel assembly. The uniform distribution of weight will produce a balanced tire.

Ballast, Liquid. Liquid, usually water solution of calcium chloride, pumped into a tire to provide more weight for added traction. (For farm and some off-the-road tires.)

Band. Two or more plies in band configuration ready to be put on the building drum for manufacture of a tire.

Band Ply. A component of a band.

Base. The rubber portion of some types of tread which does not come into contact with the road. It is a rubber layer between the actual road contact tread and carcass of the tire which helps add tread life and dissipate heat.

Bead. That part of the tire that is shaped to fit the rim. Also, the steel wire assembly which forms the core of that portion of the tire.

Bead Apex. Rubber filler above the bead wires.

Bead Base. The relatively flat surface of the tire's bead between the bead heel and toe.

Bead Core. One strand of specially treated steel wire wound into a specified number of hoops and then encased in rubber and other reinforcing materials.

Bead Failure. A failure occurring in the immediate area of the tire bead.

Bead Heel. Outer bead edge that contacts the rim flange.

Bead Movement or Bead Rocking. Movement of bead on rim usually caused by improper inflation of tire, excessive loading of tire, improper design of tire, improper seating of tire, or improper rim or tire sizing.

Bead Toe. The inner edge of the bead area.

Bead Wire. The specially treated steel wire that forms the bead core.

Bead Wrap. Fabric cover, usually square woven, which is wrapped around the bead core.

Belt. A fabric, fiberglass, Flexten, or steel cord strip which runs circumferentially around a tire usually between the tread and the plies.

Belt Separation. A tire failure in which the belts separate from the plies or tread. Usually occurs at the edge of the belts.

Belted Construction. Tire construction in which two or more belts are added to the tire.

Bias Belted Tire Construction. A tire with a bias ply carcass and stiff reinforcing belts extending from shoulder to shoulder.

Bias Ply. A tire with cords running at an acute angle to the circumferential centerline of the tire.

Bias Tire Construction. A tire construction in which adjacent plies cross each other at a bias angle.

Bleeding a Tire. Dangerous practice of letting hot air out of tires under load and after they have been running in order to reduce inflation (not recommended).

Blemished, Imperfect, Defective, etc. Superficial irregularity or imperfection. These products should have permanently stamped or molded thereon or affixed thereto and to the wrappings in which they are encased a plain and conspicuous legend or statement to the effect that such products are blemished, imperfect, or defective. Such markings by a legend such as *XX* or by a color marking or by any other code designation which is not generally understood by the public are not considered to be an adequate disclosure.

Blister. An air pocket in rubber located near the inside or outside surface of a tire.

Blowout. Instantaneous rupturing of tire body, causing complete loss of air pressure.

Body. Tire structure excepting tread and sidewall rubber.

Brake Hop. An oscillatory hopping motion of the wheel which occurs when brakes are applied in forward or reverse vehicle motion.

Brand No. A number branded into one or both sidewalls of a tire for identification purposes.

Breaker. Special cord fabric reinforcement between tire tread and cord body which reduces road shock effect on carcass.

Burst Pressure Test. Inflating tire or tube to bursting point to determine weakest point (usually done with water, for safety).

Buttress. Portion of tread running around shoulder and blending into sidewall which helps protect the sidewall from cuts.

Butyl Rubber. A synthetic rubber made from isobutylene and isoprene. It is noted for excellent weather and chemical resistance, and excellent vibration absorption and air retention.

Calcium Chloride (CaC$_{12}$). A chemical added to prevent freezing of water ballast and to add weight to certain special use tires such as farm tractors and off-road machinery.

Cap/Base Construction. A tire with a tread composed of two layers of rubber. The outer layer (cap) gives the best traction and wear properties while the inner layer (base) has the best heat resistant properties. (Same as *dual compound*.)

Carbon Black. A general name for various forms of carbon used as compounding ingredients in rubber.

Carcass. That part of a tire structure which does not include the tread and sidewall rubber.

Cargo Load. The weight of the cargo carried by a vehicle. The maximum cargo load must be included in addition to the curb weight and occupant loads in determining maximum tire load.

Carrying Capacity. Maximum rated tire load for a given inflation pressure as established by the Tire and Rim Association.

Change-Overs, New Car Take Offs. Removal of tires placed on car or truck by the manufacturer, and substitution of a different size or type. Tires that have been subjected to insignificant use necessary in moving new vehicles prior to delivery of such vehicles to franchised distributor or retailer.

Channel Wear. See *Erosion Wear*.

Checking. Minute cracking in surface of rubber caused by aging and oxidation.

Chip-Chunk. Loss of either small or substantial pieces of the tread by the cutting or breaking action of rough terrain or poor highway surfaces. Normally associated with highway tires when incorrectly used off the road.

Chipper. A narrow band of fabric or steelcord located in the bead area whose function is to reinforce the bead area and stabilize the lower sidewall.

Circumferential Breaks. A tire injury running parallel to the bead.

Circumferential Cracks. Cracks in a tire running parallel to beads. Usually consists of cracks in the grooves of the tread.

Circumferential Rib. Rib extending around circumference of tire.

Cleated Tread. Tread pattern consisting of lugs or cleats rather than ribs.

Cold Patch. Tube repair applied without heat.

Commercial Tires. Generally indicated to mean truck and industrial tires.

Concave Molded. Tires cured in a mold which produces a tread surface that is slightly depressed in the center when uninflated.

Conicity. The tendency of a tire to pull to one side due to off center tire components.

Contact Area, Gross. The total area enclosing the pattern of the tire tread in contact with a flat surface (including the area of grooves or voids) at a definite load and inflation pressure.

Contact Area, Net. The area enclosing the pattern of the tire tread in contact with a flat surface (excluding the area of grooves or other voids) at a definite load and inflation.

Contour (Tire). Outline of profile of the outside surface of a tire.

Cooler Running Tires. Tires designed to reduce internal heat generated in operation through improvements in design, fabrics, and compounding.

Cord. The twisted fiber or filament of polyester rayon, nylon, steel, or other material which gives the tire carcass and belts strength.

Cord Material. The fabric that is utilized in the ply is known as the cord material. A disclosure of the generic name of the cord material used in the ply of the tire should be made on a label or tag prominently displayed on the tire itself and affixed in such a fashion that it cannot be easily removed prior to sale.

Cracking Tread or Groove. Splitting condition in grooves of the tire tread.

Cross Ply. Sometimes used to refer to a bias ply tire.

Cross Rib Tire. A tire with deep molded tread grooves that extend radially into the shoulder.

Crown Radius. The measurement of the curvature of a tire tread between the shoulders of the tire. It indicates the relative flatness of the tire tread area.

Curb Guard. A protrusion of rubber running circumferentially around the tire just above the whitewall. Prevents whitewall scuffing on curbs.

Curb Scuffing. Abrasion of shoulder and sidewall of tire caused by rubbing against curb as in parking.

Curb Weight. The manufacturer's weight of the completed vehicle with standard equipment including cab and/or utility body and the maximum capacity of engine fuel, oil, and coolant. Air conditioning and the additional weight of an optional engine are to be included if the car is so equipped.

Curing. Process of heating or otherwise treating a rubber or plastic compound to convert it from a thermoplastic or fluid material into the solid, relatively heat-resistant state desired in the commercial product. When heating is employed, the process is called *vulcanization.*

Deflection. The difference between the unloaded and loaded section heights of a tire at a given load and inflation pressure.

Demountable Tire. Refers to an industrial tire which may be mounted and demounted from a special rim with the use of hand tools.

Denier. The weight in grams of a given length of cord before twisting. In general terms, the larger the denier the larger the cross section or diameter of the cord.

Design Rim Width. The specific rim width assigned to each tire size designation, to help determine basic tire dimensions.

Diagonal Break. A fabric break which follows the path of the cords in the plies.

Diagonal Wear. Flat spot worn across the tread at approximate 25 to 35 degree angle to the tread grooves.

Diameter, Outer Tire. Maximum circumference of a tire (in inches), divided by the constant, *pi* (3.1416).

Die Size. Refers to the dimensional size designations for retread rubber. (Example 40-80-14.) The first number gives the width of the crown in inches and 8ths of inches. The second number gives the width of the base in inches and 8ths of inches. The third number gives the gauge of the stock in 32nds of an inch.

Directional Tread. Tread design in which performance is dependent upon direction of rotation (e.g., farm tractor tires).

Disc Wheel. This is a wheel and rim assembly which is welded or riveted together for attachment to the hub with cap nuts.

DOT Number. Department of Transportation number which must be used by all tire manufacturers on all over-the-highway tires. Numbers molded in the tire sidewall identify the manufacturer, the manufacturing plant, the tire size and type, and the week of manufacture. Example: DOT MA HB ABC 037. *DOT* means the tire meets or exceeds Department of Transportation safety standard 109. *MA* is the code number assigned by DOT to the manufacturing plant. *HB* is the tire size, in this case P215/75*14. *ABC* is a group of up to four symbols, optional with the manufacturer, to identify the brand or other significant characteristics of the tire. The *037* means the tire was made during the third week of 1987 (the first two numbers designate the week, the last number indicates the year).

Double Bottom Truck. A standard tractor trailer truck unit with a second trailer attached.

Down Time. The vehicle operating time lost due to maintenance difficulties, including tire failures.

Drawbar. Bar at rear of farm tractors to which implements, trailers, and similar equipment are attached.

Drawbar Pull. Maximum amount of force a tractor is capable of exerting at the drawbar to pull a load such as a wagon, plow, tree stump. The ability of a tractor to exert its maximum pull at the drawbar is dependent partly upon ability of the tires to resist slippage.

Drive Lugs. Small metal bars on the outside of a rim base to limit circumferential movement.

Drive and Occupant Weight. Rated at 150 pounds per occupant.

Dry Ballast. A special powder put inside a tire to add weight.

Dual Bead Tires. Heavy service tires using two or more sets of bead wires in each bead rather than one.

Durometer. A device to measure the hardness of rubber. The term is also applied to the readings obtained with this device; for example, a tire tread may be defined as 60 durometer, which means that it shows this degree of hardness when tested with the durometer.

Dynamic Balance. Balancing of tire rim and wheel assembly while rotating.

Dynamic Unbalance. A balance that relates to the horizontal plane of movement (wobble) of a tire/wheel assembly, commonly used to designate two plane balance.

Dynamometer. A revolving wheel device for measuring vehicle power, tire impacts, rolling resistance skid resistance, and tire durability. Normally involves the rotation of stationary tires on metal rollers.

Equivalent Tubeless Sizes. To find tubeless drop center sizes equivalent to flat base rim tube type tires, add 1 (one) to the nominal cross section width and 2.5 to the rim diameter. Example: 10.00R20 is equivalent to 11R22.5.

Erosion Wear. Tread wear which occurs along the sides of a groove due to rib width spread during load cycle. Only occurs on deep non skid tires. Also known as *channel wear* or *river wear.*

Expansion Cycle. Refers to the attitude of a tire after leaving contact with the road as it operates on a car.

Fabric Fatigue. Deterioration of physical properties of fabric while in use, due to constant stress, high heat, overload, or a combination of these.

Face (of Tire). A term commonly used to denote the surface area of the tread of an off-road tire.

Factory-Built Repairs. Semi-cured or cured precision built repair units used by retreaders in place of hand repairs.

Feather Edge. Sharp, knifelike feathering along one edge of rib or blocks, due to scrubbing action of misaligned wheel on road.

Fiberglass Cord. A specially compounded glass which can be made into a cord fabric belt that gives support to the tread areas of a tire.

Fifth Wheel. A round metal coupling device mounted on a tractor and used to connect a semitrailer. It acts as a hingepoint to allow changes in direction of travel between tractor and trailer.

Filament. The smallest continuous element of a tire cord material.

First Line. Products should not be described as being *first line* unless the products are the best products (exclusive of premium quality products having special features) of the manufacturer or brand name distributor applying such designation.

Flash. A thin fin of excess rubber squeezed out between edges of mold pieces during curing process.

Flat Bed. A flat rim for solid (pressed on) rubber tires.

Flat Base. Tires with no taper on the bead base.

Flatspot. The area of tire tread retaining a relatively flat shape from remaining stationary while under load for several hours. Normally a temporary condition. Usual source of the temporary "thumping" action associated with nylon construction tires.

Flat Tread Profile. Tread with very slight curve from shoulder to shoulder.

Fleet Service. The professional rendering of tire maintenance service to the trucker or other user. Usually includes the periodic inspection of all rolling wheels at the trucker's place of business. Often includes emergency and road services.

Flexten. Goodyear processed aramid tire cord material.

Flotation. Ability of a tire to support a load on soft, yielding terrain.

Flow Crack. A crack caused by incomplete surface fill-out by rubber flow during tire manufacturing or retreading.

Footprint. Tread mark left by stationary tire tread in contact with ground.

Free Rolling Wheels. Wheels that are not used for traction but merely to support a load.

Front Wheel Shimmy. Abnormal side-to-side vibration of front wheels.

Front Wheel Tramp. Abnormal up-and-down vibration of front wheel, mostly at high speeds.

Full Cap. A retread process that includes replacing the shoulder area as well as the tread area.

Full Treading. When a full tread is required in retreading, a worn tire is buffed across the top of the tread and down over the shoulders as much as is necessary to receive wing stock and feather out while curing. This method will give the shoulders a finished appearance similar to that of a new tire.

Furrow Wheel. A tractor wheel that is rolling in a plowed furrow.

Glass Cord. A tire cord made from glass filaments. Usually used in tire breakers or belts.

Gouging. Chisel-like action of rocks or stubble on tires.

Grade, Line, Level, or Quality. There is no industry-wide, government, or other accepted system of quality standards or grading of tire industry products. Within the industry, however, trade terminology has developed which, when used in conjunction with consumer transactions, has the tendency to suggest that a system of quality standards or grading exists. Typical of such terminology are the expressions *line, level,* and *premium.* The exact meaning of such terms may vary from one industry member to another. Therefore, the *1st line, 100 level,* or *premium* tire of one industry member may be grossly inferior to the *1st line, 100 level,* or *premium* tire of another industry member; in the absence of an accepted system of grading or quality standards, each member can determine what *line, level,* or *premium* classification to attach to a tire.

In the absence of an accepted system of grading or quality standards for industry products, it is improper to represent, either through the use of such expressions as *line, level,* or *premium* or through the use of any other manner, that such a system exists—unless the representation is accompanied by a clear and conspicuous disclosure that no industry wide or other accepted system of quality standards or grading of industry products currently exists, and that representations as to *grade, line, level,* or *quality* relate only to the private standard of the marketer of the tire so described (e.g., *XYZ first line*).

Gripping Edge. Edge in tread design aiding traction and skid protection.

Groove. A continuous circumferential or lateral channel molded or cut in the tread rubber.

Grooved Solid Tire. Tire featuring one or more circumferential grooves.

Grommet. Metal reinforcement in hole in flat for valve stem, or metal reinforcement in valve pad.

Gross Axle Load. Total load on an axle.

Gross Axle Weight Rating (GAWR). The maximum allowable load for a specific axle, spindle, wheel, rim, and tire combination.

Gross Combination Weight (GCW). The maximum weight of a multiple vehicle combination of tractor and one or more trailers including full load of cargo, occupants, and fuel.

Gross Vehicle Weight (GVW). The maximum weight of vehicle including full load of cargo, occupants, and fuel.

Ground Drive. Operating power drawn from the wheel's contact with the ground. Power comes from contact of the wheel with the ground, and resulting frictions.

GG Ring. A molded circumferential rib in the lower tire sidewall which is used to confirm proper seating of bead area on rim.

GR-S. General purpose synthetic rubber derived from butadiene and styrene. (See *SBR.*)

Gum Strip. A thin gauge piece of rubber normally wrapped around the edge of a cut fabric or steel belt to relieve stress, facilitate handling, and prevent distortion during tire building.

Halogenated Butyl. A synthetic rubber which has the properties of high air retention and great resistance to high operating temperatures. (Used in tubeless liners.)

Hand-Built Repairs. Those units built by the repairman using a cord fabric and cushion gum.

Harshness. The projecting curved edge on a rim which retains outer edges of beads. In tire testing on an automobile, the degree to which small road irregularities are absorbed by the tires. An improvement in harshness control is apparent to the driver by a reduction in the shocks or vibrations transmitted to him.

Heat Breaks. Failure of the fabric due to excessive heat generation within the tire.

Heat Build-Up (Tire). Increase in heat of tire while being used, in excess of the heat that is dissipated.

Heat Dissipation (Tire). Removal of heat from a tire by conduction, convection, and radiation from the surface.

Heavy Gauge Rubber. Thick rubber. Gauge is the lineal measure of thickness.

Heavy Service Tubes. A designation commonly used when referring to the tubes used in truck tires.

Heel. Portion of bead fitting at junction of rim flange and bead seat.

Heel and Toe Wear. Sloping wear between ends of some tread elements (ripsaw toothlike), often resulting from shifting movement of tread units in contact with the road.

High Cis-Polybutadiene. An improved type of polybutadiene rubber which provides better wear properties and increased resistance to tread segment tearing.

Hop. The vertical oscillatory motion of a wheel between the road surface and the spring mass.

Hot Patch. Tube or tire repair that is vulcanized over the injury.

H R. Heat resistant construction. Used also on sidewall of some tires to identify this construction.

Hub. Usually referred to only in connection with disc wheels. This is the base by which either a single wheel or a dual wheel assembly is attached to the axle with cap nuts.

Hubometer. An instrument, placed on a truck hub, which calculates mileage traveled.

Hydroplaning. The action when pressure from water on the road surface lifts the tire, forcing it upward. This happens on rain slicked roads at highway speeds.

Hydrostatically Inflate. To inflate with water in place of air. (See *Liquid Ballast.*)

Impact Break. A break, usually in the shape of an X or diagonal split, which is generally visible from the inside of the tire.

Inch Ounces. A measurement of unbalance used by tire engineers. It is determined by multiplying the amount of unbalance in ounces by the radius of the tire in inches.

Inflation. The tire cold inflation pressure required for specific load and speed conditions.

Inner Liner. The layer of rubber which is laminated to the inside of a tubeless tire to insure the air retention quality of the tire body.

Kinked Bead. A bend in the tire bead that interrupts the desired bead hoop and appears as a bulge in the bead area of the tire.

Laminated Liner. A liner as used in tubeless tires which is made of two layers of rubber vulcanized together.

Latex. Milk-like liquid that comes from the rubber tree. Crude rubber is coagulated from latex.

Level (Price). Refers to the manufacturer's established list of retail prices for merchandise. (See *One Hundred Level.*)

Light Truck Tire. A tire with *LT* as part of the size designation.

Liner. The layer of rubber laminated to the first ply of a tubeless tire producing the air seal of the inside of the tire. (See *Laminated Liner.*)

Liquid Ballast. (See *Ballast, Liquid.*)

Load Base. The distance between the center of the payload and the center of the rear axle of a truck.

Load Carrying Capacity. The ability of a tire to safely carry the intended load. This information should consist of the maximum load-carrying capacity as related to various recommended air pressures and may include data which indicates the effect such varying pressures will have on the operation of the automobile.

Load Distribution. Proportion of the weight of a truck and its load that is supported by each wheel and axle.

Load Index. A numerical code associated with the maximum load a tire can carry at the speed indicated by its Speed Symbol under specified service conditions up to 210 km/h.

Load Limit. Maximum tire load at a given minimum cold inflation at a specified maximum speed.

Loadmeter. Type of scale for determining vehicle load. Used to check load distribution one wheel at a time.

Load Range. A letter (*A, B, C,* etc.), designation for standard load and extra load are used to identify a given size tire with its load and inflation limits when used in a specific type of service, as defined in the heading of Tire and Rim Association (TRA) tables.

Load Rating. The maximum load a tire is rated to carry for a given usage at a specific pressure.

Logger Tire. Special tire developed primarily for logging use.

Low Platform Trailer Tire. A small diameter truck tire used with special rims in high load trailer service. Identified with suffixes *TR* or *HC* in size designation. Example: 10.00R15TR, 11R17.5HC.

Low-Pressure Tires. Larger cross-section tires for operation at lower pressure. Increased air capacity permits lower pressure.

Low Profile Tire. A tire in which the cross section has a squat appearance. Many tires have cross sections which are essentially circular, the width of the section being practically the same as its height. In low profile tires the height of the section is about 83 percent or less of the section width.

Lubricant (Tube). A material such as vegetable oil, soap, or talc which prevents binding between tire and tube or rim.

Lug. A discontinuous projection molded in the tread rubber with no particular orientation, size, or shape, for the purpose of increasing the tractive force on snow, mud, sand, etc.

Lug Reinforcement. Supporting bar or supporting buttress design to reinforce tread lugs or cleats.

Lug Spacing. Distance between tread bars or lugs.

Lug Stability. Resistance of lug to flexing or to heel and toe wear.

Maximum Overall Tire Width. Maximum outside cross-sectional width of inflated tire without load, including sidewall, rib, and decorations.

Maximum Rated Load. Greatest load for which vehicle or tire is built.

Maximum Tire Load. The maximum load per tire shall not be greater than the applicable load specified for the proper load range and usage.

Misalignment. Maladjustment of one or more parts of steering or suspension mechanism, causing unsatisfactory operation of wheels and vehicle.

Mixing Tires. Use of different tire construction (radial, bias, bias-belted) on a vehicle. Only certain combinations are permissible on steer, drive, and trailer axles.

Modulus. A term used to denote resistance to being stretched. A measure of stiffness.

Moisture Blow. Damage caused by the presence of moisture in the tire carcass which, when subjected to heat, becomes steam and expands.

Mono-Ply Tire. A wire or fabric cord tire made with only one ply.

Mucker Tire. Flotation type of tire specially designed for use in soft ground.

Mud & Snow Tires (MS, M&S or M+S). Stands for Mud and Snow tire. A tire with a heavy bar or block tread design for maximum traction in mud or snow.

Neoprene. A synthetic rubber made by combining many molecules of chloro-butadiene (chloroprene) into long chain molecular groups. It is particularly resistant to oil, grease, heat, and ozone.

Neutral Contour. Special ply curvature in a tire design and construction that minimizes stress due to inflation pressure.

New Tread (Nu-Treads). A term used by some tire companies to denote a retreaded tire.

Non-Adjustable (NA). This marking will appear as a brand near the serial number on a tire which has already been adjusted and is no longer subject to claim.

Nondirectional Tread. Tread design which is equally effective in either direction of rotation.

Nonskid. Depth of the grooves in a tire tread.

Nonskid Depth. The groove depth of the tread (used to help indicate remaining wear left in tire).

Nylon. A family of high-strength, resilient synthetic materials, used in the manufacture of cords which are used to make plies.

Off-The-Road Tires. Tires designed primarily for use over unpaved roads or where no roads exit. Built for ruggedness and traction rather than speed.

Oil Resisting Compound (OR). Neoprene compound for use in industrial solid tires where universal type compounds show deterioration from petroleum products, acids, and animal or other fats. Also best in high temperature operations.

On-Center Feel. The lack of or presence of free play in a vehicle's steering wheel before noticeable steering response occurs.

"O" Ring. A rubber sealing ring used with some types of tubeless truck and earthmover tire rim assemblies. Designed to prevent air loss.

Original Equipment (OE). Designates equipment provided on the new vehicle by the manufacturer.

Original Equipment Tires. Understood to mean the same brand and quality tires used generally as original equipment on new current models of vehicles of domestic manufacture. A tire which was formerly but is not currently used as *Original Equipment* should not be described as *Original Equipment* without clear and conspicuous disclosure (in close conjunction with the term) of the latest actual year such tire was used as *Original Equipment*.

Out-of-Round Wear. Tire that is worn into an out-of-round condition so that tread depth minimum and maximum are 180 degrees apart. Also called *180 degree wear*.

Outside Diameter (OD). The outermost diameter of an unloaded tire when mounted and fully inflated.

Overinflation. Tire inflation above recommended pressure.

Overloading. Overload flex is excessive tire flexing or distortion caused by too much load. Tire overloading can be dangerous and is not recommended. However, note that tire load capacity can be increased in certain cases by increased inflation or control to lower speeds.

Oversizing. Mounting larger tires than size specified for a vehicle to support heavier loads, provide increased flotation, or give other performance changes.

Oversteer. Rear tires have a greater slip-angle than the front, causing the vehicle to turn in a smaller radius than desired by the driver. (See *Understeer*.)

Ozone. A form of oxygen produced by electricity. Accelerates aging and weathering in tires.

Ozone Checking. Formation of fine cracks in surface of rubber due to ozone in air.

Pay Load. Weight of commodity or load carried in any vehicle.

Ply. A layer of rubberized fabric contained in the body of the tire and extending from one bead of the tire to the other bead of the tire. The U.S. Federal Trade Commission (FTC) considers it deceptive to imply that tires possess more plies than they actually do. Accordingly, phrases such as "Super 6" or "Deluxe 8" used to describe tires of less than 6 or 8 plies, respectively, should not be used.

Ply Adhesion. Strength of attraction or adhesion between adjacent plies.

Ply Lock. Turnup of ply ends around bead so other plies lock them in place.

Ply Rating. The expression *ply rating* as used in the trade is an index of tire strength. Each manufacturer, however, has its own system of computing *ply rating*. Thus, the same *ply rating* stated by two different manufacturers is not necessarily equivalent, even though the ratings appear identical. While the expression *ply rating* may have significance to industry members, in the absence of a publicized system of standardized ratings, the use of such expressions with sales to the general public may be deceptive.

To avoid deception, the expression *ply rated* or *ply rating* should not be used unless based on actual tests utilizing technically sound procedures, with the test results in writing and available for inspection.

When ply rating is stated on the tire itself, it must be accompanied by and in identical size letters, the disclosure of the actual ply count. In addition, there must be a tag or label attached to the tire or its packaging, of such permanency that it cannot easily be removed prior to sale to the consumer. The tag or label must contain a clear and conspicuous disclosure that there is no industry wide definition of ply rating and of the basis of comparison of the claimed rating. (For example, *2-ply tire*, *4-ply rating* means this 2-ply tire is equivalent to the current or most recent 4-ply nylon cord tire.)

Ply Separation. A parting of rubber compound between adjacent plies.

Pneumatic Tire. Tire which depends on compressed air it holds to carry load. It differs from solid tires, where the tire itself carries the load.

Polybutadiene. A synthetic rubber made by combining many molecules of butadiene into long chain molecular groups. This rubber is noted for superior tread wear, heat build-up resistance, resiliency, and flexing quantities at low temperatures compared to natural rubber.

Polyester Cord. A synthetic fiber that excels in maintaining strength properties at high heat levels and eliminates flat spotting.

Polyisoprene. A synthetic rubber made by combining many molecules of isoprene into long molecular groups. This process is known as polymerization, hence the name polyisoprene. This rubber is known as "man-made natural rubber" and its properties are practically identical with natural rubber.

Polymer. A material consisting of large units (molecules) made by joining many smaller building blocks (simple molecules).

Usually used to describe synthetic rubber.

Polyurethane. A synthetic rubber made by combining many molecules of a urethane chemical group with other chemical groups such as esters, ethers, and ureas. This rubber is noted for its good wear and excellent weather resistance. It is unusual in that it is a "liquid casting" rubber and as such can be molded into complex shapes more cheaply and easily than conventional gum rubber.

Power Consumption. The energy or horsepower consumed by a tire in overcoming its inertia when operated on a vehicle.

Pressed On. Industrial solid tire using a flat base rim and applied to the wheel by hydraulic press.

Prestretched. Cord stretched sufficiently to take permanent set in order to reduce further stretching in service.

Pressure Build Up. Increase of air pressure in tire caused by temperature rise of the contained air.

Preventative Maintenance. Maintenance performed prior to any failure. Designed to lengthen product life, prevent high maintenance costs and reduce unscheduled breakdowns.

Private Brand. A special line of tires or tubes manufactured for and to the specifications of a private buyer.

Quality Grading. Refers to the legislation which requires tire manufacturers to label treadwear, traction, and temperature resistance performance criteria on the sidewall of the tires they produce.

Radial Cracking. A crack in the outer surface of a tire, usually in the mid-sidewall area, proceeding perpendicular to the bead.

Radial Ply. A tire type in which the body ply cords run from bead to bead at about a 90 degree angle to the tire centerline.

Radial Runout. In tires, a measure of out of roundness; tested by rotating the inflated tire and observing or measuring how far the surface of the tread varies from a true circle.

Rated Load. The maximum allowable load for a particular size and load range tire. The rated load is different for single versus dual applications on trucks.

Rayon. An artificial fiber made from cotton or wood pulp by chemical process.

Recapped. In general terms, same as retreading. More specifically refers to the process known as "top capping" in which rubber is applied only to the tread surface of the tire.

Regroovable. A tire with sufficient undertread so that grooves can be cut in the worn tire, thereby extending tire life.

Replacement Tire. Any tire other than those sold as original equipment.

Resilience. Capacity of rubber to recover its original size and shape after deformation.

Retreading. The process of renewing the tread on a tire by buffing the old surface and applying a new tread. It differs from recapping in that new rubber is applied to both the tread surface and shoulder area of the tire.

Revolutions Per Mile (RPM). The number of revolutions that the mounted tire will make in one mile at rated load and inflation.

Ribs. Tread projections running circumferentially around the tire.

Road Hazard. Any road or highway condition or obstacle which can damage a tire.

Road Shock. Impact of road irregularities transmitted through tires to vehicle.

Rock Drilling. A condition in which a rock has penetrated the tread rubber or fabric of a tire. Caused by the failure of tires to eject the rocks or stones picked up by the grooves.

Rolling Resistance. The resistance of a tire to free rolling.

Rubber (Natural). Substance derived from latex of rubber trees and certain shrubs.

Runout. The difference between maximum and minimum indicator readings as applied to:

a) Radial wheel runout: the difference between the maximum and minimum measurements of the wheel bead seat radii measured perpendicular to the spin axis.

b) Lateral wheel runout: the difference between the maximum and minimum measurements parallel to the spin axis on the inside vertical portion of the rim flange.

c) Radial tire runout: the difference between the maximum and minimum measurements on the tread surface and in a plane perpendicular to the spin axis while tire is mounted on a true wheel.

d) Lateral tire runout: the difference between the maximum and minimum measurements parallel to the spin axis at the widest point of each sidewall of a tire on a true running wheel.

Safety Venting. Raised rib design running laterally and circumferentially on tubes to release trapped air between tube and tire.

SBR. Styrene-Butadiene Rubber (formerly GR-S).

Scuff Rib. Raised sidewall rib to protect sidewall from curb scuffing.

Section. Cross section of a tire. Also a portion of tire showing all visible design features.

Section Height. Half the difference between the outer diameter and the nominal rim diameter.

Self Cleaning. Descriptive of a tire tread designed to eject any one or all of various loose ground cover such as dirt, stones, snow, and mud by the natural flexing action of the tire.

Separation. Pulling apart, such as ply separation (from each other) or tread separation (from plies).

Serial Number. Individual number cured onto one sidewall for identification. (See *DOT Number.*)

Shimmy. Rapid sidewise vibration of the front wheels. Usually caused by worn parts of steering mechanism. Can be caused by unbalanced tires.

Shock Pad. Extra fabric custom placed under tread extending from shoulder to shoulder to absorb road impacts. Shock pad construction differs from the breaker strip as the shock pad is wider, coming down over the shoulder of the tire to give greater protection against sidewall shock.

Shoulder. The region of the exterior of a tire formed by the joining of the tread and sidewall.

Shredded Wire. Short pieces of fine steel wire mixed into tread or undertread compound to increase the tire's resistance to cutting and penetrating objects.

Sidewall. The portion of a tire between the tread and the bead.

Single Bead. Refers to a tire built with only one wire bundle in the bead area.

Size Designation. The information which identifies tire size. Suffix letters are included, where necessary, to differentiate between tires designated for service conditions which may require different loads and inflations. For instance, *P* indicates passenger car service and *LT* indicates light truck service. The information may also indicate tires which must be used on specific rim types. (See *Tire Sidewall Markings*.)

Size Factor. The sum of the inflated tire section width and overall diameter.

Skidproof, Blowout Proof, Blow Proof. Absolute terms such as these should not be used without qualification unless the product affords complete and absolute protection from skidding, blowouts, or punctures, as the case may be, under any and all driving conditions.

Skid Resistance. Ability to maintain grip on road and to resist slide or slip, either directionally or laterally.

Snow Tires. Tires with specially designed treads that improve handling in the snow.

Society of Automotive Engineers (SAE). A group which sets standards in the automotive and petroleum industries.

Spoke Wheel (Cast Wheel). This is a wheel consisting of either three, five, or six spokes radiating from the hub, with the spokes being an integral part of the hub. A rim is attached to the outer spoke surfaces with rim clamps.

Spot Break. Localized fabric break attributed to heat.

Spot Repair. A repair made by vulcanizing rubber to a tire without replacing cord.

Spring Rate, Tire. The static rate measured by the change of load per unit vertical deflection of the tire at a specified load and inflation pressure.

Squeegee. A layer of rubber added between plies.

Squirm. The rubbing motion of the tread as the loaded tire rotates.

Stability. Ability of tires to maintain direction of vehicle on curve without causing excessive sway.

Staggered Tread Pattern. Tread design consisting of different pitch lengths to reduce noise and vibration.

Static Neutralizer. Special powder put in tires to dissipate static electrical charge built up in moving car.

Steel Belted Radial. A radial tire made with steel belts as opposed to textile belts.

Steel Wire Cord. A tire cord made from many very fine and very durable steel wires which are twisted together. Can be used to replace textile or glass cord in certain applications.

Stone Drilling. Penetration past the natural tread groove depth by a stone caught in the tread.

Stone Ejection Rib. Portion of tread rib designed to throw off stones with aid of normal tire flexing. Located about half way down in tread grooves to prevent small stones from working clear down to bottom of groove where flexing of tire cannot throw them out.

Strength Rating. Maximum load capacity of a tire.

Stud. A hard metal or plastic rivet inserted into a tire and extending slightly beyond the tread surface for the purpose of improving winter traction on ice or hard packed snow.

Studded Snow Tires. Many manufacturers offer winter tread tires with metal spikes that improve traction in the snow. Certain states, however, prohibit the use of these tires because of possible road damage. Accordingly, in advertising these tires a statement should be made that their use is illegal in certain states.

Super Low Profile. A tire in which the section height is less than 83 percent of the section width.

SWU. A marking cured onto the sidewall of a tire to indicate shredded wire under tread construction.

Tapered Bead. Tires with a taper on the base of the bead. This provides compression and a tight fit on the rim which in turn seals tubeless tires and also helps prevent tire slippage.

Tear Resistance. Ability of rubber to withstand tearing.

Test No. A number cured onto the sidewall to identify a series of test tires. Usually a digit, followed by a letter, followed by four digits.

3T. A Goodyear trademark that identifies a patented Goodyear process that sets the tire cord at its highest point of strength and resiliency.

Tire and Rim Association. Industrial association of tire and rim manufacturers. Provides technical tire and rim standards. The Tire and Rim Association determines standard tire and rim dimensions and combinations of loads and inflations recommended for the best service. Information is published in yearly editions of the *Tire and Rim Association Yearbook.*

Tire Balancing. Adding external weights around a tire/wheel assembly to compensate for unequal distribution of the tire and wheel as a unit. A small metal weight attached to the rim is used.

Tire Cycles. The basic attitudes through which a tire passes in the process of rotating on a car. There are three cycles, the normal cycle before road contact, the contraction cycle during road contact, and the expansion cycle after road contact.

Tire Dressing. Paint, black glossy or dull finish, for improving appearance of tire sidewalls.

Tire Noise. Sounds generated when a moving tire's tread contacts the surface on which it is running.

Tire Set. A temporary distortion occurring in some tires from the process of cooling in one position after being driven.

TL. Tubeless tire.

Toe. The inner part of the base of the tire bead.

Toe-In. A condition where the tires on the same axle are closer together at the front than at the back as measured at spindle height.

Ton Mile Rating. The maximum *Ton Miles Per Hour* that a tire can carry without overheating. Normally applied only to off-road tires.

Ton Miles Per Hour. Average tire load times average work day speed.

Top Treading. Only the top, or tread area, is buffed away and a tread rubber with abrupt shoulders applied. This type of treading is usually requested when tires are used in highway service where a special shoulder is not required and when appearance is secondary. This is the most economical type of treading.

Torque. The amount of force measured in a circular motion ("twist about an axis").

T R Number. Code number of tube valves and flaps set by Tire and Rim Association.

TRA. (See *Tire and Rim Association*.)

Tracking. Correct tracking is when the rear wheels of a vehicle follow the same line as the front wheels.

Traction. The adhesive friction of the tire on the surface on which it is moving.

Traction Wave. The wavy distortion a tire builds up in back of the road contact point when it runs under excessive speed. This wave will eventually destroy the tire if speed is not reduced.

Tramp. The form of wheel hop in which a pair of wheels hop in opposite phase.

Tread. Portion of tire which comes in contact with the road.

Tread Depth. The distance measured from the tread surface to the bottom of the grooves in a tire. Usually expressed in 32nds of an inch.

Tread Design. The pattern of the tread area.

Tread Life. Length of service in miles or hours of operation before tread wears out.

Tread Radius. The radius of a circle that coincides with the arc of the tread cross section. The larger the tread radius, the flatter the tread will be.

Tread Separation. Pulling away of the tread from the tire carcass.

Tread Width. The measurement across the tread face of a tire from shoulder edge to shoulder edge which defines the usable width of the tread pattern; essentially, the width of the footprint. (See *Footprint.*)

T T. Tube type tire.

Tread Wear Indicators. Raised bars of rubber molded at a height of ⅔₂ across the bottom of the tread grooves. When the tread wears down to these bars, the tire should be replaced.

Tube Growth. Increase in size of tube in service.

Tube (Inner). An airtight container placed inside tube type tire casing to hold the compressed air.

Tubeless Liner. Air diffusion resistant rubber forming inside surface of tubeless tires.

Tufsyn. A trademark for a special long wearing rubber developed by Goodyear.

Turning Radius. The distance from the center-line plane of rotation of the outermost tire on a vehicle to the center of the turning circle of the tire. Front wheels have different radii in a turn, but have a common turning center.

Two Plane Balance. Refers to dynamic (horizontal plane) and static (vertical plane) balance together.

Two Plus Two Construction. Refers to a passenger tire construction which utilizes two body plies and two belt plies.

Underinflation. Tire having less than recommended air pressure for the load being carried. Tire may build up excessive heat that may be dangerous and could result in sudden tire destruction.

Understeer. Front tires have a larger slip-angle than the rear, making the vehicle tend to turn less sharply than the wheels are pointed. Vehicle must be held into the turn. (See *Oversteer.*)

Undertread. Tread material between bottom of antiskid grooves and carcass.

Uniformity. A measure of the tire's ability to run smoothly and vibration free. Sometimes measured as tire balance or radial and lateral force variation.

Unisteel. The Goodyear name for a radial truck tire with a single wire ply and with wire belts.

Universal Compound (UC). Standard compound for industrial solid tires for use in all around service.

Vertical Deflection. Amount that a tire deflects under load.

Vulcanization. Process of combining rubber with sulphur or certain other additives under influence of heat and pressure to eliminate tackiness when warm, and brittleness when cool, and to otherwise improve the useful properties of rubber. Also known as *curing.*

Weather Checking. Hairline cracks in the sidewall surface which is usually attributable to aging time and atmospheric conditions rather than to flexing.

Wheel Alignment. Adjustment of wheel position to ensure proper orientation of wheels (and tires) to chassis and to each other.

Wheel Balance Weight. Small metal weight clamped to rim to correct unbalanced tire and/or wheel.

Wheel Base. Distance in inches between front and rear wheels at ground contact points, or distance between front and rear axles, at their centers.

Wheel Geometry. A term referring to the axis about which the wheel assembly rotates. Conditions such as bent wheels, worn bushings, and improper alignment affect wheel geometry.

Wild Wire. Wire component of a tire inadvertently protruding through exterior or interior surface.

Wire Tire. A tire consisting of wire cord plies in place of rayon, nylon, polyester, or aramid.

WSW. White sidewall tire.

TIRE VALVES

Double Bend Valve. Valve stem bent at two places for greater accessibility.

Valve. Device used to admit, retain, check, or exhaust air in a tube or mounted tubeless tire.

Valve Aperture (or Slot). Hole or slot in rim which accommodates the valve.

Valve Cap. Screw cover for end of valve stem. Protects core from dirt, provides primary seal for high pressure tire assemblies when equipped with sealing gasket.

Valve Core. Inner part of valve which may be used to increase inflation or to deflate tire. Note: A sealing valve cap is required to secure proper inflation seal.

Valve Extension. Extra length added to valve stem for greater accessibility, particularly on inside duals.

Valve Stem. Tube through which air flows in or out of tube or tubeless tire.

Valve Spud. The metal base within a heavy service tube to which various valve stems and extensions may be attached.

TIRE RIMS

Bead Seat. Flat portion of the rim on which the bead rests.

Conventional Rim. Rim accepted as standard until wide rim development.

Demountable Rim. A detachable rim used when truck tires are mounted on spoke wheels.

Drop Center Rim. Rim in which center is depressed. Usually called *DC rim.* (See *Full Drop Center Rim.*)

Flange. The projecting curved edge on a rim which retains outer edges of beads.

Full Drop Center Rim. Rim with center depression sufficiently deep to permit mounting and dismounting on tire on one piece rim. Passenger car rims are an example.

Rim. The metal support for the tire or tire and tube assembly on the wheel. The beads of a tire are seated on the rim.

Rim Back Section. The size of a rim opposite the gutter section.

Rim Base. The part of the rim which is attached to the wheel. The term is usually used in connection with rims with two loose flanges.

Rim Bruise. Damage caused by tire hitting obstruction with sufficient force to crush tire between rim flange and object hit.

Rim Diameter (Nominal or Bead Seat). Approximate diameter of the rim measured at the bottom of the flange (nominal). Bead seat diameter is the distance between intersections of bead seat line and heel line extended. True for passenger tires and most truck tires.

Rim Flange. Vertical collar of rim which retains outer edges of beads.

Rim Flange Cover. Sidewall projection over the top of the rim flange that is found in some tires.

Rim Locking Ring. Removable lock ring holding rim flange in place on some multiple piece rims.

Rim Taper. Refers to the 5 or 15 degree slope built into both sides of most rim bead seats. This slope is designed to produce compression under the tire bead and hold it firmly in place.

Rim Well. The depressed center section of a drop center or semi-drop center rim that creates a well to facilitate mounting on the vehicle.

Rim Width. The distance between the inside rim flange surfaces.

Safety Type Rim. Rim designed to hold bead in place in event of tube deflation or air loss (tubeless) during operation.

SDC Rim. Semidrop center rim whose center section is slightly depressed.

Seat, Rim. Portion of rim on which beads rest.

Side Ring (Portion of a Two Piece Rim). This is the removable flange and bead seat portion of a two piece rim. It has a gap in it and is under tension so it can be removed from and snapped back into the depression on the gutter side of a rim.

Side Ring (Portion of a Three Piece Rim). This is the solid (no gap) removable flange of a three piece rim. It is used in combination with, and applied over, a split lock ring on the gutter side of the rim. Also referred to as a side flange.

Split Base Rim. Rim forming a collar with two ends joined and locked together when assembled. To demount, rim ends are unlocked and separated.

Split Rim. A rim divided circumferentially into two similar sections. Also, a common phrase used in the truck tire market to designate a two or three piece rim.

Well Depth. Depth of the rim well as measured vertically from a straight line running from on bead seat to a point 180 degrees opposite.

Sources:

Consumer Tire Guide, Washington: Tire Industry Safety Council, 1990.

Federal Trade Commission, "Tire Advertising and Labeling Guides," 16 CFR sections 228.0 to 228.19 (1991), Washington: Government Printing Office.

National Highway Traffic Safety Administration, *Consumer Guide to Uniform Tire Quality Grading,* Washington: U.S. Department of Transportation, 1991.

Sales Training Department, *Goodyear Tire Terminology,* Cuyahoga Falls, OH: Goodyear Tire and Rubber Company, n.d.

Used Cars

Used Vehicle. Any vehicle driven more than the limited use necessary in moving or road testing a new vehicle prior to delivery to a consumer.

BUYERS GUIDE

The U. S. Federal Trade Commission's *Used Car Rule* requires car dealers to post a *Buyers Guide* on the window of each car offered for sale. The Buyers Guide lists

- what specific protection or warranty the dealer will provide, if any;
- whether the vehicle comes with no warranty ("as is") or with implied warranties only;
- a recommendation that the car be inspected by an independent mechanic before it is purchased;
- a recommendation that all promises be provided in writing; and
- what some of the major problems are that may occur in any car.

The Used Car Rule requires dealers to post the Buyers Guide on all used vehicles, including automobiles, light-duty vans, and light-duty trucks. *Demonstrator cars* also must have Buyers Guides. Buyers Guides are not required for motorcycles and most recreational vehicles. Also, individuals selling fewer than six cars a year are not required to post Buyer's Guides.

Whenever a used car is purchased from a dealer, the original or an identical copy of the Buyers Guide that appeared in the window of the vehicle should be provided to the buyer. (If the sales process was conducted in the Spanish language, the buyer is entitled to see and keep a *Spanish-language version* of the Buyers Guide.) The Buyers Guide must reflect any changes in warranty coverage that were negotiated with the dealer as part of the sale. The Buyer's Guide also becomes part of the sales contract and overrides any contrary provisions that may be in that contract.

As Is—No Warranty. About one-half of all used cars sold by dealers come "as is," which means there is no express or implied warranty. When a car is bought "as is," any repairs necessary after the sale are the responsibility of the buyer. When the dealer offers a vehicle for sale "as is," the box next to the *As Is—No Warranty* disclosure on the Buyers Guide will be checked (see illustration). If this box is checked but the dealer makes oral promises to repair the vehicle, the dealer should put those promises in writing on the Buyers Guide.

Some states (Connecticut, Kansas, Maine, Maryland, Massachusetts, Minnesota, Mississippi, New York, Rhode Island, Vermont, West Virginia, and the District of Columbia) do not permit "as is" sales for most used motor vehicles.

Implied Warranties Only. Implied warranties exist under all state laws and come with almost every purchase from a used car dealer, unless the dealer states in writing that implied warranties do not apply. Usually dealers use the words "as is" or "with all faults" to disclaim implied warranties. Most states require the use of specific words. The *warranty of merchantability* is the most common type of implied warranty. This means that the seller promises that the product will do what it is supposed to do. For example, a car will run, a toaster will toast. Another type of implied warranty is the *warranty of fitness for a particular purpose*. This applies when a vehicle is purchased on the advice of the dealer that it is suitable for a particular use. For example, a dealer who suggests a specific vehicle for hauling a trailer warrants, in effect, that the vehicle will be suitable for hauling a trailer.

If a vehicle purchased with a written warranty develops problems that the warranty does not cover, the buyer may still be protected by implied warranties. Any limitation on the duration of implied warranties must appear on the written warranty. In those states that do not permit "as is" sales by dealers, or if the dealer offers a vehicle with only implied warranties, a disclosure entitled *Implied Warranties Only* will be printed on the Buyers Guide in place of the *As Is* disclosure. The box next to this disclosure would be checked if the dealer

chooses to sell the car with implied warranties and no written warranty (see illustration).

Unexpired Manufacturer's Warranty. If the used vehicle is still covered by the manufacturer's original warranty, the dealer may include it in the "systems covered/duration" section of the Buyers Guide. This does not necessarily mean that the dealer offers a warranty in addition to the manufacturer's. In some cases, a manufacturer's original warranty can be transferred to a second owner only upon payment of a fee.

Service Contracts. Service contracts are often offered at the time of used car purchase. If the service contract is offered, the dealer must mark the box provided on the Buyers Guide, except in those states that regulate service contracts under their insurance laws. When a buyer purchases a service contract from the dealer within ninety days of buying the

BUYERS GUIDE

IMPORTANT: Spoken promises are difficult to enforce. Ask the dealer to put all promises in writing. Keep this form.

VEHICLE MAKE   MODEL   YEAR   VIN NUMBER

DEALER STOCK NUMBER (Optional)

WARRANTIES FOR THIS VEHICLE:

☐ **AS IS - NO WARRANTY**

YOU WILL PAY ALL COSTS FOR ANY REPAIRS. The dealer assumes no responsibility for any repairs regardless of any oral statements about the vehicle.

☐ **WARRANTY**

☐ FULL   ☐ LIMITED WARRANTY. The dealer will pay _____% of the labor and _____% of the parts for the covered systems that fail during the warranty period. Ask the dealer for a copy of the warranty document for a full explanation of warranty coverage, exclusions, and the dealer's repair obligations. Under state law, "implied warranties" may give you even more rights.

SYSTEMS COVERED: DURATION:

_____   _____
_____   _____
_____   _____
_____   _____
_____   _____
_____   _____
_____   _____
_____   _____

☐ SERVICE CONTRACT. A service contract is available at an extra charge on this vehicle. Ask for details as to coverage, deductible, price, and exclusions. If you buy a service contract within 90 days of the time of sale, state law "implied warranties" may give you additional rights.

PRE PURCHASE INSPECTION: ASK THE DEALER IF YOU MAY HAVE THIS VEHICLE INSPECTED BY YOUR MECHANIC EITHER ON OR OFF THE LOT.

SEE THE BACK OF THIS FORM for important additional information, including a list of some major defects that may occur in used motor vehicles.

Used car buyer's guide, side one

vehicle, federal law prohibits the dealer from disclaiming implied warranties on the systems covered in that service contract. For example, if the car is sold "as is," the car normally will not be covered by implied warranties; but if the buyer purchases a service contract covering the engine, implied warranties are thereby automatic on the engine.

Spoken Promises. The Buyers Guide warns used car buyers not to rely on spoken promises. Oral promises are difficult, if not impossible, to enforce.

Pre-Purchase Independent Inspection. The Buyers Guide suggests an independent inspection by the buyer's own choice of mechanic. The dealer may permit the buyer either to take the vehicle off the lot or to bring an independent mechanic to the used car on the lot.

Vehicle Systems. The Buyers Guide includes a list of the fourteen major systems of an automobile and some of the major problems that may occur in these systems (see illustration).

Dealer Identification and Consumer Complaint Information. The name and address of the dealership must be provided on the back of the Buyers Guide. In the space below the name and address is the name and telephone number of the person at the dealership the purchaser will contact with complaints after the sale.

DEALER WARRANTIES

When dealers offer a written warranty on a used vehicle, they must fill in the warranty portion of the Buyers Guide. Terms and conditions of written warranties can vary widely. Dealers may offer a full or limited warranty on all or some of the systems or components of the vehicle. The following information must be provided in the "Warranty" section of the Buyers Guide when the dealer offers a full or limited warranty: Percentage of the repair cost that the dealer will pay. For example, "the dealer will pay 100 percent of the labor and 100 percent of the parts...."; specific parts and systems, such as the frame, body, or brake system that are covered by the warranty will be listed.

The back of the Buyers Guide contains a list of descriptive names for the major systems of an automobile where problems may occur, duration of the warranty for each covered system (for example, "Thirty days or 1,000 miles, whichever occurs first"), and whether a deductible applies. Under another federal law, the Magnuson-Moss Warranty Act, the buyer has a right to see a copy of the dealer's warranty before a purchase. The warranty contains more detailed information than the Buyers Guide, such as a step-by-step explanation of how to obtain repairs if a covered system or component malfunctions and a statement of who is legally responsible for fulfilling the terms of the warranty. In addition, many states require that dealers (but not individuals) ensure that their vehicles will pass *state inspection* or carry a minimum warranty before they offer them for sale. The local consumer protection agency and the attorney general's office in each state have information about the requirements on individuals and on dealers.

Full Warranty. When a dealer offers a full warranty, it provides the following terms and conditions: warranty service will be provided to anyone who owns the vehicle during the warranty period when a problem is reported, and will be provided free of charge, including such costs as returning the vehicle or removing and reinstalling a system covered by the warranty, when necessary; the dealer will provide the buyer's choice of either a replacement or a full refund if the dealer is unable, after a reasonable number of tries, to repair the vehicle or a system covered by the warranty; warranty service is provided without requiring the owner to perform any reasonable duty as a precondition for receiving service, except notifying the dealer that service is needed; no limit is placed on the duration of implied warranties. The warranty need not cover the entire vehicle, but must meet the terms and conditions described here for the systems and components it covers.

Limited Warranty. If any one of the terms and conditions of the *full warranty* (see entry) is not met, the warranty is categorized as *limited*. This type of warranty is the most common applied to used cars that are sold with warranty coverage (i.e., not sold "as is"). A limited warranty states that there are some costs or responsibilities that the dealer will not assume for systems covered by the warranty.

BUYING A USED CAR FROM A PRIVATE PARTY

Many cars are available privately, such as through classified advertisements in newspapers. There are several differences between sales made by individuals and by dealers. Private sellers generally are not covered by the *Used Car Rule* and therefore do not have to use the *Buyers Guide*. Private sales usually are not covered by implied warranties of state law. A private sale probably will be on an "as is" basis. If the terms of the sale are detailed in a written contract, the seller must live up to the promises stated in the contract.

Used cars sold by individuals may be covered by a manufacturer's warranty or a separately purchased *service contract* (see entry). However, warranties and service contracts may not be transferable, or there may be limitations or cost for a transfer.

Source:
Buying a Used Car, Washington: Federal Trade Commission, March 1990.

Vehicle Sizes

(Note: Price ranges are for 1992 and are provided for comparison purposes.)

Compact Pickup Truck. Generally a two-door small truck with a load bed in the rear. It is shorter in length, narrower, and not as tall as a full-size pickup. The standard cab seats up to three. Extended-cab models with additional seating and inside storage are available. Rear- or four-wheel drive are available, and four- or six-cylinder engines are the most common power sources. Priced between $7,000 and $16,000.

Compact Utility Vehicle. These vehicles combine rugged characteristics with all the comforts of a sedan. They generally allow seating for four to six and are available in rear- or four-wheel drive configurations. Four- and six-cylinder engines are the mainstays of this segment. Most are available in two- and four-door body styles. Priced between $14,300 and $25,000.

Compact. Generally has four- to five-passenger seating. Depending on the manufacturer, front-, rear- and four-wheel drive may be available. Available engines include four- and six-cylinder models. With its relatively short wheelbase, a compact may have a better ride than a subcompact but a stiffer ride when compared to vehicles with longer wheelbases. The price range is $8,000 to $17,000.

Full-Size Pickup Truck. Generally comes as a two-door with a rear load bed and two- to three-passenger seating. Extended-cab models with additional seating and inside storage are available. Rear-wheel drive and four-wheel drive are available. Six- and eight-cylinder engines are generally used as power sources. The price range is $10,000 to $25,000.

Full-Size Utility Vehicle. Generally a cross between a station wagon and a truck. Usually uses a truck-like suspension and a wagon-like extended body in a vehicle that combines good off-road service with heavy-duty carrying and towing abilities. Most offer seating for five or more, rear- or four-wheel drive, and engines in six- and eight-cylinder configurations. Priced between $14,000 and $23,000.

Full-Size Van. Offers the largest interior of any of the vehicles. Passenger seating up to 15 is available in some models. Most full-size vans have rear-wheel drive and six- or eight-cylinder engines are available. The price range is $15,000 to $26,000.

Full-Size. The largest of the cars. Generally, five- or six-passenger seating and more trunk space than other models. Rear-wheel drive is common in this class, but front-wheel drive full-size cars are becoming more available. For the most part, four-wheel drive is not available in full-size cars. Six- and eight-cylinder engines are generally available. The price range is $17,000 to $29,000.

Luxury. The luxury car comes in a variety of sizes. It is distinguished by features and appointments which combine a level of prestige, comfort, convenience, and ride quality generally unavailable in other cars. The price range is typically $30,000 to $80,000.

Mid-Size. Offers five- or six-passenger seating with more shoulder and hip room, more trunk space, and more load-carrying capacity than smaller models. There are numerous front- and rear-wheel drive mid-size models while four-wheel drive is becoming available. Four- and six-cylinder engines are generally available. The price range is $12,500 to $27,000.

Mini-Compact. A very small, lightweight vehicle designed for economical operation in urban areas. Generally it seats from two to four passengers. Virtually all mini-compacts are front-wheel drive and use three- and four-cylinder engines of small displacement. The short wheelbase and small tires that typify mini-compacts can give them a rougher ride than large models with longer wheelbases or larger tires. The price range is $6,000 to $8,000.

Mini-Van. Combines a large interior with a relatively short vehicle length. The mini-van can be as short as a compact car while offering seating for as many as eight passengers and easy parking either on the street or in a standard garage. Front-, rear-, and four-wheel drive are available. Four- and six-cylinder engines are typical. The mini-van has a smaller engine, which may mean less towing and passing power, than a full-size van. The price range is $13,000 to $22,000.

Specialty. The specialty car, including sporty models and true sports cars, is generally a two- or four-passenger vehicle designed with performance, handling, and style as prime considerations. Specialty cars are usually two-door or hatchback models, although there are four-door vehicles in the category. Front-wheel, rear-wheel, or four-wheel drive and four-, six-, eight-, and twelve-cylinder engines can be found in these cars. Stiffer suspension components can result in a relatively harsh ride in specialty cars. The price range is $10,000 to $37,000.

Subcompact. A small vehicle designed for economical operation. Generally it is a four-passenger car. Most have front-wheel drive and a four-cylinder engine. The short wheelbase in the subcompact may mean a stiffer ride when compared to vehicles with longer wheelbases. The price range is $7,000 to $12,000.

Source:
Car and Truck Buying Made Easier, Seventh Edition, Dearborn, MI: Ford Motor Company, 1991.

Vehicle Types

Convertible. A vehicle with a retractable top that folds, along with the rear window, into a space (boot) behind the rear seat. The top is generally made of fabric stretched over a metal frame. Some convertibles have a "hardtop" which is removed completely from the vehicle for open-air driving.

Extended-Cab Truck. Offers additional passenger and storage space behind the front seats. Some offer fold-down "jump seats" for extra passengers. A few have four doors and a full-size back seat. Extended-cab versions are available in both compact and full-size trucks.

Four-Door. Available in most vehicle size classes (see *Vehicle Sizes*). Offers individual access to front and rear seats. Generally windows in the rear doors open enough for ventilation. In some models, rear-seat passenger room is increased over two-door models.

Hatchback. Available with two or four doors, this vehicle has a rear liftgate hatch which includes the back window. The space under the hatch opens into the passenger area and takes the place of the trunk. Many hatchbacks have folding rear seatbacks for increased cargo room. Hatchbacks are widely available in mini-compact, subcompact, compact, and specialty models. Availability in other size classes is more limited.

Two-Door. Available in all vehicle size classes (see *Vehicle Sizes*). Door openings in a two-door vehicle are generally longer than front-door openings in a four-door vehicle, providing more front seat entry room. In a two-door, the front seat tips forward to allow rear-seat entry. Rear passenger windows in most two-door models cannot be opened.

Van. Vans fall into two general categories: mini and full-size. Their basic rectangular shape allows for maximum interior volume. There are generally two front doors, a rear door or hatch, and one sliding or two hinged doors on the passenger side.

Wagon. In a wagon, the roof line is extended past the rear seat to the back of the car, forming a large cargo area. Wagons use a liftgate or a tailgate in the back for loading access. Wagons are generally available in all car sizes.

Source:
Car and Truck Buying Made Easier, Seventh Edition, Dearborn, MI: Ford Motor Company, 1991.

Wheelbase

The dimension measured longitudinally between front and rear wheel center lines on the same side on the vehicle. Wheelbase has an effect upon ride quality. In general terms, a longer wheelbase will contribute to a more comfortable ride. Two vehicles could be the same length bumper to bumper, but have different wheelbase lengths. A longer wheelbase can also allow for greater interior room because it allows the wheelwells to be placed away from the passenger compartment.

Source:
Car and Truck Buying Made Easier, Seventh Edition, Dearborn, MI: Ford Motor Company, 1991.

Consumer Electronics

Accessories

Accessories are devices for installation, storage, care, maintenance, and enhancement of consumer electronics products.

TERMINOLOGY

Adapter. A device that makes electric or mechanical connections
between items not originally intended for use together.

Analog to Digital Converter (ADC). Circuit that converts analog
(varying amplitude) signal to a digital (pulse type) signal.

Antenna. Used in sending and receiving electromagnetic waves.

Anti-Static. Any device used to eliminate static electricity, generally associated with phonograph records.

Audio Mixer. A unit that combines or blends several sound inputs
into one or two outputs.

Auxiliary (Aux). Refers to the connector or accessories that may be
connected to a VCR.

Cable Converter. Equipment, sometimes also called a cable decoder, which allows TVs without direct cable tuning to receive
all cable channels.

Cartridge. Device to translate (transduce) stylus motion to electrical energy in a phonograph. There are three basic types—
moving magnet, moving coil, and induced magnet. A phono
cartridge is sometimes called a *pickup*. Also, a tape container
for automatic tape systems.

Cassette. Type of tape container containing two reels. Consumer
can insert it for playback without handling the tape itself.

Circumaural. A type of headphone that almost totally isolates the
listener from room sounds.

Coaxial Cable. The standard cable consisting of a central inner
conductor and a cylindrical outer conductor. Used for most
video connections. Also used to connect the CB radio antenna
with the transceiver.

Compact Disc (CD). A 4.5-inch plastic disc containing a digital
audio recording that is played back optically on a laser-equipped
player. Has 16-bit quantization rate to "write" audio with
high-fidelity sound.

Connector. An electric or mechanical device consisting of a
mating plug and receptacle.

Converter. An auxiliary unit used with a television or radio
receiver to permit reception of channels or frequencies for
which the receiver was not originally designed, e.g., a cable
converter.

Demagnetizer. A device that removes magnetism generated in
tape heads as a consequence of playback and recording
activities.

Digital Audio Tape (DAT). Used to identify tape recorders and
players as well as tape cassettes. A highly sophisticated
recording medium whose performance equals that of a professional studio recorder. The cassette itself, only about half the
size of an analog cassette, holds two hours of recording time.

Diode. Two-element receiving tube or semiconductor device.

Dipole. Antenna fed from the center. Name often applied to "rabbit
ear" antenna.

Directional Antennas. A TV or FM antenna that picks up signals
better from a single direction than all others. Usually has two
or more sections or elements for increasing directivity.

Disk (Diskette). A round piece of magnetic-coated flexible (floppy)
plastic covered by a protective envelope and used to store data.

Filter. A device that allows certain parts of signals to pass through
and stops others.

Graphic Equalizer. A device that permits altering the total balance
of an audio component/system at several frequency levels,
usually from 5 to 12.

Infrared Remote Control. A system of controlling audio equipment from a distance without using wires or cables. It utilizes
infrared radiation to transmit the control information to a
given piece of equipment.

Lead-in Wires. Wires attaching a TV or an FM radio to an outdoor antenna.

Magnetic Tape. A ribbon of thin plastic coated with magnetic material used in both audio and video tape decks.

MATV. Master Antenna Television System, such as used in apartment buildings and motels.

Metal Tape. Tape whose coating is of iron particles; noted for its wide dynamic range and frequency response.

Micro-Cassette. Miniaturized version of the standard audio cassette.

Modem. A device used to connect a computer to a telephone line.

Monopole. Single-rod indoor TV antenna.

NiCd. Nickel Cadmium battery.

RF Converter. The unit in a VCR that places the Video and Audio signals on RF carriers so that the signals can be received by a standard TV (Channel 3 or 4).

RJ-11 Jack. The standard single-line telephone jack.

RJ-14 Jack. A two-line telephone jack.

Signal Splitter. TV/FM antenna accessory used to split the antenna signal into two (or more) paths. One type of signal splitter feeds the same signal to two connections, another separates the VHF, UHF, or FM signals.

Two-Line T-Adapter. This telephone adapter converts a 2-line RJ-14 jack into two separate one-line outlets.

Video Cassette. Magnetic tape housed in a protective container.

Videodisc. Flat disc resembling a phonograph record. Designed to display prerecorded visual information through a player attached to a standard television receiver.

Voltage Surge Suppressor. A device that protects electronic products from a sudden rise of current in an electrical circuit.

VU Meter. *Volume Unit* indicator used to show audio volume level.

Zoom Lens. An optical system for continuously changing the focus distance without changing the focus point and F value, by moving the inside lens group in the optical axis direction. A motor drive zoom lens permits remote control for adjusting the focus distance and focus point. The ratio between the shortest focus distance and the longest focus distance is called a *Zoom Ratio.*

Source:
Consumer Electronics Group, *Consumer Electronics Product Terminology Dictionary,* Washington: Electronic Industries Association, 1991.

Audio Cassette Tape

Inside a cassette tape is a magnetic tape and two reels. The consumer does not have to handle the tape itself when inserting it into a tape player. The ease by which cassette tapes can be loaded and unloaded has helped them replace most reel-to-reel tapes in the consumer market.

TYPES

Standard bias or normal tapes are reliable and usually the least expensive kind. The others, from one to four, generally have progressively better "signal-to-noise ratios" and higher prices.

Type I. (Standard [or Normal] Bias.) Sometimes known as ferric oxide, can be used on any tape deck.

Type II. High bias or chromium dioxide tapes (also known as CrO_2 or chrome equivalent). Can be used on a deck if it has separate bias/equalization switch settings.

Type III. Ferrichrome (FeCr) cassettes are a combination of a layer of ferric oxide particles and a layer of chromium dioxide particles in order to incorporate the features of each.

Type IV. This newest cassette tape is made of metal particles and called *metal tape.* A special metal switch on the tape deck usually is required to record on *metal tape.* Once recorded, however, metal tapes can be played back on any deck that can play high bias cassettes.

TERMINOLOGY

Bias. The application of an extremely high frequency signal to the tape to reduce distortion and improve performance.

Dolby Noise Reduction (NR). A system that reduces background hiss in tape recordings. Dolby reduces background hiss by 10 dB in the high frequency range. Dolby C is twice as effective (20dB) over both middle and high frequencies. (Dolby is a registered trademark of Dolby Laboratories Inc.)

Equalization (EQ). Generally refers to the action or circuitry which selectively adjusts the level of certain audio frequencies to compensate for deficiencies in the system. Also called compensation.

Equalization Switch. Tapes come with different equalization: normal, high, or metal. With this switch, the tape deck's equalization can be set to match that of the tape to get the best sound results.

High Bias Tape. Audio tape with a high frequency signal and low noise. It is coated with a specially treated iron oxide.

Standard or Normal Bias Tape. Audio tape coated with iron oxide.

Sources:
Consumer Electronics Group, *Consumer Electronics Product Terminology Dictionary,* Washington: Electronic Industries Association, 1991.
Consumer Electronics Group, *How to Choose, Use, and Care for Audio and Video Tape,* Washington: Electronic Industries Association, 1991.

Audio Equipment

The consumer electronics industry began with the first sales of consumer radios in the 1920s. Today audio continues as a strong product category. In recent years, the compact disc (CD) player has become an integral part of many audio systems.

AMAX SYMBOL

This symbol appearing on a receiver means that the receiver has met the new standards jointly established by the Electronics Industries Association (EIA) and the National Association of Broadcasters (NAB) for receiving AM broadcasts. Receivers displaying the symbol will incorporate new circuits that capture the improved sound quality now transmitted by cooperating AM radio stations. The symbol appears as follows:

A special symbol for AM stereo receivers appears as follows:

TERMINOLOGY

A-B Test. Direct comparison of the sound/picture quality of two pieces of audio/TV equipment by playing one, then the other.

Absorption Trap. A parallel-tuned circuit made of either capacitors or coils used to absorb and reduce interfering signals.

AC. Alternating current.

Acoustics. The science of sound.

Amplifiers. There are several types:

Pre-Amplifier. The first stage of an amplifier system. It boosts the amplitude of a weak signal from a source (tuner, turntable, tape deck, CD player) and/or provides for tonal adjustment so that the signal may be fed into a power amplifier. Usually contains all audio controls (also known as Control Center).

Power Amplifier. The second or final stage of an amplifier system. It regulates and increases low-level signals received from the pre-amplifier and feeds them to the speakers.

Integrated Amplifier. A pre-amplifier and power amplifier combined in one single integrated chassis.

Amplitude Modulation (AM). The type of transmission used in the standard radio broadcast band, 530 to 1705 kHz. A process which modulates the amplitude of a carrier wave according to a variation of the input voltage (signal).

Amplitude Separation. Method used to separate signals that have differences in amplitude. (For example, the sync signal is separated from the video signal by selecting the threshold level.)

Analog Recording. System of recording in which music is con-verted into electrical impulses which form "patterns" in the grooves of phonograph record masters or in the oxide particles of master tapes representing (or analogous to) musical waveforms.

Analog to Digital Converter (ADC). Circuit that converts analog (varying amplitude) signal to a digital (pulse type) signal.

Analog. A signal that is an analogy of a physical process and is continuously variable, rather than discrete.

Antenna. Used in sending and receiving electromagnetic waves.

Anti-Static. Any device used to eliminate static electricity, generally associated with phonograph records.

Audio Erase (AE). The related circuit or the magnetic head that is placed next to (ahead of) the Audio/Control head. It functions during Audio Dub mode to erase only the audio track in preparation for the new sound recording.

Audio High Density (AHD). System of digital audio recording on grooveless discs, employing an electronically guided capacitance pickup.

Audio Mixer. A unit that combines or blends several sound inputs into one or two outputs.

Audio Spectrum. The full range of audio frequencies, covering the lowest to the highest.

Automatic Gain Control (AGC). Works to maintain a constant luminance level. In television, minimizes picture differences with changes in strength of incoming signals.

Automatic Level Control (ALC). Circuit that functions similar to AGC. As applied to "audio circuit," ALC action varies the gain to maintain a relatively constant output signal over the normal range of sound levels.

Automatic Volume Control (AVC). In radio, maintains constant sound level despite undesired differences in strength of incoming signal.

Band. A range of frequencies between two definite limits.

Band Pass Filter (BPF). A circuit, commonly having inductance and capacitance, that effectively passes a given range of frequencies, whereas frequencies above and below this range are attenuated. Active filters for relatively low frequencies are often designed with op-amps which require only resistance and capacitance.

Bandwidth. The frequency difference between the highest and lowest frequencies involved. The greater the bandwidth of a transmission channel, the more information it can carry.

Base Bandwidth. The amount of bandwidth required by an unmodulated signal, such as video or audio. In general, the higher the quality of the signal, the greater the base bandwidth it requires.

Base Reflex. Type of loudspeaker system that uses a ported enclosure.

Belt Drive. Turntable drive system whose platter is rotated by a belt attached to a motor pulley.

Bias. In tape recording, the application of a high frequency signal to the tape to raise its frequency response.

Bias/Equalization Switch. See *Equalization.*

Binary Coded Decimal (BCD). Numbers based on the binary system (base 2), common in digital circuits.

Capstan. A flangeless pulley used to control speed and motion of magnetic tape through a recorder or playback unit.

Capture Ratio. The ability of a tuner or receiver to select the stronger of two signals at or near the same frequency. Expressed in decibels, the lower the figure being the better.

Carbon Fiber. A strong synthetic material that is low in mass with excellent damping characteristics, used in the manufacture of tonearms.

Cartridge. Device to translate (transduce) stylus motion to electrical energy in a phonograph. There are three basic types: moving magnet, moving coil, and induced magnet. A phono cartridge is sometimes called a *pickup*. Also, a tape container for automatic tape systems.

Cassette. Type of tape container containing two reels. Consumer can insert it for playback without handling the tape itself.

Cassette Deck. A component for recording and/or playing back analog audio signals using a tape cassette as the recording medium; it does not contain a power amplifier. A single-bay cassette deck has one tape transport and magnetic tape head assembly. A dual-bay cassette deck has two transports and two tape head assemblies.

CD-G. Music CD plus graphics. In addition to 16-bit audio, the disc has subcodes that carry textual information (such as liner notes, lyrics) and pixilated, computer-like graphics. A player with the proper adapter is needed to access the subcode information.

CD Changer. A stereo component consisting of remote controller and CD changer which allows for playback of a series of compact discs. Two-piece design.

CD-ROM. CD "Read Only Memory" format. Quantization schemes change to accommodate utilitarian data, namely text with graphics images. Multiple reference works can fit on the disc. CD-ROM is perceived primarily as a computer peripheral. It is likely that CD-R (recordable CD) and CD-E (recordable and erasable) will be more important for CD-ROM than for consumer entertainment CDs.

CE (Chip Enable). Input terminal or voltage used to enable a circuit or device to perform its function.

CEBus. The Consumer Electronics Bus is EIA/CEG's home automation standard. The CEBus Committee, comprised of both member and non-member companies, has developed the premiere standard for a unified hand control system whereby electronic products from different manufacturers can communicate with one another via existing power lines, twisted (telephone) pairs, coaxial cable, and infrared means. Standard includes "bridge" devices that convert signals from one carrier to another to enable data transmission. First demonstrated at the 1989 International Winter Consumer Electronics Show in Las Vegas.

Circumaural. A type of headphone that almost totally isolates the listener from room sounds.

Coloration. Deviation in the balance of musical sounds, audible as an accentuation of one or more parts of the audio spectrum—heavy bass, prominent mid-range, or exaggerated high frequency reproduction.

Compact Disc (CD). A 4.5-inch plastic disc containing a digital audio recording that is played back optically on a laser-equipped player. Has 16-bit quantization rate to "write" audio with high-fidelity sound.

Compact Disc Player. A turntable designed to play compact disc

(CD) recordings using a laser optical pickup. Usually requires a tuner/amplifier equipped with Tape In or AUX jacks.

Compact Stereo. A stereo system with tuner, amplifier, and often a turntable and tape recorder in the same housing. Designed for nonportable use.

Component Stereo. Stereo system composed of separate elements—such as a tuner and amplifier or receiver, turntable, and speakers—usually selected individually by purchaser.

DC. Direct current.

Decibel (dB). Unit of measure for boundaries of sound. A numerical expression of the relative loudness of sound.

Demagnetizer. A device that removes magnetism generated in tape heads as a consequence of playback and recording activities.

Digital Audio Broadcasting (DAB). Several systems currently being considered by the Federal Commission to augment current AM and FM analog broadcasting services.

Digital Audio Tape (DAT). Used to identify tape recorders and players as well as tape cassettes. A highly sophisticated recording medium whose performance equals that of a professional studio recorder. The cassette itself, about half the size of an analog cassette, holds two hours of recording time.

Digital Compact Cassette (DCC). An alternative form of digital tape recording which, unlike DATA, utilizes standard-sized compact cassettes. Expected to be introduced in 1992, DCC equipment will also be able to play back conventional analog cassettes.

Digital Recording. A system of recording in which musical information is converted into a series of pulses that are translated into a binary code intelligible to computer circuits and stored on magnetic tape or magnetic discs. Also called *Pulse Code Modulation (PCM)*.

Digital to Analog Converter (DAC). A circuit that converts digital signals to analog (varying amplitude) signals.

Digitization. The process of changing an electronic signal that is an analogy (analog) of a physical process, such as vision or hearing, into a discrete numerical form.

Direct Drive. Turntable drive system whose platter is an integral part of the motor assembly and is rotated directly by the motor.

Directional Antennas. A TV or FM antenna that picks up signals better from a single direction than all others. Usually has two or more sections or elements for increasing directivity.

Discrete. Type of quadraphonic sound reproduction in which the four original sound sources are routed directly to the respective loudspeakers without encoding and decoding.

Display. A visual representation of electrical/mechanical functions via LED, liquid crystal, or fluorescent devices. Also called readout.

Dolby. A system of noise/hiss reduction invented by Ray Dolby and widely used in consumer, professional, and broadcast audio applications.

Doppler Principle. A phenomenon of physics where a frequency can be effectively raised or lowered by a moving object.

Dynamic Headroom. Expressed in decibels, headroom relates to the ratio between the amount of power an amplifier can deliver continuously versus what it can deliver for short periods of time.

Dynamic Range. In music, the range of amplitudes from loudest passages to softest passages, expressed in decibels. The larger the figure, the more realistic or natural the sound.

Electrical Signal. The impulse that carries sound or pictures (audio or video) from a transmitter (radio or TV station) or from a disk or tape to a receiver (radio, TV set).

Emphasis. A process that boosts the high frequency component of a signal for recording.

Equalization (EQ). Generally refers to the action or circuitry which selectively adjusts the level of certain audio frequencies to compensate for deficiencies in the system. Also called compensation.

Equalization Switch. Tapes come with different equalization: normal, high, or metal. With this switch, the tape deck's equalization can be set to match that of the tape to get the best sound results.

Equalizer. Any device that alters the frequency settings of an audio signal primarily to tailor the sound to the listener's satisfaction.

Factory Service Center. Service facilities owned and operated by consumer electronic product manufacturers.

Ferric Oxide. A magnetic tape whose coating is of ferric (red iron) oxide, the original material used for magnetic recording tapes.

Ferrichrome. A tape combining a layer of ferric oxide particles and a layer of chromium dioxide particles to combine the features of each.

Fidelity. The degree to which an electronic product accurately reproduces sound. A high fidelity system (hi-fi) delivers sounds as close as possible to the original.

Filter. A device that allows certain parts of signals to pass through and stops others.

Flutter. Sound distortion resulting from fairly rapid irregularities in speed of a phonograph record or tape recording.

Frequency Generator (FG). Used in the servo circuits and relates to motor speed.

Frequency Modulation (FM). The form of modulation used for television sound transmission in most of the world, for satellite video transmission, and for videotape recording. Less susceptible to interference than AM, the FM broadcast band covers 88 to 108 MHz.

Frequency Range. Measured in Hertz (Hz), the frequency response of a radio or tape deck tells how much of the range of human hearing it can reproduce. The higher the Hertz number the better. The generally accepted hi-fidelity range for frequency response is 20-20,000 Hz.

Frequency Synthesized Tuning. Tuning method that employs a reference quartz crystal oscillator for exceptional turning accuracy—often better than 0.003 percent.

Frequency. The number of complete oscillations per second of an electromagnetic wave. The pitch of radio signal that distinguishes it from another.

Front End. The tuning, or radio-frequency, section of a radio or TV set.

Function Indicator Panel (FIP). Front display device. Also called FDP (Fluorescent Display Panel).

Graphic Equalizer. A device that permits altering the tonal balance of an audio component/system at several frequency levels, usually from 5 to 12.

Ground. A conducting path between an electrical circuit (or equipment) and the earth (or some conducting body serving in place of the earth).

Guard Band. The space between tracks on tape.

Hall Effect IC. An IC that is activated by a magnetic field.

Harmonic Distortion. Distortion that occurs when an audio component adds unwanted overtones to the original music tones.

Head. In a tape recorder, the device that makes contact with magnetic tape to convert magnetism to electrical signals or vice versa. They are used to record, erase, or play tape signals.

Head Switching. Circuits that, in conjunction with 30 Hz squarewaves (switching pulses), prevent amplified output signal from the head that is not on tape.

Hertz (Hz). The unit of frequency equal to one cycle per second (cps): one kilohertz (kHz) equals 1,000 cps; one megahertz (MHz) equal 1,000,000 cps.

Home Automation. Unified hand control system whereby electronic products from different manufacturers can communicate with one another via existing power lines, twisted (telephone) pairs, coaxial cable, and infrared means (see *CEBus*).

Infrared Remote Control. A system of controlling audio/video/home automation equipment from a distance without using wires or cables. It utilizes infrared radiation to transmit the control information to a given piece of equipment.

Integrated Circuit (IC). A combination of interconnected circuit elements inseparably associated on a base material, capable of performing a circuit function in extremely small size.

Interference. Electrical signals that have an undesirable effect on radio and TV reception.

Intermodulation Distortion (IM). Distortion caused when both high and low frequency tones in music intermodulate with each other to produce a third tone. Expressed as a percentage, the lower the percentage being the better.

IPS. Inches per second, by which tape speed is measured.

KHz. Kilohertz (kilocycles) or thousands of cycles per second.

Karaoke. Designates sing-along audio and video equipment. Karaoke players come with microphones so singers can add their voices to the recorded music. They are usually used with special Karaoke music-only audio and video tapes and discs.

Laser Beam. A tightly focused beam of laser light used to play the signals stored on laser video discs or CD recordings.

Linearity. The straightness of a frequency response curve as an indication of true or accurate sound reproduction.

Linear Tracking. A straight-line movement of a cartridge/tonearm combination in certain turntables.

Low-Mass. Low-weight phono cartridge or tonearm or tonearm/cartridge combination devices for operation with minimal downward pressure on record grooves.

Magnetic Field. The area which surrounds a magnet and is affected by it. The field created by magnets in telephones, electric motors, TVs, and other consumer electronic products usually extends for a foot or two around them.

Magnetic Tape. A ribbon of thin plastic coated with magnetic material and used in both audio and video tape decks.

Matrix. Type of quadraphonic sound system in which four channels are encoded into two channels for recording or broadcast, then decoded into four channels by the listener's equipment.

Memory. Device or circuit to hold machine-language information in electrical or magnetic form, such as a pre-set radio station frequency in a frequency-synthesized tuner or receiver.

Metal Tape. Tape whose coating is of iron particles; noted for its wide dynamic range and frequency response.

MHz. Megahertz (megacycles) or millions of cycles per second. A normal U.S. television transmission channel is 6 MHz.

Micro Components. Miniaturized audio components that provide the benefits of traditional-sized components in less space.

Modulation. The process (or result) of changing information (audio, video, data, etc.) into information-carrying signals suitable for transmission and/or recording.

Multiplex. Superimposition of two separate signals on a single channel, as in FM stereo radio.

NAMSRC. National AM Stereo Radio Committee.

Noise. Undesirable interference of picture or sound.

Noise Limiter. A circuit that reduces noise from man-made devices.

Noise Reduction System. A system that reduces background noise and tape hiss from cassette players and radios.

Open-Air. Type of stereo headphone that offers "private" listening capability but does not totally shut off sounds within the listening room.

Oxide. The material used to make audio and video tape magnetic. Oxide particles shed from tape and can clog deck heads if they are not cleaned.

PCB or PBA. Abbreviation for Printed Circuit Board or Plated Board Assembly.

Phono Cartridge. An electromechanical assembly that converts the mechanical information stored on a record into electrical signals. The stylus (needle) contacts the record surface and transfers information from the record to the cartridge.

Pinch Roller. The part of both audio and video tape decks that moves the tape forward and backward.

Pitch Control. Variable control for increasing or decreasing the speed of a tape deck or turntable.

Polyamide, Polymer, Polypropylene. Synthetic materials used for speaker cones. Noted for light weight, minimum resonance, and the proper elasticity/rigidity for fast transient response.

Pre-Emphasis. The method of placing emphasis on the higher frequency portions of the signal to improve the S/N ratio.

Preset. The "programming" of radio station frequencies in a tuner or receiver, or musical selections on a tape, for instant recall at the push of a button.

Quadraphonic or Quadrasonic. Four-channel stereo.

RACX System. A single manufacturer's complete sound reproduction system, including a rack or cabinet, packaged to sell as one unit. May be a compact or component system.

Radio Waves. Electromagnetic wave frequencies from 10 kHz to 300,000 MHz.

Receiver. An electronic device that accepts electrical signals to change into sound or pictures (audio or video). Receivers, a combination of an amplifier and a tuner, are a basic part of electronic products from radios to VCRs.

RF. Radio frequencies above 15 kHz. The high frequency for transmission of the video signal.

S/RF. Signal strength of radio frequency.

Selectivity. The ability of a radio receiver to block out adjacent channel signals. The higher the figure expressed in decibels (dB), the better the selectivity.

Sensitivity. The input signal level required by a tuner, amplifier, etc., to be able to produce a stated output. The lower the necessary input stated in υV (microvolts), the higher the sensitivity.

Separation. Extent to which two stereo channels are kept apart. Expressed as decibels, the larger the number, the better the separation and stereo effect.

Serial Copy Management System (SCMS). A proposed copying limitation system being used in digital audio tape recorders that restricts the number of generational copies which can be made from a recording. Recorder owners will be able to make a taped copy of recorded material, but not copies of the copies.

Shibata. Stylus tip configuration developed for playback of discrete four-channel records.

Short Wave. On the radio frequency spectrum, shortwave radio uses the band just above the ordinary AM radio band—from 1,600 kiloHertz (kHz) to 30,000 kiloHertz (kHz). Not as popular in the United States as AM or FM radio, shortwave radio is a much listened to and used medium in most of the rest of the world.

Signal to Noise (S/N) Ratio. Ratio between a component's output signal intensity and its accompanying noise content. Expressed in decibels, the larger the number, the better.

Simulcast. Also known as FM simulcast, this VCR feature enables the user to record the audio signals from a connected FM tuner or audio receiver onto a videotape. Due to the growing popularity of components equipped with the MTS/SAP decoders and of stereo TV broadcasts, simulcasting is not an uncommon feature.

Sonic Feedback. Sound feedback. A return of a portion of the output of a circuit or device to its input. This results in distortion.

Sound Pressure Level (SPL). Loudness level of a speaker relative to a specified input signal, stated in decibels. It is usually measured at a distance of one meter from the speaker along its front-center axis, with one watt of input.

Speaker Sensitivity. SPL output of a speaker, stated in decibels, in response to a specified input signal. It is usually measured at a distance of one meter along its front/center axis, with one watt of input.

Stereo TV Receiver. A complete television receiver that includes built-in television tuner and display, stereo amplifiers, speakers, and MTS (Multichannel Television Sound) circuitry for receiving stereo TV broadcasts.

Stereo. Short for stereophonic, stereo is the ability to create a three-dimensional sound effect using two channels of separate audio information. Also used to refer to a type of sound or a piece of audio equipment.

Stylus. Phonograph needle.

Tangential Tracking. Straight-line movement of a cartridge/tonearm combination tangent to the record grooves, for optimal tracking accuracy.

Time Delay. Audio circuitry that accepts an input signal and provides a delay in time before initiating an output signal to create a certain type of acoustical result, i.e., a "studio" or "concert hall" ambience.

Tonearm. Mechanical armlike assembly used to stabilize and position the phono cartridge and stylus when playing records.

Total Harmonic Distortion (THD). Total amount of harmonic distortion created by an audio component. Expressed as a percentage figure, the lower the better.

Track. The track made magnetically on a tape by the recording head. Audio track and control track are in upper or lower edges. Video tracks are recorded helically in the central part.

Tracking. Property of phonograph pickup to properly follow the record groove. Ability of color TV set to properly register all color tones and white.

Tracking Force. Downward force exerted by the stylus in a record groove, expressed in grams.

Transducer. Device (phono cartridge, tape head, speaker) that converts one type of energy (electrical, acoustical, magnetic, mechanical) into another.

Transistor. Active semiconductor device with three or more electrodes.

Transmitter. A device that can change sound waves into electric waves or impulses to send to a receiver—a telephone, a radio or TV broadcast, or inside a VCR.

Tuner. Portion of a radio or television set that selects the desired incoming signal.

Tuning Eye. Indicator tube that indicates whether FM or TV receiver is tuned exactly to desired incoming signal.

Turntable. A rotating platform that carries a phonograph record.

Varactor. Variable-capacitance diode used in electronic tuning systems for TV and radio, hence the name "varactor tuning."

VU Meter. Volume Unit indicator used to show volume level in tape recording.

Source:
Consumer Electronics Group, *Consumer Electronics Product Terminology Dictionary,* Washington: Electronic Industries Association, 1991.

Camcorders

A camcorder is a video camera and video cassette recorder (VCR) in one compact unit. Camcorders are purchased primarily by consumers who already own home VCR decks and are interested in a simple-to-use, lightweight portable for electronic photography. Camcorders are available in all formats—full-sized VHS and Beta as well as the compact VHS-C and 8mm. New Super VHS, Super VHS-C, ED Beta, and High Band 8mm record and playback pictures with a horizontal resolution of between 400 and 450 lines, providing a picture quality that exceeds broadcast standards.

TYPES

Compact VHS Camcorder (VHS-C). This camcorder uses the VHS format but has a smaller tape cassette—the tape itself is the same type used in standard size cassettes. This makes the camcorder smaller and lighter, but it also reduces the amount of time it can record since the smaller cassette holds less tape. After snapping the compact cassette into an adapter, the tape can be played on any VHS home deck.

Eight-Millimeter Camcorder. This is a small and lightweight camcorder. It uses a tape that is slightly larger than a standard audio cassette. The 8mm format is not compatible with home VCRs; a separate unit is needed on a TV for playback.

Standard Camcorder. A standard size VHS or Beta camcorder. The most popular of the camcorder formats and the easiest to use with a home VCR. Also called a full-size camcorder, it is the largest and heaviest camcorder.

TERMINOLOGY

AC/DC. A switch on the unit that lets you run it on either AC line power or battery power.

Adjustable Diopter. The viewfinder is adjustable and can focus to compensate for moderate nearsightedness or farsightedness.

Adjustable Viewfinder. The viewfinder is adjustable from left to right, or moves up and down and rotates.

Audio Dub. Replaces the sound track on a previously recorded tape with a new one without disturbing the video material.

Auto/Focus Infrared. Most camcorders have an infrared triangulation autofocus system. This technique involves bouncing a narrow beam of infrared light off the subject. A sensor slightly offset from the light source on the camcorder measures the angle at which the beam is reflected back; electronics inside the camcorder use that angle to calculate the distance and adjust the lens accordingly. Infrared focusing can be foiled by black or angled shiny surfaces that reflect little or no light back to the camera, by subjects too tiny to reflect the entire beam, and by off-center subjects that the beam misses entirely.

Automatic Exposure Lock. Holds the exposure setting while one recomposes the scene or pans the camcorder.

Automatic Gain Control (AGC). Works to maintain a constant luminance level.

Automatic White Balance. An electronic circuit in the color camera to control the color reproduction. This circuit automatically sets the white balance of the picture by controlling the level of the red and blue signals. White balance means that the camera will reproduce a white object in the picture as white.

Automatic White Tracking. A white balancing circuit with a sensor for constant controlling of the white balance.

Backlight Switch. This feature is most useful for scenes in which the background is brighter than the subject. By pushing a button, the user can boost the average brightness slightly to enhance detail in the foreground.

Camcorder. Camera and VCR in one compact unit.

Capstan. A flangeless pulley used to control speed and motion of magnetic tape through a recorder or playback unit.

Cassette. Type of tape container containing two reels. The consumer can insert it into a device without handling the tape itself.

Cassette Housing. The mechanical arrangement for lowering the video cassette into position for playing or recording.

Character Generator. Lets the user enter captions (or titles) across the picture on the tape being made.

Charge Couple Device (CCD). A semiconductor device used as an image pickup in consumer video cameras and camcorders.

Date/Time. Lets user record the date on the tape being made so that it will show in the picture on playback.

Digital Special Effects. Digital circuitry that lets the user store and then manipulate the video image to achieve certain special effects.

Display. A visual representation of electrical/mechanical functions via LED, liquid crystal, or fluorescent devices. Also called readout.

Dropout. A momentary loss of the playback RF signal due to dirt on the video tape or heads. Uncompensated dropout produces white or black streaks, which represent the missing information in the picture.

Dual Automatic Exposure. An exposure system that combines spot metering and center-averaged light metering to give the user the correct exposure for backlit subjects.

Dubbing. Playing a tape on one tape machine and recording (dubbing or copying) it on a second machine.

Electronic Viewfinder. A small TV monitor lets the user see what will be recorded through the lens. Frequently, various information displays are also shown on the screen of the electronic viewfinder.

Factory Service Center. Service facilities owned and operated by consumer electronics product manufacturers.

Flying Erase Heads. Erase heads on the cylinder designed to produce seamless edits—smooth, invisible transitions from one scene to the next.

Focus Lock. This feature lets the user maintain (or lock onto) a certain focus setting while recomposing the scene.

Frame Edit. Lets the user edit (delete) scenes while the tape is still inside the camera.

Gain-Up Switch. Boosts the video signal when activated by a switch to compensate for such low-light condition as a dimly lit room.

Head. In a tape recorder, the device that makes contact with magnetic tape to convert magnetism to electrical signals or vice versa. Used to record, erase, or play tape signals.

High Band. A recording method in which the carrier frequency is shifted higher in order to get high resolution.

Horizontal Aperture Correction. An electronic circuit in the color video camera used to get a sharper picture.

Horizontal Resolution. A rating of the fine detail of a TV picture, measured in lines. The more lines, the higher the resolution and the better the picture. A standard TV or VCR produces 240 lines of horizontal resolution, while about 430 lines are possible with Super VHS machines.

Image Mix. This feature allows the user to hold an image in memory so it can be superimposed on another image later.

Image Sensor. The sensor, located behind the lens on most camcorders, is like an electronic retina that converts the light into the electronic signals that make up the TV image. CCD indicates the camcorder has a charge-coupled sensor. MOS means the camcorder has a metal oxide/semiconductor sensor. TUBE means that the camcorder uses an old-fashioned tube-type sensor to convert the light into an electronic signal.

In-Camera Battery. The battery slips inside the back of the camera.

Insert. Allows the user to insert new audio/video segments into material already on tape.

Instant Review. A push of a button lets the user play back through the viewfinder the last few seconds that were shot.

Integrated Circuit (IC). A combination of interconnected circuit elements inseparably associated on a base material, capable of performing a circuit function in extremely small size.

Interlaced Scanning System. The electron beam scans the optical image. The horizontal scanning lines are divided into two fields. The first field consists of the odd lines and the second field consists of the even lines.

IPS. Inches per second, by which tape speed is measured.

Iris. Automatically adjusts the aperture and controls the amount of light that reaches the image sensor.

Lens Aperture. The maximum lens aperture (or opening) is expressed as an F-stop. The smaller the maximum aperture number, the "faster" the lens and the more light it can let in. Low light sensitivity also depends on the type and size of sensor used and on the associated electronics.

Loading. The threading of tape to the VCR's video heads.

Loading Motor. The motor that powers the VCR's mechanism for load/unload of tape with respect to the heads.

Lux. A unit of measurement (light generated by 10 candles one foot from a white surface) used to rate the amount of light needed by a video camera or camcorder to record a recognizable image—the lower the spec, the better. Although ratings are typically given in the 3- to 10-lux range, most video cameras and camcorders require over 100 lux to produce a bright, good-quality picture.

Macro Focus. A focusing range that lets the user get very close to the subject.

Macro Lens. A close-up focusing lens.

Manual Focus. Lets the user adjust the focus manually.

Memory Counter. Helps the user locate specific passages by numeric counter. The user manually sets the counter back to zero before starting to record. Upon rewinding, the camcorder will stop at this tape position.

Neutral Density Filter (ND Filter). An optical filter that reduces the amount of light entering a camera without influencing the color reproduction.

Newvicon Tube. A camera tube that has very good sharpness and low light characteristics.

NiCd. Nickel Cadmium battery.

Parallax Focus (Focusing). The viewfinder is slightly to the side of the camcorder lens so that when the user looks through the viewfinder there is a slight difference between what he sees and what the camcorder lens sees. The parallax focusing system compensates for this difference so that the viewfinder frames the subject approximately as it will appear on the tape.

Phase-Detector. This autofocus system automatically shifts focus as the subject moves closer or farther away. The camcorder will focus automatically and continually from the lens surface to infinity.

Pickup Tube. The image device is a tube-type camera that converts light from the lens into electrical signals. Newer solid-state cameras use CCD or MOS image sensors rather than a tube.

Power Zoom. The lens is motorized and zooms in or out at the touch of a button or switch.

Scanning. The horizontal and vertical movement of the electron beam in the camera or TV tube.

Self-Timer. The self-timer allows the camcorder operator to set the machine to start after a delay of about 10 seconds so that the operator can get into the picture.

Sensitivity. Ability of camcorder to capture a minimal acceptable image, measured in lux. The lower lux number indicates higher sensitivity.

Special Effects. Any feature that permits the unit to play back pictures at speeds other than normal—still, slow, scan forward or reverse, etc. Also called Tricks Mode.

Stereo. Short for stereophonic, stereo is the ability to create a three-dimensional sound effect using two channels of separate audio information.

Still Frame. A feature that lets the user pause or freeze a still frame when playing back the tape.

Super VHS (S-VHS). An improvement over the standard VHS, S-VHS's separation of the luminance and chrominance signals during record and playback, a wider luminance bandwidth and the use of high-density tape, result in sharper, more vivid picture quality. The horizontal resolution reached by S-VHS is approximately 400 lines or better—a standard VHS is 240 lines.

Through Camera Lens. The camcorder has a contrast autofocus system. A "Zone Focusing" system lets the user temporarily change the size of the central area used for focusing.

Track. The track made magnetically on a tape by the recording head. Audio track and control track are in the upper and lower edges. Video tracks are recorded helically in the central part.

Vertical Aperture Correction. The electronic circuit in the color camera used to get a sharper picture.

VHS (Video Home System). One of the two standard home VCR systems.

Vidicon. A kind of photoconductive pickup tube used for a TV camera. A vacuum tube that receives an optical image by utilizing the nature of photoconductive substance and generates an electrical signal. It has a low cost and small size.

Video Cassette. Magnetic tape housed in a protective container.

Waveform Monitor. A special oscilloscope that is designed to display the composite video signal.

White Balance. Color reproduction capability of the color camera. Depending on the color temperature of the light source, the reproduced color on the TV screen will change. The white balance circuit adjusts the red and blue signal components so that a white object is displayed on the screen as white. See *Automatic White Balance*.

Vectorscope. An instrument for checking the different chroma and luminance in waveforms.

Viewfinder Indicators. Information that can be indicated in the viewfinder—i.e., audio level monitor, battery low, end of tape warning, high-speed shutter, low light warning, moisture condensation, operating mode, time remaining on tape, shutter speed, tape counter, and focal zone.

Y/C Connections. Connections between videotape recorders and cameras, monitors, and other devices that keep luminance and chrominance separate and thus avoid cross-color and cross-luminance.

Zoom Lens. An optical system for continuously changing the focus distance without changing the focus point and F value by moving the inside lens group in the optical axis direction. A motor driven zoom lens permits remote control for adjusting the focus distance and focus point. The ratio between the shortest focus distance and the longest focus distance is called a *Zoom Ratio*.

Zoom Ratio. The longest focal length divided by the shortest. A zoom ratio of 6:1, for example, means the image at one end of the zoom range is six times the size of the image at the other end of the range. The larger the ratio, the more extreme the telephoto and wide-angle effects that are available.

Source:
Consumer Electronics Group, *Consumer Electronics Product Terminology Dictionary,* Washington: Electronic Industries Association, 1991.

Cellular Phones

A cellular phone is a mobile computerized radio telephone. Each local cellular company breaks down its geographic area of coverage into smaller areas called cells. Calls received at each tower are sent to regular phone lines through an office that coordinates the routing of calls. Calls hand off (pass from one tower to another) without interrupting cellular telephone conversations. Cellular companies also offer "roaming" privileges to their customers, so they can make and receive calls when they are outside their company's geographic area.

TYPES

Mobile. Consists of a base unit (installed in the automobile), a handset, and an antenna.

Portable. A model small enough to hold in your hand. It runs on battery power. Portables come with different amounts of talk time (as much as two hours) and standby time (some go several days) before they need recharging.

Transportable. A model which is self-contained (no installed base in the car). It can be transferred from one car to another or even used outside the car. It runs on batteries (called a *phone pack*), or it can be plugged into an automobile cigarette lighter.

FEATURES

Battery Pack. Enables you to keep the phone charged when it is being carried away from the automobile.

Buffer. Lets the phone record the numbers of callers who didn't reach you while you were away.

High Gain Antenna. Used for enhanced reception.

Pager. Alerts you to an incoming call when you were away from your car.

Scratch Pad Memory. Allows you to put a number in the phone's memory while you are talking.

Sources:
Consumer Electronics Group, *Consumers Should Know All About Auto Electronics Products,* Washington: Electronics Industries Association, 1991.
Consumer Electronics Group, *Consumer Electronics Product Terminology Dictionary,* Washington: Electronics Industries Association, 1991.

Computers, Frequency Emissions Standards

Computers emit radio signals in their operation. Because these signals may cause interference to radio and television reception, the marketing and the use of computers is regulated by the Federal Communications Commission (FCC). Under federal rules, computer users are responsible for remedying interference, including interference in neighboring homes.

Class A. Computers which have been certified for use in commercial and industrial locations. Signals from computers are more likely to be masked by electrical noise from other equipment in such an environment. These areas are also likely to have fewer radios and TVs. Accordingly, equipment marketed only for use in these locations may meet the less rigorous Class A standard.

Class B. Computers certified by the FCC as meeting the Class B standard are less likely to cause interference to radio and TV reception than those that have been certified by the manufacturer or importer to the Class A standards. Only Class B certified computers may be advertised, sold, or leased for use in residences. A similar regulatory program applies in Canada. Buyers seeking computers for use in homes (including offices at home) should shop for computers and peripherals which have been Class B certified. These devices carry a label with an FCC ID number.

Sources:
"Computers, FCC Class A, Class B, and You—or, When Is It Better to Get a B than an A?" *PC Magazine,* May 14, 1991.
Consumer Electronics Group, *Consumer Electronics Product Terminology Dictionary,* Washington: Electronic Industries Association, 1991.

Computers, PCs

Personal Computer (PC) systems are quickly becoming a consumer commodity. The Electronic Industries Association reports that in 1991 over 33 percent of the U.S. households have at least one computer, about the same penetration as home compact disc (CD) players. However, computers are complex products with a large vocabulary of technical terms associated with them. It is now common to see department store ads in the Sunday newspaper advertising a computer with "386SX, 2MG RAM, SVGA graphics, 100,000 MTBF 80Meg hard drive."

This entry will explain the terminology and grades of the products a typical consumer is most likely to encounter in purchasing a PC.

Two types of computers have come to dominate the PC market: the Apple MacIntosh and those based on the PC (the IBM PC and its clones). Because the MacIntosh is based on a proprietary technology that cannot be copied by Apple's competitors, it has not generated the large number of competing products as has the IBM PC. The IBM has an *open architecture* (one that relies on nonproprietary components) that other companies have copied to

compete against IBM. With this competition has come a level of confusion that is not present in the MacIntosh product line. Accordingly, most of the terms in this entry are related to the PC.

A computer system consists of a number of component parts. Visually, the consumer can recognize (1) a box (case) with an on-off switch and an opening for a floppy disk; (2) a TV-like monitor; (3) a keyboard; and (4) perhaps a printer. The case contains the following:

Motherboard. The place where all of the electronic components are—including the microprocessor and memory chips.

Ports. Outlets for various plugs that allow one to connect the keyboard, mouse, printers, or other peripheral devices to the motherboard.

Power Supply. Converts utility-supplied AC electricity to the direct current used by the PCs logic circuits.

Storage Devices. Floppy disks and hard disks.

Video Card. Contains the electronics needed to run the monitor.

MOTHERBOARD

The motherboard consists of 6 to 12 layers of conductive copper circuit traces glued together. It holds all the electrical components used in the computer—including the microprocessor, memory, chip set, BIOS, and bus. High-quality boards have more layers. Some of the layers serve as ground planes that isolate the radiation (electromagnetic energy or radio frequencies) from other layers. This makes the board more resistant to noise.

BIOS (Basic Input/Output System). A set of program instructions held in read-only memory (ROM) that provide software programs with a common means of activating the microprocessor and other system functions, such as the hard disks or printer ports.

Bus. *ISA (Industry Standard Architecture):* This type of bus provides a 16-bit path for data to travel from one component to the next. *EISA (Extended Industry Standard Architecture):* This architecture provides a 32-bit path. *MCA (Micro Channel Architecture):* This architecture is an alternative 32-bit bus and is being promoted by the IBM Corporation.

Chip Set. Different sets of chips on a computer motherboard serve different functions. Some sets manage the floppy disk controller or the parallel printer port, while the optional *math co-processor* speeds up mathematical calculations. Most modern PCs are built from chip sets that take all the individual circuit components and combine them into one, two, or three ASICs (application-specific integrated circuits). The more functions integrated onto a chip the fewer chips on the motherboard.

MICROPROCESSORS

The microprocessor or CPU (central procession unit) has been called the "brain" of the computer system. It is the chip that manipulates the information and around which the computer system is built. Software programs are written to take advantage of specific chip *architectures* (designs) and will not run on computers that do not use the chip architecture for which they were written. Consequently, programs written for the Apple MacIntosh computer, which uses a chip made by Motorola, will not run on IBM and compatible computers.

Both IBM personal computers (PCs) and non-IBM PC compatibles (clones) use a series of chips made by the Intel Corporation. The *architecture* or design of the Intel chip, however, has itself been cloned, and companies like American Micro Devices are now offering chips that are compatible with Intel chips. To promote its own trademarked chips from its competitor's, the Intel corporation has developed an advertising campaign whereby computer companies using Intel chips in their computers are encouraged to place an "Intel Inside" seal on their packaging. Over the years, many versions of the Intel chip have been released. These versions (known by their numbers) are explained below.

4004. Introduction date: November 15, 1971
  Clock speed: 108 kilohertz
  0.06 MIPS
  Number of transistors: 2,300 (10 microns)
  Bus width: 4 bits
  Addressable memory: 640 bytes
  Typical use: Busicom calculator
  First microcomputer chip, arithmetic manipulation

8008. Introduction date: April 1972 (developed in tandem with 4004)
  Clock speed: 200 kilohertz
  0.06 MIPS
  Number of transistors: 3,500 (10 microns)
  Bus width: 8 bits
  Addressable memory: 16 KBytes
  Typical use: Dumb terminals, general calculators, bottling machines
  Data/character manipulation

8080. Introduction date: April 1974
  Clock speed: 2 MHz
  0.64 MIPS
  Number of transistors: 6,000 (6 microns)
  Bus width: 8 bits
  Addressable memory: 64 KBytes
  Typical use: Traffic light controller, Altair computer (first PC)
  Ten times the performance of the 8008. Required six support chips versus 20 for the 8008

8085. Introduction date: March 1976
  Clock speed: 5 MHz
  0.37 MIPS
  Number of transistors: 6,500 (3 microns)
  Bus width: 8 bits
  Typical use: Toledo scale. From weight and price computed cost.
  High level of integration, operating for the first time on a single 5 volt power supply (from 12 volts previously)

8086. Introduction date: June 8, 1978
  Clock speeds: 5 MHz (0.33 MIPS)
  8 MHz (0.66 MIPS)
  10 MHz (0.75 MIPS)
  Number of transistors: 29,000 (3 microns)
  Bus width: 16 bits
  Addressable memory: 1 Megabyte
  Typical use: Portable computing
  Ten times the performance of the 8080

8088. Introduction date: June 1979

Clock speeds: 5 MHz (0.33 MIPS)
  8 MHz (0.75 MIPS)
  Internal architecture: 16 bits
  External bus width: 8 bits
  Number of transistors: 29,000 (3 microns)
  Typical use: Standard microprocessor for all IBM PCs and PC clones
  Identical to 8086 except for its 8 bit external bus

80286. Introduction date: February 1982
  Clock speed 8 MHz (1.2 MIPS)
  10 MHz (1.5 MIPS)
  12 MHz (2.66 MIPS)
  Number of transistors: 134,000 (1.5 microns)
  Bus width: 16 bits
  Addressable memory: 16 megabytes
  Virtual memory: 1 gigabyte
  Typical use: Standard microprocessor for all PC clones
  Three to six times the performance of the 8086
  Can scan the *Encyclopaedia Britannica* in 45 seconds

Intel 386 DX CPU. Introduction date: October 17, 1985
  Clock speeds: 16 MHz (5 to 6 MIPS)
  20 MHz introduced February 16, 1987 (6 to 7 MIPS)
  25 MHz introduced April 4, 1988 (8.5 MIPS)
  33 MHz introduced April 10, 1989 (11.4 MIPS)
  Number of transistors: 275,000 (1.5 microns, now 1 micron)
  Bus width: 32 bits
  Addressable memory: 4 gigabytes
  Virtual memory: 64 terabytes
  Typical use: Desktop computing
  Can address enough memory to manage an eight-page history of every person on earth
  Can scan the *Encyclopaedia Britannica* in 7 seconds

Intel 386 SX CPU. Introduction date: June 16, 1988
  Clock speeds: 16 MHz (2.5 MIPS)
  20 MHz introduced January 25, 1989 (4.2 MIPS)
  25 MHz introduced 1991
  Number of transistors: 275,000 (1.5 microns, now 1 micron)
  Internal architecture: 32 bits
  External bus width: 16 bits
  Addressable memory: 4 gigabytes
  Virtual memory: 64 terabytes
  Typical use: Entry-level desktop and portable computing

Intel 486 DX CPU.
  Introduction date: April 10, 1989
  Clock speeds: 25 MHz (20 MIPS)
  33 MHz introduced May 7, 1990 (27 MIPS)
  50 MHz introduced June 24, 1991 (41 MIPS)
  Number of transistors: 1,200,000 (1 micron, with 50 MHz at .8 micron)
  Bus width: 32 bits
  Addressable memory: 16 megabytes
  Virtual memory: 64 terabytes
  Typical use: Desktop computing and servers
  Fifty times the performance of the 8088
  Can scan the *Encyclopaedia Britannica* in 2 seconds

Intel 386 SL CPU. Introduction date: October 15, 1990
  Clock speeds: 20 MHz (4.21 MIPS)
  25 MHz introduced September 30, 1991 (5.3 MIPS)

Number of transistors: 855,000 (1 micron)
Internal architecture: 32 bits
External bus width: 16 bits
Addressable memory: 16 megabytes
Virtual memory: 64 terabytes
Typical use: First microprocessor made specifically for portables
Highly integrated; includes cache, bus, and memory controllers

Intel 486 SX CPU. Introduction date: April 22, 1991
Clock speeds: 16 MHz introduced September 16, 1991 (13 MIPS)
20 MHz (16.5 MIPS)
25 MHz introduced September 16, 1991 (20 MIPS)
Number of transistors: 1,185,000 (1 micron)
Bus width: 32 bits
Addressable memory: 4 gigabytes
Virtual memory: 64 terabytes
Typical use: Low-cost entry to Intel 486 CPU-based desktop computing.
Same as Intel 486 DX CPU with no math coprocessor on chip.
Also available in 3.3 volt versions.
Upgradable to full Intel 486 DX technology

Intel 486 DX2 CPU. Introduction date: March 3, 1992
Clock speed: 50 MHz (40 MIPS)
Number of transistors: 1.2 million (.8 micron)
Bus width: 32 bits
Addressable memory: 4 gigabytes
Virtual memory 64 terabytes
Typical use: High performance, low cost desktops
Uses "speed doubler" technology where the microprocessor core runs at twice the speed of the bus

P5. Next Generation (Intel internal code name: P5)
Introduction date: 1992
Number of transistors: over 3,000,000 (submicron)

Clock Speed. Microprocessors have an internal clock that controls the speed at which information is transferred from one component to another. Although the clock speed is not the sole factor in determining the speed of the system, computers with faster clock speeds are typically faster. Clock speed is measured in megahertz, abbreviated MHz. Modern clock speeds range from 8Mhz to over 50Mhz.

Turbo. Some computer systems have the ability to run at multiple clock speeds. When running at the highest clock speed it is computer is called running in turbo mode.

MEMORY

Circuitry and devices that hold information are referred to as memory. Computer companies often advertise their computers as having "2 megs of RAM," or "4MB RAM." These phrases refer to the amount of *random access memory* (RAM) that is installed in the computer. The computer's microprocessor temporarily stores information and data in RAM when doing its calculations and manipulations. After the microprocessor is done using it, the information may be permanently stored on storage devices like floppy disks and hard disks. When the computer is turned off, the information in RAM disappears.

RAM size is measured in Megabytes (a million bytes or characters). Four megabytes (MB) of RAM can hold 4 million characters. Accordingly, the more RAM installed in the computer, the more information that can be processed at a given time. Increased RAM can dramatically increase the speed of operation of many software programs. The larger the software program the more RAM it requires. Many advanced software applications require as much as 8 megabytes to operate; 2 megabytes is often considered minimum and 4 is becoming standard.

RAM is installed on the computer's motherboard. It typically comes on modules called SIMMs (see below), but may also come as DRAMs (Dynamic Random Access Memory).

Single In-line Memory Modules (SIMMs). Modules that carry the random access memory (RAM). Most modern system boards use SIMMs. They come in a variety of sizes, from 256K to 16MB. Currently, 1 MB and 4MB SIMMs are the most popular. The 1 MB SIMMs contain nine 10 megabit chips and are known as 1-by-9 SIMMs. 4MB SIMMs typically contain nine 4-megabit chips. SIMMs are rated at speeds of 60, 70, or 80 nanoseconds (one-billionths of a second). The faster SIMMs are more expensive and should increase system performance. However, the speed difference may be imperceptible.

FLOPPY DISKS

A floppy disk or diskette is a round piece of magnetic-coated flexible (floppy) plastic, covered by a protective envelope. It is a removable storage device that can permanently store information. Floppy disks are inserted into floppy disk drives. There are two standard sizes of floppy disks: 5.25 inch and 3.5 inch.

3.5 inch. A small disk in a hard case that is 3.5 inches square. It is often labeled MF for Micro Floppy or MFD for Micro Floppy Disk. There are two versions: one labeled DD/DD or 2DD (double sided/double density) that can hold 720K (kilobytes) of information, and a second labeled HD (high density) that can hold 1.4MB (megabytes) of information.

5.25 inch. A flexible thin disk that is 5.25 inches square. There are two versions: one labeled DD/DD (double sided/double density) that can hold 360K (kilobytes) of information and a second labeled HD (high density) that can hold 1.2MB (megabytes) of information. A single sided version is no longer in wide use.

Double Density. A type of diskette that allows twice as much data to be stored on it than on a single density diskette.

Dual or Double Sided. A diskette format using both sides of a diskette.

Floppy Disk Drive. There are as many types of floppy disk drive as there are floppy disks: 5.25 inch double density, 5.25 inch high density, 3.5 inch double density, and 3.5 inch high density. The high density drives can read double density disks, but the double density drives cannot read high density disks. Manufacturers have recently started selling *integrated dual floppy drives* that integrate both a high density 5.25 inch drive and a high density 3.5 inch drive in the same component.

Formatted. Before a diskette can be used it has to be formatted for the type of computer it will be used on. Typically the consumer formats the disk himself. Although it only takes a minute or so, formatting a disk can be a nuisance. Therefore, disk manufacturers now offer preformatted diskettes. A preformatted diskette will be marked with the name of the computer system for which it was formatted (IBM and compatibles or the Apple MacIntosh). Diskettes formatted for the IBM PC will not work on the MacIntosh.

Notched. 5.25 inch diskettes have a small notch in the upper right hand corner. If a sensor in the Floppy Disk Drive senses the notch, it allows information to be written to or erased from the disk. If it does not sense the notch, it allows information to be read from the disk but does not allow information to be copied to or erased from the disk. In 3.5 inch diskettes, the notch is covered by a metal cover attached to a spring. The cover slides back to allow information to be written to the disk.

Single Density. A type of diskette that allows half as much data to be stored on it than on a double density diskette.

TPI (Tracks per Inch). The surface of the diskette is divided into tracks that are formatted to store data. Sometimes a disk is shipped with bad tracks. These tracks cannot hold data and will decrease the total storage capacity of the diskette.

Write Protected. A diskette that has the notch covered so that information can not be written to the disk.

HARD DISKS

A hard disk, also called a fixed disk or hard drive, is a device typically installed in the computer case and can store millions of characters of information. Hard disks are graded by their storage capacity, speed, and failure rate.

Access Time. The time it takes the hard disk to access information. It is measured in milliseconds ($\frac{3}{10}$ second; abbreviated ms.). A fast hard disk will have access times below 10 milliseconds.

Interleaving. This term describes how data is placed in sectors. An interleave of 1:1 means that data is placed in sequential sections. A 1:3 interleave means that data is recorded in every third sector. It is important because the hard disk controller must get data from the hard disk. If it can't keep up with the speed of the hard disk it can slow down performance. A 1:3 ratio will give the hard disk controller more time to access data.

Mean Time Before Failure (MTBF). Hard disks are rated according to the time the disk can be expected to operate before it fails. The time is measured in hours. Early hard disks were rated at between 5,000 and 10,000 hours. Newer disks have ratings from 100,000 to 160,000 hours, or 11 to 18 years.

Megabytes. The storage capacity of a hard disk is measured in megabytes. A Megabyte is equal to 1 million characters of information. Hard disks range in storage capacity from 5MB to over 500MB. Most computers now come with at least a 40MB or 80MB hard disk. As computer software programs become more complex, they become larger and require more storage space on the hard disk. Some state-of-the-art PC word processing programs require over 15MB of storage space alone. Consequently consumers are demanding larger and larger hard disks.

HARD DISK CONTROLLERS

The hard disk controller consists of the electronics that control the flow of data between the hard disk and the motherboard. There are three types of interfaces used to connect the hard disk subsystem to the mother board:

Enhanced Small Device Interface (ESDI). An improved controller design that increases throughput by up to 40 percent.

Integrated Drive Electronics (IDE). The IDE interface is the standard interface developed for the popular IBM AT computer. It combines a hard disk's drive electronics with the drive assembly itself. It is designed to plug almost directly into the expansion bus of a PC. It is currently the most popular type of interface.

Small Computer System Interface (SCSI). A general-purpose interface designed to accommodate a variety of computer designs and system peripherals (tape drives and scanners as well as hard disks). Unlike the IDE interface it requires a separate adapter.

MODEMS

A device that connects your computer to other computers through a phone line.

Acoustic Coupler. A device that allows your home computer to be connected to a remote computer by placing a telephone handset into it.

Baud. A measure of the rate at which computer information is transferred. Standard baud rates for PC modems are 300, 1200, 9600, and 14,400—with 14,400 being the fastest.

BPS. Bits per second. The number of bits of information sent in one second. Roughly the same as baud.

External. A modem that attaches to but is separate from the computer.

Hayes Compatible. The Hayes Corporation was one of the first companies to capture a large market share for modems for PCs. By doing so, they were able to establish their technology for interfacing the modem to the computer as a defacto standard that other modem manufacturers emulate. Accordingly, many non-Hayes modems were marketed as Hayes Compatible.

Internal. A modem that installs into a slot on the computer motherboard.

MONITORS

A monitor or cathode ray tube (CRT) is a TV-like computer display with better resolution than a TV set. The quality of the image on a computer monitor screen depends both on the monitor itself and the video board installed in the computer. The video board processes the information the computer sends to the monitor to be displayed. A high quality video board (one that supports graphics, color, and high resolutions) will require a high quality monitor for maximum performance.

Dot Pitch. A measure of the space between phosphor dots on the screen. In general, the smaller the dot pitch, the sharper the image. A 17-inch monitor should have a dot pitch of .31mm or less; a 14- or 15-inch screen, .28mm or less.

Graphics. The ability to display graphical images, such as pictures and line drawings, as opposed to being limited to displaying only text and numbers.

LCD. Liquid crystal display (like the display used in most calculators).

Monochrome. Single color, usually used to indicate black and white.

Multisync. Multisync displays can work, or synchronize, with video adapters that run at multiple resolutions: 640 by 480, 800 by 600, 1024 by 768, or higher.

Non-Interlaced. Monitors work by firing beams of electrons against the inside of the screen; the beams "paint" horizontal lines across the screen, one at a time, from top to bottom. When a monitor is interlacing, the electron gun first paints the even-numbered lines and then goes back and paints the odd-numbered lines. As a result, screen flicker is more noticeable than when a monitor is not interlacing or painting each line in succession.

Pixel. The smallest picture element (dot) on a computer screen. A measure of resolution.

Refresh Rate. The vertical refresh rate is the frequency with which each line on the screen is repainted. A slow refresh rate, like interlacing, will make screen flicker more noticeable. Most people can detect a refresh rate of 60 Hz or slower by looking at the screen from the corner of their eye. Refresh rates of 70 Hz or greater are considered very good.

Resolution. Resolution refers to the number of pixels drawn on the screen—the higher the resolution, the sharper the image. High resolution monitors are capable of displaying up to 1280 by 1024 pixels. Often, monitors are "graded" by their resolution and over the years a number of PC standards have evolved which include the following:

Color Graphics Adapter (CGA). Introduced in 1981, it provides 320 by 200 pixel resolution.

Enhanced Graphics Adapter (EGA). Introduced in 1984, it provides 640 by 350 pixel resolution.

MDA. Introduced in 1981, it is a text-only technology that provides resolutions of 720 by 480 pixels.

Super Video Graphics Array (SVGA). An enhanced VGA technology that is capable of displaying 640 by 480, 800 by 600, or 1,024 by 768 pixels.

Video Graphics Array (VGA). Dating to 1987, it provides a basic graphics resolution of 640 pixels (picture elements, or dots) across by 480 pixels down, with 16 colors or gray shades. In text mode, VGA resolution is 720 by 400. It and SVGA are currently the standard video cards for most PCs.

XGA. Introduced in 1990 by IBM, it is a new standard for 1,024 by 768 resolutions. It has been met with mixed success in the marketplace.

SWEDAC. The Swedish national testing board (SWEDAC) has established guidelines that set maximum levels of allowable electromagnetic radiation for computer monitors. There are two sets of guidelines, *MPRI* and the stricter *MPRII*.

TERMINOLOGY

Chip. An integrated circuit (IC). Computers are made up of chips and other components.

CPU. Central Processing Unit. One of the main chips in a computer. Also called the *Microprocessor*.

Baud. A measure of the rate at which computer information is transferred.

Bit. A binary digit (1 or 0), the information handled by chips.

Bit Rate. The digital equivalent of bandwidth.

Board. See *Module*.

BPS. Bits per second. The number of bits of information sent in one second. Roughly the same as baud.

Byte. A single character or numeral.

Card. See "module"

CD-I. CD "interactive" is an enhanced CD-ROM. Although CD-I cannot accommodate full-motion, real-time video, it can present a series of stills for animation-like effects, along with sound effects. Since it is interactive, users will be able to respond to prompts from the software, commending CD-I's use for education or games. Not perceived as a computer peripheral, but rather as a stand-alone, add-on component to a home entertainment system.

Character. A single letter, numeral, or punctuation symbol.

Clock/Calendar. A circuit or accessory that keeps track of the time and day.

Command. An instruction that one uses to get a computer to do something.

Computer Network. Two or more computers connected to exchange information.

Control Characters. A character obtained by holding down the key marked "CTRL" while pressing another key on the keyboard.

Cursor. A position indicator on a display. Usually a square or rectangle.

Data. Information fed into or out of a computer.

Data Bank. See *Information Bank.*

Data Base. A set of data that can be retrieved by a computer, such as a mailing list.

Data Format. How data is arranged in the computer (this differs between computers).

Desktop Computer. See *Personal Computer.*

Diagnostics. A program that checks the computer for problems.

Digital Recording. A system of recording in which musical information is converted into a series of pulses that are translated into a binary code intelligible to computer circuits and stored on magnetic tape or magnetic discs. Also called Pulse Code Modulation (PCM).

Digital Video Interface (DVI). Uses the 5-inch compact disc as an information carrier. Not a Philips/Sony format nor a home entertainment component. Developed by Sarnoff Labs in the GE/RCA days and now under development by chipmaker Intel. DVI does everything that CD-I does and also adds full-motion NTSC video—up to 72 minutes worth per disc—thanks to a proprietary data-compression system. Unlike the CD-V format, DVI's video is digital, not analog. Currently, DVI is perceived as a computer peripheral.

Digitizer. A device for drawing computer pictures.

Disk Drive. A device that can store and retrieve information on a disk.

Dual Drive. Two disk drives in one box.

Dumb Terminal. A computer terminal connected to a remote computer and without a microprocessor of its own.

Electronic Mail. Sending messages between computers.

Expansion Port. See *Expansion Slot.*

Expansion Module. An interface device that is connected to a computer to expand the computer's capabilities.

Expansion Slot. A computer socket to plug in more memory or other devices.

File. A set of data.

Firmware. Software that has been permanently placed in a ROM (read-only memory) chip. Firmware is located inside a computer and in all cartridges.

Game Controllers. Devices (like joysticks) that plug into a computer and make it easier to play games.

Game Paddle. A game controller that moves an object in one of two directions.

Hardware. The actual computer equipment, as opposed to "software."

Help Screen. "Help" explanations included in a software package.

Home Computer. Any computer you would buy to take home. Typically priced under $1,000.

Information Bank. A collection of information (stocks, airline schedules, etc.) accessible by modem.

Input. Data that goes into a computer device.

Input/Output (I/O). Information into or out of a computer.

Interface. Hardware or software used to connect two computer devices.

Joystick. A game controller that moves an object around on the screen.

Keyboard Lock. Locks scanner keyboard to prevent any accidental programming.

Key Matrix. Usually refers to the function switch circuits that accept scan pulses from the MPU. When pressed, the switch returns the pulses as data to the MPU input port.

K. Kilobyte, approximately 1,000 bytes, or characters, of data.

Light Pen. A pen-like device for communication with a computer by touching it to the screen. Used to draw pictures.

Mainframe. A large computer.

Megabytes. Approximately 1,000,000 bytes, or characters, of data.

Menu. A list of choices that you have in a program.

Microcomputer. See *Personal Computer.*

Module. A device that plugs into a computer and extends its capability.

Output. Data that comes out of a computer device.

Parallel. A form of interface mainly for printers.

PCB or PBA. Abbreviation for Printed Circuit Board or Plated Board Assembly.

Personal Computer. Any computer designed for one person to use.

Peripheral. A piece of equipment that is external (peripheral) to the computer itself (disk drives, printers, etc.).

Plotter. A device that draws a picture.

Port. A computer connector that allows printers, game controllers, etc., to be added on.

Read-Only Memory (ROM). Permanently stores programs, data or languages in the computer or in cartridges.

Real-Time Clock. See *Clock/Calendar.*

Reset. A key that interrupts or restarts a computer.

RF Modulator. A device that connects a computer to a television set.

RS-232C. A type of connection (used with serial interfaces).

Save. To store a program on a disk or cassette.

Serial. A type of interface for printers, modems, and other peripherals.

Speech Synthesizer. A device added on to a computer to produce "spoken" words.

System. A set of hardware and software that works together.

Terminal. A device with a keyboard and either a display or a printer. A terminal is used to communicate with a computer or other terminals.

Trackball. A game controller using a ball to control the movement of an object on the screen.

User-Friendly. Easy to use.

User's Group. A group of computer users who exchange information.

Vertical Oscillator. The electronic circuit that creates sawtooth scanning signals synchronizing with the vertical sync signal for the vertical deflection of the CRT or the pickup tube.

Voice Recognition. A device that connects to a computer, allowing for recognition of certain words.

Voice Synthesizer. See *Speech Synthesizer.*

Sources:

Bers, Jesse, and Scott Dunn, "Super-VGA Monitors," *PC World,* March 1992: 178-185.

Consumer Electronics Group, *Consumer Electronics Product Terminology Dictionary,* Washington: Electronic Industries Association, 1991.

Computer Printers

A computer printer is a single component of a computer system. Data generated by a computer can be directed to several devices: a monitor for electronic display; a disk or cassette for storage; or a printer to produce a printed or *hard copy* of the data. There are several different types of computer printers to choose from. Which printer to pick is often determined by the consumer's needs: speed, letter quality print, image quality, price, how quiet the printer is, etc. Because of the high quality output and low noise level, the laser printer is a popular choice for office computer systems. Personal laser printers (smaller, more compact, and less expensive) are currently being marketed for the home computer system.

TERMINOLOGY

Bidirectional. Printing in both directions for increased speed.

Continuous Form. Computer paper (not single sheets).

Dots per Inch (DPI). Indicates the number of dots per inch that appear on the printed page. The more dots per inch the denser the type on the printed page. For example, typeset quality starts at about 1200 dpi. Laser printers typically provide 300 dpi. The greater the dpi the better the quality of the image.

Impact Printer. A printer that prints by impacting (hitting) a character against the paper.

Ink Jet. A printer that sprays fine droplets of ink onto the paper in order to produce text or graphics.

Laser Printer. A printer that simulates typesetting for high quality output.

Letter Quality Printer. See *Printer.*

Line Printer. See *Printer*.

Pages per Minute (PPM). Indicates the number of pages a printer can print in one minute. Standard laser printers print between 4 and 12 ppm. Dot matrix printers print considerably fewer.

Postscript. A computer language develoed by the Adobe Corporation that defines the way information will look on a printed page.

Printer. A device that produces a printed or *hard* copy of data generated by the computer.

Source:

Consumer Electronics Group, *Consumer Electronics Product Terminology Dictionary,* Washington: Electronic Industries Association, 1991.

Mobile Autosound

Amplitude Modulation (AM). The type of transmission used in the standard radio broadcast band, 550 to 1600 kHz. A process which modulates the amplitude of a carrier wave according to a variation of the input voltage (signal).

Antenna. Used in sending and receiving electromagnetic waves.

Automatic Noise Limiter (ANL). Acts as a filter, chopping holes in the received signal and substituting periods of silence, thereby reducing the static that the CB radio receiver picks up from man-made sources such as car ignition, machinery, etc.

Automatic Volume Control (AVC). In radio, maintains constant sound level despite undesired differences in strength of incoming signal.

Band. A range of frequencies between two definite limits.

Band Pass Filter (BPF). A circuit, commonly having inductance and capacitance, that effectively passes a given range of frequencies whereas frequencies above and below this range are attenuated. Active filters for relatively low frequencies are often designed with op-amps which require only resistance and capacitance.

Bandwidth. The frequency difference between the highest and lowest frequencies involved. The greater the bandwidth of a transmission channel, the more information it can carry. Also, the spread of frequencies a radar detector is sensitive to above or below the operating frequencies. For example, if the operating frequency is 10.525 GHz, a detector with a bandwidth of 10 MHz would pick up signals from 10.520 to 10.530.

Bank Scanning. Selectively scans programmed frequencies in desired banks.

Base (for CB radio). Intended for use in one place, generally a desk or table-top transceiver.

Baseband. Not modulated.

Bass Reflex. Type of loudspeaker system that uses a ported enclosure.

Beam. The electron stream in the pickup tube or TV tube. Also, a type of highly directional CB radio antenna (radiating in one general direction, but capable of providing high power gains).

Channel. Common name for a transmission frequency.

Citizens' Band (CB) Radio. Radio that operates on the 27 MHz band and is used for consumer two-way communications.

Coaxial Cable. The standard cable consisting of a central inner conductor and a cylindrical outer conductor. Used for most video connections. Also used to connect the CB radio antenna with the transceiver.

Compact Disc Player. A turntable designed to play compact disc (CD) recordings using a laser optical pickup. Usually requires a tuner/amplifier equipped with Tape In or AUX jacks.

Delay. Adds a delay to any scanner channel so that call replies will be heard before scanning is resumed.

Delta Tune. Compensates for a CB radio signal that may be slightly off frequency. Operates just like the fine tuning control on a TV set.

Demagnetizer. A device that removes magnetism generated in tape heads as a consequence of playback and recording activities.

Dolby. A system of noise/hiss reduction invented by Ray Dolby and widely used in consumer, professional, and broadcast audio applications.

Duplex System. Uses two frequencies, one for the scanner base station and one for the mobile.

Dynamike. Adjusts the CB radio microphone output to the user's voice level to achieve 100 percent modulation without distortion. Allows the user to speak at a normal level without having to shout to be heard.

Equalizer. Any device that alters the frequency settings of an audio signal primarily to tailor the sound to the listener's satisfaction.

Frequency Modulation (FM). One of the methods of signal modulation, which modulates the frequency of a carrier wave according to the amplitude of input signal. Less susceptible to interference than AM.

Frequency Range. Measured in Hertz (Hz), the frequency response of a radio or tape deck tells how much of the range of human hearing it can reproduce. The higher the Hertz number, the better. The generally accepted hi-fidelity range for frequency response is 20-20,000 Hz.

Frequency. The number of complete oscillations per second of an electromagnetic wave. The pitch of radio signal that distinguishes it from another.

Function Indicator Panel (FIP). Front display device. Also called FDP (Fluorescent Display Panel).

Graphic Equalizer. A device that permits altering the tonal balance of an audio component/system at several frequency levels, usually from 5 to 12.

Hertz (Hz). The unit of frequency equal to one cycle per second (cps): one kilohertz (kHz) equals 1,000 cps; one megahertz (mHz) equal 1,000,000 cps.

KHz. Kilohertz (kilocycles) or thousands of cycles per second.

Light-Emitting Diode (LED). A semiconductor that lights up when activated by a voltage. Used in readout displays for digital watches and calculators. Also used as indicators for radar detector functions.

Limit. Set scanner's lower and upper frequencies' limits for automatic search.

Limiter. An electronic circuit which limits the level of the output signal. Before FM demodulation, the signal passes through the limiter to remove amplitude modulation (level variation).

Lockout. Skips scanner's channels or banks not of current interest, for faster scanning cycle.

Memory. Device or circuit to hold machine-language information in electrical or magnetic form, such as a pre-set radio station frequency in a frequency-synthesized tuner or receiver.

Midrange. Speakers designed to reproduce notes between treble and bass.

Multichannel System. Various classes of units in a scanner system are given different frequencies.

Noise Reduction System. A system that reduces background noise and tape hiss from cassette players and radios.

Polyamide, Polymer, Polypropylene. Synthetic materials used for speaker cones. Noted for light weight, minimum resonance, and the proper elasticity/rigidity for fast transient response.

Preset. The "programming" of radio station frequencies in a tuner or receiver, or musical selections on a tape, for instant recall at the push of a button.

Priority. Automatically switches to the user's favorite programmed scanner frequency on channel 1 when it becomes active.

RF Gain. Adjusts the CB radio's receiver sensitivity to match the incoming signal above.

Root Mean Square (RMS). Method of measuring amplifier power.

Scan. Scans the frequencies that have been programmed on all the scanner's channels.

Single Side Band (SSB). Involves dividing each CB radio channel into a carrier and two side bands, upper and lower. Single side band offers the advantage of greater range, less interference and generally better performance.

Squelch. Circuiting that quiets the CB radio speaker until a signal is received.

Superhet. Superheterodyne CB radio circuit commonly used because of its higher sensitivity and selectivity.

SWR. Standing wave ratio. See *VSWR*.

Tweeter. High-frequency (treble) loudspeaker.

Varactor. Variable-capacitance diode used in electronic tuning systems for TV and radio; hence the name "varactor tuning."

Vernier Tuning. Continuous type fine tuning.

Voltage Standing Wave Ratio (VSWR). A rating of the efficiency of a CB radio antenna. A VSWR of 1:1 is ideal but rarely achieved. The lower the VSWR, the better.

Source:
Consumer Electronics Group, *Consumer Electronics Product Terminology Dictionary,* Washington: Electronic Industries Association, 1991.

Movie Ratings

The Motion Picture Association of America (MPAA) has established a voluntary system for rating motion pictures for content (e.g., violence, nudity, sex, drugs, etc.) The purpose of the system is to provide parents with some advance information about movies so they can decide what movies they want their children to see or not to see.

The ratings are decided by a ratings board located in Los Angeles. The board's funding comes from fees charged to producers/distributors for the rating of their films. The MPPA president chooses the chairman of the rating board. The only qualification for membership on the board is that members must have a shared parenthood experience, must be possessed of an intelligent maturity, and must have the capacity to put themselves in the role of most American parents.

Any producer/distributor who does not wish to be a part of the rating system is free to go to the market without any rating at all, or they may choose a description or symbol that is not confusingly similar to the G, PG, PG-13, R, and NC-17 rating symbols which are federally registered certification marks of the MPAA. The rating symbols (G, PG, PG-13, R, and NC-17) may only be applied by the ratings board.

RATINGS

G. General Audiences—All ages admitted. This is a film which contains nothing in theme, language, nudity and sex, violence, etc., which would, in the view of the rating board, be offensive to parents whose younger children view the film. The G rating is not a "certificate of approval," nor does it signify a children's film. Some snippets of language may go beyond polite conversation, but they are common, everyday expressions. No strong words are present in G-rated films. The violence is at a minimum. Nudity and sex scenes are not present, nor is there any drug use content.

PG. Parental Guidance suggested; some material may not be suitable for children. This is a film which clearly needs to be examined or inquired about by parents before they let their children attend. The label PG plainly states that parents may consider some material unsuitable for their children, but the parent must make the decision. Parents are warned against sending their children to PG-rated movies without parental inquiry. There may be some profanity in these films. There may be violence, but it is not deemed so strong that everyone under 17 need be restricted unless accompanied by a parent. Nor is there cumulative horror or violence that may place the film into the R category. There is no drug use content. There is no explicit sex in a PG-rated film, although there may be some indication of sensuality. Brief nudity may appear in an unrestricted film, but anything beyond that puts the film into a R rating.

PG-13. Parents are strongly cautioned. Some material may be inappropriate for children under 13. PG-13 is thus a sterner warning to parents to determine for themselves the attendance in particular of their younger children, as they might consider some material not suited for them. By the rating, parents are alerted to be very careful about the attendance of their under-teenage children. A PG-13 film is one which, in the view of the rating board, leaps beyond the boundaries of the PG rating, but does not quite fit within the restricted R category. Any drug use content will initially require at least a PG-13 rating. If nudity is sexually oriented, the film will generally not be found in the PG-13 category. If violence is rough or persistent, the film goes into the R (restricted) rating. A film's single use of one of the harsher sexually derived words, though only as an expletive, shall require the rating board to issue that film at least a PG-13 rating. A film will receive an R rating by the rating board if one such expletive is used in the film or if one of these words is used in a sexual context. However, these films can be rated less severely if, by a special vote, the rating board feels that a lesser rating would more responsibly reflect the opinion of American parents. PG-13 places larger responsibilities on parents for their children's moviegoing.

R. Restricted, under 17 requires accompanying parent or adult guardian. In the opinion of the rating board, this film definitely contains adult material. Parents are strongly urged to find out more about this film before they allow their children to accompany them. An R-rated film has adult content that may include hard language, tough violence, nudity within sensual scenes, abuse of drug or other elements, or a combination of some of the above.

NC-17. No children under 17 admitted. This rating declares that the ratings board believes that this is patently an adult film. No children will be admitted. NC-17 does not necessarily mean "obscene or pornographic" in the often accepted meaning of those words. The board does not and cannot mark films with those words. These are legal terms for the court to decide. The reasons for the application of an NC-17 rating can mean strong violence, sex, aberrational behavior, drug abuse, or any other element which, when present, most parents would want to be off-limits for viewing by their children.

Source:
Valenti, Jack, "The Voluntary Movie Rating System," New York: Motion Picture Association of America, Inc., 1991.

Multimedia

Generally speaking, multimedia refers to the integration and display of text, video, graphics, and audio. Multimedia systems are also interactive, encouraging the user to be actively involved. However, the ultimate setup and application of multimedia remains up for debate. Most computer manufacturers see multimedia as an enhanced capability for the PC, thus making the computer monitor the center of attention. The consumer electronics world tends to view multimedia as a new home entertainment box that's connected to the TV set. CD-I and CDTV are examples of this approach. The first so-called multimedia computers were introduced during 1991. Based upon 386 technology, these fully-featured models supplement hard-disk drives with the expanded capacity of internal CD-ROM (compact disc read-only memory) drives. Computer owners with 286 or faster processors can also upgrade to multimedia by adding a CD-ROM drive, as well as extra memory and storage. CD-ROM discs, while resembling CD audio discs, store large amounts of audio, text, and graphics; a disc can hold as much as 300,000 pages of information.

MULTIMEDIA PERSONAL COMPUTER (MPC)

The Multimedia Computing Marketing Council, a group of computer hardware and software companies, have issued minimum standards for MPC computers. Any computer labeled with their MPC label will be able to play MPC-labeled CD-ROM disks—including titles that use stereo sound mixed with full-motion video. To qualify for the MPC label a computer must run Microsoft Windows 3.0 with the Microsoft Multimedia Extensions

1.0 and have the following minimum hardware configuration:
386SX processor
2 megabytes of RAM
80 megabyte hard disk
VGA (Video Graphic Array) monitor
Digital sound adapter
CD-ROM drive
Musical Instrument Digital Interface (MIDI) connector

Sources:
Consumer Electronics Group, *Consumer Electronics Product Terminology Dictionary,* Washington: Electronic Industries Association, 1991.
Consumer Electronics Group, *The U.S. Consumer Electronics Industry in Review,* Washington: Electronic Industries Association, 1992.
Lewis, Peter H., "I've Got the World on a Disk," *New York Times,* March 10, 1992.

Radar

A radar detector will pick up traffic signals, serving as a reminder to keep within speed limits. Some areas have laws regulating the use of radar detectors.

TERMINOLOGY

Alarm Lamp. Amber incandescent lamp on a radar detector that illuminates when radar signals are received and blinks at an increasingly faster rate as the radar source gets closer.

Alarm Test Switch. Allows for volume adjustment on the radar detector for the audible alert and permits manual test of alarm to ensure operation readiness.

Audible Alarm. Electronic tone on radar detector that sounds when radar signals are received; and, in combination with the alarm lamp, sounds at a faster rate closer to the radar source.

Constant Radar Broadcasting. A radar gun that is on all the time and does not need to be triggered on and off as does "instant-on."

Cosine Error. The phenomenon that causes radar guns to give a lower reading than actual speed. Radar can only measure accurately the speed of an object moving directly towards or away from the antenna. If an object moves at an angle to the antenna, it will read only a portion of the speed.

Distinguishing. Radar detector gives different sounds or separate lights for the X and K bands.

Falsing. Triggering of a radar detector from something other than radar.

Highway/City Switch. *Highway* position on a radar detector ensures maximum range and sensitivity. *City* position reduces interference from non-radar signals in urban areas with minimal reduction in sensitivity.

Instant On. When a radar gun is quickly turned on.

Interference (on radar detectors). Since superheterodyne radar detectors generate a radar signal internally, this signal can sometimes be detected by other radar detectors—often called radio frequency interference.

K Band. A frequency certified by the FCC for police radar and other types of field disturbance sensors, specifically 24.15 GHz.

Leakage. The RF interference transmitted by superheterodyne radar detectors.

Line of Sight. In order for any radar gun to get a speed reading, it must have a straight view of the target car.

Mini. A small radar detector not much larger than a pack of cigarettes.

Motion Sensor. A small radar transmitter designed to detect any movement nearby. Many motion sensors operate on the same frequencies that police radar use.

Moving Radar. A type of radar gun that can clock oncoming cars while the patrol car is moving.

Mute Switch. Momentarily silences the audible alarm caused by reception of a radar signal and automatically resets the radar detector for the next radar signal after the current signal is no longer being received.

Passive. The technology most radar detectors used before superheterodyne circuitry became popular.

Photo Electric Sensor. An electronic eye on a radar detector that automatically adjusts the brightness of all indictor lights for day or night driving.

Polluting Detector. A radar detector that does not contain its internally generated signal and transmits RF interference.

Radar. Radio detecting and ranging based on the Doppler Theory. Radar limits a beam at a set frequency. When the beam is reflected off a moving object, the frequency changes. This shift is then translated into a speed reading.

Radar Sampling. A police officer using an instant-on radar gun will periodically check the speed of traffic. These "samplings" can easily be picked up by a radar detector and give prior warning to a motorist approaching a bigger activated radar gun.

Remote Detector. Also called *two-piece* detectors, remote radar detectors are designed to be permanently installed in a car with the antenna (receiver) in the grille and the control panel anywhere inside the car.

Selectivity (on radar detectors). The amount of resistance to false alerts. A radar detector has very few false alerts. This means very good selectivity.

Sensitivity (of radar detector). A detectors sensitivity is usually measured in terms of -dBm/cm². A radar detector that is rated -112 dBm/cm² is more sensitive than a detector that is rated at -108 dBm/cm².

Signal Strength. Relative proximity to the radar source; the closer the radar detector to the source, the stronger the signal strength.

Superheterodyne. Also called *active* technology. A type of radar detector technology that amplifies incoming signals several hundred times in order to make it much more sensitive and also more selective about which incoming signals are to trigger an alert.

X Band. A frequency certified by the FCC for police radar, specifically 10.525 GHz. X Band is the band most commonly used by the police.

Source:
Consumer Electronics Group, *Consumer Electronics Product Terminology Dictionary,* Washington: Electronic Industries Association, 1991.

Software

The word *software* is typically used to describe programs that tell computers what to do. Increasingly, however, it is also being applied to video and sound recordings. Computer software programs are often labeled with a numbering system that indicates the version of the program. Software companies periodically *release* new versions of their programs subsequent to the initial release. These new versions are called *upgrades*. The different versions of a program are often distinguished by an informal numbering system used by the computer software industry. The first release of a program is numbered 1.0. When minor changes are made to the program to fix mistakes (bugs) that affect the normal operation of advertised features, the subsequent release may be numbered 1.0a. When a subsequent release consists of minor enhancements, it may be numbered 1.1. Subsequent minor enhancements are numbered 1.2, 1.3, etc. When major enhancements are made to the program, the new version may be numbered 2.0. Some companies, however, have numbered the first release of their program 2.0, so this system cannot be relied upon in all cases.

GRAPHICS FILE FORMATS

Computer programs that are designed to allow the user to draw pictures rely on a number of standardized file formats for storing the electronic version of the picture. These file formats are distinguished by a three letter filename extension. Some of the most popular graphics formats include:

CGM (Computer Graphics Metafile). It is a widely supported device independent file format created by several standards organizations.

DRW (Micrografx DRAW). A file format created for Micrografx's Windows programs.

DXF (Data Exchange File). Created by Autodesk for its CADD images. Widely supported among CADD programs.

EPS (Encapsulated PostScript). A popular format designed for desktop publishing programs.

GEM (Graphics Environment Manager). Created by Digital Research for its own GEM Desktop environment.

HPGL (Hewlett-Packard Graphics Language). Created by the Hewlett-Packard Company for two-dimensional pen plotting. Supported by almost all graphics programs on the market.

IGES (Initial Graphics Exchange Specification). A nonproprietary file format created by the CADD industry.

PIC (Lotus Picture File). Created by Lotus Development Corporation for its popular spreadsheet program Lotus 1-2-3.

WMF (Windows Metafile Format). Developed the Microsoft Corporation to exchange graphics information between Microsoft Windows applications.

TERMINOLOGY

Applications Software. Software (program) designed for a specific use (such as word processing or playing games).

ASCII. American Standard Code for Information Interchange. Specifies which computer code will stand for each character, providing a standard that allows computers from different manufacturers to "talk" to each other.

Backup. An extra copy of information stored on a disk or cassette. If the program or other data stored on the first disk or cassette becomes damaged, it is still available on the backup copy.

BASIC. Beginners All Purpose Symbolic Instructional Code, the most commonly used computer language. Other popular languages include Assembler, Fortran, Logo, Pascal, and Pilot.

Boot. To start up a program.

Bug. An error. A hardware bug is an error in a computer or peripheral. A software bug is a programming error.

Bulletin Board. A free dial-up computer used to exchange messages.

Character Based. A computer software program that relies on common keyboard characters for its screen display as opposed to graphic images. See *Graphic User Interface.*

Communications Software. Allows computers to "talk" to each other.

Computer Program. A series of instructions that tell a computer to do a specific thing or series of things.

Debug. To go through a program to remove bugs (errors).

Desktop Publishing. Using a computer to lay out and typeset a newsletter, brochure, ad, or other printed materials.

Documentation. The instruction manual for a piece of hardware or software.

Graphical User Interface (GUI). Refers to the way a person instructs a computer program to execute commands. When a program uses a GUI, the user has the option to move visual symbols, called *icons* with a pointing device called a *mouse.* For example, in some programs the user deletes (erases) a file by moving the mouse cursor to a symbol that looks like a garbage can.

Load. To put data and/or programs into a computer.

Operating System. Software that oversees the operation of a computer system. All programs must be written for a specific operating system. *DOS (Disk Operating System)* is a popular operating system for IBM PCs. *CP/M (Control Program for Microcomputers)* is an operating system used on some business computers.

Program. A set of instructions that tells the computer what to do.

Programmer. A person who writes (creates) programs.

Software (Programs). Instructions that tell the computer what to do.

What You See Is What You Get (WYSIWYG). Refers to the ability of a software program to display information on the computer screen in exactly the way it will appear when printed on a printer.

Windows Compatible. The MicroSoft Corporation has developed a software program for IBM and compatible computers called *Windows.* Windows uses a graphical user interface (GUI) to buffer the user from the computer's operating system—thereby making the computer easier to use. Mirosoft allows other computer software companies to use its Windows program to develop their own applications programs like word processors and spreadsheets. When this is the case, the application program requires the Windows program before it will work on the computer. These application programs are typically labeled with a phrase like "requires Microsoft Windows." In some cases, the program may require the latest version of Windows as in the phrase "requires Windows 3.1 or higher."

Sources:

Consumer Electronics Group, *Consumer Electronics Product Terminology Dictionary,* Washington: Electronic Industries Association, 1991.

Miller, Catherine D., "Graphics File Formats," *PC Magazine,* Vol. 8, Issue 12 (June 27, 1989): 154-155.

Spars Code

The SPARS code was introduced in the mid-1980s to help identify which portions of the recording process were digital and which were analog.

Analog. Analog recording is a system of recording in which music is converted into electrical impulses which form "patterns" in the grooves of phonograph record masters or in the oxide particles of master tapes representing (or analogous to) musical waveforms.

Digital. Digital recording is a system of recording in which musical information is converted into a series of pulses that are translated into a binary code intelligible to computer *circuits* and stored on magnetic tape or magnetic discs. It is also called *Pulse Code Modulation (PCM).*

However, the Society of Professional Audio Recording Services, the code's creator, has recommended that the SPARS Code be discontinued. Advanced recording technology has led to a labyrinth of interfaces, conversions, transfers, etc. The SPARS code as presently implemented is unable to reflect the complexity of the technology, and the society believes that any attempt to revise the code would become so complex as to be meaningless. The discontinuation of the SPARS code is expected to be a slow transition. The code as it exists today has the following meanings:

DM. The release bearing this symbol was mastered digitally.

ADA. The release bearing this symbol was recorded in analog, mixed digitally, and mastered in analog.

ADD. The release bearing this symbol was recorded in analog, mixed, and mastered digitally.

DDA. The release bearing this symbol was recorded and mixed digitally and mastered in analog.

DDD. The release bearing this symbol was recorded, mixed, and mastered digitally.

These letters are found at the bottom of the SPARS symbol. The symbol for a release that was mastered digitally is provided below as an example.

An example of the symbol for a release that was recorded in analog, mixed digitally and mastered in analog follows. Notice that only the initials at the bottom of the symbol distinguishes this symbol form the previous one.

Source:
Press Release, Hollywood, CA: Society of Professional Audio Recording Services, 1992.

Speakers

Acoustic (or Air) Suspension. Type of loudspeaker system that utilizes an air-tight sealed enclosure.

Freedom from Coloration. Free from component-induced distortion often heard in the midrange voice frequencies.

Hertz (Hz). The unit of frequency equal to one cycle per second (cps): one kilohertz (kHz) equals 1,000 cps; one megahertz (MHz) equal 1,000,000 cps. The range over which most instruments emit their fundamental tones is 30 to 16,000 Herts.

Impedance. A speaker's resistance to electric current from an amplifier or receiver. It is measured in ohms. Impedance is unrelated to sound quality. A low impedance speaker (6 ohms or less) draws more current than a high impedance speaker (8 to 16 ohms). Impedance is important in matching speaker and receiver. If the speaker's impedance is too low for the receiver's circuitry, the circuitry can heat up more than it should.

Loudness. The ability to play at loud levels without breaking up or distorting.

Low-End Response. The ability of a speaker to reproduce sound at the low end of the spectrum from about 20 to 200 Hz.

Midrange. Speakers designed to reproduce notes between treble and bass.

One Way. Indicates the number of speakers in the speaker cabinet. A one way speaker system will have one speaker which may lack the ability to reproduce sound at the extreme high and low ends of the sound spectrum.

Three Way. This type of speaker system uses separate components for delivering bass, midrange (voice and most acoustic instruments), and treble (cymbals and percussion).

Tweeter. High frequency (treble) loudspeaker.

Two Way. Contains two speakers, typically a woofer and a tweeter.

Watts per Channel. Watts per channel, or watts per speaker, is a measure of the power requirements of the speaker system. The louder the speaker, the more watts required. Speaker power requirements can range from 5 to over 50 watts.

Woofer. Low frequency (bass) loudspeaker.

FTC REGULATIONS

Whenever any direct or indirect representation is made of the power output, power band or power frequency response, or distortion characteristics of sound power amplification equipment, the FTC requires that the information provided meet certain standards set by the FTC.

Sources:
Consumer Electronics Group, *Consumer Electronics Product Terminology Dictionary,* Washington: Electronic Industries Association, 1991.
Federal Trade Commission, "Power Output Claims for Amplifiers Utilized in Home Entertainment Products," 16 CFR Part 432 (1992), Washington: Government Printing Office.
"Stereo Components," Consumer Digest, Vol.28, no. 6 (November/December 1989):70.
"Mid-Priced Loudspeakers," *Consumer Reports,* Vol. 55, no. 10 (October 1990):655.

Telecommunications

Telecommunications is short for telephone communications. This field includes those devices that are connected to and use the telephone communication system to transfer information to other devices. Telephones, cellular phones, answering machines, fax machines, and computer modems are some of the devices that utilize telecommunications.

TERMINOLOGY

AC. Alternating current.

Announce Only. Telephone answering devices (TADs) with this option have the ability to play a greeting but cannot record any messages.

Audible Message Indicator. A voice or tone alerts the user that new messages have been received by the TAD.

Autodial. Frequently called numbers can be stored for instant dialing.

Auto-Disconnect. The TAD automatically stops recording whenever an extension telephone is picked up.

Automatic Greeting. A pre-recorded digital greeting that plays on the TAD if the user forgets to record a greeting or prefers not to record a greeting.

Automatic Standby. When the cordless handset on/off switch is set to "on" and the standby/talk switch is set to "talk," the cordless handset automatically resets to a "standby" mode whenever the handset is placed in the base unit.

Baby Bell. A term commonly used for one of the seven regional holding companies established when AT&T divested itself of its local telephone companies. The Baby Bells are Americom, Ameritech, Bell Atlantic, Bell South, Nynex, Pacific Telesis, Southwestern Bell, and US West.

Battery Backup. Batteries which protect or save information during a power failure.

Beeperless Remote. The ability to call from a TouchTone phone to retrieve your messages without using a beeper.

Bell Labs. Originally called Bell Telephone Laboratories; it is the research division of the Bell System.

Calling Party Control (CPC). Some phone companies send a CPC signal down the phone line when a caller hangs up. TADs with a CPC feature can hang up faster, and more reliably, than units that rely solely on voice activation (VOX).

Call Screening. The ability to listen to callers leaving a message. The user can then decide whether to answer the call personally or allow the machine to take it. All TADS have this function.

Continuous Loop. Type of tape system in which a single reel is used within an endless loop of tape.

DC. Direct current.

Digital. A recording or computer system that uses numbers to record sound or store information and will decode the numbers to produce sound or information.

Digital Chip Recording. Many TADs now use a microchip, instead of a cassette tape, to digitally record a greeting. A few models are completely tapeless, recording both greeting and incoming messages on a digital chip.

Digital Display. A display panel on the TAD shows the exact number of messages received.

Digital Personalized Greeting. The TAD outgoing greeting is recorded digitally on a RAM chip instead of on a tape.

Digital Security Code. The digital security coding system for cordless phones prevents unauthorized use of the user's telephone line and eliminates false ringing and false dialing.

Digital Signal Processing (DSP). Converts the TAD's incoming and outgoing messages to a series of electronic signals, compresses the signals, then stores the information on a memory (RAM) chip.

Display. A visual representation of electrical/mechanical functions via LED, liquid crystal, or fluorescent devices. Also called readout.

Dual Tape Answering Machine. The answering machine has two cassette tapes. One is for the outgoing greeting, and one is for incoming messages.

DX. Long distance.

FCC. Federal Communications Commission.

Feature-Phone. A telephone that has additional features.

Flashing Message Counter. An LED flashes to indicate the number of new messages received on the TAD.

Greeting Bypass. Frequent callers can bypass the user's TAD greeting to leave a message on the unit.

Handset Message Retrieval. This feature gives consumers the option of listening to TAD messages privately through the handset.

Helical Antenna. A flexible rubber antenna.

Hold/Mute. Ensures privacy when conducting off-line conversations.

Home Automation. Unified hand control system whereby electronic products from different manufacturers can communicate with one another via existing power lines, twisted (telephone) pairs, coaxial cable, and infrared means.

IC Chip/Tape Answering Machine. These answering machines provide a memory (RAM) chip for the outgoing greeting and a cassette tape to record incoming messages.

Incoming Message (ICM). A message left by a caller on a telephone answering device.

Integrated TAD. A telephone answering device and feature phone combination.

Interference. Electrical signals that have an undesirable effect on radio and TV reception and cordless phones.

Integrated Services Digital Network (ISDN). A telecommunications concept and series of standards whereby one universal digital transmission network can carry computer data, voice, and still and moving pictures (at any quality level and high fidelity sound).

K-Handset. The standard "Ma Bell" shaped telephone handset.

Light-Emitting Diode (LED). A semiconductor that lights up when activated by a voltage. Used in readout displays for telephones and TADs.

Line Selector. Choose whether the TAD answers line 1, line 2, or both.

Liquid Crystal Display (LCD). A system of readout, using nonilluminated reflective numerals, that is used on some TADs.

Magnetic Field. The area which surrounds a magnet and is affected by it. The field created by magnets in telephones, electric motors, TVs, and other consumer electronic products usually extends for a foot or two around them.

Memo/Conversation Record. User can dictate messages or record important telephone conversations on the TAD.

Memory. Device or circuit to hold machine-language information in electrical or magnetic form.

Message Transfer. TADs with this feature will call a preprogrammed number whenever a message is received. This can be used to alert the owner to new messages or to call a beeper or pager.

Micro-Cassette. Miniaturized version of the standard audio cassette.

Modem. A device used to connect a computer to a telephone line.

Multifunctional Digital Display. An easy-to-read TAD digital display shows the dialed number, time, message count, machine status, and a full operation menu.

On-Hook Dialing. A one-way speaker phone. The user can dial a number and listen to the phone line without lifting the handset.

One-Touch Operation. Features are activated by pressing one button.

Optimum Channel Memory (OCM). Provides fast cordless phone channel selection because a computerized scanning memory circuit selects and remembers the best available channels in the neighborhood.

Out-Going Message (OGM). The greeting that each telephone caller will hear when the answering device picks up the call.

Out-of-Range Alarm. An audible alarm signals the user when the cordless handset is out of normal operating range of the base unit.

Paging. The user can send a paging signal to the cordless handset from the base unit.

Pause. Users can program pause as part of an autodial number when access codes are required to dial a number.

Personal Memo. This feature allows the TAD owner to leave a message on the machine for other household members at the touch of a button.

Redial. Automatically redials the last number called by pressing a button.

Remote Access Number. A one-, two-, or three-digit number set by the manufacturer that allows the TAD user to access his answering machine when he is away from his home or office.

Remote Greeting Record. The ability to re-record your TAD's greeting remotely, from another telephone.

Remote Memo. TAD user can leave personal memos from a remote location.

Remote Room Monitoring. TAD users can call their answering machine and monitor the activity in their home or office.

Remote Security Code. Like remote access number, but this is a three-digit number and user programmable.

Remote Turn-On. A feature that allows the user to turn on the TAD from another telephone, by letting the telephone ring several times.

Ring Select. TAD users set the number of rings for the machine to answer calls.

RJ-11 Jack. The standard single-line telephone jack.

RJ-14 Jack. A two-line telephone jack.

Search. A feature that permits faster than normal tape speed while playing a tape, usually in either direction.

Short-Burst TouchTone. Some TouchTone telephones produce only a short burst of tone, no matter how long the button is pressed. Some pay phones, many cellular car phones, and office phone systems operate in this manner. Short-burst telephones may not remote many answering machines.

Single Tape Answering Machine. The answering machine has one tape which plays the outgoing greeting and records incoming messages. Sometimes referred to as the Shuttle System.

Speakerphone. A hands-free telephone.

TAD. Telephone answering device.

T-Adapter. This device plugs into a modular telephone jack, providing two outlets instead of one.

Talking Clock. Announces the time with the touch of a button.

Time and Day Stamp. A feature that records the time and day at the end of each message when it is received.

Tollsaver. When calling in to a remote TAD, Tollsaver allows the machine to answer quickly if there are new messages. If the phone rings more than three times, the user may hang up knowing that there are no new messages.

Tone/Pulse. The two methods telephones use to dial. TouchTone generates a unique tone for each button pressed. Pulse (or rotary) dialing makes clicking sounds when dialing.

Transmitter. A device that can change sound waves into electric waves or impulses to send to a receiver such as a telephone.

True Tone. A true TouchTone phone is one that emits a continuous tone as long as a button is pressed on the keypad.

Two-Line Capability. One TAD answers two separate telephone numbers.

Two-Line T-Adapter. This telephone adapter converts a two-line RJ-14 jack into two separate one-line outlets.

Voice Activation (VOX). A TAD with a VOX circuit listens to the phone line to determine when a caller is through leaving a message. After about five seconds of silence, the TAD hangs up.

Voice-Assisted Operation. A synthesized voice assists the TAD user through set up and machine operations.

Voice Line Indicator. A computer-generated voice on the TAD automatically marks after each message which line was answered.

Source:
Consumer Electronics Group, *Consumer Electronics Product Terminology Dictionary,* Washington: Electronic Industries Association, 1991.

Television

Color television represents more than 20 percent of the total factory volume of consumer electronics products. Nearly 100 percent of all U.S. households now own at least one color TV and more than 60 percent have two or more. There is also a sizable demand for black-and-white TVs (monochrome TVs). Pocketable sets with liquid crystal displays, table model sets (12-inch screen), and many sets designed for either AC or 12-volt operation (for use on boats, in trailers, and in recreational vehicles) still account for a large percentage of total TV sales.

TERMINOLOGY

A-B Test. Direct comparison of the sound/picture quality of two pieces of audio/TV equipment by playing one, then the other.

Absorption Trap. A parallel-tuned circuit made of either capacitors or coils used to absorb and reduce interfering signals.

AC. Alternating current.

AC/DC. A switch on the TV that lets one run the set on either AC line power or battery power.

Active Lines. Only those video or horizontal scanning lines that carry actual picture information, as opposed to the blanking lines and vertical sync lines.

ACTV. Advanced Compatible Television.

Adjacent Channel. A television transmission channel immediately adjacent to an existing channel.

Advanced Television (ATV). System currently being developed for the marketplace utilizing a higher horizontal resolution than the current 525 lines NTSC standard. It includes high definition television (HDTV), enhanced definition television (EDTV), improved definition television (IDTV), and artifact elimination schemes.

All-Channel Tuning. The ability of a television set to receive all assigned channels, VHF and UHF, channels 2 through 83.

Amplifier. Used to increase the voltage or power of any power signal that is fed to it, such as the multichannel television sound (MTS) broadcast signal. Most MTS stereo TVs have built-in amplifiers.

Amplitude Modulation (AM). A method of adding a signal to the carrier signal by varying the carrier's amplitude. Used in broadcasting the picture portion of television signals.

Antenna. Used in sending and receiving electromagnetic waves.

Artifacts. Visible (or audible) consequences of various television processes.

Aspect Ratio Accommodation. Techniques by means of which something shot in one aspect ratio can be presented in another.

Aspect Ratio. Ratio of the width of an image to its height, sometimes expressed as two numbers separated by a colon (e.g., 4:3) or sometimes as one number, with a colon and the number one implied (e.g., 1.85 is the same as 1.85:1). The television standard is 4:3.

ATSC. Advanced Television Systems Committee. A sort of National Television Standards Committee (NTSC) for advanced television (ATV).

ATTC. Advanced Television Test Center. Created to test different broadcast ATV systems.

Audio/Video System. Relatively expensive and large full-scale electronic component systems. Most are centered around stereo TVs, and many include electronics like CD players and stereo VCRs.

Automatic Color Control (ACC). To maintain constant color (chroma) signal levels. The burst signal is used as the ACC reference.

Automatic Color Killer (ACK). Deactivates color circuits for B/W signals—in the absence of a burst.

Automatic Fine Tuning (AFT). A circuit that compensates for a change in frequency due to tuner oscillator drift.

Automatic Frequency Control (AFC). Circuit that locks FM or TV receiver to station frequency.

Automatic Gain Control (AGC). Works to maintain a constant luminance level. In television, minimizes picture differences with changes in strength of incoming signals.

Automatic Phase Control (APC). Phase locks the chroma process circuits for stable color signals.

Band Pass Filter (BPF). A circuit, commonly having inductance and capacitance, that effectively passes a given range of frequencies whereas frequencies above and below this range are attenuated. Active filters for relatively low frequencies are often designed with op-amps, which require only resistance and capacitance.

Band Tuning (BT). Circuit that supplies tuning voltage, for terminal on the TV tuner.

Band. A range of frequencies between two definite limits.

Base Bandwidth. The amount of bandwidth required by an unmodulated signal, such as video or audio. In general, the higher the quality of the signal, the greater the base bandwidth it requires.

Beam. The electron stream inside the TV tube. Also, a type of highly directional antenna (radiating in one general direction, but capable of providing high power gains).

Bezel. The frame that covers the edge of the picture tube in some TV sets and can therefore hide edge information transmitted in an ATV system (such as ACTV I) not meant for the viewer to see.

Big-Screen TV. Big-screen sets are just like standard TVs—they just have a larger screen. Most big-screen models have screens that range from 20 inches to 27 inches (diagonally) in size, although some models have screens as large as 35 inches. A big-screen TV produces a clear, sharp picture and has conventional TV operation.

Bilingual Broadcasts. The simultaneous transmission of television programs in more than one language, using second audio program (SAP) technology. With a MTS/SAP stereo TV,

viewers can easily switch back and forth between the two audio tracks.

Black Matrix. Picture tube in which the color phosphors are surrounded by black for increased contrast.

Blur. A state of reduced resolution.

Broadcast Television. Conventional terrestrial television broadcasting, the most technically constrained delivery mechanism for ATV.

BTSC. Broadcast Television System Committee, the U.S. stereo TV standard agreed upon by the U.S. Federal Communications Committee (FCC) in 1984 and recommended by an industry EIA-sponsored committee.

Burn. An image or pattern appearing so regularly on the screen of a picture tube that it ages the phosphors and remains as a ghost image even when other images are supposed to be shown.

Burst. A short duration (8 to 10 cycles) of the 3.58 MHz subcarrier signal. It appears just after horizontal sync and locks the TV color oscillator to the station signal.

Cable-Ready, Cable-Compatible. Terms used for a TV or VCR that is capable of receiving all channels offered by cable TV—including midband and super-band channels—without the converter box that is supplied by the cable company.

Cable Labs. Cable Television Laboratories Inc. An ATV research and development center funded by U.S. cable television organizations.

Carrier. A high-frequency signal used to transport (carry) additional signals. They are isolated from one another to reduce interference.

Cathode Ray Tube (CRT). Color picture tubes used in all television systems. Electron gun generates beams that are guided to the screen illuminating small red, green, and blue phosphor targets on the surface. This then produces colors and images on screen.

CATV. Community antenna television or cable television. A delivery mechanism for ATV not necessarily as technically constrained as broadcast television.

CCIR. International Radio Consultative Committee. Also used to describe the 625-line television system used principally in Western Europe.

CEBus. The Consumer Electronics Bus is EIA/CEG's home automation standard. The CEBus Committee, comprised of both member and non-member companies, has developed the premier standard for a unified hand control system whereby electronic products from different manufacturers can communicate with one another via existing power lines, twisted (telephone) pairs, coaxial cable, and infrared means. Standard includes "bridge" devices that convert signals from one carrier to another to enable data transmission. First demonstrated at the 1989 International Winter Consumer Electronics Show in Las Vegas.

Channel. Common name for a transmission frequency.

Chip Enable (CE). Input terminal or voltage used to enable a circuit or device to perform its function

Chroma Resolution. The amount of color detail available in a television system, separate from any brightness detail.

Chrominance. A signal that carries the color information needed to produce a color picture; it is added to the luminance signal.

Clipping Circuit. A circuit that eliminates or restricts the voltage swings of the signal.

Clock Signal (CLK). The system clock or terminal of an microprocessor unit (MPU) where the clock signals may be checked.

Closed-Circuit. TV system in which camera and receiver are linked by cable or microwave.

Co-Channel Interference. Interference caused by two or more television broadcast stations utilizing the same transmission channel in different cities.

Coaxial Cable. The standard cable consisting of a central inner conductor and a cylindrical outer conductor. Used for most video connections. Also used to connect the CB radio antenna with the transceiver.

Color Bars. The video signal that is a series of colored bars. Used as a reference for brightness, contrast, color intensity, and correct color balance. Usually generated electronically.

Comb Filter. A comb filter improves resolution and reduces certain objectionable color effects.

Comparable Tuning. A requirement of the U.S. Federal Communications Committee (FCC) under the All-Channel Law; UHF channels must be as simple to tune as VHF.

Composite Signal. The television signal that consists of the video signal (luminance and chrominance), burst signal, and sync signal (horizontal and vertical).

Console. Furniture-styled TV or audio system that stands on the floor.

Convergence. Circuits that are used to align the three scanning electron beams that produce a color television picture; misaligned beams degrade the quality of the picture.

CRT. Cathode ray tube.

Dark Clip. An adjustable circuit that limits the overshoots created by signal preemphasis. If uncorrected, they cause excessive frequency swings of the FM luminance record signal. Also see *White Clip.*

DC. Direct current.

Definition. The degree of detail or sharpness of a video signal.

Degausser. Device to demagnetize color picture tube for color purity.

Detent Tuner. Manual or "click" type of TV tuner.

Digital to Analog Converter (DAC). A circuit that converts digital signals to analog (varying amplitude) signals.

Digital TV Memory. Electronic circuit that allows you to recall a stored still picture and display it simultaneously with one or more additional pictures.

Digital TV. Digital TV takes a signal, converts it into a series of numbers (1s and 0s in a specific pattern), and changes it back into a picture at the receiving end. The advantage of digital TV is that it eliminates interference, which can cause common TV problems such as ghosts and snow, and makes the picture clearer and sharper. However, in order to take full advantage of these features, the broadcast must be in digital format.

Digital Zoom. A feature that lets you magnify a portion of the picture to fill the entire screen.

Diode. A semiconductor device.

Dipole. A type of antenna.

Directional Antennas. A TV or FM antenna that picks up signals better from a single direction than all others. Usually has two or more sections or elements for increasing directivity.

Display. A visual representation of electrical/mechanical func-

tions via LED, liquid crystal, or fluorescent devices. Also called readout.

Dolby Surround Sound. A system that reproduces rear-channel information from specially recorded videotapes and discs.

Duty Cycle. The time period (or percentage) of the active portion of a given waveform (square or rectangular), as compared to the complete cycle.

Electrical Signal. The impulse that carries sound or pictures (audio or video) from a transmitter (radio or TV station) or from a disk or tape to a receiver (radio, TV set, etc.).

Electron Gun. Device in television picture tube from which electrons are emitted toward screen.

Encryption. Scrambling, considered important for signal security and pay-TV.

Enhanced or Extended Definition Television (EDTV). A form of ATV generally accepted to involve advanced encoding and/or transmission techniques but having less resolution than HDTV. Also called *Enhanced Quality Television (EQTV)*.

FCC. Federal Communications Commission.

Field. One complete vertical scan of an image. In a progressive scanning system, all of the scanning lines comprising a frame also comprise a field. In an interlaced scanning system, all of the odd-numbered or all of the even-numbered scanning lines comprise a field, and two sequential fields comprise a frame. There are 60 fields per second in American television.

Filter. A device that allows certain signals to pass through and stops others.

Flickering. Vertical roll or instability of a TV picture.

Footlambert. A measurement of light that is emitted or reflected from a surface. Used to rate the brightness of projection TV sets; the higher the rating, the brighter the picture. A rating of more than 300 footlamberts is considered very good in rear-projection televisions. There is no set standard for measuring footlamberts.

Frame. A complete television image consisting of two fields; the American NTSC broadcast system scans 30 frames per second.

Frequency Generator (FG). Used in the servo circuits and relates to motor speed.

Frequency Modulation (FM). A method of adding a signal to the carrier signal by changing the carrier's frequency. Used in broadcasting the audio portion of television signals. The form of modulation used for television sound transmission in most of the world, for satellite video transmission, and for video-tape recording. Less susceptible to interference than AM, the FM broadcast band covers 88 to 108 MHz.

Frequency. An assigned channel on which a station can transmit a signal (e.g., FM 99.3).

Fringe Area. A location that is far enough from the TV or radio broadcast signal to give consumers reception problems—especially if the location has hills, towers, or other broadcast signal spoilers.

Front End. Tuning or radio-frequency section of a radio or TV set.

Function Indicator Panel (FIP). Front display device. Also called *Fluorescent Display Panel (FDP)*.

Ghosting. A TV reception problem that occurs when the antenna picks up the original TV signal along with duplicate signals that are reflected by tall buildings and other similar obstacles.

The result is multiple images which are most noticeable around the edges of objects.

Glitch. Picture distortion.

Ground. A conducting path between an electrical circuit (or equipment) and the earth (or some conducting body serving in place of the earth).

Hall Effect IC. An IC that is activated by a magnetic field.

HD. High definition.

Hertz (Hz). The unit of measure equal to one cycle per second (cps); one kilohertz (KHz) equals 1,000 cps; one megahertz (MHz) equals 1,000,000 cps.

High Band. A recording method in which the carrier frequency is shifted higher in order to get high resolution.

High Definition Television (HDTV). High resolution television incorporating 1,000 or more horizontal lines of resolution, wide aspect ratio, and digital quality audio. (See *ATV*.)

Home Automation. Unified hand control system whereby electronic products from different manufacturers can communicate with one another via existing power lines, twisted (telephone) pairs, coaxial cable, and infrared means. (See *CEBus*.)

Horizontal Resolution. A rating of the fine detail of a TV picture, measured in lines. The more lines, the higher the resolution and the better the picture. A standard TV or VCR produces 240 lines of horizontal resolution; about 430 lines are possible with Super VHS machines.

Hue. Color set control governing color values in television picture. Also called *Tint*.

Image Enhancement. Techniques for increasing apparent sharpness without increasing actual resolution.

Image Enhancer. A device that improves color television pictures by comparing each video line element by element with the preceding and following lines. Any differences between vertically aligned elements are added to the middle-line element in the proper phase to enhance picture outlines and contrast.

Improved Definition Television (IDTV). Intermediate system designed to improve resolution of existing NTSC standard without involving new transmission standard.

In-Line. Color picture tube in which the electron guns are side-by-side, as opposed to the conventional triangular arrangement.

In Stereo. When used in TV program broadcasting, this means that the sound of the program is sent in two channels instead of one. By this method, the sound is greatly improved in both quality and clarity. However, a stereo TV is required to take full advantage of this.

Infrared Remote Control. A system of controlling audio/video/home automation equipment from a distance without using wires or cables. It utilizes infrared radiation to transmit the control information to a given piece of equipment.

Instant On. In TV, a picture appears in four seconds or less.

Instructional Television Fixed Service (ITFS). A fixed station operated by an educational organization and used primarily for the transmission of visual and aural instructional, cultural, and other types of educational material to one or more fixed receiving stations.

Integrated Circuit (IC). A combination of interconnected circuit elements inseparably associated on a base material in extremely small size, capable of performing a circuit function.

Interference. Electrical signals that have an undesirable effect on radio and TV reception.

Interlace Scanning. A process used in most television sets in which odd- and even-numbered lines of a picture are transmitted consecutively as two separate fields and superimposed to create one frame or complete picture on the TV screen.

Intermediate Frequency (IF). Frequency to which a signal is shifted within a receiver for amplification. The first stage in converting a broadcast television signal into baseband video and audio.

ITV. Instructional television or industrial television.

KHz. Kilohertz (kilocycles) or thousands of cycles per second.

Kinescope. Picture tube.

Lead-In Wires. Wires attaching a TV or an FM radio to an outdoor antenna.

Lines of Resolution. One way to characterize the clarity of a video image. The higher the number of the lines of resolution, the better the television picture.

Luminance. The part of a broadcast TV signal that causes a television's circuitry to vary light intensity from white to black with many shades of gray in between. This signal alone creates the picture on a black-and-white TV set; a color picture is produced when a chrominance signal is added to the luminance signal.

Magnetic Field. The area which surrounds a magnet and is affected by it. The field created by magnets in telephones, electric motors, TVs, and other consumer electronic products usually extends for a foot or two around them.

Master Antenna Television System (MATV). Antenna system, such as those used in apartment buildings and motels.

Memory. Device or circuit to hold machine-language information in electrical or magnetic form, such as a pre-set radio station frequency in a frequency-synthesized tuner or receiver.

MHz. Megahertz (megacycles) or millions of cycles per second. A normal U.S. television transmission channel is 6 MHz.

Microprocessor Unit (MPU). Also called a microcomputer. A large-scale integrated circuit (LSI) that performs computer-like functions. One or several are commonly used in later model VCRs for system control, clock timer functions, tuner control, servo control, etc.

Microvolt (υ1V). One millionth of a volt.

Microwave. Any electromagnetic wave of microwave frequency having a wave length from 30 centimeters to 1 millimeter.

Modulation. The process (or result) of changing information (audio, video, data, etc.) into information-carrying signals suitable for transmission and/or recording.

Monaural TV Broadcasting. Nonstereo TV with audio coming out of just one speaker.

Monitor. A separate video component that houses a picture tube and its accompanying electronics; it must be connected to a video tuner, VCR, or computer to display images.

Monitor/Receiver. A video monitor with a built-in video tuner and at least one speaker; it usually has RCA-type video inputs and outputs for connection to a VCR, video disc player, and other audio- and video-based components, avoiding the need for signal-degrading conversion of standard RF (antenna) signals.

Monochrome. Single color, usually black and white.

Monopole. Single-rod TV antenna.

Monostable Multi-Vibrator (MMV). A circuit that produces a logic low or high output of a given duration when it receives an input pulse.

Multichannel Television Sound (MTS). A common phrase for broadcast stereo TV.

Multichannel Television Sound/Second Audio Program (MTS/SAP). A process used for decoding the audio portion of stereo TV broadcasts (MTS) and an additional, mono-audio track (SAP), developed by Zenith and DBX, Inc. Some VCRs and TV sets have MTS/SAP decoders built into them; others have MTS/SAP jacks on their back panels for connection of outboard decoders.

Multipath Distortion. Distortion that occurs when signals coming directly from a radio station and signals reflected off buildings or other obstructions reach your radio or TV at slightly different times. In a television, this phenomenon creates a double image commonly known as "ghosting."

Multipix. This feature lets you display up to 9 or 12 still pictures on the screen simultaneously from different channels.

Multiplex. Superimposition of two separate signals on a single channel, as in FM stereo radio.

Muse. Multiple sub-Nyquist sampling encoding. A term originally used for a transmission scheme developed by NHK specifically for DBS transmission of HDTV.

Mute or Muting. The function or circuit which momentarily prevents passage of sound during function changes. Sound is also muted during special effects modes.

National Television Standards Committee (NTSC). The name for the standard television broadcasting system used in the United States; it produces 525 lines of horizontal resolution on the TV screen providing the TV is equipped with a comb filter.

Negative Guardband. Color picture tube in which holes in the shadow mask are slightly enlarged and phosphor areas slightly reduced, ensuring that each phosphor area is fully illuminated by the electron beam, producing higher brightness.

Negative Matrix. Combination of negative guardband and black matrix in a color tube.

Noise Blanker. See *Noise Limiter*.

Noise Limiter. A circuit that reduces noise from man-made devices.

Noise. Undesirable interference of picture or sound.

Non-Linear Emphasis. A process or the circuits that selectively boost low-level, high frequencies more than high-level, high frequencies.

Noninterlace Scanning. A digital-based process used in some newer high-end television sets to produce a sharper picture—transmits lines in sequence rather than alternating between odd- and even-numbered lines.

Open Architecture. A concept for television receivers that acknowledges an absence of ATV transmission/distribution standards and allows a receiver to deal with a multiplicity of standards and delivery mechanisms.

Overscanning. Displaying less than the complete area of an image to a viewer (i.e., scanning beyond the visible area).

PAL. Phase alternation by line. A common composite color transmission system in Europe.

Parental Lock/Channel Block. A feature found on some TVs that allows users to affix security codes to certain channels; typically used by parents to prevent children from viewing "adult" channels. Channels are blocked and unblocked using the TV set's wireless remote control.

PCB or PBA. Abbreviation for Printed Circuit Board or Plated Board Assembly.

Phase Distortion. The signal distortion caused by the different phase delays for different video frequencies.

Phase Inversion of Chroma. A process introduced in Beta VCRs to cancel the effects of signal crosstalk. Also see *Rotary Phase*.

Phase. The relative timing of the signal.

Phosphors. Chemical surfaces that illuminate in response to electron beam excitation, the actual sources of color and image on the screen.

Picture-in-Picture. Special digital effect where one image (from external source, tuner, or VCR playback) is displayed in a corner of the screen during normal viewing.

Picture Tube. The part of a TV set that receives the video signal and converts it to a picture on the screen.

Pre-Emphasis. The method of placing emphasis on the higher frequency portions of the signal to improve the S/N ratio.

Presets. The number listed indicates how many VHF, UHF, and cable channels can be selected without returning or adjusting the tuner.

Projection Television. Any indirect-view television receiver. There are currently three major types of projection TV, with screen sizes from about 35 inches to more than 10 feet across (diagonal measurement). Two-piece units employ separate screens and projector-receivers. One-piece front-projector systems have foldout or hinged drawers containing the picture source. Single-piece rear-projection systems have translucent screens which display the picture projected from the inside of the cabinet.

Pulse Generator (PG). Pulses used by the servo circuits. Phase of the PG pulses relates to motor phase (or position).

Radio Waves. Electromagnetic wave frequencies from 10 KHz to 300,000 MHz.

Raster. The beam scanned area of TV.

Receiver. An electronic device that accepts electrical signals to change into sound or pictures (audio or video). Receivers, a combination of an amplifier and a tuner, are a basic part of electronic products from radios to VCRs.

Resolution. Perceivable detail. Depends on the number of picture elements to be played back on a TV screen and regularly measured by means of the monoscope test pattern.

RF. Radio frequencies above 15 KHz. The high frequency for transmission of the video signal.

Ringing. High frequency patterns usually associated with over peaking of a video amplifier.

S-VHS Input. Special input for direct connection of S-VHS VCR or camcorder. Maintains segregation of luminance and chroma portions of signal for optimum reproduction without color fringing or dot crawl.

S/RF. Signal strength of radio frequency.

Sample and Hold. A method used in analog type servo systems for speed or phase control of the motor. A signal is measured at a specific point in time and stored (in a capacitor) for later use as a control voltage.

Sampling. The process of dealing with something continuous in discrete sections.

SAP. Second Audio Program.

Saturation. The intensity of the color.

Scan Pulses. Pulses from one or more ports of the MPU which sense the external circuits and return information via its input port(s) as data.

Scan. Scans the frequencies that have been programmed on all the scanner's channels.

Scanning Line. With a picture tube or photoconductive pickup tube of video camera, electron beams scan one line after another from left to right to catch or reproduce the image. The higher the number of these scanning lines, the more distinct the picture will be when reproduced.

Scanning. The horizontal and vertical movement of the electron beam in the camera or TV tube.

SECAM. Sequential and Memory color TV system adopted by France and most Eastern European and Middle Eastern countries.

Second Audio Program (SAP). A technology that was approved by the U.S. Federal Communications Committee (FCC) along with standard BTSC stereo TV. It is a third track of audio which can be used for a wide variety of different applications, including bilingual broadcasts and news or weather services.

Sensitivity. The input signal level required by a tuner, amplifier, etc., to be able to produce a stated output. The lower the necessary input stated in υV (microvolts), the higher the sensitivity.

Shadow Mask. A common device in which the electron beam is directed through a perforated metal mask to the desired phosphor color element on the face of the picture tube.

Sharpness Control. Means that the unit includes a control for adjusting the picture to produce softer or more defined edges.

Signal Splitter. TV/FM antenna accessory used to split the antenna signal into two (or more) paths. One type of signal splitter feeds the same signal to two connections, another separates the VHF, UHF, or FM signals.

Simulcast. Also known as FM simulcast, this VCR feature enables the user to record the audio signals from a connected FM tuner or audio receiver onto a videotape. Due to the growing popularity of components equipped with the MTS/SAP decoders and of stereo TV broadcasts, simulcasting is not an uncommon feature.

Skip. A radio frequency reflected by the ionosphere and bounced back to earth at a far distant point.

Slit Mask. Type of shadow mask using vertical slits instead of round perforations.

Slot Mask. Type of shadow mask using vertical slots.

Snow. A type of video noise or interference that typically appears on the TV screen as white specks—usually the result of a weak TV signal.

Solid State. Commonly used to indicate use of semiconductor devices in place of tubes.

Sonic Feedback. Sound feedback. Return of a portion of the output of a circuit or device to its input. Results in distortion.

Splitter. A device used to split an incoming RF signal and route it to at least two video components.

Standard. A set of rules or characteristics defining a particular television system. Some standards (such as those contained in FCC rules and regulations) are mandatory. Most (including those of the EIA, IEEE, and SMPTE) are voluntary.

Stereo Decoder. The device which allows TVs to pick up and subsequently receive the MTS stereo signal. Most stereo TVs have built in decoder circuitry; those that do not may have a provision to add a stand alone decoder to pick up the signal.

Stereo TV. A TV set or monitor/receiver that is capable of receiving and displaying programs broadcast with stereo soundtracks; it must have a built-in MTS/SAP decoder plus a stereo amplifier and at least two speakers.

Sub-Channel. A transmission path within the main transmission path.

Subcarrier. The 3.58 MHz (suppressed) CW signal used to carry color information—added to the main baseband signal prior to modulation.

Surface Acoustic Wave (SAW) Filter. A device used in TVs and monitor/receivers to eliminate adjacent-channel interference.

Surround Sound. Electronic decoder circuit used to enhance a TV stereo signal usually built into an audio receiver or VCR but also available as a separate component—best used with four speakers. A fifth speaker can be installed on top of the TV for centering the dialogue.

Synchronizing Pulses. A timing pulse of the composite signal which controls the return of the electron beam scanning of the CRT.

Telecine Equipment. Projects a movie film on a TV set. While a TV set reproduces 30 frames per second in NTSC (25 frames in PAL), a movie generally projects 24 frames per second. A specially-designed projector converts 24 frames of film picture into 30 frames (or 25 frames) for TV use.

Television Receiver. Receives broadcasts using a technology incorporating a cathode ray tube. Does not include LCD TV, projection TV, TV/VCR combinations, or audio/video systems.

Tint. Name sometimes given to hue control on color set.

Transistor. Active semiconductor device with three or more electrodes.

Transmitter. A device that can change sound waves into electric waves or impulses to send to a receiver—a telephone, a radio or TV broadcast, or inside a VCR.

Tuner. Portion of a radio or television set that selects the desired incoming signal.

Tuning Eye. Indicator tube that indicates whether FM or TV receiver is tuned exactly to desired incoming signal.

Tuning System. Usually refers to the method of changing channels; it often includes at least one MPU and remote control functions. Mechanical switch type tuners, used in early models, have been phased out and replaced by electronic (varactor) types.

TV Demodulator. The TV receiver signal processing circuits of a VCR (from RF to recovery of audio and video signals).

TV Still. This effect lets you freeze a frame from a pre-recorded tape or from a broadcast program so that you can read a list of movie or program credits while you continue to hear the sound from the tape or program.

TVI. Television interference.

Twin Lead. Standard 300 ohm TV or FM lead-in wire.

UHF (Ultra High Frequency). The band from 300 MHz to 3 GHz. In television, UHF refers to a subset of that band, the range from 470 MHz to 890 MHz, once allocated to TV channels 14 through 83.

USB. Upper side band.

Varactor. Variable-capacitance diode used in electronic tuning systems for TV and radio; hence the name *varactor tuning*.

Vertical-Sync Signal. The sync pulses on the video signal that control the vertical retrace. Frequency is: NTSC=60 Hz; PAL=50 Hz.

Vertical Frequency. The number of vertical fields per one second. NTSC=60 Hz. PAL=50 Hz.

Vertical Oscillator. The electronic circuit that creates sawtooth-scanning signals synchronizing with the vertical sync signal for the vertical deflection of the CRT or the pickup tube.

Vertical Resolution. The amount of detail that can be perceived in the vertical direction. The maximum number of alternating white and black horizontal lines that can be counted from the top of the picture to the bottom.

Vertical Retrace. The return of the electron beam from bottom to top at the end of each field.

Vertical Scanning. The vertical movement of the electron beam on the picture tube.

Vertical Sync. The sync pulses that control the vertical scanning of the TV picture: NTSC=60 Hz; PAL=50 Hz.

VHF (Very High Frequency). The range from 30 MHz to 300 MHz, within which are found U.S. television channels 2 through 13.

Video Input. A jack found on high-quality TV sets and monitor/receivers used to connect a video source, resulting in the best possible picture quality from that particular combination of components. Always located on the set's back panel; many monitor/receivers include an additional set on their front panels for easy connection of a second component, such as a camcorder.

Viewable Picture. Screen size refers to the actual size of the viewable picture area measured on a single plane basis (the measurement does not take into account the curvature of the tube.) If the indicated size is other than the horizontal dimension of the actual viewable picture area, the size designation should be accompanied by a statement clearly showing how the measurement was made.

Voltage Controlled Oscillator (VCO). An oscillator whose frequency is controlled by an external voltage.

Voltage Crystal Controlled Oscillator (VXO). Similar to a VCO except that a crystal serves as a reference and its frequency can be varied over a small range.

Wide-Band Video Amplifier. Extends the frequency response of the system to produce more detail and resolution (up to 560 horizontal lines).

Widescreen. An image with an aspect ratio greater than 1.33:1.

Wipe. A special effect that two pictures from different video sources are displayed on one screen.

XTAL. Abbreviation for crystal.

Source:

Consumer Electronics Group, *Consumer Electronics Product Terminology Dictionary*, Washington: Electronic Industries Association, 1991.

Video Cassette Recorders and Home Video

The first major in-home video program source for the television receiver since the advent of cable TV was the video cassette recorder (VCR). First introduced in 1975, it is estimated that 77 percent of all U.S. TV households contain a VCR—some households have two or even three VCRs. For home video photography, the camcorder is the choice for many consumers. Camcorders are simple to use, lightweight, and portable (see *Camcorder*).

TERMINOLOGY

AC/DC. A switch on the unit lets the user run it on either AC line power or battery power.

Additional Comb Filter. A comb filter improves resolution and reduces certain objectionable color effects.

Adjacent Track. The track on a tape that is on either side of the track being recorded or played.

Alignment Tape. A special video tape with recorded picture and sound reference signals used for VTR adjustment. All VHS VTRs have to be aligned with the master VHS video tape to allow for interchangeability between VTRs.

Analog to Digital Converter (ADC). Circuit that converts analog (varying amplitude) signal to a digital (pulse type) signal.

Artificial Vertical Sync. During special effects mode, excessive noise appears in the vertical sync which would result in picture instability. For this reason, artificial sync is generated to ensure vertical stability.

Audio Dub. Replaces the sound track on a previously recorded tape with a new one without disturbing the video material.

Auto-On. VCR turns on automatically when a tape is inserted.

Auto Index. A feature that makes it easy to find programs on a tape. Auto index electronically marks the tape every time the user starts to record so that he can find the beginning of each recording automatically during rewind or fast forward.

Auto Playback. The VCR is equipped with a feature that automatically plays back as soon as the user inserts the tape into the machine.

Auto Programming/Program Set. Indicates that the VCR has a feature that scans all channels and automatically "memorizes" those that can be IRT/OTR/STANDBY OTR. The VCR has a one-touch recording (OTR) feature that lets the user start recording instantly—at the touch of a button.

Auto Rewind/Auto Shutoff. A feature that spares the user from pressing rewind when a cassette has played to the end. After the tape is rewound, the VCR automatically shuts itself off.

Autoeject. VCR ejects the tape automatically when it reaches the end.

Automatic Color Control (ACC). To maintain constant color (chroma) signal levels. The burst signal is used as the ACC reference.

Automatic Color Killer (ACK). Deactivates color circuits for B/W signals—in the absence of burst.

Automatic Exposure Lock. Holds the exposure setting while the user re-composes the scene or pans the camcorder.

Automatic Frequency Control (AFC). Circuit that locks FM or TV receiver to station frequency.

Balanced Modulator (BM). As identified in VCR literature, a circuit designed to produce a sum or difference output of its two input frequencies. Any special characteristic of either input will appear in the output signal. This is also called a frequency converter or mixer.

Bar Code. New feature lets the user program the VCR by running a wand-like tool across a set of printed bar codes included with the VCR. The wand "reads" the information (day of week, time of day, channel, etc.) contained within the bar codes and programs the VCR with the appropriate data.

Beta or Betamax. One of two standard home VCR systems.

Binary Coded Decimal (BCD). Numbers based on the binary system , common in digital circuits.

Black Level. This level represents the dark areas of the picture on the video signal.

Blanking. The time during which the scanning beam is retracing, or non-active part of the video signals. The horizontal and vertical sync signals and the burst signal are located in this period.

Blue Screen. The VCR replaces the static that is present at the end of the a tape or on a non-receivable channel with a blank blue screen.

Blur. A state of reduced resolution.

Capacitive Electronic Disc (CED). System of video recording on a grooved disc, employing a groove-guided capacitance pickup.

Carbon Backed. A type of videotape with a carbon back coating.

Cassette Housing. The mechanical arrangement for lowering the video cassette into position for playing or recording. Early machines were loaded from the top. Motorized front loading is now commonly used.

CATV. Community antenna television or cable television. A delivery mechanism for advanced television (ATV) not necessarily as technically constrained as broadcast television.

CD-V. The V stands for video. In the 5-inch format, the gold-colored CD-V contains up to five minutes of full motion, NTSC video of the same quality found on larger, laser-optical videodisks. Although the video is recorded in analog form, the accompanying soundtrack is 16-bit digital. Besides this "music video," the disc may contain up to 20 minutes more of digital music. CD-V nomenclature has been extended to 8- and 12-inch laser videodiscs. A conventional music-CD player can extract the audio from the disc, but a "combi" player is needed to reproduce the video.

Channel. Common name for a transmission frequency.

Character Generator. Lets the user enter captions (or titles) across the picture on the tape being made.

Chroma (Chrominance). The portion of the video signal containing color information.

Chroma Crosstalk. Pickup of unwanted chroma signal from an adjacent track. Crosstalk is canceled in playback by the technique of Chroma phase rotation in VHS and Chroma phase inversion in Beta machines.

Chromium Dioxide. A tape known for its superior high-frequency output whose coating is of chromium dioxide particles.

Clamp. A process that sets the video signal at a specific DC level.

Clipping Circuit. A circuit that eliminates or restricts the excessive voltage swings of the signal.

Clogging. A condition in which VCR heads become dirty—the picture becomes snowy, the sound fuzzy.

Closed-Circuit. TV system in which camera and receiver are linked by cable or microwave.

Coaxial Cable. The standard cable consisting of a center inner conductor and a cylindrical outer conductor. Used for most video connections. Also used to connect the CB radio antenna with the transceiver.

Continuous Loop. Type of tape system in which a single reel is used within an endless loop of tape.

Control Signal. Video, audio, and control signals are put on a video tape during recording. The control signal is that signal used for controlling the video head rotation and tape speed so that the head may accurately trace on the recorded track of the tape during playback.

Control Track Signal (CTL). A 30 Hz pulse signal developed from vertical sync and recorded on the video tape. Used by the servo circuits during playback to determine tape speed, it is compared with a reference signal for proper tracking.

Converted Subcarrier. The process of low-banding the 3.58 MHz chroma signal for recording: 629 KHz in VHS, 688 KHz in Beta.

Crosstalk. The undesirable interference noise caused by the adjacent tracks which the video heads inadvertently pickup during playback.

Definition. The degree of detail or sharpness of a video signal.

Delay IRT. A feature that allows the user to delay instant recording so that he can pre-program the OTR with the desired channel or starting time information.

Delta Factor. A term used in describing *jitter (wow and flutter)* caused by variations in tape speed. Results in frequency instability during video tape playback, particularly with regard to chroma.

Deviation (DEV). A term used to describe the amount of FM carrier swing due to luminance modulation. In VHS, the upper limit is 4.4 MHz for peak white (disregarding sidebands).

Dew Sensor. The humidity sensor used in a VTR.

Digital Serve. A later servo system that uses digital technology as opposed to analog type servo control. Some VCRs use a combination of the two methods.

Digital Special Effects. Digital circuitry that lets the user store and then manipulate the video image to achieve certain special effects.

Digital TV Memory. This feature allows the user to recall a stored still picture and display it simultaneously with one or more additional pictures.

Digital Zoom. A feature that lets the user magnify a portion of the picture to fill the entire screen.

Digital. Using a contrast system termed *piezo,* it keeps adjusting the focus until the contrast of the video images is at a maximum. Some camcorders use a digital autofocus system. Camcorders with the feature utilize digital circuitry to achieve the optimum focus.

Dihedral. A term that applies to the adjustment or accuracy of the VCR's head cylinder or scanner which holds the video heads. Eccentricity must be minimized for optimum performance.

Display. A visual representation of electrical/mechanical functions via LED, liquid crystal, or fluorescent devices. Also called readout.

Double Limiter. The electronic circuit in the playback process of the VTR that prevents overmodulation.

Dropout. A momentary loss of the playback RF signal due to dirt on the video tape or heads. Uncompensated dropout produces white or black streaks, which represent the missing information, in the picture.

Drum. The assembly on a VCR that contains the video head assembly.

Dual Azimuth/4 Video Head. Special design four-head system that spaces heads next to each other on the head drum (as opposed to 180 degrees apart). Provides jitter-free and noise-free images when in still frame or slow-motion.

Dubbing. Playing a tape on one tape machine and recording (dubbing or copying) it on a second machine.

ED-Beta. Extended definition Betamax. A consumer/professional videocassette format developed by Sony offering 500-line horizontal resolution and Y/C connections. An improvement over standard Beta, ED-Beta's separation of the luminance and chrominance signals during record and playback, a wider luminance bandwidth, and the use of high-density tape result in sharper, more vivid picture quality.

Edit Switch. A switch that boosts the high frequency components of the video signal in an attempt to compensate for degradation of picture quality resulting from copying or dubbing a tape from the camcorder to a second VCR.

Electrical Signal. The impulse that carries sound or pictures (audio or video) from a transmitter (radio or TV station) or from a disk or tape to a receiver (radio, TV set, etc.).

Electronics to Electronics (E-E). The picture monitored while recording or the related circuits that permit monitoring.

Emphasis. A process that boosts the high frequency component of the signal for recording.

Encryption. Scrambling, considered important for signal security and pay-TV.

Fast Play. This feature lets the user play the tape at twice the normal playback speed.

Fidelity. The degree to which an electronic product accurately reproduces sound. A high fidelity system (hi-fi) delivers sounds as close as possible to the original.

Fine Editing. Lets the user synchronize new recorded material with material already on tape without a noticeable transition.

Flag Waving. The term applied to a picture that has signal time base errors. This usually appears as a movement (or hook) in the top of the picture during tape playback.

Flying Erase Head. An extra video head which is located on the rotary cylinder used to erase the video signal during the editing process. Designed to produce seamless edits—smooth, invisible transitions from one scene to the next.

Frame Advance. A feature that enables the user to advance video frames one at a time.

Head Switching. Circuits that, in conjunction with 30 Hz squarewaves (switching pulses), prevent amplified output signal from the head that is not on tape.

Head. In a tape recorder, the device that makes contact with magnetic tape to convert magnetism to electrical signals or vice versa. They are used to record, erase, or play tape signals.

Hi-Fi. When the VCR has true high-fidelity stereo sound capability—the top of the line in sound quality for VHS and Beta machines and a match for the sound quality of the best movie soundtracks. To take full advantage of a hi-fi VCR, the user needs to connect the VCR to a good hi-fi system or stereo TV set to hear better audio from prerecorded tapes. Even then, the user won't hear hi-fi sound on most TV programs unless the broadcasts are in high-fidelity stereo and unless the VCR has the capability to receive them.

Hi8. A high band video recording system used to improve the resolution of 8mm format VCRs. (See *Super VHS.*)

High Quality (HQ). A desirable feature that can improve picture quality. VHS models with HQ have at least two possible picture enhancements: white clip level extended by 20 percent, which improves definition; detail enhancer; chrominance noise reduction; and luminance noise reduction.

Horizontal Resolution. A rating of the fine detail of a TV picture, measured in lines. The more lines, the higher the resolution and the better the picture. A standard TV or VCR produces 240 lines of horizontal resolution; 430 lines are possible with Super VHS machines.

Horizontal Sync Signal (HSS). Signal that is derived from the composite video signal.

Inches Per Second (IPS). Tape speed is measured by this.

Infrared Remote Control. A system of controlling audio/video/ home automation equipment from a distance without using wires or cables. It utilizes infrared radiation to transmit the control information to a given piece of equipment.

Insert. Allows the user to insert new audio/video segments into material already on tape.

Interference. Electrical signals that have an undesirable effect on radio and TV reception.

Jitter. Horizontal sway of playback picture caused by uneven rotation of the rotary heads, capstan, etc., or by friction of the tape as it is running. The effect of *wow and flutter* during playback. Also see *Delta Factor.*

Laser-Optical. System of video recording on grooveless discs and employing a laser-optical-tracking pickup.

Laser Beam. A tightly focused beam of laser light used to play the signals stored on laser video discs or CD recordings.

Laserdisc Players. A device which has the ability to process digital signals from optical discs to reproduce digital video in combination with stereo sound (laser video) and may be capable of playing both digital audio compact discs and 8 inch and 12 inch laser videodiscs (combi-player).

Laserdisc. The standard industry designation for optical laser-read video discs and videodisc players.

Linear Stereo. When the VCR can record stereo and play back stereo tapes by using the linear audio tracks on the tape. Many stereo VCRs also have Dolby noise-reduction circuitry that helps to reduce background hiss in the audio on the linear track.

Loading Motor. The motor that powers the VCR's mechanism for load/unload of tape with respect to the heads. A cassette loading motor is used in front machines to drive the carriage assembly.

Loading. The threading of tape to the VCR's video heads.

Low-Frequency Noise Canceller. This circuit eliminates noise components including the switching noise from the playback luminance signal on a VTR.

Magnetic Tape. A ribbon of thin plastic coated with magnetic material used in both audio and video tape decks.

Memory. Device or circuit to hold machine-language information in electrical or magnetic form, such as a pre-set radio station frequency in a frequency-synthesized tuner or receiver.

Metal Tape. Tape whose coating is of iron particles; noted for its wide dynamic range and frequency response.

Microprocessor Unit (MPU). Also called a microcomputer. A large-scale integrated circuit (LSI) that performs computer-like functions. One or more are commonly used in later model VCRs for system control, clock timer functions, tuner control, servo control, etc.

Mistracking. The symptom caused by the video head when it traces either no track or the improper track.

Modulation. The process (or result) of changing information (audio, video, data, etc.) into information-carrying signals suitable for transmission and/or recording.

Monitor Receiver. Similar to a TV set except that it has additional and separate audio and video outputs on the back.

Mosaic. This feature gives the user the ability to make the video image appear as small blocks of color.

Multipix. This feature lets the user display up to 9 or 12 still pictures on the screen simultaneously from different channels.

Noise Limiter. A circuit that reduces noise from man-made devices.

Noise. Undesirable interference of picture or sound.

Number of Functions. The figure indicates the number of functions that can be performed on the remote control.

On-Screen Programming. An X indicates that the VCR has a useful feature that "guides" the user with a series of prompts on the TV screen to help him enter and display the appropriate programming information. Many VCRs include a "help" function as part of the on-screen programming to make the programming task as easy as possible.

One Touch Recording. See *Auto Programming.*

OTR. One-touch recording.

Over-Modulation. On the playback picture, the white and black spike noise occurring at the vertical edge portion of the video signal.

Oxide. The material used to make audio and video tape magnetic. Oxide particles shed from tape and can clog deck heads if they are not cleaned.

PAL. Phase alternation by line. A common composite color transmission system in Europe.

Peaking Circuit. The electronic circuit of the video head amplifier. The peak frequency is the frequency at which the heads deliver the maximum output. It is determined by a capacitor at each playback amplifier input.

Phase Compensator. Used in several places in the video recording and playback circuits to correct any phase errors introduced by the filters of the frequency response shapers.

Phase Distortion. The signal distortion caused by the different phase delays for different video frequencies.

Phase Inversion of Chroma. A process introduced in Beta VCRs to cancel the effects of signal crosstalk. Also see *Rotary Phase.*

Phase. The relative timing of the signal.

Pinch Roller. The part of both audio and video tape decks that moves the tape forward and backward.

Pixels. Picture elements. The smallest dots that can be transmitted for any given bandwidth and scanning system.

Power-Off Eject. Enables cassette ejection when VCR power is off. Push *Eject,* the VCR turns on, ejects the tape, and turns off.

Pre-emphasis. The method of placing emphasis on the higher frequency portions of signal to improve the S/N ratio.

Presets. The number listed indicates how many VHF, UHF, and cable channels can be selected without returning or adjusting the tuner.

Program. A set of instructions that tells the VCR what to do.

Programming Capability (Events/Days). The figure to the left of the slash is the maximum number of programs, called events, that the user can automatically record on the unattended VCR. The figure to the right of the slash indicates the maximum number of days over which the user can tape those programs.

Pulse Generator (PG). Pulses used by the servo circuits. Phase of the PG pulses relates to motor phase (or position).

Quick Start System. This feature permits a picture to appear on the screen in 1.5 seconds after *Play* is pressed—much faster than with conventional VCRs.

Receiver. An electronic device that accepts electrical signals to change into sound or pictures (audio or video). Receivers, a combination of an amplifier and a tuner, are a basic part of electronic products from radios to VCRs.

Recording Speeds. Using the slower speed allows the user to get more material on the tape, but picture quality generally will not be as high as it would be at the faster speed.

Recording Times (Min.). The maximum record time in minutes. For VHS models, that would be the longest time the user could record with a T-160 tape. For 8mm models, the time listed; 120 minutes is the maximum time using the longest available cassettes. For VHS-C models, the maximum time is 20 minutes if the user tapes at the fast speed (SP), 60 minutes if the slow speed (EP) is used.

Remote Programming. Means the VCR can be programmed via the remote control.

RF Converter. The unit in a VCR that places the video and audio signals on RF carriers so that the signals can be received by a standard TV (Channel 3 or 4).

RF. Radio frequencies above 15 KHz. The high frequency for transmission of the video signal.

Ringing. High-frequency patterns usually associated with over peaking of a video amplifier.

Rotary Phase of Chroma. The process of rotating chroma phase by 90 degrees, at a horizontal line rate, in VHS. See *Chroma Cross Talk.*

Rotary Transformer. A device used to magnetically couple signals to and from the video heads, thus eliminating the need for slip-rings and brushes.

Safety Device. A sensor or other component, working in conjunction with an MPU or other logic devices, which prevents operation of the VCR in the event of a potential problem that may cause damage to the tape and/or the mechanism.

Safety Tab. The record inhibit tab on the video cassette. If the safety tab on the cassette has been removed, the system control microprocessor will prevent recording on that tape.

Search. A feature that permits faster than normal tape speed while playing a tape, usually in either direction.

Sensitivity. The input signal level required by a tuner, amplifier, etc., to be able to produce a stated output. The lower the necessary input stated in μV (microvolts), the higher the sensitivity.

Servo Control. The servo control system controls the speed and the phase of VTR head rotation, or tape speed, by detecting variations and feeding back signals to the control circuit to correct and regulate.

Servo. An electromechanical device whose output is constantly monitored and regulated so that it matches or follows an external reference.

Signal Splitter. TV/FM antenna accessory used to split the antenna signal into two (or more) paths. One type of signal splitter feeds the same signal to two connections, another separates the VHF, UHF, or FM signals.

Signal to Noise (S/N) Ratio. Ratio between a component's output signal intensity and its accompanying noise content; expressed in decibels, the larger the number, the better.

Skip. Remote control has a button the user can press to fast forward the tape 30 seconds ahead (the typical length of a single commercial).

Slow Motion. Allows the user to advance the tape slowly. VAR means that the user can select among variable slow-motion playback speeds.

Solarization. This feature, sometimes called *postarization* or *digital art*, allows the user to produce a surrealistic, high-contrast, brightly-colored image.

Special Effects. Any feature that permits the VCR to play back pictures at other than normal speed: still, slow, scan forward or reverse, etc. Also called *Tricks Mode*.

Speed. The number of times faster than normal speed (in SP or EP/SLP) that the user can search (or scan) the tape while still being able to see a picture.

Still-Frame. Playback of material can be visually stopped on a single frame.

Strobe. This function allows the user to freeze and display several images simultaneously.

Strobe/Multi-Strobe. This function allows the user to freeze and display several frames from several channels simultaneously.

Super VHS (S-VHS). An improvement over the standard VHS, S-VHS's separation of the luminance and chrominance signals during record and playback, a wider luminance bandwidth, and the use of high-density tape, result in sharper, more vivid picture quality. The horizontal resolution reached by S-VHS is approximately 400 lines or better—compared to 240 lines by a standard VHS.

Surround Sound Processor. A component which incorporates a signal decoder device and has the ability to produce multichannel sound from a monaural or stereophonic two channel source. It may also enhance the sound through techniques such as time delay.

System Control (Syscon). The electronic circuits in a VCR that provide control of the mechanism and electrical switching functions.

Tape Heads. Electrical assemblies that convert magnetism to electrical signals or vice versa when they contact magnetic tape. They are used to record, erase, or play tape signals.

Three-Quarter-Inch VCR. This system uses a cassette (case) that contains both a supply reel and a takeup reel. One of the advantages of the cassette system is that the cassette can be stopped halfway and taken out without rewinding to the end of the tape.

Time-Remaining Indicator. Displays the amount of time remaining in hours and minutes on a tape.

Time Base Error. Relates to the difference between the VCR's playback video signal and an external reference, specifically with regard to sync timing errors. Also see *Flag Waving*.

Track. The track made magnetically on a tape by the recording head. Audio track and control track are in upper or lower edges. Video tracks are recorded helically in the central part.

Tracking Control. Provided in order to control the video heads rotation phase to trace accurately on the recorded tracks on the tape during playback.

Tracking. Ability of color TV set to properly register all color tones and white.

Transmitter. A device that can change sound waves into electric waves or impulses to send to a receiver—a telephone, a radio or TV broadcast, or inside a VCR.

Tricks Mode. See *Special Effects*.

TV Demodulator. The TV receiver signal processing circuits of a VCR (from RF to recovery of audio and video signals).

TV Still. This effect lets the user freeze a frame from a pre-recorded tape or from a broadcast program so that he can read a list of movie or program credits while continuing to hear the sound from the tape or program.

TVCR. Used to denote TV-VCR combinations. Personal video-video products designed for viewing by one person; it usually refers to battery portable TV-VCR combinations having 3-inch to 5-inch liquid crystal display screens, but it can be used for any small-screen TV or TV combination.

U-Standard. Offers standards of ¾ inch video cassette recorder under the agreement concluded by three companies—JVC, Matsushita Electric (National/Panasonic) and Sony—whose aim is to define the condition of color TV signal magnetic recording method and maintain the interchangeability of tapes between ¾ inch VCRs.

Unified Remote. Enables the user to control both the VCR and a TV (from the same manufacturer) with a single remote device.

VCR. Video cassette recorder.

Vertical Sync Signal (VSS). Vertical synchronizing pulses, extracted from the composite video signal.

Video-to-Video (V-V). The picture produced when a tape is played back (also refers to the playback signal path).

Video Cassette Player (VCP). A magnetic tape device that can play, but not record, videocassettes.

Video Cassette Recorder. A video recorder that uses magnetic tape housed in a protective container. Video cassette types for home use are Beta, VHS, and 8mm.

Video Cassette. Magnetic tape housed in a protective container.

Video Dub. A feature that allows the user to insert new video segments.

Video Head. A video head is a tiny electromagnet that "writes" information on the tape when recording and "reads" information from the tape during playback. Recording requires at least two video record/playback heads. Additional heads are used for special visual effects such as slow motion or for playback at the slowest speeds. VHS models with hi-fi have two extra heads devoted exclusively to audio.

Video High Density (VHD). System of video recording on grooveless discs, employing an electronically guided capacitance pickup.

Video Home System (VHS). One of the two standard home VCR systems.

Video In. A composite video signal input for a VTR or monitor.

Video Noise Reduction. Indicates the machine has chrominance noise reduction, an HQ feature that reduces color "noise": spots, streaks, and patches. Luminance noise reduction, another HQ feature, is intended to reduce the snow-like noise in the picture.

Video Out. A composite video signal output from a VTR or monitor.

Video Player. Any device that plays back recorded video information.

Video Signal. The electric signals containing frequencies of DC to about 4 MHz that are produced by a TV camera to reproduce the images on a TV set.

Videodisc. Flat disc resembling a phonograph record. Designed to display prerecorded visual information through a player attached to a standard television receiver.

VISS. Sophisticated search feature allows the user to go directly to a predesignated point (address) manually placed anywhere on the tape. It can be used with the tape moving in either direction in Fast Forward, Rewind, or Scan/Search mode.

VTR. Video tape recorder.

VU Meter. *Volume Unit* indicator used to show volume level in tape recording.

Waveform Monitor. A special oscilloscope that is designed to display the composite video signal.

Wipe. A special effect whereby two pictures from different video sources are displayed on one screen.

Wow and Flutter. Frequency deviation of playback signal caused by variation of tape speed, video head rotation, etc. It is expressed as a percentage of change from the desired signal frequency. The phenomenon occurring at a relatively slower period is called Wow; those of a relatively faster period are called Flutter. The signal gets distorted and flutter appears on the picture and sound.

Y/C Connections. Connections between videotape recorders and between videotape recorders and cameras, monitors, and other devices that keep luminance and chrominance separate and thus avoid cross-color and cross-luminance.

Source:
Consumer Electronics Group, *Consumer Electronics Product Terminology Dictionary,* Washington: Electronic Industries Association, 1991.

Videotape

Videotape is a magnetic recording medium inside a plastic housing known as a cassette. The magnetic tape used in videotape is a thin, plastic film base coated with a fine powder that can hold or react to a magnetic field. Glue or a binder holds the magnetic particles to the plastic film. All VCRs operate in much the same way, but each tape cassette is different. The different formats are as follows:

Beta (or Betamax). The Beta format is licensed by the Sony Corporation.

Hi-8. A high-resolution imaging technology that uses advanced metal tape cassettes.

S-VHS-C. The compact format for S-VHS.

S-VHS. Super-VHS. A new and improved quality VHS format which offers line resolution 80 percent greater than standard VHS VCRs, resulting in brighter colors and greater image clarity. To get the full enhanced picture effect, a special S-VHS TV monitor and special tapes are needed.

VHS-C. A compact VHS recording format.

VHS. The VHS format is licensed by J.V.C. Corporation and has come to dominate the marketplace.

Each format has a registered logo with which all videotape cassettes in the marketplace are labeled.

All full size camcorders use standard VCR-size tapes that correspond to the VCRs on which they can be played. For example, VHS camcorders use the same tape as VHS VCRs. Compact camcorders, 8mm, Hi-8, and VHS-C use specially designed mini-cassettes which are about the same size as an audio cassette.

GRADES

In addition to the logo, there is information on the label indicating the quality or grade of the tape. The consumer may find words like *everyday* or *high grade* or explanations of the best uses for a tape. The explanations and abbreviations used on labels vary from manufacturer to manufacturer. Although there is no industry standard, the following abbreviations are often used on tape labels:

EHG or HGX. Extra high grade.

HG. High Grade. A premium tape with higher quality control. May be packaged in a dust free case. Also, may have a smoother surface, making it easier to pass over the heads of the camera or cassette player. May also have a stronger film that doesn't stretch and thereby distort the image on the film.

Hi-Fi. Used for Hi-Fi VCRs that need the best audio reproduction.

HQ. High quality.

HS. High standard.

PRO. Grade for professional use.

SHG. Super high grade.

STD. Standard. Videotape conforming to the quality standards of the licenser of the technology: Sony or J.V.C.

TERMINOLOGY

Camcorder. Has a camera and VCR combined. They are smaller than table top VCRs and can be carried easily.

Frequency-Response Range. Tapes with high F-R ranges will give sharper images.

S/N Range. Highest signal-to-noise ratio. Tapes with higher ratios produce recordings that are less grainy and have the best color reproduction.

Time (T). Used to indicate the number of minutes of recording time. For example, a videotape labeled T-120 will record for 2 hours at the fastest speed (SP—Standard Play), 4 hours at middle speed (LP—Long Play), and 6 hours at slow speed (ELP, SLP, EP—Extended Long Play, Super Long Play, or Extended Play).

VIDEOCASSETTE RECORDING TIME

Videocassette	Recording Time (in minutes)		

VHS

	Cassette Recording Speeds		
	SP	LP	EP
T-30	30	60	90
T-60	60	120	180
T-90	90	180	270
T-120	120	240	360
T-160	160	320	480

BETA

	Cassette Recording Speeds		
	X1(a)	X2	X3
L-125	15	30	45
L-250	30	60	90
L-500	60	120	180
L-750	90	180	270
L-830	(b)	200	300

(a) X1 speed was original Beta consumer recording speed. It's available today as a recording speed only on professional Beta VCRs. X1 speed is available on some home VCRs as a playback speed only.

(b) Recording at X1 speed with L-830 not recommended.

Sources:

Consumer Electronics Group, *Consumer Electronics Product Terminology Dictionary,* Washington: Electronic Industries Association, 1991.

Costello, M. and Heiss, M., *How to Select & Use Home Video Equipment,* Tucson, AZ: HP Books, 1984.

How to Choose, Use, and Care for Audio and Video Tape, Electronic Industries Association, Washington, 1991.

Health & Beauty

Alcohol

Ethyl (Ethanol). Alcohol widely used as a solvent in such cosmetics as after-shave lotion, cologne, deodorant, mouthwash, and shampoo. Also used externally as an *antiseptic* (see entry). *Absolute alcohol* is ethyl alcohol with additives which make it unfit for drinking. *Denatured alcohol* is ethyl alcohol made unfit for drinking through the addition of various perfumes and other substances.

Isopropyl (Isopropanol). An alcohol used as an antibacterial agent, solvent, or as a denaturant (i.e., to make alcohol unfit for drinking). Prepared from propylene and used in a wide variety of cosmetic products.

Rubbing. Contains not less than 68.5 percent and not more than 71.5 percent (by volume) of absolute alcohol (see *Alcohol, Ethyl*), with denaturants (substances to make the alcohol unfit for drinking) such as perfume oils.

Wood (Methyl Alcohol or Methanol). Solvent obtained through destructive distillation of wood. Used as a fuel (for chafing dishes, etc.) and in the manufacture of other products such as formaldehyde and paint.

Sources:
Nonprescription Medicines: A Consumer's Dictionary of Terms, New York: Council on Family Health, 1992.

Winter, Ruth, *A Consumer's Dictionary of Cosmetic Ingredients,* New York: Crown Publishers, Inc., 1989.

American Dental Association (ADA)

The American Dental Association seeks to improve and maintain the standards and qualities of certain materials, instruments, and equipment used in the practice of dentistry and to promote the truthful advertising and labeling of dental products. Through its Council on Dental Materials, Instruments, and Equipment, the ADA maintains three evaluation programs for the acceptance, certification, or recognition of dental materials, instruments, and equipment. These programs differ from one another in the mechanisms used in evaluation.

COUNCIL ON DENTAL MATERIALS, INSTRUMENTS, AND EQUIPMENT

ACCEPTANCE PROGRAM

The Acceptance Program applies to materials, instruments, and equipment for which evidence of safety and usefulness has been established by guidelines. These guidelines request biological, laboratory, and/or clinical evaluations where appropriate and where specifications do not exist. Evaluations of products are based on information submitted according to the established guidelines. Products accepted under this program are classified as follows:

Acceptable. Those products classified as *Acceptable* have met the criteria established in the appropriate ADA guidelines. Acceptable products are granted the *Seal of Acceptance*, a statement on their acceptance by the council. In addition, the product is added to the *List of Accepted Dental Materials, Instruments, and Equipment*.

Provisionally Acceptable. *Provisionally Acceptable* products lack sufficient evidence to justify classification as *Acceptable,* but show reasonable evidence of safety and usefulness including clinical feasibility. These products may not display the *Seal of Acceptance* but are authorized to use a suitable statement to define specifically the area of usefulness of products classified as *Provisionally Acceptable.* They are also added to the *List of Accepted Dental Materials, Instruments, and Equip-*

ment. Products are reviewed for renewal of provisional acceptance status every year for a maximum of three years.

CERTIFICATION PROGRAM

Under the certification program, a manufacturer certifies that a product complies with the appropriate specification of the ADA. All ADA specifications have been approved by the American National Standards Institute as American National Standards. After a manufacturer makes a certification request, the ADA procures a sample which is tested in the council's laboratory according to the specifications. Products complying with the specifications under this program may be classified as follows:

Certified. Those products classified as *Certified* have met the requirements established in the appropriate ANSI/ADA specification. Certified products are granted the *Seal of Certification* and are added to the *List of Certified Dental Materials, Instruments, and Equipment*.

Provisionally Certified. Products which do not meet all the specification requirements but are determined to be safe and effective are listed as *Provisionally Certified*. These products may not display the *Seal of Certification* but are authorized to use a suitable statement. They are also added to the *List of Certified Dental Materials, Instruments, and Equipment*.

RECOGNITION PROGRAM

This program, which has been terminated, applied to materials, instruments, and equipment for which neither certification program specifications or acceptance program guidelines had been developed. Evaluations were based on laboratory and/or clinical information substantiating the safety and effectiveness as claimed. Study protocols varied considerably depending on the nature of each product and the claims made for the product. Products of obvious safety and efficacy were not eligible for the program. Products that met the program requirements were granted the *Seal of Recognition*, along with a statement of their recognition by the council, and were added to the *List of Recognized Dental Materials, Instruments, and Equipment*. Products previously in this

category will be reassigned to the remaining programs.

COUNCIL ON DENTAL THERAPEUTICS

ACCEPTANCE PROGRAM

Through its acceptance program, begun in January 1930, the Council on Dental Therapeutics of the ADA evaluates the safety and efficacy of over-the-counter and prescription therapeutic drugs used in the diagnosis, treatment, or prevention of dental disease. The council evaluates the safety and efficacy of submitted products according to criteria delineated in various council guidelines. The council also reviews available scientific literature as well as comments from voluntary consultants, and from the ADA's Research Institute and Departments of Chemistry and Toxicology. In addition, the council reviews and approves prior to use all labeling, package inserts, advertising, and promotional material for accepted products. Provided a product is in full compliance with council provisions, council acceptance of that product is valid for a period of three years. Thereafter, the product distributor may submit data in support of council reacceptance of the product every three years. Products accepted under this program are classified as *Accepted* and are granted use of the *Seal of Acceptance*.

Source:
Clinical Products in Dentistry; A Desktop Reference, Chicago, IL: American Dental Association, 1992.

Condoms

Condoms are one of the oldest forms of birth control and for decades have been used to prevent *sexually transmitted diseases* (STDs). They are also called *safes* or *prophylactics*. The condom is a sheath that covers the entire penis. It acts as a barrier, or wall, to keep semen, blood, and vaginal fluids from passing from one

Seals of the American Dental Association.

person to another. These fluids can harbor organisms such as *HIV* (*human immunodeficiency virus*), the virus that causes AIDS.

Condoms currently marketed in the United States are made of either latex (rubber) or natural membrane (lambskin). Neither is 100 percent effective.

Date MFG. This is the date the condom was made, not the expiration date. However, the Food and Drug Administration (FDA) requires that all condoms to which a spermicide has been added be labeled with the expiration date of the spermicide. New York State requires an expiration date on all condoms sold in that state. The expiration date is usually labeled with the abbreviation *EXP*.

For Disease Prevention. A condom package should say that the condoms are to prevent disease. If the package doesn't say anything about preventing disease, the condoms may not provide the protection needed, even though they may be the most expensive ones available.

Latex Condoms. Made of latex (rubber) and recommended for disease protection.

Lubricants. Some condoms are lubricated with dry silicone, jelly, or cream. Lubricants may help prevent condoms from breaking during use and may prevent irritation that might increase the chance of infection.

Natural Membrane Condoms (Lambskin). These condoms have different permeability characteristics and less uniformity than those made of latex and may allow HIV, which is tinier than sperm or bacteria, to pass through. For this reason, lambskin condoms are not considered as effective as latex condoms in reducing the risk of STDs, including AIDS.

Spermicides. Spermicides kill sperm and are sometimes added to condoms. Their packages are required to be labeled with the expiration date of the spermicide, and they should not be used after that date.

Source:

Willis, Judith Levine, "Latex Condoms Lessen Risks of STDs," *FDA Consumer*, Vol. 24, No. 7 (September 1990): 32-36.

Contact Lenses

TYPES

Bifocal Contacts. Bifocal contacts come in two types, alternating-vision and simultaneous-vision. *Alternating-vision lenses*, like bifocal eyeglasses, include two zones, one for near vision and one for far vision. Alternating-vision lenses are either weighted or flat on the bottom to keep them from rotating. Even with the weighting, it may be difficult for the wearer to use the proper zone on the lens. *Simultaneous-vision lenses* have multiple zones for both close and distance vision, spread throughout the lens. The brain receives light rays from both near and far objects simultaneously and then sorts out which to recognize. The result is that many objects in the wearer's field of vision will be somewhat blurry, thereby blurring overall visual acuity.

Disposable Lenses. Disposable lenses are extended-wear lenses

designed to be thrown away after seven days of wear. They are safer than *extended-wear lenses* (see entry) because they are disposed of before harmful levels of contaminants can build up, but oxygen deprivation to the cornea remains a problem.

Extended-Wear Lenses. In response to user's objections to the demanding care regimen required by *soft lenses* (see entry), manufacturers have developed extended-wear lenses which can be worn around the clock. Many ophthalmologists recommend wearing the lenses during the day, but only occasionally during the night. The Food and Drug Administration (FDA) recommends using extended-wear lenses no longer than seven days without removing them to let the eyes rest overnight. Extended-wear lenses are not believed to be as safe as gas-permeable, rigid lenses or soft lenses. However, the FDA approved the first extended-wear, rigid gas-permeable lens in December 1986.

Frequent-Replacement Lenses. These lenses are a compromise, made of a slightly thicker and more durable materials than *disposable lenses* (see entry), and designed to be replaced at regular intervals (e.g., once a month or once every two or three months). The lenses must be removed, cleaned, and disinfected every night, but they may not require the weekly enzyme treatment recommended for soft lenses. The cost per lens of frequent-replacement lenses is about a quarter of the cost of a single lens designed to be worn for a year. Industry experts predict that 80 percent of soft lens wearers will be using this type of lens by the mid-1990s.

Monovision Contacts. Presbyopia (farsightedness) which affects nearly everyone over the age of 40, is a condition in which the lens of the eye loses the elasticity it needs to adjust for close vision. If the person also requires correction for distance vision, an option is monovision contacts. When using monovision contacts, one eye wears a contact lens that corrects for close vision and the other eye wears a contact lens that corrects for distance. The brain adjusts to this type of visual information, although some loss in depth perception can be expected, and vision correction may not be adequate for driving.

Rigid Lenses. When originally introduced in the mid-1970s, these lenses were made of impermeable plastic and covered the cornea (the transparent layer over the iris and pupil). Because the plastic material was impermeable to oxygen, they were made smaller than the iris to allow some oxygen to reach the cornea. Today, rigid lenses are made from a more flexible, gas-permeable material which allows up to four times as much oxygen to reach the cornea as do *soft lenses* (see entry). These lenses are sometimes called *RGP* lenses (rigid gas-permeable). Some experts feel that rigid lenses are the safest and healthiest lenses for daily wear. Gas-permeable rigid lenses are easier to clean than other contact lens types, and they can provide sharper vision for some patients, especially those with astigmatism, in which irregular curvature of the cornea causes blurred vision. Rigid lenses require an adjustment period from a few days to three weeks, and they are more difficult to fit.

Soft Lenses. Consisting primarily of water, soft lenses are pliable and a good medium for delivering oxygen to the cornea, although rigid gas-permeable lenses can allow up to four times more oxygen to reach the cornea. Soft lenses have a sticky, gelatinous surface which attracts contaminants from the environment and protein deposits from tears. As time passes, the plastic from which soft lenses are made deteriorates, becoming thicker, pitted and less pliable. Soft lenses must be cared for according to manufacturer's directions, and after a year of wear, will need to be replaced. Some experts feel that soft lenses are less safe for daily wear than rigid, gas-permeable lenses, but are safer than extended wear lenses. *Toric soft lenses* are weighted at the bottom to keep them from rotating on the eye, to adjust for mild to moderate astigmatism (oval, rather than round, cornea). Toric lenses are also available in *disposable* and *frequent-replacement* styles (see entries).

Sources:

Carr, Teresa, "The Better to See You," *American Health,* Vol. XI, No. 6 (July/August 1992): 64-67.

Tolber, Margaret, and Lippman, Richard E., "Are Your Contact Lenses as Safe as You Think?" *FDA Consumer,* Vol. 21 No. 3 (April 1987): 16-19.

Drugs

Under current law, all new drugs need proof that they are effective, as well as safe, before they can be approved by the Food and Drug Administration (FDA) for marketing. The review process has engendered an official vocabulary. Some of these terms have found their way onto product labels and into advertisements and commercials. For example, the phrase "clinical studies have shown…" relates to an official FDA approval process.

TERMINOLOGY

Bioavailability. Rate and extent to which a drug is absorbed or is otherwise available to the treatment site in the body.

Bioequivalence. Scientific basis on which generic and brand-name drugs are compared. To be considered bioequivalent, the bioavailability of two products must not differ significantly when the two products are given in studies at the same dosage under similar conditions. Some drugs, however, are intended to have a different absorption rate. The FDA may consider a product bioequivalent to a second product with a different rate of absorption if the difference is noted in the labeling and doesn't affect the drug's safety or effectiveness or change the drug's effects in any medically significant way.

Clinical Studies. Clinical, or human, studies aim to distinguish a drug's effect from other influences—for example, a spontaneous change in disease progression or in the effect of a *placebo* (an inactive substance that looks like the test drug). Such studies conducted in the United States must be under an approved Investigational New Drug Application (IND) under the guidance of an institutional review board, and in accord with FDA rules on human studies and informed consent of participants.

Drug Product. The finished dosage form (tablet, capsule, etc.) that contains a drug substance, generally, but not necessarily, in association with other active or inactive ingredients.

Drug Substance. The active ingredient intended to diagnose, treat, cure, or prevent disease or affect the structure or function of the body, excluding other inactive substances used in the product.

Effectiveness. The desired measure of a drug's influence on a disease condition. Effectiveness must be proven by substantial evidence consisting of adequate and well-controlled investigations, including human studies by qualified experts, that prove the drug will have the effect claimed in its labeling.

Generic. A version of a drug that is equivalent of the pioneer or brand-name drug and is not marketed until the pioneer drug's patent exclusivity has expired. These "copies" are often marketed under just the generic name of the drug—for example, Diazepam.

Investigational New Drug Application (IND). An application that a drug sponsor must submit to FDA before beginning tests of a new drug on humans.

New Drug Application (NDA). An application requesting FDA approval to market a new drug for human use.

Orphan Drug. "Orphans" are drugs and other products for treating rare diseases. They may offer little or no profit to the manufacturer, but may benefit people with the rare diseases. To foster orphan product development, the Orphan Drug Act (1983) allows drug companies to take tax deductions for about three-quarters of the cost of their clinical studies. Firms also are given exclusive marketing rights for seven years for any orphan products that are approved.

Pioneer. The first version of a drug, which is marketed under a brand name. For example, Valium is the brand name for the first marketed version of the anti-anxiety drug diazepam.

Pre-Clinical Studies. Studies that test a drug on animals and other nonhuman test systems.

Raw Data. Researcher's records of patients, such as patient charts, hospital records, X-rays, and attending physician's notes.

Safety. No drug is completely safe or without the potential for side effects. Before a drug may be approved for marketing, the law requires the submission of results of tests adequate to show the drug is safe under the conditions of use in the proposed labeling. Thus, "safety" is determined case by case and reflects the drug's risk vs. benefit relationship.

Sources:

Farley, Dixie, "How FDA Approves New Drugs," *FDA Consumer,* Vol. 21, No. 10 (Dec. 1987-Jan. 1988): 7-13.

Yorke, Jeffrey, "FDA Ensures Equivalence of Generic Drugs," *FDA Consumer,* Vol. 26, No. 7 (September 1992).

Eyeglasses

TERMINOLOGY

Antireflective Coatings. Lenses coated to help reduce glare.

Designer Frame. A frame that was designed by a well-known designer. Does not necessarily mean a frame of superior quality.

Photochromatic Lenses. Photochromatic lenses are glass lenses that lighten or darken in response to the intensity of the light.

They are now available as plastic lenses.

Scratch-Resistant Coating. Plastic lenses scratch more easily than glass lenses. To improve performance, the plastic lenses can be coated to make them as scratch-resistant as glass lenses.

Shatter-Resistant Lenses. The lens cannot shatter when hit by a steel ball weighing 0.56 ounces dropped from a distance of 50 inches. Does not mean that the lens is unbreakable.

UV Protection. Lenses that protect against excess UV light, a known source of cataracts.

Source:
Bold, Kathy, "Buyer's Guide to Better Eyeglasses, *Consumers Digest,* Vol. 27, No. 1 (January/February, 1988): 58-60.

Fragrances

TYPES

Perfume. Strongest, most concentrated and lasting form of fragrance. A blend of natural *essential oils* and/or *synthetics* and *fixatives* (see entries), a perfume may contain as many as 300 different elements. Perfume balance is achieved with the addition of alcohol which acts as the carrier. The amount of alcohol added to the original blend determines the strength of the fragrance.

Toilet Water. Next in strength to perfume, toilet water contains the fragrance of the original perfume in a more dilute form, making it lighter and more subtle.

Cologne. Cologne is the lightest form of fragrance. The first cologne to be introduced was the citrus type of fragrant "water" first created in the city of Cologne, Germany, in the seventeenth century. Many citrus type colognes still exist, but a majority of colognes are diluted versions of perfume. Cologne is less concentrated with perfume oils than toilet water.

TERMINOLOGY

Floral Bouquet. A blended bouquet of individual flower fragrances, or notes, which are given balance and body by a combination of fixatives like *civet, ambergris,* and *musk.* See *Fragrance Ingredients.*

Fruity. Citrus quality of oranges and lemons, and a mellow peachlike aroma.

Modern Blend. These fragrances are also known as *aldehydes.* This category includes any fragrance which combines features of other fragrance categories, but cannot be classified in any other category.

Note. Distinctive odor or component of a fragrance. *Body-note* describes the main characteristic of the fragrance. *Top-note* is the most volatile part of a fragrance and provides its first impression. *Bottom-note* is the residual fragrance, its longest lasting component. *Dry-out* is the last impression of the fragrance, sometimes with evidence of the characteristics of the fixative.

Oriental Blend. Mixtures of musk, ambergris, civet, and other such exotic ingredients.

Single Florals. Features the scent of a single flower such as a rose, carnation, violet, or lilac.

Spicy. Combination of pungent spice ingredients like cinnamon, clove, and ginger. Often used in combination with spicy flower aromas.

Woodsy/Mossy. Sandalwood, rosewood, cedar, and other aromatic woods are combined with earthy oak moss and fern to create scents in this category.

FRAGRANCE INGREDIENTS

Synthetics. Aromatic chemicals that offer fragrance types not provided by nature. Certain fragrances such as lily of the valley and gardenia must be produced synthetically, since their flowers do not yield oil. Natural oils are combined with synthetics to develop new fragrances.

Fixatives. Equalize the evaporation rate of all of the fragrant elements. The fixative is what makes a perfume "lasting." Fixatives come from animals, mosses, and resins. The following are animal fixatives:

Civet is a yellowish-brownish substance developed in the scent glands of both the male and female civet cat, which is native to India, China, and Haiti. The scent is highly unpleasant until it is blended with other fragrance ingredients.

Musk comes from the male musk deer, native to Tibet, China, and India. A drop of musk no larger than the head of a pin can scent a large area for many weeks.

Ambergris is a solid, fatty substance which results from an upset digestive system of the whale. Ambergris looks much like marble, and can be found floating on the surface of the ocean almost anywhere. Next to pearls, ambergris is the most precious product, by weight, taken from the sea.

Alcohol. Primarily in the form of ethyl alcohol, the carrier for other fragrance ingredients. To complete a fragrance product, the natural and synthetic oils and fixatives must be diluted in alcohol. The alcohol used by perfumers is specially prepared and aged.

EXTRACTION METHODS—ESSENTIAL OILS

The five methods of extracting essential oils for fragrance production are:

Distillation. An ancient process whereby the fragrance-producing materials are placed in a still and the essential oil is extracted by means of steam. The heat breaks open the cells of the petals, leaves, roots, etc., releasing the essential oil, which floats on top while the water settles to the bottom.

Extraction. The fragrance-producing materials are placed in large tanks, and a volatile solvent such as benzene or petroleum ether is pumped in. After repeating this process three times, the solvent has extracted the natural fragrance oil. The mixture is then put into a stirring apparatus in dark cellars to prevent its being disturbed by light and air. The *concrete,* a waxy substance, is extracted; then alcohol extracts the liquid flower oil again, which is concentrated in vacuum stills.

Enfleurage. In this process both sides of sheets of glass are coated with grease. The flower petals are then spread on the grease-coated surfaces and the sheets of glass are placed between wooden frames in tiers. The petals are removed by hand and changed again and again until the fat has absorbed all the odor it can. The glass is then removed from the frames and washed with a solvent which separates the essential oil from the fat.

Maceration. Similar to enfleurage, this method uses warm fats instead of cold fats. The flowers are mixed and stirred in the fats. The flower oils are absorbed by the fats. When all odors are obtained, the mixture is put on a perforated screen and allowed to drain, thus separating the flowers from the remaining strained fat containing the essential oil.

Expression. In this method, the oil is squeezed out by physically pressing the fruit of the plant. It may be accomplished by mechanical pressure, by hand, or by a combination of both.

Source:
"The History, The Mystery, The Enjoyment of Fragrance," New York: The Fragrance Foundation, undated.

Health and Beauty Products

Many health and beauty products share a large vocabulary of terms that are used to label the various products. The following terminology is frequently encountered by consumers.

TERMINOLOGY

Active Ingredients. Ingredients in medicines that provide therapeutic benefit.

Acute. Describing an experience that comes on rapidly and lasts a short time; sharp, as in acute pain. Differs from chronic, which describes a long-lasting or frequently recurring experience.

Adverse Reaction. Side effect. Any unintended, abnormal reaction to a medicine taken at normal doses.

Alkaline Bath. Bath water to which sodium bicarbonate has been added; used to treat some skin disorders.

Allergen. A substance that causes an *allergic reaction* (see entry) in those individuals who are sensitive, but does not affect others. Examples are plant pollens and animal danders.

Allergic Reaction. Abnormal bodily response to an ingredient in a medication or a natural substance such as ragweed, pollen, or bee venom. Symptoms vary widely, but may include a rash (often itchy), hives, sneezing, wheezing, runny nose, or serious reactions leading to collapse. See *Anaphylaxis*.

Aloe Vera. A substance extracted from the leaves of a lily-like plant of South African origin. Contains 99.4 percent water and 0.5 percent amino acids and carbohydrates. Used in many cosmetic and sunscreen products for its alleged soothing and softening effects. According to the American Medical Association (AMA), there is no scientific evidence of the benefits claimed for aloe vera.

Analgesic. Medication that relieves painful symptoms, especially headache, muscle soreness, and stiffness. Most nonprescription analgesics also reduce fever. Some analgesics may be applied topically to relieve itching or muscle pain.

Analgesic Liniment. Liquid rubbed onto the skin. It mildly stimulates nerve endings for warmth, coolness, or tingling mild pain (or sometimes all three at once), blocking or distracting the user from more bothersome pain.

Anaphylaxis. Severe hypersensitivity reaction to an allergen, such as bee venom or a drug. Symptoms may include rash, swelling, breathing difficulty, and collapse. A severe form is called *anaphylactic shock*. See *Allergic Reaction*.

Anesthetic. Medication that deadens sensation or feeling. Over-the-counter anesthetic agents are limited to topical applications.

Antacid. Preparation that neutralizes excess hydrochloric acid found in the stomach. Over-the-counter antacids relieve symptoms such as heartburn, sour stomach, or acid indigestion caused by excess acid.

Antiarthritic. Medication that helps relieve arthritis symptoms, such as swelling, redness, and pain.

Antibacterial. In the context of products for external use, usually on the skin. Describes the ability of the product to limit the growth or effect of bacteria and other microorganisms. See also *Antibiotic*.

Antibiotic. Medication that kills or limits the growth and multiplication of bacteria and other microorganisms. Most nonprescription antibiotics are applied topically. Prescription antibiotics are usually, but not always, taken internally.

Antidiarrheal. Medication that lessens or controls diarrhea.

Antiemetic. See *Vomiting Medication*.

Antiflatulent. Agent that reduces intestinal gas. Antiflatulents are sometimes combined with antacids in a single product to relieve gas and other symptoms commonly occurring with gas, such as heartburn, sour stomach, or acid indigestion.

Antifungal. Agent that destroys or prevents the growth of fungi. Usually applied topically. Fungal infections include jock itch, athlete's foot, and ringworm.

Antihistamine. Drug that minimizes allergy symptoms by blocking the action of histamine, a substance in the body that affects nasal and other tissues and may cause runny nose, congestion, sneezing, and itching. Some antihistamines are also used as sleep aids because they induce drowsiness.

Antimicrobial Soap. Soap containing an ingredient that kills or inhibits growth and reproduction of bacteria.

Antiperspirant. Product that reduces underarm wetness. Usually combined with a *deodorant* (see entry). Most frequently used antiperspirant chemical in the U. S. is aluminum chlorhydrate. Antiperspirants are classified by the Food and Drug Administration (FDA) as *drugs*, not *cosmetics* (see entries).

Antipyretic. See *Fever Reducer*.

Antiseptic. Agent that slows or stops the growth of bacteria, but may not actually kill them. Often used to reduce bacteria in a wound and lessen the chance of infection.

Antispasmodic. Drug that reduces muscle spasms of the gastrointestinal tract, airways and genitourinary tract.

Antitussive. See *Cough Suppressant*.

Artificial. In cosmetics and health care products, used to label products not duplicated in nature. Even if a product such as a cologne uses all natural ingredients, it must be called *artificial* if it has no equivalent in nature.

Artificial Tears. Product used to relieve dryness of the eyes. So-called because these salty formulations mimic natural tears and coat and lubricate dry mucous membranes. They help the eye hold moisture and/or thicken the tear fluid. Sometimes used to keep contact lenses wet while in the eye.

Astringent. Substance that causes skin or mucous membranes to pucker and shrink by reducing their ability to absorb water. Often used in preparations such as shaving lotion and skin cleansers because it has a drying effect on the skin surface. It also reduces swelling and helps stop bleeding.

Bactericidal. Describing a drug that kills bacteria.

Bacteriostatic. Describing a drug that stops the growth or multiplication of bacteria.

Balm. Soothing or healing preparation applied to the skin.

Barrier Agent. Water-repellent or oil-repellent substance added to lotion or cream to provide a barrier against irritation from water, wind, or irritating chemicals.

Batch Code or Lot. Series of numbers and/or letters on over-the-counter medication labels indicating the manufacturer and where and when a particular bottle of medicine was manufactured.

Bronchial Muscle Relaxant (Bronchodilator). Medication that relaxes the smooth muscles lining the airways leading to the lungs. Helps to widen airways, facilitate normal breathing, and eliminate bronchial spasms.

Bronchoconstrictor. Substance that causes the airways in the lungs to narrow or constrict. An attack of asthma may be caused by the release of bronchoconstrictor substances such as histamine.

Buffered. Describing a special formulation of a product that minimizes chemical irritation in the stomach.

Bulk Forming Laxative. Product that promotes bowel movement by increasing the stool's volume, water, and fiber content, making the stool softer and easier to evacuate.

Calorie. Unit of heat content used to compute the energy value of foods. One calorie is the amount of heat needed to raise the temperature of one kilogram of water one degree Celsius.

Caplet. Form of medication shaped like a capsule, but solid like a tablet.

Capsule. Medicine-containing shell of gelatin or other material that can dissolve in the stomach, releasing the capsule's content.

Caries. Dental cavities.

Cathartic. Drug that stimulates bowel action to help induce a bowel movement.

Certified Color. See heading *Color, Food, Drug, and Cosmetics.*

Cheilitis. *Dermatitis* (see entry) of the lips, typically caused by a reaction to lipstick in susceptible individuals.

Child-Resistant Packaging. Packaging designed to resist opening by young children. Intended to reduce the likelihood of accidental ingestion of packaging contents and possible poisoning.

Chronic. Long-lasting or frequently recurring condition.

Colors. See heading *Color, Food, Drug, and Cosmetics.*

Constipation. Condition in which bowel movements are infrequent or incomplete, sometimes accompanied by a sensation of abdominal pressure.

Contraceptive Cream or Jelly. Substance used as a means of preventing pregnancy, applied topically in the vagina and sometimes used with a diaphragm.

Contraindication. Factor in a person's current condition, medical history, or genetic make-up referenced in labeling to inform that a particular drug may increase risk of an adverse effect (from a product containing that drug), indicating the product should not be used.

Cosmetic. Product designed to beautify or enhance a person's physical appearance. Includes products for the hair, skin, nails, and facial features.

Cough Suppressant. Substance, also known as an *antitussive,* that suppresses or inhibits the act of coughing. Most antitussives act directly to inhibit the brain's cough-control center.

Counterirritant. Agent applied directly to the skin to stimulate nerve endings to feel warmth, coolness, or pain, distracting the user from more bothersome pain.

Decongestant. Oral or topical medication that helps clear up congestion and unclog nasal passages, to allow freer breathing and better drainage.

Demulcent. Oil, salve, or other agent that soothes and relieves skin discomfort. It helps tissues retain moisture and helps insulate from sun and wind.

Dental Floss. Thin string used in the removal of plaque and food particles between the teeth and along the gum line. It may be *waxed* or *unwaxed.* Waxed dental floss is easier to pull between the teeth, but if used prior to using an anticavity (fluoride) rinse the flossing can coat the teeth with wax, shielding them from the rinse.

Dentifrice. Paste or powder for use with a toothbrush in cleaning teeth.

Deodorant. Controls perspiration odor by inhibiting growth of microorganisms. Usually combined with an antiperspirant to control flow of perspiration.

Depilatory. Chemical in cream, wax, or lotion used for hair removal. Chemically removes hair by dissolving it.

Dermatitis. Inflammation of the skin. See also *Cheilitis.*

Dermatitis, Allergic Contact (ACD). Inflammation of the skin caused by direct contact with a substance to which the skin is sensitive. (Common example is poison ivy.) Cannot spread on a person's body or be spread to another person. Spread is caused by contact with the irritant substance.

Dermatitis, Atopic. Chronic inflammation of the skin.

Detergent. Water-soluble cleaning agent that differs from *soap* (see entry) in that it is not prepared from fats or oils. Most are made from petroleum derivatives.

Directions for Use. Instructions printed on a medicine label giving specific directions for use, including how much of (dosage) and how frequently a drug should be taken and by whom.

Diuretic. Drug used to remove excess fluids from the body by increasing the flow of urine.

Dosage Instructions. See *Directions for Use.*

Douche. Liquid preparation used to cleanse the vagina internally.

Drug. Substance taken by mouth, by injection, or by suppository, or applied locally, to prevent or treat a disorder.

Drug Interaction. The modification of the effect of one drug by another, in a way that diminishes, negates, or enhances the effectiveness or safety of both drugs.

Dysmenorrhea. Painful menstruation.

Elixir. Sweetened liquid, generally containing alcohol, that forms a base for many medicines, such as those used to treat coughs.

Emetic. Substance ipecac that induces vomiting. Used in the treatment of certain types of poisonings.

Emollient. Agent that soothes or softens the skin.

Enteric Coating. Coating on a medicine allowing the medicine to bypass the stomach and dissolve in the intestine, thereby helping to lessen stomach upset and irritation.

Epilatory. Waxlike product for hair removal. Product is softened by heat, applied (to the skin surface with hair to be removed) when cooled slightly, allowed to cool and harden further, and then pulled off the skin, removing the hair with it.

Essential Oil. Oily liquid resulting from processing plant material, with characteristic taste and smell of the original plant. Stronger than *Extract* (see entry).

Expectorant. Medication that helps thin and loosen phlegm (thick mucus of the respiratory passages), making it easier to cough up bronchial secretions.

Expiration Date. The date prior to which the product can be expected to retain its full strength as stated on the label, according to the manufacturer.

Extract. Solution that results from passing alcohol or an alcohol/water mixture through a substance. Not as strong as *Essential Oil* (see entry).

Eyewash. Sterile solution used to bathe the eye or dilute and flush out irritating foreign matter.

FDA (Food and Drug Administration). A branch of the U. S. federal government's Department of Health and Human Services. The FDA is responsible for reviewing data required to establish safety, effectiveness, and proper labeling and manufacturing practices for all nonprescription and prescription medicines prior to marketing. It also regulates foods, cosmetics, and medical devices.

Federal Food and Cosmetic Act, 1938 (FD&C Act). The primary law governing drugs sold in the United States. Among other things, prohibits the sale of drugs contaminated, misbranded, or otherwise dangerous to health; establishes minimum standards of strength, quality, and purity for many drugs, and sets up specifications for drug labeling.

Federal Trade Commission (FTC). The federal agency in the United States responsible for preventing unfair and deceptive advertising.

Fever Reducer. Medication that lowers elevated body temperature; sometimes called an *antipyretic*.

Fiber. Nondigestible food content that adds roughage to the diet and bulk to the stool. Used to promote regular bowel movement.

First Aid. Immediate care given to an injured or ill person before treatment by medically trained personnel.

Flag. Symbol, phrase, or notation on a package alerting consumers to significant product changes, including new ingredients, dosage instructions, or warnings.

Generic Drug. Drug not protected by a trademark. The generic name is distinct from a brand name chosen by a manufacturer for a particular product.

Gingivitis. Condition in which the gums are red, swollen, and bleeding. It most often results from poor oral hygiene and development of plaque on the teeth. If untreated, gingivitis can cause infection and tooth loss.

Glycerol. Sweet, colorless preparation made from the glycerol found in fats; used as a moisturizing agent for chapped skin, in suppositories and as a sweetening agent in drugs.

Hemorrhoidal Ointment. Preparation used to relieve the itching, pain, and swelling of dilated veins under the skin of the anus, known as hemorrhoids.

Homeopathy. Alternative, and controversial, remedies made from solutions of herbs, minerals, animal extracts, and other natural substances. The theory is that small amounts of a disease-causing microorganism can be used to cure people suffering from the disease.

Hydrogenation. Process of adding hydrogen gas under pressure to liquid oils. Used in cosmetic and food production to convert liquid oils to semisolids at room temperature.

Hypoallergenic. Describing products from which most of the cosmetic ingredients known to be allergens have been removed to minimize chance of allergic reaction. The individual manufacturer decides the testing method used to determine the hypoallergenic quality of a product. Therefore, each manufacturer's use of *hypoallergenic* is unique, and is not necessarily related to the use of the term by another manufacturer (even if the products are similar).

Imitation. In the context of cosmetics, used to label products containing all or some non-natural ingredients.

Inactive Ingredients. Substances not therapeutically active, such as starch, added to medicines to provide bulk, flavor, color, or for other nontherapeutic purpose.

Indications for Use. The medical condition for which a medication is intended.

Inhaler. Device for administering a drug through the mouth or nose. Inhalers are used principally in the treatment of respiratory disorders, such as asthma and upper respiratory infections related to the common cold.

Jojoba Oil. Oil used in cosmetics such as shampoos and lotions and obtained from the beanlike seeds of the desert shrub, *Simondsia chinensis*.

Laxative. Agent that promotes bowel movement by softening or increasing the bulk of the stool, lubricating the intestinal tract, or stimulating muscle contractions of the intestine.

Lotion. Liquid preparation applied to large areas of skin. Common ingredients are mineral oil, stearic acid, lanolin, and beeswax.

Nonallergenic. Formerly used to label products to indicate that they contained no allergenic ingredients. Widely replaced by *hypoallergenic* (see entry).

Medication. Remedy having preventive, relieving, or curative properties.

Menthol, Mentholated. A mild local anesthetic used in body rubs, after-shave lotions, and other cosmetics. Imparts a "cool" feeling to the skin. Obtained from peppermint or other mint oils or by *hydrogenation* (see entry) of certain essential oils.

Mineral Supplement. Tablet, capsule, or liquid that provides additional inorganic nutrients from sources outside the diet. Often used to augment the diet in combination with vitamins.

Miotic. Drug that constricts (narrows) the pupils.

Mucolytic. Drug that thins and breaks up mucus secretions in the air passages.

Mucus. Clear, thick secretion from, for example, the lining of the oral cavity, airways, digestive tract, or vagina.

Mydriatic. Drug that dilates (widens) the pupils.

Nasal Decongestant Spray. Medicine in spray form used to reduce nasal swelling and congestion and allow the user to breathe more easily.

Natural Cosmetics. See *Organic Cosmetics.*

Nonprescription Medicine. Medicine available over-the-counter without a doctor's prescription. See *Over-the-Counter (OTC) Medicine.*

Nonsedating. Not containing ingredients which may cause drowsiness.

Ointment. Semisolid preparation or salve, applied externally, usually containing a drug.

Ophthalmic Products. Medicines for the eyes. Those available over-the-counter are used in treating minor ailments such as tear insufficiency, sties, or mild conjunctivitis.

Organic Cosmetics. Describes products made only from animal or vegetable product ingredients.

Otic Solution. Ear drops. Used to relieve minor ear discomfort by softening ear wax.

Over-the-Counter (OTC) Medicine. Medicine available without a doctor's prescription. Used for the temporary relief, prevention, or cure of self-recognizable conditions.

Persistent. To continue to exist past a usual, expected amount of time, as in a symptom such as pain.

pH. Scale of 1 to 14 used to measure acidity and alkalinity. Neutral (distilled water) is 7; greater than 7 is alkaline; less than 7 is acid.

Pharmacist. Person who dispenses prescription medicines and offers advice on the choice and use of nonprescription medicines.

Pharmacy. Drugstore. A retail store selling prescription and nonprescription medicines.

Photosensitivity. Condition which develops in connection with use of drug or cosmetic, causing skin sensitivity to sunlight. The result is rash, hyperpigmentation, and swelling.

Plaque. Buildup of a film of acid forming bacteria and material from saliva on the teeth. Believed to be a main cause of gingivitis (inflamed gums), the formation of tartar, and dental cavities.

Potency. Term referring to the relative strength of a drug.

Prescription Drug. Medicine available from a pharmacy only with a doctor's written order and instructions for use.

Primary Self-Care. Treatment of routine health disorders with home remedies or use of nonprescription medicines as directed in the labeling without professional supervision or involvement.

Pupil. Part of the eye. The black, circular opening in the center of the iris (colored portion of the eye) through which light enters.

Rhinitis. Inflammation of the membranes lining the nose. Usually occurs as a result of a cold or allergy.

Rx. Symbol for prescription, the order of a physician for medication, including name of person for whom the medication is intended and dosage instructions. Also refers to drugs available only by prescription.

Rx to Over-the-Counter. Describes the shift of prescription medicines by the Food and Drug Administration (FDA) from prescription to over-the-counter (nonprescription) status.

Safety-Coated. Describes a tablet with a smooth coating which helps the user to swallow the medication.

Saponin. Any of a number of natural glycosides (natural or synthetic compounds derived from sugars) that occur in plants such as soapwort and sarsaparilla. Characterized by their ability to foam in water, producing fine bubble lather.

Self-Medication. Self-care by the use of nonprescription medicines as directed by the labeling.

Sensitivity. Adverse reaction, usually allergic, to a drug.

Side Effect. Unintended, but sometimes not unexpected, effect on the body apart from the principal and intended action of the medication.

Sleep Aid. Agent that causes drowsiness and aids in falling asleep. Over-the-counter sleep aids are usually antihistamines.

Smelling Salts. Unusual-smelling preparation, such as ammonia.

Spasm. Sudden involuntary muscle contraction.

Sterile Dressing. Wound covering, treated to be free of bacteria.

Stimulant. Agent that increases the activity of a body part or system. Caffeine, for example, is a central nervous system stimulant.

Stimulant Laxative. Laxative that stimulates intestinal contractions as an aid in bowel movement.

Suppository. Form of medicine inserted into the vagina or rectum.

Systemic. Having a generalized effect; causing physical or chemical changes throughout the body.

Tablet. Solid form of medication taken orally.

Tamper-Resistant Packaging. Packaging designed to make it apparent to the user if someone tampered with the package after it was sealed in the factory.

Tartar. Hard deposit that forms on the teeth, especially near the gum line.

Topical. Used to describe the application of a drug directly to the external site on the body where it is intended to have its effect.

Toxic Reactions. Symptoms, sometimes severe, caused by a drug as the result of an overdose or adverse reaction.

United States Pharmacopeia (USP). Reference work containing monographs covering standards for the strength and purity of drug ingredients and directions for making medicinal preparations. *USP* is often used on nonprescription labels after the name of an ingredient to show that the ingredient meets specifications set forth in the *United States Pharmacopeia.*

Vasoconstrictor. Agent that causes a narrowing of the blood vessels. Cold, stress, nicotine, and certain drugs are vasoconstrictors.

Vitamin Supplement. Tablet, capsule, or liquid that provides essential organic nutrients from sources outside the body. Often used to augment the diet.

Vomiting Medication. Medication that prevents or helps to relieve vomiting. Called *antiemetic medication.* To induce vomiting, see *Emetic.*

Yeast Infection Medication. Medication used to treat an infection caused by a yeast organism affecting the vagina, skin, or mouth, causing itching, peeling, or discharge.

Sources:
Newman, Jennifer, "Homeopathy, Diluted or Deluded?" *American Health,* Vol. 11, No. 3 (April 1992): 47.
Nonprescription Medicines: A Consumer's Dictionary of Terms, New York: Council on Family Health, 1992.
Winter, Ruth, *A Consumer's Dictionary of Cosmetic Ingredients,* New York: Crown Publishers, Inc., 1989.

Shampoo

The skin's glands secret an oily substance called sebum. The sebum coats the shaft of the hair and, due to its oily nature, attracts dirt and dead skin cells. The more dirt and dead skin cells that build up on the hair, the dirtier the hair becomes. Shampoos contain *sufficants* (see entry) that surround and entrap the oil on the hair and enable it to be rinsed off with water.

Conditioner. Replaces the oils that the shampoo removes with other oils, emollients, and conditioning agents that are designed to make the hair more manageable after it has been shampooed.

For Dry Hair. May contain more additives that bring moisture to the hair and oils to lubricate the hair.

For Oily Hair. May contain less additional additives designed to add moisture or lubricants that add oil to the hair.

Hypoallergenic. Describing products from which most of the cosmetic ingredients known to be allergens have been removed to minimize chance of allergic reaction. The individual manufacturer decides the testing method used to determine the hypoallergenic quality of a product. Therefore, each manufacturer's use of *hypoallergenic* is unique and is not necessarily related to the use of the term by another manufacturer (even if the products are similar).

Moisturizing Formula for Dry, Color Treated, Permed, or Damaged Hair. The sufficants used in the formula may not be as powerful or harsh as those used in shampoos for normal hair. Also may contain additives that bring moisture to the hair and oils that lubricate the hair.

pH Adjusted. The acidity or alkalinity of the shampoo has been adjusted, usually to a range of pH 5 to 8.

Shampoo, Dandruff. Shampoos that contain dry skin dissolvers to remove flakes of dead scalp tissue.

Shampoo, Dry. Typically, a water-absorbent powder such as talc and a mild alkali additive to clean the hair without the addition of water.

Shampoo, Herbal. Shampoos containing *saponins,* a class of substances found in plants. Claimed to be effective in reducing scaliness of the scalp.

Sufficant. The active detergent that removes dirt and sebum, an oily substance that is secreted by the scalp.

Sources:
Nonprescription Medicines: A Consumer's Dictionary of Terms, New York: Council on Family Health, 1992.
"Shampoos and Conditioners," *Consumer Reports,* Vol. 57, No. 6 (June 1992): 395-397.
Winter, Ruth, *A Consumer's Dictionary of Cosmetic Ingredients,* New York: Crown Publishers, Inc., 1989.

Soap

A cleanser, usually a mixture of sodium salts of fatty acids (for bar soaps) or potassium (for liquid soaps).

Castile Soap. A fine, hard, mild soap, white, cream-colored, or green; it is named for the region of Spain where it originated and is made from olive oil and sodium hydroxide.

Hypoallergenic. Describing products from which most of the cosmetic ingredients known to be allergens have been removed to minimize chance of allergic reaction. The individual manufacturer decides the testing method used to determine the hypoallergenic quality of a product. Therefore, each manufacturer's use of *hypoallergenic* is unique and is not necessarily related to the use of the term by another manufacturer (even if the products are similar).

Neutral Soaps. Soaps that have a pH around 10, which is actually alkaline, when dissolved with water.

Non-Comedogenic. Means the soap will not clog pores and promote comedones (blackheads).

Pumice. An abrasive used in some soaps to help remove greasy dirt.

Softens the Skin. The soap may contain emollients (an agent that soothes or softens the skin) such as bath oil, moisturizing cream, lanolin, and vitamin E.

Sources:
Nonprescription Medicines: A Consumer's Dictionary of Terms, New York: Council on Family Health, 1992.
"Soaping Up," *Consumer Reports,* Vol. 55, No. 10 (October 1990): 644-647.

Sunglasses

Products are rated according to their ability to protect against ultraviolet rays. Ultraviolet A (UVA) rays are longer and are considered to be less harmful than ultraviolet B (UVB) rays. Both types are believed to cause cataracts, and UVB rays are believed to contribute to retina damage. The American National Standards Institute (ANSI) has established the following criteria for grading sunglasses. Sunglasses that follow the ANSI guidelines carry the ANSI symbol on their label.

Cosmetic. Blocks at least 70 percent of UVB rays and at least 20 percent of UVA rays. Considered adequate for nonharsh sunlight.

General Purpose. Blocks at least 95 percent of UVB rays and at least 60 percent UVA rays. Considered adequate for boating and hiking.

Special Purpose. Blocks at least 99 percent of UVB rays and at least 60 percent of UVA rays. Recommended for ski slopes and beaches.

FDA GUIDELINES

The U.S. Food and Drug Administration (FDA) defines a sunglass as a spectacle lens that protects the human eye from bright sunlight. The agency has proposed a revised voluntary standard for sunglasses. Summarized, the characteristics recommended by the FDA standard include:

UVB-Blocking. Sunglasses must block 99 percent of UVB. A UVB-blocking sunglass is adequate to protect the eyes in moderately bright sunlight, such as is found in low-altitude, urban areas in temperate to northern latitudes.

UV-Blocking. Blocks 99 percent of both UVA and UVB. A UV-blocking sunglass is adequate to protect human eyes in intensely bright sunlight, such as is found in low-elevation snow fields and non-equatorial beaches. Such sunglasses should block 60 to 90 percent of visible light to adequately reduce glare and increase visual comfort. Adequate traffic signal recognition should be provided by these sunglasses.

To be adequate to protect the eyes during prolonged daily use in extremely bright sunlight, such as is found in high-elevation snow fields and equatorial sand beaches, a UV-blocking sunglass should block 92 to 97 percent of visible light and have side-shields (or be goggles). Side shields are needed in extremely bright sunlight to prevent reflected UV and visible light from entering the eye.

Sources:
Brooks, Andrii, "Eyes Don't Need Sun," *New York Times*, May 25, 1991.
Pine, Devera, "Color Tips for a Hot Season," *FDA Consumer*, Vol. 26, No. 5 (June 1992): 20-25.

Sunscreens

It is the ultraviolet radiation from the sun that causes tanning by stimulating melanocyte cells in the skin to release melanin, which is the skin's darkening protective pigment. These ultraviolet rays are a combination of three types: UVA, UVB, and UVC. Currently, UVC rays are not considered a threat because they are absorbed by the ozone in the atmosphere before they reach the skin. However, the increasing deterioration of the ozone layer may make UVC rays a factor in sunscreens in the future. Both UVA and UVB types darken the skin, although UVB works more quickly and is most responsible for the burn that goes with tanning. With UVA, tanning and burning occur more slowly, but the rays penetrate more deeply. UVA is present in sunlight throughout the day, while the more intense and quicker burning UVB is mostly present at midday. The reddening effect of sunburn is the skin's response to exposure to excessive sunlight. To shield itself against further exposure, the skin releases its melanin. The less melanin available—that is, the fairer the complexion—the less protection that skin will have. Following is a listing of skin types and their reactions.

Type I. Always burns, never tans (Celtic).

Type II. Burns easily and tans minimally.

Type III. Burns moderately; tans gradually to light brown (average Caucasian).

Type IV. Burns minimally; tans well to moderately brown (olive skin).

Type V. Rarely burns; tans profusely to dark (brown skin).

Type VI. Never burns; deeply pigmented (black skin).

SPF FACTOR

The manufacturers of sun protection products use *Sun Protection Factor* (*SPF*) numbers to denote the relative protective qualities of sunscreens. Sunscreen numbers range from 2 to 15 (although some go higher) and appear in bold numerals on sunscreen packages. The higher the number, the greater the protection. SPF-15, for example, means that the user can spend 15 hours in the sun and absorb the same amount of tanning rays that would be absorbed in one hour without a sunscreen. SPF-2 means the user can spend two hours in the sun and absorb the rays that would be absorbed in an hour without a screen. The SPF number is developed under laboratory conditions; protection under actual sun exposure conditions is estimated to be 1-2 numbers lower than the package rating. SPF of 12 or more is recommended for adequate protection from aging and cancer causing effects of UV rays. The rating values together with some common sunscreen terminology include:

SPF 2 to 4. Minimal protection from sun burning; permits suntanning; recommended for people who rarely burn and tan easily and deeply.

SPF 4 to 6. Moderate protection from sun burning; permits some suntanning; recommended for people who tan well with minimal burning.

SPF 6 to 8. Extra protection from sun burning; permits limited suntanning; recommended for people who burn moderately and tan gradually.

SPF 8 to under 15. Maximal protection from sun burning; permits little or no suntanning; recommended for people who always burn easily and tan minimally.

SPF 15 or greater. Ultra-protection from sunburn, offers most protection; permits no suntanning; recommended for people who burn easily and never tan. Some sunscreens are available with values of 50 or more. However, higher SPF value sunscreens contain more active ingredients and therefore increase the possibility of an allergic reaction.

Waterproof. Must retain its SPF value after 80 minutes in water.

Water-Resistant. Must retain its SPF value after 40 minutes in water.

Sweatproof. Must retain its SPF value after 30 minutes of nonstop sweating.

Oil-Free or Gel. A type of sunscreen that is absorbed into the skin as opposed to sitting on top of the skin, thereby lessening the threat of an allergic reaction.

PABA. A chemical sunscreen that is an ingredient in many lotions. It has been found to cause an allergic reaction in up to 5 percent of the population. Many sunscreens are now advertised as "contains no PABA" or "PABA Free."

Chemical Sunscreens. Sunscreen ingredients that absorb UV rays.

Physical Sunblocks. Sunscreen ingredients that reflect the UV rays rather than absorb them. Micronized titanium dioxide is a commonly used physical sunblock.

The FDA is currently revising its sunscreen regulations. Anticipated changes include a ceiling of 30 on all SPF values and an increase in the lengths of time used to define waterproof, water-resistant, and sweatproof.

TAN ACCELERATOR LOTIONS

Lotions, creams, and powders that supposedly pre-release melanin—the skin's darkening protective pigment—in the skin and allow faster tanning if used a day or so before going out in the sun.

BRONZERS

Promoted as a way to get a tan without the sun. These products contain FDA-approved additives (such as dihydroxyacetone) that interact with protein on the skin's surface to produce a color when applied to the skin. Though bronzers can give the skin a golden color, they do not provide any protection against the sun. Also they can be difficult to apply; thus, the resulting "tan" may be uneven, and the chemicals in the bronzers may react differently on various areas of the body, producing a tan of many shades.

Sources:
Murray, Linda J., "The Ultimate Sunscreen Report," *Self,* July 1992: 120-125.
Pine, Devera, "Color Tips for a Hot Season," *FDA Consumer,* Vol. 26, No. 5 (June 1992): 20-25.
Thompson, Richard C., "Out of the Bronzed Age," *FDA Consumer,* Vol. 21, No. 5 (June 1987): 21-23.

Tampons

ABSORBENCY

The ability of a tampon to absorb menstrual fluids is measured in *fluid absorbed in grams.*

Absorbency Term	Ranges of Fluid Absorbed in Grams
Junior Absorbency	Under 6
Regular Absorbency	6 to 9
Super Absorbency	9 to 12
Super Plus Absorbency	12 to 15

Toxic Shock Syndrome (TSS). A rare but serious disease that can affect any person at any age. However, it occurs mainly in tampon users under 30—especially those 15 to 19 years old—during or just after a menstrual period. Scientists believe TSS requires the presence of *Staphylococcus aureus,* a bacterium that commonly exists on the skin and sometimes causes infections. *S. aureus* can be present in other body areas, including the vagina. Sometimes, certain strains of the bacterium give off a toxin (poison) that gets into the body, probably through the bloodstream. Tampons themselves have not been found to cause TSS, although the majority of reported TSS cases are among tampon users. Scientists are trying to learn what other factors are involved. A menstruating female's chance of getting TSS is about 1 to 17 in 100,000 each year.

Source:
U. S. Department of Health and Human Services, *Toxic Shock Syndrome and Tampons,* Washington: Government Printing Office, 1991.

Wigs and Hairpieces

Included in this entry are any kind or type of lady's wig, wiglet, fall, chignon, or other hairpiece and any kind or type of man's toupee or other hairpiece. Federal Trade Commission (FTC) guidelines state that the label for the product should disclose the composition of the hair (man-made hair, imitation hair, simulated hair, etc.) and the percentage of each type of hair fiber contained in the product. The label should also disclose if the hair has a foreign origin ("Human Hair from Europe," "Asian," "Oriental," etc.). Other guidelines also apply that are designed to give the consumer an accurate understanding of the quality of the product.

Custom-made. Terms like "Custom-made," "Customized," or "Personalized" indicate that the product is designed and structured on the basis of actual personal measurements of the purchaser, and dyed or made of a mixture of precolored hair stock to match a color meeting the personal requirement of the purchaser.

Hair Composition. The type of hair fiber contained in the piece. It may consist of, or be a combination of, three basic types of fiber: human hair, animal hair, and artificial hair.

Hair, Natural Hair, Real Hair, etc. Indicates that the product is made of human hair and does not contain either animal hair or artificial hair.

Handmade. The entire process of joining or stitching the hair to the foundation is performed by hand.

Source:
Federal Trade Commission, "Guides for Labeling, Advertising, and Sale of Wigs and Other Hairpieces," 16 CFR Part 252 (1992), Washington: Government Printing Office.

Housewares & Appliances

Air Conditioners

Air conditioning units provide three functions: (1) they "condition" the air by removing dust and dirt as the air is drawn through a filter; (2) they lower humidity, making the air more comfortable; and (3) they cool the air.

TERMINOLOGY

Consumer Central Air Conditioner. A unit powered by a single phase electric current, which is rated below 65,000 BTUs per hour, and which is not contained within the same cabinet as a furnace whose rated capacity is above 225,000 BTUs per hour, and which is either a "heat pump" or a "cooling only" unit. (BTU stands for British Thermal Unit, a unit of energy measurement.) Basically, a unit designed to cool the whole house by tying into the existing ductwork.

Cooling Capacity. A room air conditioner's cooling capacity is the amount of heat and moisture that it transfers from the room to the outdoors. This capacity is expressed in BTUs (British Thermal Units) per hour (BTU/hr). A unit with a cooling capacity of 6,000 BTUs/hr would transfer 6,000 BTUs of heat every hour. The more heat the unit removes from a room in one hour, the higher its BTU/hr rating, and the greater its cooling capacity. Cooling capacities for current models range from 4,200 to 35,000 BTU/hr.

Energy Efficiency Rating (EER). Room air conditioner efficiency is expressed as EER, which is computed by dividing BTU/hr (British Thermal Units per hour, the cooling capacity) by the watts of power used. The higher the EER, the more energy efficient the air conditioner. E.g., a model under 6,000 BTU/hr with a 10.0 EER will use 20 percent less energy than the same capacity model with an 8.0 EER. Bright yellow EnergyGuide labels (see *Energy Efficiency Labeling*) are affixed to all room air conditioners. This label shows the model's EER, which is measured according to test procedures prescribed by the Federal Trade Commission (FTC). The label also shows the unit's cooling capacity and how the unit compares in efficiency to other models of similar capacity.

Room Air Conditioner. An encased assembly designed as a unit for mounting in a window or through the wall. Its purpose is to deliver conditioned air to a room. It includes a prime source of refrigeration and may include a means for ventilating and/or heating.

Seasonal Energy Efficiency Ratio (SEER). Central air conditioners are rated on their average efficiency over the entire cooling season. The higher the SEER the more efficient the system. E.g., a system rated 8 uses 25 percent less energy than a system rated 6. A SEER of 12 or more is excellent.

Sources:

Federal Trade Commission, "Cooling Performance and Cost for Central Air Conditioners," 16 CFR Part 305 (1992), Washington: Government Printing Office.

Federal Trade Commission, "Room Air Conditioners," 16 CFR Part 305 (1992), Washington: Government Printing Office.

1990 Consumer Selection Guide for Room Air Conditioners, Chicago: Association of Home Appliance Manufacturers.

"What to Know About Air-Conditioners," *Consumers' Research Magazine,* Vol. 74, No. 6 (June 1991): 20-23.

Baby Cribs

Full-Size. A bed for infants with interior dimensions of approximately 28 by 52 inches. Crib construction (spacing of spindles, height of guardrails, etc.) is governed by regulations issued by the U.S. Consumer Products Safety Commission (CPSC).

Non-Full-Size Crib. Either smaller or larger than a full-size crib.

Portable Crib. A non-full-size baby crib. The legs may be removed or adjusted to provide a play pen or play yard for a child.

Specialty Crib. An unconventionally shaped (circular, hexagonal, etc.) non-full-size baby crib incorporating a special mattress or other unconventional components.

Undersize Crib. A non-full-size baby crib with an interior length dimension smaller than about 50 inches or an interior width smaller than about 26 inches, or both.

Oversize Crib. A non-full-size baby crib with an interior length dimension greater than 55 inches or an interior width dimension greater than about 31 inches, or both.

Source:

Consumer Product Safety Commission, "Requirements For Full-Size Baby Cribs," 16 CFR Part 1508 (1992), Washington: Government Printing Office.

Consumer Product Safety Commission, "Requirements for Non-Full-Size Baby Cribs," 16 CFR Part 1509 (1992), Washington: Government Printing Office.

Bedding Materials

Many states regulate the manufacture, repair, and renovation of all mattresses, pillows, bolsters, feather beds, comforters, all types of upholstered furniture, and other filled bedding. The information in this entry comes from the bedding and upholstery law and regulations of the Commonwealth of Pennsylvania. Their laws are typical of those currently in force within the United States. Typically, all feathers, down, wool, hair, and shoddy are required to be sterilized and disinfected before being used as filling material. Likewise, all secondhand mattresses, pillows, bolsters, feather beds, comfortables, cushions, and upholstered furniture must be sterilized and disinfected before being resold. The filling material of secondhand articles can not again be used as filling material until after it has been sterilized. All secondhand filling material used in making or renovating upholstered furniture must be sterilized and disinfected before being used. The type of filling material used in the bedding (e.g., goose down, chicken feather, new curled horse tail hair, etc.) must be disclosed on a label that is attached to the bedding. Examples of tags used in Pennsylvania follow.

TERMINOLOGY USED IN PENNSYLVANIA REGULATIONS

Acetate Fibers or Cellulose Acetate. Manmade fibers, monofilaments, and continuous filament yarns composed of acetylated cellulose with or without lesser amounts of nonfiber forming material.

Acrylic Fibers or Polyacrylic Fibers. Manmade fibers made from any long chain polymers or copolymers which contain 85 percent or more of acrylonitrile and which are formed into a filament.

Arolac, Azlon, or Casein Protein Base Fibers. Manmade fibers and filaments made from modified proteins or derivatives of such proteins with or without lesser amounts of nonfiber forming material. The term azlon shall be used for labeling purposes

UNDER PENALTY OF LAW
THIS TAG MAY NOT BE REMOVED
EXCEPT BY THE CONSUMER

ALL NEW MATERIAL
CONSISTING OF

REG. NO. PA —	PER. NO.
	Certification is made by the manufacturer that the materials in this article are described in accordance with law.
	CONTENTS STERILIZED

A white tag is used for new bulk filling materials required to be sterilized, such as material derived from animal or fowl and for articles containing such types of materials.

UNDER PENALTY OF LAW
THIS TAG MAY NOT BE REMOVED
EXCEPT BY THE CONSUMER

ALL NEW MATERIAL
CONSISTING OF

REG. NO. PA —	
	Certification is made by the manufacturer that the materials in this article are described in accordance with law.

A white tag for new bulk filling materials not required to be sterilized, such as vegetable fibers, rubber synthetic fibers, and articles containing these types of materials.

UNDER PENALTY OF LAW
THIS TAG MAY NOT BE REMOVED
EXCEPT BY THE CONSUMER

ALL SECONDHAND MATERIAL

REG. NO. PA —   PER. NO. PA —

| | **CONTENTS DISINFECTED** |
| | Certification is made that the materials in this article are described in accordance with law. |

A yellow tag for articles of secondhand nature and secondhand bulk filling materials.

UNDER PENALTY OF LAW
THIS TAG MAY NOT BE REMOVED
EXCEPT BY THE OWNER

This is A RENOVATED Article and Contains the Same Material Received From the Owner to Which Has Been Added:

REG. NO. PA —   PER. NO. PA —

| | **CONTENTS DISINFECTED** |
| | This article must not be sold, it is the property of and must be returned to: |

OWNER _____

ADDRESS _____

A yellow tag for renovated articles to be returned to the owner.

UNDER PENALTY OF LAW
THIS TAG MAY NOT BE REMOVED
EXCEPT BY THE LESSEE

This is a RENTAL Article and contains the same material received from the manufacturer and has been disinfected as required by law.

REG. NO. PA —   PER. NO. PA —

| | **CONTENTS DISINFECTED** |
| | This article must not be sold, it is the property of and must be returned to: |

A yellow tag for articles to be leased.

regardless of the source of the protein.

Bulk Filling Materials. Bulk materials intended for use in mattresses, pillows, bolsters, feather beds, and other filled bedding of any description. The term applied to cushions and all types of upholstered furniture, except cotton rolls, shredded synthetic foam, and other filling materials which are sold at retail to be used and consumed in the home of the purchaser for his personal use.

Cardboard, Fiberboard, or Corrugated Cardboard. Sheets of material composed of paper, wood pulp, or other materials with or without resin bonding and labeled with their appropriate name.

Cattail Plant Fibers. The fibers from the cattail plant, *Apacynaceae typhaceae*. The material shall be labeled cattail fibers.

Cellulose Fiber. The fibers obtained from wood pulp and compressed into pads. The label designation shall be cellulose fiber pad.

Cemented Shredded Latex Foam Rubber. Shredded latex foam rubber which has been cemented together.

Cemented Shredded Sponge Rubber. Shredded sponge rubber which has been cemented together.

Cemented Shredded Synthetic Foam. Shredded synthetic foam which has been cemented together.

Coconut Husk Fiber or Coconut Coir. The fibrous material obtained from the husks or outer shell of the coconut. Either term may be used on the tag.

Colored. A material which has been artificially dyed or colored.

Comforter. Any cover, quilt, or quilted article made of any material and stuffed or filled with any of the filling materials defined in this section.

Cotton. This term shall not be used by itself.

Cotton Felt or Blend Cotton Felt. Felt made from staple cotton, cotton linters, cotton wastes, or mixtures of any of those. The label designation shall be cotton felt or blended cotton felt.

Cotton Linters. The fibrous growth removed from the cotton seed subsequent to the process of ginning. The term cotton linters may be used on the tab but the term linters alone shall not be used.

Cotton Waste. Cotton material recovered from various machine operations used in the manufacture of cotton yarn other than cotton itself. When unfelted, this material shall be designated on the tag as cotton waste.

Creped Cellulose Fiber. The material formed of layers of composed and creped cellulose fiber.

Crushed Feathers. Feathers which have been processed by a curling, crushing, or chopping machine which has changed the original form of the feathers without removing the quill. The term also includes all of the material components resulting from such processing. Such material or percentage thereof shall be designated on the label as "crushed" and shall be followed by the designation of "waterfowl feathers," "goose feathers," "duck feathers," "chicken feathers," "turkey feathers," and so forth. When the species of the crushed waterfowl feathers or crushed landfowl feathers or a percentage thereof is designated on the label, a minimum of 80 percent of the crushed waterfowl feathers or crushed landfowl feathers or a percentage thereof so designated must be of that species.

Curled Hair. This term shall apply when any hair has been put through a curling process. The appropriate designation as to origin shall appear on the label along with this term.

Cushion. Any bag or case, transparent or opaque, and stuffed or filled with any of the materials defined in this section, to be used for resting, reclining, or sleeping purposes. This term includes any preformed article made of materials defined in this section and used for reclining, resting, or sitting purposes.

Disinfection. The direct application of chemical or physical means to kill pathogenic agents.

Down. The soft undercoat of waterfowl consisting of the light fluffy filament growing from one quill point but without any quill shaft. The species of the down or a percentage thereof may be designated on the label. When the species of the down or a percentage thereof is designated on the label, a minimum of 80 percent of the down or percentage thereof so designated must be of that species. An article labeled down or a percentage thereof shall contain a minimum of 80 percent of down, plumules and down fiber so designated.

Excelsior. The fine shredded thread or ribbon-like fiber of wood. This term does not include waste products such as sawdust, shavings, or similar materials. The term wood wool is prohibited and the label designation shall be excelsior.

Feather Fiber. The detached barbs of feathers which are not joined or attached to each other.

Feathers. The terms "waterfowl feathers," "landfowl feathers," "goose feathers," "duck feathers," "chicken feathers," "turkey feathers," and so forth shall mean the feathers of the desig-

nated fowl which are whole in physical structure with the natural form and curvature originally found in the feathers. The species of the waterfowl feathers or percentage thereof, goose or duck, may be designated on the label. The species of the landfowl feathers or percentage thereof, chicken or turkey, shall be designated on the label. When the species of the waterfowl or landfowl feathers or percentage thereof is designated on the label, a minimum of 80 percent of the waterfowl feathers or landfowl feathers or a percentage or down mixtures shall be represented to contain a certain percentage of feathers, crushed feathers, or down unless it in fact contains the stated percentage with due regard to the tolerances set forth in the definitions of down, feathers, and crushed feathers.

Felt. Any material which has been carded into layers or sheets by a garnetting or felting machine. This term shall not be used by itself but in conjunction with the name of the materials from which it is made. This term does not include felt scraps or repicked felt.

Felted Mixtures. Felt made from other than reprocessed fibers and containing the name and percentage of the fibers present, or made from reprocessed fibers containing the names and percentages of fibers present and labeled as felt made from reprocessed fibers. A tolerance of 10 percent shall be allowed.

Foam. A polymerized material consisting of a mass of thin-walled cells produced chemically or physically. This term shall be placed on the tag along with the name of the organic base from which it is made.

Garnetted Clippings. Any new material which has been made into fabric and subsequently cut up, torn up, broken up, or ground up and which has been run through a garnetting machine and processed to a fibrous state so as to contain not more than 10 percent yarn or 2 percent fabric. The label designation shall be garnetted clippings.

Glass Fiber. Fibers made of spun glass. This term shall appear on the tag.

Hair. The coarse, filamentous, epidermal outgrowth of such animals as horses, cattle, hogs, and goats. This term shall not be used by itself but in conjunction with its particular source as follows:

Body Hair. The short soft hair removed from the bodies of animals.

Goat Hair. The hair from any species.

Hog Hair. The bristles and body hair of swine.

Horse Hair. The hair of the manes or tails of horses.

Hair and Fiber Blends. The use of filling material of any origin in a mixture with hair. The kind and percentage by weight of each component of the mixture shall be designated on the label, and a tolerance of 10 percent shall be allowed.

Hair Blends. The use of two different origins of hair in a blend or mixture. The kind and percentage by weight of each shall be stated on the label, and a tolerance of 10 percent shall be allowed.

Hair Pad. Hair which is interwoven or punched on burlap or any other woven material or otherwise fabricated into a pad. Percentages of component materials shall reflect the hair and fiber content only.

Hay. Grass, properly cured, dried, and free from dust, dirt, burrs, sticks, or other objectionable material. This term shall be designated on the tag.

Jute. The fiber obtained from various species of corchorus plants.

Jute Pad. A pad made of jute fibers.

Jute Waste. The by-product of rope or cordage, reclaimed rope ends, or other fabricated material which have not previously been used for bailing or other purposes.

Kapok. The fibrous growth contained in the pod of the Kapok tree, *Ceiba pentenda*. This term shall be designated on the tag, and the use of the term silk floss is prohibited.

Latex Foam Rubber. Natural or synthetic rubber latex which has been converted from a liquid state to a stable foamy mass and molded or otherwise assembled into suitable shapes for commercial use.

Mattress. Any quilted pad, mattress, mattress pad, crib pad, mattress protector, bunk quilt, or box spring stuffed or filled with any of the filling materials defined in this section, to be used on a couch or other bed for sleeping or reclining purposes.

Milkweed. The fibrous growth attached to the seed within the pod of the milkweed plant, *Asclepias*.

Moss. The material derived from the epiphyte *Tillandsia useoides*.

New. Any material which has not been previously used for any purpose including by-products produced in the manufacture of new textile materials or fabrics and material reclaimed from new fabrics.

Nylon Fibers. Manmade fibers made from any long synthetic polymeric amide which has recurring amide groups as an integral part of the main polymer chain and which is formed into a filament. This term or the term polymide fiber may be used on the tag.

Palm Fiber. The fibrous material obtained from the leaf of the palm, palmetto, or palmyra tree.

Person. Persons, partnerships, companies, corporations, or associations.

Pillow, Bolster, Feather Bed, or Sleeping Bags. Any bag, case, or covering made of any material, transparent or opaque, and stuffed or filled with any of the filling materials defined in this section, to be used on a bed, couch, divan, sofa, lounge, or other article of furniture for sleeping or reclining purposes.

Polyester Fibers. Manmade fibers made from a long chain synthetic polymer which contains 85 percent or more of the polymeric ester produced from the reaction of terephthalic acid and ethylene glycol or other dihydric alcohols and dicarboxylic acids or produced from hydroxy acids and which is formed into a filament. This term shall be used on the tag.

Polyethylene Fibers. Manmade fibers made from long chain polymers of ethylene and made into a filament. This term shall be used on the tag.

Polyurethane Fibers. Manmade fibers made from the copolymerization of diisocyanates and alcohols of diisocyanates and polyesters and formed into filaments. This term shall be used on the tag.

Polyvinyl Fibers. Manmade fibers made from copolymerization of vinyl chloride and vinyl acetate, vinyl chloride, and acrylonitrile, after chlorinated polyvinyl chloride, and copolymers of vinylidene chloride and other monomers, and made into filaments. This term shall be used on the tag.

Quill Feathers. The wing and tail feathers of any fowl. This term shall be designated on the tag.

Rayon. Manmade fibers, monofilaments, and continuous filament yarns composed of regenerated cellulose, with or without lesser amounts of nonfiber-forming materials. The terms cellulose or rayon fibers may be used on the tag.

Redwood Bark Fibers. The fibers obtained from the bark of the California redwood tree, *Sequoia sempervirens*.

Reprocessed Fibers. Fibers reclaimed from any spun, knitted, or woven product which is new. This term applies equally to fibers reclaimed from garnetted clippings, yarns, or nappers. The names of the reprocessed fibers shall be set forth on the tag and the percentages of each given if more than one fiber is present.

Reprocessed Jute. Jute fibers reclaimed from unused fabric, cordage, or other similar material. This term shall be designated on the tag.

Resin Treated Cotton Felt. Cotton impregnated with vinyl or other resins.

Rubberized Hair or Rubberized Curled Hair. Any hair treated with natural or synthetic latex. When hair is rubberized, the label designation shall be rubberized hair, or if curled, rubberized curled hair, with the appropriate designation indicating its origin.

Rubberized Hair Pieces. Trimmings and pieces of rubberized hair of indefinite size. The material shall be designated on the label as rubberized hair pieces or rubberized curled hair pieces, whichever term is applicable. When shredded, this material shall be labeled shredded rubberized hair. The term curled shall not be used.

Sea Grass. Any material obtained from maritime plants or seaweeds. This term shall appear on the tag.

Secondhand. Any materials previously used for any purpose. Manufacturing process shall not constitute prior use.

Shredded Clippings. Any new fabric made from new materials which has been subsequently cut up, ground up, torn up, or broken up and which contains more than 10 percent yarn or 2 percent fabric. This term shall be designated on the label.

Shredded Latex Foam Rubber. Latex foam rubber which has been subjected to a shredding process.

Shredded Sponge Rubber. Sponge rubber which has been subjected to a shredding process.

Shredded Synthetic Foam. Synthetic foams which have been subjected to a shredding process.

Shoddy. Any material made from secondhand rags, clothing, yarn, fabric, clippings, or nappings by a process of grinding, tearing, or breaking up. This material shall be sterilized. A yellow label shall be used with this designation on all secondhand material consisting of shoddy.

Silk Waste. The by-products recovered from various machine operations necessary in the manufacture of threads of natural silk. This term shall appear on the tag.

Sisal. The fiber obtained from the agave plant. This term applies only to new material. If the material is made of waste or reclaimed fibers, the term, "reprocessed sisal fibers" is used on the tag.

Sisal Shoddy. Reclaimed used cordage or other sisal material which has been fabricated and used for baling or other purposes and which shall be sterilized before use.

Sponge Rubber. Natural or synthetic solid rubber expanded into a cellular foam and molded or otherwise assembled into suitable shapes for commercial use.

Staple Cotton. The fibrous growth removed from the cotton seed by ginning. This term may be used on the tab.

Starch Fibers. Fibers made from long chains of amylose acetate units or regenerated amylose. This term shall be used on the tag.

Steel Wool. Fibrous material made from very fine steel wire. Either this term or the term steel fiber may appear on the tag.

Sterilization. Any process which destroys bacteria—micro-organisms—not necessarily bacterial spores.

Straw. The stalk or stem of grain such as wheat, rye, oats, rice, and the like after threshing. This term shall be designated on the tag. The kind of straw need not be designated but, if so indicated, shall be a true statement. The straw shall be free from chaff, beards, bristles, husks, glumes, dirt, or other extraneous matter.

Stripped Feathers. The barbs of feathers stripped by any process from the quill shaft but not separated into feather fiber.

Synthetic Fibers. Any other synthetic fiber not defined in this section.

Synthetic Foam. Material made or synthetic products other than synthetic rubber and produced in a resilient foam-like state. This term shall not be used by itself. The label designation shall include terms describing the recurring units or groups of the polymerized product. E.g., the foam derived from polyesters and diiocyanate shall be termed polyurethane foam.

Tampico Tula. The fibers from the leaves of plants such as *Agave iophantha* or *Hesperaloe funifera*. The term *tampico* shall be used on the tag, and if curled, the term *curled tampico* may be used.

Tanners Wool. The growth of wool removed from tanned sheep skins. This term shall be designated on the tag and classed as a new material.

Tow. The fibrous coarse straw-like part of a plant recovered as a by-product in securing commercial fibers and shall be further designated by the plant origin.

Upholstered Furniture. Any article of furniture stuffed or filled with any of the filling materials defined in this section, to be used for sitting, resting, or reclining purposes.

Wood Fiber. Wood comminuted or reduced to a splintered or fragment piece of finer texture than excelsior.

Wool Blend. The by-products recovered from the various machine operations necessary in the manufacture of wool yarn or the by-product of the tanned sheep hide industry, except tanners' wool. This term includes wool noils and may be used on the tag.

Wool or Virgin Wool. Fleece of sheep or lamb scoured or scoured and carbonized and free from kemp and vegetable matter. This term shall not apply to the by-product of any process of manufacture or sustained prior use. Either term may be used on the tag.

Source:
Bedding and Upholstery Law Act No. 249, May 27, 1937, as Amended May 22, 1953 and August 23, 1961, Commonwealth of Pennsylvania, Department of Labor and Industry, Bureau of Occupational and Industrial Safety.

Carpet

Broadloom. A method by which carpet is produced: on continuous rolls with no seams.

Fibers. The material of which the carpet is made. Natural fibers include wool and cotton. Man-made fibers include nylon, polyester, acrylic, and olefin. Nylon is the most frequently used carpet fiber.

Seconds. Carpets that have an imperfection.

Soil or Stain Resistant or Retardant. The fibers of the carpet have a protective coating to resist soil and stains.

Source:
"Buying Wall-to-Wall Home Carpeting," *Consumers' Research Magazine,* Vol. 75, No. 3 (March 1992): 26.

Carpet Cushion

Bonded Foam. Bonded foam cushions are made by combining shredded pieces of urethane through a fusion process into a single sheet of material. Bonded foam grades are also measured by density.

Fiber. There are three basic types of fiber carpet cushion: natural fiber (such as animal hair and jute), synthetic carpet fiber (like nylon, polypropy!ene, and polyester), and resinated recycled textile fiber (synthetic fibers recycled from textile manufacturing processes). The grade of fiber cushion is determined by its weight in ounces per square yard. Fiber cushions tend to have a firm "walk" or "feel."

Mechanically Frothed Urethane Foam. Frothed urethane foam cushions are made from a process originally developed to apply cushioned backings to carpet. The urethane foam cushioning is applied to a sheet of nonwoven material, forming a carpet cushion product with a typically higher density and firmer feel.

Prime Urethane Foam. There are three types of prime urethane carpet cushion: conventional prime, grafted prime, and densified prime cushion. Conventional prime and grafted prime urethane cushion are manufactured by a chemical mixing reaction process. There are many types of prime urethane available today with a variety of density and firmness. The best products are those which combine the right balance of properties for comfort and durability. In densified prime, the chemical structure is modified during the manufacturing process to produce a product with specific performance characteristics. Grades of densified prime urethane are determined by the foam density (weight of the material per cubic foot).

Sponge Rubber. There are two specific types of sponge rubber carpet cushion: flat sponge (smooth or flat surface) and rippled sponge (rippled or waffled surface). Flat sponge offers a firm feel; rippled sponge is softer. Grades are measured by weight in ounces per square yard.

TYPES

Class 1. Light and moderate traffic (such as living rooms, dining rooms, bedrooms, recreational rooms, and corridors).

Class 2. Heavy duty traffic (for heavy traffic use at all levels, specifically for public areas such as lobbies and corridors in multi-family facilities). Also recommended for stairs and hallways. Class 2 cushion may be used in Class 1 applications.

Source:
The Supporting Facts About Carpet Cushion, Riverside, CT: Carpet Cushion Council, 1991.

Certification Seals, Appliances

The Association of Home Appliance Manufacturers (AHAM) has certification programs for the following types of products:

Refrigerators and Freezers
Room Air Conditioners
Dehumidifiers
Humidifiers
Room Air Cleaners

Products that meet the certification standards of AHAM may display the AHAM seal. The AHAM certification seal is the consumer's assurance that the performance factors stated on the seal are determined and accurately stated in accordance with the applicable American National Standard. Representative examples of AHAM seals appear below:

Source:
Mackay, Alane, letter to editors, Alexandria: Virginia: Association of Home Appliance Manufacturers, 1992.

Child Resistant

Packaging designed to make it difficult for children under the age of five to obtain the substance inside within a reasonable time. It does not mean packaging which all such children cannot open within a reasonable time.

Source:
Annual ASTM Book of Standards, Designation D3475-88, Philadelphia: ASTM.
Consumer Products Safety Commission, 16 CFR section 1700.01 (1992), Washington: Government Printing Office.

Cleaners

All-Purpose Cleaners. A cleaner designed and promoted as appropriate for a wide variety of cleaning chores—cars, counter tops, tile, pans, stoves, etc. Distinguished from cleaners that are tailored for specific jobs like floor cleaners or toilet-bowl cleaners.

Source:
"All-Purpose Cleaners," *Consumer Reports,* Vol. 53, No. 8 (August 1988): 519.

Coffee Makers, Electric

Cup Capacity Rating. The cup capacity rating represents the number of 5 ounce poured cups of beverage which can be brewed with the vessel filled to the maximum cup mark applied by the manufacturer.

Source:
ANSI/AHAM CM-1-1986, Chicago: Association of Home Appliance Manufacturers, 1986.

Cookware

Cookware is made from a variety of materials. Choice of cookware is dependent on the particular needs of the user.

Aluminum. Aluminum cookware accounts for over half of all cookware sold today, mainly because aluminum is an excellent heat conductor. Heat spreads quickly and evenly across the bottom, up the sides, and across the cover to completely surround the food. Most aluminum pots and pans are coated with nonstick finishes or treated using a process that alters and hardens the structure of the metal. Aluminum cookware was linked by some doctors to Alzheimer's disease, but after reviewing existing data, the FDA formally announced in May 1986 that the agency "has no information at this time that the normal dietary intake of aluminum, whether from naturally occurring levels in food, the use of aluminum cookware, or from aluminum food additives or drugs, is harmful." Aluminum cookware is graded by "gauge," the thickness of the metal. Gauge is described by a number. For example, an 8-gauge aluminum is 0.125 inch thick. A 20-gauge aluminum is 0.032 inch thick. Accordingly, the smaller then gauge number, the thicker the aluminum.

Anodized Aluminum. Anodization involves a series of electrochemical baths that thicken the oxide film that forms naturally on aluminum. This supplemental coating hardens the metal, making it more scratch resistant. Also, food does not stick easily to the surface, making the pans easier to clean. Anodized aluminum cookware does not react to acidic foods.

Cast Iron. Cast iron is strong, inexpensive, and an even conductor of heat. Foods cooked in unglazed cast iron pans may contain twice the amount of iron as they would otherwise. This iron is an important nutrient.

Ceramic and Enameled. Cast iron is often finished with porcelain enamel, a highly durable glass that is stain and scratch resistant. It also does not pick up food odors.

Copper. Copper is an excellent conductor of heat and, therefore, is especially good for top-of-the range cooking. However, copper cookware is usually lined with tin or stainless steel. The U.S. Food and Drug Administration (FDA) cautions against using unlined copper for general cooking because the metal is relatively easily dissolved by some foods with which it comes in contact and, in sufficient quantities, can cause nausea, vomiting, and diarrhea.

Heat-Resistant Glass. Cookware made of this type of material has an inert nonporous surface that won't absorb food odors or flavors. For easy cleaning, both glass and ceramic ovenware are available with nonstick interiors. It may be made of clear or tinted transparent material or opaque white (commonly called "opal" glass).

Non-Stick Coatings. These coatings are made from a tough, nonporous material called perfluorocarbon resin. This material is a stable, noncorrosive plastic that offers a non-stick cooking surface. The trademarked material Teflon is an example of such a coating. Silverstone and Excalibur nonstick coatings, which are made of three layers of the same plastic used on Teflon, is extremely durable.

Stainless Steel. Stainless steel cookware accounts for 43 percent of the cookware sold. It is very durable and will not corrode or tarnish permanently. It has a hard, tough, nonporous surface that is resistant to wear. Unlike aluminum, stainless steel does not conduct heat evenly. Therefore, most stainless steel cookware is made with copper or aluminum bottoms. Manufacturers caution against allowing acidic or salty foods to remain in stainless steel for long periods. Although there are no known health hazards from leaching of the metal, undissolved salt will pit steel surfaces.

Source:
Blumenthal, Dale, "Is That Newfangled Cookware Safe?" *FDA Consumer*, October 1990: Washington, U.S. Food and Drug Administration.
"A Tour of Cookware Materials," *Consumers Research Magazine*, Vol. 72, No. 4: 32-36.

Curtains and Draperies, Glass Fibers

CARE LABELING

Most glass fibers currently used in weaving fabrics for producing curtains and draperies become increasingly brittle with enlargement of the denier of the fibers. When these fabrics are handled, as by washing, sewing, or hanging, minute glass particles may break off and become lodged in the exposed skin of the individuals handling them. Likewise, when certain articles, such as garments or bed sheets, are washed with glass fiber curtain or drapery fabrics or washed in a container previously used for washing such fabrics, minute glass particles may become embedded in such articles and transmitted to the exposed skin of the user or wearer. In either case, skin irritation may result. Therefore, these products are labeled with the warning that skin irritation may result to the exposed skin of the person handling glass fiber products and from body contact with clothing or other articles, such as bed sheets, which have been washed (1) with glass fiber products or (2) in a container previously used to wash glass fiber products, unless the container has been cleaned of all fibers.

Source:
Consumer Products Safety Commission, 16 CFR Sections 413.1 to 413.6 (1992), Washington: Government Printing Office.

DEHUMIDIFICATION REQUIRED IN PINTS PER 24 HOURS

Condition Without Dehumidification During Warm and Humid Outdoor Conditions.	Area—Sq.Ft.				
	500	1,000	1,500	2,000	2,500
Moderately damp—space feels damp and has musty odor only in humid weather.	10	14	18	22	26
Very damp—space always feels damp and has musty odor. Damp spots show on walls and floor.	12	17	22	27	32
Wet—space feels and smells wet. Walls or floor sweat, or seepage is present.	14	20	26	32	38
Extremely wet—Laundry drying, wet floor, high load conditions.	16	23	30	37	44

Dehumidifiers

Capacity. A measure of the ability of a dehumidifier to remove moisture from its surrounding atmosphere. The capacity of a dehumidifier is the amount of water, stated in pints, collected per 24 hours of continuous operation under controlled test conditions. Values in the table below indicate dehumidification capacity required (in pints per 24 hours) based on the area of the space to be dehumidified and the conditions that would exist in that space when a dehumidifier is not in use.

Dehumidification variables also include such other factors as climate, laundry equipment, number of family members, number of doors and windows, and degree and intensity of area activity.

Source:
ANSI/AHAM DH-1-1980, Chicago: Association of Home Appliance Manufacturers, 1988.

Dinnerware

Bone China. Vitrified china that differs because bone ash, or its commercial equivalent, is used in its basic mixture. The bone ash gives the china a characteristic whiteness. Bone china was first made in England in the mid 1800s by the addition of ox bone ash.

Earthenware. Also called pottery, made of ordinary clays and generally fired at lower temperatures. Earthenware chips easily leaving the clay exposed, which is unsightly and can be harmful by harboring bacteria. It is generally thick, opaque, and porous because it is not vitrified. Made from clays that cannot withstand the extreme heat that helps produce the translucency of fine china.

Fine China. Sometimes incorrectly called porcelain. Ware that is translucent and vitrified. A fine china plate gives off a bell-like ring when struck with a pencil.

Ironstone. A heavy earthenware.

Porcelain. Refers to fine dinnerware and also to decorative accessories. Differs from china primarily in the manufacturing process. In most respects, they are alike.

Stoneware. Harder than semivitreous ware. Nonporous it does not have the translucence of china or the strength.

Super Ceramics. A unique combination of contemporary designs on an advanced ceramic body with a lustrous glaze. Chinastone combines the beauty of fine china with the strength of stoneware. Microwave and dishwasher safe.

Vitrified China. Nonporous. Fine china fired at extremely high temperatures. It is far stronger, thinner, and more translucent than ware fired at lower temperatures and for shorter periods of time.

TERMINOLOGY

Belleek. An ivory-colored porcelain with an iridescent glaze produced only in Belleek, Ireland.

Bisque or Biscuit Ware. The "body" of the ware after the first firing—before glazing. Word origin said to had been derived from its similarity in appearance to a sailor's sea biscuit.

Buffet/Place Setting. Consists of a dinner plate, teacup, and saucer.

Causal China. Durable and versatile china for frequent use. Typically microwaveable and dishwasher safe.

Ceramic. A term that has come to mean any molded and fired clay ware.

Complete Place Setting. A 5-piece setting that consists of a teacup, a saucer, and dinner, salad/dessert, and butter plates. Ideal for all entertaining needs.

Crazing. Minute cracks in the glaze. Caused by differences in the rates of expansion and contraction between body and glaze.

Firing. Refers to a point when the ceramic ware goes into the kiln. Firing can take place at temperatures over 2200 degrees F. Firing at high temperatures helps to give ceramic ware strength and high translucence.

Five-piece Serving Set. Consists of a 16 inch oval platter, a large open vegetable bowl, a cream pitcher and a covered sugar bowl.

Glaze. A glass-like coating that is fired onto the ware, producing a glossy surface. A dinnerware glaze should be lustrous and free from bubbles and other imperfections.

Hand-Enameled. Color applied to china that is hand-painted or hand-transferred.

Open Stock. Refers to the fact that individual pieces of a pattern may be purchased at any time and that they will be available to store customers as long as they are in production.

Overglaze. Decorations are applied on top of the glaze and fired into it. When properly fired, the ware can be safely used in a dishwasher with a mild detergent.

Pottery. Used to describe informal, decorative clay accessories or dinnerware. Frequently rustic in appearance, it chips easily and thus is rather limited in its uses.

Services for 4, 8, or 12. A 20-piece set for four consists of four 5-piece complete place settings; a 45-piece service for eight or a 65-piece service for 12 consists of two or three 20-piece sets, respectively, and a 5-piece serving set.

Translucency. Light can pass through the ware. Held to the light, a translucent plate will clearly reveal the shape of a hand behind it.

Vitrify. To change into glass or a glasslike substance by fusion due to heat.

Washability. Refers to its ability to be washed safely in the dishwasher.

Source:
Glossary of Fine China and Crystal Terms, Lawrenceville, NJ: Lenox China, 1988.

Electric Blankets

Electromagnetic Field. Electromagnetic fields are a form of energy that radiates from electric blankets and many other household appliances as a consequence of alternating electri-

Federal Trade Commission

Dishwasher
Capacity: Standard

Pt. 305, App. K

(Name of Corporation)
Model(s) MR328, XL12, NA83

ENERGYGUIDE

Estimates on the scale are based
on a national average electric
rate of 4.97¢ per kilowatt hour
and a natural gas rate of
36.7¢ per therm.

Only standard size
dishwashers are used
in the scale.

Electric Water Heater

Model with
lowest
energy cost
$50

$60
THIS MODEL

Model with
highest
energy cost
$84

Gas Water Heater

Model with
lowest
energy cost
$19

$27
THIS MODEL

Model with
highest
energy cost
$42

Estimated yearly energy cost

Estimated yearly energy cost

Your cost will vary depending on your local energy rate and how you use the product. This energy cost is based on U.S. Government standard tests.

How much will this model cost you to run yearly?

with an electric water heater

Loads of dishes per week		2	4	6	8	12
Estimated yearly $ cost shown below						
Cost per kilowatt hour	2¢	$8	$15	$23	$31	$47
	4¢	$15	$31	$46	$62	$92
	6¢	$23	$46	$69	$92	$139
	8¢	$31	$62	$92	$123	$189
	10¢	$39	$77	$116	$154	$231
	12¢	$47	$92	$139	$185	$278

with a gas water heater

Loads of dishes per week		2	4	6	8	12
Estimated yearly $ cost shown below						
Cost per therm (100 cubic feet)	10¢	$2	$5	$7	$9	$14
	20¢	$5	$11	$16	$22	$33
	30¢	$7	$14	$21	$27	$41
	40¢	$9	$19	$28	$36	$55
	50¢	$12	$23	$35	$45	$68
	60¢	$19	$28	$42	$54	$82

Ask your salesperson or local utility for the energy rate (cost per kilowatt hour or therm) in your area, and for estimated costs if you have a propane or oil water heater.

Energy efficiency label.

cal current. Some consumers are concerned that this type of energy may increase the risk of certain types of cancer or otherwise contribute to health risks. Although there are no studies to confirm this link, some manufacturers are labeling their electric blankets with phrases like "engineered to eliminate over 95 percent of its own electromagnetic field." When this phrase is found on the packaging of electric blankets, it is often accompanied by a small line drawing of a bird flying in front of a circle that appears to represent the sun.

Source:
"Cutting the Magnetic Field," *Consumer Reports*, Vol. 56, No. 10 (October 1991): 697.

Energy Efficiency Labeling

Consumer appliance products must be labeled with information indicating their estimated annual energy costs or energy efficiency ratings, according to regulations of the Federal Trade Commission (FTC). The following is a list of appliances covered by these regulations: refrigerators, refrigerator/freezers, and freezers; dishwashers, gas, electric, and oil water heaters; room air conditioners; automatic, semi-automatic, and other clothes washers; furnaces; central air conditioners; air-source and water-source heat pumps; and fluorescent lamp ballasts.

LABELING REQUIREMENTS

Format. An example of the energy efficiency label, called the EnergyGuide, accompanies this entry. The label should measure 5⁵⁄₁₆ in by 7⅜ in., and should be printed in bright yellow with black lettering. White "windows" may be used for tables displaying yearly cost. Labels may be adhesive (to be affixed prominently to the appliance) or hang tags, which should be attached to the appliance prominently and securely. Information required on the label differs for each type of appliance. Every EnergyGuide includes the following categories of information: headlines as shown on the illustration; model number, capacity or size, data on estimated annual energy cost and energy efficiency ratings (see below); and a statement prohibiting removal of the label before consumer purchase.

Estimated Annual Energy Cost and Energy Efficiency Rating. Procedures for determining these factors for appliances covered by these regulations are specified in the regulations. Reports of test results must be filed with the Federal Trade Commission to support costs and efficiency ratings listed on appliance labels. A statement that the estimated costs and energy efficiency ratings are based on U.S. government standardized tests must appear on the label.

Ranges of Costs and Efficiency Ratings. Each year in the *Federal Register*, the Federal Trade Commission (FTC) publishes ranges of annual energy costs and energy efficiency ratings for each appliance covered by the labeling regulations.

Fluorescent Lamp Ballasts and Luminaires. Fluorescent lamp ballasts and luminaires must be stamped with a capital E inside a circle, to indicate that information on estimated annual energy cost and energy efficiency ratings is available, and that these products are covered by the FTC energy efficiency labeling regulations. Estimated annual energy costs and energy efficiency ratings must be available in writing to the consumer purchasing these products.

Source:

Federal Trade Commission, "Rules for Using Energy Costs and Consumption Information Used in Labeling and Advertising for Consumer Appliances Under the Energy Policy and Conservation Act," 16 CFR Part 305 (1992), Washington: Government Printing Office.

Feather and Down Products

This term includes all pillows, cushions, comforters, sleeping bags, wearing apparel, and similar products which are filled with feathers or down. These products should be labeled as to the kind or type of filling material it contains. When the filling material consists of a mixture of more than one kind or type, then the proportion of each should be disclosed in the order of predominance, the largest proportion first.

TERMINOLOGY

100 Percent Down, All Down, Pure Down. Contains only down.

Has a higher content of down than products labeled only as *down product.*

Crushed Feathers. Feathers which have been processed by a curling, crushing, or chopping machine which has changed the original form of the feathers without removing the quill. The term also includes the fiber resulting from such processing.

Damaged Feathers. Feathers which have been broken, damaged by insects, or otherwise materially injured.

Down Fibers. Detached barbs from down and plumules and the detached barbs from the basal end of waterfowl quill shafts.

Down Product. Consists primarily of down and plumules (minimum 70 percent). May contain varying amounts of other types of feathers.

Down. The undercoating of waterfowl, consisting of clusters of light, fluffy filaments (i.e., barbs) growing from the quill point but without any quill shafts.

Feather Fiber. Detached barbs of feathers which are not joined or attached to each other.

Feathers. The plumage or out-growth forming the contour and external covering of fowl. They are whole and have not been processed in any manner other than by washing, dusting, chemical treatment, and sanitizing.

Filling Material. The contents of a product including feathers and down of any kind or type.

Nonwaterfowl Feathers or Land-Fowl Feathers. Feathers derived from chickens, turkeys, and other land fowl.

Plumules. Downy waterfowl plumage with underdeveloped soft and flaccid quill, with barbs indistinguishable from those of down.

Quill Feathers. Feathers which are over 4 inches in length or which have a quill point exceeding ⁶⁄₁₆ of an inch in length.

Residue. Quill pith, quill fragments, trash, or foreign matter.

Tan-O-Quil-QM. A process developed by the Clothing and Organic Materials Laboratory and described in Technical Report 69-37-CM, "Tan-O-Quil-QM Treatment for Feathers and Down" (dated August 1968).

Waterfowl Feathers. Feathers derived from ducks and geese.

Source:

16 CFR Sections 253.1 to 253.11 (1992), Washington: Government Printing Office.

Flatware

Flatware (eating utensils like knives, forks, spoons, etc.) is typically of three varieties: silver, silverplate, or stainless—although ceramics, plastics, wood, and other materials are also used.

Silver. Because of the high cost of silver, *silver*ware is often sold in jewelry stores. See *Jewelry/Silver.*

Silverplate. See *Jewelry/Silver.*

Stainless. Steel is an alloy of carbon and iron that corrodes easily. However, by adding other elements to the composition (most notably chromium and nickel), its corrosive properties improve considerably. This improved metal is called stainless steel. The chromium gives the steel hardness and better resistance to stains and corrosion. Nickel gives it a bright finish. Consequently, stainless steel has become a standard material for making flatware.

However, stainless steel is not *stainproof*. Finished flatware has an oxide film that protects it from most staining and corrosion. Once the film is penetrated, however, the flatware will continue to stain, pit or corrode. Such common things as tea, coffee, vinegar, salad dressing, mustard, eggs, and salt, if present on flatware for prolonged periods of time, may stain, pit, or corrode stainless steel flatware. Minerals in tap water and chemicals in dishwasher detergent may also harm stainless steel surfaces.

The proportion of chromium and nickel used in the composition will affect the quality of the flatware. Higher quantities of chromium result in improved properties. E.g., a stainless steel consisting of 18 percent chromium and 8 percent nickel is heavier and more stain resistant than a metal with only 13 percent chromium. Some stainless steels are named for the percentages of chromium and nickel in the alloy. E.g., "18/8" is the name of the steel just mentioned. Stainless steels are also numbered according to a system developed by the American Iron and Steel Institute (AISI). Common AISI grades of stainless steel include: 304, 302, and 316.

Source:
Product Literature, Oneida, NY: Consumer Products Division, Stainless Flatware, Oneida LTD Silversmiths, 1992.

Furniture

Material Used in Construction. All kinds and types of chairs, tables, cabinets, desks, sofas, bedsteads, chests, and mirror frames are labeled with the type of material used in the construction. E.g., veneer construction is disclosed by such phrases as the following: veneer construction; veneered tops, fronts, and end panels; or [wood name] veneered, 5-ply construction with solid parts of [wood name]. Solid wood construction is disclosed in similar ways, e.g., walnut veneers and pecan solids. The stuffing used in cushions and construction should also be completely and accurately disclosed. E.g., it is considered misleading to describe shredded or flaked foam rubber stuffing as *foam rubber* without disclosing that it is shredded or flaked, or to describe any non-latex foam cushion as *foam* without disclosing the kind of foam used, such as *urethane foam*.

New. Composed entirely of unused material and parts. Furniture which has the appearance of being new but which contains used materials or parts—such as springs, latex foam rubber stuffing, or hardware—should be conspicuously disclosed.

Made in the U.S.A. Furniture that was manufactured in the United States is typically so labeled, followed by the name and address of the domestic manufacturer. Furniture manufactured in the United States should not be unqualifiedly described with such terms as "Danish," "Spanish," "English," etc., that might suggest foreign origin, unless the fact that the furniture was manufactured in the United States is clearly and conspicuously disclosed in advertising or on the product. However, manufacturers of furniture made in the U.S.A. will typically label furniture with such well-known terms as "French Provincial," "Italian Provincial," "Chinese Chippendale," and "Mediterranean" when used to describe the style of the furniture. In this case, the general public would not infer that the furniture was made outside of the U.S.A.

Discontinued. The manufacturer has discontinued its manufacture or the industry member offering it for sale will discontinue offering it entirely after clearance of his existing inventories.

Source:
16 CFR Sections 250.0 to 250.13 (1992), Washington: Government Printing Office.

Gas Ranges

High Speed Burner. Most gas ranges have cooktop burners that deliver approximately 9,000 BTU of heat per hour at the highest setting. High speed burners deliver 12,000 BTU or more of heat per hour and therefore are able to heat more quickly.

Source:
"Gas Ranges," *1991 Buying Guide Issue, Consumer Reports,* Vol. 55, No. 12: 79-80.

Glassware

Casual Crystal. Hand-blown casual or informal crystal is designed specifically for more casual entertaining where fine crystal is not appropriate.

Crystal Suite. Consists of water goblet/large wine glass, wine glass, champagne glass (flute or dessert/champagne glass). Iced beverage glass may be substituted for water goblet/large wine glass.

Etched Glass. Delicate designs on crystal created by coating the parts not to be etched with wax and dipping the piece in an acid bath.

Flute Champagne Glass. Popular, slender shape retains the effervescence of champagne.

Hand-Blown. The breath of a master craftsman blown through a pipe to create fine crystal.

Heavily Cut Crystal. Intricately and expertly cut with diamond wheels, then carefully polished for maximum light refraction, sparkle, and beauty.

Lead Crystal. Lead helps to increase the brilliance, weight, and reflectiveness of crystal and softens it for easier cutting. Has a clear bell-like "ring" when one taps the rim.

Source:
Glossary of Fine China and Crystal Terms, Lawrenceville, NJ: Lenox China, 1988.

Glue

Aliphatic Glues. Also known as *carpenter glues*. Used primarily for food. They have a yellow-brown color.

Carpenter Glue. See *Aliphatic Glues.*

Catalyzed Acrylic Glue. A strong glue that is good at sticking to oily surfaces.

Contact Cement. Flexible adhesives that bond quickly to a surface (on contact). However, they are not as strong as many other glues.

Epoxy Glue. A very hard, strong, and water-resistant glue. It typically comes in two tubes. The first tube contains a resin and the second a hardener. The resin and hardener must be mixed together to create the glue.

Instant Glue. See *Super Glue.*

Model Airplane Glue. See *Plastic Cement.*

Plastic Cement. Also known as *model airplane glue*, it cures slowly when applied to large areas.

Resin Glue. Used primarily for wood. Creates a strong bond that is water resistant.

Silicone Rubber. A glue with good elasticity, water-resistance, and gap-filling abilities.

Super Glue. Super glues are made from cyanoacrylate adhesives (CAs). These glues can have tensile strength of over 1,000 pounds per square inch. Also called *instant glue*.

Urethane. A viscous, sticky substance that forms a tough, rubbery foam.

Viscosity. The flowing properties of the glue. A super glue may have a viscosity that flows very easily or one that is thick and slow. The viscosity of the glue may affect the ability of the glue to provide a proper bond.

White Glues. An inexpensive glue primarily used for wood or other porous surfaces.

Source:

Hand, A.J., "What to Know About Super Glues," *Consumers' Research Magazine,* Vol. 73, No. 11 (November 1990): 32-33.

"Which Glue for the Job," *Consumer Reports,* Vol. 53, No. 1 (January 1988): 46-51.

Heating Systems

Heating systems include forced-air furnaces and hot water/steam boilers, and central heat pumps.

Annual Fuel Utilization Efficiency (AFUE) Percentage. The measure of a heating unit's efficiency. It is the amount of each dollar spent on fuel that actually goes to heating the house as opposed to being wasted because of inefficiencies of the heating system. E.g., a system rated at 93 percent would convert 93 cents of a fuel dollar to heat used to heat the house. The remaining 7 cents would be wasted as heat by-products. The Federal Trade Commission (FTC) requires manufacturers to make the AFUE ratings of their heating products available to consumers.

Heating Capacity. The measure of the amount of heat that can be generated by a heating system. It is measured in BTUs (British Thermal Units) per hour rounded to the nearest 1000 BTUs/hr. Heating capacities of typical residential heating systems are generally under 120,000 BTU/hr.

High Efficiency Heating Systems. This term is used to describe systems that have AFUE percentages above those of conventional heating systems. Conventional systems have ratings of between 78 and 85 percent. High efficiency units have AFUE percentages as high as 97 percent. Older furnaces may have AFUE percentages as low as 60 percent.

CENTRAL HEAT PUMPS

Central heat pumps provide both cooling in the summer and heating in the winter.

Coefficient of Performance (COP). A heat pump rating based on the ratio of heat delivered to energy consumed. Ratings are provided for two outdoor temperatures: 17 degrees F and 47 degrees F. The higher the COP number (2 or greater at 17 degrees F and 3 or more at 47 degrees F), the more efficient the unit.

Heating Season Performance Factor (HSPF). A measure of heating performance over the entire heating season. It is a ratio of the estimated seasonal heating output divided by the seasonal power consumption. An average new heat pump has an HSPF ratio of about 6.8. The higher the HSPF the more efficient the unit.

Seasonal Energy Efficiency Ratio (SEER). Central heat pump cooling efficiency is rated on the average efficiency over the entire cooling season. The higher the SEER the more efficient the system. E.g., a system rated 8 uses 25 percent less energy than a system rated 6. Its cooling capacity is rated in BTU/hrs. See *Air Conditioners.*

Sources:

Federal Trade Commission, "Determinations of Capacity," 16 CFR 305.7 (1992), Washington: Government Printing Office.

"High-Efficiency Heating Systems," *Consumer Research Magazine,* Vol. 73, No. 2 (February 1990): 19-22.

"The Most Efficient Heating Systems," *Consumer Research Magazine,* Vol. 72, No. 1 (January 1989): 25-28; original source: *Saving Energy and Money with Home Appliances,* Washington: American Council for an Energy-Efficient Economy (ACEEE).

Knives

Knives are graded according to the material used for the blade and the profile to which the blade is ground. The smaller the angle of the bevel the sharper the blade.

Flat-Ground. Uniformly thinned from the back of the blade to the edge and from the heel of the blade to the point.

High-Carbon Steel. Formerly, high quality knife blades were made of steel with a high carbon content. These blades can be resharpened by the consumer to a fine edge. However, carbon steels rust, darken, or stain, and are therefore more difficult to maintain. Low carbon steel blades are harder to sharpen and do not hold their edge very well. The vast majority of knives are now made of stainless steel.

Hollow-Ground Blade. This type of blade is designed to minimize resistance when cutting. It is concaved from the edge to a line halfway up the blade.

Stainless Steel. Presently, high quality knives are primarily made of stainless steel (a carbon steel to which other alloying elements, like chromium, have been added to improve corrosion resistance). These knives hold an edge nearly as well as carbon steel blades.

Taper-Ground. Eliminates a "shoulder" at the cutting bevel, minimizing the blade's resistance and making it easier to resharpen.

Source:
Overton, Mac, "The Mystique of the Blade," *Consumers' Digest,* Vol. 26, No. 1 (January/February): 1987.

Ladders

Ladders are constructed from wood, metal, and fiberglass. The two most common types of ladders are stepladders and extension ladders. Ladders are graded by their ability to carry a load. The load includes both the weight of the ladder user and the materials carried: paint, tools, etc.

Type I. Heavy Duty. Rated up to 250 pounds load.

Type II. Medium. Rated up to 225 pound load.

Type III. Light Duty. Rated up to 200 pounds load.

EXTENSION LADDERS

Total Length of Sections. A ladder so labeled is measured by adding the total length of each section. E.g., a ladder with two 10 foot sections would have a total length of sections of 20 feet. A ladder labeled "17 foot extension ladder" would indicate the length measurement is based on *working length.*

Working Length. The working length of a ladder, however, would exclude footage lost in overlapping of the sections. Accordingly, a ladder with a total length of sections of 20 feet may have a working length of only 17 feet.

Source:
16 CFR Sections 418.1 to 418.6 (1992), Washington: Government Printing Office.
Consumer Products Safety Commission (CPSC), *A Consumer's Guide to Safe Ladder Selection Care and Use,* Washington: Government Printing Office, 1980.

Lightbulbs

Energy Saving Incandescent Lamps. A type of lamp that uses a more efficient filament or inert gases in the bulb and thereby uses less electricity.

Fluorescent Lamps. Glass tubes filled with mercury gas and coated on the inside with phosphors. When electricity is passed between the filaments at each end of the tube, the mercury gas is activated and emits UV (ultraviolet) radiation. This radiation is absorbed by the phosphor coating, which converts it to visible light.

Halogen Lamp or Quartz-Halogen. A type of lamp whereby the filament is encased in a small halogen-filled quartz chamber inside the lamp. The chamber redeposits evaporating tungsten back onto the filament causing it to burn brighter and last longer.

Incandescent Lamps. A type of lamp that consists of a tungsten filament enclosed in a vacuum-sealed bulb. When electric current runs through the filament, it becomes white hot and gives off light. The tungsten filament dissipates over time and eventually breaks.

IR (Infrared) Halogen Lamp. A halogen lamp that reflects wasted heat energy back onto the filament, thereby increasing the efficiency of the lamp.

Long-Life Bulb. An incandescent lamp that uses a heavier filament that does not dissipate and break as quickly.

Source:
16 CFR Section 409.01 (1992), Washington: Government Printing Office.
Murdoch, Guy, "Lighting Options for the Home," *Consumers' Research Magazine,* Vol. 74, No. 2 (February 1991): 21-24

Linens, Bed

Bed linen is a term applied to sheets and pillow cases. However, few bed linens made today are actually made of linen. Linen is a cloth made of fibers from the stem of the flax plant. Although long-lasting and easy to care for, linen is very expensive. Therefore, most bed linens are made of cotton or a blend of cotton and a synthetic material. (See *Textiles and Apparel/Cotton.*)

In the United States bed linens have uniform sizes that have been standardized by the major manufacturers. These sizes appear in the table that follows.

Standard Mattress	Flat	Sheet	Pillow	Pillowcase
Crib	27x52	38x52		
Cot	30x75	63x96	20x26	20x30
Twin	39x75	66x96	20x26	20x30
Extra-long twin	39x80	66x102	20x26	20x30
Full	54x75	81x96	20x36	20x30
Extra-long full	54x80	81x102	20x26	20x30
Queen	60x80	90x102	20x30	20x34
King	76x80	108x102	20x36	20x40
Calif. King	72x84	108x102	20x36	20x40

In practice, however, linens from different manufacturers may vary somewhat from the standards. Some general rules are the following:

Sheets. Should be at least 24 inches wider and longer than the mattress.

Fitted Sheets. These sheets need a "box" deeper than the mattress. Standard U.S. mattresses are 6 to 8 inches deep. Therefore a box of 9 inches deep will be sufficient for most mattresses.

Pillowcases. Should be at least four inches longer than the pillow.

Source:
Lechaux, Dominique, "Bed Linens," *Martha Stewart Living,* April/May 1992: 38-42.

Linens, Table

Cut Size. Represents the actual dimensions of the finished products. The finished sizes of the products are usually smaller than the *cut size* of the materials from which they are made.

Finished Size. The size of the tablecloth after hemming and finishing.

Source:
16 CFR Sections 404.1 to 404.3 (1992), Washington: Government Printing Office.

Mattresses

Mattresses are advertised with such terms as *firm, soft, extra-firm,* etc. These terms relate to how the mattress feels when one lies on it. They have no official meaning and are only relative to a single manufacturer's product line. Therefore, they cannot be used to compare mattresses from different manufacturers.

Standard U.S. mattresses are 6 to 8 inches deep with the following horizontal dimensions:

Standard Mattress	Size
Crib	27x52
Cot	30x75
Twin	39x75
Extra-long twin	39x80
Full	54x75
Extra-long full	54x80
Queen	60x80
King	76x80
Calif. King	72x84

Source:
Lechaux, Dominique, "Bed Linens," *Martha Stewart Living,* April/May 1992: 38-42.

Microwave Ovens

Microwaves ovens use microwave, a form of electrical and magnetic energy, to cook food. Microwaves should not be con-

fused with x-rays, which are much more powerful. Microwaves can pass through glass, paper, plastic, and similar materials but are reflected by metal. Microwaves are absorbed by food where they cause the food molecules such as water to vibrate. This vibration produces the heat that cooks the food. Microwave ovens are regulated by the Food and Drug Administration and are required to meet a radiation safety standard. This standard limits microwave leakage to 5 milliwatts per square centimeter (mW/cm^2) at about 2 inches from the oven. In comparison, medical applications use up to 1,000 mW/cm^2 without ill effects. FDA tests have shown that actual microwave emission is under 2mW/cm^2.

TERMINOLOGY

Active Packaging. Some microwave food packaging designed to be used in the microwave is made of microwave-absorbing *heat susceptors* that induce high temperatures which help to cook or brown the food. The food-contact surface of heat-susceptor packaging is usually a metallized polyethylene terephthalate (PET) film laminated to paperboard with adhesive. This metallized film absorbs the microwave energy in the oven and consequently acts as a frying pan that actively participates in the cooking. The Food and Drug Administration (FDA) is currently studying heat susceptors to determine if some of the materials used in the packaging—such as adhesives, polymers, paper, and paperboard—migrate into the food. Although current reports show no health hazard due to substances migrating from heat-susceptor and dual ovenable packaging (entry follows), the FDA continues to work with industry to obtain more conclusive safety information. Only a small percentage of microwave packages use susceptors.

Dual Ovenables. Plastic utensils or convenience food packaging prepared for use in either the conventional or microwave oven.

Microwave Safe. A term generally used to refer to utensils that can safely be used in microwave ovens. In general, it is not good to use conventional metal pans or aluminum foil because these materials reflect the microwaves and cause uneven cooking. However, some new metal cookware is specially configured for use in microwave ovens. Hot food melts some plastic containers, such as margarine tubs, and the melted plastic may find its way into the food. In addition not all glass and ceramics are microwave-safe. To test if a certain kind of glass is appropriate for heating foods likely to become very hot, like fatty foods, use the following test. Microwave the empty container for one minute and check the surface temperature. It is *unsafe* for use in the microwave oven if it is warm, *good for reheating* if it is lukewarm, and *good for cooking* if it is cool.

Passive Packaging. Packaging which uses materials which are transparent to microwaves. The waves pass through the materials to cook the food. These materials are heated solely from the cooking food, so they do not get much hotter than the food.

Wattage. The power of a microwave oven is determined by its wattage, which can vary from 200 watts to over 750 watts. Ovens with higher wattage cook food faster. Accordingly, some microwaveable packaged foods are labeled with heating directions by wattage. The Campbell Microwave Institute suggests the following test for gauging a microwave oven's output: Fill a glass measuring cup with exactly 1 cup of tap water. Microwave, uncovered, on "high" until water begins to boil. If boiling occurs in less than 3 minutes the wattage is 600 to 700; if 3 to 4 minutes, 500 to 600, and if more than 4 minutes, the wattage is less than 500 watts.

SIZES

Big. Typically 23 inches wide and 17 inches deep with an average cooking-compartment floor size of 16 by 15 inches.
Mid-Sized. Typically 22 inches wide and 14 inches deep with an average cooking-compartment floor size of 15 by 12 inches.
Small. Usually just large enough to hold a 10-inch dinner plate.

Sources:
Farley, Dixie, *Keeping Up with the Microwave Revolution,* Washington: Department of Health and Human Services, 1991.
"Large Microwave Ovens," *Consumer Reports,* Vol. 55, No. 11 (November 1990): 733-737.

Pacifiers

A pacifier is an article consisting of a nipple that is intended for a young child to suck upon and usually includes a guard or shield and a handle or a ring. It is not designed to facilitate a baby's obtaining fluid. In general, the pacifier must be large and sturdy enough so as not to fit within a baby's mouth. Pacifiers are labeled as follows: Warning: Do Not Tie Pacifier Around Child's Neck as it Presents a Strangulation Danger.

Source:
Consumer Product Safety Commission, "Requirements for Pacifiers," 16 CFR Part 1511 (1992), Washington: Government Printing Office.

Padlocks

There are two types of padlocks: *Type P01,* key operated; and *Type P02,* combination operated. The grades of padlocks are determined by strength levels. A number of different tests are used to determine strength levels, including forcing tests, surreptitious entry tests (picking, drilling, etc.), cycle tests, and environmental tests. There are 6 grades with Grade 1 the lowest and Grade 6 the highest. For example, Grade 1 withstands a tensile force of 1,225 lbf, whereas Grade 6 withstands a force of 2,700 lbf. In some cases, a rating beyond 1 through 6 may be used by some manufacturers. For example, a padlock designated as Grade 3 may also have the parenthetical designation (F5S3). This would mean the padlock met the requirements for forcing test of Grade 5. Users not overly concerned with surreptitious entry but wanting relatively high resistance to forcing would find such a padlock more useful than one rated Grade 3.

Source:
"Standard Performance Specification for Padlocks," Designation F 883-84, *Annual Book of ASTM Standards,* Volume 15.07, Philadelphia: American Society for Testing and Materials, 1990.

Polish

Polish is defined as a temporary coating that enhances the appearances and may protect the substrate to which it is applied. The following terms relate to application and performance of different types of polish.

TERMINOLOGY

Abrasion Resistance. Ability of the polished finish to withstand scuff marks compared to the unpolished finish (used in relation to shoe polish).
Bloom. A condition in which moisture has condensed upon and is being trapped by a polish film, rendering a haze over the surface (used in relation to furniture polish).
Buffable. Capable of improvement in gloss or general appearance, or both, of a polish film by a mechanical action.
Buffing-Type Floor Polish. Requires buffing to maintain or enhance appearance, or both.
Build-up. Condition where new polish film deposits over old, with little or no self-cleaning.
Cleaning. When used in connection with polish, the removal of marks, dust, film, and other extraneous material from the surface.
Crock, Dry and Wet. The degree of polish rub-off obtained during rubbing tests between a cloth (dry or wet, respectively) and the polished surface (usually used in relation to polished shoes).
Detergent Resistance. The degree to which a polish film exhibits no deterioration when spotted or cleaned with a solution of a nonabrasive detergent (with no ammonia).
Dry Bright Polish. A polish that dries to a gloss without buffing.
Gloss Retention. Ability of applied polish to retain a gloss under normal wear conditions (but not including exposure to water).
Haze. Film that reflects unclear or foggy images, usually a sign of incompatibility between the surface finish and applied substance (polish or spilled liquid).
Healing. The ability of a polish film to return to original state after being disturbed by fingerprints, marks, etc. (Usually refers to furniture polish.)
Powdering. Partial or total disintegration of the polish resulting in a fine, light-colored material.
Self-Polishing-Type Floor Polish. Dries to a shine.
Service Life. Period of time under use conditions to change the appearance of a surface treated with floor polish sufficiently to require retreatment.
Slip Resistance. Friction across a surface, usually referring to a shoe on a floor.
Smear Resistance. The ability of a polished surface to remain unscuffed when touched.
Spray Buffing. Restorative maintenance of a previously polished floor by the action of a suitable floor polishing machine immediately following the mist-spraying of an appropriate product onto the surface whereby the wet application is buffed to dryness.
Tack. Sticky, gummy character of a polish film, rendering the surface conducive to dust accumulation, fingerprinting, etc. (Usually refers to furniture polish.)

Volatile Solvent. Any nonaqueous liquid that has the distinctive property of evaporating readily at room temperature and atmospheric pressure.

Water Beading. Surface property that causes the formation of discrete water droplets on the polished surface.

Water Spotting. Change in appearance of surface resulting solely from the action of cool water.

Water-Emulsion Floor Polish. An emulsion-based floor polish in which water is the continuous or external phase. It falls into two categories: polymer-emulsion, a water-emulsion containing a predominance of synthetic emulsion polymers; and wax-emulsion, a water emulsion containing a predominance of natural or synthetic waxes, or both.

Weatherability. Ability of a polish to resist the effect of exposure to weather elements. Used in reference to automobile and related polishes.

Source:
"Standard Definitions of Terms Relating to Polishes and Related Materials," Designation D2825-88, *Annual Book of ASTM Standards,* Philadelphia: American Society for Testing Materials, 1990.

Ranges, Electric

TERMINOLOGY

Continuous Cleaning Oven. Soil on oven surfaces is gradually reduced, resulting in a presentably clean condition on porous porcelain enamel, during normal baking or roasting operations.

Conventional Oven. A cooking compartment in which heat is utilized through radiation, convection, and conduction, unassisted by any other means.

Forced Convection Oven. A fan or other means is used to circulate the heated air within the cooking compartment. Circulating air reduces cooking time.

Oven Space, Actual. The actual size of the cooking compartment.

Oven Space, Usable. The space available for baking.

Porcelain Enamel. A substantially vitreous or glassy inorganic coating (for oven surfaces) bonded to a metal by fusion at a temperature above about 800 degrees F. *General Purpose* is formulated for range applications that has excellent hardness, color retention, and a high resistance to rust, stains, and acids. *Continuous Cleaning* is a type of porcelain enamel or ceramic coating having a textured granular surface that is designed to provide for the continuous removal, during normal baking operations, of cooking oils deposited on the interior of the oven surface.

Pyrolytic Self Cleaning. A cooking compartment which uses a process whereby the cooking soil is reduced to light ash during a separate high temperature cycle. The remaining ash is removed with a damp cloth.

Source:
ANSI/AHAM ER-1-1986, Chicago: Association of Home Appliance Manufacturers, 1986.

Room Air Cleaner

Clean Air Delivery Rate (CADR). This term describes the measure of air cleaner performance for portable household electric cord-connected room air cleaners. The practical limits of measurability are: dust, 10 to 350 CADR; tobacco smoke, 10 to 300 CADR; pollen, 25 to 450 CADR.

Source:
American National Standard Method for Measuring Performance of Portable Household Electric Cord-Connected Room Air Cleaners, ANSI/AHAM AC-1-1988, Chicago, IL: Association of Home Appliance Manufacturers, 1988.

Smoke Detectors

Smoke detectors work by sensing the rising smoke from a fire and sounding a piercing alarm.

TYPES

Ionization Chamber Detector. Uses a radioactive source to produce electrically charged molecules (ions) in the air. This sets up an electric current within the detector chamber. When smoke enters the chamber, it attaches itself to the ions and reduces the flow of electric current, thus setting off the alarm.

Photoelectric Detector. Activates when the smoke is dense enough to deflect a beam of light.

POWER SOURCES

Battery Operated. Generally operates for one year before requiring the battery to be replaced. Designed with a safety-feature to signal when it is time to replace the battery. When the battery begins to lose power and needs replacement, the detector will begin to emit "beeps" every minute or so and will keep this up for a week or longer.

Household Current. Operates on household current, and therefore has power as long as there is current in the circuit to which it is connected. This type of smoke detector is vulnerable to power failure.

Source:
U.S. Consumer Product Safety Commission (CPSC), *What You Should Know About Smoke Detectors,* 1985. Washington: Government Printing Office.

Sump, Effluent, and Sewage Pumps

The Sump and Sewage Pump Manufacturers Association has established voluntary product standards for pumps. Manufacturers of sump, effluent, and sewage pumping equipment may indicate adherence to these standards by stating in specifications and product description: *Tested and rated in accordance with SSPMA Standards.* Manufacturers licensed through the Association may also affix the *SSPMA Certified* seal to products bearing their name or brand name, or incorporate the seal design in the description of any product to indicate adherence to SSPMA Standards and Procedures.

TERMINOLOGY

Sump Pump. A pump powered by an electric motor for the removal of clear water drainage from a sump, pit, or low point in a residential, commercial, or industrial property.

Effluent Pump. A pump powered by an electric motor for the removal of natural or artificial pretreated liquid waste discharge from an on-site sewage disposal system.

Sewage Pump. A pump powered by an electric motor for the removal of wastewater containing solids of up to 2 inches in diameter.

TYPES

Pedestal (Type P). A pump with the pumping element located in the sump, pit, or low point and the motor mounted on a tube or column extending vertically upward from the pumping element.

Submersible (Type S). A pump with the entire pumping unit located in the sump, pit, or low point and designed so the motor and pumping element can be submerged.

Horizontal (Type H). A pump comprised of a horizontally mounted self-priming pumping unit located at or above the floor level adjacent to a sump, pit, or low point.

SPECIFICATION NUMBERS

Pumps are classified with reference to the parts which are submerged or in contact with the liquid being pumped. The table that appears on the opposite page explains the specification numbering system.

Source:

Sump, Effluent, and Sewage Pump Standards, Winnetka, IL: Sump and Sewage Pump Manufacturers Association, 1985.

Tools

Drop Forged. Drop forging is a production method whereby a hot piece of metal is placed in a forge. A large hammer is dropped onto the metal. The force and weight of the hammer forces the metal into a die that forms the shape of the tool. In the process, small air bubbles and other discontinuities are forced from the interior structure of the metal thereby creating a uniform structure that adds strength to the finished forging. A dropped forged tool is stronger than one which has been cast.

Cast. In the casting process, metal is simply poured into a mold and than allowed to cool. Air bubbles and cavities, which weaken the metal, are more likely to form in castings.

Source:
McClintock, Mike, "Picking Proper Tools," *Consumers' Research Magazine,* Vol. 69, No. 2 (February 1986): 33-34.

Wallcovering

Wallcovering is classified on its durability in tests for abrasion resistance, blocking resistance, breaking strength, coating adhesion, cold cracking resistance, colorfastness, crocking resistance, heat aging resistance, scrubbability, stain resistance, tear resistance, and washability. Based on these criteria, wallcovering is classified in the following categories.

CATEGORIES

I, Decorative Only. Can be hung without damage.

II, Decorative with Limited Serviceability. More washable and colorfast than Category I wallcoverings.

III, Decorative with Medium Serviceability. For use where abrasion resistance, stain resistance, scrubbability, and increased colorfastness are necessary.

IV, Decorative with High Serviceability. For heavy consumer and light commercial use.

V, Medium Commercial Serviceability. Used where better wearing qualities are required and exposure to wear is greater than normal.

VI, Full Commercial Serviceability. For use in heavy traffic areas.

FLAMMABILITY RATINGS

Wallcoverings labeled with a flammability rating are tested and classified as a *Class A, B, or C Interior Finish* in accordance with the NFPA Life Safety Code.

TERMINOLOGY

Adam Design. The two Scottish Adams brothers, Robert and James, were architects who designed buildings, interiors, and furnishings in England during the late 18th century. Their style is recognized by such classical motifs as urns, lozenge forms, plaques, and dainty scrollwork.

Advancing Colors. Warm colors such as red, yellow, and orange; and dark colors which make surfaces appear closer or larger.

American Single Roll. A single roll of wallcovering that comes in a wide variety of lengths and widths ranging from 18 to 36 inches in width and from 4 to 8 yards in length. Regardless of length or width, each single roll contains 34 to 36 square feet of wallcovering.

Bleeding. In printing, a spreading of pigment beyond the design outline, or the appearance of one color through another.

Blooming. A hazy or foggy appearance due to the incompatibility of some of the compounds in the coating or plastic sheeting.

Bolt. A roll of fabric or wallcovering of a given length.

Borax. A colloquialism of the home furnishings trades, denoting cheap or in bad taste.

Caen-Stone. A wallcovering that resembles a cream-colored building stone that comes from Caen in France.

Type	Pump Housing (Class)	Component Materials
P — Pedestal	B — Bronze	1
S — Submersible	C — Cast Iron	2
H — Horizontal	A — Aluminum	3
	M — Molded Material	4
	R — Corrosion-Resistant Material	5
	X — Unlisted Materials	6

The specification number for a particular pump shall be listed in the following manner:

Submersible

Type	Pump Housing	Impeller	Control Housing	Motor Housing	Other Wetted Components
S	B	4	6	2	6

"SB-4626" means:
S — Type — Submersible
B — Class — Bronze
4 — Impeller — Molded Material
6 — Control Housing — Unlisted Material
2 — Motor Housing — Cast Iron
6 — Other Components — Unlisted Material

Pedestal

Type	Pump Housing	Impeller	Shaft at Journal	Column	Other Wetted Components
P	A	5	5	3	6

"PA-5536" means:
P — Type — Pedestal
A — Class — Aluminum
5 — Impeller — Corrosion-Resistant Materials
5 — Shaft at Journal — Corrosion-Resistant Materials
3 — Column — Aluminum
6 — Other Components — Unlisted Materials

Horizontal

Type	Pump Housing	Impeller	Shaft	Control Housing	Other Wetted Components
H	C	2	6	1	6

"HC-2616" means:
H — Type — Horizontal
C — Class — Cast Iron
2 — Impeller — Cast Iron
6 — Shaft — Unlisted Materials
1 — Control Housing — Bronze
6 — Other Components — Unlisted Materials

Specification numbers for pumps.

Cellulose Paste. The adhesive often applied to prepasted wallcoverings. It is non-staining, odorless, vermin-proof, mildew-retardant, mixes easily, and will not ferment.

Coatings. A thin protective surface layer, usually of vinyl, which is applied to wallcoverings to provide washability and durability.

Color Run. The amount of rollage of a particular design produced of a single color combination. Subsequent runs of that same design and color may be slightly different. (This is why it is important for purchasers to retain the run number in case additional rollage is needed.)

Commercial. Manufactured in quantity to serve low-priced markets.

Contract Wallcoverings. Wallcoverings produced for commercial use and normally available in 48 or 54 inch widths.

Cool Colors. Blue, green, and violet, or any color to which blue has been added.

Cork. Cork of various textures, usually laminated to a backing,

145

which can be used as a wallcovering. It absorbs sound, insulates, provides visual contrast, and can be used as a bulletin board.

Correlated. Wallcoverings and fabrics designed to be used together. They are known as correlates or companions.

Crocking. Coloring that rubs off and causes discoloration.

Double Cut Seam. Type of seam used in situations where it is necessary to overlap two strips of wallcovering and yet avoid a raised ridge. One example would be when a border is being used as a chairrail with coordinated wallcoverings above and below the border/wallcovering. A straightedge is placed at the center of the overlap and, with a razor knife or blade, a cut is made through both layers. The top cutoff section is removed and then the bottom cutoff portion is removed leaving a tightly butted seam.

Engraving. Machine printing of wallcovering with etched-out rollers to obtain subtle and fine effects.

Etching. A process in which a copper shell is slowly revolved in an acid bath.

Euro-Roll. An imported roll of wallcovering ranging in width from 20 to 21 inches but always 5½ yards in length that contains approximately 28 square feet.

Flock. Wallcoverings made by shaking finely chopped fibers over a pattern printed in varnish or other sticky material to give the appearance of velvet or damask.

Gray Goods. Raw woven cloths before any processing.

Hot Spots. Shiny spots on wallcovering caused by chemical reactions.

Impregnate. The saturating of a piece of cloth with a special coating.

Ink Embossed. The ink colors are applied at the time that the wallcoverings are being embossed.

Inlay Embossing. During the embossing of vinyl, ink is inserted into the valleys.

Job-Lot. Discontinued patterns which are often sold at reduced prices.

Lincrusta. A permanent wallcovering coated with a wood flour and linseed oil mixture on a paper backing which is molded instead of printed.

Line. Merchandise belonging to one group or series offered by a manufacturer. In wallcovering, name collections appearing periodically every year or two.

Lining Paper. Plain material, often paper, usually applied horizontally and used under wallcoverings to assure a smoother surface and better adhesion.

Machine Printing. The method by which most modern wallcoverings are produced. It employs a rotary press and a series of cylinders which turn out wallcoverings at high speeds.

Matching. Hanging strips of wallcovering so that the design will be in the correct relation to the preceding strips. The types of match are random, straight, and drop.

Matte Finish. A dull finish.

Mildew-Resistant. The wallcovering is protected to resist fungi (mildew) growth on the decorative surface.

Moire. Wallcoverings having a watered silk-sheen effect.

Mylar. A hard plastic film that offers an impressive appearance along with durability.

Non-Metallic Substrate. Any substrate such as paper or fabric that doesn't contain metal.

Off Grades. Not first quality goods.

Pad Grounds. Wallcovering which has been printed in one operation, with the design printed on a wet background. It is not lightfast or washable.

Peelable. The decorative surface may be dry-peeled from the substrate, leaving a continuous layer of the substrate on the wall.

Plastic-Bonded Wallcoverings. Made with a protein size and added plastic. They are washable but can be stained with certain liquids.

Plastic-Coated Wallcoverings. Washable and stain-resistant wallcoverings which feature a thick plastic coating.

Prepasted. Wallcovering that has had adhesive applied to the back of it by the manufacturer. Dipping a strip in water before hanging activates the paste.

Pretrimmed. Rolls of wallcovering from which the selvage has been trimmed at the factory.

Production Run. The production of one pattern in one combination of colors from the beginning to end on one machine.

Repeat. The distance from the center on one motif or pattern to the center of the next.

Run. The number of times an individual wallcovering is made. Colors and other features can be slightly different from run to run.

Scrubbable. Any wallcovering that can be safely washed with a sponge and detergent while still on the wall.

Sculptured Wallcovering. Molded wallcovering of a solid material, usually synthetic, to produce real texture and shadows.

Shading. An effect that can sometimes appear along the seams of non-patterned or textured wallcoverings due to heavier ink coverage at one edge that the other during printing. This effect can be eliminated or reduced by reversing each strip as it is hung by alternating the top and bottom. Dark edges will thus butt to dark edges and light to light, minimizing the shading.

Single Roll. The standard commercial length of wallcovering. American-made, containing about 35 square feet of surface after trimming, regardless of the width. Wallcovering is usually packaged in double or triple rolls, but prices are quoted by the single roll.

Size. A sealer used to prepare the wall before the wallcovering is applied.

Skin. An ungrounded, nonwashable type of wallpaper of the lowest price grade.

Stain-Resistant Wallcovering. A wall covering on which a coat of plastic or vinyl has been added to make the surface stain-resistant and maintenance-free.

Stock. Different qualities and grades of paper or the man-made materials. Also, the inventory on hand.

Strippable. Can be dry-stripped without leaving appreciable residue or otherwise damaging the wall.

Substrate. The backing of a wallcovering. It becomes laminated to the design layer.

Swatch. A sample cutting of wallcovering or fabric.

Tonal Value. The relative strength of color.

Turnover. The cycle of inventory depletion and replenishment.

Ungrounded Papers. A pattern printed on raw stock as it comes from the paper mills, without a ground color.

Vinyl Coating. Either the liquid vinyl or flexible film applied to a wallcovering backing material. It gives strength, durability, and scrubbability.

Wall Fabric. A durable surface on a cotton backing used to cover walls.

Wall Primer. The preparatory coat of primer given to walls before hanging wallcoverings.

Wallcoverings. Coverings applied to walls for decoration, scrubbability, and to hide imperfections.

Wallpaper. A wallcovering made of paper.

Washable. A wallcovering that can be cleaned with a sponge, mild soap, and water. Also called *Scrubbable*.

LABELING

When a wallcovering is tested in accordance with ASTM standardized test methods, the packaging may contain the following phrase: Conforms to ASTM F 793, Category _____ (descriptive phrase) (name and address of manufacturer or distributor).

Source:
"Standard Classification of Wallcovering by Durability Characteristics," Designation F 793-82, *Annual Book of ASTM Standards,* Philadelphia: American Society for Testing and Material, 1990.
Terminology, St. Louis: National Decorating Products Association, 1992.

Water Treatment Units

Home water treatment units are typically used for the following purposes: to remove chemicals or particles that affect the taste or appearance of drinking water; to remove harmful organisms, such as bacteria; and/or to remove chemical pollutants, such as pesticides or industrial solvents. Listed below are descriptions of many common types of water treatment units.

Physical Filters. Physical filters are simple units designed to remove particles such as grit, sediment, dirt, and rust from the water. They often are made of fabric, fiber, ceramic, or other screening material. Some filters can remove even small organisms like cysts and bacteria, and small particles like asbestos fibers. Because filters cannot remove all disease-causing organisms from water, they are inadequate to treat microbiologically unsafe water.

Activated Carbon Filters. Generally, filters in this category can remove some organic chemical contaminants that may cause undesirable tastes, odors, and colors from water. Some inorganic chemicals, such as chlorine, also may be reduced by activated carbon filters. However, the filters usually will not remove most inorganic chemicals, such as salts or metals.

Certain specially-prepared activated carbon filters can remove lead from drinking water. If lead is present in drinking water, the consumer wishing to use an activated carbon filter should ask the salesperson for a written assurance of its effectiveness against lead.

Although most municipal drinking water is disinfected to remove harmful bacteria, drinking water usually carries harmless levels of bacteria. These bacteria can collect and multiply on an activated carbon filter. Therefore, activated carbon filters should be maintained properly and replaced periodically.

Carbon filters (registered as bacteriostatic by the Environment Protection Agency) are marked by the presence of the pesticide silver in the filter. Registration, as required by the *Federal Insecticide, Fungicide, and Rodenticide Act,* does not indicate recommendation, approval, or endorsement of the product by EPA. Studies on the effectiveness of bacteriostatic filters have shown unpromising results as to their ability to control bacterial growth. Further, a bacteriostatic carbon filter is not adequate to treat water that is microbiologically unsafe, such as fecally contaminated water.

Reverse Osmosis (RO) Units. These units remove substantial amounts of most inorganic chemicals such as salts, metals (including lead), asbestos, minerals, nitrates, and some organic chemicals, by allowing tap water to pass through a membrane and collecting the filtered water in a storage tank. Alone, RO units are not recommended for use on microbiologically unsafe water. Typically, about 75 percent of tap water put into the RO system is wasted, so it may take 4 gallons or more of tap water to get 1 gallon of RO filtered water. Also, the tap on the tank where the treated water is stored flows much more slowly than the tap on a regular faucet. The most common membranes used in RO units are subject to decay and filters must be replaced periodically.

Distillation Units. This type of system comes in many different shapes and sizes, but all vaporize the water and then condense it. This process removes most dissolved solids, such as salts, metals, minerals, asbestos fibers, particles, and some organic chemicals. Distillation units, however, may not remove all chemical pollutants, and some bacteria may pass through. Although distillation may be an effective water treatment, the process of heating the water will add to energy use.

Ultraviolet (UV) Disinfection Units. Systems in this category may destroy bacteria, inactivate viruses, and leave no taste or odor in the water. However, UV units are not effective in removing most chemical pollutants from water, and the Environmental Protection Agency questions whether UV is effective against spores and cysts in water.

Source:
Federal Trade Commission, "Buying A Home Water Treatment Unit," *Facts for Consumers,* Washington: Government Printing Office, 1989.

Jewelry

Clocks

MOVEMENTS

Battery Clock. Alexander Bain designed the first battery clock shortly before 1838. Later he made use of an *earth battery,* consisting of copper and zinc plates sunk in the ground. The modern battery clock is more properly applied to a portable electric clock which depends on a dry cell or battery for its electric power. The cell may be used for driving a quartz-crystal oscillator and integrated electronic circuits, or for rewinding at intervals, driving a small electric motor, or periodic impulsing of a pendulum or balance.

Digital Clock. Any clock which indicates the time by a display of numerals rather than by a dial. Examples may be found at all stages of mechanical timekeeping; many early astronomical clocks in Italy had digital presentation in addition to dials. The *ticket* or *flick* clock was the first digital clock to be produced in commercial quantities. It was invented and made in the United States and features a glass cylinder containing two sets of celluloid *tickets* bearing numbers. The tickets are arranged to flick over one by one to indicate the time. The modern digital clock is all-electronic and uses either neon indicators, light-emitting diodes, or liquid crystal displays for the digital presentation.

Electric/Synchronous Clock. Synchronous clocks were developed in the United States by Henry E. Warren, who obtained his first patent in 1918. There was no general application for this type of clock until alternating-current power supplies were available to large numbers of consumers and the frequency could be maintained at a fixed and accurately maintained value. A rotor is kept synchronously in step with the generator at the electricity generating station, and gearing is used to drive the clock hands. Often worm drives are employed to achieve great reduction with the minimum number of wheels, immersed in oil baths to achieve silent running, as the early rotors ran at high speeds. Later models used a greater number of poles in the field magnet to reduce the rotor speed and, together with the use of plastic gears, minimized the noise levels without the need for lubrication. Strictly speaking, these are not clocks, but time indicators, for there is no means of measuring time within the synchronous clock mechanism.

Key-Wind Clock. In key-wind clocks, energy to operate the clock mechanism is stored in a spring that is wound by a key. The key may be either permanently attached to the spring shaft or, as with mantel and chime clocks, removable. Most key-wind movements are designed to supply enough energy to run the clock for 30 hours (a full day plus a six-hour grace period) or eight days (a full week plus a day's grace period) before rewinding is necessary. The winding knob or key turns, coiling up the mainspring that drives the gears. The gears are turned as the mainspring uncoils. Each gear turns at a different speed. The hour, minute, and second hands are attached to gears that turn at a predetermined rate of speed to indicate the proper time. The ticking comes from the escapement which allows the gears to turn or "escape" one tooth at a time. It is this stop-and-go control that creates the characteristic "tick-tock" sound.

Quartz Electronic Clock. A tiny quartz crystal, vibrating at a high frequency (ranging from 32,768 times per second to 4,194,303 times per second), permits the time-keeping mechanism to perform with great precision, accurate to plus or minus one clock minute a year. Electronic movements work on battery energy and require no outside source of energy (such as winding or plug-in electricity) at all. The vibrations of the quartz crystal are translated by a *chip* (a tiny microcomputer) into impulses that drive a motor that moves the hands.

TERMINOLOGY

Analog. Traditional look of a watch, clock, or other timepiece. Time is determined by the angular positioning of hands on a dial.

Anniversary Clock. Brass-and-crystal clock that features a visible movement in constant motion. So-called when it was invented because it needed winding just once a year on its anniversary.

Arabic Numerals. Most familiar numeral style (1, 2, 3, etc.) used on clock dials.

Beat. Term used to describe the tick-tock of a mechanical timepiece. A clock is said to be *in beat* if the spacing between the tick and the tock are equal. If they are not equally spaced, the clock is out of beat and will generally stop after a short run.

Beveled Glass. Glass with an angled surface beginning about ¾ inch from the edge, and used in the clock case.

Bezel. Front section of the clock case including the grooved rim into which the crystal is set (also applies to watches).

Big Ben Gong. Deep sounding chime that announces the hour; patterned after the large bell in the clock tower of the House of Parliament in London.

Bim-Bam. Descriptive term for clock chime which sounds only at the hour and half hour.

Bob. Weight at the lower end of a clock pendulum.

Bow Top. Design feature of some wall, shelf, and grandfather clock cases. Characterized by a curved top section.

Bracket Clock. Unit with handle on top. Originally designed to enable it to be carried from room to room. Also called *Carriage Clock.*

Burl. Decorative pattern in the wood grain caused by a series of irregularities that add to the character of the wood.

Cabinet or Case. Wooden enclosure of the movement, dial, and pendulum.

Cable-Driven. Movement powered by weights hanging on cables wound with a key or crank.

Carriage Clock. See *Bracket Clock.*

Center Shaft. Shaft to which the minute hand is attached, geared to make one revolution every 60 minutes.

Chain-Driven. Traditional grandfather clock movement, driven by weights hung from chains with engaged sprockets.

Chapter Ring. A decorative ring on the clock face upon which the hours are indicated. A feature on most traditional design mantel clocks.

Chime Melody. Tune played by the clock movement in portions, to mark the quarter hour, half hour, three-quarter hour and hour.

Chime Rods. Tuned rods which, when struck by small hammers powered by the clock movement, produce the chime melody and strike the hour.

Chip. Small silicon square onto which integrated circuits are imprinted. An integral part of the quartz movement.

Crown. The top of the clock.

Crystal. Glass or plastic piece that covers the dial for protection.

Day Ring. Divided ring on the lunar dial to indicate the days in the 29½ day lunar cycle.

Dial. The face of the clock. A decorative plate on which the hours are located.

Digital. Time display that uses no hands but shows the time in digits (numerals) on a readout screen.

Drop Case. Clock with a lower case, which usually houses a swinging pendulum. An example is a schoolhouse clock.

Finial. A decorative accessory, usually in wood or brass, forming the upper extremity of a column or structure. Often used to complement design on grandfather clock cabinets.

Frets. Removable grill panels in the side of a grandfather clock to help create better sound and allow easy access to movement.

Grandfather Clock. A floor clock or tall case clock.

Grandmother Clock. A floor clock similar to, but smaller than a grandfather design. Usually less that 80 inches in height.

Hands. Indicators for the measurement of hours, minutes, and seconds on the dial.

Inlaid Veneers. Thin layers of wood applied to form a decorative pattern.

Key-Wind. A spring-driven clock that is wound with a key or crank.

Light Emitting Diode (LED). Numbers telling the hours and minutes light up on a readout screen.

Liquid Crystal Display (LCD). Most frequently used in quartz timepieces. Time is continuously displayed in digits.

Lunar Dial. Extra feature on some clocks to indicate the correct phase of the 29½ day lunar cycle (i.e., cycle of the moon) on each day. Typically, a dial at the top of the clock face. Also called a *Moon Dial.*

Lyre. A decoration on the pendulum resembling an ancient musical instrument.

Marquetry. Decorative inlay of wood, ivory, and other materials.

Minute Track. Square or circular track on the face of the clock or watch. It is divided into 60 equal segments to measure minutes. It may appear on the outer perimeter of the dial or in the dial center.

Moon Dial. See *Lunar Dial.*

Movement. Timekeeping mechanism of the clock, which also produces the strike and chime.

Pediment. Any decorative frontal structure above the cornice of a clock.

Pendulum. A swinging rod and weight suspended below the clock movement. It accurately determines the rate of operation of the movement.

Pilaster. Decorative part used to create the effect of columns in the clock cabinet.

Pinch-Waisted. Traditional clock style with the crown and base wider than the part of the clock enclosing the pendulum.

Quartz. Electronic transistorized movements that work on battery energy and require no winding or external source of electricity. A tiny quartz crystal, vibrating at high frequency, permits the clock mechanism to perform with extraordinary precision.

Regulator. Mechanism that can be adjusted to make the clock more accurate.

Roman Dial. Roman numerals (e.g., I, II, III) are frequently used in traditional style carriage, mantel, and grandfather clocks.

Schoolhouse Clock. Traditional wood cabinet wall clock with a round or octagonal clock case and lower pendulum cabinet. Said to be a true Early American design because it was commonly found on classroom walls in American Colonial days.

St. Michael's Chimes. Chimes copying those originally installed in the St. Michael Church steeple in Charleston, SC, in 1764.

Scroll. Decorative ornament resembling a partially opened parchment scroll.

Snooze Alarm. An alarm that has a temporary shut-off feature. After being turned off, the alarm repeats, at certain intervals.

Straight Sided. A style of clock cabinet even in width from crown to base.

Strike. Chime or gong to indicate the hour.

Tambour. A style of clock whose shape is supposedly derived from Napoleon's hat.

Tempus Fugit. Latin phrase meaning "time flies," and often engraved on a decorative panel on the clock dial. A feature of many mantel and grandfather clocks.

Three-Sided Glass. Clock cabinet with a glass door and two glass side panels.

Timetrain. The series of gears in the clock movement that operates the minute and hour hands, and the second hand where applicable. The timetrain is responsible for activating the chimetrain in the movement.

Triple Chimes. Movement that plays three different chimes.

Tubular Bell Chime. Long hollow tubes which, when struck by small hammers powered by the clock movement, produce the chime melody and strike the hour.

Vacuum Fluorescence. Digital readout that develops a variety of colors with the most popular being blue.

Weight. Heavy metal piece that provides power to the movement.

Weight-Driven. A type of clock movement in which power is provided by gravitational effect of heavy weights.

Westminster Chimes. Famous tune played by the chime in the Victorian clock towers in the House of Parliament in London.

Whittington Chimes. Chimes originally rung in the church of St. Mary Le Bow in London. Legend has it that a young Dick Whittington, escaping the drudgeries of his master's housekeeper, thought he heard the church's chimes call out his name and advise him to turn back. He did, and eventually became Lord Mayor of London.

Winchester Chimes. Melodious chimes originating around 1093 from the Winchester Cathedral's central tower in Hampshire, England.

Source:

Granger, Patricia, et. al., *Industry Handbook of Clock Terminology,* Naperville, IL: Clock Manufacturers & Marketing Association, 1986.

Diamonds

A diamond is a natural mineral consisting essentially of pure carbon crystallized in the isometric system. Diamonds are found in many colors. A diamond is the hardest substance known to man. The Mohs scale, which is a scale of hardness used in mineralogy, assigns its maximum hardness number, 10, to diamond. Other properties of diamond are specific gravity of approximately 3.52; and refractive index of 2.42. In addition to meeting the above requirements, the U.S. Federal Trade Commission (FTC) requires that the "unqualified" use of the term diamond cannot be used to describe a stone unless it has been symmetrically fashioned with at least seventeen polished facets.

TERMINOLOGY

Blue White. A diamond that shows no other color or trace of color than blue (or bluish) when viewed under normal daylight or its equivalent.

Brilliant and Full Cut. A round diamond which has at least thirty-two facets plus the *table* (the largest and topmost facet) above the *girdle* (the widest circumference of the diamond) and at least twenty-four facets below plus the *culet* (*point*).

Gem Diamond. A diamond meeting the FTC requirement of having been symmetrically fashioned with at least seventeen polished facets.

Perfect Diamond. A diamond without flaws, cracks, carbon spots, clouds, or other blemishes or imperfections of any sort when examined in normal daylight, or its equivalent, by a trained eye under a ten-power, corrected diamond eye loupe or other equal magnifier.

Rough Diamond. An uncut or unfaceted object or product meeting the requirements of the above definition of diamond. Only 20 percent of all rough diamonds are suitable for cutting in gem diamonds.

GRADES

The Gemological Institute of America (GIA) has established a grading system for diamonds based on carat weight, color, clarity, and cut. These four factors are referred to in the industry as the *Four C's.*

Carat Weight. The unit of weight used for diamonds is the metric carat equal to 0.2 grams. Weight is the most objective of the Four C's, since loose diamonds can be weighed on a balance. Mounted diamonds cannot, but their weights can be estimated from careful measurements and calculations.

Color. This has two meanings in the diamond industry. A diamond said to have *fine color* frequently has no visible color. The term *fancy color* describes naturally colored diamonds with distinct tints. Artificially colored diamonds are called *treated,* or *enhanced.* The following *Color Grading* chart provides an illustration of GIA's color grading system and equivalent terms. Although a diamond may be any color of the spectrum, grading a cut stone for color means deciding on the amount by which it deviates from the whitest possible (truly colorless). Completely colorless, icy-white diamonds are rare, and therefore, more valuable. White diamonds with a tinge of blue—known as *blue white*—are rarer still. The best way to see the true color of a diamond is to look at it against a white surface. Although most diamonds are a shade of white, they do come in all colors—pale yellow, canary, pink, red, green, blue, and brown. These are called *fancies,* and they are valued for their depth of color, just as white diamonds are valued for their lack of color. The famous Hope Diamond is blue, and the well-known Tiffany Diamond is canary.

Clarity. This refers to the presence of internal features in a stone, called inclusions, and external characteristics, called blem-

Gemological Institute of America (GIA)		Old World Terms		
Colorless	D	Finest White	Jager	Colorless
	E			
	F		River	
Near Colorless	G	Fine White	Top Wesselton	Stones in these grades will face up colorless (i.e., slight traces of color will not be apparent in mounted stones to other than the trained eye.)
	H	White	Wesselton	
	I	Commercial White	Top Crystal	
	J	Top Silver Cape	Crystal	Small stones in this range will face up colorless when mounted but large ones will be tinted.
Faint Yellow	K	Silver Cape	Top Cape	
	L			
	M	Light Cape	Cape	Mounted stones in these grades will display a yellowish tint even to the untrained eye.
Very Light Yellow	N		Low Cape	
	O	Cape		
	P			
	Q			
	R			
Light Yellow	S	Dark Cape	Very Light Yellow	
	T			
	U			
	V			
	W			
	X			
	Y			
	Z			
Fancy Yellow	Z+			

Color grading chart for diamonds

ishes. The fewer the inclusions, the clearer and more brilliant the diamond. Truly flawless diamonds are extremely rare. It is possible to find in virtually all diamonds the minute crystals, feathers, and clouds that are called inclusions. A complete discussion can be found in the *Clarity* section, which follows.

Cut. This includes a diamond's style and make, which can enhance color and minimize the appearance of inclusions. *Style* is the basic facet design, while *make* means proportions and finish. Diamonds are cut according to an exact mathematical formula. To be called a diamond, the stone must have at least 17 polished facets, which are the small, flat polished planes cut into a diamond. The greater the number of facets, the more light is reflected back to the viewer's eye. This reflection is called *brilliance,* and is extremely important in evaluating the quality of a diamond. A *full-cut diamond* has 58 facets. The widest circumference of a diamond is the *girdle.* Above the girdle are 32 facets plus the *table,* the largest and topmost facet. Below the girdle there are 24 facets plus the *culet,* or *point.* Cut also deals with the shape of the diamond. Traditional shapes are round and fancy, a term which includes emerald, marquise, pear, oval, heart, and star. Few diamonds are properly cut. The vast majority are *spread.* This means that the cutter has compromised the proper proportions and has cut the stone to weigh more than it would if cut to proper proportions. When this is the case, beauty and brilliance are sacrificed for size.

CLARITY

Clarity refers to the presence of internal features in a stone, called inclusions, and external characteristics, called blemishes. Most of the following descriptions are most applicable to round brilliants in typical jewelry sizes: characteristics may be more visible in large stones and fancy shapes. When a clarity grade is assigned, consideration is given to the size, number, position, nature, and color or relief of the various clarity characteristics.

Flawless (FL). Flawless diamonds show no blemishes or inclu-

sions when examined by a skilled grader under 10x magnification. The following do not disqualify a stone from the flawless category: An extra facet on the pavilion which cannot be seen face-up; naturals totally confined to the girdle, which neither thicken the girdle nor distort its outline; internal graining which is not reflective, white, or colored, and does not significantly affect transparency.

Internally Flawless (IF). Stones which show no inclusions and only insignificant blemishes under 10x. Normally what separates *IF* from *FL* stones are characteristics that can be removed by minor repolishing (light surface graining is an exception).

Very Very Slightly Included (VVS1 and VVS2). *VVS* diamonds contain minute inclusions that are difficult for even a skilled grader to locate under 10x. In *VVS1*, they are extremely difficult to see, visible only from the pavilion, or are small and shallow enough to be removed by minor repolishing. In *VVS2*, they are very difficult to see.

Very Slightly Included (VS1 and VS2). VS stones contain minor inclusions ranging from difficult (*VS1*) to somewhat easy (*VS2*) for a trained grader to see under 10x. Small included crystals, small feathers, and distinct clouds are typical.

Slightly Included (SI1 and SI2). *SI* stones contain noticeable inclusions which are easy (*SI1*) or very easy (*SI2*) to see under 10x. In some SIs, inclusions can be seen with the unaided eye.

Imperfect (I1, I2, and I3). *I*-grade diamonds contain inclusions which are obvious to a trained grader under 10x magnification, can often be easily seen face-up with the unaided eye, seriously affect the stone's potential durability, or are so numerous they affect transparency and brilliance.

Sources:
Christie, Andrew, *Private Correspondence,* New York: Gemological Institute of America, March 23, 1992.
Federal Trade Commission, "Guides of the Jewelry Industry," 16 CFR 23.0, Washington: Government Printing Office, 1992.
"How to Buy a Diamond" (pamphlet), New York: Tiffany & Co., 1992.
"What You Should Know About Buying a Diamond" (pamphlet), New York: Jewelers of America, Inc., 1992.

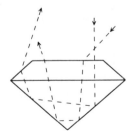
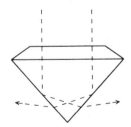

The diamond at left is properly proportioned to reflect light and maximize brilliance. Many diamonds are cut to maximize weight, resulting in loss of brilliance and fire.

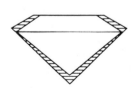
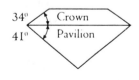

The diamond at left is properly cut, while the diamond at right is spread. The shaded area should have been cut away, as it reduces the diamond's brilliance.

Gemstones

To qualify as *gemstones,* minerals must possess: beauty (affected by color, transparency, and brilliance), which is brought out by cutting; durability (the stone's hardness and toughness); and rarity (taking into consideration size and quality). Some organic materials also are used in jewelry. These include pearl, coral, amber, and jet. The most popular organic gem is the pearl (the birthstone for June). Other popular gemstones include:

Alexandrite
Amber
Amethyst, birthstone for February
Amertrine
Aquamarine, birthstone for March
Cat's Eye Chrysoberyl
Citrine
Coral
Diamond, birthstone for April
Emerald, birthstone for May
Garnet, birthstone for January
Iolite
Jade
Kunzite
Lapis Lazuli
Opal, birthstone for October
Peridot, birthstone for August
Ruby, birthstone for July
Sapphire, birthstone for September
Spinel
Tanzanite
Topaz, birthstone for November
Tourmaline
Tsavorite
Turquoise, birthstone for December
Zircon

NATURAL, SYNTHETIC, AND IMITATION STONES

As their names indicate, natural stones are found in nature; synthetic stones are made in a laboratory. Except for their origin, synthetics are essentially the same as natural stones in their composition and properties, such as hardness and brilliance. By contrast, imitation stones only resemble natural stones in appearance. They may be glass, plastic, or less costly stones.

The following guide provides an easy-to-understand shorthand system for labeling synthetic gemstones. Each of the broad non-natural material categories has been assigned a code consisting of two or more letters. Each code identifies the nature of materials from which it was made.

The appropriate code is to be used by the industry on every tag, stone paper, container, invoice, and/or memorandum each time a seller offers for sale or sells one of these materials to a buyer within the trade.

All non-natural materials must be properly represented. However, codes and abbreviations are not sufficient when dealing with the consuming public. According to U.S. Federal Trade Commis-

sion (FTC) guidelines, a synthetic or imitation stone cannot be offered for sale without disclosing that it is not natural. For example, a ruby made in a laboratory having the same composition as a natural stone must be described as *synthetic, created, laboratory-grown,* or *man-made.* Similarly, a stone that does not have the same composition as the natural stone must be described as *imitation* or with a similar word. In either case, consumers must be clearly informed if the stone is not natural. In order to clearly disclose the nature of these products, and to make it perfectly clear that these are not natural stones, full words (not codes) must be used in all advertising and promotion, stone papers, containers, sales slips, invoices, and/or memorandums. For example, the word(s) *synthetic* or *laboratory-grown, imitation, assembled,* or some other word or phrase of like meaning must be used in place of or in addition to abbreviations or code symbols.

Trade names used to promote various products must be accompanied by a specific reference to the actual composition of the material(s) the product contains.

Synthetic or Laboratory-Grown Materials (SYN or LG). These tag codes may be used to describe *synthetic* or *laboratory-grown* material which has essentially the same optical, physical, and chemical properties as a naturally occurring counterpart. The code names may not be used as nouns; thus a stone must not be referred to as *a synthetic* or *a laboratory-grown.* In all cases, the name of the material must also be used; thus a stone must be referred to as *synthetic emerald, laboratory-grown ruby,* etc. The tag codes may not be used with the consuming public; only full descriptions are acceptable. Synthetic or laboratory-grown materials are stable in color and composition under normal wear. The jeweler has the option to call these materials either *synthetic* or *laboratory-grown.*

Imitation Products, Simulants, or Substitutes (IMIT). Used for a manufactured product fabricated in such material as glass, ceramic, or plastic, designed to imitate or resemble the appearance but not duplicate the characteristic properties of a natural gemstone. These materials require special care, and household chemicals, cosmetics, abrasives, and sudden shocks should be avoided. *IMIT* is also the tag code for a simulant, which is defined as a man-made single crystal product that is used to simulate the appearance, but not duplicate the properties, of the natural gemstone it imitates. This category also includes non-single crystal materials such as imitation lapis lazuli and imitation coral.

Assembled Materials or Composite (ASBL). Used to tag products made of multiple layers or combinations of manufactured and/or natural materials fused, bonded, or otherwise joined together to imitate the appearance of a natural gemstone, to create a unique design, or to generate unusual color combinations. The *ASBL* coded stones require special care, and household chemicals, cosmetics, abrasives, and sudden shocks should be avoided.

UNITS OF MEASUREMENT

Gemstones may be measured by weight or size, or both. The basic unit for weighing gemstones is the *carat,* which is equal to one-fifth of a gram. (Alternative spelling is *karat,* used primarily when referring to gold jewelry.) Carats are divided into 100 units, called *points*. E.g., a half-carat gemstone would weigh .50 carats or 50 points. When gemstones are measured by dimensions, the size is expressed in millimeters. E.g., cultured pearls are measured in millimeters. A common size of cultured pearls in necklaces is six to seven millimeters.

GEMSTONE ENHANCEMENTS

Gemstone enhancements refer to the way some gems are altered or treated to improve their appearance or durability. It includes any process other than cutting and polishing that improves the appearance (color/clarity/phenomena), durability, or availability of a gemstone. The treatment may or may not be permanent and the treated stone may require special care. Depending on the stone, enhancement may or may not affect its value.

The Jewelers of America, an industry consortium, has published *The Gemstone Enhancement Manual* which contains an easy-to-understand shorthand system for labeling. The manual was developed by a coalition of jewelry industry leaders representing the various trade organizations, gemological scientists, and the trade press. Each item has been assigned a code consisting of one or more letters, indicating the possibility of enhancement and identifying the pertinent process. This code is to be used by the industry on every tag, stone paper, container, invoice and/or memorandum each time a seller offers for sale or sells a gemstone to a buyer within the trade.

To communicate with the consumer about traditionally enhanced gemstones, many jewelers distribute information by stocking Consumer Information Leaflets. These leaflets are available for most gemstones.

The *Gemstone Enhancement Manual* was submitted to the Federal Trade Commission on behalf of the jewelry industry. Its main provisions are presented below.

LABELING ENHANCEMENTS

All gemstones can be divided into three basic categories:

A (Those which are not routinely enhanced). The *A* symbol used alone indicates either a gemstone that is not currently known to be enhanced (e.g., alexandrite and garnet), or one that is so rarely enhanced that to give it an *E* symbol would mislead the public (e.g., colorless, near-colorless, or faint yellow diamonds that have not been laser-drilled or altered in any other way).

E (Those which are normally enhanced). The *E* symbol indicates that the gemstone is routinely enhanced. The type of traditional enhancement covered by this symbol is indicated on the following chart and is addressed within the text of the Consumer Information Leaflets. E.g. the *E* designation for aquamarine means only the treatment that is described in the manual, i.e., heat treatment. In the case of emerald, the *E* designation refers to oiling with colorless oil. Since many traditional enhancements are difficult or impractical to prove definitively, the approach taken in this manual is, unless otherwise indicated, to assume that such enhancement has been done to that particular gemstone. This assumption has been made in order to protect both the seller and the consumer. The *E* symbol may be used only for those gemstones and for

those enhancements as prescribed on the chart. However, nothing precludes the seller from using the specific enhancement code in place of the *E* symbol. (E.g., an *H* can be used for an aquamarine in place of an *E*.)

F (Those which are altered in a non-traditional manner). Those gemstones and treatments not covered under the *A* or *E* symbols are addressed in a specific manner. [E.g., *Ruby (F)* has surface cavities filled with a foreign matter such as glass.] Within the industry, this gemstone must be labeled with the letter *F*. This information must be provided to the consuming public in writing. Abbreviations and codes are not sufficient.

N (Exception to above). The *N* symbol is used in the event that a particular gemstone has received no enhancement and the seller will provide a guarantee that there has been none. That gemstone must be accompanied by documentation to support the fact that the gemstone is not enhanced. The supporting documentation may be supplied by an independent source, such as a laboratory, or provided by the seller of the gemstone as his/her personal guarantee of no enhancement. The *N* symbol does not appear on the chart and should only be used in accordance with these instructions.

ENHANCEMENT CODES

Defined below are the specific Enhancement Codes used in the Gemstone Enhancement/Alteration Information Chart. Multiple enhancement techniques are sometimes applied to the same material. The most significant process should be listed first. E.g., Diamond (*IL*; *Impregnation/Infusion* and *Lasering*).

B (Bleaching). The use of chemicals or other agents to lighten or remove a gemstone's color.

C (Coating). The use of such surface treatments as lacquering, enameling, inking, foiling, or sputtering of films to improve appearance, provide color, or add other special effects.

D (Dyeing). The introduction of coloring matter into a gemstone to give it new color, intensify present color, or add color uniformity.

F (Filling). The filling of surface breaking cavities or fractures with glass, plastic, or another foreign substance to improve appearance and/or add weight.

H (Heating). The use of heat to achieve desired alteration of color, clarity, and/or phenomena.

I (Impregnation/Infusion). General introduction or infusion of any foreign substance.

L (Lasering). The use of a laser and chemicals to reach and alter inclusions in diamonds.

O (Oiling). The penetration of colorless oil into voids and fissures which reach the surface to improve overall appearance.

R (Irradiation). The use of a high-energy or subatomic particle bombardment to alter a gemstone's color. Often followed by a heating process.

S (Stabilization). The use of a colorless bonding agent (commonly plastic) within a gemstone to improve durability and appearance.

U (Surface Diffusion). The use of high temperature and chemicals resulting in the shallow penetration of color and/or asterism (starlike figure produced by transmitted or reflected light) on or just below the surface of a gemstone.

ENHANCEMENT DESIGNATIONS

The column in the Information Chart labeled *Frequency Used* represents a reasonable estimate of how commonly a particular enhancement process is utilized in the trade. The columns *Frequency Used* and *Stability* refer specifically to the enhancement process applied to the material. The *Care Required* column relates to special care that may be necessary to preserve the enhancement applied to the material. special advice relates to the need for any special care required by the specific gemstone variety, irrespective of enhancement.

ENHANCEMENT FREQUENCY DESIGNATIONS
Rarely
Occasionally
Commonly
Usually
Always
Unknown

ENHANCEMENT STABILITY DESIGNATION
Excellent
Very Good
Good
Fair
Poor
Variable

SPECIAL CARE DESIGNATIONS
Normal
Special
Extra Special

Sources:
Federal Trade Commission, *About Fine Jewelry: Facts for Consumers,* Washington: Government Printing Office, June 1989.
The Gemstone Enhancement Manual, New York: Jewelers of America, 1990.

GEMSTONE ENHANCEMENT/ALTERATION CHART

The *A* symbol indicates a gemstone which is not currently known to be enhanced, or one that is very rarely enhanced. The *E* symbol indicates a gemstone which is routinely and traditionally enhanced. The *N* symbol may be used for any gemstone that the seller guarantees has not been enhanced or treated.

Gemstone	Tag Code	Enhancement Method	Frequency Used	Stability	Care Required	Special Advice
Alexandrite	A	None	....	....	Normal	
Amazonite	E or I	Waxed/Parafined to improve appearance	Usually	Good	Special	Avoid heat, chemicals and ultrasonic
	O	Oiled to improve appearance	Occasionally	Good to Fair	Special to extra special	Avoid heat, chemicals and ultrasonic
	S	Plastic and other agents to improve appearance	Unknown	Very Good	Normal	
Amber	E or H	Heated to improve appearance, add "sun spangles" or deepen color	Occasionally	Very Good to good	Special	Avoid chemicals and ultrasonic
	D	Dyed to surface treated to add color	Rarely	Viable	Special	Avoid repolishing surface, chemicals, and ultrasonic
Amethyst	A	None	....	....	Normal	
	H	Heated to lighten color	Occasionally	Excellent	Normal	
Andalusite	A	None	....	....	Normal	
Aquamarine	E or H	Heated to improve color	Usually	Excellent	Normal	
Ametrine	A	None			Normal	
(Bi-color Quartz)	R	Limited information available at this time	Unknown	Unknown	Normal	
Beryl						
Blue ("Maxie Type")	R	Irradiated blue from pale pink or colorless	Always	Poor	Extra Special	Color fades, avoid light or heat

GEMSTONE ENHANCEMENT/ALTERATION CHART (Continued)

Gemstone	Tag Code	Enhancement Method	Frequency Used	Stability	Care Required	Special Advice
Pink	E or H	Heated from orangy colors	Commonly	Excellent	Normal	
Yellow-Green	A	None	....	....	Normal	
Red	A	None	....	....	Normal	
Yellow	R	Produced by irradiation	Usually	Variable	Normal to special depending on method	Certain stones may fade in light or heat
Chalcedony						
Agate	E or D	Dyed	Usually	Excellent	Normal	General comment-Dyes used in this category are stable to light and heat
Black (Onyx)	E or D	Dyed	Always	Excellent	Normal	
Banded	E or D	Dyed	Usually	Excellent	Normal	
Blue	E or D	Dyed	Usually	Excellent	Normal	
Green	E or D	Dyed	Usually	Excellent	Normal	
Carnelian	E or H	Heated to produce color	Usually	Excellent	Normal	
	E or D	Dyed to produce color	Commonly	Excellent	Normal	
Jasper	A	None	....	....	Normal	
Chrysoprase	A	None	....	....	Normal	
Chrysoberyl						
Cat's Eye	A	None	....	....	Normal	
Transparent Varieties:						
Yellow	A	None	....	....	Normal	
Brown	A	None	....	....	Normal	
Green	A	None	....	....	Normal	
Citrine	E or H	Produced by heating various types of quartz	Usually	Excellent	Normal	
Coral						
Black	A	None	....	....	Special	Avoid chemicals, cosmetics, and ultrasonic
White	E or B	Bleached	Commonly	Good	Special	Avoid chemicals, cosmetics, and ultrasonic: material may discolor in time
Pink	A	None	....	....	Special	Same as above
Orange	A	Nonc	....	....	Special	Same as above
"Gold"	B	Bleached from black coral	Usually	Very Good	Special	Same as above
Red	D	Dyed	Occasionally	Variable	Special to extra special depending on type of dye	Certain material may fade in light or heat. Avoid chemicals, cosmetics, and ultrasonic

GEMSTONE ENHANCEMENT/ALTERATION CHART (Continued)

Gemstone	Tag Code	Enhancement Method	Frequency Used	Stability	Care Required	Special Advice
Diamond						
Colorless to	A	None	....	....	Normal	
Faint yellow	L	Laser drilled to improve appearance	Occasionally to commonly	Very good	Normal	
	C	Coated to disguise off-color	Rarely	Poor to very good depending on method	Variable	Recutting, steam cleaning, ultrasonic, and occasionally alcohol may adversely affect color and appearance
	F	Filling of surface cavities or fractures with a foreign substance	Occasionally	Very good	Special to normal	Recutting or extreme heat will affect appearance
Colored	R	Irradiated and/or heated to induce "fancy" colors	Occasionally	Excellent to very good	Normal except green	Avoid heating treated green stones as the color may change
	C	Coated to "fancy" color	Rarely	Good to fair	Special	Recutting, steaming, and ultrasonic may adversely affect color and appearance
Emerald	E or O	Oiled with colorless oil to improve appearance	Usually	Fair to good	Special	Avoid temperature changes, steaming, chemicals, and ultrasonic
	D	Dyed with dye and/or colored oil	Occasionally	Variable	Special	Same as above
	S	Stabilized with colorless bonding agent to improve durability and appearance	Occasionally	Very good to good	Special to normal	Avoid temperature changes and chemicals
Garnets						
Almandite	A	None	....	....	Normal	Avoid sudden temperature change
Demantoid	A	None	....	....	Normal	Same as above
Grossularite	A	None	....	....	Normal	Same as above
Pyrope	A	None	....	....	Normal	Same as above
Rhodolite	A	None	....	....	Normal	Same as above
Spessartite	A	None	....	....	Normal	Same as above
Tsavorite	A	None	....	....	Normal	Same as above
Hermatite	A	None	....	....	Normal	
Iolite	A	None	....	....	Normal	
Ivory & Bone	E or B	Bleached to whiten and remove discoloration	Commonly	Good	Special	Avoid chemicals and ultrasonic; may discolor in time
	D	Dyed for artistic purposes	Occasionally	Good	Special	Same as above
	I	Impregnated with wax	Occasionally	Good	Special	Same as above
Jade						
Jadeite	E or I	Impregnated with colorless wax	Commonly	Very good to good	Normal to special	Avoid ultrasonic

GEMSTONE ENHANCEMENT/ALTERATION CHART (Continued)

Gemstone	Tag Code	Enhancement Method	Frequency Used	Stability	Care Required	Special Advice
	D	Dyed to imitate natural colors	Occasionally	Variable	Special	Avoid stong light, chemicals, and ultrasonic; may discolor in time
Nephrite	A	None	....	....	Normal	
	D	Dyed selectively to alter color for artistic purposes in carvings	Rarely	Unknown	Special	Avoide chemicals, ultrasonic, and strong light
Kunzite	E or H	Heated to improve color from certain locations	Unknown	Unknown	Special	May fade; avoid strong lignt and ultrasonic
	R	Irradiated to darken color	Occasionally	Fair	Special	Same as above
Lapis Laxuli	E or I	Impregnated with colorless wax or oil	Commonly	Very good to good	Normal to special	Avoid ultrasonic
	D	Dyed to provide color and/or uniformity	Commonly	Variable	Special	Avoid chemicals and ultrasonic
Malachite	A	None	....	....	Special	Avoid chemicals and ultrasonic
	C	Coated with wax	Occasionally	Fair to Good	Special	Avoid chemicals and ultrasonic
	S	Stabilized to improve durability and appearance	Unknown	Unknown	Special	Same as above
Moonstone	A	None	....	....	Normal	
Opal						
White, near colorless & colorless	A	None	....	....	Special	Avoid heat, chemicals, and ultrasonic with all opals
	D	Dyed or modified with colored plastic	Rarely	Good	Special	Same as above and avoid repolishing
	O	Oiled to hide crazing	Rarely	Fair	Special	Avoid heat, chemicals, and ultrasonic
	S	Stabilization with plastic to hide crazing	Rarely	Good	Special	Same as above
	C	Coated with a dark substance to improve play-of-color	Rarely	Fair	Special	Same as above
Black, Gray, and Semi-black	A	None	....	....	Special	Same as above
	O	Oiled to mask crazing	Rarely	Fair	Special	Same as above
	D	Smoke treatment	Rarely	Fair to Good	Special	Same as above and avoid repolishing
	S	Stabilization with plastic to hide crazing, improve appearance or durability	Rarely	Good	Special	Avoid heat, chemicals and ultrasonic
Boulder	A	None	....	....	Special	Same as above
	O	Oiled to mask crazing	Rarely	Fair	Special	Same as above

GEMSTONE ENHANCEMENT/ALTERATION CHART (Continued)

Gemstone	Tag Code	Enhancement Method	Frequency Used	Stability	Care Required	Special Advice
	S	Stabilization with plastic to hide crazing, improve appearance or durability	Rarely	Good	Special	Same as above
Matrix	A	None	....	....	Special	Avoid heat, chemicals and ultrasonic
	D	Special type takes dye-sugar treatment to produce black and play of color	Occasionally	Fair	Special	Same as above and avoid repolishing
Pearl						
Natural	E or B	Bleached to improve color and appearance	Usually	Very Good	Special	Avoid cosmetics and household chemicals
	D	Dyed black (other than chemical treatment with heat)	Rarely	Unknown	Special	Same as above
	D	Chemical treatment combined with heat to produce gray to black	Rarely	Very good to good	Special	Avoid chemicals, cosmetics, and ultrasonic
Cultured	E or B	Bleached to improve color and uniformity	Usually	Excellent	Speical	Same as above
	E or D	Dyed to give rose or blue tints	Usually	Good	Special	Same as above
	D	Dyed blue and blackish	Occasionally	Variable	Special	Same as above
	D	Dyed all colors (fresh water)	Usually	Variable	Special	Same as above
	R	Irradiated to produce blue and gray colors	Occasionally	Good	Special	Same as above
	D	Chemical treatment combined with heat to produce gray to black	Commonly	Good	Special	Same as above
Peridot	A	None	....	....	Special	Avoid sudden temperature change and harsh chemicals
Rhodonite	A	None	....	....	Normal	
Ruby	E or H	Heated to improve color and appearance	Usually	Excellent	Normal	
	D	Dyed with colored oil to improve appearance	Rarely	Fair	Special	Avoid household chemicals and ultrasonics
	F	Surface cavities filled with a foreign material, including glass	Rarely	Fair to good	Special	Foreign material is fragile and may fall out, avoid heat and ultrasonic
	U	Difusion of color or asterism into the surface	Rarely	Good	Special	Avoid repolishing or recutting
Sapphire	E or H	Heated to produce, intensify or lighten color and/or improve color uniformity	Usually	Excellent	Normal	

GEMSTONE ENHANCEMENT/ALTERATION CHART (Continued)

Gemstone	Tag Code	Enhancement Method	Frequency Used	Stability	Care Required	Special Advice
	U	Diffusion of color or asterism into the surface, usually blue	Rarely	Good	Special	Avoid repolishing or recutting
	R	Irradiation to provide temporary intense yellow or orange color	Occasionally	Very Poor	Extra Special	Fades quickly in light or heat
Serpentine	D	Dyed various colors	Commonly	Fair to good	Special	Dye may fade
Sodalite	A	None	....	....	Normal	
	D	Dyed	Rarely	No data	Special	Dye may fade
Spinel	A	None	....	....	Normal	
Spodumene						
Green	R	Iradiated to produce green color	Rarely	Poor	Extra special	Color fades in light or heat
Tanzanite (Zoisite)	E or H	Heated to produce violet-blue color	Usually	Excellent	Special	Avoid sudden temperature changes and ultrasonic
Topaz						
Blue	R	Irradiated and heated to produce blue color	Usually	Excellent	Normal	
Yellow/Orange	R	Irradiated to intensify color	Occasionally	Variable	Special	Avoid heat and strong light
Pink	E or H	Heated chromium bearing pinkish-brown to orange stones	Usually	Excellent	Normal	
Tourmaline						
Chrome Vanadium	A	None	....	....	Normal	
Cat's Eye	A	None	....	....	Normal	
Yellow/Orange	A	None	....	....	Normal	
	H	Heated to improve color; reported	Unknown	Unknown		
	R	Irradiated to improve color; reported	Unknown	Unknown		
Green, Blue	E or H	Heated to improve color	Commonly	Excellent	Normal	
	R	Irradiated to blue color; reported	Unknown	Unknown		
Pink, Redand Purple	E or H	Heated to improve color	Occasionally	Excellent	Normal	
	R	Irradiated to intensify color	Commonly	Good	Normal	
	S	Stabilized with colorless bonding agent to improve durability and appearance	Occasionally	Variable	Normal	

GEMSTONE ENHANCEMENT/ALTERATION CHART (Continued)

Gemstone	Tag Code	Enhancement Method	Frequency Used	Stability	Care Required	Special Advice
Turquoise	S	Stabilized with plastic to create or improve color and durability	Commonly	Good	Normal	
	I	Impregnated with oil or wax to enhance or create color	Commonly	Poor to fair	Special	Avoid hot water and household chemicals
	D	Dyed to improve color	Rarely	Poor	Extra Special	Same as above
Zircon						
Yellow, Green, and Brown	A	None	....	....	Special	Avoid harsh abrasives
Blue, Red, and Colorless	E or H	Brwonish crystals are heated to these colors	Always	Good	Special	Same as above

Jewelry, Gold

Guidelines established by the U.S. Federal Trade Commission (FTC) in cooperation with the jewelry industry state that the word *gold,* used by itself, means "all gold" or 24 karat (24K) gold. The *karat* is used to describe the fineness of gold, and each karat equals $\frac{1}{24}$ part. (The alternative spelling, *carat*, is commonly used in reference to gemstones, and designates a weight of 0.2 grams or approximately 3.086 grains troy.) Karat may be abbreviated K, k, kt. (Carat, car., or ct.) Because 24K gold is soft, it is usually mixed with other metals to increase its hardness and durability. The *karat* marking describes what proportion of gold is mixed with other metals and is based on a total of 24 parts. For example, if fourteen parts of gold are mixed with ten parts of base metal, the combination is called 14 karat (14K) gold. The higher the karat rating, the higher the proportion of gold in the object. The lowest karat gold that can be marketed as gold in the United States is 10 karat. The karat quality is not required to be marked, but most jewelry has its karat quality designated. A karat quality mark must be accompanied by the U.S. registered trademark of the person or company that will stand behind the mark, according to the requirements of the National Gold and Silver Stamping Act.

GRADES

10 Karat Gold. 10 parts pure gold and 14 parts alloy. The lowest karat gold that can be sold as *gold* in the U.S.

14 Karat Gold. 14 parts pure gold and 10 parts alloy.

18 Karat Gold. 18 parts pure gold and 6 parts alloy.

20 Karat Gold. 20 parts pure gold and 4 parts alloy.

24 Karat Gold. Pure gold.

Fine Gold. 24 karat gold.

Gold. Composed throughout of fine (24 karat) gold.

Red Gold. Gold alloyed with copper, the proportion of copper varying between 25 and 50 percent. The more copper the darker the red. Sometimes referred to as *pink gold.*

White Gold. A gold alloy that usually contains 10 to 20 percent nickel, plus zinc, copper, and perhaps platinum or manganese. It contains no silver, and little or no palladium.

TERMINOLOGY

Fool's Gold. Common name for iron pyrite, which is sometimes mistaken for gold. Iron pyrite is hard and brittle, while gold is soft and malleable.

Gold Electroplate or Gold Electroplated. A product or part of a product surfaced by an electrolyte process with coating or plating of gold alloy of not less than 10 karat fineness, the minimum thickness throughout of which is equivalent to $\frac{7}{1000000}$ of an inch of fine gold.

Gold Filled, Gold Plate, Gold Plated, Gold Overlay, Rolled Gold Plate. These terms are applied to a product or a part of a product that has been plated with a gold alloy that is not less than 10 karat fineness. In the case where the plating constitutes at least $\frac{1}{20}$ of the weight of the metal in the entire article, the term is immediately preceded by a designation of the karat fineness of the plating (as, e.g., *14K Gold Filled, 14K GF, 14K Gold Plated, 14K GP,* and *14K Gold Overlay*). When the plating consists of less than $\frac{1}{20}$ of the weight of the metal in the article, the terms *Gold Plate, Gold Plated, Rolled Gold Plate,* and *Gold Overlay* may be used only if the karat fineness designation is immediately preceded by a fraction which accurately discloses the portion of the weight of the metal that is the plating (e.g. $\frac{1}{40}$ *14K Rolled Gold Plate,* and $\frac{1}{40}$ *14K R G P*).

Gold Filled. Bonding a layer (or layers) of gold alloy to a base metal and then rolling or drawing the metal to the thickness desired. The gold content must be $\frac{1}{20}$ or more of the total weight of the metal in the piece.

Gold Flashed or Gold Washed. A product that meets the minimum fineness of *Gold Electroplate* but has a minimum thickness less than $\frac{7}{1000000}$ of an inch.

Gold Tubing or Gold-Hollow Center. A product which is composed throughout of gold alloy but contains a concealed hollow center or interior.

Heavy Gold Electroplate or Heavy Gold Electroplated. A product electrolytically surfaced with a minimum thickness throughout of $^{100}/_{1000000}$ of an inch of fine gold.

Karat (K, k, or kt). One 24th part of pure gold. 20 karat gold is 20 parts pure gold and 4 parts alloy, 18 karat gold is 18 parts pure gold and 6 parts alloy, etc. Each karat equals $\frac{1}{24}$ purity.

Plated, Gold Filled (GF), Gold Overlay. Terms used to describe jewelry that has a layer of at least 10 karat gold mechanically bonded to a base metal. If such jewelry is marked with one of the terms listed above, the term itself must follow the karat quality of the gold used (*14K Gold Overlay,* e.g.). If the layer of karat gold constitutes less than $\frac{1}{20}$ of the total weight of the object, any markings must state the actual percentage of karat gold, such as $\frac{1}{40}$ *14K Gold Overlay.* Mechanically plated jewelry often lasts a long time but, depending on use, its coating can eventually wear away.

Rolled Gold Plate (RGP). The same type of gold covering on a base metal as *Gold Filled,* except that the quantity of karat gold is less than $\frac{1}{20}$ of the total metal weight. Must be identified with a fraction indicating the quantity of gold.($\frac{1}{40}$ *18K RGP,* e.g.).

Roman Gold. A finish on gold jewelry produced by matting or frosting the surface, then electroplating it with pure gold. This provides a soft matte finish with a rich yellow color.

Solid Gold. Refers to any karat gold if the inside of the item of jewelry is not hollow. The proportion of gold in the piece of jewelry is still determined by the karat mark. Refers to a jewelry item solidly of gold or of a gold alloy (e.g., *14K Solid Gold* or *Solid 14K Gold*).

Troy Ounce. From the troy system of weight used for measuring precious metals, based on a pound of 12 ounces and an ounce of 20 pennyweights or 480 grains. Precious metals are measured in troy ounces worldwide.

Vermeil. Sterling silver jewelry plated with a coating of gold $^{120}/_{100000}$ of an inch thick to produce "vermeil."

Source:
Federal Trade Commission, "Guides of the Jewelry Industry," 16 CFR 23.0, Washington: Government Printing Office, 1992.

Jewelry Terminology

Anodizing. Forming a coat of stable oxide compound on a metal surface. It is done electrochemically, mostly to aluminum, titanium, and their alloys. The coating protects the metal from further oxidation, corrosion, and discoloring.

Antiquing. A process whereby metal objects are chemically treated to take on a color or patina associated with age.

Art Nouveau. Late 19th and early 20th century style of art that found its way into jewelry. It is generally depicted as curved, flowing, asymmetrical forms, recurring and intertwining as leaves, flowers, and insects.

Baguette. A rectangular-shaped small diamond often used to enhance the setting of a larger stone.

Burnish. Cold-working the metal surface to make it smooth.

Channel Setting. Type of setting often used in mounting a number of smaller stones of uniform size in a row. Stones are not held by individual prongs but rather continuous strips of metal forming a channel into which are fitted the outer edges of the row of stones.

Colored Stone. Any precious or genuine stone other than diamond used as a component in jewelry; sometimes used to describe synthetics, glass, plastic, or similar imitation stones.

Cubic Zirconia. Also called *CZ.* A diamond imitation having high dispersion and refraction, but weighing 70 percent more than diamond.

Engravable. Any item with a relatively flat, thick area suitable for engraving.

Estate Jewelry. Used jewelry, usually from a deceased person's estate, re-entering the market.

Fancy Cut. A diamond cut other than round—such as baguette, emerald, triangle, pearl, star.

Fine Jewelry. There is no commercial or legal definition for the phrase *fine jewelry.* However, many retailers use the term to describe karat gold jewelry, gemstones, and higher-priced watches.

Florentine Finish. A textured surface for gold and silver produced by engraving a series of parallel lines in one direction, then cross-hatching them more lightly at a 90 degree angle.

Hand made or Hand wrought. The entire shaping and forming of the product from raw materials, and finishing and decoration were accomplished by hand labor and manually controlled methods which permit the maker to control and vary the construction, shape, design, and finish of each part of each individual product.

Hand-Polished, Hand-Engraved, Hand-Finished, or Hand-Forged. The operation described was accomplished by hand labor and manually controlled methods which permit the maker to control and vary the type, amount, and effect of such operation on each part of each individual product.

Hardness. One component of a gem's overall durability. It measures how well a stone resists scratching.

Matte Finish. A finish that gives a metal a grainy, sandblasted look.

Melee. A general term for small cut gems, usually weighing 0.20 carats or less.

Patina. A green film formed by oxidation on copper and bronze; can be formed naturally over a period of time through exposure to air, but can be hastened or artificially induced by coloring agents. Popular in costume jewelry.

Pave. A type of setting in which a number of small stones are set as closely together as possible to appear as an all-diamond surface without any metal showing.

Platinum Group Metals. Platinum and other rare metallic elements that occur in association with it, including iridium, palladium, ruthenium, rhodium, and osmium.

Platinum. A precious metal used in fine jewelry. It has a silvery appearance and usually is alloyed with a related metal called iridium.

Quality Mark. Any letter, figure, numeral, symbol, sign, word, or term, or any combination thereof, which has been stamped, embossed, inscribed, or otherwise placed, on any jewelry product. The quality mark indicates the product composition or surface (on which there has been plated or deposited any precious metal or alloy) of any precious metal or alloy. Included are the words gold, karat, carat, silver, sterling, platinum, iridium, palladium, ruthenium, rhodium, or osmium, or any abbreviation thereof, whether used alone or in conjunction with the word filled, plated, overlay, electroplated, or any abbreviation thereof.

Real Jewelry. The U.S. Federal Trade Commission (FTC) considers it an unfair trade practice to use the words *real, genuine, natural,* or similar terms to describe any article or articles which are manufactured or produced synthetically or artificially.

Rhinestone. Defined as quartz from the gold washings along the Rhine River in Baden; but generally used to refer to glass used in jewelry.

Satin Finish. A finely textured metal finish, resembling a satin sheen. It is produced by scratching a series of tiny parallel lines on the surface with a wire brush.

Seamless. Without a seam, generally referring to a ring or piece of tubing made from one piece of metal, cupped, drawn, and cut.

Simulated Stones. Imitation stones of glass, paste, or plastic.

Solitaire. The mounting of a single gemstone.

Textured Finishes. Any finish other than high polish; includes Florentine, bark, satin, hammered, woven, nugget, granulated, bright-cut, etc.

Tiffany Setting. A four- or six-prong setting generally round in shape and flaring out from the base to the top, having long slender prongs that hold the stone.

Total Weight. Generally used for diamond jewelry but can be applied to any jewelry with small stones. It refers to the combined carat weight of all the stones in the piece.

White Metal. Various alloys of tin, antimony, and copper used in the rubber mold or spincasting process; common in costume jewelry.

Sources:
American Jewelry Manufacturers, *A Findings Glossary,* April 1988.
Accent, December 1991.
Federal Trade Commission, "Guides of the Jewelry Industry," 16 CFR 23.0, Washington: Government Printing Office, 1992.

Pearl

A pearl is a solidified mass consisting of concentric layers of a crystalline substance called *nacre* (carbonate of lime and organic material) formed within the body of certain mollusks (typically the pearl oyster). When a foreign body is placed inside the mollusk's shell, the mantle (a membrane which secretes shell-forming fluid) is irritated. By responding to the irritation with abnormal secretions, the mollusk engages in the pearl-making process. When the irritant is placed in the mollusk by man, the resulting pearl is referred to as *cultured;* when the irritant lodges in the mollusk by accident, the resulting pearl is referred to as *natural.*

Cultured pearls are harvested in pearl farms in the sea or freshwater lakes, then sorted, graded, drilled, and threaded. Most at

present come from China, Hong Kong, Japan, and India. Mollusks produce pearls in a variety of tints: creamy white, pink, gold, blue-gray, and black. Pearls lose their luster if they are not handled and worn. *Baroque* pearls are irregular in shape. *Artificial* or *simulated* pearls are glass beads with a coating of pearly varnish. The difference can easily be discerned by rubbing the bead against your tooth: a natural pearl makes a grating sound whereas a varnished glass pearl is smooth and slips over the tooth.

GRADING OF CULTURED PEARLS

Seven factors listed below are considered in grading and pricing cultured pearls. Except for size, each category is represented by a numerical grade based on a given range. From these, the grader then calculates a composite number grade which is descriptive and comparative, rather than evaluative, e.g., a pearl necklace grade 40 is not worth exactly half as much as one graded 80.

Color. Body color, overtone, and orient (the shimmering iridescent characteristic of pearl).

Luster. The quality of the light reflections from the pearl's surface.

Spotting. The extent and severity of surface blemishes.

Shape. Round, symmetrical, or baroque (irregular), with subcategories in each.

Size. Pearl diameter is measured in millimeters. A common size for cultured pearls is 6 to 7 millimeters. Pearl weight is measured as follows: one pearl grain equals 0.25 carat; for large quantities or "lots," one momme equals 75 pearl grains (equal to 3.75 grams, or 0.13 ounces, or 18.75 carats).

Make. The quality of the craftsmanship in matching and assembling pearls in necklaces or jewelry.

Nacre Thickness. The thickness of the solidified mollusk secretion.

TYPES

Akoya. The most familiar type of cultured pearl, grown in true pearl oysters off the coasts of Japan. Akoya pearls are known for lovely orient and warm color. They rarely grow more than 9 mm in size.

Biwa Cultured Pearl. A cultured pearl, originally non-nucleated, grown in a freshwater mussel from Lake Biwa in Japan. Only those actually produced there should be called biwas. Others are simply freshwater cultured pearls.

Blister Pearl, Cultured. A cultured pearl that grows attached to the mollusk's shell. A hemispherical nucleus is usually used. Since they must be cut loose, one side is flat and has no pearly coating. (See also *Mabe Cultured Pearl.*)

Burmese. Large cultured pearls (10 mm and larger) grown in large oysters off the coasts of Burma. Warmer in color tone than South Sea cultured pearls, Burmese pearls are rare and costly.

Cultured Pearl. The composite product created when a nucleus (usually a sphere of calcareous mollusk shell) planted by man inside the shell or in the mantle of a mollusk is coated with nacre by the mollusk. Cultured pearls are so nearly identical to natural pearls that x-ray testing may be required to tell them apart.

Fresh Water Pearl. Cultivated in mollusks other than oysters found in fresh water lakes and rivers. Fresh water pearls generally are elongated in shape and have a milky translucent appearance.

Keshi. Tiny pearls, some only slightly bigger than a grain of sand, which form naturally in many cultured pearl oysters.

Mabe Cultured Pearls. Large hemispherical or *blister* cultured pearls grown around a pear-shaped or half-round nucleus against the inside shells of oysters instead of within the body. Less expensive than round cultured pearls and, because of their hemispherical shape, used mounted in jewelry as earrings, rings, and brooches.

Mother-of-Pearl. White pearly oyster shell which is easily carved into beads and pendants.

Natural Pearls. Natural pearls form in several types of freshwater and saltwater mollusks—such as mussels, oysters, and abalone. Usually a tiny worm, microscopic bacterium, or other foreign material gets inside the shell and irritates the animal. The mollusks secrete soothing substances that cover the intrusion. Successive coats get smoother and smoother.

One-Year Pearl. Cultured pearl with extremely thin layer of nacre over the nucleus.

Oriental Pearl. A natural pearl taken from a salt water mollusk, with the distinctive appearance of pearls obtained from mollusks inhabiting the Persian Gulf. This term cannot be used to identify or refer to any cultured or imitation pearl.

Saltwater Pearls. Pearls from oceans, bays and gulfs.

Seed Cultured Pearls. Small pearls less than one-quarter grain in weight.

South Sea. Large cultured pearls (10 mm and larger) grown in large oysters off the coasts of Australia. Usually silvery in appearance and sometimes not as lustrous as fine Akoya pearls, South Sea pearls are rare and costly.

TERMINOLOGY

Bib. Multiple strands of pearls, each shorter than the one below, nested together in one necklace.

Black Pearl. A natural colored formation of concentric layers of nacre, with colors varying from jet black to light gray, as well as dark brown to bronze.

Choker. A necklace 14 to 15 inches in length.

Dog Collar. Multiple strands of pearls fitting closely around the neck.

Graduated. A necklace composed of pearls which taper downward in size from large pearls in the center.

Imitation Pearl. A manufactured product composed of any material (or materials) which simulates in appearance a pearl or cultured pearl.

Matinee. A necklace 22 to 23 inches in length.

Momme. A term used by pearl dealers to express the weights of large lots of cultured pearls. One momme equals 75 pearl grains (which makes it 3.75 grams, about 0.13 ounces, or 18.75 carats). Freshwater cultured pearls nucleated without a bead (about 95 percent of total freshwater production) are sold by the momme.

Opera. A necklace 30 to 36 inches in length.

Orient. Iridescent colors seen on or just below the surface of a pearl or cultured pearl. It is caused by layers of tiny crystals that form the pearl's surface, which break up white light into spectral colors.

Paua Shells. Large, iridescent abalone shells from northeast Australia that have bright blue and green pearly coatings and produce quality mother-of-pearl.

Pearl Grain. A unit of weight used to describe the size of natural pearls. One pearl grain equals 0.25 carat (0.05 gram or a little less than 0.002 ounce). About 567 pearl grains equal one ounce.

Princess. A necklace 18 inches in length.

Sautoir or Rope. Any pearl necklace longer than opera length.

Uniform. A necklace which appears to be composed entirely of pearls of the same size, though there generally is a slight difference in size between the center and the end pearls for a more proportionate look.

Sources:

Federal Trade Commission, "Guides of the Jewelry Industry," 16 CFR 23.0, Washington, D.C.: Government Printing Office, 1992.

Christie, Andrew, Private Correspondence, Gemological Institute of America, New York, March 23, 1992.

"A Glossary of Beads," *American Jewelry Manufacturer,* March, 1990.

"What You Should Know About Cultured Pearls" (pamphlet), New York: Jewelers of America, Inc., 1992.

Silver

GRADES

Britannia. An alloy of silver that must be at least 95.84 percent pure silver by weight.

Coin. An alloy composed of 900 parts per 1,000 of silver, i.e., 90 percent silver. Cannot legally be called sterling.

Commercial. Silver that is 999 fine or higher.

Danish. Silverware made in Denmark is $830/1000$ fine silver if made to minimum Danish standards: $925/1000$ fine silver is made for export.

Fine. Metal that is 999 parts pure silver per 1,000; essentially pure silver.

German. Another name for *nickel silver*. A composition of nickel, copper, and zinc, it contains no silver.

Nickel Silver. A composition of nickel, copper and zinc. It contains no silver. Also known as *German Silver*.

Pure Silver. Fine silver.

Silver. Jewelry marked *silver* must contain 92.5 percent silver under jewelry industry guidelines.

Sterling. Must be $925/1000$ (92.5 percent) fine silver and $75/1000$ (7.5 percent) copper. This proportion is fixed by law.

TERMINOLOGY

Beading. Ornamentation, as along a border, with a continuous row of tiny hemispheres.

Bright-Cut Engraving. Engraving in which metal is removed by beveled cutting tools to form reflective facets.

Chasing. An incised, fine design created by hammering the outer surfaces using small, sharp tools that do not cut away any metal.

Die. A metal stamp used to create an ornamental design.

Electroplating. Electrical method of coating a base metal with a thin layer of silver.

Fluting. Parallel concave vertical panels. The term is also loosely used to refer to convex ornamentation of this sort, which is more properly called reeding.

Gardrooning. Ornamentation, usually on a border, with parallel raised ovals resembling twisted rope.

Matting. Deliberate dulling of a surface with fine punches or scratches.

Patina. The quality or glow of the metal after it has been worn.

Plate. In British usage, solid silver of sterling standard or higher, not to be confused with *plated silver* in British usage or *silver plate* in American usage.

Plated Silver. In British usage, electroplate.

Reeding. Narrow vertical convex panels.

Repousse. High-relief ornamentation produced by hammering from the back or from the inside.

Sheffield Plate. Originally made by bonding sheet silver to copper, rolling and manufacturing the bonded metals into hollow-ware. Imitations are made by electroplating silver on copper and are sometimes erroneously advertised as Sheffield plate.

Silver Filled. A mechanical bonding with a silver alloy of at least 92.5 percent fineness. The bonding must be at least $\frac{1}{20}$ of the metal in the article. It can also be called silver overlay, but never silver plate.

Silver Plate. Thin sheets of silver and copper fused together. For a product to be marked as plated or coated with silver, all significant surfaces of the product or part must contain a plating or coating of silver which is of substantial thickness.

Silver Plated Ware. Made by electroplating fine silver on a base metal alloy—usually nickel silver or Britannia metal, sometimes brass or copper.

Threaded. Bordered with fine raised lines.

Troy Ounce. The standard unit of measure for precious metals. There are 14.583 troy ounces in an avoirdupois pound.

Vermeil. Sterling silver jewelry plated with a coating of gold $^{120}\!/_{1000000}$ of an inch thick to produce "vermeil."

Sources:

The Encyclopedia of Collectibles, Silhouettes to Swords, Alexandria, VA: Time-Life Books, 1980.

Federal Trade Commission, "Guides of the Jewelry Industry," 16 CFR 23.0, Washington: Government Printing Office, 1992.

Watches

Analog. Traditional look of a watch, clock, or other timepiece. Time is determined by the angular positioning of hands on a dial.

Antimagnetic. This means that the inner workings of the watch are made from metals that will not attract each other magnetically—a benefit that offers greater accuracy because the inner parts will work independently. A watch is tested for its resistance to magnetism by placing it in a demagnetized condition in an electrical field of not less than 60 Gauss for at

least five seconds in a vertical position, and for at least five seconds in a horizontal position. If the daily rate of the watch has not been changed by more than 15 seconds as a result of the exposure, it is considered to have passed the test.

Arabic Numerals. Most familiar numeral style (1, 2, 3, etc.) used on watch dials.

Automatic or Self-Winding. Watches that "wind themselves" as the wearer moves his/her wrist. The wearer's arm actions cause a weight behind the movement to rotate, winding the mainspring. These watches can also be wound manually.

Base Metal. Watchcases that have this label are not made of gold, silver, silver plate, gold plate, etc. The kind of metal used should be clearly marked as in *Aluminum, Stainless Steel, Chromium Plated Steel,* etc. When watchcases are composed of parts having different metallic compositions, they may be marked with such terms as, *Base Metal Back, 14 K Gold Filled Bezel.*

Bezel. Outer section of the watch case including the grooved rim into which the crystal is set.

Chip. Small silicon square onto which integrated circuits are imprinted. An integral part of the quartz watch movement.

Chronograph. Watches that include a stopwatch feature; some measure fractions of a second. Some are used to calculate speeds, distances, and altitudes.

Chronometer. A watch (or clock) with special mechanism for ensuring accuracy. Used in demanding environments (such as at high altitude, while sailing, skin-diving, or participating in other physical activities). Used in determining longitude at sea or for any purpose where very exact measurement of time is required.

Crystal. Glass or plastic piece that covers the dial for protection.

Day Ring. Divided ring on the lunar dial to indicate the days in the 29 ½ day lunar cycle.

Dial. The face of the watch featuring a decorative plate on which the hour indicators are located.

Digital. Time display that uses no hands but shows the time in digits (numerals) on a readout screen.

Digital Watch. Any watch which indicates the time by a display of numerals rather than by a dial. The digital watch is all-electronic and uses either neon indicators, light-emitting diodes, or liquid crystal displays for the digital presentation.

Electronic. Watches powered by batteries rather than a mechanical spring. The batteries send electronic impulses through a small bar of synthetic quartz crystal which vibrates more than 32,000 times per second. Those vibrations are channeled through other watch parts to result in one impulse per second.

Hands. Decorative indicators which indicate the measurement of hours, minutes, and seconds on the dial.

Jeweled. This applies to the gemstones—usually synthetic sapphires or rubies—that serve as bearings inside a mechanical watch. Highly polished jewels reduce friction and offer more assurance of accuracy and wear. Most experts agree that 17 jewels are sufficient in a mechanical watch. However, before a watch can be labeled *jeweled* it must contain at least seven jewels, each of which serves the purpose of protecting against wear from friction by providing a mechanical contact with a moving part at a point of wear. A manufacturer cannot refer to the number of jewels contained in a watch unless each and every one of these jewels serves the purpose of protecting against wear.

Light-Emitting Diode (LED). Numbers telling the hours and minutes light up on a readout screen.

Liquid Crystal Display (LCD). Most frequently used in quartz timepieces. Time is continuously displayed in digits.

Lunar Dial. Extra feature on some watches to indicate the correct phase of the 29½ day lunar cycle (i.e., cycle of the moon) on each day. Typically, a dial at the top of the watch face. Also called a *Moon Dial*.

Mechanicals. Traditional *wind-up* watches. They work because of a mainspring inside the watch which the wearer winds by turning the crown on the side of the watch. The spring gradually unwinds and turns tiny interlocking wheels which move the watch hands to measure seconds, minutes, and hours.

Minute Track. Square or circular track on the face of the watch. It is divided into 60 equal segments to measure minutes. It may appear on the outer perimeter of the dial or in the dial center.

Movement. Timekeeping mechanism of the watch.

Quartz. Term used to describe electronic transistorized timekeeping movements that work on battery energy and require no winding or external source of electricity. A tiny quartz crystal, vibrating at high frequency, permits the clock mechanism to perform with precision.

Quartz Electronic Watch. A tiny quartz crystal, vibrating at a high frequency (ranging from 32,768 times per second to 4,194,303 times per second), permits the time-keeping mechanism to perform with great precision, accurate to plus or minus one clock minute a year. Electronic movements work on battery energy and require no outside source of energy (such as winding or plug-in electricity). The vibrations of the quartz crystal are translated by a *chip* (a tiny microcomputer) into impulses that drive a motor that moves the hands.

Roman Dial. Roman numerals (e.g.,I, II, III) used on some watch faces and in traditional style carriage, mantel, and grandfather clocks.

Shock Resistant. Watches that are able to resist damage from a 3-foot fall to a hardwood surface can be labeled *shock resistant*. A watch should be tested for shock resistance in a room having a temperature between 18 and 25 degrees C. A wrist watch which does not have a permanently affixed band should be tested without the band or strap. According to current U.S. Federal Trade Commission (FTC) guidelines, the test for shock resistance should be conducted as follows: One hour after the watch has been fully wound, its daily rate in each of the following three positions should be determined by observing it for two minutes in each position: horizontal with the dial facing down; vertical with three o'clock to the watch's left; and vertical with three o'clock pointed downwards. Shocks equal to that which the watch would receive if it were dropped from a height of three feet onto a horizontal hardwood surface should be applied as follows: (1) The first shock should be applied to the middle of the watch at a position directly opposite the crown and in a direction which is parallel to the plane of the watch; (2) The second shock should be applied to the crystal, and in a direction which is perpendicular to the plane of the watch. Five minutes after the last shock, the daily rate of the watch in each of the three positions described above should be determined by observing it for two minutes in each position. The differences in daily rate before and after the shock should be determined for each position. The residual effect of the shocks will be equal to the greatest of these differences. A watch will be considered to have passed the test if, after application of the shocks, it does not stop; the residual effect does not exceed 60 seconds per day; and an examination of the watch does not disclose any physical damage which would affect its operation or appearance, e.g., hands bent or out of position, cracked crystal, or automatic or calendar devices inoperable or out of alignment.

Skin Diver's, Navigator's, Railroad. These terms are often used to describe watches that possess the ruggedness, accuracy, dependability, or other features, required by persons engaged in those activities.

Spring-Driven. A watch that is driven by a mainspring that is wound using a knob and stem mechanism. The winding knob turns, coiling up the mainspring that drives the gears. The gears are turned as the mainspring uncoils. Each gear turns at a different speed. The hour, minute, and second hands are attached to gears that turn at a predetermined rate of speed to indicate the proper time. The ticking comes from the escapement which allows the gears to turn or "escape" one tooth at a time. It is this stop-and-go-control that creates the characteristic "tick-tock" sound.

Swiss-Made or Made in Japan. Names of countries appear on watches to disclose origin of manufactured parts and to disclose the country where the watch movement was assembled. If the movement has been assembled in the same country in which parts constituting 50 percent or more (in terms of the cost to the assembler of all the parts of the movement) have been manufactured, the name of the country alone should be used to designate the origin of the movement. If the watch movement has been assembled in one country and parts constituting 50 percent or more (in terms of the cost to the assembler of all the parts of the movement) have been manufactured in a single other country, the names of both such countries, and no other, should be used to designate the origin of the movement. Appropriate forms of disclosure include "Assembled in France from Swiss parts," or "Japanese parts, assembled in the United States." If the watch movement has been assembled in one country but parts constituting 50 percent or more (in terms of the cost to the assembler of all the parts of the movement) have not been manufactured in a single other country, only the name of the country of assembly should be used, accompanied by a disclosure that the parts are partially foreign, imported, or domestic, as the case may be. Appropriate forms of disclosure include "Movement assembled in the United States from domestic and imported parts" or "Movements assembled in France from foreign parts" or "Assembled in Germany with parts from foreign countries."

Watch. A timepiece or time-keeping device for measuring or indicating time which is designed to be worn on or about the person.

Watchcase, or Case. Any case, covering, or housing of any quality or description for a watch as defined above. The case includes the back, center, lugs, bezel, pendant, crown, bow, cap, and other parts, and includes a watch band which has been permanently affixed. Unless otherwise stated, either term applies to the case whether marketed separately or together with the movement or works.

Water Resistant. A watch may be described or designated as water resistant if it can be submerged 80 feet in fresh water—or 75 feet in salt water—without leaking or losing accuracy. A watch should be tested for water resistance by immersing it completely for at least five minutes in water under atmospheric pressure of 15 pounds per square inch and for at least another five minutes in water under an additional pressure of at least 35 pounds per square inch (total pressure of 50 pounds per square inch). If the watch does not admit any water or moisture, it will be considered to have passed the test.

Sources:

Federal Trade Commission, *Guides for the Watch Industry,* Washington: Government Printing Office, as amended August 18, 1970.

Granger, Patricia, et. al., *Industry Handbook of Clock Terminology,* Naperville, IL: Clock Manufacturers and Marketing Association, 1986.

Product Literature, Washington: American Watch Association, 1992.

"What You Should Know About Buying a Fine Watch" (pamphlet), New York: Jewelers of America, Inc., 1992.

Materials

Asphalt

Asphalt paving mixes may be designed and produced from a wide range of aggregate blends, each suited to specific uses. The aggregate composition may vary from coarse to fine particles. For a general classification of mix compositions, the Asphalt Institute recommends consideration of mix designations and nominal maximum size of aggregate ranging as follows: 37.5 mm (1½ inch); 25.00 mm (1 inch); 19.0 mm (¾ inch); 12.5 mm (½ inch); 9.5 mm (⅜ inch); 4.75 mm (No. 4); and 1.18 mm (No. 16).

Coarse Aggregate. All mineral material retained on the 2.36 mm (No. 8) sieve. It consists of crushed stone, crushed slag, or crushed or uncrushed gravel.

Fine Aggregate. All mineral matter that passes the 2.36 mm (No. 8) sieve. It consists of natural sand or manufactured material derived by crushing stone, slag, or gravel and includes mineral filler and mineral dust.

Mineral Aggregates. Mineral aggregates used for asphalt mixtures are required to meet grading and quality standards.

Special Local Aggregates. There are a number of local types of aggregate which often do not pass the stand test but which make excellent asphalt mixtures.

Source:
Introduction to Asphalt, Manual Series No. 5 (MS-5), eighth edition, College Park: The Asphalt Institute, 1986.

Bolt Head Markings

In the heat treatment of a bolt, the bolt is first heated to a temperature of between 1,500 to 1,550 degrees F. It is held at this temperature for a period of time (the length depends on the size of the bolt) and is then quickly quenched in oil. At this point the bolt is fully hardened (over 50 on the Rockwell scale). The bolt is then tempered (heated a second time) to relieve the stress caused by the oil quenching and to reduce the bolt's hardness to the required level. This tempering is often at a temperature between 900 to 1,100 degrees F. Final hardness is determined by a Rockwell Hardness Tester. Using this tester, a specific amount of pressure is applied to the bolt through a diamond tipped tool. The deeper the tool penetrates into the bolt, the softer it is. Although the Rockwell Hardness Tester has several scales, bolts are usually measured on the C scale—the lower the C reading, the lower is the bolt's hardness.

Bolt hardness cannot be judged by physical appearance alone. Bolts that have been heat-treated are often black in appearance; however, many heat-treated bolts are sent to platers to receive a corrosion-resistant coating. This coating can give the bolt a bright, silvery finish. The hardness of a bolt can best be determined by the markings on its head. Generally, the more lines on the bolt's head, the higher is its minimum hardness. The figure that follows shows several different bolt head markings. In addition to the markings shown, a bolt may have a manufacturer's symbol (for identification purposes) stamped on it. The consumer can usually find bolts of the four more common markings: no lines, SAE Grade 1 and 2; 3 lines, SAE Grade 5; 6 lines, SAE Grade 8; and sometimes 5 lines, SAE Grade 7. The figure also shows the minimum and maximum hardness (Rockwell C scale) of the bolts. Although the heat-treater tries to harden a bolt to somewhere in the middle of this minimum and maximum range, some bolts can be on the high or low end and still pass for the given grade. This means that a Grade 5 bolt (at maximum hardness) can be harder than a Grade 7 (at minimum hardness). However, on *average*, the higher the Grade or the more lines on the bolt's head, the harder it will be.

Grade marking	Specification	Tensile Strength (min.), psi.	Rockwell Hardness Min.	Rockwell Hardness Max.
	SAE–Grade 1	60,000	B 70	B 100
	SAE–Grade 2	74,000 60,000	B 80 B 70	B 100 B 100
	ASTM A-307	60,000	B 69	B 100
	SAE 3	100,000	—	—
	SAE 5 ASTM A-449	120,000 105,000	C 25 C 19	C 34 C 30
BB	ASTM 354BB	105,000	C 18	C 30
A-325	ASTM A-325	120,000	C 23	C 34
	SAE– Grade 5.1	120,000	C 23	C 40
	SAE– Grade 5.2	120,000	C 26	C 36
BC	ASTM A-354-BC	125,000	C 26	C 36

Grade Marking	Specification	Tensile Strength (min.), psi.	Rockwell Hardness Min.	Rockwell Hardness Max.
	SAE–Grade 6	133,000	C 28	C 36
	SAE 7	133,000	C 28	C 34
	ASTM A-354-BD SAE–Grade 8	150,000	C 33	C 38
	SAE 8.2	150,000	C 35	C 42
A-490	ASTM A-490	150,000	C 32	C 38
	Exceeds SAE–Grade 8	185,000	C 36	C 40
A-490	Specification underlined Atmospheric corrosion resistant	Varies	—	—

Source:

Anderson, Robert Clark, *Inspection of Metals, Visual Examination,* Metals Park, OH: American Society for Metals, 1983.

Brick

A brick is a solid masonry unit of clay or shale, formed into a rectangular prism while plastic, and then burned or fired in a kiln.

TERMINOLOGY

Acid-Resistant. Brick suitable for use in contact with chemicals, usually in conjunction with acid-resistant mortars.

Adobe. Large roughly molded, sun-dried clay brick of varying sizes.

Angle. Any brick shaped to an oblique angle to fit a salient corner.

Arch. 1) Wedge-shaped brick for special use in an arch. 2) extremely hard-burned brick from an arch of a scove kiln.

Building. Brick for building purposes not especially treated for texture or color. Formerly called common brick.

Clinker. A very hard-burned brick whose shape is distorted or bloated due to nearly complete vitrification.

Common. See *Building Brick.*

Dry-Press. Brick formed in molds under high pressures from relatively dry clay (5 to 7 percent moisture content).

Economy. Brick whose nominal dimensions are 4 by 4 by 8 inches (see figure).

Eight by Eight. Brick whose nominal dimensions are 4 by 8 by 8 inches (see figure).

Engineer (or Engineered). Brick whose nominal dimensions are 4 by 3.2 by 8 inches. (See figure)

Facing Brick. Brick made especially for facing purposes, often treated to produce surface texture. They are made of selected clays, or treated, to produce desired color.

Fire. Brick made of refractory ceramic material which will resist high temperatures.

Floor. Smooth dense brick, highly resistant to abrasion, used as finished floor surfaces.

Gauged. 1) Brick which has been ground or otherwise produced to accurate dimensions. 2) A tapered arch brick.

Hollow. Hollow bricks are bricks that are cored between 25 and 40 percent, i.e., are 60 percent solid. They are used in all types of commercial and residential construction. There are different types based on appearance characteristics and different grades based on durability characteristics. Technically, these bricks are a masonry unit of clay or shale whose net cross-sectional area in any plane parallel to the bearing surface is not less than

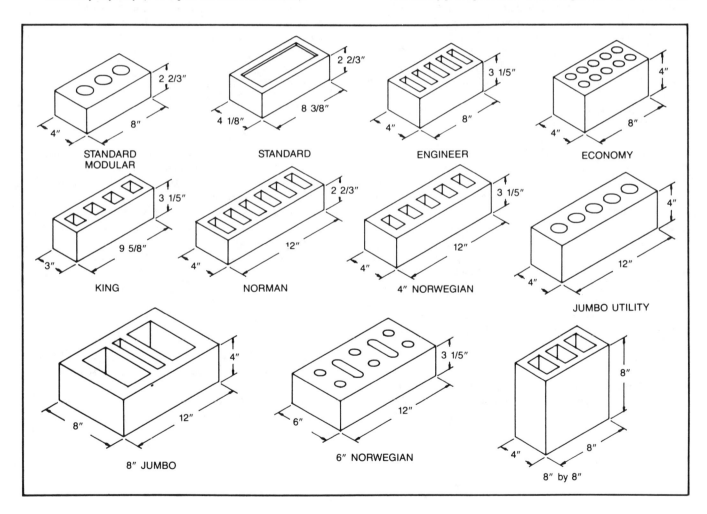

Brick sizes (nominal dimensions)

60 percent of its gross cross-sectional area measured in the same plane.

Jumbo. A generic term indicating a brick larger in size than the standard. Some producers use this term to describe oversized brick of specific dimensions manufactured by them (see figure).

Jumbo Utility. A brick whose nominal dimensions are 4 by 4 by 12 inches (see figure).

King. Brick whose nominal dimensions are 3 by 3.2 by 9⅝ inches.

Norman. Brick whose nominal dimensions are 4 by 2⅔ by 12 inches (see figure).

Norwegian. The 4 inch Norwegian: Brick whose nominal dimensions are 4 by 3.2 by 12 inches. The 6 inch Norwegian: Brick whose nominal dimensions are 6 by 3.2 by 12.

Paving. Vitrified brick especially suitable for use in pavements where resistance to abrasion is important.

Roman. Brick whose nominal dimensions are 4 by 2 by 12 inches.

Salmon. Generic term for underburned brick which is more porous, slightly larger, and lighter colored than hardburned brick. Usually pinkish-orange color.

Sewer. Low-absorption, abrasive-resistant brick intended for use in drainage structures.

Soft-Mud. Brick produced by molding relatively wet clay (20 to 30 percent moisture), often a hand process. When the insides of the molds are sanded to prevent stickiness of clay, the product is called sandstruck brick. When the molds are wetted to prevent sticking, the product is called waterstruck brick.

Standard. Brick whose nominal dimensions are 4½ by 2⅔ by 8⅜ inches.

Standard Modular. Brick whose nominal dimensions are 4 by 2⅔ by 8 inches.

APPEARANCE DESIGNATIONS

HBS. For use in exposed exterior and interior masonry walls and partitions where wider color ranges and greater variation in size is permitted.

HBX. For general use in exposed exterior and interior masonry walls and partitions where narrow color range and minimum permissible variation in size are required.

HBA. Manufactured to produce characteristic architectural effects resulting from nonuniformity in size, color, and texture of the individual units.

HBB. For general use where color and texture are not a consideration and where a greater variation in size is permitted.

GRADES

Severe Weathering (SW). For use where a high and uniform degree of resistance to frost action and disintegration by weathering is desired and where the exposure is such that hollow brick may be frozen when permeated with water.

Moderate Weathering (MW). For use where a moderate and somewhat nonuniform degree of resistance to frost action is permissible or where they are unlikely to be permeated with water when exposed to temperatures below freezing.

Negligible Weathering (NW). For use where a negligible resistance to weathering is required.

Sources:
Technical Notes on Brick and Tile Construction, No. 2, McLean, VA: Brick Institute of American, revised edition, 1975.
Technical Notes on Brick and Tile Construction, No. 41, McLean, VA: Brick Institute of American, revised edition, 1983.

Brick, Hollow

Hollow bricks are bricks that are cored between 25 and 40 percent, i.e., 60 percent solid. They are used in all types of commercial and residential construction. There are different types based on appearance characteristics and different grades based on durability characteristics.

TYPES

HBS. For use in exposed exterior and interior masonry walls and partitions where wider color ranges and greater variation in size is permitted.

HBX. For general use in exposed exterior and interior masonry walls and partitions where narrow color range and minimum permissible variation in size are required.

HBA. Manufactured to produce characteristic architectural effects resulting from nonuniformity in size, color, and texture of the individual units.

HBB. For general use where color and texture are not a consideration and where a greater variation in size is permitted.

GRADES

Severe Weathering (SW). For use where a high and uniform degree of resistance to frost action and disintegration by weathering is desired and where the exposure is such that hollow brick may be frozen when permeated with water.

Moderate Weathering (MW). For use where a moderate and somewhat nonuniform degree of resistance to frost action is permissible or where they are unlikely to be permeated with water when exposed to temperatures below freezing.

Source:
Technical Notes on Brick and Tile Construction, No. 41, McLean, VA: Brick Institute of American, revised edition, 1983.

Brick, Modular

The nominal dimension of modular bricks are equal to the manufactured dimensions plus the thickness of the mortar joint, (usually ⅜ or ½ inch). They are designed in such a way so that they will fit together simply and easily with the other parts of the construction.

Source:
Technical Notes on Brick and Tile Construction, No. 15, McLean, VA: Brick Institute of America, May 1988.

Brick, Salvaged or Preused

Bricks obtained from demolished buildings which stood 40 to 50 years or more. It may be impossible to salvage brick from new construction because bricks set in Portland cement mortars absorb the mortar, making it nearly impossible to completely clean the particles from the surfaces. In general, walls using salvaged brick are weaker and less durable than walls constructed of new brick masonary.

Source:
Technical Notes on Brick and Tile Construction, No. 15, McLean, VA: Brick Institute of America, May 1988.

Brick, Veneer Construction

Consists of a nominal 3-inch thick exterior brick tied to a backup system with metal ties in such a way that a 1-inch clear space is provided between the veneer and the backup system

Source:
Technical Notes of Brick and Tile Construction, No. 15, McLean, VA: Brick Institute of America, May 1988.

Carbon and Alloy Steels

CLASSIFICATION

Classification is the systematic arrangement or division of steels into groups on the basis of some common characteristic. Steel can be classified on the basis of (a) composition, such as carbon or alloy steel; (b) finishing methods, such as hot rolled or cold rolled steel; or (c) product form, such as bar, plate, sheet, strip, tubing, or structural shape.

DESIGNATION

Grade, type, and *class* are terms used to classify steel products. Within the steel industry, they have very specific uses: *grade* is used to denote chemical composition; *type* is used to indicate deoxidation practice; and *class* is used to describe some attribute, such as strength level or surface smoothness. Designation is the specific identification of each *grade, type,* or *class* of steel by a number, letter, symbol, name, or suitable combination that is unique to a particular steel. Chemical composition is by far the most widely used basis for designation, followed by mechanical property specifications. The most widely used system for designating carbon and alloy steels is that of the American Iron and Steel Institute (AISI) and the Society of Automotive Engineers (SAE). These are two separate systems, but they are nearly identical and are carefully coordinated by the two groups. The numerical designations summarized in the table below are used by both AISI and SAE. The *xx* in the last two (or three) digits of these designations indicates that the carbon content (in hundredths of a percent) is to be inserted. For more detailed information on individual designations, please consult the source cited below.

Carbon Steels. These types of steels contain less than 1.65 percent manganese, 0.60 percent silicon, and 0.60 percent copper. They comprise the 1*xxx* groups in the AISI-SAE system.

*10*xx *Plain Carbon Steels.* They contain a maximum of 1.00 percent manganese. The range and limits of chemical composition depend on the product form.

*11*xx *Resulfurized Carbon Steel.* This group of steels are

THE AISI-SAE SYSTEM OF DESIGNATIONS

Numerals and digits(a)	Type of steel and/or nominal alloy content	Numerals and digits(a)	Type of steel and/or nominal alloy content	Numerals and digits(a)	Type of steel and/or nominal alloy content
Carbon steels		**Nickel-chromium-molybdenum steels**		**Chromium steels**	
10xx	Plain carbon (Mn 1.00% max)	43xx	Ni 1.82; Cr 0.50 and 0.80; Mo 0.25	50xxx	Cr 0.50
11xx	Resulfurized	43BVxx	Ni 1.82; Cr 0.50; Mo 0.12 and 0.25; V 0.03 min	51xxx	Cr 1.02 } C 1.00 min
12xx	Resulfurized and rephosphorized			52xxx	Cr 1.45
15xx	Plain carbon (max Mn range — 1.00 to 1.65%)	47xx	Ni 1.05; Cr 0.45; Mo 0.20 and 0.35	**Chromium-vanadium steels**	
		81xx	Ni 0.30; Cr 0.40; Mo 0.12	61xx	Cr 0.60, 0.80 and 0.95; V 0.10 and 0.15 min
Manganese steels		86xx	Ni 0.55; Cr 0.50; Mo 0.20		
13xx	Mn 1.75	87xx	Ni 0.55; Cr 0.50; Mo 0.25	**Tungsten-chromium steel**	
Nickel steels		88xx	Ni 0.55; Cr 0.50; Mo 0.35	72xx	W 1.75; Cr 0.75
23xx	Ni 3.50	93xx	Ni 3.25; Cr 1.20; Mo 0.12	**Silicon-manganese steels**	
25xx	Ni 5.00	94xx	Ni 0.45; Cr 0.40; Mo 0.12	92xx	Si 1.40 and 2.00; Mn 0.65, 0.82 and 0.85; Cr 0.00 and 0.65
Nickel-chromium steels		97xx	Ni 0.55; Cr 0.20; Mo 0.20		
31xx	Ni 1.25; Cr 0.65 and 0.80	98xx	Ni 1.00; Cr 0.80; Mo 0.25	**High-strength low-alloy steels**	
32xx	Ni 1.75; Cr 1.07			9xx	Various SAE grades
33xx	Ni 3.50; Cr 1.50 and 1.57	**Nickel-molybdenum steels**		**Boron steels**	
34xx	Ni 3.00; Cr 0.77	46xx	Ni 0.85 and 1.82; Mo 0.20 and 0.25	xxBxx	B denotes boron steel
Molybdenum steels		48xx	Ni 3.50; Mo 0.25	**Leaded steels**	
40xx	Mo 0.20 and 0.25	**Chromium steels**		xxLxx	L denotes leaded steel
44xx	Mo 0.40 and 0.52	50xx	Cr 0.27, 0.40, 0.50 and 0.65		
Chromium-molybdenum steels		51xx	Cr 0.80, 0.87, 0.92, 0.95, 1.00 and 1.05		
41xx	Cr 0.50, 0.80 and 0.95; Mo 0.12, 0.20, 0.25 and 0.30				

(a) "*xx*" in the last two (or three) digits of these designations indicates that the carbon content (in hundredths of a percent) is to be inserted.

produced for applications requiring good machinability.

12xx Resulfurized and Rephosphorized Carbon Steel. This group of steels (like resulfurized carbon steel) are produced for applications requiring good machinability.

15xx Plain Carbon Steels. They have a nominal manganese content of between 0.90 and 1.5 percent, but no other alloying additions.

Alloy Steels. Alloy steels contain carbon, manganese, silicon, or copper in quantities greater then those in carbon steels, or they have specified ranges or minimums for one or more of the alloying elements. The alloying additions enhance mechanical properties, fabricating characteristics, or some other attribute of the steel. The alloy steels include the following: manganese, nickel, nickel-chromium, molybdenum, chromium-molybdenum, nickel-chromium-molybdenum, nickel-molybdenum, chromium, chromium-vanadium, tungsten-chromium, silicon-manganese, high-strength low-alloy, boron, and leaded steels. In the AISI-SAE system of designations, the major alloying elements in a steel are indicated by the first two digits of the designation. The amount of carbon, in hundreds of a percent, is indicated by the last two (or three) digits. The table above lists only the general information for the different alloy steel groups; for more specific information on the chemical composition of individual AISI-SAE designations, please consult the source cited below.

Source:
Boyer, Howard, and Timothy L. Gall, *Metals Handbook Desk Edition,* Metals Park, OH: American Society for Metals, 1984.

Doors, Steel Fire

Steel fire doors are covered by four ratings determined by exposure limitations of the door itself. The maximum requirement for any steel fire door is an exposure rating of 3 hours. The other ratings are 1½ hours, ¾ hour, and ⅓ hour (20 minutes). In general doors carry three fourths of the rating of the surrounding wall. Therefore, a 3 hour fire door is used in a 4 hour rated wall, a 1½ hour fire door in a 2 hour rated wall, and a ¾ hour fire door in a 1 hour rated wall.

Louvers are permitted in 1½ hour and ¾ hour fire doors. The louver must meet specifications and be no larger than 24 inch by 24 inch. Louvers are not permitted in doors with glass lights or fire exit devices, and should not be used where smoke control is a consideration. Louvers are not permitted in ⅓ hour (20 minute) rated doors. Louvers are not permitted to be installed in the upper half of a labeled door. There are additional requirements for labeling, latching, hinges, etc. Consult the Steel Door Institute for more detailed information.

CLASSIFICATIONS

Fire door openings are classified by their locations in the building. The location determines the length of exposure protection required, based on the potential fire hazard of that particular area. The five opening classifications are shown below along with the

four door ratings and maximum amount of glass in square inches allowed for each classification.

Class A. Openings are in walls separating buildings or dividing a single building into fire areas. Doors for these openings require a fire protection rating of 3 hours, and no glass is permitted.

Class B. Openings in enclosures of vertical communication through buildings. These could be stairwells or elevator shafts. Boiler room doors are generally categorized as Class B openings as well. Doors for these areas require a fire protection rating of 1½ hours, and glass areas may not exceed 100 square inches per individual door leaf. A minimum 6 inch stile is required between visible glass and the edge of the door, unless the manufacturer has specific approval for a smaller stile dimension.

Class C. Openings in corridors and room partitions. Doors for these areas require a fire protection rating of ¾ hour, and the glass area cannot exceed 1,296 square inches per light (pane), with no dimension exceeding 54 inches. A minimum 6 inch stile is required between the edge of the door and visible glass or, in the case of multiple light (pane) doors, between the visible glass area, unless the manufacturer has specific approval to provide a smaller stile dimension.

Class D. Openings in exterior walls which are subject to severe fire exposure from the outside of the building. These doors require a fire protection rating of 1½ hours; and, as in Class A openings, no glass is permitted.

Class E. Openings are in exterior walls which are subject to moderate or light fire exposure from the outside of the building. A typical example would be a door leading to an exterior fire escape. Doors for these openings require a fire protection rating of ¾ hour with glass areas not exceeding 1,296 square inches per light (pane).

One-Third Hour (20 Minute). These doors have no class designation. Used for the protection of openings between living quarters and corridors and where smoke control is a primary concern.

Source:
Basic Fire Door Requirements, Technical Data Series, SDI 118-88, Cleveland: Steel Door Institute, 1991.

Doors, Steel (Types)

The nomenclature appearing below was adopted by the Steel Door Institute as their official standard. The SDI encourages the adoption of this nomenclature by the rest of the construction industry.

DOOR DESIGN NOMENCLATURE

F. Flush.
L*. Louvered (bottom).
TL*. Louvered (top).
LL*. Louvered (top and bottom).
V. Vision Line.
VL*. Vision Line and Louvered.

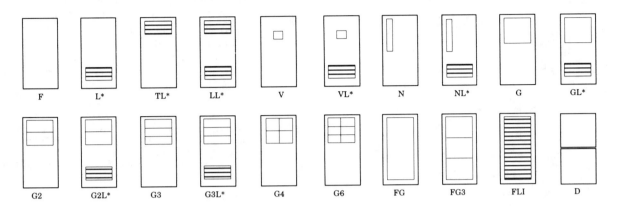

Steel door designs

N. Narrow Line.
NL*. Narrow Line and Louvered.
G. Half Glass (options G2, G3, G4 and G6).
GL*. Half Glass and Louvered (options G2L* and G3L*).
FG. Full Glass (option FG3).
FLI. Full Louver (installed).
D. Dutch Door.

* Louvered door designs: specify design, louver size, and/or free area requirements.
   Add Suffix I to indicate Inserted Louver.
   Add Suffix P to indicate Pierced Louver.
   Add Suffix A to indicate Air Condition Grille.

Sources:
American National Standard Nomenclature for Steel Doors and Steel Door Frames, ANSI/SDI-A123.1-1989 (revision of ANSI A123.1-1982), New York: American National Standards Institute, Inc., 1989.
The Standard Steel Door and Frame Story, Cleveland: Steel Door Institute, 1992.

Doors, Steel (Construction)

TYPES

Steel door construction can be categorized into three groups:
Full Flush. In these doors a pan type or enclosed type grid construction is used, and no seams are visible on the face of the door. They may have exposed seams on the vertical edges where the two pans join or interlock.
Seamless. The construction of these doors may be similar to those in the full flush category. However, no seams occur on the door face, and no visible seams occur on the vertical edges. The top and bottom of the door may have a flush end closure or may be closed with a recessed channel end closure.
Stile and Rail. The structural elements of this door are composed of tubular stiles and rails which are usually mitered and continuously welded at the joint. The stiles and rails surround

and hold in place a panel which is either in the same plane as the perimeter member or recessed no more than the thickness of the face members of the panel.

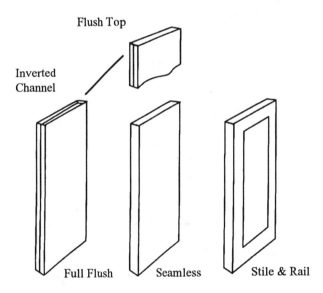

The three basic door constructions

INTERNAL CONSTRUCTION

There are a number of basic types of internal construction. These include vertical steel stiffened, mineral core, grid systems, polystyrene foam, honeycomb, and polystyrene. Any number of other materials could be used to constitute a core construction. The importance of the core construction is that it provides adequate reinforcing for the door to allow it to perform its day-to-day function:

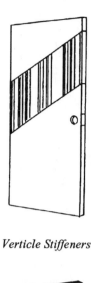

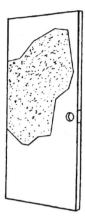

Verticle Stiffeners   *Mineral Core*

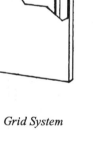

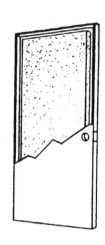

Grid System   *Polystyrene Slab*

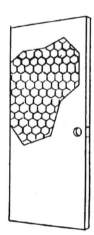

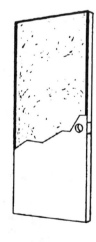

Honeycomb   *Polyurethane Foam*

Internal door construction

Grade I. Standard-duty 1⅜ inches and 1¾ inches (Level C). Model 1: Full flush design. Model 2: Seamless design.

Grade II. Heavy-duty 1¾ inches (Level B). Model 1: Full flush design. Model 2: Seamless design.

Grade III. Extra heavy-duty 1¾ inches (Level A). Models 1 & 1A: Full flush design. Models 2 & 2A: Seamless design. Model 3: Stile and rail flush panel.

Source:

American National Standard, Recommended Specifications Standard Steel Doors and Frames, ANSI/SDI-100-91 (revision of ANSI/SDI-100-85), New York: American National Standards Institute, Inc., 1991.

The Standard Steel Door and Frame Story, Cleveland: Steel Door Institute, 1992.

Fallout Shelters

A structure which, when properly installed, has a protection factor against fallout gamma radiation of at least 40. *Protection factor* is the relative reduction in the amount of radiation that would be received by a person in a shelter compared with the amount which he would receive if unprotected. For example, an unprotected person would receive 40 times more radiation than a person in a shelter with a protection factor of 40.

Blast-Resistant. Capable of withstanding an overpressure of at least 25 pounds per square inch (psi).

Custom Built or Custom Made. Designed and built for the particular purchaser.

Limited Blast-Resistant. Capable of withstanding an overpressure of at least 5 pounds per square inch.

Overpressure. 5 pounds per square inch (psi). Overpressure would occur at a range of about 8½ miles from a 10 megaton, and about 18 miles from a 100 megaton, explosion. 30 psi overpressure would occur at a range of about 2½ miles from a 1 megaton, and about 5 miles from a 100 megaton, explosion.

Guaranteed Fallout Proof. This claim is a representation that complete protection against fallout is afforded under all conditions, and constitutes a misrepresentation of fact. Therefore, the use of this term would be contrary to Federal Trade Commission (FTC) regulations.

Source:

Federal Trade Commission, "Guides for Advertising Fallout Shelters," 16 CFR sections 229.0 to 29.15 (1992), Washington: Government Printing Office.

Glass

Glass is a hard, brittle, amorphous substance produced by fusion, usually consisting of mutually dissolved silica and silicates that also contains sods and lime. It may be transparent, translucent, or opaque.

Annealed Glass. Glass that has been subjected to a slow, controlled cooling process during manufacture to control residual stresses so that it can be cut or subjected to other fabrication. Regular polished plate, float, sheet, rolled, and some patterned surface glasses are examples of annealed glass.

Carved Glass. A decoration glazing material in which a permanent visible design has been produced by polishing, grinding, or otherwise removing portions of the surface.

Dalle Glass or Dalle de Verre (Including Faceted Glass). A decorative composite glazing material made of individual pieces of glass which are imbedded in a cast matrix of concrete or epoxy.

Glazing Material. Glass, including annealed glass, organic coated glass, tempered glass, laminated glass, wired glass, or a combinations of these. This term is used for glass used for a particular purpose, as the term *siding* is applied to wood and other materials.

Laminated Glass. Glazing material composed of two or more pieces of glass—each piece being either tempered glass, heat strengthened glass, annealed glass, or wired glass—bonded to an intervening layer or layers of resilient plastic material.

Leaded Glass. A decorative composite glazing material made of individual pieces of glass whose perimeter is enclosed by lengths of durable metal such as lead or zinc. The pieces of glass can be clear, colored, beveled, painted, or flashed and etched.

Low-E. *E* is emissivity: the ability of glass to reradiate the heat it absorbs. Low-E values represent better heat reradiation. The lower the emissivity (E) of the glass, the better its insulation quality.

Low-E Glazing. There are two types of Low-E glazing: Pyrolitic, which is applied during manufacture of the glass, and Sputtered, which is sprayed on finished glass They are used on the interior pane of double and triple thermal pane systems. In insulated glass, Low-E glazing improves U-value (thermal transmission) from 0.49 to 0.32, and increases R-value (thermal resistance) from 2.04 to 3.12. In wood windows with insulated glass, it improves U-value from 0.45 to 0.30 and increases R-value from 2.22 to 3.33. In storm sashes or doors (single glazing), it improves U-value from 1.04 to 0.75 and increases R-value from 0.96 to 1.33.

Organic-Coated Glass. A glazing material consisting of a piece of glass that is coated and bonded on one or both sides with an applied polymeric coating, sheeting, or film.

Plate Glass. A transparent glass that gives a clear and undistorted vision and reflection, manufactured either by floating hot glass in ribbon form upon a heated liquid or by grinding and polishing a ribbon of glass formed between two rolls. Also known as *float glass.*

R-Value. A measure of thermal resistance: how well material stops/resists heat flowing through it. High R-Values represent a greater ability to stop/resist heat absorption.

Shatterproof. Manufactured or treated in such a way as to prevent shattering and dispersal of particles of the glass if it should break.

Superwindows. Window units with high R-values. Refers to units such as a double paned window with argon gas instead of air in the space between the panes.

Tempered Glass. A piece of specially heat-treated or chemically treated glass that cannot be cut, drilled, ground, or polished

after treatment without fracturing. When fractured at any point, if highly-tempered, the entire piece breaks into small particles.

U-Value. Measures thermal transmission: The heat flow through material or assembly from inside air to outside air. Low-U values represent greater resistance to transmission of interior heat to outside.

Window Glass. A transparent glass which has been drawn or rolled, has glossy, fire-polished surfaces and has a characteristic waviness of its surfaces which is visible when viewed at an acute angle or in reflected light. Sometimes referred to as *sheet* or *shock glass.*

Wired Glass. A single piece of annealed glass that contains wire embedded in the body of the glass.

Sources:

Consumer Product Safety Commission, "Safety Standard for Architectural Glazing Materials," 16 CFR Part 1201 (1992), Washington: Government Printing Office.
"Looking at the New Superwindows," *Consumer Research Magazine,* Vol. 73, no. 7 (July 1990).
"Thermal Integrity and Durability of Wood Windows and Doors," *Technical Bulletin,* Woodwork Institute of California, 1988.

Insulation, Home

Insulation is any material mainly used to slow down heat flow. It may be mineral or organic, fibrous, cellular, or reflective (aluminum foil). It may be in a rigid, semirigid, flexible, or loose-fill form. The term home insulation applied to insulation used in old or new homes, condominiums, cooperatives, apartments, modular homes, or mobile homes. The term does not include pipe insulation or any kind of duct insulation, except for duct wrap.

R-value. Measures resistance to heat flow. The higher the R value, the greater the insulating power. See ASTM C 177-85.

TYPES

Fibrous Glass. A mineral fiber made from molten silica. It can be installed by blowing, or it can be purchased in batts or blankets with or without a vapor barrier attached to the insulation.

Plastic Foam. This type of insulation is usually of one of the following types: polystyrene (which is used in board form and called *bead board*); polyurethane (which may be used in board form or may be sprayed in place); or urea formaldehyde (which is generally foamed in place between studs in the walls. Many building codes require that some plastic foam insulations be used only when they are protected from potential ignition sources. Manufacturers also treat polyurethane and polystyrene (beadboard) with flame retardant chemicals to make them less combustible. Urea formaldehyde foams can release formaldehyde vapors into the home, causing a variety of health problems—including irritation of the eyes, nose, and throat, coughing, shortness of breath, nausea, skin irritation, headaches, and dizziness. Persons with respiratory problems or allergies may suffer more serious reactions, especially persons allergic to formaldehyde.

Cellulose Insulation. Generally made from ground-up or shredded paper. Cellulose insulation must meet the Consumer Product Safety Commission (CPSC) standard for flammability and corrosiveness. This type of insulation is normally treated with chemicals to make it smolder- and fire-resistant.

Light Fixtures Type-IC. A type of light fixture that has been tested and listed by manufacturers for installation under insulated surfaces.

R-Value. An *R* stands for Resistance to the flow of heat and is a measure of insulating power. The R-value of any material is a measure of how good an insulator is; that is, how well it resists the flow of heat into a home in summer or out of it in winter. The higher the R-value, the greater the insulating power. Every type of insulation has a different R-value per inch of thickness; therefore, different thicknesses of various materials can provide the same total insulating (R) value. The R-value for each product should be marked on its package.

Sources:
A Homeowner's Guide to Insulation and Energy Savings, Toledo, OH: Owens-Corning Fiberglas Corp.
Consumer Product Safety Commission, "Interim Safety Standard for Cellulose Insulation," 16 CFR 1209 (1992), Washington: Government Printing Office.
"Home Insulation Safety," *Product Safety Fact Sheet,* No. 91 (revised July 1980), Washington: U.S. Consumer Product Safety Commission.

Marble, Cultured

Cultured marble is a man-made material that has the appearance of natural marble. (Natural marble for building materials is referred to as *dimension stone.*) It is a blend of polyester resin and crushed marble, glass frit, or alumina trihydrate fillers. The materials are mixed, molded, and then cured to a specified hardness. They can be cast into virtually any shape, design, or color, resulting in seamless one-piece construction such as bathtubs, shower receptacles, and lavatories. Other cultured products include cultured onyx and cultured granite. The Cultured Marble Institute maintains a certification program together with the national Association of Home Builders Research Foundation. Products meeting industry standards for workmanship and finish, structural integrity, wear and cleanability, colorfastness, flammability, and resistance to staining chemicals, cigarette burns, aging, and water temperature changes may bear the certification labels of these organizations.

Source:
ANSI Z124.1, Z124.2, and Z124.3, New York: American National Standards Institute.
Product Literature, Chicago: Cultured Marble Institute, 1992.

Mortar

Selection of a particular mortar type is usually a function of the needs of the finished structural element. Where high winds are expected, a high lateral strength is required; hence, a mortar with high tensile bond strength is chosen. For load bearing walls, high compressive strength may be the governing factor, or considerations of durability, color, flexibility, etc., may be of utmost concern. Factors which improve one property of mortar often do so at the expense of others.

Type N Mortar. A medium-strength mortar suitable for general use in exposed masonry above grade. It is specifically recommended for parapet walls, chimneys, and exterior walls that are subject to severe exposure.

Type S Mortar. Tests indicate that the tensile bond strength between brick and Type S mortar approaches the maximum obtainable with cement-lime mortars. Type S mortar also has reasonably high compressive strength. It is recommended for use in reinforced masonry, for unreinforced masonry where maximum flexural strength is required, and for use where mortar adhesion is the sole bonding agent between facing and backing.

Type M Mortar. Type M mortar has high compressive strength and somewhat greater durability than other mortar types. It is specifically recommended for unreinforced masonry below grade and in contact with earth such as foundations, retaining walls, walks, sewers, and manholes.

Type O Mortar. A low-strength mortar suitable for general interior use in nonloadbearing masonry. It may be used for loadbearing walls of solid masonry where compressive stresses do not exceed 100 pounds per square inch, provided that exposures are not severe. In general, Type O Mortar is not used where it will be subject to freezing.

Dirt Resistant Mortar. Where resistance to staining is desired, aluminum trestearate, calcium stearate, or ammonium stearate is added to the construction mortar in the amount of 3 percent of the weight of the Portland cement.

Source:
Technical Notes on Brick and Tile Construction, Reston, VA: Brick Institute of America.

Paint

Acrylic. A synthetic polymer used in high-performance latex or water-based paint. As the paint's binder, acrylic resins enable the coating to last longer and retain its color.

Adhesion. The ability of dry paint to remain on the surface without blistering, flaking, or cracking. Adhesion is probably the single most important property of paint. Wet adhesion, the ability of dry paint to adhere to the surface in spite of wet conditions, is particularly important for exterior house paints.

Binder. The binder cements the pigment particles into a uniform paint film and also makes the paint adhere to the surface. The nature and amount of binder determine most of the paint's performance properties—washability, toughness, adhesion, and color retention. Acrylic polymers are the binder of choice in producing quality high-performance latex paints.

Color Retention. The ability of paint to keep its original color and resist fading.

Consistency. The resistance of a paint to flow. A paint with high consistency flows slowly; with low consistency, it flows readily.

Durability. The degree to which paint withstands the destructive effects of the environment to which it is exposed, especially harsh weather conditions. Durability has two aspects: Its protective properties safeguard the substrate from degradation; its decorative properties allow the paint to retain its attractive appearance.

Elasticity. The ability of paint to expand and contract with the substrate without suffering damage or changes in its appearance. Expansion and contraction are usually caused by temperature fluctuations. Some substrates such as yellow pine expand at different rates depending on their grain type. Elasticity is a key to durability. Acrylic binders are noted for their elasticity.

Extender. A less-expensive ingredient than pigment (titanium dioxide) that fills out and extends the pigment's capabilities. Extender cannot be used without pigment. Some common extenders are clays, calcium carbonate, and silicas.

Fading. Lightening of the paint's color, usually caused by exposure to light or heat.

Hiding Power. The ability of paint to hide or obscure a surface, color, or stain over which it has been uniformly applied. Hiding power is provided by the paint's pigment.

Latex Paint. Water-based paint made with synthetic binders such as 100 percent acrylic, vinyl acrylic, terpolymer, or styrene acrylic. Unlike oil-based paint, latex paint dries fast, flows smoothly, and cleans up easily with water. High-performance latex paints contain 100 percent acrylic polymers.

Mildewcide. Chemical agent in quality paints that destroys mildew—a common problem in humid climates.

Peeling. The detachment of paint from the surface in ribbons or sheets. Like flaking, the result of loss of adhesion.

Pigment. This powder-like substance is one of paint's basic components (the other is the binder). The pigment gives the paint its color and hiding power. Titanium dioxide (TiO_2) is the most important pigment used to provide hiding in paint.

Pigment Volume Concentration (PVC). The ratio of the volume of pigment to the volume of total nonvolatile material (i.e., pigment and binder) present in a coating. The figure is usually expressed as a percentage.

Polymer. This binder is produced from petrochemical feedstocks. The binder's polymer particles are small in size and carried in water. The binder polymers and water mix is known as emulsion.

Spattering. Droplets of paint that spin or mist off the roller as paint is being applied.

Thinner. The thinner and binder together form the paint's vehicle. Water, the thinner used in latex paints, evaporates as the paint dries, allowing a smooth paint application. Turpentine or spirits are the thinners in oil-based paints.

Volatile Organic Content (VOC). Any carbon compound that evaporates under standard test conditions. Essentially, all paint solvents except water are VOCs. Federal and state governments are beginning to limit the amount of volatile organics found in paint because of concerns about possible environmental and health effects.

Volume Solids. The volume of pigment plus binder divided by the total volume, expressed as a percent. High volume solids mean a thicker dry film, improved hiding, and high durability.

Washability. Ease with which washing will remove dirt from the paint's surface without causing damage.

Source:
National Decorating Products Association, St. Louis, MO, 1992, original source *Glossary of Paint Terms*, Rohm and Hass Paint Quality Institute.

Paint, Lead Containing

Paint or other similar surface coating materials containing lead or lead compounds and in which the lead content (calculated as lead metal) is in excess of 0.06 percent by weight of the total nonvolatile content of the paint or the weight of the dried paint film. Because of health risks associated with lead poisoning, the Consumer Product Safety Commission (CPSC) has banned lead paints and consumer products, such as toys and furniture, that bear lead-containing paint.

Source:
Consumer Product Safety Commission, "Ban of Lead-Containing Paint and Certain Consumer Products Bearing Lead-Containing Paint," 16 CFR Part 1303 (1992), Washington: Government Printing Office.

Roofing, Asphalt

A dark brown to black cement material in which the predominating constituents are bitumens, which occur in nature or are obtained in petroleum processing. Bitumens are substances comprised principally of high molecular weight hydrocarbons soluble in carbon disulfide. Bitumens are found in asphalt, tar, pitch, and related materials.

GRADES

Cold-Laid Plant Mixture. Plant mixtures that may be spread and compacted at atmospheric temperatures.

Hot-Laid Plant Mixture. Plant mixtures that are spread and compacted at elevated temperatures. To dry the aggregate and obtain sufficient fluidity of the asphalt (usually asphalt cement), both must be heated prior to mixing—giving origin to the term *hot mix.*

TYPES

Type I (Dead Level). Used on inclines up to ½ inch per foot slope.

Type II (Flat). Used on inclines ranging from ½ to 1½ inches per foot slope.

Type III (Steep). Used on inclines ranging from 1½ to 3 inches per foot slope.

Type IV (Special Steep). Used on inclines ranging from 2 to 6 inches per foot slope.

Source:
NRCA/ARMA Manual of Roof Maintenance and Repair, Rosemont, IL: National Roofing Contractors Association, 1988.

Roof Membranes

BUILT-UP BITUMINOUS

The continuous semiflexible component of a roof system with the primary function of excluding water is known as a built-up bituminous membrane. The membrane consists of two or more alternate plies of felts, fabrics, or mats that are often saturated and sometimes coated with bituminous materials, assembled in place, and adhered to each other with alternate layers of bituminous products. Bitumen is a class of amorphous, black or dark colored, and solid, semi-solid, or viscous cementatious substances composed principally of high molecular weight hydrocarbons, soluble in carbon disulfide, and found in asphalts, tars, pitches, and asphaltites. It is also a generic term used to denote any material composed principally of bitumen.

SINGLE-PLY

Materials that are to be used as sheet-applied roofing membranes. There are three groups of single-ply products defined by their chemical nature:

VULCANIZED ELASTOMERS
Also know as *thermosets*. Distinguished by the fact that it can only be bonded to itself (e.g., to seam overlapping sheets) by the use of an adhesive.

EPDM (Ethylene, Propylene, and Diene Monomer). Sheets range in thickness from 30 to 60 mils and are usually black or white in color. Exhibit a high degree of ozone, ultraviolet, weathering, and abrasion resistance and good low-temperature flexibility.

Neoprene (Chloroprene Rubber). Sheets vary in thickness from 30 to 120 mils. Available plain or with a reinforcing fabric. Have excellent resistance to weather, heat, oils, solvents, and abrasion. Allows fabrication of field splices that achieve high seam strength to provide a reliable continuous weatherproofing membrane.

NON-VULCANIZED ELASTOMERS
Also known as *uncured elastomers*. They are not physically cured during manufacture but may cure or vulcanize naturally over some period of time upon exposure to the elements. Once cured, they behave like vulcanized elastomers.

Chlorosulfonated Polyethylene (CSPE). A synthetic rubber that may be reinforced with polyester scrim or laminated to felt backing materials. They have a thickness of 30 to 60 mm. Exhibits strong resistance to weathering and to a broad range of chemicals and pollutants, as well as being inherently ozone resistant.

Chlorinated Polyethylene (CPE). May be nonreinforced or reinforced with thicknesses ranging from 40 to 48 mm. Exhibits strong resistance to oils and chemicals, excellent weatherabil-

ity, and ozone resistance. Also resistant to bitumen and can therefore be installed directly over existing asphalt or coal tar pitch roofs.

Polyisobutylene (PIB). The 60 mm PIB membrane is laminated to a 40 mm non-woven synthetic fleece backing with an unbacked prefabricated sealing edge for the side laps. Exhibits good resistance to weathering, ultraviolet light, and radiant heat.

NBP. Range in thickness from 30 to 45 mm. Used extensively for weather and waterproofing applications since the mid 1960s. Exhibit excellent tear and puncture resistance, good weatherability, remain flexible at low temperature, and have a low water vapor permeability. They are resistant to most chemicals but are sensitive to aromatic hydrocarbons.

THERMOPLASTIC MATERIALS
Distinguished from thermosets in that there is no cross-linking or vulcanization. Can be welded together with heat or solvent and develop welds bond strengths that equal or surpass the strength of the base material.

Polyvinyl Chloride (PVC). Usually 40 to 48 mm thick. Some available that have provided up to 20 years of service life as exposed roofing. Resistant to bacterial growth, industrial chemical atmospheres, and extreme weather conditions. Chemically incompatible with bituminous materials.

Ethylene Interpolymers (EIP). Generally reinforced with polyester fabric and are usually 32 mm thick. Possess good resistance to fire, chemicals, and oils and have high tear strength.

MODIFIED BITUMEN ROOFING MEMBRANES

Composite sheets consisting of bitumen, modifiers, and reinforcements. Exhibit the thermoplastic quality of being softened by heat but are separated into their own category because of the differences in chemical makeup.

RATINGS

Windstorm Rating (I60, I90). The *I* in the windstorm rating refers to the Class I fire rating possessed by the roof assembly. The number 60 or 90 refers to the wind pressure in pounds per square foot that the roof assembly was subjected to.

Fire Spread Below the Roof Deck. A Class I fire rating means that the building owner is not required to install automatic sprinklers below the deck.

Fire Spread Across the Roof Cover. Can be IA, IB, or IC depending on the length of spread under ASTM-E108 fire testing.

Source:
The Roofing Materials Guide, Vol. 16, Feb. 1988, Rosemont, IL: National Roofing Contractors Association. Portions originally from *Single-Ply Roofing: A Professional's Guide to Specifications*, Single-Ply Roofing Institute.

SCR Brick

SCR stands for Structural Clay Research and is the trademark of the Structural Clay Products Institute, Brick Institute of America. This product combines the beauty and permanence of a finished ceramic surface with the load bearing properties of clay masonry.

PRODUCTS

SCR Acoustical. A side-construction two-celled facing tile having a perforated face backed with glass wool for acoustical purposes.

SCR Brick. Brick whose nominal dimensions are 6 by 2⅔ by 12 inch.

SCR Building Panel. Prefabricated, structural ceramic panels approximately 2½ inch thick.

GRADES

Grade S (Select). For use with comparatively narrow mortar joints.

Grade G (Ground Edge). For use where variations of face dimensions must be very small.

TYPES

Type I (Single-Faced Units). For use where only one finished face will be exposed.

Type II (Two-Faced Units). For use where two opposite finished faces will be exposed.

Type FTX. Smooth-face tile suitable for general use in exposed exterior and interior masonry walls and partitions and adapted for use where tile low in absorption, easily cleaned, and resistant to staining are required and where a high degree of mechanical perfection, narrow color range, and a minimum variation in face dimensions are desired.

Type FTS. Smoother or rough-textured facing tile suitable for general use in exposed exterior and interior masonry walls and partitions and adapted for use where tile of moderate absorption, moderate variation in face dimensions, and medium color range may be used and where minor defects in surface finish (including small handling chips) are not objectionable.

Source:
Technical Notes on Brick and Tile Construction, No. 22 (May/June 1965), Structural Clay Products Institute.

Shell Home

A home that does not include such features as wiring, plumbing, heating, interior trim and finish, or other essential components.

Source:
Consumer Product Safety Commission, 16 CFR sections 230.1 to 230.9 (1992), Washington: Government Printing Office.

Door Insulating System Index (DISI)

The purpose of the Door Insulating System Index (DISI) is to establish a standard method of rating the energy loss through a door assembly. The index is a single number that combines the energy losses due to both the transmission through the door and the infiltration of outside air around the perimeter (crack) of the door. Both must be combined to determine the total energy loss. The system was designed to provide a meaningful method of comparing the insulating efficiency of insulated steel doors and frames as a unit.

DISI Number. The total BTU loss for one day divided by 1,000. The lower the index number, the more efficient the door system. The maximum acceptable DISI number is 5.0 for an insulated steel door system.

Source:
Door Insulating System Index (DISI) for Insulated Steel Door Systems, *ISDSI-109-89*, revised 11-8-89. Cleveland: Insulated Steel Door Systems Institute.

Vulcanized

Subjected to a chemical reaction in which the physical properties of a rubber are changed in the direction of decreased plastic flow, less surface tackiness, and increased strength. This is done by reacting the rubber with sulfur or other suitable agents.

Source:
Standard Designation D907-89, "Adhesives," *Annual ASTM Book Of Standards*, Philadelphia: American Society for Testing and Materials, 1989.

Sports & Hobbies

Archery

TARGET ARCHERY

Target archery is practiced both outdoors and indoors. Standard targets are circular, with five concentric color zones, from the center outward: gold or yellow, red, light blue, black, and white. The two standard sizes for targets used outdoors are 122 cm (approximately 48 inches) and 80 cm (approximately 31 inches); targets used indoors are slightly smaller, 60 cm (approximately 23 inches) and 40 cm (approximately 15 inches). The color zones are each divided by a thin line into two zones of equal width, creating ten equal scoring zones. The center of the target is referred to as the "bull's eye" or "gold." Each competitor shoots a round, which is a specific number or arrows shot from specified distances. These specifications are developed by the Federation Internationale de Tir a l'Arc (FITA), the International Archery Federation, which is made up of a national amateur archery association member from each participating country.

FIELD ARCHERY

Field archery relates to marksmanship and the bow's use as a hunting instrument. Outdoor and indoor field archery competitions exist, each with its own targets and rules.

Indoor field archery rounds are: *National Field Archery Association (NFAA) Indoor Championship, NFAA Freeman, and the Flint Bowman Indoor Round.* Both Championship and Freeman use a screened blue square target surface with inner scoring rings of white and pale blue. For the Championship Round, five ends of four arrows each are shot at 16 cm targets 20 yards away. Freeman is 60 arrows shot as in three games, at distances of 10, 15, and 20 yards. Scoring for both is 5 points for the inner ring, 4 for the next

white ring, 3 for the inner blue ring, and 2 for the outer blue ring. Flint Bowman uses the standard 20 cm and 35 cm field targets, placed in two rows, one above the other, and uses the same scoring as the field round.

The three types of rounds in outdoor field archery are the field round, the hunter's round, and the animal round. Each uses its own type of targets and has its own style of action.

Field Round. Federation Internationale de Tir a l'Arc (FITA) outdoor *field round* (defined as twice around a *unit* or 14 target course), four target faces are used: 65 cm (approximately 25 inches), 50 cm (approximately 19 inches), 35 cm (approximately 13 inches), and 20 cm (approximately 7 inches). The spot, or center, is two black rings with a white *X* in the middle ring. Next there are two white inner rings and two black outer rings. Each contestant shoots four arrows at each of the fourteen targets in the unit from various distances.

Hunter's Round. The *hunter's round* targets are the same size as those used for the *field round,* but the target face has two white rings with a black *X* in the center ring and two outside black rings (The *X* ring is only used to break ties.)

Animal Round. To simulate the hunting experience, the targets are in the shape of animals. The largest targets simulate large animals like black bear, deer, moose, elk. The medium size targets simulate such animals as the wolf, small deer, mountain lion. The smallest targets simulate such animals as the coyote, jack rabbit, and crow. There are two scoring zones on each target: a "high scoring" oblong zone representing the animal's vital parts; the section between the high scoring area and the "hide and hair" or "feathers" is the low scoring area.

VARIATIONS

Archery Golf. The game closely follows the rule for regular golf, but usually has some special rule. The object is to play the number of holes from tee to target in as few shots as possible.

Clout Shooting. The archer shoots a high trajectory, aiming the arrow to strike a flag-marked bull's eye on a 48 ft. target on the ground.

Roving. The forerunner of field archers, originally featuring groups of archers shooting at casually selected natural targets in fields and woods. Marks of stone or wood, called rovers, were placed on the field and the archers shot from one to the next. As practiced today, one member of the group chooses the target and all try to hit it, with the one coming closest choosing the next target.

EQUIPMENT

Bow. Device made of a piece of flexible material with a string connecting the two ends, used to propel an arrow. The *compound bow* is a hand-held, hand-drawn bow that uses a pair of cables and wheels to store more energy. The *longbow* has limbs that bend toward the archer, and is favored by a small group of enthusiasts for its grace and historic significance. The *recurve bow* has curved tipped limbs that bend away from the archer when the bow is held in shooting position.

Arrows. Arrow *shafts* may be made of aluminum, fiberglass, a compination of graphite and fiberglass, or wood. *Fletching* is the term used for the natural feathers or plastic vanes that are bonded to the arrow shaft to stabilize its flight. *Nock* is an attachment at the end of the arrow which, when placed on the bowstring, holds the arrow in place. *Points* come in many different styles, depending on the style of target and type of competition.

Accessories. *Finger tabs* are usually made of leather or smooth vinyl, shaped to the outline of the three fingers used to draw the arrow, with a notch for the arrow nock, and are often used by target archers. *Gloves*, preferred by hunters, fit snugly over the first three fingers of the shooting had. *Armguards* prevent the string from scraping the inside of the bow arm. *Release aids* are mechanical devices which replace the archer's fingers on the bowstring, thereby protecting the archer's fingers. Release aids allow the archer to shoot a lighter-spined arrow for optimum performance, but they are not permitted in official competitions. *Bow sights* affix to the bow and aid the archer in sighting the target. *Stabilizers* are weights extended forward or backward from the bow to absorb vibration and allow the archer to hold steadier on the target. *Quiver* is a device used to hold arrows.

Source:
The ABC's of Archery, Gainesville, FL: Archery Manufacturers Association, undated.

BB Guns

Technically, BB guns are non-powder guns which propel a projectile using compressed gas, compressed air, a mechanical spring action, or a combination of those. Air guns and pellet guns are also of the non-powder variety. It is recommended that these guns not be labeled for use by persons less than 8 years of age.

Adult Guns. The two categories are described as follows: *Rifle*—a single-shot gun capable of attaining a muzzle velocity of 550 ft/s when firing projectiles 4.5 mm or smaller or 400 ft/s when firing projectiles larger than 4.5 mm, has a rifle barrel, a minimum overall length of 36 inches, a minimum weight of 5.3 lbs, a rear sight adjustable for wind and elevation, a hooded front sight or is designed for telescopic sight use, and has an adjustable or two-stage trigger; and *Hand Gun*—capable of attaining a muzzle velocity of 320 ft/s when firing projectiles 4.5 mm or smaller or 280 ft/s when firing a projectile larger than 4.5 mm, has a rifled barrel, a minimum overall barrel length of 6 inches, a minimum weight of 1.75 pounds, a rear sight adjustable for wind and elevation, a front sight, and an adjustable or two-stage trigger. The recommended labeling is: CAUTION: THIS AIR GUN IS RECOMMENDED FOR ADULT USE ONLY. CARELESS USE MAY RESULT IN SERIOUS INJURY OR DEATH. DANGEROUS WITHIN _____ YARDS.

General Purpose Guns. Guns not classified as *Match-Precision, Adult,* or *Training*. It is recommended that the packaging for guns that cannot attain a muzzle velocity of 350 ft/s when firing 4.5 mm projectiles, or 275 ft/s when firing larger projectiles, be labeled as follows: CAUTION: NOT A TOY, ADULT SUPERVISION REQUIRED. MISUSE OR CARELESS USE MAY CAUSE SERIOUS INJURY, PARTICULARLY TO THE EYE. MAY BE DANGEROUS UP TO _____ YARD. If the gun can attain those muzzle velocities, the label is recommended to read as follows: CAUTION: NOT A TOY. ADULT SUPERVISION REQUIRED. MISUSE OR CARELESS USE MAY CAUSE SERIOUS INJURY OR DEATH. MAY BE DANGEROUS UP TO _____ YARDS AWAY.

Match Precision Guns. Match precision guns fall into two broad categories: *Rifle*—which is capable of firing a five-shot group at a target 32.8 feet away so that the centers of all five fall within a 0.30 inch circle; and *Hand Gun*—which can fire a five shot group at the same target and have all five shots fall within a 0.40 inch circle. The recommended packaging labeling for these guns is: CAUTION: THIS AIR GUN IS DESIGNED FOR USE BY EXPERIENCED SHOOTERS AND IS INTENDED FOR MATCH COMPETITION OR TARGET RANGE USE. CARELESS USE MAY RESULT IN SERIOUS INJURY OR DEATH. DANGEROUS WITHIN _____ YARDS.

Training Guns. Special purpose guns intended for use in organized educational shooting programs. The recommended labeling is: CAUTION: NOT A TOY. THIS AIR GUN IS DESIGNED ESPECIALLY FOR CONTROLLED AND SUPERVISED TRAINING USE ONLY. CARELESS USE MAY RESULT IN SERIOUS INJURY OR DEATH. DANGEROUS WITHIN _____ YARDS.

Source:
Standard Consumer Safety Specification for Non-Powdered Guns, Designation: F 589-78, *Annual Book of ASTM Standards,* Philadelphia: ASTM, 1990.

Bicycles

The Consumer Product Safety Commission defines a bicycle as a two-wheeled vehicle having a rear drive wheel that is solely human-powered.

ROAD BIKES

Multi-speed, drop handlebars. Two types are available:

Racing. Tight geometry, responsive, thin tires, lightweight.

Touring. Longer wheel base, heavier, more relaxed geometry, tires thinner than mountain bikes, but typically not as narrow as racing bikes. Designed to be comfortable on long rides. Can be equipped with racks and panniers.

OFF-ROAD BIKES

All-terrain, multi-speed, upright handlebars. Two types are available:

BMX. Name derived from *bicycle motorcross.* Youth bike, modified frame, small wheels and frame, competition handlebars and seat.

Mountain. Sturdy, long wheel base, typically sized smaller than a road bike. Wide knobby tires. Designed for off-road use. Suitable for hilly terrain with rocks, branches, mud, water crossings, etc.

MISCELLANEOUS

Cruiser. Single speed. May have hand brakes or coaster brakes. Often used as a rental bike at resort locations.

Human Powered Vehicles (HPV). Fully enclosed, highly streamlined tandem recumbents used by a small group of racing enthusiasts.

Hybrid. Also know as *city bike* or *cross bike.* Combines some of the responsiveness of a road bike with the off-road capabilities of a mountain bike. Modified upright handlebars. May have slick tires for road use or slightly knobby, medium width tires for off-road use. Fastest selling bikes of 1990s.

Sidewalk Bicycle. A bicycle with a seat height of no more than 25 inches.

Tandem. Bicycle built for two (or more) riders. Available in either road or mountain styles.

Track Bicycle. A bicycle designed and intended for sale as a competitive machine having tubular tires, single crank-to-wheel ratio, and no free-wheeling feature between the rear wheel and the crank.

TIRES

Clincher Tire. A tire, sometimes called a *wire-on,* that has a lip or bead which expands under pressure to grip the flanges of the rim. It is made of a synthetic material and the cords are usually made of nylon. They are relatively rugged with good puncture resistance.

Tubular Tire. Also called a *sewup.* A more expensive tire preferred by racers. Gives a better ride. The extremely light tube is actually sewn into the casing.

FRAMES

Aircraft Quality. Used to indicate that the frame material is the same as that used in airframes, as for bikes made with chrome-moly (a steel with chromium and molybdenum added for increased strength) frames.

Butted. A practice whereby the ends of the tubes in the frame are butted or made thicker than the midsection by reducing the inside diameter. Components of a frame may be *single butted,* with only one end of the tube frame butted; or *double butted,* with both ends of the tube butted.

Dead. The ride produced by a frame that has little or no spring.

Live. The ride produced by a frame that has more resilience and spring.

Lugless. Tubes of the frame have been joined together in such a way as to have no lugs or fillets to help reinforce the joints. The lug is a pressed steel sleeve that spans the tubes. A fillet joint has reinforcement, and is quite strong. Fillet joints have outperformed equivalent lugged joints. Both types outperform welded bikes with no lugs or fillets.

Sources:

Consumer Product Safety Commission, "Requirements for Bicycles," 16 CFR Part 1512 (1992), Washington: Government Printing Office.

Dempsy, *The Bicycler's Bible,* Blue Ridge Summit, PA: Tab Books, 1977.

Jones, Susan H., National Organization of Bicyclists, Baltimore, Maryland, Letter to the editor, April 1992.

Walton, Bill, and Bjarne Rostaing, *Bill Walton's Total Book of Bicycling,* New York: Bantam Books, 1985.

Binoculars

Binoculars are labeled to indicate power, objective diameter, and field width. Examples of binocular labeling are 8x23 6.3°, 10x50 7°, 7x35 7°, etc.

Power. The number before the *x* stands for the binocular's power. Binoculars labeled 8 magnify an object 8 times, binoculars labeled 10 magnify 10 times, etc.

Objective Size. The number after the *x* stands for the objective size and is the diameter in millimeters of the front lenses. Larger lenses allow more light and help to view objects at dusk or indoors.

Exit Pupil. The power and objective size determine the exit pupil size: a measure of the size of the focused beam of light that projects the image to the pupil (user's eye). The larger the exit pupil, the better the image will appear in low light. The exit pupil size is calculated by dividing the objective size by the power. E.g., a 10x50 set of binoculars would have a pupil size of 5 (50 divided by 10).

Field Width. The last number indicates the field width, or how much of an object can be seen through the lenses. It is measured in degrees of field. E.g., a person using an 8 power binocular may be able to see just the head of an actor on a stage;

by using another set of binoculars with a larger field width, the actor's whole body may be visible. However, in both cases the image would still only be magnified 8 times. The field width is determined by the eyepieces and not by the objectives: binoculars with wide lenses do not necessarily have wide field widths.

FTC GUIDELINES

In the past, the term *binoculars* has caused some controversy among manufacturers and distributors. Some contended that the term applied to any two-tubed viewing instrument, whether prismatic or nonprismatic, while others contended that only a fully prismatic instrument is a binocular. The confusion affects the labeling of instruments having bulges on the tubes (which simulate prismatic instruments but which were not prismatic instruments) as binoculars. A Federal Trade Commission (FTC) investigation resulted in the development of guidelines to help with the labeling of these instruments.

Binocular. Used to describe any product which is fully prismatic.

Binocular-Nonprismatic. Used to describe any nonprismatic product.

Binocular-Mirror-Prismatic or Binocular-Partially Prismatic. Used to describe products which have a combination mirror and prism system.

Binocular-Nonprismatic Mirror. Used to describe a nonprismatic product having a mirror reflecting system.

Field Glasses. Used to describe straight tube nonprismatic products.

Field Glasses-Nonprismatic. Used to describe nonprismatic products having bulges on the tubes.

Sources:
Federal Trade Commission, 16 CFR Sections 402.1 to 402.5 (1992), Washington: Government Printing Office.
"How to Size Up Binoculars," *Consumer Reports,* Vol. 54, No. 7 (July 1989): 444-450.

Bowling Balls

Core Design. Refers to the inside construction of the ball and the placement of weight within the ball.

Cover Material. The surface of the ball that contacts the lanes and the pins. Typically made of either urethane or polyester. Urethane surfaces are more abrasive, providing more adhesion on lane surfaces.

Hardness. The hardness of a bowling ball cover cannot be softer than 72 durameter *D,* the allowable limit as regulated by the American Bowling Congress.

Hook Potential. A measurement of the possibility for a bowling ball to hook on a lane. It is determined by the cover material and the core design of the ball.

Three-Piece Ball. The most common way to manufacture bowling balls until the late 1980s. They have a flat or pancake shaped weight block, usually placed under the ball's label between a bowler's thumb and finger holes. This weight block, located near the surface of the bowling ball, is just a small portion of the ball's inner core which is more than 80 percent of the ball's total diameter. The core is surrounded by a veneer or outer shell of urethane or plastic, approximately ½ to ¾ inch thick.

Two-Piece Ball. These balls, which are coming to dominate the market, have a solid *core* design, which serves as the ball's weight block. The core is significantly smaller in most cases than balls of three-piece construction. The design puts more of the weight of the ball in the center which improves hook potential.

Source:
Woman Bowler, May/June 1992: 72-75.

Brassieres, Athletic

Brassieres are classified according to use in athletics, sports, and other physical activities.

Supportive. Intended to constrain the breasts and limit the displacement of breast tissue during physical activity. Applicable for noncontact sports, such as recreational jogging.

Protective. Intended to provide safety from external objects impacting the breasts. *Type 1* protective brassieres protect against low impact objects like basketballs. *Type 2* protect against higher impact objects like those found in hockey and fencing.

Source:
Standard Classification of Brassieres, Designation: F753-82, *Annual Book of ASTM Standards,* Philadelphia: ASTM, 1990.

Cameras

Bridge or New Concept Camera. A camera that is more sophisticated than simple non-adjustable cameras and single lens reflex (SLR) cameras. This camera has a distinctive look, resembling a hand-held video camera more than a traditional camera.

Point and Shoot Camera. A camera that cannot be adjusted by the user. The user simply points and shoots.

Singles Lens Reflex (SLR) Camera. A camera with interchangeable lenses; the photographer sees through the viewfinder exactly what the camera lens will capture on film.

FOCUSING

Active Auto Focus (Active AF). An autofocusing system whereby the camera emits a near-infrared beam or ultrasonic wave that is reflected off the subject. This type of system is less costly than a passive AF system and will work in total darkness. However, it will not work through glass, and it has a limited range.

Auto Focus (AF). The camera adjusts the focusing distance automatically without the aid of the user.

Autofocus Range (AF Range). The range of light levels within which the autofocusing system will operate.

Continuous Autofocusing Mode. The camera continuously checks and readjusts its focus to the target of the autofocusing mechanism. Also called *servo* or *follow-focus mode.*

Focus Priority. The camera will not allow the shutter to release until the image is in focus. A *Release Priority* system overrides the *focus priority system,* allowing the shutter to be released whether or not the subject is in focus.

Manual Focusing. The operator focuses the camera by turning focusing rings on the lens.

Passive Auto Focus (AF). Passive phase matching system that analyzes the scene image to determine the focusing distance. Will work at any distance but is not as effective in dim lighting and with low-contrast subjects.

Predictive Auto Focus (AF) or Focus Tracking. A system whereby the camera adjusts its focus to a moving subject by calculating where it expects the subject to be and sets the lens to that point of focus. Designed to compensate for shutter-release time lag.

Single-Shot Autofocusing Mode. When the shutter button is depressed, the camera focuses on whatever is centered in the viewfinder. It will lock onto that range until the shutter button is either pressed or released.

Trap Focus or Freeze Focus. A system that automatically releases the shutter when the subject reaches a predetermined distance from the camera.

EXPOSURE

Aperture Priority (AP). Allows the user to set the aperture while the camera automatically sets the corresponding shutter speed.

Automatic Exposure (AE). The camera automatically adjusts the exposure setting.

Center Weighted Average. The meter reads the image area and centers its focus on the central area.

Meter Manual Exposure Control. Allows the user to set both the shutter speed and the aperture.

Multizone Metering System. The camera adjusts its setting based on meter readings from several areas.

Program AE. The camera sets both the shutter speed and lens aperture for proper exposure. It does not allow the user to control the settings.

Shutter Priority AE. Allows the user to set the shutter speed.

Spot Metering. The camera reads only a small portion of the scene (typically indicated by a small circle within the viewfinder) when adjusting its exposure.

Through the Lens Metering (TTL). The meter reads the light coming through the lens and adjusts its exposure accordingly.

FLASH

Automatic Flash Exposure Control. The camera automatically provides proper exposure.

Rear Curtain Sync. The flash fires as the shutter closes. Used for shooting moving objects. Records ghost-image streaks as the subject moves across the screen.

Slow Sync Flash. Uses slow shutter speeds. Used to take pictures with a flash at night.

Through the Lens (TTL) Flash Metering. The camera reads the light coming through its lens and automatically adjusts the flash exposure.

LENS

Zoom Lens. A lens that can be varied in focal length while automatically maintaining sharp focus at any object distance.

OTHER

Autowinder. Threads, advances, and rewinds the film automatically.

Depth of Field Preview. Adjusts the lens to show how much of background and foreground will be sharp, given the lens aperture setting.

Diopter Adjustment. Adjusts the viewfinder for moderate near- or farsightedness so that many eyeglass wearers can focus and shoot without their glasses on.

DX Film Speed Reader. Reads the checkered code on 35 mm film cartridges to set film speed.

Film Prewind. The camera automatically unwinds the film before the first picture is taken. As pictures are shot, the film is wound back into the light-tight container. Prevents the film that has already been used from being exposed if the camera is accidentally opened.

Sources:
"Autofocus Terms Explained," *Popular Photography,* Vol. 98, no. 6 (June 1991): 60-61.
DeBat, Alfred, "The New Space-Age Cameras," *Consumers' Digest,* Vol. 30, no. 3 (May/June 1991).
"The Ultimate 35mm Camera Buyer's Guide," *Photograhic,* (December 1991): 79-81.
"What's What in Zoom Lens Terms," *Popular Photography,* Vol. 98, no. 4 (April 1991): 58.

Coins

Proof. A specially made coin distinguished by sharpness of detail and usually with a brilliant mirror like surface. Proof refers to the method of manufacture and is not a condition. Normally the term implies perfect mint state (unless otherwise noted and graded as below).

Mint State. The terms *mint state (MS)* and *uncirculated (Unc.)* are used to describe coins showing no trace of wear. Such coins may vary to some degree because of blemishes, toning, or slight imperfections as described in the following subdivisions.

Perfect Uncirculated (MS-70). Perfect new condition, showing no trace of wear. The finest quality possible, with no evidence of scratches, handling, or contact with other coins. Very few regular issue coins are ever found in this condition.

Choice Uncirculated (MS-65). An above average uncirculated coin which may be brilliant or lightly toned and has very few contact marks on the surface or rim. MS-67 through Ms-62 indicate a slightly higher or lower grade of preservation.

Uncirculated (MS-60). Has no trace of wear but may show a number of contact marks, and the surface may be spotted or lack some luster.

Choice About Uncirculated (AU-50). Barest evidence of light wear on only the highest points of the design. Most of the mint luster remains.

About Uncirculated (AU-50). Has traces of light wear on many of the high points. At least half of the mint luster is still present.

Choice Extremely Fine (EF-45). Light overall wear shows on the highest points. All design details are very sharp. Some of the mint luster is evident.

Extremely Fine (EF-40). Design is lightly worn throughout, but all features are sharp and well defined. Traces of luster may show.

Choice Very Fine (VF-30). Light even wear on the surface and highest parts of the design. All lettering and major features are sharp.

Very Fine (VF-20). Shows moderate wear on high points of the design. All major details are clear.

Fine (F-12). Moderate to considerable even wear. Entire design is bold with overall pleasing appearance.

Very Good (VG-8). Well worn with main features clear and bold, although rather flat.

Good (G-4). Heavily worn with design visible but faint in areas. Many details are flat.

About Good (AG-3). Very heavily worn with portions of lettering, date, and legends worn smooth. The date may be barely readable.

Damaged coins, such as those which are bent, corroded, scratched, holed, nicked, stained, or mutilated, are worth less than those without defects. Flawless, uncirculated coins are generally worth more than values quoted in some books. Slightly worn coins (*sliders*) which have been cleaned and conditioned (*whizzed*) to simulate uncirculated luster are worth considerably less than perfect pieces. Unlike damage inflicted after striking, manufacturing defects do not always lessen values. Examples are colonial coins with planchet flaws and weakly struck designs, early silver and gold with weight adjustment *file marks,* and proofs with *lint marks* (dust or other foreign matter which may mar the surface during striking).

Source:
American Numismatic Association, Official Grading Standards for U.S. Coins, *Colorado Springs: ANA, 1992.*
Yeoman, R.S., *A Guide Book of United States Coins,* 46th edition, Racine, WI: Western Publishing Co., 1993.

Crayons

Basic Colors. The generic or spectrum colors: red, orange, yellow, green, blue, and purple.

Inert Reinforcing Agents. Substances that contribute to desirable working characteristics without altering the color of the crayon.

Molded Crayons. Molded crayons should not break, warp, or melt under moderate forces of pressure or friction. The color is equally intense from both ends of the crayons, and it resists water.

Molded Hard Crayons. Molded hard crayons have greater resistance to breakage, warpage, and melting than molded crayons. They also have less flaking and piling, yield an even and intense distribution of color, and last longer than molded crayons.

Molded Washable Crayons. Molded washable crayons have the same characteristics as molded crayons except that they do not resist water, and markings made with them are removable from nonporous surfaces with minimum effort.

Oil Pastel Crayons. These crayons have a soft marking texture which yields color evenly without scratching. When they are applied wet with a petroleum vehicle such as linseed oil or turpentine, oil color effects can be achieved.

Pressed Crayons. They are compacted under pressure and have greater resistance to breakage, melting, flaking, and piling than molded crayons. They yield an even, intense distribution of color and last longer than molded crayons under terms of identical use.

Source:
American National Standard for Crayons, ANSI Z356.1-1981, New York: American National Standards Institute, Inc.

Explosives

Blasting Agents. Examples include ammonium nitrate-fuel oil and certain water-gels.

High Explosives. Explosive materials which can be caused to detonate by means of a blasting cap when unconfined (e.g, dynamite and flash powders).

Low Explosives. Explosive materials which can be caused to deflagrate, i.e., to burn rapidly, when confined (e.g., black powder, safety fuses, igniters, fuse lighters, and "special fireworks" defined as Class B explosives by U.S. Department of Transportation regulations in 49 CFR part 173.)

MAGAZINES

A magazine is a space in which explosives are stored. The Bureau of Alcohol, Tobacco, and Firearms recognizes 5 types of magazines based on the type of explosive being stored.

Type 1. Permanent magazines for the storage of high explosives.

Type 2. Mobile and portable indoor and outdoor magazines for the storage of high explosives.

Type 3. Portable outdoor magazines for the temporary storage of high explosives while attended (e.g., a "day-box").

Type 4. Magazines for the storage of low explosives.

Type 5. Magazines for the storage of blasting agents.

Source:
Bureau of Alcohol, Tobacco, and Firearms, US Department of the Treasury, 27 CFR Sections 47 (1991), Washington: Government Printing Office.

Eye Protectors, Athletic

The types listed in this section apply to eye protectors designed for use by players of racket sports. Eye protectors significantly reduce potential injury to the eye due to impact and penetration by both rackets and balls.

Type I. A protective lens with the lens and frame frontpiece moulded as one unit. Frame temples or other devices, such as straps, to affix the lens/frontpiece may be separate pieces.

Type II. A protector with a lens, either plain or prescription, mounted in a frame that was manufactured as a separate unit.

Type III. A protector without a lens.

Type IV. A full face shield.

Source:

Standard Specification for Eye Protectors for Use by Players of Racket Sports, Designation: F 803-83, *Annual Book of ASTM Standards*, Philadelphia: ASTM, 1990.

Firearms

The National Rifle Association has established standards for labeling the condition of new and used firearms.

FIREARMS MANUFACTURED AFTER 1898

New. Not previously sold at retail, in same condition as current factory production.

New-Discontinued. Same as new, but discontinued model.

Perfect. A second-hand firearm in new condition in every respect.

Excellent. A second-hand firearm in new condition, used but little, no noticeable marring of wood or metal, bluing perfect (except at muzzle or sharp edges).

Very Good. A second-hand firearm in perfect working condition, no appreciable wear on working surfaces, no corrosion or pitting, only minor surface dents or scratches.

Good. A second-hand firearm in safe working condition, minor wear on working surfaces, no broken parts, no corrosion or pitting that will interfere with proper functioning.

Fair. A second-hand firearm in safe working condition, but well worn, perhaps requiring replacement of minor parts or adjustments, which should be indicated; no rust, but may have corrosion pits which do not render article unsafe or inoperable.

FIREARMS MANUFACTURED BEFORE 1899

Factory New. All original parts; 100 percent original finish; in perfect condition in every respect, inside and out.

Excellent. All original parts; over 80 percent original finish; sharp lettering, numerals, and design on metal and wood; unmarred wood; fine bore.

Very Good. All original parts; none-to-30 percent original finish; original metal surfaces smooth with all edges sharp; clear lettering, numerals, and design on metal, wood slightly scratched or bruised; bore disregarded for collectors firearms.

Good. Some minor replacement parts; metal smoothly rusted or lightly pitted in places, cleaned, or reblued; principal lettering, numerals, and design on metal legible; wood refinished, scratched, bruised, or minor cracks repaired; in good working order.

Fair. Some major parts replaced; minor replacement parts may be required; metal rusted, may be lightly pitted all over, vigorously cleaned, or reblued; rounded edges of metal and wood; principal lettering, numerals, and design cracked or repaired when broken; in fair working order or can be easily repaired and placed in working order.

Poor. Major and minor parts replaced; major replacement parts required and extensive restoration needed; metal deeply pitted; principal lettering, numerals, and design obliterated, wood badly scratched, bruised, cracked, or broken; mechanically inoperative; generally undesirable as a collector's firearm.

TERMINOLOGY

Antique Firearm. Any firearm manufactured in or before 1898.

Auto-Loading (Automatic) Pistols. A shot is fired each time the trigger is pulled, with some of the energy of each shot actuating the pistol's mechanism to place a fresh cartridge in firing position. The so-called double-action feature of some automatic pistols does not place a fresh cartridge in firing position, as does the double-action mechanism of a revolver, but does offer a second chance to ignite the primer of a cartridge that misfired.

Caliber. The diameter of the barrel measure from land to land. In the example below (1) indicates the grooves, (2) the lands, and (3) the caliber.

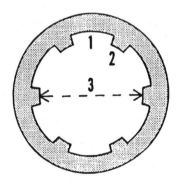

Carbine. A short-barreled rifle whose barrel is generally not longer than 22 inches and is characterized by light weight.

Double-Action Revolver. Can be fired single action or as a self-cocking revolver; pulling the trigger cocks and fires the gun.

Firearms. A weapon (and all components and parts thereof) not over .50 caliber which will (or is designed to or may be readily converted to) expel a projectile by the action of an explosive.

Handgun. Any firearm including a pistol or revolver designed to be fired by the use of a single hand.

Machinegun. A *machinegun, machine pistol, sub-machinegun, or automatic rifle* is a firearm originally designed to fire or is capable of being fired fully automatically by a single pull of the trigger.

Muffler or Silencer. Any device for silencing, muffling, or diminishing the report of a portable firearm. The term is also used to describe any combination of parts designed (or redesigned) and intended for use in assembling or fabricating a firearm silencer or firearm muffler, and any part intended only for use in such assembly or fabrication.

Pistol. A hand-operated firearm having a chamber integral with, or permanently aligned with, the bore.

Revolver. A hand-operated firearm with a revolving cylinder containing chambers for individual cartridges.

Rifle. A shoulder firearm discharging bullets through a rifled barrel (i.e., a barrel with spiral grooves cut into the inner surface to make the bullet spin when fired) at least 16 inches in length, including combination and drilling guns.

Short-Barreled Rifle. A rifle having one or more barrels less than 16 inches in length, and any weapon made from a rifle (whether by alteration, modification, or otherwise) if such weapon as modified has an overall length of less than 26 inches.

Short-Barreled Shotgun. A shotgun having one or more barrels less than 18 inches in length, and any weapon made from a shotgun (whether by alteration, modification, or otherwise) if such weapon as modified has an overall length of less than 26 inches.

Shotgun. A weapon designed (or redesigned, made, or remade) and intended to be fired from the shoulder and to use the energy of the explosive in a fixed shotgun shell to fire through a smooth bore either a number of ball shot or a single projectile for each single pull of the trigger.

Single-Action Revolver. Must be cocked by hand before each firing.

Single-Shot Pistols. Only one shot can be fired prior to reloading.

Sporting Type Sight Including Optical. A telescopic sight suitable for daylight use on a rifle, shotgun, pistol, or revolver for hunting or target shooting.

Sources:

American Rifleman, Washington: National Rifle Association of America, 1992.

Bureau of Alcohol, Tobacco, and Firearms, 27 CFR Section 47 (1991), Washington: Government Printing Office.

Thomas, Charles C., *The New Handbook of Handgunning,* Springfield, IL: Charles C. Thomas, 1980.

Golf Balls

TERMINOLOGY

Compression. Golf ball makers who employ wound ball technology sort and test their balls prior to offering them for sale to consumers. Balls with lower compression are labeled *90s* and those with higher compression *100s.*

Cover Material. A golf ball is typically made with either a soft cover (balata, lithium balata), or hard cover (surlyn or zinthane).

The hard cover balls are more durable. The soft cover balls are preferred for their spin and control.

Dimple Pattern. Refers to the arrangement of the dimples on the outer cover of the ball. A good dimple design can improve distance and spin. Patterns include:

Icosahedral. 20 triangles.

Octahedral. 8 triangles, also called Atti.

Dodecahedral. 12 pentagons.

Double Dimple. Triangular design.

Icosahedral Multiple Parting Line. 12 pentagons within 20 triangles.

Interlock. 80 small triangles within 20 large triangles.

Slice-Proof or Cut-Proof. The cover is made of a tougher material (surlyn) that is less likely to be cut by a poor hit or impact with a rock.

Spin Rate. Spin rates are measured in revolutions per minute (RPMs) and can range from 7,000 to over 9,000 RPMs in manufacturer's tests of a full 9-iron.

Three Piece Golf Ball. This type of ball is constructed of a larger solid rubber center around which denser rubber windings are wound. A strong outer cover is the final layer.

Trajectory. Refers to the arch the ball makes when in flight. A low-trajectory ball stays close to the ground. A high-trajectory ball has a bell-shaped flight pattern. A carry-trajectory ball will reach its highest point toward the end of its flight. Different golfers tend to hit the ball in different trajectories. Balls are designed to take advantage of a golfer's natural trajectory.

Two Piece Golf Ball. This type of ball is constructed of a high-energy solid core with a strong outer cover.

Sources:

Golf, Vol. 34, No. 3 (March 1992): 18.

Mattes, J.B., "Can You Buy Spin?" *Golf,* Vol. 30, No. 9 (September 1988): 106.

Golf Clubs

Cavity Back Design. Additional metal is used around the back perimeter of the iron to add weight and balance. This design results in a scooped-out cavity in the center of the back of the club.

Flex. The ability of the shaft of the club to flex (or bend) during the swing. A shaft's flex is measured on a deflection board. Golf club shafts can have a flex ranging from extra stiff to ladies.

X. Extra stiff.

S. Stiff

R. Regular.

A. Semi-flexible.

L. Ladies.

With few exceptions, only professional golfers swing hard enough to use extra-stiff shafts. Stiff shafts are for single-digit handicappers who generate high clubhead speeds (95 mph or above). Other golfers generally use regular (*R*), semi-flexible (*A*), or flexible (*L*) ranges.

Flow Weighting. The progressive placement of clubhead weight from near the toe on long irons to near the heel on short irons.

Forged Irons. Golf clubs made by stamping red-hot metal bars between a pair of dies.

Investment-Cast Irons. Made by pouring molten steel into a mold.

Laminated Woods. Clubheads cut from blocks formed by glueing together several thin sheets of wood, usually maple.

Muscleback. A design feature usually found on forged irons, where weight is concentrated in a bulge along the back of the clubhead.

Perimeter Weighting. The weight of a club head is distributed out toward its edges.

Persimmon Woods. Clubheads cut from a solid block of wood from the persimmon tree.

Progressive Offset. *Offset,* setting the clubface slightly behind the hosel, allows an extra split-second for the club to get square at impact. In this case, the amount of *offset* is greatest in the long irons and reduces to very little in the short irons.

Radiused (Cambered) Soles. Rounded bottoms on more recent iron designs, compared with the flat soles of classic irons, help players adjust to uneven lies and get through rough more easily.

Sole Weighting. Placing more weight toward the bottom of the clubhead, which promotes higher shot trajectory.

Source:
"Equipment Glossary," *Golf,* Vol. 30, No. 3 (March 1988): 107.

Headgear and Helmets

Protective headgear for sporting and leisure activities is certified by both the Snell Memorial Foundation and the National Operating Committee on Standards for Athletic Equipment (NOCSAE). A voluntary standard for determining shock-attenuation characteristics of football helmets has also been established by the American Society for Testing and Materials (ASTM).

SNELL MEMORIAL FOUNDATION

The goals of the foundation are to prevent head injures or fatalities in recreational and competitive sports and to educate the public about head injury/fatality prevention. To further this cause, Snell Memorial Foundation has established standards for protective headgear. The headgear for which standards exist are: bicycling headgear, harness racing and other equestrian sports headgear, motorcycles and other automotive vehicles headgear, and competitive automotive sports headgear. Helmets are submitted voluntarily by the manufacturers for certification. If the helmet passes the certification test series, Snell adds it to its list of certified helmets. They do not rate helmets other than to say whether or not they are certified, and all test data and information is confidential. Once a helmet is certified, the manufacturer orders certification decals from Snell to be affixed to the inside the certified helmets. These decals are sequentially numbered, and change when a new standard is issued. Helmets certified to a standard are still certified to that standard when an updated standard is issued; however, to become certified to the updated standard the helmets must pass certification testing to the new standard. Participation in the Snell program is strictly voluntary. Manufacturers are not obliged to seek certification or to continue it, but while a manufacturer does participate, the Snell Memorial Foundation demands full compliance. The Snell Foundation currently maintains three laboratories.

NOCSAE

The National Operating Committee on Standards for Athletic Equipment (NOCSAE) is comprised of representatives from a number of groups which have an interest in athletic equipment. These include manufacturers, reconditioners, equipment managers, and sports medicine organizations. NOCSAE has established voluntary safety standards for football, baseball, and lacrosse helmets. Helmets that meet the NOCSAE standards bear the seal *Meets NOCSAE Standard,* which is permanently branded or stamped on the outside rear portion of the helmet. This seal is a registered trademark of NOCSAE, as is the name NOCASE itself. Manufacturers test their own and competitors' helmets as they are produced.

The National Athletic Equipment Reconditioners' Association (NAERA) became a member of NOCSAE, and a revision of the NOCSAE Football Helmet Standard was issued in 1977 to provide for recertification of helmets. National Collegiate Athletic Association (NCAA) rules mandated the use of certified helmets beginning with the 1978 season, and the National Federation of State High School Associations required them beginning with the 1980 season.

Sources:
NOCSAE Manual, Kansas City: National Operating Committee on Standards for Athletic Equipment, undated.
Snell Memorial Foundation, Inc., Post Office Box 493, St. James, NY 11780.
Standard Test Method for Shock-Attenuation Characteristics of Protective Headgear for Football, Designation: F 429-79, *Annual Book of ASTM Standards,* Philadelphia: ASTM, 1984.

Kiddie Ride

A *kiddie ride* is an amusement ride designed primarily for use by children up to 12 years of age.

Source:
ASTM, Standard Definitions of Terms Relating to Amusement Rides and Devices, Designation: F747-82, *Annual Book of ASTM Standards, Philadelphia:* 1990.

Life Jackets

The U.S. Coast Guard approves life jackets that conform to an Underwriters Laboratories safety standard. Life jackets are judged by their ability to turn a person face up in the water and by how high above the water they keep the mouth. Life jackets are classified as Class I, II, III, or V, according to their design.

Type I. Good for rough water. Especially good at turning an unconscious person face up.

Type II. Best for use in calm water. Consists of two compartments over the chest and one behind the head.

Type III. Designed to keep a conscious person face up in the water with the mouth at least two inches above the water.

Type V. A new inflatable type of design.

Source:
"Life Jackets," *Consumer Reports*, Vol. 53, No. 7 (July 1988): 433.

Model Railroads

Gauge. The distance between the inside surfaces of the two rails that form the track. According to the American Railway Engineering Association, the gauge is measured ⅝ of an inch below the top of the rail.

Narrow Gauge. Wheels spaced to run on rails only 3 feet apart. A model train based on narrow gauge track will often have *n3* after its gauge initial as in *Gn3*. The number indicates the distance in feet between the rails. An exception is *Nn3* track. In the United States, this gauge is really 40" wide, not 36 inches (3 feet).

O-27. Track that requires a 27" diameter to make a curve.

Scale Model Railroading. Model railroading with trains that are accurate scale replicas of real trains.

Scale. The length of an element on the prototype (in model railroading, it is the full sized trains or track gauge) divided by the length of the same element on the model. For example, an HO locomotive is, in all dimensions, 1/87 the size of a real one.

Scale Designations. Scale model railroads are made to the following standard scales, which are sometimes referred to as gauges. *G* or *Gauge 1* is the biggest, and *Z* is the smallest.

Scale (gauge) Designation	Proportion to prototype	Track Gauge
Z	1:220	6.5 mm
N	1:160	9.0 mm
HO	1:87	16.5 mm
S	1:64	⅞ inch
O	1:48	1¼ inch
Gn3	1:22.5	1¾ inch

Standard Gauge. Wheels spaced to run on rails 4 feet 8½ inches apart. This is a track gauge that is nearly universal throughout North America and much of the rest of the world.

Toy Trains. Model railroading with trains that are not accurate scale replicas of real trains.

Sources:
Kelly, Jim, "Scales and Gauges," *Your Introduction to Model Railroading*, Waukesha, WI: Kalmbach Publishing Co., 1991.
Shoe, Steve, "Scale Vs. Gauge," *MIRA Reporter*, (January 1992): Model Railroad Industry Association.

Mouthguards

A resilient device or appliance placed inside (or inside and outside) the mouth, to reduce mouth injuries, particularly to teeth and surrounding structures. Principally used as protective equipment for sports.

Type I. Stock.

Type II. Mouth-formed.

Type III. Custom fabricated over a model.

Source:
ASTM, Standard Practice for Care and Use of Mouthguards, Designation: F 697-80, *Annual Book of ASTM Standards*, Philadelphia: ASTM, 1990.

Nontoxic Art and Craft Materials

The Art and Craft Materials Institute, Inc. (formerly The Crayon, Water Color, and Craft Institute, Inc.) sponsors a certification program for children's art materials. The program certifies that products are non-toxic and meet voluntary standards of quality and performance.

Products in the certification program which have earned the Certified Product (CP) or Approved Product (AP) seal include crayons, water colors, tempera colors, finger paints, chalks, modeling materials, block printing inks and media, drawing inks and media, etching inks and media, screen printing inks and media, school pastes and adhesives, acrylic and oil paints and media, marking crayons, and other art materials. Products bearing the AP seal are non-toxic, even if ingested, inhaled, or absorbed. Those bearing the CP seal are non-toxic, even if ingested, inhaled, or absorbed, and meet or exceed specific quality standards of material, workmanship, working qualities, and color.

Products added to the expanded certification program include acrylic and oil colors, pigments, ceramic clays, glazes and colors, screen printing, drawing and other inks, oils, varnishes, solvents, and media. A Health Label (HL) seal has been added to the program and signifies that products bearing this seal are certified to be properly labeled in a program of toxicological evaluation by a medical expert. Some non-toxic products bear the HL Health Label seal with the wording *Non-Toxic* or *No Health Labeling Required* or with no cautionary labeling. Products requiring cautions bear the Health Label (HL) seal with appropriate cautionary labeling and safe use instructions.

Source:
Promotional material supplied by the Art and Craft Materials Institute, Inc., 100 Boylston Street, Suite 1050, Boston, MA 02116.

Paper

Acid Free. The pH value is a measure of the strength of the acidity or alkalinity of paper on a scale of 0 to 14. Papers with a high acidity (pH over 7) are more likely to decompose over time. Papers labeled *acid free* typically have a pH value of 7 or lower. A pH of 7 is considered neutral because it represents a balance between acidity and alkalinity. (See the entry *Paper, Permanent Records.*)

Bleaching. Paper producers use chlorine to bleach wood pulp before it is made into paper. It takes between 110 and 176 pounds of chlorine to produce every ton of conventionally bleached wood pulp. Unfortunately, the chlorine combines with organic molecules in the wood to produce organochlorines, long-lasting substances—including dioxin—that are harmful to the environment. Accordingly, many consumers are now requesting paper that was bleached with less harmful substances, such as hydrogen peroxide or oxygen.

Coated. Coatings of clay and other materials on base paper provide a smooth, glossy surface for quality print production. Types and grades include the following: No. 1 and No. 2 coated, machine coated, dull coated, and cast coated.

Cotton Fiber. The cellulose fibers derived from the cotton plant.

Cotton Linters. The shorter fibers left behind after the ginning operation. Used in hand- and mouldmade papermaking.

Cotton Rags. Fibers reclaimed from cotton rags discarded during the manufacture of cotton thread; the rags must be broken down to free the fibers. Although not used much in papermaking today, cotton rags produce a paper with good strength. These papers are called *rag* paper.

De-Inking. The process used to remove clay fillers and inks from collected waste paper. Mills de-ink incoming waste in order to use higher percentages of postconsumer fiber in papermaking. Environmentalists are concerned that the sludge produced in the process is toxic, containing heavy metals from removed inks. To avoid the harmful environmental affects of traditional inks, some printers now use vegetable- or soy-based inks instead of those made with petroleum.

Grain. Represents the alignment of fibers during manufacturing. Papers tear more easily with (as opposed to against) the grain.

Handmade. Made by scooping pulp up from a vat and placing it onto a mold by hand.

Laid. Indicates the type of mesh used to cover the paper mold; it also indicates the texture of the paper. Traditionally, a laid mesh is one constructed of long parallel wire lines held together with less heavy *chain* wires running at right angles to them. This type of mesh produces a paper with distinctive lines in its texture that can be distinguished when the paper is held up to light.

Linen. The fibers from linen rags. They are long and tubular and give the paper a hard and strong, yet smooth and silky, quality.

Long Grain. Describes fibers running parallel with the longest side of a sheet.

Machinemade. Made on a flat bed papermaking machine designed for mass producing paper.

Mouldmade. A mechanization of the *handmade* process. A quicker process for making paper of handmade texture and quality.

Short Grain. Describes fibers running along the shortest side of a sheet.

Sizing. A chemical treatment applied to the paper to help it resist water and moisture.

Waterleaf. Used to describe paper that does not contain any size.

Watermark. A distinguishing mark impressed on the substance of a sheet of paper during manufacture. It is typically only noticeable when the paper is held up to the light.

Weight. The weight in pounds of 500 sheets of a given type of paper.

Woven. Indicates the type of mesh used to cover the paper mold. A woven mesh produces a very smooth paper with an even distribution of pulp. The texture of the paper looks like that of a woven fabric with warp and weft threads.

Sources:

Leibman, Dena, "Paper Puzzle," *Friends of the Earth,* Volume 22, no. 6 (June/July 1992): 8.

Lem, Dean Phillip, *Graphics Master 2,* second edition, Los Angeles: Dean Lem Associates, 1977.

Turner, Silvie, *A Guide to Choosing Fine Paper,* New York: Design Press, 1991.

Paper, International (ISO) Sizes

The International Standards Organization (ISO) has established three standard series of paper sizes designated A, B, and C. These standards are used extensively in Europe. The A series is for general purposes, such as stationery and publications. The B series is for posters, and the C series is for envelopes. The base size in each series is designated 0—as in A0, B0, and C0. The next smallest size is equal to half of the area of the preceding size. For example, A1 is half the size of A0. Sheets larger than the base size maintain the same proportions and are given a prefix indicating the size. For example, 2A0 is twice as large as A0.

A SERIES

Size	Millimeters
4A0	1682 x 2378
2A0	1189 x 1682
A0	841 x 1189
A1	594 x 841
A2	420 x 594
A3	297 x 420
A4	210 x 297
A5	148 x 210
A6	105 x 148
A7	74 x 105
A8	52 x 74
A9	37 x 52
A10	26 x 37

B SERIES

Size	Millimeters
B0	1000 x 1414
B1	707 x 1000

(B Series continued)

Size	Millimeters
B2	500 x 707
B3	353 x 500
B4	250 x 353
B5	176 x 250
B6	125 x 176
B7	88 x 125
B8	62 x 88
B9	44 x 62
B10	31 x 44

C SERIES

Size	Millimeters
C0	917 x 1297
C1	648 x 917
C2	458 x 648
C3	324 x 458
C4	229 x 324
C5	162 x 229
C6	114 x 162
C7	81 x 114
C8	57 x 81

Source:
Lem, Dean Phillip, *Graphics Master 2,* second edition, Los Angeles: Dean Lem Associates, 1977.

Paper, Standard Sizes (U.S.)

Packaging for paper and envelopes is often marked with a number that indicates its standard size; as in *No. 10* envelopes.

PAPER SIZES

3 x 6
3½ x 6¼
3¾ x 6⅞
4 x 5½
4 x 6
4 x 9
4¾ x 6¼
5 x 7
5 x 8
5½ x 7½
5½ x 8½
6 x 9
7 x 10
7½ x 10
8 x 10
8½ x 11
9 x 12

ENVELOPE SIZES

Commercial. Used for business letters and standard correspondence.

Number	Size
5	3¹⁄₁₆ x 5½
6	3⅛ x 6
6¼	3½ x 6
6½	3⁹⁄₁₆ x 6¼
6¾	3⅝ x 6½
7	3¾ x 6¾
7½	3¾ x 7⅝
7¾ (Monarch)	3⅞ x 7½
Data Card	3½ x 7⅝
8⅝ (Check)	3⅝ x 8⅝
9	3⅞ x 8⅞
10	4⅛ x 9½
10½	4½ x 9½
11	4½ x 10⅜
12	4¾ x 11
14	5 x 11½

Announcement. Used to hold announcements, such as change of address notices, weddings, promotions, etc.

Number	Size
A-2	4⅜ x 5⅝
A-6	4¾ x 6½
A-7	5¼ x 7¼
A-8	5½ x 8⅛
A-10	6¼ x 9⅝
Slim	3⅞ x 8⅞

Baronial. A formal type of announcement envelope

Booklet. Used to hold direct mail sales literature and other types of correspondence that are not too bulky.

Catalog. Designed to hold sales catalogs, magazines, etc.

Coin. Used to hold coins and paper currency.

Metal Clasp. Used to handle bulky materials and when the envelop will be used again and again.

Policy. An envelope developed for holding insurance policies, wills, or other legal documents.

Remittance. Often used by oil companies for returning payment for credit card purchases.

Ticket. Used for holding tickets to the theater, sporting events, etc.

Wallet Flap. Stronger than standard envelopes, it is used for bulky material.

Window. Has an opening in the front that allows an address printed on the correspondence inside to show through. Most often used for mailing bills.

Source:
Lem, Dean Phillip, *Graphics Master 2,* second edition, Los Angeles: Dean Lem Associates, 1977.

Paper, Permanent Records

GRADES

Type I, Maximum Permanence. Used for documents expected to last several hundred years. Has a pH level from 7.5 to 9.5. *Grade 1* is for ordinary use. *Grade 2* is for high reference use where the copies will be handled frequently.

Type II, High Performance. Used for documents expected to last over 100 years. Has a pH level from 6.5 to 8.5. *Grade 1* is for ordinary use. *Grade 2* is for high reference use where the copies will be handled frequently.

Type III, Medium Performance. Used for documents expected to last 50 to 100 years. Has a minimum pH of 5.5. *Grade 1* is for ordinary use. *Grade 2* is for high reference use where the copies will be handled frequently.

TERMINOLOGY

Alkaline-Filled Paper. An alkaline paper (7.5 to 9.5 pH) that contains a reserve buffering capacity that can neutralize the acidic gases which are in the paper and which tend to made it yellow and brittle.

Bond. A grade of writing paper used for letterheads, forms, or other applications requiring permanence, strength, and durability. Three types of bond paper are available.

Ledger Paper. Has high strength, high tearing resistance, erasability, water and ink resistance, uniformity of surface, and smoothness.

Neutral Sized Paper. Paper treated with a synthetic material that allows it to be manufactured with a pH of 7.0 or higher.

Source:
Paper; Packaging; Flexible Barrier Materials; Business Copy Products, ASTM D 3290-86, *Annual Book of ASTM Standards,* Volume 15.09, Philadelphia, PA: American Society for Testing and Materials, 1989.

Photographic Film

35 mm. Indicates the size of the film. 35 mm means that the film is 35 millimeters wide.

ANSI Paper Speed (Formerly ASAP). Photographic papers differ in the ratio of the exposures required to produce a tone just perceptibly removed from white and one which is just a full black. The papers upon which photographs are printed have differing contrast grades that correspond to an established American National Standards Institute (ANSI; formerly American Standards Association) paper speed.

Number of paper	Contrast	Grade ANSI Paper Speed	Contrast
0	Extra Soft	1600	Lowest
1	Soft	1000	
2	Normal	500	
3	Hard	300	
4	Extra Hard	200	
5	Ultra Hard	160	Highest

Chrome. Generally, films ending in the word *chrome* are color slide films.

Color Negative Film. Color film used for prints.

Color Transparency Film. Color film used for slides; it is also known as reversal film.

Color. Generally, films ending in the word color are color negative material.

Emulsion. Describes the thin layer of light-sensitive chemicals which have been coated on film or paper for use in cameras or darkrooms. The normal chemistry of emulsions consists of crystals of compound silver salts or halides; all of them are inherently receptive to the blue wave lengths of light and UK radiation. By the use of additives, sensitivity can be extended to all colors of the spectrum and infrared.

EXP. EXP stands for exposures. When found on a film box, it is usually preceded by a number that stands for the number of pictures (or exposures) that one can get from that roll of film. Common numbers include 24 EXP (24 exposures) and 36 EXP (36 exposures).

Expiration Date. Film ages and should be processed before its expiry date. Old film may be slower than expected and may also produce a color cast. Most film boxes have the expiry number printed on them; e.g., the numbers *1/1993 467-45* appearing on a box of film. *1/1993* indicates that January 1993 is the expiry date and *467-45* indicates the manufacturer's batch number.

Film Speed (DX) Recognition. Modern 35 mm cameras offer such features as automatic loading, rewinding, and frame advance. Modern film containers have a bar code near the slit opening where the film comes out. The camera has sensors that reads this code and automatically adjusts its light meter to the appropriate speed for the film.

Fixers. Fixers dissolve away similar halides or salts in the emulsion that have not been affected by light. After their removal, light cannot alter the image.

Glossy. A smooth paper stock that is coated with several layers of baryta to produce a very smooth finish. When this is coated with emulsion, a paper with a glossy stock surface is produced.

ISO Numbers. The speed of the film (its sensitivity to light) is represented by ISO numbers. The faster the film (the less light it requires) the higher its ISO number. ISO numbers for color film range from 100 to 16000. 100 would be used in dim light while ISO 400 (4 times more sensitive) would be used in normal daylight. Black and white film is categorized as slow (ISO 64-100); medium (ISO 125-400), the most popular; and fast (ISO 400 to 3200). ISO stands for International Standards Organization—a group that sets standards for all sorts of consumer and industrial products and processes. The number of the individual standard for film speeds is ISO 6-1974. In addition to the International Standards Organization, other organizations have established standards for film speeds: ASA (American Standards Association, which is the former name of ANSI, the American National Standards Institute); BS (British Standards); and DIN (German Standards). Although each national group maintains their own standard, most are in agreement with the International Standards Organization standard.

Multigrade Papers. Ones that use the same emulsion for all contrasts.

Root Mean Square (RMS). RMS refers to the grain size of the chemical on photographic film.

RMS Value	Graininess classification
45, 50, 55	Very Coarse
33, 36, 39, 42	Coarse
26, 28, 30	Moderately Coarse
21, 22, 24	Medium
16, 17, 18, 19, 20	Fine
11, 12, 13, 14, 15	Very Fine
6, 7, 8, 9, 10	Extremely Fine
less than 5.5	Micro Fine

Sources:

Hedgewe, John, *Complete Guide to Photography*, New York: Sterling Publishing Co., Inc., 1991.

Jacobson, et.al., *The Manual of Photography*, eighth edition., Boston: Focal Press, 1988.

Langford Michael, *The Masters Guide to Photography*, New York: Alfred A. Knopf, 1982.

Photo Lab Index, Lifetime Edition, Dobbs Ferry, NY: Morgan & Morgan, 1985.

Pinkard, Bruce, *The Photographer's Bible*, New York: ARCO, 1983.

Postage Stamps

Stamp condition is classified into the six grades below based on how well the design is centered, color, how clear the impression is, and whether perforation teeth are bent, broken, or whole. On used stamps, placement and heaviness of the cancellation influence the grade. An uncanceled stamp is graded higher if in mint condition—never mounted and with original gum intact.

Superb
Extra Fine
Very Fine
Fine
Average
Below Average

TERMINOLOGY

Bisect. A stamp cut by a postmaster for use at half face value.

Block. A group of at least four stamps, two across and two deep, that are still attached to each other.

Cachet. A decorative embellishment on an envelope.

Cancellation. A mark on a stamp showing it has been used.

Canceled to Order (CTO). Stamps canceled as a service to collectors, without having passed through the mail.

Cinderella. A stamp not for postage, such as a Christmas seal.

Commemorative. A stamp sold for a limited period of time, honoring a person, place, or event.

Corner Block. A block from the corner of a sheet with the selvage still attached

Cover. An envelope with postal markings and stamps intact.

Definitives. The regular stamps of a country.

Imperforate (Imperf). A stamp issued without perforations.

Issue. A stamp or group of stamps put out as a single series.

Margin Block. A block of stamps from the edge of a sheet with the selvage still attached.

Mint. The condition of a stamp. It has not been used or hinged and has its original gum.

N.H. Never hinged, i.e., never mounted.

O.G. Original gum/adhesive.

Overprint. Anything printed over the design of a stamp to change its validity (e.g., to make an ordinary stamp valid for airmail).

Perforation Number. The number of perforation holes for every two centimeters along the edge of a stamp.

Phantom. Stamp of nonexistent country—a fraud or joke.

Postmaster's Provisionals. Stamps created by a postmaster in lieu of government issues.

Precancel. Stamp issued with the cancellation already applied.

Proof. An impression taken as a test from the plate.

Reprint. A stamp printed from its original plates after it is no longer valid for postage.

Selvage. The border of a sheet of stamps.

Semipostal. Stamps sold for more than postal value in order to earn money for charity.

SE-Tenant. Two attached stamps that are different. Some are the result of an error, but others are made intentionally for issues containing different designs.

Sheet. A group of unseparated stamps, usually 50 or more.

Tied On. This is said of a stamp on a cover that has been canceled so that part of the mark is on the stamp and part is on the envelop.

Ungummed. A stamp issued without gum, as opposed to a stamp that has lost its original adhesive.

Unused. Condition of a stamp that has not been used for postage but may have been hinged and may lack original gum.

Source:

The Encyclopedia of Collectibles: Silhouettes to Swords, Alexandria, VA: Time-Life Books, 1980

Skis, Alpine

TERMINOLOGY

Contact Length. That portion of the ski that actually touches the snow.

Damping. Represents the reduction of the longitudinal and torsional vibrations of a ski within a set period of time. If a ski has little or no dampening, it will vibrate, resulting in nervous or unpredictable handling characteristics. A ski with too much dampening lacks liveliness and the inherent dynamics necessary for a well-handling ski.

Flex. Flex is the force required to displace a ski by one centimeter. It is measured in Newtons (N)/centimeter and is typically measured along the length of the ski at standard points. The flex will differ at each point. The relationship of the different values is called the *flex balance* or *flex pattern*. The *flex pattern* of a ski has a direct influence on its torsional rigidity. That is, stiff flexing skis will generally have greater torsion rigidity, and vice versa. By combining different materials and varying their dimensions the relationship between flex and torsion may be controlled. The guidelines which follow describe which flex patterns apply to various terrain and snow conditions:

Hardpack slope (smooth, hard to icy). Balanced, even flex pattern from ski tip to tail (medium to stiff flex).

Hard slope (undulating, bumpy). Balanced, even flex pattern from ski tip to tail (medium flex).

Soft snow consistency (smooth to bumpy, deep snow, spring snow). Balanced, even flex pattern from ski tip to tail (soft to medium flex).

Moguls (hard to soft). Flex pattern medium to soft with tip and tail area softer for better adaptation to the terrain.

Backcountry (irregular, difficult conditions). Balanced, even flex pattern from ski tip to tail (soft to medium flex).

Projected Length. The total length of the ski.

Sidecut or Waist Design. Refers to the outside dimensions of the ski. Skis with deep sidecuts are wider at the tops (the shovels) and taper in at the middle and towards the back of the ski (the heels). Skis with deep sidecuts, such as slalom skis, are generally quick-turning and maneuverable; skis with shallow sidecuts, such as downhill racing skis, are usually stable. For larger turn radii and higher speeds, a wider tail for increased directional control and tracking will be best.

Torsion. Measured in Newton meters (Nm)/degrees, torsional rigidity represents the ability of a ski to resist twist along its longitudinal axis. Skis high in torsion offer better edge grip and precision on steep, icy slopes due to their resistance to edge angle distortion under load. However, strong, technical skiing skills are required to reach optimum ski performance. Skis low in torsion, though more forgiving, offer less carving precision and stability at moderate to high speeds. This is due to their tendency to deform when on edge, resulting in inability to maintain consistent pressure. Therefore, skis low in torsion will have a greater tendency to slide than skis high in torsion.

SKI CONSTRUCTION

Materials used in skis include carbon (graphic) fiber, ceramic fiber, kevlar, polyethylene, and titanal (a high-strength aluminum/magnesium/titanium alloy). These materials are used in the following ski construction types:

Braided. A technique whereby fiberglass is woven around a ski core.

Hybrid. The skis are composed of a number of different materials (e.g., wood, fiberglass, metal, etc.).

Laminate. Layers of materials are put together in a sandwich-like construction.

One-Piece Cap. The top sheet and sidewalls are replaced with a one-piece molded cap which may be glued to the ski or injected over it.

Reaction Injection Molding (RIM). Liquid is injected into a form and allowed to expand and set into a semi-dense foam.

Torsion Box. The load-carrying materials surround the core. Usually results in a stiff ski.

BINDINGS

The binding is the mechanism that connects the boots to the ski. The function of the binding is to firmly retain the boot to the ski while enabling it to be released from the ski should the skier get into trouble, thereby minimizing the chance that the ski will act as a lever and twist or bend the skier's leg. Release in all directions is usually controlled by an adjustment screw, which regulates the force on the release spring. The release setting is usually shown by a scale that ranges from 1 to 10 with the higher numbers indicating a firmer retention level. Alpine skies are also graded according to the attachment strength of the bindings to the skis.

Class A. Skis with high screw-retention strengths.
Class B. Skis with intermediate screw-retention strengths.
Class C. Skis with acceptable screw-retention strengths.
The American Society for Testing and Materials has established a standard that requires ski manufacturers to put a permanent line on both sidewalls or top surface of each ski that corresponds with the mark on the side surface of each ski and with a similar mark on the side surface of the boot sole. The location of the mark on the ski shall be determined by the ski manufacturer in accordance with established test procedures and results. The mark on the ski consists of a line at least 0.5 cm in length from 0.03 to 0.10 cm in width in contrasting color to the surface on which it is located.

Sources:
"Buyer's Guide '91: Skis, Boots, Bindings, Skiwear, Eyewear, and More," *Skiing,* Vol. 43, No. 1 (September 1990): 95-210.
Head Ski Division, Head Sports, Inc.
Standard Specification for Binding Mounting Area Dimensions on Alpine Skis, Designation: F 473-76 (Reapproved 1988), *Annual Book of ASTM Standards,* Philadelphia: ASTM, 1990.
Standard Specifications for Boot Sole Dimensions of Adult Alpine Ski Boots, Designation: F 944-85, *Annual Book of ASTM Standards,* Philadelphia: ASTM, 1990.
Standard Specification for Static Screw-Retention Strength of Binding Mounting Area on Alpine Skis, Designation: F474-76 (Reapproved 1983), *Annual Book of ASTM Standards,* Philadelphia: ASTM, 1990.

Standard Terminology for Geometry of Alpine Skis, Designation: F 472-86, *Annual Book of ASTM Standards,* Philadelphia: ASTM, 1990.
United Ski Industries Association, 8377-B Greensboro Drive, McLean, VA.

Sleeping Bags

SIZES

Cut Size. The cut size of a sleeping bag is considerably larger than the finished size. The dimensions of the cut size are accurate measurements of the yard goods used in construction of the sleeping bags. The finished size gives the length and width of the finished products. An example of a size marking when the product has a finished size of 33x68 inches and a cut size of 36x72 inches is—Finished size 33x68 inches, cut size 36x72 inches.

Mummy (MU). A sleeping bag design that is narrow at the feet and wider at the shoulders. This form-fitting shape leaves little excess air inside. The tapered cut takes less material to make, saving weight, and packing smaller into backpacks.

TERMINOLOGY

Fill. This term refers to the type of material used to insulate the sleeping bag. Fill materials are made of either down or a synthetic material. Down is more expensive but is the warmest material. However, it loses its effectiveness if it becomes wet. Synthetic fill is less expensive and performs better when wet. However, it is also heavier and bulkier (see *Feathers and Down, Textiles*).

Ripstop Nylon. Has heavy threads woven every quarter inch or so that prevent minor rips from running and form a reinforcing web to distribute stress.

Shell. The outer material of the sleeping bag. Many shells are made of nylon. Some are specially designed to be both waterproof and breathable.

Temperature Ratings. Many sleeping bag manufacturers give their products ratings, such as "good to -20 degrees F." These ratings are not based on an established standard and may vary widely among manufacturers.

Sources:
Federal Trade Commission, "Guides for Advertising Sleeping Bags," 16 CFR section 400.1 (1992), Washington: Government Printing Office.
Hamel, John P., "Sleeping Bags," *Backpacker,* Vol. 19, No. 2 (April 1991): 76-77. (*Backpacker* publishes an annual buyers guide issue.)

Spa, Residential

A spa is a hydrotherapy unit of irregular or geometric shell design.

Hot Tub. A spa constructed of wood with sides and bottoms formed separately; and the whole shaped to join together by pressure from the surrounding hoops, bands, or rods; as distinct from spa units formed of plastic, concrete, metal, or other materials.

Hydrotherapy Units. Units that may have a therapeutic use but which is not drained, cleaned, or refilled for each individual. It may include hydrotherapy jet circulation, hot water, cold water mineral baths, air induction bubbles, or any combination thereof. Industry terminology for spa includes *therapeutic pool, hydrotherapy pool, whirlpool, hot spa,* etc.

Permanent Residential Spa. A spa in which the water heating and water circulating equipment is not an integral part of the product. The spa is intended as a permanent plumbing fixture, not intended to be moved.

Residential Portable Spa. There are two types of portable spas.
Self Contained. A spa in which all control, water heating, and water circulating equipment is an integral part of the product. Self-contained spas may be permanently wired or cord connected.
Non-Self Contained Spas. A spa in which the water heating and circulating equipment is not an integral part of the product. Non-self contained spas may employ separate components such as an individual filter, pump, heater, and controls, or they may employ assembled combinations of various components.

Source:
Standard for Public Swimming Pools, American National Standard, ANSI/NSPI-1 1991, Alexandria, VA: National Spa and Pool Institute.

Swimming Pools

Aboveground Pool—Type 0. A removable pool of any shape that has a minimum water depth of 36 inches and maximum water depth of 48 inches at the wall. The wall is located on the surrounding earth and may be readily disassembled or stored. Diving and the use of a water slide are prohibited.

Inground Swimming Pool. Any pool whose sides rest in partial or full contact with the earth.

Onground Residential Swimming Pool—Type 0. A removable pool whose walls rest fully on the surrounding earth and has an excavated area below the ground level where diving and the use of a water slide are prohibited.

Public Pool. A nonresidential pool operated by an owner, lessee, operator, licensee, or concessionaire.
Class A Public Pool. A pool intended for use for accredited competitive aquatic events.

Residential Pool. Any permanent or nonportable pool that is intended for noncommercial use as a swimming pool by not more than three families and their guests and that is over 24 inches in depth, has a surface area exceeding 250 square feet and/or a volume over 3,250 gallons.
Type 0. Any residential pool where the installation of diving equipment is prohibited.
Type I-V. Residential pools suitable for the installation of diving equipment by type.

COVERS

Something that covers, protects, or shelters a swimming pool, spa, or hot tub.

Hard Top Cover. Rests on the lip of the pool, not a flotation cover, used as a barrier to users, for maintenance, and thermal protection.

Safety Cover. As defined by ASTM in ES 13-89, a barrier intended to be completely removed before entry of users that, when properly installed, reduces the risk of drowning of children under five years of age, by inhibiting their access to the contained body of water, and by providing for the removal of any substantially hazardous level of collected surface water.

Solar Cover. When placed on a pool increases the water temperature by solar activity, and reduces evaporation.

Thermal Cover. An insulating cover used to help prevent evaporation and heat loss.

Winter Cover. Secured around the perimeter of a pool that provides a barrier to debris, when the pool or spa is closed for the season.

FILTERS

A filter is a device that removes undissolved particles from water by recirculating the water through a porous substance (a filter medium or element).

Cartridge Filter. A filter that utilizes a porous element that acts as a filter medium. The cartridge is disposable.

Diatomaceous Earth Filter. A filter that utilizes a thin coating of diatomaceous earth (DE) over a porous fabric as its filter medium that periodically must be replaced.

Permanent Medium Filter. A filter that utilizes a medium (e.g., sand) that under normal use will not have to be replaced.

Vacuum Filter. A filter that operates under a vacuum from the suction of a pump.

LINERS

The plastic membrane constructed of vinyl or vinyl compounds that acts as a container for the water.

Expandable Liner. A liner that is constructed of a material that has the capability of stretching into a shape other than the original construction dimensions.

Hopper Liner. the liner that is used to obtain greater depth by geometrical pattern construction on the liner bottom or floor to fit a predetermined size and shape.

Winterized Liner. A plastic liner that is manufactured with sufficient plasticizers to withstand exposure to its rated lowest temperature of -20 degrees F.

SLIDES

Tamper Proof. Means that tools are required to alter or remove portions of the slide such as guards, treads, etc.

Source:
Consumer Product Safety Commission, "Safety Standard for Swimming Pool Slides," 16 CFR Part 1207 (1992) Washington: Government Printing Office.
Standard for Public Swimming Pools, American National Standard, ANSI/NSPI-1 1991, Alexandria, VA: National Spa and Pool Institute.

Tennis Racquets

Boron. An expensive racquet material that is stiffer than graphite, yet lighter in weight.

Comfort. An assessment of how much shock, vibration, and racquet twisting occurs and the nature of the sensory feedback on all shots.

Composite. Refers of the structural design of the racquet. Various materials are combined together to create the racquet.

Control. The racquet's ability to direct the ball to where it is intended to be hit.

Graphite. A material made of carbon fiber, it is extremely light, stiff, and strong. Graphite also damps the vibrations in the frame caused by the ball's impact. Today, graphite is the most widely used material in racquets.

Head-Heavy (HH). A racquet that has more weight in the top half of the frame. This type is generally considered better for baseline play.

Head-Light (HL). A racquet that has its balance point in the lower half of the frame (expressed in inches from the racquet's center). Because most of its weight is in the lower half of the racquet, it is quicker at the net and on serves.

Maneuverability. The relative ease with which the racquet can be brought into motion and its relative mobility on all strokes.

Metal and Graphite. Last longer than wood racquets and are more durable. First made of aluminum and are now also made of fiberglass and graphite.

Oversized Racquet. Introduced in 1976, to give players greater power and control and to make tennis easier to learn. The traditional wooden racquet has a hitting area that measures approximately 68 square inches. The early oversized racquets' hitting areas measured 110 square inches. Today, popular sizes range from 90 square inches (midsize) to 135 square inches (super oversized). Newer materials, such as kevlar, boron, and boron and ceramic, allow the oversized racquet to be bigger but not heavier.

Power. The potential a racquet has to transfer energy to the ball.

Traditional. A racquet that has a face of 70 square inches.

Widebody. A frame with a wider beam, which makes the racquet stiffer. Because it flexes less, it delivers more power without additional weight. Many widebodies also have larger "sweet spots" (the hitting area). Today almost all manufacturers make only this style of racquet.

Wood. Made of laminated wood. Deteriorate easily. Were in general use prior to 1970.

STRINGS

Gauge. Refers to the thickness of the string. The higher the number, the thinner the string. Today, the most common gauges are 15, 15L, 16, and 17. The thinner the string the more desirable, since thin strings enable the ball to sink farther into the string bed, giving the player more control and potential for spin.

Gut Strings. Made from cattle or sheep intestines. Superior to nylon in its playing characteristics but more expensive, more fragile, less durable, and less resistant to damage by moisture and humidity than synthetics.

Hybrids. Use main and cross strings of different materials for specific purposes.

Monofilaments. Single strands of fiber.

Multifilament. Multiple strands of fiber.

Multiple Filament Cores with Outer Wraps. Used for cushioned response.

Synthetics. Man-made materials used for racquet strings. Nylon is the most commonly used synthetic material. Other synthetic materials include kevlar and Zyex.

Textured Outer Wraps. For spin.

Sources:

Chirls, Stuart, "How to Choose a String," *Tennis,* Vol. 28, No. 4 (August 1992): 92-93.

Day, Karen, "Racquet Smarts: What You Need to Know Today," *Tennis,* Vol. 24, No. 4 (August 1988): 61-66.

"Racquet Glossary," *Tennis,* Vol. 27, No. 11 (March 1992): 40.

Tennis Racquets: 30 Years of Change, North Palm Beach, FL: The American Tennis Industry Federation, 1992.

Tents

Tents are graded or classified by how appropriate they are for different weather conditions during the year.

Four Season Tents. Often identical to a three season tent except that the netting sidewalls have been replaced with nylon fabric to retain heat generated by warm bodies inside. Also feature sturdier construction designed to bear more severe weather conditions.

Mountaineering/High-Altitude. Designed primarily to survive the extremities of weather at high altitudes.

Summer/Screen Tents. Often consist of a net canopy, serviceable floor, and minimal rain protection. Designed to provide shade and ventilation.

Three Season Tents. Tents that will handle anything but frigid, blustery winter weather. Typically has netting in the side walls. However, lacks the ventilation necessary to be comfortable on very hot and humid nights.

Water Repellent Fabrics. Tents made of these fabrics keep the water out. The drawback is that the material does not breathe and let interior moisture from wet clothes and bodies escape. Some tent designs include a breathable inner canopy and waterproof outer fly. This allows body heat to drive interior moisture through the canopy while rain is stopped by the outer fly.

Source:

Hamel, John P., "Tents," *Backpacker,* Vol. 19, No. 2 (April 1991): 91-93. (*Backpacker* publishes an annual buyers guide issue.)

Toys

The American Society for Testing and Materials defines a toy as an object that is designated, manufactured, or marketed as a plaything for children through the age of 14 years, including miniature imitations for play use of objects intended primarily for specific purpose.

Normal Use. Play modes that conform to the instructions that accompany the toy, that have been established by tradition or custom, or that are evident from an examination of the toy.

Point, Hazardous. An accessible point that presents an unreasonable risk of injury during normal use or reasonably foreseeable abuse.

Projectile. An object propelled by means of a discharge mechanism capable of storing and releasing energy under the control of the operator.

Projection, Hazardous. A projection that, because of its material, configuration, or both, may present a puncture hazard if a child should fall onto it.

Reasonably Foreseeable Abuse. Conditions to which a child may subject a toy that are not normal use conditions, such as deliberate disassembly, dropping, or using the toy for a purpose for which it was not intended.

Rigid. Any material that has a Young's modulus in tension of greater than 100,000 pounds per square inch.

Small Objects. No toy (including removable, liberated components, or fragments of toys) intended for children under 36 months of age should be small enough, without being compressed, to fit entirely within a specified cylinder that represents the mouth cavity of a child. Balloons, books, and other articles made of paper; writing materials such as crayons, chalk, pencils, and pens; phonograph records; modeling clay and similar products; fingerpaints, water colors, and other paint sets are exempt from this test.

AGE LABELING

Toymakers follow the age grading guidelines of the Consumer Products Safety Commission (CPSC) and the industry's voluntary safety standard, ASTM F963. In general, age labeling is intended to provide guidance to consumers for selection of appropriate toys for children. It takes into consideration both the average abilities and interests of various age groups and the safety aspects of the toys themselves. When establishing the age appropriateness for a toy, manufactures take the following factors into consideration:

- The physical ability of a child to manipulate and play with the specific features of a toy.
- The mental ability of a child to understand how to use the toy.
- The toy must meet play needs and interests at different levels of development.
- The toy must be safe for the intended user.

Age grades are indicators of *average* development: they do not necessarily reflect suitability for the exceptional child. A parent remains the best judge of whether the child is at the appropriate development stage for safe play with a particular toy. However, manufacturers can assist parents and other purchasers in the appropriate selection of toys by incorporating descriptive labeling to identify potential safety concerns if the toy is accessible to children outside the recommended age group. For example, if a toy contains small play pieces and is labeled for older children (such as an action figure set) the manufacturer should consider including a statement on the retail packaging that the toy contains small pieces.

Sources:

Promotional material supplied by the Toy Manufacturers of America, Inc., 200 Fifth Avenue, Suite 740, New York, NY, 10010.

Standard Consumer Safety Specification on Toy Safety, Designation: F963-86, *Annual Book of ASTM Standards,* Philadelphia: American Society for Testing and Materials, 1986.

Textiles & Apparel

Care Labeling

The U.S. Federal Trade Commission (FTC) has issued regulations that require manufacturers and importers of textile wearing apparel to provide regular care instructions at the time such products are sold to purchasers through the use of care labels. These labels must state what regular care is needed for the ordinary use of the product. In general, labels for textile wearing apparel must have either a washing instruction or a dry-cleaning instruction. Following below is a glossary of standard terms used on care labels.

Care Label. A permanent label or tag, containing regular care information and instructions, that is attached or affixed in such a manner that it will not become separated from the product and will remain legible during the useful life of the product.

MACHINE LAUNDERING METHODS

Machine Wash. A process by which soil may be removed from products or specimens through the use of water, detergent, or soap, agitation and a machine designed for this purpose. When no temperature is given, e.g., *warm* or *cold*, hot water up to 150 degrees F can be regularly used.

Warm. Initial water temperature setting 90 to 110 degrees F (hand comfortable).

Cold. Initial water temperature setting same as cold water tap up to 85 degrees F (30 degrees C).

Do Not Have Commercially Laundered. Do not employ a laundry which uses special formulations, sour rinses, extremely large loads, or extremely high temperatures or which otherwise is employed for commercial, industrial, or institutional use. Employ laundering methods designed for residential use or use in a self-service establishment.

Small Load. Smaller than normal washing load.

Delicate Cycle or Gentle Cycle. Slow agitation and reduced time.

Durable Press Cycle or Permanent Press Cycle. Cool down rinse or cold rinse before reduced spinning.

Separately. Launder alone.

With Like Colors. Launder with colors of similar hue and intensity.

Wash Inside Out. Turn product inside out to protect face of fabric.

Warm Rinse. Initial water temperature setting 90 to 110 degrees F.

Cold Rinse. Initial water temperature setting same as cold water tap, up to 85 degrees F.

Rinse Thoroughly. Rinse several times to remove detergent, soap, and bleach.

No Spin or Do Not Spin. Remove material start of final spin cycle.

No Wring or Do Not Wring. Do not use roller wringer, or wring by hand.

HAND LAUNDERING METHODS

Hand Wash. A process by which soil may be manually removed from products or specimens through the use of water, detergent, or soap, and gentle squeezing action. When no temperature is given, e.g., *warm* or *cold,* hot water up to 150 degrees F can be regularly used.

Warm. Initial water temperature setting 90 to 110 degrees F (hand comfortable).

Cold. Initial water temperature setting same as cold water tap up to 85 degrees F.

Separately. Launder alone.

With Like Colors. With colors of similar hue and intensity.

With No Wring or Twist. Handle to avoid wrinkles and distortion.

Rinse Thoroughly. Rinse several times to remove detergent, soap, and bleach.

Damp Wipe Only. Surface clean with damp cloth or sponge.

DRYING, ALL METHODS

Tumble Dry. Use machine dryer. When no temperature setting is given, machine drying at a hot setting may be regularly used.

Medium. Set dryer at medium heat.

Low. Set dryer at low heat.

Durable Press or Permanent Press. Set dryer at *permanent press* setting.

No Heat. Set dryer to operate without heat.

Remove Promptly. When items are dry, remove from dryer immediately to prevent wrinkling.

Drip Dry. Hang dripping wet with or without hand shaping and smoothing.

Line Dry. Hang damp from line or bar in or out of doors.

Line Dry in Shade. Dry away from direct sunlight.

Line Dry Away from Heat. Dry away from heat.

Dry Flat. Lay out horizontally for drying.

Block to Dry. Reshape to original dimensions while drying.

Smooth by Hand. While wet, remove wrinkles; straighten seams and facings.

IRONING AND PRESSING

Iron. Ironing is needed. When no temperature is given, iron may be regularly used at the highest temperature setting.

Warm Iron. Medium temperature setting.

Cool Iron. Lowest temperature setting.

Do Not Iron. Item not to be smoothed or finished with an iron.

Iron Wrong Side Only. Article turned inside out for ironing or pressing.

No Steam or Do Not Steam. Steam in any form should not be used.

Steam Only. Steaming without contact pressure should be used.

Steam Press or Steam Only. Use iron at *steam setting*.

Iron Damp. Articles should feel moist when ironed.

Use Press Cloth. Use a dry or a damp cloth between iron and fabric.

BLEACHING

Bleach When Needed. All bleaches may be used when necessary.

No Bleach or Do Not Bleach. No bleaches may be used.

Only Non-Chlorine Bleach, When Needed. Only the bleach specified may be used when necessary. Chlorine bleach may not be used.

WASHING OR DRY-CLEANING

Wash or Dry-Clean, Any Normal Method. Can be machine washed in hot water, can be machine dried at a high setting, can be ironed at a hot setting, can be bleached with all commercially available bleaches, and can be dry-cleaned with all commercially available solvents.

DRY-CLEANING, ALL PROCEDURES

Dry-Clean. A process by which soil may be removed from products in a machine which uses any common organic solvent (e.g., petroleum, perchlorethylene, fluorocarbon) located in any commercial establishment. The process may include moisture addition to solvent up to 75 percent relative humidity, hot tumble drying up to 160 degrees F and restoration by steam press or steam-air finishing.

Professionally Dry-Clean. Use the dry-cleaning process, but modi-

fied to ensure optimum results either by a dry-cleaning attendant or through the use of a dry-cleaning machine which permits such modifications. Such modifications or special warnings must be included in the care instructions. Do not use bulk or coin-operated cleaning, which cannot be modified.

Petroleum, Fluorocarbon, or Perchlorethylene. Employ solvents specified to dry-clean the item. These solvents are used to remove stains that are not water soluble.

Shortcycle. Reduced or minimum cleaning time, depending upon solvent used.

Minimum Extraction. Least possible extraction time.

Reduced Moisture or Low Moisture. Decreased relative humidity. The dry-cleaner should decrease humidity for fabrics that may shrink with normal drycleaning moisture.

No Tumble or Do Not Tumble. Do not tumble dry. Especially for loosely woven fabrics that may suffer thread slippage.

Tumble Warm. Tumble dry up to 120 degrees F.

Tumble Cool. Tumble dry at room temperature.

Cabinet Dry Warm. Cabinet dry up to 120 degrees F.

Cabinet Dry Cool. Cabinet dry at room temperature.

Steam Only. Employ no contact pressure when steaming. Do not press or iron the garment when steaming. Fabrics with nap or pile are crushed by pressing.

No Steam or Do Not Steam. Do not use steam in pressing, finishing, steam cabinets, or wands.

LEATHER AND SUEDE CLEANING

Leather Clean. Have cleaned only by a professional cleaner who uses special leather or suede care methods. With other methods, leather may dry out and stiffen, and colors may bleed.

Sources:

Fair Claims Guide for Consumer Textile Products, Silver Spring, MD: International Fabricare Institute, 1988.

Federal Trade Commission, "Care Labeling of Textile Wearing Apparel and Certain Piece Goods as Amended," 16 CFR Part 423 (1992), Washington: Government Printing Office.

Singer Sewing Reference Library: Clothing Care and Repair, Minnetonka, MN: Cy DeCosse Inc., 1985.

Clothing Finishes

Antistatic. Chemical substances that absorb moisture to reduce static electricity and keep clothing from clinging.

Antiseptic. Chemical agents that inhibit bacterial growth to reduce perspiration damage and inhibit odors.

Crease-Resistant. Fabric is resistant to wrinkles, but is stiffer and less absorbent.

Flame-Retardant or Flame-Resistant. Fabric resists ignition or retards burning. It is required by law for children's sleepwear and other items of clothing. No finish is flame-proof.

Permanent Press or Durable Press. Chemical treatment or heat-set process adds resistance to wrinkles during wearing and washing. Creases and pleats can be set using this process.

Preshrunk. Shrinkage is controlled but the garment may shrink slightly.

Sizing. Starch-like substance added to a fabric to give extra body or stiffness. Sizing may also add extra strength or weight. Sizing may be temporary.

Water-Repellent. Fabric is treated with silicones to cause it to resist water. Finish is not permanent, but may be reapplied.

Source:
Singer Sewing Reference Library: Clothing Care and Repair, Minnetonka, MN: Cy DeCosse Inc., 1985.

Colorfastness

Colorfastness is the resistance of a material to change in any of its color characteristics, to transfer its colorants to adjacent materials, or both, as a result of the exposure of the material to any environment that might be encountered during the processing, testing, storage, or use of the material.

The American Association of Textile Chemists and Colorists has developed tests rating colorfastness on a scale of 1 to 5 with 5 being the most colorfast. This rating process results in assigned grades for different properties:

COLORFASTNESS TO LIGHT

Grade 9. Superlative.
Grade 8. Outstanding.
Grade 7. Excellent.
Grade 6. Very good.
Grade 5. Good.
Grade 4. Fairly Good.
Grade 3. Fair.
Grade 2. Poor.
Grade 1. Very poor.

ALTERATION IN LIGHTNESS, HUE, AND SATURATION OF COLOR

Grade 5. Negligible or not changed.
Grade 4. Slightly changed.
Grade 3. Noticeably changed.
Grade 2. Considerably changed.
Grade 1. Much changed.

DEGREE OF STAINING

The degree of staining on undyed textiles in colorfastness tests.
Grade 5. Negligible or not staining
Grade 4. Slightly stained.
Grade 3. Noticeably stained.
Grade 2. Considerably stained.
Grade 1. Heavily stained.

MOST OTHER PROPERTIES

Grade 5. Excellent.
Grade 4. Good.

Grade 3. Fair.
Grade 2. Poor.
Grade 1. Very poor.

Source:
"Nomenclature for Subjective Rating Processes," *AATCC Technical Manual*, Research Triangle Park, NC: American Association of Textile Chemists and Colorists, 1992.

Cotton

Cotton has the highest wear resistance of all the principal textile fibers. It is highly absorbent and dries quickly, allowing moisture to pass through the fabric. Cotton fibers are classified according to their staple, or length: short, long, and extra-long. Extra-long staple cotton is considered the finest. Clothing and other items made of 100 percent cotton may shrink up to 5 percent in laundering.

American Upland. A short- to long-staple cotton that makes up 90 percent of the world's crop.

Combed Cotton. Cotton which has been processed through a *comber* which removes short fibers and trash components. When this combed product is spun into yarn, the resultant yarn is of higher uniformity and tenacity.

Cotton Count. An indirect yarn numbering system generally used for yarn spun *on the cotton system*. The cotton count is the number of 840 yd. lengths of yarn per pound.

Egyptian. An extra-long staple cotton with a brownish color. It is fine and lustrous.

Flannel. A loosely woven, heavy cotton noted for its softness. It has a napped (raised) finish and considerable variation in weight and texture.

Gray Goods. A rough, unfinished cotton straight from the loom.

Long Staple Cotton. Cotton fiber which is not less than 1⅛ inch in length of staple.

Muslin. A firm cotton cloth with a plain weave, it is one of the oldest staple cotton cloths.

Pima. A fine but strong, brownish-in-color, extra-long staple cotton.

Sea Island. A silky, white, extra-long staple cotton grown in the West Indies. It is considered the highest quality cotton.

Thread Count. The number of threads per square inch. The higher the count, the finer the quality of the fabric. The highest count made in the United States is 310. Typical thread counts average 200.

Unbleached Cotton. A cotton fabric to which no finish has been applied. Although good for the environment because they are not treated with chemicals, they do not wear well or maintain their appearance after repeated launderings.

THE COTTON SYMBOL

Cotton Incorporated, a research and marketing organization representing the interests of over 45,000 cotton producers worldwide, has a trademarked logo, called the *Seal of Cotton*, used to identify cotton content in textiles. An example of the symbol follows:

GRADES

Cotton grades are based on (1) color, which may vary in degrees from white to yellow; (2) amount of foreign matter present (leaf, burr, etc.); and (3) preparation of fiber (quality of ginning). The U.S. Department of Agriculture has established grading practices for cotton. Cotton is compared to a set of samples maintained by the Department of Agriculture, and grades are assigned as follows:

White Cotton
Good Middling
Strict Middling
Middling
Strict Low Middling
Low Middling
Strict Good Ordinary
Good Ordinary

Light Spotted Cotton
Good Middling Light Spotted
Strict Middling Light Spotted
Middling Light Spotted
Strict Low Middling Light Spotted
Low Middling Light Spotted
Strict Good Ordinary Light Spotted

Spotted Cotton
Good Middling Spotted
Strict Middling Spotted
Middling Spotted
Strict Low Middling Spotted
Low Middling Spotted
Strict Good Ordinary Spotted

Tinged Cotton
Strict Middling Tinged
Middling Tinged
Strict Low Middling Tinged
Low Middling Tinged

Yellow Stained Cotton
Strict Middling Yellow Strained
Middling Yellow Stained

American Pima Cotton
Grade No. 1

Grade No. 2
Grade No. 3
Grade No. 4
Grade No. 5
Grade No. 6
Grade No. 7

Sources:
A Direct Marketer's Guide to Labeling Requirements Under the Textile and Wool Acts, Washington: Federal Trade Commission, undated.
Agricultural Marketing Service, U.S. Department of Agriculture, "Official Cotton Standards of the United States for the Grade of American Upland Cotton," 7 CFR sections 28.402 to 28.507 (1987), Washington: Government Printing Office.
Cotton Incorporated, 1370 Avenue of the Americas, New York, NY, 10019.
Lechaux, Dominique, "Bed Linens," *Martha Stewart Living* (April/May 1992): 38-42.

Fur Products

The Federal Trade Commission has established guidelines for the advertising and labeling of fur products. Information required on the label is set out in the following sequence.

- That the fur product contains or is composed of natural, pointed, bleached, dyed, tip-dyed, or otherwise artificially colored fur, when such is the fact;
- That the fur product contains fur which has been sheared, plucked, or letout, when such is the fact;
- That the fur contained in the fur product originated in a particular country (when so used the name of the country should be stated in the adjective form), when such is the fact;
- The name or names of the animal or animals that produced the fur;
- That the fur product is composed in whole of backs or in whole or in substantial part of paws, tails, bellies, gills, ears, throats, heads, scrap pieces, or waste fur, when such is the fact;
- The name of the country of origin of any imported furs used in the fur product;
- The name or registered number (provided by the FTC to the manufacturer) of the manufacturer or dealer.

NAMES

Within the regulations, the FTC has established a *Name Guide;* a list of animal names that can be used in labeling furs. Only the designated names can be used. In addition, the FTC prohibits labeling a fur with a name in an adjective form that connotes a false geographic origin of the animal. For example, such designations as *Sable Mink, Chinchilla Rabbit,* and *Aleutian Mink* cannot be used. However the use of the following terms is permitted.

Persian Lamb. Used to describe the skin of the young lamb of the Karakul breed of sheep or top-cross breed of such sheep, having hair formed in knuckled curls.

Broadtail Lamb. This term is used to describe the skin of the prematurely born, stillborn, or very young lamb of the Karakul breed of sheep or top-cross breed of such sheep, having flat light-weight fur with a moire pattern.

Persian-Broadtail Lamb. Used to describe the skin of the very young lamb of the Karakul breed of sheep or top-cross breed of such sheep, having hair formed in flattened knuckled curls with a moire pattern.

Mouton Lamb. Used to describe the skin of a lamb which has been sheared, the hair straightened, chemically treated, and thermally set to produce a moisture repellent finish; e.g., Dyed Mouton Lamb.

Shearling Lamb. Used to describe the skin of a lamb which has been sheared and combed.

Broadtail-Processed Lamb. Used to describe the skin of a lamb which has been sheared, leaving a moire hair pattern on the pelt having the appearance of the true fur pattern of "Broadtail Lamb"; e.g., Dyed Broadtail-Processed Lamb, Fur origin: Argentina.

ARTIFICIAL COLORING AND ALTERATIONS

Where a fur or fur product is pointed or contains bleached, dyed, or otherwise artificially colored fur, those facts are disclosed as a part of the required information in labeling, invoicing, and advertising.

Pointing. The process of inserting separate hairs into furs or fur products for the purpose of adding guard hairs, either to repair damaged areas or to simulate other furs.

Bleaching. The process for producing a lighter shade of a fur, or removing off-color spots and stains by a bleaching agent.

Dyeing. Includes the processes known in the trade as *tipping* the hair or fur, *feathering,* and *beautifying.* It is the process of applying dyestuffs to the hair or fur, either by immersion in a dye bath or by application of the dye by brush, feather, spray, or otherwise, for the purpose of changing the color of the fur or hair, or to accentuate its natural color. When dyestuff is applied by immersion in a dye bath or by application of the dye by brush, feather, or spray, it may respectively be described as *vat dyed, brush dyed, feather dyed,* or *spray dyed,* as the case may be. When dyestuff is applied only to the ends of the hair or fur, by feather or otherwise, it may also be described as *tip-dyed.* The application of dyestuff to the leather or the skin (known in the trade as *tipping,* as distinguished from tip-dyeing the hair or fur as described) which does not affect a change of, nor accentuate the natural color of, the hair or fur, shall not be considered as *dyeing.* When fluorescent dye is applied to a fur or fur product it may be described as *brightener added.*

Artificial Coloring. Any change or improvement in color of a fur or fur product in any manner other than by pointing, bleaching, dyeing, or tip-dyeing, and shall be described in labeling, invoicing, and advertising as *color altered* or *color added.*

Natural. Where a fur or fur product is not pointed, bleached, dyed, tip-dyed, or otherwise artificially colored it is described as *natural.*

Color Altered. Where any fur or fur product is dressed, processed, or treated with a solution or compound that changes or improves the color of the fur fiber, that fur product is described in labeling, invoicing, and advertising as *color altered* or *color added.*

Pieces. Where fur products, or fur mats and plates, are composed in whole or in substantial part of paws, tails, bellies, sides, flanks, gills, ears, throats, heads, scrap pieces, or waste fur, that fact is disclosed on the labeling, invoicing, and advertising. The same is true when a fur product is made of the backs of skins.

Where fur products, or fur mats and plates, are composed wholly or substantially of two or more of the parts set out above or one or more of such parts and other fur, disclosure of that fact is made by naming the parts or other fur in order of predominance by surface area.

The terms *substantial part* and *substantially* mean 10 percent or more in surface area.

Used Fur. When fur in any form has been worn or used by an ultimate consumer it shall be designated *used fur* as a part of the required information in invoicing and advertising.

When fur products or fur mats and plates are composed in whole or in part of used fur, such fact shall be disclosed as a part of the required information in labeling, invoicing and advertising; e.g., Leopard, Used Fur, or Dyed Muskrat, Contains Used Fur.

Damaged Fur. A fur which, because of a known or patent defect resulting from natural causes or from processing, is of such a nature that its use in a fur product would decrease the normal life and durability of such product. When damaged furs are used in a fur product, full disclosure of such fact shall be made as part of the required information in labeling, invoicing, or advertising such product; e.g., Mink, Fur origin: Canada, Contains Damaged Fur.

Second-Hand Fur Products. When a fur product has been used or worn by an ultimate consumer and is subsequently marketed in its original, reconditioned, or rebuilt form with or without the addition of any furs or used furs, the labeling requirements of the act are applicable. The product is also designated *Second-Hand, Reconditioned-Second-Hand,* or *Rebuilt-Second-Hand,* as the case may be.

Repairing, Restyling, and Remodeling. When fur products owned by and to be returned to the ultimate consumer are repaired, restyled, or remodeled and used fur or fur is added to the product, labeling of the fur is not required. However, the person adding the used fur or fur must give to the owner an invoice disclosing the information required under the act and regulations respecting the used fur or fur added to the fur product, subject, however to the provisions regarding country of origin requirements.

Source:
Federal Trade Commission, "Rules and Regulations Under Fur Products Labeling Act," 16 CFR part 31 (1992), Washington:Government Printing Office.

Hosiery

Includes hosiery for men, women, and children, including all types and kinds of hose, stockings, socks, anklets, and other related products.

PANTYHOSE

All-in-One Pantyhose. A pantyhose garment which includes a true knitted-in panty, constructed of heavier weight nylon or cotton. Eliminates *panty lines* that can show through clothing. (Also known as *Panty/Pantyhose.*)

Control Top. Pantyhose with spandex added to the panty portion to flatten the tummy and control bulges. Control top panty hose is available in several variations of firmness. It was once considered a favorite of only the weight or figure conscious customer. Today, because of the comfort factor involved, control top pantyhose account for a substantial portion of the pantyhose market.

Demi-Toe. Stocking or pantyhose with a nude, sheer heel and reinforced toe. A popular fashion with sling back shoes.

Finger Island. A reinforcement just under the waistband of all nude pantyhose to give protection against fingernail punctures when pulling up the pantyhose.

Firm Support. Support pantyhose that give more support because heavier weights (usually 70) of spandex are used.

Girdle Top. Pantyhose with a sewn-on girdle, for the firmest possible tummy control.

Knit-in Waistband. This type of waistband is made of spandex and nylon and is inserted into the top of the garment while on the knitting machine. It is not attached later. It is non-binding and does not get tighter, and thus uncomfortable, during wear.

Light Support. Pantyhose made with a low denier spandex in the leg, usually 40 denier or lower spandex, to give light compression on the wearer.

Non-Run. Stockings or panty hose with a special interlocking stitch that prevents runs (but not holes). Also called *run-proof* and *run-less*. Special processes under which the hosiery are manufactured are all designed to give the stockings or pantyhose extra life.

One-Piece Pantyhose. Pantyhose that is knit in a continuous operation beginning at one toe and ending at the other, eliminating the seams of a conventional style.

Panty/Pantyhose. A pantyhose garment that includes a true knitted-in panty, constructed of heavier weight nylon or cotton. Eliminates *panty lines* that can show through clothing. (Also known as *All-in-One Pantyhose.*)

Pantyhose. Both panty and stockings in a one piece waist-high garment that extends from the waist to the toes.

Runguard. Acts as a deterrent to runs from the foot into the leg, or from the panty into the leg. It can be made of heavier yarn, or can be a change of stitch from plain to mesh.

Runs. Stitches that have unchained due to broken stitches.

Runblocks. Mesh stitches that act as a deterrent to runs around the crotch seams. These stitches are usually used in all-nude constructions.

Sheer Support. A term used to describe support pantyhose which are considerably more sheer than the original support garments, due to improvements in yarns and manufacturing techniques.

Sheer-to-the-Waist. Pantyhose without visible panty lines or reinforcement in the panty portion. It is an all-sheer garment from waist to toe.

Sheers, Dress. Dress sheers are hosiery fashioned generally of 15 or 20 denier yarn, to be worn for daytime glamour.

Sheers, Evening. Hosiery fashioned of wisp weight 10, 12, or 15 denier yarn, to be worn for special occasions.

Silken Sheer. Category of soft, silky well-fitting pantyhose made from DuPont nylon and fine denier Lycra spandex.

U Seams. Pantyhose that are sewn one leg blank to another with a continuous U-seam to join the legs. These garments have no crotch (gusset) sewn in.

TERMINOLOGY

Athletic Socks. Hosiery designed for active sports, often having a ribbed striped top and plain foot construction. Usually knit of cotton, wool, acrylic, or combinations thereof.

Bruised Fabric. Sheer nylons cannot stand coming in contact with any hard surface and contacted by another hard object. This action will bruise the fabric sufficiently to cause a rupture when placed under strain.

Crew Socks. Another name for mid-calf socks. Hosiery with a rib-to-ankle or deep elastic construction and plain foot. The ribbed top joins the lower leg portion about one to two inches above the top of the heel. It is one of the most popular styles for both men and women.

Cuffed. Socks folded over at the top, usually just above the ankle.

Cushioned. Any construction with a terry pile surface on one side and a ribbed or plain knit surface on the other. In most cushioned athletic socks, the terry forms the inside of the foot portion of the sock. Some of the more complex constructions feature added layers of cushioning under certain areas of the foot, depending upon the sports activity for which the socks are intended.

Denier. Denier is the weight-per-unit-length of the yarn used to manufacture knit fabric, including hosiery. (It is numerically equal to the weight, in grams, of 9,000 meters of yarn.) The lower the denier, the lighter and finer the yarn, and the sheerer the garment. Hosiery knit of higher denier yarns tend to be more durable.

Double-Reinforcement. Two (usually nylon or polyester) thread lines knitted into portions of the sock foot where added abrasion resistance is desired, usually at the heel and/or toe.

Dress Socks. Light to medium weight men's and boy's styles, usually in dark, solid colors. Lengths may vary from mid- to over-the-calf. May be ribbed or filament. When ribbed, dress socks are traditionally ribbed from top to toe, versus ribbing only in the top in casual styles. Though filament socks are considered dress socks, the majority of dress socks are ribbed from top to toe.

Executive Length. Men's over-the-calf dress socks.

Fair Isle. Any Nordic or snowflake patterning.

Fancies. Fancies are men's socks of any length bearing multicolor designs. Examples of this type of sock include stripes, herringbones, argyles, and other fashion styles.

Filament Socks. Sheer, dark-toned men's dress or formal hosiery made usually of filament yarns.

Fishmouth Toe. A method for closing a toe pocket in which the seam runs parallel to the bottom of the foot rather than across the top of the toe.

Five-Eighths Hose. Hosiery which reach five-eighths of the way from the ankle to the knee. (Also called *golf socks*.)

Flammability. The test to determine if fabric will ignite under controlled conditions.

Flat Knit. The second most widely used construction for hosiery. Sock fabric is knitted on a single cylinder machine to produce a fine, smooth surface with a jersey-like appearance. Used for casual socks of all types, some varieties of work socks, for children's hosiery, and in socks where the distinction is achieved by the yarn or by treatments such as embroidery, appliqués, or small neat patterns. The smooth surface of flat knits also makes them appropriate for heat transfers. Also refers to *tricot* or *raschel knit* (as opposed to circular knit).

Flock Design. Applied to a boot, usually soft and fuzzy in appearance.

Footsocks. Hosiery with a top which does not extend above the ankle bone. Also known as *footies*.

Footed Sock. A sock knitted to conform to foot shape, as contrasted with a tube sock.

Full-Fashioned. Full-fashioned stockings are knitted flat, and the two sides are united afterwards by a seam up the back. As a result of decreasing stitches over the calf to make the hose narrower in the ankle, small *fashion markings* or loops are visible running parallel to either side of the seam. The popularity of the full-fashioned stocking, at a peak immediately after World War II, has declined since the introduction of seamless hosiery.

Glimmer. This term refers to a light reflection from the yarn, mainly from a *trilobal yarn* which gives the glimmer effect by reflecting the light.

Gore. The center of the heel or toe pocket, created in the knitting process, sometimes giving the appearance of a seam.

Graduated Support. This type of support hosiery is more comfortable because there are no sudden changes in the tightness of the spandex going up and down the leg.

Gusset. A term that means crotch panel in pantyhose.

Half Hose. Short hosiery of a length to cover from the ankle halfway between the ankle and the knee, with rib cuff and plain leg and foot. Standard for men.

Irregulars. Hosiery with imperfections that make them unsuitable for selling as first quality. The Federal Trade Commission defines irregulars as all hosiery which is not of first quality but which contains only minor imperfections limited to irregularities in dimensions, size, color, or knit, and without the presence of any obvious mends, runs, tears, or breaks in the fabric or any substantial damage to the yarn or fabric itself.

Knee-Highs. Short women's hosiery that comes up to just below the knee. They are styled with elastic tops and stay up without the help of garters.

Lycra Spandex. A registered trademark of the DuPont Company for their spandex fiber. Used in sheer hosiery, socks, and half-hose for its stretch and recovery properties, providing better fit and shape retention, comfort, and/or support.

Matte. Hosiery with a dull finish; minus shine or luster.

Mesh Knit. A hosiery fabric produced in a variety of tiny patterns. Upon close inspection it looks like lots of fine zig-zag lines. Actually, the knit is a variety of tiny patterns with loops interlocked. This kind of construction helps prevent runs, but a snag in a mesh stocking will generally leave a hole. There are

variations of mesh stitches, but for the most part, because the mesh stitch isn't as sheer, it is seldom used in the leg portion of the panty hose. The runguard, however, does use the mesh stitch. (See *Runguard*.)

Micro-mesh. A seamless mesh stocking where the loops are knotted in one direction only. Because of this, the stocking can run in one direction—from the foot up towards the *welt*. (See *Welt*.)

Mid-Calf/Crew. Hosiery with a top extending beyond ankle length but not beyond the largest part of the calf.

Mock Rib. A surface texture variation used in flat knit socks to simulate the look of a rib.

Mock Seams. A false seam sewn into the back of a seamless stocking of circular knit hosiery.

Neats. Solid color socks with tiny evenly spaced patterns such as dots or fleur-de-lis.

Needle Count. The total number of needles used in knitting a sock or sheer hosiery product. The higher the needle count the closer the stitches and the finer the fabric.

Nude Heel. Pantyhose or stocking without reinforcement in the heel area. The exact same knitting is used as in the boot or leg of the stocking or pantyhose.

Nylon. Man-made fiber introduced in 1938. It is the first and the oldest of the true synthetics. Chemically, nylon is a man-made polyamide fiber derived from coal, air, and water. This fiber is famous for its strength, abrasion resistance, dimensional stability, soft hand, elasticity, and easy-washing and quick-drying characteristics. There are two basic types of nylon used in hosiery. They are Type 6 and Type 6,6. The 6 nylon is softer and has less memory when textured than Type 6,6. Most of the yarns used in ladies' hosiery are made of Type 6,6 nylon to impart the maximum memory to the fabric. In socks, it is used primarily in men's dress socks and as a reinforcement with other fibers. Another use for nylon in socks is the stretch filament nylon plaited with other fibers to obtain multi-sizes.

One Size. Term applied to pantyhose or stockings that fit most sizes from very small to large.

Opaque. Stockings or pantyhose made of yarns which give them a heavier appearance, usually 40 denier or greater in weight.

Over-the-Calf. Men's and boys' socks that extend above the fattest part of the calf.

Pouch Heel. A simulated or "false" heel in what is fundamentally a shaped tube sock. The heel effect is created in boarding. Unlike the tube, a pouch heel sock usually has a *fishmouth toe*. (See *Fishmouth Toe*.)

Proportioned Fit. Stockings or pantyhose specially designed to have different circumferences (foot, ankle, calf, and thigh) and lengths for each size wearer.

Reinforced. Toe and heel areas often are strengthened (usually with nylon or polyester) to improve abrasion resistance and therefore increase durability.

Rolldown, Rolled Cuff, Rolled Top. A top which is turned over on itself and sewn down, often during the knitting operation. Traditionally a women's style, but also used in men's athletic socks.

Run-Resistant. Stockings or pantyhose knit with micro-mesh or tuck stitch patterns that resist runs in an upward direction.

Sandalfoot. Hosiery with invisible heel and toe reinforcement for wear with open shoes and sandals. This nude toe and heel hosiery is not as strong as hosiery with conventional reinforcement.

Seamless. Stockings knit in one operation on circular machines (one continuous operation) so that no seaming is required up the back. (See *Full-Fashioned.*)

Seconds. Hosiery with major imperfections which make them unsuitable for sale even as irregulars. The U.S. Federal Trade Commission (FTC) defines seconds as all hosiery which is not of first quality, does not qualify as *irregulars* and which contains runs, obvious mends, irregularities, substantial imperfections, or defects in material, construction or finish.

Seven-Eighths Hose. Socks which reach seven-eighths of the way from the ankle to the knee. (Also called *golf hose.*)

Spandex Sheers. A category of sheer hosiery styles. The leg yarn is composed of sheer nylon and single covered light-weight spandex (20 denier or finer) to give this hosiery good fit, sheerness, and softness. Spandex sheers do not give leg support, but the spandex does enhance fit and comfort.

Spectator Socks. A casual men's or women's sports sock designed to coordinate with ready-to-wear casual clothing but not engineered to provide optimum performance when used in active sports. This type of sock varies in length from footsocks to over-the-calf.

Sports Socks. Any sock with sport styling, whether designed for active sports participation or for spectator wear. (See *Athletic Socks.*)

Stocking. A knitted, close-fitting covering for the foot and leg.

Stretch Hosiery. Stockings knit of processed nylon filament yarn treated to give permanent stretchability. Stretch stockings "change" size to fit each foot, leg length, and volume perfectly. They are extremely desirable to the woman whose dimensions are at either end of the fit range.

Stretch Socks. Socks which are made from stretch yarn such as Ban-Lon, Flexcel, Fluflon, Helanca, Superloft, or Synfoam. A stretch sock can be adapted to fit a range of foot sizes.

Super Toe. A construction in which the fabric in the toe has considerable more density than normal. The addition of density in the forward part of the foot is so gradual that no change in appearance is visible. The wear life achieved is significantly improved over the normal nude toe.

Support Hosiery. Socks or other hosiery made of nylon or polyester with spandex or other elastic fiber added to give support to the leg. Support hosiery has spandex in the legs to reduce leg fatigue. The principle of support is to provide graduated compression to the leg. A total support pantyhose is one that has control in the panty portion as well as support in the legs.

Terry. A looped pile construction used inside most athletic socks and some work socks.

Thermal Socks. Winter-weight boot length socks favored by skiers, skaters, or anyone who spends time outdoors in cold weather. They can be made of heavy duty Orlon acrylic, wool, Thermax, silk, polypropylene, or Hollofil yarns, or a blend of fibers.

Thigh-Highs. Stockings that just reach the thigh and are held up by elastomer bands.

Tights. A heavy, opaque one-piece garment from hip to toe worn with leotards for dance, exercise, etc. It is usually made with

40 denier yarn and over and is sometimes made of yarn other than nylon.

Tube Socks. Hosiery knit in the shape of a tube, usually on multi-feed machines. Tube socks are nonreciprocated (without a knit-in heel) and are primarily used as men's and boys' spectator or athletic socks.

Ultra Sheer. A fine denier fiber which gives the ultimate in sheerness. It is usually 20 denier or less.

Unboarded. Hosiery not subjected to preboarding or boarding operations in its manufacture. In appearance it is wrinkled and shapeless until stretched over the leg and body.

Unbranded. Applied to hosiery that is not marketed throughout the country under a recognizable name. Usually not nationally advertised.

Vivanna. A registered BASF trademark for a yarn used in shiny tights and the panty of some styles to give it sheen. Sometimes this yarn is referred to as "bright" nylon.

Welt. A fabric knitted separately and machine-sewn to the top of the sock, or a hem at the top of a stocking knit in heavier denier yarn and folded double to give strength for supporter fastening.

Wool. Wool is the soft, curly hair of a sheep which is spun into yarn. The wool family includes Shetland (Scottish) and Merino (Spanish) wool which are soft and of high quality. Most woolen yarn used in socks is made from standard grades produced in the U.S., Australia, and elsewhere. (Alpaca and cashmere are animal hairs and are sometimes called wool.) Wool is warm, sturdy, and durable. It has a crisp, resilient hand and has excellent insulating properties.

Woolen. Yarns produced by the woolen system of spinning. Generally containing very short fibers, unevenly distributed and not parallel to each other.

Work Socks. Designed to meet the needs of people who work outdoors or in heavy industry. There are many styles available including cushioned and flame-resistant socks for fishermen and foundry workers.

Sources:
Federal Trade Commission, "Guides for the Hosiery Industry," 16 CFR part 22 (1992), Washington: Government Printing Office.
Glossary of Sock and Sheer Hosiery Terms, Charlotte, NC: National Association of Hosiery Manufacturers, 1992.

Labeling Requirements, Textiles

All textile and wool products regulated by the U.S. Federal Trade Commission (FTC) must identify, on the label and on most packaging:

Where the product was processed or manufactured
Its fiber content
The name of the manufacturer (or company in the line of distribution). In lieu of its name, a company may have a registered identification number, issued by the Commission, that represents the company's name.

Any required information that is omitted and/or falsely represents the fiber and origin disclosures is a violation of Federal law. All fiber (natural or manufactured), yarns, fabrics, and household textile articles must be labeled. Household textile articles include articles of wearing apparel, draperies, floor coverings, furnishings, bedding, and other wool or textile articles customarily used in a household. A partial listing of common articles covered by the U.S. FTC regulations includes:

Wearing apparel
Bedding, including bedspreads, blankets, comforters, covers, mattresses, pads, pillowcases, pillows, quilts, and sheets
Curtains, casements, and draperies
Towels and wash cloths
Dish cloths
Slip covers
Afghans and throws
Sleeping bags
Hammocks
Furniture Scarves

The U.S. Federal Trade Commission (FTC) has established the following generic names for manufactured fibers. In most cases the generic names of all fibers present in the amount of five percent or more are used when naming fibers.

Acetate
Acrylic
Anidex
Aramid
Azlon
Glass
Metallic
Modacrylic
Novoloid
Nylon
Nytril
Olefin
Polyester
Rayon
Rubber
Saran
Spandex
Vinal
Vinyon

TERMINOLOGY

All or 100%. Where a textile fiber product is comprised wholly of one fiber, other than any fiber ornamentation, decoration, elastic, or trimming as to which fiber content disclosures is not required, either the word *All* or the term *100%* may be used in labeling, together with the correct generic name of the fiber and any qualifying phrase, when required; e.g., *100% Cotton, All Rayon, Exclusive of Ornamentation, 100% Acetate, Exclusive of Decoration, All Nylon, Exclusive of Elastic,* etc.

Coated Fabric. Any fabric which is coated, filled, impregnated, or laminated with a continuous-film-forming polymeric composition in such a manner that the weight added to the base fabric is at least 35 percent of the weight of the fabric before coating, filling, impregnation, or lamination.

Ornamentation. Any fibers or yarns imparting a visibly discernible pattern or design to a yarn or fabric.

Virgin or **New.** The terms *virgin* or *d* as descriptive of a textile fiber product shall not be used when the product is not composed wholly of new or virgin fiber which has never been reclaimed from any spun, woven, knitted, felted, bonded, or similarly manufactured product.

Source:
A Direct Marketer's Guide to Labeling Requirements Under the Textile and Wool Acts, Washington: Federal Trade Commission, undated.
Federal Trade Commission, "Rules and Regulations Under the Textile Fiber Products Identification Act," 16 CFR part 303 (1992), Washington: Government Printing Office.

Leather

Alligator. Leather made from the skins of all aquatic species with a grain similar to that of the American alligator which cannot be legally killed.

Alligator-Grained. Leather of various types, such as calf, sheep or cattlehide, embossed to resemble the grain of alligator hide.

Calf Leather. Leather made from the skins of young cattle. It has a finer grain, is lighter in mass, and more supple than cowhide or kip leathers. (See *Cowhide* or *Kip*.)

Chamois. A soft, absorbent leather made from the inner side of a sheepskin.

Capeskin Leather. Fine-grained leather (superior to the skin of wool sheep) for gloves and garments. Originally made from the skin of goats from the Cape of Good Hope, now loosely applied to all hair sheep.

Bridle Leather. A strap leather.

Buckskin. Leather from deer and elk skins. Only the outer cut of the skin from which the surface grain has been removed may be defined as *genuine buckskin*.

Buffalo Leather. Made from domesticated water buffalo of the Far East, not from American bison.

Carpincho Leather. Leather from the skin of the carpincho, a large South American rodent. Used to make gloves and often classified as *pigskin*.

Collar Leather. Made from very light cattlehides and used for covering horse collars.

Cordovan. Leather made from the tight, firm portion of horse buttocks. Has very fine pores and is very durable.

Cowhide. Leather made from skins of cows, although sometimes loosely used to designate leather from any animal of the bovine species (such as oxen).

Crushed Leather. Leather made from chrome-vegetable retanned kidskins with the grain accentuated by boarding.

Doeskin. White leather from sheep or lambskin tanned with alum or formaldehyde or both.

Elk Leather. Designates chrome-tanned cattlehide for workshoes, hunting boots, and some children's shoes. More properly, *elk-finished cowhide*. Leather from elkhide is *buckskin*.

Fang Leather. Any leather with a distinctive finish, whether natural or the result of processing.

Fancy Leather. Hides and skins of value primarily because of grain or distinctive finish, whether natural or the result of processing.

French Kid. Leather tanned from kidskin by an alum or vegetable process.

Full Grain. Has the original grain surface of the skin.

Garment Leather. Leather for coats, jackets, hats, and breeches made most commonly from sheep, cabretta, pig, or goat skins, cattle, or horse hides.

Glove Leather. For either dress gloves or work gloves.

Grain. The outer or hair side of a hide or skin.

Grained Leather. Any leather on which the original natural grain, through any method, process, or manipulation, has been changed or altered.

Kid. Originally referring to leathers made from the skins of immature goats, the term is now loosely applied to glove and shoe leather made from goatskins.

Kip. Skin from a bovine animal in size between a calf and a cow. Also loosely applied to untanned hide of a calf, lamb, or other young or small animal.

Kosher Hide. Hide of an animal slaughtered according to Jewish religious customs.

Lambskin. From either lambskins or sheepskins.

Mocha Leather. Leather from any variety of hair sheep. After the grain has been removed by a liming process, the fine fibers below the grain are sueded.

Sole Leather. Leather for the soles of shoes. There are two types: *Finder,* which is less flexible and suitable for shoe repair. *Factory,* which is more flexible and more suitable for use in shoemaking machinery.

Split Leather. The portion of hide or skin, split into two or more thicknesses, other than the grain or hair side. Splits are usually named according to their sequence of production, such as *main, second,* or *slab* split (in case of upholstery leather), or for the use to which they are to be put, such as *flexible* (for innersoles); *glove, waxed* (for inexpensive shoe-uppers); *bag and case* (finished with pyroxylin or pigment finish); *sole,* etc.

Suede Finish. A finish produced by running the surface of leather on a carborundum or emery wheel to separate the fibers in order to give the leather a nap. The grain side of the leather may be suede-finished, but the process is most often applied to the flesh surface. The term *suede* is applied to the flesh surface of the leather. The term *suede* is applied to chrome or alum-tanned leather, while *ooze* is applied to vegetable-tanned suede. The term *sueded* when used alone refers to leather only. The term denotes a finish, not a type of leather.

Top Grain. The first cut taken from the grain side of a split hide from which nothing except the hair and associated epidermis have been removed.

Wallaby. Leather from skins of the wallaby, small and medium-sized kangaroo.

Water-Repellent. A leather that has been treated with any of a variety of chemicals to reduce the ability of water to spread on or wet the surface. Treatments can be for grain or suede leathers.

Water-Resistant. A term formerly applied to leather heavily stuffed with oils, greases, and waxes, used primarily in work shoes and boots. Currently, the term may also, and more commonly, include upper leathers treated with any of a variety of chemicals to reduce the penetration or absorption of liquid water.

Waterproof. The leather is impermeable to water and moisture.

Sources:

Federal Trade Commission, "Guides for Shoe Content Labeling and Advertising, 16 CFR 231 (1992) Washington: Government Printing Office.

Federal Trade Commission, "Guides for the Luggage and Related Products Industry," 16 CFR 24 (1992), Washington: Government Printing Office.

Federal Trade Commission, "Misbranding and Deception as to Leather Content of Waist Belts," 16 CFR 405 (1992), Washington: Government Printing Office.

Federal Trade Commission, "Guides for the Ladies' Handbag Industry," 16 CFR 247 (1992), Washington: Government Printing Office.

Standard Definition and Terms Relating to Leather, Designation D 1517-80, Annual book of ASTM Standards, Philadelphia: American Society for Testing and Materials, 1989.

Life Expectancy, Consumer Textiles

Consumer textiles should perform satisfactorily for the normal life of the product. If the product becomes damaged because of poor workmanship on the part of the manufacturer, the consumer may, in certain cases, be entitled to a replacement product, refund, or price adjustment. Types of damage that are the responsibility of the manufacturer include severe general color loss in the care process, shrinkage that makes an item unusable, color change because of the decomposition of fluorescent brighteners, and failure of attached trims to withstand the care process. Generally the manufacturer is only responsible if the damage is not due to failure of the consumer, drycleaner, or launderer to follow proper care instructions.

TYPES OF DAMAGE

Appearance Change. Pilling, puckering, or permanent wrinkles in the fabric.

Change in Body or Hand. Changes in the feel of the fabric such as stiffness or limpness.

Color Change. A change in color of any kind.

Crocking. A transfer of color from the surface of a colored fabric to an adjacent area of the same fabric or to another surface by rubbing action.

Delamination. The separation of a layered fabric.

Dimensional Change. Changes in the length or width of a garment. Terms such as *preshrunk* and *shrinkage controlled* relate to special processing of fabrics for reduction of dimensional loss. The degree of control is usually expressed in residual percentage based on the initial dimensions of the product.

Fading. Loss of color due to cleaning or laundering, heat, light exposure, etc. Also includes loss of color due to atmospheric gases such as ozone and nitrous oxide. Fading from nitrous oxide is commonly referred to as *fume fading*. Acetate fabrics,

TABLE 1. AVERAGE LIFE EXPECTANCY OF TEXTILE ITEMS IN YEARS

APPAREL
Bathing Suits 2
Bathrobes
   Lightweight 2
   Heavy or quilted 3
   Wool 3
Blazers
   Cotton and blends 3
   Imitation suede* 3
   Wool 4
Coats and Jackets (Outerwear)
   Children's 2
   Cotton and blends 3
   Down 3
   Fur 10
   Imitation fur or suede* 3
   Leather and suede 5
   Plastic 2
   Wool 4
Blouses 3
Choir Robes 6
Dresses
   Casual 2
   Office 3
   Silk 2
   Evening
      High Fashion 3
      Basic 5
Formal Wear 5
Gloves
   Fabric 1
   Leather 2
Rainwear & Windbreakers
   Film & plastic coated 2

Fabric, lined & unlined 3
Rubber and plastic 3
Shirts
   Dress 3
   Sports 2
   Wool or silk 2
Ski Jackets
   (including down) 2
Skirts 2
Slacks
   Lounging and active sport 2
   Dress 3
Socks 1
Sport Coats
   Cotton and synthetic blends 3
   Imitation suede* 3
   Wool and wool blends 4
Suits
   Cotton and synthetic 2
   Summer-weight wool 3
   Imitation suede* 3
   Silk 3
   Washable 2
   Winter-weight wool 4
Sweaters 3
Ties 1
Underwear
   Foundation garments 1
   Panties 1
   Slips 2
Uniforms 1
Vests 2

HOUSEHOLD FURNISHINGS
Bedspreads 6
Blankets
   Heavy wool and
      synthetic fibers 10
   Lightweight 5
   Electric 5
Comforters 5
   Down 5
Curtains
   Sheer 3
   Glass fiber 3
Draperies
   Lined 5
   Unlined 4
   Sheer 3
   Glass fiber 4
Sheets & Pillow Cases 2
Slipcovers 3
Table Linen
   Fancy 5
   Other 2
Towels 3
Upholstery Fabrics 5

*Nonwoven only. Life expectancy for coated or flocked articles is two years.

TABLE 2. CLAIMS ADJUSTMENT VALUES CRITERIA

Life Expectancy rating of article in years (from Table I)						Adjustment Values Percent of Replacement Cost Depending on Condition		
1	**2**	**3**	**4**	**5**	**10**			
Age of Article						**Excellent**	**Average**	**Poor**
0-4 mo.	0-4 mo.	0-4 mo.	0-4 mo.	0-4 mo.	Less than 1 Year	100%	100%	100%
4-7 mo.	4-7 mo.	4-10 mo.	4-13 mo.	4-16 mo.	2-4 yrs.	75%	75%	60%
7-9 mo.*	7-13 mo.*	10-19 mo.	13-25 mo.	16-31 mo.	4-6 yrs.	70%	60%	45%
9-11 mo.*	13-19 mo.	19-28 mo.	25-37 mo.	31-46 mo.	6-8 yrs.	50%	40%	30%
11-13 mo.*	19-25 mo.	28-37 mo.	37-49 mo.	46-61 mo.	8-11 yrs.	30%	20%	15%
13 mo. & older	25 mo. & older	37 mo. & older	49 mo. & older	61 mo. & older	11 years & older	20%	15%	10%

*Use only with "Average" column in figuring Adjustment Value.

especially blues and purples, are particularly susceptible to fume fading, usually turning a reddish color. All color types are susceptible to the effects of ozone. Fading from atmospheric contaminants is considered a fabric failure unless circumstances of exposure are unreasonably severe. Although colors should be resistant to perspiration, excessive acidity or alkalinity in an individual's perspiration is a condition against which there can be no assurance of colorfastness.

ADJUSTMENT VALUE

To help in determining a fair adjustment value for damaged products, the accompanying tables have been developed as a general guide. They help to determine the *average life expectancy* of a textile product, and the *adjusted value* (measured in percent of replacement cost depending on the condition of the product). E.g., a high fashion cocktail dress has a life expectancy of 3 years (Table 1). If it is 20 months old and in excellent condition, it has an adjustment value of 50% (Table 2). If the replacement cost is $200, the adjustment would be the adjustment value (50%) times the replacement cost ($200) which equals $100. Tables 1 and 2 can also be used as Income Tax Deduction guidelines for determining the *fair market value* of used textile products contributed to charitable organizations.

Source:
Fair Claims Guide for Consumer Textile Products, Silver Spring, MD: International Fabricare Institute, 1988.

Made in the USA

The U.S. Federal Trade Commission (FTC) has adopted regulations that require manufacturers of textile and wool products identify the country-of-origin on clothing and other textile products. According to these regulations, manufacturers must include the following:

Disclose country-of-origin information on labels for textile and wool products;

Place these labels in the necks of garments that have necks and in other conspicuous locations for garments without necks;

Individually label all textile or wool products in packages (certain hosiery products are excepted) and if consumers cannot see the labeling through the package, label the packages containing the products as well; and

Include country-of-origin information in all descriptions of textile and wool products in mail-order catalogs and mail-order promotional material.

All textile and wool products covered by the FTC regulations are required to have labels disclosing country-of-origin information. This information is in addition to information concerning the percentage of each fiber in a product and the name of the manufacturer or a way of identifying the manufacturer.

To determine country-of-origin information, the FTC requires that manufacturers go back only one step in the manufacturing process. For example, a manufacturer of yarn would look back to the source of its fiber and a manufacturer of garments would look back to either the source of its cloth or its yarn.

In labeling textile and wool products made entirely in the United States, manufacturers must use the words *Made in U.S.A.,* or other clear and equivalent terms, such as *Crafted with Pride in the U.S.A.* and *Made in New York, U.S.A.*

In labeling imported products, manufacturers must use the name of the country where the product was made, as determined by the U.S. Customs Services; e.g., *Made in Korea.*

In labeling products made in the United States from foreign materials, manufacturers must disclose that the products include imported materials by using words such as *Made in U.S.A. of imported fabric* or equivalent terms.

In labeling products partially manufactured in the United States and partially manufactured in a foreign country, the manufacturers must disclose, in general terms, the domestic and foreign origins of the products; e.g., *sewn in U.S.A. of imported components.* However, if the manufacturer is required by the U.S. Customs Service to label products in order to bring them into the United States, the manufacturer may use that country-of-origin information to comply with the FTC regulations.

In locating the labels on textile and wool garments, manufacturers must place the labels in the inside center of the necks of those garments that have necks. If the product has a brand label already affixed to that spot, the manufacturers may place the country-of-origin label next to the brand label, provided it is still conspicuous. For all other textile and wool products, manufacturers must disclose the country of origin in another conspicuous place.

Packages of textile and wool products intended to remain intact and unbroken until sold to consumers must be labeled with all the required information, unless consumers can read a product label through the package. Packaging used only for shipping or delivering products to consumers and packaging that is used as a protective cover until the product is displayed does not have to be labeled.

Finally, companies selling textile or wool products through the mail or by telephone must disclose country-of-origin information in their mail-order catalogs and in any promotional materials. This information will tell consumers if the product was made in the United States or was imported, or is some combination of the two. Promotional material designed solely to attract consumers to a store to purchase the products does not have to contain the disclosures.

CERTIFICATION MARKS

The Crafted With Pride in the U.S.A. Council advocates the usage of the labels below on products made in the U.S.A.

Made in the USA may be used as long as the product is produced in the U.S. of U.S. components. *Crafted With Pride in U.S.A.* may be used solely to identify U.S. produced fiber, yarn (including sewing thread), textiles for apparel, and home furnishings, as well as merchanise in the latter two product groups, but only if the fibers are domestically made.

Sources:
Federal Trade Commission, *News Release,* Washington: Federal Trade Commission, 1985.
Product Literature, New York: Crafted with Pride in the U.S.A. Council, Inc., 1992.

Mill, Textiles

The word Mill in the corporate, business, or trade name of any concern handling textiles signifies that the concern actually owns and operates or directly and absolutely controls the manufacturing facility in which all textile materials which are sold under that name are produced. For example, a distributor who furnishes yarns and other materials to a knitting mill for manufacture into garments according to the distributor's specifications is not a mill because it does not exercise direct and absolute operational control over the milling operations.

Source:
Federal Trade Commission, "Guides for Avoiding Deceptive Use of Word 'Mill' in the Textile Industry," 16 CFR part (1992), Washington: Government Printing Office.

Shoes

Acrylonitrile-Butadiene Styrene (ABS). Used in women's heels because of its high impact strength.

Air Cure-Vulcanization. Without the aid of applied heat. Also known as self-cure or self-Vulcanization.

Anatomic. Relating or conforming to the physical structure of the foot.

Aniline Finish. Usually used on full-grain leathers to produce a transparent, mirrored look with a high polish.

Bench-Made. Handmade by a single craftsman working at a shoemaker's bench.

Breathability. The ability of a material to absorb and pass off foot moisture. In other words, its ventilation ability.

Brushed Leather. Buffed to create a rough or course nap.

Custom Made. Made especially for an individual.

Custom Molded. Made over casts of the individual foot.

Double Sole. An outsole consisting of two full layers of leather.

Ethylene-Vinyl Acetate (EVA) Copolymers. Have increased flexibility, elongation, and impact over polyethylenes used for outsoles, midsoles, and wedges.

Flexible Sole. Made of leather which has been treated to increase its ability to bend easily.

Full Iron Bottom. A full sheet metal bottom surface from heel to toe.

Goodyear Welt. A shoe constructed with an insole rib to which both the welt and upper are secured by a strong flexible chainstitch.

Hard Toe. A hard reinforcement place under the toe-end to give a good appearance and firmness.

Hypoallergenic. Less inclined to produce dermatitis; in shoes, usually an absence of rubber and rubber cements as well as of chromate salts.

Neoprene. An elastomer, polychloroprene, formed by adding hydrogen chloride to monovinylacetylene. Widely used in footwear for outsoles, heels, and welting to impregnate cellulose fibers for insoles and contours, and as an adhesive.

Oil Repellency. Resists wetting by oily liquids.

Oil Resisting. Ability to resist the deteriorating effect or penetration of oil.

Ozone Resistance. Ability to withstand the deteriorating effects of ozone.

Polyurethane Resins (PU). Widely used as a finish for patent leathers and for the outer, breathable layer of shoe upper materials for adhesives, heel lifts, and outsoles.

Polyvinyl Chloride (PVC). Used for unit soles or direct molded outsoles.

Safety Shoe. Incorporates special features to protect the wearer; e.g., non-slip soles, non-conductive, puncture resistant, safety toe, etc.

Speed Lacing. The rows of eyelets and rings in which the shoelaces are threaded are replaced with plastic or metal rings for easier threading of the laces and improved fit. Used in sports shoes.

Variable Lacing. Creates more fit options because the eyelets are staggered horizontally to allow for greater width adjustment. Users can customize their fit by skipping eyelets to create more volume inside the shoe. Used in sports shoes.

Sources:
Brunick, Tom, "Glossary: The Ins and Outs of Shoes," *Tennis,* Vol. 27 no. 12 (April 1992): 79-80.
Federal Trade Commission, "Guides for Shoe Content Labeling and Advertising," 16 CFR part 231 (1992), Washington: Government Printing Office.
Schachter, Ruth J., ed., *The Dictionary of Shoe Industry Technology,* Philadelphia: Footwear Industries of America, 1986.

Silk

GRADES

Silk is graded in its bulk form before it is made into consumer products. The grading system sets standards of size deviation, evenness, neatness, cleanliness, tenacity, elongation, cohesion, and conditioned weight. The grading standards are established by the International Silk Association.

TERMINOLOGY

Crepe Yarns. Yarns with as many as 30-70 twists per inch used in the weaving of crepes and chiffons.

Denier. A yarn numbering system based on the relationship of a known length to a weight. As the number increases so does the coarseness of the yarn.

Filament. A single fiber extruded to an indefinite length.

Organzine. Combines two 13-15 denier yarns each with 16 turns per inch in the opposite direction.

Scoop. A term used to describe the rustling, crunchy sound associated with silk. It is achieved by treating the silk with dilute acetic or tartaric acids. Although not an indication of quality, it is highly valued by consumers.

Sewing Threads. Strong, tightly-twisted yarns. Made by twisting 13-15 denier yarns together and then combining several of them by twisting in the opposite direction.

Spun Silk. Made from silk wastes. Spun silks are used for velvets and other pile fabrics, knitted goods, lace, blended fabrics, etc. These silks are numbered according to the cotton system.

Tram Silk. Combines two or three 13-15 denier yarns with 3-5 twist per inch.

Source:
Cowan, Mary L. and Martha E. Jungerman, *Introduction to Textiles,* Second Edition, New York: Appleton-Century-Crofts, 1969: 18-23.

Symbols, International

Washing Symbol. Gives washing instructions: 60 degrees C (140 degrees F) means you may safely wash in hot water; 30 degrees C (86 degrees F) indicates special cold water washing is necessary.

Drying Symbol. Indicates the garment may be tumble-dried.

Triangle. Instructions pertain to chlorine bleaching.

Iron. Gives ironing instructions: one dot indicates cool iron; two dots a medium iron; three dots mean a hot iron may be safely used.

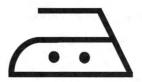

Circle. Gives drycleaning instructions: *A* indicates all normal drycleaning methods; *P* specifies perchlorethylene cleaning; *F* indicates the *Solvent F* process.

X Through Symbol. Means do not wash, tumble dry, bleach, iron, or dryclean.

Source:
Clothing Care and Repair, Singer Sewing Reference Library, Minnetonka MN: Cy DeCosse Inc., 1985.

Terminology, Apparel

Ample. A term used to indicate clothes for the *queen-size* or *outsize* wearer. (See *Outsize.*)

Fast or Colorfast. Used to describe fabrics that hold their colors after cleaning or exposure to the elements.

Finishing. Any treatment applied to fabric or cloth that enhances its appearance or serviceability.

Fit. Fit is the combination of yarn and construction that determines the adaptability of apparel to the human form. Stretch and recovery of yarns and knit construction contribute to a garment's fit.

Full Fashioned. A knitting process where stitches are used to shape the fabric to the contour of the body when seamed.

Latitude of Fit. Textured yarns and spandex yarns have more fit latitude than monofilament ultra sheer yarns. Fit latitude means the lower end of the size matrix and the upper end of the size matrix can be better fit when a style employs a yarn said to have *fit latitude.*

Mercerized. A cotton yarn which has been treated with a solution of caustic under conditions of caustic concentration and temperature which effect a permanent or irreversible swelling of the cellulose. It makes the fabric smooth and lustrous and improves dye penetration. Named for John Mercer, an English calico printer who invented the process in 1844.

Momme. A Japanese unit of weight used in the silk industry.

Moth Proofing. A treatment given to a wool fabric to prevent it being destroyed by moth larvae.

Natural Fibers. Cotton, wool, or silk.

Outsize. Proportioned to accommodate the heavier person or the taller than average figure.

Plain Knit. Similar to a jersey or hand-knit stitch. Plain knit gives a smooth, sheer surface.

Plied Yarn. When strands of single yarns are combined, twisted together, or air entangled, the resulting yarn is called *plied.*

Private Label. Merchandising products under the name of a retail operation, as opposed to manufacturer's brand names. Private label programs, sometimes called private brands, can include all varieties of men's or women's clothing.

Queen Size. Clothes sized to fit the heavier woman. Queen size is usually considered an extension of standard garments into a larger size. Outsize, on the other hand, is considered a separate category of merchandise altogether. (See *Outsize.*)

Sanforized. Mechanically preshrunk to ensure that the finished article doesn't reduce in size when laundered.

Shrinkage. A reduction in size that takes place when a fabric is washed and dried, or when hosiery is finished.

Tebalized. A registered trade mark for a special crease or crush resistant finish applied to a variety of fabrics including pile fabrics.

Sources:
Flusser, Alan, *Clothes and the Man: The Principles of Fine Men's Dress,* New York: Villard Books, 1988.
Glossary of Sock and Sheer Hosiery Terms, Charlotte, NC: National Association of Hosiery Manufacturers, 1992.
Hardingham, Martin, *The Fabric Catalog,* New York: Pocket Books, 1978: 146.

Terminology, Textiles

Acetate. Fiber produced from cellulose, acetic acid, and other chemicals.

Acrylic Fiber. A generic term denoting a man-made fiber that is characteristically warm and lightweight. It is spun into yarn and is used in men's, women's, and children's casual, dress, and athletic socks and in other apparel items. Acrylic has good shapekeeping properties and resilience; it is soft, easy-care, and low-shrinkage. Acrylic holds rich colorations. Trademarks include *Orlon* (DuPont).

Alpaca. Extremely fine, soft, and costly yarn derived from the hair of a domesticated Peruvian llama. Often used for insulated coats and shell-stitched sweaters. (See also *Mohair.*)

Angora. A yarn made from the hair of the Angora rabbit. It is prized for its soft feel and fluffy look is often used in blends. Angora is now often simulated by the use of specialty acrylic fibers.

Antron Nylon. A registered trademark of the DuPont Company for trilobal nylon. Antron combines luster, strength, and coloration properties.

Barathea. Silk, rayon, cotton, or wool with pebble effect used primarily in neckwear and evening wear.

Bare Spandex. Spandex that has not been wrapped with another fiber.

Batiste. A thin, finely woven fabric of cotton or other fibers named for Baptiste of Damrai, a French weaver of fine linen. Batiste is generally used for shirts and underwear.

Bengaline. A ribbed fabric of silk, worsted blends, and either wool or cotton used in men's suits and trousers.

Blends. The combination of two or more types of fiber in one yarn to achieve improved performance or styling effects.

Broadcloth. A fabric that is closely woven with the rib running *weftwise* (crosswise). It is often made of lustrous cotton, polyester, or other fibers.

Bulk. This term is usually used when referring to textured multifilament yarn. Mutifilament twisted yarn with low turns produces *low bulk* or lean yarn. High twist multifilament yarn produces *high bulk* yarn. The degree of bulk can be built into the yarn by the throwster (yarn making equipment) as desired.

Calico. An plain-woven printed cotton cloth.

Camel's Hair. A fabric of soft, wool-like texture. Varies in color from light tan to brownish black.

Cashmere. Luxuriously soft, expensive yarn made from the undercoat of the Cashmere (Kashmir) goat.

Challis. A napped fabric of lightweight worsted wool, spun rayon, or blends.

Chambray. A fabric woven with colored warp and white filling, resulting in a frosted colored surface; made in cotton or spun rayon with a small plain-weave effect.

Chino. A khaki-colored cotton and polyester cloth used in sportswear.

Cleerspan. A registered trademark for spandex by Globe Manufacturing Company.

Coated Fabric. Any fabric that is coated, filled, impregnated, or laminated with a continuous film-forming polymeric composition is such a way that the weight added to the base fabric is at least 35 percent of the weight of the fabric before the coating.

Compact Synthetic Fills. Materials, used as insulators, in outdoor apparel that offer good warmth for their thickness. They are made of ultra-fine filaments of polyolefin plastic which form tiny air pockets. They perform well when wet, and they dry quickly.

Core-Spun Yarn. A yarn made by spinning fibers around a filament of a previously spun yarn, thus concealing the core and allowing for properties of both fibers to be combined. Core-spun yarns are used in sewing thread, blankets, and socks and to obtain novelty effects in fabrics.

Course. A series of adjacent loops forming a horizontal line across the knitted fabric. Small horizontal stitches mean more yarn has been used, resulting in finer fabric, greater elasticity, and longer wear.

Covered Yarn. A core usually composed of one spandex or rubber fiber, wrapped with a filament or spun yarn.

Crepe. A crinkled-surface lightweight fabric made of silk, cotton, polyester, wool, or blends.

Creslan. Registered trademark for an acrylic fiber by American Cyanamic.

Crochet. A knitting process that creates a fabric by a series of interlocking loops rather than rows of stitches. Needlework that is used to form an ornamented design on hosiery, for example, whether it is sheer or "wool-like" in texture.

Decitex. The metric measuring system used to indicate weight per unit length of yarns in Europe. (It is numerically equal to the weight, in grams, of 10,000 meters of yarn.)

Denim. A sturdy twill-weave fabric. Named for de Nimes, France, where it was first produced.

Double-Covered Spandex. Spandex that has been wrapped in both directions with nylon or polyester continuous filament yarn or other textile fibers.

Double-Knit. A double-faced material knitted with solid colors on both sides or with a pattern on one side.

Elasticized. Fabrics which have elastic threads running through them, or which have been treated to give them elastic qualities.

Fabric Recovery. The ability of fabric to recover from the fully extended state to the original flat state before extending again.

Fabric Stretch. The amount of stretch in fabric from the relaxed state to the fully extended stretch.

Fabric. Any woven, knitted, felted, or other material that is produced from, or in combination with, any natural or manufactured fiber, yarn, or their substitute.

Fiber. A unit of matter, either natural or man-made, which forms the basic element of fabrics and other textile structures. A fiber is characterized by having a length at least 100 times its diameter or width. The term refers to units which can be spun into yarn or made into fabric by various methods including weaving, knitting, braiding, felting, twisting, and webbing. The resulting fabric is the structural element of textile products.

Filament Count. The number of individual filaments that make up a thread or yarn.

Filament Yarn. A yarn composed of long strands of synthetic fiber which continue the entire length of the yarn. The basic yarns used in women's hosiery are all filament yarns. To describe the size of filament yarns, the term *denier* (weight-per-unit-length) is used.

Filament. Finished fiber characterized by continuous length. It is extruded either as monofilament yarn, which is composed of one single strand, or multifilament yarn which is made up of several filaments bundled together.

Flat Yarn. This term is often used by knitters and coverers to indicate raw yarn they use. Flat yarns have no stretch unless they are textured. They are also used as the alternate course (see *Course*) in many sheer spandex styles. (Also see *Raw Yarn.*)

Float Loop. In commercial knittings, when a needle is not raised, the yarn which should have been associated with the needle goes behind the needle and appears as a *float*. The spandex elastic in the waistband is *floated* into the garment.

Generic Fiber Name. A name that the U.S. Federal Trade Commission (FTC) assigns to a man-made fiber. This name must be used when disclosing information required under the Wool and Textile Acts.

Glospan. A registered trademark for spandex by Globe Manufacturing Company.

Greige. The term *greige goods* applies to any fabric as it comes off the knitting machine before bleaching, scouring, or dyeing.

Gauge. The closeness of needles, one to another, in a knitting machine. On a 51-gauge machine there are 51 needles to 1½ inches. On a 60 gauge machine there are 60 needles to 1½ inches. Two-thirds of gauge is equal the number of needles per inch. (See *Needle Count.*)

Hand or Handle. The tactile qualities of a fabric, e.g., softness, firmness, elasticity, fineness, resilience, and other qualities perceived by touch.

High Twist. A yarn spinning process in which more twist is used than is needed for normal processing to provide desired aesthetic properties such as harshness, brightness, or to reduce hairiness on the yarn surface.

High-Bulk Yarn. Qualitative term to describe a highly-twisted textured yarn. A *bulked yarn* develops more bulk than stretch in the finished fabric.

High-Loft Synthetic (HLS). Refers to insulating materials used in outdoor apparel (fills). They come in two basic types: continous filaments and short, crimped hollow-core fibers. They are less expensive, easier to care for, and offer better insulating properties when wet than down fills.

Ingrain Yarns. An already dyed yarn.

Intarsia. A geometric pattern knitted-in either with a different stitch or a different color from the background. In intarsia knitting, both sides of the fabric look alike.

Jacquard. An intricate process for knitting patterns, designs, or textures into the fabric, and the method by which the decorative patterns are produced. Jacquard equipment is necessarily slower than conventional knitting machines and the lower productivity is reflected in the cost.

Lisle. Made of yarn composed of two or more plies of combed, long staple cotton fiber.

Lycra Spandex. A registered trademark for spandex fiber of the DuPont Company .

Man-Made Fiber. A class name for various fibers (including continuous filaments) produced from fiber-forming substances:

1) polymers synthesized from chemical compounds: acrylics, nylon, polyester, polyethylene, polyurethane, and polyvinyl fibers; 2) modified or transformed natural polymers: alginic and cellulose-based fibers such as acetates and rayons; 3) minerals: glass. Man-made fibers offer uniform quality for consistency in color, hand, and performance.

Manufactured Fiber. Any fiber derived by a manufacturing process from any substance that, at any point in the process, is not a fiber.

Marls. Multicolored yarns in which each component strand is a different color.

Mesh. An open knit used primarily to achieve a hand-knit, textured look.

Metallic Yarn. A manufactured yarn usually made of metallic-coated polyester plastic. Often used for ornamentation.

Microfiber. A generic term applied to fabircs with ultra-fine fibers and weave. When used in outdoor wear, materials made with microfibers shed wind and rain but are not waterproof without a coating or laminate.

Mohair. The hair of the Angora goat, characterized by a soft and silky texture and rich luster. (See also *Angora*.)

Monofilament Yarn. Yarn made of one single filament of fiber.

Multifilament Yarn. Yarn made of several filaments twisted or bundled together.

Natural Fiber. Any fiber that exists as such in its natural state, such as cotton, silk, wool, or flax (linen).

Needle Count. The total number of needles used in knitting a sock or sheer hosiery product. The higher the needle count the closer the stitches and the finer the fabric.

Nutria. A beaverlike fur named for the South American water-dwelling rodent of the same name.

Nylon. A tough and durable manmade fabric.

Nylon Taffeta. Taffeta is a plain-weave nylon fabric weighing 1.5 to 3 ounces per square yard. It is tightly woven and quite wind-resistant.

Olefin. Man-made fibers derived from polypropylene or polyethylene.

Open-End Spun Yarn. Yarn-making process in which fibers are twisted and wrapped around each other by the use of a rapidly rotating rotor. This process is much faster than ring-spinning. (See *Ring-Spun Yarn*.)

Orlon Acrylic. A registered trademark of the DuPont Company for their acrylic fiber. Used in socks for its combination of softness, durability, rich color clarity, comfort, and easy care.

Oxford. A soft, porous, and heavy fabric with twice as many warp as weft threads. It was first produced in Scotland in the nineteeth century.

Percale. A finely combed, closely woven fabric noted for its fine texture and finish.

Pilling. When a fiber exceeds it abrasion level and the fibers begin to break and form a small ball of fiber on the fabric surface.

Plain Weave. A simple crossing over and under of warp (lengthwise) and weft (widthwise) threads. It is the oldest and most common of fabric weaves.

Pointelle. An open, lacy-look knit similar to crochet.

Polyester. Polyester is a man-made fiber which has abrasion-resistance, excellent washability, and is fast-drying. It is readily heat-settable and dyeable.

Polypropylene. A petrochemical-based man-made fiber.

Raw Yarn. Filament yarn which has no stretch (untextured).

Rayon. A generic term for filaments made from various solutions of modified cellulose by pressing or drawing the cellulose solution through an orifice and solidifying it in the form of a filament. Rayon has a soft hand, high moisture absorbency and retention, and good dyeability and washability.

Ring-Spun Yarn. Yarn prepared by drafting and twisting together individual fibers with the use of rings to achieve a desired yarn size.

Rip-Stop Nylon. One of the lighter nylon fabrics that is tough for its weight. *Ripstop* refers to double threads cross-hatching the fabric for increased tear resistance. Plain ripstop is windproof, but not rain resistant unless coated with or laminated to a waterproofing agent.

Semi-Boarded. These garments are not subjected to a full heat setting operation. In appearance they are slightly wrinkled and shapeless until stretched over the leg and body. This operation is sometimes called the Intech Process.

Shetland. Originally a soft, warm shaggy yarn made only from wool of Shetland sheep. Now often used to describe yarns that offer Shetland characteristics.

Silk. The filaments obtained from the cocoons of various types of silkworms.

Single Covered Spandex. Spandex that has been wrapped in one direction with nylon or other yarn.

Skein-Relaxed. A method of applying bulk to a yarn by the controlled application of heat. This softens yarn texture and hand.

Slub Yarns. Any yarn made in an irregular diameter to achieve a nubby or knotted effect.

Spandex. A generic term denoting a man-made elastomeric fiber used in place of rubber. Spandex was developed by DuPont in 1959, offering the unique capacity for stretch and recovery. It can stretch to over five times its relaxed strength and fully recover. Spandex is used in support and light support hosiery products to provide the energy to shape and compress the leg. Spandex yarns are often covered with nylon yarns to protect the spandex.

Spun Yarns. Short lengths of fibers, of various lengths, are twisted together to form spun yarns. These yarns are more bulky than continuous filament yarns.

Staple. Short lengths of fiber that are spun together to form yarn.

Stitch. A stitch is the basic repeating unit of the yarn pattern in forming a knitted fabric, consisting of the needle loop and the sinker loop.

Stretch Yarns. Continuous filament yarns (e.g., nylon) that have been textured to give them elasticity.

Textile Fiber Product. This is an industrial term used to describe any fiber, yarn, or fabric, whether in the finished or unfinished state, used in household textile articles. Any household textile article made in whole or in part of yarn or fabric. Items subject to the Wool Products Labeling Act are not referred to as *textile fiber products*.

Textured Yarns. Yarns modified so they have desirable properties such as improved *hand* (feel), increased softness, and greater fit latitude.

Textures. A general term that includes all knitted-in patterns.

Typical textures include cable, herringbone, basketweave, fisherman, and pointelle.

Texturizing. A method of processing continuous filament yarns using heat and twist to give them bulk, elasticity, and/or better recoverability or *memory.*

Thread Count. The number of threads per square inch. The higher the count, the finer the quality of the fabric. The highest count made in the United States is 310. Typical thread counts average 200.

Trilobal Yarn. Contrary to a round cross section of yarn, trilobal yarn has a cross section with three lobes. It reflects light and gives the finished product a glimmer or brilliance.

Twist. The number of turns about its axis per unit of length of a yarn. Normally, no more twist is placed in a yarn than is needed for strength and abrasion resistance. (See also *High Twist.*)

Ventilation. A knitting operation that allows fabrics to breath. It is often utilized in pantyhose for cotton crotch panels or cotton soles.

Wind-Resistant. Outerwear apparel that offers resistance to wind with a tighter weave, more fabric layers, fabric coatings (e.g., urethane), or waterproof/breathable membranes sandwiched between layers (e.g., Gore-Tex).

Waterproof/Non-Breathable. Refers to fabrics for outdoor apparel that block rain and snow, but don't allow water vapor emanating from the body to pass through. Typically a nylon coated with an impermeable barrier of polyurethane, neoprene rubber, or other similar materials.

Waterproof/Breathable. Refers to fabrics for outdoor apparel that keep water out but allow some personal water vapor to pass through. These fabrics are generally constructed of nylon treated with a vapor-permeable agent or laminated to a breathable membrane.

Worsted Count. An indirect numbering system generally used for yarns spun on the worsted system; the number of 560 yd. lengths of yarn per pound.

Worsted. Yarns produced by the worsted system of spinning. Generally contain long fibers arranged in parallel and well-distributed order.

Wrapped Yarn. A yarn composed of one fiber as a core, wrapped with a filament or spun yarn of another. For example, spandex is frequently wrapped with nylon to improve strength and durability.

Yarn Count. A numerical designation expressing relationship of length to weight.

Yarn. A generic term for filament, either natural or manufactured, twisted or laid together to form a continuous strand suitable for weaving, knitting, braiding, felting, webbing, or otherwise fashioning into a fabric.

Sources:
A Direct Marketer's Guide to Labeling Requirements Under the Textile and Wool Acts, Washington: Federal Trade Commission, undated.
Flusser, Alan, *Clothes and the Man: The Principles of Fine Men's Dress,* New York: Villard Books, 1988.
Getchell, Dave, et. al., "Backpacker's Guide to Functional Outdoor Apparel," *Backpacker,* Vol. 19, no. 6 (September 1991): 39-42.
Glossary of Sock and Sheer Hosiery Terms, Charlotte, NC: National Association of Hosiery Manufacturers, 1992.

Wool

SHEEP

The Merino sheep is valued for its wool, and together with the Rambouillet, a related breed, offers the highest quality wool. However, the Merino sheep has deep folds in its skin which make shearing difficult. For this reason, sheep breeders have succeeded in developing three types of Merino sheep:

Type A. Has highly folded skin.

Type B. An intermediate stage.

Type C. Has soft skin folds, mostly in the neck areas, and is therefore more easily shorn.

Other sheep used for wool include the Lincoln and Leicester breeds which offer much coarser, stronger, and more lustrous wool used for carpet blends, braids, buntings, etc.

GRADES

Historically, commercial wool-sorters graded wool by comparing it to the wool from pure blood Merino sheep. The grade was expressed by a number that defined the fiber fineness of the wool. The finer the wool, the higher the number. This method of grading is referred to as the English system. More recently, complex machinery and processing methods have made it necessary to measure the fiber diameter more accurately in microns to determine the grade. Obviously, the finest wools have the smallest diameters.

Grade	English	Microns
Fine	80s, 70s, 64s	16-22
Half-Blood	62s, 60s, 58s	22-26.5
Three-Eighths Blood	56s	26.5-29.25
Quarter-Blood	50s, 48s	29.25-32.5
Low-Quarter Blood	46s	32.5-34.5
Common	44s	34.5-36
Braid	40s, 36s	36-40

WOOLMARK

The International Wool Secretariat and Wool Bureau Inc. (United States) have established quality standards for strength, colorfastness, and fiber content. Products that meet these standards are labeled with the *Woolmark* symbol or the *Wool Blend* symbol (for fabrics with at least 60 percent wool) shown below.

Woolmark Symbol

Wool Blend Symbol

LABEL REQUIREMENTS

The Wool Products Labeling Act requires every wool product to be marked with stamp, tag, label, or other means of identification that shows the following:

Fiber Content. The generic names and percentages by weight of the constituent fibers present in the wool product, exclusive of ornamentation.

Total Weight. The maximum percentage of the total weight of the wool product by any non-fibrous loading, filling, or adulterating matter.

Name. The name or registered identification number issued by the U.S. Federal Trade Commission (FTC) of the manufacturer of the wool product.

Country. The name of the country where the wool product was processed or manufactured.

TERMINOLOGY

All Wool or 100% Wool. Where the fabric or product is composed wholly of one kind of fiber, either the word *all* or the term *100%* may be used with the correct fiber name; as for example, *100% Wool, All Wool, 100% Recycled Wool, All Recycled Wool.* If any such product is composed wholly of one fiber with the exception of fiber ornamentation not exceeding 5%, such terms as *all* or *100%* may be used, provided it is immediately followed by the phrase *exclusive of ornamentation,* or by a phrase of like meaning.

Fiber Trademark. A word or words to identify a particular fiber produced or sold to distinguish it from fibers of the same generic class produced or sold by others.

Fur Fiber. Used to describe the hair or fur fiber or mixtures thereof of any animal or animals other than the sheep, lamb, Angora goat, Cashmere goat, camel, alpaca, llama, and vicuna.

Lambswool. The first clip taken from a sheep up to seven months old. Lambswool has a soft hand. (See *Hand.*)

Merino. A fine grade of wool from sheep originating in Spain.

Mohair and Cashmere. In labeling the fiber content of a product containing either hair of the Angora goat (known as *mohair*) or hair or fleece of the Cashmere goat (known as *cashmere*), the term *mohair* or *cashmere* may be used in lieu of the word *wool.* However, the respective percentage of *mohair* or *cashmere* must be given. Furthermore, *mohair* or *cashmere* where used must be qualified by the word *recycled* when the fiber referred to is *recycled wool.* The following are examples:

50% Mohair, 50% Wool; 60% Recycled Mohair, 40% Cashmere; or *60% Cotton, 40% Recycled Cashmere.*

Ornamentation. Any fibers or yarns giving a visible pattern or design to a yarn or fabric. The fiber content of such ornamentation may be disclosed, e.g., *70% Recycled Wool 30% Acetate, Exclusive of 4% Metallic Ornamentation.* Where the fiber ornamentation exceeds 5 percent it shall be included in the statement of required percentages of fiber content.

Other Fibers. Fibers in amounts less than 5 percent are designated as *other fibers.*

Pile Fabrics. The fiber content of pile fabrics (or products made from piled products) may appear on the label or mark of identification. The label should show the fiber content of the face or pile and of the back or base. The label should identify the ratio between the face and the back, e.g., *100% Wool Pile, 100% Cotton Back (Back constitutes 60% of fabric and pile 40%).*

Reclaimed Fibers. Where a wool product is composed in part of various man-made fibers recovered from textile products containing undetermined quantities of such fibers, the percentage content of the fibers recovered from such products may be disclosed on the required stamp, tag, or label in aggregate form as *man-made fibers.* This should be followed by the naming of such fibers in the order of their predominance by weight, e.g., *60% Wool; 40% Man-made fibers: Rayon, Acetate, Nylon.*

Recycled Wool. The resulting fiber when wool has been woven or felted into a product which, without ever having been utilized in any way by the ultimate consumer, subsequently has been made into a fibrous state, or the resulting fiber when wool or reprocessed wool has been spun, woven, knitted, or felted into a wool product which, after having been used in any way by the ultimate consumer, subsequently has been made into a fibrous state.

Specialty Fibers. In setting forth the required fiber content of a product containing specialty fibers (camel, alpaca, llama, and vicuna), the name of the specialty fiber may be used in lieu of the word *wool,* provided, the percentage of each named specialty fiber is given, and if that fiber has been *recycled,* the label should reflect that fact, e.g., *55% Alpaca, 45% Camel Hair;* or *50% Recycled Camel Hair, 50% Wool;* or *60% Recycled Alpaca, 40% Rayon;* or *35% Recycled Llama, 35% Recycled Vicuna, 30% Cotton;* or *60% Cotton, 40% Recycled Llama.*

Superimposed or Added Fibers. Where a wool product is made of one fiber or a blend of fibers with an additional fiber added in certain distinct sections for reinforcing or other purposes, the product may be labeled according to the principal fibers, with a reference to the added fiber, giving the percentage of the principal fiber (by weight) and indicating the area or section which contains added fiber. An example of this type of fiber content label for products having reinforcing fibers added is as follows: *55% Recycled Wool, 45% Rayon, Except 5% Nylon added to toe and heel.*

Unknown Reclaimed Fibers. Where a wool product is composed in part of wool or recycled wool and in part of unknown fibers reclaimed from any spun, woven, knitted, felted, braided, bonded, or otherwise manufactured or used product, the required fiber content disclosure may set forth (1) the percentages of wool or recycled wool, (2) the generic names and the percentages of all other known fibers, and (3) the percentage of the unknown and indeterminable reclaimed fibers. E.g., *75% Recycled Wool; 25% Unknown Reclaimed Fibers* or *35 % Recycled Wool; 30% Acetate; 15% Cotton; 20% Undetermined Reclaimed Fibers.*

Unknown Recycled Fibers and Undetermined Recycled Fibers. Used in describing unknown and indeterminable reclaimed fibers that have been recycled.

Virgin Wool. Natural wool that is being used for the first time in a fabric. Composed wholly of new or virgin fiber which has not been reclaimed from any manufactured or used product.

Wool Product. Any product, or portion of a product, which contains wool or recycled wool.

Wool. The fiber from the fleece of sheep or lamb, or hair of the Angora rabbit or goat (mohair) or Cashmere goat (and may include the so-called specialty fibers from the hair of the camel, alpaca, llama, and vicuna) which has never been reclaimed from any woven or felted wool product.

Woolen Cut Count. An indirect yarn numbering system based on the number of 300 yd. lengths per pound.

Woolen Run Count. An indirect numbering system generally used for yarns spun on the woolen system; the count represents the number of 1,600 yd. lengths of yarn per pound.

Sources:

Federal Trade Commission, "Rules and Regulations Under the Wool Products Labeling Act of 1939," 16 CFR sections 300.1 to 300.35 (1992), Washington: Government Printing Office.

Cowan, Mary L., and Martha E. Jungerman, *Introduction to Textiles,* Second Edition, New York: Appleton-Century-Crofts, 1969: 18-23.

Wood

Architectural Woodwork

Architectural woodwork is exterior and interior woodwork exposed to view in finished buildings, including all exposed wood, plywood, hard plastics, and wood doors. The Architectural Woodwork Institute (AWI) has established voluntary standards for grading architectural woodwork. The AWI is a not-for-profit association representing architectural woodwork manufacturers in the U.S. and Canada. If no quality grade is selected in architectural specifications using the AWI standards, then it will be assumed that *Custom Grade* is intended.

Premium Grade. The highest grade available in both material and workmanship. Wood of this quality is intended for the finest work. This is the most expensive grade and is most often used in selected spaces within a building, or for selected items.

Custom Grade. The middle or normal grade in both material and workmanship. This grade is intended for high-quality, conventional work. Also used when no quality grade is specified.

Economy Grade. The lowest grade in both material and workmanship. Intended for work where price outweighs quality considerations.

Source:
Architectural Woodwork Quality Standards, Guide to Specifications and Quality Certification Program, 4th Ed., Arlington, VA: Architectural Woodwork Institute, 1985.

Fiberboard, Medium Density

Medium density fiberboard (MDF) is used in furniture, cabinet work, millwork, and other interior applications. The technology used to manufacture medium density fiberboard is a combination of that used in the particleboard industry and that used in the hardboard industry. It is manufactured from lignocellulosic fibers combined with a synthetic resin or other suitable binder. The panels are manufactured to a density of 31 to 55 pounds per cubic foot by the application of heat and pressure. The process results in a substantial interfiber bond created by the added binder. Other materials may have been added during manufacturing to improve certain properties.

LABELING

Each panel shall be marked with the information that follows. Alternatively, the fiberboard shipment or order shall be accompanied by the above information in written form.

Manufacturer's name and/or trademark
ANSI Standard A208.2
Density in pounds per cubic foot (pcf)
Thickness in fractions of an inch.
For example: ANSI/A208.2, 45 pcf, ⅝ inch thick.

Formaldehyde Emission. A voluntary standard exists that sets an upper limit on the amount of formaldehyde emitted from MDF under certain dynamic conditions. The maximum emission permitted by the standard is 0.3 ppm when measured under the prescribed test condition. Fiberboard that meets this standard is identified either on the board itself or in accompanying written material as meeting the levels in the standard. Additional government standards are found in 24 CFR 3280.208.

Sources:
Medium Density Fiberboard for Interior Use, ANSI/A208.2-1986, Approved October 16, 1986, Gaithersburg, MD: National Particleboard Association, 1992.
Voluntary Standard for Formaldehyde Emission From Medium Density Fiberboard (MDF), Gaithersburg, MD: National Particleboard Association, 1992.

Fire Endurance

The lumber and truss industries have developed fire assembly through-penetration ratings. Penetrations include metal pipe or conduit, non-metallic pipe or conduit, insulated pipe, and cable or cable trays. These firestop systems are tested in accordance with ASTM E 814, and receive an *F-* or *T-rating* upon successful completion. An *F-rating* means that the firestop remains in the opening during the *fire and hose stream test* without allowing the passage of flame to the unexposed side of the firestop for the prescribed period of time. A *T-rating* means that the assembly met the *F-rating* requirements and also did not allow the temperature of any thermocouple on the unexposed surface of the firestop to rise more than 325 degrees F above its initial temperature. Refer to Underwriters Laboratory (UL) listings for complete details.

Source:

ASTM Annual Book of Standards, Designation E-814, Philadelphia: American Society for Testing and Materials, 1990. For further information: Underwriters Laboratories, 1285 Walt Whitman Rd., Melville, NY 11747-3081.

Flame Spread Ratings

Flame spread ratings are often confused with *fire endurance ratings* (see heading). Flame spread is solely a measure of the surface burning characteristics of a material. A low flame spread material will not necessarily improve the performance of a fire endurance assembly. Flame spread requirements are typically included in the code for interior finish materials. Different maximum flame spread rates are permitted depending upon the building occupancy, location of the material in the building, and the presence of sprinklers.

Flame spread rating is the generally accepted measurement for fire rating of wood materials. It compares the rate of flame spread on a particular species of wood with the rate of flame spread on untreated red oak. (Untreated red oak has a flame spread rate of 91. Woods with lower flame spread rate numbers are more flame resistant, woods with higher flame spread rate numbers are less flame-resistant.)

Most authorities accept the following classes of flame spread:

Classification	Flame Spread
Class I or A	0 - 25
Class II or B	26 - 75
Class III or C	76 - 200

Flame spread ratings for specific species of wood are listed in the following table.

Wood Species (Untreated)	Flame Spread Classification
Birch, Yellow	105 - 110
Cedar, Western Red	70
Cherry	76
Cypress	145 - 150
Elm	76
Fir, Dougla	70 - 100
Gum, Red	140 - 155
Maple, Soft	109 - 113
Maple, Hard	104
Oak, Red	91
Oak, White	77 - 100
Pecan	84
Pine, Eastern White	84
Pine, Idaho White	72
Pine, Northern, White	120 - 215
Pine, Ponderosa	105 - 230
Pine, Southern Yellow	129 - 195
Poplar, Yellow	170 - 185
Redwood	70 - 95
Spruce, Northern	65
Spruce, Western	100
Walnut, Black	131 - 138

Many species may be treated with chemicals to reduce flammability and retard the spread of flame over the surface. This usually involves impregnating the wood, under pressure, with salts and other chemicals. The species listed have been treated and tested with the following results:

Wood Species (Treated)	Flame Spread Classification
Ash	60
Basswood	35
Fir, Douglas	FR-S*
Gum, Red	FR-S*
Lauan	FR-S*
Maple, Soft	25
Oak, Red	25
Oak, White	Untreatable
Pine, Southern Yellow	FR-S*
Poplar, Yellow	25
Redwood	FR-S*

*FR-S denotes that the *flame spread, fuel contributed,* and *smoke developed* values applicable to a particular species are 25 or less and that the species has been subjected to tests of 30 minute duration, during which the flame spread did not exceed the equivalent of 25. In addition, there was no evidence of significant combustion.

Source:

Architectural Woodwork Quality Standards, Guide Specifications and Quality Certification Program, 4th Edition, Arlington, VA: Architectural Woodwork Institute, 1985. Original source for treated wood table, *Building Materials Directory,* Melville, NY: Underwriters Laboratories, Inc., 1989.

Flooring, Hardwood Surface Finishes

There are two principal types of finishes used on wood floors: *penetrating seals* and *surface finishes*. Each requires about the same care. A third classification known as an *irradiated polymer*, or *acrylic impregnated*, is used primarily in commercial applications. *Varnish, shellac,* and *lacquer* finishes are rarely used today, and generally are not considered as durable as the more modern finishes. Shellacs are the softest and show water spots. Varnishes are harder and will show ambering over time. Lacquers are hard and brittle and scratch easily.

PENETRATING SEALS

This finish is widely used on residential floors. The sealer soaks into the wood pores and hardens to seal the floor against dirt and certain stains. It delivers a low-gloss satin finish.

SURFACE FINISHES

These finishes are blends of synthetic resins, plasticizers, and other film-forming ingredients. All are durable, moisture-resistant and available in high-gloss, semi-gloss, satin, and matte, except moisture-cured urethane, which is generally available only in gloss finish. These finishes are recommended for kitchens where there is exposure to water splashing or spills.

Moisture-Cured Urethane. The hardest finish. Non-yellowing and generally available only in gloss finish.

Polyurethane. The most common finish. Tends to amber slightly as it ages.

Swedish Finish. Clear and fast drying and resists yellowing. Generally harder than polyurethane.

Water-Based Finish. Fast drying, durable, non-yellowing, and non-flammable at time of application.

Source:
Wood Floor Care Guide, Memphis, TN: Oak Flooring Institute, revised, June 1991.

Flooring, Prefinished Beech and Pecan

This flooring is furnished prefinished, and usually in the grade of *Tavern & Better*.

GRADES

Prime Grade. The face is selected for appearance after finishing, but sapwood and natural variations of color are permitted. The minimum average length is 3½ ft. Bundles are 1¼ ft. and longer.

Standard Grade. It is of such nature as to make and lay a serviceable floor without cutting, but purposely containing typical wood characteristics which are to be properly filled and finished. The minimum average length is 1¼ ft. with bundles 1¼ ft. and longer.

Tavern Grade. An economical floor with a rustic finish. It lays without cutting. Bundles are 1¼ ft and up with a average length of 3 ft.

Tavern & Better. A combination of *Prime, Standard,* and *Tavern* to contain the full product of the board, except that no pieces are lower than *Tavern Grade*. The minimum average length is 3 ft. with bundles 1¼ ft. and longer.

Source:
Official Flooring Grading Rules, Memphis, TN: National Oak Flooring Manufacturers Association, revised effective June 26, 1989.

Flooring, Prefinished Oak

White and red oak are separated in each grade. Grades are established after the flooring has been sanded and finished.

GRADES

Prime Grade. The face is selected for appearance after finishing, but sapwood and natural variations of color are permitted. The minimum average length is 3½ ft. Bundles are 1¼ ft. and longer.

Standard & Better Grade. A combination of *Prime* and *Standard* to contain the full product of the board except that no pieces are to be lower than *Standard Grade*. The minimum average length is 3 ft.. with bundles 1¼ ft. and longer.

Standard Grade. It is of such nature as to make and lay a serviceable floor without cutting, but purposely containing typical wood characteristics which are to be properly filled and finished. The minimum average length is 1¼ ft. with bundles 1¼ ft. and longer.

Tavern Grade. An economical floor with a rustic finish. It lays without cutting. Bundles are 1¼ ft. and up with a average length of 3 ft..

Tavern & Better Grade. A combination of *Prime, Standard,* and *Tavern.* The bundles are 1¼ ft. and up with an average length of 3 ft.

Source:
National Oak Flooring Manufacturers Association, *Official Flooring Grading Rules,* Memphis, TN: National Oak Flooring Manufacturers Association, revised effective June 26, 1989.

Flooring, Unfinished Birch, Beech, and Hard Maple

The National Oak Flooring Manufacturers Association recognizes ¾, 25⁄32, and 33⁄32 inch as acceptable thicknesses for the manufacture of maple flooring. However, other sizes are produced.

GRADES

First Grade. The face is practically free of all defects but the varying natural color of the wood is not considered a defect. Bundles are 1¼ ft. and longer through 8 ft., as the stock will produce. Bundles under 4 ft. do not comprise over 45 percent of the total footage. Up to 25 percent of the total footage may be 2 ft. bundles and up to 5 percent 1¼ ft. bundles.

Second Grade. Has a variegated appearance. Will allows tight, sound knots and slight imperfections in dressing, but must lay without waste. The bundles are 1¼ ft. and longer through 8 ft. Bundles under 4 ft. do not comprise over 55 percent of the total. Up to 27 percent of the total footage may be 2 ft. bundles and up to 10 percent 1¼ ft. bundles.

Third Grade. Has a rustic appearance. All wood characteristics of species. It is a serviceable, economical floor after filling. Bundles are 1¼ ft. and longer up to 8 ft. Bundles under 4 ft. comprise less than 75 percent and those under 1¼ ft. less than 45 percent.

Second & Better Grade. A combination of *First* and *Second grades* developing in a strip without crosscutting for each grade. The lowest grade pieces admissible are not less than *Second Grade*. Standard lengths in this grade are equivalent to *Second Grade*.

Third & Better Grade. A combination of *First, Second, and Third Grades* developing in a strip without crosscutting. No piece is of a lesser quality than standard *Third Grade*. Bundles are 1¼ ft. and longer with not over 60 percent of the total under 4 ft.

First Grade White Hard Maple. This is a special stock, selected for uniformity of color. It is almost ivory white and is the finest grade of hard maple flooring that can be produced.

First Grade Red Beech & Birch. Special grades produced from all red faced stock selected for color.

Source:
Official Flooring Grading Rules, Memphis TN: National Oak Flooring Manufacturers Association, revised effective June 26, 1989.

Flooring, Unfinished Oak

Appearance alone determines the grades of oak flooring since all grades are equally strong and serviceable. Flooring that is practically free of defects and made up mostly of heartwood is known as *Clear,* though it still may contain minor imperfections. *Select* is almost clear, but contains more of the natural characteristics such as knots and color variations. The *Common* grades have more markings than either of the other two grades and are often specified because of these natural features and the character they bring to the installation. Grades are sometimes combined (*Select* and *Better*). Short pieces produced in manufacturing are generally graded *No. 1 Common and Better Shorts* or *No. 2 Common Shorts.* For quarter sawn grades, the face of the piece is principally radial (see illustration).

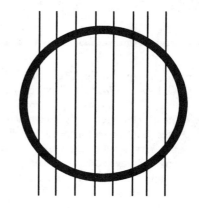

Plain Swan

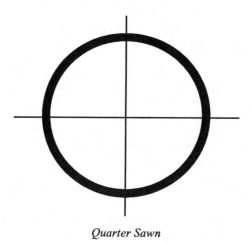

Quarter Sawn

GRADES

Clear Quarter Sawn. It has the best appearance. The face is practically clear, admitting an average of ⅜ in. of bright sapwood. Color is not considered. Bundles are 1¼ ft. and up. The average length is 3¾ ft. It is the best grade.

Select Quarter Sawn. It has an excellent appearance. The face may contain sap, small streaks, pin worm holes, burls, slight imperfections in working, and small tight knots which do not average more than one to every 3 ft. Bundles are 1¼ ft. and up. The average length is 3¼ ft.

Clear Plain Sawn. The same as *Clear Quarter Sawn* but the bundles may contain both plain and quartered pieces.

Select Plain Sawn. The same as *Select Quarter Sawn* but the bundles may contain both plain and quartered pieces.

No. 1 Common. The quality is such that it will lay a good residential floor. It has a variegated appearance. Light and dark colors; knots, flags, worm holes, and other character marks allowed to provide a variegated appearance after imperfections are filled and finished. Bundles 1¼ ft. and up.

Average length 2¾ ft.

No. 2 Common. May contain sound natural variations of the forest product and manufacturing imperfections. The purpose of this grade is to furnish an economical floor suitable for homes, general utility use, or where character marks and contrasting appearance is desired. Bundles are 1¼ ft. and up. The average length is 2½ ft.

1¼ Ft. Shorts. Pieces 9 to 18 in. long, bundled together.

No. 1 Common & Better Shorts. A combination grade of *Clear, Select,* and *No. 1 Common.*

No. 2 Common Shorts. Same as *No. 2 Common.*

Source:
Official Flooring Grading Rules, Memphis, TN: National Oak Flooring Manufacturers Association, revised effective June 26, 1989.

Flooring, Unfinished Pecan

GRADES

First Grade. Has excellent appearance, natural color variation, limited character marks, and unlimited sapwood. The bundles are 2 ft. and longer, with not over 25 percent 2 and 3 ft.

First Grade Red. Same as *First Grade* except that the face is all heartwood.

First Grade White. Same as *First Grade* except the face is all bright sapwood.

Second Grade. Has a variegated appearance with varying sound wood characteristics of species. This grade will admit wood with tight sound knots, pin worm holes, streaks, light stain, and slight imperfections in working. The floor shall lay without cutting. The bundles are 1¼ ft. and longer.

Second Grade Red. Same as *Second Grade* except that the face is all *heartwood.*

Third Grade. Has a rustic appearance. It is serviceable and economical after filling. The bundles are 1¼ ft. and longer.

Third & Better Grade. A combination of *First, Second,* and *Third Grades.*

Source:
Official Flooring Grading Rules, Memphis, TN: National Oak Flooring Manufacturers Association, revised effective June 26, 1989.

Hardboard

Hardboard is made from wood chips converted to fibers which are permanently bonded under heat and pressure into a panel. The wood comes not only from logs, but also from wood chips and board trimmings, which were once wastes of the lumber industry. The wood fibers are combined with other additives that improve certain properties. Hardboard, made from wood fibers, should not be confused with *particleboard* (see entry) which is made from wood chips and particles which are not refined into a distinct fiber.

The hardboard production process has 8 steps:

1) Removing bark.
2) Reduction of the wood to thumbnail size chips.
3) Cooking the chips to soften them and dissolve natural resin.
4) Shredding the chips into fibers. (Chemicals may be added at this stage to improve strength and impart moisture resistance. Fibers leaving this refining stage are conveyed either by water or air, depending on the subsequent forming process being used.)
5) Forming the fibers into a mat. (Either a wet process or dry process is used. The *wet process* employs a continuously traveling mesh screen, onto which the soupy pulp flows. Water is drawn off through the screen and then through a series of press rolls, similar to an old fashioned washing machine. The *dry process* is similar but air is used instead of water. Air-formed mats emerge much thicker and softer than wet-formed ones and require more care in loading onto the press.)
6) Pressing in hydraulic presses to weld the fibers back together. *Smooth one side (S1S)* board is delivered to the presses on a wire mesh screen. *Smooth two sides board (S2S)* is hot-pressed between two smooth plates. At this stage some boards are tempered to increase hardness, strength, and water resistance.
7) Humidifying to prevent post-press warping or buckling.
8) Trimming to shape the boards into standard sizes.

GRADES

Tempered Grade (Class 1). Impregnated with siccative (substances to absorb moisture) material, stabilized by heat, or processed with special additives to impart substantially improved properties of stiffness, strength, hardness, and resistance to water and abrasion as compared with *Standard Grade.*

Standard Grade (Class 2). High strength and water resistance. Substantially same form as when it comes from press, except for humidification and trimming to size.

Service-Tempered Grade (Class 3). Impregnated with siccative material, stabilized by heat, or processed with special additives to impart substantially improved properties of stiffness, strength, hardness, and resistance to water and abrasion, as compared with *Service Grade.*

Service Grade (Class 4). Good strength, but somewhat less strong than *Standard Grade.* Substantially same form as from press, except for humidification and trimming to size.

Industrialite Grade—Medium Density Hardboard (Class 5). Moderate strength, lower unit weight than other types.

TYPES

Smooth-One-Side (S1S). With impression of screen on one side.

Smooth-Two-Sides (S2S). Produced from substantially dry fiber mat pressed between two smooth platens.

HARDBOARD SIDING

The American Hardboard Association maintains a voluntary quality conformance program. Products are tested at an independent laboratory in accordance with Product Standard ANSI/AHA 135.6 and stamped with the following mark:

CONFORMS

ANSI/AHA 135.6

Source:
Today's Hardboard, Palatine, IL: American Hardboard Association, 1992.

Hardwood

Hardwood refers to the botanical grouping of the wood rather than its physical properties, although the majority of hardwoods are in fact harder than softwoods. Hardwoods are generally more durable than softwoods and offer a wider choice of color. Hardwood is graded according to a system published by the National Hardwood Lumber Association. The grades are based on the number of defects in the wood and the number of high quality boards, clear of worm holes, knots, and other defects, that can be cut from the board. There are eight standard grades, although *Firsts and Seconds* are usually combined as one grade (abbreviated *FAS* or *1S & 2S*). When this is the case, the percentage of *Firsts* in the combined grade cannot be less than as follows:

Hardwood Species	Minimum Percent Firsts in Combined Grade Firsts and Seconds
Poplar	40%
Philippine Mahogany	40%
African and Tropical American Mahogany	35%
Tupelo, Sycamore, Plain Oak, Chestnut, Red Gum, Sap Gum, Black Gum, Cottonwood, Magnolia, Locust, Hackberry, Willow and Aspen	33⅓%
Cherry, Soft Elm, Buckeye, Box Elder, Quartered Oak and Quartered Gum	25%
Hard Maple, Soft Maple, Red Alder, White Ash, Beech, Birch, Black Ash and Basswood	20%

Other combination grades are *Selects and No. 1 Common,* and *No. 3A Common and No. 3B Common.* Some of the main features of the grading system are as follows:

GRADES

Firsts. This grade allows pieces that will yield just under 92 percent clear-face cuttings.

Seconds. Allows pieces that will yield between 83 and 92 percent clear-face cuttings.

Selects. Widths of 4 in. or wider and lengths of 6 to 16 ft., admitting 30 percent 6 to 11 ft., of which one-sixth may be 6 and 7 ft. This grade admits pieces of 2 and 3 ft. surface measure that will yield 91⅔ percent clear face in one cutting.

No. 1 Common. Widths of 3 in. and wider, admitting 5 percent of 3 in. widths. Lengths of 4 to 16 ft., admitting 10 percent of 4 to 7 ft., of which one-half may be 4 and 5 ft. No piece is admitted which contains pith in the aggregate exceeding one-half its length.

No. 2 Common. Widths of 3 in. and wider with lengths of 4 to 16 ft., admitting 30 percent of 4 to 7 ft., of which one-third may be 4 and 5 ft. There is no restriction as to pith when outside of the required cutting area.

Sound Wormy. Of the same quality as *No. 1 Common* except that the natural characteristics of wormholes, bird pecks, stain, and sound knots not exceeding ¾ in. in diameter are admitted. Other sound defects which do not exceed in extent or damage the defects described are admitted in the cuttings.

No. 3A Common. Widths of 3 in. and wider and lengths of 4 to 16 ft., admitting 50 percent 4 to 7 ft., of which one-half may be 4 and 5 ft.

No. 3B Common. Widths 3 in. and wider and lengths 4 to 16 ft., admitting 50 percent 4 to 7 ft., of which one-half may be 4 and 5 ft.

Below Grade. Lumber poorer in quality than the lowest grade.

Source:
Rules for the Measurement and Inspection of Hardwood and Cypress, Memphis, TN: National Hardwood Lumber Association, 1986.

Hardwood, Endangered Species

The destruction of the world's rain forests is leading to a severe shortage of tropical hardwoods. To conserve valuable resources many experienced woodworkers recommend using only those woods grown on plantations or managed forests. The following species are most at risk:

Afrormosia
Brazilwood
Bubinga
Cocobolo
Ebony
Goncalo Alves
Jelutong
Kingwood
Lauan, Red
Mahogany, Brazilian
Lignum Vitae

Obeche
Padauk, African
Purpleheart
Ramin
Rosewood, Brazilian
Rosewood, Indian
Satinwood
Teak
Tulip
Utile

Source:

Jackson, A., D. Day, S. Jennings, *The Complete Manual of Woodworking,* New York: Alfred A. Knopf, 1989.

Lumber, Terms & Abbreviations

TERMINOLOGY

Air-Dried. Seasoned by exposure to the atmosphere, in the open or under cover, without artificial heat. It takes about 1 year to dry every inch of thickness for hardwoods, and about half that time for softwoods.

All-Heart. Of heartwood throughout; that is, free of sapwood.

Annual Ring. Growth put on in a single year.

Bark Pocket. Patch of bark partially or wholly enclosed in the wood. Classified with pitch pockets.

Blemish. Anything marring the appearance of lumber.

Bow. See *Warp.*

Boxed Pith. Where the pith is enclosed within the four sides of the piece.

Bright. Unstained.

Characteristics. Distinguishing features which by their extent and number determine the quality of a piece of lumber. Examples include grain quality and defects such as wormholes, knots, and bird pecks.

Check. Lengthwise grain separation, usually occurring through the growth rings as a result of seasoning.
Surface Check. Occurs on a surface of a piece.
Small Surface Check. Not over ⅟₃₂ in. wide and not over 4 in. long.
Medium Surface Check. Not over ⅟₃₂ in. wide and over 4 in. long, but not over 10 in. long.
Large Surface Check. Over ⅟₃₂ in. wide or over 10 in. long.
End Check. Occurs on an end of a piece.
Through Check. Extends from one surface through the piece to the opposite surface or to an adjoining surface.

Chipped Grain. Area where the surface is chipped or broken out in very short particles below the line of cut. Not classed as *torn grain* (see entry) and, as usually found, is not considered unless in excess of 25 percent of the surface involved.

Clear. Free or practically free of all blemishes, characteristics, or defects.

Compression Wood. Abnormal wood that forms on the underside of leaning and crooked coniferous trees. It is characterized,

aside from its distinguishing color, by being hard and brittle and by its relatively lifeless appearance.

Cutting. Resulting pieces after crosscutting and/or ripping.

Decay. Disintegration of wood substance due to action of wood-destroying fungi. Also known as *dote* and *rot.*
Advanced (or Typical) Decay. Older stage of decay in which disintegration is readily recognized because the wood has become punky, soft, spongy, stringy, shaky, pitted, or crumbly. Decided discoloration or bleaching of the rotted wood is often apparent.
Incipient Decay. Early stage of decay in which disintegration has not proceeded far enough to soften or otherwise change the hardness of the wood perceptibly. Usually accompanied by a slight discoloration or bleaching of the wood.
Pocket Rot. Typical decay which appears in the form of a hole, pocket, or area of soft rot, usually surrounded by apparently sound wood.
Water-Soak or Stain. Water-soaked area in heartwood, usually interpreted as the incipient stage of certain wood rots.

Degrades. Pieces which, on reinspection, prove of lower quality than the grade in which they were grouped.

Diagonal Grain. A deviation of the grain from a line parallel to the edges, which results from sawing a piece of lumber at an angle other than parallel with the bark.

Double-End Trimmed. Trimmed reasonably square by a saw on both ends.

Dry. Seasoned; not green.

Earlywood. The part of the annual growth ring laid down in the early part of the growing season.

Edge. The narrow faces of rectangular-shaped lumber.

Edge-Grained (Vertical Grain). Annual rings which form an angle of 45 degrees or more with the surface of the piece.

Free of Heart Centers (F-O-H.C.). Where the pith is not enclosed within the four sides of the piece.

From Red Heart. A stage of incipient decay characterized by a reddish color in the heartwood, which does not make the wood unfit for the majority of yard purposes. (Not to be confused with natural red heartwood in some species.)

Grain. Appearance produced by the arrangement of wood fibers of the species. Fibers form a pattern of rings during the annual growth cycle of the species (see *Annual Rings*).
Flat Grain. Pattern which forms an angle of less than 45 deg. with the surface of the piece.
Medium Cross Grain. Slope of grain more than 1 in. in a length of 15 in., but not more than 1 in. in a length of 8 in.
Slight Cross Grain. Slope of grain not more than 1 in. in a length of 15 in.
Slash Grain. See *Flat Grain.*
Spiral Grain. Fibers that extend spirally about instead of vertically along the length of a tree.
Steep Cross Grain. Slope of grain more than 1 in. in a length of 8 in.
Straight Grain. Slope of grain limited to 1 in. in each 20 in. of length.
Tangential Grain. See *Flat Grain.*

Green. Not fully seasoned.

Growth Ring. The growth of new wood put on in a single year.

Gum Pocket. An opening between growth rings which usually contains or has contained resin or bark, or both.

Gum Seam. Check or shake filled with gum.

Gum Spot. Accumulation of gumlike substance occurring as a small patch. May occur in conjunction with a bird peck or other injury to the growing wood.

Gum Streak. Well-defined accumulation of gum in a more or less regular streak. Classified with pitch streaks.

Hardwood. Refers to the botanical grouping (which includes oak, cherry, maple, mahogany, etc.) of the wood rather than to its physical properties, although the majority of hardwoods are in fact harder than softwoods. Hardwoods are generally more durable than softwoods and offer a wider choice of color.

Heart Face. Face side free of sapwood.

Heart Shake. See *Shake,* and *Pith Shake.*

Heartwood. Inner core of the tree trunk comprising the annual rings containing nonliving elements; usually darker in color than sapwood.

Hit-and-Miss. Series of surfaced areas, with skips not over ⅟₁₆ in. deep between them.

Hit-or-Miss. To skip or to surface a piece for a part or the whole of its length, with no spots cut down more than ⅟₁₆ in.

Holes. Holes may extend partially or entirely through a piece and be from any cause. To determine the size of a hole, average the maximum and minimum diameters, unless otherwise specified.

  Pin Hole. Not over ⅟₁₆ in. in diameter.

  Medium Hole. Over ⅟₁₆ in., but not over ¼ in. in diameter.

  Large Hole. Over ¼ in. in diameter.

Honeycomb (Decay). Honeycomb is indicated by large pits in the wood.

Kiln-Dried. Seasoned in a chamber by means of artificial heat.

Knot. Branch or limb embedded in the tree and cut through in the process of lumber manufacture. Classified according to size, quality, and occurrence. To determine the size of a knot, average the maximum length and maximum width, unless otherwise specified.

  Pin Knot. Not over ½ in. in diameter.

  Small Knot. Over ½ in., but not over ¾ in. in diameter.

  Medium Knot. Over ¾ in. but not over 1½ in. in diameter.

  Large Knot. Over 1½ in. in diameter.

Knot Occurrence.

  Branch Knots. Two or more knots grouped together, the fibers of the wood being deflected around the entire unit. A group of single knots is not a knot cluster.

  Knot Cluster.

  Single Knot. Occurs by itself, the fibers of the wood being deflected around it.

  Spike Knot. A knot sawed in a lengthwise direction.

Knot Quality.

  Decayed Knot. Softer than the surrounding wood, and containing advanced decay.

  Encased Knot. Its rings of annual growth are not intergrown with those of the surrounding wood.

  Hollow Knot. Apparently sound except that it contains a hole over ¼ in. in diameter.

  Intergrown Knot. Partially or completely intergrown on one or two faces with the growth rings of the surrounding wood.

  Loose Knot. Not held tightly in place by growth or position, and cannot be relied upon to remain in place.

  Fixed Knot. Will hold its place in a dry piece under ordinary conditions; can be moved under pressure, though not easily pushed out.

  Pith Knot. Sound knot except that it contains a pith hole not over ¼ in. in diameter.

  Sound Knot. Solid across its face, as hard as the surrounding wood, shows no indication of decay, and may vary in color from the natural color of the wood to reddish brown or black.

  Star-Checked Knot. Having radial checks.

  Tight Knot. So fixed by growth or position as to retain its place.

  Firm Knot. Solid across its face, but containing incipient decay.

  Water-Tight Knot. Its rings of annual growth are completely intergrown with those of the surrounding wood on one surface of the piece, and it is sound on the surface.

Latewood. The part of the annual ring that develops in the latter part of the growing season and produces thicker-walled cells, creating denser and usually darker wood that is less able to conduct sap but adds support to the tree.

Loosened Grain. Small portion of the wood loosened but not displaced.

Machine Burn. Darkening or charring due to overheating by machine knives.

Machine Gouge. Groove due to the machine cutting below the desired line of cut.

Mismanufactured. Includes all defects or blemishes produced in manufacturing. See *Chipper Grain, Hit-and-Miss, Hit-or-Miss, Loosened Grain, Machine Burn, Machine Gouge, Mismatched Lumber, Raised Grain, Skip, Torn Grain,* and *Variation in Sawing.*

Mismatched Lumber. Worked lumber that does not fit tightly at all points of contact between adjoining pieces, or in which the surface of adjoining pieces are not in the same plane.

  Slight Mismatch. Mismatch variation not over ⅟₆₄ in.

  Medium Mismatch. Mismatch variation over ⅟₆₄ in., but not over ⅟₃₂ in.

  Heavy Mismatch. Mismatch variation over ⅟₃₂ in.

Mixed Grain. Any combination of edge grain and flat grain.

Moisture Content. Weight of the water in wood expressed in percentage of the weight of ovendry wood.

Peck. Channeled or pitted stress or pocket as sometimes found in cedar and cypress. Wood with this condition is referred to as *pecky.*

Pitch. Accumulation of resin in the wood cells in a more or less irregular pattern.

  Light Pitch. Lightly evident presence of pitch.

  Medium Pitch. Trace of pitch slightly more evident than light pitch.

  Heavy Pitch. Very evident presence of pitch showing by its color and consistency.

  Massed Pitch. Clearly defined accumulation of solid pitch in a body by itself.

Pitch Pocket. An opening between growth rings which usually contains or has contained resin or bark, or both.

Very Small Pitch Pocket. Not over ⅛ in. in width and not over 2 in. in length.

Small Pitch Pocket. Not over ⅛ in. in width and not over 4 in. in length or not over ¼ in. in width and not over 2 in. in length.

Medium Pitch Pocket. Not over ⅛ in. in width and not over 8 in. in length; or not over ⅜ in. in width and not over 4 in. in length

Large Pitch Pocket. Width or length exceeds the maximum permissible for medium pitch pocket.

Closed Pitch Pocket. Does not show an opening on both sides of the piece.

Open (Through) Pitch Pocket. Is cut across on both sides of the piece.

Pitch Seam. Shake or check filled with pitch.

Pitch Streak. Well-defined accumulation of pitch in a more or less regular streak.

Small Pitch Streak. Not over one-twelfth of the width by one-sixth of the length of the surface on which it occurs.

Medium Pitch Streak. Larger than a small pitch streak but not over one-sixth of the width or one-third of the length of the surface on which it occurs.

Large Pitch Streak. Over one-sixth of the width or one-third of the length of the surface on which it occurs.

Pith. Small soft core in the structural center of a log.

Boxed Pith. Where the pith is within the four faces of an end of a piece.

Pith Fleck. Narrow streak resembling pith on the surface of a piece, usually brownish, up to several inches in length, resulting from burrowing of larvae in the growing tissue of the tree.

Raised Grain. Roughened condition of the surface of dressed lumber in which the hard summerwood is raised above the softer springwood but not torn loose from it.

Remanufacture. Manufacture of wood into such products as doors, windows, furniture, frames, moulding, boxes, and cabinetry. Used in reference to *Factory* and *Shop* grades available in most wood products (see entries).

Sapwood. Outer layers of growth in a tree, exclusive of bark, which contains living elements which conduct or store nutrients; usually lighter in color than heartwood.

Saw Butted. Trimmed by a saw on both ends.

Seasoning. Evaporation or extraction of moisture from green or partially dried wood.

Shake. A lengthwise grain separation between or through the growth rings. May be further classified as follows:

Fine Shake. A barely perceptible opening.

Slight Shake. More than a perceptible opening but not over 1/32 in. wide.

Medium Shake. Over 1/32 in. but not over ⅛ in. wide.

Open Shake. Over ⅛ in. wide.

Oup Shake. Does not completely encircle the pith.

Oound Shake. Completely encircles the pith.

Ring Shake. Partially or completely encircles the pith.

Shell Shake. Where both ends of a shake which has been cut across occur on one face or edge of a piece.

Through Shake. Extends from one surface through the piece to the opposite surface or to an adjoining surface.

Pith Shake (Heart Check). Extends across the rings of annual growth in one or more directions from the pith toward, but not to, the surface of a piece.

Side Cut. Where the pith is not enclosed within the four sides of the piece.

Skip. Area on a piece whose surface did not finish smoothly, classified as follows:

Light Skip. Area not over 6 times the width of the piece that failed to surface smoothly.

Shallow (Small) Skip. Area not over 6 times the width of the piece that failed to surface by not over 1/32 in.

Deep (Heavy) Skip. Area not over 12 times the width of the piece that failed to surface by not over 1/16 in.

Slope of Grain. Cross grain or deviation of the fiber from a line parallel to the sides of the piece, and may consist of diagonal grain, spiral grain, or both.

Smoke-Dried. Seasoned by exposure to the heat and smoke of fire maintained beneath or within the stack of lumber.

Softwood. One of the group of trees which have needle-like or scale-like leaves. The term has no specific reference to the softness of the wood.

Sound. Free of decay.

Split. Lengthwise separation of the wood extending from one surface through the piece to the opposite surface or to an adjoining surface.

Short Split. Length docs not exceed either the width of a piece or one-sixth of its length.

Medium Split. Length exceeds the width of a piece, but does not exceed one-sixth of its length.

Long Split. Length exceeds one-sixth of the length of a piece.

Springwood. The part of the annual growth ring laid down in the early part of the growing season, characterized by more or less open and porous tissue, and marking the inner part of each annual ring.

Stain. Discoloration on or in lumber other than its natural color.

Light Stain. Slight difference in color which will not materially impair the appearance of the piece if given a natural finish.

Medium Stain. Pronounced difference in color which, although it does not obscure the grain of the wood, is customarily objectionable in a natural but not in a painted finish.

Heavy Stain. Difference in color so pronounced as practically to obscure the grain.

Summerwood. Denser fibrous outer portion of each annual ring, usually without conspicuous pores, formed late in the growing period (not necessarily in summer).

Texture. The relative size of the wood's cells. *Fine-Textured Woods* have small closely spaced cells, while *Coarse-Textured Woods* have relatively large cells.

Torn Grain. Part of the wood torn out in dressing; classified as follows:

Slight Torn Grain. Not over 1/32 in. deep.

Medium Torn Grain. Over 1/32 in., but not over 1/16 in., deep.

Heavy Torn Grain. Over 1/16 in., but not over ⅛ in., deep.

Deep Torn Grain. Over ⅛ in. deep.

Unsound. Decayed.

Variation in Sawing. A deviation from the line of cut. *Slight Variation* is not over 1/16 in. scant in 1 in. lumber; ⅛ in. in 2 in.;

$\frac{3}{16}$ in. in 3 to 7 in.; and ¼ in. in 8 in. and up.

Wane. This is bark or lack of wood from any cause on the edge or corner of a piece.

Slight Wane. Not over ¼ in. wide on the surface on which it appears for one-sixth of the length and one-fourth of the thickness of the piece.

Medium Wane. Over ¼ in., but not over ½ in. wide on the surface on which it appears, for one-sixth of the length and one-fourth of the thickness of the piece.

Large Wane. Over ½ in. wide on the surface on which it appears, or over one-sixth of the length or one-fourth of the thickness of the piece, or both.

Warp. Any variation from a true or plane surface, including *Bow, Crook, Cup* (definitions follow) or any combination thereof.

Bow. Deviation flatwise from a straight line from end to end of a piece, measured at the point of greatest distance from the straight line.

Crook. Deviation edgewise from a straight line from end to end of a piece, measured at the point of greatest distance from the straight line; and classified as *Slight, Small, Medium,* and *Large.* Based on a piece 4 in. wide and 16 ft. long, the distance for each degree of crook shall be: *Slight Crook,* 1 in.; *Small Crook,* 1½ in.; *Medium Crook,* 3 in.; and *Large Crook,* over 3 in. For wider pieces it shall be ⅛ in. less for each additional 2 in. of width. Shorter or longer pieces may have the same curvature.

Cup. Deviation flatwise from a straight line across the width of a piece, measured at the point of greatest distance from the line; and classified as *Slight, Medium,* and *Deep.* Based on a piece 12 in. wide, the distance from each degree of *Cup* shall be: *Slight Cup,* ¼ in.; *Medium Cup,* ⅜ in.; and *Deep Cup,* ½ in. Narrower or wider pieces may have the same curvature.

LUMBER ABBREVIATIONS

AAR. Association of American Railroads.
AD. Air dried.
ALS. American Lumber Standards.
AW&L. All widths and lengths.
BD. Board.
BD FT. Board foot (feet).
BDL. Bundle.
BEV. Bevel.
BH. Boxed heart.
BM. Board measure.
B&S. Beams and stringers.
BSND. Bright sapwood, no defects.
BTR. Better.
CB. Center beaded.
C/L. Carload.
CLF. Hundred lineal feet.
CLG. Ceiling.
CLIB. California Lumber Inspection Bureau.
CLR. Clear.
CM. Center matched.
CS. Caulking seam.
CSG. Casing.

CV. Center vee.
CWT. Hundredweight.
DET. Double end trimmed.
DF. Douglas fir.
DF-L. Douglas fir-larch.
DIM. Dimension.
DKG. Decking.
D/S or DS. Drop siding.
E. Edge or Elaticity (see *MOE*).
EB1S. Edge bead one side.
EB2S. Edge bead two sides.
E&CB2S. Edge & center bead two sides.
EV1S. Edge vee one side.
EV2S. Edge vee two sides.
E&CV1S. Edge & center vee one side.
E&CV2S. Edge & center vee two sides.
EE. Eased edges.
EG. Edge (vertical) grain.
EM. End matched.
ES. Englemann spruce.
F or Fb. Extreme fiber stress in bending.
FAS. Free along side (vessel).
FBM or FT BM. Feet board measure.
FCPW. Flat car paper wrapped.
FG. Flat or slash grain.
FLG. Flooring.
FOB. Free on board (named point).
FOHC. Free of heart center.
FRT. Freight.
FT. Foot.
FT SM. Feet surface measure.
G/S. Gradestamped.
HB. Hollow bark.
Hem-Fir. Hemlock-true firs.
HEM. Hemlock.
H&M. Hit and miss.
H or M. Hit or miss.
IC. Incense cedar.
IN. Inch or Inches.
IND. Industrial.
IWP. Idaho white pine.
J&P. Joists and planks.
JTD. Jointed.
KD. Kiln dried.
L. Larch.
LF. Light framing.
LFVC. Loaded full visible capacity.
LGR. Longer.
LGTH. Length.
LIN. Lineal.
LNG. Lining.
LP. Lodgepole pine.
M. Thousand.
MBF. Thousand board feet.
MBM. Thousand (ft.) board measure.
MC. Moisture content.
MG. Mixed grain.
MLDG. Moulding.

MOE or E. Modulus of elasticity.
MOR. Modulus of rupture.
MSR. Machine stress rated.
NBM. Net board measure.
N1E. Nose one edge.
PAD. Partly air dried.
PARA. Paragraph.
PART. Partition.
PAT. Pattern.
PET. Precision end trimmed.
PLIB. Pacific Lumber Inspection Bureau.
PP. Ponderosa pine.
P&T. Posts and timbers.
PW. Paper wrapped.
RC. Red cedar.
RDM. Random.
REG. Regular.
RGH. Rough.
RIS. Redwood Inspection Service.
R/L or RL. Random lengths.
R/S. Resawn.
R/W or RW. Random widths.
RW/L. Random widths and random length.
SB1S. Single bead one side.
SDG. Siding.
SEL. Select.
SG. Slash or flat grain.
S/L or SL. Shiplap.
SM. Surface measure.
SP. Sugar pine.
SQ. Square.
STK. Stock.
STND. Stained.
STPG. Stepping.
STR. Structural.
S&E. Side and edge.
S1E. Surfaced one edge.
S2E. Surfaced two edges.
S1S. Surfaced one side.
S2S. Surfaced two sides.
S4S. Surfaced four sides.
S1S&CM. Surfaced one side and center matched.
S2S&CM. Surfaced two sides and center matched.
S4S&CS. Surfaced four sides and caulking seam.
S1S1E. Surfaced one side, one edge.
S1S2E. Surfaced one side, two edges.
S2S1E. Surfaced two sides, one edge.
S4SEE. Surfaced four sides, eased edges.
TAD. Thoroughly air dried.
TBR. Timber.
T&G. Tongue and groove.
T&T. Truck and trailer.
VG. Vertical (edge) grain.
WCLIB. West Coast Lumber Inspection Bureau.
WDR. Wider.
WF. White fir.
WRC. Western red cedar.
WT. Weight.

WTH. Width.
WW. White woods.
WWPA. Western Wood Products Association.

Sources:
Recommended Lumber Terminology and Invoice Procedure, Portland, OR: Western Wood Products Association, revised 1981.
U.S. Department of Commerce, *NBS Voluntary Product Standard, PS 20-70, American Softwood Lumber Standard,* Washington: Government Printing Office, amended 1986.

Millwork

The Woodwork Institute of California (WIC) publishes voluntary standards designed to assist the architectural and design profession (primarily in California and Nevada) in selecting and specifying grades of materials for architectural millwork (doors, windows, cabinets, railings, counters, etc.). The WIC recommends discontinuing the use of lumber grades such as *B&Btr., C Select, A Grade, FAS,* or similar lumber terms to specify the quality of architectural millwork. WIC recommends that architectural millwork be specified simply as *Economy, Custom,* or *Premium Grade,* as the project may require. The WIC has established three alternative grades for practically all items of architectural millwork products:

Economy. This grade establishes a standard to meet the requirements of lower cost residential and commercial construction where economy is the principal factor, and for use in storage room and utility areas.

Custom. This grade includes all the requisites of high quality millwork and is suitable for all normal uses in high grade construction, such as higher quality residential, school, and commercial buildings.

Premium. This grade, as the name implies, is superior in quality of materials and craftsmanship, with a corresponding increase in cost. It is intended primarily for the best of hardwood construction, but any species of wood may be specified.

Detailed information on the specific requirements of each grade are given in the source cited below. The WIC has a certification program and provides *WIC Certified Compliance Labels* for products that meet all requirements for the grade specified.

Source:
Manual of Millwork, Fresno, CA: Woodwork Institute of California, 1992.

Plywood

The plywood grades that are summarized in this entry apply to products manufactured by member mills of the American Plywood Association (APA). Products meeting the APA's quality standards are marked with the association's trademarks. With the exception of *Plyron* and some *APA Performance Rated Panels,* all of the APA grades are produced under the provisions of the voluntary commodity standard, *U.S. Product Standard PS-1-83 for Construction and Industrial Plywood,* developed cooperatively by the U.S. Department of Commerce and the construction and industrial plywood industry. More detailed information can be found in the source cited.

GRADE TERMINOLOGY

The term *grade* may refer to *panel grade* or to *veneer grade. Panel grades* are generally identified in terms of the veneer grade used on the face and back of the panel (e.g., *A-B, B-C,* etc.), or by a name suggesting the panel's use (e.g., *APA Rated Sheathing, Underlayment*). *Veneer grades* define veneer appearance in terms of natural, unrepaired growth characteristics and the allowable number and size of repairs that may be made during manufacture. The highest quality veneer is *A,* the lowest, *D.* The minimum grade permitted in exterior plywood is *C. D* veneer is used only in panels intended for interior use or for applications protected from permanent exposure to the weather. Examples of typical APA registered trademarks appear below.

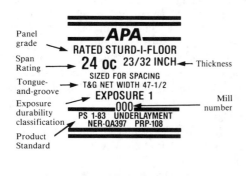

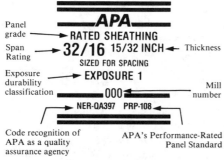

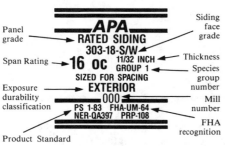

EXPOSURE DURABILITY

APA trademarked panels may be produced in four exposure durability classifications:

Exterior. The panels have a fully waterproof bond and are designed for applications subject to permanent exposure to the weather or to moisture.

Exposure 1. Have a fully waterproof bond and are designed for applications where long construction delays may be expected prior to providing protection, or where high moisture conditions may be encountered in service. Made with the same exterior adhesives used in *Exterior* panels; however, because other compositional factors may affect bond performance, only *Exterior* panels should be used for permanent exposure to the weather.

Exposure 2. Identified as *Interior Type with Intermediate Glue* under *U. S. Product Standard PS-1-83 for Construction and Industrial Plywood.* This grade is intended for protected construction applications where only moderate delays in providing protection from moisture may be expected.

Interior. Panels which lack further glueline information in their trademarks are manufactured with interior glue and are intended for interior applications only.

SPECIES GROUP NUMBER

Plywood manufactured under *U.S. Product Standard PS-1-83 for Construction and Industrial Plywood* may be made from over 70 species of wood. These species are divided according to strength and stiffness properties into five groups with *Group 1* being the strongest and stiffest, *Group 5* having the least strength and stiffness.

Group 1—Wood Species
Apitong
Beech, American
Birch, Sweet
Birch, Yellow
Douglas Fir 1
Kapur
Keruing
Larch, Western
Maple, Sugar
Pine, Caribbean
Pine, Ocote
Pine, Southern Loblolly
Pine, Southern Longleaf
Pine, Southern Shortleaf
Pine, Southern Slash
Tanoak
Group 2—Wood Species
Cedar, Port Orford
Cypress
Douglas Fir 2
Fir, Balsam
Fir, California Red
Fir, Grand
Fir, Noble
Fir, Pacific Silver

Fir, White
Hemlock, Western
Hemlock, Western Lauan
Hemlock, Western Almond
Hemlock, Western Bagtikan
Hemlock, Western Mayapis
Hemlock, Western Red
Hemlock, Western Tangile
Hemlock, Western White
Maple, Black
Megkulang
Meranti, Red
Mersawa
Pine, Pond
Pine, Red
Pine, Virginia
Pine, Western
Spruce, Black
Spruce, Red
Spruce, Stika
Sweetgum
Tamarack
Yellow Poplar
Group 3—Wood Species
Alder, Red
Birch, Paper
Cedar, Alaska
Fir, Subalpine
Hemlock, Eastern
Maple, Bigleaf
Pine, Jack
Pine, Lodgepole
Pine, Ponderosa
Pine, Spruce
Redwood
Spruce, Engelmann
Spruce, White
Group 4—Wood Species
Aspen, Bigtooth
Aspen, Quaking
Cativo
Cedar, Incense
Cedar, Western Red
Cottonwood, Eastern
Cottonwood, Black(Western Poplar)
Pine, Eastern White
Pine, Sugar
Group 5—Wood Species
Basswood
Poplar, Balsam

SPAN RATING

Some American Plywood Association (APA) trademarked panels carry numbers in their trademarks called *Span Ratings*. These denote the maximum recommended center-to-center spacing, in inches, of supports over which the panel should be placed in construction applications.

APA Rated Sheathing. Span ratings appear as two numbers separated by a slash, such as $^{32}/_{16}$, $^{48}/_{24}$, etc. The left hand number denotes the maximum recommended spacing of supports when the panel is used for roof sheathing with the long dimension or strength axis of the panel across three or more supports. The right-hand number indicates the maximum recommended spacing of supports when the panel is used for subflooring with the long dimension or strength axis of the panel across three or more supports.

APA Rated Sturd-I-Floor. Panels designed for single-floor applications under carpet and are manufactured with span ratings of 16, 20, 24, 32, and 48 in.

APA Rated Siding. Produced with span ratings of 16 and 24 in. Panels and lap siding may be installed directly to studs or over nonstructural wall sheathing, or over nailable panel or lumber sheathing. Panels rated 16 may be installed directly to studs spaced 16 in. apart. Panels rated 24 may be used direct to studs 24 in. on center. When used over nailable structural sheathing, the span rating refers to the maximum recommended spacing of vertical rows of nails rather than to stud spacing.

VENEER GRADES

Grade N. Intended for natural finish. It is smoothly cut, 100 percent heartwood or 100 percent sapwood, free from knots, knotholes, pitch pockets, open splits, other open defects, and stain. Not more than two pieces in 48 in. widths and not more than three pieces in wider panels. Well matched for color and grain. Synthetic fillers may be used to fill small cracks, splits, openings, and chipped areas. (This grade is not listed as an American Plywood Association grade but is listed in *U.S. Product Standard PS-1-83 for Construction and Industrial Plywood.*)

Grade A. Smooth, paintable, not more than 18 neatly made repairs (boat, sled, or router type and parallel to grain) permitted. May be used for natural finish in less demanding applications. Synthetic repairs permitted.

Grade B. Solid surface. Shims, circular repair plugs, and tight knots to 1 in. across grain permitted. Some minor splits permitted. Synthetic repairs permitted.

Grade C (Plugged). Improved *Grade C* veneer with splits limited to ⅛ in. width and knotholes and borer holes limited to ¼ x ½ in. Admits some broken grain. Synthetic repairs permitted.

Grade C. Tight knots to 1½ in. Knotholes to 1 in. across grain and some to 1½ in. if total width of knots and knotholes is within specified limits. Synthetic or wood repairs. Discoloration and sanding defects that do not impair strength permitted. Limited splits allowed. Stitching permitted.

Grade D. Knots and knotholes to 2½ in. width across grain and ½ in. larger within specified limits. Limited splits allowed. Stitching permitted. Exposure durability limited to *Interior, Exposure 1,* and *Exposure 2* panels.

APA PERFORMANCE-RATED PANELS

The American Plywood Association (APA) specifies the following performance ratings for plywood panels.

Sheathing. Designed for subflooring, wall sheathing, and roof sheathing, but also used for a broad range of other construction.

Sturd-I-Floor. Designed as combination subfloor-underlayment. Provides smooth surface for application of carpet and possesses high concentrated and impact load.

Structural 1 Rated Sheathing. Unsanded grade for use where cross-panel strength and stiffness or shear properties are of maximum importance, such as panelized roofs, diaphragms, and shear walls.

Siding. For exterior siding, fencing, etc. Special surface treatments are available such as V-groove, channel-groove, deep-groove, brushed, rough-sawn, and texture-embossed. Span rating or stud spacing and face grade classification are indicated in the trademark.

APA SANDED & TOUCH-SANDED PLYWOOD

The American Plywood Association (APA) specifies the following classifications for sanded and touch-sanded plywood.

A-A. Used where appearance of both sides is important for interior applications such as built-ins, cabinets, furniture, partitions; and exterior applications such as fences, signs, boats, shipping containers, tanks, ducts, etc.

A-B. For use where appearance of one side is less important but where two solid surfaces are necessary.

A-C. Used where appearance of one side is important in exterior applications such as soffits, fences, structural uses, boxcar and truck linings, farm buildings, tanks, trays, commercial refrigerators, etc.

A-D. For use where appearance of only one side is important in interior applications such as paneling, built-ins, shelving, partitions, flow racks, etc.

B-B. Utility panels with two solid sides.

B-C. Utility panel for farm service and work buildings, boxcar and truck linings, containers, tanks, agricultural equipment, and/or as a base for exterior coatings and other exterior uses.

B-D. Utility panel for backing, sides of built-ins, industry shelving, slip sheets, separator boards, bins, and other interior or protected applications.

C-C Plugged. For use as an underlayment over structural subfloor, refrigerated or controlled atmosphere storage rooms, pallet fruit bins, tanks, boxcar and truck floors and linings, and other exterior applications.

C-D Plugged. For open soffits, built-ins, cable reels, walkways, separator boards and other interior or protected applications.

Underlayment. For application of carpet. Possesses high concentrated and impact load resistance.

SPECIALTY PANELS

B-B Plyform Class 1. APA proprietary concrete form panels designed for high reuse.

Decorative. Rough sawn, brushed, grooved, or other faces. For paneling, interior accent walls, built-ins, counter facing, exhibit displays, etc.

High Density Overlays (HDO). Plywood panel manufactured with a hard, semi-opaque resin-fiber overlay on both sides. Ex-

tremely abrasion resistant and ideally suited to scores of punishing construction and industrial applications, such as concrete forms, industrial tanks, work surfaces, signs, agricultural bins, exhaust ducts, etc.

Marine. Designed plywood panel made only with Douglas fir or western larch, solid jointed cores, and highly restrictive limitations on core gaps and face repairs. Ideal for boat hulls and other marine applications.

Medium Density Overlay (MDO). Manufactured with smooth, opaque, resin-treated fiber overlay providing ideal base for paint on one or both sides. Excellent material choice for shelving, factory work surfaces, paneling, built-ins, signs, and numerous other construction and industrial applications.

Plyron. APA proprietary panel with hardboard face on both sides. Faces may be tempered, untempered, smooth, or screened. For countertops, shelving, cabinet doors, concentrated load flooring, etc.

TREATED PLYWOOD

Fire-Retardant-Treated Plywood. Pressure-treated with fire retardant. Each panel shall be labeled or marked by an approved independent testing agency, such as Underwriters Laboratories, Inc. After treatment, plywood shall be dried to an average moisture content of 15 percent or less. The plywood shall be all-veneer *APA Rated Sheathing* (or better).

Preservative-Treated Plywood. Pressure-treated with creosote, pentachlorophenol, or water-borne preservatives, as required for coastal water, wood foundation, ground contact, or above ground exposure. After treatment it is dried to a moisture content of 18 percent or less. It is marked by an approved inspection agency. The plywood shall be all veneer *APA Rated Sheathing* (or better).

Sources:

APA Product Guide: Grades and Specifications, Tacoma, WA: American Plywood Association, revised June 1990.

Office of Product Standards Policy, National Institute of Standards and Technology, *U.S. Product Standard PS 1-83 for Construction and Industrial Plywood,* Washington: U.S. Department of Commerce, 1983.

Pressure Treated Lumber

There are three broad classes of wood preservatives used in modern pressure treating processes. (See *Trade Names* in this section for information on trademarked names for these preservatives.)

Water-Borne Preservatives. For residential, commercial, marine, agricultural, recreational, and industrial applications.

Creosote and Creosote/Coal Tar Mixtures. For railroad ties, pilings, and utility poles. Wood preserved with these oilborne chemicals may be labeled *Treated with Creosote Solutions, Treated with Creosote-Petroleum* or *Treated with Creosote.*

Pentachlorophenol or Penta. For industrial applications and utility poles.

WATER-BORNE PRESERVATIVES

For most residential, commercial, and marine applications water-borne preservatives approved by the U.S. Environmental Protection Agency (EPA) are preferred. The most commonly used water-borne preservative, known as *CCA,* is *chromated copper arsenate.* There are three types of *CCA* preservatives (see entry which follows), but all contain inorganic arsenic to protect the wood from insect attack and decay. The inorganic arsenic penetrates deeply into the wood where it remains for a long time. Consequently wood pressure-treated with these preservatives should not be used for beehives, food storage containers, or other applications where it might come into direct or indirect contact with food or drinking water.

Chromated Copper Arsenate (CCA). There are three types of *CCA: CCA-Type-A, Type-B,* and *Type-C.* They differ by their composition, although all three are composed of arsenic, hexavalent chromium, and copper. *Type C* has 34 percent arsenic and 47.5 percent hexavalent chromium; *Type B* has 45.1 percent arsenic and 35.3 percent hexavalent chromium. *Type A* has 65.5 percent and 16.4 percent, respectively. All three have between 18.1 and 19.6 percent copper. (See Trade Names below.)

Industrial Applications. The use of the other water-borne wood preservatives listed below is generally limited to industrial applications.

Chromated Zinc Chloride (CZC)
Ammoniacal Copper Zinc Arsenate (ACZA)
Ammoniacal Copper Arsenate (ACA)
Acid Copper Chromate (ACC)

RETENTION LEVELS

The American Wood-Preservers' Association (AWPA) has developed a labeling system for different levels of preservative retention in treated lumber, based on the intended use for the wood. Retention levels refer to the amount of preservative that remains in the cell structure after the pressure treatment process is completed. Retentions are expressed in *pounds of preservative per cubic foot of wood;* the higher the number, the harsher the condition to which the wood may be exposed. For CCA-treated lumber and plywood, the following retentions have been established.

Retentions (lbs./cu. ft.)	Uses/Exposure
0.25	Above ground
0.40	Ground contact and fresh water
0.60	Wood foundation
2.50	Salt water

The number of the applicable AWPA standard or standards to which the wood conforms is often printed on the label. AWPA standard numbers for softwood lumber and plywood appear below:

C1. All timber products, preservative treatment by pressure process.

C2. Lumber, timbers, bridge ties, and mine ties.
C3. Piles.
C4. Poles.
C5. Fence posts.
C6. Crossties and switch ties.
C9. Plywood.
C11. Wood blocks for floors and platforms.
C14. Wood for highway construction.
C15. Wood for commercial and residential construction.
C16. Wood used on farms.
C17. Playground equipment.
C18. Marine construction.
C22. Permanent wood foundation.
C23. Round poles and posts used in building construction.
C24. Sawn timber piles for residential and comercial construction.
C25. Sawn crossarms.
C28. Standard for preservative treatment of structural glued laminated members.
C29. Lumber to be used for the harvesting, storage, and transportation of foodstuffs.
C30. Lumber and timbers for cooling towers.

TYPICAL QUALITY MARKS FOR TREATED LUMBER

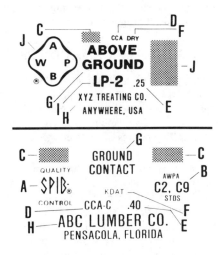

A Trademark of the Southern Pine Inspection Bureau

B The applicable American Wood Preservers' Association Standard

C Year of treatment

D The preservative used for treatment

E Retention Level

F Dry or KDAT if applicable

G Proper exposure conditions

H Treating company and plant location

I The applicable American Wood Preservers' Bureau Quality Procedure

J Trademark of the American Wood Preservers' Bureau or trademark of the AWPB certified agency

TRADE NAMES

Wolmanized. Wolmanized lumber is wood that has been pressure-treated with Wolman preservative, a trademarked *Type C CCA preservative* (see entry) produced by the Hickson Corporation.

Wolmanized Extra. Similar to *Wolmanized* lumber, this wood has been pressure-treated with a preservative which contains a specially formulated water repellent to protect against long-term weather exposure. *Wolmanized Extra* is a Hickson Corporation trademark.

Outdoor Wood. A Hickson Corporation trademark, *Outdoor Wood* is top grade lumber which is treated with Wolman preservative and water repellent, and dried after treatment.

SupaTimber. SupaTimber is lumber pressure treated with *CCA preservative* (see entry above). A trademark of Chemical Specialites, Inc.

UltraWood. UltraWood is lumber pressure treated with a *CCA preservative* that also has been treated with a water repellent. A trademark of Chemical Specialites, Inc.

D-Blaze. A trademark of Chemical Specialites, Inc. *D-Blaze* is a *FRT* (fire-retardant treated) lumber which has been tested by Underwriters Laboratories and has been awarded the UL classification *FRS*, which signifies a 25 or less rating for flame spread, smoke development, and fuel contributed (see *Flame Spread Rating*). When tested for 30 minutes there is no evidence of significant progressive combustion.

THE EPA CONSUMER INFORMATION SHEET

In voluntary participation with the Environment Protection Agency (EPA), the pressure-treated wood industry provides the following information for pressure-treated wood product literature and labels to make consumers aware of the EPA's recommendations for safe use and handling of pressure-treated wood:

This wood has been preserved by pressure treatment with an EPA-registered pesticide containing chromated copper arsenate (CCA) to protect it from termite attack and decay. Wood treated with CCA should be used only where such protection is important. CCA penetrates deeply into, and remains in the pressure-treated wood for a long time. Exposure to CCA may present certain hazards. Therefore, the following precautions should be taken both when handling the treated wood and in determining where to use or dispose of the treated wood.

Use site precautions for CCA pressure-treated wood.

Wood pressure-treated with CCA preservatives may be used inside residences as long as all sawdust and construction debris are cleaned up and disposed of after construction.

Do not use treated wood under circumstances where the preservative may become a component of food or animal feed. Examples of such sites would be structures or containers for storing silage or food.

Do not use treated wood for cutting-boards or countertops.

Only treated wood that is visibly clean and free of surface residue should be used for patios, decks, and walkways.

Do not use treated wood for construction of those portions of beehives which may come into contact with the honey.

Treated wood should not be used where it may come into direct or indirect contact with public drinking water, except for uses involving incidental contact such as docks and bridges.

Handling Precautions for CCA Pressure-Treated Wood

Dispose of treated wood by ordinary trash collection or burial. Treated wood should not be burned in open fires or in stoves, fireplaces, or residential boilers because toxic chemicals may be produced as part of the smoke and ashes. Treated wood from commercial or industrial use (e.g., construction sites) may be burned only in commercial or industrial incinerators or boilers in accordance with state and federal regulations.

Avoid frequent or prolonged inhalation of sawdust from treated wood. When sawing and machining treated wood, wear a dust mask. Whenever possible, these operations should be performed outdoors to avoid indoor accumulations of airborne sawdust from treated wood.

When power-sawing and machining, wear goggles to protect eyes from flying particles.

After working with the wood, and before eating, drinking, and use of tobacco products, wash exposed areas thoroughly.

If preservatives or sawdust accumulates on clothes, launder before reuse. Wash work clothes separately from other household clothing.

Sources:

American Wood Preservers' Association, Southern Pine Marketing Council, *Pressure Treated Southern Pine,* Kenner, LA: Southern Forest Products Association, 1991.
Product Literature, Charlotte, NC: Chemical Specialties, 1992.
Specification Guide for Wolmanized Pressure-Treated Lumber, Atlanta: Hickson Corporation, 1992.

Redwood Lumber

Redwood is graded by appearance and durability, with criteria defined by the Redwood Inspection Service. There are over 30 different grades. The basic grades are given below. Other specialized grades exist for glued panels, moldings, timbers, expansion joints, foundations, lattice and flat battens, garden furniture material, bench lumber, laminating grades, lath, etc. For durability and resistance against insects and decay, redwood is graded by its color. Reddish-brown heartwood from the inner portion of the tree contains extractives that render it resistant to decay. The cream-colored sapwood that develops in the outer growth layer of the tree does not possess the heartwood's resistance to decay and insects. Architectural grades *Clear All-Heart, Clear,* and *B Grade,* are normally sold kiln-dried (pre-shrunk and stress free). Garden grades *Construction Heart, Construction Common, Merchantable Heart,* and *Merchantable* are offered seasoned or unseasoned and are frequently specified for decks, fences, and garden uses. For construction where the wood will be on or near soil (such as posts, bulkheads, or patio grids) the durable heartwood grades are used, *Clear All Heart, Select Heart, Construction Heart,* or *Merchantable Heart.* For above ground construction where insect or decay problems are slight, one of the sapwood-containing grades is usually specified, such as *Clear, B Grade, Select, Construction Common,* or *Merchantable.*

TERMINOLOGY

See also *Lumber, Terms & Abbreviations.*

Bright Sapwood, No Defect (BSND). Bright sapwood is permitted in each piece in any amount.

Double End Trimmed (DET). Trimmed reasonably square by a saw on both ends.

Dressed Lumber. Has been surfaced to attain smoothness and uniformity of size on one side (*S1S*), two sides (*S2S*), one edge (*S1E*), two edges (*S2E*), or any combination of these.

Edge. Either the narrow face of rectangular-shaped pieces, the corner of a piece at the intersection of two longitudinal faces, or (usually in stress grades) that part of the wide face nearest the corner of the piece.

Edge Grain (EG). See *Vertical Grain.*

Flat Grain (FG). Cut tangent to annual growth rings exposing a face light-figured or "marbled."

Free of Heart Centers (FOHC). Without pith (the center core of the log).

Mixed Grain (MG). May be either (or both) vertical and flat grain.

Precision End Trimmed (PET). Trimmed square and smooth on both ends to uniform lengths.

Resawn Face. Produced by resawing rough or dressed lumber to yield a surface suitable for use where a saw-textured appearance is intended.

Rift Grain. See *Vertical Grain.*

Rough Lumber. Has not been dressed but has been sawed, edged, and trimmed at least to the extent of showing saw marks in the wood on the four longitudinal surfaces of each piece for its overall length.

S-Dry. Nineteen percent moisture content or less. Applies to all redwood grades except *Clear All Heart* and *Clear.* Manufactured *rough* or *dressed.*

Saw-Textured. One or more faces resawn for a rough textured effect. The saw-textured surface increases redwood's natural finish-holding ability, resists or obscures smudges and scuffs, and is recommended for exterior siding and less formal interior applications.

Slash Grain (SG). See *Flat Grain.*

Surfaced. Unless otherwise specified, boards and patterns are sold with a smooth-planed surface, emphasizing the wood's grain and color.

Trim. Cross-cutting a piece to a given length.

Vertical Grain (VG). Lumber milled so that a cross section of the annual growth rings appears with grain lines parallel on the face of the board.

Worked to Pattern. In addition to being *dressed,* has been matched, shiplapped, patterned, or molded.

MANUFACTURING IMPERFECTIONS

See also **Lumber, Terms & Abbreviations.**

Standard A. Very light torn grain, occasional slight chip marks, very slight knife marks.

Standard B. Very light torn grain, very light raised grain, very light loosened grain, slight chip marks, average of one slight chip mark per lineal foot but not more than two in any lineal foot, slight knife marks, very slight mismatch.

Standard C. Medium torn grain, light raised grain, light loosened grain, very light machine bite, very light machine gouge, very light machine offset, light chip marks if well-scattered, occasional medium chip marks, very slight knife marks, very slight mismatch.

Standard D. Heavy torn grain, medium raised grain, very heavy loosened grain, light machine bite, light machine gouge, light machine offset, medium chip marks, slight knife marks, very light mismatch.

Standard E. Torn grain, raised grain, very heavy loosened grain, medium machine bite, machine gouge, medium machine offset, chip marks, knife marks, light wavy dressing, light mismatch.

Standard F. Very heavy torn grain, raised grain, very heavy loosened grain, heave machine bite, machine gouge, heavy machine offset, chip marks, knife marks, medium wavy dressing, medium mismatch.

GRADES

Clear All Heart. Finest architectural heartwood grade, normally Certified Kiln Dried (also available unseasoned), well manufactured, free of defects one face (reverse face may have slight imperfections). Available surfaced or saw-textured. Used for siding, paneling, trim, cabinetry, molding, soffits, millwork, decks, hot tubs, gardens, industrial storage and processing tanks.

Clear. Same general quality as *Clear All Heart* except contains sapwood in varying amounts. Normally Certified Kiln Dried (also available unseasoned.) Some imperfections not permitted in *Clear All Heart.* Available surfaced or saw-textured. Used for siding, paneling, trim, cabinetry, molding, soffits. Also quality decking, garden shelters, and other above-ground outdoor applications.

B Grade. Quality grade containing sapwood, limited knots, and other characteristics not permitted in *Clear All Heart* and *Clear.* Normally Certified Kiln Dried, but also unseasoned. Available surfaced or saw-textured. Used for siding, paneling, trim, fascia, molding, and other architectural uses. Quality decking, garden shelters, and other above-ground outdoor applications.

Construction Heart. A heartwood grade containing knots of varying sizes and other slight imperfections. Available seasoned or unseasoned. This highly useful grade can be ordered surfaced or rough. Used for decks, posts, retaining walls, fences, garden structures, stairs, or other outdoor uses especially on or near soil. Also industrial and farm uses.

Merchantable Heart. An economical heartwood grade that allows slightly larger knots than construction grades with holes limited to size of knots. Allow *checks* (see *Lumber, Terms & Abbreviations*), some splits and some manufacturing flaws. Unseasoned, surfaced, or rough. Used for fences, retaining walls, garden structures, especially on or near soil. Industrial and farm applications requiring insect and decay resistance.

Construction Common. Same general characteristics as *Construction Heart,* but permits sapwood in varying amounts. Unseasoned or seasoned, it can be surfaced or rough. Also available saw-textured. Used seasoned or unseasoned for decking, fence boards, and other above ground garden uses that do not require heartwood's insect and decay resistance.

Merchantable. Has the same characteristics as *Merchantable Heart* but contains sapwood in varying amounts. This economical grade is available unseasoned, can be ordered surfaced or rough. Used for fence boards, railings, and other above-ground outdoor and garden uses. Also subflooring, and temporary construction.

Select Heart. A tight-knotted heartwood grade resistant to insects and decay, with face free of *splits* or *shake* (see *Lumber, Terms & Abbreviations*). It is suitable for high quality construction without waste. Usually unseasoned. This durable grade is available surfaced or rough. Used for decks, posts, garden structures, curbing, retaining walls, industrial uses, farm structures.

Select. Same general characteristics as *Select Heart,* but contains sapwood in varying amounts, some imperfections on the back side not permitted in *Select Heart.* Usually unseasoned. This economical grade is available surfaced or rough. Used for decking, fence boards, garden structures, and other above-ground uses where durability is not a factor.

Stress Grades. Lumber grades having assigned working stress and modulus of elasticity values in accordance with accepted basic principles of strength grading.

Foundation Grade. Selected from 2-in. or thicker *Construction Heart* or better for durability and ability to resist insect and fungus attacks.

Select Fence Boards. Intended for use as privacy fencing where it is exposed. Pieces of this grade are of sound wood. Where they occur, characteristics are limited to assure a good appearance.

Redwood Deck Heart and **Redwood Deck Common.** Suited for residential or non-residential exterior patio deck uses where specific design values are required in combination with an attractive appearance. Manufactured in 2 in. thicknesses, in 4 and 6 in. widths. Generally of the same quality as *Construction Heart* and *Construction Common.* The primary difference is the inclusion of slope of grain requirements and knot measurement based upon equivalent displacement rather than average diameter.

REDWOOD GRADEMARKS

Standard grademarks include grade name and symbol of authorized grading agency. Grademarks may be on seasoned or unseasoned lumber on face, edge, or end of piece, *Certified Kiln Dried*

marks lumber kiln dried to accepted standards. The lumber may display the trademark of the California Redwood Association if the mill is a member and adheres to the Association's standards for quality. Examples of the grade marks appear below:

Sources:

Redwood Lumber Grades and Uses, Novato, CA: California Redwood Association, 1988.

Standard Specifications for Grades of California Redwood Lumber, Novato, CA: Redwood Inspection Service, December 1990.

Shakes and Shingles, Cedar

The product grades summarized in this entry are approved by the Cedar Shake and Shingle Bureau (also referred to as the Red Cedar Shingle and Handsplit Shake Bureau). Products bearing the bureau's trademark label have met the bureau's standards of in-plant inspection. The terms *Certigrade, Certi-Split, Certi-Guard,* and *Certi-Last* are registered trademarks of the bureau. The differences between shingles and shakes are in the method of manufacture and the method of installation. Shakes are primarily hand-split, with a thicker butt and a more rustic look. They are installed with greater surface exposed. Shingles have a thinner butt and are sawn on both surfaces. They are installed at reduced surface exposure, resulting in a tighter, more formal look.

An example of a Cedar Shake & Shingle Bureau label accompanies this entry.

CERTIGRADE RED CEDAR SHINGLES

No. 1 Blue Label. The premium grade of shingles for roofs and sidewalls. They are 100 percent heartwood, 100 percent clear of defects such as knots, wormholes, decay, checks, crimps, flat-grain, cross-grain, and sapwood. They are 100 percent edge grain.

No. 2 Red Label. A good grade for many applications. Not less than 10 in. clear on 16 in. shingles and 11 in. clear on 18 in. shingles. Flat grain and limited sapwood are permitted.

No. 3 Black Label. A utility grade for economy applications and secondary buildings. Not less the 6 in. clear on 16 in. shingles and 18 in. shingles, 10 in. clear on 24 in. shingles.

No. 4 Undercoursing. A utility grade for starter course undercoursing.

16" x 5/2"   (407mm x 5/51mm)

16" x 5/2"   (406mm x 5/50mm)

Examples of two of the registered trademark labels of the
Cedar Shake & Shingle Bureau

Rebutted and Rejoined. Has the same specifications as above for No. 1 and No. 2 grades but machine trimmed for parallel edges with butts sawn at right angles. For sidewall application where tightly fitting joints are desired. Also available with smooth sanded face.

CERTIGROOVE RED CEDAR SHAKES

No. 1 Machine Grooved. Machine grooved shakes are manufactured from shingles and have striated faces and parallel edges. Used double-coursed on exterior sidewalls.

CERTI-SPLIT RED CEDAR SHAKES

No. 1 Hand Split & Resawn. These shakes have split faces and sawn backs. Cedar logs are first cut into desired lengths. Blanks or boards of proper thicknesses are split and then run diagonally through a bandsaw to produce two tapered shakes from each blank.

No. 1 Taper-Sawn. These shakes are sawn on both sides. Nos. 2 and 3 are also available.

No. 1 Tapersplit. Produced largely by hand, using a sharp-bladed steel froe (wedge-shaped cleaving tool) and a mallet. The natural shingle-like taper is achieved by reversing the block, end-for-end, with each split.

No. 1 Straight-Split. Produced by machine or in the same manner

as tapersplit shakes except that, by splitting from the same end of the block, the shakes acquire the same thickness throughout.

SPECIALTY PRODUCTS

Fancy-Butt Red Cedar Shingles. These shingles are 5 in. wide and 16 or 18 in. long. A 96 piece carton will cover 25 square feet at 7½ in. exposure.

Panels. Western Red Cedar shingles available in 4- and 8-ft. panelized form.

Fire-Retardant Cedar Shakes and Shingles. *No. 1-Certigrade* shingles and *No. 1 Certisplit* shakes are available pressure-impregnated with fire-retardants to meet testing standards developed by Underwriters Laboratories. *Certi-Guard* is the Cedar Shake and Shingle Bureau registered trademark for fire-retardant shakes and shingles.

Pressure Preservative Treated. *Certi-Grade* shingles and *Certi-Split* shakes are pressure-treated with 0.40 *CCA preservative* (see entry), and are labeled *Certi-Last,* the Cedar Shake and Shingle Bureau registered trademark for treated shingles and shake. These products are suitable in areas of high humidity where premature decay may occur.

Source:
Design and Application Manual for New Roof Construction, Bellevue, WA: Cedar Shake and Shingle Bureau, 1991.

241

Siding, Wood

Solid wood has long been used as a siding materials. Few restrictions are placed on its use by building codes. Only New Jersey requires a gradestamp for wood siding. However, all Western species of wood used for siding are listed under at least one industry-recognized grade rule published by a certified rules-writing agency, such as the Western Wood Products Association (WWPA), West Coast Lumber Inspection Bureau (WCLIB), or the National Lumber Grades Authority (NLGA) for Canadian cedar.

TERMINOLOGY

No Prior Selection (NPS). This term has no standard definition, and is used by some manufacturers as a marketing term.

Select Tight Knot (STK). Some manufacturers market siding under this term, but it is a marketing term only, and not a grade designation overseen by a certifying agency.

PATTERNS

Trim Board-on-Board and Board-and-Batten. Boards may be surfaced smooth, rough, or saw-textured.

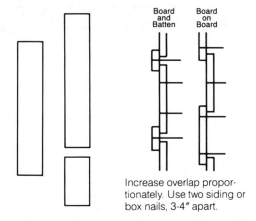

Increase overlap proportionately. Use two siding or box nails, 3-4″ apart.

Bevel or Bungalow. Bungalow (also referred to as *Colonial*) is slightly thicker than Bevel. Either can be used with the smooth or saw-faced surface exposed. Provides a traditional-style appearance.

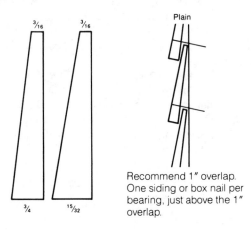

Recommend 1″ overlap. One siding or box nail per bearing, just above the 1″ overlap.

Dolly Varden. Slightly thicker than bevel, with a rabbeted edge. Surface smooth or saw textured, providing traditional-style appearance.

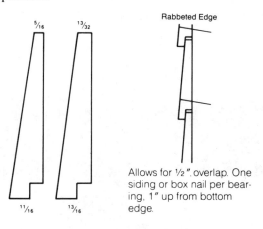

Allows for ½″ overlap. One siding or box nail per bearing, 1″ up from bottom edge.

Drop. Available in thirteen patterns, rough and saw textured surfaces, tongue and groove or shiplapped.

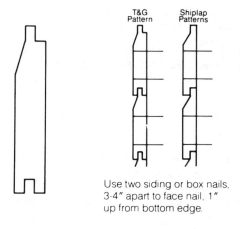

Use two siding or box nails, 3-4″ apart to face nail, 1″ up from bottom edge.

Tongue and Groove. Available in different patterns, and can be used to achieve different effects.

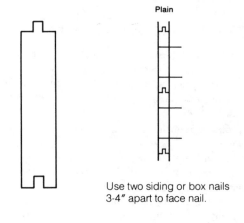

Use two siding or box nails 3-4″ apart to face nail.

Channel Rustic. One-half inch overlap and 1 to 1¼ in. channel when installed. Available smooth, rough, or saw textured.

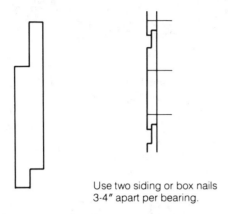

Use two siding or box nails
3-4″ apart per bearing.

Log Cabin. At its thickest point, 1½ in. thick. Informal, rustic appearance.

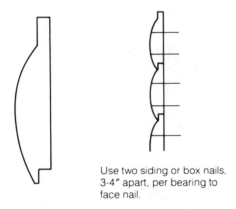

Use two siding or box nails,
3-4″ apart, per bearing to
face nail.

Source:
Natural Wood Siding: Selection, Installation, and Finishing Technical Guide, Portland, OR: Western Wood Products Association and Western Red Cedar Lumber Association, 1990.

Softwood Lumber Standard

The *American Softwood Lumber Standard, PS 20-70,* is a voluntary standard developed by the U.S. Department of Commerce in cooperation with producers, distributors, and users of softwood lumber (see also *Southern Pine* and *Softwood Lumber, Western*). The purpose is to establish voluntary standards for the size, grade, and inspection of softwood lumber. The standard establishes a common basis for uniform industry-wide inspection and grade marking practices. The guidelines contained in *PS 20-70* are not intended for use as grading rules. Instead, *PS 20-70* provides a common basis of understanding for the classification, measurement, grading, and grade marking of rough and dressed sizes of lumber.

GRADE MARKS

Grading rules for the different species of lumber are developed by various lumber inspection agencies. These agencies belong to the American Lumber Standards Committee which approves grading rules and grade marks issued by member organizations. It has two standing committees: National Grading Rule Committee and the Board of Review. Grading rules of the various agencies may vary in terminology but generally conform to the structure of *PS 20-70*. Most grade stamps, except those for rough lumber or heavy timbers, contain five basic elements:

a. The trademark certifies agency quality supervision.
b. Mill Identification—firm name, brand, or assigned mill number.
c. Grade Designation—grade name, number, or abbreviation.
d. Species Identification—indicates species individually or in combination.
e. Condition of Seasoning at time of surfacing:
   S-DRY—19 percent max. moisture content
   MC 15—15 percent max. moisture content
   S-GRN—over 19 percent moisture content (unseasoned)

Typical grade stamps of inspection agencies belonging to or affiliated with the American Lumber Standards Committee include:

California Lumber Inspection Service
San Jose, California
Approved as an inspection agency including mill supervisory service under the WCLIB rules, the WWPA rules, the RIS rules, the National Grading Rule portion of the NLGA rules for Canadian lumber, and for Boards, Scaffold Plank, and the NGR portions of the SPIB rules. Approved to supervise fingerjointing.

Northeastern Lumber Manufacturers Association, Inc.
Cumberland Center, Maine

Approved for the rules they publish, and as an inspection agency including mill supervisory service under: the NSLB rules, the NGR portions of the WCLIB rules, the WWPA rules and the NLGA rules for Canadian lumber, for Selects and Common Boards, 4/4 Shop, Heavy Shop, for Posts, Timbers, Beams, and Stringers under the WWPA rules, for Posts, Timbers, Beams and Stringers under the WCLIB rules. Approved to supervise machine stress rated lumber.

Northern Softwood Lumber Bureau
Cumberland Center, Maine
(formerly Northern Hardwood and Pine Manufacturers Association, Inc.)

Approved for rules they publish, and as an inspection agency including mill supervisory service under the NGR portions of the WCLIB rules, the WWPA rules, and the NLGA rules for Canadian lumber.

Pacific Lumber Inspection Bureau, Inc.
Bellevue, Washington

Approved as an inspection agency including mill supervisory service under the WCLIB rules, the WWPA rules, the RIS rules and the NLGA rules for Canadian lumber. Approved to supervise machine stress rated lumber.

Redwood Inspection Service
Novato, California

Approved for rules they publish, and as an inspection agency including mill supervisory service under the WCLIB rules, and the WWPA rules.

Southern Pine Inspection Bureau
Pensacola, Florida

Approved for the rules they publish, and as an inspection agency including mill supervisory service under the NGR portions of the NELMA rules, the WWPA rules, the WCLIB rules, and the NLGA rules for Canadian lumber. Approved to supervise fingerjointing and machine stress rated lumber.

Timber Products Inspection
Conyers, Georgia

Approved as an inspection agency including mill supervisory service under the RIS rules, the SPIB rules, the WCLIB rules, the WWPA rules, the NGR portions of the NELMA rules, the NLGA rules for Canadian lumber, and the NSLB rules. Also approved for Posts, Timbers, Beams, and Stringers under the NELMA rules. Approved to supervise fingerjointing and machine stress rated lumber.

MILL 10
NO. 2
DOUG FIR   S-DRY

West Coast Lumber Inspection Bureau
Portland, Oregon

Approved for rules they publish and as an inspection agency including mill supervisory service under the RIS rules, the WWPA rules, the NLGA rules for Canadian lumber, the Scaffold, Boards, Radius Edge Decking, Finish and NGR portions under the SPIB rules. Approved to supervise fingerjointing and machine stress rated lumber.

Western Wood Products Association
Portland, Oregon

Approved for the rules they publish and as an inspection agency including mill supervisory service under: the WCLIB rules, the NLGA rules for Canadian lumber, for Studs under the RIS rules, and for Scaffold and the NGR portion of the SPIB rules. Approved to supervise fingerjointing and machine stress rated lumber.

CANADIAN NATIONAL LUMBER GRADES AUTHORITY

The following Canadian agencies have been accredited by the Board of Review of the American Lumber Standards Committee as inspections agencies including mill supervisory service under the National Lumber Grades Authority for Canadian Lumber.

A.F.P.A® 00
S — P — F
S-DRY STAND

Alberta Forest Products Association
Edmonton, Alberta

Approved to supervise fingerjointing and machine stress rated lumber.

C L® A   C L® A 100
S-P-F   SPRUCE PINE FIR
100   NO. 1   S-DRY
No. 2
S-GRN.

Canadian Lumbermen's Association
Ottawa, Ontario

Approved to provide supervisory service under the NGR portion of the NELMA rules.

Cariboo Lumber Manufacturers Association
Williams Lake, British Columbia

Approved to supervise fingerjointing and machine stress rated lumber.

CFPA® 00
S-P-F   S-DRY
CONST

Central Forests Products Association
Hudson Bay, Saskatchewan

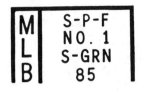

Maritime Lumber Bureau
Amherst, Nova Scotia

Approved to provide supervisory service under the NGR portion of the NELMA rules.

CQFI®   S-P-F
    S-GRN
100   № 1

Council of Forest Industries of British Columbia
Vancouver, British Columbia

Approved to supervise fingerjointing and machine stress rated lumber.

O.L.M.A.® 01-1
CONST.   S-DRY
SPRUCE - PINE - FIR

Ontario Lumber Manufacturers Association
Toronto, Ontario

Approved to supervise machine stress rated lumber. Approved to provide supervisory service under the NGR portion of the NELMA rules.

ILMA® S-DRY 1
00   S—P—F

Interior Lumber Manufacturers Association
Kelowna, British Columbia

Approved to supervise fingerjointing and machine stress rated lumber.

NLGA RULE
No 1
S-GRN
HEM-FIR-N

Pacific Lumber Inspection Bureau
Bellevue, Washington

Approved to supervise machine stress rated lumber.

No 1
S-DRY
D FIR (N)

MacDonald Inspection
Coquitlam, British Columbia

Approved to supervise fingerjointing and machine stress rated lumber.

Quebec Lumber Manufacturers Association
Quebec, Quebec

Approved to supervise fingerjointing and machine stress rated lumber. Approved to provide supervisory service under the NGR portion of the NELMA rules.

CLASSIFICATIONS

Softwood lumber is classified according to use, manufacturing, and size classifications.

Use Classifications

Yard Lumber. Lumber of those grades, sizes, and patterns, which is generally intended for ordinary construction and general building purposes.

Structural Lumber. Lumber that is 2 or more in. in nominal thickness and width for use where working stresses are required.

Factory and Shop Lumber. Lumber that is produced or selected primarily for remanufacturing purposes.

Manufacturing Classifications

Rough Lumber. Lumber which has not been dressed (surfaced) on all opposing faces but which has been sawed, edged, and trimmed at least to the extent of showing saw or other primary manufacturing marks in the wood on the four longitudinal surfaces of each piece for its overall length. Lumber may be dressed (surfaced) as: *S1E,* surfaced one edge; *S2E,* surfaced two edges; *S1S,* surfaced one side; *S2S,* surfaced two sides; *S1S1E,* surfaced one side one edge; *S1S2E,* surfaced one side two edges; *S2S1E,* surfaced two sides one edge; *S4S,* surfaced four sides. Dressed (surfaced) lumber is classified according to the surfaced width or thickness.

Worked Lumber. In addition to being dressed, has been matched, shiplapped, or patterned. *Matched lumber* has been worked with a tongue on one edge of each piece and a groove on the opposite edge to provide a close tongue-and-groove joint by fitting two pieces together; when end-matched, the tongue and groove are worked in the ends also. *Shiplapped lumber* has been worked or rabbeted on both edges of each piece to provide a close-lapped joint by fitting two pieces together. *Patterned lumber* is shaped to a pattern or to a molded form, in addition to being dressed, matched, or shiplapped, or any combination of these.

Size Classifications

Boards. Less than 2 in. in nominal thickness and 2 or more in. in nominal width. Boards less than 6 in. in nominal width may be classified as *strips.*

Dimension. From 2 in. up to, but not including, 5 in. in thickness, and 2 or more in. in nominal width. Dimension may be classified as framing, joists, planks, rafters, studs, small timbers, etc.

Timbers. 5 or more in. nominally in least dimension. Timbers may be classified as beams, stringers, posts, caps, sills, girders, purlins, etc.

GRADING PROVISIONS

Yard Lumber

Grading is based upon the uses for which the grade is designed.

Select

Lumber of good appearance and finishing qualities.

    (a) Suitable for natural finishes.

        (i) Practically clear.

        (ii) Generally clear and of high quality.

    (b) Suitable for paint finishes.

        (i) Adapted to high-quality paint finishes.

        (ii) Intermediate between high-finishing grades and common grades, and partaking somewhat of the nature of both.

Common

Lumber which is suitable for general construction and utility purposes.

    (a) For standard construction use.

        (i) Suitable for better-type construction purposes.

        (ii) Well adapted for good standard construction.

        (iii) Designed for low-cost temporary construction.

    (b) For less exacting construction purposes.

        (i) Low quality.

        (ii) Lowest quality.

Structural Lumber

Structural lumber factors are working stress and modulus of elasticity (MOE) values. These are established and contained in grading rules developed in accordance with appropriate ASTM standards and other technically sound criteria.

Factory and Shop Lumber

The end use of factory and shop lumber produced from different species and in the several regions varies considerably; accordingly, the American Lumber Standard grade classifications are those promulgated by the several agencies which formulate and publish grading rules approved by the Board of Review.

Sources:

ALSC Agencies Typical Grade Stamps, Germantown, MD: American Lumber Standards Committee, 1992.

National Institute of Standards and Technology, *Voluntary Product Standard PS 20-70, American Softwood Lumber Standard,* Washington: U.S. Department of Commerce, amended 1986.

Softwood Lumber, Western

Softwood comes from one of the group of trees which have needle-like or scale-like leaves. The term has no specific reference to the softness of the wood. The grades of lumber summarized in this entry are approved by the Western Wood Products Association (WWPA), which maintains detailed grading rules for the various products. The WWPA follows the guidelines established in the U.S. Department of Commerce's Voluntary Product Standard *PS 20-70* for American Softwood Lumber, which was developed in cooperation with producers, distributors, and users of softwood lumber (see *Softwood Lumber Standard*).

    Grading of lumber is by visual inspection and is a judgment of appearance and suitability to end-use rather than strength. Natural characteristics and manufacturing imperfections are taken into account. The WWPA publishes a series of 4-color pamphlets (cited below) that visually display the appearance of the different grades. Lumber graded under supervision of the WWPA is certified and marked with the association's trademark symbol.

MOISTURE CONTENT (MC)

Moisture content indicates the condition of seasoning at time of surfacing.
MC-15. 15 percent maximum moisture content.
Surfaced Dry (S-DRY). 19 percent maximum moisture content.
Surfaced Green (S-GRN). Over 19 percent moisture content (unseasoned)
DRY. Indicates that a product was either kiln- or air-dried to a moisture content specified by grade.

GRAIN PATTERNS

VG. Vertical grain.
FG. Flat grain.
MG. Mixed grain.

GRADE STAMPS

Grade stamping often is not done on appearance grades of lumber, except on the ends or back, to avoid impairing the surface. But when used, the grade stamp contains five elements identifying the manufacturer, grade, species, moisture content, and certification agency, as is shown below:

a. WWPA Certification Mark: Certifies agency quality supervision. The WWPA Certification Mark is a registered trademark.
b. Mill Identification: Firm name, brand, or assigned mill number. WWPA can be contacted to identify an individual mill whenever necessary.
c. Grade Designation: Grade name, number, or abbreviation.
d. Species Identification: Indicates species individually or in combination. Other species identification marks are shown in the species list that accompanies this entry.
e. Condition of Seasoning at time of surfacing:
    S-DRY—19 percent max. moisture content
    MC 15—15 percent max. moisture content
    S-GRN—over 19 percent moisture content (unseasoned)

Common grade abbreviations found on grade stamps include:

CONST   Construction.
STAND   Standard.
UTIL   Utility.
STUD   Stud.
SEL STR Select Structural.
B & BTR Grade B and Better.
SEL   Select.
COM   Common.

DIMENSION LUMBER (FRAMING LUMBER)

Dimension lumber is surfaced lumber of nominal thicknesses from 2 to 4 in. It is used for structural framing, including studs, joists, rafters, 4x4 in. posts, and 4 in. thick beams. National Grading Rules classify dimension lumber in three width categories and four use categories. *Structural Light Framing* and *Light Framing* are 2 to 4 in. wide. *Studs* are 2 to 6 in. wide. *Structural Joists & Planks* are 5 in. wide and wider. Western softwood species commonly manufactured into dimension lumber include Douglas fir, larch, Western hemlock, Engelmann spruce, cedars, all pines, and true firs. Some species are grouped together.

Structural Light Framing
Select Structural. The highest grade, where good appearance is required along with strength and stiffness.
No. 1. This grade is recommended where good appearance is desired but is secondary to strength and stiffness.
No. 2. Recommended for most general construction uses.
No. 3. Appropriate for general construction where high strength is generally not a factor.
Economy. No design values are assigned to this grade, and it should not be used in structural applications.

Light Framing
Construction. The highest grade. Indicates a piece widely used for general framing, with good appearance but graded primarily for strength and serviceability.
Standard Grade. Customarily used for the same purposes, or in conjunction with *Construction Grade,* providing good strength and excellent serviceability.
Utility Grade. Recommended where economies are desired for studding, blocking, plates, and bracing.
Stud Grade. Selected pieces suitable for all stud uses including load-bearing walls. Restrictions on crook, wane, and edge knots make this one of the most popular grades for wall construction. Lengths, however, are limited to 10 ft.
Economy. No design values are assigned to this grade, and it should not be used in structural applications.

Structural Joists & Planks
Select Structural. The highest grade. It indicates a piece recommended where good appearance is required along with strength and stiffness.
No. 1. This grade is recommended where good appearance is desired but is secondary to strength and stiffness.

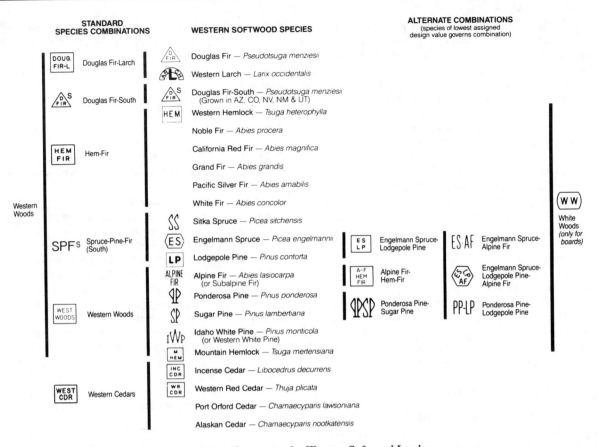

Marketing Categories for Western Softwood Lumber

No. 2. Recommended for most general construction uses.

No. 3. Appropriate for general construction where high strength is generally not a factor.

Economy. No design values are assigned to this grade, and it should not be used in structural applications.

APPEARANCE LUMBER

The lumber in the *Appearance Lumber* category is intended for applications where strength is not the primary consideration. Lumber in this category is often referred to as *Board Lumber*. Western softwood species commonly manufactured into board lumber include Douglas fir, Western larch, Ponderosa pine, lodgepole pine, sugar pine, Engelmann spruce, Idaho white pine, Western red cedar, incense cedar, Western hemlock, and the true firs. Many of these species are grown, harvested, manufactured, and marketed together. Some have similar appearance and performance properties which make them interchangeable in use. This applies to Western hemlock and the true firs which are grouped together as *Hem-Fir*. Similar marketing groupings include: *Western cedars* (incense and Western red cedar) and *white woods* (Engelmann spruce, any true firs, any hemlocks, and any pines).

Selects (all species)

B & BTR. The ultimate in appearance. It is the highest quality of

Select grade lumber and many pieces are absolutely clear.

C Select. Recommended for all finishing uses where fine appearance is essential. Its appearance ranks only slightly less than *B & BTR* grade.

D Select. Has many of the appearance features of *C Select* and is suitable where the needs for finishing are less exacting.

Finish (usually available only in Douglas fir and Hem-Fir)

Superior. The highest grade of *Finish* lumber. Many pieces are absolutely clear.

Prime. Exhibits a fine appearance although less restrictive than *Superior* grade.

E Finish. Can be ordered where pieces can be crosscut or ripped to obtain cuttings of *Prime* or better quality.

Special Western Red Cedar Pattern Grades

Clear Heart. Exposed width is all heartwood, free from imperfections. Used where highest quality is indicated.

A Grade. Has only minor imperfections.

Common Boards (primarily in pines, spruces, and cedars)

No. 1 Common. Not usually carried in stock in large quantities but may be ordered when the ultimate in fine appearance of knotty material is required.

No. 2 Common. Intended primarily for use in paneling, shelving, and other uses calling for knotty lumber with fine appearance.

No. 3 Common. Widely used for shelving, paneling, and siding as well as fences, boxes, crating, sheathing, and industrial applications.

No. 4 Common. More widely used than any other grade for general construction such as subfloors, roof and wall sheathing, concrete forms, low-cost fencing, crating, and similar uses.

No. 5 Common. Intended for use in economical construction where appearance and strength are not basic requirements.

Alternate Boards (primarily in Douglas fir and Hem-Fir)

Select Merchantable. Intended primarily for use in housing and light construction where it is exposed as paneling, shelving, and where knotty type lumber with the finest appearance is required.

Construction. Recommended for subfloors, roof and wall sheathing, concrete forms, and similar types of construction.

Standard. The most widely used grade for general construction purposes where seldom left exposed.

Utility. Judged primarily on serviceability instead of appearance to provide a low-cost lumber for general construction purposes.

Economy. Suitable for low-grade sheathing, crating, bracing, temporary construction, and similar uses.

FACTORY AND SHOP GRADE LUMBER

Factory and Shop Grades provide the remanufacturer with an opportunity to buy industrial lumber, intended for the recovery of clear pieces, at an economical price. These grades, available primarily in Douglas fir, Hem-Fir, Ponderosa pine, and sugar pine, are especially well suited for remanufacture to obtain clear, standard-size cuttings that are based on typical U.S. joinery and millwork cutting sizes. Grades include *Moulding Stock, Clear Door, Factory Select (No. 3 Clear), No. 1 Shop, No. 2 Shop, No. 3 Shop,* and *Fingerjoint Shop Common.* Factory lumber is usually sold as random width 4 to 25 in. and random length 6 to 20 ft., and in thicknesses from ⁴⁄₄ to ¹⁶⁄₄.

INDUSTRIAL LUMBER

Mining Timbers. Designed primarily for use as shoring and bracing materials in mines and tunnels. The grades are designed for serviceability, not necessarily appearance. There are two grades: *No. 1 Mining* and *No. 2 Mining.* Both are graded full length. No design values are applied. Nominal sizes are 5 in. and thicker, and 5 in. and wider.

Scaffold Plank. Shipped rough & unseasoned in Douglas fir-larch 1¼ in. and thicker, 8 in. and wider, in two grades (*Scaffold No. 1* and *Scaffold No. 2*) with applied design values.

Foundation Lumber. Commonly used for sill plates. It is available only in Western red cedar and incense cedar, in sizes 2 in. and thicker, 4 in. and wider. There is only one grade, *Foundation.* It is selected from heartwood (naturally decay resistant) and must be free of heart center and free of sapwood. It is manufactured rough sawn or surfaced.

Stress-Rated Boards. Available from lumber manufacturers in all species to provide a range of products suitable for special applications when *Board Lumber* is to have applied design

values. Several such uses include light trusses, belt rails, horizontal bracing, rafters, and box beams for mobile and factory built homes.

Source:

Western Lumber Product Use Manual, Portland, OR: Western Wood Products Assoc., revised November 1991.

Sound Transmission Class

Sound transmission ratings are closely aligned with fire endurance ratings for assemblies. This is due to the fact that flame penetration and sound penetration follow similar, least-resistant paths. Sound striking a wall or ceiling surface is transmitted through the air in the wall or ceiling cavity. It then strikes the opposite wall surface, causing it to vibrate and transmit the sound into the adjoining room. Sound also is transmitted through any openings going into the room, such as air ducts, electrical outlets, window openings, and doors. This is *airborne sound transmission.*

The Sound Transmission Class method of rating airborne sounds evaluates the comfortability of a particular living space. The higher the STC, the better the airborne noise control performance of the structure. An STC of 50 or greater is generally considered a good airborne noise control rating. The following table describes the privacy afforded by each STC rating:

STC Rating	Privacy Afforded
25	Normal speech easily understood.
30	Normal speech audible but not intelligible.
35	Loud speech audible and fairly understandable.
40	Loud speech barely audible but not intelligible.
45	Loud speech barely audible.
50	Shouting barely audible.
55	Shouting not audible.

Source:

Southern Pine Marketing Council, *Southern Pine Use Guide,* Kenner, LA: Southern Forest Products Association, 1991.

Southern Pine

Southern pine lumber and timber products have been used since colonial times. About half of all Southern pine lumber is now pressure-treated to increase its longevity and design versatility. Another quarter of total production is used in trusses and other structural framing applications. The grades summarized in this entry are approved by the Southern Pine Inspection Bureau (SPIB). Strength and stiffness values for Southern pine products in current SPIB rules have been approved by the Board of Review of the American Lumber Standards Committee. The voluntary standard, *PS-20-70* (see *Softwood Lumber Standard*), developed by the U.S. Department of Commerce and the softwood industry, provides for a National Grading Rule (NGR) with simplified grade names and sizes to assure uniformity, efficiency, and economy in the use of dimension lumber. The NGR was incorporated in the *SPIB Standard Grading Rules for Southern Pine Lumber, 1991 Edition*, published by the Southern Pine Inspection Bureau. Please consult this publication for official grading rules.

GRADE MARKS

Lumber inspected by an agency certified by the Board of Review of the American Lumber Standards Committee is marked with symbols. Examples of two typical lumber grademarks appear below.

Inspection Service:
Southern Pine Inspection Bureau

Symbol for members of SFPA (optional)

Lumber grade

Mill identification number

Kiln dried (Max. 19% M.C.)   Surfaced Dry

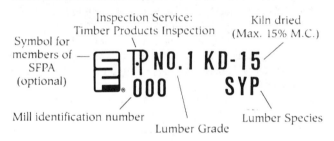

Inspection Service:
Timber Products Inspection

Kiln dried (Max. 15% M.C.)

Symbol for members of SFPA (optional)

Mill identification number

Lumber Grade

Lumber Species

PRODUCTS AND GRADES

Dimension Lumber: 2-4 in. thick, 2 in. and wider.

Dense Select Structural, Dense Select, and Non-Dense Select Structural. High quality, relatively free of characteristics which impair strength or stiffness. Recommended for uses where high strength, stiffness, and good appearance are desired.

No. 1 Dense, No. 1, and No. 1 Non-Dense. Recommended for general utility and construction where high strength, stiffness, and good appearance are desired.

No. 2 Dense, No. 2, and No. 2 Non-Dense. Recommended for most general construction uses where moderately high design values are required. Allows well-spaced knots of any quality.

No. 3. Assigned design values meet a wide range of design requirements. Recommended for general construction purposes where appearance is not a controlling factor. Many

pieces included in this grade would qualify as *No. 2* except for a single limiting factor.

Stud (2 to 6 inches wide only). Suitable for stud uses including use in load-bearing walls. Composite of *No. 3* strength and *No. 1* nailing edge characteristics.

Construction (2 to 4 in. wide only). Recommended for general framing purposes. Good appearance, but graded primarily for strength and serviceability.

Standard (2 to 4 in. wide only). Recommended for same purposes as *Construction* grade. Characteristics are limited to provide good strength and excellent serviceability.

Utility (2 to 4 inches wide only). Recommended where a combination of economical construction and good strength is desired. Used for such purposes as studding, blocking, plates, bracing, and rafters.

Economy. Usable lengths suitable for bracing, blocking, bulkheading, and other utility purposes where strength and appearance are not controlling factors.

Timbers. 5 in. by 5 in. and larger
Note: SR in grade name stands for Stress Rated.

Dense Select Structural Stress Rated (SR) and Select Structural SR. Recommended where high strength, stiffness and good appearance are desired.

No. 1. Dense Stress Rated (SR), No. 1 SR, No. 2 Dense SR, and No. 2 SR. No. 1 and *No. 2* are similar in appearance to corresponding grades of 2 in. thick *Dimension Lumber.* Recommended for general construction uses.

Square Edge & Sound No. 1, No. 2, and No. 3. Non-stress rated, but economical for general construction purposes such as blocking, fillers, etc.

Machine Stress Rated (MSR) Lumber. 2 in. and less in thickness, 2 in. and wider.

1200f-1.2E thru 300f-2.6E. MSR lumber has been evaluated by mechanical stress rating equipment. It is distinguished from visually stress-graded lumber in that each piece is non-destructively tested. MSR lumber is also required to meet certain visual grading requirements.

Machine Evaluated Lumber (MEL). 2 in. and less in thickness, 2 in. and wider.

M-10 thru M-27. Well-manufactured material evaluated by calibrated mechanical grading equipment which measures certain properties and sorts the lumber into various strength classifications. Also required to meet certain visual requirements.

Scaffold Plank. 2 and 3 in. thick, 8 in. and wider.

Dense Industrial 72 and Dense Industrial 65. Design values calculated using ASTM standards D245 and D2555.

Machine Stress Rated Lumber. 2400f-2.0E and MSR:2200f-1.8E. Dressed to standard dry size prior to machine stress rating, and visually graded to assure that characteristics affecting strength are no more serious than the limiting characteristics for each grade.

Stadium Grade. 2 in. thick, 4 to 12 in. wide.
No. 1 Dense and *No. 1.* For outdoor seating.

Prime & Merchantable Dimension. 2 to 4 in. thick, 2 to 6 in. wide.

Prime Dense and Prime. Grade based on *No. 1 Dimension Lumber* characteristics except that holes, skip, and wane are closely limited to provide a high-quality product.

Merchantable Dense and Merchantable. Grade based on *No. 2 Dimensional Lumber* characteristics except that holes, skip, and wane are closely limited.

Marine Framing. 2 to 20 in. thick, 2 to 20 in. wide.

Any Grade of Dimension Lumber or Timbers. All four longitudinal faces must be free of pith and/or heartwood. Application of the product requires pressure treatment by an approved treating process and preservative for marine usage.

Seawalls. 2 to 4 inches thick, 6 to 14 inches wide.

Any grade of Dimension Lumber. Provides three heart-free faces for use as a seawall. Application of the product requires pressure treatment by an approved treating process and preservative for marine usage.

Decking, Heavy Roofing, and Heavy Shiplap. 2 to 4 in. thick, 2 in. and wider.

Dense Standard Decking. High-quality product, suitable for plank floor where face serves as finish floor. Has a better appearance than *No. 1 Dense Dimension Lumber* because of additional restrictions on pitch, knots, pith, and wane.

Dense Select Decking and Select Decking. An excellent decking grade that can be used face side down for roof decking or face side up for floor decking.

Dense Commercial Decking and Commercial Decking. An economical roof decking which conforms to *No. 2 Dimension Lumber* characteristics.

Industrial Lumber. 4 in. and less in thickness, 12 in. and less in width.

Industrial 86. Appearance is same as *B&Btr. Finish.* Larger sizes conform to *Dense Structural 86* except for dense grain requirement.

Industrial 72. Appearance is same as *C Finish.* Larger sizes conform to *Dense Structural 72* except for dense grain requirement.

Industrial 65. Appearance is same as *D Finish.* Larger sizes conform to *Dense Structural 65* except for dense requirement.

Structural Lumber. 2 in. and thicker, 2 in. and wider.

Dense Structural 86, 72 and 65. Premier structural grades. Provides good appearance with some of the highest design values available in any softwood species.

Radius Edge Decking. 1¼ in. thick, 4 to 6 in. wide.

Premium. High-quality product, recommended where smallest knots are desired and appearance is of utmost importance. Excellent for painting or staining.

Standard. Slightly less restrictive than premium grade. A very good product to use where appearance is not the major factor. Excellent for painting or staining.

Boards. 1 to 1½ in. thick, 2 in. and wider.

Industrial 55. Graded as per *No. 1 Dimension.*

Industrial 45. Graded as per *No. 2 Dimension.*

No. 1. High quality with good appearance characteristics. Generally sound and tight-knotted. Largest hole permitted is ¹⁄₁₆ in. Superior product suitable for a wide range of uses including shelving, crating, and form lumber.

No. 2. Good-quality sheathing, fencing, shelving, and other general purpose uses.

No. 3. Good, serviceable sheathing, usable for many economical applications without waste.

No. 4. Admits pieces below a *No. 3* grade which can be used without waste, or which contain less than 25 percent waste by cutting.

Finish. ⅜ to 4 in. thick, 2 in. and wider.

B&B. Highest recognized grade of Finish. Generally clear, although a limited number of pin knots are permitted. Finest quality for natural or stain finish.

C. Excellent for painted or natural finish where requirements are less exacting. Reasonably clear, but permits limited number of surface checks and small tight knots.

C&BTR. Combination of *B&Btr.* and *C* grades. Satisfies requirements for high-quality finish.

D. Economical, serviceable grade for natural or painted finish.

Flooring, Drop Siding, Paneling, Ceiling and Partition, OG Batts, Bevel Siding, Misc. Millwork.

B&B, C, C&BTR, and *D.* See *Finish Grades* for face side; reverse side wane limitations are lower.

No. 1. No. 1 Flooring and Paneling not provided under SPIB Grading Rules as a separate grade, but if specified, will be designated and graded as *D. No. 1 Drop Siding* is graded as *No. 1 Boards.*

No. 2. Graded as *No. 2 Boards.* High utility value where appearance is not a factor.

No. 3. More manufacturing imperfections allowed than in *No. 2,* but suitable for economical use.

PRESSURE TREATED SOUTHERN PINE

Before using treated Southern pine either above ground or in contact with the ground, check the treated quality mark or end tag on each piece of lumber. It will indicate *above ground* for uses such as decking not in direct contact with the soil. It will read *ground contact* for treated Southern pine that will touch the soil, or be buried in the ground. (See *Pressure Treated Lumber.*)

Source:
Southern Pine Marketing Council, *Southern Pine Use Guide,* Kenner, LA: Southern Forest Products Association, 1991.

Wood Imitations

Simulated Wood Grain Finish. A panel having a wood surface which has been stamped, rolled, pressed, or processed in such manner as to change the natural wood grain design.

Hardwood Plywood with Simulated Wood Grain on Vinyl Overlay.
A panel made of hardwood plywood but having a vinyl film
surface simulating a wood finish.

Simulated Wood Surface on Plywood. Plywood with a vinyl film
surface simulating a wood finish.

Simulated Wood Finish. A panel that has an exposed surface of
plastic, metal, vinyl, hardboard, particleboard, or other material not possessing a natural wood grain structure but which
has an appearance simulating that of a wood grain. Depending
on the composition, typical descriptions would include *simulated walnut finish on plastic face, vinyl surface with simulated pecan finish, simulated birch finish on hardboard,
mahogany grain plastic,* or other nondeceptive phrases.

Source:
Federal Trade Commission, 16 CFR sections 243.0 to 243.3 (1992), Washington: Government Printing Office.

Wood Names

Voluntary industry and government standards require that labels
identifying the type of wood in products should not be misleading.
The following guidelines apply:

Walnut. Is not used to describe wood other than genuine solid
walnut (genus *Juglans*). The term *black walnut* is applied only
to the species *Juglans nigra*.

Mahogany. This term is not used to describe wood other than
genuine solid mahogany (genus *Swietenia* of the *Meliaceae*
family). The wood of the genus *Swietenia* may be described by
the term *mahogany* with or without a prefix designating the
country or region of its origin, such as *Honduras mahogany,
Costa Rican mahogany, Brazilian mahogany,* or *Mexican
mahogany.* The term may also be used to describe solid wood
of the genus *Khaya* of the *Meliaceae* family, but only when
prefixed by the word *African.* In naming the seven
nonmahogany Philippine woods *Tanguile, Red Lauan, White
Lauan, Tiaong, Almon, Mayapis,* and *Bagtikan,* the term
mahogany may be used but only when prefixed by the word
Philippine, due to the long standing usage of that term.

Maple. The terms *hard maple, rock maple, bird's eye maple,
Northern maple,* or other terms of similar nature should not be
used to describe woods other than those known under the
lumber trade names of *Black Maple* (*Acer nigrum*) and *Sugar
Maple* (*Acer saccharum*).

Source:
Federal Trade Commission, 16 CFR sections 243.3 to 243.4 (1992), Washington: Government Printing Office.

Wood Particleboard

Particleboard is a generic term for a panel made from lignocellulosic materials (usually wood) primarily in the form of discrete
pieces or particles (flakes, shavings, slivers, fibers, etc.) as
distinguished from fibers (see *Hardboard*), combined with a
synthetic resin or other binder and bonded together under heat and
pressure in a hot press by a process in which entire interparticle
bond is created by the added binders, and to which other materials
may have been added during manufacture to improve certain
properties.

Particleboards are further defined by the method of pressing.
When pressure is applied in the direction perpendicular to the
faces as in a conventional multi-platen hot-press, they are defined
as *flatplaten pressed.* When the applied pressure is parallel to the
faces, they are defined as *extruded.*

GRADE NOMENCLATURE

The grading system sponsored by the National Particleboard
Association describes 15 grades, subdivided into 2 types based on
the type of resin bonding system employed.

Particleboard grades have 3 parts—a first digit, a letter designation, and a final digit or letter. The first digit indicates the type
of bonding system used:

Type 1. A system, e.g., ureaformaldehyde, which enables the
product to meet all applicable property requirements specified
for the relevant Type 1 grade. There are 9 grades of Type 1
particleboard. General uses include high density industrial
products for the high density grades (*1-H-1, 1-H-2, 1-H-3*),
commercial and industrial applications for the medium density grades (*1-M-1, 1-M-2, 1-M-3*), and door cores for the
lower density grades (*1-LD-1* and *1-LD-2*). The grades differ
in strength, screwholding ability, and hardness.

Type 2. A system, e.g. phenolformaldehyde, which enables the
products to meet all applicable property requirements specified for the relevant Type 2 grade. There are 6 grades of Type
2 particleboard. General uses include exterior industrial products for the high density grades (*2-H-1* and *2-H-2*), and siding,
sheathing, and flooring for the medium density grades (*1-M-
1, 1-M-2, 2-M-3,* and 2-M-W. The *W* indicates that the product
is made from wafers).

The letter designations have the following meanings:

H. High nominal density (above 50 lbs per cubic ft).
M. Medium nominal density (40-50 lbs per cubic ft).
LD. Lower nominal density (less than 40 lbs per cubic ft).
D. Manufactured Home Decking. There are four grades of home
decking particleboard. Grade *1-D-3* differs from *1-D-2* by
having a higher modulus of rupture and modulus of elasticity.

The final digit or letter indicates the grade identification within a
particular description. For instance, *1-M-2* indicates *Type 1 medium density particleboard, Grade 2.* Typically, a higher grade
number indicates a stronger material.

LABELING

All particleboard which is represented as conforming to ANSI
standards must be identified with the following information:
Manufacturer's name or trademark

ANSI A208.1

The Grade

The lot number or date of production

With respect to D grade products the words *MANUFACTURED HOME DECKING*

With respect only to particleboard intended for use as underlayment, the word *UNDERLAYMENT*

With respect only to Type 2 products intended for exterior application, the words *EXTERIOR GLUE*

The label must be stamped on each panel of *D* grade particleboard, and particleboard intended for use as underlayment. For all other grades, the information can be either stamped on the board or provided in a written statement in a unit label, invoice, or other commercial document.

Source:

American National Standard, Wood Particleboard, ANSI/208.1-1989, Gaithersburg, MD: National Particleboard Association, published 1992, approved February 1, 1989.

Wood Veneer

Wood veneer is a thin layer of more valuable or beautiful wood used on the face of a panel for overlaying an inferior wood or other core material.

Source:

Federal Trade Commission, 16 CFR section 243 (1992), Washington: Government Printing Office.

Yard
& Garden

Bark Mulch Products

The National Bark and Soil Producers Association has defined 10 categories of bark products for uniform specification. The product categories do not reflect product trade names used by individual producers. These nomenclature recommendations are voluntary and use of the NBSPA certification mark given below indicates voluntary acceptance of product nomenclature recommended by the Association.

DECORATIVE BARK PRODUCTS

Consists of products mechanically screened for uniform size and containing cambium or wood content equal to 15 percent or less of total product weight.

Southern Pine Bark Nuggets. Particle size ranging from 1.25 inches to 3.50 inches in diameter.

Southern Pine Bark Mini-Nuggets. Particle size ranging from 0.5 inch to 1.5 inches in diameter.

West Coast Large Bark. Particle size ranging from 1.75 inches to 3 inches in diameter.

West Coast Medium Bark. Particle size ranging from 0.5 inch to 2 inches in diameter.

West Coast Pathway Bark. Particle size ranging from 0.25 inch to 0.5 inch in diameter.

BARK MULCH PRODUCTS

Consists of products mechanically screened or shredded and with cambium or wood content limited in accordance to the terms set forth below.

Southern Pine Mulch. Particle size less than 1.5 inches in length.

West Coast Bark Mulch. Particle size less than 1 inch in length.

Hardwood Bark Mulch. Particle size less than 3 inches in length with cambium and wood content equal to 15 percent or less of total product weight.

Cypress Mulch A. Particle size less than 3 inches in length with wood fiber content equal to 15 percent or less of total product weight.

Cypress Mulch. Particle size less than 3 inches in length.

Source:
Uniform Nomenclature for Quality Bark Products, Clifton, VA: National Bark and Soil Producers Association, 1992.

Christmas Trees

The standards contained in this subpart are applicable to sheared or unsheared trees of the coniferous species which are normally marketed as Christmas trees. The majority of the Christmas trees marketed are of the following species: Douglas Fir (*Pseudotsuga menziesii*); Balsam Fir (*Abies balsamea*); Red Fir (*Abies magnifica*); White Fir (*Abies concolor*); Fraser Fir (*Abies fraseri*); Grand Fir (*Abies grandis*); Noble Fir (*Abies procera*); White Spruce (*Picea glauca*); Blue Spruce (*Picea pungens*); Eastern Red Cedar (*Juniperus virginlana*); Red Pine (*Pinus resinosa*); White Pine (*Pinus strobus*); Virginia Pine (*Pinus virginiana*); Scotch Pine (*Pinus sylvestris*).

TREE GRADES

U.S. Premium.
- The trees have characteristics typical of the species;
- Butt trimmed (all barren branches have been removed and the trunk has been smoothly cut at approximately right angles to the trunk), except for trees graded on the stump;
- Normal taper (the tree forms a cone, the base of which is from 40 to 100 percent of its height);
- Fresh (the needles are green, pliable, and firmly attached without more than slight shedding);
- Clean;
- Healthy (the needles have a fresh, natural appearance characteristic of the species);
- Well shaped (the tree is not flat on one side and the branches are of sufficient number and length to form a conical outline tapering from the lowest whorl of branches to the top);
- Heavy density (see table below);
- Handle length (the part of the trunk between the base of the tree and the lowest complete whorl of foliated branches), unless otherwise specified, shall be not less than 6 inches or more than 1½ inches for each foot of tree height. For trees graded on the stump, handle length will not be a requirement.
- Three faces with not more than 1 minor defect (slight imperfections in the development of the tree or defects resulting from handling); Remaining face may not have more than 1 minor defect (see below).

U.S. No. 1. This grade differs from *U.S. Premium* in that the tree is not as clean; it only has medium density and may contain more defects (three faces with not more than 2 minor defects—remaining face may not have more than 1 noticeable defect).

U.S. No. 2. This grade differs from *U.S. No. 1* by requiring not less than light density and allowing more defects (two adjacent faces with not more than 3 minor defects—remaining faces may not have more than 2 noticeable defects).

Culls. Individual trees which fail to meet the requirements of the U.S. *No. 2 grade.*

SIZE

The size of trees is stated in foot increments. Unless otherwise specified, the following color codes are used to designate the the respective sizes of Christmas trees.

Color	Size
Lime	3 feet or less
Orange	Over 3 to 4 feet
Blue	Over 4 to 5 feet
Red	Over 5 to 6 feet
Yellow	Over 6 to 7 feet
Green	Over 7 to 8 feet
White	Over 8 to 9 feet
Pink	Over 9 feet

DENSITY

Density means the amount of foliage on the tree. It is measured by the percentage of the main stem that is covered and not visible.

| Name | Percentage of main stem not covered Density | | |
	Heavy	Medium	Light
Red Cedar	90 to 100	70 to 90	50 to 70
Balsam Fir	80 to 100	60 to 80	40 to 60
Douglas Fir	90 to 100	70 to 90	50 to 70
Fraser Fir	70 to 100	50 to 70	40 to 50
Red Fir	60 to 100	50 to 60	40 to 50
White Fir	70 to 100	50 to 70	40 to 50
Grand Fir	80 to 100	60 to 80	40 to 60
Noble Fir	60 to 100	50 to 60	40 to 50
Red Pine	70 to 100	60 to 70	40 to 60
Scotch Pine	90 to 100	70 to 90	50 to 70
Virginia Pine	90 to 100	70 to 90	50 to 70
White Pine	90 to 100	70 to 90	50 to 70
Spruce (all)	80 to 100	60 to 80	40 to 60

MINOR DEFECTS

Slight uneven density. Slight, visible crook in the main stem (4 inches or less from the vertical). Slight insect or disease damage. One broken whorl branch near the main stem. Slight physical damage. Slight amount of foreign material or vines. Multiple leader stems. Branch over 10 inches longer than other branches on corresponding whorl. Slightly abnormal curling of needles. Less than ¼ of branches are missing in a given whorl. Only a slight loss of needles.

NOTICEABLE DEFECTS

Moderately uneven density. Main stem visibly curved more than 4 but less than 6 inches from vertical. Moderate insect or disease damage. Broken leader or more than 1 broken whorl branch adjacent main stem. Moderate physical damage. Moderate amount of foreign material or vines. Crows nest. Moderately abnormal curling of needles. Weak lower branches affecting up to ¾ of branches on bottom whorl. Handle not proportional to height of tree. One fourth but less than ½ of the branches are missing in a given whorl. Hole in the tree or space considerably out of proportion with the uniform branch characteristics of the balance of the tree.

Source:
Agricultural Marketing Service, USDA, "United States Standards for Grades of Christmas Trees," 7 CFR Sections 51.3085 to 51.3105 (1992), Washington: Government Printing Office.

Fertilizer

FERTILIZER GRADE

The minimum guarantee of available plant food expressed in terms of total nitrogen (not ammonia), available phosphoric acid or phosphorus, and soluble potash or potassium. The numerals—nitrogen(N), available phosphoric acid (P_2O_5) and soluble potash (K_2O), or available phosphorus (P) and soluble potassium (K)—appearing as the grade must coincide with the guaranteed analysis statement. Only one set of numerals may be used in the grade designation.

TERMINOLOGY

Acid Forming Fertilizer. Capable of increasing the residual acidity of soil.

Bulk Fertilizer. Fertilizer delivered to the purchaser either in solid or liquid state in a non-package form to which a label cannot be attached.

Coated Slow Release Fertilizer. A product containing sources of water soluble nutrients, the release of which is controlled by a coating applied to the fertilizer.

Composting. The biological decomposition of organic matter. It may be accomplished by mixing and piling in such a way to promote aerobic and/or anaerobic decay. The process inhibits pathogens, viable weed seeds, and odors.

Fertilizer. Any material or mixture which supplies the necessary plant nutrients—usually nitrogen, phosphorus, and potash.

Fertilizer Analysis. The percentage by weight of the components found in a fertilizer. For example, a fertilizer with a 10-6-4 analysis contains 10 percent nitrogen (N), 6 percent phosphoric acid (P_2O_5) and 4 percent potash (K_2O).

Fertilizer Formula. The quantity and grade of the crude stock materials used in making a fertilizer mixture.

Fertilizer Grade. The guaranteed minimum analysis of the major plant nutrients found in a fertilizer.

Fertilizer Ratio. A ratio of the basic weights of the major nutrients found in a fertilizer. For example, a fertilizer having an analysis of 18-6-6 would have a 3:1:1 ratio, or 3 parts of N to 1 part of P and 1 part K.

Filler. A substance added to fertilizer materials to provide bulk, prevent caking, or serve some purpose other than providing essential plant nutrients.

Granular Fertilizer. One in which 95 percent or more of the product is retained on a series of sieves within the range of U.S. No. 4 (4.75 mm opening) to and including U.S. No. 20 (0.850 mm opening), and in which the largest particle passes through a sieve having an opening not larger than four times that of the sieve which retains 95 percent or more of the product.

Liquid Fertilizer. A fluid in which the plant nutrients are in true solution.

Natural Inorganic Fertilizer. A mineral nutrient source that exists in or is produced by nature and may be altered from its original.

Natural Organic Fertilizer. Materials derived from either plant or animal products containing one or more elements (other than carbon, hydrogen, and oxygen) which are essential for plant growth. These materials may be subjected to biological degradation processes under normal conditions of aging, rainfall, sun-curing, air-drying, composting, rotting, enzymatic, or anaerobic/aerobic bacterial action, or any combination of these. These materials shall not be mixed with synthetic material or changed in any physical or chemical manner from their initial state except by manipulations—such as dying, cooking, chopping, shredding, ashing, hydrolysis, or pelleting.

Non-Acid Forming Fertilizer. Not capable of increasing the residual acidity of the soil.

Organic Fertilizer. A material containing carbon and one or more elements other than hydrogen and oxygen essential for plant growth.

Pelletized Fertilizer. A form, uniform is size and usually of globular shape, containing one or more nutrients produced by one of several methods, including (a) solidification of a melt while falling through a countercurrent stream of air, (b) dried layers of slurry applied to recycling particles, (c) compaction, (d) extrusion, and (e) granulation.

Polymer Coated Fertilizer. A coated slow release fertilizer consisting of fertilizer particles coated with a polymer (plastic) resin. It is a source of slowly available plant nutrients.

Primary Nutrients. These include the following plant foods: Nitrogen (N); available phosphoric acid (P_2O_5) or phosphorus (P); and soluble potash (K_2O) or potassium (K).

Secondary and Micro Plant Nutrients. Those other than the primary nutrients that are essential for the normal growth of plants and that may need to be added to the growth medium. Secondary plant nutrients include calcium, magnesium, and sulfur; micro plant nutrients include boron, chlorine, cobalt, copper, iron, manganese, molybdenum, sodium, and zinc.

Slurry Fertilizer. A fluid mixture that contains dissolved and undissolved plant nutrient materials and requires continuous mechanical agitation to assure homogeneity.

Suspension Fertilizer. A fluid containing dissolved and undissolved plant nutrients. The suspension of the undissolved plant nutrients may be inherent with the materials or produced with the aid of a suspending agent of nonfertilizer properties. Mechanical agitation may be necessary in some cases to facilitate uniform suspension of undissolved plant nutrients.

Synthetic. Any substance generated from another material or materials by means of a chemical reaction.

Unit. 20 pounds of plant food or 1 percent of a ton.

Source:
"Official Terms and Definitions," *Official Publication Number 45*, Raleigh, NC: Association of American Plant Food Control Officials.

Gladiolus Bulbs

These standards apply to corms (bulbs) of the genus *Gladiolus* that are characteristically flattened in shape, consisting of solid corms (bulbs) propagated by a new corm which grows on top of the old corm (bulb) or by cormels (bulblets) which form between the old and new corms. (See Figure I.) To allow for variations in quality caused by grading and handling, a percentage of the bulbs may fail to meet all of the requirements of the grade.

SIZE

Size	Diameter (in.) Min.	Max.	Circumference (cm) Min.	Max.
Jumbo	Over 1¾		Over 14	
1	1½	1¾	12	14
2	1¼	1½	10	12
3	1	1¼	8	10
4	¾	1	6	8
5	½	¾	4	6
6	¼	½	2	4
7	under ¼		under 2	
Large	1⅛	1¾	10	14
Medium	¾	1¼	6	10
Small	¼	¾	2	6

GRADES

U.S. Fancy. Gladiolus corms which are mature (firm with a well-healed base scar and dry neck) and well cured; well filled (compact and plump); clean; and well trimmed (the tops are not more than 1 inch in length). They are free from mold, shattered corms, thrips, freezing, nut sedge, grass roots, rogues, and decay. They are free from damage by any means.

U.S. No. 1. Gladiolus corms which meet the requirements of *U.S. Fancy*, except for increased tolerances for defects.

U.S. Fancy Mixture. Gladiolus corms which meet the requirements of *U.S. Fancy*, except for rogues (a distinctly different cultivar from that labeled for the entire lot).

Source:
Agricultural Marketing Service, "United States Standards for Grades of Gladiolus Corms (Bulbs)," 7 CFR Sections 51.4240 to 51.4246 (1992), Washington: Government Printing Office.

Grass Seed

There are many species of grasses, but only a few are well-adapted to turf areas. Each grass has its own texture, color, growth characteristics, and maintenance levels. Some grasses perform exceptionally well under a wide variety of conditions, while others are restricted to specific situations. One grass might be excellent in shade, while another might be the answer in full sunlight. For these reasons, many grasses are blended so that the best of each can contribute to the overall vitality and beauty of the lawn.

However, some grasses do not perform well in blends. Bentgrass, for instance, tends to dominate a mixture and forms extensive patches—on golf greens, it is ideal. Coarse grasses such as Tall Fescue can make an acceptable grass alone; but, unless it dominates a mixture, it can form unsightly clumps. Grasses must be blended properly, or the resulting lawn can become an endless source of dissatisfaction. Once a problem grass is established, it may be practically impossible to eradicate.

On each seed package is an analysis label containing important information about the seed itself. A typical seed label appears below:

FINE-TEXTURED GRASSES
90% Common Kentucky Bluegrass   80% Germination
COARSE KINDS - None Claimed
OTHER INGREDIENTS
1.69% Crop
7.96% Inert Matter
0.35% Weed Seed
120 Sheep Sorrel seeds per pound

An analysis of this label revels the following information:

Purity. The percent by weight of each component. Purity is an indication of quantity, not quality. All Pure seeds are not capable of growth. In the above label, the component Common Kentucky Bluegrass makes up 90 percent of the package. The remaining 10 percent is material that was not removed from the seed.

Germination. The 80 percent germination listed above represents the percentage of pure seed (90 percent) which is capable of growth. All seeds do not germinate at the same rate. Therefore, plants which are slower to emerge in the laboratory stand a lesser chance of surviving under less than ideal conditions.

Pure Live Seed. By multiplying the purity percentage by the germination, the amount of seed actually capable of growth can be determined. (90% x 80% = 72% Pure Live Seed.)

Crop. The 1.69 percent crop listed in the label could be Bentgrass, clover, Tall Fescue, or Timothy, the percent by weight of seeds grown as an agricultural crop. It must be specified by name if in excess of 5 percent by weight. Bentgrass and Tall Fescue, by themselves, would be listed as a crop, but they are undesirable in a Bluegrass lawn. If 2 percent crop was Bentgrass, this would be equal to 181,000 seeds per pound. By weight, 1.69 percent of the package is seed that is undesirable when blended with Common Kentucky Bluegrass.

Inert. The 7.95 percent inert listed on the label is any substance not capable of growth. It could be broken seed which could not be cleaned out, or it might be a filler added to take up space. When multiplied by 2 (to determine volume), it could represent 15-20 percent of the package which will not grow under any conditions.

Weeds. The .35 percent weed is the weight of undesirable (generally broadleafed) plants which were not cleaned out. By being unidentified, the difficulty or ease of control is not pointed out. One harmless Needlegrass seed weighs the same as 32 obnoxious Chickweed seeds. Both would be listed as 0.27 percent on the package. If 0.1 percent weed was Chickweed, this would be equal to 560,000 plants in 10,000 sq. ft. lawn.

Noxious Weeds. The number per pound or per ounce of weed seeds (such as Sheep Sorrel) considered undesirable by a state because they are difficult to control with weed controls and proper cultural practices. Most noxious weeds are problems in farm fields, but not in home lawns. *Poa annua* is extremely undesirable in lawns, but only considered as noxious in a few states. Even when labeled, consumers often do not recognize it as a problem since it would be called Annual Bluegrass.

SEED COUNT

Grass seed varieties are listed on the seed label under two broad classifications: (a) Coarse Textured Grasses (Tall Fescue), and (b) Fine Textured Grasses (Bluegrass). Within these categories are many grasses which vary greatly in number of seeds per pound. It is extremely important to remember that seed varieties listed on a package are listed by weight and not by seed count. While it only takes 226,800 Ryegrass seeds to make a pound, Highland Bentgrass requires 9,072,000. The difference in seed size and weight accounts for the tremendous variation in the actual number of seeds per pound. Ryegrass seeds are fairly large and heavy, while Bentgrass seeds are very small and light.

The importance of seed count should always be considered when analyzing a seed label. For instance, assume that a seed blend was 80 percent Kentucky Bluegrass and 20 percent Highland Bentgrass. These two grasses do not make a good blend, but because the Bentgrass is in such small proportion, this *appears* to be a fairly good mixture. By calculating actual seed count, a pound of this blend would have 1,714,824 Bluegrass seeds and 1,814,400 seeds of Highland Bentgrass. In other words, even though the percentage of Bentgrass appears insignificant on the label, it actually comprises over 50 percent of the mixture. Avoiding undesirable grasses will eliminate future problems. This can be achieved by learning the fundamentals of seed label analysis.

TERMINOLOGY

Acidity (Acid Soil). A soil which has a pH below 7.0.

Aerification (Aeration). When referring to lawns, the process of improving the movement of air, water, and nutrients into the soil by removing thatch, slicing the soil, or removing plugs of soil.

Algae. Microscopic plants generally found growing on the soil surface in areas of poor sunlight, poor drainage, or low fertility.

Alkalinity (Alkaline Soil). A soil which has a pH above 7.0.

Alternate. An orderly growth with a leaf or seed arranged first on one side and then the other, along a stem or spike.

Ammoniacal. An immediate release source of nitrogen used in some fertilizers.

Analysis. The statement on a package listing the ingredients and their percentage by weight.

Annual. Any plant which germinates, matures, produces seed, and dies within one growing season.

Asexual. Without sex. Propagation is by sod, stolons, or offshoots.

Auricles. Projecting arms of a grass leaf, located at the collar, which may or may not clasp the stem.

Axil. The point where the leaf grows from the stem.

Bahiagrass. A coarse-textured, warm-season grass which spreads by tillers and some *rhizomes.* (See entry.)

Barrier. A chemical boundary located below the soil surface to prevent the germination or growth of undesirable plants.

Bentgrass. A cool season grass of fine to medium texture which grows from *stolons.* (See entry.)

Bermudagrass. A grass of fine to medium texture which grows from vigorous *rhizomes* and *stolons.* (See entries.)

Biennial. A plant which completes its life cycle in two years. Forms a rosette the first season and produces flowers and seeds the second.

Blade. The wide or expanded part of a grass leaf extending from the sheath.

Bluegrass. A cool season grass of medium-fine texture, reproducing vegetatively by *rhizomes* and *tillers.* (See entries.)

Broad-Leaved. Referring to dicot plants which emerge from the seed with two leaves.

Bud. The underdeveloped state of a stem or flower generally covered with overlapping leaves.

Bulb. A thickened or fleshy underground stem usually made up of overlapping food-storing scales.

Capillary Action. Movement of water and nutrients between soil particles and between the cells of any organism.

Capsule. A closed receptacle, containing seeds, composed of two or more parts.

Carrier. The material added to a product to facilitate its distribution.

Centipedegrass. A coarse-textured, *stoloniferous* (see entry) grass which grows best on acid soil.

Certified Seed. Seed grown under inspection by a certifying agency and, when mature, approved as to its genetic identity, purity, and high quality standards.

Chaff. The husks of grain or other waste material separated from pure seed during cleaning.

Chlorophyll. The green pigment in plants which is vital for photosynthesis.

Chlorosis. The result of poor *chlorophyll* (see entry) production in green plants, which causes a yellowish color.

Clay Soil. Indicates a soil type consisting of clay as ⅔ to ¾ of the content.

Clone. A clump of grass having the same genetic makeup.

Clusters. The grouping of flowers or leaves on a plant.

Collar. A narrow band marking the place where the blade and the sheath join.

Compacted Soil. A condition where the soil particles are packed tightly together, forcing out all air and moisture.

Compost. A decomposed mixture of plant and animal waste to which lime, fertilizer, or soil may have been added.

Contact Herbicide. A herbicide that kills weeds by direct contact rather than by *translocation* (see entry).

Contaminant. Any undesirable plant in turf or undesirable seeds in a blend.

Control. To limit population and spread of a pest to tolerable levels.

Conversion. Gradually changing an old turf into turf of a more desirable grass without total renovation.

Cotyledon. The first leaf, or leaves, that emerge from the seed plant.

Crop. A term used on a seed label—meaning any plant grown for profit.

Crown. The above-ground base of a grass plant from which all growth begins.

Culm. The stem of grasses and sedges.

Cultivar. A variety of plants, which retain their distinguishing features when reproduced.

Cultivate. Preparing the soil for seeding.

Debris. When used in a lawn or garden context, the accumulation of unwanted material in turf or seed bed.

Decay (Decompose). The breakdown of living matter into chemical forms.

Dentrification. The biochemical reduction of nitrogen in the nitrate or nitrate forms to elemental nitrogen.

Density. In referring to a lawn, the thickness of turf measured by the number of plants in a given area.

Desiccation. The drying out of turf—usually used in reference to *winter desiccation*—when there is lack of snow cover to protect the turf from drying winds.

Dichondra. A vining, broadleaf plant which is used successfully as a ground cover in California.

Dicot (Dicotyledon). A plant emerging from the seed with two leaves.

Disease. In referring to a lawn, a condition caused by parasitic organisms, resulting in damage to the grass plant.

Disease Organism. The parasite (usually a fungus) which causes injurious effects to a grass plant.

Disease Tolerance. The ability of a plant to resist a disease.

Dormant. A reduction of growth and other normal life functions of perennial plants caused by stress or seasonal changes.

Dry Wilt. A condition caused by a lack of moisture in the soil.

Duff. An organic layer consisting of partially decomposed vegetative matter such as leaves, roots, stems, and stolons.

Ecology. The study of the inter-relationships of organisms to one another and to the environment.

Environment. All the external conditions which affect the growth of an organism.

Epidemic. A disease outbreak among a population at one time.

Epidermis. The outermost layer of cells or tissue of a plant.

Erosion. The wearing away of the soil by wind, water, or ice.

Eutrophication. A condition occurring in bodies of water where the water is deficient in oxygen and aquatic plants are abundant. This process is accelerated by the surface runoff of nutrients such as nitrogen and phosphorus.

Evaporation. The process by which a liquid is changed to a vapor or gaseous form.

Evapotranspiration. Water transpired by plants plus that which has evaporated from the soil.

Field Capacity. The remaining water content of a soil after it has been saturated and drained for a specific length of time.

Fescue. Cool season grasses of fine and coarse textures reproducing vegetatively by tillers or rhizomes.

Foliage. The leaf covering of a plant.

Fungi. Plants lacking chlorophyll that cannot produce their own food; parasitic forms cause turf diseases.

Fungicide. Any chemical which controls or destroys the growth of a fungus.

Germination. The beginning of visible growth of a plant as it emerges from the seed.

Ground Cover. A low-growing plant used in place of turf, e.g., *dichondra* (see entry), an ivy.

Grub. The larva stage of various beetles, one of the insect invaders of turf.

Guard Cells. A pair of cells which regulate the opening and closing of the *stoma* (see entry).

Habit (Growth). The general pattern or style of plant growth.

Habitat. The environment which supplies the needs for plant or animal life.

Herbicide. A chemical used to destroy or inhibit plant growth.

Humus. Decomposed organic matter.

Hybrid. A plant produced by the crossing of two species with different characteristics.

Hygroscopic. Refers to a condition where water is held so tightly by soil particles that it is unavailable to plants.

Hyphae. A thread of fungal growth.

Impregnate. To force particles of one substance between the particles of another.

Inert. Any substance which does not take an active part in a chemical reaction. When used on a seed label, anything in a seed blend that is not classified as a seed.

Infestation. The spread of harmful weeds, diseases, or insects in a lawn.

Inflorescence. The flower cluster of a plant and its mode of arrangement.

Inorganic. Natural or synthetic elements or chemicals of non-living material.

Insecticide. Any chemical which destroys insects.

Insoluble. Any chemical which cannot be dissolved by a given liquid.

Internode. The portion of a stem or other plant parts between two nodes.

Irregular. An arrangement of leaves, stems, or seeds which have no pattern or uniform order.

Larva. The immature, wormlike stage of insect development.

Lateral Growth. The sideward, rather than upward, growth of a plant or leaves.

LD. The lethal dose of a pesticide. An *LD 50* indicates a lethal dose that will kill 50 percent of a given population of test animals under stated conditions.

Leaching. The removal of materials in solution by the passage of water through soil.

Lesion. A scar or mark on a plant caused by a disease or injury.

Ligule. An upright projection of tissue at the junction of the blade and sheath of a grass leaf.

Lime. Generally refers to calcium oxide (CaO) in various forms, including ground limestone (calcium carbonate), hydrated lime (hydroxides), and burnt lime (calcium oxide).

Loam. A soil which is made up of sand, *silt* (see entry) and clay.

Lobe. A rounded or divided segment of a leaf.

Maintenance. When referring to a lawn, the upkeep or care of turf.

Margin. The edge or border of a leaf or blade.

Mat. The interwining of stems, leaves, or *stolons* (either living or dead) at or below the soil surface.

Methylene Ureas. A term used to describe a ureaformaldehyde polymer whose structural characteristics control the solubility of nitrogen, and therefore, its rate of release.

Microorganism. Any of a range of small-sized organisms ranging from protozoa and bacteria to fungi.

Midrib (Midvein). The central or main rib or vein of a leaf.

Monocot. Any plant emerging from the seed with only one leaf, such as grass.

Moss. A low-growing, simple plant found in shady, moist areas of turf generally lacking in sunlight, drainage, and fertility.

Mulch. A covering, such as straw, used to protect seedlings, preserve moisture, and prevent erosion.

Mutation. A genetic change in an offspring which results in distinct permanent characteristics that differ from those of the parent.

Mycelium. The mass of interwoven, threadlike filaments of a fungus growing in and among grass blades.

Net Venation. The veins of a broadleaf plant branching in all directions to form a net-like pattern.

Nitrification. The soil process by which nitrites are changed to nitrates through the aid of bacteria.

Nitrogen (N). One of three major nutrients necessary for healthy plant growth. Used by the plant for chlorophyll production and plant and leaf growth.

Nitrogen Availability Index (NAI). The percentage of water-insoluble nitrogen which becomes available to the plant in 1 to 4 weeks. The higher the NAI, the more rapid release of nitrogen.

Node. The joint where the leaf is attached to the stem.

Noxious Weed. Any plant which has been declared by law to be harmful or dangerous.

Nutlet. A small, reproductive growth on the roots of sedges and other plants.

Nutrient. Any food or material that nourishes or promotes plant growth.

Nymph. The immature stage in the life cycle of certain insects.

Opposite. Two leaves at a node growing across from one another.

Organic. Any substance formed from decaying living matter.

Osmosis. An interchange of materials between two solutions which are separated by a semi-permeable membrane.

Overseed. Seeding into a thin, existing turf.

Panicle. An irregularly branched and rebranched flower cluster.

Parallel Venation. Principal veins of a leaf parallel to each other and to the longitudinal axis of the leaf.

Parasite. An organism which takes its food from the living tissues of a host organism.

Pathogen. An organism causing a disease.

Peat. Partially decomposed organic matter entering the first stage of coal formation.

Percolation. When used in a gardening context, the movement of water through the soil.

Pesticide. Any chemical agent used to control pests. This would include *fungicides, herbicides, insecticides, nematocides*, etc.

Petiole. The stalk which supports the leaf.

Phosphorus (P$_2$O$_5$). One of the three major plant nutrients necessary for healthy growth. Used in root growth, plant development and seed formation.

Photosynthesis. The process by which plants containing chlorophyll convert sunlight, carbon dioxide, and water into chemical energy for their own use.

Plugging. A method of starting a turf area by inserting small cores of grasses at given intervals.

Post-Emergence Control. Applying a herbicide which destroys a growing plant.

Potash (K$_2$O). One of three major plant nutrients necessary for overall healthy growth.

Pre-Emergence Control. Applying a herbicide which prevents the germination or growth of a plant.

Protoplasm. The life-giving substance of all organisms.

Pupa. The intermediate stage of insect development between the larva and adult.

Purity. The percent, by weight, of pure seed of each component in the seed blend.

Pustules. A small blister-like elevation found on grass blades and generally associated with fungi.

Renovate. When referring to a lawn, to rebuild turf using an existing turf as the seedbed.

Residual. The length of time a chemical remains effective after application.

Resilience. The ability of a grass blade to return to an upright position after bending.

Respiration. A process by which living plants and animals use oxygen for metabolism. This term is often mistaken for inhaling or the breathing of oxygen.

Rhizome (Rootstock). The underground stem which is capable of producing a new plant.

Roguing. The physical removal of unwanted plants from seed fields.

Root System. The underground downward growth of a plant; it anchors the plant to the soil and absorbs moisture and nutrients from the soil for use by the entire plant.

Root Zone. The area of the soil where roots develop, grow, and mature.

Rosette. A plant having a circular cluster of leaves.

Ryegrass. Annual or perennial types of cool-season grasses of fine and coarse textures.

St. Augustine. A coarse-textured, warm-season grass which spreads by stolons.

Salt Tolerance. The ability of a plant to withstand salt water or salt-laden soil.

Sandy Soil. A broad term used to indicate a soil type with ⅔ to ¾ sand.

Saprophyte. An organism which lives on a host without taking food from it.

Saturation. A condition when soil is holding its total capacity of water.

Scalp. When referring to a lawn, to cut the turf from the soil, to mow overly close, or to cut into the grass crowns.

Sedge. A family of plants resembling grass, but having a solid triangular stem.

Seed. The reproductive structure of a plant containing the embryo (young plant), food supply, and protective coat.

Seed Bed. Soil that is properly tilled and prepared for seeding.

Seed Coat. The outer layer of the seed structure which holds the embryo and food supply and protects the young plant until germination.

Seed Count. The number of seeds in a pound.

Seedpod. A dried case or capsule containing a seed or seeds.

Selective Herbicide. A weed killer capable of controlling one type of weed without damaging other types of plants.

Serrated. The saw-toothed pattern on the margin of a leaf.

Sessile. A condition where a plant has flowers or leaves without a stalk.

Sheath. The tubular lower portion of a grass leaf which surrounds the stem.

Silt. A finely textured soil or sediment usually deposited by water.

Sod. The grass-covered surface of the ground.

Soil. The natural medium for plant growth, usually containing inorganic and organic materials.

Soil Amendments. Any material added and worked into the soil to improve productivity.

Soil Porosity. Describes the availability of pores or cavities for nutrient and moisture storage.

Soil Sterilant. A chemical which will destroy all vegetation and seeds in the soil.

Solution. A liquid containing a dissolved substance.

Spatulate. A leaf which gradually widens from the base to a rounded end, resembling a spatula.

Species. A class of organisms having common characteristics designated by a common name.

Spore. The reproductive structure of a fungus functioning as a seed.

Spray Drift. The movement of airborne spray particles from the spray nozzle outside the intended contact area.

Sprigging. Establishing new turf by planting *stolons* (see entry) in the soil.

Stand. A group of plants growing together in one area.

Stem. The part of a plant which develops buds and shoots and supports a leaf or flower.

Stolon (Runner). A *runner* is a stem growing along the soil surface which is capable of taking root and starting a new plant at each node.

Stoloniferous (Creeping). The spreading of plants by stolons.

Stoma. Minute openings for transpiration on the surface of leaves and stems, which are opened and closed by guard cells.

Stress. When referring to a plant, a condition under which a plant suffers due to lack of moisture, food, extreme heat, or any combination of the three.

Sub-Irrigation. Supplying moisture to the root zone from beneath the surface.

Subsoil. The stratum of weathered material that underlies the surface soil.

Surfactant. A material that improves the emulsifying, spreading, wetting, and other surface modifying properties of chemical formulations.

Synthetic. Any material created by artificial means; not from nature.

Syringing. Adding moisture to a plant through the leaf to reduce or prevent water loss and cool the plant.

Systemic Pesticide. A chemical which is absorbed by the plant roots and thus internally prevents disease or insect damage.

Taproot. A long, single, vertical-growing root.

Tensiometer. Instrument used for measuring the pressure of soil water.

Thatch. The accumulation layer of undecomposed plant parts between the living plant parts and the soil surface.

Tillers. A sprout or stalk that forms its own leaves and originates at the base of the parent plant.

Tolerance. When referring to a plant, the degree to which a plant endures a stress.

Top Dressing. A prepared mixture spread over and worked into the turf. It is apt to be formulated of sand, compost, organic matter, and fertilizer.

Topsoil. The upper layer of soil which, ideally, contains rich, fertile, organic matter.

Trace Elements. Small amounts of certain elements essential for healthy plant growth.

Translocate. To move about in the plant in solution.

Transpiration. The exchange of gases and water vapor between the plant and the atmosphere.

Turf. The upper stratum of soil bound by grass and plant roots into a thick mat.

Turgidity. When referring to a plant, the expansive force in a blade, caused by the presence of water, permitting it to stand erect.

Urea. A water-soluble nitrogen compound used in fertilizers made from carbon dioxide and ammonia.

Ureaform (Ureaformaldehyde). A water-insoluble source of nitrogen used in fertilizers. Made by combining heated urea and formaldehyde.

Vascular System. Transports the nutrients and water to all parts of the plant.

Vermiculite. A micaceous mineral silicate which expands with heat and has absorption qualities.

Vertical Mowing. Cutting perpendicular into the turf to lift or cut stolons to control gain, or to remove thatch.

Viable. When referring to a seed, describes one which is capable of germinating.

Vining. Plants whose stems creep along the surface of the ground.

Volatize. The state of changing from a liquid to a gas at ordinary temperatures when exposed to the air.

Weed. Any plant growing where it is not wanted.

Wet Wilt. The inability of a plant to absorb enough moisture through the roots to equal the rapid loss of moisture through the leaves.

Whorl. A circular arrangement of three or more leaves or flowers around a single plant.

Winterkill. Injuries of turf resulting from environmental stresses during the cold part of the year.

Zoysia. A warm-season grass which spreads slowly by *stolons* and *rhizomes* (see entries).

Source:
The Scotts Company, 14111 Scottslawn Road, Marysville, OH, 43041.

Lawn Mowers

Mulching Mower. A lawn mower that holds the clippings in the deck area to be cut several times by the whirling blade. By the time they are discharged, the clippings have been chopped into small pieces. These grass particles easily fall between the growing grass blades and quickly decompose. This alleviates the need to bag the clippings and send them to a landfill.

Source:
Gibson, H.E., "Mulching Mowers," *Flower and Garden,* Vol. 36, no. 3 (June-July 1992): 68-69.

Nursery Products

The term *nursery products* includes all types of trees, small fruit plants, shrubs, vines, ornamentals, herbaceous annuals, biennials and perennials, bulbs, corms, rhizomes, and other products intended for outdoor planting. Not included are florists' or greenhouse products.

Lining-Out Stock. All plant material coming from propagating houses, beds, or frames, and young material (such as seedlings, rooted or unrooted cuttings, grafts, or layers) of suitable size to transplant either in the nursery row or in containers for "growing on."

Nursery-Grown Stock. Plants propagated and grown under cultivation, or plants transplanted from the wild and grown under cultivation, for at least one full growing season.

Source:
Federal Trade Commission, "Guides for the Nursery Industry," 16 CFR Sections 18.0 to 18.8 (1992), Washington: Government Printing Office.

Peonies in the Bud, Cut

GRADES

U.S. No. 1. Peonies of similar varietal characteristics which have fresh, strong, unbroken, and fairly straight stems. The stems are also well trimmed in that all lateral or side buds and all foliage on the lowest 6 to 8 inches of the stem have been neatly removed. The buds are symmetrical (not lopsided or otherwise deformed) and the buds and foliage are bright (not badly wilted, limp, or flabby). The buds are firm and the calyxes have expanded to the extent that the true color of the outer petals is exposed. The buds and stems are free from decay and freezing injury and from damage caused by dirt, discoloration, moisture, disease, insects, mechanical, or other means. Each bud is not less than 1 inch in diameter and, unless otherwise specified, the overall length of bud and stem is not less than 24 inches. However, in no case shall the overall length be less than 20 inches.

U.S. No. 2. Peonies of similar varietal characteristics which have fresh, fairly well trimmed, and unbroken stems that are not badly curved or crooked. The buds are fresh and firm with calyxes normally expanded but not overmature. They are free from puff balls, bull heads, and wood heads. The buds and stems are free from decay and from damage caused by freezing and from serious damage caused by dirt, discoloration, moisture, disease, insects, mechanical, etc. Each bud is not less

than ⅞ inch in diameter; and, unless otherwise specified, the overall length of bud and stem is not less than 20 inches. However, in no case shall the overall length be less than 16 inches.

Unclassified. Peonies which have not been classified in accordance with the foregoing grades. The term *unclassified* is not a grade within the meaning of these standards but is provided as a designation to show that no grade has been applied to the lot.

Source:
Agricultural Marketing Service, "United States Standards for Grades of Cut Peonies," 7 CFR sections 51.4475 to 51.4496 (1992), Washington: Government Printing Office.

Soil Products

The National Bark and Soil Producers Association has developed soil nomenclature & labeling guidelines for the purpose of (1) establishing industry labeling and nomenclature guidelines for organic soil products by defining those products that are most commonly produced and sold to the lawn and garden and horticulture markets in the United States, (2) promoting uniform and informative labeling of product contents, and (3) identifying for the consumer those products that provide an acceptable growing medium for plant materials. In order to quality for the licensing of the NBSPA product certification logo mark (see entry *Bark Products*) each licensee must agree to comply with the following soil product labeling guidelines:
• Product names, soil characteristics, and label terminology must conform to the product definitions of the guideline.
• Product names that incorporate or refer to a single specific material must be comprised of 100 percent of that material.
• Product names that list a specific material as "First mentioned" among other materials must be comprised of more than 50 percent of that product by volume.
• Product names that list a component material or materials on other than a first-mentioned basis must be comprised of at least 10 percent of the named materials by volume and such materials shall be listed in the name in the declining order of their volume content.
• Product names which indicate a specific animal manure by name, picture, graphic, drawing, or other means (e.g., cow, sheep, poultry, etc.) shall contain more than 50 percent of that specific animal manure as part of its total manure content by volume.
• A product label shall appear on each product bag. Product labels shall list the component materials of a product in declining order by present of volume, except that all materials that are less then 2 percent of total product volume, individually, shall be grouped together under the category *other trace materials,* and the specific percentage of product volume of each listed material need not be given on the product label.

TERMINOLOGY

Compost. Material derived from the biological decomposition of organic matter accomplished by mixing and piling in such a way as to promote aerobic and/or anaerobic decay without synthetic fertilizer materials and adjuncts, other than those used to promote decomposition, and which minimizes pathogens, viable weed seeds, and odors.

Humus. Material suitable for soil conditioning that is derived primarily from the decomposition of animal or vegetable matter.

Manure. Dried, pulverized, shredded, composted, or otherwise processed, manipulated, or treated animal manures are the excreta of animals together with whatever organic bedding or other materials are needed to follow good dairy barn, feedlot, poultry house (etc.) practice in order to maintain proper sanitary conditions, to conserve plant food elements in the excreta, and to absorb the liquid portion without the addition of other material.

Peat. Naturally occurring material suitable for soil conditioning and formed chiefly from the decomposition of organic matter in a water-saturated environment.

Peat Moss. Naturally occurring material formed chiefly from the partial decomposition of moss plants and organic matter in a water-saturated environment.

Planting Mix. A mixed or blended material suitable for holding and growing indoor and/or outdoor plants, and made primarily from natural soils, peat, humus, compost, and/or manure. It may include fertilizer, pesticides, and/or additives intended as soil conditioners (e.g., perlite, vermiculite, sand, peat moss, charcoal).

Potting Soil. Material suitable for holding and growing potted plants and made primarily from natural materials, such as bard, peat, humus, compost, and/or manure. It may include fertilizers, pesticides, and/or additives intended as soil conditioners (e.g., perlite, vermiculite, sand, peat moss, charcoal).

Professional Potting Soil. Material suitable for holding and growing potted plants and made primarily from peat moss, peat, humus, compost, and/or manure. It may include fertilizer, pesticides, and/or additives intended as soil conditioners (e.g., perlite, vermiculite, sand, charcoal). It is a blended product which has a high percentage of sphagnum, vermiculite, and other lightweight materials and is considered a premium quality potting soil with a high porosity.

Sludge. The solid precipitate, resulting from water or sewage treatment processes, that contains human waste matter.

Top Soil. Material suitable for growing outdoor plants, such as grass and shrubs, generally high in organic matter and made chiefly from natural materials—such as soils, peat, humus, compost, and/or manure.

Source:
Nomenclature and Labeling Guidelines for Quality Soil Products, Clifton, VA: National Bark and Soil Producers Association, 1992.

Turfgrass Sod

The American Sod Producers Association has developed the following voluntary standards to assist in providing a common consensus in the sod industry. The ASPA has developed two alternative sets of standards:

GRADES (ALTERNATIVE 1)

No. 1 Quality Premium. The turf is of sufficient density so that no surface soil is visible when mowed to a height of 1½ inches. Maximum mowing height shall be 2½ inches. At the time of sale, the turf shall contain no more than 1 percent undesirable grasses or clover and not more than two weeds per 50 sq. yds.

Commercial Grade. Turfgrass sod being sold as *Commercial Grade* shall meet the density and mowing requirements of No. 1 sod. It may however contain up to 10 percent undesirable grass species and 10 weeds per 50 sq. yds. Any grass other than the species shown on the sales slip shall be deemed as an undesirable. Annual Bluegrass shall be included in this classification.

GRADES (ALTERNATIVE 2)

Premium Grade. Shall contain only the species and variety of turfgrass shown on the sales slip, and no weeds or foreign grasses. It may have no visible signs of disease or insect stress. The turfgrass sod shall be neatly mowed and be mature enough that when grasped at one end, it can be picked up and handled without damage.

Standard Grade. May have no visible broadleaf weeds when viewed from a standing position, and the turf shall be visibly consistent, with no obvious patches of foreign grasses. In no case may the total amount of foreign grasses or weeds exceed 2 percent of the total canopy. The turfgrass sod shall be neatly mowed and be mature enough that when grasped at one end it can be picked up and handled without damage.

Commercial Grade. Any turfgrass sod which fails to meet the *Standard Grade* specifications.

TERMINOLOGY

Approved Turfgrass Sod. Superior sod grown from approved seed of known origin or from plantings of approved grass certified sod. It is inspected by the official certification agency of the state to assure overall high quality and freedom from noxious weeds as well as excessive amounts of other crop and weedy plants at time of harvest. It may be either one variety or composed of a mixture of two or more varieties or species. However, all seed or original plant material in a mixture must be approved.

Bluegrass Blend. Seeded using a blend of two or more varieties of Kentucky Bluegrass. The names of these varieties and the percentages in the original seed blend should be available on request.

Certified Turfgrass Sod. Superior sod grown from certified, high-quality seed of known origin or from plantings of certified grass seedlings or stolons. It is inspected by the certification agency of the state to assure satisfactory genetic identity and purity, overall high quality, and freedom from noxious weeds as well as excessive amounts of other crop and weedy plants at time of harvest. It may be of either one variety or composed of a mixture of two or more varieties or species. However, all seed or original plant material in a mixture must be certified. The turfgrass sod must meet the published state standards for certification.

Field Turfgrass Sod. This class of sod may include all sod not covered in the above classes. It may consist of sod lifted from pastures or meadows, which may have been grown primarily for forages. May also be termed *Pasture Turfgrass Sod*.

Mineral Sod. In some geographic areas, the soil types may be termed *mineral, muck, peat,* or *organic,* in reference to the basic composition of the farm's soil. When combined with turfgrass sod, the product may be called *Mineral Sod, Muck Sod, Peat Sod,* or *Organic Sod*. While this may cause some initial confusion, the overall condition of the turfgrass sod and its basic classification, as defined above, are generally considered to be of much greater importance. These terms do not refer to the class of turfgrass sod.

Nursery Turfgrass Sod. Any turfgrass sod planted on cultivated agricultural land and grown specifically for sod purposes. It shall have been mowed regularly and carefully and otherwise maintained from planting to harvest to maintain reasonable quality and uniformity. May also be termed *Cultivated Turfgrass Sod*.

Pasture Sod. Any turfgrass sod that has not been sown and maintained as a nursery sod crop.

Variety. Any turfgrass sod in which one variety of any species makes up an excess of 90 percent of the turf shall be sold as that variety. Any turfgrass sod grown from a mixture of turfgrass species, such as Kentucky Bluegrass and fine leafed Fescue, shall be labeled as such and the species identified. Percentages by weight of each sown variety shall be available on request.

Source:

Guideline Specifications to Turfgrass Sodding, Rolling Meadows, IL: American Sod Producers Association, revised 1988.

Food
Overview

Acidified Foods

Acidulants or acidifiers are acids that many foods use as flavor-enhancing agents, as preservatives to inhibit growth of microorganisms, as antioxidants to prevent discoloration or rancidity, and to adjust the acidity in some foods.

Acid Foods. Foods that have a natural pH of 4.6 or below.

Low-Acid Foods. Foods, other than alcoholic beverages, with a finished equilibrium pH greater than 4.6 and a water activity (a_w) greater than 0.85. However, tomatoes and tomato products having a finished equilibrium pH less than 4.7 are not classified as low-acid foods.

Acidified Foods. Low-acid foods to which acid(s) or acid food(s) are added; these foods include, but are not limited to, beans, cucumbers, cabbage, artichokes, cauliflower, puddings, peppers, tropical fruits, and fish. They have a water activity greater than 0.85 and a finished equilibrium pH of 4.6 or below. These foods may be called *pickles* or *pickled* _____.

Water Activity (a_w). A measure of the free moisture in a product, and it is the quotient of the water vapor pressure of the substance divided by the vapor pressure of pure water at the same temperature.

Source:
Food and Drug Administration, "Acidified Foods," 21 CFR part 114 (1991), Washington: Government Printing Office.

Contains Sulfites

Sulfites are a group of food preservatives that retard the spoilage and discoloration of numerous foods and beverages and may occur naturally in some foods and beverages. Sulfites are also used to preserve certain prescription medications and drugs that are given intravenously. The Food and Drug Administration (FDA) has determined that sulfites may cause breathing difficulties or even death, especially among people with asthma. For that reason, the FDA requires any packaged food containing detectable quantities of sulfites to be labeled as containing sulfites on the ingredient label. Foods in grocery stores and restaurants are no longer permitted to contain sulfites, except for grapes and potatoes, which are currently being reviewed and require labels on the grocery shelf.

SULFITING AGENTS IN MEAT PRODUCTS

The presence of sulfiting agents (sulfur dioxide, sodium sulfite, sodium bisulfite, potassium bisulfite, sodium metabisulfite, and potassium metabisulfite) in or on sulfite labeling ingredients used in the preparation of meat or poultry food products must be declared on the label of the product if the concentration of sulfiting agent(s) in the finished food is 10ppm or higher. However, some finished meat and poultry food products may be comprised of multiple separable components, e.g., potatoes or apple cobbler in frozen dinner. For these products, if a separable component contains 10ppm or more sulfiting agent(s), the sulfiting agent(s) must be declared even though the total product contains less than 10ppm of sulfiting agent(s).

Sources:
Harte, John, Cheryl Holdren, Richard Schneider, Christine Shirley, *Toxics A to Z: A Guide to Everyday Pollution Hazards,* Berkeley, Los Angeles and Oxford: University of California Press, 1991.

Lecos, Chris W., "An Order of Fries—Hold the Sulfites," *FDA Consumer,* Vol. 22, no. 2 (March 1988): 9-11.

Standards and Labeling Division, Food Safety and Inspection Service, USDA, *Standards and Labeling Policy Book,* Washington: Government Printing Office, June 1991.

Dating Terms

Expiration Date. The final date one should eat a food. Infant formulas have an expiration date.

Freshness Date. Similar to the expiration date, but safety is not an issue. Bakery products often have a freshness date.

Pack Date. The day the food was packaged. Most foods have coded pack dates for the manufacturer's information in case of product recall.

Pull or Sell Date. This is the final date the product should be sold. It allows for some storage time at home. Refrigerated dough products, luncheon meats, and milk have sell dates.

Source:
Labels: The Buyer's Guide to Healthful Foods (pamphlet), Chicago: The American Dietetic Association, 1989.

Dietary Fiber

Comprised of components of plant materials that are resistant to human digestive enzymes. These components are predominantly nonstarch polysaccharides and lignin and may include, in addition, associated substances. To date, the best documented and most widely accepted nutritional role for dietary fibers is for normal bowel function and health. It is estimated that current dietary fiber intakes of 10 to 15 grams per day (6 to 7 grams per 1000 kilocalories) in the United States are less than optimal for meeting needs for normal bowel function and health.

Naturally occurring fibers in food are usually a mixture of insoluble fibers, such as cellulose and lignin; soluble fibers, such as pectins, gums, and mucilages; and combinations of soluble and insoluble fibers, such as hemicelluloses. The proportions and types of fiber subcomponents vary among foods, e.g., oatmeal contains relatively large amounts of soluble fiber, while whole wheat bread contains relatively large amounts of insoluble fiber. Fiber content also varies within a food item or food group depending on maturity of the plant, storage and ripening conditions, and food processing techniques used, if any.

DIETARY FIBER AND CANCER

The FDA has tentatively found that a basis does not exist on which to authorize the use on foods, including dietary supplements, of health claims relating to an association between ingestion of dietary fiber and reduction in risk of cancer. While data support an association between consumption of fiber-rich plant foods and reduced risk of cancer, the FDA tentatively finds that it cannot attribute this effect to the fiber itself.

DIETARY FIBER AND CARDIOVASCULAR DISEASE

The FDA has tentatively found that a basis does not exist on which to authorize the use on foods, including dietary supplements, of health claims relating to the association between dietary fiber and cardiovascular disease. While an association appears to exist between consumption of fiber-rich foods and reduced risk of cardiovascular disease, the FDA tentatively finds that it cannot attribute this effect to the fiber itself.

Source:
"Fiber: Something Healthy to Chew On," *FDA Consumer* (June 1985).

Dietary Supplements

Any vitamin and/or mineral preparation offered in tablet, capsule, wafer, or other similar uniform unit form; in powder, granule, flake, or liquid form; or in the physical form of a conventional food but which is not a conventional food; and which purports or is represented to be for special dietary use by humans to supplement their diets by increasing the total dietary intake of one or more of the essential vitamins and/or minerals.

Source:
Consumer Product Safety Commission, "Poison Prevention Packaging," 16 CFR 1700, 1992: Washington, Government Printing Office.

Fat Substitutes

Fat substitutes are designed to replace the fat in foods. Simplesse was the first fat substitute approved by the Food and Drug Administration. It is a product of the NutraSweet Company, a subsidiary of Monsanto Company of St. Louis, Missouri. (NutraSweet also makes aspartame, the sugar substitute widely used in low-calorie beverages and other products.) Simplesse is made from egg white and milk protein which are blended and heated in a process called microparticulation—the protein is shaped into microscopic round particles that roll easily over one another. The aim of the process is to create the feel of a creamy liquid with the texture of fat. On February 23, 1990, the FDA affirmed Simplesse as "generally recognized as safe" (GRAS) for use as a thickener or texturizer in frozen desert products. Approval for use in other products is pending. Simplesse cannot be used in cooking because baking or frying causes it to lose its creaminess.

Source:
Segal, Marian, "Fat Substitutes, A Taste of the Future," a pamphlet reprinted from the December 1990 issue of *Consumer Magazine,* DHHS Publication No. (FDA) 91-2245, Washington: Government Printing Office.

Food Additives

In the broadest sense, a food additive is any substance added to food. Legally the term refers to "any substance the intended use of which results or may reasonably be expected to result—directly or indirectly—in its becoming a component or otherwise affecting the characteristics of any food." This definition includes any substance used in the production, processing, treatment, packaging, transportation, or storage of food. Sucrose, corn syrup, dextrose, salt, black pepper, caramel, carbon dioxide, citric acid, modified starch, sodium bicarbonate, yeast, and yellow mustard account for 95 percent by weight of all additives used in the United States.

Direct Additive. If a substance is added to a food for a specific purpose in that food, it is referred to as a direct additive. For example, the low-calorie sweetener aspartame, which is used in beverages, puddings, yogurt, chewing gum, and other foods, is considered a direct additive. Many direct additives are identified on the ingredient label of foods.

Indirect Food Additives. Those that become part of the food in trace amounts due to its packaging, storage, or other handling. For instance, minute amounts of packaging substances may find their way into foods during storage. Food packaging manufacturers must prove to the U.S. Food and Drug Administration (FDA) that all materials coming in contact with food are safe, before they are permitted for use in such a manner.

Natural Additives. Additives manufactured from natural sources such as soybeans and corn, which provide lecithin to maintain product consistency, or beets, which provide beet powder used as food coloring.

Artificial Additives. Man-made additives that are not found in nature.

USES OF ADDITIVES

To Maintain Product Consistency. *Emulsifiers* give products a consistent texture and prevent them from separating. *Stabilizers* and *thickeners* give smooth uniform texture. *Anticaking agents* help substances, such as salt, to flow freely.

To Improve or Maintain Nutritional Value. Vitamins and minerals are added to many common foods such as milk, flour, cereal, and margarine to make up for those likely to be lacking in a person's diet or lost in processing. All products containing added nutrients must be appropriately labeled.

To Maintain Palatability and Wholesomeness. *Preservatives* retard product spoilage caused by mold, air, bacteria, fungi, or yeast. Bacterial contamination can cause food-born illness, including life-threatening botulism. *Antioxidants* are preservatives that prevent fats and oils in baked goods and other foods from becoming rancid or developing an off-flavor. They also prevent fresh-cut fruits, such as apples, from turning brown when exposed to air.

To Provide Leavening or Control Acidity/Alkalinity. Leavening agents that release acids when heated can react with baking soda to help cakes, biscuits, and other goods to rise during baking. Other additives help modify the acidity and alkalinity of foods for proper flavor, taste, and color.

To Enhance Flavor or Impart Desired Color. Many spices and natural and synthetic flavors enhance the taste of foods. Colors, likewise, enhance the appearance of certain foods to meet consumer expectations. Many substances added to food may seem foreign when listed on the ingredient label, but are actually quite familiar. For example, ascorbic acid is another name for vitamin C, alphatocopherol is another name for

vitamin E, and beta-carotene is a source of vitamin A. Although there are no easy synonyms for all additives, it is helpful to remember that all food is made up of chemicals. Carbon, hydrogen, and other chemical elements provide the basic building blocks of everything in life.

COLOR ADDITIVES

A color additive is any dye, pigment, or substance that can impart color when added or applied to a food, drug, or cosmetic or when applied to the human body. Color additives may be used in foods, drugs, cosmetics, and certain medical devices, such as contact lenses. Food colors are tested by the FDA before being listed as acceptable for use in food. Only seven synthetic colors are certified. Many other food colors from natural sources are also available. However, many of these natural food colors have not undergone toxicity testing. When the letters *FD&C* precede a color, it means the color can be used in a food, drug, or cosmetic. When *D&C* precedes the color, it means it can only be used in drugs or cosmetics, but not in food. *Ext. D&C* before a color means that it is certified for external use only in drugs and cosmetics. Colors permitted for use in foods are classified as either *certified* or *exempt from certification.*

Certified. Certified colors are man-made, with each batch being tested by the manufacturer and FDA to ensure that they meet strict specifications for purity. There are nine certified colors approved for use in the United States. One example is FD&C Yellow No. 6, which is used in cereals, bakery goods, snack foods, and other foods. The Nutrition Labeling and Education Act of 1990 requires that any certified color added to food be listed in the ingredient statement by its common or usual name.

Exempt From Certification. Color additives that are exempt from certification include pigments derived from natural sources such as vegetables, minerals, or animals, e.g., caramel color is produced commercially by heating sugar and other carbohydrates under strictly controlled conditions for use in sauces, gravies, soft drinks, baked goods, and other foods. colors exempt from certification also must meet certain legal criteria for specifications and purity.

REGULATION

The Food Additives Amendment to the FD&C Act, passed in 1958, requires FDA approval for the use of an additive prior to its inclusion in food. It also requires the manufacturer to prove an additive's safety for the ways it will be used. The Food Additives Amendment exempted two groups of substances from the food additive regulation process.

Prior-Sanctioned Substances. All substances that FDA or the USDA had determined were safe for use in a specific food prior to the 1958 amendment. Examples of prior-sanctioned substances are sodium nitrite and potassium nitrite used to preserve luncheon meats.

GRAS (Generally Recognized as Safe). Those whose use is generally recognized by experts as safe, based on their extensive history of use in food before 1958 or based on published scientific evidence. Salt, sugar, spices, vitamins, and monosodium glutamate are classified as GRAS, along with several hundred other substances.

GMP (Good Manufacturing Practices). Regulations that limit the amount of food and color additives used in foods. Manufacturers use only the amount of an additive necessary to achieve the desired effect.

Safe. No food additive is deemed safe if it is found to induce cancer when ingested by man or animal.

Source:

Food Additives, Washington: Food and Drug Administration in cooperation with Food Education Foundation, 1992.

Harte, John, Cheryl Holdren, Richard Schneider, Christine Shirley, *Toxics A to Z: A Guide to Everyday Pollution Hazards*, Berkeley, Los Angeles and Oxford: University of California Press, 1991.

Food Irradiation

Food irradiation is a process whereby food is treated with ionizing radiation for the purpose of preventing illness from food-borne bacteria. The process damages the genetic material of the bacteria so that the organisms can no longer survive or multiply. Irradiation does not make food radioactive and does not increase human exposure to radiation. Absorbed radiation is measured in units called *Grays.* The amount of Grays refers to the level of energy absorbed by a food from ionizing radiation that passes through the food in processing. 1,000 Grays = 1 kiloGray (1 kGy). In the past, the term *rad* was commonly used. It stands for *radiation absorbed dose.* 100 rad = 1 Gy. Food irradiation is regulated by the U.S. Food and Drug Administration. The FDA has established rules governing which products can be irradiated and for what purposes. It has also limited the Gray dose permitted to be used in the process.

LABELING

The label and labeling of retail packages of foods irradiated bears the above logo along with either the statement *treated with radiation* or the statement *treated by irradiation.* For irradiated foods not in package form, the required logo and phrases are displayed to the purchaser with either (1) the labeling of the bulk container plainly in view or (2) a counter sign, card, or other appropriate device bearing the information that the product has been treated with radiation. As an alternative, each item of food may be individually labeled. In either case, the information must be prominently and conspicuously displayed to the consumer.

Source:

Blumenthal, Dale, "Food Irradiation: Toxic to Bacteria, Safe for Humans," *FDA Consumer* (November 1990).

Food and Drug Administration, "Irradiation in the Production, Processing and Handling of Food," CFR part 179 (1991), Washington: Government Printing Office.

Food Labeling

In response to the Nutrition Labeling and Education Act of 1990, the Food and Drug Administration (FDA) and the U.S. Department of Agriculture's Food Safety and Inspection Service (FSIS) each issued proposed regulations on November 27, 1991 regulating the use of terms on labels for foods. The purpose of the regulations is to make the nutrition information on food packages more truthful and useful to consumers. The final regulations were to be issued by a congressionally-mandated November 8, 1992 deadline. However, just prior to the deadline the U.S. Department of Agriculture, which regulates meat and poultry products, objected to a proposed labeling format that shows consumers how a product's fat, saturated fat, and cholesterol fit into a healthy diet. The dispute between FDA and USDA continued past the mandated deadline and was finally settled on December 2, 1992 when the President stepped in to break the stalemate. The most significant changes expected in the regulations have been incorporated into this entry. The regulations apply to all packaged foods, which must bear the new labels by May 1994. The rules do not apply to fresh meat, poultry, fish and produce.

FAT AND CHOLESTEROL

Cholesterol Free. Foods containing little or no cholesterol can contain saturated fats at levels that can contribute to high blood cholesterol which, in turn, can contribute to atherosclerotic cardiovascular disease. Unfortunately, many consumers believe that a *Cholesterol Free* food would also be low in saturated fat. Therefore, cholesterol content claims are only permitted when the foods also contain levels of saturated fats that are below a specified threshold. The use of *Cholesterol Free,* and *Low Cholesterol* claims on foods that contain more than 2 grams of saturated fatty acids is prohibited.

Fat Free. Less than 0.5 grams of fat per serving, providing that it has no added ingredient that is fat or oil.

Low Fat. 3 grams or less of fat per serving and 50 per grams of the food must have less than 3 grams of fat.

Reduced Fat. No more than half the fat of an identified comparison, e.g., "Reduced fat, 50 percent less fat than our regular brownie. Fat content has been reduced from 8 grams to 4 grams." To avoid trivial claims, the reduction must exceed 3 grams of fat per serving.

Low in Saturated Fat. May be used to describe a food that contains 1 gram or less of saturated fat per serving and not more than 15 percent of calories from saturated fat.

Reduced Saturated Fat. No more than 50 percent of the saturated fat than the food with which it's compared. Foods with a reduction of 25 percent or greater may have a comparative claim using the term *less*. If *reduced saturated fat* or a comparative claim is used, it must indicate the percent reduction and the amount of saturated fat in the food with which it's compared. The reduction of saturated fat must exceed 1 gram.

SOURCE OF AND SUBSTITUTE FOODS

Substitute Food. One that may be used interchangeable with another food that it resembles, i.e., it is organoleptically, physically, and functionally (including shelf life) similar to and is not nutritionally inferior to the food, unless it is labeled as an "imitation."

Source, Good Source of, Important Source of. The food contains 10 to 19 percent of the Reference Daily Intake (RDI) or the Daily Reference Value (DRV). Any high-fiber claim for a food containing more than 3 grams of fat per serving and per 100 grams of the food must be accompanied by a declaration of total fat.

RELATIVE TERMS

High, Rich In, Major Source Of. The food contains 20 percent or more of the RDI or the DRV.

Less and Reduced. These terms are synonymous. To make the claim there must be a reduction of at least 25 percent of the nutrient. The actual percentage of the reduction would have to be included, e.g., "50 percent less fat."

More. The food contains at least 10 percent more of the RDI for protein, vitamins, or minerals or of the DRV for dietary fiber or potassium (expressed as a percent of the Daily Value) than the comparable food. Could be used to show that a food contains more of a desirable nutrient, such as fiber or potassium, than does a comparable food.

More (Complex Carbohydrates). More may also be used to describe the level of complex carbohydrates in a food, provided that the food contains at least 4 percent more of the DRV for carbohydrates than the reference food, and the difference between the two foods is only complex carbohydrates.

More (Unsaturated Fat). More may be used to describe the level of unsaturated fat in a food, provided that the food contains at least 4 percent more of the DRV for unsaturated fat then the comparable food, that the level of total fat is not increased, and that the level of transfatty acids does not exceed 1 percent of the total fat.

LIGHT

Light or Lite. The food has at least ⅓ fewer calories than a comparable food. Any other use of the term *light* must specify if it refers to the look, taste, or smell, e.g., "Light in Color."

Light (Salt). May be used to describe a salt substitute if the sodium content of the product has been reduced by at least 50 percent compared to ordinary table salt.

Light (Common Usage). If a manufacturer can demonstrate that the word "light" has been associated, through common use, with a particular food (e.g., light brown sugar or light molasses) to the point where it attained common recognition in the marketplace, it will be exempt from the requirements.

CALORIES

Calorie Free, No Calories, Trivial or Negligible Source of Calories, or Dietarily Insignificant Source of Calories. Contains less than 5 calories per serving. If the food naturally doesn't have calories, the label should disclose that fact, e.g., "soda water, a calorie-free food."

Fewer Calories. Contains at least 25 percent fewer calories, with a minimum reduction of more than 40 calories per serving.

Low Calorie, Few Calories, Contains a Small Amount of Calories, Low Source of Calories, Low in Calories. Does not provide more than 40 calories per serving and per 100 grams of food.

Reduced Calorie, Reduce in Calories, Calorie Reduced. The food has been specifically processed, altered, formulated, or reformulated to reduce its calorie content by ⅓ or more, with a minimum reduction of more than 40 calories per serving.

SUGAR

Less Sugars. The food contains at least 25 percent less sugars per serving than the reference food that it resembles and for which it is being substituted.

No Added Sugars, Without Added Sugars, No Sugars Added. No amount of sugar is added during processing or packaging. The product does not contain ingredients containing added sugars, such as jam, jelly, and concentrated fruit juice. The sugars content has not been increased above the amount naturally present in the ingredients by some means such as the use of enzymes. The food to which it is being compared normally contains added sugars.

Sugar Free, No Sugars, Zero Sugars. The food contains less than 0.5 grams of sugars per serving.

SODIUM AND SALT

Less Sodium. The food contains at least 25 percent less sodium, with a minimum reduction of more than 140 mg per serving when compared with the food it resembles.

Low Sodium, Low in Sodium, Little Sodium, Contains a Small Amount of Sodium, Low Source of Sodium. The food contains 140 mg or less sodium per serving and per 100 grams of food.

Reduced Sodium, Reduced in Sodium, Sodium Reduced. The food has been specifically processed, altered, formulated, or reformulated to reduce its sodium content by 50 percent or more, with a minimum reduction of more than 140 mg per serving.

Salt Free. The food is "sodium free"; it contains less than 5 milligrams (mg) of sodium per serving.

Sodium Free, No Sodium, Zero Sodium, Trivial Source of Sodium. Contains less than 5 mg of sodium per serving.

Unsalted, Without Added Salt, No Salt Added. No salt is added during processing. The food that it resembles and for which it substitutes is normally processed with salt. If the food is not sodium free, such claims are immediately accompanied each time they are used by the statement "Not a Sodium Free food" or "Not for Control of Sodium in the Diet."

Very Low Sodium, Very Low in Sodium. Contains 35 mg or less sodium per serving and per 100 grams of food.

FRESH

Fresh Frozen, Frozen Fresh. The food was quickly frozen while still fresh, i.e., the food had been recently harvested when frozen. *Quickly frozen* means frozen by a freezing system, such as blast-freezing (sub-zero Fahrenheit temperature with fast moving air directed at the food), that ensures the food is frozen quickly, even to the center of the food, and that virtually no deterioration has taken place.

Fresh. The food has not been frozen of subjected to any form of thermal processing or any other form of preservation.

Freshly Prepared, Freshly Baked, Freshly Roasted, etc. The food is recently made or prepared and has not been frozen or subjected to any form of thermal processing or any other form of preservation.

LEAN

Extra Lean. Used on a meat product that contains less than 4.9 grams fat, less than 1.8 grams saturated fat, and less than 94.5 mg cholesterol per 100 grams.

Lean. The term lean may be used on the label of a meat product that contains less than 10.5 grams fat, less than 3.5 grams saturated fat, and less than 94.5 mg cholesterol per 100 grams.

NURTIENTS AND HEALTH CLAIMS

Dietary Supplement. A food, other than a conventional food, that supplies a component with nutritive value to supplement the diet by increasing the total dietary intake of that substance. A dietary supplement includes a food for special dietary use within the meaning that is in conventional food form.

Disqualifying Nutrient Levels. The levels of total fat, saturated fat, cholesterol, or sodium in a food above which the food will be disqualified from making a health claim. These levels are 11.5 grams of fat, 4.0 grams of saturated fat, 45 milligrams of cholesterol, or 360 milligrams of sodium—per reference amount commonly consumed, per label serving size, and per 100 grams. Any one of the levels (on a per reference amount commonly consumed, a per label serving size, or a per 100 gram basis) will disqualify a food from making a health claim.

Health Claim. Any claim made on the label or in labeling of a food, including a dietary supplement, that expressly or by implication, including "third party" endorsements, written statements (e.g., a brand name including a term such as "heart"), symbols (e.g., a heart symbol), or vignettes, that characterizes the relationship of any substance to a disease or health-related condition. Implied health claims include only those statements, symbols, vignettes, or other forms of communication that a manufacturer intends to assert, or that would be likely to be understood, as a direct beneficial relationship between the presence or level of any substance in the food and a health or disease-related condition.

Nutritive Value. A value in sustaining human existence by such processes as promoting growth, replacing loss of essential nutrients, or providing energy.

Reference Amounts. The Food and Drug Administration calculated the amount of food customarily consumed per eating occasion and established reference amounts for different product categories of food.

Reference Daily Intake (RDI). The terms *Reference Daily Intake (RDI)* and *Reference Daily Values (DRVs)* replace the term U.S. Recommended Daily Allowances (RDA) for protein, vitamins, and minerals that have been used for many years. RDIs would provide consumers a basis to compare the protein, vitamin and mineral content of foods, based on the National Academy of Sciences' Recommended Dietary Allowances. Generally, the amount of nutrients required to cover the needs of almost all healthy people. DRVs would provide a similar basis to compare certain other food components—total fat, saturated and unsaturated fat, cholesterol, carbohydrates, dietary fiber, sodium, and potassium—that are especially important in affecting health, but which have not been addressed by the National Academy. To present these numbers as simply as possible, labels will just refer to the percentage content of all these components as *Percent of Daily Value.*

Serving Size or Serving. An amount of food customarily consumed per eating occasion by persons 4 years of age or older; it is expressed in a common household measure that is appropriate to the food. When the food is specially formulated or processed for use by infants or by toddlers, a serving or serving size means an amount of food customarily consumed per eating occasion by infants up to 12 months of age or by children 1 through 3 years of age. The term portion means an amount of food that is not typically expressed in a serving size, i.e., a food customarily used only as an ingredient in the preparation of other foods, e.g., ¼ cup flour or ¼ cup tomato sauce. Declaration of the number of servings per container need not be included in nutrition labeling of raw fruit, vegetables, and fish.

Substance. A component of a conventional food or of a dietary supplement of vitamins, minerals, herbs, or other nutritional substances.

Source:

Proposed amendments to 21 CFR Part 101, et al. and 9 CFR Parts 317, 320, and 381, published on Wednesday, November 27, 1991, in the Federal Register.

Foods, Chemical Preservative

Any chemical that when added to food tends to prevent or retard deterioration. The term does not include common salt, sugars, vinegars, spices, or oils extracted from spices, substances added to food by direct exposure to wood smoke, or chemicals applied for their insecticidal or herbicidal properties. To be acceptable for food use, a chemical preservative should comply with established purity specifications. Chemical preservatives may be disclosed on food labels by statements such as, _____*added as a preservative,* or *preserved with* _____. (The blank is filled in with the common or usual name of the preservative ingredient.)

Source:
Food and Drug Administration, *Compliance Policy Guides*, Guide 7120.13, Reissued 02/01/89: Washington, National Technical Information Service.

Information Panel

For packaged foods, the information panel is the part of the label immediately contiguous and to the right of the *Principal Display Panel*. Like the *Principal Display Panel*, the *Information Panel* contains information required by federal regulations.

Source:
Food and Drug Administration, "Information Panel of Package Form Food," 21 CFR 101.2, Washington, U.S. Government Printing Office, 1991.

Kosher

The Hebrew word *Kosher* means "clean or fit to eat according to dietary laws prescribed in the Torah." The Torah is the whole body of Jewish religious literature, including the Scripture, the Talmud, etc. *Trephah,* a Hebrew term describing animals found non-kosher due to physical damages or imperfections, is commonly used to describe all foods that are non-kosher. All kosher meat comes from animals that have split hooves, chew their cud, and have been slaughtered in the manner prescribed by the Torah. The Biblical authority regarding dietary laws is found in Genesis 32:33, Exodus 12:15, and 23:19, Leviticus 3:17 and 11, and Deuteranomy 14. These passages are interpreted differently by many Jewish scholars. Accordingly, in practice there are different interpretations as to what Kosher means and what practices are required before a product can be labeled as Kosher.

SYMBOLS

The use of the letter "U" inside the letter "O" is authorized by the Union of Orthodox Jewish Congregations of America. The letter "K" inside the letter "O" (symbol for kosher) indicates that the food complies with the Jewish dietary laws and has been processed under the direction of a rabbi. These symbols are not required, regulated, or enforced by the Food and Drug Administration (FDA).

UNITED STATES DEPARTMENT OF AGRICULTURE (USDA) POLICIES

Products prepared by federally inspected meat packing plants identified with labels bearing references to Kosher or Rabbinical markings must be handled under Rabbinical supervision. The Federal Meat and Poultry Inspection Program does not certify to kosher preparation of products; instead, it accepts the statements and markings in this regard offered and applied under the supervision of the Rabbinical authority. The word *Kosher* may be used only on the labeling of meat and poultry products prepared under Rabbinical supervision. Application for approval must identify the Rabbinical authority under whose supervision the product is to be prepared. Qualification of the word by such terms as "style" or "brand" does not negate the requirement.

Parvemargarine. A nondairy product used in Kosher products as a substitute for margarine, butter, and other such foods which might have a dairy background.

Sources:
Standards and Labeling Division, Food Safety and Inspection Service, USDA, *Standards and Labeling Policy Book,* Washington: Government Printing Office, June 1991.
Union of Orthodox Jewish Congregations of America, *The Kashruth Guide,* New York: Union on Jewish Orthodox Jewish Congregations of America, 1991.

Packaged Foods

All packaged foods labels must provide at least the following: the name of the product; the name and location of the manufacturer, packer, or distributor; and the net contents or net weight. Regulations adopted by the Food and Drug Administration (FDA) in 1973 require manufacturers to provide nutrition information on their product labels only if one or more nutrients are added to the food or if a nutritional claim is made about the product. Slightly more than half of all packaged foods today carry nutrition information, many of them voluntarily. At the time of writing of this book, nutrition labeling of foods is under review by the FDA and USDA, and proposed regulations have been published but have not yet gone into effect.

Many foods, but not all, list all the ingredients on the label. Consumers interested in knowing the ingredients used in a food will usually find at least most of them on the label. The FDA requires the ingredient present in the largest amount, by weight, to be listed first, the next largest second, and so forth. The Federal Food, Drug, and Cosmetic Act requires a listing of all ingredients by their "common or usual names" for all so-called nonstandardized foods. Most are nonstandardized.

STANDARDIZED FOODS

There are about 300 foods on the market today—from ice cream to peanut butter—for which the Food and Drug Administration (FDA) has established a *standard of identity,* or *food standard.* These products have specified mandatory ingredients that, under the law, do not have to be identified on the ingredient list. Only the optional ingredients must be listed. However, as a matter of practice even the mandatory ingredients are listed on the labels of most standardized foods. Many of the foods in the *Fruits* and *Vegetables* sections in this book have been standardized by the FDA in Title 21 of the *Code of Federal Regulations.*

TERMINOLOGY

Acidulants or Acidifiers. Acids that have many food uses: as flavor-enhancing agents, as preservatives to inhibit growth of microorganisms, as antioxidants to prevent discoloration or rancidity, and to adjust the acidity in some foods.

Anti-Caking Agents. Substances used to prevent powdered or granular foods from absorbing moisture and becoming lumpy. They help products like table salt and powdered sugar flow freely.

Antioxidants. Preservatives that prevent or delay discoloration in foods, such as cut potatoes and sliced apples. They also help keep oils and fats from turning rancid. Examples of some antioxidants are BHA, BHT, and propyl gallate.

Bran. Outer tough coating of cereal grains (such as wheat, rye and oats) that is separated in the refining process but is included in whole-grain products. It may also be added to cereals and other grain products.

Calorie. A unit of measure of the amount of fuel or energy a food provides to the body. Food energy comes from three primary sources: fat, carbohydrates, and protein. (Alcohol also provides calories, but no other nutrients.) The nutrition label on packaged foods includes the amount of calories in a specific serving of the product.

Carbohydrates. Sugars and starches that supply energy and help the body use fats efficiently. Carbohydrates are present in varying amounts in many foods. Foods with complex carbohydrates are recommended for a healthful diet—namely, whole-grain breads and cereals and dried peas and beans. Fruits contain mostly simple carbohydrates (sugars) and fiber.

Cholesterol. Fat-like substances found in foods of animal origin (meat, poultry, and dairy products), but not in foods from plants. Cholesterol is essential to body functions, but because the body can make what it needs, the amount in some people's diets is often excessive, increasing the risk of heart disease.

Complex Carbohydrates. Complex carbohydrates, or polysaccharides, are made mostly of long strands of simple sugars. They are found in grains, fruits, legumes (peas and beans), and other vegetables. Complex carbohydrates include starches and three types of dietary fiber—cellulose, hemicellulose, and gums. It is recommended that complex carbohydrates should make up about 55 percent of the calories in our daily diet, with fat making up 30 percent or less, and protein the remainder. In an 1,800-calorie daily diet, 55 percent represents about 250 grams of complex carbohydrates or nearly 1,000 calories.

Dietetic. At least one ingredient has been changed or restricted. The food may have fewer calories or less slat, sugar, or fat. Read the label to see what has been changed. Some dietetic cookies have less sugar but more fat.

Emulsifiers. Widely used in food processing, these agents stabilize fat and water mixtures so they will not separate. For example, in mayonnaise, egg yolks act as emulsifiers to keep the oil from separating from the acids (vinegar or lemon juice). Lecithin, derived from soybeans, acts as an emulsifier in such foods as chocolate and margarine.

Fats. A major source of energy; they a play a key role as carriers of fat-soluble vitamins (A, D, E, and K). Fat is a constituent of most foods of plant and animal origin.

Fatty Acids. The major constituents of fat. Fats in foods are a mixture of saturated and unsaturated fatty acids. Fats with a high proportion of saturated fatty acids are solid or nearly solid at room temperature and are found in larger amounts in foods

of animal origin. Fats with mostly unsaturated fatty acids are liquid at room temperature and may be mono-unsaturated or polyunsaturated. Unsaturated fatty acids become more saturated by a process called hydrogenation. Olive oil and peanut oil are especially high in mono-unsaturated fatty acids. Polyunsaturated fatty acids are found in large amounts in plant oils, such as safflower, sunflower, corn, soybean, and cottonseed oils. (For more details, see the February and March 1987 issues of *FDA Consumer*.)

Fiber. Provides bulk or roughage in the diet. Fiber is derived from such plant-derived foods as cereal grain products, vegetables, fruits, seeds, and nuts. *Dietary fiber* is the amount left after digestion by the body.

Flavor Enhancers. Help bring out the natural flavor of foods. Some examples of flavor enhancers are Monosodium glutamate (MSG), disodium guanylate, and disodium inosinate.

Flavors. Naturally occurring and artificial agents used to give more taste to food. Flavoring agents include extracts from spices and herbs as well as others that are man-made.

Grains. Hard seeds of cereal plants, such as wheat, rice, corn, and rye. Whole grains contain the entire seed of the plant.

Humectants. Chemicals, such as glycerol, propylene glycol, and sorbitol, that are added to foods to help retain moisture, fresh taste, and texture. Often used in candies, shredded coconut, and marshmallows.

Hydrogenated and Partially Hydrogenated. Labeling terms that describe the process of adding hydrogen to an unsaturated fat to make it saturated, e.g., oils may be hydrogenated to various degrees to make them suitable for use in products such as margarine. The more an oil is hydrogenated, the more saturated fatty acids it contains.

Ingredient List. List that appears on the label of packaged food to show the added components of the product. The ingredient (and sometimes standard) used in the greatest amount, by weight, is listed first, next largest is second, and so forth.

Leavening Agents. Substances such as yeasts and baking powders that are used to make foods light in texture by forming carbon dioxide gas in the dough.

Natural. Term that appears on many products but has little meaning. Such labeling is objectionable, says FDA, when a product contains artificial ingredients, but is described as being *natural*.

Niacin. A water-soluble B vitamin that is important for the health of all body cells. The body needs it to use oxygen to produce energy.

Preservatives. Substances that keep foods from spoiling and becoming rancid or developing off-colors and flavors. (For a more detailed explanation and listing of preservatives, see "Food Preservatives: A Fresh Report" [April 1984] *FDA Consumer*.)

Refined Flour. Type of flour produced by milling grains to a fine white consistency. Refining removes bran, fiber, and some other nutrients. Enriched flour has iron and three B vitamins added to levels required by FDA.

Riboflavin. A water-soluble B vitamin that helps the body obtain energy from food and aids in the proper functioning of the nervous system, in growth, and in digestion.

Sequestrants. Chemicals used to bind trace amounts of metal impurities that can cause food to become discolored or rancid.

Sodium. A chemical in some foods. Essential for regulating body fluids and muscle function; excessive amounts have been linked with an increased risk of high blood pressure. Since July 1986, FDA has required sodium content in nutrition labeling. Some 70 sodium compounds are used in foods. Salt is the largest single source of sodium in the human diet but is not synonymous with sodium. Salt is sodium chloride and is about 40 percent sodium.

Stabilizers and Thickeners. Substances that give foods a smooth, uniform texture. They also protect foods from adverse conditions, such as wide temperature fluctuations and physical shock during distribution. The most common thickening agents are starches (cornstarch and wheat starch) and modified food starches. Other types include carrageenan, locust bean gum, agar, sodium alginate, gelatin, and pectin.

Unsweetened. In some cases, the Food and Drug Administrations regulations allow manufacturers to inform consumers that a product contains no added sweeteners without necessarily implying that the product has been reduced in calories.

Sources:
Consumer Fact Sheet, The Sugar Association, Washington, 1992.
Food and Drug Administration, "A Simple Guide to Complex Carbohydrates," a pamphlet reprinted from the April 1989 issue of *Consumer Magazine* and revised March 1991, DHHS Publication No. (FDA) 91-2230, Washington: Government Printing Office.
Lecos, Chris, "Food Labels, Test Your Food Label Knowledge," *FDA Consumer,* Vol. 22, no. 2 (March 1988): 16-20.

Packaging Terms

Aseptic Packaging. This is a three-step process in which the food is heated until sterile; in a separate process, the container (usually a multi-layered material made of plastic, paper, and aluminum foil) is also sterilized. In the last step, the sterilized food is put in the sterile container in a sterile atmosphere. Products packaged this way are *shelf-stable*—they can be stored on a shelf for up to two years.

Canned. A food is considered canned if it has been hermetically sealed and so processed by heat as to prevent spoilage. Foods that are in metal containers of the types normally used for canning and that are stored and displayed under conditions which do not suggest or imply that the article is other than a canned food need not be labeled *canned*. If packed in glass or plastic bottles or jars and stored or displayed under refrigeration which might cause consumers to believe it is fresh, the label designation should include the word *canned* or *pasteurized,* as the case may be.

Dried or Dehydrated. A food which is dried or dehydrated should be labeled with a designation which includes one of these words, unless the name is one like *raisins* which consumers recognize as indicating a dried product.

Dual-Ovenable Tray. Typically constructed form either paper-board or polyester and can be used in either a microwave or conventional oven.

Freeze Dried. A food which has been freeze dried may be designated with *dried* or *freeze dried*.

Suscepter Packaging. For food to brown it must come into contact with hot air or a very hot surface, like a frying pan. Because microwave ovens cook food from the inside out, they are unable to give food the crisp brown appearance of fried food. Suscepter packaging is the microwave's frying pan. A very thin layer of metal is deposited on plastic or paper; the hot surface browns the food.

Sources:
Folkenberg, Judy, "The Big Chill, How Safe Are Sous-Vide Refrigerated Foods?" *FDA Consumer,* Vol. 23, no. 7 (September 1989): 33-36.
Food and Drug Administration, *Compliance Policy Guides*, Guide 7120.06, 10/01/80: Washington, National Technical Information Service.

Principal Display Panel

When applied to a food package this term means the part of a label that is most likely to be displayed, presented, shown, or examined under customary conditions of display for retail sale. The principal display panel should be large enough to accommodate all the mandatory label information required to be placed on the package in a manner that is clear and easy to read.

Source:
Food and Drug Administration, Principal Display Panel of Package Form Food, 21 CFR 101.1, Washington, U.S. Government Printing Office, 1991.

Residues

A residue is something left behind after a process has been completed. For example, residues can remain in fat, internal organs, or other tissues after food animals have been treated with veterinary drugs to cure or prevent disease or to promote health. Chemical residues are unintended leftovers, not direct food additives approved for a specific purpose. Illegal residues are usually preventable. *Illegal levels* of residues are any amount greater than the legal limit. Legal limits for residues are expressed in terms of parts per million or parts per billion—equivalent to a few drops of water in an Olympic-sized swimming pool. Limits are set with a margin of safety usually at least 100 times stricter than the level at which health effects can be observed. Violations detected by the Federal Safety and Inspection Service (FSIS) are usually only slightly above legal limits—barely measurable differences.

The Environmental Protection Agency (EPA) registers pesticides and sets legal limits for pesticide residues in food. The Food and Drug Administration (FDA) approves animal drugs, sets legal limits for animal drug residues in food, regulates commercial animal feed, and estimates consumer exposure to residues by analyzing "marketbaskets" of food purchased around the country. The experts believe residues are a public health *concern* rather than an acute health risk.

ORGANIC FARMING

Because of the health concerns over residues, many food producers are using organic food production techniques. For many years the definition of *organic farming* was defined by voluntary consensus standards and third party certification programs created by growers. For example, officials of the Association of American Plant Food Control Officials recommend that at least 50 percent of a fertilizer weight and plant nutrients be *natural* or *organic* to earn the *organic* or *organic base* label. However, in the fall of 1993, the Organic Foods Production Act will go into effect. The promulgation under the act of rules and regulations regarding organic practice will set mandatory minimum standards on all organic producers and handlers.

Source:
Food Safety and Inspection Service, USDA, *Meat and Poultry Safety: Questions and Answers About Chemical Residues* (pamphlet no. FSIS-38 September 1990), Washington: U.S. Department of Agriculture.
Organic Foods Production Association of North America, *OFPANA Reports* (February 1992): 4-5.

Solid Pack, Canned Fruit

Canned fruits designated in labeling as "solid pack" does not contain any added liquid packing medium. If any water at all is added in packing the food, the term "solid pack" would not appear at any place on the label.

Source:
Food and Drug Administration, *Compliance Policy Guides*, Guide 7120.05, Revised 02/01/89: Washington, National Technical Information Service.

Sous-Vide Refrigerated Foods

Sous-vide is French for "under vacuum." It refers to a process developed in France whereby fresh raw ingredients are sealed in a plastic pouch and the air is vacuumed out. The pouch is then cooked under precise conditions and immediately refrigerated. The consumer takes the food home and reheats it in a pot of boiling water—it then is ready to eat. The process is also known as *vacuum-packed* refrigerated foods or *new generation* refrigerated foods. Some processors replace some of the air with nitrogen or carbon dioxide. Foods produced in this manner are known as modified-atmosphere refrigerated foods.

The process is very new in the United States, and few food companies have yet adopted it. Very few restaurants serve food

prepared this way, and supermarkets have just begun carrying vacuum-packed refrigerated foods—including such products as pasta, vegetables, fish, chicken, and beef. Experts predict that vacuum-refrigerated foods may one day replace canned and frozen items as the mainstay in supermarkets, mainly because they taste better and fresher. Vacuum-packed refrigerated foods are spared the extreme cold of frozen foods and intense heat used to process canned foods, both of which damage the cell structure of the food.

There is some concern, however, that the process may present a potential bacterial problem. Because the technology relies on an oxygen-free or near-oxygen-free environment, it provides a breeding ground for harmful bacteria to thrive, especially the organisms responsible for botulism, listeriosis, an *Yersinia* poisoning—all potentially deadly forms of food poisoning. However, other countries have managed the risks well. In Europe, where vacuum-packed refrigerated foods are common, there has been virtually no food poisoning caused by the technology.

The technology is especially attractive to restaurants because meals can be prepared in advance at an off-site location, thereby reducing the need for large kitchens and highly paid chefs. It has been estimated that two or three highly skilled chefs can prepare food for 50 restaurants.

To guard against the risk of bacterial contamination of vacuum-packed refrigerated foods, the Food and Drug Administration recommends the following precautions:

Keep Foods Refrigerated. As soon as you get home, put refrigerated foods in the refrigerator. Don't delay getting home, and avoid running numerous errands on a hot summer day while foods requiring refrigeration are left to heat up in the car.

Look at the Expiration Date. Throw away food not used by the expiration date.

Heat Well. When you heat vacuum-packed refrigerated food, follow the packaged instructions for time and temperature.

Source:
Folkenberg, Judy, "The Big Chill, How Safe Are Sous-Vide Refrigerated Foods?" *FDA Consumer,* Vol. 23, no. 7 (September 1989): 33-36.

U.S. Grades

The U.S. Department of Agriculture (USDA) Grade Standards are developed in cooperation with broad segments of the industry, consumer groups, and the public at large in accordance with the Administrative Procedures Act. The official standards of quality are correlated closely with the *standards of identity* promulgated by the Food and Drug Administration.

The use of official standards, with a few exceptions, is not mandatory. Their main value is as a marketing aid to be used by producers, dealers, wholesale commission merchants, and retailers. They provide a common language among producers and dealers for trading purposes for a commodity and facilitate the development of standardization in buying procedures for many organizations. They are also useful to retailers in buying and selling and to consumers in buying.

The USDA maintains a system of *inspection* and a system of *grading*. Both are available at practically all major shipping points and major and secondary markets in all of the states. In many cases, the USDA has cooperative agreements with state departments of agriculture and other marketing services.

Grading practices can influence the marketability of a product. For example, although meat is graded in carcass or wholesale cut quantities, the grade stamp is applied in such a way as to carry through to the consumer. Similarly, butter is graded in churn lots, but the pound print generally carries the grade designation for the consumer's benefit. In contrast, a bushel of U.S. No. 1 wheat loses its identity when it is processed into flour or breakfast food, for which there are no official grade standards.

Detailed information on the grade requirements for most fruits, vegetables, nuts, meats, dairy products, and seafood can be found in the sections of this volume that follow.

MEAT AND POULTRY

USDA inspectors check meat and poultry to ensure that safely prepared, properly labeled products reach consumers. Food safety inspection of meat and poultry products is a mandatory, taxpayer-subsidized activity to protect public health and prevent economic deception. The official USDA inspection mark or stamp is proof that the product was inspected. The inspection stamp can be found on processed meat and on poultry products such as canned beef stew and chicken franks. The stamps include the number of the plant in which the product was produced. The plant number is preceded with the letters "EST." for "establishment" on processed meats, and with the letter "P" on poultry. This data makes it easy for USDA to refer to the plant that produced the product should a problem occur. Although it is not part of the inspection stamp, the name and address of the company that made the product must also appear on the label. The lot or batch number may also appear on the label. These numbers tell on what day and on what shift the products were produced. Examples of typical inspection marks appear below.

Unlike inspection, grading of meat and poultry is a voluntary, producer-subsidized activity aimed at quality rather than safety. Information on the U.S. grades for meats can be found in Section 17—*Meat and Poultry*.

FRUITS AND VEGETABLES

The Agricultural Marketing Service (AMS) of the USDA is responsible for the inspection of fresh fruit, vegetables, and related products (including such items as tree nuts and peanuts) and of processed fruit, vegetables, and a group of other products (such as honey, maple syrup, coffee, and spices).

The use of the inspection services (like the use of the U.S. grades) is not compulsory, except in instances in which federal or state marketing agreements and orders may require that marketing of a commodity be limited to specified grades and in which inspection for compliance with the prescribed grades is compulsory.

Fresh Fruits and Vegetables

Most of the grade standards for fresh fruit and vegetables are designed for wholesale trading. With the more widespread use of prepackaged fresh fruit and vegetables, however, there has been a need for grade standards that are adapted especially to the retail level of trading. Accordingly, several retail grades, known as *consumer standards,* have been developed. Only a few vegetables and fruit are marked as to U.S. grade when displayed at retail, even though most of the transactions up to the retail level may have been made on the basis of these grades and the wholesale containers may have carried the mark.

The grades for fresh fruit and vegetables generally are designed by numbers, names, or a combination of the two. The basic trading grade is *U.S. No. 1*. Premium grades are established for some commodities. The following grade nomenclature is used:

U.S. Fancy. Premium quality; it covers only the top quality range produced.

U.S. No. 1. The chief trading grade; it represents good, average quality that is practical to pack under commercial conditions. It covers the bulk of the quality range produced.

U.S. No. 2. Intermediate quality between U.S. No. 1 and U.S. No. 3; it is noticeably superior to U.S. No. 3.

U.S. No. 3. The lowest merchantable quality practical to pack under normal conditions.

The basic grade designation in the series of consumer standards is *U.S. Grade A,* the premium grade is *U.S. Grade AA,* and the lower grade is *U.S. Grade B. Unclassified* products in the trading standards become *Off-grade* in consumer standards.

Grade Marks. The approved shield mark with the appropriate U.S. grade designation is used on containers, labels, or otherwise indicated on the package when (1) the product has been packed under continuous inspection as provided by the Inspection Service; (2) the plant in which the product is packed is maintained under good commercial sanitary practices; and (3) the product has been certified by an inspector as meeting the requirements of U.S. Grade A, U.S. Grade No. 1, or a higher U.S. grade as shown within the shield. The shields with approved grade designation for use should be similar in form and design to the examples in figures 1 and 2 below.

→ Blue

→ White

→ Red

Figure 1

Figure 2

Inspection Legends. The approved, continuous inspection legends may be used on containers, labels, or otherwise indicated on the package when (1) the product has been packed under continuous inspection provided by the Inspection Service; (2) the plant in which the product is packed is maintained under good commercial sanitary practices; and (3) the product meets the requirements of such quality, grade, or specification as may be approved by the administrator. The continuous inspection legends approved for use should be similar in form and design to the examples in figures 3 and 4.

**PACKED UNDER
CONTINUOUS
INSPECTION
OF THE
U. S. DEPT. OF
AGRICULTURE**

Figure 3

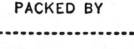

PACKED BY

**UNDER CONTINUOUS
FEDERAL-STATE
INSPECTION**

Figure 4

Combined Grade and Inspection Legends. The grade marks illustrated by figures 1 and 2 and the inspection legends illustrated by figures 3 and 4 may be combined into a consolidated grade and inspection legend for use on products which meet the requirements of both of these. See figure 5.

PACKED BY

**UNDER CONTINUOUS
FEDERAL-STATE
INSPECTION**

Figure 5

Packer Identification. The packer's name and address, assigned code number, or other mark identifying the packer appears on any container bearing grade marks or inspection legends. An example of an approved packer identification is illustrated in figure 6.

**PACKER NO. 01
PACKED UNDER CONTINUOUS
FEDERAL - STATE INSPECTION**

Figure 6

Other Identification Marks. Products may be inspected on a lot inspection basis and identified by an official inspection mark similar in form and design to figure 7. The use of this mark or other comparable identification marks may be required by the administrator whenever he determines that such identification is necessary in order to maintain the identity of lots which have been inspected and certified.

U S DEPT OF AGRICULTURE
INSPECTED
DEC 18 1972
545

Figure 7

Processed Fruits and Vegetables

As with fresh fruits and vegetables, grading and inspection of processed fruit and vegetable products is voluntary. Three types of official inspection service are available for processed products.

Lot Inspection. At the request of the seller or buyer, specific lots are inspected and certified as to U.S. grade or as meeting the applicant's specifications.

Continuous Inspection. Available to processors who meet high standards of sanitation for plant and equipment. Inspectors are stationed in the plant all the time it is operating. The inspector checks sanitation, observes preparation of all raw materials, selects samples of the product at random, and issues daily reports. When final inspection of the finished product is completed, he issues certificates, as requested, showing the final grade of each lot packed. All products packed are eligible for labeling with the U.S. grade and with a statement as to continuous inspection.

Pack Certification. Available to processors whose plants meet the sanitary standards and use acceptable raw material. An inspector is assigned to the plant during the processing season to inspect and certify each lot of the product as it is packed. He also observes preparation of the raw material and checks the cleanliness of the plant. He does not have to be present all the time during the processing operations, as is required under continuous inspection.

Grade designations for processed fruit appear as a combination of letter and name. The top grade is *U.S. Grade A or U.S. Fancy.* The lower grades are *U.S. Grade B or U.S. Choice* and *U.S. Grace C or U.S. Standard.* Processed vegetables carry the same designation, except that the second grade is *U.S. Grade B or U.S. Extra Standard.*

EGGS AND DAIRY PRODUCTS

The USDA also offers voluntary inspection and grading services for many manufactured dairy products: butter; cheddar, Swiss,

process, and cottage cheese; nonfat dry milk; dry whole milk; etc. The grades generally are designated by letters or by names.

For eggs, resident graders classify eggs as consumer grades, procurement grades, and wholesale grades, or according to contract specifications. When eggs are classified as consumer grades to be packaged with official identification, each egg is candled for quality and sorted for weight. When cartoned eggs are officially graded, the grade mark is printed on the carton or on a label used to seal the carton. Please see the section in this volume entitled *Dairy Products* for more detailed information on egg grades. Although the grading of shell eggs is voluntary, egg product inspection is mandatory. Examples of the Grade Marks for eggs appear in figure 8.

Figure 8

Sources:

Agricultural Marketing Service, USDA, "Regulations," 7 CFR sections 51.46 to 51.52 (1992), Washington: Government Printing Office.

Agricultural Marketing Service, USDA, "Regulations Governing Inspection and Certification," 7 CFR sections 52.1 to 52.208 (1991), Washington: Government Printing Office.

Lennartson, Roy W., "What Grades Mean," *Yearbook of Agriculture,* Washington: U.S. Department of Agriculture, 1959.

Beverages

Apple Juice, Frozen Concentrated

Frozen concentrated apple juice is prepared from the unfermented, unsweetened, unacidified liquid obtained from the first pressing of sound, clean, mature, fresh apples. The juice is clarified and concentrated. The apple juice concentrate is packed and frozen in accordance with good commercial practice and maintained at temperatures necessary for the preservation of the product. It may contain additional ingredients that are permissible under the Federal Food, Drug, and Cosmetic Act.

GRADES

U.S. Grade A or U.S. Fancy. When reconstituted, the color is bright and transparent. It has a light golden appearance that is not darker than USDA's Honey Color Standards White designation. It is practically free from sediment, residues, dark specks, or any other defects which affect appearance or palatability. It has a fine, distinct, fruity flavor and bouquet. It is free from astringent flavors, flavors due to overripe apples, oxidation, caramelization, or ground or musty flavors. It is also free from objectionable flavors or objectionable aromas of any kind.

U.S. Grade B or U.S. Choice. When reconstituted the color is slightly dull or slightly turbid. It may be light golden to light amber in appearance but not darker than the USDA's Honey Color Standards Light Amber designation. It is reasonably free from defects. It has a normal flavor and bouquet. It may be slightly astringent or may be slightly affected by overripe apples, oxidation, caramelization, or ground or musty flavors. However, it is free from objectionable flavors or aromas of any kind.

Substandard. Fails to meet the requirements of U.S. Grade B.

Source:
Agricultural Marketing Service, USDA, 7 CFR sections 52.6321 to 52.6332 (1991), Washington: Government Printing Office.

Beer

Beer is commonly understood to be a beverage made from barley although certain other grains including corn and wheat are also used. The barley is soaked in water until it sprouts. It is then dried in a kiln. The resulting substance (malt) is cooked in hot water. Hops (the dried ripe cones of the female flowers) are added as an agent of flavoring and preservation. Yeast is introduced to bring about fermentation.

Alcohol Free. Contains no alcohol.

Ale. English style top fermented beers. Usually copper-colored, but sometimes darker.

Bock. A strong bottom-fermented beer.

Bottled By or For. If malt beverages are bottled or packed for a person other than the actual bottler or packer, the bottle may contain the words *bottled for* or *distributed by*.

Domestic Ales. All brands defined as ales or cream ales brewed in the United States independent of price level or brewing process.

Dry Beer. Developed by Asahi Brewing in Japan, dry beer is characterized by a total lack of malt-sweet taste and little aftertaste.

Economy. Defined by rock-bottom price level and, generally, regional distribution.

Imports. Includes all brands that are imported into the United States.

Lager. A bottom fermented beer.

Low Alcohol or Reduced Alcohol. Malt beverages containing less than 2.5 percent alcohol by volume.

Low-Calorie. Beers with reduced-calorie content.

Malt Liquor. Brands which have a higher alcohol content than standard lagers.

Non-Alcoholic. Malt beverages that look and taste similar to beer, but have less than 0.5 percent alcohol by weight.

Popular. Defined by price level and wide or national distribution. May include some brands that were previously premium-priced, but have recently been discounted to be more competitive.

Premium. Defined by price level. Not as expensive as Super Premium.

Super Premium. Defined mainly by its high price level.

Sources:

Bureau of Alcohol, Tobacco, and Firearms, 27 CFR chapter 1 (1991), Washington: Government Printing Office.

Jackson, Michael, *The World Guide to Beer*, New York: Ballantine Books, 1977.

Product Literature, Golden, Colorado: Coors Brewing Company, 1990.

Beverage Bases

The article is one to which only water need be added to make a finished beverage. If ingredients other than water must be added to make the beverage, the name is accompanied by a conspicuous statement concerning the ingredient or ingredients which must be added. There are on the market complete beverage bases, that is, articles to which it is necessary to add only water to make a finished beverage. The purchaser should be able to readily distinguish, by means of the name or accompanying statement, between such articles and those to which sugar must be added by the purchaser before beverages can be made from them.

Source:

Food and Drug Administration, *Compliance Policy Guides,* Guide 7101.01, Washington: National Technical Information Service (NTIS), 1988.

Champagne

Champagne is a wine produced only from certain grapes, grown in a precisely delimited area of France known as the Champagne Region. No wine produced outside the delimited Champagne Region can properly claim to be Champagne.

Only three varieties of grapes are used to make Champagne: Pinot Noir, a red grape which gives the wine body and fullness of flavor; Chardonnay, a white grape which gives lightness to the final blend; and Pinot Meunier, another red grape which contributes freshness.

After pressing, the juice, known as must, is transferred first to purifying vats and then to the Champagne firms where the juice ferments for several weeks and becomes wine. Next, various wines are blended to produce a style distinctive of the winery. This blend, or *cuvee,* is often made of up to 20 or 30 still wines from the Champagne Region. Both red and white grapes may be used, and

the proportion used of each determines the style (appellation) of the Champagne (see *Styles,* below).

After blending, natural fermenting agents (yeast) and a small quantity of cane sugar are added to the blend before bottling. This *liqueur de tirage* is what causes the second fermentation within the bottle which is known as the *méthode champenoise.* Within the stoppered bottle yeasts act on the sugar to produce carbonic gas (carbon dioxide). The gas remains imprisoned in the bottle, gradually mixing with the wine. Later on, when the bottle is opened, it will appear as streams of tiny bubbles in the glass—the distinctive feature of Champagne.

EUROPEAN COMMUNITY LABELING RULES

Newly promulgated regulations for Champagne under European Community Regulations call for nine specifics on all bottle labels:

Brand Name

Champagne Appellation. Style of champagne.

Degree of Sweetness. 5 levels: extra-brut (driest), brut, semi-sweet, sec, demi-sec (sweetest).

Volume. 9 levels from 18.7 centiliter quarter-bottle to 15 liter (Nebuchadnezzar).

Alcohol Content 10-13 percent; 11-13 percent for vintage Champagne.

Professional Registration. See below.

Elaborator's Identity. Name of person/society or code number.

Village or Town of Elaboration.

Country of Origin. France.

PROFESSIONAL REGISTRATION

Récoltants Manipulants (RM). Vine growers who are not members of cooperatives but produce and sell their own Champagne. They are also allowed to use the following designations on their labels: *viticulteur à... propriétaire à....*

Récoltant-Coopérateur (RC). Growers who bring their grapes, must, or wine to cooperatives and receive an equal volume (though not the same) of must or wine at some stage in the elaboration process and sell Champagne under their own label. Newcomers to this category will have this status from December 9, 1988, the others not later than January 31, 1990.

Sociétés de Récoltants (SR). Entities comprising several growers from the same family (parents and children, brothers and sisters). They elaborate and sell Champagne made from grapes or wines produced by their members. However, they are not allowed to buy grapes outside the family. The effective date for this category is the same as for the equally new RC category.

Négociants-Manipulants (NM). Entities buying part or all of the grapes, must or wine they need to make their own branded Champagne. They are allowed to have up to three primary brands, or up to six if they take over previously existing brands.

Coopératives de Manipulation (CM). Cooperative entities which produce and market Champagne under their own proprietary labels.

Marques Auxiliaires (MA). *Designates a marque d'acheteur* or *Buyer's Own Brand* (private label). It applies to brands not

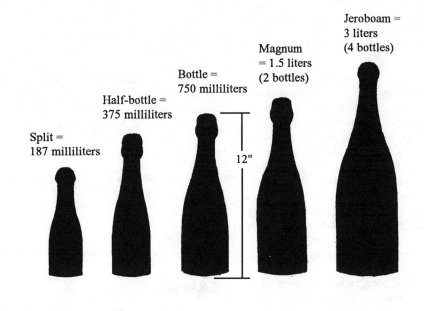

Jeroboam =
3 liters
(4 bottles)

Magnum
= 1.5 liters
(2 bottles)

Bottle =
750 milliliters

Half-bottle =
375 milliliters

Split =
187 milliliters

12"

Methuselah =
6 liters
(8 bottles)

Salmanazar =
9 liters
(12 bottles)

Balthazar =
12 liters
(16 bottles)

Nebuchadnezzar =
15 liters
(20 bottles)

Champagne bottle terminology

belonging to the producer, e.g., Champagnes produced for a wholesaler, retailer, restaurants, etc.)

STYLES

Vintage. In an exceptional year Champagne is blended from the wines of only that year's harvest, although from many different vineyards and pressings, and the year of the crop is shown on the label. By law, at least 20 percent of a vintage year's wines must be held in reserve for future blending.

Non-Vintage. A blend of wines from the current year's harvest combined with reserve wines from harvests of previous years. Considered to be most representative of a House's *style* of blending, the use of reserve wines permits the cellar-master to compensate for any variations caused by adverse climactic conditions.

Prestige Cuvee. Top-of-the-line connoisseur Champagne blended from the first pressing of grapes, grown in the highest-rated vineyards, and aged *on the yeasts* longer than either vintage or non-vintage Champagnes. Known as deluxe Champagne, super Champagne, or *Tête de cuvee,* these are superior blends of rare and costly wines.

Blanc de Blancs. Blended exclusively with wines from white Chardonnay grapes. Available in non-vintage, vintage, and prestige *cuvee* bottlings.

Rose (Pink). Derives its color from the skins of black grapes and varies from a pale salmon shade to a rich berry color. Also available in non-vintage, vintage, and prestige *cuvee* bottlings.

Degree of Dryness. Depending on the dosage, Champagne may be quite dry (extra-brut or brut), semi-sweet (extra-dry), or quite sweet (sec and demi-sec). Brut is dryer than extra-dry, and is considered the most versatile of Champagnes.

Light Bodied. Blended with a high proportion of white Chardonnay wines.

Full-Bodied. Blended with a high proportion of black Pinot Noir or Pinot Meunier wines.

Medium-Bodied. Blended with approximately equal proportions of white and black grape wines.

TERMINOLOGY

Méthode Champenoise. The second fermenting of Champagne in the bottle after natural fermenting agents (yeast) and a small quantity of cane sugar are added to the blend before bottling. This term is also used on the bottles of wine fermented by the Champagne method although not from wineries in the Champagne Region. If the name of any country or state other than France appears on the label, or if the phrase *Méthode Champenoise* is used, the wine is not authentic Champagne.

Dosage. Second fermentation causes the formation of a deposit (spent yeasts) which adheres to the inside surface of the bottle. This sediment is removed by a process know as *remuage* whereby over a period of months the bottle is gradually shaken, turned, and tilted until it is vertical in an inverted position. At this point the sediment has collected into the neck of the bottle where it is deposited against the cork. This sediment is removed by a process known as *dégorgement* whereby the neck of the bottle is placed in a freezing solution.

This causes the sediment to freeze within a small block of ice. Turning the bottle upright and removing the cellar cork causes internal pressure to eject the ice pellet and with it the sediment. A mixture of cane sugar and Champagne is added to the bottle after the sediment has been removed to replace the wine lost in disgorging. This mixture is called the *dosage,* and the proportion of sugar used determines if the Champagne will be extra brut or brut (dry); semi-sweet; or sec or demi-sec (sweet).

Source:
Product Literature, New York: Champagne News and Information Bureau, 1992.

Coffee

GRADING

Coffee beans are brewed and then graded for aroma and taste by a process called *cupping*. The *cupping process* consists of a systematic procedure that enables the *cupper* to evaluate the taste and aroma of coffee. The coffee grades are not numbered as in Grade 1, Grade 2, etc., but rather *described* using a controlled vocabulary. Because cupping is primarily used by professionals when buying or blending coffees, its procedures are rigorously followed by those in the coffee trade. Some of the terms used by cuppers to describe coffee include:

BOUQUET (COMPLEXITY)
Fragrance. Sweetly floral, sweetly spicy.
Aroma. Fruity, herby.
Nose. Caramelly, nutty, malty.
Taints. Earthy, grassy, hidy, musty.
Aftertaste. Carbony, chocolaty, spicy, turpeny.

LIQUORING (BALANCE)
Taste. Acidy, bland, harsh, mellow, pungent, sharp, soury, winey.
Faults. Fermented, rancid, rubbery, woody.

MOUTHFEEL (DEPTH)
Body. Creamy, heavy.

TERMINOLOGY

Mountain Grown, Premium, Gourmet, Fancy, etc. These terms have no official definitions and have little meaning.

Blends. A mix of two or more types of coffee beans.

Roasted. Coffee beans are roasted and become darker the longer they roast. Coffees may be called unroasted, American Roast, French Roast, and Italian Roast, with Italian Roast the darkest. Different coffee beans reach their peak flavor at different roasting times and temperatures.

100% Columbian. Consists only of coffee beans from Columbia. Is not necessarily an indication of high quality.

Decaffeinated. Coffee made from beans from which the caffeine has been removed by soaking the unroasted beans in solvents such as methylene chloride.

Water Processed. A term used to refer to the Swiss Water Process decaffeination system which uses charcoal filters instead of solvents to dissolve the caffeine. However, all decaffeinated coffee can be called water processed.

Natural Decaffeination. Used to describe coffee decaffeinated by soaking the beans in ethyl acetate, which occurs naturally in some fruits, instead of methylene chloride, a man-made substance.

Instant Coffee. The beans go through a process whereby the flavors are condensed into a liquid which is either freeze-dried (the liquid is frozen and then dried in a vacuum and low heat) or spray-dried (the coffee is atomized with hot air).

High Yield Coffee. A type of coffee that purportedly requires less coffee per cup than a traditional ground coffee.

Sources:

Correspondence, The Specialty Coffee Association of America, One World Trade Center, Suite 800, Long Beach, CA, 1992.

"Ground Coffee," *Consumer Reports,* Vol. 56, no. 1 (January 1991): 30-41.

Lingle, Ted R., *The Coffee Cupper's Handbook: A Systematic Guide to the Sensory Evaluation of Coffee's Flavor,* Washington: Coffee Development Group, 1986.

Lockhart, E.E., "Chemistry of Coffee," Publication No. 25, New York: The Coffee Brewing Center, 1969.

Sivetz, Michael, and Norma W. Desrosier, *Coffee Technology,* Westport, Connecticut: AVI Publishing Co., 1979.

Cognac

Legend has it that Cognac was first discovered 400 years ago by a knight remembered today as the Chevalier de la Croix Marron. Betrayed by his wife, he murdered her and her lover and then dreamt of burning in hell twice for his sins. The next morning he ordered that the wine he had been distilling once, making a brandy that was indifferent to taste, be distilled twice. Thus, the double-distillation process that distinguishes Cognac from all other brandies was discovered. All Cognacs are brandy, but only the best, twice-distilled brandies made in the Cognac region can be called Cognac. All Cognacs are blends of spirits of different ages and different vintages. Creating the final product is the job of a master blender who combines the different spirits to produce a harmonious whole. Generally, the older the average age of the Cognac in the final blend, the higher the price. Unlike wines, Cognacs do not age in the bottle, only in wood. Therefore, a Cognac that has aged 3 years in oak is a 3-year-old Cognac even if it has been sitting in a wine cellar for 100 years.

GRADES

The various qualities of Cognacs are often indicated by stars: one, two, or three, in ascending quality. In 1975 French law decreed that a three star Cognac must have spent at least 2½ years aged in wood. Cognacs are also labeled by a lettering system to indicate quality.

C. Cognac.

E. Extra or Especial.

F. Fine.

O. Old.

P. Pale.

S. Superior.

V. Very.

X. Extra.

VO, VSOP, or Reserve. Cognac aged in wood at least 4½ years.

Accordingly, Cognac labels contain designations like the following:

VS (Historically Three Stars). The average aging period of the Cognac is 5 to 9 years.

VSOP (Very Superior Old Pale) or Réserve. The average age of Cognac used in the blend is above 12 years.

XO, Napoleon, VVSOP, Vieille Réserve, Grande Réserve, Royal and Vieus. Cognacs that are older and therefore contain a very high percentage of Cognac that has been aged 20, 30, 40 years or more.

Grande Champagne. The grapes used to produce the Cognac come entirely from the Cognac region's top vineyards. Fine Champagne is a blend of Grande and Petite Champagne, with at least 50 percent of the blend coming from Grande Champagne.

Source:

Product Literature, New York: Cognac Information Bureau, 1992.

Distilled Spirits

Bond, Bonded, Bottled in Bond, Aged in Bond. The distilled spirits are composed of the same kind of spirits from the same class of materials, are produced in the same distilling season by the same distiller at the same distillery, are stored for at least four years in wooden containers, are unaltered from their original condition by the addition of other substances, are reduced in proof by the addition of pure water only to 100 degrees of proof, and bottled at 100 degree of proof.

Brandy. An alcoholic distillate from the fermented juice, mash, or wine of fruit, or from the residue thereof, produced at less than 190 degree proof in such manner that the distillate possesses the taste, aroma, and characteristics generally attributed to the product, and bottled at not less than 80 degree proof.

Gin. A product obtained by original distillation from mash, or by redistillation of distilled spirits, or by mixing neutral spirits, with (or over) juniper berries and other aromatics, or with (or over) extracts derived from infusions, percolations, or maceration of such materials, and includes mixtures of gin and neutral spirits. It shall derive its main characteristic flavor from juniper berries and be bottled at not less than 80 degree proof. Gin produced exclusively by original distillation or by redistillation may be further designated as *distilled. Dry gin*, Geneva gin, and *Old Tom Gin* are types of gin known under such designations.

Grain Spirits. Neutral spirits distilled from a fermented mash of grain and stored in oak containers.

Neutral Spirits or Alcohol. The distilled spirits produced from any material at or above 190 degree proof, and, if bottled, bottled at not less than 80 degree proof.

Proof Gallon. A gallon of liquid at 60 degree F which contains 50 percent by volume of ethyl alcohol having a specific gravity of 0.7939 at 60 degree F.

Proof. The relative strength of an alcoholic liquor with reference to the arbitrary standard for proof spirit, taken as 100 proof. One degree of proof equals one-half of 1 percent of alcohol. An 80 proof product contains 40 percent alcohol; a 90 proof product, 45 percent.

Pure. The word pure cannot be used unless it refers to a particular ingredient or is part of the name of the producer or bootlegger.

Vodka. Neutral spirits so distilled so as to be without distinctive character, aroma, taste, or color.

Source:

Bureau of Alcohol, Tobacco, and Firearms, "Standards of Identity for Distilled Spirits," 27 CFR Section 5.22 (1991), Washington: Government Printing Office.

Grape Juice, Canned

Canned grape juice is the unfermented liquid obtained from properly matured fresh grapes. The grape juice is prepared without concentration, without dilution, is packed with or without the addition of sweetening ingredients, and is sufficiently processed by heat to assure preservation of the product in hermetically sealed containers (either metal or glass).

TYPES

Type I. Concord type (prepared from grapes of the slip-skin varieties of the Concord type of the *Labrusca* species).

Type II. Any type other than Concord type (prepared from a single variety of grapes other than Concord type).

Type III. Blended type (prepared from two or more varieties of grapes).

STYLES

Unless specifically designated as *sweetened,* canned grape juice is considered as *unsweetened.*

Style I. Unsweetened (without added sweetening ingredient).

Style II. Sweetened (with added sweetening ingredient).

GRADES

U.S. Grade A or U.S. Fancy. Canned grape juice from which tartrate crystals have been removed. Type I products possess a bright purple or bright reddish-purple color. Types II and III products have a bright color characteristic of the varietal type from which it was prepared. The juice is practically free from defects but may possess a slight amount of sediment and residue of an amorphous nature and not more than a trace of sediment and residue of a nonamorphous nature. It is practically free from tartrate crystals and is free from particles of skin, particles of pulp, particles of seed, and from any other defects. The flavor is a distinct and normal flavor, typical of

well-matured grapes. The canned grape juice is free from any trace of scorching, caramelization, objectionable flavors, and objectionable odors of any kind.

U.S. Grade B or U.S. Choice. The quality of canned grape juice from which tartrate crystals have been removed. It possesses a reasonably good color, meaning that for Type I juice, a purple or reddish-purple color which may be slightly dull purple, slightly dull bluish-purple, or slightly dull reddish-purple, but which is not off-color. For Types II and III, a color typical of canned grape juice characteristic of the varietal type or varietal types from which prepared. It may be slightly dull but is not off-color. The juice is reasonably free from defects, meaning that the it may possess a slight amount of sediment and residue of an amorphous or non-amorphous nature, a slight amount of tartrate crystals, and not more than a trace of particles of skin, particles of pulp, particles of seed, and other defects. The flavor is normal and typical of reasonably well-matured grapes, and the canned grape juice may be slightly astringent but is free from any trace of scorching, caramelization, and objectionable flavors and odors of any kind.

U.S. Grade D or Substandard. Fails to meet the requirements of U.S. Grade B or U.S. Choice.

Source:

Agricultural Marketing Service, USDA, United States Standards for Grades of Canned Grape Juice, 7 CFR sections 52.1341 to 52.1352 (1991), Washington: Government Printing Office.

Grape Juice, Frozen Concentrated Sweetened

Frozen concentrated sweetened grape juice is prepared from unfermented single-strength grape juice. Single-strength grape juice, natural grape essence, or a combination of both may be mixed to the concentrate and packed with the addition of nutritive sweetening ingredient, with or without ascorbic acid. Edible fruit acid may be added to adjust the flavor. The product is then frozen and maintained at temperatures necessary for its preservation.

TYPES

Type I. Prepared from grapes of the slip-skin varieties of the Concord type of the *Labrusca* species. Not less than 50 percent of the total soluble solids of the finished concentrate is derived from the grapes.

Type II. Prepared from a mixture of Type I with one or more varieties other than Type I. Not less than 50 percent of the total soluble solids of the finished concentrate are derived from the grapes, of which, not less than one-half are derived from Type I grapes.

GRADES

U.S. Grade A or U.S. Fancy. The reconstituted product possesses a good color. For Type I products that means a bright reddish-purple color characteristic of a grape juice prepared from Concord type grape juice. For Type II it means a bright color characteristic of a grape juice beverage prepared from Type I juice and from varietal types of juice other than Type I. It is practically free from defects such as sediment and other residue, from tartrate crystals, particles of skin, particles of seed, and from other defects. The flavor is fine, distinct, and normal, free from any objectionable flavors and objectionable odors of any kind.

U.S. Grade B or U.S. Choice. Reconstitutes properly and of which the reconstituted product possesses a reasonably good color which may be slightly dull but which is not off-color. It is reasonably free from defects and possesses a reasonably good flavor typical of reasonably well matured grapes free from objectionable flavors and objectionable odors of any kind.

Substandard. Fails to meet the requirements of U.S. Grade B or U.S. Choice.

Source:
Agricultural Marketing Service, USDA, 7 CFR sections 52.2451 to 52.2464 (1991), Washington: Government Printing Office.

Grapefruit Juice

Grapefruit juice is the unfermented juice, intended for direct consumption, obtained by mechanical process from sound, mature grapefruit (*Citrus paradise macfadyen*) from which seeds and peel (except embryonic seeds and small fragments of seeds and peel which cannot be separated by good manufacturing practice) and excess pulp are removed and to which may be added not more than 10 percent by volume of the unfermented juice obtained from mature hybrids of grapefruit.

STYLES

Unsweetened
Sweetened (Sweetener added)

COLOR

White or amber
Pink or red

GRADES

U.S. Grade A. Has a good color which is representative of juice from mature, well-ripened grapefruit. The juice may show fading and lack of luster. It is practically free from defects normally expected in grapefruit juice.

U.S. Grade B. The color of grapefruit juice may be slightly, but not materially, affected by scorching, oxidation, or caramelization. The presence of defects does not seriously affect the appearance or drinking quality of grapefruit juice. The grapefruit juice is materially but not seriously affected by bitterness, terpene, processing, storage, or container flavors.

Substandard. Fails to meet the requirements for U.S. Grade B.

Sources:
Agricultural Marketing Service, USDA, United States Standards for Grades of Grapefruit Juice, 7 CFR sections 52.1221 to 52.1230 (1991), Washington: Government Printing Office.Food and Drug Administration, HHS, Grapefruit Juice, 21 CFR Section 146.132 (1991), Washington: Government Printing Office.

Grapefruit-Orange Juice

Juice prepared from a combination of unfermented juices obtained from mature fresh grapefruit (*Citrus paradisi*) and mature sweet oranges (*Citrus sinensis*). Up to 10 percent of the juice of oranges from the mandarin group (*Citrus reticulata*), however, may be added. It is recommended that the minor juice ingredient (either orange or grapefruit) provide not less than 25 percent, by weight, of the total soluble fruit solids present in the finished product.

TYPES

Single Strength Type. Composed of single strength grapefruit juice and orange juice, with or without added grapefruit juice concentrate and/or orange juice concentrate.

Reconstituted Type. Composed of grapefruit juice concentrate and orange juice concentrate and water, with or without added single strength grapefruit juice and/or single strength orange juice.

STYLES.

Unsweetened
Sweetened (Sweetener added)

GRADES

U.S. Grade A or U.S. Fancy. Shows no coagulation. The juice mixture has a yellow-orange color that is bright and typical of the freshly extracted juice of oranges and either white fleshed grapefruit or red or pink fleshed grapefruit. It is free from browning due to scorching, oxidation, caramelization, or other causes. The juice may not contain more than 12 percent free and suspended pulp. Any other defects present, such as small seeds and particles of membrane, core, and peel, may no more than slightly detract from the appearance or drinking quality of the juice. For refrigerated juice or juice not subjected to high temperatures prior to refrigerating the flavor is fine, distinct, and substantially typical of freshly extracted grapefruit juice. For canned juice or juice that has been subjected to high temperatures, "good flavor" means a fine, distinct grapefruit juice and orange juice flavor which is free from off flavors and off odors of any kind.

U.S. Grade B or U.S. Choice. May show only a slight coagulation. The juice has a fairly typical color that may range from light yellow to light amber, may be dull or show evidence of slight browning, but is not off color. It is reasonably free from defects, meaning the juice may not contain more than 18 percent free and suspended pulp, and that any other defects present may no more than materially detract from the appearance or drinking quality of the juice. It has a flavor less desirable than "good flavor" because of excess bitterness, terpenic, processing, storage, or container flavors but is not seriously objectionable and is free from off flavors and off odors of any kind.

Substandard. The quality of grapefruit-orange juice that fails to meet the requirements of U.S. Grade B.

Source:

Agricultural Marketing Service, USDA, United States Standards for Grades of Grapefruit Juice and Orange Juice, 7 CFR sections 52.1281 to 52.1293 (1991), Washington: Government Printing Office.

Lemon Juice, Canned

Canned lemon juice is the undiluted, unconcentrated, unfermented juice obtained from sound, mature lemons of one or more of the high acid varieties. The fruit is prepared by sorting and washing prior to extraction of the juice to assure a clean and sanitary product. The product is sufficiently processed with heat to assure preservation in hermetically sealed containers. The flavor of the product is evaluated after preparing as follows:

Lemon juice - 30 ml
Sugar - 26 gm
Water - 160 ml

GRADES

U.S. Grade A or U.S. Fancy. Has a good color which is bright and typical of fresh, properly processed lemon juice. It is practically free of browning caused by such factors as scorching, oxidation, and storage conditions. It is practically free of such defects as particles of membrane, core, or skin, from seeds or seed particles, and any other defects that affect the wholesomeness or detract from the appearance or utility of the product. It has the distinct flavor of freshly extracted canned lemon juice that is free of any trace of terpenic, oxidized, scorched, or caramelized flavors and is free of any other abnormal flavors.

U.S. Grade C or U.S. Standard. Has fairly good color that may be only fairly bright, but is not off-color. It is reasonably free of browning due to scorching, oxidation, improper storage, or any other causes. The product is fairly free of defects and has a normal flavor; it may have a slightly caramelized or slightly oxidized flavor, but it is free of off-flavors of any kind.

Substandard. Fails to meet the requirements of U.S. Grade C.

Sources:

Agricultural Marketing Service, USDA, 7 CFR sections 52.5481 to 52.5492 (1991), Washington: Government Printing Office.
Food and Drug Administration, HHS, Lemon Juice, 21 CFR Section 146.144 (1991), Washington: Government Printing Office.

Lemonade, Frozen Concentrated

Frozen concentrate for lemonade is the product prepared from lemon juice and one or more nutritive sweetening ingredients. It may contain added lemon oil or concentrated lemon oil (or their extracts or emulsions) and may or may not contain water in sufficient quantities to standardize the product. The product contains not less than 48 percent by weight of soluble solids. The lemon juice is produced from fresh, sound, ripe, and thoroughly cleansed fruit of one or more of the high acid varieties of the species *Citrus limon (limonia)*. This juice may be fresh or frozen or fresh concentrated or frozen concentrated. The concentrate for lemonade is processed in accordance with good commercial practice and is frozen and maintained at temperatures sufficient for the preservation of the product. If properly labeled, any color materials permissible under the provisions of the Federal Food, Drug, and Cosmetic Act may be added.

U.S. Grade A or U.S. Fancy. Mixes readily into a lemonade that possesses an amount of pulp, cloud, and juice sacs so as to substantially reflect the appearance of lemonade prepared from freshly expressed lemon juice. It possesses a good color that reflects the appearance of fresh lemonade or, if colored, possesses a bright, attractive, light-red color typical of colored lemonade. It is practically free from defects so that there may be present not more than an average of one seed or portion of seed for each quart of prepared lemonade. The appearance and drinking quality of the lemonade is otherwise not materially affected by objectionable material, harmless extraneous material, any other defects. Possesses a fine, distinct, and substantially typical flavor of fresh lemonade free from terpenic, oxidized, rancid, or other off-flavors.

U.S. Grade B or U.S. Choice. Mixes readily into a lemonade that reasonably reflects the appearance and color of fresh lemonade. It is reasonably free from defects, meaning that there may be present not more than an average of two seeds or portions of seeds for each quart of lemonade, and the appearance and drinking quality is otherwise not seriously affected. It possesses a reasonably good flavor practically free from off-flavors.

Substandard. Fails to meet the requirements of U.S. Grade B or U.S. Choice.

Sources:

Agricultural Marketing Service, USDA, 7 CFR sections 52.1421 to 52.1431(1991), Washington: Government Printing Office.
Food and Drug Administration, HHS, Frozen Concentrate for Lemonade, 21 CFR Section 146.120 (1991), Washington: Government Printing Office.

Limeade, Frozen Concentrated

Frozen concentrate for limeade is the product prepared from lime juice and one or more nutritive sweetening ingredients to which may be added oil derived from limes for added flavor. It may or may not contain water in sufficient quantities to standardize the product. The lime juice is produced from fresh, sound, mature, and thoroughly cleansed fruit of one or more of the varieties of the species *Citrus aurantifolia*. Such juice may be fresh or frozen or may be fresh juice concentrate or frozen concentrate. The concentrate for limeade is processed in accordance with good commercial practice and is frozen and maintained at temperatures sufficient for the preservation of the product. If properly labeled, any artificial color permissible under the provisions of the Federal Food, Drug, and Cosmetic Act may be added.

GRADES

U.S. Grade A or U.S. Fancy. Mixes readily into a limeade that possesses an amount of pulp and cloud so as to substantially reflect the appearance of limeade prepared from freshly expressed lime juice. It possesses a good, bright, characteristic color. If artificially colored, it possesses a bright, attractive, light green color typical of artificially colored limeade. It is practically free from defects and possesses a fine, distinct flavor free from terpenic, oxidized, rancid, or other off flavors.

U.S. Grade B or U.S. Choice. Mixes readily into a limeade that possesses at least a slight, but not an excessive, amount of pulp and cloud so as to reasonably reflect the appearance of fresh limeade. Possesses a reasonably good, characteristic color that reflects the color of fresh limeade, but is not dark or otherwise discolored for any reason. If artificially colored, possesses a reasonably bright color that is reasonably free from defects. Possesses a reasonably good flavor fairly typical of limeade prepared from freshly expressed lime juice and is practically free from terpenic, oxidized, rancid, or other off flavors and is free from abnormal flavors of any kind.

Substandard. Fails to meet the requirements of U.S. Grade B or U.S. Choice.

Source:
Agricultural Marketing Service, USDA, 7 CFR sections 52.2521 to 52.2530 (1991), Washington: Government Printing Office.

Orange Juice

Orange juice is the unfermented juice obtained from mature oranges of the species *Citrus sinensis*. Seeds (except embryonic seeds and small fragments of seeds that cannot be separated by good manufacturing practice) and excess pulp are removed. The juice may be chilled, but it is not frozen.

Frozen Orange Juice. Orange juice that has been frozen.

Pasteurized Orange Juice. The orange juice is so treated by heat as to reduce substantially the enzymatic activity and the number of viable microorganisms. Either before or after such heat treatment, all or part of the product may be frozen.

Orange Juice with Preservative. A preservative is added to inhibit spoilage. It may be heat-treated to reduce substantially the enzymatic activity and the number of viable microorganisms.

Reduced Acid Frozen Concentrated Orange Juice. A process that uses anionic ion-exchange resins to reduce acidity.

Frozen Concentrated Orange Juice. Prepared by removing water from the juice of mature oranges. The finished food is of such concentration that when diluted according to label directions the diluted article will contain not less than 11.8 percent by weight of orange juice soluble solids, exclusive of the solids of any added optional sweetening ingredients. The dilution ratio shall be not less than 3 plus 1. The term *dilution ratio* means the whole number of volumes of water per volume of frozen concentrate required to produce orange juice. The name of the food concentrated to a dilution ratio of 3 plus 1 is *frozen concentrated orange juice* or *frozen orange juice concentrate*. The name of the food concentrated to a dilution ratio greater than 3 plus 1 is *frozen concentrated orange juice, ____ plus 1* or *frozen orange juice concentrate, ____ plus 1*, the blank being filled in with the whole number showing the dilution ratio, e.g., *frozen orange juice concentrate, 4 plus 1*.

GRADES

U.S. Grade A. No coagulation, good color when compared with the USDA Orange Juice Color Standards as points of reference. It is practically free from defects such as juice cells, pulp, seeds or portions of seeds, specks, particles of membrane, core, peel, or any other distinctive features that adversely affect the appearance or drinking quality of the orange juice. It has very good flavor when evaluated based upon characteristics normal to each type of product. If the orange juice comes from concentrate, it has the appearance of fresh orange juice, reconstitutes properly, and has very good color. It is practically free from defects and has a very good flavor that is fine, distinct, and substantially typical of orange juice free from off flavors of any kind.

U.S. Grade B. It may have slight coagulation and reasonably good color. Any defects present do not seriously affect the appearance or drinking quality of the orange juice. It has good flavor. If the orange juice comes from concentrate, it has the appearance of fresh orange juice, reconstitutes properly, has good color, is reasonably free from defects, and has good flavor.

Substandard. Orange juice that fails to meet the requirements for Grade B.

STYLES

Unsweetened.

Sweetened. (Not applicable to reduced acid frozen concentrated orange juice.)

Sources:
Agricultural Marketing Service, USDA, 7 CFR sections 52.1551 to 52.1559 (1991), Washington: Government Printing Office.
Food and Drug Administration, HHS, Lemon Juice, 21 CFR sections 146.135 to 146.154 (1991), Washington: Government Printing Office.

Tangerine Juice, Canned

Canned tangerine juice is the undiluted, unconcentrated, unfermented juice obtained from mature fresh fruit of the Mandarin orange (*Citrus reticulata*), which fruit has been properly washed. It is packed with or without the addition of sweetening ingredients and is sufficiently processed by heat to assure preservation of the product. It is packed in containers which are hermetically sealed.

GRADES

U.S. Grade A or U.S. Fancy. Shows no coagulation. Possesses a bright yellow to yellow-orange color typical of freshly extracted juice and is free from browning due to scorching, oxidation, caramelization, or other causes. It may contain not more than 7 percent free and suspended pulp, and there may be present not more than 0.025 percent by volume of recoverable oil. It does not contain seeds or seed particles or other defects that more than slightly affect the appearance of the products. It possesses a fine, distinct canned tangerine juice flavor which is free from traces of scorching, caramelization, oxidation, or terpene. It is free from off flavors of any kind.

U.S. Grade C or U.S. Standard. May show slight coagulation. It possesses a typical yellow to yellow-orange color that may be slightly amber or show evidence of slight browning, but is not off-color. It may contain not more than 10 percent free and suspended pulp, and there may be present not more than 0.035 percent by volume of recoverable oil. It does not contain seeds or seed particles or other defects that materially affect the appearance of the product. It possesses a good, normal canned tangerine juice flavor which may have a slightly caramelized or slightly oxidized flavor but is free from off flavors of any kind.

U.S. Grade D or Substandard. Fails to meet the requirements of U.S. Grade C or U.S. Standard.

Source:
Agricultural Marketing Service, USDA, 7 CFR sections 52.2071 to 52.2082 (1991), Washington: Government Printing Office.

Tea

BLACK TEAS

Assam. Grown in northeastern India, descendent of wild tea found in the province of Assam in the 1830s. Bright colored infusion with a distinct, full bodied, rich malt taste. Almost always used in blends.

Cachar. Product of Assam's Surma Valley in India. Grayish-black leaf, thick and sweet infusion. Most common variety of Indian tea.

Ceylon. Produced in Sri Lanka. Rich flavor, bright infusion, light golden color, pungent.

China Black. From the Anhewi Province, a blend of traditional China teas. Mild flavor, strong aroma of Keemun teas.

Ching Wo. Not often seen outside of China, it is found in specialty shops and considered the finest South China tea. Tightly rolled, long leaf with a delicate flavor and bright reddish color.

Coronation. A blend of India and Ceylon teas originally prepared to commemorate the 1953 coronation of Queen Elizabeth II.

Hearty, full-bodied tea with distinct character of Ceylon and strong taste of Assam.

Darjeeling. The "champagne" of teas, grown in the foothills of the Himalayas. Gold tip Darjeeling is superior. Delicate, full-bodied tea with a rich amber color, muscatel flavor, with a pleasant, lingering aftertaste.

Dooars. From a district in India and generally produced for blending. A black leaf, soft and mellow infusion.

Dragonmoon. A blend of Darjeeling and Assam teas.

Earl Grey. Oil of Bergamot, derived from a citrus fruit, is the fragrance of this tea.

English Breakfast. A blend of India and Ceylon teas. The name is a North American invention.

Hu-Kwa. Named for a wealthy Chinese merchant, this is also the name of America's first commercial clipper ship.

Irish Breakfast. Assam and Ceylon tea blend.

Jasmine. From Foochow, made with a blend of Hyson green tea and China black tea. It is scented with white jasmine flowers. The blossoms are scattered on beds of hot, just-fired tea leaves. When the buds are removed, the scent remains. Sometimes, in finer blends, the blossoms are retained with the tea.

Keemun. From China and Taiwan, the finest of China's black teas. Sometimes blended into English Breakfast.

Kenya. High-grown tea from Africa. Tippy tea made of black leaves with rich aroma and brisk flavor. Reddish-black infusion, which is slightly fragrant and flavorful.

Lapsang Souchong. South China tea originating in Fujian Province. Sometimes blended with Assam and Ceylon. Distinctively large, black, slightly curled leaf. The infusion is rich and smoky with a strong aroma.

Lemon. A blend of high-grown Ceylon teas with lemon peel and essence added.

Nilgiri. The name of this tea means *blue mountains*. It grows in southern India at high elevations. Mostly used for blending.

Orange Pekoe. A large leaf tea often confused for a blend. Also a brand name for some companies. Generally a high-grown leaf with flavor that varies from very delicate to bland.

Russian. Grown in the foothills of the Caucasian Mountains bordering Russia and Turkey on tea plantations dating back to 1848. Long leaf, like a China tea. Thin, light liquor with a somewhat flat flavor.

Russian Blend. Traditional Russian combination of three parts Lapsang Souchong to one part Orange Pekoe.

Russian Caravan. A blend of China black and oolong teas, said to be more flavorful because it was carried by land and not exposed to moist sea air, which lessens flavor.

Yunnan. From southwestern province of China. Long golden leaves are delicately twisted to make a golden infusion.

OOLONG TEAS

Black Dragon. From China's Amoy, Foochow, and Canton provinces as well as Taiwan. A delicate, fruity infusion with a light color.

China Oolong. From both China and Formosa, generally a blend of 50 percent each. Large brown leaf, gentle infusion, fragrance of sun-ripened fruit.

Formosa Oolong. Originated in Indochina. Astringent like

Darjeeling with no bitterness.

Mainland Oolong. From China, often scented with jasmine and gardenia with a nutty taste.

Pouchong. From China and Taiwan. Sometimes called Pao-Chung.

GREEN TEAS

Gunpowder. A grade of tea in which leaves are rolled into small round pellets. It is also a brand name. The Chinese call it Siaou Chu, and it is grown in China's Anhwel Province and Taiwan. The smaller the pellets, the younger the leaves and the finer the quality. The color is yellow-green.

Gyokuro. Also known as *Pearl Dew*. This is the finest grade of exported Japanese tea, made from the tender tips of plants grown in shaded gardens. It is treated by hand, is expensive, and, outside of Japan, is found only in specialty stores. It also has a high caffeine content.

Hyson. Bears the name of a wealthy East India merchant who first introduced it to England. The name translates to *flourishing spring*. It is a pan-fried, older, large, bluish-black leaf that is hard and twisted. The infusion is fragrant, light, mellow, and often bitter.

Imperial. A type of Ceylon, China, or India green tea. Made from rolled older leaves after the gunpowder grade is sifted out.

Matcha. Also known as *Tencha*. The Japanese powdered tea used exclusively for the tea ceremony. Young leaves of mature plants are used to make this thick and bitter infusion.

Pingsuey. One of the most prominent green teas from China's Chekiang Province. Named for the market town where it is sold, the name means *ice water*. A light and sweet infusion with a blue-green color.

Runchi. Chinese green tea with a brassy flavor produced in the Indian district of the same name.

Sencha. The most common Japanese tea. Popular in Japanese restaurants in the West with sushi.

Shou-Mei. China green, sun dried, minimally processed with a bitter taste. It is known as *Old Man's Eyebrows*.

Spider Leg. Japanese tea named for the plant's long, thin, twisted leaves.

Young Hyson. A tea grade that has become a brand name. The name translates to mean *before the rains*.

WHITE TEAS

White teas are very rare teas that are highly prized and produced exclusively in China. They are primarily from the Fukien province. They are generally taken without a meal. All white teas are pale golden and slightly sweet. Names include:

Yin-Chen. Known as *Silver Needles*.

Pai-Mu-Ta. Known as *White Peony*.

Ying-Mei. Known as *Noble Beauty*.

Silvery Tip Pekoe.

GRADING

Like coffee, tea is not graded by a numbering system like Grade 1, Grade 2, etc., but rather by a vocabulary of terms that are generally used by tea tasters. Teas are judged on: pungency (a sharp and slightly acrid but not bitter taste); body (is the tea strong and bold?); color; purity; and flavor (which could be delicate or bitter, robust or mild, subtle or sharp, fruity or spicy, smoky or wine-like, etc.). The following terms are among those used by professionals when tasting tea:

Agony of the Leaves. The unfolding of the leaves when subjected to boiling water.

Aroma. The smell of the tea leaf and infusion associated with the tea's flavor and fragrance.

Baggy. An undesirable taint in the dry leaf, as well as in the liquor of the tea.

Bakey. The result of a tea that is too high fired, too much moisture removed.

Banji. Two leaves without a dormant bud; sterile.

Biscuity. The pleasant aroma occasionally sensed in the leaf or liquor of well-fired Assam tea grown in northeastern India.

Black Tea. Any tea that has been well-fermented before being fired as opposed to green or oolong teas.

Blend. A mixture of different growths.

Blistered. Swollen or hollow leaves that carry bubblelike cavities which result from drying too quickly during firing.

Bloom. A desirable leaf with a sheen to it, which means it is not overly processed and was carefully sorted.

Body. A liquor with fullness and strength, not thin.

Bold. A large leaf, which might have benefited from cutting, or a rich and well-pronounced tasting infusion.

Bright. Sparkling reddish infusion that can have a copper look.

Brisk. Tea that has been well-fired, resulting in a pungent, lively taste.

Broken. Tea that has been broken while being rolled or cut, used to define grades.

Brownish. The color of tea that has been excessively fired at high temperatures after improper withering or bad plucking. It can also refer to the natural color of a tippy tea.

Burnt. An infusion that has a taste of tea prepared at too high a temperature.

Caffeine. The stimulating component of tea, less than 1 grain per cup as opposed to 1.5 grains in coffee.

Character. A desirable property of the infusion that allows a well-trained taster to define the origin of the tea leaf, as in, "This is the character of an Assam tea from India."

Chunky. Broken teas too large in size.

Clean. A leaf free of debris and other grades, or an infusion of an inferior tea that does not have an aftertaste.

Color. The hue of the infusion.

Colory. A bright and appealing infusion.

Common Tea. A thin and nondescript infusion with little flavor.

Coarse. An infusion with undesirable taste resulting from irregular firing or coarse leaves.

Coppery. Bright, copper-colored infusion, which is the sign of a well-prepared black tea.

Creaming Down. A film from the milk that rises to the top of the testing cup and results in a thick liquor of certain high-grade teas. It is considered to be a reaction of the tannin content with the caffeine.

Curly. A leaf with an appearance of whole leaf grades, instead of twisted or wiry leaves.

Dark. A poor tea's color.

Dull. An infusion that lacks brightness and is unclear; also a dry leaf that has been improperly processed.

Dust. The smallest sifting grade that is like a powder and generally of poor taste.

Earthy. Tea that has been stored in damp quarters and has a musty taste.

Even. Tea leaf that is consistent in size and once infused delivers a bright liquor.

Fannings. Small, grainy, particle grade often used in industrial teas.

Flaky. A leaf that is improperly processed and is flat and fragile.

Flat. An infusion that is not brisk or pungent, with little discernible aroma.

Full. Substantial, colorful, and strong tea that isn't bitter.

Fully Fired. An infusion made from over-fired tea.

Golden Tip. The orange-colored tip looked for in black tea.

Gone Off. Moldy or old tea which is not desirable because of its deteriorated quality.

Green. The color of an infused leaf that is not well-withered or rolled. Not to be confused with green tea.

Green Tea. Tea that is not fermented.

Gray. The color of a black tea leaf that has been overprocessed.

Hard. Pungent; a quality looked for in Assam teas of India.

Harsh. A bitter infusion common in improperly withered or immature tea, also resulting from coarse tea leaves.

Heady. Distinctively potent.

Heavy. A thick infusion which is strong and colory, not overly brisk.

High-Fired. Tea that is processed under high temperatures. It can also refer to tea that is dried too long and has lost flavor.

Infusion. The liquor resulting from steeped or soaked leaves, bark, berries, etc.

Malt. Tea with slight malt aroma that is the desirable result of high firing.

Mature. Not flat or raw.

Metallic. Coppery taste.

Mixed. An unblended tea that is poorly manufactured with leaves that are not uniform in color.

Muddy. A dull-looking infusion.

Mushy. Tea that is too soft because it is packed in a moist container.

New. Tea that has not had time to mellow so it tastes raw when infused.

Nose. Aroma of tea.

Orange Pekoe. A common, long, thin, wiry leaf sometimes containing a tip.

Plain. An infusion that has a dull look and sour taste.

Point. Characteristics of a leaf that, when combined, cause a strong flavor that penetrates a blend. Also brightness and acidity of the infusion.

Pungent. Sharp, astringent taste. Not bitter.

Ragged. Uneven leaf.

Rasping. Coarse flavor.

Rawness. Bitter flavor.

Roughness. A harsh infusion.

Round. Strong and good color, not rough.

Sappy. Full, juicy infusion.

Self-Drinking. Unblended tea that is full of flavor, aroma, and body.

Smoky. The smoke flavor pervasive in certain infusions such as Lapsang Souchong from China.

Stalk. A tea with stalks in it that is usually the result of a coarse leaf and hard rolling.

Standing Up. When tea holds its original color and flavor in a quality-control test.

Strength. Thick, pungent, and brisk.

Sweet. A light infusion.

Sweetish. A tainted infusion.

Tainted. Strangely flavored tea, which may have been infected by microorganisms during manufacture or storage; a tea affected by a strong aroma from another herb or chemical.

Tannin Content. The chemical component of tea that provides astringency.

Tarry. A smoky aroma.

Theol. The essential oil of tea.

Thick. Full, strong taste in mouth.

Tip. The bud of the tea plant.

Tippy Teas. Tea with golden buds, which have been harvested from young leaves.

Uneven. Irregular tea leaf resulting from poor sorting. In infusions it means that the leaf turns different colors as a result of uneven processing.

Weak. A thin infusion.

Well Twisted. Tightly rolled leaf ideal in withered tea.

Wiry. Well twisted Orange Pekoe.

Woody. Poor flavor that is reminiscent of hay or grass.

Source:

Food and Drug Administration, "Regulations Under the Tea Importation Act," 21 CFR part 1220 (1991), Washington: Government Printing Office.

Information supplied by the Tea Association of the U.S.A., Inc., 230 Park Ave., New York, NY 10169.

Tomato Juice

GRADES

U.S. Grade A. Has a good, distinct tomato juice flavor and odor characteristic of good quality tomatoes. The juice is not materially affected by stems, leaves, crushed seeds, cores, immature tomatoes, or the effects of improper trimming or processing. The color is bright and characteristic of tomato juice made from mature red tomatoes and is not affected by caramelization, oxidation, or other similar causes. The juice flows readily and has a normal amount of insoluble tomato solids in suspension, and there is little solids separation. It is practically free from dark specks or scale-like particles, seeds, particles of seed, tomato peel, core material, or other similar substances, and any defects present do not more than slightly affect the appearance or drinking quality of the product.

U.S. Grade B. Has color that is typical of red tomato juice which may be slightly affected by caramelization, oxidation, or other similar causes. The consistency is such that the juice flows readily and has a normal amount of insoluble tomato solids in suspension; and there is not a marked degree of solids separation. Any defects present may be noticeable, but are not so large, so numerous, or of such contrasting color as to seriously affect the appearance or drinking quality. Has a characteristic tomato juice flavor which may be materially, but not seriously, affected by stems, leaves, crushed seeds, cores, immature tomatoes, or the effects of improper trimming or processing.

Substandard. Fails to meet the requirements for U.S. Grade B.

Source:

Agricultural Marketing Service, USDA, 7 CFR sections 52.3621 to 52.3629 (1991), Washington: Government Printing Office.

Tomato Juice, Concentrated

Concentrated tomato juice means the product prepared from clean, sound, whole tomatoes of the red or reddish varieties. The product contains not less than 20 percent but less than 24 percent of natural tomato soluble solids. When packed in hermetically sealed containers, it is sufficiently processed by heat, before or after sealing, to assure preservation.

GRADES

U.S. Grade A or U.S. Fancy. When properly reconstituted, it has a good color typical of canned tomato juice made from well ripened red tomatoes. The reconstituted tomato juice flows readily and has a normal amount of insoluble tomato solids in suspension which have little tendency to settle out. The product is practically free from defects such as dark specks or scale-like particles, seeds, particles of seed, tomato peel, core material, or other similar substances. Has a good, distinct canned tomato juice flavor and odor characteristic of good quality tomatoes. The reconstituted juice is not adversely affected by such defects as stems, leaves, crushed seeds, cores, immature tomatoes, or the effects of improper trimming or processing.

U.S. Grade C or U.S. Standard. When properly reconstituted, it has a fairly good color. The reconstituted tomato juice flows readily and has a normal amount of insoluble tomato solids in suspension which do not have a marked tendency to settle out. It is fairly free from defects and has a fairly good flavor. The reconstituted juice may be affected adversely, but not seriously, by stems, leaves, crushed seeds, cores, immature tomatoes, or the effects of improper trimming or processing.

Substandard. Fails to meet the requirements of U.S. Grade C.

Source:

Agricultural Marketing Service, USDA, 7 CFR sections 52.5201 to 52.5210 (1991), Washington: Government Printing Office.

Water, Bottled

Bottled water is a highly regulated drinking water supply. Bottled drinking water must meet established quality standards. These are based on the maximum contaminant levels set under the Environmental Protection Agency's Safe Drinking Water Act. Because bottled water is considered a *food* by the U.S. Food and Drug Administration, its production is also required to meet established criteria for sanitation and quality control. All bottled water, including mineral water, must be processed and packaged in accordance with the FDA Good Manufacturing Practices (GMPs) as well as any other regulations prescribed by local governments or country of origin.

Many terms are used on the labels of water products: pure, premium, crystal pure, filtered, distilled, glacial, spring, etc. However, these terms have not been defined by the FDA. The definitions in this entry are taken from the International Bottled Water Association's Model Bottled Water Regulation. Prepared by the Association's membership, it is designed to be used as model *regulation* or *legislation* in states or municipalities. The following states have enacted the IBWA Model Code as the basis for regulation:

Arizona
California
Connecticut
Florida
Hawaii
Louisiana
Massachusetts
New Hampshire
New Jersey
New York
Ohio
Oklahoma
Pennsylvania
Texas
Wyoming

Some changes have been made in the model in each state to fit certain standards, procedures, etc., specific to the state.

TERMINOLOGY

Artesian Water. Bottled water from a well tapping a confined aquifer in which the water level stands above the water table.

Bottled Water. Water that is placed in a sealed container or package, and is offered for sale for human consumption or other consumer uses. Bottled water may be with or without natural or added carbonation, and may be prepared with added flavors, extracts, and/or essences derived from a spice or fruit and comprising less than one percent by weight of the final product. Said products shall contain no sweeteners, acidulants, or additives other than said flavors, extracts, or essences.

Carbonated Water. Bottled water containing carbon dioxide.

Club Sodas and Seltzer Waters. These products are considered soft drinks and not bottled water.

Distilled Water. Bottled water which has been produced by a process of distillation and meets the definition of purified water in the most recent edition of the *United States Pharmacopeia*.

Drinking Water. Bottled water obtained from an approved source that has at minimum undergone treatment consisting of filtration processes such as activated carbon and/or particulate and has been treated with ozone or an equivalent disinfection process.

Fluoridated Water. Bottled water containing fluoride. The label shall specify whether the fluoride is naturally occurring or added. Any water which meets the definition of this paragraph shall contain not less than 0.8 milligrams per liter fluoride ion and otherwise comply with the Food and Drug Administration (FDA) quality standards in Section 103.35(d)(2) of Title 21 of the Code of Federal Regulations (CFR).

Mineral Water. Bottled water coming from an approved source tapped at one or more boreholes or natural springs, originating from a geologically and physically protected underground water source. Mineral water shall be clearly distinguishable from other types of water by its specific content of minerals and trace elements which in the original state at the point of emergence remain constant. The total dissolved solids (TDS) of natural mineral water shall appear on the label of the bottle and be stated in milligrams per liter. *Mineral Water* shall meet the requirements of *Natural Water*.

Natural Water. Bottled spring, mineral, artesian well or well water which is derived from an underground formation and is not derived from a municipal or public water supply. The water has not been modified by blending with water of another type or by the addition or deletion of dissolved solids, except as it relates to ozonation or equivalent disinfection and filtration.

Purified Water. Bottled water produced by distillation, deionization, reverse osmosis, or other suitable process and that meets the definition of purified water in the *United States Pharmacopeia*. Water which meets this definition and is vaporized, then condensed, may be labeled *distilled water*. Water can be purified by: distillation, where water is vaporized, then condensed leaving the water free of dissolved minerals; deionization, where water is passed through resins which remove most of the dissolved minerals; or reverse osmosis, where water is forced under pressure through membranes which remove 90 percent of the dissolved minerals.

Spring Water. Bottled water derived from an underground formation from which water flows naturally to the surface of the earth. *Spring Water* meets the requirements of *Natural Water*.

Sparkling Water. See *Carbonated Water*.

Well Water. Bottled water from a hole bored, drilled, or otherwise constructed in the ground which taps the water of an aquifer. *Well Water* meets the requirements of *Natural Water*.

Source:
"How Good is Bottled Water?" *Consumers' Research Magazine*, Vol. 74, no. 6, (June 1991): 10.
International Bottled Water Association Model Bottled Water Regulation, Alexandria, VA: International Bottled Water Association, revised 1/23/92.

Whisky

Blended Whisky. A mixture which contains straight whisky or a blend of straight whiskies at not less than 20 percent on a proof gallon basis, excluding alcohol derived from added harmless coloring, flavoring, or blending materials, and, separately, or in combination, whisky or neutral spirits. A blended whisky containing not less than 51 percent on a proof gallon basis of one of the types of straight whisky shall be further designated by that specific type of straight whisky; e.g., blended rye whisky.

Bourbon Whisky, Rye Whisky, Wheat Whisky, Malt Whisky, or Rye Malt Whisky. Whisky produced at not exceeding 160 degree proof from a fermented mash of not less than 51 percent corn (bourbon), rye, wheat, malted barley, or malted rye grain, respectively, and stored at not more than 125 degree proof in charred new oak containers. Also includes mixtures of such whiskies of the same type.

Canadian Whisky. Whisky which is a distinctive product of Canada, manufactured in Canada in compliance with the laws of Canada regulating the manufacture of Canadian whisky for consumption in Canada. If such product is a mixture of whiskies, the mixture is *Blended Canadian Whisky*.

Corn Whisky. Whisky produced at not exceeding 160 degree proof from a fermented mash of not less than 80 percent corn grain, and stored at not more than 125 degree proof in used or uncharred new oak containers (if stored) and not subjected in any manner to treatment with charred wood. Also includes mixtures of such whisky.

Irish Whisky. Whisky which is a distinctive product of Ireland, manufactured either in the Republic of Ireland or in Northern Ireland, in compliance with their laws regulating the manufacture of Irish whisky for home consumption. If the product is a mixture of whiskies it is called *Blended Irish Whisky*.

Light Whisky. Whisky produced in the United States at more than 160 degree proof, on or after January 26, 1968, and stored in used or uncharred new oak containers. Also includes mixtures of such whiskies. If light whisky is mixed with less than 20 percent of straight whisky on a proof gallon basis, the mixture shall be designated *Blended Light Whisky*.

Mash. Whisky distilled from bourbon (rye, wheat, malt, or rye malt) mash is whisky produced in the United States at not exceeding 160 degree proof from a fermented mash of not less than 51 percent corn, rye, wheat, malted barley, or malted rye grain, respectively, and stored in used oak containers. Also includes mixtures of such whiskies of the same type. Whisky conforming to the standard of identity for corn whisky must be designated *Corn Whisky*.

Scotch Whisky. Whisky which is a distinctive product of Scotland, manufactured in Scotland in compliance with the laws of the United Kingdom regulating the manufacture of Scotch whisky for consumption in the United Kingdom. If the product is a mixture of whiskies, such mixture is *Blended Scotch Whisky*.

Spirit Whisky. A mixture of neutral spirits and not less than 5 percent on a proof gallon basis of whisky, or straight whisky, or straight whisky and whisky, if the straight whisky component is less than 20 percent on a proof gallon basis.

Straight Whisky. Whiskies stored in prescribed oak containers for a period of two years or more may be designated as *straight*. Examples are *Straight Bourbon Whisky* or *Straight Corn Whisky*. Straight whisky includes mixtures of straight whiskies of the same type produced in the same state.

Whisky. An alcoholic distillate produced at less than 190 degree proof, stored in oak containers, bottled at not less than 80 degree proof, with the taste, aroma, and characteristics generally attributed to whisky.

Source:
Bureau of Alcohol, Tobacco, and Firearms, "Standards of Identity for Distilled Spirits," 27 CFR section 5.22 (1991), Washington: Government Printing Office.

Wine

Aperitif Wine. Wine having an alcohol content not less than 15 percent by volume, compounded from grape wine containing added brandy or alcohol, flavored with herbs or other natural flavors and possessing the taste, aroma, and characteristics of aperitif. Vermouth is a type of aperitif compounded from grape wine.

Berry Wine. Fruit wine produced from berries.

Carbonated Wine. Wine made effervescent with carbon dioxide other than that resulting from the secondary fermentation of the wine within a closed container, tank, or bottle.

Champagne. A type of sparkling light wine which derives its effervescence solely from the secondary fermentation of the wine within glass containers of a gallon or less as long as it has the taste, aroma, and characteristics attributed to champagne.

Champagne Style. A sparkling light wine that has the characteristics of champagne but may have been fermented in containers larger than a gallon. May also be labeled *New York* (or *American, California,* etc.) *Champagne-bulk process.*

Citrus Wine. Wine produced with citrus fruit, e.g., *orange wine, grapefruit wine,* etc.

Contains Sulfites or Contains (a) sulfiting agent(s). This phrase appears on a label when sulfur dioxide or a sulfiting agent is detected at a level of 10 or more parts per million.

Crackling Wine. Also called *petillant* or *frizzante*. Sparkling light wine not as effervescent as champagne but with enough carbon dioxide to produce a slow and steady flow of gas bubbles through the wine. If fermented in containers larger than a gallon it is designated *crackling wine—bulk process.*

Dessert Wine. Wine having an alcoholic content of 14 to 24 percent by volume. When grape brandy or alcohol is added so that the alcohol content exceeds 17 percent it may be designated as *sherry*, depending on its taste, aroma, and characteristics. Similarly those with alcohol content of 18 percent or more may be termed *angelica, Madeira, muscatel,* or *port* if characteristic of those wines. Those wines having the taste, aroma, and characteristics of the above but with alcohol contents between 14 and 17 percent may be designated as *light* as in *light muscatel.*

Estate Bottled. This term is used on a wine labeled only if the winery grew all the grapes on land owned or controlled by the winery, crushed the grapes, fermented, finished, aged, and bottled the wine on the premises.

Fruit Wine. Wine produced with fruit. Fruit wine containing no added brandy or alcohol may be designated as *natural*. If produced solely from one type of fruit, the word *wine* is qualified by the name of the fruit, e.g., *peach wine, apple wine,* etc. Fruit wines derived solely from apples or pears may be designated *cider* or *perry*, respectively.

Grape Names. Wine is also labeled with the type of grape predominantly used, with the generic name of the type of wine (e.g., *angelica, burgundy, claret, chablis, champagne, chianti, malaga, marsala, madeira, moselle, mort, Rhine wine, sauterne, haute sauterne, sherry, tokay*) or with a name with geographic significance. Examples of nongeneric names which are also distinctive designations of specific grape wines are: *Bordeaux Blanc, Bordeaux Rouge, Graves, Medoc, Saint-Julien, Chateau Yquem, Chateau Margaux, Chateau Lafite, Pommard, Chambertin, Montrachet, Rhine, Liebfraumilch, Rudesheimer, Forster, Deidesheimer, Schloss, Hohnnisberger,* and *Lagrima* and *Lacryma Christi.*

Grape Wine. The fermented juice of ripe grapes.

Imitation Wine. Any wine containing synthetic materials; made from a mixture of water and the residue remaining after the thorough pressing of grapes, or that has acquired its taste, aroma, or color by treatment with synthetic methods or materials of any kind.

Raisin Wine. Wine made from dried grapes.

Retina Wine. Grape table wine fermented or flavored with resins.

Sake. Wine made from rice.

Sparkling Wine. Grape wine made effervescent with carbon dioxide solely from the fermentation of the wine within a closed container, tank, or bottle.

Table Wine. Wine having an alcoholic content not exceeding 14 percent by volume. Also called *light wine, red table wine, light white wine, sweet table wine,* etc.

Vintage Wine. Wine labeled with the year of harvest of the grapes.

Source:
Bureau of Alcohol, Tobacco, and Firearms, 27 CFR Chapter 1 (1991), Washington: Government Printing Office.

Dairy Products

Butter

For purposes of these grades, *butter* means the food product usually known as butter and which is made exclusively from milk or cream, or both, with or without common salt, and with or without additional coloring matter. It contains not less than 80 percent by weight of milkfat. The term *cream,* when used in this grade, means cream separated from milk produced by healthy cows. The cream is pasteurized at a temperature of not less than 185 degree F for not less than 15 seconds, or it is pasteurized by other approved methods giving equivalent results.

GRADES

The U.S. grade of butter is determined on the basis of classifying first the flavor characteristics and then the characteristics in body, color, and salt. Flavor is the basic quality factor in grading butter and is determined by taste and smell. The grade descriptions which follow are intended only as a general consumer guide. For more detailed information, please consult the source cited below.

U.S. Grade AA. Possesses a fine and highly pleasing butter flavor. It is made from sweet cream of low natural acid to which a culture (starter) may or may not have been added. Butter of all U.S. grades is free of foreign materials and visible mold.

U.S. Grade A. Possesses a pleasing and desirable butter flavor. May possess any of the following flavors to a slight degree: acid, aged, bitter, coarse, flat, smothered, and storage. May possess feed flavor to a definite degree.

U.S. Grade B. Possesses a fairly pleasing butter flavor. It may possess any of the following flavors to a slight degree: malty, musty, neutralizer, scorched, utensil, weed, and whey. It may also possess any of the following flavors to a definite degree: acid, aged, bitter, smothered, storage, and old cream; feed flavor to a pronounced degree.

BUTTER, WHEN USED TO LABEL FOODS

The word butter is often used in product labels to help describe the product—for example, *butter cookies, butter shortbread,* etc. When a product name contains the word butter, all of the shortening ingredients should be butter. If a product contains both butter and shortening and has a sufficient amount of butter to give a characteristic butter flavor to the product, it is typically named *butter flavored _____.*

Source:

Agricultural Marketing Service, USDA, United States Standards for Grades of Butter, 7 CFR 58.2621 (1992), Washington: Government Printing Office.

Food and Drug Administration, *Compliance Policy Guides,* Guide 7102.03, Reissued 03/08/88, Washington: National Technical Information Service.

Buttermilk, Dry

Dry buttermilk (made by the spray process or the atmospheric roller process) is the product resulting from drying liquid buttermilk; the buttermilk is derived from the churning of butter and is pasteurized prior to condensing at a temperature of 161 degrees F for 15 seconds. Dry buttermilk has a protein content of not less than 30.0 percent. Dry buttermilk neither contains nor is derived from nonfat dry milk, dry whey, or products other than buttermilk; it does not contain any added preservative, neutralizing agent, or other chemical.

GRADES

This product is graded according to a very technical system whereby penalty points are assessed for such factors as edibility, poor appearance, or defects in workmanship. The more penalty points assessed the lower the grade. The grade descriptions which follow are intended only as a general consumer guide. For more detailed information, please consult the source cited below.

U.S. Extra Grade.

Flavor (applies to the reconstituted product). Sweet, pleasing, and has no unnatural or offensive flavors.

Physical Appearance. Possesses a uniform cream to light brown color, is free from lumps (except for those that readily break up with slight pressure), and is practically free from visible dark particles.

Bacterial Estimate. Not more than 50,000 per gram standard plate count.

Milkfat Content. Not less than 4.5 percent.

Moisture Content. Not more than 4.0 percent.

Scorched Particle Content. Not more than 15.0 mg for the spray process and 22.5 mg for the roller process.

Solubility Index. Not more than 1.25 ml for the spray process and 15.0 ml for the roller process.

Titratable Acidity. Not less than 0.10 percent or more than 0.18 percent.

Protein Content (dry buttermilk only). Not less than 30.0 percent.

Protein Content (dry buttermilk product only). Less than 30.0 percent.

U.S. Standard Grade.

Flavor (applies to the reconstituted product). Should possess a fairly pleasing flavor, but may possess slight unnatural flavors, although it has no offensive flavors.

Physical Appearance. Possesses a uniform cream to light brown color, is free from lumps (except for those that readily break up with moderate pressure), and is reasonably free from visible dark particles.

Bacterial Estimate. Not more than 200,000 per gram standard plate count.

Milkfat Content. Not less than 4.5 percent.

Moisture Content. Not more than 5.0 percent.

Scorched Particle Content. Not more than 22.5 mg for the spray process and 32.5 mg for the roller process.

Solubility Index. Not more than 2.0 ml for the spray process and 15.0 ml for the roller process.

Titratable Acidity. Not less than 0.10 percent or more than 0.20 percent.

Protein Content (dry buttermilk only). Not less than 30.0 percent.

Protein Content (dry buttermilk product only). Less than 30.0 percent

Source:
Agricultural Marketing Service, USDA, United States Standards for Grades of Dry Buttermilk and Dry Buttermilk Product, 52 CFR Subpart Q (1992), Washington: Government Printing Office.

Cheese, Bulk American

Bulk American cheese is cheese which is packaged in bulk form and in which no single piece of cheese, whatever its shape, weighs

less than 100 pounds. The following varieties are included: cheddar, washed curd cheese, granular cheese, and Colby cheese.

DEGREE OF CURING

Fresh (Current). Cheese which is in the early stages of the curing process, usually 10 to about 90 days old.

Cured (Aged). Cheese which has the more fully developed flavor and body attributes which are characteristic of the curing process; it is generally cured for over 90 days.

GRADES

This product is graded according to a very technical system whereby penalty points are assessed for such factors as edibility, poor appearance, or defects in workmanship. The more penalty points assessed the lower the grade. The grade descriptions which follow are intended only as a general consumer guide. For more detailed information, please consult the source cited below.

U.S. Extra Grade. Has a pleasing flavor. A sample drawn from the cheese should be firm and sufficiently compact. It also meets the standards for finish, body, and texture.

U.S. Standard Grade. The flavor is pleasing but may possess certain flavor defects to a limited degree. The body and texture is such that the cheese is sufficiently compact enough to allow a plug to be drawn for examination; however, it may have large and connecting mechanical openings. In addition to four sweet holes, the plug sample may have scattered yeast holes and other scattered gas holes. The finish and surface appearance may be rough or soiled.

U. S. Commercial Grade. The flavor may possess certain defects to specified degrees. A plug drawn from the cheese may appear loosely knit with large and connecting mechanical openings. The finish and appearance may have a pronounced rough and soiled surface.

Source:
Agricultural Marketing Service, USDA, 7 CFR sections 58.2455 to 48.2463 (1992), Washington: Government Printing Office.

Cheese, Cheddar

Cheddar cheese is cheese made by the cheddar process or by another procedure which produces a finished cheese having the same physical and chemical properties as the cheese produced by the cheddar process. It is made from cow's milk with or without the addition of coloring matter and with common salt. It contains not more than 39 percent of moisture, and in the water-free substance, contains not less than 50 percent of milkfat.

TYPES OF PACKAGING

Bandaged and Paraffin-Dipped. The cheese is bandaged and dipped in a refined paraffin, amorphous wax, microcrystalline wax, any combination of such, or any other suitable substance. The coating is a continuous, unbroken, and uniform film adhering tightly to the entire surface of the cheese.

Rindless. The cheese is properly wrapped in a wrapper or covering which will not impart any color or objectionable odor or flavor to the cheese. The wrapper is sealed with a sufficient overlap or satisfactory closure to prevent air leakage. The wrapper or covering is of sufficiently low permeability to water vapor and air as to prevent the formation of rind and to prevent the entrance of air during the curing and holding periods.

GRADES

The determination of U.S. grades of cheddar cheese, according to the degree of curing, is based on the following quality factors: (a) flavor, (b) body and texture, (c) color, and (d) finish and appearance. The rating of each quality factor is established on the basis of characteristics present in any vat of cheese. The final U.S. grade is established on the basis of the lowest rating of any one of the quality characteristics. The grade descriptions which follow are intended only as a general consumer guide. For more detailed information, please consult the source cited below.

U.S. Grade AA

Flavor. Fine, highly pleasing, and free from undesirable flavors and odors. May possess very slight feed flavors.

Body and Texture. A plug drawn from the cheese should be firm and appear solid, smooth, compact, and close; it should be translucent, although it may have a few small mechanical openings. May possess limited sweet holes in accordance with the degree of curing, but it is free from other gas holes.

Color. May be colored or uncolored. If colored, it should be a medium yellow-orange. May possess numerous tiny white specks associated with aged cheese. Very slight seaminess is permitted.

Finish and Appearance. If bandaged and paraffin-dipped, the rind is sound, firm, smooth, and provides a good protection to the cheese. The bandage is evenly placed on the end of the cheese and is free from unnecessary overlapping and wrinkles, but it should not be burst or torn. The surface is smooth, bright, and has a good coating of paraffin or wax that adheres firmly to all surfaces of the cheese. There may be mold under the bandage and paraffin, but it must be within certain limited tolerances for the degree of curing. There should be no indication that mold has entered the cheese. The cheese is free from high edges, huffing, and lopsidedness. If rindless, the wrapper or covering adequately and securely envelops the cheese, is neat, unbroken, and fully protects the surface, but it may be slightly wrinkled. The cheese is free from huffing and lopsidedness. It may have very slight mold under the wrapper or covering in medium and cured classifications. However, there should be no indication that mold has entered the cheese.

U.S. Grade A

Flavor. Pleasing and free from undesirable flavors and odors. May possess feed, acid, and bitter flavors—within limited tolerances.

Body and Texture. A plug drawn from the cheese appears reasonably solid, compact, and close; it should be translu-

cent, although it may have a few mechanical openings that are not large and connecting. It may not have more than two sweet holes on a plug and must be free from other gas holes.

Color. May be colored or uncolored. If colored, it should be a medium yellow-orange. May possess numerous tiny white specks, associated with aged cheese. May possess seaminess and waviness to a limited degree.

Finish and Appearance. If bandaged and paraffin-dipped, the rind is sound, firm, smooth, and provides a good protection to the cheese. The bandage may be slightly uneven, overlapped, or wrinkled, but it is not burst or torn. The surface is practically smooth, bright, and has a good coating of paraffin or wax that adheres firmly to all surfaces of the cheese. According to the degree of curing, certain tolerances for mold and other defects are allowed. There should be no indication that mold has entered the cheese. The cheese is free from huffing, but it may have slightly high edges and may be slightly lopsided. If rindless, the wrapper or covering adequately and securely envelops the cheese, is neat, unbroken, and fully protects the surface; it may be slightly wrinkled. The cheese is free from huffing but may be slightly lopsided and may have very slight mold under the wrapper or covering (in medium and cured classifications). There should be no indication that mold has entered the cheese.

U.S. Grade B

Flavor. May possess certain undesirable flavors to a limited degree in accordance with the aging of the cheese.

Body and Texture. A plug drawn from the cheese may be loose and open and may have numerous sweet holes, scattered yeast holes, and other scattered gas holes. It may possess various other body characteristics in accordance with the degree of curing, but pinny gas holes are not permitted.

Color. May be colored or uncolored.

Finish and Appearance. If bandaged and paraffin-dipped, the rind is sound, may be slightly weak, but is free from soft spots, rind rot, cracks, and openings of any kind. The bandage may be uneven and wrinkled, but not burst or torn. The surface may be rough and unattractive, but it possesses a fairly good coating of paraffin or wax. The paraffin may be scaly or blistered. Surface mold and certain other characteristics are permitted in accordance with the degree of curing, but there should be no indication that mold has entered the cheese. May be huffed, lopsided, and have high edges. If rindless, the covering or wrapper adequately and securely envelops the cheese, is fairly neat, unbroken, and protects the surface, but it may be wrinkled. The cheese may be huffed, lopsided, and have slight mold under the wrapper or covering in medium and cured classifications. There should be no indication that mold has entered the cheese.

U.S. Grade C

Flavor. May possess somewhat objectionable flavors and odors with increased tolerances in accordance with the degree of curing.

Body and Texture. May be loose with large and connecting mechanical openings and may possess various gas holes and body characteristics—within certain limitations and varying with the degree of curing. The cheese, however, is sufficiently compact to permit the drawing of a plug.

Color. May be colored or uncolored, but not to the extent that the color is particularly unattractive.

Finish and Appearance. If bandaged and paraffin-dipped, the rind may be weak and possess characteristics such as soft spots, rind rot, cracks, and openings—varying with the degree of curing. The bandage may be uneven and wrinkled but not burst or torn. May have a very rough, unattractive appearance, and the paraffin may be scaly and blistered. Surface mold and other characteristics are permitted, varying with the degree of curing. There should be no evidence that mold has entered the cheese. May be huffed, lopsided, and have high edges to a degree which is not permitted in the higher grades. If rindless, the wrapper or covering adequately and securely envelops the cheese, is unbroken, and protects the surface; it may be wrinkled and soiled. The cheese may be huffed, lopsided, and have mold under the wrapper or covering. However, there should be no indication that mold has entered the cheese.

Source:

Agricultural Marketing Service, USDA, 7 CFR 58.2501 to 58.2506 (1992), Washington: Government Printing Office.

Cheese, Colby

Colby cheese is cheese made by the Colby process or by any other procedure which produces a finished cheese having the same physical and chemical properties as Colby process. The physical attributes of Colby cheese are as follows: uncolored to orange in color; a mild to mellow flavor similar to mild cheddar cheese; and softer bodied and more open textured than cheddar. The cheese is made from cow's milk with or without the addition of coloring matter. It contains added common salt, contains not more than 40 percent of moisture, and, in the water-free substance, contains not less than 50 percent of milkfat.

TYPES

Bandaged and Paraffin-Dipped. The cheese is bandaged and dipped in a refined paraffin, amorphous wax, microcrystalline wax, or other suitable substance. Such coating is a continuous, unbroken, and uniform film adhering tightly to the entire surface of the cheese.

Rindless. The cheese is properly wrapped in a wrapper or covering which will not impart any color or objectionable odor or flavor to the cheese. The wrapper or covering is sealed to prevent air leakage. The wrapper or covering is of sufficiently low permeability to water vapor and air as to prevent the formation of rind and to prevent the entrance of air during the curing and holding periods.

GRADES

The determination of U.S. grades of Colby cheese is based on the following quality factors: (a) flavor, (b) body and texture, (c) color, and (d) finish and appearance. The cheese is graded no sooner than 10 days of age. The cheese is held at no lower than 35 degrees F during this period. The final U.S. grade is established on the basis of the lowest rating of any one of the quality factors. The grade descriptions which follow are intended only as a general consumer guide. For more detailed information, please consult the source cited below.

U.S. Grade AA

Flavor. Is fine and highly pleasing, free from undesirable flavors and odors. May be lacking in flavor development or may possess a characteristic Colby cheese flavor. May possess a very slight acid or feed flavor but is free from any undesirable flavors and odors.

Body and Texture. A plug drawn from the cheese is firm. It has numerous small mechanical openings evenly distributed throughout the plug. It is relatively free from blind areas and does not possess sweet holes, yeast holes, or other gas holes. The texture may be definitely curdy or may be partially broken down if more than 3 weeks old.

Color. Has a uniform, bright, attractive appearance. May be colored or uncolored, but the color is uniform.

Finish and Appearance. If bandaged and paraffin-dipped, the rind is sound, firm, smooth, and provides a good protection to the cheese. The bandage is evenly placed on the end and over the entire surface of the cheese, is free from unnecessary overlapping and wrinkles, and is not burst or torn. The cheese surface is smooth, bright, and has a good coating of paraffin or wax that adheres firmly to the entire surface of the cheese. The cheese is free from mold under the bandage and paraffin and is free from high edges, huffing, and lopsidedness; it may possess a soiled surface to a very slight degree. If rindless, the wrapper or covering is practically smooth and properly sealed with adequate overlapping at the seams. The wrapper or covering is neat and adequately and securely envelops the cheese, but it may be slightly wrinkled. When vacuum packaging is used, allowance is made for wrinkles caused by crimping or sealing. The cheese is free from mold under the wrapper or covering and is not huffed or lopsided.

U.S. Grade A

Flavor. Is pleasing and free from undesirable flavors and odors. May be lacking in flavor development, or it may possess a slight, characteristic Colby cheese flavor. May possess a very slight bitter, slight acid, or feed flavor, but it does not possess undesirable flavors and odors.

Body and Texture. A plug drawn from the cheese should be reasonably firm. It has numerous mechanical openings, but the openings are not large and connecting. It should not possess more than two sweet holes per plug, and the plug should be free from other gas holes. The body may be very slightly, loosely knit and definitely curdy or partially broken down if more than 3 weeks old.

Color. Has a fairly uniform, bright, attractive appearance.

May be colored or uncolored, but the color is uniform. Very slight waviness is permitted.

Finish and Appearance. If bandaged and paraffin-dipped, the rind is sound, firm, smooth, and provides a good protection to the cheese. The bandage may be slightly uneven, overlapped, or wrinkled, but it is not burst or torn. The surface is practically smooth, bright, and has a good coating of paraffin or wax that adheres firmly to all surfaces of the cheese. The cheese is free from mold under the bandage. May possess the following characteristics: to a very slight degree—a soiled surface and surface mold; and to a slight degree—a rough surface, irregular bandaging, lopsidedness, and high edges. If rindless, the wrapper or covering is practically smooth and properly sealed with adequate overlapping at the seams. It can also be sealed by any other satisfactory type of closure. The wrapper or covering is neat and adequately and securely envelops the cheese. It may be slightly wrinkled, but it fully protects the surface of the cheese and does not detract from the cheese's initial quality. The cheese is free from mold under the wrapper or covering and is not huffed, but it may be slightly lopsided.

U.S. Grade B

Flavor. Possess a fairly pleasing, characteristic Colby cheese flavor; it may possess a very slight onion flavor; a flat, bitter, fruity, utensil, whey-taint, yeasty, malty, old milk, weedy, barny, and lipase flavor to a slight degree; and an acid and feed flavor to a definite degree.

Body and Texture. A plug drawn from the cheese may be loosely knit and open and may have numerous sweet holes, scattered yeast holes and other scattered gas holes; it may possess various other body defects: pinny gas holes and scattered yeast holes. The cheese may possess the following characteristics: to a slight degree—coarse, short, mealy, weak, pasty, crumbly, gassy, slitty, corky and loosely knit; and to a definite degree—curdy, and sweet holes.

Color. The color may possess the following characteristics to a slight degree: wavy, mottled, salt spots, dull, or faded. It may be colored or uncolored, and the color may be slightly unnatural. In addition, rindless Colby cheese may have, to a slight degree, a bleached surface.

Finish and Appearance. If bandaged and paraffin-dipped, the rind is reasonably sound, may be slightly weak, but is free from soft spots, rind rot, cracks, and openings of any kind. The bandage may be uneven and wrinkled, but it is not burst or torn. The surface may be rough and unattractive, but it possesses a fairly good coating of paraffin or wax. The paraffin may be scaly or blistered, with very slight mold under the bandage or paraffin but there should be no indication that mold has entered the cheese. May possess the following characteristics: to a slight degree—a soiled surface, surface mold, defective coating, checked rind, weak rind, and sour rind; and to a definite degree—a rough surface, irregular bandaging, lopsidedness, and high edges. If rindless, the wrapper or covering is unbroken but may be wrinkled. The wrapper or covering adequately and securely envelops the cheese. The following characteristics may be present: to a very slight degree—mold under the wrapper, but not entering the cheese; to a slight degree—a soiled surface, surface mold, lopsidedness; and to a definite degree—a rough surface and wrinkled wrapper or cover.

Source:
Agricultural Marketing Service, USDA, 7 CFR sections 58.2475 to 58.2479 (1992), Washington: Government Printing Office.

Cheese, Monterey Jack

Monterey cheese is cheese made by the Monterey process or by any other procedure which produces a finished cheese having the same physical and chemical properties as the cheese produced by the Monterey process. The physical attributes of Monterey cheese are as follows: white to light cream in color; a mild to mellow flavor; a semisoft body which contains more moisture and is softer than Colby; a texture which is similar to Colby; and mechanical holes that are evenly dispersed. The cheese is made from cow's milk. It contains added common salt, contains not more than 44 percent of moisture, and, in the water-free substance, contains not less than 50 percent of milkfat.

TYPES OF SURFACE PROTECTION

Bandaged and Paraffin-Dipped. The cheese is bandaged and dipped in a refined paraffin, amorphous wax, microcrystalline wax, or other suitable substance. This coating is a continuous, unbroken, and uniform film adhering tightly to the entire surface of the cheese.

Paraffin-Dipped. The cheese is dipped in a refined paraffin, amorphous wax, microcrystalline wax, or any other film adhering tightly to the entire surface of the cheese.

Rindless. The cheese is properly wrapped in a wrapper or covering which will not impart any color or objectionable odor or flavor to the cheese. The wrapper or covering is sealed to prevent air leakage. The wrapper or covering is of sufficiently low permeability to water vapor and air as to prevent the formation of rind and to prevent the entrance of air during the curing and holding periods.

GRADES

The determination of U.S. grades of Monterey cheese is based on rating the following quality factors: (a) flavor, (b) body and texture, (c) color, and (d) finish and appearance. The cheese is graded no sooner than 5 days of age. The final U.S. grade is established on the basis of the lowest rating of any one of the quality factors. The grade descriptions which follow are intended only as a general consumer guide. For more detailed information, please consult the source cited below.

U.S. Grade AA

Flavor. Has a fine and highly pleasing flavor and is free from undesirable flavors and odors. It possesses a characteristic

Monterey cheese flavor, although it may be lacking in flavor development. May also possess a very slight acid or feed flavor, but it is free from any undesirable flavors and odors.

Body and Texture. A plug drawn from the cheese should be reasonably firm. It has numerous small mechanical openings evenly distributed throughout the plug. It should not possess sweet holes, yeast holes, or other gas holes. The texture may be definitely curdy or may be partially broken down if more than 3 weeks old.

Color. The cheese has a natural, uniform, bright, attractive appearance.

Finish and Appearance. If bandaged and paraffin-dipped, the rind is sound, firm, smooth, and provides a good protection to the cheese. The bandage is evenly placed on the end and over the entire surface of the cheese, is free from unnecessary overlapping and wrinkles, and is not burst or torn. The cheese surface is smooth, bright, and has a good coating of paraffin or wax that adheres firmly to the entire surface of the cheese. The cheese is free from mold under the bandage and paraffin and is free from high edges, huffing, and lopsidedness; it may possess soiled surface to a very slight degree. If paraffin-dipped, it has a good coating of paraffin or wax that adheres firmly to the entire surface. The cheese is free from mold under the paraffin and is free from high edges, huffing, rough surfaces, and lopsidedness; it may possess a soiled surface to a very slight degree. If rindless, the wrapper or covering is practically smooth and properly sealed with adequate overlapping at the seams. The wrapper is neat but may be slightly wrinkled.

U.S. Grade A

Flavor. The flavor is a pleasing, characteristic flavor free from undesirable flavors and odors. May possess a slightly characteristic Monterey cheese flavor or may be lacking in flavor development. May possess very slight bitter, slight acid, or feed flavor, but it does not possess undesirable flavors and odors.

Body and Texture. A plug drawn from the cheese should be reasonably firm. It has numerous mechanical openings, but the openings are not large and connecting. It should not possess more than two sweet holes per plug. Also, the plug should be free from other gas holes. The body may be definitely curdy or partially broken down if more than 3 weeks old.

Color. The cheese should have a natural, fairly uniform, bright, attractive appearance.

Finish and Appearance. If bandaged and paraffin-dipped, the rind is sound, firm, smooth, and provides good protection to the cheese. The bandage may be slightly uneven, overlapped, or wrinkled, but it is not burst or torn. The surface is practically smooth, bright, and has a good coating of paraffin or wax that adheres firmly to all surfaces of the cheese. The cheese should be free from mold under the bandage. It may possess the following characteristics: to a very slight degree—soiled surface and surface mold; and to a slight degree—rough surface, irregular bandaging, lopsidedness and high edges. If par-

affin-dipped, the rind is sound, firm, smooth, and provides a good protection to the cheese. The cheese surface is practically smooth, bright, and has a good coating of paraffin or wax that adheres firmly to all surfaces of the cheese. The cheese should be free from mold under the paraffin. It should be free from huffing, but it may possess a soiled surface and surface mold to a very slight degree and a rough surface, high edges, and lopsidedness to a slight degree. If rindless, the wrapper or covering is properly sealed with adequate overlapping at the seams. The wrapper or covering is neat and adequately and securely envelops the cheese, but it may be slightly wrinkled. The cheese should be free from mold under the wrapper or covering and should not be huffed, but it may be slightly lopsided.

U.S. Grade B

Flavor. Should possess a fairly pleasing characteristic Monterey cheese flavor, but it may be lacking in flavor development. May possess a very slight onion and sour flavor; a flat, bitter, fruity, utensil, whey-taint, yeasty, malty, old milk, weedy, barny and lipase flavor to a slight degree; and an acid and feed flavor to a definite degree.

Body and Texture. A plug drawn from the cheese may be open and may have numerous sweet holes, scattered yeast holes, and other scattered gas holes. It may possess various other body defects. Pinny gas holes are not permitted. A plug drawn from the cheese may have numerous mechanical openings varying in size and dispersement and may possess the following characteristics to a slight degree: coarse, short, mealy, weak, pasty, crumbly, gassy, slitty, and corky. It may possess the following characteristics to a definite degree: curdy and sweet holes.

Color. It has a natural color but may possess the following characteristics to a slight degree: wavy, acid-cut, unnatural, mottled, salt spots, dull, or faded. In addition, rindless Monterey cheese may have a bleached surface to a slight degree.

Finish and Appearance. If bandaged and paraffin-dipped, the rind is reasonably sound, may be slightly weak, but is free from soft spots, rind rot, cracks, and openings of any kind. The bandage may be uneven and wrinkled, but it is not burst or torn. The surface may be rough and unattractive, but it possesses a fairly good coating of paraffin or wax. The paraffin may be scaly or blistered, with very slight mold under the bandage or paraffin, but there should be no indication that mold has entered the cheese. May possess the following characteristics: to a slight degree—a soiled surface, surface mold, defective coating, checked rind, weak rind, and sour rind; and to a definite degree—a rough surface, irregular bandaging, lopsided and high edges. If paraffin-dipped, the rind is sound, firm, smooth, and provides a good protection to the cheese. The cheese surface may be rough and unattractive, but it possesses a fairly good coating of paraffin or wax. The paraffin may be scaly or blistered, with very slight mold under the paraffin, but there should be no indication that mold has entered the cheese. May possess the following characteristics: to a slight degree—a soiled surface, surface mold, defective coating, checked rind, weak rind, and sour rind; and to a definite degree—a rough surface, lopsidedness and high edges. If rindless, the wrapper or covering is fairly smooth and properly sealed with adequate overlapping at the seams. The wrapper or covering is fairly neat and adequately and securely envelops the cheese. When vacuum packaging is used, allowances are made for wrinkles caused by crimping or sealing. The following characteristics may be present: to a very slight degree—mold under the wrapper, but not entering the cheese; to a slight degree—a soiled surface, surface mold, lopsidedness; and to a definite degree—a rough surface and wrinkled wrapper or cover.

Source:
Agricultural Marketing Service, USDA, 7 CFR sections 58.2465 to 58.2471 (1992), Washington: Government Printing Office.

Cheese, Swiss (Emmentaler)

Swiss cheese is cheese made by the Swiss process or by any other procedure which produces a finished cheese having the same physical and chemical properties as cheese produced by the Swiss process. It is prepared from milk and has holes, or eyes, developed throughout the cheese by microbiological activity. It contains not more than 41 percent of moisture, and its solids contain not less than 43 percent of milkfat. It is not less than 60 days old. For the purpose of these grades, the words *Swiss* and *Emmentaler* are interchangeable.

STYLES

Rind. The cheese is completely covered by a rind sufficient to protect the interior of the cheese.

Rindless. The cheese is properly enclosed in a wrapper or covering which will not impart any objectionable flavor or color to the cheese. The wrapper or covering is sealed with a sufficient overlap or satisfactory closure to exclude air. The wrapper or covering is of sufficiently low permeability to water vapor and air as to prevent the formation of a rind through contact with air during the curing and holding periods.

GRADES

The grade descriptions which follow are intended only as a general consumer guide. For more detail please consult the source cited below.

U.S. Grade A

Flavor. Has a pleasing, desirable, and characteristic Swiss cheese flavor that is consistent with the age of the cheese. It is free from undesirable flavors.

Body. The body is uniform, firm, and smooth.

Eyes and Texture. The cheese is properly set and possesses well-developed round or slightly oval-shaped eyes which are uniformly distributed. The majority of the eyes are $^{11}/_{16}$ to $^{13}/_{16}$ inch in diameter. The cheese may possess the

following eye characteristics: to a very slight degree—dull, rough, and shell. It may possess the following texture characteristics: to a very slight degree—checks and picks.

Finish and Appearance. The rind is sound, firm, smooth, and provides good protection to the cheese. The surface of the cheese may exhibit mold to a very slight degree. There should be no indication that mold has penetrated into the interior of the cheese. If rindless, the blocks of Swiss cheese should not be less than 6½ inches or more than 8½ inches in height. They should be reasonably uniform in size and well shaped. The wrapper or covering adequately and securely envelops the cheese, is neat, unbroken, and fully protects the surface of the cheese, but it may be slightly wrinkled. The surface of the cheese may exhibit mold to a very slight degree. There should be no indication that mold has penetrated into the interior of the cheese.

Color. The color is natural, attractive, and uniform.

U.S. Grade B

Flavor. Has a pleasing, desirable, and characteristic Swiss cheese flavor that is consistent with the age of the cheese. It is free from undesirable flavors. The cheese may possess an acid, bitter, feed, flat, and utensil flavor to a slight degree.

Body. The body is uniform, firm, and smooth. The cheese may possess a slight weak body.

Eyes and Texture. The cheese possesses well-developed round or slightly oval-shaped eyes. The cheese may possess the following eye characteristics: to a very slight degree—dead eyes, nesty and small eyed; and to a slight degree—dull, frog-mouth, one sided, overset, rough, shell, underset, and uneven. The cheese may possess the following texture characteristics: to a slight degree—checks, picks, and streuble.

Finish and Appearance. The rind is sound, firm, smooth, and provides good protection to the cheese. The cheese may exhibit the following characteristics: to a slight degree—huffed, mold, soiled, uneven, and wet rind. There should be no indication that mold has penetrated into the interior of the cheese. If rindless, the blocks of Swiss cheese should not be less than 6½ inches or more than 8½ inches in height. The wrapper or covering adequately and securely envelops the cheese, is neat, unbroken, and fully protects the surface, but it may be slightly wrinkled. The cheese may exhibit the following characteristics: to a slight degree—huffed, mold, uneven, and wet surface. There should be no indication that mold has penetrated into the interior of the cheese.

Color. The cheese may possess, to a slight degree, a bleached surface.

U.S. Grade C

Flavor. Possesses a characteristic Swiss cheese flavor which is consistent with the age of the cheese. The cheese may possess the following flavors: to a slight degree—barny, flat, fruity, rancid, metallic, old milk, onion, sour, weedy, whey-taint, and yeasty; and to a definite degree—acid, bitter, feed, and utensil.

Body. It is uniform and may possess the following characteristics: to a slight degree—coarse, pasty, and short; and to a definite degree—the cheese may be weak.

Eyes and Texture. The cheese may possess the following eye characteristics: to a slight degree—afterset, cabbage, collapsed, irregular, large eyed, and small eyed; and to a definite degree—dead eyes, dull, frog mouth, nesty, rough, one sided, overset, shell, underset, and uneven. The cheese may possess the following texture characteristics: to a slight degree—gassy, splits, and sweet holes; and to a definite degree—checks, picks and streuble.

Finish and Appearance. The rind is sound and provides good protection to the cheese. The cheese may exhibit the following characteristics: to a slight degree—checked rind, and soft spots; and to a definite degree—huffed, mold, soiled, uneven, and wet rind. There should be no indication that mold has penetrated into the interior of the cheese. If rindless, the wrapper or covering adequately and securely envelops the cheese, is unbroken, fully protects the surface, and may be wrinkled. The cheese may exhibit a very slight soiled surface and contain soft spots to a slight degree. The cheese may possess the following characteristics: to a definite degree—huffed, mold, uneven, and wet surface. There should be no indication that mold has penetrated into the interior of the cheese.

Color. The cheese may possess the following color characteristics: to a slight degree—acid cut, bleached, colored spots, dull or faded, mottled and pink ring; and to a definite degree—bleached surface.

Source:
Agricultural Marketing Service, USDA, "United States Standards for Grades of Swiss Cheese, Emmentaler Cheese," 7 CFR sections 58.2570 to 58.2578 (1992), Washington: Government Printing Office.

Cream

Heavy Whipping Cream. A cream which contains not less than 36 percent milkfat. It is pasteurized or ultra-pasteurized and may be homogenized. It may contain nutritive sweeteners and flavoring ingredients.

Light Cream. A cream which contains between 18 and 30 percent milkfat. It is pasteurized or ultra-pasteurized and may be homogenized. It is also known as *coffee cream* or *table cream*. It may contain nutritive sweeteners and flavoring ingredients.

Light Whipping Cream. A cream which contains between 30 and 36 percent milkfat. It is pasteurized or ultra-pasteurized and may be homogenized. It may include nutritive sweeteners and characterizing flavoring ingredients.

Sweetened. Contains no characterizing flavoring ingredients, but nutritive sweetener is added.

Source:
Food and Drug Administration, Milk and Cream, 21 CFR Part 131 (1992), Washington: Government Printing Office.

Eggnog

Eggnog. A milk product consisting of a mixture of milk or milk products (with at least 6.0 percent butterfat), at least 1.0 percent egg yolk solids, sweetener, and flavoring. Emulsifier and not over 0.5 percent stabilizer may be added.

Eggnog Flavored Milk. A milk product consisting of a mixture of at least 3.25 percent butterfat, at least 0.5 percent egg yolk solids, sweetener, and flavoring. Emulsifier and a maximum of 0.5 percent stabilizer may be added.

Source:
Food and Drug Administration, *Compliance Policy Guides*, Guide 7106.02, 10/01/80, Washington: National Technical Information Service.

Eggs

The U.S. standards for quality of individual shell eggs contained in this entry are applicable only to eggs that are the product of the domesticated chicken hen and are in the shell.

Interior egg quality specifications for these standards are based on the apparent condition of the interior contents of the egg as it is twirled before a candling light. Any type or make of candling light may be used that will enable the particular grader to make consistently accurate determination of the interior quality of shell eggs.

The grade descriptions which follow are intended only as a general consumer guide. For more detail please consult the source cited below.

TERMINOLOGY

Dirty. An individual egg that has an unbroken shell with adhering dirt or foreign material, prominent stains, or moderate stains covering more than 1/32 of the shell surface, if localized, or 1/16 of the shell surface, if scattered.

Check. An individual egg that has a broken shell or crack in the shell, but its shell membranes are intact and its contents do not leak. A *check* is considered to be lower in quality than a *dirty*.

Leaker. An egg that has a crack or break in the shell and shell membranes to the extent that the egg contents are exposed, are exuding, or are free to exude through the shell.

Loss. An egg that is unfit for human food because it is smashed or broken; its contents are leaking; it was overheated, frozen, or contaminated; or it is an incubator reject.

GRADES

AA Quality. The shell must be clean, unbroken, and practically normal. The air cell must not exceed 1/8 inch in depth, may show unlimited movement, and may be free or bubbly. The white must be clear and firm so that the yolk is only slightly defined when the egg is twirled before a candling light. The yolk must be practically free from apparent defects.

A Quality. The shell must be clean, unbroken, and practically normal. The air cell must not exceed ⅛ inch in depth, may show unlimited movement, and may be free or bubbly. The white must be clear and at least reasonably firm so that the yolk outline is only fairly well defined when the egg is twirled before a candling light. The yolk must be practically free from apparent defects.

B Quality. The shell must be unbroken, may be abnormal, and may have slightly stained areas. Moderately stained areas are permitted if they do not cover more than ⅟₃₂ of the shell surface, if localized, or ⅟₁₆ of the shell surface, if scattered. Eggs having shells with prominent stains or adhering dirt are not permitted. The air cell may be over ³⁄₁₆ inch in depth, may show unlimited movement, and may be free or bubbly. The white may be weak and watery so that the yolk outline is plainly visible when the egg is twirled before a candling light. The yolk may appear dark, enlarged, and flattened, and may show clearly visible germ development, but there is no blood due to such development. May show other serious defects that do not render the egg inedible; blood or meat spots (aggregating not more than ⅛ inch in diameter) may be present.

CONSUMER GRADES

U.S. Consumer Grade AA. Consists of eggs which are at least 72 percent AA quality. The remaining tolerance of 28 percent may consist of at least 10 percent A quality and the remainder may be B quality. Not more than 7 percent (9 percent for Jumbo size) *Checks* are permitted, and not more than 1 percent *Leakers, Dirties,* or *Loss* (due to meat or blood spots) in any combination are permitted.

U.S. Consumer Grade A. Consist of eggs which are at least 82 percent A quality or better. Within the maximum tolerance of 18 percent which may be below A quality, not more than 1 percent may be B quality due to air cells over ⅛ inch, blood spots (aggregating not more than ⅛ inch in diameter), or serious yolk defects. Not more than 7 percent (9 percent for Jumbo size) *Checks* are permitted, and not more than 1 percent *Leakers, Dirties,* or *Loss* (due to meat or blood spots) in any combination are permitted.

U.S. Consumer Grade B. Consists of eggs which are at least 90 percent B quality or better. Not more than 10 percent may be *Checks* and not more than 1 percent may be *Leakers, Dirties,* or *Loss* (due to meat or blood spots) in any combination.

U.S. WEIGHT CLASSES FOR CONSUMER GRADES FOR SHELL EGGS

Size	Per 30 per dozen (oz.)	Individual dozen (lbs.)	Eggs per dozen (oz.)
Jumbo	30	56	29
Extra Large	27	50½	26
Large	24	45	23
Medium	21	39⅓	20
Small	18	34	17
Peewee	15	28	—

When establishing a weight class, a lot average tolerance of 3.3 percent for individual eggs in the next lower weight class is permitted as long as no individual case within the lot exceeds 5 percent.

Source:
Agricultural Marketing Service, USDA, 7 CFR sections 56.200 to 56.232 (1992), Washington: Government Printing Office.

Half-and-Half

Consists of a mixture of milk and cream which contains between 10.5 and 18 percent milkfat. It is pasteurized or ultra-pasteurized and may be homogenized. It may also include nutritive sweeteners and characterizing flavoring ingredients. The presence of any characterizing flavoring is found on the label.

Sweetened. No characterizing flavoring ingredients are used, but nutritive sweeteners are added.

Sour Half-and-Half, Cultured Half-and-Half. Results from the souring, by lactic acid-producing bacteria, of pasteurized half-and-half.

Acidified Sour Half-and-Half. Results from the souring of pasteurized half-and-half with acidifiers and with or without the addition of lactic-acid producing bacteria.

Cultured. Indicates the use of bacterial cultures.

Source:
Food and Drug Administration, "Milk and Cream," 21 CFR part 131 (1992), Washington: Government Printing Office.

Ice Cream

Ice cream contains at least 1.6 pounds of total solids to the gallon, weights not less than 4.5 pounds to the gallon, and contains not less than 20 percent total milk solid which is composed of not less than 10 percent milkfat. In no case should the content of milk solids (not fat) be less than 6 percent. Whey should not, by weight, be more than 25 percent of the milk solids (not fat). Optional characterizing ingredients, optional sweetening ingredients, stabilizers, and emulsifiers as approved by the Food and Drug Administration may be used.

OFFICIAL IDENTIFICATION.

The official symbol to be used to identify product meeting the USDA standard for ice cream is as follows:

> MEETS USDA
> INGREDIENT STANDARD
> FOR ICE CREAM

Ice cream manufacturing plants using this symbol are USDA approved, and the ice cream bearing the symbol is manufactured under continuous resident or continuous nonresident USDA inspection service. The dairy ingredients used in such ice cream come from USDA approved plants.

Source:
Agricultural Marketing Service, USDA, "United States Standards for Ice Cream," 7 CFR sections 58.2825 to 58.2827 (1992), Washington: Government Printing Office.

Margarine

Margarine (or oleomargarine) is a food in plastic form or liquid emulsion containing not less than 80 percent fat. Margarine contains only safe and suitable ingredients. It is produced from one or more of the following optional ingredients:

Edible fats and/or oils whose origin is vegetable or rendered animal carcass fats.

It is combined with one or more of the following additional optional ingredients to form a solidified or liquid emulsion:

Water, milk, milk products, suitable edible protein which includes (but not limited to) the liquid, condensed, or dry form of whey, whey modified by the reduction of lactose and/or minerals, nonlactose containing whey components, albumin, casein, caseinate, vegetable proteins, or soy protein isolate. These ingredients are added in amounts not greater than reasonably required to accomplish the desired effect. The ingredients are pasteurized and then may be subjected to the action of one or more harmless bacterial starters.

To the above ingredients, one or more of the following optional ingredients may be added:

1. Vitamin D in such quantity that the finished oleomargarine contains not less than 1,500 International Units of vitamin D per pound.
2. Salt (sodium chloride), or potassium chloride for dietary margarine or oleomargarine.
3. Nutritive carbohydrate sweeteners.
4. Emulsifiers which include (but is not limited) mono- and diglycerides of fatty acids esterified with the following acids: acetic, acetyltartaric, citric, lactic, tartaric, and their sodium and calcium salts, 0.5 percent; such mono- and diglycerides in combination with the sodium sulfoacetate derivatives thereof, 0.5 percent; polyglycerol esters of fatty acids, 0.5 percent; 1.2-propylene glycol esters of fatty acids, 2 percent; lecithin, 0.5 percent.
5. Preservatives which include (but not limited to) the following: Sorbic acid, benzoic acid and their sodium, potassium, and calcium salts, individually, 0.1 percent, or in combination, 0.2 percent, expressed as the acids; calcium disodium EDTA, 0.0075 percent; propyl, octyl, and dodecyl gallates, BHT, BHA, ascorbyl palmitate, ascorbyl stearate, all individually or in combination, 0.02 percent; stearyl citrate, 0.15 percent; isopropyl citrate mixture, 0.02 percent.
6. Color additives. Provitamin A (beta-carotene) is considered a color additive.
7. Flavoring substances. If the flavoring ingredients impart to the food a flavor other than that of butter, the characterizing flavor should be included in the name of the food.
8. Acidulants.
9. Alkalizers.

Margarine contains vitamin A in such quantity that the finished margarine contains not less than 15,000 International Units per pound.

Each of the optional ingredients used should be declared on the label. The term *milk* means milk from cows. If any milk other than cow's milk is used in whole or in part, the animal source is identified in conjunction with the word milk in the ingredient statement. Colored margarine is subject to the Federal Food, Drug, and Cosmetic Act.

Source:
Food and Drug Administration, "Margarine," 21 CFR part 166 (1991), Washington: Government Printing Office.

Milk Products

Cream. The liquid milk product high in fat that separated from milk. It may be adjusted by adding the following: milk, concentrated milk, dry whole milk, skin milk, concentrated skim milk, concentrated skim milk, or nonfat dry milk. Cream contains not less than 18 percent milkfat.

Pasteurized. Pasteurization is a method of destroying disease-producing bacteria and checking the activity of fermentative bacteria in milk, beer, etc., by exposing the liquid to high temperatures. When used to describe a dairy product, pasteurized means that every particle of the dairy product has been heated to one of the temperatures specified in the table below and held continuously at or above that temperature for the specified time:

Temperature	Time
145[a]	30 minutes
161[a]	15 seconds
191	1 second
204	0.05 second
212	0.01 second

[a]If the dairy ingredient has a fat content of 10 percent or more or if it contains added sweeteners, the specified temperature is increased by 5 degrees F.

Ultra-Pasteurized. Thermally processed at or above 280 degrees F for at least 2 seconds, either before or after packaging. Produces a product which has an extended shelf life under refrigerated conditions.

Milk. The FDA defines milk as the lactela secretion, practically free from colostrum, obtained by the complete milking of healthy cows. Milk that is in final package form for beverage use is pasteurized or ultra-pasteurized; it does not contain less than 8.25 percent milk solids (not fat) and not less than 3.25 percent milkfat.

Homogenized. The term homogenized means that milk or a milk product has been treated to insure breakup of the fat globules to such an extent that, after 48 hours of quiescent storage at 40 degrees F, no visible cream separation occurs on the milk; the fat percentage of the top 100 ml of milk in a quart does not differ by more than 10 percent from the fat percentage of the remaining milk—as determined after thorough mixing.

Vit. An abbreviation for the word vitamin.

Nutritive Carbohydrate Sweeteners. An optional ingredient to milk products. It includes beet or cane sugar (sucrose), invert sugar, brown sugar, refiner's syrup, molasses, high fructose corn syrup, fructose, fructose syrup, maltose, maltose syrup, dried maltose syrup, malt extract, dried malt extract, malt syrup, dried malt syrup, honey, maple sugar, dextrose anhydrous, dextrose monohydrate, glucose syrup, dried glucose syrup, lactose, cane syrup, maple syrup, sorghum syrup, and table syrup.

Reconstituted or Recombined. Milk or milk products which result from the reconstituting or recombining of milk constituents with water.

Concentrated Milk. A fluid product, unsterilized and unsweetened, resulting from the removal of a considerable portion of the water from the milk. When combined with water, the result is a product conforming with the milkfat and milk solids (not fat) levels of milk.

Lactose-Reduced Milk. Milk treated by the addition of enzymes in order to convert sufficient amounts of the lactose to glucose and/or galactose so that the remaining lactose is less than 30 percent of the lactose in ordinary milk.

Low Sodium Milk. Milk treated by a process of passing the milk through an ion exchange resin. It effectively reduces the sodium content of the product to less than 10 mg in 100 ml.

Hermetically Sealed Container. A container that is designed and intended to be secure against the entry of microorganisms and thereby maintain the commercial sterility of its contents after processing.

Aseptic Processing. The product has been subjected to sufficient heat processing and has been packaged in a hermetically sealed container to maintain the commercial sterility of the product under normal non-refrigerated conditions.

Aseptically Processed Milk. Hermetically sealed in a container and thermally processed in order to render the product free of microorganisms capable of reproducing in the product under normal non-refrigeration conditions of storage and distribution. The product is free of viable microorganisms (including spores) of public health significance.

Grade A Milk and Milk Products. Products labeled Grade A have been produced in accordance with the standards detailed in the Pasteurized Milk Ordinance developed by the U.S. Department of Health and Human Services. The ordinance is the basic standard used in the voluntary Cooperative State-PHS Program for Certification of Interstate Milk Shippers—a program participated in by all 50 States, the District of Columbia, and U.S. Trust Territories. The Ordinance states that only Grade A pasteurized, ultra-pasteurized, or aseptically processed milk and milk products shall be sold to the final consumer or to restaurants, soda fountains, grocery stores, or similar establishments. In an emergency, the sale of pasteurized milk and milk products which have not been graded, or the grade of which is unknown, may be authorized by the regulatory agency; in which case, such milk and milk products are labeled *ungraded.*

ACIDIFIED LOWFAT

Milk produced by souring one or more of the optional dairy ingredients with one or more of the acidifying ingredients. It contains between 0.5 and 2.0 percent milkfat and not less than 8.25 percent milk solids (not fat). It has a titratable acidity of not less than 0.5 percent, expressed as lactic acid. It may be homogenized and is pasteurized or ultra-pasteurized.

Sweetened. Nutritive carbohydrate sweetener is added.

_____% Milkfat. The blank is filled in with the actual fat content measured in multiples of ½.

Vitamin A Added. May be added in an amount of 2,000 International Units per quart.

Vitamin D Added. May be added in an amount of 400 International Units per quart.

Flavorings. If the product contains any flavoring ingredient, the name of the ingredient is listed on the label and be made part of the name—as in *kefir cultured lowfat milk,* or *acidophilus cultured lowfat milk.*

ACIDIFIED SKIM MILK

Produced by souring one or more of the optional dairy ingredients (cream, milk, partially skimmed milk, or skim milk—used alone or in combination) with one or more of the acidifying ingredients (acetic acid, adipic acid, citric acid, fumaric acid, glucono-delta-lactone, hydrochloric acid, lactic acid, malic acid, phosphoric acid, succinic acid, and tartaric acid). It contains less than 0.5 percent milkfat and not less than 8.25 percent milk solids (not fat). It has a titratable acidity of not less than 0.5 percent, expressed as lactic acid. It is pasteurized or ultra-pasteurized and may be homogenized.

Vitamin A Added. Contains 2,000 International Units of vitamin A per quart.

Vitamin D Added. Contains 400 International Units of vitamin D per quart.

Flavorings. If the product contains any flavoring ingredient, the name of the ingredient is listed on the label and may be made part of the name—as in *acidified kefir skim milk,* or *acidified acidophilus lowfat milk.*

Sweetened. Nutritive carbohydrate sweetener is added.

CONCENTRATED MILK

Concentrated milk, or condensed milk, is a liquid obtained by the partial removal of water from milk. Concentrated milk contains not less than 7.5 percent milkfat and not less than 25.5 percent total milk solids. It is pasteurized, but is not processed by heat so as to prevent spoilage. It may be homogenized. Vitamin D may be added in the amount of 25 International Units per fluid ounce. Other optional ingredients include flavoring ingredients, with or without coloring.

CULTURED MILK

Cultured milk is produced by culturing cream, milk, partially skimmed milk, or skim milk (alone or in combination) with characterizing microbial organisms. Cultured milk contains not less than 3.25 percent milkfat and not less than 8.25 percent milk solids (not fat); it has a titratable acidity of not less than 0.5 percent, expressed as lactic acid. It is pasteurized or ultra-pasteurized prior to the addition of the microbial culture and may be homogenized.

Vitamin A Added. Contains 2,000 International Units of vitamin A per quart.

Vitamin D Added. Contains 400 International Units of vitamin A per quart.

CULTURED SKIM MILK

Cultured skim milk (cultured nonfat milk) is produced by culturing one or more of the optional dairy ingredients (cream, milk, partially skimmed milk, or skim milk—used alone or in combination) with characterizing microbial organisms. Contains less than 0.5 percent milkfat and not less than 8.25 percent milk solids (not fat); it has a titratable acidity of not less than 0.5 percent, expressed as lactic acid. It is pasteurized or ultra-pasteurized prior to the addition of the microbial culture and may be homogenized.

Vitamin A Added. Contains 2,000 International Units of vitamin A per quart.

Vitamin D Added. Contains 400 International Units of vitamin D per quart.

Sweetened. Nutritive carbohydrate sweetener is added.

Flavorings. If the product contains any flavoring ingredient, the name of the ingredient is listed on the label and may be made part of the name—as in *kefir cultured nonfat milk,* or *acidophilus cultured nonfat milk.*

Cultured Skim Milk Buttermilk. When characterizing ingredients and lactic acid-producing organisms are used.

EVAPORATED MILK

Milk from which the water has been partially removed. It contains not less than 7.5 percent milkfat and not less than 25 percent of total milk solids. It is homogenized, sealed in a container, and processed by heat to prevent spoilage.

Vitamin D or Vitamin D Added. Evaporated milk contains added vitamin D in an amount of 25 International Units per fluid ounce.

Vitamin A or Vitamin A Added. Evaporated milk may optionally contain not less than 125 International Units per fluid ounce of vitamin A.

EVAPORATED SKIMMED MILK

Skim milk from which the water has been partially removed. It contains not less than 20 percent of milk solids and not more than 0.5 percent of milkfat (unless otherwise indicated). It is sealed in a container and processed by heat to prevent spoilage. It may be homogenized.

Vitamins A and D or Vitamins A and D Added. Evaporated skimmed milk contains 25 International Units per ounce of vitamin D and 125 International Units per ounce of vitamin A.

Contains_____% Milkfat. If the milkfat content is over 0.5 percent, the blank is filled in with the fraction ½ or multiple thereof which is closest to the actual milkfat content.

LOWFAT MILK

Milk from which milkfat has been removed. There are four standardized milkfat contents for lowfat milk: ½, 1, 1½, or 2 percent. Lowfat milk is pasteurized or ultra-pasteurized. It contains added vitamin A and not less than 8¼ percent milk solids (not fat). It may be homogenized.

_____% Milkfat. The blank is filled in with a fraction that is a multiple of ½ and indicates closest the actual fat content.

Vitamin A or Vitamin A Added. Vitamin A has been added in an amount not less than 2,000 International Units per quart.

Vitamin D or Vitamin D Added. Indicates the optional addition of 400 International Units of vitamin D per quart.

With Added Milk Solids Not Fat. Contains not less than 10 percent milk-derived nonfat solids.

LOWFAT DRY MILK

Pasteurized lowfat milk from which all the water has been removed. It contains between 5 and 20 percent by weight of milkfat and not more than 5 percent by weight of moisture on a milk solids (not fat) basis.

Vitamin A or Vitamin A Added. Contains added vitamin A in the amount of not less than 2,000 International Units per quart.

Vitamin A and D or Vitamins A and D Added. Unlike vitamin A, the addition of vitamin D is optional. If included it is in an amount of 400 International Units per quart.

Contains_____% Milkfat. The blank is filled in with the whole number that is closest to the actual fat content of the food.

DRY WHOLE MILK

Dry whole milk (made by the spray process or by the atmospheric roller process) is the product obtained by removal of water only from pasteurized milk which may have been homogenized. Alternatively, dry whole milk may be obtained by blending fluid, condensed, or dried nonfat milk with liquid or dried cream or with fluid, condensed, or dried milk, as appropriate—provided the resulting dry whole milk is equivalent in composition to that obtained by drying. It contains the lactose, milk proteins, milkfat, and milk minerals in the same relative proportions as the milk from which it was made. It may be optionally fortified with either vitamins A or D or both.

Vitamin A Added. Vitamin A Added dry whole milk contains 2,000

International Units of vitamin A per quart.

Vitamin D Added. Contains 400 International Units of vitamin D per quart.

Contains_____% Milkfat. The blank contains the whole number that is closest to the actual fat content of the food.

GRADES

The grade descriptions which follow are intended only as a general consumer guide. For more detailed information, please consult the source cited below.

U.S. Extra

Flavor (applies to the reconstituted product). Sweet, pleasing, and desirable. It may possess a slight feed flavor and a definite cooked flavor. It is free of undesirable flavors.

Physical Appearance. Should be white or light cream color, free from lumps that do not break up under slight pressure, and practically free from visible dark particles. The reconstituted product should be free from graininess.

Bacterial Estimate. Not more than 50,000 per gram standard plate count.

Coliform Estimate. Not more than 10 per gram.

Milkfat Content. Not less than 26.0 percent, but less than 40.0 percent.

Moisture Content. Not more than 4.5 percent (as determined by weight of moisture on a milk solids not fat basis).

Scorched Particle Content. Not more than 15.0 mg for the spray process and 22.5 mg for the roller process.

Solubility Index. Not more than 1.0 ml for the spray process and 15.0 ml for the roller process.

U.S. Standard

Flavor (applies to the reconstituted product). Has a sweet and pleasing flavor. It may possess the following flavors: to a sight degree—bitter, oxidized, scorched, stale, and storage; and to a definite degree—feed and cooked. It should be free from undesirable flavors.

Physical Appearance. Should be white or light cream color, but it may possess a slight unnatural color. It should be free from lumps that do not break up under moderate pressure; it is reasonably free from visible dark particles. The reconstituted product should be reasonably free from graininess.

Bacterial Estimate. Not more than 100,000 per gram standard plate count.

Coliform Estimate. Not more than 10 per gram.

Milkfat content. Not less than 26.0 percent, but less than 40.0 percent.

Moisture Content. Not more than 5.0 percent (as determined by weight of moisture on a milk solids, not fat, basis).

Scorched Particle Content. Not more than 22.5 mg for the spray process and 32.5 mg for the roller process.

Solubility Index. Not more than 1.5 ml for the spray process and 15.0 ml for the roller process.

NONFAT DRY MILK

The product resulting from the removal of fat and water from milk; it contains lactose, milk proteins, and milk minerals in the same relative proportion as in the fresh milk from which made. It contains not over 5 percent by weight of moisture. The fat content is not over 1½ percent by weight, unless otherwise indicated.

Instant Nonfat Dry Milk. Nonfat dry milk which has been produced in such a manner as to substantially improve its dispersing and reconstitution characteristics over that produced by the conventional processes.

Contains _____% Milkfat. If the fat content is over 1½ percent, the blank contains the percentage to the nearest one-tenth percent of fat.

Fortified with Vitamins A and D. Contains 2000 International Units per quart of vitamin A and 400 International Units per quart of vitamin D.

GRADES

The U.S. grades of nonfat dry milk—spray process—are determined on the basis of flavor, physical appearance, bacterial estimate on the basis of standard plate count, milkfat content, moisture content, scorched particle content, solubility index, and titratable acidity. The grade descriptions which follow are intended only as a general consumer guide. For more detailed information, please consult the source cited below.

U.S. Extra

Flavor (applies to the reconstituted product). Sweet, pleasing, and desirable but may possess the following flavors: to a slight degree—chalky, cooked, feed and flat.

Physical Appearance. Possess a uniform white to light cream natural color, is free from lumps (except those that readily break up with very slight pressure), and is practically free from visible dark particles. The reconstituted product is free from graininess.

Bacterial Estimate. Not more than 50,000 per gram standard plate count.

Milkfat Content. Not more than 1.25 percent.

Moisture Content. Not more than 4.0 percent.

Scorched Particle Content. Not more than 15.0 mg.

Solubility Index. Not more than 1.2 ml, except for that product classified as U.S. High Heat and which may have not more than 2.0 ml.

Titratable Acidity. Not more than 0.15 percent.

U.S. Standard

Flavor (applies to the reconstituted product). Possess a fairly pleasing flavor. However, it may possess the following flavors: to a slight degree—bitter, oxidized, stale, storage, utensil, and scorched; and to a definite degree—chalky, cooked, feed, and flat.

Physical Appearance. May possess a slight unnatural color, is free from lumps (except those that break up readily under slight pressure), and is reasonably free from visible dark particles. The reconstituted product is reasonably free from graininess.

Bacterial Estimate. Not more than 100,000 per gram standard plate count.

Milkfat Content. Not more than 1.50 percent.

Moisture Content. Not more than 5.0 percent.

Scorched Particle Content. Not more than 22.5 mg.

Solubility Index. Not more than 2.0 ml, except U.S. High Heat may have not more than 2.5 ml.

Titratable Acidity. Not more than 0.17 percent.

NONFAT SKIM MILK

Milk from which sufficient milkfat has been removed to reduce its milkfat content to less than 0.5 percent. It is pasteurized or ultra-pasteurized and contains added vitamin A. It contains not less than 8-1/4 percent milk solids and may be homogenized.

With Added Milk Solids Not Fat. Contains not less than 10 percent milk-derived nonfat solids.

Vitamin A Added. Contains 2,000 International Units of vitamin A per quart.

Vitamin D Added. Contains an optional 400 International Units of vitamin D per quart.

SWEETENED CONDENSED MILK

Obtained by the partial removal of water from a mixture of milk and nutritive carbohydrate sweeteners. The finished food contains not less than 8 percent by weight of milkfat and not less than 28 percent by weight of total milk solids. It is pasteurized and may be homogenized.

SWEETENED CONDENSED SKIMMED MILK

Obtained by the partial removal of water from a mixture of skim milk and nutritive carbohydrate sweeteners. Contains not more than 0.5 percent by weight of milk fat, unless otherwise indicated, and not less than 24 percent by weight of total milk solids. It is pasteurized and may be homogenized. It may also include flavoring ingredients.

Sources:
Food and Drug Administration, "Milk and Cream," 21 CFR part 131 (1992), Washington: Government Printing Office.
Public Health Service, Food and Drug Administration, *Grade "A" Pasteurized Milk Ordinance* (1989), Washington: Department of Health and Human Services.

Sour Cream

Sour cream (also called cultured sour cream) results from the souring, by lactic acid-producing bacteria, of pasteurized cream. Sour cream contains at least 18 percent milkfat. If nutritive sweeteners or bulky flavoring ingredients have been added, it must contain at least 14.4 percent milkfat. Sour cream has a titratable acidity of not less than 0.5 percent, calculated as lactic acid.

Sweetened. Nutritive sweetener has been added in an amount sufficient to characterize the food without the addition of characterizing flavoring.

Cultured Cream. Bacterial cultures may be declared by the word *cultured* followed by the name of the substrate, e.g., *cultured cream.*

SOUR CREAM, ACIDIFIED

Acidified sour cream results from the souring of pasteurized cream with safe and suitable acidifiers, with or without addition of lactic acid producing bacterial.

Source:
Food and Drug Administration, "Milk and Cream," 21 CFR part 131 (1992), Washington: Government Printing Office.

Yogurt

Yogurt is produced by culturing cream, milk, partially skimmed milk, or skim milk (alone or in combination) with a characterizing bacterial culture that contains the lactic acid-producing bacterial, *Lactobacillus bulgaricus* and *Streptococcus thermophilus.* Yogurt may also contain sweeteners and flavoring ingredients. Before the addition of bulky flavors, it contains not less than 3.25 percent milkfat and not less than 8.25 percent milk solids (not fat). It has a titratable acidity of not less than 0.9 percent, expressed as lactic acid. It may be homogenized and is pasteurized or ultra-pasteurized prior to the addition of the bacterial culture.

Contains Active Yogurt Cultures. Yogurt labeled with this phrase has not been heat-treated after culturing and contains living yogurt cultures.

Flavoring. The label contains the name of any characterizing flavoring included.

Heat-Treated After Culturing. Yogurt may be heat-treated after culturing is completed in order to destroy viable microorganisms and extend the shelf life of the food.

Liquid Yogurt. Fruit and yogurt are blended into a drinkable liquid.

Lowfat and Nonfat. The FDA recognizes three standardized yogurt products. Yogurt made from whole milk has at least 3.25 percent milkfat. Lowfat yogurt is made from lowfat milk or part skim milk and has between 2 and 5 percent milkfat. Nonfat yogurt is made from skim milk and contains less than 0.5 percent milkfat.

Made with Active Cultures. All yogurts are made with active cultures. Only those that are not heat-treated, however, retain the active cultures.

Sundae or Fruit-on-the-Bottom. The fruit is on the bottom. If one was to look at the yogurt from the bottom up, it would resemble an ice cream sundae. The liquid part of the yogurt, the whey, may float on top of the solid curds. Consumers can mix them together to make it smooth and creamy.

Sweetened. Nutritive carbohydrate sweetener is added without the addition of characterizing flavor.

Swiss or Custard. Fruit and yogurt are mixed together and poured into individual servings. A stabilizer such as gelatin may be added for firmness or body. In some custard-style yogurt products, the fruit is placed on top of the yogurt to make a marbled effect as it settles to the bottom.

Vitamin A or Vitamin A Added. If added, vitamin A is present in the amount of 2,000 International Units per quart.

Vitamin D or Vitamin D Added. If added, vitamin D is present in the amount of 400 International Units per quart.

Source:
Williams, Rebecca D., "Yogurt: The Curds and Whey to Health," *FDA Consumer,* Vol. 26 no. 5 (June 1992): 28.
Food and Drug Administration, "Milk and Cream," 21 CFR part 131, 1992: Washington, Government Printing Office.

Fruits

Apple Butter

Apple butter is a fruit butter prepared from clean, sound, whole-some, mature apples (either fresh, frozen, canned and/or dried) and other ingredients. The apples are prepared by cooking, with or without added water, and the skins, seeds, and cores are screened out. The soluble solids are not less than 43 percent.

GRADES

This product is graded according to a technical system whereby penalty points are assessed for such factors as edibility, poor appearance, or defects in workmanship. The more penalty points assessed the lower the grade. The grade descriptions which follow are intended only as a general consumer guide. For more detailed information, please consult the source cited below.

U.S. Grade A or U.S. Fancy. Possesses a good color that may be moderately reddish brown or moderately dark brown. It has a good consistency. The apple particles are evenly divided and the product is fine grained and smooth. It is practically free from black specks, dark scale-like particles, particles of carpel tissue, peel, stem, seed-coat, and blossom-end material. It possesses a flavor and aroma characteristic of apple butter properly prepared and processed from good quality ingredients.

U.S. Grade C or U.S. Standard. Possesses a dark brown or light brown color which may be somewhat lacking in luster. May possess a thick consistency. The apple particles are evenly divided. The product may be slightly coarse, but the apple particles are neither hard nor excessively grainy. It is fairly free from defects and possesses an apple butter flavor and odor that may be excessively sweet or excessively tart. The product may be excessively spiced or lacking in proper spicing or may

be excessively caramelized, but it is not seriously objection-able for any reason.

Substandard. Fails to meet the requirements of U.S. Grade C or U.S. Standard.

Source:

Agricultural Marketing Service, USDA, 7 CFR sections 52.2801 to 52.2812 (1991), Washington: Government Printing Office.

Apples

This product is graded according to a technical system whereby penalty points are assessed for such factors as edibility, poor appearance, or defects in workmanship. The more penalty points assessed the lower the grade. The grade descriptions which follow are intended only as a general consumer guide. For more detailed information, please consult the source cited below.

U.S. Extra Fancy. Apples of one variety which are mature but not overripe. They have been carefully handpicked, are clean, and are fairly well formed. They are free from decay, internal browning, internal breakdown, scald, scab, bitter pit, Jonathan spot, freezing injury, visible water core, broken skins, and bruises. The apples are also free from injury caused by russeting, sunburn, sprayburn, limb rubs, hail, drought spots, scars, disease, insects, or other means. See color requirements below.

U.S. Fancy. Apples of one variety which are mature (but not overripe), carefully handpicked, clean, and fairly well formed. They are free from decay, internal browning, internal break-down, bitter pit, Jonathan spot, scald, freezing injury, visible water core, broken skins, and bruises (except those which are incident to proper handling and packing). The apples are also free from damage caused by russeting, sunburn, sprayburn, limb rubs, hail, drought spots, scars, stem or calyx cracks, disease, insects, and invisible water core. See color requirements below.

U.S. No. 1. The requirements of this grade are the same as for U.S. Fancy except for color, russeting, and invisible water core. In this grade, less color is required for all varieties with the exception of the yellow and green varieties (other than Golden Delicious). Apples of this grade are free from excessive damage caused by russeting; the aggregate area of an apple which may be covered by smooth net-like russeting cannot exceed 25 percent, and the aggregate area of an apple which may be covered by smooth solid russeting cannot exceed 10 percent. However, in the case of the Yellow Newtown or similar varieties, the aggregate area of an apple which may be covered with smooth solid russeting cannot exceed 20 percent. There is no requirement in this grade pertaining to invisible water core. See color requirements below.

U.S. No. 1 Early. Apples which meet the requirements of U.S. No. 1 grade except for color and maturity and which meet a minimum size requirement. Apples of this grade have no color requirements, need not be mature, and cannot be less than 2 inches in diameter. This grade is provided for varieties such as Duchess, Gravenstein, Red June, Twenty Ounce, Wealthy, Williams, Yellow Transparent, and Lodi, or other varieties which are normally marketed during the summer months.

U.S. No. 1 Hail. Apples which meet the requirements of U.S. No. 1 grade except that hail marks where the skin has not been broken and well-healed hail marks where the skin has been broken are permitted.

U.S. Utility. Apples of one variety which are mature but not overripe. The have been carefully handpicked, are not seriously deformed, and are free from decay, internal browning, internal breakdown scald, and freezing injury. The apples are also free from serious damage caused by dirt or other foreign matter, broken skins, bruises, russeting, sunburn, sprayburn, limb rubs, hail, drought spots, scars, stem or calyx cracks, visible water core, disease, insects, or other means.

COMBINATION GRADES

Combinations of the above grades may be used as follows:

Combination U.S. Extra Fancy and U.S. Fancy
Combination U.S. Fancy and U.S. No. 1
Combination U.S. No. 1 and U.S. Utility

Combinations other than these are not permitted in connection with the U.S. apple grades. When combination grades are packed, at least 50 percent of the apples in any lot meet the requirements of the higher grade in the combination.

COLOR REQUIREMENTS

Color requirements (in percent) for specified U.S. Grades of Apples by Variety.

Variety	U.S. Extra Fancy	U.S. Fancy	U.S. No. 1
Solid Red:			
Black Ben	66	40	25
Gano	66	40	25
Winesap	66	40	25
Other similar varieties(1)	60	40	25
Red Sport varieties (2)	66	40	25
Striped or partially red:			
Jonathan	66	33	25
MacIntosh	50	33	25
Cortland	50	33	25
Other similar varieties (3)	50	33	25
Rome Beauty	50	33	15
Stayman	50	33	15
York Imperial	50	33	15
Baldwin	50	25	15
Ben Davis	50	25	15
Delicious	50	25	15
Mammoth Blach Twig	50	25	15
Turley	50	25	15
Wagener	50	25	15
Wealthy	50	25	15
Willow Twig	50	25	15
Northern Spy	50	25	15
Other similar varieties (4)	50	25	15
Hubbardston	50	15	10
Stark	50	15	10
Other similar varieties	50	15	10
Red June	50	15	(5)
Red Gravenstein	50	15	(5)
Williams	50	15	(5)
Other similar varieties	50	15	(5)
Gravenstein	25	10	(5)
Duchess	25	10	(5)
Other similar varieties(6)	25	10	(5)
Red-cheeked or blushed:			
Maiden Blush	(7)	(5)	(8)
Twenty Ounce	(7)	(5)	(8)
Winter Banana	(7)	(5)	(8)
Other similar varieties	(7)	(5)	(8)
Green varieties	(9)	(9)	(9)
Yellow varieties	(9)	(9)	(9)
Golden Delicious	(10)	(10)	(9)

(1) Arkansas Black, Beacon, Detroit Red, Esopus Spitzenburg, King David, Lowry, Minjon.
(2) When Red Sport varieties are specified as such, they meet the color requirements specified for Red Sport varieties.
(3) Haralson, Kendall, Macoun, Snow (Fameuse).
(4) Bonum, Early McIntosh, Limbertwig, Milton, Nero, Paragon, Melba.
(5) Ting of Color.
(6) Red Astrachan, Smokehouse, Summer Rambo, Dudley.
(7) Blush Cheek.
(8) None.

(9) Characteristic ground color.

(10) 75 percent or more of the surface of the apple shows white or light green predominating over the green.

Source:

Agricultural Marketing Service, USDA, United States Standards for Grades of Apples, 7 CFR sections 51.300 to 51.323 (1991), Washington: Government Printing Office.

Apples, Canned

Canned apples is the product prepared from sound, fresh apples of proper maturity and ripeness. The fruit is packed with or without any of the following ingredients: water, salt, spices, nutritive sweetening ingredients, and any other ingredients permissible under the provision of the Federal Food, Drug and Cosmetic Act. It is sufficiently processed by heat to assure preservation of the product in hermetically sealed containers.

STYLES

Sliced. Cut longitudinally and radially from the core axis.

GRADES

This product is graded according to a technical system whereby penalty points are assessed for such factors as edibility, poor appearance, or defects in workmanship. The more penalty points assessed the lower the grade. The grade descriptions which follow are intended only as a general consumer guide. For more detailed information, please consult the source cited below.

U.S. Grade A or U.S. Fancy. Possess similar varietal characteristics and a normal flavor and odor; it is free from objectionable flavors and odors. The slices, internally and externally, possess a reasonably uniform, bright color characteristic of apples of similar varieties. They are practically uniform in size: at least 90 percent of the drained weight of the product consists of whole or practically whole slices of 1¼ inch. They are practically free from harmless extraneous matter, from damaged or seriously damaged slices, and from carpel tissue. They possess a tender texture and not more than 5 percent of the drained weight of the product consists of mushy apples.

U.S. Grade C or U.S. Standard. Possess similar varietal characteristics and a normal flavor and odor. The slices may vary noticeably in color and may possess a slight (but not markedly) brown, pink, or gray cast. However, they are practically free from internal discoloration. They are fairly uniform in size and are fairly free from defects. They possess a fairly good character; the slices may be variable in texture, with not more than 15 percent of the drained weight of the product consisting of slices that are too hard, too soft, or mushy.

Substandard. Fail to meet the requirements of U.S. Grade C or U.S Standard.

Source:

Agricultural Marketing Service, USDA, 7 CFR sections 52.2161 to 52.2173 (1991), Washington: Government Printing Office.

Apples, Dehydrated

Dehydrated (low-moisture) apples are prepared from clean, sound, fresh or previously dried (or evaporated) apples (see *Apples, Dried*). The peels and cores have been removed, and the apples have been cut into segments. The dried (or evaporated) apple segments may be cut further into smaller segments. Practically all of the moisture is removed to produce a very dry texture. The sulfur dioxide content of the finished product may not exceed 1,000 parts per million. No other additives may be present.

STYLES

Pie Pieces. Consist predominantly of parallel-cut, irregularly shaped pieces, approximating ³⁄₁₆ inch (5 mm) or less in thickness and ¾ inch (19 mm) or longer in their longest dimension.

Flakes. Consist predominantly of parallel-cut, irregularly shaped pieces, approximating ³⁄₁₆ inch (5 mm) or less in thickness and less than ¾ inch (19 mm) in their longest dimension.

Wedges. Fairly thick sectors, approximating no more than ⅝ inch (16 mm) at their greatest thickness.

Sauce Pieces. Small popcorn-like units of varying shapes and sizes, not otherwise conforming to the style of flakes. Practically all of the units will pass through ⁹⁄₁₆ inch (11.3 mm) square openings. Sauce pieces of this style are considered finely cut when practically all of the units will pass through ³⁄₈ inch (9.5 mm) square openings.

GRADES

This product is graded according to a technical system whereby penalty points are assessed for such factors as edibility, poor appearance, or defects in workmanship. The more penalty points assessed the lower the grade. The grade descriptions which follow are intended only as a general consumer guide. For more detailed information, please consult the source cited below.

U.S. Grade A. The moisture content of the finished product is not more than 3 percent by weight. It has a normal flavor and odor free from objectionable flavors or objectionable odors of any kind. Has a good color, a reasonably uniform, bright light yellow to yellow-white color which, upon cooking, is a reasonably bright color. Fairly uniform in size, it is practically free from units damaged by pieces of peel, bruises or other discoloration, bitter pit, corky tissue, water core, or damaged by other means. They have a good texture; the units are brittle and, upon cooking, the textures of the respective styles are as follows:

Pie Pieces or Wedges. The units are reasonably uniform in

tenderness and texture and are practically free from any tough (or leathery) units; there is no more than moderate disintegration except for small pieces that may have been present.

Flakes. The units are reasonably uniform in tenderness and texture and are practically free from any tough (or leathery) units; there may be considerable disintegration of the pieces but not to the degree of a grainy applesauce consistency.

U.S. Grade B. The moisture content of the finished product is not more than 3.5 percent by weight. They have a normal flavor and odor. The color is fairly uniform, bright light yellow-amber or light yellow to yellow-white. Upon cooking, the color may be variable, but it is typical of cooked dehydrated apples that have been properly prepared and processed. They are fairly uniform in size, are reasonably free from defects, and have a reasonably good texture.

Substandard. Fail to meet the requirements of U.S. Grade B.

Source:
Agricultural Marketing Service, USDA, 7 CFR sections 52.2341 to 52.2351 (1991), Washington: Government Printing Office.

Apples, Dried

Dried apples are prepared from sound, properly ripened fruit of the common apple (*Malus pumila*). They have been washed, sorted, trimmed, peeled, cored, and cut into segments. The prepared apple segments are dried to remove the greater portion of moisture and to produce a semi-dry texture. The product may be sulfured sufficiently to retard discoloration. The dried apples are sorted and/or cleaned to assure a clean, sound, wholesome product.

STYLES

Pie Pieces. Irregularly shaped segments of approximate parallel thickness.

Slices or Rings. Circular sections or partial circular sections with open or solid centers. They are cut at approximate right angles to the core and are of approximate parallel thickness.

Wedges. Cut longitudinally and radially from the core.

Cuts. Segments of irregular shapes or irregular thicknesses, or both, which are not predominantly of a single style of pie pieces, slices, rings, or wedges.

GRADES

This product is graded according to a technical system whereby penalty points are assessed for such factors as edibility, poor appearance, or defects in workmanship. The more penalty points assessed the lower the grade. The grade descriptions which follow are intended only as a general consumer guide. For more detailed information, please consult the source cited below.

U.S. Grade A or U.S. Fancy. The moisture content of the finished product is not more than 24 percent by weight. The apples possess similar varietal characteristics, a normal flavor and odor, and a good, uniform, bright light yellow to white color. The apples are nearly uniform in size and practically free from defects. They possess a good texture that is generally pliable, although there may be present a few hard and dry units.

U.S. Grade B or U.S. Choice. The moisture content of the finished product is not more than 24 percent by weight. They possess similar varietal characteristics and a normal flavor and odor. They possess a reasonably good, bright yellow to white color (or other reasonably uniform, bright characteristic color). They are nearly uniform in size and reasonably free from defects. They possess a good texture that may vary in pliability, but they are reasonably free from hard and dry units.

U.S. Grade C or U.S. Standard. The moisture content of the finished product is not more than 24 percent by weight. The apples may possess dissimilar varietal characteristics. They possess a normal flavor and odor and a fairly good yellow to white color or other characteristic color; the color may be variable, but it cannot be so variable or dark as to materially affect the appearance or edibility of the product. They are fairly uniform in size and are fairly free from defects They possess a fairly good texture which may vary in degrees of pliability, including hard and dry units.

Substandard. Fail to meet the requirements of U.S. Grade C or U.S. Standard.

Source:
Agricultural Marketing Service, USDA, 7 CFR sections 52.2481 to 52.2489 (1991), Washington: Government Printing Office.

Apricots

To allow for variations in quality caused by grading and handling, a percentage of the apricots may fail to meet all of the requirements of the grade.

GRADES

This product is graded according to a technical system whereby penalty points are assessed for such factors as edibility, poor appearance, or defects in workmanship. The more penalty points assessed the lower the grade. The grade descriptions which follow are intended only as a general consumer guide. For more detailed information, please consult the source cited below.

U.S. No. 1. Apricots of one variety which are mature but not soft, overripe, or shriveled. They are well formed, free from decay, cuts, skin breaks, and worm holes. They are free from damage caused by limb rubs, russeting, growth cracks, dirt, scab, scale, hail, disease, insects, or mechanical means.

U.S. No. 2. Apricots of one variety which are mature but not soft, overripe, or shriveled. They are free from decay, worm holes, and from serious damage caused by limb rubs, growth cracks, dirt, scale, hail, disease, insects, or mechanical means. This grade has a higher tolerance for defects than does *U.S. No. 1.*

Unclassified. Apricots which do not meet the requirements of the foregoing grades.

Source:
Agricultural Marketing Service, USDA, 7 CFR sections 51.2925 to 51.2932 (1992), Washington: Government Printing Office.

Apricots, Canned

Canned apricots are prepared from mature apricots and prepared in one of the styles specified below. They are sealed in a container and before or after sealing are processed by heat to prevent spoilage. The food may be seasoned with one or more optional ingredients permitted in the USDA's standards of identity for canned apricots.

STYLES

Halves. Pitted apricots cut approximately in half along the suture from stem to apex.

Slices. Cut into thin sectors or strips.

Whole. Unpitted apricots with stems removed.

Pieces or Irregular. Irregular in size and shape.

Unpeeled. When the apricots are unpeeled, the name of the style is preceded or followed by the word *unpeeled.*

Peeled. When the apricots are peeled, the name of the style is preceded or followed by the word *peeled.*

PACKING MEDIA

The apricots are packed in either water, fruit juice(s) and water, or fruit juice(s). When a sweetener is added as a part of any such liquid packing medium, the density range of the resulting packing medium, expressed as percent by weight of sucrose, is designated by the appropriate name for the respective density ranges.

Slightly Sweetened Water. The density of the solution is 10 percent or more, but less than 16 percent. Also called *extra light syrup, slightly sweetened fruit juice(s),* and *slightly sweetened fruit juices(s).*

Light Syrup. The density of the solution is 16 percent or more, but less than 21 percent. Also called *lightly sweetened fruit juice(s) and water* or *lightly sweetened fruit juice(s).*

Heavy Syrup. The density of the solution is 21 percent or more, but less than 25 percent. Also called *heavily sweetened fruit juices(s)* or *heavily sweetened fruit juice(s).*

Extra Heavy Syrup. The density of the solution is 25 percent or more, but not more than 40 percent. Also called *extra heavily sweetened fruit juice(s) and water* or *extra heavily sweetened fruit juice(s).*

ARTIFICIALLY SWEETENED

The packing medium used is water artificially sweetened with saccharin, sodium saccharin, or a combination of both. This packing medium may be thickened with pectin; it may contain any mixture of any edible organic salt or salts and any edible organic acid as a flavor-enhancing agent. If the packing medium is thickened with pectin, the label bears the statement "thickened with pectin." When any organic salt or acid is added, the label bears the common or usual name of each ingredient.

GRADES

This product is graded according to a technical system whereby penalty points are assessed for such factors as edibility, poor appearance, or defects in workmanship. The more penalty points assessed the lower the grade. The grade descriptions which follow are intended only as a general consumer guide. For more detailed information, please consult the source cited below.

U.S. Grade A or U.S. Fancy. Have similar varietal characteristics and a normal flavor and odor. The color is typical and characteristic of well-matured apricots. Pale yellow areas may not exceed one-fourth of the outer surface area and are free from brown color due to oxidation, improper processing, or other causes. The apricots are at least reasonably uniform in size; they are practically free from pit material, loose pits, harmless extraneous material, short stems, peel, minor blemishes, major blemishes, and crushed or broken units. The product is uniformly tender with a fleshy texture. The apricots may be soft, but they hold their original conformation and size without material disintegration.

U.S. Grade B or U.S. Choice. Have a color typical of reasonably well-matured apricots. They may have pale yellow areas not exceeding one-half of the outer surface area or may have light greenish-yellow areas not exceeding one-fourth of the outer surface area. However, they are free from brown color due to oxidation, improper processing, or other causes. They are at least fairly uniform in size and symmetry and are at least reasonably free from defects. The texture is fairly fleshy, and the units are reasonably thick. However, the tenderness may be variable within the unit or among the units. The apricots may be soft to slightly firm, but they are not mushy. They may be slightly ragged.

U.S. Grade C or U.S. Standard. Have at least a fairly good color. They may have pale yellow and light greenish-yellow areas that cannot exceed one-half of the outer surface area or have light green areas that cannot exceed one-fourth of the outer surface areas. The units may have a slight brown color due to oxidation, improper processing, or other causes. They are at least fairly uniform in size and symmetry; they are at least fairly free from defects. The character may be variable in fleshiness, but the texture is fairly fleshy. The units may be lacking uniformity of tenderness, may be very soft to moderately firm, and may be markedly ragged with frayed edges.

Substandard. Fails to meet the requirements of U.S. Grade C or U.S. Standard.

Source:
Agricultural Marketing Service, USDA, 7 CFR sections 52.2641 to 52.2657 (1991), Washington: Government Printing Office.
Food and Drug Administration, HHS, 21 CFR sections 145.115 to 145.116 (1991), Washington: Government Printing Office.

Apricots, Dried

Dried apricots are the halved and pitted fruit of the apricot tree (*Prunus armeniaca*) from which the greater portion of moisture has been removed. Before packing, the dried fruit is processed to clean the fruit and may be sulfured sufficiently to retain a characteristic color. Slabs are apricots that have been mashed, broken, or mutilated to the extent that they have lost their normal contour and have become definitely flattened at the edge or rim. A half that has a slightly torn edge is not considered a slab. The moisture content of the finished product is not more than 26 percent by weight for sizes No. 1, No. 2, and No. 3 and for slabs, and not more than 25 percent by weight for other sizes.

SIZES

No. 1 Size (Jumbo Size). 1⅜ inches or more in diameter.
No. 2 Size (Extra Fancy Size). 1¼ to 1⅜ inches in diameter.
No. 3 Size (Fancy Size). 1⅛ to 1¼ inches in diameter.
No. 4 Size (Extra Choice Size). 1 inch to 1⅛ inches in diameter.
No. 5 Size (Choice Size). ¹³⁄₁₆ to 1 inch in diameter.
No. 6 Size (Standard Size). Less than ¹³⁄₁₆ inch in diameter.

GRADES

This product is graded according to a technical system whereby penalty points are assessed for such factors as edibility, poor appearance, or defects in workmanship. The more penalty points assessed the lower the grade. The grade descriptions which follow are intended only as a general consumer guide. For more detailed information, please consult the source cited below.

Grade A or U.S. Fancy. Possess similar varietal characteristics and a practically uniform, bright color that is characteristic of fully ripe apricots. The fruit may possess pale yellow areas around the stem that do not exceed an area equivalent to one-eighth of the outer surface side. Not more than 10 percent by weight may be slabs, immature, possess pits or pieces of pits, or damaged by discoloration, sunburn, hail marks, scab disease, insect injury, or other similar defects; not more than 10 percent by weight may be affected by mold, decay, insect infestation (no live insects are permitted), imbedded dirt, or other foreign material.

Grade B or U.S. Choice. Possess similar varietal characteristics and a reasonably uniform, bright, typical color. The apricots are firm but may not have reached the fully ripe stage. The fruit may possess pale yellow areas around the stem end, but they cannot exceed an area equivalent to one-fourth of the outer surface side. Not more than 15 percent may be slabs or otherwise defective.

U.S. Grade C or U.S. Standard. Possess similar varietal characteristics and a fairly uniform, typical color. The apricots may be hard, but they are not tough or possess a green or other color indicative of immature fruit. The fruit may be pale yellow in color and may possess light green areas around the stem end of the fruit, but they cannot exceed an area equivalent to one-quarter of the outer surface side of the unit. Not more than 20 percent may be slabs or otherwise defective

U.S. Grade D or Substandard. Wholesome and edible fruit that fails to meet the requirements of U.S. Grade C or U.S. Standard but does meet minimum standards.

Source:
Agricultural Marketing Service, USDA, 7 CFR sections 52.5761 to 52.5773 (1991), Washington: Government Printing Office.

Apricots, Frozen

Frozen apricots are prepared from sound, mature, fresh, peeled or unpeeled fruit of any commercial variety of apricot; they are sorted, washed, and may be trimmed to assure a clean and wholesome product. The apricots are properly drained of excess water before they are placed into containers. They may be packed with the addition of nutritive sweetening ingredient(s) (including syrup and/or syrup containing pureed apricots), suitable antioxidant ingredient(s), and/or any other ingredient(s) permissible under the provisions of the Federal Food, Drug, and Cosmetic Act. The apricots are prepared and frozen in accordance with good commercial practice and are maintained at temperatures necessary for the preservation of the product.

STYLES

Halves. Cut in half with the pits removed.
Quarters. Halves cut into two approximately equal parts.
Slices. Halves cut into sectors smaller than quarters.
Diced. Cut into cubes.
Cuts. Cut in such a manner as to change the original conformation.
Machine-pitted. Mechanically pitted in such a manner as to substantially destroy the conformation of the fruit in removing the pit.

GRADES

This product is graded according to a technical system whereby penalty points are assessed for such factors as edibility, poor appearance, or defects in workmanship. The more penalty points assessed the lower the grade. The grade descriptions which follow are intended only as a general consumer guide. For more detailed information, please consult the source cited below.

U.S. Grade A or U.S. Fancy. Have similar varietal characteristics, a normal flavor and odor, and a good color that internally and externally is bright, nearly uniform, and typical of well-ripened apricots. They are uniform in size and practically free of such defects as peel (in peeled apricots), short stems, minor blemishes, crushed or broken units (except in cuts or machine-pitted styles), and from any other defects which affect the appearance or edibility of the product. Halves style apricots are uniformly intact and may be soft, but they hold their original conformation and size without material disintegration. Not more than a total of 5 percent may be firm or very soft. Quarter, slice, and dice-cut apricots are reasonably intact and may be soft but not mushy. Not more than a total of 5 percent may be firm or very soft. The character of machine-pitted apricots may vary from slightly firm to very soft.

U.S. Grade B or U.S. Choice. Have similar varietal characteristics and a normal flavor and odor. Internally and externally the frozen apricots have a color that is reasonably bright, fairly uniform, and typical of reasonably well-ripened apricots. They are reasonably uniform in size and symmetry and reasonably free of defects. They have a uniform, tender, and fleshy texture. The apricots are reasonably intact. Not more than 10 percent may be very soft or very firm. Machine-pitted apricots may be variable in texture from firm to very soft.

U.S. Grade C or U.S. Standard. Have similar varietal characteristics and a normal flavor and odor. The apricots are not materially darkened and are fairly uniform in size and symmetry. They are fairly free of defects; and, regardless of style, the frozen apricots may be firm or mushy. Not more than a total of 10 percent may be very firm units.

Substandard. Fails to meet the requirements of U.S. Grade C or U.S. Standard.

Source:
Agricultural Marketing Service, USDA, 7 CFR sections 52.5521 to 52.5531 (1991), Washington: Government Printing Office.

Apricots, Dehydrated

Dehydrated (low-moisture apricots) are prepared from clean, sound, and fresh (or previously dried) apricots which are then cut, chopped, or otherwise prepared into various sizes and shapes. They are processed by dehydration whereby practically all of the moisture is removed to produce a very dry texture. They are packaged to assure retention of the low-moisture characteristics of the product. The product is given a sulfur treatment to retain the characteristic color, but no other additives may be present.

STYLES

Nugget. Processed to produce popcorn-like or foam-textured units of irregular shapes that will pass through ⅝ inch square openings.

Pieces. Irregular shaped, cut or chopped pieces that will pass through ⅝ inch square openings.

Diced. Cube-shaped units with a square dimension on one surface.

Slices. Parallel-cut strips of irregular shapes and thicknesses.

GRADES

This product is graded according to a technical system whereby penalty points are assessed for such factors as edibility, poor appearance, or defects in workmanship. The more penalty points assessed the lower the grade. The grade descriptions which follow are intended only as a general consumer guide. For more detailed information, please consult the source cited below.

U.S. Grade A or U.S. Fancy. Possess a normal flavor and odor. The color ranges from bright reddish-orange to bright orange-amber. When cooked it has a reasonably bright, typical color. The apricots are uniform in size and practically free from

defects. The texture may vary from partially pliable to brittle, but the apricots are otherwise uniform in texture.

U.S. Grade B or U.S. Choice. Possess a normal flavor. The color overall may vary considerably, ranging from slightly dull orange to dull amber. When cooked it may be slightly dull. The apricots are fairly uniform in size and reasonably free from defects. The texture may vary from partially pliable to brittle and may lack uniformity of texture.

Substandard. Fails to meet the requirements of U.S. Grade B or U.S. Choice.

Source:
Agricultural Marketing Service, USDA, 7 CFR sections 52.3871 to 52.3883 (1991), Washington: Government Printing Office.

Berries, Canned

Canned berries include boysenberries, dewberries, blackberries, and loganberries. The food is sealed in a container and before or after sealing is processed by heat to prevent spoilage.

PACKING MEDIA

The berries are packed in either water, fruit juice(s) and water, or fruit juice(s). When a sweetener is added as a part of the liquid packing medium, the density range of the resulting packing medium (expressed as percent by weight of sucrose) is designated by the appropriate name for the respective density ranges.

Slightly Sweetened Water. The density of the solution (depending on the type of berry) is 10 percent or more, but less than 16 percent. Also called *extra light syrup, slightly sweetened fruit juice(s),* and *slightly sweetened fruit juices(s).*

Light Syrup. The density of the solution (depending on the type of berry) is 14 percent or more, but less than 21 percent. Also called *lightly sweetened fruit juice(s) and water* or *lightly sweetened fruit juice(s).*

Heavy Syrup. The density of the solution (depending on the type of berry) is 19 percent or more, but less than 27 percent. Also called *heavily sweetened fruit juices(s)* or *heavily sweetened fruit juice(s).*

Extra Heavy Syrup. The density of the solution (depending on the type of berry) is 24 percent or more, but not more than 35 percent. Also called *extra heavily sweetened fruit juice(s) and water* or *extra heavily sweetened fruit juice(s).*

GRADES

This product is graded according to a technical system whereby penalty points are assessed for such factors as edibility, poor appearance, or defects in workmanship. The more penalty points assessed the lower the grade. The grade descriptions which follow are intended only as a general consumer guide. For more detailed information, please consult the source cited below.

U.S. Grade A or U.S. Fancy. The berries possess similar varietal characteristics. The canned berries possess a color typical of well-ripened berries and are uniform and bright in color. They are uniform in size with not more than 15 percent of the blackberries less than $^{20}\!/_{32}$ inch in diameter. The berries are practically free from defects such as leaves, stems or portions of stems, and caps or portions of caps. The berries possess a firm, tender texture that is characteristic of well-ripened berries; they are practically intact. The berries and accompanying liquor are nearly free from detached seed cells. Not more than 5 percent of the blackberries may be crushed. Not more than 10 percent of dewberries, boysenberries, loganberries, or other similar types may be crushed. The product is free from objectionable odors and flavors of any kind.

U.S. Grade B or U.S. Choice. Possess similar varietal characteristics, and a color typical of reasonably well-ripened berries. They may be somewhat lacking in luster and may range in color from the lighter shades to the darker hues of reasonably well-ripened berries. They are nearly uniform in size and any variation in size does not seriously affect the appearance of the product. Not more than 15 percent of the blackberries are less than $^{18}\!/_{32}$ inch in diameter. They are reasonably free from defects and possess a reasonably good character and tender texture. The berries and accompanying liquor are nearly free from detached seed cells. Not more than 10 percent of the blackberries may be crushed, and not more than 15 percent of dewberries, boysenberries, loganberries, or other similar types may be crushed. They have a normal flavor and odor.

U.S. Grade C or U.S. Standard. The berries possess similar varietal characteristics and a color typical of fairly well-ripened berries. The color may be variable, but it is not off-color. The canned berries may be variable in size and, with respect to canned blackberries, not more than 15 percent are less than $^{18}\!/_{32}$ inch in diameter. They are fairly free from defects and may possess a fairly tender texture. Not more than 20 percent of the berries may be crushed. They have a normal flavor and odor.

Substandard. Fails to meet the requirements of U.S. Grade C or U.S. Standard.

Source:
Agricultural Marketing Service, USDA, 7 CFR section 52.551 (1991), Washington: Government Printing Office.
Food and Drug Administration, Canned Berries, 21 CFR 145.120 (1991), Washington: Government Printing Office.

Berries, Frozen

Frozen berries are prepared from the properly ripened, fresh fruit of the plant (genus *Rubus*). They are stemmed and cleaned, may be packed with or without packing media, and are frozen and stored at temperatures necessary for the preservation of the product.

TYPES

Blackberries
Boysenberries
Dewberries

Loganberries
Youngberries
Other similar types, such as Nectaberries

TYPES OF PACK

Frozen berries are often packed with added sugar or added sugar and water. Sugar packs are usually designated by the amount of fruit to sugar; for example, "6+1" means that at the time of packing, 1 pound of sugar was added to 6 pounds of berries.

GRADES

This product is graded according to a technical system whereby penalty points are assessed for such factors as edibility, poor appearance, or defects in workmanship. The more penalty points assessed the lower the grade. The grade descriptions which follow are intended only as a general consumer guide. For more detailed information, please consult the source cited below.

U.S. Grade A or U.S. Fancy. The berries are of similar varietal characteristics. They possess a uniform, typical color and not more than 10 percent may vary markedly from the intensity and luster of the characteristic color of well-ripened berries. The berries are nearly free from defects such as leaves, stems, and caps; from undeveloped berries; and from berries damaged by blemishes, insect, or other similar injury. The berries are mature and ripe, but not overripe. They are fleshy, tender, and virtually intact. The accompanying liquor is practically free from detached seed cells. They possess a normal flavor and odor free from objectionable odors and flavors.

U.S. Grade B or U.S. Choice. They possess a reasonably uniform, typical color. Not more than 15 percent may vary markedly from the color of reasonably well-ripened berries, provided not more than 5 percent are definitely off-color for any reason. The berries are reasonably free from defects and are not more than slightly immature or slightly overmature.

U.S. Grade D or Substandard. Fails to meet the requirements of U.S. Grade B or U.S. Choice.

Source:
Agricultural Marketing Service, USDA, 7 CFR sections 52.5881 to 52.5892 (1991), Washington: Government Printing Office.

Blueberries, Canned

TYPES

Native or Wild Type
Cultivated Type

GRADES

This product is graded according to a technical system whereby penalty points are assessed for such factors as edibility, poor appearance, or defects in workmanship. The more penalty points assessed the lower the grade. The grade descriptions which follow are intended only as a general consumer guide. For more detailed information, please consult the source cited below.

U.S. Grade A or U.S. Fancy. The blueberries possess similar varietal characteristics and a good color that is a practically uniform, bright, dark blue-purple color typical of ripe blueberries. The berries are practically free from defects such as cap stems, whole leaves, large stems, and other leafy material. They are reasonably firm, fleshy, nearly whole, and practically intact with not more than 10 percent crushed, mushy, or broken. They possess a normal flavor and odor and are free from objectionable odors and flavors of any kind.

U.S. Grade B or U.S. Choice. They possess similar varietal characteristics and a reasonably uniform dark blue-purple color typical of reasonably well-matured blueberries. They are fairly free from defects and may be lacking in firmness and fleshy texture, but they are whole and reasonably intact with not more than 15 percent crushed, mushy, or broken. They have a normal flavor and odor.

U.S. Grade C or U.S. Standard. The blueberries possess similar varietal characteristics and a fairly good blue-purple color, but they are not off-color for any reason. They are fairly free from defects and are fairly whole and intact with not more than 30 percent crushed, mushy, or broken. They possess a normal flavor and odor.

U.S. Grade D or Substandard. Fails to meet the requirements of U.S. Grade C or U.S. Standard.

Blueberries

These standards apply only to selected and hybrid varieties of the highbush blueberry (*Vaccinium australe* and *Vaccinium corymbosum*) produced under cultivation, but not to other species of the genus *Vaccinium* or to the true huckleberries of the genus *Gaylussacia*. To allow for variations in quality caused by grading and handling, a percentage of the blueberries may fail to meet all of the requirements of the grade.

GRADES

This product is graded according to a technical system whereby penalty points are assessed for such factors as edibility, poor appearance, or defects in workmanship. The more penalty points assessed the lower the grade. The grade descriptions which follow are intended only as a general consumer guide. For more detailed information, please consult the source cited below.

U.S. No. 1. Blueberries of similar varietal characteristics which are clean and well-colored. More than one-half of the surface of the individual berry is blue, bluish-purple, purple, or bluish-black. They are not overmature, soft, or wet with juice from crushed, leaking, or decayed berries. They are not affected by decay.

Unclassified. Blueberries which have not been classified in accordance with the foregoing grade. The term *unclassified* is not a grade within the meaning of these standards but is provided as a designation to show that no grade has been applied to the lot.

SIZE

The following size classifications are used in specifying size of blueberries:

Extra Large. Less than 90 berries per standard 2 gill cup.
Large. 90 to 129 berries per standard 2 gill cup.
Small. 190 to 250 berries per standard 2 gill cup.

Source:
Agricultural Marketing Service, USDA, 7 CFR sections 51.3475 to 51.3487 (1992), Washington: Government Printing Office.

Blueberries, Frozen

Frozen blueberries are prepared from sound, properly ripened, fresh fruit of the blueberry bush (genus *Vaccinium*), including species or varieties often called huckleberries, but not of the genus *Gaylussacia*. They are cleaned and stemmed, properly washed, packed with or without packing media, and frozen and maintained at temperatures necessary for the preservation of the product.

TYPES

Native or Wild
Cultivated

GRADES

This product is graded according to a technical system whereby penalty points are assessed for such factors as edibility, poor appearance, or defects in workmanship. The more penalty points assessed the lower the grade. The grade descriptions which follow are intended only as a general consumer guide. For more detailed information, please consult the source cited below.

U.S. Grade A or U.S. Fancy. The berries possess similar varietal characteristics. They are practically free from defects such as leaves, large stems, green berries, undeveloped berries, edible berries other than blueberries, and from berries damaged by insect, pathological, or any other injury. The blueberries are reasonably firm, fleshy, whole and intact with not more than 6 percent crushed, mushy, or broken. They are free from objectionable flavors and odors. They possess a practically uniform, bright, dark blue-purple color typical of ripe berries. Not more than 5 percent are a red-purple color.

U.S. Grade B or U.S. Choice. Possess similar varietal characteristics. The blueberries are a reasonably uniform dark blue-purple color with not more than 10 percent a red-purple color. They are reasonably free from defects. The blueberries may be lacking in firmness and fleshy texture, but they are reasonably whole and intact with not more than 10 percent crushed, mushy, or broken.

U.S. Grade C or U.S. Standard. Possess similar varietal characteristics. May be moderately variable in color but are not dull or off-color; not more than 20 percent are red-purple. They are fairly free from defects and are fairly whole and intact with not more than 20 percent crushed, mushy, or broken.

U.S. Grade D or Substandard. Fails to meet the requirements of U.S. Grade C or U.S. Standard.

Source:
Agricultural Marketing Service, USDA, 7 CFR section 52.611 (1991), Washington: Government Printing Office.

Canned Fruits for Salad

Canned fruits for salad (or canned salad fruits or canned fruit salad) is the product consisting of units of properly prepared apricots, yellow clingstone peaches, pears, pineapple, cherries, and/or grapes in the forms and proportions specified in USDA regulations. The product is packed in a suitable liquid medium with or without the addition of nutritive sweetening ingredients, artificial sweetening ingredients, or other ingredients. It is processed by heat to assure preservation of the product in hermetically sealed containers.

GRADES

This product is graded according to a technical system whereby penalty points are assessed for such factors as edibility, poor appearance, or defects in workmanship. The more penalty points assessed the lower the grade. The grade descriptions which follow are intended only as a general consumer guide. For more detailed information please consult the source cited below.

U.S. Grade A or U.S. Fancy. Each fruit ingredient possesses similar varietal characteristics and a reasonably uniform typical color that is bright and characteristic of well-ripened fruit. None may be no more than slightly affected by pink staining and may not be dull or off-color. The fruit is uniform in count and size and practically free from defects such as loose or attached peel, main stems, grape capstems, pit or core material, broken or severed units, excessive trimming, and other defects and blemishes typical for each fruit ingredient. The individual fruits may lack the distinctive flavor and odor of each fruit ingredient, but the product is free from objectionable flavors and odors of any kind

U.S. Grade B or U.S. Choice. Each fruit ingredient possesses similar varietal characteristics and a fairly uniform and fairly good, typical color that is characteristic of at least fairly well-ripened fruit. The fruit ingredients may be more than slightly affected by pink staining but not to the extent that the appearance is materially affected. None of the fruit ingredients may be off-color. The fruit may be irregular in count but are fairly uniform in size and reasonably free from defects. The cherries, or grapes if present, may be only fairly firm as long as the appearance or edibility is not materially affected. The product possess a normal flavor and odor.

Substandard. Fails to meet the requirements of U.S. Grade B or U.S. Choice.

Source:
Agricultural Marketing Service, USDA, 7 CFR sections 52.3831 to 52.3845 (1991), Washington: Government Printing Office.

Cantaloupes

This product is graded according to a technical system whereby penalty points are assessed for such factors as edibility, poor appearance, or defects in workmanship. The more penalty points assessed the lower the grade. The grade descriptions which follow are intended only as a general consumer guide. For more detailed information, please consult the source cited below.

U.S. No. 1. Cantaloupes which have reached proper maturity. They have good internal quality. They are not overripe or so soft as to yield readily to slight pressure. The cantaloupe does not lack turgidity and is not flabby, spongy, or pliable under moderate pressure. They are well formed and free from decay. There are no discolored or bleached sunken areas of the surface. It does not have a tough skin nor a leathery flesh that is off-color. They are free from damage caused by liquid in the seed cavity, sunburn, hail, dirt, surface mold, disease, insects, scars, cracks, sunken areas, ground spot, bruises, or mechanical or other means.

U.S. Commercial. Cantaloupes which are mature but not overripe, soft, or wilted. They are well formed and free from decay, wet slip, and sunscald. They are also free from damage caused by liquid in the seed cavity, sunburn, hail, dirt, surface mold, disease, aphids or other insects, scars, cracks sunken areas, ground spot, bruises, or mechanical or other means.

Unclassified. Cantaloupes which have not been classified in accordance with any of the foregoing grades. The term *unclassified* is not a grade within the meaning of these standards but is provided as a designation to show that no grade has been applied to the lot.

Source:
Agricultural Marketing Service, USDA, 7 CFR sections 51.475 (1991), Washington: Government Printing Office.

Cherries, Maraschino

These cherries have been dyed red, impregnated with sugar, and packed in a sugar syrup flavored with oil of bitter almonds or a similar flavor.

Source:
Food and Drug Administration, *Compliance Policy Guides*, Guide 7110.16, 10/01/80: Washington, National Technical Information Service.

Cherries, Sweet (Canned)

TYPES

Light. Of the light sweet varietal group (including such varieties known as Royal Anne).

Dark. Of the dark sweet varietal group (including such varieties known as Bing, Black Republican, Schmidt, and Lambert).

STYLES

Unpitted. Stemmed cherries without the pits removed.
Pitted. Stemmed cherries with the pits removed.

GRADES

This product is graded according to a technical system whereby penalty points are assessed for such factors as edibility, poor appearance, or defects in workmanship. The more penalty points assessed the lower the grade. The grade descriptions which follow are intended only as a general consumer guide. For more detailed information, please consult the source cited below.

U.S. Grade A or U.S. Fancy. The quality of canned sweet cherries that are practically free from defects such as portions of stems or pits; from damaged, misshapen, and blemished cherries; and from any other defects which detract from the appearance or edibility of the product. The cherries are thick-fleshed and tender; they are not soft or noticeably flabby. They possess a normal flavor and odor free from objectionable flavors and odors of any kind. In light sweet cherries, the basic background color is a pinkish-yellow to pale amber color. In dark sweet cherries, the basic background color is a typical deep red to purple-red or purple-black.

U.S. Grade B or U.S. Choice. They are reasonably free from defects. The cherries are reasonably thick-fleshed and tender and are not more than slightly soft or markedly flabby. They possess a normal flavor and odor. In light sweet cherries, the basic background color is a pinkish-yellow to amber color which may be no more than slightly dull. In dark sweet cherries, the basic background color is a typical deep red to purple-red or purple-black which may be no more than slightly dull.

U.S. Grade C or U.S. Standard. In light sweet cherries, the basic background color and blush may be variable or may be slightly dull but is not off-color. In dark sweet cherries, the cherries may possess a slightly dull deep red to slightly dull purple-red color or slightly dull purple-black color that may be variable but is not off-color. They are fairly uniform in size and fairly free from defects. They may be lacking in thickness of flesh. They may be variable in tenderness and texture, ranging from firm to soft; but they are characteristic of canned sweet cherries from slightly immature to slightly over-mature cherries. Not more than 10 percent may be markedly flabby. In unpitted style, serious processing cracks may be present. They possess a normal flavor and odor.

Substandard. Fail to meet the requirements of U.S. Grade C or U.S. Standard and is the quality of canned sweet cherries that may or may not meet the minimum standard of quality for canned cherries issued pursuant to the Federal Food, Drug, and Cosmetic Act.

Source:
Agricultural Marketing Service, USDA, 7 CFR sections 52.821 to 52.836 (1991), Washington: Government Printing Office.

Cherries, Red Tart Pitted (Frozen)

GRADES

This product is graded according to a technical system whereby penalty points are assessed for such factors as edibility, poor appearance, or defects in workmanship. The more penalty points assessed the lower the grade. The grade descriptions which follow are intended only as a general consumer guide. For more detailed information, please consult the source cited below.

U.S. Grade A or U.S. Fancy. Cherries of which not more than five cherries per sample unit may be less than $\frac{9}{10}$ inch (14 mm) in diameter. They possess a good red color that is bright and typical of properly ripened cherries. They are practically free from pits, mutilated cherries, and cherries blemished by scab, hail injury, discoloration, scar tissue, or by other means. They have a good character; the cherries are thick-fleshed, have a firm, tender texture, and possess a normal flavor.

U.S. Grade B or U.S. Choice. Cherries of which not more than ten cherries per sample unit may be less than $\frac{9}{10}$ inch (14 mm) in diameter. Possess a reasonably good red color, are reasonably free from pits, and are reasonably free from defects. They have a reasonably good character; the cherries may be reasonably thick-fleshed and slightly soft. Possess a normal flavor.

U.S. Grade C or U.S. Standard. Possess a fairly good red color, are fairly free from pits, and are fairly free from defects. They have a fairly good character; the cherries may be thin-fleshed, soft (but not mushy), or slightly tough (but not leathery). The cherries possess a normal flavor.

Substandard. Fails to meet the requirements of U.S. Grade C or U.S. Standard.

Source:
Agricultural Marketing Service, USDA, 7 CFR sections 52.801 to 52.812 (1991), Washington: Government Printing Office.

Cherries, Red Tart Pitted (Canned)

GRADES

This product is graded according to a technical system whereby penalty points are assessed for such factors as edibility, poor appearance, or defects in workmanship. The more penalty points assessed the lower the grade. The grade descriptions which follow are intended only as a general consumer guide. For more detailed information, please consult the source cited below.

U.S. Grade A or U.S. Fancy. Cherries that have a uniform color that is bright and typical of canned red tart pitted cherries which have been properly prepared and processed. They are practically free from pits, mutilated cherries, or cherries blemished by scab, hail injury, discoloration, scar tissue, or by other means. The cherries are thick-fleshed and have a firm, tender texture and a normal flavor and odor.

U.S. Grade B or U.S. Choice. The cherries are reasonably thick-fleshed and may be slightly soft. They are reasonably free from pits and defects. They have a fairly uniform color which may range from a slight yellowish-red to a slightly mottled reddish brown. They have a reasonably good character. They have a normal flavor and odor.

U.S. Grade C or U.S. Standard. Has a fairly uniform color which may range from a brownish cast to mottled shades of brown. They are fairly free from pits and defects. They may be thin-fleshed, soft (but not mushy), or slightly tough (but not leathery). They have a normal flavor and odor.

Substandard. Fails to meet the requirements of U.S. Grade C or U.S. Standard.

Source:
Agricultural Marketing Service, USDA, 7 CFR sections 52.801 (1991), Washington: Government Printing Office.

Cherries, Sulfured

Sulfured cherries are prepared from properly matured whole cherries (*Prunus avium* or *Prunus cerasus*) of similar varietal characteristics and are packed, with or without the addition of a hardening agent, in a solution of sulfur dioxide of sufficient strength to preserve the product.

STYLES

Unstemmed and Unpitted. Whole cherries with pits. Not less than 80 percent of the cherries have the stems attached.

Stemmed and Unpitted. With pits and not more than 0.5 percent have stems attached.

Stemmed and Pitted. Not more than 0.5 percent of all the cherries have stems attached and all but 2 per each 40 ounces are pitted.

Unstemmed and Pitted or Cocktail. Whole cherries of which not more than 7 percent are cherries without the stems firmly attached and all but 2 per each 40 ounces are pitted.

GRADES

This product is graded according to a technical system whereby penalty points are assessed for such factors as edibility, poor appearance, or defects in workmanship. The more penalty points assessed the lower the grade. The grade descriptions which follow are intended only as a general consumer guide. For more detailed information, please consult the source cited below.

U.S. Grade A or U.S. Fancy. The cherries are clean and are practically free from loose pits, leaves, detached stems, bark, fruit spurs, dirt, or other foreign material. They possess a uniform color typical of well-bleached sulfured cherries. They are practically free from defects such as misshapen cherries, cherries damaged by mechanical injury, blemished by discoloration, rain or solution cracks, bird pecks, pathological injury, or insect injury. They have a firm fleshy texture, retain their approximate original shape, are not shriveled or watery, and do not show more than slight collapsed areas of flesh.

U.S. Grade B or U.S. Choice. Cherries that are clean and that possess a reasonably uniform color typical of reasonably well-bleached sulfured cherries. They are fairly free from defects. They are reasonably firm but may have slightly lost their original shape, may be slightly shriveled, or may show moderate collapsed areas of flesh.

U.S. Grade D or Seconds. Cherries that are clean but fail to meet the requirements of U.S. Grade B or U.S. Choice.

U.S. Combination. Cherries that are clean. Not less than 90 percent possess at least a reasonably good color and a reasonably good character. The 90 percent must be free from misshapen cherries, cherries seriously damaged by mechanical injury, and seriously blemished cherries. Unless otherwise specified, at least 50 percent possess a good color and a good character. This 50 percent must be free from blemished cherries or seriously blemished cherries, misshapen cherries, and cherries damaged by mechanical injury or cherries seriously damaged by mechanical injury.

Source:
Agricultural Marketing Service, USDA, 7 CFR sections 52.741 to 52.755 (1991), Washington: Government Printing Office.

Cherries, Sweet (Frozen)

Frozen sweet cherries are prepared from the clean, sound, properly matured, fresh fruit of any commercial variety of sweet cherries. They are sorted, washed, and drained, may be packed with or without the addition of nutritive sweetening ingredient(s), are frozen in accordance with good commercial practice, and are maintained at temperatures necessary for the preservation of the product.

TYPES

Light Sweet Type. Napoleon or Royal Ann variety.
Dark Sweet Type. Bing or Lambert varieties.

STYLES

Pitted. Whole, stemmed cherries with pits removed.
Unpitted. Whole, stemmed cherries without the pits removed.

GRADES

This product is graded according to a technical system whereby penalty points are assessed for such factors as edibility, poor appearance, or defects in workmanship. The more penalty points assessed the lower the grade. The grade descriptions which follow are intended only as a general consumer guide. For more detailed information, please consult the source cited below.

U.S. Grade A or U.S. Fancy. Possess similar varietal characteristics, a normal flavor, and a reasonably uniform color that is bright and typical of well-ripened sweet cherries. Not more than 10 percent, by count, of cherries may vary markedly from this color because of discoloration due to oxidation, improper processing, or because of not using well-ripened sweet cherries. The cherries possess a good appearance with respect to size and symmetry. They are practically free from harmless extraneous material, pits, and seriously damaged cherries. The cherries possess a tender, fleshy texture.

U.S. Grade B or U.S. Choice. Possess similar varietal characteristics, a normal flavor, and a color that is reasonably bright and typical of well-ripened sweet cherries. Not more than 20 percent, by count, of cherries may vary markedly from this color. They possess a reasonably good appearance with respect to size and symmetry. The cherries are reasonably free from defects. The texture is fleshy; the tenderness may be variable from slightly soft to slightly firm. Not more than 15 percent, by count, of the cherries may be overripe or immature.

Substandard. Fails to meet the requirements of U.S. Grade B or U.S. Choice.

Source:
Agricultural Marketing Service, USDA, 7 CFR sections 52.3161 to 52.3172 (1991), Washington: Government Printing Office.

Cherries, Sweet

To allow for variations in quality caused by grading and handling, a percentage of the sweet cherries may fail to meet all of the requirements of the grade.

GRADES

This product is graded according to a technical system whereby penalty points are assessed for such factors as edibility, poor appearance, or defects in workmanship. The more penalty points assessed the lower the grade. The grade descriptions which follow are intended only as a general consumer guide. For more detailed information, please consult the source cited below.

U.S. No. 1. Sweet cherries which have similar varietal characteristics. They have reached the stage of growth which will insure the proper completion of the ripening process. They are fairly well-colored with 95 percent of the surface of the cherry showing characteristic color. They are well formed and clean. They are free from decay, insect larvae or holes caused by them, undeveloped doubles, and sunscald. They are not soft, overripe, or shriveled. The minimum diameter of each cherry is not less than ¾ inch.

U.S. Commercial. Sweet cherries which meet the requirements for the U.S. No. 1 grade except for minimum diameter and except for increased tolerances for defects. The diameter of each cherry is not less than ⅝ inch.

Source:
Agricultural Marketing Service, USDA, 7 CFR sections 51.2646 to 51.2660 (1992), Washington: Government Printing Office.

Cranberries, Frozen

Frozen cranberries is the product prepared from the sound, mature berries of the cultivated cranberry plant. The product is prepared by sorting and cleaning to assure a wholesome product. The prepared product is frozen and stored at temperatures necessary for preservation.

GRADES

This product is graded according to a technical system whereby penalty points are assessed for such factors as edibility, poor appearance, or defects in workmanship. The more penalty points assessed the lower the grade. The grade descriptions which follow are intended only as a general consumer guide. For more detailed information, please consult the source cited below.

U.S. Grade A or U.S. Fancy. Possess a good color that is a pink or red color characteristic of the variety. The cranberries are practically free from such defects as harmless vines, leaves, fine stems, minor and major blemishes, and from any other defects which affect the appearance or edibility. The cranberries may be slightly soft to moderately firm with only a small number mushy or hard. There is no grit or silt present.

U.S. Grade B or U.S. Choice. Possess a reasonably good color. The character of the cranberries may be slightly soft to moderately firm with twice the number of mushy or hard berries as are present in Grade A. There is no grit or silt present that affects the appearance or edibility of the product.

U.S. Grade C or U.S. Standard. They are fairly free from defects. The berries are fairly well-colored; 75 percent or more of the surface of the individual cranberry is a pink or red color characteristic of the variety. The cranberries may be very soft to very firm with up to 6 times the number of mushy or hard berries as are present in U.S. Grade A. There is not more than a trace of grit or silt present.

Substandard. Fails to meet the requirements of U.S. Grade C or U.S. Standard.

Source:
Agricultural Marketing Service, USDA, 7 CFR sections 52.6281 to 52.6290 (1991), Washington: Government Printing Office.

Cranberries, Fresh

These standards apply only to the commonly cultivated cranberry (*Vaccinium macrocarpon*). To allow for variations in quality caused by grading and handling, a percentage of the cranberries may fail to meet all of the requirements of the grade.

GRADES

This product is graded according to a technical system whereby penalty points are assessed for such factors as edibility, poor appearance, or defects in workmanship. The more penalty points assessed the lower the grade. The grade descriptions which follow are intended only as a general consumer guide. For more detailed information, please consult the source cited below.

U.S. No. 1. They are of similar varietal characteristics which are clean and mature. Cranberries that show more than a slight amount of green color are considered immature. They are firm and not soft or decayed. They are free from damage caused by moisture, bruises, freezing, scarring, sunscald, foreign material, disease, insects, or mechanical or other means. The color of the individual cranberries are at least fairly well-colored with 75 percent of the surface showing pink or red color characteristic of the variety. The cranberries in the container are fairly uniform in color. The diameter of each cranberry is not less than 13/32 of an inch.

Source:
Agricultural Marketing Service, USDA, 7 CFR sections 51.2775 to 51.2783 (1992), Washington: Government Printing Office.

Cranberries for Processing

These standards apply only to the commonly cultivated cranberry (*Vaccinium macrocarpon*). The primary purpose of these standards is for classifying cranberries intended for manufacture of strained sauce. This product is graded according to a technical system whereby penalty points are assessed for such factors as edibility, poor appearance, or defects in workmanship. The more penalty points assessed the lower the grade. The grade descriptions which follow are intended only as a general consumer guide. For more detailed information, please consult the source cited below. To allow for variations in quality caused by grading and handling, a percentage of the cranberries may fail to meet all of the requirements of the grade.

U.S. No. 1. The fresh cranberries are clean, mature, fairly well-colored with 75 percent of the surface of the individual cranberry showing pink or red color characteristic of the variety. They are not soft or decayed. They are free from worms, worm holes, and damage caused by bruises, scars, freezing, sunscald, foreign material, disease, insects, or mechanical or other means.

Source:
Agricultural Marketing Service, USDA, 7 CFR sections 51.3030 to 51.3037 (1992), Washington: Government Printing Office.

Dewberries and Blackberries

To allow for variations in quality caused by grading and handling, a percentage of the berries may fail to meet all of the requirements of the grade.

GRADES

This product is graded according to a technical system whereby penalty points are assessed for such factors as edibility, poor appearance, or defects in workmanship. The more penalty points assessed the lower the grade. The grade descriptions which follow are intended only as a general consumer guide. For more detailed information, please consult the source cited below.

U.S. No. 1. The dewberries or blackberries are firm, well-colored (the whole surface of the berry is a blue or black color), well-developed (the berries are not misshapen owing to anthracnose injury, frost injury, lack of pollination, insect injury, or other causes), and not overripe. They are free from caps (calyxes), mold and decay, and from damage caused by dirt or other foreign matter, shriveling, moisture, disease, insects, or mechanical or other means.

U. S. No. 2. Dewberries fail to meet the requirements of the U.S. No. 1 grade. The berries do not contain more than 10 percent, by volume, of berries which are seriously damaged by any cause, including not more than 2 percent which are affected by mold or decay.

Unclassified. Dewberries or blackberries which have not been classified in accordance with either of the foregoing grades. The term *unclassified* is not a grade within the meaning of these standards but is provided as a designation to show that no grade has been applied to the lot.

Source:
Agricultural Marketing Service, USDA, 7 CFR sections 51.4270 to 51.4277 (1992), Washington: Government Printing Office.

Figs, Canned

STYLES

Style I. Whole.
Style II. Whole and split (or broken).
Style III. Split (or broken) and whole.
Style IV. Split (or broken).

GRADES

This product is graded according to a technical system whereby penalty points are assessed for such factors as edibility, poor appearance, or defects in workmanship. The more penalty points assessed the lower the grade. The grade descriptions which follow are intended only as a general consumer guide. For more detailed information, please consult the source cited below.

U.S. Grade A or U.S. Fancy. Possess similar varietal characteristics, a normal flavor and odor, and a practically uniform, bright light amber or light greenish-yellow color. The canned figs are practically uniform in size and practically free from such defects as harmless extraneous material (such as leaves and stems), from split (or broken) figs, severed figs, and from figs blemished with scab, scars, bruises, and discoloration. They are free from caprified figs, and from figs damaged by mechanical, pathological, insect injury, or similar injury. The figs are well-matured and fleshy; they have a fairly uniform, tender texture.

U.S. Grade B or U.S. Choice. Possess similar varietal characteristics, a normal flavor and odor, and a fairly bright light green color that may lack a definite yellow cast but is typical of properly prepared and processed figs. The figs are reasonably uniform in size and are reasonably free from defects. They have a reasonably uniform and tender texture.

U.S. Grade C or U.S. Standard. Canned figs that possess similar varietal characteristics, a normal flavor and odor, and a fairly good color that may possess a green, slightly milky, or a light brown color; the figs may vary moderately in such typical color. The figs are fairly uniform in size and fairly free from defects. The figs may be variable in texture from very soft to firm but are not excessively mushy nor excessively firm.

Substandard. Fail to meet the requirements of U.S. Grade C or U.S. Standard.

Source:

Agricultural Marketing Service, USDA, 7 CFR sections 52.2821 to 52.2835 (1991), Washington: Government Printing Office.

Figs, Dried

Dried figs are the fruit of the fig tree (*Ficus carica*) from which the greater portion of moisture has been removed. The dried figs are prepared from clean, sound fruit and are sorted and thoroughly cleaned to assure a sound, wholesome product. The figs may or may not be sulfured or otherwise bleached.

COLOR TYPES

White. White figs (or white type figs) are white to dark brown in color and include such varieties as Adriatic, Calimyrna, and Kadota.

Black. Black figs (or black type figs) are black or dark purple in color as in the Mission varieties.

STYLES

Style I, Whole. Dried figs in any of the following types of packs:

Style I(a), Whole, Loose. Whole dried figs, not materially changed from their original dried form, that are packed without special arrangement in a container.

Style I(b), Whole, Pulled. Whole dried figs which are changed from their original dried form by purposely flattening and shaping and are placed in a definite arrangement in a container. The dried figs may or may not be split slightly across the eye but are not split to the extent that the seed cavity is materially exposed.

Style I(c), Whole, Layered. Whole dried figs which are changed from their original dried form by purposely flattening and shaping and are placed in a staggered-layer arrangement in a container. The figs are split across the base to the extent that the seed cavity may be materially exposed.

Style II, Sliced. Dried whole figs that have been cut into slices not less than ¼ inch in thickness and that are not showing more than two cut surfaces.

SIZES

The sizes of Style I(a), whole, loose, dried figs for the respective varieties are as follows:

Adriatic or Kadota

No. 1 (Jumbo Size). 1⁷⁄₁₆ inches or larger in width.

No. 2 (Extra Fancy Size). 1⁵⁄₁₆ inches to, but not including, 1⁷⁄₁₆ inches in width.

No. 3 (Fancy Size). 1³⁄₁₆ inches to, but not including, 1⁵⁄₁₆ inches in width.

No. 4 (Extra Choice Size). 1¹⁄₁₆ inches to, but not including, 1³⁄₁₆ inches in width.

No. 5 (Choice Size). ¹⁵⁄₁₆ inch to, but not including, 1¹⁄₁₆ inches in width.

No. 6 (Standard Size). Less than ¹⁵⁄₁₆ inch in width.

Calimyrna

No. 1 (Jumbo Size). 1⁹⁄₁₆ inches or larger in width.

No. 2 (Extra Fancy Size). 1⁶⁄₁₆ inches to, but not including, 1⁹⁄₁₆ inches in width.

No. 3 (Fancy Size). 1³⁄₁₆ inches to, but not including, 1⁶⁄₁₆ inches in width.

No. 4 (Extra Choice Size). 1¹⁄₁₆ inches to, but not including, 1³⁄₁₆ inches in width.

No. 5 (Choice Size). ¹⁵⁄₁₆ inch to, but not including, 1¹⁄₁₆ inches in width.

No. 6 (Standard Size). Less than ¹⁵⁄₁₆ inch in width.

Black Mission

No. 1 (Jumbo Size). 1⁵⁄₁₆ inches or larger in width.

No. 2 (Extra Fancy Size). 1³⁄₁₆ inches to, but not including, 1⁵⁄₁₆ inches in width.

No. 3 (Fancy Size). 1¹⁄₁₆ inches to, but not including, 1³⁄₁₆ inches in width.

No. 4 (Extra Choice Size). ¹⁵⁄₁₆ inch to, but not including, 1¹⁄₁₆ inches in width.

No. 5 (Choice Size). 1³⁄₁₆ inch to, but not including, ¹⁵⁄₁₆ inch in width.

No. 6 (Standard Size). Less than 1³⁄₁₆ inch in width.

GRADES

This product is graded according to a technical system whereby penalty points are assessed for such factors as edibility, poor appearance, or defects in workmanship. The more penalty points assessed the lower the grade. The grade descriptions which follow are intended only as a general consumer guide. For more detailed information, please consult the source cited below.

U.S. Grade A or U.S. Fancy. A well-matured, dried fig which is well-developed and in which the interior shows very good sugary tissue development that is syrupy and gumlike in consistency and texture. Has a clean and distinct dried fig flavor and odor. It is free from any flavors or odors that are characteristic of scorching or caramelization and is free from other slight abnormal flavors or odors. Free from foreign material.

U.S. Grade B or U.S. Choice. A reasonably well-matured, dried fig which is reasonably well-developed and in which (1) the interior shows good sugary tissue development that is gummy but slightly fibrous in consistency and texture, or (2) one third or less of the interior of the fig may be entirely lacking in sugary tissue, if the remainder of the interior of the fig is syrupy and gumlike in consistency and texture. Has a clean and distinct dried fig flavor and odor; it may possess very slight flavors or odors that are characteristic of slight scorching or caramelization. May possess other very slight abnormal flavors or odors.

U.S. Grade C or U.S. Standard. Figs which are fairly well-developed and in which (1) the sugary tissue in the interior of the fig is gummy and fibrous in consistency and texture, or (2) one-third or less of the interior of the fig may be entirely lacking in sugary tissue, if the remainder of the interior of the fig is gummy but slightly fibrous in consistency and texture, or (3) more than one-third but less than one-half of the interior of the fig may be entirely lacking in sugary tissue, if the remainder of the interior of the fig is syrupy and gum-like in consistency and texture. Have a clean and distinct dried fig flavor and odor which may possess slight flavors or odors that are characteristic of scorching or caramelization. It may not possess any flavor in amounts resulting in objectionable or any off-flavors.

Fruit Cocktail, Canned

GRADES

This product is graded according to a technical system whereby penalty points are assessed for such factors as edibility, poor appearance, or defects in workmanship. The more penalty points assessed the lower the grade. The grade descriptions which follow are intended only as a general consumer guide. For more detailed information, please consult the source cited below.

U.S. Grade A or U.S. Fancy. The product is practically free from defects such as peach and pear peel, pits, capstems, crushed or broken grapes, broken cherry halves, unevenly colored cherry halves, blemished units, or from any other defects which detract from appearance or edibility. Each fruit ingredient has a practically uniform, typical color that is bright and characteristic of at least reasonably well-ripened fruit. They product may be no more than slightly affected by pink staining, and none of the fruit ingredients are dull or off-color. Each fruit ingredient is reasonably uniform in texture and tenderness with no more than slight disintegration. The liquid media is reasonably clear in that the liquid drained from the fruit cocktail is reasonably bright in color without any tinge of pink color or dullness of color and may contain fine fruit particles which do not materially affect the appearance of the product.

U.S. Grade B or U.S. Choice. The product is reasonably free from defects. Each fruit ingredient has a color of at least fairly well-ripened fruit although each may be more than slightly affected by pink staining or may be slightly dull in color, but not to the extent that the appearance is materially affected. The charac-

ter of the fruit may range from a firm to soft texture. There is no serious disintegration. The liquid drained from the fruit cocktail may be slightly pink or slightly dull in color but is not off-color for any reason and may contain fruit particles which materially affect, but do not seriously affect, the appearance of the product.

Substandard. Fails to meet the requirements of U.S. Grade B or U.S. Choice.

Source:
Agricultural Marketing Service, USDA, 7 CFR sections 52.1051 to 52.1065 (1991), Washington: Government Printing Office.

Grapefruit, Frozen

Frozen grapefruit is prepared from the matured fruit of the grapefruit tree (*Citrus paradisi*). After the fruit has been washed and peeled, it is separated into segments by removing the core, seeds, and membrane. It may be packed with or without packing media. The fruit is frozen and stored at temperatures necessary for the preservation of the product.

GRADES

This product is graded according to a technical system whereby penalty points are assessed for such factors as edibility, poor appearance, or defects in workmanship. The more penalty points assessed the lower the grade. The grade descriptions which follow are intended only as a general consumer guide. For more detailed information, please consult the source cited below.

U.S. Grade A or U.S. Fancy. Not less than 75 percent of the grapefruit consists of segments that are whole or almost whole. The grapefruit may possess not more than a slight variation from the typical color of properly matured grapefruit or pink grapefruit. The product is practically free from such defects as seeds, portions of covering membrane, and damaged units. The grapefruit is moderately firm and fleshy; the segments possess a well-developed, juicy, cellular structure; the product is fairly free from loose cell sacs; and not more than 5 percent of the grapefruit consists of soft, fibrous, or ricey segments.

U.S. Grade B or U.S. Choice. Not less than 50 percent of the grapefruit consists of segments that are whole or almost whole. The grapefruit may be variable in color, is fairly bright, and is not off-color. It is reasonably free from defects. The grapefruit is fairly firm and fleshy, and not more than 15 percent of the grapefruit consists of soft or fibrous segments.

U.S. Broken. Less than 50 percent of the grapefruit consists of segments that are whole or almost whole. It is reasonably free from defects and possesses a reasonably good character.

U.S. Grade D or Substandard. Fails to meet the requirements of U.S. Grade B or U.S. Choice and U.S. Broken.

Source:
Agricultural Marketing Service, USDA, 7 CFR section 52.1171 (1991), Washington: Government Printing Office.

Grapefruit, Canned

Canned grapefruit is prepared from clean, sound, and mature grapefruit (*Citrus paradisi*).

GRADES

This product is graded according to a technical system whereby penalty points are assessed for such factors as edibility, poor appearance, or defects in workmanship. The more penalty points assessed the lower the grade. The grade descriptions which follow are intended only as a general consumer guide. For more detailed information, please consult the source cited below.

U.S. Grade A or U.S. Fancy. Has an average drained weight of not less than 53 percent of the water capacity of the container, of which not less than 65 percent by weight of the drained grapefruit consists of whole or practically whole segments. Has a practically uniform, bright, typical color free from any noticeable tinge of amber. The canned grapefruit is practically free from seeds, from portions of albedo or tough membrane, from damaged units, and from other similar defects. The grapefruit segments are moderately firm and fleshy. The segments or portions possess a juicy, cellular structure free from dry cells, ricey cells, or fibrous cells that materially affects the appearance or eating quality of the product.

U.S. Grade B or U.S. Choice. Has an average drained weight of not less than 53 percent of the water capacity of the container, of which not less than 50 percent by weight of the drained grapefruit consists of whole or practically whole segments. Has a fairly bright color which may be variable but is not off-color for any reason. It is reasonably free from defects. The grapefruit segments may be affected, but not seriously so, by dry cells, ricey cells, or fibrous cells that may detract from the appearance or eating quality of the product.

U.S. Broken. Has an average drained weight of not less than 53 percent of the water capacity of the container, of which less than 50 percent weight of the drained grapefruit consists of whole or practically whole segments. It has a reasonably good color and is free from defects.

Substandard. Fails to meet the requirements of U.S. Grade B or U.S. Choice and U.S. Broken.

Grapefruit, Florida

This product is graded according to a technical system whereby penalty points are assessed for such factors as edibility, poor appearance, or defects in workmanship. The more penalty points assessed the lower the grade. The grade descriptions which follow are intended only as a general consumer guide. For more detailed information, please consult the source cited below.

U.S. Fancy. The fruit is mature, well formed, of similar varietal characteristics, and has a smooth texture. The fruit is firm and is not soft, noticeably wilted, or flabby. The skin is not spongy or puffy. The fruit is yellow in color with practically no trace of green color. Not more than one-tenth of the surface, in the aggregate, may be affected by discoloration. It is free from ammoniation, bruises, buckskin, caked melanose, cuts that are not healed, decay, growth cracks, scab, sprayburn, and wormy fruit. The fruit is free from injury caused by green spots, oil spots, scale, scars, skin breakdown, and thorn scratches. It is also free from damage caused by dirt or other foreign material, disease, dryness or mushy condition, hail, insects, sprouting, sunburn, and other means.

U.S. No. 1. The fruit is firm, mature, well formed, and of similar varietal characteristics. The fruit has a fairly smooth texture and is fairly well-colored. Not more than one-third of the surface, in the aggregate, may be affected by discoloration. It is free from bruises, cuts that are not healed, decay, growth cracks, and wormy fruit. The fruit is free from damage caused by ammoniation, buckskin, caked melanose, dirt or other foreign material, disease, dryness or mushy condition, green spots, hail, insects, oil spots, scab, scale, scars, skin breakdown, sprayburn, sprouting, sunburn, thorn scratches, and other means.

U.S. No. 1 Bright. The requirements for this grade are the same as for U.S. No. 1 except that no fruit may have more than one-fifth of Its surface, in the aggregate, affected by discoloration.

U.S. No. 1 Golden. The requirements for this grade are the same as for U.S. No. 1 except that not more than the number of fruits permitted in section 51.761, Tables I and II, shall have more than one-third of their surface, In the aggregate, affected by discoloration.

U.S. No. 1 Bronze. The requirements for this grade are the same as for U.S. No. 1 except that all fruit must show some discoloration. Not less than the number of fruits required in section 51.761, Tables I and II, shall have more than one-third of their surface, in the aggregate, affected by discoloration. The predominating discoloration on these fruits shall be of rust mite type.

U.S. No. 1 Russet. The requirements for this grade are the same as for U.S. No. 1 except that not less than the number of fruits required in section 51.761, Tables I and II, shall have more than one-third of their surface, In the aggregate, affected by any type of discoloration.

U.S. No. 2. The fruit is fairly firm, mature, and of similar varietal characteristics. It is not more than slightly misshapen or rough textured. The fruit may be slightly colored, but not more than one-half of the surface, in the aggregate, may be affected by discoloration. It is free from bruises, cuts that are not healed, decay, growth cracks, and wormy fruit. The fruit is free from serious damage caused ammoniation, buckskin, caked melanose, dirt or other foreign material, disease, dryness or mushy condition, green spots, hail, insects, oil spots, scab, scale, scars, skin breakdown, sprayburn, sprouting, sunburn, thorn scratches, or other means.

U.S. No. 2 Bright. The requirements for this grade are the same as for U.S. No. 2 except that no fruit may have more than one-fifth of its surface, in the aggregate, affected by discoloration.

U.S. No. 2 Russet. The requirements for this grade are the same as for U.S. No. 2 except that not less than the number of fruits required can have more than one-half of their surface, in the aggregate, affected by discoloration.

U.S. No. 3. Consists of grapefruit which is mature. It may be misshapen and poorly colored. However, not more than 25 percent of the surface may be of a solid dark green color. It has a rough texture, but is not seriously bumpy. It can be slightly spongy. The fruit is free from cuts that are not healed, decay, and wormy fruit. It is free from very serious damage caused by ammoniation, bruises, buckskin, caked melanose, disease, dryness or mushy condition, growth cracks, hail, insects scab, scale, scars, skin breakdown, sprayburn, sprouting, sunburn, and other means.

Unclassified. Consists of grapefruit which have not been classified in accordance with any of the foregoing grades. The term *unclassified* is not a grade within the meaning of these standards but is provided as a designation to show that no grade has been applied to the lot.

Grapefruit, Texas

Grapefruit in this category comes from Texas and states other than Florida, California, and Arizona. It is graded according to a technical system whereby penalty points are assessed for such factors as edibility, poor appearance, or defects in workmanship. The more penalty points assessed the lower the grade. The grade descriptions which follow are intended only as a general consumer guide. For more detailed information, please consult the source cited below.

U.S. Fancy. The fruit is mature, smooth textured, well formed, well-colored, and of similar varietal characteristics. The fruit is not soft, noticeably wilted, or flabby. The skin is not spongy or puffy. The fruit is yellow in color with practically no trace of green color. Not more than one-tenth of the surface, in the aggregate, may be affected by discoloration. It is free from ammoniation, bruises, buckskin, cuts not healed, skin breakdown, decay, growth cracks, scab, sprayburn, and wormy fruit. It is not injured by green spots, oil spots, scale, scars, and thorn scratches.

U.S. No. 1. The fruit is firm, mature, of similar varietal characteristics, and fairly well-colored. Except for a l inch circle, in the aggregate, of green color, the yellow color predominates over the green color. In addition, not more than one-half of the surface, in the aggregate, may be affected by other discolorations. The skin is not materially rough, coarse, or thick for the variety. The fruit may be slightly soft, but not bruised; the skin is not spongy or puffy. The fruit may not have the shape characteristic of the variety, but it is not elongated, pointed, or otherwise deformed. It is free from bruises, cuts not healed, caked melanose, growth cracks, sprayburn, decay, and wormy fruit.

U.S. No. 1 Bright. The requirements for this grade are the same as for U.S. No. 1 except that no fruit may have more than one-tenth of its surface, in the aggregate, affected by discoloration.

U.S. No. 1 Bronze. The requirements for this grade are the same as for U.S. No. 1 except that all fruit must show some discoloration. Not less than the number of fruits required

in section 51.628, Tables I and II, shall have more than one-half of their surface, in the aggregate, affected by discoloration. The predominating discoloration on these fruits shall be of rust mite type.

U.S. Combination. U.S. Combination consists of a combination of U.S. No. 1 and U.S. No. 2 grapefruit: Provided, That the number of U.S. No. 2 fruits specified in section 51.628, Tables I and II, are not exceeded.

U.S. No. 2. The fruit is fairly firm, mature, and of similar varietal characteristics. It may be slightly discolored; however, not more than two-thirds of the surface, in the aggregate, may be affected by discoloration. The fruit may not be more than slightly misshapen or slightly rough textured. It is free from bruises, cuts not healed, growth cracks, decay, and wormy fruit. The fruit cannot be seriously damaged by any other cause.

U.S. No. 2 Russet. The requirements for this grade are the same as for U.S. No. 2 except that not less than the number of fruits required in section 51.628, Tables I and II, shall have more than two-thirds of their surface, in the aggregate, affected by discoloration.

U.S. No. 3 The fruit is fairly mature and of similar varietal characteristics. It may be misshapen, slightly spongy, or have rough texture. It cannot be seriously lumpy or cracked. The fruit may be poorly colored; however, not more than 25 percent of the surface may be of a solid dark green color. It is free from cuts not healed, decay, and wormy fruit. It cannot be very seriously damaged by any other cause.

Grapes, Canned

Canned grapes are prepared from the light seedless varietal types and are stemmed.

GRADES

This product is graded according to a technical system whereby penalty points are assessed for such factors as edibility, poor appearance, or defects in workmanship. The more penalty points assessed the lower the grade. The grade descriptions which follow are intended only as a general consumer guide. For more detailed information, please consult the source cited below.

U.S. Grade A or U.S. Fancy. They possess similar varietal characteristics and a normal flavor. The grapes have a practically uniform, bright light green to greenish-yellow color, typical of well-developed Thompson seedless grapes that have been properly prepared and processed. Not more than 10 percent may possess a noticeably dull color. The grapes are practically uniform in size so that largest 5 percent of the grapes are not more than twice the weight of the smallest 5 percent. The grapes are practically free from defects such as main stems, harmless extraneous vegetable material, attached or loose capstems, mutilated grapes, and any other defects that affect the appearance or edibility of the product. The grapes are reasonably uniform in texture, generally thick-fleshed, and tender, but not soft or flabby. Not more than 5 percent may be affected by serious processing cracks.

U.S. Grade B or U S. Choice. Possess similar varietal characteristics and a normal flavor. The grapes have a reasonably uniform, bright color typical of Thompson seedless grapes. The presence of grapes with a noticeably dull color or a brownish cast does not seriously affect the appearance or edibility of the product. The grapes may vary in size as to appearance and weight, provided such variation does not seriously affect the appearance. The product is reasonably free from defects, and the grapes are fairly uniform in texture. They may be slightly soft, but not flabby. No more than 10 percent may be affected by serious processing cracks.

Substandard. Fails to meet the requirements of U.S. Grade B or U.S. Choice.

Source:
Agricultural Marketing Service, USDA, 7 CFR sections 52.4021 to 52.4034 (1991), Washington: Government Printing Office.

Grapes, American (Eastern Type) Bunch

To allow for variations in quality caused by grading and handling, a percentage of the grapes may fail to meet all of the requirements of the grade.

GRADES

This product is graded according to a technical system whereby penalty points are assessed for such factors as edibility, poor appearance, or defects in workmanship. The more penalty points assessed the lower the grade. The grade descriptions which follow are intended only as a general consumer guide. For more detailed information, please consult the source cited below.

U.S. Fancy Table Grapes. Bunches of grapes of one variety (except when designated as assorted varieties). The grapes are juicy, palatable, and have reached that stage of development at which the skin of the berry easily separates from the pulp. They show full color characteristic of the variety. The berries are firm and do not yield more than slightly to moderate pressure. They are firmly attached to capstems, and are not split, shattered, crushed, dried, or wet. They are free from decay, mold, mildew, berry moth, russeting, and hail. The grapes are free from damage caused by freezing, disease, insects, or other means. At least 50 percent of the bunches in each container are compact (the bunches are well-filled and have no open spaces), the remainder fairly compact (the berries are not as closely spaced as in compact). They are not excessively small. Not less than 90 percent, by count, of the berries (exclusive of dried berries) on each bunch may have a minimum diameter, unless otherwise specified, of 9/16 inch.

U.S. No. 1 Table Grapes. Bunches of grapes of one variety (except when designated as assorted varieties). They are mature and fairly well-colored with not less than 75 percent showing full color (25 percent may be partially or poorly colored but not

characteristic of immature berries). The berries are firm, are firmly attached to capstems, and are not split, shattered, crushed, dried, or wet. They are free from decay, mold, and berry moth. The grapes are also free from damage caused by freezing, russeting, hail, mildew, other disease, insects, or other means. For packages which contain 5 pounds or less of grapes, at least 50 percent of the bunches are fairly compact. Bunches should not be excessively small. Not less than 90 percent, by count, of the berries (exclusive of dried berries) on each bunch may have a minimum diameter, unless otherwise specified, of 9/16 inch.

U.S. No. 1 Juice Grapes. Bunches of grapes of one variety (except when designated as assorted varieties) which are mature and fairly well-colored. The berries are firm, are firmly attached to capstems, and are not split, shattered, crushed, dried, or wet. They are free from mold, decay, and berry moth. The grapes are also free from serious damage caused by freezing, russeting, hail, mildew, other disease, insects, or other means.

Unclassified. Grapes which have not been classified in accordance with any of the foregoing grades. The term *unclassified* is not a grade within the meaning of these standards but is provided as a designation to show that no grade has been applied to the lot.

Source:
Agricultural Marketing Service, USDA, 7 CFR sections 51.3610 to 51.3624 (1992), Washington: Government Printing Office.

Grapes, Juice (European or Vinifera Type)

To allow for variations in quality caused by grading and handling, a percentage of the grapes may fail to meet all of the requirements of the grade.

GRADES

This product is graded according to a technical system whereby penalty points are assessed for such factors as edibility, poor appearance, or defects in workmanship. The more penalty points assessed the lower the grade. The grade descriptions which follow are intended only as a general consumer guide. For more detailed information, please consult the source cited below.

U.S. No. 1 Juice Grapes. Bunches of well-developed grapes of one variety which are fairly well-colored, mature, and are not weak, loose at capstems, shattered, split, crushed, or wet. They are free from waterberry, redberry, mold, and decay. The grapes are also free from damage caused by freezing, heat, sunburn, mildew, other disease, insects, or other means. There is no color requirements in this grade for white varieties when the grapes test not less than 20 percent soluble solids in juice. Not more than a total of 15 percent, by weight, of the berries may be raisining or raisined, and not more than 5 percent may be raisined. However, any amount of raisining may be permitted if the percentage of raisining is specified in connection with the grade. Bunches cannot be excessively straggly or damaged by dried berries or immature shot berries. Stems cannot be moldy or damaged by freezing.

U.S. No. I Mixed Juice Grapes. Grapes of mixed varieties of the same color which meet the remaining requirements of U.S. No. 1 Juice Grapes.

U.S. No. 2 Juice Grapes. Grapes of one variety which are mature and are not detached from the capstems, split, crushed, or wet. They are free from raisined berries, sunburned or dried berries, waterberry, redberry, mold, or decay; they are free from serious damage caused by heat, freezing, or other means.

No. 2 Mixed Juice Grapes. Mixed varieties of the same color which meet the remaining requirements of U.S. No. 2 Juice Grapes.

Unclassified. Grapes that are mature and do not include an excess of 10 percent, by weight, of berries which are affected by decay.

Source:
Agricultural Marketing Service, USDA, 7 CFR sections 51.4290 to 51.4307 (1992), Washington: Government Printing Office.

Kiwifruit

This product is graded according to a technical system whereby penalty points are assessed for such factors as edibility, poor appearance, or defects in workmanship. The more penalty points assessed the lower the grade. The grade descriptions which follow are intended only as a general consumer guide. For more detailed information, please consult the source cited below.

U.S. Fancy. The fruit has similar varietal characteristics and is mature. It is not soft, overripe, or shriveled. The fruit is carefully packed, clean, and well formed (has the shape characteristic of the variety and slight bumps or other roughness are permitted, providing they do not detract from the appearance). The fruit is free from worm holes, broken skins that are not healed, sunscald, freezing injury, internal breakdown, and decay. It is also free from injury caused by bruises, leaf or limb rubs, discoloration, hail, growth cracks, scab, scars, heat, sprayburn, sunburn, scale, insects, other diseases, and mechanical or other means.

U.S. No. 1. The fruit in this grade differs from U.S. Fancy in that it need only be fairly well formed (has the shape characteristic of the variety but slight bumps or other roughness are permitted, providing they do not materially detract from the appearance of the product). There is also a higher tolerance for defects from both natural causes and grading and handling.

U.S. No. 2. This grade is of a lower quality than U.S. No. 1 in that the fruit need only be fairly clean. It cannot badly misshapen (to the point that its appearance is seriously affected as opposed to materially detracted). There is also a higher tolerance for defects from both natural causes and grading and handling.

Source:
Agricultural Marketing Service, USDA, 7 CFR sections 51.2335 to 51.2341 (1992), Washington: Government Printing Office.

Lemons

To allow for variations in quality caused by grading and handling, a percentage of the lemons may fail to meet all of the requirements of the grade.

GRADES

This product is graded according to a technical system whereby penalty points are assessed for such factors as edibility, poor appearance, or defects in workmanship. The more penalty points assessed the lower the grade. The grade descriptions which follow are intended only as a general consumer guide. For more detailed information, please consult the source cited below.

U.S. No. 1. Lemons which are firm and fairly well formed (has a normal shape and is not flattened on one side). Lemons that have a moderately thick neck at the stem end are considered acceptable. The lemons are reasonably smooth and not materially affected by protrusions or lumpiness of the skin or by grooves or furrows. They have stems which are properly clipped. They are free from decay, contact spot (an area which bears evidence of having been in contact with decay or mold), internal evidence of Alternarla development (includes red or brown staining of the tissue under the button in the core), unhealed broken skins, hard or dry skins, exanthema, growth cracks, internal decline (endoxerosis), red blotch, membranous stain or other internal discoloration. They are free from damage caused by bruises, dryness or mushy condition, scars, oil spots, scale, sunburn, hollow core, peteca, scab, melanose, dirt or other foreign material, other disease, insects, or other means. The lemons are fairly well-colored; the area of yellow color exceeds the area of green color. Lemons which meets all the requirements of this grade except those relating to color may be designated as *U.S. No. 1 Green,* if the lemons are of a full green color, or as *U.S. No. 1 Mixed Color,* if the lemons fail to meet the color requirements of either *U.S. No. 1 or U.S. No. 1 Green.*

U.S. Combination. A combination of U.S. No. 1 and U.S. No. 2 lemons. At least 40 percent, by count, of the lemons meet the requirements of U.S. No. 1 grade.

U.S. No. 2. Lemons which are fairly firm, reasonably well formed (not decidedly flattened), and fairly smooth (not badly folded, badly edged, or very decidedly lumpy). The stems are properly clipped. The lemons are free from decay, contact spot, internal evidence of Alternaria development, unhealed broken skins, hard or dry skins, exanthema, internal decline (endoxerosis), and red blotch. They are free from serious damage caused by bruises, membranous stain or other internal discoloration, dryness or mushy condition, scars, oil spots, scale, sunburn, hollow core, peteca, growth cracks, scab, melanose, dirt or other foreign material other disease, insects, or other means. The lemons are fairly well-colored. Lemons which meets all of the above requirements of this grade except those relating to color may be designated as *U.S. No. 2 Green,* if the lemons are of a full green color, or as *U.S. No. 2 Mixed Color,* if the lemons fail to meet the color requirements of either *U.S. No. 2 or U.S. No. 2 Green.*

Unclassified. Lemons which have not been classified in accordance with any of the foregoing grades. The term *unclassified* is not a grade within the meaning of the standards but is provided as a designation to show that no grade has been applied to the lot.

Source:
Agricultural Marketing Service, USDA, 7 CFR sections 51.2795 to 51.2821 (1992), Washington: Government Printing Office.

Limes, Persian (Tahiti)

This product is graded according to a technical system whereby penalty points are assessed for such factors as edibility, poor appearance, or defects in workmanship. The more penalty points assessed the lower the grade. The grade descriptions which follow are intended only as a general consumer guide. For more detailed information, please consult the source cited below.

U.S. No. 1. Consists of Persian limes which are firm (not soft or flabby), fairly well formed (the fruit shows normal characteristic shape for the Persian variety and is not materially flattened on one side), and fairly smooth textured. The fruit is comparatively free from lumpiness and the pebbling is not abnormally coarse. Coarse pebbling is not objectionable; it is indicative of good keeping quality and is characteristic of the fruit, especially that from young trees. The fruit is free from decay, stylar end breakdown or other internal discoloration, broken skins which are not healed, bruises (except those incident to proper handling and packing), and hard or dry skins. It is also free from damage caused by freezing, dryness or mushy condition, sprayburn, exanthema (ammoniation), scars, thorn scratches, scale, sunburn, scab, blanching, yellow color, discoloration, buckskin, dirt or other foreign material, disease, insects, or mechanical or other means. At least three-fourths of the surface of the fruit, in aggregate area, must show a good green color characteristic of the Persian lime. The fruit has a juice content of not less than 42 percent, by volume.

U.S. No. 1, Mixed Color. Limes which fail to meet the U.S. No. 1 grade requirements because of blanching.

U.S. No. 1, Turning. Limes which fail to meet the U.S. No. 1 or U.S. No. 1 Mixed Color grade requirements because of yellowing caused by the ripening process

U.S. Combination. Consists of a combination of U.S. No. 1 and U.S. No. 2 limes. At least 60 percent, by count, of the limes meet the requirements of U.S. No. 1 grade.

U.S. No. 2. Consists of Persian limes which are fairly firm, are not badly deformed, and are not excessively rough textured. They are free from decay, stylar end breakdown or other internal discoloration, broken skins which are not healed, bruises (except those incident to proper handling and packing), and hard or dry skins. The limes are also free from serious damage caused by freezing, dryness or mushy condition, sprayburn, exanthema (ammoniation), scars, thorn scratches, scale, sunburn, scab, blanching, yellow color, discoloration, buckskin, dirt or other foreign material, disease, insects, or mechanical or other means. At least one-half of the surface of the fruit, in

aggregate area, must show a good green color characteristic of the Persian lime. The fruit has a juice content of not less than 42 percent, by volume.

U.S. No. 2, Mixed Color. Limes which fail to meet the U.S. No. 2 grade requirements because of blanching.

U.S. No. 2, Turning. Limes which fail to meet the U.S. No. 2 or U.S. No. 2 Mixed Color grade requirements because of turning yellow or yellow color, caused by the ripening process.

Unclassified. Persian limes which have not been classified in accordance with any of the foregoing grades. The term *unclassified* is not a grade within the meaning of these standards but is provided as a designation to show that no grade has been applied to the lot.

Source:
Agricultural Marketing Service, USDA, 7 CFR sections 51.1000 to 51.1016 (1992), Washington: Government Printing Office.

Melon Balls, Frozen

Melon balls are spheres of melon flesh prepared from suitable varieties of sound, fresh cantaloupe (*Cucumis melo*) melons and/or sound, fresh honeydew (*inodorus*) melons to which melon balls prepared from sound, fresh melons of a definitely different but suitable variety may be added. The balls are prepared and washed in a manner to assure a clean and wholesome product. They are properly drained before filling into containers. They may packed with a suitable fruit and/or vegetable garnish, a nutritive or nonnutritive sweetening ingredient(s), or any other ingredient permissible under the provisions of the Federal Food, Drug, and Cosmetic Act. The melon balls are prepared and frozen in accordance with good commercial practice and maintained at temperatures necessary for the preservation of the product.

TYPES

Cantaloupe

Honeydew

Mixed Cantaloupe and Honeydew. Not less than 50 percent, by weight, of units derived from cantaloupe melons and not less than 33⅓ percent derived from honeydew melons.

Mixed Honeydew and Cantaloupe. Not less than 50 percent derived from honeydew melons and not than 33⅓ percent derived from cantaloupe melons.

Other Types. Derived from a single variety of melon or mixture of melon types.

GRADES

This product is graded according to a technical system whereby penalty points are assessed for such factors as edibility, poor appearance, or defects in workmanship. The more penalty points assessed the lower the grade. The grade descriptions which follow are intended only as a general consumer guide. For more detailed information, please consult the source cited below.

U.S. Grade A or U.S. Fancy. Possess a pleasant flavor and odor normally expected of well-ripened melons. (The flavor and odor of any garnish used should be normal.) The melon balls have a bright overall appearance and possess a reasonably uniform, typical color. The melons are practically uniform in size and shape. They are practically free from defects such as exterior and interior rind, melon seeds, membrane material, and from any other defects which detract from the appearance or edibility of the product. The melon balls possess a tender texture that is typical of mature, well-ripened melons. Not more than 10 percent may be excessively soft, mushy, excessively frayed, fibrous, tough, or rubbery—provided not more than 5 percent, by count, are tough or rubbery.

U.S. Grade B or U.S. Choice. Possess a flavor and odor expected of reasonably well-ripened melons of the variety or varieties used. This flavor and odor may be slightly flat, but it is free from objectionable flavors or odors of any kind. (The flavor and odor of any garnish used should be normal.) The melon balls have a reasonably uniform, bright appearance that is typical of reasonably well-ripened melon flesh. The fruit is reasonably uniform in size and shape and reasonably free from defects. It possess a fairly tender texture. Not more than 20 percent are excessively soft, mushy, excessively frayed, fibrous, tough, or rubbery—provided that not more than 10 percent, by count, are tough or rubbery.

Substandard. Fails to meet the requirements of U.S. Grade B or U.S. Choice.

Source:
Agricultural Marketing Service, USDA, 7 CFR sections 52.5361 to 52.5371 (1991), Washington: Government Printing Office.

Melons, Honeydew and Honeyball Type

This product is graded according to a technical system whereby penalty points are assessed for such factors as edibility, poor appearance, or defects in workmanship. The more penalty points assessed the lower the grade. The grade descriptions which follow are intended only as a general consumer guide. For more detailed information, please consult the source cited below.

U.S. No. 1. Melons which are mature, firm, and well formed (has a normal shape). They are free from decay and from damage caused by dirt, aphid stain, rust spots, bruises, cracks, broken skin, sunscald, sunburn, hail, moisture, insects, disease, or other means.

U.S. Commercial. Melons which meet the requirements of U.S. No. 1 grade except there is an increased tolerances for defects.

U.S. No. 2. Melons which are mature, firm, and fairly well formed. They are free from decay and from serious damage by any cause.

Unclassified. Melons which have not been classified in accordance with any of the foregoing grades. The term *unclassified* is not a grade within the meaning of these standards but is provided as a designation to show that no grade has been applied to the lot.

Source:
Agricultural Marketing Service, USDA, 7 CFR sections 51.3740 to 51.3749 (1992), Washington: Government Printing Office.

Nectarines

This product is graded according to a technical system whereby penalty points are assessed for such factors as edibility, poor appearance, or defects in workmanship. The more penalty points assessed the lower the grade. The grade descriptions which follow are intended only as a general consumer guide. For more detailed information, please consult the source cited below. To allow for variations in quality caused by grading and handling, a percentage of the tangerines may fail to meet all of the requirements of the grade.

U.S. Fancy. Nectarines of one variety which are mature but not soft or overripe. They are well formed, clean, and free from decay, broken skins which are not healed, worms, and worm holes. The nectarines are free from injury caused by bruises, growth cracks, hail, sunburn, sprayburn, scab, bacterial spot, scale, split pit, scars, russeting, other disease, insects, or mechanical or other means. In the case of the John Rivers variety, each nectarine should show some blushed or red color. In the case of other varieties, at least one-third of its surface must show a red color characteristic of the variety.

U.S. Extra No. 1. This grade is similar to U.S. Fancy (except in the case of John Rivers variety, 50 percent of which must show some blushed or red color). In the case of other varieties, at least 75 percent of the nectarines must show some blushed or red color. Also, there is a higher tolerance for defective units.

U.S. No. 1. This grade is similar to U.S. Extra No. 1 except at least 75 percent of the nectarines must show some blushed or red color. There is no color requirements for nectarines of the John Rivers variety in this grade.

U.S. No. 2. Nectarines of one variety which are mature but not soft or overripe. They are not badly misshapen, are clean, and are free from decay, broken skins which are not healed, worms, and worm holes. The nectarines are free from serious damage caused by bruises, growth cracks, hail, sunburn, sprayburn, scab, bacterial spot, scale, split pit, scars, russeting, other disease, insects, or mechanical or other means. There are no color requirements for nectarines in this grade.

Unclassified. Nectarines which have not been classified in accordance with any of the foregoing grades. The term *unclassified* is not a grade within the meaning of these standards but is provided as a designation to show that no grade has been applied to the lot.

Source:
Agricultural Marketing Service, USDA, 7 CFR sections 51.3145 to 51.3160 (1992), Washington: Government Printing Office.

Oranges, Coloring

It is a common practice to color the skins of oranges in certain orange growing areas of the country because of climatic or cultural conditions which cause the oranges to mature while still green in color. The coloring of the skins is done in one of two ways: (1) adding a color to the skin of the orange, Citrus Red No. 2, if they are not intended or used for processing and if they meet the maturity standards for the states in which they are grown, and (2) subjecting the orange to ethylene gas by a commercial process. This hastens the blanching process which apparently takes place normally after picking. Artificially colored oranges received in bulk and sold at a retail establishment are not required to bear a label statement declaring the use of artificial coloring—provided the oranges are displayed to the purchaser with either the labeling of the bulk container plainly in view or a counter card, sign, or other appropriate device bears prominently and conspicuously the fact that the oranges are artificially colored. In no case can the coloring be used to conceal any inferiority or defect.

Source:
Food and Drug Administration, *Compliance Policy Guides*, Guide 7110.21, 10/01/80: Washington, National Technical Information Service.

Oranges, Texas

These standards apply only to the common or sweet orange group from Texas and states other than Florida, California, and Arizona. Also included are citrus varieties belonging to the Mandarin group (except tangerines for which separate U.S. Standards are issued). To allow for variations in quality caused by grading and handling, a percentage of the oranges may fail to meet all of the requirements of the grade.

GRADES

This product is graded according to a technical system whereby penalty points are assessed for such factors as edibility, poor appearance, or defects in workmanship. The more penalty points assessed the lower the grade. The grade descriptions which follow are intended only as a general consumer guide. For more detailed information, please consult the source cited below.

U.S. Fancy. As applied to common oranges, the fruit is mature and firm; it is not soft, noticeably wilted, or flabby. As applied to oranges of the Mandarin group (Satsuma, King, and Mandarin), the fruit is not extremely puffy, although the skin may be slightly loose. The fruit is mature. In both cases, the fruits in any container are similar in color and shape. The fruit is yellow or orange in color with practically no trace of green color. Not more than one-tenth of the surface, in the aggregate, may be affected by discoloration. The fruit is well formed and smooth textured. It is free from ammoniation, buckskin, caked melanose, creasing, cuts not healed, decay, growth cracks,

scab, skin breakdown, sprayburn, undeveloped segments, and wormy fruit. The fruit is not injured by green spots, oil spots, scale, scars, thorn scratches, and split, rough, wide, or protruding navels.

U.S. No. 1. Consists of oranges which are mature, firm, well formed, and of similar varietal characteristics. The fruit has a fairly smooth texture. Not more than one-third of the surface, in the aggregate, may be affected by discoloration of any kind. Early and midseason varieties are fairly well-colored. Except for a 1 inch circle in the aggregate of green color, the yellow or orange color predominates over the green color. For Valencia and other late varieties, less than 50 percent, by count, are fairly well-colored, and the remainder are reasonably well-colored. All varieties are free from bruises, cuts not healed, caked melanose, decay, growth cracks, sprayburn, undeveloped segments, and wormy fruit.

U.S. No. 1 Bright. The requirements for this grade are the same as for U.S. No. 1 except that no fruit may have more than one-tenth of its surface, in the aggregate, affected by discoloration.

U.S. No. 1 Bronze. The requirements for this grade are the same as for U.S. No 1 except that all fruit shows some discoloration. The predominating discoloration on these fruits is of a rust mite type.

U.S. Combination. Consists of a combination of U.S. No. 1 and U.S. No. 2 oranges.

U.S. No. 2. Consists of oranges which are fairly firm, mature, and of similar varietal characteristics. They are reasonably well-colored. Not more than one-half of the surface, in the aggregate, may be affected by discoloration. The oranges are not more than slightly misshapen or slightly rough. The fruit is free from bruises, cuts not healed, decay, growth cracks, and wormy fruit.

U.S. No. 2 Russet. The requirements for this grade are the same as for U.S. No. 2 except that not less than the number of fruits required in section 51.689, Tables I and II, shall have more than one-half of their surface, in the aggregate, affected by discoloration.

U.S. No. 3. The oranges are mature and of similar varietal characteristics. The fruit may be misshapen, slightly spongy, or rough textured. The fruit is not seriously lumpy or cracked. It may be poorly colored; however, not more than 25 percent of the surface may be of a solid dark green color. It is free from cuts not healed, decay, and wormy fruit.

Oranges, California and Arizona

This product is graded according to a technical system whereby penalty points are assessed for such factors as edibility, poor appearance, or defects in workmanship. The more penalty points assessed the lower the grade. The grade descriptions which follow are intended only as a general consumer guide. For more detailed information, please consult the source cited below.

U.S. Fancy. The oranges are mature, well-colored, firm, well formed, and of similar varietal characteristics (the oranges in any container are similar in color and type). The fruit is at least light orange in color, with not more than a trace of green at the stem end, and not more than 15 percent of the remainder of the surface of the fruit shows green color. The fruit does not yield to more than slight to moderate pressure, and it shows the normal shape characteristic of the variety. The fruit has a smooth texture; the skin is of fairly fine grain for the variety; the pebbling is not pronounced; and any furrows radiating from the stem end are shallow. The fruit is free from decay, broken skins which are not healed, hard or dry skins, exanthema, growth cracks, bruises (except those incident to proper handling and packing), and dryness or mushy condition. The fruit is also free from injury caused by creasing, scars, oil spots, scale, sunburn, dirt or other foreign material, disease, insects, or mechanical or other means; it is free from split, rough, wide, or protruding navels.

U.S. No. 1. The oranges are mature, firm, well formed, of fairly smooth texture, and of similar varietal characteristics. The fruit is free from decay, broken skins which are not healed, hard or dry skins, exanthema, growth cracks, and bruises (except those incident to proper handling and packing). It is also free from damage caused by dryness or mushy condition, creasing, scars, oil spots, scale, sunburn, dirt or other foreign material, disease, insects, or mechanical or other means; the fruit is free from split, rough, wide, or protruding navels. Each fruit is well-colored, except Valencia oranges which are at least fairly well-colored (the yellow or orange color predominates the fruit).

U.S. Combination. A combination of U.S. No. 1 and U.S. No. 2 oranges. At least 40 percent, by count, of the oranges meet the requirements of U.S. No. 1 grade.

U.S. No. 2. Oranges of similar varietal characteristics which are mature, fairly well-colored, and fairly firm. The fruit may yield to moderate pressure, but it is not soft. The fruit is fairly well formed; it is not of the shape characteristic of the variety, but it is not decidedly flattened, pointed, extremely elongated, or otherwise badly deformed. The fruit may have a slightly rough texture, but the skin is not decidedly rough, badly folded, badly ridged, or decidedly lumpy. A heavily pebbled skin is considered slightly rough. The fruit is free from decay, broken skins which are not healed, hard or dry skins, exanthema, and growth cracks. It is free from serious damage caused by bruises, dryness or mushy condition, split or protruding navels, creasing, scars, oil spots, scale, sunburn, dirt or other foreign material, disease, insects, or mechanical or other means.

Unclassified. Oranges which have not been classified in accordance with any of the foregoing grades. The term *unclassified* is not a grade within the meaning of these standards but is provided as a designation to show that no grade has been applied to the lot.

Source:
Agricultural Marketing Service, USDA, 7 CFR sections 51.1085 to 51.1109 (1992), Washington: Government Printing Office.

Oranges and Tangelos, Florida

The standards contained in this part apply only to the common or sweet orange group, varieties, and hybrids of varieties belonging to the mandarin group, except tangerines, and to the citrus fruit commonly known as tangelo—a hybrid between tangerine or mandarin orange (*Citrus reticulata*) with either the grapefruit or pomelo (*C. paradisi* and *C. grandis*). Separate U.S. Standards apply to tangerines.

GRADES

This product is graded according to a technical system whereby penalty points are assessed for such factors as edibility, poor appearance, or defects in workmanship. The more penalty points assessed the lower the grade. The grade descriptions which follow are intended only as a general consumer guide. For more detailed information, please consult the source cited below.

U.S. Fancy. The fruit is mature, firm, well-colored, well formed, and of similar varietal characteristics (similar in color and shape). For common oranges and tangelos, the fruit is not soft, noticeably wilted, or flabby. For oranges of the Mandarin group (Statsumas, King Mandarin), the fruit is not extremely puffy, although the skin may be slightly loose. Not more than one-tenth of the surface, in the aggregate, may be affected by discoloration. The fruit is smooth textured; the skin is thin. It is yellow or orange in color with practically no trace of green color. The fruit is free from ammoniation, bruises, buckskin, caked melanose, creasing, cuts not healed, decay, growth cracks, scab, split navels, sprayburn, undeveloped segments, and wormy fruit. It is free from injury caused by green spots, oil spots, scale, scars, skin breakdown, thorn scratches, and rough, wide, or protruding navels. The fruit is also free from damage caused by dirt or other foreign material, disease, dryness or mushy condition, hail, insects, woodiness, sunburn, and other means.

U.S. No. 1 Bright. The requirements for this grade are the same as for U.S. No. 1 except that no fruit may have more than one-fifth of its surface, in the aggregate, affected by discoloration.

U.S. No. 1 Color. The fruit is firm, mature, well formed, and of similar varietal characteristics. Early and midseason varieties are fairly well-colored. Except for an aggregate area of green color which does not exceed the area of a circle 1 inch in diameter, the yellow or orange color predominates over the green color. For Valencia and other late varieties, not less than 50 percent, by count, are fairly well-colored and the remainder is reasonably well-colored. Not more than one-third of the surface, in the aggregate, may be affected by discoloration. The fruit has a fairly smooth texture; the skin is fairly thin and not coarse for the variety and size.

U.S. No. 1 Golden. The requirements for this grade are the same as for U.S. No. 1 except that a portion of the fruit has more than one-third of its surface, in the aggregate, affected by discoloration.

U.S. No. 1 Bronze. The requirements for this grade are the same as for U.S. No. 1 except that all fruit must show some discoloration.

U.S. No. 1 Russet. The requirements for this grade are the same as for U.S. No. 1 except that a portion of the fruit has more than one-third of its surface, in the aggregate, affected by any type of discoloration.

U.S. No. 2 Bright. The requirements for this grade are the same as in U.S. No. 2 except that no fruit may have more than one-fifth of its surface, in the aggregate, affected by discoloration.

U.S. No. 2. The fruit is mature, fairly firm, reasonably well-colored, and of similar varietal characteristics. Not more than one-half of the surface, in the aggregate, may be affected by discoloration. Common oranges and tangelos may be slightly soft, but not bruised. For Mandarin oranges, the skin is not extremely puffy or extremely loose. For both types, the yellow or orange color predominates over the green color on at least two-thirds of the fruit surface, in the aggregate. The fruit is not more than slightly misshapen. It does not have a characteristic shape, but it is not appreciably elongated, pointed, or otherwise deformed. The fruit is not more than slightly rough textured; the skin does not have a smooth texture, but it is not materially ridged, grooved, or wrinkled.

No. 2 Russet. The requirements of this grade are the same as for U.S. No. 2 except that a portion of the fruit has more than one-half of its surface, in the aggregate, affected by discoloration.

U.S. No. 3. Mature. The fruit is decidedly elongated, pointed, or flatsided. It is poorly colored; however, not more than 25 percent of the surface may be of a solid dark green color. It has a rough texture but is not seriously lumpy. The fruit is slightly spongy; the fruit is puffy or slightly wilted but not flabby.

Unclassified. Oranges or tangelos which have not been classified in accordance with any of the foregoing grades. The term *unclassified* is not a grade within the meaning of these standards but is provided as a designation to show that no grade has been applied to the lot.

GRADES BASED ON JUICE CONTENT

U.S. Grade AA Juice (Double A*)*. Each lot of fruit contains an average of not less than 5 gallons of juice per standard packed box of 1⅗ bushels.

U.S. Grade A Juice. Each lot of fruit contains an average of not less than 4½ gallons of juice per standard packed box of 1⅗ bushels.

Source:
Agricultural Marketing Service, USDA, 7 CFR sections 51.1140 to 51.1179 (1992), Washington: Government Printing Office.

Peaches

Peaches are graded according to a technical system whereby penalty points are assessed for such factors as edibility, poor appearance, or defects in workmanship. The more penalty points assessed the lower the grade. The grade descriptions which follow are intended only as a general consumer guide. For more detailed information, please consult the source cited below.

U.S. Fancy. Peaches of one variety which are mature (have reached the stage of growth which will insure a proper completion of the ripening process) but not soft or overripe, well formed (the shape may be slightly irregular but not unpleasingly so), and which are free from decay, bacterial spot, cuts which are not healed, growth cracks, hail injury, scab, scale, split pits, worms, worm holes, leaf or limb rub iniury (the scarring is not smooth, not light colored, or aggregates more than ¼ inch in diameter); and free from damage caused by bruises, dirt or other foreign material, other disease, insects or mechanical or other means. In addition to the above requirements, each peach shall have not less than one-third of its surface showing blushed pink or red color. (A 10 percent tolerance is allowed for variations [except for color] incident to handling and grading as long as no more than 5 percent are seriously damaged and no more than 2 percent are soft, overripe, or decayed.)

U.S. Extra No. 1. Any lot of peaches may be designated U.S. Extra No. 1 when the peaches meet the requirements of U.S. No. 1 grade, provided that, in addition to the requirements for U.S. No. 1, 50 percent, by count, of the peaches in any lot shall have not less than one-fourth of the surface showing blushed pink or red color.

U.S. No. I. Peaches of one variety which are mature but not soft or overripe, well formed, and which are free from decay, growth cracks, cuts which are not healed, worms, worm holes, and free from damage caused by bruises, dirt, or other foreign material, bacterial spot, scab, scale, hail injury, leaf or limb rubs, split pits, other disease, insects, or mechanical or other means.

U.S. No. 2. Peaches of one variety which are mature but not soft or overripe, are not badly misshapen, and are free from decay, cuts which are not healed, worms, and worm holes. They are also free from serious damage caused by bruises, dirt or other foreign material, bacterial spot, scab, scale, growth cracks, hail injury, leaf or limb rubs, split pits, other disease, insects, or mechanical or other means.

Unclassified. Peaches which have not been classified in accordance with any of the foregoing grades. The term *unclassified* is not a grade within the meaning of these standards but is provided as a designation to show that no definite grade has been applied to the lot.

Source:
Agricultural Marketing Service, USDA, 7 CFR sections 51.1210 to 51.1223 (1992), Washington: Government Printing Office.

Peaches, Dehydrated

Dehydrated, low-moisture peaches, hereinafter referred to as low-moisture peaches, are prepared from clean and sound fresh or previously dried peaches which are cut, chopped, or otherwise prepared into various sizes and shapes; are prepared to assure a clean, sound, wholesome product. Low-moisture peaches are processed by dehydration whereby practically all of the moisture is removed to produce a very dry texture. They are packaged (including kind of container and proper closure) to assure retention of the low-moisture characteristics of the product. The product shall have been subjected to sulfur treatment sufficiently to retain a characteristic color but no other additives may be present.

STYLES

Nugget. Processed to produce popcorn-like or foam-textured units of irregular-shapes that will pass through ⅝ inch square openings.

Pieces. Irregularly shaped cut or chopped pieces that will pass through ⅝ inch square openings.

Diced. Partial cube-shaped units with a square dimension on one surface.

Slices. Parallel-cut strips of irregular shapes and thicknesses.

GRADES

This product is graded according to a technical system whereby penalty points are assessed for such factors as edibility, poor appearance, or defects in workmanship. The more penalty points assessed the lower the grade. The grade descriptions which follow are intended only as a general consumer guide. For more detailed information, please consult the source cited below.

U.S. Grade A or U.S. Fancy. Possess a normal characteristic flavor and odor that is free from objectionable flavors or odors of any kind. A flavor and odor indicative of proper sulfur treatment is not considered objectionable unless it can be detected after cooking. The overall color ranges from deep rich yellow or yellow-orange to deeper orange-amber and, upon cooking, is a reasonably bright typical color. The peaches are reasonably uniform in size and practically free from defects such as damaged units and other defects or injury that affect the appearance or eating quality. The units may vary in texture from partially pliable to brittle but are otherwise reasonably uniform.

U.S. Grade B or U.S. Choice. Possess a normal flavor and odor. The over-all color may vary considerably ranging from slightly dull yellow or slightly dull yellow-orange to darker orange and dark amber and, upon cooking, may be slightly dull but is typical of cooked low-moisture peaches. The peaches are fairly uniform in size and reasonably free from defects. The texture of the units may vary from partially pliable to brittle and may lack uniformity.

Substandard. Fails to meet the requirements of U.S. Grade B or U.S. Choice.

Source:
Agricultural Marketing Service, USDA, 7 CFR sections 52.391 to 52.3922 (1991), Washington: Government Printing Office.

Peaches, Frozen

Frozen peaches are prepared from sound, mature, fresh peaches which are peeled, pitted, washed, cut, and may be trimmed to

assure a clean and wholesome product. The peaches are properly drained of excess water before filling into containers. They may be packed with the addition of a nutritive sweetening ingredient(s), including syrup and/or syrup containing pureed peaches and any other ingredient(s) permissible under the provisions of the Federal Food, Drug, and Cosmetic Act. Peaches are prepared and frozen in accordance with good commercial practice, and are maintained at temperatures necessary for the preservation of the product.

TYPES

Yellow Freestone. Freestone peaches of the yellow-fleshed varieties which may have orange or red pigments emanating from the pit cavity.

White Freestone. Freestone peaches that are predominately white fleshed.

Red Freestone. Freestone peaches that have substantial red coloring in the flesh.

Yellow Clingstone. Clingstone peaches of the yellow or orange fleshed varieties.

STYLES

Halved. Cut approximately in half along the suture from stem to apex.

Quartered. Halved peaches cut into two approximately equal parts.

Sliced. Cut into sectors smaller than quarters.

Diced. Cut into approximate cube-shaped units.

Mixed. Pieces of irregular sizes and shapes. Cut or broken into pieces of irregular sizes and shapes and which do not conform to a single style of halves, quarters, or slices.

GRADES

Peaches are graded according to a technical system whereby penalty points are assessed for such factors as edibility, poor appearance, or defects in workmanship. The more penalty points assessed the lower the grade. The grade descriptions which follow are intended only as a general consumer guide. For more detailed information, please consult the source cited below.

U.S. Grade A or U.S. Fancy. Possess similar varietal characteristics and a normal flavor. Have a good color that is bright, reasonably uniform, and typical of well-ripened peaches, with not more than 10 percent of the thawed peaches possessing a slight tinge of green or slight tinge of brown color due to oxidation, improper processing, or other causes, and none may possess a pronounced green or brown color. The peaches are practically uniform in size and symmetry and practically free from such defects as leaves and stems, pit material, peel, and blemishes. Soft-ripe fruit vary from soft to slightly firm with not more than 10 percent very soft, mushy, firm and rubbery, or tough. Firm-ripe fruit may vary from slightly firm to firm, with not more than 10 percent soft, very soft, and rubbery or tough.

U.S. Grade B or U.S. Choice. Possess similar varietal characteristics and a normal flavor. Have a reasonably good color with not more than a total of 20 percent affected by green or brown color. The peaches are reasonably uniform in size and symmetry and reasonably free from defects. Soft-ripe fruit peaches may vary from soft to slightly firm with not more than 20 percent very soft, mushy, firm, and rubbery or tough. Firm-ripe fruit peaches may vary from slightly firm to firm, with not more than 20 percent mushy, soft, very soft, rubbery or tough, and hard.

U.S. Grade C or U.S. Standard. Possess similar varietal characteristics and a normal flavor. The peaches may possess slight tinges of green or brown color and not more than 15 percent may be materially affected by brown color or may possess a pronounced green color. They are fairly uniform in size and symmetry and fairly free from defects. For soft-ripe fruit not less than 50 percent may vary from very soft to firm and the remainder may be mushy, firm, rubbery or tough, and hard. For firm-ripe fruit not less than 50 percent may vary from slightly firm to firm. The remainder may be mushy, very soft, soft, rubbery or tough, and hard. For mixed soft-ripe and firm-ripe fruit, not less than 50 percent, by weight, of the thawed drained peaches vary from very soft to firm. The remainder may be mushy, tough or rubbery, and hard.

Substandard. Fails to meet the requirements of U.S. Grade C or U.S. Standard.

Source:
Agricultural Marketing Service, USDA, 7 CFR sections 52.3551 to 52.3563 (1991), Washington: Government Printing Office.

Peaches, Fresh Freestone for Canning, Freezing or Pulping

These peaches are graded according to a technical system whereby penalty points are assessed for such factors as edibility, poor appearance, or defects in workmanship. The more penalty points assessed the lower the grade. The grade descriptions which follow are intended only as a general consumer guide. For more detailed information, please consult the source cited below.

U.S. No. 1. Fresh freestone peaches of similar varietal characteristics which are mature, fairly well formed, and firm, firm-ripe, or ripe, but not hard or soft. They are free from decay, worms, worm holes, and split pits, and free from damage caused by scab, bacterial spot, other disease, insects, bruises, or other means. Color shall not be greener than yellowish-green.

U.S. No. 2. Fresh freestone peaches of similar varietal characteristics which are mature, not badly misshapen, which may be firm, firm-ripe, or ripe, but not hard or soft. They are free from decay, worms, worm holes, and from serious damage by split pits, scab, bacterial spot, other disease, insects, bruises, or other means. Color shall not be greener than yellowish-green.

U.S. No. 3. Fresh freestone peaches which meet the requirements of the U.S. No. 2 grade except that there is no requirement for shape, and peaches may be hard.

Culls. Peaches which fail to meet the requirements of U.S. No. 3 grade.

Source:
Agricultural Marketing Service, USDA, 7 CFR sections 51.3695 to 51.3712 (1992), Washington: Government Printing Office.

Pears, Canned

Canned pears are prepared from properly prepared, mature pears. The canned pears are peeled and the term *canned pears* includes canned pears, canned spiced pears, and canned artificially sweetened pears.

STYLES

Halves or Halved. Peeled pears, with cores and stems removed, cut longitudinally from stem to calyx into approximate halves.

Quarters or Quartered. Peeled pears with cores and stems removed, cut longitudinally from stem to calyx into approximate quarters.

Slices or Sliced. Peeled pears, with cores and stems removed cut longitudinally from stem to calyx into approximate equal segments smaller than quarters.

Dice or Diced Canned Pears. Peeled pears, with cores and stems removed, cut into approximate cubes.

Whole Canned Pears. Peeled, cored, or uncored whole pears with or without stems removed.

Pieces or Irregular Pieces. Peeled and cored pears that are irregular in shapes and sizes.

GRADES

Canned pears are graded according to a technical system whereby penalty points are assessed for such factors as edibility, poor appearance, or defects in workmanship. The more penalty points assessed the lower the grade. The grade descriptions which follow are intended only as a general consumer guide. For more detailed information, please consult the source cited below.

U.S. Grade A or U.S. Fancy. Possesses a characteristic, practically uniform color that is a typical light yellow-white or light greenish-white or light beige-white. Any skin pigment on the individual pears may affect no more than slightly the overall color of the product. For halves, quarters, and wholes, each unit is reasonably symmetrical and the weight of the largest full-size unit does not exceed that of the smallest by more than 50 percent. The weight of each half is not less than three-fifths ounce; and the weight of each quarter is not less than three-tenths ounce. For slices, not more than 10 percent, by count, of the units vary noticeably from the uniform shape of slices. Diced units are fairly symmetrical and not more than 10 percent may be of such size as to pass through $5/16$ inch square openings. Overall the product is practically free from harmless extraneous vegetable material, peel, external stems, interior stems, seeds, core material or portions thereof, and from blemished units, improperly, insufficiently, or unevenly trimmed units for the applicable style, and from any other defects which detract from the appearance or edibility of the product. The texture is fleshy and free from noticeable graininess or toughness. The units are tender, uniformly intact, and pliable, but firm enough to possess well-defined edges with no visible breaking down of the flesh.

U.S. Grade B or U.S. Choice. Possesses a normal flavor and odor and a reasonably good color which may show a very slight tint of pink, may be light tan (or beige), may show a lack of uniformity, or may vary in translucency. Halves, quarters, and whole style units may vary in symmetry with the weight of the largest full-size unit not exceeding that of the smallest by more than 75 percent. The weight of each half is not less than three-fifths ounce, and the weight of each quarter is not less than three-tenths ounce. For slices, not more than 15 percent, by count, may vary noticeably from the uniform shape of slices. For diced, not more than 15 percent may be of such size as to pass through ⁵⁄₁₆-inch square openings. The product may possess a texture of moderate graininess and variable tenderness. The units may be slightly firm or slightly ragged with slightly frayed edges or slightly soft but not mushy or, in the case of diced style, disintegrated. Overall, the product is reasonably free from defects.

U.S. Grade C or U.S. Standard. Possesses a normal flavor and odor with a color that may be dead white (or chalky) or may have a slight pink or brown cast (but not a definitely pink or brown color), and is not off-color for any reason. For halves, quarters, and wholes, the units may vary in symmetry but the weight of the largest full-size unit may be not more than twice that of the smallest. The weight of each half is not less than three-fifths ounce, and the weight of each quarter is not less than three-tenths ounce. The shape of sliced and diced units may vary noticeably but not more than 20 percent of diced units may be of such size as to pass through ⁵⁄₁₆ inch square openings. The units may possess a texture of marked graininess, may be lacking uniformity of tenderness, may be markedly firm, markedly ragged with frayed edges, or may be soft. For slices and diced styles, not more than 20 percent, by weight, may be disintegrated or mushy. Are fairly free from defects.

Substandard. Pears that fail to meet the applicable requirements of U.S. Grade C or U.S. Standard.

Source:
Agricultural Marketing Service, USDA, 7 CFR sections 52.1611 to 52.1624 (1991), Washington: Government Printing Office.

Pears, Dried

Dried pears are the halved fruit of the pear tree (*Pyrus communis*) (which may or may not be cored) from which the external stems and calyx cups have been removed, and from which the greater portion of the moisture has been removed. Before packing, the dried fruit is processed to cleanse the fruit and may be sulfured sufficiently to retain a characteristic color. *Slabs* are pears that have been mashed or mutilated to the extent that they have lost their normal shape. A half that has a slightly torn edge is not considered a slab.

SIZES

No. 1 (Jumbo). 1⅞ inches or more in width.
No. 2 (Extra Large). 1¾ to 1⅞ inches.
No. 3 (Large). 1½ to 1¾ inches.
No. 4 (Medium). 1⅜ to 1½ inches.
No. 5 (Small). 1⅛ to 1⅜ inches.
No. 6 (Extra Small). Less than 1⅛ inches in width.

GRADES

Dried pears are graded according to a technical system whereby penalty points are assessed for such factors as edibility, poor appearance, or defects in workmanship. The more penalty points assessed the lower the grade. The grade descriptions which follow are intended only as a general consumer guide. For more detailed information, please consult the source cited below.

Grade A or U.S. Fancy. Possesses similar varietal characteristics and a practically uniform, bright, and translucent color characteristic of ripe pears but that is not darker than pear yellow. The pears have been cut lengthwise in half and the halves are practically whole and symmetrical. Not more than 10 percent may be slabs, immature, or scraps; may be affected by russet or similar discoloration; may be damaged by discoloration, sunburn, hailmarks, limb-rubs, hard end, black end, external stems and calyx cups, scab, disease, insect injury, or other similar defects; or may be affected by mold, decay, insect infestation (no live insects are permitted), imbedded dirt, or other foreign material.

U.S. Grade B or U.S. Choice. Possesses similar varietal characteristics and a reasonably uniform, bright, and translucent color that is not darker than pear yellow. The color is characteristic of pears that are firm and but may not have reached the fully ripe stage. The pears have been cut lengthwise in half and the halves may tend to be oval in shape but not so irregular as to be misshapen. Not more than 15 percent may be slabs or otherwise defective.

U.S. Grade C or U.S. Standard. Possesses similar varietal characteristics. The halves are fairly bright and fairly translucent and are of any normal color not darker than dark amber. The pears are fairly well-matured which means they may be hard but not immature. Not more than 20 percent may be slabs or otherwise defective.

U.S. Grade D or Substandard. Wholesome and edible fruit that fails to meet the requirements of U.S. Grade C or U.S. Standard, provided that not more than 5 percent by weight of the total fruit may be affected by mold, decay, insect infestation (no live insects are permitted), imbedded dirt, or other foreign material.

Source:
Agricultural Marketing Service, USDA, 7 CFR sections 52.5841 to 52.5849 (1991), Washington: Government Printing Office.

Pears, Winter

These standards apply to varieties such as Anjou, Bosc, Winter Nelis, Comice, Flemish Beauty, and other similar varieties. To allow for variations in quality caused by grading and handling, as many as 10 percent of the pears may fail to meet all of the requirements of the grade.

GRADES

Winter pears are graded according to a technical system whereby penalty points are assessed for such factors as edibility, poor appearance, or defects in workmanship. The more penalty points assessed the lower the grade. The grade descriptions which follow are intended only as a general consumer guide. For more detailed information, please consult the source cited below.

U.S. Extra No. 1. Pears of one variety which are mature, but not overripe. They are carefully handpicked and do not show evidence of rough handling or of having been on the ground. They are clean (free from excessive dirt, dust, spray residue or other foreign material), well formed (any slight irregularities of shape do not appreciably detract from the general appearance), free from decay, internal breakdown, scald, freezing injury, worm holes, black end (an abnormally deep green color around the calyx, or black spots usually occurring on the one-third of the surface nearest to the calyx, or by an abnormally shallow calyx cavity), hard end, and drought spot. They are free from injury caused by russeting, limbrubs, hail, scars, cork spot, sunburn, sprayburn, stings or other insect injury, or injury by mechanical or other means. They are also free from damage caused by bruises, broken skins, or disease.

U.S. No. 1. Pears of one variety which are mature (but not over-ripe), carefully handpicked, clean, fairly well formed (may be slightly abnormal in shape but not to an extent which detracts materially from the appearance of the fruit), free from decay, internal breakdown, scald, freezing injury, worm holes, black end, and from damage caused by hard end, bruises, broken skins, russeting, limbrubs, hail, scars, cork spot, drought spot, sunburn, sprayburn, stings or other insect injury, disease, or injury by mechanical or other means.

U.S. Combination. A combination of U.S. No. 1 and U.S. No. 2 may be packed. When such a combination is packed, at least 50 percent of the pears in any container meet the requirements of U.S. No. 1.

U.S. No. 2. Pears of one variety which are mature, but not overripe, carefully handpicked, clean, not seriously misshapen, free from decay, internal breakdown, scald, freezing injury, worm holes, black end, and from damage caused by hard end or broken skins. The pears are also free from serious damage caused by bruises, russeting, limbrubs, hail, scars, cork spot, drought spot, sunburn, sprayburn, stings or other insect injury, disease, or injury by mechanical or other means.

Unclassified. Pears which have not been classified in accordance with any of the foregoing grades. The term *unclassified* is not a grade, but is provided as a designation to show that no grade has been applied to the lot.

Source:
Agricultural Marketing Service, USDA, 7 CFR sections 51.1300 to 51.1323 (1992), Washington: Government Printing Office.

Pears, Summer and Fall

These standards apply to varieties such as Bartlett, Hardy and other similar varieties. A small percentage (not more than 10 percent) of the pears in a lot may vary somewhat from the quality standards of a grade.

GRADES

Summer and fall pears are graded according to a technical system whereby penalty points are assessed for such factors as edibility, poor appearance, or defects in workmanship. The more penalty points assessed the lower the grade. The grade descriptions which follow are intended only as a general consumer guide. For more detailed information, please consult the source cited below.

U.S. No. 1. Pears of one variety which are mature, but not over-ripe (that is, are not dead ripe, very mealy or soft, or past commercial utility), carefully handpicked (do not show evidence of rough handling or of having been on the ground), clean (free from excessive dirt, dust, spray residue or other foreign material), fairly well formed (may be slightly abnormal in shape but not unpleasingly so), free from decay, internal breakdown, scald, freezing injury, worm holes, black end (an abnormally deep green color around the calyx, or black spots usually occurring on the one-third of the surface nearest to the calyx), and from damage caused by hard end, bruises, broken skins, russeting, limbrubs, hail, scars, drought spot, sunburn, sprayburn, stings or other insect injury, disease, or injury by mechanical or other means.

U.S. Combination. A combination of U.S. No. 1 and U.S. No. 2 may be packed. When such a combination is packed, at least 50 percent of the pears in any container meet the requirements of U.S. No. 1.

U.S. No. 2. Pears of one variety which are mature, but not over-ripe, carefully handpicked, clean, not seriously misshapen (excessively flattened or elongated), are free from decay, internal breakdown, scald, freezing injury, worm holes, black end, and from damage caused by hard end or broken skins. The pears are also free from serious damage caused by bruises, russeting, limbrubs, hail, scars, drought spot, sunburn, sprayburn, stings or other insect injury, disease, or injury by mechanical or other means.

Unclassified. Pears which have not been classified in accordance with any of the foregoing grades. The term *unclassified* is not a grade within the meaning of these standards, but is provided as a designation to show that no grade has been applied to the lot.

Source:
Agricultural Marketing Service, USDA, 7 CFR sections 51.1260 to 51.1280 (1992), Washington: Government Printing Office.

Pears for Canning

Pears for canning are graded according to a technical system whereby penalty points are assessed for such factors as edibility, poor appearance, or defects in workmanship. The more penalty points assessed the lower the grade. The grade descriptions which follow are intended only as a general consumer guide. For more detailed information, please consult the source cited below.

U.S. No. 1. Pears of one variety which are mature, handpicked (do not show evidence of having been on the ground), firm (the pear is fairly solid and yields only very slightly to moderate pressure, and is not wilted, shriveled, rubbery or flabby), well formed, free from scald, hard end, black end, internal breakdown, decay, worms, and worm holes. They are also free from damage caused by broken skins, limbrubs, sprayburn, sunburn, scab, russeting, bruises, hail, frost, drought spot, disease, insects, and from injury by mechanical or other means. Unless otherwise specified, the pears shall not be further advanced in ripening than yellowish green color. Tree-ripened pears and pears grown from late blooms shall not be considered as meeting the requirements of this grade.

U.S. No. 2. Pears of one variety which are mature, handpicked, firm, not seriously deformed, free from scald, hard end, black end, internal breakdown, decay, worms, and worm holes, and free from serious damage by any other cause. Unless otherwise specified, the pears shall not be further advanced in ripening than yellowish green color. Tree-ripened pears and pears grown from late blooms shall not be considered as meeting the requirements of this grade.

Culls. Pears which do not meet the requirements of either of the foregoing grades.

Source:
Agricultural Marketing Service, USDA, 7 CFR sections 51.1345 to 51.1359 (1992), Washington: Government Printing Office.

Pineapples

These standards are applicable to fresh pineapples with or without tops, provided that pineapples with tops attached or with tops removed may not be commingled in the same container.

GRADES

Pineapples are graded according to a technical system whereby penalty points are assessed for such factors as edibility, poor appearance, or defects in workmanship. The more penalty points assessed the lower the grade. The grade descriptions which follow are intended only as a general consumer guide. For more detailed information, please consult the source cited below.

U.S. Fancy. Have similar varietal characteristics, and are mature, well formed, and have the stems removed. The tops have similar varietal characteristic color, a single stem, are moderately straight, and are well-attached to fruit, and are not more than 1½ times the length of the fruit. The fruit is free from

fresh cracks, evidence of rodent feeding, freezing injury, and decay. The tops are free from crown slips, freezing injury, and decay. The fruit is free from injury by bruising, sunburn, gummosis, internal breakdown, insects, healed cracks, and from injury by mechanical or other means. The tops are free from injury by discoloration and insects.

U.S. No. 1. This grade is similar to U.S. Fancy except that the tops are not more than moderately curved and not more than twice the length of the fruit. Also the tops may not necessarily be free from crown slips.

U.S. No. 2. The pineapples meeting this grade need only be fairly well formed (i.e., the fruit is not excessively lopsided, or excessively flattened at the shoulders or sides). It may have more than one fairly well-developed stem and otherwise lacks the features of U.S. No. 1.

Source:
Agricultural Marketing Service, USDA, 7 CFR sections 51.1485 to 51.1510 (1992), Washington: Government Printing Office.

Pineapple, Canned

Guidelines for labeling and grading canned pineapple are as follows:

STYLES

Whole. Whole fruit peeled and cored into reasonably symmetrical pineapple cylinders with both ends cut perpendicular to the cylinder axis.

Slices. Uniformly cut circular slices or rings cut across the axis of the peeled, cored pineapple cylinders.

Half Slices. Uniformly cut, approximately semicircular halves of slices.

Broken Slices. Arc-shaped portions which are not required to be uniform in size and/or shape.

Spears. Predominantly 65 mm (2.5 inch) or longer, slender sectors cut radially and lengthwise from peeled cored pineapple cylinders.

Tidbits. Predominantly 8 to 13 mm (0.31 to 0.51 inch), reasonably uniform wedge-shaped sectors cut from slices or portions thereof.

Chunks. Short, thick units cut from slices and/or from peeled, cored pineapple which are predominantly more than 13 mm (0.51 inch) in both thickness and width, and less than 38 mm (1.5 inch) in length.

Cubes. Reasonably uniform, cube-shaped units, predominantly 14 mm (0.55 inch) or less in the longest edge dimension.

Crushed. Finely cut, finely shredded or grated, or small diced pieces of canned pineapple.

GRADES

Canned pineapple is graded according to a technical system whereby penalty points are assessed for such factors as edibility, poor appearance, or defects in workmanship. The more penalty points assessed the lower the grade. The grade descriptions which follow are intended only as a general consumer guide. For more detailed information, please consult the source cited below.

U.S. Grade A. The units are of practically uniform ripeness, are reasonably firm with fruitlets appearing as a compact structure, and are reasonably free from porosity. There is not more than 11 g (0.4 ounce) of core material contained in one pound of drained fruit. The color of the canned pineapple units or mass is bright and is characteristic of properly ripened and properly processed pineapple of similar varieties. There may be slight variations in shades of such characteristic color in the units, within each unit or within the mass, and white radiating streaks may be present, provided that such variations do not materially affect the appearance or edibility of the product.

U.S. Grade B. The units are of reasonably uniform ripeness, the fruitlets are reasonably compact in structure, are fairly free from porosity, and there is not more than 31 g (1.1 ounce) of core material contained in one pound of drained fruit. The color of the canned pineapple units or mass may be no more than slightly dull but is characteristic of properly ripened and properly processed pineapple of similar varieties. There may be marked variations in shades of the pineapple units.

U.S. Grade C. The units are of fairly uniform ripeness, the fruitlets are fairly compact in structure, the units are fairly free from porosity, and there is not more than 31 g (1.1 ounce) of core material contained in one pound of drained fruit. The color of the canned pineapple units or mass may be dull, but is characteristic of properly ripened and properly processed pineapple of similar varieties. There may be marked variations in shades of such characteristic color in the units, within each unit, or within the mass, and white radiating streaks may be present which may seriously affect the appearance or edibility of the product.

Substandard. Fails to meet the requirements for U.S. Grade B or U.S. Grade C.

PACKING MEDIA DESIGNATIONS

Extra Heavy Syrup. Extra heavily sweetened pineapple juice and water, or extra heavily sweetened pineapple juice.

Heavy Syrup. Heavily sweetened pineapple juice and water, or heavily sweetened pineapple juice.

Light Syrup. Lightly sweetened pineapple juice and water, or lightly sweetened pineapple juice.

Slightly Sweetened Water. Extra light syrup, slightly sweetened pineapple juice and water, or slightly sweetened pineapple juice.

In Water (except Crushed Style)

In Pineapple Juice

In Pineapple Juice and Water

In Clarified Pineapple Juice

Artificially Sweetened

Source:
Agricultural Marketing Service, USDA, 7 CFR sections 52.1711 to 52.1723 (1991), Washington: Government Printing Office.

Pineapple, Frozen

Frozen pineapple is prepared from the properly ripened fruit of the pineapple plant (*Ananas sativus* or *Ananas comosus*) which is peeled, cored, trimmed, and washed. It may be packed with or without packing media, and is frozen and stored at temperatures necessary for the preservation of the product.

STYLES

Whole Slices. Whole, practically unbroken slices of pineapple that have been cut, at a right angle to the longitudinal axis, into approximately equal units.

Half Slices. Portions of whole slices of pineapple that are so matched in size and thickness that two portions are approximately equivalent to a slice.

Broken Slices. Portions of slices of pineapple, if such portions are approximately of the same thickness and diameter.

Crushed. Frozen crushed pineapple is pineapple that has been cut, shredded, or crushed into fine pieces.

Tidbits. Small, wedge-shaped sections.

Chunks. Pieces of pineapple which do not conform to any of the foregoing styles, which need not be symmetrical nor uniform in size, and which do not exceed 1½ inches in any dimension.

GRADES

Frozen pineapple is graded according to a technical system whereby penalty points are assessed for such factors as edibility, poor appearance, or defects in workmanship. The more penalty points assessed the lower the grade. The grade descriptions which follow are intended only as a general consumer guide. For more detailed information, please consult the source cited below.

U.S. Grade A or U.S. Fancy. Whole slices, crushed, tidbits, or chunks that possess a practically uniform, bright, characteristic yellow color in the applicable style. Fruit is practically uniform in size and symmetry, practically free from defects, and possesses a good character. (In relation to whole slices, tidbits, and crushed pineapple, good character means practically uniform ripeness and not more than 2.5 percent by weight of core material of fibrous stock. In the case of whole slices and tidbits, the fruit is reasonably firm and the fruitlets appear as a compact structure, reasonably free from porosity. For chunks of this grade, normally more of the fibrous portions around the core hole have been removed than is the case with other styles. The fruit is reasonably firm and the fruitlets appear as a compact structure, reasonably free from porosity, and they possess a normal flavor and odor.)

U.S. Grade B or U.S. Choice. Whole slices, crushed, tidbits, or chunks that possess a reasonably uniform, good, characteristic yellow color, are reasonably uniform in size and symmetry, and are reasonably free from defects. Possess a reasonably uniform, reasonably good character, and a normal flavor and odor. (Reasonably uniform, good, characteristic yellow color means that the frozen pineapple may have considerable variation of such color in the mass or of the units. Reasonably good character has the following meanings: With respect to whole slices, tidbits, and crushed, the fruit is of reasonably uniform ripeness, and there may be present not more than 5 percent, by weight of the pineapple, that is core material or fibrous stock. In the case of whole slices and tidbits, the fruitlets are reasonably compact in structure and fairly free from porosity. With respect to chunk style, the fruit is of reasonably uniform ripeness and normally has had more of the fibrous portions around the core hole removed than is the case with other styles of pack. The fruitlets are reasonably compact in structure and fairly free from porosity.)

U.S. Grade C or U.S. Standard. Half slices and broken slices that are fairly uniform in size and symmetry, possess a fairly uniform, fairly good, characteristic yellow color or better, and are fairly free from defects. They possess a fairly good character and a normal flavor and odor. (Fairly uniform, fairly good characteristic yellow color means that the individual units of the frozen pineapple may vary markedly from a uniform, typical yellow color and may be slightly dull in color. Fairly good character has the following meaning with respect to half slices and broken slices: the texture may be variable; there may be present not more than 5 percent, by weight of the pineapple, core material of fibrous stock; and the fruitlets may be flaccid and loosely constructed.)

U.S. Grade D or Substandard. Whole slices, crushed, tidbits, or chunks that fail to meet the requirements of U.S. Grade B or U.S. Choice. Also half slices or broken slices that fail to meet the requirements of U.S. Grade C or U.S. Standard.

Source:
Agricultural Marketing Service, USDA, 7 CFR section 52.1741 (1991), Washington: Government Printing Office.

Pineapple Juice

This entry covers pineapple juice and pineapple juice from concentrate.

GRADES

Pineapple juice is graded according to a technical system whereby penalty points are assessed for such factors as edibility, poor appearance, or defects in workmanship. The more penalty points assessed the lower the grade. The grade descriptions which follow are intended only as a general consumer guide. For more detailed information, please consult the source cited below.

U.S. Grade A. Possesses a bright typical varietal color ranging from light yellowish beige to a golden amber or golden pinkish cast typical of freshly pressed and properly processed juice from mature, well-ripened pineapple. Possesses a distinct varietal flavor that is typical of freshly extracted pineapple juice or typical of reconstituted juice (pineapple juice from concentrate). Practically free from defects such as excess pulp, dark specks, pieces of shell, seeds, or other coarse or hard substances that are objectionable, or particles that might affect the appearance or palatability of the juice.

U.S. Grade B. Possesses a color which may be slightly dull (but not

off-color), yet normal for freshly pressed juice. Possesses a flavor that may be slightly caramelized but is not off-flavor. Any defects present do not more than materially affect the appearance or palatability of the juice. Reasonably free from defects.

Substandard. Fails to meet the requirements for U.S. Grade B.

Source:
Agricultural Marketing Service, USDA, 7 CFR sections 52.1761 52.1769 (1991), Washington: Government Printing Office.

Plums, Frozen

Frozen plums are prepared from clean, sound, fresh fruit of any commercial variety of plums (exclusive of Damson) which are sorted, washed, drained, and pitted. They may be packed with or without the addition of a nutritive sweetening ingredient, and are frozen in accordance with good commercial practice and maintained at temperatures necessary for the preservation of the product.

COLOR TYPE

Purple or Blue. Such as Italian prune plum variety.

Red. Such as Satsuma or Santa Rosa varieties.

Yellow-Green. Such as Yellow Egg, Jefferson, and Reine Claude varieties.

STYLES

Halved. Cut longitudinally into approximate halves.

Whole Pitted. Not excessively crushed or broken in removing the pits.

Crushed and Broken. Most of the plums are crushed or broken in removing the pits.

GRADES

These plums are graded according to a technical system whereby penalty points are assessed for such factors as edibility, poor appearance, or defects in workmanship. The more penalty points assessed the lower the grade. The grade descriptions which follow are intended only as a general consumer guide. For more detailed information, please consult the source cited below.

U.S. Grade A or U.S. Fancy. Possesses similar varietal characteristics and a normal flavor. Internally and externally, possesses a practically uniform, bright, typical color practically free from any brown color due to oxidation, improper processing, or other causes. Practically uniform in size and free from defects such as leaf, stem, or crushed or broken units. The units possess a tender, fleshy texture, typical of well-ripened, properly processed frozen plums.

U.S. Grade B or U.S. Choice. Possesses similar varietal characteristics and a normal flavor. Internally and externally, possesses a reasonably uniform, bright, typical color reasonably free from any brown color. Reasonably uniform in size and reasonably free from defects. The texture is reasonably fleshy and the units are reasonably tender, or the tenderness may be variable from slightly soft to slightly firm.

Substandard. Fail to meet the requirements of U.S. Grade B or U.S. Choice.

Source:
Agricultural Marketing Service, USDA, 7 CFR sections 52.2911 to 52.2921 (1991), Washington: Government Printing Office.

Plums, Canned

This entry describes labeling and grading guidelines for canned plums.

TYPES

Purple Plum Groups
Green-Yellow Plum Groups

STYLES

Whole, Unpeeled, Unpitted
Whole, Peeled, Unpitted
Whole, Unpeeled, Pitted
Whole, Peeled, Pitted
Halves, Unpeeled, Pitted
Halves, Peeled, Pitted

GRADES

Canned pears are graded according to a technical system whereby penalty points are assessed for such factors as edibility, poor appearance, or defects in workmanship. The more penalty points assessed the lower the grade. The grade descriptions which follow are intended only as a general consumer guide. For more detailed information, please consult the source cited below.

U.S. Grade A or U.S. Fancy. Have similar varietal characteristics, normal flavor and odor, a good, practically uniform color, are at least reasonably uniform in size, and practically free from defects such as stems, leaves, crushed or broken units, and pits or loose pits. For the applicable style, practically free from blemished and seriously blemished units and from any other defects not specifically mentioned which detract from the appearance or edibility. The units are thick-fleshed and tender, may be soft but hold their apparent original conformation, and otherwise possess a good texture of both skin and flesh characteristic of canned plums processed from well-ripened plums.

U.S. Grade B or U.S. Choice. Have similar varietal characteristics, normal flavor and odor, a reasonably good and reasonably uniform color, and are at least fairly uniform in size and reasonably free from defects. The units may be reasonably fleshy. They may vary in texture from soft to slightly firm, and otherwise possess a reasonably good texture of both skin and flesh.

U.S. Grade C or U.S. Standard. Have similar varietal characteristics, normal flavor and odor, a fairly good color, are fairly uniform in size, and are fairly free from defects. The units may be thin-fleshed, may possess a fairly good texture of both skin and flesh, may vary in texture from very soft to slightly tough, but are not so soft as to show material disintegration. They may possess shriveled areas that materially affect, but do not seriously affect, the appearance of the product.

Substandard. Canned plums that fail to meet the requirements of U.S. Grade C or U.S. Standard.

Source:
Agricultural Marketing Service, USDA, 7 CFR sections 52.1781 to 52.1811 (1991), Washington: Government Printing Office.

Plums and Prunes, Fresh

Plums and prunes are graded according to a technical system whereby penalty points are assessed for such factors as edibility, poor appearance, or defects in workmanship. The more penalty points assessed the lower the grade. The grade descriptions which follow are intended only as a general consumer guide. For more detailed information, please consult the source cited below.

U.S. Fancy. Plums or prunes of one variety which are well formed, clean, mature but not overripe, soft, or shriveled. They are free from decay, sunscald (injury caused by the sun in which softening or collapse of the flesh is apparent), heat injury, sunburn, split pits, and hail marks, and free from damage caused by broken skins, growth cracks, drought spots, gum spots, russeting, scars, other disease, insects, or injury by mechanical or other means. Italian type prunes shall be well colored (95 percent of the surface of the prune is purple) and, unless otherwise specified, shall be not less than 1¼ inches in diameter.

U.S. No. 1. Plums or prunes of one variety which are well formed, clean, mature but not overripe, soft, or shriveled. They are free from decay and sunscald, and free from damage caused by broken skins, heat injury, growth cracks, sunburn, split pits, hail marks, drought spots, gum spots, russeting, scars, other disease, insects, or injury by mechanical or other means. Italian type prunes shall be fairly well colored (at least ¾ of the surface of the prune is purple) and, unless otherwise specified, shall be not less than 1¼ inches in diameter.

U.S. Combination. A combination of U.S. No. 1 and U.S. No. 2 plums or prunes, provided that at least 75 percent, by count, meet the requirements of U.S. No. 1 grade.

U.S. No. 2. Plums or prunes of one variety which are not badly misshapen, which are clean, mature (but not overripe, soft, or shriveled), and which are free from decay and sunscald, and free from serious damage caused by broken skins, heat injury, growth cracks, sunburn, split pits, hail marks, drought spots, gum spots, russeting, scars, other disease, insects, or injury by mechanical or other means.

Unclassified. Plums or prunes which have not been classified in accordance with any of the foregoing grades. The term *unclassified* is not a grade within the meaning of these standards but is provided as a designation to show that no grade has been applied to the lot.

Source:
Agricultural Marketing Service, USDA, 7 CFR sections 51.1520 to 51.1537 (1992), Washington: Government Printing Office.

Prunes, Dried and Canned

Labeling and grading guidelines for canned dried prunes are included in this entry. Canned dried prunes are available either pitted or unpitted.

TYPES

Sweet. Include such varieties as French, Imperials, Sugar, and *Robe de Sergent.*

Tart. Includes the Italian variety.

GRADES

Canned dried prunes are graded according to a technical system whereby penalty points are assessed for such factors as edibility, poor appearance, or defects in workmanship. The more penalty points assessed the lower the grade. The grade descriptions which follow are intended only as a general consumer guide. For more detailed information, please consult the source cited below.

U.S. Grade A or U.S. Fancy. The color of the skins of the prunes may be black, blue-black, or reddish brown. However, not more than 5 percent may possess a dull chocolate brown surface color or abnormal darkening of the flesh due to caramelization or fermentation. The prunes are practically uniform in size and practically free from such defects as growth cracks, splits, breaks in the skin, or skin damage. The prunes are thick-fleshed and not more than 5 percent by count of prunes have fibrous or tough skins, and not more than 10 percent may be soft or hard in texture.

U.S. Grade B or U.S. Choice. The color of the skins of the prunes may be black, blue-black, or reddish brown. However, not more than 10 percent may possess a dull chocolate brown surface color or abnormal darkening of the flesh due to caramelization or fermentation. The prunes are reasonably free from defects, possess a reasonably good, tender, fleshy texture, and not more than 10 percent may have fibrous or tough skins and not more than 15 percent may be soft or hard in texture.

U.S. Grade C or U.S. Standard. The color of the skins of the prunes may vary in shades of typical colors. Not more than 15 percent by count of the prunes may possess a dull chocolate brown surface color or may possess abnormal darkening of the flesh due to caramelization or fermentation. The prunes are fairly free from defects. The prunes may vary in thickness and texture of flesh, or may possess fibrous or tough skins, but not more than 20 percent may be soft or hard in texture. The prunes possess a normal flavor.

U.S. Grade D or Substandard. Dried prunes that are wholesome and edible but fail to meet the requirements of U.S. Grade C or U.S. Standard.

Source:
Agricultural Marketing Service, USDA, 7 CFR sections 52.5601 to 52.5616 (1991), Washington: Government Printing Office.

Prunes, Dehydrated, Low-moisture

Dehydrated, low-moisture prunes, hereinafter referred to as low-moisture prunes, are prepared from clean and sound fresh prune-plums or clean and sound previously dried prunes. They are pitted and otherwise prepared into various sizes and shapes. The prunes are prepared to assure a clean, sound, wholesome product, and are processed by dehydration whereby practically all of the moisture is removed to produce a very dry texture. They are packaged (including kind of container and proper closure) to assure retention of the low-moisture characteristics of the product.

MOISTURE CONTENT OF LOW-MOISTURE PRUNES

Nugget-Type. 2.5 percent moisture.

Pieces. 2.5 percent moisture.

Whole Pitted. 4.0 percent moisture.

STYLES

Nugget. Processed to produce foam-textured units of irregular shapes of such size that practically all of the units will pass through 0.625 inch (⅝ inch) square openings.

Pieces. Irregularly shaped cut or chopped pieces of such size that practically all of the units will pass through 0.625 inch (⅝ inch) square openings.

Whole Pitted. Substantially whole units except for mechanical marking or damage from pitting.

GRADES

This product is graded according to a technical system whereby penalty points are assessed for such factors as edibility, poor appearance, or defects in workmanship. The more penalty points assessed the lower the grade. The grade descriptions which follow are intended only as a general consumer guide. For more detailed information, please consult the source cited below.

U.S. Grade A or U.S. Fancy. Possesses a normal flavor and odor. The color of nugget-type prunes may range from characteristic light chocolate brown to darker brown but the overall color impression is reasonably uniform. Pieces or whole pitted prunes may vary from characteristic blue-black typical of the exterior skin color, and chocolate brown to darker brown typical of the interior color. The prunes are reasonably uniform in size and practically free from defects. They possess a good texture varying from partially pliable to brittle and, after cooking:

Nugget-Type. The cooked mass has a reasonably uniform

texture and finish that is coarse or grainy with practically no hard particles.

Pieces. The cooked product is practically free from hard, firm, or tough units and there is no more than moderate disintegration except for small pieces that may have been present.

Whole Pitted. The cooked product is practically free from hard or tough units and substantially retains the semblance of whole pitted prunes except for small pieces that may have been present.

U.S. Grade B or U.S. Choice. Possesses a normal flavor and odor. The color of nugget-type prunes may vary noticeably in shades of brown color. In the style of pieces or whole pitted prunes the units may possess a variable dull blue-black to very dark brown color that are fairly uniform in size and count for the applicable style. The prunes are reasonably free from defects and possess reasonably good texture, varying in texture from partially pliable to brittle. They may lack uniformity of texture and, after cooking:

Nugget-Type. The cooked mass has a fairly uniform texture and finish that may range from fine and grainy to coarse and grainy. Hard particles may be noticeable but not objectionable.

Pieces. The cooked product is fairly free from hard, firm, or tough units and may disintegrate generally into a coarse, sauce-like consistency.

Whole Pitted. The cooked product is fairly free from hard or tough units and may consist of ragged or broken larger pieces and whole pitted units intermingled with slight amount of mushiness from small pieces which may have been present.

Substandard. Fails to meet the requirements of U.S. Grade B or U.S. Choice.

Source:
Agricultural Marketing Service, USDA, 7 CFR sections 52.3231 to 52.3243 (1991), Washington: Government Printing Office.

Prunes, Dried

Dried prunes are prepared from sound, properly matured prune plums from which the greater portion of moisture is removed by drying. The dried prunes are cleaned to assure a wholesome product. They may be treated with water or steam, and a safe and suitable preservative may be added.

TYPES

Type I. French or Robe, or a mixture of French and Robe.
Type II. Italian.
Type III. Imperial or Sugar, or a mixture of Imperial and Sugar.
Type IV. Any other types, or mixtures of any types other than mixtures in Type I and Type III.

STYLES

Whole Unpitted. Pits have not been removed.

Whole Pitted. Pits have been removed.
Extra Large. Average not more than 43 prunes per pound.
Large. Average not more than 53 prunes per pound.
Medium. Average not more than 67 prunes per pound.
Small. Average not more than 85 prunes per pound.

GRADES

Dried prunes are graded according to a technical system whereby penalty points are assessed for such factors as edibility, poor appearance, or defects in workmanship. The more penalty points assessed the lower the grade. The grade descriptions which follow are intended only as a general consumer guide. For more detailed information, please consult the source cited below.

U.S. Grade A or U.S. Fancy. Except for mixed types, possess similar varietal characteristics, are fairly uniform in size and average 85 prunes or less per pound, are reasonably uniform in moisture, and not more than a total of 10 percent may be damaged or affected by such defects as off-color, poor texture, end cracks, skin damage, fermentation, scars, mold, dirt foreign material, insect infestation, or decay.

U.S. Grade B or U.S. Choice. Not more than a total of 15 percent may be damaged or affected by defects.

U.S. Grade C or U.S. Standard. Not more than a total of 20 percent may be damaged or affected by defects.

Substandard. Fails to meet requirements for U.S. Grade C or U.S. Standard.

Source:
Agricultural Marketing Service, USDA, 7 CFR sections 52.3181 to 52.3188 (1991), Washington: Government Printing Office.

Raisins, Processed

Processed raisins are dried grapes of the *Vinifera* varieties, such as Thompson Seedless (Sultanina), Muscat of Alexandria, Muscatel Gordo Blanco, Sultana, Black Corinth, or White Corinth. The processed raisins are prepared from clean, sound, dried grapes. They are properly stemmed and capstemmed—except for cluster or uncapstemmed raisins. They are properly seeded in seeded styles and are sorted, cleaned, or both. Except for cluster or uncapstemmed raisins, they are washed in water to assure a wholesome product. Raisins that have not been detached from the main bunch are referred to as *Layer (or Cluster) Raisins.*

TYPE I—SEEDLESS RAISINS

SIZE

Select Size. No more than 60 percent, by weight, of all the raisins will pass through round perforations $\frac{22}{64}$ inch in diameter, but not more than 10 percent, by weight, of all the raisins may pass through round perforations $\frac{20}{64}$ inch in diameter.

Small or Midget Size. 95 percent, by weight, of all the raisins will pass through round perforations $\frac{24}{64}$ inch in diameter, and not less than 70 percent, by weight, of all raisins will pass through round perforations $\frac{22}{64}$ inch in diameter.

GRADES

U.S. Grade A. The raisins have similar varietal characteristics and a good typical color. They have a good characteristic flavor and show development characteristics of raisins prepared from well-matured grapes. Not less than 80 percent of the raisins are well matured or reasonably well matured. They contain not more than 18 percent moisture for all varieties of seedless raisins—except the Monukka variety, which may contain not more than 19 percent moisture.

U.S. Grade B. The quality of seedless raisins that have similar varietal characteristics. They have a reasonably good typical color and a good characteristic flavor. They show development characteristics of raisins prepared from reasonably well-matured grapes with not less than 70 percent of raisins that are well matured or reasonably well matured. Contains not more than 18 percent of moisture for all varieties—except the Monukka variety, which may contain not more than 19 percent.

U.S. Grade C. The quality of seedless raisins that have similar varietal characteristics and a fairly good typical color. They have a fairly goood flavor and show development caracteristics of raisins prepared from fairly well-matured grapes. Not less than 55 percent of raisins that are well matured or reasonably well matured. Contain not more than 18 percent moisture for all varieties of seedless raisins—except the Monukka variety.

TYPE II—GOLDEN SEEDLESS RAISINS

The color ranges from yellow or golden to light amber color with a predominating yellow or golden color and not more than 1.2 of 1 percent of all the raisins are definitely dark berries.

Grades. Except for color, the grades of Golden Seedless Raisins are the same as for Seedless Raisins.

TYPE III—RAISINS WITH SEEDS

Includes natural, dipped, vine-dried, or similarly processed raisins.

SIZES

Raisins with seeds—except layer or cluster:

Seeded Select Size. Not more than 70 percent, by weight, of the raisins will pass through round perforations $\frac{34}{64}$ inch in diameter, and not more than 5 percent, by weight, of the raisins will pass through round perforations $\frac{22}{64}$ inch in diameter.

Seeded Small or Midget Size. All of the raisins will pass through round perforations $\frac{34}{64}$ inch in diameter, and not less than 90 percent, by weight, of all the raisins will pass through round perforations $\frac{22}{64}$ inch in diameter.

Seeded Mixed Size. A mixture which does not meet either the requirements for select size or for small (or midget) size.

Unseeded 4 Crown. The raisins will not pass through round perforations $\frac{42}{64}$ inch in diameter.

Unseeded 3 Crown. The raisins will pass through round

perforations $\frac{42}{64}$ inch in diameter but will not pass through round perforations $\frac{34}{64}$ inch in diameter.

Unseeded 2 Crown. The raisins will pass through round perforations $\frac{34}{64}$ inch in diameter but will not pass through round perforations $\frac{24}{64}$ inch in diameter.

Unseeded 1 Crown. The raisins will pass through round perforations $\frac{24}{64}$ inch in diameter.

Raisins with seeds—layer or cluster:

3 Crown Size or Larger. In layer or cluster raisins with seeds, this means that the raisins, exclusive of stems and branches, are such a size that they will not pass through round perforations $\frac{34}{64}$-inch in diameter.

GRADES

U.S. Grade A. The quality of raisins that have similar varietal characteristics and a good typical color. They have a good characteristic flavor and show development characteristics of raisins prepared from well-matured grapes.

U.S. Grade B. The quality of raisins that have similar varietal characteristics. They have a reasonably good typical color and a good characteristic flavor. They show development characteristics of raisins prepared from reasonably well-matured grapes.

U.S. Grade C. The quality of raisins that have similar varietal characteristics and a fairly good typical color. They have a fairly good flavor and show development characteristics of raisins prepared from fairly well-matured grapes.

Substandard. The quality of raisins that fail to meet the requirements of U.S. Grade C.

TYPE IV—SULTANA RAISINS

GRADES

U.S. Grade A. The quality of Sultana Raisins that have similar varietal characteristics and a good typical color. They have good characteristic flavor and show development characteristics of raisins prepared from well-matured grapes. They have not less than 80 percent raisins that are well matured or reasonably well matured and contain not more than 18 percent moisture.

U.S. Grade B. The quality of Sultana Raislns that have similar varietal characteristics and a reasonably good typical color. They have a good characteristlc flavor and show development characteristics of raisins prepared from reasonably well-matured grapes.

U.S. Grade C. The quality of Sultana Raisins that have similar varietal characteristics and a fairly good typical color. They have a fairly good flavor and show development characteristics of raisins prepared from fairly well-matured grapes. They contain not more than 18 percent, by weight, of moisture.

Substandard. The quality of Sultana Raisins that fail to meet the requirements of U.S. Grade C.

TYPE V—ZANTE CURRANT RAISINS

Includes unseeded and seeded.

GRADES

U.S. Grade A. The quality of Zante Currant Raisins that have similar varietal characteristics, a good typical color, and a good characteristic flavor. They show development characteristics of raisins prepared from well-matured grapes. Not less than 75 percent the of raisins are well matured or reasonably well matured. They contain not more than 20 percent of moisture.

U.S. Grade B. The quality of Zante Currant Raisins that have similar varietal characteristics and a reasonably good typical color. They have a good characteristic flavor and have development characteristics of raisins prepared from reasonably well-matured and/or fairly well-matured grapes. Contains not more than 20 percent of moisture.

Substandard. The quality of Zante Currant Raisins that fail to meet the requirements of U.S. Grade B.

TYPE VI—MIXED TYPES OR VARIETIES

A mixture of two or more different types (varieties) of raisins including sub-types other than: (1) mixtures containing layer or cluster raisins with seeds; (2) mixtures containing unseeded-capstemmed and unseeded-uncapstemmed raisins with seeds; and (3) mixture of seeded and unseeded raisins with seeds.

Source:
Agricultural Marketing Service, USDA, 7 CFR sections 52.1841 to 52.1858 (1991), Washington: Government Printing Office.

Raspberries

Raspberries are graded according to a technical system whereby penalty points are assessed for such factors as edibility, poor appearance, or defects in workmanship. The more penalty points assessed the lower the grade. The grade descriptions which follow are intended only as a general consumer guide. For more detailed information, please consult the source cited below.

U.S. No. 1. Raspberries of one variety which are well colored (the whole surface of the berry shows a color characteristic of a mature berry); are well developed (not misshapen), not soft, overripe, or broken; are free from cores, sunscald, mold, and decay, and from damage caused by dirt or other foreign matter, shriveling, moisture, disease, insects, or injury by mechanical or other means.

U.S. No. 2. Raspberries of one variety which fail to meet the requirements of the U.S. No. 1 but which do not contain more than 10 percent, by volume, of berries in any lot which are seriously damaged by any cause, including not more than 2 percent for berries which are affected by mold or decay.

Unclassified. Raspberries which have not been classified in accordance with either of the foregoing grades. The term *unclassified* is not a grade within the meaning of these standards but is provided as a designation to show that no grade has been applied to the lot.

Source:
Agricultural Marketing Service, USDA, 7 CFR sections 51.4320 to 51.4328 (1992), Washington: Government Printing Office.

Raspberries, Canned

Labeling and grading guidelines for canned raspberries are presented in this entry.

COLOR TYPES

Red. Such as the New Washington, Latham, and Lloyd George varieties.

Reddish Purple. Such as the Columbian and Sodus varieties.

Black. Such as the Logan and Cumberland varieties.

GRADES

Canned raspberries are graded according to a technical system whereby penalty points are assessed for such factors as edibility, poor appearance, or defects in workmanship. The more penalty points assessed the lower the grade. The grade descriptions which follow are intended only as a general consumer guide. For more detailed information, please consult the source cited below.

U.S. Grade A or U.S. Fancy. Possess similar varietal characteristics and normal flavor. Possess a bright and typical color of well-ripened raspberries for the varietal type that have been properly processed. They are practically uniform in that not more than 5 percent, by weight, of the drained raspberries may vary markedly from this typical color. The variation in size of the raspberries does not materially affect the appearance and not more than 10 percent are less than 9/16 inch in diameter. They are practically free from defects such as harmless leaves, caps, and stems, undeveloped berries, damaged berries, and any other defects that affect the appearance or edibility of the product. The raspberries are thick fleshed and well ripened and the presence of detached drupelets does not more than slightly affect the appearance of the product. Not more than 10 percent, by weight, of the drained raspberries may be broken or mashed.

U.S. Grade B or U.S. Choice. Possess similar varietal characteristics and normal flavor. The raspberries possess a reasonably bright and typical color. They are reasonably uniform in that not more than 15 percent, by weight, may vary markedly from this typical color. The variation in size of the raspberries does not affect the appearance of the product and not more than 15 percent may be less than ½ inch in diameter. They are reasonably free from defects. The raspberries are reasonably thick fleshed and well ripened and the presence of detached drupelets does not materially affect appearance. Not more than 15 percent, by weight, of the drained raspberries may be broken or mashed.

U.S. Grade C or U.S. Standard. Possess similar varietal characteristics, normal flavor, and possess a fairly good color which may be variable but not off-color. The canned raspberries may be variable in size and not more than 25 percent may be less than 7/16 inch in diameter. They are fairly free from defects. The raspberries are fairly thick-fleshed and fairly well-ripened. The presence of detached drupelets does not seriously affect appearance and not more than 20 percent of the drained raspberries may be broken or mashed berries.

Substandard. Fails to meet the requirements of U.S. Grade C or U.S. Standard.

Source:
Agricultural Marketing Service, USDA, 7 CFR sections 52.3311 to 52.3324 (1991), Washington: Government Printing Office.

Raspberries, Frozen

Frozen raspberries are prepared from the properly ripened fresh fruit of the plant (genus *Rubus*). The raspberries are stemmed and cleaned, may be packed with or without packing media, and are frozen and stored at temperatures necessary for the preservation of the product.

COLORS

Red raspberries are red to reddish purple in color.

GRADES

Frozen raspberries are graded according to a technical system whereby penalty points are assessed for such factors as edibility, poor appearance, or defects in workmanship. The more penalty points assessed the lower the grade. The grade descriptions which follow are intended only as a general consumer guide. For more detailed information, please consult the source cited below.

U.S. Grade A or U.S. Fancy. Possess similar varietal characteristics and a bright, practically uniform, typical color. None of the raspberries possesses a gray cast or darkening. They are practically free from defects such as caps, sepal-like bracts, stems, undeveloped raspberries, and damaged raspberries. The raspberries are mature, well developed, and practically intact. They are fleshy and tender, and the raspberries and accompanying liquor, if any, are practically free from detached seed cells. They possess a normal flavor and odor.

U.S. Grade B or U.S. Choice. Possess similar varietal characteristics, a reasonably bright, reasonably uniform, typical color, and may possess a slight gray cast or slight darkening. The berries are reasonably free from defects and are reasonably mature, reasonably well-developed, and reasonably intact. The raspberries are reasonably fleshy and reasonably tender, and the raspberries and accompanying liquor, if any, are reasonably free from detached seed cells. They possess a normal flavor and odor.

U.S. Grade D or Substandard. Fail to meet the requirements of U.S. Grade B or U.S. Choice.

Source:
Agricultural Marketing Service, USDA, 7 CFR sections 52.1871 to 52.1886 (1991), Washington: Government Printing Office.

Strawberries

To allow for variations in quality caused by grading and handling, a percentage of the strawberries may fail to meet all of the requirements of the grade.

GRADES

Strawberries are graded according to a technical system whereby penalty points are assessed for such factors as edibility, poor appearance, or defects in workmanship. The more penalty points assessed the lower the grade. The grade descriptions which follow are intended only as a general consumer guide. For more detailed information, please consult the source cited below.

U.S. No. 1. Strawberries of one variety or similar varietal characteristics with the cap (calyx) attached, which are firm and not overripe or undeveloped and which are free from mold or decay and free from damage caused by dirt, moisture, foreign matter, disease, insects, or injury by mechanical or other means. Each strawberry has not less than three-fourths of its surface showing a pink or red color. Unless otherwise specified, the minimum diameter of each strawberry is not less than ¾ inch.

U.S. Combination. A combination of U.S. No. 1 and U.S. No. 2 strawberries, except for size, provided that at least 80 percent, by volume, of the strawberries meet the requirements of U.S. No. 1. Unless otherwise specified, the minimum diameter of each strawberry is not less than ¾ inch.

U.S. No. 2. Strawberries which are free from decay and free from serious damage caused by dirt, disease, insects, mechanical or other means. Each strawberry has not less than one-half of its surface showing a pink or red color. Unless otherwise specified, the minimum diameter of each strawberry is not less than ⅝ inch. This grade also has a higher tolerance for defects such as soft, badly deformed, and badly bruised berries.

Unclassified. Strawberries which have not been classified in accordance with any of the foregoing grades. The term *unclassified* is not a grade within the meaning of these standards but is provided as a designation to show that no grade has been applied to the lot.

Source:
Agricultural Marketing Service, USDA, 7 CFR sections 51.3115 to 51.3124 (1992), Washington: Government Printing Office.

Strawberries, Frozen

Frozen strawberries are prepared from sound, properly ripened fresh fruit of the strawberry plant by stemming, proper washing, sorting, and proper draining, may be packed with or without packing medium, and are then frozen in accordance with good commercial practice and maintained at temperatures necessary for the preservation of the product.

STYLES

Whole Strawberries. Retain approximately their original conformation.

Slices or Sliced. Produced by slicing whole strawberries into two or more slices.

Small. Less than ⅝ inch in diameter.

Medium. ⅝ to 1¼ inches in diameter.

Large. More than 1¼ inches in diameter.

GRADES

Frozen strawberries are graded according to a technical system whereby penalty points are assessed for such factors as edibility, poor appearance, or defects in workmanship. The more penalty points assessed the lower the grade. The grade descriptions which follow are intended only as a general consumer guide. For more detailed information, please consult the source cited below.

U.S. Grade A or U.S. Fancy. Possess similar varietal characteristics and a good, characteristic, normal flavor and odor free from objectionable flavors or odors of any kind. The strawberries possess characteristic pink to red color which is not more than slightly affected by a dull, gray, or reddish-brown cast. They are practically free from defects such as grit, sand, or silt, caps, sepal-like bracts, stems, short stems, and damaged strawberries, weeds, weed seeds, grass, and leaves. The strawberries possess a good character and are reasonably firm; the appearance and eating quality of the product are not materially affected by disintegration or seediness.

U.S. Grade B or U.S. Choice. Possess similar varietal characteristics and a normal flavor and odor free from objectionable flavors or odors of any kind. The strawberries possess a characteristic pink to red color which is not materially affected by dull, gray, or reddish-brown cast. They are reasonably free from defects and are fairly firm. The appearance and eating quality of the product are not seriously affected by seediness or disintegration.

U.S. Grade C or U.S. Standard. Possess similar varietal characteristics, may be lacking in good characteristic normal flavor and odor, but is free from objectionable flavors or odors. Possess a predominant characteristic pink to red color but may show a dull, gray, or slightly dark color (but not to the extent that the appearance or eating quality is seriously affected). They are fairly free from defects and possess a fairly good and firm character.

Substandard. Fail to meet the requirements of U.S. Grade C or U.S. Standard.

Source:
Agricultural Marketing Service, USDA, 7 CFR sections 52.1981 to 52.1993 (1991), Washington: Government Printing Office.

Tangerines

See also *Tangerines, Florida.*

Tangerines are graded according to a technical system whereby penalty points are assessed for such factors as edibility, poor appearance, or defects in workmanship. The more penalty points assessed the lower the grade. The grade descriptions which follow are intended only as a general consumer guide. For more detailed information, please consult the source cited below.

U.S. Fancy. Tangerines which are mature and firm. The flesh is not soft, and the skin has not become materially separated from the flesh. They are well formed and free from soft bruises, bird pecks, unhealed skin breaks, and decay. They are free from damage by ammoniation, creasing, dryness or mushy condition, green spots, oil spots, pitting, scale, sprouting, sprayburn, sunburn, unsightly discoloration, buckskin, melanose, scars, scab, dirt or other foreign materials, disease, insects, or mechanical or other means. The ground color of each fruit is a deep tangerine color with practically no trace of yellow. Not more than ⅟₁₆ of the surface in the aggregate of each fruit may have a light shade of brown discoloration caused by rust mite or any other cause.

U.S. No. 1. Tangerines which are mature, firm, and well formed. They are free from soft bruises, bird pecks, unhealed skin breaks, and decay. They are also free from damage by ammoniation, creasing, dryness or mushy condition, green spots, oil spots, pitting, scale, sprouting, sprayburn, sunburn, unsightly discoloration, buckskin, melanose, scars, scab, dirt or other foreign materials, disease, insects, or mechanical or other means. Each fruit may have not over 1 inch of green color in the aggregate, and the remainder of the surface shows a good tangerine color with some portion of the surface showing a reddish tangerine blush. Not more than one-third of the surface in the aggregate of each fruit may have a light shade of brown discoloration caused by rust mite or any other cause.

U.S. No. 1 Bronze. The requirements for this grade are the same as for U.S. No. 1 except for discoloration. In this grade at least 75 percent, by count, of the fruit shows some discoloration, and more than 20 percent, by count, of the fruit has more than one-third of the surface of each fruit affected with bronzed russeting. This discoloration must be cause by thrip or wind scars or rust mite. Otherwise, no discoloration may exceed the amount allowed in the U.S. No. 1.

U.S. No. 2. Tangerines which are mature and fairly firm. The flesh may be slightly soft but is not bruised or badly puffy, and the skin has not become seriously separated from the flesh. They are fairly well formed and are free from soft bruises, bird pecks, unhealed skin breaks, and decay. They are free from serious damage by ammoniation, creasing, dryness or mushy condition, green spots or oil spots, pitting, scale, sprouting, sprayburn, sunburn, unsightly discoloration, buckskin, melanose, scars, scab, dirt or other foreign materials, disease, insects, or mechanical or other means. A good yellow or reddish color predominates over the green color on at least one-half of the surface, and there is practically no lemon color. In this grade not more than two-thirds of the surface in the aggregate of each fruit may be affected with discoloration.

U.S. No. 2 Russet. The requirements for this grade are the same as for U.S. No. 2, except that more than 20 percent, by count, of the fruit has in excess of two-thirds of the surface in the aggregate affected with light brown discoloration.

U.S. No. 3. Tangerines which are mature, not flabby, and not seriously lumpy and which are free from unhealed bird pecks, unhealed skin breaks, and decay. They are free from very serious damage by bruises, ammoniation, creasing, dryness or mushy condition, pitting, scale, sprouting, sprayburn, sunburn, unsightly discoloration, melanose, scars, scab, dirt or other foreign materials, disease, insects, or mechanical or other means.

Source:
Agricultural Marketing Service, USDA, 7 CFR sections 51.1770 to 51.1793 (1992), Washington: Government Printing Office.

Tangerines, Florida

Florida tangerines must meet standards set by the state for maturity. In addition, these tangerines are graded according to a technical system whereby penalty points are assessed for such factors as edibility, poor appearance, or defects in workmanship. The more penalty points assessed the lower the grade. The grade descriptions which follow are intended only as a general consumer guide. For more detailed information, please consult the source cited below.

U.S. Fancy. Not more than one-tenth of the surface, in the aggregate, may be affected by discoloration. Tangerines are firm, the flesh is not soft, the fruit is not badly puffy, and the skin has not become materially separated from the flesh of the tangerine. The ground color of each fruit is a deep tangerine color with practically no trace of yellow. They are mature and well formed. They are free from defects caused by insects, injury, weather, or disease.

U.S. No. 1. Not more than one-third of the surface, in the aggregate, may be affected by discoloration. Fairly well-colored. The surface may have green color which does not exceed the aggregate area of a circle 1¼ inches in diameter, and the remainder of the surface has a yellow or better ground color with some portion of the surface showing reddish tangerine blush. The fruiit is firm, mature, and well formed and is free from defects caused by injury, weather, insects, or disease.

No. 1 Bronze. The requirements for this grade are the same as for U.S. No. 1 except that all fruit must show some discoloration. The predominating discoloration on these fruits is rust mite.

U.S. No. 1 Russet. The requirements for this grade are the same as for U.S. No. 1 except that there is a higher tolerance for fruit with more than one-third of their surface, in the aggregate, affected by any type of discoloration.

U.S. No. 2. Not more than one-half of the surface, in the aggregate, may be affected by discoloration. The flesh may be slightly soft but is not bruised or badly puffy, and the skin has not become seriously separated form the flesh. It is fairly well formed, mature, and reasonably well-colored. A good yellow or reddish tangerine color predominates over the green color on at least one-half of the surface, and each fruit shows practically no lemon color. Free from defects caused by

weather, insects, or disease.

U.S. No. 2 Russet. The requirements for this grade are the same as for U.S. No. 2 except that there is a higher tolerance for fruit with one-half of their surface, in the aggregate, affected by discoloration.

U.S. No. 3. Mature. Not flabby and not seriously lumpy. Free from bruises, decay, unhealed skin breaks, and wormy fruit. Free from serious damage caused by insects, the weather, and other causes which seriously detracts from the appearance or the edible quality of the fruit.

Source:
Agricultural Marketing Service, USDA, 7 CFR sections 51.1810 to 51.51.1835 (1992), Washington: Government Printing Office.

Watermelons

Watermelons are graded according to a technical system whereby penalty points are assessed for such factors as edibility, poor appearance, or defects in workmanship. The more penalty points assessed the lower the grade. The grade descriptions which follow are intended only as a general consumer guide. For more detailed information, please consult the source cited below.

U.S. Fancy. The watermelon has reached the stage of development at which the flesh is at least fairly sweet and shows the characteristic color of a mature watermelon for the variety. The watermelon has the characteristic shape but not necessarily the perfect shape of the variety. They may be tapered at the ends or slightly constricted. It has not reached such an advanced stage of maturity that the flesh becomes mealy, less juicy, or has an insipid taste. They are free from anthracnose, decay, sunscald, whiteheart, and damage by any means.

U.S. No. 1. Mature watermelons of similar varietal characteristics which are fairly well formed and are not overripe. They are free from anthracnose, decay, sunscald, and damage by any means.

U.S. No. 2. Mature watermelons of similar varietal characteristics which are not overripe or badly misshapen (bottlenecks or gourdnecks). They are free from anthracnose, decay, sunscald, and serious damage by any means.

OPTIONAL INTERNAL QUALITY REQUIREMENTS

Very Good Internal Quality. The combined juice from the edible portion of a sample of watermelons selected at random contains not less than 10 percent soluble solids.

Good Internal Quality. The combined juice from the edible portion of a sample of watermelons selected at random contains not less than 8 percent soluble solids.

Source:
Agricultural Marketing Service, USDA, 7 CFR sections 51.1970 to 51.1987 (1992), Washington: Government Printing Office.

Meat & Poultry

Artificial Color

Labels of products which are artificially colored either by artificial colors or natural colors must bear a statement to indicate the presence of the coloring, e.g., *artificially colored* or *colored with annatto*. Products whose true color is disguised by packing media (such as colored pickling solutions) must also have labels that include a statement indicating the presence of the color. The statement must appear in a prominent and conspicuous manner contiguous to the product name. Products which have a component (e.g., breading, sauce, sausage, etc.) that is artificially colored do not have to have names that are qualified to indicate the presence of the color. However, in all cases, the presence of the coloring must appear in the ingredients statement. Whenever FD&C Yellow No. 5 is used, it must be declared in the ingredients statement by *FD&C Yellow No. 5* or *Yellow 5*. Some products (e.g., chorizos and some other sausages) are expected to be characterized by coloring. In these situations, the presence of the coloring need only be indicated in the ingredients statement.

Source:
Standards and Labeling Division, Food Safety and Inspection Service, USDA, *Standards and Labeling Policy Book,* Washington: Government Printing Office, June 1991.

Baby Food

The following rules govern the labeling of baby food products:
High Meat Dinner. At least 26 percent meat.
High Meat Poultry Dinner. At least 18.75 percent cooked poultry meat, skin, fat, and giblets.
Meat and Broth. At least 61 percent meat.

Poultry and Rice. At least 5 percent cooked, deboned poultry meat.
Poultry with Broth. At least 43 percent cooked poultry, meat, skin, and giblets.
Vegetable with Meat. At least 8 percent meat.
Wine, MSG, Nitrites, and Nitrates. Not acceptable in baby and toddler foods.
With Fresh Ham or Bacon. Ham or bacon without nitrates or nitrites must show in ingredients statement as ham or bacon (water, salt, sugar, etc., without nitrates or nitrites).

Source:
Standards and Labeling Division, Food Safety and Inspection Service, USDA, *Standards and Labeling Policy Book,* Washington: Government Printing Office, June 1991.

Bacon

The term *bacon* is used to describe the cured belly of a swine carcass. If meat from other portions of the carcass is used, the product name must be qualified to explain this, e.g., *Pork Shoulder Bacon. Certified* refers to products treated to eliminate trichinae.

PRODUCTS

Back Bacon. Boneless pork loin with wide fat back attached.
Country Style. Means product is dry cured.
Canned, Prefried. In *Canned Prefried Bacon* such as *Bacon Crumbles,* the following criteria should be applied: (1) *M/SP Index* of 0.4 or more (M/SP = Moisture/[Salt x Protein]); (2) *Brine Ratio* of 9.0 or less (Brine ratio = moisture/salt); (3) *Brine Concentration* of 10 percent or more (Brine concentration = Salt/[Moisture + Salt]); and (4) Maximum 40 percent yield.

Canned—Pasteurized. A shelf stable item with at least 7 percent brine concentration (salt/[moisture + salt]).

Cooked. Not to yield more than 40 percent bacon, that is 60 percent shrink required. BHA and BHT may be used as antioxidants in pre-cooked bacon at a level of 0.01 percent individually or 0.02 percent collectively, based on fat content.

Honey Cured. At least 3 percent honey in the pickle pump solution.

Thick or Thin Sliced. Slices must be qualified by approximately the size of the slice, or range of slices, such as *Sliced approximately ⅛ inch,* or the thickness of the slice must be visible in product stack packed.

Bacon and Pork Sausage. Product is formulated with a high percentage of bacon (usually bacon ends and pieces) with at least 20 percent pork.

Bacon Arkansas and Arkansas Style Bacon. Produced from the pork shoulder blade Boston roast. (The pork shoulder blade Boston roast includes the porcine muscle, fat and bone, cut interior of the second or third thoracic vertebrae and posterior of the atlas joint [first cervical vertebrae], and dorsal of the center of the humerus bone.) For *Arkansas Bacon*, the neck bones and rib bones are removed by cutting close to the underside of those bones. The blade bone (scapula) and the dorsal fat covering, including the skin (clear plate), are removed, leaving no more than ¼ inch of the fat covering the roast. The meat is then dry cured with salt, sugar, nitrites, and spices, and smoked with natural smoke. The meat may not be injected or soaked in curing brine, nor may any artificial or liquid smoke be applied to the meat. Product that is prepared outside the state of Arkansas, but in the manner prescribed, may be identified as *Arkansas Style Bacon*. The true product name must be shown as *Boneless Cured Pork Shoulder Butt.*

Bacon Bar. Same requirements as *Canned Prefried Bacon,* but packaged in bar shape.

Bacon Dressing for Stuffing. At least 8 percent bacon.

Bacon Squares. The label must show true product name *Pork Jowl Bacon.*

Beef Bacon. Cured and smoked beef product sliced to simulate regular bacon. It is prepared from various beef cuts and offered with a variety of coined names including *Breakfast Beef, Beef Bacon,* etc. A common or usual name is required, e.g., *Cured and Smoked Beef Plate,* and should be shown contiguous to the coined name.

Canadian Style Bacon (Made in USA). Made from a trimmed boneless pork loin. (On the shoulder end, the cross section of the longissimus dorsi muscle is equal to or larger than the combined cross sectional areas of the splenius and semispinalis capitis muscles. The ham end is removed anterior to the ilium. The exposed faces are approximately perpendicular with the skin surface. The dorsal and ventral side on each end of the Canadian Style Bacon is not more than 1.0 inch different in length. The belly is removed adjacent to the longissimus dorsi muscle.) All bones and cartilage are removed. The tenderloin and the flesh overlying the blade bone are excluded. The surface fat (and false lean when necessary) are trimmed to 0.3 inches thick at any point. The fat on the ventral and dorsal sides is neatly beveled to meet the lean. The term *Canadian Style Bacon,* when featured on the label as a product name or part of a product name (i.e., as a description, etc.), may stand alone without an additional qualifier indicating the true geographical origin of the product. *Chunked and Formed* and *Water Added* products are permitted provided proper labeling is applied. Uncooked and/or unsmoked Canadian Style Bacon is also permitted, provided labeling describes the product as uncooked and/or unsmoked.

Canadian Style Bacon Made With/From Pork Sirloin Hips. *Canadian Style Bacon* products (1) made exclusively from the sirloin hip portion of a pork loin, or (2) which include the sirloin hip portion of a pork loin in addition to the portion of the pork loin that has traditionally been used to prepare Canadian Style Bacon. The sirloin is obtained by removing a 5- to 7-inch section of the pork loin immediately in front of the hip or pelvic bone. The sirloin hip is obtained by removing the half of the sirloin which comprises the posterior end of the pork loin. The tenderloin is not included, and surface fat is trimmed to 0.3 inches in thickness. The labeling for these Canadian Style Bacon products must bear a qualifying statement adjacent to the product name, clarifying that pork sirloin hips are included or that the product is made entirely from pork sirloin hips, e.g., *Canadian Style Bacon—Includes Pork Sirloin Hips* or *Canadian Style Bacon—Made from Pork Sirloin Hips.*

Dixie Bacon. True product name such as *Pork Jowl Dixie Bacon, Cured and Smoked* should appear on the label.

Dixie Square. Same as for *Dixie Bacon.*

Source:

Standards and Labeling Division, Food Safety and Inspection Service, USDA, *Standards and Labeling Policy Book,* Washington: Government Printing Office, June 1991.

Beef

GRADES

There are eight quality grade designations:

Prime
Choice
Select
Standard
Commercial
Utility
Cutter
Canner

All eight designations are applicable to steer (castrated male) and heifer (young female) carcasses. Except for Prime, the same designations apply to cow (mature female) carcasses.

The quality grade designations for bullock (young bull) carcasses are Prime, Choice, Select, Standard, and Utility. The designated grades of bullock beef are not necessarily comparable in quality or cutability with similar grades of beef from steers, heifers, or cows. The Prime, Choice, Select, and Standard grades are restricted to beef from young cattle. The Commercial grade is restricted to beef from cattle too mature for Prime, Choice, Select, and Standard. The Utility, Cutter, and Canner grades may include beef from animals of all ages.

For steer, heifer, and cow beef, the quality of the meat is based on evidence of maturity. It is evaluated by considering its marbling and firmness as observed in a cut surface (usually a ribeye on either side of the carcass). The maturity of the carcass is mainly determined by evaluating the size, shape, and ossification of the bones and cartilages and the color and texture of the lean flesh.

In steer, heifer, and cow beef, the color and texture of the flesh undergo progressive changes with advancing maturity. In the very youngest carcasses considered as *beef*, the lean flesh will be very fine in texture and light grayish red in color. In progressively more mature carcasses, the texture of the lean will become coarser and the color of the lean will become darker red. In very mature beef, the lean flesh will be very coarse in texture and very dark red in color. (Bullock beef is sometimes darker in color than steers and heifers of similar age; they are therefore graded according to separate standards which take this difference into consideration.)

In determining the maturity of a carcass in which the skeletal evidence of maturity is different from that indicated by the color and texture of the lean, slightly more emphasis is placed on the characteristics of the bones and cartilages than on the characteristics of the lean. In determining compliance with the maximum maturity limits for the Prime, Choice, Select, and Standard grades for steer, heifer, and cow carcasses, color and texture of the lean are considered only when the factors indicate a slightly more advanced degree of maturity than that specified as maximum for these grades, and provided further that the lean is considerably finer in texture and lighter in color than normal for the grade and maturity involved.

The accompanying chart shows the relationship between meat marbling, animal maturity, and carcass quality grade. This chart assumes that the firmness of the meat is comparably developed with the degree of marbling. The maturity (as shown in this chart) increases from left to right, A through E.

GRADES: STEER, HEIFER, AND COW

Prime. Minimum quality characteristics are described for two maturity groups (A and B) which cover the entire range of maturity permitted in the Prime grade. Beef produced from cows is not eligible for the Prime grade.

A Group. In carcasses throughout the range of maturity included in this group, a *minimum slightly abundant* amount of marbling is required (see chart), and the ribeye muscle is moderately firm, light red in color, and fine in texture.

B Group. The minimum degree of marbling required increases with advanced maturity throughout this group from *minimum slightly abundant to maximum slightly abundant* (see chart), and the ribeye muscle is firm. The lean tends to be fine in texture.

Choice. Minimum quality characteristics are described for two maturity groups (A and B) which cover the entire range of maturity permitted in the Choice grade.

A Group. In carcasses throughout the range of maturity included in this group, a *minimum small* amount of marbling is required (see chart), and the ribeye muscle may be slightly soft, moderately light red in color, and fine in texture.

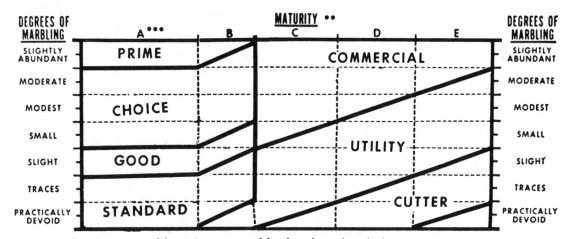

*Assumes that firmness of lean is comparably developed with the degree of marbling and that the carcass is not a "dark cutter."
**Maturity increases from left to right (A through E).
***The A maturity portion of the Figure is the only portion applicable to bullock carcasses.

Relationship between marbling, maturity, and carcass quality grade •

B Group. The minimum degree of marbling required increases with advanced maturity throughout this group from a *minimum small* amount to a *maximum small* amount (see chart), and the ribeye muscle is slightly firm. The lean tends to be fine in texture.

Select. Minimum quality characteristics are described for two maturity groups (A and B) which cover the entire range of maturity permitted in the Select grade.

A Group. In carcasses throughout the range of maturity included in this group, a *minimum slight* amount of marbling is required (see chart), and the ribeye muscle may be moderately soft, slightly light red in color, and fine in texture.

B Group. The minimum degree of marbling required increases with advanced maturity throughout this group from a *minimum slight* amount to a *maximum slight* amount (see chart), and the ribeye muscle is slightly soft. The lean tends to be fine in texture.

Standard. Minimum quality characteristics are described for two maturity groups (A and B) which cover the entire range of maturity permitted in the Standard grade.

A Group. In carcasses throughout the range of maturity included in this group, a *minimum practically devoid* amount of marbling is required (see chart), and the ribeye muscle may be soft, slightly dark red in color, and fine in texture.

B Group. The minimum degree of marbling required increases with advanced maturity throughout this group from a *minimum practically devoid* amount to a *maximum practically devoid* amount (see chart), and the ribeye muscle may be moderately soft. The lean is moderately fine in texture.

Commercial. Commercial grade beef carcasses are restricted to those with evidences of more advanced maturity than permitted in the standard grade. Maturity groups C, D, and E.

C Group. The minimum degree of marbling required increases with advanced maturity throughout this group from a *minimum small* amount to a *maximum small* amount (see chart), and the ribeye muscle is slightly firm, moderately dark red, and slightly coarse in texture.

D Group. The requirements for this group are determined by interpolation between the requirements indicated for C Group and E Group (i.e., the requirements are somewhere between C and E Group).

E Group. The minimum degree of marbling required increases with advanced maturity throughout this group from a *minimum moderate* amount to a *maximum moderate* amount (see chart), and the ribeye muscle is firm.

Utility. Carcasses within the full range of maturity classified as beef are included in the Utility grade. Thus, five maturity groups are recognized.

A Group. In carcasses throughout the range of maturity included in this group, the ribeye muscle is *devoid* of marbling, slightly dark red in color, fine in texture, and may be soft and slightly watery,.

B Group. The requirements for this group are determined by interpolation between the requirements indicated for A Group and C Group.

C Group. The minimum degree of marbling required increases with advanced maturity throughout this group from a *minimum practically devoid* amount to a *maximum practically devoid* amount (see chart), and the ribeye muscle may be moderately soft.

D Group. The requirements for this group are determined by interpolation between the requirements indicated for C Group and E Group.

E Group. The minimum degree of marbling required increases with advanced maturity throughout this group from a *minimum slight* amount to a *maximum slight* amount (see chart), and the ribeye muscle is slightly firm.

Cutter. Carcasses within the full range of maturity classified as beef are included in the Cutter grade. Thus, five maturity groups are recognized.

A Group. In carcasses throughout the range of maturity included in this group, the ribeye muscle is *devoid* of marbling, slightly dark red in color, fine in texture, and may be very soft and watery.

B Group. The requirements for this group are determined by interpolation between the requirements indicated for A Group and C Group.

C Group. In carcasses throughout the range of maturity included in this group, the ribeye muscle is *devoid* of marbling, dark red in color, slightly coarse in texture, and may be very soft and watery.

D Group. The requirements for this group are determined by interpolation between the requirements indicated for C Group and E Group.

E Group. the range of maturity in this group extends to include carcasses from the oldest of animals produced. The minimum degree of marbling required increases with advanced maturity throughout this group from a *minimum practically devoid* amount to a *maximum practically devoid* amount (see chart), and the ribeye muscle is very dark red in color, coarse in texture, and is soft and slightly watery.

Canner. The Canner grade includes only those carcasses that are inferior to the minimum requirements specified for the Cutter grade.

GRADES: BULLOCK

Prime. For the Prime grade, the minimum degree of marbling required is a minimum slightly abundant amount for carcasses throughout the range of maturity (A group only) permitted in the bullock class. The ribeye muscle is moderately firm and, in carcasses having the maximum maturity for this class, the ribeye is light red in color.

Choice. For the Choice grade, the minimum degree of marbling required is a *minimum small* amount for carcasses throughout the range of maturity (A group only) permitted in the bullock class. The ribeye muscle may be slightly soft; and, in carcasses having the maximum maturity for this class, the ribeye is moderately light red in color.

Select. For the Select grade, the minimum degree of marbling required is a *minimum slight* amount for carcasses throughout the range of maturity (A group only) permitted in the bullock class. The ribeye muscle may be moderately soft; and, in carcasses having the maximum maturity for this class, the ribeye is slightly light red in color.

Standard. For the Standard grade, the minimum degree of marbling required is a *minimum practically devoid* amount for carcasses throughout the range of maturity (A group only) permitted in the bullock class. The ribeye muscle may be soft; and, in carcasses having the maximum maturity for this class, the ribeye is slightly dark red in color.

Utility. The Utility grade includes only those carcasses that do not meet the minimum requirements specified for the Standard grade.

TERMINOLOGY—GENERAL

Artificial Marbling-Beef Steaks. Beef injected with melted beef fat, butter, or shortening must contain a statement on the label to indicate the added substance, e.g, *Injected With Beef Fat* or *Product May Appear To Be Of A Higher Quality Than The Actual Grade.*

Basterna. Cured, dried cut of beef coated with a spice crust. The label must show true product name such as *Cured and Dried Beef with Spices.*

Beef a la Deutsch. A product made with beef, vegetables, and sauce. Must show true product name such as *Gravy with Vegetables and Beef* or *Beef and Gravy with Vegetables.*

Beef a la King. At least 20 percent cooked beef.

Beef a la Mode. At least 50 percent beef. Sliced beef (marinated in wine, cognac, vegetable stock) with carrots, onions, and other ingredients covered with wine sauce.

Beef Almondine with Vegetables. At least 18 percent cooked meat on the ready-to-serve basis. Product must contain almonds.

Beef and Dumplings with Gravy. At least 25 percent meat and not more than 25 percent water blanched dry dumplings.

Beef and Gravy. At least 50 percent cooked beef. Alternatively, if labeled *Gravy and Beef,* at least 35 percent cooked beef.

Beef Blood Glaze. A coating of beef blood is permitted on cured products (such as ham, hamette, etc.) if the product name is prominently qualified to reflect the coating. Nitrite is not permitted in the glaze.

Beef Brisket (Canned). Minimum of 5.5 percent brine concentration.

Beef Burgundy or Bourguignonne. At least 50 percent beef. Product contains beef cubes, mushrooms, onions, and red wine or burgundy gravy. Other vegetables may include carrots, shallots, tomato paste, and potatoes. Other acceptable names include *Beouf a la Bourguignonne, Beef Burgundy Style, Beef Burgundy,* and *Burgundy Beef.*

Beef Burgundy with Noodles. At least 50 percent beef in the beef burgundy. Total product should not contain more than 50 percent cooked noodles.

Beef Concentrate and Salt. Broth derived from cooking fresh beef containing 3 to 4 percent solids is centrifuged and evaporated to approximately 60 percent solids under vacuum. The water fraction is salted to a level of 25.5 percent of the water weight. No need for refrigeration.

Beef Consomme. Requires beef as an ingredient and a minimum protein content of at least 3 percent in the finished product.

Additional optional ingredients are gelatin, beef extract, tomato puree, hydrolyzed plant protein, and seasoning.

Beef Gravy Mix. At least 15 percent dried beef.

Beef Greavess. Must have a true product name, such as *Cooked Beef Tissue Solids.* This product is usually high temperature rendered beef fat. However, if partially defatted beef fatty tissue is used, the product cannot be rendered above 120 degrees F.

Beef Heart. The following terms are used to identify product from beef hearts: *Beef Hearts* refers to untrimmed beef hearts with bone intact; *Beef Hearts, Bone Removed* refers to untrimmed beef hearts with bone removed; *Beef Heart Meat* refers to beef hearts with auricles (heart cap) and bone removed.

Beef Marsala. At least 50 percent beef. Product contains beef cubes, marsala wine sauce, and usually mushrooms and onions. White wine may be used, but it may not replace marsala wine.

Beef Oriental or Oriental Beef. At least 12 percent meat and oriental style vegetables and sauce. The label must show true product name such as *Beef Oriental with Vegetables.*

Beef Powder, Beefs, or Beef Juice. When added to sauces, should be listed in ingredients statement by their common or usual names. Beefs, or products of, are not an approved ingredient in sausage or uncooked meat products.

Beef Roast (Beef Fat Added). A beef roast wrapped with a layer of fat is labeled *Beef Roast, Beef Fat Added* or *Beef Chuck Roast, Beef Fat Added* or similar names. If the fat is placed over bones or tends to cover bones, the words *Bone-in* must be shown with the product name.

Beef Roulade. At least 50 percent cooked meat. Usually a thin strip of flank meat wrapped around vegetables and cooked.

Beef Slices a la Pizzaiola. At least 50 percent cooked beef. Label must show true product name as *Beef in Pizza Sauce.*

Beef Stroganoff. A dish with a creamy sauce prepared with beef cut into narrow strips or cubes and sauteed. Product labeled *Beef Stroganoff* should be prepared with a formula which includes at least 45 percent uncooked beef or 30 percent cooked. In addition, beef stroganoff must contain at least 10 percent sour cream *or* 7.5 percent sour cream and 5 percent wine *or* 9.5 percent whole milk, 2 percent sour cream, and 2.5 percent wine.

Beef Stroganoff with Noodles. Meat and sauce portion must meet the standard for Beef Stroganoff. Total product shall contain no more than 50 percent cooked noodles.

Beef Suet. Hard fat from kidneys and loin, mainly used for tallow. May be labeled *Beef Fat* or *Beef Suet.*

Beef Sukiyaki. At least 30 percent meat based on total product. Consists of thinly sliced beef and various vegetables cooked in a flavored beef stock. This is not a stew as the vegetables and components are mixed during the cooking process. Vegetables used with this food are celery, bean sprouts, leeks, onions, mushrooms, chinese cabbage, carrots, spinach, water chestnuts, bamboo shoots, and bean curds.

Beef Tongues (Cured and Canned). This product consists of thoroughly trimmed, short cut tongue.

Beef Wellington. Is made with beef tenderloin that is roasted very rare. It is then spread with a liver pate, covered with pastry, and baked in a hot oven until pastry is brown. At least 50 percent cooked meat and no more than 30 percent pastry.

Beevett. A term used to identify meat of large calves approaching one year of age, labeled as *Beevett Beef.*

Bresaola. Dry cured beef which is rubbed with spices and wine.

Calf Livers, Hearts. Large calf livers and hearts may be designated as *beef livers* and *beef hearts.*

Chipped Beef. Beef that is dried, chipped, or sliced and may be cured or smoked. It may be chunked, ground, chopped, and formed. If so, must be qualified, e.g., *Chipped Beef, Chunked and Formed.*

Creamed Beef (Chipped or Dried). At least 18 percent dried beef.

Dried or Air Dried. Product name is *Air Dried Beef* or *Dried Beef.* It is usually cured by rub and/or stitch pump followed by cover pickle for 4 to 8 weeks with several overhauls, followed by 3 to 10 days in a smokehouse or drying chamber.

Gravy and Swiss Steak. Not less than 35 percent cooked beef. Product labeled *Swiss Steak* must be floured or dusted before searing, or may have flour added to gravy.

Hydrolyzed Beef Stock. A beef stock which has been treated with acid, alkali, or enzymes to digest the protein. The protein molecules are broken down into amino acids, peptides, polypeptides, and peptones. As the digestion is carried out for longer periods of time, more and more of the larger molecules are broken down into amino acids, with free alpha-amino groups. By analyzing these alpha-amino nitrogens one can determine the degree of hydrolysis. One hundred percent hydrolysis would mean that all the nitrogen (protein) is in the form of amino acids. Ten percent of hydrolysis would mean that only ten percent of the nitrogen is in the form of free amino acids, while the rest is still present in polymeric form. The label should indicate the degree of hydrolysis. This is determined from the ratio of amino nitrogen to total nitrogen. A product labeled *Fifty percent Hydrolyzed Beef Stock* must, therefore, have fifty percent of the total nitrogen present as amino nitrogen.

Injected Beef. Beef injected or containing phosphates, regardless of injection, must have complete detailed processing procedures approved. Product labeled *Beef for Cooking, Cooked Beef, Beef for Broiling* followed immediately by a qualifying statement which reads *Injected with up to ____ percent of a solution of water, salt, etc.* Cooked product must reach an internal temperature of 145 degrees F.

Injected With or Dipped In. Instead of or preceding ingredient statement, products should state these processes in conjunction with product name, e.g., *Corned Beef Brisket injected with a solution of water, salt,* etc.

Minced Beef. Must meet the ground beef standard.

TERMINOLOGY—GROUND BEEF

Beef Patties. Consist of chopped fresh and/or frozen beef with or without the addition of beef fat and/or seasonings. Binders or extenders, mechanically separated (species) and/or partially defatted beef fatty tissue may be used without added water or with added water only in amounts such that the product characteristics are essentially that of a meat pattie.

Chopped Beef or Ground Beef. Consists of chopped fresh and/or frozen beef with or without seasoning and without the addition

of beef fat. Does not contain more than 30 percent fat, and shall not contain added water, phosphates, binders, or extenders. Cheek meat is permitted up to 25 percent and, if in excess of natural proportions, its presence is declared on the label. Beef of skeletal origin, or from the diaphragm or esophagus (weasand) may be used. Heart meat and tongue meat as organ meats are not acceptable ingredients.

Fabricated Steak. Fabricated beef steaks, veal steaks, beef and veal steaks, or veal and beef steaks, and similar products, such as those labeled *Beef Steak, Chopped, Shaped, Frozen, Minute Steak, Formed, Wafer Sliced, Frozen, Veal Steaks, Beef Added, Chopped-Molded-Cubed-Frozen, Hydrolyzed Plant Protein, and Flavoring* are prepared by comminuting and forming the product from fresh and/or frozen meat, with or without added fat, of the species indicated on the label. The product shall not contain more than 30 percent fat and shall not contain added water, binders, or extenders. Beef cheek meat may be used in the preparation of fabricated beef steaks only. Beef of skeletal origin, or from the diaphragm or esophagus (weasand) may be used. Heart meat and tongue meat as organ meats are not acceptable ingredients.

Ground Beef and Pork. Mixtures of fresh ground pork and beef must be treated for possible live trichinae.

Ground Beef Chuck. Derived from all or part of the primal part of the beef carcass commonly referred to as the *Beef Chuck.*

Ground Beef Round. Must be derived from all or part of the primal part of the beef carcass commonly referred to as the *Beef Round.* Generally, shank meat may be added but may not exceed the natural proportion of the beef carcass, which is considered to average 6 percent. Higher quantities of shank meat may be used if the shank meat remains attached during the cutting and boning of the boneless chuck or round, or if the processor can demonstrate that a higher percentage is applicable.

Ground Beef—Seasoned. Ground beef or chopped beef may contain seasoning substances such as salt, sweetening agents, flavorings, spices, MSG, HVP, etc., provided in condimental proportions. Paprika or other such substances which might influence the coloration of the product are not included in the acceptable seasoning category.

Hamburger. Consists of chopped fresh and/or frozen beef with or without the addition of beef fat and/or seasoning. Does not contain more than 30 percent fat, and shall not contain added water, phosphates, binders, or extenders. Cheek meat is permitted. Beef of skeletal origin, or from the diaphragm or esophagus (weasand) may be used. Heart meat and tongue meat as organ meats are not acceptable ingredients.

Hamburger and Soy Products. Combinations of ground beef or hamburger and soy products may be descriptively labeled, e.g., *Hamburger and Textured Vegetable Protein Product* or *Ground Beef and Isolated Soy Protein Product* if the combination product is not nutritionally inferior to hamburger and ground beef. If the combination products are nutritionally inferior, they are to be labeled as *Imitation Ground Beef, Imitation Hamburger, Beef Patty,* or *Beef Patty Mix.*

Partially Defatted Beef Fatty Tissue. A beef byproduct derived from the low temperature rendering (not exceeding 120 degrees F) of fresh beef fatty tissue. Such product shall have a pinkish color and a fresh odor and appearance.

TERMINOLOGY—STEAK

Chinese Pepper Steak. At least 30 percent cooked steak. A Chinese-style dish usually served with rice. Beef steak is cut in thin strips, browned, and added to a sauce. Vegetables are also added to the sauce; green pepper strips are always used and other vegetables may include celery, onions, scallions, red pepper, bean sprouts, tomatoes, or water chestnuts.

Delmonico, Boneless Club Steak. These terms are synonymous and are restricted as a designation to the meat served from the anterior portion of the beef short lean extending from the T-bone area up to and including the 13th rib.

Dipped in a Solution of Papain. When steaks or other meat cuts are dipped in approved proteolytic enzymes, a prominent statement such as *Tenderized in a Solution of Water and Papain* shall show contiguous to the product name.

Dipped Steaks. Steaks made from a solid piece of meat may be dipped in a solution of water and flavoring. The resulting gain shall not be more than 3 percent above the weight of the untreated product. A prominent statement, such as *Dipped in a Solution of _____*, will accompany the product name.

Country Style. This term is popular in the southern region of the United States. Country Style Steak resembles a *Gravy and Swiss Steak* product. Characteristics of this product are: It is prepared from the steaking portions of beef (usually from the round) and braised. The meat is mechanically "tenderized" and floured prior to browning. The meat is browned by sauteing or oven browning (but not flame browned or cooked in water). When the product name is shown as *Gravy and Beef Steak* at least 35 percent cooked steak must be used. When the product name is shown as *Beef Steak with Gravy,* at least 50 percent cooked steak must be used.

Flank Steak. The flat oval-shaped muscle embedded in the inside of the clod or upper end of the flank. It is practically free of fat and often labeled *London Broil.*

Salisbury Steak. At least 65 percent meat and limited to 30 percent fat in finished product. It must be an unbreaded cooked product; the meat block may contain 25 percent pork, with the remainder being beef; partially defatted chopped beef and pork may be used at 12 percent of the beef or pork; and up to 12 percent extenders may be used. The extenders include (but are not limited to) cereal, bread crumbs, cracker meal, soy flour, soy protein concentrate, and textured vegetable protein. Isolated soy protein is also permitted, but 6.8 percent isolated soy protein is the equivalent of 12 percent of the other extenders. Meat byproducts are not permitted, but beef heart meat is permitted. Permitted liquids include (but are not limited to) water, broth, milk, cream, skim milk, and reconstituted skim milk (9 parts water to 1 part nonfat dry milk). Product not cooked which conforms to the above may be labeled *Patties for Salisbury.*

Sandwich Steak. A product composed of thinly sliced beef. The label must show true product name such as *Wafer Beef Slices Chopped and Formed.*

Swiss Steak, Swiss Steak and Gravy. Not less than 50 percent cooked beef.

Teriyaki Style Steak. A slice of beef marinated in a soy solution and then cooked.

Beef Skirt Steaks. Beef Skirt Steaks consists of strips approximately 3 inches in width by 12 to 14 inches in length of the heavy muscular portion of the beef diaphragm, with the serous membranes removed. The label must show true product name *Beef Skirt Steak Diaphragm.*

Source:

Agricultural Marketing Service, USDA, "Application of Standards for Grades of Carcass Beef," 7 CFR 54.104 (1992), Washington: Government Printing Office.
Food Safety and Inspection Service, USDA, "Miscellaneous Beef Products," 9 CFR 319.15 (1992), Washington: Government Printing Office.

Beefalo

The term *beefalo* cannot substitute for beef in labeling. It can be featured as a further labeling term such as *beef from beefalo.* The terms *calf* and *veal* apply to meat from young beefalo animals on the same basis as they are used with meat from other young bovines.

Source:

Standards and Labeling Division, Food Safety and Inspection Service, USDA, *Standards and Labeling Policy Book,* Washington: Government Printing Office, June 1991.

Burritos

A Mexican-style sandwich-like product consisting of a flour tortilla, various fillings, and at least 15 percent meat or 10 percent cooked poultry meat. The product is rolled and has tucked ends. Fillings may contain, in addition to meat or poultry meat, such major ingredients as beans, potatoes, cheese, rice, tomatoes, and chilies.

Examples of product names are: *Beef Burrito, Turkey Burrito, Chicken Fajita Burrito,* and *Chili Verdi with Beans Burrito.* If ingredients, such as rice or beans are declared in the product name, they must appear in the proper order of predominance. Ingredients cannot be mentioned in the product name unless all other ingredients present in amounts equal to or above the declared ingredient are included in the name, e.g., *Beans, Beef, Tomato, Onion, and Rice Burrito.*

The use of *Red Chili* or *Green Chili* or a similar designation of the chili content in a star-burst, flag, or similar display, separated from the product name, is acceptable. If such designations are used as part of the descriptive name, the presences of the chilies must appear in the correct order of predominance, and all other ingredients present in amounts equal to or greater than the chilies must appear in the product name.

Source:

Standards and Labeling Division, Food Safety and Inspection Service, USDA, *Standards and Labeling Policy Book,* Washington: Government Printing Office, June 1991.

Cheese

When _cheese_ is declared in the ingredients statement of a fabricated product, cheddar cheese must be used.

The term _cheese_ may be shown in the name of a fabricated product such as _Ham and Cheese Loaf_ provided the common names of the cheeses used are declared in the ingredients statement. Imitation and substitute cheeses are not considered cheese.

When a cheese product and a meat food or poultry product are packaged together, the product name shown on the label must show the name of each. For example, if slices of ham and slices of a cheese product are packaged together, the product name should include ham and the name of the cheese product, such as _Ham and Pasteurized Processed American Cheese_. Alternatively, the _Pasteurized Processed American Cheese_ could be qualified contiguous to product name, such as _Ham and Cheese (Pasteurized Processed American Cheese)_. The name _Ham and Cheese_ would be acceptable if the cheese product was cheddar cheese.

When substitute or imitation cheese is used in products where real cheese is expected, such as in products designated _cordon bleu,_ the name of the product must be changed or qualified to indicate the presence of the ersatz cheese. There is no limit on the amount of ersatz cheese used.

TERMINOLOGY

Cheese, Pasteurized Processed. An acceptable name for pasteurized processed cheddar cheese. Other types of processed cheese are listed such as _Pasteurized Processed Swiss Cheese._

Cheese (Pasteurized Processed Cheese Food or Spread). Not considered a cheese, but a _cheese food_ product. It cannot be used in meat food products where cheese is an expected ingredient, such as _Cheesefurters_ or _Veal Cordon Bleu._

Cheesefurter. A meat food product consisting of a mixture of meat and cheese resembling a sausage.

Cheesewurst or Cheddarwurst. Such names are not considered common or usual names or descriptive names and must be accompanied by a true descriptive name, e.g., _Smoked Sausage with Cheese._

Cheese Products Containing Meat. Must have over 50 percent meat.

Cheese Sauce. A sauce containing a characterizing cheese ingredient. All ingredients of the sauce should show in parentheses following _Cheese Sauce._

Cheese Smokies. A cooked smoked sausage. Same cheese requirements as _Cheesefurter._

Cheese, Swiss or Gruyère. The term _Gruyère_ pertains to a cheese that closely resembles _Swiss Cheese_ both in its appearance and on the basis of analysis. The Food and Drug Administration (FDA) advises that Gruyere cheese is a suitable substitute for Swiss cheese, since it would give the same character to a finished food product such as _Cordon Bleu_. Gruyère has smaller holes than Swiss Cheese.

Source:
Standards and Labeling Division, Food Safety and Inspection Service, USDA, _Standards and Labeling Policy Book,_ Washington: Government Printing Office, June 1991.

Chili

The following are common terms used to label chili products:

Brick Chili or Condensed Chili. Requires 80 percent meat, with cereal limited to 16 percent.

Reconstituted Chili. Chili with reconstitution directions should meet the standard for _chili_ when reconstituted.

Chili with Heart Meat. When beef heart meat, cheek meat, or head meat is used in excess of 25 percent of the meat block, it must be reflected in the product name, e.g., _Chili with beef and beef heart meat._

Beef. When beef appears in the product name, the product must include beef as the only meat. _Beef chili_ may not contain beef fat or other beef byproducts.

Chili Gravy with Meat. Requires at least 40 percent fresh meat and no more than 8 percent cereals.

Chili Con Carne. The terms _Chili_ or _Chili Con Carne_ may be used interchangeably.

CHILI WITH BEANS

Brick Chili with Beans or Condensed Chili with Beans. Requires 50 percent meat, with cereal limited to 16 percent.

Beef. When beef appears in the product name, beef must be the only meat used. _Beef Chili with Beans_ may not contain beef fat or other beef byproducts.

Chili with Beans. Usually contains beans up to 25 percent of the product. About one-fourth of these beans may be incorporated in the product as ground beans; they should be listed in the ingredients statement as ground beans.

Chili con Carne with Beans. The terms _Chili with beans_ or _Chili con carne with beans_ may be used interchangeably.

TYPES

Chili Colorado. The chili peppers used must be exclusively of the red variety. If a prepared chili powder is used it must be prepared exclusively from red chili peppers. The word _Colorado_ is used for red; the term _Rojo_ is used more in Spain, Puerto Rico, and Cuba.

Chili-Mac. At least 26 percent meat, and must include a true product name, such as _Bean, Macaroni, and Beef in Sauce._

Chili Peppers or Chilies. May be listed in the ingredients statement as _red pepper, cayenne pepper,_ or _spice._

Chili Pie. Product as _Chili Pie with Chili, Onions, Corn Chips, and Cheese_ must have (in the chili component of the total product) at least 40 percent fresh meat.

Chili Pups. Emulsion stuffed in casing and smoked. Requires true product name such as _Chili Con Carne and Ground Beans Product._ At least 60 percent fresh meat in total formulation.

Chili Relleno. At least 12 percent fresh meat. Sometimes called _Chili Pepper Relleno._ (_Relleno_ means stuffed.)

Chili Sauce with Meat. Must contain at least 6 percent meat.

Chili Spaghetti. Contains at least 16 percent meat. Requires true product name such as *Beans and Spaghetti with Beef in Tomato Sauce.*

Chili Verde. The chili peppers used must be exclusively of the green chili or verde chili varieties. If a prepared chili powder is used, it must have been prepared exclusively from green chili or verde chili peppers.

Source:
Standards and Labeling Division, Food Safety and Inspection Service, USDA, *Standards and Labeling Policy Book,* Washington: Government Printing Office, June 1991.

Corned Beef

Canned, Cooked with Natural Juices. Canned product labeled *Cooked Corned Beef with Natural Juices* is limited to 10 percent added solution before cooking. If the added solution is greater than 10 percent, the label must indicate the total added solution, e.g., *Cooked Corned Beef and Water product _____percent of weight is added ingredients.* See also *Cooked Corned Beef with added substances.*

Cooked Corned Beef (or Cured Pork) Products with Added Substances. Cooked corned beef products (and cooked cured pork products) whose weights after cooking exceed the weight of the fresh uncured beef (or pork) must be labeled to indicate the presence and the amount of the additional substances. Examples of acceptable product names are *Cooked Corned Beef and _____ percent Water* or *Cooked Cured Pork and Water Product _____ percent of Weight is Added Ingredients.* (The ingredients of the added solution may be incorporated into the product name, e.g., *Cooked Cured Pork and Water Product _____ percent of Weight is Added Water, Salt, Sodium Phosphates, and Sodium Nitrite.*) The actual percentage is determined by subtracting the weight of the fresh beef (or pork) from the weight of the finished product.

Corned Beef and Cabbage. At least 25 percent cooked corned beef.

Corned Beef Family Style. The term *Family Style* has been accepted for display bags or like devices used to identify chunks of *Corned Beef Brisket* or like products. The pieces weigh individually from 3 to 4 pounds. The term *Family Style* is related to the size or weight of the corned beef and is intended to convey that the piece is a suitable amount for use by an average (or larger) family.

Corned Beef Hash. When canned corned beef is used as an ingredient of corned beef hash, it should be identified in the ingredient statement as *cooked corned beef.*

Corned Beef Loaf. Must meet cured meat loaf standard using corned beef.

Corned Beef Patties. Patties made from only corned beef.

Gray Corned Beef. Not a cured product, but one that contains water, salt, sugar, flavorings, etc. It should be labeled as *Gray Corned Beef, Gray Corned Beef Rounds,* etc. The label must show an ingredient statement rather than a curing statement as shown on other corned beef labels.

Wafer Thin Sliced (Chopped, Pressed, and Cooked). It is permissible for this product to be ground prior to the application of the curing ingredients, then pressed and cooked.

Source:
Standards and Labeling Division, Food Safety and Inspection Service, USDA, *Standards and Labeling Policy Book,* Washington: Government Printing Office, June 1991.

Cured Meats

Cured Beef Patties. A cured beef patty (alternatively spelled pattie) which was ground and then cured. *Corned Beef Seasoned* may appear on a label to qualify *Cured Beef Patty* in smaller letters.

Cured Meat Products, Labeling of Mechanically Reduced. The traditional names of cured meat products, e.g., bacon, may be used even though mechanical reduction (chopping or chunking) has taken place before the product has acquired the characteristics expected of the product. The mechanical reduction must be noted in the product name in a qualifier to the product name, e.g., *Chopped Bacon* or *Bacon-chopped and formed.*

Cured Meat Products, Packed in Brine. Cured meat products (such as pork tails, pork snouts, and cured boneless beef brisket) that contain 120-200 ppm nitrite and are packed and sold in brine solution do not require a handling statement, e.g., *keep refrigerated,* provided the finished product has at least 10 percent brine concentration. The packing medium must contain sufficient salt to maintain the 10 percent brine concentration in the product.

Cured Meats as Ingredients. When products contain cured meats at levels of 10 percent or less of the total formula, they may be labeled to feature the common or usual name of the cured meat in the ingredient statement without the use of a *cured with* statement listing the curing solution ingredients. At levels above 10 percent, the ingredients of the cured meat ingredient must be identified either by a *cured with* statement listing the ingredients in parentheses with the common name of the cured meat ingredient or by using a composite ingredient statement.

Cured Uncooked Beef. Cured, uncooked, unsmoked beef tongues and cured unsmoked beef (other than corned beef briskets) may be labeled as such if they contain not more than 10 percent added substances. Corned beef brisket may be labeled as such if it contains no more than 20 percent added substances.

Dry Cured. Product labeled as *dry cured* are not be injected with a curing solution or processed by immersion in a curing solution.

Dry Salt Cured. May contain a curing solution injected directly into the tissue but not through the circulatory system before it is covered with a dry curing mixture. It may be momentarily moistened to facilitate initial salt penetration but shall not be immersed in a curing solution.

Source:
Standards and Labeling Division, Food Safety and Inspection Service, USDA, *Standards and Labeling Policy Book,* Washington: Government Printing Office, June 1991.

Egg and Meat Products

Egg Foo Young with Meat. Must contain at least 12 percent meat.
Egg Foo Young with Poultry. Must contain at least 3 percent poultry meat.
Egg Roll with Meat. Must contain at least 10 percent meat.
Egg Roll with Poultry. Must contain at least 2 percent poultry meat.
Egg Roll. Acceptable crunchy vegetables are bamboo shoots, bean sprouts, cabbage, carrots, celery, green peppers, snow peas, and water-chestnuts.
Eggs Benedict. Must contain at least 18 percent cured smoked ham. A poached egg on a toasted English Muffin, topped with a slice of ham and covered with hollandaise sauce.
Fresh Eggs. For breakfast-type foods with eggs as components, the egg portions may be referred to in the product names and the ingredients statement as *Fresh U.S. Grade A Large.* The eggs involved are received in shells or broken and blended and not in dry or frozen form.

Source:
Standards and Labeling Division, Food Safety and Inspection Service, USDA, *Standards and Labeling Policy Book,* Washington: Government Printing Office, June 1991.

Enzymes

Enzymes, Proteolytic. A three percent pickup of enzymes is the maximum permitted pickup on dipped items such as steak and solid pieces of meat. Labeled as *Tenderized with Papain.* Trimmings from this method may be used in fresh meat products up to 25 percent of the formula, provided the finished product is immediately frozen and distribution is limited to institutional use only. The transmittal form should state the conditions and means of inspectional control. Meat from this method may be used in cooked ground beef products up to 25 percent of the formula without showing the ingredients of the solution.
Enzyme-Treated Product. Product from carcasses of animals injected with papain. Liver, heart, tongue, cheek, and head meat, trimmings, boneless beef, tenderloin, tails, tripe, and cuts of meat not showing an imprint reading *Tenderized with papain* shall be properly identified and kept separate from other product. Kidneys must be segregated and properly labeled. Containers for these products must bear a label showing, in addition to the other required labeling, a statement such as *Tenderized with papain* prominently displayed contiguous to the product name. The processor will furnish retail dealers handling such product with labels bearing the statement *Tenderized with papain* prominently displayed contiguous to the product name for use on consumer packages.

Source:
Standards and Labeling Division, Food Safety and Inspection Service, USDA, *Standards and Labeling Policy Book,* Washington: Government Printing Office, June 1991.

Extra

The terms *extra* or *more (component) than* may be used on meat products when the following guidelines are followed:
(1) There is at least a 10 percent increase in the particular component of interest over the amount that is found in the usual or regular formulation.
(2) In the situation where production of the regular product formulation ceases, the *extra* or *more (component) than* product label would be given a six-month temporary approval.
(3) A comparison to a similar product on the market may be made to support the *extra* or *more/than* claim, provided suitable market basket data are submitted with the label application that establish the similarity of formulations and show the increased amount of the component over the usual amount.

Source:
Standards and Labeling Division, Food Safety and Inspection Service, USDA, *Standards and Labeling Policy Book,* Washington: Government Printing Office, June 1991.

Foie Gras Products

Goose liver and duck liver foie gras (fat liver) are obtained exclusively from specially fed and fattened geese and ducks. Products in which *foie gras* is used are classified into the following three groups based on the minimum duck liver or goose liver foie gras content:

(1) French Product Name	English Product Name
Foie gras d'oie entier	Whole goose foie gras
Foie gras de canard entier	Whole duck foie gras

These are products in which goose liver or duck liver foie gras are the only animal tissues present. They may contain added substances such as seasonings and cures, and when truffles are featured in the product name, they are required at a minimum 3 percent level.

(2) French Product Name	English Product Name
Foie gras d'oie	Goose foie gras
Foie gras de canard	Duck foie gras
Bloc de foie gras d'oie	Block of goose foie gras
Bloc de foie gras de canard	Block of duck foie gras
Parfait de foie gras d'oie	Parfait of goose foie gras
Parfait de foie gras de canard	Parfait of duck foie gras

These products are composed of a minimum 85 percent goose liver or duck liver foie gras, although *parfaits* may contain mixtures of goose liver and/or duck liver foie gras. These products may also contain a wrapping or stuffing consisting of the lean or fat of pork, veal, or poultry, pork liver, and/or aspic jelly. When these ingredients are used, their presence must be indicated in a product name qualifier. Truffles, when featured in the product name, are required at a minimum 3 percent level.

(3) <u>French Product Name</u>   <u>English Product Name</u>
    Pâte dé foie d'oie   Pate of goose liver
    Pâte dé foie de canard   Pate of duck liver
    Galantine de foie d'oie   Galantine of goose liver
    Galantine de foie de canard   Galantine of duck liver
    Puree de foie d'oie   Puree of goose liver
    Puree de foie de canard   Puree of duck liver

These products must contain a minimum of 50 percent duck liver and/or goose liver foie gras and may also contain a wrapping or stuffing of the lean or fat of pork, veal, or poultry, pork liver, aspic jelly, extenders, and/or binders. When these ingredients are used, their presence must be indicated in a product name qualifier. Truffles, when featured in the product name, are required at a minimum 1 percent level.

In all groups, an English translation of the term *foie gras* is not required, although all other product name terms must be translated into English. The kinds of poultry liver(s) used must be indicated in the product name. Also, other species and/or binders used must be indicated in a product name qualifier immediately following the product name, while the ingredient statement must follow the product name or qualifier as the case may be.

Source:
Standards and Labeling Division, Food Safety and Inspection Service, USDA, *Standards and Labeling Policy Book,* Washington: Government Printing Office, June 1991.

Game Meats

Certain game meat products containing over three percent raw meat (cattle, sheep, swine, goat, horses or other equine) are subject to inspection. The game meat used in these products must be derived from carcasses slaughtered under the Food Safety and Inspection Service. The following products composed of meat from game animals are not governed by to the Federal Meat Inspection Act:
* Products made entirely with meat from game animals or animals other than cattle, sheep, swine, goat, or horse or other equine.
* Products made with meat from game animals with 3 percent or less of meat or edible portion from cattle, sheep, swine, goat, or up to 30 percent meat fats, provided the only reference to meat or meat byproduct on the labeling is in the statement of ingredients or referred to as *flavored with.*
* Custom prepared products composed of meat from game animals and up to 30 percent animal fat.

INSPECTION REQUIREMENTS

Buffalo and venison are subject to federal or state inspection;

however, venison may also be produced under the supervision of inspection officials of a country approved to export meat products into the United States. All other game meat used must be derived from carcasses slaughtered under the Food Safety and Inspection Service.

Source:
Standards and Labeling Division, Food Safety and Inspection Service, USDA, *Standards and Labeling Policy Book,* Washington: Government Printing Office, June 1991.

General

Fresh, Not Frozen. The word *fresh* may not be used in conjunction with the product name of: (1) any cured product, e.g., corned beef, smoked cured turkey, and prosciutto; (2) any canned, hermetically sealed, shelf-stable, dried, or chemically preserved product; and (3) any poultry, poultry part, or any edible portion thereof that has been frozen or previously frozen at or below 0 degrees F. Generally, trademarks, company names, fanciful names, etc., containing the word *fresh* are acceptable, even on products produced in a manner described above, provided the term is used in such a manner that it remains clear to the purchaser that the product is not fresh. Further processed meat and poultry products, such as nuggets, dinners, etc., sold in the refrigerated state, may be labeled as *fresh* even when made from components processed in a manner described above.

New and Similar Terms. Terms such as *new, new and improved,* and similar terms may be used within the following guidelines: The terms may only be used for a period of six months from the date of the initial approval except as noted below. Extensions to the six-month period may be granted if processors can demonstrate that production or distribution delays precluded the use of the approved labeling as scheduled or if processors can demonstrate that labeling inventory needs for the six-month period were overestimated due to poor sales. The processors must maintain records to support their claims. Up to an additional six months approval for the use of *new* can be granted, but no further extension will be considered. In those situations where it is customary to distribute *new* products to various geographical regions, each geographic area may receive a temporary approval for six months if the processor can assure adequate controls over the segregation and distribution of the products. In situations where it is customary to test market products in no more than approximately 15 percent of the intended total marketing area before total distribution begins, labeling for the test market area can receive an initial temporary approval and also be included in the six-month temporary approval given to the labeling of the product distributed to the total marketing area. Processors must be able to assure that only 15 percent of the total market is involved in test marketing.

Aged. The term *Aged* on a label must be qualified, such as *Aged 65 days. Aged _____ Days* may also be approved and in this case the blank is filled in by the establishment at the time the product is labeled. In either case, a partial quality control program is required. Aging time on cured products such as ham cannot include the required curing time.

Approximate. The word *approximate* is not acceptable on labels with reference to serving size. It is acceptable on bacon or like products to denote thickness of slice.

Awards. Replicas of medals or other award design designs may not be used on labeling unless the circumstances involved are plainly evident. This would include the identification of the kind of award, when received, and where it took place.

Bonus Offer or Money Savings Claim. Claims suggesting or stating that a product or a line of products are being sold at a price that is less than the customary price for that product or similar products may be used under the following conditions: The company initiating the claims must be capable, upon request, of verifying that the cost of the product to the retailer has been reduced sufficiently to enable the retailer to pass the price reduction on to the consumer. This may entail the keeping, maintaining, or securing of invoices and other records through all levels of commerce.

Broiled. Permitted labeling when a product has been subject to direct heat. Has no standard regarding the degree of doneness.

Certified. With the exception of the term *Certified Pork,* the term *certified* implies that the United States Department of Agriculture (USDA) and Agriculture Marketing Service (AMS) have officially evaluated a meat product for class, grade, or other quality characteristics. When used under other circumstances, the term should be closely associated with the name of the organization responsible for the certification process, e.g., *XYZ Company's Certified Meat,* or *Our Certified Meat.*

Coin Names. Words (such as *Daintee, Cola, Picnic,* etc.) are approved for labels provided the product label also contains the true product name (*Pork Shoulder*).

Cold Smoke. Product that is smoked without the use of heat.

Color Added. Where approved colors are permitted to be added to product's surface and the coloring changes the natural color of the product, the product name shall be qualified as *Color Added* or *Artificial Color Added,* as the case may be.

Completely Cooked. This is approved for use on labels identifying ham commodities reaching an internal temperature of 158-162 degrees F during processing. This heat results in a product that is relatively dry, quite pliable with the tissues separating readily, and with the fat rendered to a marked extent.

Coupons. When enclosed in consumer packages, coupons do not contain an expiration date or allow purchasers at least six months for redemption from date of first sale. If coupon is enclosed inside a consumer sized package, the label must clearly and conspicuously disclose the presence of the coupon, its conditions, and limitations.

Dry Aged. Fresh meat is held (without vacuum packing) for various periods of time (usually 10 days to 6 weeks) under controlled temperatures (34 to 38 degrees F), humidity, and airflow to avoid spoilage and ensure flavor enhancement, tenderness, and palatability. [There are different approaches to humidity levels in the cooler for dry aging. Some processors employ low humidity (from 70 to 75 percent) so that exposed surfaces of the meat remain dry. Others use humidities up to

85 to 90 percent to purposely develop a mold growth on the outside of the meat and reduce evaporation losses. Ultraviolet light may be used to reduce microbial levels in the aging room.] The number of days fresh meat has been aged does not have to appear on the label when the product is identified as *Dry Aged,* as in *Dry Aged Beef.*

Foreign Meat and Solid Intact Labels. Meat and poultry products imported into the USA must carry labels naming the country of origin so they are not represented as being of American origin. This is done through wording such as *Product of Argentina,* shown immediately under product name.

Foreign Names. Foreign names for most meat food products are permitted, provided wording appears which gives the common or English name of the product.

Green Weight. Weight of the raw article prior to cooking or the addition of added substances.

Guarantee Statements. Any guarantee statement must be complete enough to advise the consumer as to the steps to be taken if not satisfied. An acceptable statement would be *Satisfaction guaranteed or your money refunded—return unused portion in the package to your dealer.*

Ingredients Statement. The order of predominance shall be based on the amounts of ingredients used in product preparation rather than the amounts in the finished product. Ingredients statements consisting of a component listing must have the components listed in order of predominance.

Jumbo. The term *Jumbo* may be used on labels if it is stated in the possessive such as *Our Jumbo* or using the firm's name. An exception to this is made when the term is used on franks where there are no more than 8 to the pound. The term *Jumbo* may not be used to qualify a net weight statement.

Keep Frozen. Phrases such as *Do Not Thaw* or *Do Not Defrost* are synonymous to *Keep Frozen.*

Legends. Products (or containers) consisting of mixed meat and poultry ingredients (or products) bear either the official meat inspection legend or poultry inspection legend, depending on which ingredients (or products) are present in the greater amounts. If meat and poultry exist in equal proportions, either official legend may be used. If meat and poultry exist in exact proportions and both appear in the product name, the official legend use must reflect the ingredient (or product) appearing first in the name.

Legends, Dual Inspection. Containers of products intended for sale to household consumers can bear only the official mark of inspection of the product enclosed.

Marinated. To be labeled *marinated* the product must be a mixture in which food is either soaked, massaged, tumbled, or injected to improve taste, tenderness, or other sensory attributes (such as color or juiciness). Time in a marinade depends on many factors such as: thickness and size of meat and strength of marinade. Therefore, marinade should be only that amount necessary to affect finished product. Limited to 10 percent pickup in red meat, 8 percent pickup in boneless poultry, and 3 percent in bone-in poultry.

Meat. The term *meat* may be used in the product name to identify the use of pork, beef, lamb, etc., or the species name may be shown.

Source:
Standards and Labeling Division, Food Safety and Inspection Service, USDA, *Standards and Labeling Policy Book,* Washington: Government Printing Office, June 1991.

Geographic Statements

Country, Ranch, and Farm in Trade, Branch, and Fanciful Names. In general, such terms as *farm* or *country* cannot be used on labels in connection with products unless those products are actually prepared on the farm or in the country. However, tradenames, brandnames, or fanciful names that include the words country, ranch, or farm, such as *Country Kitchen, Ranch House, Hickory Farms,* or *Carabeef Ranch Brand* are not governed by this requirement in the regulations unless the terms are used alone in conjunction with the product name (as in *Country Stew*). When the term is used in this context, the product must be prepared in the country (or on the ranch or farm, as the case may be).

Geographic and Related Terms. Any label representation that expresses or implies a particular geographical origin of the product or any ingredient of the product is only used when:

1. A truthful representation of geographical origin, e.g., *Virginia Ham* for a ham produced in the state of Virginia; or

2. A trademark or trade name which:

    a. has been so long and exclusively used by a manufacturer or distributor that it is generally understood by consumers to mean the product of the particular manufacturer or distributor, e.g., *Swiss Chalet;* or

    b. is so arbitrary or fanciful that it is generally understood by the consumer not to suggest geographical origin, e.g., *Moon Sausage;* or

    c. a part of the name required or allowed by an applicable Federal law, regulation or standard, e.g., *Frankfurter, Vienna;* or

3. A name whose market significance is generally understood by consumers to connote a particular class, kind, type or style of product or preparation rather than to indicate geographical origin of the product, e.g., *Mexican Style Dinner, Italian Style Pizza.* Such terms must be qualified with the word *style* or *type* unless specifically approved by the Food Safety and Inspection Service administrator as a generic term, e.g., *Lebanon Bologna, Genoa Salami, Milan Salami.*

Any geographical representation that does not meet these guidelines should be qualified by the word *brand* (provided that it is not used in such a way as to be false or misleading). A qualifying statement identifying the place where the product was actually made is required in proximity to the brand name, e.g., *Milwaukee Brand Bacon, Made in Chicago, Illinois.* The word *brand* must be in the same size and style of type as the geographical term. If the product has a foreign brand name, it may be identified as having been made in this country, e.g., *Scandinavian Brand Bacon, Made in U.S.A..*

Southern. This term is restricted to use only in areas south of the Mason-Dixon Line and east of the Mississippi River as well as Arkansas, Louisiana, and Missouri, which are also considered southern states.

Source:
Standards and Labeling Division, Food Safety and Inspection Service, USDA, *Standards and Labeling Policy Book,* Washington: Government Printing Office, June 1991.

Gravies

Gravies. At least 25 percent meat stock or broth, or 6 percent meat. One percent mono- and diglycerides allowed in gravies.

Gravy and Beef. At least 35 percent cooked beef when the word *beef* appears in the same size lettering as *gravy.* When the *beef* lettering is no larger than one-half the size of lettering of *gravy,* must contain at least 25 percent cooked beef.

Gravy and Dressing with Pork or Gravy and Pork with Dressing. At least 14 percent cooked pork.

Gravy and Yankee Pot Roast. At least 35 percent cooked beef, cooked with or without vegetables.

Gravy and Swiss Steak. At least 35 percent cooked meat.

Gravy and Poultry Salisbury Steak. Not more than 65 percent gravy and at least 35 percent poultry salisbury steak.

Source:
Standards and Labeling Division, Food Safety and Inspection Service, USDA, *Standards and Labeling Policy Book,* Washington: Government Printing Office, June 1991.

Ham

The upper part of a hog's leg (technically, all tissues posterior to the junction of the tuber coxae and the lumbar vertebrae) may be classified as *ham* regardless of the method of separation from the carcass. Usually cured by salting, drying, smoking, etc. When not cured, the ham is described as *fresh.* Detached hock, feet, skin, and fat cannot be so classified.

TERMINOLOGY

A la King. At least 20 percent ham (on a *cooked* basis).

Boiled. A fully cooked, boneless product which must be cooked in water and may be processed in a casing or can. The product may be of various shapes and may be partially cooked in boiling water (optional).

Capacolla. Product made with ham instead of pork shoulder butts. It is labeled *Ham Capacolla.*

Capacolla, Cooked. Ham which has been cured and then cooked.

Certified Pork. Pork that has been treated for trichinae by one of the approved methods.

Chopped. Chopped ham with shank meat permitted to the extent of not more than 25 percent over that normally present in the boneless ham. Also known as *Chopped, Pressed, Cooked, Smoked, or Sliced.*

Cooked. Product cooked in conventional manner. If labeled *Completely Cooked,* it should reach an internal temperature of 158 degrees F.

Croquettes. At least 35 percent cooked ham. If chopped ham is used the product name must be *Chopped Ham Croquettes.*

Fresh or Uncured. Ham that does not contain a cure must be labeled either *Fresh* or *Uncured.* This also applies to cooked product.

Ham and Cheese Loaf. Cheese is chopped into small cubes and combined with finely ground ham.

Ham and Cheese Salad. At least 25 percent ham (cooked basis).

Ham and Cheese Spread. At least 25 percent ham (cooked basis).

Ham and Dumplings and Sauce or Gravy. At least 18 percent cooked ham.

Ham Chowder, Condensed. At least 10 percent cooked ham.

Ham Half. Permitted on labels for semi-boneless ham products which have had the shank muscles removed. The two halves of the finished product have approximately an equal amount of bone. The term *No Slices Removed* is also suitable for use with a ham item referred to as *Half Ham.*

Ham Omelet. At least 18 percent cooked ham.

Ham Salad. At least 35 percent cooked ham. Chopped ham may be used without it appearing in the product name.

Ham Shortcake. At least 25 percent cooked ham.

Hamcola. Not an acceptable product name; should be accompanied by true product name such as *Boneless Cooked Ham Coated with Spices.*

Parma Ham, Prosciutto di Parma. When labeled *Parma Ham* and/or *Prosciutto di Parma,* the ham would have to be produced in the region of Parma, Italy, in accordance with Italian law, which defines the denomination of origin, the territorial limits of production, characteristics of the product, and the method of manufacture.

Pepperam. A peppered ham that is coated with spices.

Pressed. Same as *chopped ham.*

Quarter, Semi-Boneless (No Slices Removed). The product consists of a ham prepared as a *Regular Semi-Boneless, Half Ham* which is sectioned again to result in four pieces just about equal not only in weight but also in content of bone.

Regular. The skin-on-ham produced by separating it from the side of the hog at a point ranging from 2½ to 2¾ inches ahead of the exposed knob end of the aitch bone.

Scotch Style. A cured, uncooked, boned and rolled whole ham either tied or in a casing.

Shankless. When the term *shankless* is used in reference to a ham, it indicates that the shank has been removed by a cut through the joint at a right angle to the femur bone. The distal tip of the semitendinosus muscle may be severed above its tendinosus attachment, leaving an extension approximately 2 inches long. The extension is considered an integral part of the ham's body and is usually folded over the femur's end.

Smithfield. This is an aged, dry-cured ham made exclusively in Smithfield, Virginia. The use of the words *brand* or *style,* e.g., *Smithfield Brand Ham, Smithfield Style Ham,* does not eliminate this requirement.

Trimmings. Ham trimmings, to be labeled as ham, contain no excess shank meat and have a fat content not in excess of 35 percent or consist of at least 65 percent lean meat as determined by chemical analysis.

Virginia. Must either be processed in the state of Virginia or labeled as *Virginia Brand, made in (city and state).*

Westphalian or Westphalian Style. Ham is cut with bone in, the hip bone cut out, cured in a combination of dry and pickle cure but not a pickle alone. It is smoked in a medium warm (no greater than 100 degrees F) smokehouse until a shining red brown or chestnut color is acquired. Beechwood may be used and will impart the characteristic Westphalian flavor. Other hard woods are also acceptable. Juniper berries are permitted.

Source:

Standards and Labeling Division, Food Safety and Inspection Service, USDA, *Standards and Labeling Policy Book,* Washington: Government Printing Office, June 1991.

Head Meat

The following guidelines apply to the use and labeling of beef cheek meat and/or beef head meat, and pork cheek meat and/or pork head meat. *Beef cheek meat* and *pork cheek meat* refer to beef and pork cheeks from which the glandular material has been removed. *Beef head meat* and *pork head meat* refer to muscle tissue remaining on the beef and hog skull after removal of the skin, cheeks, tongue, and lips. The meat normally attached to and considered as part of the tongue trimmings when detached from the tongue trimmings may also be included as beef head meat or pork head meat although it can be labeled as *beef* or *pork.*

When beef cheek meat and/or beef head meat are included in boneless beef, their presence must be specifically declared. Examples include *Boneless Beef—Contains Beef Cheek Meat and Beef Head Meat, Boneless Beef Heat Meat, Boneless Beef—Ingredients. Beef, Beef Head Meat, Beef Cheek Meat,* or *Boneless Beef—20 percent Beef Head Meat, 25 percent Beef Cheek Meat.*

Beef cheek meat and/or beef head meat may be used in unlimited quantities and identified as *beef* in meat food products unless restricted by regulatory standards for specific products, i.e., chopped beef, ground beef, hamburger, fabricated beef, chili con carne, chili con carne with beans, and corned beef hash.

Source:

Standards and Labeling Division, Food Safety and Inspection Service, USDA, *Standards and Labeling Policy Book,* Washington: Government Printing Office, June 1991.

Honey

The word *honey* may be used on a product label if at least one of the following conditions is met: (1) the product contains at least 3 percent honey; (2) the honey contains at least 80 percent solids or is U.S. Grade C or above; or (3) when other sweeteners (sugar, dextrose, maltose, invert sugar, corn syrup solids, and similar ingredients) are used, the quantity may not exceed one-half that of the honey, e.g., if 3 percent honey is used, then no more than 1.5 percent of all other sweeteners may be used. For a product to be identified as *Honey Glazed,* it must contain a ratio of honey to other sweeteners of no less than 2:1 (if dried honey is used, the ratio is to be no less than 1.6:1). When honey is included in a breading, a honey claim may be made regardless of the quantity of honey used.

TERMINOLOGY

Honey Cured. May be shown on the labeling of a cured product if (1) the honey used contains at least 80 percent solids or is U.S. Grade C or above; (2) honey is the only sweetening ingredient (or when other sweetening ingredients are used in combination with honey, they do not exceed one-half the amount of honey used); and (3) honey is used in an amount sufficient to flavor and/or affect the appearance of the finished product.

Sugar Cured. Used on the labeling of a cured product if (1) the sugar used is cane sugar or beet sugar; (2) sugar is the only sweetening ingredient (or when other sweetening ingredients are used in combination with sugar, they do not exceed one-half the amount of sugar used); and (3) sugar is used in an amount sufficient to flavor and/or affect the appearance of the finished product.

Honey and Sugar Cured or Sugar and Honey Cured. Used on labeling if (1) the honey and sugar are of the nature described above; (2) the honey and sugar are the only sweetening agents (or when other sweetening ingredients are used in combination with the honey and sugar, they do not individually exceed either the amount of honey or sugar used and collectively do not exceed one-half the total amount of honey and sugar); and (3) the honey and sugar are used in amounts sufficient to flavor and/or affect the appearance of the finished product.

Source:
Standards and Labeling Division, Food Safety and Inspection Service, USDA, *Standards and Labeling Policy Book,* Washington: Government Printing Office, June 1991.

Imitation

A label for a product which is an imitation of another food should bear the word *Imitation* immediately preceding the name of the food imitated. Immediately thereafter, the word *Ingredients* must appear, followed by the names of the ingredients arranged in descending order of predominance. Cuts of meat in their natural form containing excess moisture cannot be labeled *imitation* (e.g., ham, corned beef brisket, tongue).

IMITATION FLAVORS

Imitation beef flavor, imitation mushroom flavor, flavor base for gravies, and similar substances which enhance, fortify, or help to simulate a flavor are usually composed of food additives and, as such, are not *artificial flavors* for labeling purposes. *Imitation flavors* can be composed of such ingredients as flour, fats, oils, salt, hydrolyzed vegetable protein, vegetable gums, thiamine hydrochloride, beta alanine, disodium inosinate, glutamic acid, and a host of other ingredients. These flavorings must be identified on labels by showing each individual ingredient by its common name. Class names such as amino acids are not acceptable. Each specific amino acid must be listed.

Source:
Standards and Labeling Division, Food Safety and Inspection Service, USDA, *Standards and Labeling Policy Book,* Washington: Government Printing Office, June 1991.

Jerky

Jerky products are meats sliced into thin strips and preserved. Strips may be cured or uncured, air or oven dried, and smoked or unsmoked. A reference to the particular type of drying method is not a labeling requirement.

TYPES

Beef Jerky. Produced from a single piece of beef. May also be classified as *Natural Style Beef Jerky* provided this product name is accompanied by the explanatory statement *Made from solid pieces of beef* or comparable terminology.

Beef Jerky, Chunked and Formed. Produced from chunks which are molded and formed and cut into strips.

Beef Jerky, Ground and Formed or Chopped and Formed. Produced as described, molded, and formed and cut into strips.

Binders and Extenders. Jerky products containing binders or extenders must show the true product name, such as *Beef and Soy Protein Concentrate Jerky, Ground and Formed.*

Species (or Kind) Jerky Sausage. The word *jerky* can only appear on labels for products in which the meat has been chopped or ground and then stuffed into casings, when the word *Sausage* appears immediately contiguous to *jerky* whenever it is shown. *Sausage* must be in type at least one-third as high as *jerky* in the same color ink and on the same background. The words *stick, piece,* etc., cannot be used as substitutes for *sausage* in the product name. *Sausage* means that the product has been chopped.

Source:
Standards and Labeling Division, Food Safety and Inspection Service, USDA, *Standards and Labeling Policy Book,* Washington: Government Printing Office, June 1991.

Lamb, Yearling Mutton, and Mutton

Sheep (ovine) carcasses are classified as *lamb, yearling mutton,* or *mutton,* depending upon their maturity as indicated by their muscular and skeletal systems. Typical lamb carcasses have a light red color and fine texture of lean. Yearling mutton carcasses have a slightly dark red color and slightly coarse texture of lean. Mutton carcasses have a dark red color and coarse texture of lean.

GRADES

The quality grade of an ovine carcass is based on separate evaluations of two general considerations—the quality or the palatability-indicating characteristics of the lean and the conformation of the carcass. The quality of the lean is evaluated by its texture, firmness, and marbling, as observed in a cut surface, in relation to the apparent maturity of the animal. Conformation is the manner of formation of the carcass with reference to the development of the muscular and skeletal systems. Superior

conformation implies a high proportion of edible meat to bone and a high proportion of the weight of the carcass in the more demanded cuts. The quality standards are intended to apply to all ovine carcasses without regard to the sex condition of the animal at time of slaughter. However, males which are uncastrated are discounted in quality grade in accord to their development.

The chart below shows the relationship between flank fat streakings, maturity, and quality.

GRADES: LAMB

Prime. Lamb carcasses having minimum conformation qualifications for the Prime grade tend to be thickly muscled throughout, are moderately wide and thick in relation to their length,

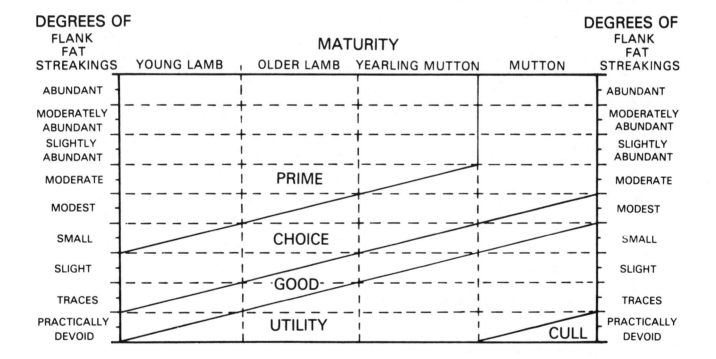

Relationship between flank fat streakings, maturity, and quality

and have moderately plump and full legs, moderately wide and thick backs, and moderately thick and full shoulders.

Young Lamb. The minimum degree of flank fat streakings required for such carcasses increases with advancing maturity throughout this group from *minimum small* to *maximum small* (see chart). Inside flank muscles are a slightly dark pink color.

Older Lamb. The minimum degree of flank fat streakings required for such carcasses increases with advancing maturity throughout this group from *minimum modest* to *maximum modest* (see chart). Inside flank muscles are a light red color.

Choice. Lamb carcasses having minimum conformation qualifications for the Choice grade are slightly thick muscled throughout, tend to be slightly wide and thick in relation to their length, and tend to have slightly plump and full legs, slightly wide and thick backs, and slightly thick and full shoulders.

Young Lamb. The minimum degree of flank fat streakings required for such carcasses increases with advancing maturity throughout this group from *minimum traces* to *maximum traces* (see chart). Inside flank muscles are a moderately dark pink color.

Older Lamb. The minimum degree of flank fat streakings required for such carcasses increases with advancing maturity throughout this group from *minimum slight* to *maximum slight* (see chart). Inside flank muscles are a moderately light red color.

Good. Lamb carcasses having minimum conformation qualifications for the Good grade are slightly thin muscled throughout, are moderately narrow in relation to their length, and have slightly thin, tapering legs and slightly narrow and thin backs and shoulders.

Young Lamb. The minimum degree of flank fat streakings required for such carcasses increases with advancing maturity throughout this group from *minimum practically devoid* to *maximum practically devoid* (see chart). Inside flank muscles are a dark pink color.

Older Lamb. The minimum degree of flank fat streakings required for such carcasses increases with advancing maturity throughout this group from *minimum traces* to *maximum traces* (see chart). Inside flank muscles are a slightly dark red color.

Utility. The Utility grade includes those lamb carcasses whose characteristics are inferior to those specified as minimum for the Good grade.

Source:
Agricultural Marketing Service, USDA, "Lamb, Yearling Mutton, and Mutton Carcasses," 7 CFR 54.122 (1992): Washington: Government Printing Office.

Lard

Manteca, Manteca Pura. A Spanish term. When either *Manteca* or *Manteca Pura* is used as a product name, the English designa-

tion, *lard* or *rendered pork fat,* as appropriate, follows in close proximity in the same size and style of type.

Continuous Process Lard. Acceptable name for *lard,* rendered by a low temperature process separating the oil from the fatty tissue by means of heat and centrifugal force.

Lard, Refined. This term is applied to open-kettle rendered, prime steam, or dry-rendered lard put through a filter press, with or without a bleaching agent.

Source:
Standards and Labeling Division, Food Safety and Inspection Service, USDA, *Standards and Labeling Policy Book,* Washington: Government Printing Office, June 1991.

Lasagna

Lasagna is a pasta dish made with wide flat noodles. Sauce is an expected ingredient of lasagna products and its declaration in the product name is optional. Other terms used on lasagna labels are defined as follows.

TERMINOLOGY

Cheese Lasagna with Meat. 12 percent meat.

Lasagna with Meat and Sauce. 12 percent meat.

Lasagna with Meat Sauce. 6 percent meat in total product.

Lasagna with Poultry. 8 percent poultry meat.

Lasagna with Tomato Sauce, Cheese, and Pepperoni. 8 percent pepperoni.

Meat Lasagna. 12 percent meat.

Poultry Lasagna. 8 percent poultry meat.

Source:
Standards and Labeling Division, Food Safety and Inspection Service, USDA, *Standards and Labeling Policy Book,* Washington: Government Printing Office, June 1991.

Liver Products

Any product with liver in its name must contain a minimum of 30 percent liver.

TERMINOLOGY

Liver, Chopped. At least 50 percent liver.

Liver and Onions. At least 45 percent liver.

Liver and Onions and Eggs. At least 40 percent liver.

Liver Spread (Streich Leberwurst). At least 30 percent liver in total formulation.

Source:
Standards and Labeling Division, Food Safety and Inspection Service, USDA, *Standards and Labeling Policy Book,* Washington: Government Printing Office, June 1991.

Luncheon Meat

The meat components of *Luncheon Meat* are identified in the ingredients statement on the label as *beef, pork, beef tongue meat, pork tongue meat, beef heart meat,* and *pork heart meat. Beef* and *pork* in the ingredients statement on labels for luncheon meats mean lean meat with overlying fat and the portions of sinew, nerve, and the blood vessels which normally accompany muscle tissue and which are not separated in the process of dressing. It does not include bone and skin. Up to 10 percent of the meat portion of the formula can consist of cured and smoked meat trimmings. They do not require special declaration in the ingredients statement but are included under pork and beef. Heart or heart muscle, tongues, or tongue meat and cheek meat can be included in Luncheon Meat under the following restrictions:

- Hearts or heart meat or tongues or tongue meat must be declared individually by species in the ingredients statement on the label.
- No restriction on the percentage limits of hearts, heart meat, tongues, and tongue meats in the formulation.
- The terms *heart meat* and *tongue meat* refer to the muscle tissue remaining after heart caps, glands, nodes, connective tissue, etc., are trimmed away.

Water added to Luncheon Meat during manufacture cannot exceed 3 percent by weight of the total ingredients. This is controlled by weighing ingredients and not by analysis. Care must be used to see that water is not added indirectly through the use of undrained hearts and tongues.

The only ingredients permitted in Luncheon Meat are curing ingredients, sweetening agents, spices, and flavoring. All of these substances must be declared in the ingredients statement by name except the various flavorings and spices which need not be named individually. Spices refers to natural spices and not to extracts.

Source:
Standards and Labeling Division, Food Safety and Inspection Service, USDA, *Standards and Labeling Policy Book,* Washington: Government Printing Office, June 1991.

Macaroni

Macaroni and Beef in Sauce. At least 12 percent beef.
Macaroni and Cheese with Ham. At least 12 percent cooked ham.
Macaroni and Noodle Type Products. A pasta product may be declared in the ingredients statement by one of the following specific names if it meets the applicable size and shape requirements specified below:

Name	Shape	Size (dia. in inches)
Macaroni	Tube-shaped	0.11 to 0.27
Spaghetti	Tube-shaped or Cord-shaped (not tubular)	0.06 to 0.11
Vermicelli	Cord-shaped (not tubular)	Not more than 0,.06
Noodles	Ribbon-shaped	

A macaroni product should be declared in the ingredients statement by the generic name *Macaroni Product* if it does not conform to any of the shape and size requirements specified above. The noodle product should be declared by the generic name *Noodle Product* if it is made with eggs and/or egg yolks and does not conform to the shape and size requirements specified above.
Macaroni Salad with Meat (or Poultry). At least 12 percent cooked meat or poultry meat.

Source:
Standards and Labeling Division, Food Safety and Inspection Service, USDA, *Standards and Labeling Policy Book,* Washington: Government Printing Office, June 1991.

Meals

Breakfasts (Containing Meat). At least 15 percent cooked meat or poultry (or meat or poultry food product) based on the total net weight of breakfast.
Dinners and Suppers, Frozen. Frozen products labeled as *dinner* or *supper* must weigh at least 10 ounces and shall contain at least 3 of the following: meat, poultry, cheese, eggs, vegetables, fruit, potatoes, or rice or other cereal-based products (other than bread or rolls). This is not intended to include products such as casseroles and stews that have all of the components combined. Sauces and gravies are not considered as one of the components.

They may also contain other servings of food such as soup, bread or rolls, appetizer, beverage, and dessert, and these components may be included in the minimum 10 ounces net weight requirement. If meat is featured in the product name, e.g., *Beef Dinner,* the requirement is 25 percent or 2.5 ounces cooked meat. If a meat food product is featured in the product name, e.g., *Beef Burgundy Dinner,* then 25 percent or 2.5 ounces meat food product is needed.

If poultry is featured in the name, e.g., *Chicken Dinner,* the standard is 18 percent or 2 ounces cooked deboned poultry meat, whichever is greater. However, if a poultry food product is featured in the product name, e.g., *Chicken a la King Dinner,* then 25 percent or 2.5 ounces of poultry food product, whichever is greater, is needed.

The meat requirement for products with net weights greater than 10 ounces may be established exclusive of the appetizer, bread, and dessert, provided the remaining components weigh not less than 10 ounces.

The name for dinner and supper products shall consist of or include a listing of each of the dish components in descending order of predominance by weight, for example, *Fried Chicken Dinner—Fried Chicken, Mashed Potatoes, Peas, and Carrots.* Dinner or supper identification may appear on side panels without the complete product name shown, e.g., *Fried Chicken Dinner* or *Beef Dinner.*
Entree (Principal Dish or Main Course). Product labeled *entree* should fall into one of the following categories: (1) *all meat or*

meat food product—100 percent meat or meat food product; (2) *meat or meat food product and one vegetable* or *meat or meat food product and gravy*—50 percent cooked meat or meat food product; (3) m*eat and vegetable with gravy*—30 percent cooked meat portion and meat and gravy portion at least 50 percent, e.g., *Salisbury Steak with Potatoes and Gravy;* or (4) *Meat or entree portion of dinner*—25 percent cooked meat or meat food product, e.g., *Meat Loaf Dinner* would require 25 percent meat loaf.

Serving Suggestion. *Serving Suggestion, Serve as Suggested, Picture does not represent contents of package,* and similar phrases must accompany all vignettes which illustrate ingredients that reasonably could be but are not in the package as sold, or which illustrate the nature of the product after preparation. Such vignettes that are not so identified are misleading.

Servings or Portions. When a label contains statements or claims identifying the number of servings, it must be qualified to identify the size of the serving. For example: *Three 2-oz. servings* or *One 6-oz. serving* or *Three portions, 2 ounces,* etc., all in the same size print.

Snacks (Hor d'oeuvres). At least 15 percent cooked meat or 10 percent cooked bacon. The label must show true product name such as *Liver Pate on Toast.*

Source:
Standards and Labeling Division, Food Safety and Inspection Service, USDA, *Standards and Labeling Policy Book,* Washington: Government Printing Office, June 1991.

Meat, Processed Foods

Meat Casseroles. Must contain at least 25 percent meat or 18 percent cooked meat.

Meat Curry. Must contain at least 50 percent meat.

Meat Cuts Specifications. Labels for meat cuts with names plus numbers that refer to specifications in the *Meat Buyers' Guide* from the National Association of Meat Purveyors shall be approved with the understanding that the product is certified by the Livestock Division as meeting the required specification.

Meat Food Products Containing Poultry Ingredients. Meat food products containing poultry ingredients in amounts that exceed 20 percent of the total livestock and poultry product portion of the meat food product must have product names that indicate the presence of the poultry ingredients, e.g., *Beef and Chicken Chili* or *Chili made with Beef and Chicken.*

Meat food products containing poultry ingredients in amounts at 20 percent or less of the total livestock and poultry product portion of the meat food product must have product names that are qualified to indicate the presence of the poultry ingredients, e.g., *Beef Stew—Turkey Added.* However, meat food products that do not meet specified minimum livestock ingredient requirements because poultry ingredients are replacing any part of the required livestock ingredients must have product names that indicate the presence of the poultry

ingredients, e.g., *Beef and Turkey Stew* or *Stew Made with Beef and Turkey.*

Meat Foldover Mit Dressing. Must contain at least 50 percent meat (chopped and formed).

Meat Pies (or Vegetable Meat Pies). Must contain at least 25 percent meat (meat in gravy may be counted).

Meat Pie Filling. Must contain at least 37 percent meat.

Meat Ravioli. Must contain at least 10 percent meat in ravioli.

Meat Ravioli in Sauce. Must contain at least 10 percent meat in ravioli and at least 50 percent ravioli in total product.

Meat Ravioli in Meat Sauce. Must contain at least 10 percent meat in ravioli and at least 50 percent ravioli in total product. At least 6 percent meat in sauce.

Meat Sauce. Must contain at least 6 percent ground meat.

Meat Spreads. Must contain at least 50 percent meat or 35 percent cooked meat. When another major component considered a significant source of protein (such as cheese) is added, the requirement is reduced to 25 percent cooked meat. Must show true product name, such as *Sausage and Cheese Spread.*

Source:
Standards and Labeling Division, Food Safety and Inspection Service, USDA, *Standards and Labeling Policy Book,* Washington: Government Printing Office, June 1991.

Meat By-Products

The term *by-products* on meat product labels is accompanied by the name of the species from which the byproduct was derived and individually named, e.g., *beef by-products (heart, kidney, liver).* They may also be listed by species, e.g., *calf liver, beef heart,* etc.

Beef Bile. Acceptable as an edible meat by-product.

Blood Pudding. Non-specific product made with livestock blood. Product name must be followed by an ingredients statement.

Bung. Large intestine used as a casing.

Derma. When the term *derma* is used in the product name, only natural casing or skin must be used.

Diaphragm. This is the muscle and connective tissue separating the chest and abdominal cavity. Steaks cut from the diaphragm are often referred to as *Beef Skin and Steaks.*

Giblets. The liver, heart, and gizzard of a poultry carcass. Although often packaged with them, the neck of a bird is not a giblet.

Head Meat. After removal of the cheeks, lips, snout, skin, and tongue from the head, there remains small pockets and areas on the skull to which muscle tissue is attached. This muscle may be removed and used in products and declared on labeling as beef or pork as the case may be. However, there are a few standardized products in which the regulations limit the amount of this meat that may be used and require that it be specifically declared on the label, e.g., chili, chili with beans, and corned beef hash. See *Beef Cheek Meat and Beef Headmeat.*

Headcheese. A jellied product consisting predominantly of pork by-products and seasoning ingredients. It must contain some product from the head. Extenders like cereal, soy derivatives,

369

nonfat dry milk, etc., are not permitted ingredients of head-cheese. Headcheese in natural casings should be processed by heating to an internal temperature of at least 150 degrees F.

Heart Breads. That portion of the thymus gland or sweetbread that lies in the chest cavity. Less desirable than the portion in the neck.

Heart Cap. Blood vessels and auricles at the top of an untrimmed heart.

Hearts/Heart Meat. Must be listed separately by species in all products. May not be labeled as *beef, pork,* etc. Hearts/heart meat (including the heart cap) is considered meat only for purposes of calculating the meat-to-textured vegetable protein ratios.

Hog Stomachs. Must bear mark of inspection regardless of intended use.

Intestines. Intestines can be prepared as edible products and must bear the mark of inspection.

Morcella Blood Pudding. The product is made from pork fat, beef blood, and/or pork blood and may contain meat.

Sheep (Lamb) Brains, Hearts, Tongues. Sheep brains, hearts, and tongues are practically indistinguishable from lamb brains, hearts, and tongues, respectively; therefore, brains, hearts, and tongues from ovine carcasses may be designated as either sheep or lamb.

Tongue-Cheek Trimmings. Labeling terminology for the various kinds of tongue and cheek trimmings are as follows:

- *(Species) salivary glands, lymph nodes, and fat (cheeks)* identifies the tissues remaining after trimming cheeks.
- *(Species) tongue trimmings* identifies all tissues except cartilage and bone that are obtained by converting long-cut to short-cut tongues. This conversion is done by making a transverse cut anterior to the epiglottis, removing the soft palate and epiglottis, and cutting through the hyoid bone. Approximately 1½ inches of the bone is left with the tongue. *(Species) tongue trimmings* may also be used to identify salivary glands, lymph nodes, and fat from which the muscle tissue has not been removed.
- *(Species) salivary glands, lymph nodes, and fat (tongue),* must be preceded by the name of the species from which derived.
- Trimmings from the tongue itself should be identified as *tongue meat,* preceded by the name of the species from which derived.

Tongue Spread. At least 50 percent fresh tongues or 35 percent cooked tongues.

Windpipes. This term includes larynx, trachea, and bronchi.

Source:
Standards and Labeling Division, Food Safety and Inspection Service, USDA, *Standards and Labeling Policy Book,* Washington: Government Printing Office, June 1991.

Meat Loaf

These products are uncooked or cooked pork, beef, or lamb and other ingredients formed into a loaf. Ingredients such as cracker meal, oatmeal, bread crumbs, nonfat dry milk, soy ingredients (untextured), milk, and whole eggs are not required in the product name. May contain head meat, cheek meat, heart meat, and tongue meat under label declaration in ingredients statement only. May not include more than 12 percent extenders and binders. Partially defatted chopped beef or pork may be used up to 25 percent and declared as meat in the ingredients statement. Must contain at least 65 percent meat. Onion, tomato juice, water, and other liquid extenders are not directly controlled by labeling or other regulations.

Loaf. A *loaf* (other than meat loaf) consists of meat in combination with any of a wide range of nonmeat ingredients. These products are not identified with the terms *Meat Loaf, Beef Loaf,* or the like, but with designations, such as *Olive Loaf, Pickle and Pimiento Loaf, Honey Loaf, Luxury Loaf,* and others descriptive names.

Meat Loaf, Canned (Perishable). Canned perishable products in the loaf category must:

- Adequately label the product's perishable labeling requirements.
- Be cured with at least 1 ounce nitrate per 100 pounds product and 0.5 percent dextrose or 1 percent sugar.
- Show a brine concentration of not less than 3.5 percent in finished product. Products that contain cereal, starch, or other extenders must have not less than 6.1 percent brine concentration.
- Be cooked to an internal temperature of not less than 150 degrees F.

Meat Loaf, Canned (Sterile Packed). No head, cheek, heart, or tongue meat permitted. Other requirements same as uncanned cured meat loaf. Binders and extenders must be shown in the product name such as *Meat Loaf, cereal added.*

Meat Foldover Mit Dressing. At least 50 percent meat (chopped and formed).

Meat Loaf, Cured. Such a product can contain in addition to cures and seasonings, up to 3 percent ice or water. Extenders or binders are not permitted.

Meat Pasty. At least 25 percent meat.

Source:
Standards and Labeling Division, Food Safety and Inspection Service, USDA, *Standards and Labeling Policy Book,* Washington: Government Printing Office, June 1991.

Meat Product Terminology

Agnelotto See Dry Aged. This Italian term describes ravioli dumplings stuffed with at least 10 percent minced meat. Labeling must show a true product name, such as *Dumpling Stuffed With Meat.*

Alcapurrias. A Spanish term for a Puerto Rican meat turnover containing at least 8 percent cooked beef. Product labeled as Alcapurrias must be made only in Puerto Rico. If pork used, then identify as *Pork-Alcapurrias.* If made outside of Puerto Rico, the true product name must be shown in English, such as *Beef Turnover.*

Arroz Con Pollo. A Spanish term for a product containing at least 15 percent cooked chicken meat. Must show true product name *Rice with Chicken.*

Au Gratin Potatoes and Bacon. At least 8 percent fully cooked bacon (based on 40 percent yield).

Baby Back Ribs. The portion of the pork ribs removed from the loin dorsal to the scribe line. This desciption of the cut must be provided with the information for label approval.

Beans with Bacon in Sauce. At least 12 percent smoked bacon.

Beans with Barbecued Meats and Sauce Products. Product consisting of a combination of beans and barbecued meats and sauce must not contain less than 8.4 percent meat in total formula.

Beans with Frankfurters in Sauce. At least 20 percent franks.

Beans with Ham in Sauce. At least 12 percent ham.

Beans with Meat in Sauce. At least 12 percent meat.

Beans with Meatballs in Sauce. At least 20 percent meatballs.

Bialy. A Jewish roll or bread. Approval granted for labeling term *Pizza on a Bialy.*

Blintzes. Originally a Jewish term for a filled delicate pancake resembling the crepe of France. The standard for crepes is applied to this product.

Boingghetti. This label must show a true product name, *Spaghetti with Chicken Sauce.* At least 6 percent cooked chicken meat.

Bolo. Contains beef and pork, water, nonfat dry milk, and flavoring. The label must show a true product name, such as *Beef and Pork, Water and Nonfat Dry Milk Product.*

Bone-In Meat Food Products. Label must declare *Bone-In.*

Bread Stuffing. If product contains over 3 percent meat, it must be processed under inspection. Product name should be *Bread Stuffing with Meat* or *Bread Stuffing with Pork,* etc.

Breading Mixtures (with Paprika). Paprika may be added to breading mixtures for the purpose of enhancing or influencing the color. However, the statement *Breading Colored with Paprika* need not be shown when paprika is listed in its correct position in the ingredient statement.

Brochette. Meat broiled on a skewer. Must have qualifying statement under product name, such as *Beef Cubes on a Skewer.*

Brociola (Braciola or Brasiola). An Italian term for a rolled and tied product formulated from pork, cheese, salt, flavoring, and parsley. May also be made from beef. Species must be identified in product name.

Burger. Meat or poultry products labeled with the term *burger* must conform to the standard for *hamburger* (9 CFR 319.15[b]) and *poultry burgers* (9 CFR 381.160).

Burritos with Sauce or Gravy. At least 50 percent burritos.

Butt. Must be used in conjunction with primal part name.

Buttcola. Used as a coin name only; must be accompanied by true product name such as *Boneless Cooked Pork Shoulder Butt.*

Calzone, Calzini. An Italian term for a turnover-like product made with dough stuffed with meat or poultry, cheese, and seasonings and baked. Must contain 25 percent meat or 14 percent poultry meat. The label must show a true product name, such as *Sausage and Cheese Filling in Dough.*

Canned Chopped Beef or Pork. Cured products with no more than 3 percent water in formula.

Cannelloni. A pasta product having at least 10 percent meat or 7 percent cooked poultry meat. Cannelloni is an Italian term used to describe a product having the same characteristics as ravioli with the exception that the pasta is in a tubular form. The label must show a true product name such as *Beef Cannelloni.*

Cappelleti with Meat in Sauce. A macaroni-like product containing at least 12 percent meat.

Casserole. To be labeled *casserole,* the product must contain at least 25 percent meat or 18 percent cooked meat.

Catsup. When permitted in meat food products, catsup is listed in the ingredients statement either as catsup or tomato catsup. Not permitted in sausage or ground (chopped) beef patties. When used with prepared meat patties, product name must reflect the use, e.g., *Beef Patties with Catsup.*

Cha Shu Bow. A Chinese term for a steamed bun with a dry roasted pork filling requiring 15 percent cooked pork. Label must show true product name such as *Steamed Bun with a Pork and Cabbage Filling.*

Charol, Charoil. A natural smoke flavoring.

Chevon. A French term for goat meat used for food.

Chimichanga. A Mexican specialty from the state of Sonora. They are made by wrapping a flour tortilla around a filling and fried until brown and crisp. Must contain at least 15 percent meat or 10 percent poultry meat.

Chinese Pepper Steak. Contains at least 30 percent cooked beef. A Chinese main dish usually served with rice. Beef steak is cut into thin strips, browned in fat or oil, and added to a soy-flavored sauce. Vegetables are also added to the sauce. Green pepper strips are always used, and other vegetables may be included.

Chitterlings. Approved label must be accompanied with a reference to the species of food animal from which the product is secured. Hog bungs may be labeled *Pork Chitterlings.* The purge under normal conditions should not exceed 20 percent of the net weight of frozen chitterlings.

Chohinita Pibil. A Mexican term for a product consisting of pork filling wrapped in banana leaves and baked. The leaves are removed prior to serving. Requires true product name to appear on the lable, such as *Pork Filling wrapped in Banana Leaves.*

Chopette. May be used as part of product name, e.g., *Pork Chopette,* but product must conform to standard for *Fabricated Steak* (see entry).

Chopped, Pressed, Cooked, Smoked, Sliced. Products such as beef, chicken, and turkey with this qualifying phrase may be formulated with unlimited water. However, the finished product must be returned to the *green weight* (see index).

Chopped Egg and Ham Salad. Must contain at least 12 percent bacon (or 9 percent fully cooked bacon).

Chopped Ham. A total of 15 percent shank meat is permitted. This is 3 percent above the normal proportion of 12 percent shank meat found in a whole ham.

Choron Sauce. A French term for a bearnaise sauce containing tomato puree or paste served with grilled meat or poultry.

Chow Mein with Meat. Must contain at least 12 percent fresh meat.

Chulent (Cholent). Must contain at least 25 percent fresh meat. A meal-in-one dish of Jewish cuisine made in various ways. The name can stand without qualification.

Club or Delmonico Steak. These terms are restricted to meat from the anterior portion of the beef short loin extending from the T-bone area up to and including the 13th rib.

Coppa. An Italian term for Pork Shoulder Butts, Uncooked, Dry-Cured.

Corn Meal Mush with Bacon. Must contain at least 15 percent cooked bacon.

Cottage Butt. Must be qualified as a *pork shoulder butt.*

Country Brand. To be followed by *Made in City and State.*

Cracklings. See *Pork Cracklings.*

Creamed Cheese with Chipped Beef. Consists of cream cheese, chipped beef, cream, and chopped onions, with the most component not less than 12 percent of the total formulation.

Creole. A French term which applies to many dishes made with tomatoes, spices, and green peppers. Must contain at least 25 percent fresh meat.

Crepe Filling (Meat or Poultry). At least 40 percent cooked meat or 20 percent cooked meat if filling has one other characterizing ingredient such as cheese. At least 14 percent cooked meat when the filling has two other characterizing ingredients such as cheese and mushrooms. Percentages based on total product.

Crepes (Meat or Poultry). At least 20 percent cooked meat when the filling contains no other major characterizing component. At least 10 percent cooked meat when the filling contains only one other major characterizing component (Cheese and Meat). At least 7 percent cooked meat when the filling contains two or more other major characterizing components (Cheese, Ham, Mushrooms). These percentages are based on the total weight of the product.

Croissant (Filled). Crescent-shaped roll requiring 18 percent cooked meat. Labeling must show a true product name, such as *Croissant with a ham and cheese sauce filling.*

Croquette. At least 35 percent cooked meat, based on total formulation. Beef, ham, etc., must appear as part of product name.

Croute. A French term for a a product enclosed in a pastry shell or covered with crust.

Cube. Meat cut into uniform cubes such as *Beef Cubes for Stew.*

Cubed. Acceptable on labels of meat products such as steaks or patties that have been cubed (tenderized) in a cubing machine. The word *Cube* is not acceptable.

Curried Sauce with Meat (Poultry) and Rice Casserole. At least 35 percent cooked meat or poultry meat based on the sauce and meat portion only.

Cushion (Ham). That portion of the posterior, rounded, and more fleshy side of the ham.

Daisy. Must be accompanied by true product name, such as *Cured Pork Shoulder Butt.*

Delmonico Beef Steak. See *Club Steak.*

Deviled Meat Food Product or Potted Meat Food Product. Product is made from mostly meat by-products with some meat. The product name, *Deviled Meat Food Product,* need not appear all on one line. However, the name must be displayed in a prominent manner and must be featured in the same size, style, and color print on the same background.

Deviled Poultry. A semisolid cured poultry food product made from finely comminuted poultry in natural proportions and containing condiments. Deviled poultry may contain poultry fat provided that the total fat content shall not exceed 35 percent of the finished product and the moisture content shall not exceed that of the fresh unprocessed poultry. When skin is in excess of natural proportions, skin must be included in the product name, e.g. *Deviled (Kind) with (Kind) Skin Added.*

Duck, Salted. Product labeled as such should reach an internal temperature of 155 degrees F during processing.

Dumplings with Beef. Must contain at least 18 percent meat in total formulation.

Dutch Brand Loaf. Nonspecific loaf, but name must be qualified with *Made in USA.*

Easter Nola. Salami that is made with pork that is coarsely chopped and mildly seasoned with black pepper and garlic.

Empanadillas. A Spanish term for a turnover containing 25 percent fresh meat or poultry (raw basis). The species or kind is part of the product name. They may vary in size from large to hors d'oeuvre size.

Enchilada (Poultry). Must contain at least 10.5 percent poultry meat.

Enchilada (Meat). A Mexican style product containing at least 15 percent meat. Consists of a tortilla which has been filled with a variety of fillings and then rolled. The species must appear in the product name, e.g., *Beef Enchilada.*

Enchilada, Sonora Style. Consists of two or more tortillas stacked pancake style with filling spread between each tortilla.

Enchilada with Beef Chili Gravy or Enchilada Prepared with Meat and Sauce. At least 50 percent of the product must be enchilada.

Faggots. A sausage made with a combination of beef, veal, and pork cured with salt, nitrates, and sugar. Sheep or hog casings are used and sausage is linked in pairs, each about 6 inches long. Classed as cooked smoked sausage.

Fajitas. A Spanish term, which translated is "little belts" or strips of meat. Fajitas are strips of seasoned or marinated meat or poultry meat which has been cooked. Fajitas may also be a sandwich-like product, requiring 15 percent strips of cooked meat or poultry meat (excluding the marinade) and topped with onions, peppers and sauce and rolled in a flour tortilla. Fajita, including the name of the meat or poultry, may stand alone, e.g., *Beef Fajita, Chicken Fajita.*

Filet Mignon. Beef tenderloin cut into steaks against the grain and broiled. Sometimes wrapped in certified bacon strips in which case the product name must be qualified, such as *bacon wrapped.*

Flank Steak. See *Steak, Flank.*

Flanken in the Pot. Must contain at least 25 percent beef. Product is made from beef plates and may contain such components as matzo balls, noodles, and vegetables. True product name, such as *Flanken in the Pot with Matzo Balls, Noodles and Vegetables,* must be used.

Fresh Kielbasa. Acceptable name for *kielbasa* when made without cures.

Fried Noodles with Pork. Must contain at least 12 percent fresh pork in total formulation.

Fried Products. Frying medium need not be shown on the label.

Fried Rice with Meat. Must contain at least 10 percent meat, and may contain eggs and vegetables.

Fried Rice. This term has a long association with a rice product in which the rice is boiled. Accordingly, the term *fried* in the name is considered acceptable.

Fries. Beef testicles may be labeled as *Beef Fries*. They are not permitted to be used as an ingredient in meat food products.

Fritters (Meat). Must contain at least 35 percent fresh meat in total formulation, and can contain up to 65 percent breading. Can be labeled as *breaded* provided the breading (coating) does not exceed 30 percent. Textured vegetable protein and soy derivatives can be included when properly labeled. Fritters containing pork should be trichinae treated.

Frizzes. An acceptable name for a product similar to pepperoni but not smoked.

Galantine or Galatine. A molded roll or shape of meat, poultry, or game stuffed with forcemeat (finely ground meat or poultry, usually containing binders), coated with aspic jelly, and served cold. Not permitted in sausages, luncheon meat, meat loaves, etc.

Gelatin in Poultry Rolls. If gelatin or some other binder comprises more than 3 percent of the formula, the name of the product must be qualified by wording such as *Gelatin Added*.

German Potato Salad. Salad traditionally prepared with bacon as an ingredient at 7 to 8 percent of the formula. Only the bacon ingredient is specified by labeling regulations.

German Potato Salad with Bacon. Must have at least 14 percent cooked bacon in total formulation.

Giblet Gravy (Kind). Requires 7.25 percent giblets. Must contain an equal number of livers, hearts, and gizzards.

Gnocchi. Italian term describing dumplings made of wheat or potato flour rolled into rope-like strips about ¾ inch thick and cut into pieces ¾ inch long.

Goetta. An oatmeal product prepared with a formula containing not less than 50 percent meat and meat by-products. The cereal component should consist of oats or oat products and just enough water to prevent product from sticking and burning during the preparation process. The term *Old Fashioned* when noted on a label for Goetta refers to the round shape.

Goose Breast Uncooked, Smoked. Becasue this product is cold smoked, the 155 degrees F requirement for processing is waived. The product is labeled *uncooked*.

Goose Liver or Goose Liver Sausage. At least 30 percent cooked goose liver. When pistachio nuts are added, product name must be qualified, such as *pistachio nuts added*.

Gorditas, Meat and Potato. Must contain at least 15 percent cooked meat based on the weight of the total product.

Gothaer Cervelat. Originated in Gotha, Germany, a sausage usually made of very lean pork finely chopped and cured.

Gumbo. A Creole word for okra. Now recognized as a dish or a soup thickened with okra. To qualify, the dish must have okra as an ingredient. Product identified as *Creole style _____ Gumbo* does not contain okra; however, it must contain a roux (flour, milk or water, etc.) or gumbo file (dried, powdered, young leaves and leaf buds of sassafras).

Haggis, Scottish. Made of grated sheep's liver and sheep's heart combined with oatmeal, suet, and seasoning, usually stuffed into a pig's or sheep's stomach and boiled. A meat pudding, formed like a sausage.

Ham and Cheese Salad. Must contain at least 25 percent cooked ham.

Hors d'oeuvres (Meat). Must contain at least 15 percent cooked meat or 10 percent bacon (cooked basis). True product name must be shown, such as *Puffed Pastry Wrapped Frank*.

Hot Dog, Chili Sauce with Meat. Must contain at least 6 percent meat.

Hot Dog, Chili with Meat. Must contain at least 40 percent meat. Sausages and bologna rework not permitted.

Jalepeno Loaf. A nonspecific loaf containing sufficient jalapenos to characterize the product. (Jalapeno is a variety of chili pepper.)

Jambalaya. Must contain at least 25 percent cooked ham including one other meat or seafood. A New Orleans dish involving rice and ham and usually tomatoes (shrimp or other shellfish, other meat or poultry), together with seasonings. Must show true product name such as *Ham and Shrimp Jambalaya*.

Jardiniere. Must contain at least 50 percent cooked meat based on the total product. This is a French term, which translated means "in the manner of the gardener." The term applies to dishes made with diced garden vegetables which have been cooked with meat. Jardiniere should be followed by a true product name, such as *Beef with Vegetables*.

Jellied Beef or Pork Loaf. When gelatin is added to beef or pork loaf type products, the product name should reflect this (e.g., *Jellied, Cooked Beef Loaf*).

Jellied Chicken Loaf. Made of seasoned chopped chicken and cooked to at least 160 degrees F and mixed with gelatin.

Jellied Corned Beef Loaf. Cooked corned beef is chopped, seasoned, and mixed with gelatin and then molded.

Juniper Berries. Juniper berries and twigs are added to the fire from which dry cured hams are smoked.

Kabobs (Meat). This product normally consists of chunks of beef with slices of onion, pepper, and tomatoes interlaced between. Must show true product name, such as *Beef Cubes, Onions, Peppers, and Tomatoes on a Wood (or Metal) Skewer*.

Katrifitas. The product consists of dough containing yucca made to resemble a meat turnover with a special meat filling. There must be at least 25 percent raw meat (beef) in total formulation, and the label must include a true product name such as *Katrifitas, Beef Turnover made with Yucca Shell*, or similar wording.

Kippered Beef. A cured dry product similar to beef jerky but not as dry.

Kiska, Kisba, Kishka, or Stuffed Derma. Ingredients statement is part of the product name. This is a meat product which may be prepared two different ways:

1. With meat by-products, including beef blood, pork snout, pork liver, pork cheeks, etc., packaged in fully labeled packages or individually banded. When beef blood is used, it must be shown as part of product name.

2. With more than 30 percent animal fat, mixed with farinaceous materials containing no other meat by-products and ordinarily stuffed into beef casings and cooked. Product containing 30 percent or less fat is not governed by the labeling regulations.

Knishes. Must contain at least 15 percent cooked meat or poultry or 10 percent bacon (cooked basis). The type of meat or poultry should be identified in a true product name such as *Chicken Knishes*.

Kreplach. Must contain at least 20 percent meat. The type of kreplach should be identified in a true product name such as *Beef Kreplach.*

Kubbee. Other acceptable names are *Kubbe, Kibbe, Kabeda, Kilin, Kibbes, Kibby, Kabbo, or Kabe.* A product popular in Syria and Lebanon which must contain at least 25 percent meat based on total formulation, and must contain soaked cracked wheat. True product name must appear, such as *Fried Cracked Wheat and Beef Balls, Baked Stuffed Wheat and Beef Patty.* Products may be shaped like a hamburger and fried or shaped into balls and fried.

Kurma. Must contain at least 50 percent meat or at least 35 percent poultry meat.

Lamb Curry. Must contain at least 50 percent fresh meat.

Lau-Lau. A Hawaiian dish made with pork and fish, wrapped in tara leaves. Must contain at least 25 percent meat, and must have a true product name on the label, such as *Pork and Fish Stuffed Tara Leaves.*

Lentil Soup with Bacon, German Style. Acceptable name for a lentil soup containing only bacon. The bacon requirement is 4.0 percent for condensed and 2.0 percent for ready-to-eat.

Lima Beans with Ham or Bacon in Sauce. Must contain at least 12 percent ham or bacon.

Lobster Sauce. May refer to an Oriental style sauce originally intended to be served with lobster. The sauce so used contains no lobster, but the characterizing ingredients include ground pork, soy sauce, garlic, and scallions. May also refer to a sauce that contains lobster.

London Broil. Name applied only to cooked dish. Products including the expression *London Broil* on labels must be prepared with beef flank steak. Uncooked product must be labeled to indicate this, e.g., *Beef Flank Steak for London Broil.* If prepared from another cut, the identity of that cut must accompany the term London Broil, e.g., *Sirloin Tip London Broil.*

Macaroni with Ham or Beef. Must contain at least 12 percent cooked meat.

Manicotti (with Meat). Must contain at least 10 percent fresh meat. An Italian pasta main dish consisting of rectangular-shaped pasta spread with a filling of meat (such as sausage or ground beef) and/or cheeses (such as ricotta or mozzarella). The pasta is rolled, the edges are pressed together to seal, and covered with grated parmesan cheese and tomato sauce. A true product name must be shown, such as *Beef Manicotti in Sauce.*

Marengo, Veal or Poultry. Must contain at least 35 percent cooked meat or poultry meat. Chicken or veal in a sauce containing tomatoes, mushrooms, onions, and wine. Must show true product name, such as *Chicken Marengo.*

Masa. This is a basic component in foods such as tortillas, tacos, burritos, tamales, etc. The basic ingredient of masa is whole corn, usually white, which is processed by soaking or cooking for a short time in hot lime water. The term *masa* is acceptable for labeling purposes to identify this material. *Masa Harina* is a dried masa and may be declared as such.

Meat Curry, Lamb or Beef. Must contain at least 50 percent meat.

Mesquite. Mesquite wood or sawdust will be classified as hardwood and is acceptable for use in processing meat products.

Mince Meat. Must contain at least 12 percent fresh meat or 9 percent cooked meat or heart meat. Products marketed as mince meat which contain beef suet as the only ingredient of animal origin are not considered to be meat food products. When 2 percent or more cooked meat is present in the formula, it is considered to be a meat food product. In addition to *mince meat* the product name should include the kind of meat, e.g., *Mince Meat with Beef* or *Mince Meat with (Species) Heart Meat.* The mince meat with less than 2 percent cooked meat lacks character due to the grinding and mixing, and is not considered to be a meat food product. The meat is present for flavor purposes only, and is not referred to in the product name but must be declared in the ingredients statement.

Mofongo. Pork skins and plantain type products with at least 20 percent pork skins in total formulation. Must show true product name, such as *Pork Skin Filling Wrapped in Plantain.*

Mostaccioli. This is a macaroni product, round in shape and grooved with the ridges running lengthwise. It is hollowed, and the tubes are about the same as the end of a man's little finger. May be declared in the ingredient statement as *Mostaccioli, A Macaroni Product.*

Mousaka, Moussake, Musaka. Must contain at least 25 percent meat; mousaka is a casserole containing layers of meat and eggplant. A true product name is required such as *Eggplant and Meat Casserole.*

Mousse, Meat. A finely emulsified paste made from meat or poultry which contains eggs, egg yolks, or egg whites and which usually contains milk, cream, or milk products. Must show true product name, such as *Pork Mousse.*

Mulligatawny Soup. At least 2 percent cooked poultry meat and enough curry powder and pepper to characterize the product. The label must show a true product name, such as *Chicken Mulligatawny Soup.*

New England Boiled Dinner. Must contain at least 25 percent cooked Corned Beef.

Noodle Chicken Vegetable Dinner or Noodle Chicken Dinner with Vegetables. Canned or in glass jars, with a minimum of 6 percent cooked chicken.

Nugget Labeling. Nuggets are irregularly shaped, usually bite-sized meat and/or poultry products, which are usually breaded and deep fat fried and intended to be used as finger foods. There are a number of different types of nuggets. Products made from a solid piece of meat or poultry may use the term *nugget* as part of the product name without further qualification, e.g., *Chicken Nugget, Beef Nugget.* Products made from chopped and formed meat or poultry may use the term *nugget* as part of the product name, provided a qualifying statement describing such process is shown contiguous to the product name, e.g., *Chicken Nugget, Chopped and Formed* or *Beef Nugget, Chopped and Formed.* Products made from chopped meat or poultry and containing binders, extenders and/or water may use the term *nugget* as a fanciful name, provided a descriptive name immediately follows. An example of a descriptive name would be *Breaded Nugget Shaped Chicken Patties.* Products described above which are breaded are labeled as such and the breading is limited to 30 percent.

Paella con bacalao. Must contain at least 35 percent cooked meat or poultry meat and seafood and no more than 25 percent cooked rice. Since this is a Spanish term, the label must show true product name, such as *Beef and Fish with Rice.*

Pancetta. A rolled, cured, spiced pork belly. Trichinae treatment required, and curing alone is not an acceptable method for trichinae treatment.

Papain. Meat and poultry products that are dipped in a solution containing the enzyme papain shall show in conjunction with product name a statement, such as *Tenderized with a solution of (list ingredients of solution).* Carcasses of animals treated with papain by antemortem injection shall be roller branded *Tendered with Papain.*

Partially Defatted Chopped Beef or Pork (PDCB, PDCP). Partially defatted chopped beef is not permitted in hamburger, ground, or chopped beef. If used in products (such as taco mix or patty mix) which later may be used in preparing other products (such as tacos or patties), the PDCB or PDCP must always be declared in the ingredients statement of the mix.

Partially Defatted Cooked Beef or Pork Fatty Tissue. This product may be used as an ingredient in beef patties (cooked and uncooked), potted meat food product, sauces, gravies, imitation sausage, and nonspecific loaves. No limit on quantity is made. It is believed to be self-limiting.

Pastelles. Must contain at least 10 percent fresh meat. Product is always made with pork in Puerto Rico. The term is Spanish and the label must show the type of meat used, such as *Pork Pastelles.*

Pastellillos. Puerto Rican-style product containing at least 8 percent cooked meat. Species must be used with the Spanish term as part of the product name, e.g, the label must show a name such as *Pork Pastellillos.*

Pasties. Must contain at least 25 percent fresh meat, and the label must show the type of meat, as in *Beef Pasties.*

Pastitsio. This Greek term, translated, means casserole. Must contain at least 25 percent fresh meat or 18 percent cooked. When the product contains macaroni, ground beef, tomato paste, wine, white sauce, and Parmesan cheese, it may be labeled *Greek Style Pastitsio.*

Pastrami, Beef. Cooked beef cured with spices. The product must be smoked or treated with smoke flavoring. It is generally made from the plate but other cuts can be used. *Pastrami, Water Added* is not permitted. The term *Unsmoked Cooked Pastrami* must be used when the product is not smoked or does not contain smoke flavoring.

Pastrami, Turkey. A cured turkey product that is cooked. It must be smoked or treated with smoke flavoring. The term *Unsmoked Cooked Turkey Pastrami* must be used when the product is not smoked or does not contain smoke flavoring.

Pate de foie. Spread that must contain at least 30 percent liver. Translated from French, *pate* means paste, *foie* means liver.

Patties (Jamaican Style). See entry under *styles* for *Jamacian Style Patties.*

Paupiette. A French name for thinly slices pieces of meat stuffed and rolled. Must contain at least 50 percent cooked meat.

Paws, Chicken. An acceptable name for the lower portion of the chicken foot remaining after cutting the chicken leg into two parts just below the spurpoint. The toe nails must always be removed.

Pork, Phosphated Trimmings in Loaves. Trimmings from preparation of pork cuts, cured with approved phosphates besides other curing ingredients, may be used without limitation in loaves other than meat loaves. When such trimmings are used, phosphates may be listed in the ingredients statement using the term *sodium phosphates* or other applicable generic terms.

Protein Fat Free (PFF) Controlled Cured Pork Products. Qualifying statements, e.g., *Ham—Water Added,* may be used in place of *PFF controlled cured pork products* without qualifying statements, e.g., *Ham,* to meet the minimum meat requirements of various products. However, the amounts of the PFF controlled cured pork products with qualifying statements used will need to be increased. For example, if a standard requires a certain amount of Ham and a processor wishes to use "Ham—Water Added," a greater amount of the "Ham—Water Added" will be needed to meet the standard. The magnitude of the additional amount is directly related to the relationship between the respective PFF values.

Picadillo. A Spanish term describing a Mexican-style hash usually made with beef, garlic, onions, vinegar, and raisins. Must contain at least 35 percent cooked meat, and the label must show true product name, such as *Beef Hash.*

Pickled Products, Dry Packed. Products that are pickled and dry packed should be qualified with the name of the pickle as part of the product name, such as *Knockwurst Pickled with Vinegar,* or *Knockwurst, Pickled.* The weight of the package shall be the weight of the product less the weight of the pickle that will weep out of the product.

Picnic, Pork. When used in reference to pork, picnic is not an acceptable term unless accompanied by a more descriptive name, such as *Pork Shoulder Picnic.*

Pie, English Style or Australian Style. Must contain at least 25 percent meat or meat byproduct. Contains gravy and no vegetables with a puff pastry top.

Pie Filling, Meat or Poultry. Must contain at least 37.5 percent meat, or 18.75 percent cooked poultry meat.

Pie, Meat or Poultry. Must contain at least 25 percent meat. Meat in the gravy may be counted. Poultry pies require at least 14 percent cooked poultry meat.

Pimiento. A cone-shaped thick walled Spanish sweet red pepper. Other varieties of sweet red peppers are to be listed as sweet red peppers. To use *pimiento* in a product name, pimientos must be the variety of sweet red peppers used.

Piroshki. A Russian or Jewish dish made of thin rolled dough or pastry that is filled and either steamed, baked, or fried. Resembling small turnovers, pockets, or raviolis, they must contain at least 10 percent cooked meat.

Potato and Crackling Ring. Must contain at least 25 percent pork crackling.

Poultry Curry. Must contain at least 35 percent cooked poultry meat.

Poultry Salad. Must contain at least 25 percent cooked poultry (natural proportions of skin and fat). See *Salads.*

Premier Jus or Oleo Stock. Premier Jus is not an acceptable name unless accompanied by the term *Oleo Stock.* The product obtained by rendering at low heat the fresh fat (killing fat) or heart, caul, kidney, and mesentery collected at the time of slaughter of bovine animals. The raw material does not include cutting fats.

Pulled Pork. Refers to pork removed from bones by hand or by mechanical means. The meat must retain its natural striated muscle fiber structure, (i.e., it can be shredded, chunked, etc.) and may not be ground, chopped, or comminuted.

Ravioli, Meat. Must contain at least 10 percent meat in ravioli.

Ravioli, Meat—Genoa or Genoese Style. Must contain at least 10 percent fresh meat and must contain some (species) brains.

Reconstituted Skim Milk. The ratio of water to nonfat dry milk cannot exceed 9:1.

Relleno de papa. A Puerto Rican product with 8 percent cooked meat. The label must show true product name, such as *Potato Balls with Beef,* or *Potato Dough with a Beef Filling.*

Rendered Beef Fat Tissue Solids. This designation has been approved as identification for the solid phase resulting from the processing of ground beef fat by means of a high temperature (180 degrees F) continuous wet rendering system.

Rice and Beef. Must contain at least 12 percent meat.

Risotto. An Italian term for a rice dish. Must show a true product name, such as *Leg of Chicken Stuffed with Italian Rice.*

Romano Cheese. Must show kind of milk, such as (*Caprino*) *Romano Cheese made with goat's Milk,* (*Pecornia*) *Romano cheese made from sheep's milk,* or (*Vaccino*) *Romano Cheese made from cow's milk.* The words in parenthesis are not required to be shown on the label.

Rumaki. Rumaki is a combination of chicken livers, water chestnuts, and bacon which must contain at least 50 percent chicken livers. Served as an hors d'oeuvre or appetizer.

Salad, German Potato. Product is traditionally prepared with bacon as an ingredient at 7 to 8 percent of the total formula. Products labeled as *German Potato Salad* are not been considered to be governed by labeling regulations. However, product labeled as *German Style Potato Salad with Bacon* requires at least 15 percent cooked bacon, which is amenable to the Federal Meat Inspection Regulations.

Salad, Poultry. When titanium dioxide is used as a whitener, a qualifying phrase should appear under the product name stating that the product has been *Artificially Whitened* or *Artificially Lightened.*

Salads. Must contain at least 35 percent cooked meat or meat food product, e.g., corned beef, ham. Products such as *Ham water added* or *Corned Beef and water product* may be used if adjusted to account for the amount of added substances. Cracker meal, bread crumbs, and similar ingredients may be included in meat or poultry salads at a level of 2 percent computed on the basis of the total formula. If used over 2 percent, a product name qualifier is required.

Salt as a Cure. Dry processed hams, pork shoulders, and bacon are ordinarily cured with mixtures that contain mostly salt along with sugar and nitrates plus nitrites. However, some processors use salt alone in preparing their products. The salt in contact with the meat provides the desired cured color, taste, and necessary product protection. Salt is an acceptable cure when used singly in the curing and salt equalization of dry processed hams, pork shoulders, and bacon. The cured products must have a 10 percent brine concentration.

Samosa. This product, resembling a meat turnover, consists of a spiced vegetable and meat mixture within a dough crust. It originated in India and is also associated with Pakistan. Must contain at least 25 percent meat. Product must show a true product name such as *Beef Turnover.*

Sassafras Smoked. Will be permitted unless during the smoking process safrole (a colorless or faintly yellow liquid from sassafras oil) is steam distilled. If this happens, safrole would be considered an additive to a meat product and thus prohibited. Sassafras smoking is acceptable if the heat or burning is sufficient to oxidize the safrole. Processor must document that finished product contains no detectable amounts of safrole, isosafrole, or dehydrosafrole.

Satay. Meat product that can be prepared two ways:
1. Meat is cut into one inch cubes that are dipped into a spicy sauce, skewered, and roasted over an open fire (similar to kabobs, except no vegetables or fruit are added to the skewer). Must show true product name, such as *Beef Cubes on stick.*
2. Alternatively, the meat is cut into one inch cubes that are dipped into a spicy sauce and then canned. Must show true product name, such as *Beef Cubes in Spicy Sauce.*
The term is appropriate for use with chicken, beef, lamb, pork and other food items, since it refers more to a preparation method than to the nature of the finished product.

Sauce with Meat or Meat Sauce. Must contain at least 6 percent ground meat.

Sauerbraten. A German term for a product consisting of cooked beef in a vinegar flavored sauce. The beef is marinated in vinegar sauce. The beef and sauce are partially cooked separately, then combined to complete the cooking. Must contain at least 50 percent cooked beef. *Gravy with Sauerbraten* must contain at least 35 percent cooked meat.

Sauerkraut Balls with Meat. Must contain at least 30 percent meat or meat food product.

Sauerkraut with Franks and Juice. Must contain at least 20 percent franks.

Scalloped Potatoes and Ham. Must contain at least 20 percent cooked ham.

Scalloped Potatoes and Sausage. Must contain at least 20 percent cooked sausage.

Scalloped Potatoes Flavored with Sausage. At least 3 percent sausage.

Scaloppini. Must contain at least 35 percent cooked meat or poultry meat. Thin slices of cooked veal, sometimes beef or poultry, seared or fried. Must show true product name, such as *Veal Scaloppini, Chicken Scaloppini.*

Schickenwurst. A German term to describe a two part product. One part is an emulsion prepared from pork and beef cuts. The second component consists of chunks of ham measuring from 2 to 3 inches in size. The two parts are mixed, stuffed into large casings, and smoked while being cooked. The final product appears as a luncheon sausage with large pieces of red ham meat held together by a light pink binder. The ham sections comprise at least 50 percent of the product and the item has a distinct smoked flavor. This product is very similar in appearance to the product sold as *Ham Bologna.*

Scrambled Eggs with Bacon. Must contain at least 10 percent cooked bacon.

Shepherds Pie (With or Without Vegetables). Must contain at least 25 percent meat in total formulation. Shepherds Pie is a meat food product consisting of chopped, minced, or cubed beef or lamb, seasoned with gravy or sauce, with or without vegetables, and baked with a covering layer or surrounding border of seasoned mashed potatoes. The label must show true product name, such as *Beef Shepherds Pie*.

Shu-Mai. A Chinese product that resembles a dumpling, and is similar to a meat ravioli. Must contain at least 10 percent meat. The label must show true product name such as *Pork dumpling*.

Sliced Dried Beef in Jars. Acceptable fill is 2 ounces in a 4 fluid ounce glass, 2½ ounces in a 5 fluid ounce glass, and 5 ounces in a 9⅝ fluid ounce glass.

Sloppy Joe. A name that must be qualified by a true product name, such as *Barbecue Sauce with Beef*. The meat content depends on the name of the product. Heart meat and tongue meat can be used, but not to satisfy the minimum meat requirement.

Sofrito with Pork. A sauce containing 6 percent smoked pork.

Souffle, Meat or Poultry. Must contain at least 18 percent cooked meat or poultry meat.

Souse. This nonspecific product can be made with all pork by-products.

Soy Sauce. May be shown as such in ingredients statement without sublisting. If no salt is listed in the ingredients statement and soy sauce is an ingredient of the product, the ingredients statement must read *Soy Sauce (contains salt)*.

Spanish Rice with Beef. Must contain at least 20 percent cooked beef.

Spiced Beef. A cured, spiced, and cooked product.

Sticks, Meat. An extended pattie-like product, meat sticks are usually breaded. No more than 10 percent extenders and 30 percent breading are permitted. When whole egg, tomato, and nonfat dry milk are used, the label must indicate the addition, e.g., *Breaded Meat Stick—Nonfat Dry Milk Added*. The infant finger food type of stick is usually packed in jars. It conforms to the sausage standard and must show a true product name such as *Meat Stick. Nonspecific dry or semi-dry sticks* that do not meet the sausage standard must be followed by the ingredients statement. If products meet the sausage standard, they may be identified as *Smoked Sausage*.

Stromboli. An Italian term for a sandwich-like product. Minimum requirement is 25 percent fresh meat or 18 percent cooked meat. The label must show a true product name, such as *Pepperoni and Cheese Wrapped in Dough*.

Studzienina. An Italian term for a type of souse. The label must show the true product name, *Souse*.

Stuffed Cabbage with Meat in Sauce. Must contain at least 12 percent meat. *Stuffed Cabbage with Poultry in Sauce* must contain at least 8 percent cooked poultry.

Stuffed Peppers with Meat in Sauce. Must contain at least 12 percent meat. Stuffed Peppers with Poultry in Sauce must contain at least 8 percent cooked poultry.

Sukiyaki. Must contain at least 30 percent beef. Product is a mixture of vegetables such as mushrooms, leeks, and celery, cut up and cooked briefly with thin slices of beef and soy sauce.

Sweet and Sour Pork, Beef, or Poultry. Requires at least 25 percent uncooked meat or poultry meat or 18 percent cooked meat or poultry meat. Requires sufficient traditional sweet and sour ingredients (fruit, fruit juices, vinegar, etc.) to impart sweet and sour characteristics.

Sylita. A Danish variety of *Head Cheese*. The label must show the true product name *Head Cheese*.

Taco. Must contain at least 15 percent meat.

Taco Filling, Meat or Poultry. Must contain at least 40 percent raw poultry meat or fresh meat. The label must show true product name such as *Taco Filling with Meat, Beef Taco Filling,* or *Taco Meat Filling*.

Tallow. Acceptable product name for the meat food product consisting of rendered beef fat or mutton fat or both.

Tamales. Must contain at least 25 percent meat. Tamales prepared with meats other than beef and pork must show the ingredient in the product name, such as *Chicken Tamales* or *Chicken and Beef Tamales*. When inedible wrappings are used, their presence must be indicated in the product name or as a qualifier to the product name. The wrapping cannot be included as part of the net weight.

Taquitos. A Mexican dish requiring at least 15 percent meat. Cooked meat is cut into strips or shredded and placed in center of tortilla, and the tortilla is then rolled around the beef product.

Tasajo Salted Beef. A Spanish term for a product that is stitch-pumped and cured in salt brine for 72 hours or more, after which it is dried with circulated warm air for a period of at least 20 days. If the item is dipped in a tallow mixture, a statement must be shown contiguous to the product name identifying the constituents of the dipping mixture.

Teawurst or Teewurst. A cooked or uncooked product processed with or without curing and cold smoked two to five days. It is ground or coarsely chopped and is characterized by a soft spreadable texture. Typical meat ingredients include pork, beef, pork bellies, and bacon. Fresh pork bellies may be used in place of pork fat and bacon.

Tempura. A Japanese dish consisting of ingredients (such as shrimp, fish, vegetables, meat, poultry, etc.), each dipped in an egg batter and deep fried. The label must show true product name such as *Chicken Tempura, Pork Tempura,* etc.

Tenderay. The term *Tenderay* is appropriate for display on labeling materials and for application by marking devices in establishments operating under Federal Meat Inspection when the carcasses involved are from the better grades of beef (those meeting the specifications for commercial grade or better). The carcasses should be held following slaughter for at least 44 hours (at a temperature of 65 to 68 degrees F in an atmosphere having a relative humidity of 80 to 85 percent) and exposed to active ultra-violet rays during this period to inhibit the growth of surface mold and bacteria. The hold period may be reduced to 24 hours for the beef cuts known as ribs and trimmed loins. All processors wishing to use the *Tenderay* term must submit request for approval to the Federal Meat Inspector with transmittal forms identifying in detail how the meats involved will be handled.

Teriyaki, Meat or Poultry. Cubes or slices of meat or poultry meat which have been marinated in a sauce containing soy sauce, some kind of sweetener, and usually ginger, garlic, or wine. When the marinated product is combined with additional sauce the product name must reflect the sauce, e.g., *Beef Teriyaki with Sauce*. For uncooked products, see *Teriyaki Products*.

Teriyaki Products. Meat and poultry teriyaki products are not required to be cooked, provided a prominent statement is on the principal label display panel informing the consumer that the product is not cooked, e.g., *Ready to Cook.*

Tetrazzini, Poultry or Beef. Must contain at least 15 percent poultry or cooked beef. It is made with diced cooked poultry or meat in a rich cream sauce containing sherry. This is added to cooked spaghetti or noodles in a casserole and usually topped with bread crumbs or grated cheese.

Tocino. Spanish word for salt pork or bacon.

Tocino (Filipino or Philippine Style). Refers to the thinly sliced piece of meat taken from either the hind leg or shoulder portion of the pork carcass, and treated with salt, sugar, and nitrite and/or nitrates. Optional ingredients (ascorbic acid; condiments such as spices, monosodium glutamate, and phosphates) may be added. Presence of acceptable color agents such as annatto, beet powder, and paprika must be indicated on the label with the phrase *artificially colored.* A true product name must be shown on the label, such as *Sliced Marinated Cured Pork Shoulder Butt.*

Tocino, Poultry. A name for a tocino product made from poultry. The name must be followed by a true descriptive product name such as *Chicken Tocino, Sliced, Marinated, Cured Chicken Thigh Meat.*

Tortellini with Meat. Must contain at least 10 percent meat.

Tortilla with Meat. Must contain at least 10 percent meat. Tortilla is a thin, flat, unleavened masa cake which is baked on both sides.

Tostada with Meat. A tortilla usually topped with refried beans, meat, cheese, and fresh vegetables. Must contain at least 15 percent meat.

Tropic Cure Pork Products. Pork products when ready for shipment from the official establishment must have a moisture protein ratio not in excess of 3.25:1, and a salt content not less than 6 percent.

Truffles. Meat food products such as *Liver Pate with Truffles* or *Sandwich Spread with Truffles* would be expected to be prepared with at the least 3 percent truffles. Labels of product containing less than 3 percent truffles should indicate the amount of truffle content in the name such as *Liver Pate with 2 percent truffles.* If the name does not feature truffles and they are mentioned only in the list of ingredients, we have no minimum requirement, provided the illustration does not show truffles.

Turbinado. Partially refined sugar, which shall be identified in the ingredient statement as *Turbinado sugar.*

Turnovers. 25 percent meat or 14 percent poultry meat. Similar to pies except the dough is folded. Cheese may be substituted for meat or poultry meat in an amount not to exceed 50 percent under the conditions outlined below. Cheese must be part of the product name such as *Beef and Cheese Turnover* or *Chicken and Cheese Turnover.* Imitation cheese, substitute cheese, cheese food, and cheese spreads are not acceptable replacement for cheese.

Tzimmes. The true product name is *Beef and Vegetables* (or similar wording), when at least 50 percent beef is present in product. *Vegetables with Beef* (or similar wording) is acceptable when at least 35 percent raw beef is used.

Unskinned Pork Jowls. When permitted in product must be labeled as *Unskinned Pork Jowls.*

Variety Meats in Franks. Cooked sausages with variety meats (meat by-products). Must contain not less than 15 percent red skeletal meat based on *total meat block* weight. The meat block includes meat, meat by-products, and, if applicable, poultry.

Vegetable and/or Fruit with Poultry. Must contain at least 25 percent cooked poultry.

Welsh Rarebit Sauce with Cooked Ham. Must contain at least 20 percent cooked ham in total formulation.

Wheat Pilaf with Crisp Bacon. Meat food product is formulated with water, wheat, bacon, and condiments.

Whey Products. Common names for whey products in dry form that may be used in meat food products are *dried whey, reduced lactose whey, reduced minerals whey,* and *whey protein concentrate.* They may be used as binders and thickeners in sausage and bockwurst at up to 3.5 percent, in chile con carne and pork or beef with barbecue sauce at up to 8 percent, and in soups, stews, and non-specific loaves in amounts sufficient for purpose. They may also be used in batters, gravy mixes, and breadings.

Wiener Schnitzel. A German term for a veal cutlet prepared by dipping in egg, flour, and bread crumbs and frying to a golden brown.

Wine Flavored or Wine Cured. Must have enough wine to give a wine flavor characteristic to the product.

Wine in Meat and Poultry Products. Meat and poultry products formulated with cooking wine may not declare *Cooking Wine* on the label, but must show the type of wine (e.g., Burgundy Wine, Sauterne Wine, etc.). The ingredients of cooking wines are not required to be sublisted.

Won Ton Soup, Meat. Must contain at least 3 percent cooked meat or 5 percent uncooked meat.

Won Ton Soup, Poultry. Must contain at least 2 percent cooked poultry meat. The name of the poultry must be shown in the product name, e.g., *Chicken Won Ton Soup.*

Yankee Pot Roast. See entry under *Gravies* for *Gravy and Yankee Pot Roast.*

Yearling. The term *yearling* (as in *yearling beef*) may be used to describe an animal of either sex that is too old to be classified as a calf or lamb but less than two years of age. A partial quality control program for carcass segregation and product identification is required to insure that no comingling occurs between qualifying and non-qualifying products.

Source:
Standards and Labeling Division, Food Safety and Inspection Service, USDA, *Standards and Labeling Policy Book,* Washington: Government Printing Office, June 1991.

Meatballs

Meatballs are uncooked or cooked pork, beef, veal, and lamb and other ingredients in ball form.

- Product must contain at least 65 percent meat.
- Binders and extenders are limited to 12 percent. When

isolated soy protein is used, 6.8 percent is the equivalent to 12 percent of the other binders or extenders. The permitted binders and extenders include cereal, bread crumbs, cracker meal, soy flour, soy protein concentrate, isolated soy protein, and textured vegetable protein.
- Cheeks, hearts, and tongues are not allowed, but product may contain head meat, cheek meat, heart meat, and tongue meat, when declared in the ingredients statement.
- Partially defatted chopped (species) may be used up to 25 percent of the meat block. PDC (species) can be identified as (species) in the ingredients statements.

TERMINOLOGY

Albondigas. Spanish term meaning meatball. Label must show a true product name in English such as *Meatball*.

Meatball Stew. At least 25 percent meat.

Meat Balls in Sauce. Requires a 50 percent minimum of meatballs, by weight, in finished product.

Stroganoff, Meatball. At least 45 percent cooked meatballs. Sauce portion shall comply with the *Stroganoff Sauce* standard.

Stroganoff Sauce with/and Meatballs. At least 31 percent cooked meatballs. Sauce portion shall comply with the *Stroganoff Sauce* standard.

Stroganoff Sauce. The sauce must contain at least 10 percent sour cream or a combination of at least 7.5 percent sour cream and 5 percent wine or 2 percent sour cream, 2.5 percent wine and 9.5 percent whole milk.

Swedish Style. At least 65 percent fresh meat. *Swedish Meatballs* or *Swedish Style Meatballs* are small in size and usually contain 2 or 3 different varieties of meat, nutmeg and/or allspice, potatoes, and milk. *Swedish Brand Meatballs Made in USA* is any meatball.

Turkey. At least 65 percent raw turkey meat. Skin is permitted in natural proportions of meat used; if in excess, it shall be reflected in the product name.

With Water Chestnuts. Water chestnuts are not a common or usual ingredient in formula for meatball products. Labels for meatball items that contain water chestnuts should bear a true product name, such as *Meatballs with Water Chestnuts*.

Source:
Standards and Labeling Division, Food Safety and Inspection Service, USDA, *Standards and Labeling Policy Book,* Washington: Government Printing Office, June 1991.

Natural

The term *natural* may be used on labeling for meat products and poultry products, provided that the product does not contain any artificial flavor or flavoring, coloring ingredient, or chemical preservative, or any other artificial or synthetic ingredient. In addition, the product and its ingredients are not more than minimally processed. Minimal processing may include those traditional processes used to make food edible or preserve it or make it safe for human consumption, e.g., smoking, roasting, freezing, drying, and fermenting. It may also include those physical processes which do not fundamentally alter the raw product and/or which only separate a whole, intact food into component parts, e.g., grinding meat, separating eggs into albumen and yolk, and pressing fruits to produce juices.

Relatively severe processes, such as solvent extraction, acid hydrolysis, and chemical bleaching would clearly be considered more than minimal processing. Thus, the use of a natural flavor or flavoring which has undergone more than minimal processing would place a product in which it is used outside the scope of these guidelines.

However, the presence of an ingredient which has been more than minimally processed would not necessarily preclude the product from being promoted as natural. Exceptions of this type may be granted on a case-by-case basis if it can be demonstrated that the use of such an ingredient would not significantly change the character of the product to the point that it could no longer be considered a natural product. In such cases, the natural claim must be qualified to clearly and conspicuously identify the ingredient, e.g., *contains refined sugar*.

All products claiming to be natural or a natural food should be accompanied by a brief statement which explains what is meant by the term *natural*, i.e., that the product is a natural food because it contains no artificial ingredients and is only minimally processed. This statement should appear directly beneath or beside all natural claims or, if elsewhere on the principal display panel, an asterisk should be used to tie the explanation to the claim.

NATURAL SMOKED COLOR

Used when products are smoked and not artificially colored. The use of artificial smoke materials can, by means of a number of processing operations, result in a color characteristic being acquired by frankfurters, bologna, etc. The term *Natural Smoked Color* can be used to properly identify this point.

Source:
Standards and Labeling Division, Food Safety and Inspection Service, USDA, *Standards and Labeling Policy Book,* Washington: Government Printing Office, June 1991.

Negative Labeling Terms

Negative ingredient statements on meat and poultry product labels are used under the following circumstances:
- If it is not clear from the product name that the ingredient is not present. For example, the use of *no beef* on the label of Turkey Pastrami would clarify that the product, although labeled pastrami, does not contain beef.
- If the manufacturer or packager can demonstrate that the statements are beneficial for health, religious preference, or other similar reasons. For example, highlighting the absence of salt in a product would be helpful to those persons on sodium-restricted diets.

- If the claims are directly linked to the product packaging, as opposed to the product itself. For example, flexible retortable pouches could bear the statement *No Preservatives, Refrigeration, or Freezing Needed With This New Packaging Method.*
- If such claims call attention to the absence of ingredients because they are prohibited in a product by regulation or policy. The statements must clearly and prominently indicate this fact, so as not to mislead or create false impressions. For example, *USDA federal regulations prohibit the use of preservatives in this product,* would be an acceptable statement on a ground beef label.
- To indicate the absence of an ingredient when that ingredient is expected or permitted by regulation or policy. This could also apply to ingredients which are not expected or permitted by regulation or policy if the ingredient could find its way into the product through a component. For example, the use of *no preservatives* on the label of a container of spaghetti with meat and sauce (which by regulation does not permit the direct addition of preservatives) would be acceptable if it contained an ingredient, such as vegetable oil, which could contain antioxidants but did not.

Source:
Standards and Labeling Division, Food Safety and Inspection Service, USDA, *Standards and Labeling Policy Book,* Washington: Government Printing Office, June 1991.

Omelets

The following guidelines apply to omelets prepared with meat and poultry.
Bacon. Must contain at least 9 percent cooked bacon.
Chicken Livers. Must contain at least 12 percent cooked liver.
Corned Beef Hash. Must contain at least 25 percent corned beef hash.
Creamed Beef. Must contain at least 25 percent creamed beef.
Ham. Must contain at least 18 percent cooked ham.
Omelet, Florentine. Must contain at least 9 percent cooked meat and must contain spinach.
Omelet, Denver or Western Style. Must contain at least 18 percent ham along with onions and green and/or red peppers.
Sausage and Cheese or Pepperoni, (Cheese and Sauce). Must contain at least 9 percent sausage in total product.
Sausage. Must contain at least 12 percent dry sausage.

Source:
Standards and Labeling Division, Food Safety and Inspection Service, USDA, *Standards and Labeling Policy Book,* Washington: Government Printing Office, June 1991.

Pizza

The following guidelines apply to pizza prepared with meat, poultry, and processed products.
Bacon. Must contain at least 9 percent cooked bacon.
Chili with Beans. Must contain at least 25 percent chili with beans.

Meat Pattie Crumble. Must contain at least 15 percent pattie crumbles (fresh) or 12 percent cooked.
Meat. Must contain at least 15 percent meat.
Pizza, Chicago Style. Acceptable labeling for a product which has been manufactured by first placing the cheese on the crust, then following with the meat and then the sauce. Condimental quantities of a grated cheese may then be placed on the top. The product usually has deep dish characteristics.
Pizza, Combination or Deluxe. In a combination pizza such as *Sausage and Pepperoni Pizza,* the component declared last, must be present at least at 25 percent of its required level in a pizza containing a single meat component.
Pizza, Pan Style. Pizza that is marketed in a pan and features a thick crust.
Pizza Burger. It can be two patties with cheese (usually Romano) and/or tomato or pizza sauce between the patties.
Pizza Containing Cheese Substitutes. Labels which contain cheese in a ratio less than one part cheese to nine parts cheese substitute must contain additional qualifying information. Example: *Pizza—Sausage, Cheese Substitute, and Cheese*; Combination Pizza—Sausage, Pepperoni, Imitation Cheese, and cheese.
Pizza Pups. Product has two crusts, filled with a mixture of pork, tomato puree, and condimental substances. The finished product is approximately 8 inches long, 2½ inches wide, and ¾ inch thick. The label must show a true product name, such as *Pork and Sauce Filling in a Crust.*
Pizza Roll. When the name appears on a label, there must be a contiguous statement identifying the major components of the product or a complete ingredient listing. There are two major types of pizza rolls. One is a cooked sausage-like meat food product that contains cheese, usually contains peppers, and has no water limitation. The second type consists of a roll-shaped dough enclosure with various fillings. A manufacturer of the latter type of product has asserted trademark protection of the term *pizza roll.*
Pizza Sauce with Sausage. Must contain at least 6 percent sausage.
Pizza Topping Mix. A nonspecific product, including those products which indicate the type of meat or poultry in the product name (e.g., *Chicken and Pork Pizza Topping* or *Beef Pizza Topping*). Antioxidants are permitted, and water, extenders, and binders are acceptable.
Poultry. Must contain at least 12 percent cooked poultry meat.
Sausage. Must contain at least 12 percent cooked sausage or 10 percent dry sausage (such as pepperoni).

Source:
Standards and Labeling Division, Food Safety and Inspection Service, USDA, *Standards and Labeling Policy Book,* Washington: Government Printing Office, June 1991.

Pork

Andouille. French term for a product made with pork and/or pork by-products, stuffed in large intestines. It is sold cooked or uncooked. It must be accompanied by a true product name such as *sausage* or *pudding* depending on the formulation. If beef is used, it must show in the product name, such as *Beef Andoulle Sausage* or *Beef Andoulle Pudding*.

Bier Schinken. A German term, which translated means "Beer Ham." If the product is made of all pork, it may be labeled *Bier Schinken.*

Bohemian Peesky. Made of salt-cured pork trimmings, seasoned with garlic, pepper, and salt. Label must show true product name such as *Seasoned Salt Cured Pork.*

Cala, Calle, Callie. Names for the lower portion of pork shoulder. Must be qualified as *Pork Shoulder Product.*

Capacollo (Capicola, Capocolla, Capacola, Capicollo, Cappicola), Cooked. Italian terms for boneless pork shoulder butts which are cured and then cooked. The curing process may be dry curing, immersion curing, or pump curing. The cured product is coated with spices and paprika before cooking. This product shall always be labeled with *Cooked* as part of the product name. *Water added* is permitted.

Center Cut Pork Chops. Chops cut from center cut pork loin.

Center Cut Pork Loin, Bone-In. This term refers to the pork loin with the blade and the sirloin portions removed by straight cuts made approximately perpendicular to the split surface of the backbone and the length of the loin. The sirloin is removed anterior to the hip bone cartilage, exposing the gluteus medius. The blade portion shall be removed to leave no more than 11 ribs present.

Center Cut Pork Loin, Boneless. This term refers to the center cut pork loin from which the tenderloin, all bones, and all cartilages have been removed. On the blade end, the longissimus dorsi (LD) shall be approximately equal to or larger than the spinalis dorsi, and the rhomboideus shall not be present. The sirloin is removed anterior to the hip bone cartilage, exposing the gluteus medius.

Center Slice. When the term *Center Slice* is used on labels for slices of ham from smoked and cooked, smoked, or water cooked hams, product must be sliced from an area of original ham positioned about 1 inch on each side of a center cut.

Chicharrones. A French term that must be accompanied by the name *Fried Pork Skins.*

Chipped Ham. An acceptable name for wafer-thin sliced ham.

Cutlet, Pork. Term used for a product consisting of pork temple meat, inside masseter muscles, and the small piece of lean from the tip of pork jaws. These are flattened and knitted together in cutlet-size product by means of cubing or Frenching machines or by hand pounding with cubing hammers. The term *cutlet* relates to thin slices of meat. They can be identified as sliced pork meat product when the designation clearly states the specific part of the carcass from which the meat in the product is derived (*Pork Loin Cutlets*). All of the terms should be conspicuously displayed on labels.

Kassler. Product is from cubed and smoked pork loin. Must be labeled with a true product name, such as *Smoked Pork Chop.*

Pork and Dressing with Gravy. Must contain at least 30 percent pork.

Pork and Dressing. Must contain at least 50 percent cooked pork.

Pork Burger. This product must meet the standard for *hamburger* (see entry), with pork being substituted for beef. Antioxidants are not permitted.

Pork Cracklings. Must be prepared from fatty tissues from which the skin has been detached. In the event the skin is not removed from the product prior to rendering, then a descriptive name must be used to informatively identify the product (e.g., *Pork Cracklings, Fried-Out Pork Fat with Attached Skin*).

Pork Cutlets. A piece of lean muscle trimmed from the tip of jaw bones, temporal meat, and from lean cheek meat free of fat and glands, either Frenched by hand pounding or processed through a Frenching machine.

Pork Fat. Must be declared as such in the ingredients statement. Clear fatbacks and clear shoulder plates must be declared as *Pork Fat.* Pork fat may be declared as pork in the ingredients statement if it contains visible lean and it is used in a standardized product which has a fat limitation.

Pork Jowls. May be declared as pork if skinned.

Pork Loin, Short Cut. This product consists of the loin remaining following the production of *Long Cut* ham. This means the butt portion of the loin remains with the ham product.

Pork Pate. Crown on the top of the head, tissues from which the skin has been removed containing approximately 35 to 40 percent lean tissue. Should be identified as *pork* in the ingredient statement on the label.

Pork Skin Braciolo. This product is made only with pork skins.

Pork Skin Residue After Gelatin Extraction. This material consists of back fat skins from which the gelatin has been extracted by means of soaking the skin in acid and subsequent low temperature cooking for the extraction of gelatin. It is not permitted in sausage but may be used in imitation sausage, potted meat food product, loaves (other than meat loaves), and other non-specific products.

Pork Skins, Fried. When prepared from the skin of smoked pork bellies, it may be labeled as *Fried Bacon Skins, Fried Bacon Rinds,* or *Fried Pork Skins.* The kind of skin used must be stated on the transmittal form when submitted for label approvals.

Pork Skins. Not permitted in salami, bologna, frankfurters, Vienna sausage, and braunschweiger. When packed in vinegar pickle, they are not permitted to be artificially colored. When pork skin, either attached to fat and/or muscle tissue or detached from fat and/or muscle tissue, is used to manufacture meat or poultry products, it must be specifically listed in the formulation on the label approval application form and in the ingredients statement on the label, e.g., *Pork Skins, Unskinned Pork Jowls, Unskinned Pork Shoulder Trimming, Unskinned Pork Fat,* and *Unskinned Pork Bellies.* Detached skin refers to the portion of skin from which most of the underlying fat is removed, e.g., skin from bacon intended for slicing, skin from closely skinned hams, shoulder cuts, fat backs, etc. If removal of skin portions is incidental to removal of a considerable proportion of underlying fat from ham, shoulder, back, etc., preparatory to rendering such fat, portions of skin so removed should not be regarded as detached skin and may be included with fats and rendered into lard. Ham facings are not regarded as detached skin.

Pork with Dressing and Gravy. May contain at least 30 percent cooked pork.

Porkette. A pork product. May also be used for products other than fabricated pork steaks if used with a true descriptive name.

Pot Sticker. A fanciful name for a type of dumpling which requires 10 percent meat or 7 percent poultry meat. When this product name appears, a full descriptive name is required, e.g., *Chinese-Style Dumpling with Pork and Cabbage Filling* or *Pork and Vegetable Dumpling*.

Prosciutto Cotto, Cooked Ham. The product name *Prosciutto Cotto, Cooked Ham* is used on labeling to identify a regular pickle-cured cooked ham. Prosciutto Cotto is the Italian name for cooked ham. *Cooked Prosciutto* is used on labeling to identify a dry-cured prosciutto ham that is cooked.

Prosciutto. *Italian for ham, dry cured.* The product name *Prosciutto* is used on labeling to identify a dry-cured ham.

Source:

Standards and Labeling Division, Food Safety and Inspection Service, USDA, *Standards and Labeling Policy Book,* Washington: Government Printing Office, June 1991.

Poultry

CHICKEN CLASSES

Rock Cornish Game Hen or Cornish Game Hen. A young immature chicken (usually 5 to 6 weeks of age), weighing not more than 2 pounds ready-to-cook weight, which was prepared from a Cornish chicken or the progeny of a Cornish chicken crossed with another breed of chicken.

Rock Cornish Fryer, Roaster, or Hen. The progeny of a cross between a purebred Cornish and a purebred Rock chicken, without regard to the weight of the carcass involved; however, the use of *fryer, roaster,* or *hen* applies only if the carcasses are from birds with ages and characteristics that qualify them for such designation.

Broiler or Fryer. A young chicken (usually under 13 weeks of age), of either sex, that is tender-meated with soft, pliable smooth-textured skin, and flexible breastbone cartilage.

Roaster or Roasting Chicken. A bird of this class is a young chicken (usually 3 to 5 months of age), of either sex, that is tender-meated with soft, pliable, smooth-textured skin, and breastbone cartilage that may be somewhat less flexible than that of a broiler or fryer.

Capon. A capon is a surgically unsexed male chicken (usually under 8 months of age) that is tender-meated with soft, pliable, smooth-textured skin.

Hen, Fowl, or Baking or Stewing Chicken. A bird of this class is a mature female chicken (usually more than 10 months of age) with meat less tender than that of a roaster or roasting chicken and nonflexible breastbone tip.

Cock or Rooster. A cock or rooster is a mature male chicken with coarse skin, toughened and darkened meat, and hardened breastbone tip.

TURKEY CLASSES

Fryer-Roaster Turkey. A young immature turkey (usually under 16 weeks of age), of either sex, that is tendermeated with soft,

pliable, smooth-textured skin, and flexible breastbone cartilage.

Young Turkey. A young turkey is a turkey (usually under 8 months of age) that is tender-meated with soft, pliable smooth-textured skin, and breastbone cartilage that is somewhat less flexible than in a fryer-roaster turkey. Sex designation is optional.

Yearling Turkey. A fully matured turkey (usually under 15 months of age) that is reasonably tender-meated and with reasonably smooth-textured skin. Sex designation is optional.

Mature Turkey or Old Turkey (Hen or Tom). A mature or old turkey is an old turkey of either sex (usually in excess of 15 months of age) with coarse skin and toughened flesh.

For labeling purposes, the designation of sex within the class name is optional, and the two classes of young turkeys may be grouped and designated as *young turkeys*.

DUCK CLASSES

Broiler Duckling or Fryer Duckling. A young duck (usually under 8 weeks of age) of either sex, that is tender-meated and has a soft bill and a soft windpipe.

Roaster Duckling. A young duck (usually under 16 weeks of age), of either sex, that is tender-meated and has a bill that is not completely hardened and a windpipe that is easily dented.

Mature Duck or Old Duck. A mature duck or an old duck is a duck (usually over 6 months of age), of either sex, with toughened flesh, hardened bill, and hardened windpipe.

GEESE CLASSES

Young Guinea. A young guinea may be of either sex, is tender-meated, and has a flexible breastbone cartilage.

Mature Guinea or Old Guinea. A mature guinea or an old guinea may be of either sex, has toughened flesh, and a hardened breastbone.

PIGEON CLASSES

Squab. A squab is a young, immature pigeon of either sex, and is extra tender-meated.

Pigeon. A pigeon is a mature pigeon of either sex, with coarse skin and toughened flesh.

UNITED STATES STANDARDS FOR QUALITY OF READY-TO-COOK POULTRY AND SPECIFIED POULTRY FOOD PRODUCTS

A Quality. The carcass or part is free of deformities that detract from its appearance or that affect the normal distribution of flesh. Slight deformities, such as slightly curved or dented breastbones and slightly curved backs, may be present. The carcass has a well developed covering of flesh considering the kind, class, and part.

Breast. The breast is moderately long and deep, and has sufficient flesh to give it a rounded appearance with the flesh carrying well up to the crest of the breastbone along its entire length.

Leg. The leg is well fleshed and moderately thick and wide at the knee and hip joint area, and has a well-rounded, plump appearance with the flesh carrying well down toward the hock and upward to the hip joint area.

Drumstick. The drumstick is well fleshed and moderately thick and wide at the knee joint, and has a well-rounded, plump appearance with the flesh carrying well down toward the hock. The thigh is well to moderately fleshed.

Wing. The wing is well to moderately fleshed.

The carcass or part, considering the kind, class, and part, has a well-developed layer of fat in the skin. The fat is well distributed so that there is a noticeable amount of fat in the skin in the areas between the heavy feather tracts. The carcass or part has a clean appearance, especially on the breast. The carcass or part is free of pinfeathers, diminutive feathers, and hair, which are visible to the grader.

The carcass is free of broken bones and has not more than one disjointed bone. The wing tips may be removed at the joint, and in the case of ducks and geese, the parts of the wing beyond the second joint may be removed, if removed at the joint and both wings are so treated. The tail may be removed at the base. Cartilage separated from the breastbone is not considered as a disjointed or broken bone.

Discolorations due to bruising shall be free of clots (discernible clumps of red or dark cells). Evidence of incomplete bleeding, such as more than an occasional slightly reddened feather follicle, is not permitted. Flesh bruises and discolorations of the skin, such as "blue back," are not permitted on the breast or legs of the carcass, or on these individual parts, and only lightly shaded discolorations are permitted elsewhere.

With respect to consumer packaged poultry, parts, or specified poultry food products, the carcass, part, or specified poultry food product is practically free from defects which result from handling or occur during freezing or storage.

B Quality. The carcass or part may have moderate deformities, such as a dented, curved, or crooked breast, crooked back, or misshapen legs or wings, which do not materially affect the distribution of flesh or the appearance of the carcass or part. The carcass has a moderate covering of flesh considering the kind, class, and part.

Breast. The breast has a substantial covering of flesh with the flesh carrying up to the crest of the breastbone sufficiently to prevent a thin appearance.

Legs. The leg is fairly thick and wide at the knee and hip joint area, and has sufficient flesh to prevent a thin appearance.

Drumstick. The drumstick has a sufficient amount of flesh to prevent a thin appearance with the flesh carrying fairly well down toward the hock.

Thighs. The thigh has a sufficient amount of flesh to prevent a thin appearance.

Wings. The wing has a sufficient amount of flesh to prevent a thin appearance.

The carcass or part has sufficient fat in the skin to prevent a distinct appearance of the flesh through the skin, especially on the breast and legs.

The carcass or part may have a few nonprotruding pinfeathers or vestigial feathers which are scattered sufficiently so as not to appear numerous. Not more than an occasional protruding pinfeather or diminutive feather should be in evidence.

A carcass may have exposed flesh, provided that no part on the carcass has more than one-third of the flesh exposed, and the meat yield of any such part on the carcass is not appreciably affected. A part may have no more than one-third of the flesh normally covered by skin exposed. A moderate amount of meat may be trimmed around the edges of a part to remove defects.

Parts may be disjointed, but are free of broken bones. The carcass may have two disjointed bones, or one disjointed bone and one nonprotruding broken bone. Parts of the wing beyond the second joint may be removed at a joint. The tail may be removed at the base. The back may be trimmed in an area not wider than the base of the tail and extending from the tail to the area halfway between the base of the tail and the hip joints.

The carcass or part is free of serious defects. Discoloration due to bruising are free of clots (discernible clumps of red or dark cells). Evidence of incomplete bleeding is no more than very slight. Moderate areas of discoloration due to bruises in the skin or flesh and moderately shaded discoloration of the skin, such as "blue back," are permitted.

With respect to consumer packaged poultry, parts, or specified poultry food products, the carcass, part, or specified poultry food product may have moderate defects which result from handling or occur during freezing or storage. The skin and flesh should have a sound appearance, but may lack brightness. The carcass or part may have a few pockmarks due to drying of the inner layer of skin (derma). However, no single area of overlapping pockmarks may exceed that of a circle one-half inch in diameter. Moderate areas showing layers of clear pinkish or reddish colored ice are permitted.

C Quality. A part or carcass that does not meet the requirements for A or B quality may be of C quality if the flesh is substantially intact and other specific requirements are met.

POULTRY ROAST

A Quality. The deboned poultry meat used in the preparation of the product should be from young poultry. Bones, tendons, cartilage, blood clots, and discolorations should be removed from the meat. All pinfeathers, bruises, hair, discolorations, and blemishes, should be removed from the skin, and where necessary, excess fat should be removed from the skin covering the crop area or other areas. Seventy-five percent or more of the outer surface of the product should be covered with skin, whether attached to the meat or used as a wrap. The skin should not appreciably overlap at any point. The combined weight of the skin and fat used to cover the outer surface and that used as a binder should not exceed 15 percent of the total net weight of the product. The product should be fabricated in such a manner that it can be sliced after cooking and each slice can be served with minimal separation. Seasoning or flavor enhancers, if used, should be uniformly distributed. Product should be fabricated or tied in such a manner that it will retain its shape after defrosting and cooking. Packaging should be neat and attractive. Product should be practically free of weepage after packaging and/or freezing, and if frozen, shall have a bright, desirable color.

TERMINOLOGY

Grade Mark for Poultry. Indicates the quality grades of poultry (*U.S. Grade A, B,* or *C*). The shield design contains the letters *USDA*, the U.S. grade of the product, and if not shown elsewhere, the class of poultry. Any letter grade on a consumer package or individual carcass indicates the product was graded by a licensed grader of the federal or federal-state grading service, and may not be applied otherwise. Letter grades on bulk packaging or shipping containers only indicate that the product is equal to that particular U. S. grade.

Boneless Breast Trimmings. Boneless breast trimmings (turkey or chicken) are defined as trimmings that are removed from the breast portion only. When a product is formulated with boneless breast trimmings, the amount of skin should be indicated in order to determine that the meat requirement is met for a standardized product and that the product is properly labeled. Trimmings from the ribs may be identified as white turkey or white chicken trimmings, or white turkey or white chicken rib meat (excluding skin).

Buffalo Style Chicken Wings. These are chicken wings that are coated with a mild, hot or spicy sauce. The sauce is sometimes sold in a separate container.

Buffalo Style Wings or Buffalo Wings. These are fanciful names that require a descriptive name, e.g., *chicken wings coated with sauce.* The sauce may be mild, hot, or spicy.

Butterball. A disclaimer statement required (i.e., *No butter added*). *Butterball* labeled products are only applicable to whole birds or poultry parts (bone-in or boneless) to which solutions have been added.

Capon. A surgically unsexed male chicken (usually under 8 months of age) that is tender-meated with soft, pliable, smooth-textured skin.

Chicarrones de pollo (Puerto Rican Term). An acceptable name for *Marinated Cut-up Fried Chicken* sold in Puerto Rico. When product is destined for sale only in Puerto Rico, *Chicarrones de pollo* can be the product name. When destined for sale in other places, *Chicarrones de pollo* must be explained with true product name.

Chicken, Aloha. Acceptable as a coin name which must be followed by a true product name such as *Chicken and Sauce with Rice.* The standard for the product is 22 percent cooked poultry meat.

Chicken and Noodles Au Gratin. A French term for a product containing at least 18 percent cooked chicken meat.

Chicken Cordon Bleu. A French term for a product containing not less than 60 percent chicken breast meat (sliced); 5 percent ham or Canadian style bacon; cheese (either Swiss, Gruyere, mozzarella, or pasteurized processed Swiss). Contains not more than 30 percent batter and breading (if used).

Chicken Enchiladas. Contains at least 15 percent raw or 10.5 percent cooked chicken meat.

Chicken Enchilda Suiza. Must be shown with a true product name such as *Chicken Enchilada with Cream Sauce.* The product consists of chicken enchiladas with a cream sauce. The sauce used must be made with sour cream, heavy cream, or whipping cream in an amount sufficient to characterize the sauce.

Chicken, Fried. Any breaded chicken product which has been fried.

Chicken Paprika. A Hungarian dish with sauce that must contain either sour or sweet cream and enough paprika to give a pink color. Must contain at least 35 percent chicken.

Chopped Chicken Livers Combined with Other Characterizing Components. Must contain at least 30 percent cooked livers (e.g., *Chopped Chicken Livers with Eggs and Onions*).

Chopped Chicken Livers. Must contain at least 50 percent cooked chicken livers in total product. Wheat flour and similar ingredients are acceptable.

Cutlet, Poultry. May be fabricated (as opposed to using whole pieces of poultry meat). However, in such cases the term *cutlet* must be properly and distinctly qualified to describe the product, such as: *Turkey Cutlet from Turkey Loaf, Chicken Cutlet from Chicken Roll,* or *Turkey Cutlet, Chopped and Formed.*

Poultry Bacon. Bacon products prepared from poultry are acceptable. The product may be designated as *(Kind) Bacon.* However, a true descriptive name must appear contiguous to *(Kind) Bacon* without intervening type or design, in letters at least one-half the size of the letters used in the *(Kind) Bacon* and in the same style and color and on the same background. An example of an acceptable designation is *Turkey Bacon— Cured Turkey Breast Meat, Chopped and Formed.* The descriptive name can serve alone as the product name.

Poultry Breasts. When poultry breasts with ribs are boned and the resulting product contains portions of the scapula (shoulder) muscles and/or muscle overlying the vertebral ribs, they must be labeled to indicate that fact. Proper names for such products are *Boneless Breast with Rib Meat, White Chicken Meat,* or *White Turkey Meat,* or if the skin is left intact, *White Boneless Chicken* or *White Boneless Turkey.* Product labeled *Boneless Breast* without further qualification may not contain scapula or rib meat.

Poultry Cooked. With the exception of cooked, cured, smoked poultry breakfast strips, cooked, uncured poultry products must reach an internal temperature of 160 degrees F before removal from the cooking chamber. Correspondingly, cooked, cured poultry products must reach an internal temperature of 155 degrees F before removal from the cooking chamber.

Poultry Meat, Raw. The nomenclature for poultry meat obtained from other than young poultry shall include the class designation such as *Yearling Turkey Meat* or *Mature Chicken Meat.*

Poultry Parts. Specific net weights packages for poultry parts, usually those containing legs or wings, sometimes include a single part, such as a drumstick or thigh, to make the stated weight. The name on the label must reflect this practice, e.g. *Chicken Legs—Chicken Thigh added to make weight.* The single part must be cut at the joint. Wing tips are not permitted as added parts.

Poultry Products Containing Livestock Ingredients. Poultry products containing livestock ingredients (in amounts that exceed 20 percent of the total livestock and poultry product portion of the poultry product) must be descriptively labeled to indicate the presence of the livestock ingredients, e.g., *Chicken and*

Beef Stew or *Stew made with Chicken and Beef.* Poultry products containing livestock ingredients in lesser amounts (20 percent or less of the total livestock and poultry product portion of the poultry product) must have names that are qualified to indicate the presence of the livestock ingredients, e.g., *Chicken Stew—Beef Added.* However, poultry products that do not meet specified minimum poultry ingredient requirements because livestock ingredients are replacing any part of the required poultry ingredients must be descriptively labeled to indicate the presence of livestock ingredients, e.g. *Turkey and Pork Chop Suey.*

Poultry Products. In poultry products where *meat* appears in the product name, such as *White Meat Chicken Roll* and *Dark Meat Turkey Loaf,* skin and attached fat are permitted in greater than natural proportions. However, the ingredients statement must have the poultry skin or poultry fat listed. When skin and attached fat appear in the ingredient statement, their placement should be in the correct order of predominance and determined by the amount present over the permitted natural proportions.

Poultry Puffs. Must contain at least 15 percent cooked poultry meat. *Chicken* or *Turkey Puffs* are classified as hors d'oeuvres and must show a true product name, such as *Breaded Chicken and Rice Balls.*

Poultry Roast. May be formulated with up to 10 percent liquids without a qualifying statement. If more than 10 percent liquid is used, the name must be qualified with a statement, such as *containing up to* x *percent____.*

Poultry Salami Products. Poultry sausages prepared to resemble salami and offered to consumers as a salami shall bear product names as follows: *(Kind) Salami* (e.g., *Turkey Salami*) shall be the product name when the moisture-to-protein ratio in the finished product does not exceed 1.9:1. This product resembles a dry salami made from red meats. *Cooked (Kind) Salami* (e.g., *Cooked Turkey Salami*) shall be the product name when the product is cooked and the moisture-to-protein ratio is above 1.9:1. This product resembles a *cooked salami* made from red meats.

Poultry Tenders and Poultry Tenderloins. Any strip of breast meat from the kind of poultry designated.

Titanium Dioxide. When used in poultry salads, a qualifying phrase should appear under the product name stating that the product has been *Artificially Whitened* or *Artificially Lightened.*

Turkey, Hickory Smoked. Product is exposed to natural smoke during the cooking process, and returned to green weight or less. It is usually cured, but this is not a requirement. Cooked to an internal temperature of 160 degrees F (155 degrees F if cured).

Turkey Chops. Prepared by cutting the frozen breast into slabs with each cut being made perpendicular to the long axis of the keel bone (sternum). The larger slabs are split in half through the center of the sternum, resulting in two individual servings of meat with a piece of bone on one side and a thin layer of skin on the other. The smaller pieces at each end of the breast are left intact as individual servings. *Steak* is not a suitable name because a *turkey steak* is boneless by definition.

Turkey Loaf, Cured, Chopped, Canned. May contain seasonings,

cures, and no more than 3 percent water at formulation. Binders and extenders are not permitted.

Turkey Salisbury Steak. Must contain at least 55 percent turkey meat in natural proportions (light and dark) or 65 percent turkey with skin and fat in natural proportions (skin 10 percent, turkey meat 55 percent). Maximum amount of binders and extenders is 12 percent.

Sources:

Agricultural Marketing Service, USDA, "Grading of Poultry Products and Rabbit Products," 7 CFR part 70 (1992), Washington: Government Printing Office.

Standards and Labeling Division, Food Safety and Inspection Service, USDA, *Standards and Labeling Policy Book,* Washington: Government Printing Office, June 1991.

Quiche Products

The term *quiche* does not have to be qualified to indicate it is a custard cheese pie. However, when characterizing ingredients (such as bacon, ham, chicken, onion, etc.) are used either alone or in combination, the ingredients are either clearly identified as part of the product name or prominently displayed elsewhere on the principal display panel (PDP) of the label, e.g., *Bacon Quiche* or *Ham and Onion Quiche.*

Similarly the characterizing ingredients in quiches bearing fanciful names are identified as part of the product name or highlighted elsewhere on the principle display panel (e.g., *Quiche Bercy—made with ham and wine*). Since *Quiche Lorraine* is widely recognized, the characterizing ingredients do not have to be identified as part of the product name or elsewhere on the principle display panel.

Meat and poultry quiches must contain at least 8 percent cooked meat or poultry and sufficient cheese so that the combined total at least comprises 18 percent of the finished product. Quiche Lorraine must contain cooked bacon and/or ham and the only cheeses are Swiss and/or Gruyère. If other characterizing ingredients (excluding cheese), such as onions, peppers, or olives, are used in addition to the meat or poultry ingredient in Quiche Lorraine or in any other quiche, the combination of these other characterizing ingredients and the meat or poultry ingredients must comprise at least 8 percent of the total product and the cooked meat or poultry portion must be at least 5 percent of the total product.

Source:

Standards and Labeling Division, Food Safety and Inspection Service, USDA, *Standards and Labeling Policy Book,* Washington: Government Printing Office, June 1991.

Rare, Medium, and Well Done

There is no objective basis for determining particular temperature that will produce beef products considered to be properly identified by the terms *rare, medium,* and *well-done.* Therefore, if they appear on labels in relation to meats, they should be shown in conjunction with possessive terms to clearly indicate that it is a labeling declaration about degree of doneness that is associated with the producer or distributor, e.g., *Our Rare Beef* or *Jones Packing Company's Medium Cooked Beef.*)

Source:
Standards and Labeling Division, Food Safety and Inspection Service, USDA, *Standards and Labeling Policy Book,* Washington: Government Printing Office, June 1991.

Sandwich

The following are guidelines for labeling prepared sandwiches.

Sandwich, Open. Must contain at least 50 percent cooked meat. Product must show true product name, such as *Sliced Roast Beef on Bread.*

Sandwich, Closed. Must contain at least 35 percent cooked meat and no more than 50 percent bread.

Dinners, Meat or Poultry Sandwiches. Some dinner products consist of a frankfurter, hamburger, or sliced poultry meat packaged with a sliced bun for consumption as a sandwich and packaged with beans, french fries, and other foods. These articles are made by federally inspected plants, and it has been determined that consumers purchase such articles on the basis that they are meat or poultry *dinners.* Therefore, the product should be defined as meat *dinner* or poultry *dinner.*

Source:
Standards and Labeling Division, Food Safety and Inspection Service, USDA, *Standards and Labeling Policy Book,* Washington: Government Printing Office, June 1991.

Sauce

The following are guidelines for labeling of sauces used with meats.

Barbecue Sauce with Chicken. Must contain at least 15 percent cooked chicken meat.

Barbecue Sauce with Meat. Must contain at least 35 percent cooked meat. When the name of the product shows meat in smaller letters (not more than one-half size) of the largest letter in product name, 25 percent cooked meat is required.

Bolognese. A meat sauce which may be labeled as *Bolognese Sauce* or *Bolognese Meat Sauce.*

Burgundy Sauce with Beef and Noodles. Must contain at least 25 percent cooked beef, with up to 10 percent cooked noodles and enough wine to characterize the sauce. A claim that identifies the use of shredded meat or shredded poultry meat is permitted. However, if ground meat or ground poultry meat is also used, its presence must also be identified in the name, e.g., *Shredded Beef and Ground Beef Burrito.*

Creamed Sauce with Meat or Creamed Meat Products. These products may include chipped beef, cooked beef, sausage, ham, franks, meatballs, etc., and must contain at least 18 percent meat or meat products (cooked basis). The kind of meat product should be reflected in the product name (e.g. *Creamed Cured Beef, Chopped, Pressed, Cooked*).

Creole Sauce. Must contain green peppers, tomatoes, and spices.

Mock Turtle Soup. May be made with beef and beef by-products. At least 10 percent beef is required.

Worcestershire Sauce. When used in a product it must be shown as *Worcestershire Sauce* in the ingredients statement. It cannot be listed as flavoring. However, the ingredients do not have to be listed.

Source:
Standards and Labeling Division, Food Safety and Inspection Service, USDA, *Standards and Labeling Policy Book,* Washington: Government Printing Office, June 1991.

Sausage

Sausages. (Species) sausages, which may be cooked, cured, or smoked (or any combination), must comply with standards before processing if the product name is to include *(Species) Sausage.* For example, fresh beef sausage which is cured and cooked may be labeled *Cured, Cooked Beef Sausage.* Prior to this processing, these products could not contain more than the 3 percent water permitted by the standard. Cooked cured sausages or smoked cured sausages containing up to 10 percent added water in the finished product and prepared from one species may be labeled as *Cooked Cured Sausage* or *Smoked Sausage* or as *Cooked Cured Sausage Made with (Species)* or *Smoked Sausage Made with (Species).* Semi-dry and dry sausages made from a single species may be labeled *(species) sausage,* e.g., *beef sausage.*

Sausage Names. Other names for sausage are: *wurst* (German), *kielbasa* (Polish), *Kobacica* (Croatian), *salchica* (Spanish), *korv* (Swedish), *loukaniko* (Greek), *naknik* (Jewish), *salcicca* (Italian), *ispin* (Irish), *saucisse* (French), or *sucuk* (Turkish).

SAUSAGE CLASSIFICATION

Fresh Sausage. Made of fresh, uncured meat (generally cuts of fresh pork and sometimes beef). Its taste, texture, tenderness, and color are related to the ratio of fat to lean. Trimmings from primal cuts such as pork, loin, ham, and shoulders are often used. Must be kept under refrigeration and thoroughly cooked before serving. Bratwurst is in this class. Binders and extenders are permitted except where regulations do not permit the use of such ingredients.

Uncooked Smoked Sausage. Has all the characteristics of fresh sausage except it is smoked, producing a different flavor and color. It sometimes contains fresh meat and must be thoroughly cooked before serving. Kielbasa is in this class. If a mixture of pork and other meats, regardless of size, it must be treated for trichinae.

Cooked Smoked Sausages. Usually made from cured meats which are chopped or ground, seasoned, smoked, and cooked. The use of cure contributes to flavor, color, and preservation of the product. It comes in all shapes and sizes—short, thin, long, and chubby. The largest and most popular of all categories, the skinless varieties, have been stripped of their casings after cooking. These include weiners and smoky links.

Cooked Sausages. Usually prepared from fresh, uncured meats, although sometimes cured meats are used. Often variety meat or organ meat such as liver is used. The product may be smoked and is always ready to serve. Liver sausage is the most popular in this group.

Dry and Semi-Dry Sausages. Dry sausages may or may not be characterized by a bacterial fermentation. When fermented, the intentional encouragement of a lactic acid bacteria growth is useful as a meat preservative as well as producing the typical tangy flavor. The meat ingredients, after being mixed with spices and curing materials, are generally held for several days in a curing cooler. Afterward, the meat is stuffed into casings and is started on a carefully controlled air-drying process. Some dry sausage is given a light preliminary smoke, but the key production step is a relatively long, continuous air-drying process. Principal dry sausage products are salami (coarsely cut) and cervelat (finely cut). They may be smoked, unsmoked, or cooked. Italian and French dry sausage are rarely smoked, but other varieties usually are. Dry sausage requires more production time than other types of sausage and results in a concentrated form of meat. Medium-dry sausage is about 70 percent of its green weight when sold. Less-dry and fully-dried sausage range from 80 to 60 percent of original weight at completion. Semi-dry sausages are usually heated in the smokehouse to fully cook the product and partially dry it. Semi-dry sausages are semi-soft sausages with good keeping qualities due to their lactic acid fermentation. Although dry and semi-dry sausages originally were produced in the winter for use in the summer, the term *summer sausage* now refers to semi-dry sausages.

MOISTURE PROTEIN RATIO (MPR)

Moisture Protein Ratio (MPR)-pH. Nonrefrigerated or shelf stable sausages must have an MPR of 3.1:1 or less and a pH of 5.0 or less, unless commercially sterilized. This does not apply to products containing more than 3.5 percent binders or 2 percent isolated soy protein. The MPR for the following products is given below:

Thuringer	3.7:1
Tropic Cure Pork	3.25:1
Genoa Salami	2.3:1
Sicilian Salami	2.3:1
Roast Beef, Canned	2.25:1
Kippered Beef	2.03:1
Ukrainian Sausage	2.0:1
Dry Salami	1.9:1
Italian Salami	1.9:1
Sausage, Dry	1.9:1
Farmer Summer Sausage	1.9:1
Frizzes	1.6:1
Pepperoni	1.6:1
Meat, Dried	1.04:1
Chipped Beef	1.04:1
Jerky	0.75:1

TYPES

Alessandri. An Italian term for a dry sausage. A true product name must be shown, such as *Alessandri Sausage.*

Apennino. An Italian term for a dry sausage originating in the Alpine Region of northern Italy. Must show true product name, such as *Apennino Brand Sausage—Made in USA.*

Arles or D'Arles. A dry sausage that must show a true product name such as *Arles Sausage.* It is similar to Milano Salami and is made of coarsely chopped meat and corded crisscross style.

Bangers. A sausage-like product prepared with meat and varying amounts of rusk or other cereals. Must show percentage of rusk (or other cereal) adjacent to product name in prominent lettering. May be labeled *British, Scottish,* or *Irish Style.*

Beerwurst, Bierwurst. A cooked smoked sausage with the same requirements as *beef salami* (see *Salami, Beef*), with the exception that pork may be used.

Berliner Blood Sausage. A cooked blood sausage containing diced bacon. After cooking, it is dried and smoked. Ham fat, snouts, and lips are not permitted. See *Blood Sausage.*

Berliner. A cooked smoked sausage usually made from coarsely cut cured pork in large casings. When beef is used it should not exceed 50 percent of the meat block. Pork stomachs or beef tripe not permitted.

Blockwurst. A semi-dry sausage.

Blood and Tongue Sausage. Same as blood sausage except cured and cooked pork or beef tongues are used.

Blood Sausage/Pudding. A cooked sausage formulated with blood and some meat. Usually contains pork skins and/or pork jowls. May also contain sweet pickled ham fat, snouts, and lips. If it does not contain meat, it must be labeled as *Blood Pudding.*

Bologna or Cooked Smoked Sausage. There are three types of bologna: *Standard,* which is 4 to 5 inches in diameter for slicing; *Ring,* which is about 2 inches in diameter in a casing horseshoe-shaped or tied in a ring; and *Ham Bologna,* which may have large chunks of ham mixed in with the standard bologna emulsion. Ham bologna must have at least 50 percent ham, although it may be made with all ham emulsion.

Boudin. A French term for a meat sausage or pudding usually made with chicken and veal or chicken and pork. Should be labeled *Boudin Sausage* (if it meets the sausage standard) or *Boudin Pudding.* May contain by-products and rice and is usually uncured.

Bratwurst. A fresh, uncured, uncooked, unsmoked sausage that may not contain more than 3 percent water at time of formulation. As a sausage, it may not contain eggs, milk, vegetables, or cheese. It may contain extenders up to 3.5 percent, and may contain antioxidants.

Bratwurst, Cooked. An uncured, unsmoked, finely comminuted sausage, permitted to contain 10 percent water based on the finished product. Chicken has been approved in cooked bratwurst, when identified in the product name. Antioxidants are not permitted.

Bratwurst, Cured. Products that meet the requirement for bratwurst but also contain cures must use *Cured* on the label.

Bratwurst, Poultry. Same requirements as for *Bratwurst*. There is no limitation on beef fat when properly identified in product name.

Breakfast Link Sausage. Regular fresh sausage which does not have to be made with pork.

Breakfast Links. A fresh sausage made with pork.

Brotwurst. A cured and cooked sausage that may be smoked.

Brown and Serve Sausage, Canned. A cooked sausage, usually without cure, and not more than 8 percent water. The weight of the sausage at canning does not exceed the weight of fresh uncured meat ingredients plus the weight of curing and seasoning ingredients.

Brown and Serve Sausage. The standard is based on one of the four options listed: (1) the MPR (see *Moisture Protein Ratio*) is no more than 3.7:1—fat limited to 35 percent and 10 percent added water at formulation; (2) no more than 10 percent added water at formulation and a yield of no greater than 80 percent; (3) no more than 8.8 percent added water at formulation and a yield no greater than 85 percent; or (4) must show fresh sausage standard before cooking. The label must show true product name, such as *Brown and Serve Pork Sausage*.

Butifarr Sausage. An uncured sausage. Labeling requires an additional product name

Cacciatore. Cacciatore is an Italian term, meaning hunter or sportsman. Used to describe a dry sausage, which must be labeled as *Cacciatore Sausage*.

Calabrese. An Italian term for a salami originating in southern Italy. Usually made entirely of pork seasoned with hot peppers.

Casing, Artificial. Frankfurters packaged in retail containers with the artificial casing left on must bear a prominent statement, such as *Remove casing before eating,* contiguous to the product name on the label.

Casing, Collagen. Collagen casings are prepared from beef hides specially processed and formed into casings. For classification purposes, they are *edible casings* but are not considered *natural casings*.

Cervelat or Cured and Cooked Sausage. Often a semi-dry or dry summer sausage. Hog stomachs, beef tripe, and extenders are permitted.

Chorizo, Fresh. Fresh chorizos (uncured, uncooked) shall not contain more than 3 percent added water. These products may contain vinegar. The vinegar used must have strength of no less than 4 grams of acetic acid per 100 cubic centimeters at a temperature of 20 degrees C.

Chorizo. A Spanish term used to describe a cooked, dry, or semi-dry, cured pork sausage. Sausage standard applicable. Seasoned with Spanish pimento and red pepper. Partially defatted pork fatty tissue is acceptable.

Chorizo in Lard, Canned. Canned chorizos not thermally processed but packed hot, usually in lard, have a standard for the chorizos of an MPR (see *Moisture Protein Ratio*) of 1.8:1 and a pH of not more than 5.5. An alternative standard is a water activity (Aw) of 0.92.

Chorizo in Lard. Must contain at least 55 percent chorizo.

Chourico. A Portugese term for sausage.

Chub. An acceptable name to denote a short, usually plump, meat food product, unsliced in casing.

Cocktail Frankfurters. A small frankfurter normally about 2 inches long and ½ inch in diameter.

Coney or Coney Island. Generally recognized as pertaining to a frankfurter in a bun with meat sauce and not considered a geographic term.

Coney Sauce or Coney Island Sauce. A coined name for hot dog chili sauce with meat, which is not considered a geographic term. This name must be accompanied by the true product name, e.g., *Hot Dog Chili Sauce with Meat.*

Corn Dog or Korn Dog. A coined name that must be accompanied by a true product name, e.g., *Batter Wrapped Franks on a Stick.* Limited to 65 percent batter and a minimum of 35 percent frankfurter.

Corn Dog or Korn Dog (Poultry). Sausage made from cooked poultry such as poultry franks or poultry frankfurters must show the *kind* of the poultry used in conjunction with the coined name, as in *Chicken* (or *Turkey*) *Corn Dogs.* The name of the kind of poultry should be shown in type size at least one-third the size of the largest letter of the coined name. A descriptive name such as *Batter Wrapped Chicken Frank on a Stick* must accompany the coined name. If the descriptive name is at least one-third the size of the coined name, the kind name need not precede the coined name.

Cotegino. An acceptable name for a Portugese sausage. The meat block is formulated with pork, pork by-products, and/or pork skins, and cured. Binders which are permitted must be reflected in the product name. It is limited to 3 percent added moisture at time of formulation.

Cotto Salami. A cooked salami.

Dinner Dog. A coined name that must be accompanied by the true product name such as *A Meat and Soy Protein Concentrate Product.*

Farmer Sausage Cervelat. Usually a semi-dry sausage, but may be made in dry form of equal parts of pork and beef delicately seasoned without garlic.

Farmer Summer Sausage. Special type of sausage made of beef and pork, salt, spices, nitrite or nitrate, and heavily smoked. It is classed as *cervelat* (see entry), and no extenders are permitted. It is dry with an MPR (see *Moisture Protein Ratio*) of 1.9:1. The word *Farmer* is considered a generic term, and labels can be approved without any qualifying words such as *Style* or *Brand*. Such labels are not required to bear a statement identifying the place of manufacture. Must be trichinae treated.

Fleischkaese. Acceptable name for a cured, cooked sausage in loaf form.

Fresh Farm or Country Style. When sausage products are labeled *fresh farm style* or *country style,* they must be prepared with natural spices with the exclusion of oleoresins, essential oils, or other spice extractives. Sugar is the sweetening agent for *farm style* or *country style.*

Fresh Polish Sausage. Is a name for an uncooked product made without cures.

Gelbwurst. See *Sausage, German with milk.*

Genoa or Genoa Salami. A dry sausage product with an MPR (see

Moisture Protein Ratio) not in excess of 2.3:1. It is prepared with all pork or with a mixture of pork and a small amount of beef. The meat is given a coarse grind and enclosed in a natural casing. No smoke is used in its preparation.

Goteborg. A Swedish dry sausage made of coarsely chopped beef and sometimes pork. Mildly seasoned with thyme. It has a somewhat salty flavor and is heavily smoked, usually in long casings, and is air dried.

Heat and Eat Sausage. Not the same as *Brown and Serve Sausage.* Product must comply with cooked sausage regulations, such as limitation of 10 percent added water and not more than 3.5 percent binder.

Holstein or Holsteiner. Same as *farm style sausage,* except that it is stuffed into wide casings and heavily smoked, usually in long casings, and is air dried. No extenders permitted.

Jagwurst. A cooked sausage made from a fine emulsion with cubes of lean meat rather than fat (as in *mortadella*). It is the same as *yachtwurst* (the Americanized name for the item).

Junior Meat Snacks. Must conform to the sausage standards going into the jar before processing. Limited to 3.5 percent extenders.

Kalberwurst. Product is similar to *Bockwurst* with no limit on water or milk.

Kielbasa. A cooked, cured sausage, *Kolbassy* is a Czechoslovakian spelling; other variations include *Kielbassy, Kolbasa,* and *Kolbase* (see entry). Made from coarsely ground pork or coarsely ground pork with added beef or mutton. The meat mix shall be predominantly pork when beef or mutton is included. *Beef Kielbasa* may be prepared by using only beef as the meat ingredient. The finished product may contain up to 10 percent added water. Kielbasa is usually highly seasoned and can contain up to 156 ppm sodium nitrite.

Knackwurst, Knockwurst, or Knoblouch. Oversized frankfurters.

Kolbase, Hungarian Style. Finely ground cured beef and pork seasoned and stuffed into casings and smoked. Classed as a cooked, smoked sausage.

Krakow. Acceptable name for a cooked sausage similar to *Berliner* (see entry).

Kuemmelwurst. A cooked sausage of the ring variety, with whole caraway seeds. Usual ingredients are beef, pork, salt, caraway, flavorings, and cure. Also called *carawaywurst.*

Landjaeger Cervelat. A semi-dry sausage that originated in Switzerland. It is about the size of a large frankfurter but pressed flat, smoked, and dried, giving it a black appearance.

Lebanon Bologna. A coarse-ground, fermented, semi-dry sausage. If the product has an MPR (see *Moisture Protein Ratio*) and a pH of 5.0 or less, no refrigeration is required. It is made of 3.1:1 or less with beef. No extenders or hearts are permitted in the product.

Leona. A coarse-ground, cooked sausage.

Linguica. A Portuguese-type sausage containing pork to the exclusion of other meat and meat by-products and usually containing condiments, such as vinegar, cinnamon, cumin seed, garlic, red pepper, salt, and sugar. Usually contains nonfat dry milk. Paprika and cures are acceptable.

Links. This designation falls into four categories: (1) *links* without further qualification refers to an all-pork fresh sausage in links; (2) *links sausage* can be used to designate any sausage-type formulation, usually cured and smoked in links; (3) *links, cereal, and nonfat dry milk added* are usually formulated with meat and meat products cured and smoked, and approved with understanding each link is banded with an approved band label; or (4) *links, a pork and textured vegetable protein product* followed immediately by an ingredients statement is acceptable. Such names as *Links, Top's Links,* and *Joe's Links* are coin names and must be followed immediately by true product name.

Little Smokies. A smoked, small variety sausage link made with beef and pork.

Liverwurst or Pâté de Foie-Style Liverwurst. Must meet liver sausage requirements.

Lola and Lolita. Italian terms for dry sausage products consisting of mildly seasoned pork and containing garlic. *Lolita* comes in 14 ounce links, while *Lola* comes in 2½ pound links.

Longaniza. A fresh sausage product. If it is prepared otherwise, the product name must indicate its nature, such as *Cured Longaniza.*

Longaniza or Puerto Rican Style Longaniza. A Puerto Rican sausage made from pork which may contain beef, but does not contain annatto. Added fat is not permitted.

Loukanika. A cooked fresh Greek sausage. It is usually made with lamb and pork, oranges, allspice, whole pepper, and salt.

Lyons Sausage. A French term for a dry sausage made exclusively of pork (four parts finely chopped lean and one or two parts small diced fat) with spices and garlic. It is stuffed into large casings, cured, and air-dried.

Merguez, Mergues, or Merghez Sausage. A hot and spicy fresh sausage originating in North Africa and common in France. It contains hot pepper and/or paprika. The meat component must contain beef and may contain lamb or mutton when labeled as *Merguez Sausage.* When pork is used as part of meat component, the product is labeled as *Merguez Sausage with Pork.* When pork is the only meat ingredient, the product is labeled *Pork Merguez Sausage.*

Mettwurst. An uncooked, cured, smoked sausage in which by-products and extenders are not permitted. Beef heart meat is acceptable. Water is limited to 3 percent and the fat content to 50 percent.

Mettwurst, Cooked. May contain up to 10 percent water based on finished product, and must be cooked.

Metz Sausage. Cured lean beef and pork and bacon are finely chopped, seasoned, and stuffed into beef middles. It is air-dried for five days, then given a cool smoke. Classed as a semi-dry sausage.

Mortadella. Normally a cooked sausage but can be dry or semi-dry. It is similar to salami and cervelat except that it has large chunks of pork fat. Red sweet peppers are acceptable up to 5 percent and pistachio nuts up to 1 percent and are shown as added in the true product name.

Mortadella, Canned. Canned items designated *Mortadella* must be labeled with the phrase *Perishable, Keep Under Refrigeration* and must have an MPR (see *Moisture Protein Ratio*) not in excess of 3.85:1.

Mortadella, Poultry. A dry, semi-dry, or cooked sausage formulated with poultry which may contain extenders and/or binders. The sausage must contain large chunks of pork fat, which is indicated as *pork fat added* in the product name. Red sweet peppers are permitted up to 5 percent and pistachio nuts up to 1 percent. If product is canned and the product is to be refrigerated, the MPR (see *Moisture Protein Ratio*) must not exceed 3.85:1 and the internal temperature upon cooking must have reached 160 degrees F. The product must be labeled *Perishable, Keep Under Refrigeration* or similar wording.

Mortadella Without Fat Cubes or Chunks. Must meet the standard for *Mortadella*. Product must be qualified to indicate the absence of fat cubes or chunks, e.g., *Mortadella without Fat Cubes* or *Mortadella without Fat Chunks.*

Myvacet (Distilled Acetylated Monoglycerides). Acceptable for use as a coating on sausage casings. Sausages so coated show, adjacent to the product name, a qualifying statement disclosing the presence of the compound, such as *Summer Sausage Coated with a Solution of Distilled Acetylated Monoglycerides.*

Pepperoni with Poultry. Poultry may be added to pepperoni if properly labeled. If the meat block contains 20 percent or less poultry, the product is labeled *Pepperoni with (Kind) Added.* When poultry is added to over 20 percent of the meat and poultry block, the product is labeled *Pork and (Kind) Pepperoni,* and an MPR (see *Moisture Protein Ratio*) of 1.6:1 is applied. If the amount of poultry exceeds that of the meat, the product label reads, e.g., *Turkey and Pork Pepperoni.* This would carry a poultry legend.

Pepperoni. A dry sausage prepared from pork or pork and beef. If beef is used with pork, the formulation may not contain more than 55 percent beef and still be called pepperoni. Combinations containing more than 55 percent beef are called *beef and pork pepperoni.* Pepperoni made with beef must be called *beef pepperoni.* Pepperoni must be treated for destruction of possible live trichinae and must have an MPR (see *Moisture Protein Ratio*) of not more than 1.6:1. Antioxidants are permitted in pepperoni. The casing, before stuffing, or the finished product, may be dipped in a potassium sorbate solution to retard mold growth. Extenders and binders are not permitted in pepperoni. Hearts, tongues, and other by-products are not acceptable ingredients.

Peppers and Cooked Sausage in Sauce. At least 20 percent cooked sausage in total formulation.

Pfefferwurst. A German term for a product which conforms to the sausage standard and contains whole pepper corn. Pork livers, pork stock, and beef blood are not acceptable ingredients.

Phosphates in Sausages. If trimmings containing phosphates are used in formulating sausage products, and the usage rate of these trimmings does not exceed 10 percent of the meat block, the trimmings may be used without declaration of the phosphates in the ingredients statement.

Pimiento Sausage. Pimientos permitted when declared in product name as *Pimiento Sausage.*

Pinkelwurst. A German term for a cooked product that is stuffed in a casing with a diameter of 1½ to 2 inches and a length of about 10 to 12 inches. It is formulated with beef fat, pork fat, onions, oat groats, water, and sufficient spice to satisfy seasoning requirements. The product is cooked in water to an internal temperature of more than 152 degrees F.

Puerto Rican Style Longaniza. An acceptable labeling for sausage made from pork which may contain beef and does contain annatto. Added fat is not permitted, although up to 3 percent

lard may be used as a carrier for annatto. When annatto is used it should be included in the ingredients statement as *annatto.*

Salami. A dry sausage that requires an MPR (see *Moisture Protein Ratio*) of 1.9:1 or less. Extenders and binders are permitted. May be cooked to shorten drying period.

Salami, Beef Casing. Refers to a salami stuffed into beef casings.

Salami, Beef. A cooked, smoked sausage, usually mildly flavored, and coarsely ground beef in large casings. Cereals and extenders are permitted, does not have to be labeled cooked. May contain fat.

Salami, Cooked. Must be labeled to include the word *Cooked* regardless of the type and size of its packaging, unless it is one of the following: a salami with a moisture protein ratio of no more than 1:9 to 1; *Genoa Salami* with a moisture protein ratio of no more than 2.3:1; or *Sicilian Salami* with a moisture protein ratio of no more than 2.3:1. Labeled as *Kosher Salami, Kosher Beef Salami, Beef Salami, Beer Salami,* and *Salami for Beer.*

Salami, Cotto. A cooked smoked sausage, usually beef and pork, coarsely ground and cured, mildly flavored, in large casings and with whole peppercorns. It is smoked and cooked in dry heat. If unsmoked, some smoke flavoring must be added.

Salami, German Brand Made in U.S.A. A dry sausage with an MPR (see *Moisture Protein Ratio*) of 1.9:1. It is made with beef and pork and seasoned with garlic. Less highly flavored but usually more heavily smoked than *Italian Salami* (see entry). It is tied with loops of twine that give a scalloped appearance.

Salami, Italian. Nonfat dry milk has been approved for use in this dry salami consisting of about 80 percent finely chopped pork to which a small amount of pork fat may be added. The remainder consists of chopped beef seasoning, salt, and curing agent. It is easily distinguished by its covering of a white mold. The nonfat dry milk can comprise 3.5 percent of the finished product. The product should have an MPR (see *Moisture Protein Ratio*) not in excess of 1.9:1 to insure the fat content and dryness properties associated with this dry salami will be maintained.

Salami, Milan or Milano. A dry sausage with a maximum MPR (see *Moisture Protein Ratio*) of 1.9:1. It is an Italian-type salami made with beef, pork fat, spiced with garlic, and has a distinctive cording.

Salami, Sicilian Brand Made in U.S.A. An acceptable name for an uncooked dry sausage which is uncooked and contains no garlic. Antioxidants are permitted. Trichinae treatment required.

Salchichon. A Spanish term meaning "large sausage" which may only be used for casing sausage products 3 inches in diameter or more. Product must show a true product name.

Salcina, Portuguese Brand Made in U.S.A. Sausage usually containing pork, green onions, parsley, vinegar, salt, sugar, spices, and garlic.

Salpicao. A type of smoked sausage. The label must show true product name, such as a *Smoked Sausage.* No more than 3 percent water at formulation.

Salsiccia. An Italian term for a fresh pork sausage in which paprika is permitted. It is a rope style sausage made of finely cut pork trimmings and highly spiced.

Sarno. A type of dry smoked sausage. The label must show true product name such as *Smoked Sausage.* Coarsely chopped beef, pork, and garlic is not permitted. The product is smoked and air dried.

Sausage, German with Milk. Whole milk is a permitted ingredient in the following meat food products when the ingredients statement is shown immediately under the name of the product 'or the milk is shown in a qualifying statement contiguous to the product name: *Speckblutwurst, Kalbsbratwurst, Langblutwurst, Blutwurst, Gelbwurst, Zengenwurst, (Brand) Tongue* and *Blood Pudding, Kalbslebenwurst (Swiss Liver Sausage).* The latter should be considered on the same basis as *Bockwurst,* e.g., no limit on water or milk. Milk is a characterizing ingredient in German sausages and not an extender.

Sausage, Polish. A sausage that is cured, cooked, and usually smoked. Pork and pork by-products shall at least 50 percent of the meat and meat by-products ingredients. If beef is predominant ingredient, product name would be *Beef and Pork Polish Sausage.* Green peppers are permitted up to 4 percent in total formulation.

Sausage, Pork and Bacon. Up to 50 percent bacon permitted provided that the bacon is brought back to green weight before use, the product is trichinae treated, and the product name either is *Pork and Bacon Sausage* or *Pork Sausage and Bacon.* To differentiate between these two products, the standard will be to use *Pork Sausage and (with) Bacon* on the label when the product contains 10 to 20 percent bacon, and to use *Pork and Bacon Sausage* on the label when the bacon is more than 20 percent but not more than 50 percent.

Sausage, Pork. Does not include the use of pork cheeks. When such an item is offered as *Whole Hog,* tongues, hearts, and cheeks may be used in the natural proportion as found in the hog carcass.

Sausage, Potato or Potato Brand Sausage, Potato Ring and Potato Brand Ring. A cooked or uncooked meat food product with the following requirements: Must contain at least 45 percent meat and no by-products; water is limited to 3 percent at formulation; extenders or binders are limited to 3.5 percent of the finished product, except that 2 percent of isolated soy protein shall be deemed to be equivalent of 3.5 percent of any one of the other binders or extenders; must contain at least 18 percent potatoes.

Sausage or Ring, Potato, Swedish Style. A cooked or uncooked meat food product with the following requirements: Must contain at least 65 percent meat and no by-products; water is limited to 3 percent at formulation; no extenders or binders permitted; must contain at least 18 percent potatoes.

Sausage, Poultry. Sausage products made from poultry must be labeled to indicate kind, such as *Chicken Sausage, Turkey Bologna,* etc. Products containing more than one kind of poultry or red meat must declare added ingredient in the product name, such as *Chicken Bologna, Beef Added* and *Turkey Franks, Chicken Hearts Added.* Binders and extenders in poultry sausage shall be shown in product name, such as *Chicken Sausage, Sodium Caseinate Added.* The basic meat sausage standards apply to poultry except for added water and fat.

Sausage, Romanian Brand. An uncooked smoked sausage made with cured lean pork. Requires trichinae treatment.

Sausage with Fruits and Vegetables. Sausage-type products that contain unexpected ingredients that significantly alter the character of the product may be descriptively labeled as *(Characterizing Ingredient) Sausage,* e.g., *Cherry Pecan Sausage* or *Wild Rice Sausage,* or with other equally descriptive names such as *Sausage with Wild Rice.* For fresh sausages, the sausage portion of the product, prior to the addition of the characterizing ingredient(s), must meet any applicable standards including fat and added water limitations, moisture/protein ratios, and use of binders and extenders. For cooked, smoked, dry, etc., sausages, the finished sausage type product must meet the standard that was applicable to the sausage prior to the addition of the characterizing ingredients. The unexpected ingredient must be present in sufficient quantity or form to characterize the sausage-type product in flavor, texture, or other sensory attributes. However, there are no minimum use levels.

Sausage, Galician. Cured beef and pork, seasoned and stuffed into beef rounds. It is then smoked at a high temperature. Cooling is done in a blast of air which produces the characteristic wrinkled appearance of Galician sausage.

Sausage, Greek. Must contain orange peel.

Sausage, Summer. May be a semi-dry or cooked sausage. Meat by-products and extenders are permitted.

Sausage, Ukrainian. A dry sausage made from lean pork and/or veal chunks. The product contains large amounts of garlic which dominates the flavor. It is cooked and smoked at high temperatures (around 180 to 185 degrees F) for four to five hours and then air dried. The water activity (Aw) of the finished product shall not exceed 0.92 or a moisture/protein ratio of 2.0:1 or less.

Sausage, Vienna—Packed in Beef Broth. Must contain 80 percent sausage to be in compliance prior to inclusion in can. Broth component to have an MPR (see *Moisture Protein Ratio*) of not more than 135:1. A manufacturer holds trademark rights to the terms *Vienna* and *Vienna Beef.*

Sausage with Sauerkraut in Sauce. Must contain at least 40 percent sausage.

Saveloy. A cooked smoked sausage which is English in origin and similar to Bologna made of beef and pork. The label must show a true product name such as *Sausage.*

Serkelki or Serdelowa. A cooked smoked pork sausage of Polish origin. Must show a true product name such as *Smoked Sausage.*

Smearwurst. It is a cooked sausage, similar to *Mettwurst.* The label must show a true product name such as *Sausage.*

Smoked Sausage, Country Style. An uncured or cooked smoked sausage with natural spices and sugar. It is made with beef and pork. Trichinae treatment required.

Smoked Thuringer Links. A cooked smoked sausage made with pork only.

Smoky Snax. A smoked sausage. The label must show true product name such as *Smoked Sausage* or *Dry Sausage.*

Soppresate. An acceptable name for a dry salami with an MPR (see *Moisture Protein Ratio*) of 1.9:1. This is an Italian salami that is lightly flavored with garlic and generally hotly seasoned with paprika and black or red peppers. It is smoked to varying degrees depending on regional tastes.

Soujouk. A Turkish term for sausage made from beef and which is very dry and highly spiced with an MPR (see *Moisture Protein Ratio*) of 2.04:1. The product is usually flattened or resembles a dry salami or ring bologna. The label must show a true product name such as *Dried Beef Sausage*.

Southern Hots. A name for a cooked smoked sausage made in the southern U.S. (South of the Mason-Dixon line is regarded as *southern*.) Must be accompanied by a true product name such as *Smoked Sausage*.

Speckwurst. Product should conform to sausage standard without the use of by-products, except chunks of fat are usually present.

Texas Hots. A coined name for a smoked sausage made in Texas. The label must show true product name such as *Smoked Sausage*.

Thuringer. A semi-dry sausage which may not contain binders or extenders (such as cereal, vegetable starch, starch vegetable flour, soy flour, soy protein concentrate, isolated soy protein, nonfat dry milk, calcium reduced dry skim milk, dried milk). It has an MPR (see *Moisture Protein Ratio*) of 3.7:1, and is usually smoked. It complies with the following factors: Pork fat as such may comprise up to 10 percent of the total ingredients. Heart meat (beef or pork) may comprise up to 50 percent of meat ingredients. Tongue meat (beef or pork) may comprise up to 10 percent of meat ingredients. Cheek meat (beef or pork) may comprise up to 50 percent of meat ingredients. *Cooked Thuringer* can contain up to 10 percent added water. Acceptable product names for uncooked thuringer include *Beef Summer Sausage—Thuringer Cervelat* and *Summer Sausage—Thuringer Cervelat*.

Touristen Wurst. A semi-dry type of sausage. The MPR (see *Moisture Protein Ratio*) is 3.7:1.

Trichinae Treatment. All sausage and meat food products containing pork that are not cooked or understood to be cooked prior to serving must be treated by one of the prescribed methods.

Turkey Braunschweiger. The product name must be shown on the label as *Turkey Liver Sausage*. No by-products other than liver are permitted in the product.

Weisswurst. An acceptable name for fresh sausage. It is usually made of pork or veal and must be thoroughly cooked before eating. A German term which means white sausage, it is similar to bratwurst. Weisswurst with milk should be labeled *kalbsbratwurst*. Weisswurst with milk and eggs should be labeled *bockwurst*.

White Hots. A cooked smoked sausage that may be qualified as *Weisswurst* or *Bockwurst Style*. Product usually made of pork, beef, and/or veal. By-products and additives permitted. No cure permitted.

Whole Hog Sausage. Must contain all primal parts of a hog. Hearts, and tongues, in natural proportions, are permitted ingredients when declared in the ingredients statement. Other meat by-products not permitted in whole hog sausage.

Source:

Standards and Labeling Division, Food Safety and Inspection Service, USDA, *Standards and Labeling Policy Book,* Washington: Government Printing Office, June 1991.

Smoked Products

The guidelines for approving labels for products prepared with natural smoke and/or smoke flavor (natural or artificial) are as follows:

1. Meat or poultry products which have been exposed to smoke generated from burning hardwoods, hardwood sawdust, corn cobs, mesquite, etc., may be labeled as *Smoked* or with terms such as *Naturally Smoked* to indicate that the traditional smoking process is used.

2. Meat or poultry products which have been exposed to natural liquid smoke flavor which has been transformed into a true gaseous state by the application of heat or transformed into vapor by mechanical means, e.g., atomization, may be labeled *Smoked*.

3. Meat or poultry products may be labeled *Smoked* if natural liquid smoke flavor is applied by spraying, dipping, liquid flooding, or similar processes prior to or during heat processing. In such cases, the natural liquid smoke flavoring must be transformed into a true gaseous state by the heat of processing.

4. Meat or poultry products to which smoke flavor (natural or artificial) has been directly applied to the exposed product surface, e.g., massaging or margination, or incorporated into the product by such means as injection, must be labeled to identify the smoke flavor as part of the product name, e.g., *Ham-Natural Smoke Flavor Added* and in the ingredients statement.

5. Meat or poultry products that are smoked as provided for in 1, 2, and 3 above, and also treated with smoke flavor as described in 4, may only be labeled *Smoked* or with terms such as *Naturally Smoked,* as appropriate, if it is clearly disclosed that the product is also treated with smoke flavor. The presence of the smoke flavor must be identified as part of the product name, e.g., *Smoked Ham— Smoke Flavoring Added* and in the ingredients statement.

TERMINOLOGY

Hickory Smoked. Product may be labeled as *hickory smoked* only if the processor provides appropriate certification to a government inspector that such sawdust or wood used for smoking is 100 percent hickory.

Smoked Beef Round. Consists of beef rounds which are soaked for approximately one-half hour in a solution consisting of water and salt. After removal from the solution they are stuffed into plain casings to secure a round shape. They are then smoked and heated until an internal temperature of 140 to 145 degrees F is reached.

Smoke Flavoring. The use of smoke flavoring (natural or artificial) in a component of a meat or poultry food product, e.g., ham in a ham salad, does not require that the product name be qualified to indicate the presence of the smoke flavoring. However, the smoke flavoring must be declared in the ingredients statement on the meat or poultry product labels.

Source:
Standards and Labeling Division, Food Safety and Inspection Service, USDA, *Standards and Labeling Policy Book,* Washington: Government Printing Office, June 1991.

Soups

Soups declaring in the product name that they are made with meat stock are meat food products and contains at least 25 percent meat stock with an MPR (see *Moisture Protein Ratio*) of not less than 67:1 for *condensed soup,* 135:1 for *ready-to-eat soup.* For beef bouillon, the requirement is at least 50 percent beef stock and an MPR of 67:1. Soups made with meat contain not less than 10 percent meat for condensed soup, and not less than 5 percent meat for ready-to-eat soup. Soups containing smoked meats contain not less than 4.0 percent smoked meat (condensed soup), or 2.0 percent smoked meat (ready-to-eat soup). Soups made with cooked sausages contain at least 4.0 percent cooked sausage.

SOUP PRODUCTS

Bean & Ham Shank. When soup is made from ham shanks, they must be shown in the true product name such as *Bean and Ham Shank Soup.*

Blood. Must contain at least 1 percent blood, and must be made under inspection.

Chowders. Follow standard for soups.

Consomme. A broth cooked with vegetables and then strained. Must have an MPR (see *Moisture Protein Ratio*) of 135:1.

Italian Style Minestrone. Soup must contain zucchini, and the meat used must be identified in the true product name.

Pepper Pot. Must contain at least 20 percent scalded tripe.

Petite Marmite. A French term for a soup made with meat, chicken, and vegetables.

Scotch Broth. Must contain at least 3 percent mutton in a thick mutton broth.

Vegetable. Vegetable soups made with soup stock are not governed by the labeling regulations for product containing meat.

Source:
Standards and Labeling Division, Food Safety and Inspection Service, USDA, *Standards and Labeling Policy Book,* Washington: Government Printing Office, June 1991.

Spaghetti

The following guidelines apply to prepared spaghetti and spaghetti sauce products.

Sauce with Meat. Must contain at least 6 percent meat.

Sauce with Meatballs. Must contain at least 35 percent cooked meatballs.

Spaghetti Sauce with Meat Stock. Consists mainly of tomatoes with seasoning. Must contain 5 percent fresh beef and 12.5 percent concentrated meat stock.

Spaghettios in Cheese Sauce with Ground Beef. Must contain at least 12 percent meat.

With Franks and Sauce. Must contain at least 12 percent franks.

With Meat and Sauce. Must contain at least 12 percent meat.

With Meatballs and Sauce. Must contain at least 12 percent meat.

With Meatballs. Must contain at least 12 percent meat or 18 percent meatballs.

Source:
Standards and Labeling Division, Food Safety and Inspection Service, USDA, *Standards and Labeling Policy Book,* Washington: Government Printing Office, June 1991.

Stew

Beef Tripe Stew. There are two versions of this product. One is of Mexican origin and merchandised in association with the term *Menudo.* Corn is a prominent ingredient in its formula. The standard for an item of this nature requires that it contain not less than 33 percent beef tripe computed on the basis of the uncooked tripe in relation to total ingredients. The second product is popular in Puerto Rico. It is referred to as *Mondungo* and is made with 25 percent raw beef tripe. The remainder consists principally of potatoes, a squash with a pumpkin-like appearance and flavor, and a native vegetable called *tanier.* When the vegetables are not distinguishable, this second product can be labeled as *Dominican Style Mondungo.*

Brunswick Stew. Must contain at least 25 percent (fresh basis) of at least two kinds of meat, one of which may be poultry. Must contain corn as one of the vegetables.

Burgoo. A thick soup or stew made from a combination of meats and vegetables. If it is labeled *Burgoo Soup,* the meat soup standard is applicable; if labeled *Burgoo Stew,* apply the stew standard. Product must contain more than one kind of meat or poultry.

Carbonnade. A French term for a product that contains at least 50 percent meat. May be beef, pork, or mutton. Usually made with cheaper cuts of meat. Contains beer or wine. Product slowly cooked, either slowly cooked, either braised or stewed. Label must show true product name, such as *Beef Carbonnade.*

Cassoulet. A French term for a product which contains at least 25 percent meat. A complex stew consisting of dried white beans and a combination of pork, lamb, game, and sausages. The ingredients are cooked, then put into a casserole, usually covered with crumbs, and baked. Label must show true product name, such as *Beans and Bacon in Sauce.*

Chop Suey, American. Must contain at least 25 percent fresh meat in total formulation. A stew-like dish prepared with beef, pork, or veal. Vegetables include onion and celery. Macaroni, noodles, or rice are usually incorporated in the product, although recipes suggest serving chop suey over one of these.

Chop Suey. Vegetables with meat. Must contain at least 12 percent fresh meat.

Goulash, Hungarian Style. Must contain paprika and at least 25 percent meat or 12 percent poultry meat. No noodles, potatoes, or dumplings.

Goulash. A stew like product with at least 25 percent meat or 12 percent poultry meat. Unless designated *Hungarian,* generally means stew, whether veal, pork, beef, turkey, etc., are used. Product may be just meat and gravy or meat and gravy with vegetables served with or without rice, potatoes, or noodles.

Irish Stew. Does not require a geographical qualifying statement nor the words, *Style, Type,* or *Brand.* Usually it contains lamb or mutton but beef may be used. Must meet the stew standard. Vegetables include onions, carrots, potatoes, and turnips. Dumplings are often used. Beans are not acceptable in *Irish Stew.*

Mondongo. See *Beef Tripe Stew.* A mixture of one or more of the following: beef tripe, cattle feet with or without hide on, chitterlings, beef intestines.

Mulligan Stew. Must contain at least 25 percent fresh meat or meat and poultry. Mulligan stew is a mixture of vegetables and meat combined in a gravy or sauce. The label must have a true product name, such as a *Chicken and Meat Mulligan Stew.*

Navarin. Navarin is a stew containing lamb or mutton and vegetables and considered a national dish of France. Must meet the meat stew standard of 25 percent meat.

Vegetable Stew with Meatballs. Must contain at least 12 percent meat.

Vegetable Stew with Meat. Must contain at 12 percent meat.

Vegetable Stew with Meat Sauce or Gravy. Must contain at least 6 percent meat.

Vegetable Stew with Sauce and Meat. Must contain at least 12 percent meat.

Vegetable Stew with Poultry. Must contain at least 6 percent cooked poultry meat.

Source:
Standards and Labeling Division, Food Safety and Inspection Service, USDA, *Standards and Labeling Policy Book,* Washington: Government Printing Office, June 1991.

Styles

Amandine. A French term for a product which must contain sufficient almonds to characterize.

Barbecue (Infrared Cooked). Product must indicate heat source as *infrared cooked* in lettering not less than one-half as large as the largest letter in the word *barbecue.*

Beef, Chinese-Style. Contains grain alcohol and soy sauce.

Cajun Brand Made in ____. Refers to any products not having to meet the standards for *Cajun* or *Cajun Style.*

Cajun Style/Cajun Recipe. Acceptable identification for products containing onion/onion powder/dehydrated onion, garlic/garlic powder/dehydrated garlic, white pepper, red pepper, and black pepper.

Cajun. Refers to product made in Louisiana.

Cornish Style Pastry. Must contain at least 25 percent beef.

Product consists of a round or square of piecrust with a filling of chopped beef, potatoes, and onions.

Country Style Chicken. Cut up chicken in which wishbone is left whole.

Deli or Delicatessen Style. Although there is not a recognizable *Deli Style* as such, the terminology has been permitted on labeling for ready-to-eat meat products that consumers would normally expect to find in a delicatessen.

Hickory Smoked. Product labeled *Hickory Smoked* must use hickory wood exclusively.

Italian Recipe. Verification of authenticity of phrase *Italian Recipe* must accompany application for approval of labeling terminology.

Italian Style. Used for products containing anise or fennel or Italian type cheese (such as mozzarella, parmesan, provolone, ricotta, romano) or at least three of the following: basil, garlic, marjoram, olive oil, or oregano.

Jamaican Style Patties. At least 25 percent meat enclosed in a crust. The label must show true product name such as *Beef Turnover.*

Jamaican Style. May be used to identify meat and poultry food products made with allspice, garlic, onion, red pepper, and thyme. The name of the product must be further qualified with a statement, such as *with Jamaican Style Seasoning,* e.g., *Jamaican Style Chicken Wings with Jamaican Style Seasonings.*

Mexican Style Dinners. Dinners or entrees labeled *Mexican Style* must include items such as tamales and enchiladas making up 25 percent of the entree. The individual product standard must also be met.

Mexican Style. Acceptable for products that contain at least four of the following: jalapeno peppers, chili peppers, green chilies, cumin, cayenne pepper, red or green peppers, chili powder, jalapeno powder, Monterey jack cheese, or cheddar cheese. A garnish (decoration) of cheese in or on the sauce of Mexican style foods does not require the presence of the cheese to be declared in the product name or qualifying statement.

Nacho Style, Nacho Flavor, and Similar Terms. Acceptable terminology for products possessing the commonly expected flavor characteristics associated with *Nachos,* a Mexican hors d'oeurve. The characterizing flavor components generally include, but are not limited to, cheese (cheddar or Monterey jack), tomato (e.g., tomato solids, tomato powder), spices, or other natural seasonings and flavorings (usually garlic and onion), and chili peppers (mild or hot). Romano and parmesan cheese are also often present, but they may not be used to satisfy the above cheese requirement.

Old Fashion or Old Fashioned. The terms *Old Fashion* or *Old Fashioned* are considered subjective in nature and may be used unqualified on labels for meat and/or poultry products with the exception of *old fashioned loaf* (see entry).

Oven Prepared. Defined as fully cooked in an oven and ready to eat, regardless of use on poultry or meat items.

Oven Ready. Defined as ready to cook, regardless of use on poultry or meat items.

Poultry, Cantonese-Style. Sauteed in soy sauce which, by rapid cooking at a high temperature, gives the product a brownish character.

Surf and Turf. A coined name on a product containing beef and seafood which must be followed immediately by the true product name, such as *Beef Rib and Lobster Tail.*

Source:
Standards and Labeling Division, Food Safety and Inspection Service, USDA, *Standards and Labeling Policy Book,* Washington: Government Printing Office, June 1991.

Substitute Products

If a product fails to comply with a standard only because the meat or poultry content is lower than required and the product has generic identity as a nonmeat product (e.g., pizza, stew, pies), then the product may be designated by the nonmeat term in the standardized name (e.g., *Pizza, Stew, Pie*)—provided the meat/poultry content of the product is conspicuously disclosed contiguous to the product name along with a statement of the amount of meat/poultry in the standarized product. For example, *Pizza (contains 5 percent sausage; Sausage Pizza contains 12 percent sausage).* Such products may not be nutritionally inferior to the standardized product it resembles. If a product is nutritionally inferior to the standardized product it resembles, it must be labeled *imitation.*

Source:
Standards and Labeling Division, Food Safety and Inspection Service, USDA, *Standards and Labeling Policy Book,* Washington: Government Printing Office, June 1991.

Thawing

The USDA Food Safety and Inspection Service (FSIS) regulates the labeling of *Safe Thawing Instructions* on consumer packages. Thawing instructions which appear on the label of a frozen meat or poultry product must be given in accordance with FSIS recommendations for safe thawing procedures. These procedures are as follows:
1. Thawing product in the refrigerator.
2. Thawing product in cold water, changing water every 30 minutes until product is thawed.
3. Thawing product in a microwave oven for less than two hours. Cook immediately.

Upon request, alternative thawing procedures may be considered. However, scientific evidence which thoroughly establishes the safety of an alternative thawing procedure must be presented with the procedure when it is submitted for review.

Source:
Standards and Labeling Division, Food Safety and Inspection Service, USDA, *Standards and Labeling Policy Book,* Washington: Government Printing Office, June 1991.

Tomato Products

Declaration of tomato product in the statement of ingredients for meat products is as follows:

Whole tomatoes—shown as *Tomatoes*
Tomato Puree—shown as *Tomato Puree*
Tomato Paste—shown as *Tomato Paste*

Tomato paste or puree and water may be declared as *Tomato* or *Tomatoes* provided paste or puree is made from whole tomatoes, the finished tomato product has a solid content of not less than 6.2 percent, a specific gravity of 1.0263 at 25 degrees C, or a refractive index of 1.3412 at 20 degrees C. Tomato paste and water may be declared as tomato puree provided paste is made from whole tomatoes, the finished product has a solid content of not less than 8 percent but less than 24 percent.

Tomato Juice. Cannot be made from puree or paste.

Tomato Sticks, Pudding or Ring. A non specific sausage-like product containing tomatoes.

Tomato and Bacon Spread. Must contain at least 25 percent cooked bacon.

Source:
Standards and Labeling Division, Food Safety and Inspection Service, USDA, *Standards and Labeling Policy Book,* Washington: Government Printing Office, June 1991.

Turkey Ham

Product otherwise conforming to the standard for turkey ham but weighing more than the original weight of the turkey thigh meat used prior to curing shall be descriptively labeled as follows:
1. The product name must include in addition to *Turkey Ham,* words that specify the amount of the additional substances, e.g., *and ___ percent Water, With ___ percent Water Added,* or *Turkey Ham and Water Product ___ percent of Weight is Added Ingredients.* (The ingredients of the added solution may be incorporated into the product name, e.g., *Turkey Ham and Water Product ___ percent of Weight is Added Water, Salt, Dextrose, Sodium Phosphate, and Sodium Nitrite.*) The blank filled in with the percent determined by subtracting the original weight of the turkey thigh meat from the weight of the cooked finished product. *Turkey Ham and 12 percent Water* is an example.
2. In retail and non-retail size packaging, the qualifying statements described in (1), i.e., *With ___ percent Water Added,* or *and___ percent Water,* or *___ percent of Weight is Added Ingredients,* and similar statements must be shown in lettering that is either not less than ⅜ inch in height or is at least one-third the size of the letters used in the product name, and in the same color and style and on the same background as the product name. Full length of the product labeling is not required.
3. The *Turkey Ham* portion of the product name must be qualified with the statement *Cured Turkey Thigh Meat.* This may be

effected by using an asterisk as long as there is not type or other designs between the total product name and the qualifying statement. Other means of qualifying *Turkey Ham* will be evaluated based on clarity. Alternatively, the total name as described in (1) and (2) may be qualified with a statement that includes *Cured Turkey Thigh Meat* and the amount of added water, e.g., *Cured Turkey Thigh Meat and 12 Percent Water.* A product complying with the standard for Turkey Ham, containing added water and descriptively labeled as stated above, must be produced under a Partial Quality Control (PQC) program approved by the Processed Products Inspection Division (PPID) prior to the use of the approved label.

Small amounts of ground turkey thigh meat may be added as a binder in turkey ham products without declaration provided the ground turkey thigh meat is made from trimmings that are removed from the turkey thighs during the boning and trimming process. The amount of ground turkey thigh meat that may be used can represent no more than the amount that was trimmed and in no case more than 15 percent of the weight of the turkey thigh meat ingredients at the time of formulation. Products containing any

ground turkey thigh meat not removed during the boning and trimming processes or products containing more than 15 percent ground turkey thigh meat must be labeled to indicate the presence of the ground turkey thigh met, e.g., *a portion of ground turkey thigh meat added.* The provision regarding the required use of terminology such as *Chunked and Formed, Chopped and Formed,* and *Ground and Formed* will continue to be followed.

Source:
Standards and Labeling Division, Food Safety and Inspection Service, USDA, *Standards and Labeling Policy Book,* Washington: Government Printing Office, June 1991.

Veal and Calf

Differentiation between veal, calf, and beef carcass is made primarily on the basis of the color of the lean—although such factors as texture of the lean; character of the fat; color, shape, size,

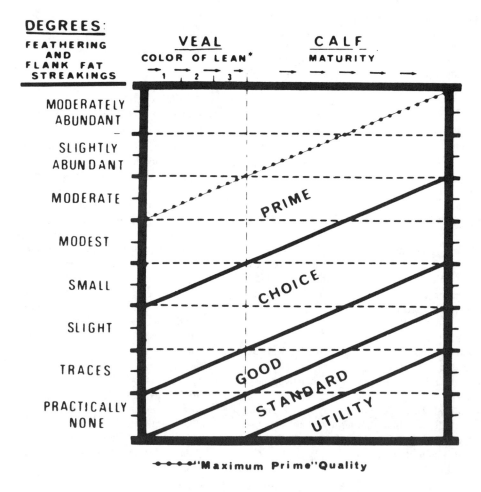

*Quality grade equivalent of various degrees of feathering and flank fat streakings in relation to color of lean (veal) or maturity (calf). *Color of lean flesh: 1. light grayish pink, 2. grayish pink, 3. dark grayish pink.*

and ossification of the bones and cartilages; and the general contour of the carcass are also given consideration. Typical veal carcasses have a grayish pink color of lean that is very smooth and velvety in texture, and they also have a slightly soft, pliable character of fat and marrow. By contrast, typical calf carcasses have a grayish red color of lean and a flakier type of fat. Calf carcasses with maximum maturity for their class have lean flesh that is usually not more than moderately red in color. Carcasses with evidences of more advanced maturity than described here are classified as beef.

Class determination is based on the apparent sex condition of the animal at time of slaughter. Hence, there are three different classes of veal and calf—steers, heifers, and bulls. While recognition may sometimes be given to these different classes on the market, the characteristics of such carcasses are not sufficiently different from each other to warrant the development of separate standards for them. Therefore, the grade standards which follow are equally applicable to all classes of veal and calf carcasses.

GRADES

Veal and calf carcasses are graded on a composite evaluation of two general factors—conformation and quality. These factors are concerned with the proportions of lean, fat, and bone in the carcass and the quality of the lean. Conformation is the manner of formation of the carcass; its thickness and fullness. The quality of lean is usually evaluated by giving equal consideration to the following:

1.   The amount of feathering of fat intermingled within the lean between the ribs
2.   The quantity of fat streakings within and upon the inside flank muscles

In addition, consideration also may be given to other factors if, in the opinion of the grader, this will result in a more accurate quality assessment. Examples of such factors include firmness of the lean, and the distribution of feathering. Conformation and quality often are not developed to the same degree in a carcass, and it is obvious that each grade will include various combinations of development of these two characteristics. In each of the grades a superior development of quality is permitted to compensate, without limit, for a deficient development of conformation—on a one-to-one basis. The reverse type of compensation—a superior development of conformation for an inferior development of quality—is not permitted in the *Prime* and *Choice* grades.

The chart on the preceding page depicts the quality grade equivalent of various degrees of feathering and flank fat streakings in relation to color of lean (veal) or maturity (calf).

GRADES: VEAL

Prime. Veal carcasses with minimum conformation for this grade tend to be moderately wide and thick in relation to their length. They are slightly thick-fleshed and have a slightly plump appearance. Legs tend to be slightly thick and bulging. Loins and backs tend to be moderately full and plump. Shoulders and breasts tend to be moderately thick. The degree of feathering or fat streakings for minimum *Prime* quality increases from a minimum small amount for carcasses having the lightest color of lean to a maximum small amount for carcasses with a dark grayish pink color of lean.

Choice. Veal carcasses with minimum conformation for this grade tend to be slightly wide and thick in relation to their length. They tend to be slightly thin-fleshed and have little or no evidence of plumpness. Loins, backs, and legs are slightly thin and nearly flat. Shoulders and breasts tend to be slightly thin. The degree of feathering or fat streakings associated with minimum *Choice* quality for veal increases from minimum traces for carcasses having the lightest color of lean to maximum traces for carcasses with a dark grayish pink color of lean. The lean flesh is slightly soft regardless of its color.

Good. Veal carcasses with minimum conformation for this grade are rangy, angular, and narrow in relation to their length. They are thinly fleshed. Legs are thin and tapering and slightly concave. Loins and back are depressed. Shoulders and breasts are thin. The degree of feathering or fat streakings associated with minimum *Good* quality for veal increases from minimum to practically devoid for carcasses having the lightest color of lean to maximum practically devoid for carcasses with a dark grayish pink color of lean. The lean flesh is moderately soft regardless of its color.

Standard. Veal carcasses with minimum conformation for this grade are very rangy and angular and very narrow in relation to their length. They are very thinly fleshed. Legs are very thin and moderately concave. Loins and backs are very depressed. Shoulders and breasts are very thin. Refer to the chart for the degree of feathering and fat streakings associated with *Standard* quality. The lean flesh is soft regardless of its color.

Utility. This grade includes veal carcasses whose characteristics are inferior to those specified as minimum for the *Standard* grade.

GRADES: CALF

Prime. Calf carcasses with minimum conformation for this grade tend to be moderately wide and thick in relation to their length. They are moderately thick-fleshed and have a moderately plump appearance. Legs tend to be moderately thick and bulging. Loins and backs tend to be moderately thick. The degree of marbling required for minimum *Prime* quality increases from minimum practically devoid for the very youngest carcasses classified as calf to a maximum moderate amount for carcasses with maturity at the juncture of the calf and beef classes. The lean flesh is moderately firm regardless of maturity.

Choice. Calf carcasses with minimum conformation for this grade tend to be slightly wide and thick in relation to their length. They are slightly thick-fleshed and have a slightly plump appearance. Legs tend to be slightly thick but have little evidence of plumpness. Loins and backs are very slightly full and plump. Shoulders and breasts are slightly thick. The degree of marbling required for minimum *Choice* quality increases from minimum practically devoid for carcasses at midpoint calf maturity to a maximum slight amount for carcasses with maturity at the juncture of the calf and beef classes. Marbling is not required for *Choice* quality in carcasses which are less than midpoint calf maturity. The lean flesh is slightly firm regardless of maturity.

Good. Calf carcasses with minimum conformation for this grade tend to be rangy, angular, and narrow in relation to their length. They tend to be thinly fleshed. Legs are thin and tapering and very slightly concave. Loins and backs are slightly shallow and depressed. Shoulders and breasts are thin. The minimum degree of marbling required for *Good* quality decreases from typical traces for carcasses with maturity at the juncture of the calf and beef classes to minimum practically devoid for carcasses midway in maturity within the more mature half of the range of maturity included in the calf class. In less mature carcasses, marbling is not required for *Good* quality. The lean flesh is moderately soft regardless of maturity.

Standard. Calf carcasses with minimum conformation for this grade are rangy, angular, and narrow in relation to their length. They are very thinly fleshed. Legs are very shallow and depressed. Shoulders and breasts are very thin. Marbling ranges from minimum practically devoid to maximum slight amount. The lean flesh is soft regardless of maturity.

Utility. This grade includes those calf carcasses whose characteristics are inferior to those specified as minimum for the *Standard* grade.

Sources:

Agricultural Marketing Service, USDA, "Veal and Calf Carcasses," 7 CFR 54.112 (1992), Washington: Government Printing Office.

Standards and Labeling Division, Food Safety and Inspection Service, USDA, *Standards and Labeling Policy Book,* Washington: Government Printing Office, June 1991.

Veal Products

The following guidelines apply to labeling of processed products containing veal.

Veal Birds. Product is similar to a turnover made with meat and no more than 40 percent stuffing. Categories of products are as follows:

Veal Birds. Must contain at least 60 percent veal

Veal Birds Beef Added. Must contain at least 60 percent veal and beef of which 20 percent may be beef

Veal and Beef Birds. Must contain at least 60 percent veal and beef of which up to 50 percent may be beef

Veal Birds (Made from Patties). Birds made from patties bear a true product name descriptive of patty used, such as *Veal Birds Made with Veal Patties—Beef added.* The patty portion contains 70 percent meat.

Veal Cordon Bleu. A French term. The standard requires at least 60 percent veal and 5 percent ham, Canadian bacon, or cooked cured pork loin and cheese (either Swiss, Gruyere, mozzarella,

or pasturized processed Swiss). If the product is breaded it must be shown in product name. When the product is made with other than solid pieces of meat, *Chopped and Formed* must be shown contiguous to product name. Beef is not permitted in this product. Veal that has been injected with water and phosphates and used for Veal Cordon Bleu should be labeled *Veal Roll Cordon Bleu* or other descriptive names as appropriate.

Veal Cutlet. Must be a solid piece of meat from the round, although slice thickness may vary. However, combining several thin slices to represent a single cutlet is not permitted.

Veal Drumstick, Breaded. May not contain more than 15 percent water, or more than 10 percent extenders.

Veal Fricassee. Must contain at least 40 percent meat.

Veal and Peppers in Sauce. Must contain at least 30 percent cooked veal.

Veal Parmagiana. There now exists the following categories of products.

Breaded Veal Parmagiana. The product name for a solid piece of veal that is breaded and topped with cheese and tomato sauce. Breaded cooked veal to represent 50 percent of finished product.

Breaded Veal Parmagiana, Chopped and Formed Beef (or Beef Fat) Added. The product name for chopped veal with up to 20 percent beef and/or beef fat added that is formed, breaded, and topped with cheese and tomato sauce. The *Chopped and Formed Beef Added* statement is shown one-third the size of *Veal* contiguous to product name. Breaded cooked patty to represents 40 percent of the finished product.

Breaded Veal Parmagiana Made with Veal Patties, Beef (or Beef Fat) Added. The product name for a veal patty containing at least 70 percent fresh meat (in unbreaded patty) of which 20 percent may be beef or beef fat. The patty is breaded and topped with cheese and tomato sauce. The entire qualifying statement in the product name is to be shown one-third the size of *Veal* contiguous to product name. The breaded cooked patty represents 40 percent of finished product.

Breaded Veal and Beef Patty Parmagiana. Minimum meat patty requirement is 50 percent.

If the product is breaded, the name reflects this fact. The cheese component of the product does not have to be shown in the name of the product. A specific kind of cheese is not required, although romano, mozzarella, and parmesan are the usual types used. No specific spelling of the word *Parmagiana* is required. Name applies to a *Cooked Product Assembled, Ready to Heat and Eat.*

The labeling of Veal Parmagiana made from veal patty includes veal patty in the product name, e.g., *Breaded Veal Parmagiana Made with Veal Patties* or *Breaded Veal Patty Parmagiana.* The ingredients of the veal patty do not have to be part of the product name.

Veal Patties. May contain up to 20 percent beef, and/or beef fat of the meat block. Beef and/or beef fat must show in the true product name such as *Veal Patties, Beef Added* or *Veal Patties, Beef Fat Added.* Beef and/or beef fat in excess of 20 percent of meat block must show as *Veal, and Beef Fat Patties.*

Veal Scaloppini. This veal and sauce product must contain at least 35 percent cooked sliced veal.

Source:
Standards and Labeling Division, Food Safety and Inspection Service, USDA, *Standards and Labeling Policy Book,* Washington: Government Printing Office, June 1991.

Vegetable and Meat Products

The following are guidelines for labeling processed products.

Vegetable Beef Pie. Must contain at least 25 percent meat.

Vegetable Declaration on Labels. Onion, garlic, celery, and parsley unqualified mean fresh, frozen, or canned. Processed onion or garlic must be qualified in a manner such as *dried* or *dehydrated onion* or may be shown as *onion flakes* or *powdered.* It is usually not necessary to show vegetables as whole, diced, sliced, granulated, powdered, or pureed; however, whenever the name of the vegetable is necessary to describe a food, then the name of the vegetable should be modified to show the form of its degree of processing. Onion or garlic juice to which water has been added is shown in a manner such as *Onion Juice with Water Added.* Celery seed may be listed as a spice. Celery salt is shown as *Celery Salt.* Oil of celery may be listed as flavoring.

Vegetable Gum. Common or usual name of each must be declared, such as *Guar Gum.*

Vegetable Ham Casserole. Must contain at least 25 percent ham.

Vegetable Pie with Meat. Must contain at least 12 percent meat.

Vegetable Protein Product (VPP). A vegetable protein product fortified in accordance with Food and Nutrition Service Regulations. The ingredients of such must be sublisted.

Source:
Standards and Labeling Division, Food Safety and Inspection Service, USDA, *Standards and Labeling Policy Book,* Washington: Government Printing Office, June 1991.

Vinegar in Meat Products

Must contain at least 4 grams of acetic acid per 100 cubic centimeters (approximately 4 percent acetic acid). This strength is referred to as *40 grain vinegar.* Cider vinegar, which during the course of manufacture has developed an excess of acetic acid over 4 percent, may be reduced to a strength not less 4 percent. Cider vinegar so reduced is not regarded as adulterated but must be labeled as to its nature as *diluted* or *water added cider vinegar.* However, when vinegar of any concentration (not less than 4

percent acetic acid) is used in a food product, the only labeling requirement is *vinegar.* Statements such as *diluted* or *water added* are not required.

Source:
Standards and Labeling Division, Food Safety and Inspection Service, USDA, *Standards and Labeling Policy Book,* Washington: Government Printing Office, June 1991.

Wild Boar

Wild Boar is an acceptable label term for a product, provided the words *Wild Boar* are directly followed by the statement *Meat from Feral Swine,* which must appear prominently on the principal display panel. If the statement *Meat from Feral Swine* does not directly follow the term *Wild Boar,* then an asterisk may be included with the term *Wild Boar* and the statement *Meat from Feral Swine* should appear prominently elsewhere on the principal display panel. *Wild Boar from Feral Swine, Wild Boar Meat from Feral Swine,* and *Wild Boar (byproduct) from Feral Swine* are also acceptable product names.

In order to obtain approval for a product label bearing the name *Wild Boar from Feral Swine* (or similar acceptable names), the manufacturer must provide a statement describing and verifying the following physical and environmental characteristics typical of wild boar: color patterns such as white stripes or spots, longer bristly haircoat, elongated snout with visible tusks, a razorback body shape, and wild boar males which are uncastrated. (Both males and females come under the term *Wild Boar.*) The purchased hogs should be obtained from a nonrestrictive environment which permits foraging for uncultivated feed, natural selection and breeding, and farrowing without confinement. A letter should be submitted with *Wild Boar from Feral Swine* labels describing the environment where such swine live and their method of capture or entrapment. These same criteria would also apply to imported *Wild Boar Meat from Feral Swine* and arrangements should be made through Foreign Programs for slaughter and export from approved establishments.

In multi-ingredient products, such as *Beans in Sauce with Wild Boar,* the *Wild Boar* part of the product name must be followed by an asterisk and a statement *(Meat or meat byproduct) from Feral Swine* must appear somewhere on the principal display panel. The ingredient wild boar, wild boar meat, or wild boar byproduct, must be listed as *Wild Boar ([Meat or meat byproduct] From Feral Swine)* in the ingredient statement in its proper order of predominance.

Source:
Standards and Labeling Division, Food Safety and Inspection Service, USDA, *Standards and Labeling Policy Book,* Washington: Government Printing Office, June 1991.

Nuts

Almonds, in the Shell

To allow for variations in quality caused by grading and handling, a percentage of the almonds may fail to meet all of the requirements of the grade.

GRADES

Almonds are graded according to a very technical system whereby *penalty* points are assessed for such factors as edibility, poor appearance, or defects in workmanship. The more penalty points assessed, the lower the grade. The grade descriptions which follow are intended only as a general consumer guide. For more detailed information, please consult the source cited below.

U.S. No. 1. Almonds in the shell which are of similar varietal characteristics and free from loose extraneous and foreign material. The shells are clean and are fairly bright and uniform in color. They are free from damage caused by discoloration, adhering hulls, broken shells, or other means. The kernels are well dried, firm, and brittle, not pliable or leathery. They are free from decay, rancidity, and from damage caused by insects, mold, gum, skin discoloration, shriveling, brown spot, etc. Unless otherwise specified, the almonds are not less than $^{28}/_{64}$ of an inch in thickness.

U.S. No. 1 Mixed. Almonds in the shell which meet the requirements of *U.S. No. 1* grade, except that two or more varieties of sweet almonds are mixed.

U.S. No. 2. Almonds in the shell which meet the requirements of *U.S. No. 1* grade, except that an additional tolerance of 20 percent shall be allowed for almonds with shells damaged by discoloration.

U.S. No. 2 Mixed. Almonds in the shell which meet the requirements of *U.S. No. 2* grade, except that two or more varieties of sweet almonds are mixed.

Unclassified. Almonds in the shell which have not been classified in accordance with any of the foregoing grades. The term *unclassified* is not a grade but is provided as a designation to show that no definite grade has been applied to the lot.

Source:
Agricultural Marketing Service, USDA, 7 CFR sections 51.2075 to 51.2092 (1992), Washington: Government Printing Office.

Almonds, Shelled

To allow for variations in quality caused by grading and handling, a percentage of the shelled almonds may fail to meet all of the requirements of the grade. The grades are differentiated based on the amount of tolerance allowed.

GRADES

Shelled almonds are graded according to a very technical system whereby *penalty* points are assessed for such factors as edibility, poor appearance, or defects in workmanship. The more penalty points assessed, the lower the grade. The grade descriptions which follow are intended only as a general consumer guide. For more detailed information, please consult the source cited below.

U.S. Fancy. Shelled almonds of similar varietal characteristics which are whole, clean, and well dried. They are free from decay, rancidity, insect injury, foreign material, doubles, split or broken kernels, particles, and dust. Also free from injury caused by chipped and scratched kernels, and from damage caused by mold, gum, shriveling, brown spot, or other means.

U.S. Extra No. 1. Has a higher tolerance for defects than *U.S. Fancy*.

U.S. No. 1. Has a higher tolerance for defects than *U.S. Extra No. 1*.

U.S. Select Sheller Run. Shelled almonds of similar varietal characteristics which are whole, clean, and well dried. They are free from decay, rancidity, insect injury, foreign material, doubles, split or broken kernels, particles, and dust, and from damage caused by chipped and scratched kernels, mold, gum, shriveling, brown spot, or other means.

U.S. Standard Sheller Run. The same as *U.S. Select Sheller Run* except for a higher tolerance for defects.

U.S. No. 1 Whole and Broken. In this grade not less than 30 percent, by weight, of the kernels are whole. Doubles are not considered as whole kernels in determining the percentage of whole kernels. Unless otherwise specified, the minimum diameter is not less than $20/64$ of an inch.

U.S. No. 1 Pieces. Shelled almonds which are not bitter and which are clean, well dried, and free from decay, rancidity, insect injury, foreign material, particles, and dust, and from damage caused by mold, gum, shriveling brown spot, or other means. Unless otherwise specified, the minimum diameter is not less than $8/64$ of an inch.

Mixed Varieties. Any lot of shelled almonds consisting of a mixture of two or more dissimilar varieties which meet the other requirements of the above grades; no lot of any of these grades may include more than 1 percent of bitter almonds mixed with sweet almonds.

Unclassified. Shelled almonds which have not been classified in accordance with any of the foregoing grades. The term unclassified is not a grade but is provided as a designation to show that no definite grade has been applied to the lot.

Source:
Agricultural Marketing Service, USDA, 7 CFR sections 51.2105 to 51.2132 (1992), Washington: Government Printing Office.

Brazil Nuts, in the Shell

To allow for variations in quality caused by grading and handling, a percentage of the nuts may fail to meet all of the requirements of the grade.

GRADES

Brazil nuts are graded according to a very technical system whereby *penalty* points are assessed for such factors as edibility, poor appearance, or defects in workmanship. The more penalty points assessed, the lower the grade. The grade descriptions which follow are intended only as a general consumer guide. For more detailed information, please consult the source cited below.

U.S. No. 1. Whole Brazil nuts in the shell which are free from loose extraneous and foreign material and meet one of the size classifications below. The shell is free from surface moisture, and the kernel is firm and crisp, not pliable or leathery. The shells are clean and free from damage caused by splits, breaks, punctures, oil stain, mold, or other means. The kernel fills at least one-half of the capacity of the shell. They are free from rancidity, mold, decay, and from damage caused by insects, discoloration, or other means.

Extra Large. Not more than 15 percent, by count, of the Brazil nuts pass through a round opening $78/64$ inch in diameter, including not more than 2 percent which pass through a round opening $74/64$ inch in diameter; or count does not exceed 45 nuts per pound.

Large. Not more than 15 percent, by count, of the Brazil nuts pass through a round opening $73/64$ inch in diameter, including not more than 2 percent which pass through a round opening $60/64$ inch in diameter; or count does not exceed 50 nuts per pound.

Medium. Not more than 15 percent, by count, of the Brazil nuts pass through a round opening $59/64$ inch in diameter, including not more than 2 percent which pass through a round opening $50/64$ inch in diameter; or count is not less than 51 nuts per pound but not more than 65 nuts per pound. When size is based on count per pound, the 10 smallest nuts per 100 weigh at least 6 percent of the total weight of the 100 nut sample.

Unclassified. Brazil nuts in the shell which have not been classified in accordance with the foregoing grade. The term unclassified is not a grade but is provided as a designation to show that no definite grade has been applied to the lot.

Source:
Agricultural Marketing Service, USDA, 7 CFR sections 51.3500 to 51.3511 (1992), Washington: Government Printing Office.

Hazelnuts (Filberts, in the Shell)

GRADES

Hazelnuts, also called filberts, are graded according to a very technical system whereby *penalty* points are assessed for such factors as edibility, poor appearance, or defects in workmanship. The more penalty points assessed, the lower the grade. The grade descriptions which follow are intended only as a general consumer guide. For more detailed information, please consult the source cited below.

U.S. No. 1. The hazelnuts are of a similar type and are dry. The shells are well formed and not misshapen. They are clean, bright, and free from blanks (a hazelnut containing no kernel or a kernel filling less than one-fourth the capacity of the shell) and broken or split shells (a shell having any crack which is open and conspicuous for a distance of more than one-fourth the circumference of the shell). Also free from damage caused by stains, adhering husk, or other means. The kernels fill one-half or more of the shell and are not badly misshapen so as to have an unpleasant appearance. The hazelnuts are free from rancidity, decay, mold, and insect injury. Also free from damage caused by shriveling, discoloration, or other means.

SIZE

The size is specified in connection with the grade in terms of minimum diameter, minimum and maximum diameters, or in accordance with one of the size classifications below:

Size	Maximum*	Minimum**
Round type varieties		
Jumbo	no maximum	$^{56}/_{64}$
Large	$^{56}/_{64}$ inch	$^{49}/_{64}$
Medium	$^{49}/_{64}$	$^{45}/_{64}$
Small	$^{45}/_{64}$	no minimum
Long type varieties		
Jumbo	no maximum	$^{47}/_{64}$
Large	$^{48}/_{64}$	$^{44}/_{64}$
Medium	$^{45}/_{64}$	$^{34}/_{64}$
Small	$^{35}/_{64}$	no minimum

* Will pass through a round opening of the following size.
** Will not pass through a round opening of the following size.

Source:

Agricultural Marketing Service, USDA, 7 CFR sections 51.1995 to 51.2009 (1992), Washington: Government Printing Office.

Mixed Nuts

Mixed nuts consist of a mixture of four or more of the following optional shelled tree nut ingredients:
Almonds
Black walnuts
Brazil nuts
Cashews
English walnuts (alternatively walnuts)
Hazelnuts (Filberts)
Pecans
Other suitable tree nuts
Mixed nuts may also include one or more shelled peanut ingredients (Spanish, Valencia, Virginia, or similar varieties).

Each kind of nut used should be present in a quantity not less than 2 percent and not more than 80 percent by weight. If the percentage of a single tree nut ingredient or the total peanut content by weight of the finished food exceeds 50 percent but not 60 percent, the statement *contains up to 60 percent* or *contains 60 percent _____* or *60 percent_____* shall immediately follow the name *Mixed Nuts.* The blank is to be filled in with the appropriate name of the predominant nut ingredient, e.g., *contains up to 60 percent pecans.*

Peanuts. If the Spanish variety of peanuts is used, it shall be declared as *Spanish peanuts.* Other varieties of peanuts shall be similarly named on the product label.
Unblanched (unshelled). If the peanut ingredients are unblanched, the label has the statement *Peanuts unblanched, Peanuts skins on,* or words with similar meaning.

Vegetable Oil. Vegetable oils used shall be declared by the words *Vegetable oil* or *Hydrogenated vegetable oil,* or alternatively *_____ oil* or *Hydrogenated _____ oil,* as the case may be.

Preservatives. When antioxidant preservatives are used in the mixed nuts, the label bears the statement *_____ added as a preservative* or *_____ added to inhibit rancidity,* the blank is filled in with the name or names of the preservative(s) used.

Source:
Food and Drug Administration, HHS, Tree, Nut, and Peanut Products, 21 CFR part 164 (1991), Washington: Government Printing Office.

Peanut Butter

Peanut butter is a food prepared by grinding either blanched peanuts (in which the germ may or may not be included) or unblanched peanuts (including the skins and germ). Safe and suitable seasoning and stabilizing ingredients may be added to the ground peanuts. However, the seasoning and stabilizing ingredients do not exceed 10 percent of the weight of the finished food. To the ground peanuts, cut or chopped, shelled, and roasted peanuts may be added. During processing, the oil content of the peanut ingredient may be adjusted by the addition or subtraction of peanut oil. The fat content of the finished food shall not exceed 55 percent.

Unblanched Peanuts. If peanut butter is prepared from unblanched peanuts, the name shows that fact by some such statement as *Prepared from unblanched peanuts (skins left on).* This statement appears prominently and conspicuously immediately preceding or following the words *Peanut Butter.*

Optional Ingredients. The label of peanut butter gives, by their common names, the optional ingredients used.

Hydrogenated Vegetable Oil. If hydrogenated vegetable oil is used, the label statement of optional ingredients includes the words *Hydrogenated _____ oil* or *Hardened _____ oil.* The blank is filled in either with the names of the vegetable sources of the oil or, alternatively, with the word *vegetable,* e.g., *Hydrogenated peanut oil* or *Hardened peanut and cottonseed oils* or *Hydrogenated vegetable oil.*

GRADES

Peanut butter is graded according to a very technical system whereby *penalty* points are assessed for such factors as edibility, poor appearance, or defects in workmanship. The more penalty points assessed, the lower the grade. The grade descriptions which follow are intended only as a general consumer guide. For more detailed information, please consult the source cited below.

U.S. Grade A or U.S. Fancy. Has good color, consistency, flavor, and aroma, has uniform dispersion of any added ingredient(s), is practically free from defects.

U.S. Grade B or U.S. Choice. Has reasonably good color, consistency, flavor, and aroma, has reasonably uniform dispersion of any added ingredient(s), is reasonably free from defects.

Substandard. Fails to meet the requirements of *U.S. Grade B.*

TEXTURES OF PEANUT BUTTER

Smooth. Has a very fine, very even texture with no perceptible grainy peanut particles.

Medium. Has a definite grainy texture with perceptible peanut particles approximating not more than $^{1}/_{16}$ inch in any dimension.

Chunky or Crunchy. Has a partially fine or partially grainy texture with substantial amounts of peanut particles larger than 1⁄16 inch in any dimension.

TYPES

Stabilized. Stabilized peanut butter is prepared by any special process and/or with any suitable added ingredient(s) designed to prevent oil separation.

Nonstabilized. Nonstabilized peanut butter is prepared without special process or added ingredient(s) to prevent oil separation.

STYLES

Regular Pack. Regular pack peanut butter is a stabilized type peanut butter prepared from peanuts from which the skins have been removed and to which salt and suitable nutritive sweetener(s) have been added.

Specialty Pack. Specialty pack peanut butter is any type or style of peanut butter that is not described above. This style includes, but is not limited to, peanut butter that is made from unblanched peanuts and to which salt and/or a nutritive sweetener may or may not have been added.

Source:
Food and Drug Administration, HHS, Tree Nut and Peanut Products, 21 CFR part 164 (1991), Washington: Government Printing Office.

Peanuts, in the Shell—Cleaned Virginia Type

GRADES

These peanuts are graded according to a very technical system whereby *penalty* points are assessed for such factors as edibility, poor appearance, or defects in workmanship. The more penalty points assessed, the lower the grade. The grade descriptions which follow are intended only as a general consumer guide. For more detailed information, please consult the source cited below.

U.S. Jumbo Hand Picked. Cleaned peanuts in the shell which are mature (firm and well developed), dry, and free from loose peanut kernels, dirt, or other foreign material. Also free from pops (fully developed shells which contain practically no kernels), paper ends (peanuts which have very soft and/or very thin ends), and from damage caused by cracked or broken shells, discoloration, or other means. The kernels are free from damage from any cause. In addition, the peanuts will not pass through a screen having 37⁄64 by 3 inch perforations. Unless otherwise specified, the unshelled peanuts in any lot do not average more than 176 count per pound. (A limited tolerance of 10% is allowed for variations incident to grading and handling.)

U.S. Fancy Hand Picked. Consist of cleaned peanuts in the shell

which are mature, dry, and free from loose peanut kernels, dirt, or other foreign material. Also free from pops (fully developed shells which contain practically no kernels), paper ends (peanuts which have very soft and/or very thin ends), and from damage caused by cracked or broken shells, discoloration, or other means. The kernels are free from damage from any cause. In addition, the peanuts will not pass through a screen having 32⁄64 by 3 inch perforations. Unless otherwise specified, the unshelled peanuts in any lot do not average more than 225 count per pound.

Unclassified. Peanuts which fail to meet the requirements of either of the foregoing grades. The term unclassified is not a grade within the meaning of these standards but is provided as a designation to show that no definite grade has been applied to the lot.

Source:
Agricultural Marketing Service, USDA, 7 CFR sections 51.1235 to 51.1242 (1992), Washington: Government Printing Office.

Peanuts, Shelled Runner Type

To allow for variations in quality caused by grading and handling, a percentage of the peanuts may fail to meet all of the requirements of the grade.

GRADES

These peanuts are graded according to a very technical system whereby *penalty* points are assessed for such factors as edibility, poor appearance, or defects in workmanship. The more penalty points assessed, the lower the grade. The grade descriptions which follow are intended only as a general consumer guide. For more detailed information, please consult the source cited below.

U.S. No. 1 Runner. Shelled runner type peanut kernels of similar varietal characteristics which are whole and free from foreign material, damage and minor defects. The kernels will not pass through a screen having 16⁄64 by 3⁄4 inch openings.

U.S. Runner Splits. Shelled runner type peanut kernels of similar varietal characteristics which are split or broken (more than 1⁄4 of the peanut kernel is broken off), but are free from foreign material, damage, and minor defects, and which will not pass through a screen having 17⁄64 inch round openings.

U.S. No. 2 Runner. Shelled runner type peanut kernels of similar varietal characteristics which may be split or broken, but are free from foreign material, damage, and minor defects, and which will not pass through a screen having 17⁄64 inch round openings. This grade has a higher tolerance for defects than grade *U.S. No. 1 Runner* or *U.S. Runner Splits*. Accordingly, there may be more peanuts that are damaged, off-sized, or otherwise contain minor defects.

Source:
Agricultural Marketing Service, USDA, 7 CFR sections 51.2710 to 51.2721 (1992), Washington: Government Printing Office.

Peanuts, Shelled Spanish Type

To allow for variations in quality caused by grading and handling, a percentage of the peanuts may fail to meet all of the requirements of the grade.

GRADES

These peanuts are graded according to a very technical system whereby *penalty* points are assessed for such factors as edibility, poor appearance, or defects in workmanship. The more penalty points assessed, the lower the grade. The grade descriptions which follow are intended only as a general consumer guide. For more detailed information, please consult the source cited below.

U.S. No. I Spanish. Peanut kernels which are whole and free from foreign material, damage, and minor defects and which will not pass through a screen having $15/64$ by $3/4$ inch openings.

Spanish Splits. Peanut kernels which are split or broken, but are free from foreign material, damage, and minor defects, and which will not pass through a screen having $16/64$ inch round openings.

U.S. No. 2 Spanish. Peanut kernels which may be split or broken, but are free from foreign material, damage, and minor defects, and which will not pass through a screen having $16/64$ inch round openings. This grade has a higher tolerance for defects. Accordingly, there may be more peanuts that have minor defects or are off-size.

Source:
Agricultural Marketing Service, USDA, 7 CFR sections 51.2730 to 51.2741 (1992), Washington: Government Printing Office.

Peanuts, Shelled Virginia Type

To allow for variations in quality caused by grading and handling, a percentage of the peanuts may fail to meet all of the requirements of the grade.

GRADES

These peanuts are graded according to a very technical system whereby *penalty* points are assessed for such factors as edibility, poor appearance, or defects in workmanship. The more penalty points assessed, the lower the grade. The grade descriptions which follow are intended only as a general consumer guide. For more detailed information, please consult the source cited below.

U.S. Extra Large Virginia. Peanuts of similar varietal characteristics which are whole and free from foreign material, damage, and minor defects and which will not pass through a screen having $20/64$ by 1 inch openings. Unless otherwise specified, the peanuts in any lot do not average more than 512 per pound.

U.S. Medium Virginia. Kernels of similar varietal characteristics which are whole and free from foreign material, damage, and minor defects and which will not pass through a screen having

$18/64$ by 1 inch openings. Unless otherwise specified, the peanuts in any lot do not average more than 640 per pound.

U.S. No. 1 Virginia. Kernels of similar varietal characteristics which are whole and free from foreign material, damage, and minor defects and which will not pass through a screen having $15/64$ by 1 inch openings. Unless otherwise specified, the peanuts in any lot do not average more than 864 per pound.

U.S. Virginia Splits. Kernels of similar varietal characteristics which are free from foreign material, damage, and minor defects and which will not pass through a screen having $20/64$ inch round openings. Not less than 90 percent, by weight, are splits.

U.S. No. 2 Virginia. Kernels of similar varietal characteristics which may be split or broken (more than one-fourth of the peanut kernel is broken off), but are free from foreign material, damage, and minor defects, and which will not pass through a screen having $17/64$ inch round openings. This grade has a higher tolerance for defects. Accordingly a lot of *No. 2* peanuts may have a higher percentage of peanuts with minor defects or which are off-size.

Source:
Agricultural Marketing Service, USDA, 7 CFR sections 51.2750 to 51.2763 (1992), Washington: Government Printing Office.

Pecans, in the Shell

To allow for variations in quality caused by grading and handling, a percentage of the pecans may fail to meet all of the requirements of the grade.

GRADES

Pecans are graded according to a very technical system whereby *penalty* points are assessed for such factors as edibility, poor appearance, or defects in workmanship. The more penalty points assessed, the lower the grade. The grade descriptions which follow are intended only as a general consumer guide. For more detailed information, please consult the source cited below.

U.S. No. 1. Pecans in the shell which are free from loose, extraneous, or foreign material and which have shells that are fairly uniform in color and free from damage by any cause. The kernels are also free from damage by any cause.

U.S. No. 2. The requirements for this grade are the same as for *U.S. No. 1* except that there is no requirement for uniformity of color of shells and there are increased tolerances for defects.

SIZES

Size classification	Number of nuts per pound
Oversize	55 or less
Extra large	56 to 63
Large	64 to 77
Medium	78 to 95
Small	96 to 120

KERNEL COLOR CLASSIFICATION

Light.
Light Amber.
Amber.
Dark Amber.

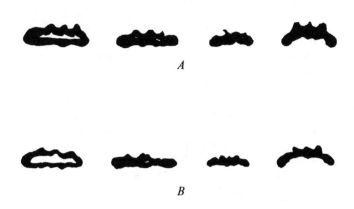

A

B

C

Pecan cross section illustration. (A) Well developed. Lower limit. Kernels having less meat content than these are not considered well developed. (B) Fairly well developed. Lower limit for U.S. No. 1 grade. Kernels having less meat content than these are not considered fairly well developed and are classed as damaged. (C) Poorly developed. Lower limit, damaged but not seriously damaged. Kernels having less meat content than these are considered undeveloped and are classed as seriously damaged.

Source:
Agricultural Marketing Service, USDA, 7 CFR sections 51.1400 to 51.1415 (1992), Washington: Government Printing Office.

Pecans, Shelled

To allow for variations in quality caused by grading and handling, a percentage of the pecans may fail to meet all of the requirements of the grade.

GRADES

This product is graded according to a very technical system whereby *penalty* points are assessed for such factors as edibility,

poor appearance, or defects in workmanship. The more penalty points assessed, the lower the grade. The grade descriptions which follow are intended only as a general consumer guide. For more detailed information, please consult the source cited below.

U.S. No. 1. The shelled pecans are well dried (the portion of kernel is firm and crisp, not pliable or leathery); fairly well developed (the kernel has at least a moderate amount of meat in proportion to its width and length); fairly uniform in color and not darker than amber skin color; free from damage or serious damage by any cause; free from pieces of shell, center wall, and foreign material; and fairly uniform in size.

U.S. No. 1 Halves and Pieces. The requirements for this grade are the same as those for *U.S. No. 1,* except at least 50 percent, by weight, are half-kernels, and both halves and pieces will not pass through a ⁵⁄₁₆ inch round opening.

U.S. No. 1 Pieces. The requirements for this grade are the same as those for *U.S. No. 1* except there is no requirement for uniformity of color or for the percentage of half-kernels.

Size classification for halves	Number of halves per pound
Mammoth	250 or less
Junior mammoth	251-300
Jumbo	301-350
Extra large	351-450
Large	451-550
Medium	551-650
Small (topper)	651-750
Midget	751 or more

| Size classification for pieces | Diameter in inches | |
	Maximum*	Minimum**
Mammoth pieces	No limitation	⁸⁄₁₆
Extra large pieces	⁹⁄₁₆	⁷⁄₁₆
Halves and pieces	No limitation	⁵₁₆
Large pieces	⁸⁄₁₆	⁵⁄₁₆
Medium pieces	⁶⁄₁₆	³⁄₁₆
Small pieces	⁴⁄₁₆	²⁄₁₆
Midget pieces	³⁄₁₆	¹⁄₁₆
Granules	²⁄₁₆	¹⁄₁₆

*Will pass through round opening of following diameter.
**Will not pass through round opening of following diameter.

Source:
Agricultural Marketing Service, USDA, 7 CFR sections 51.1430 to 51.1451 (1992), Washington: Government Printing Office.

Pistachio Nuts, in the Shell

These standards are applicable to pistachio nuts in the shell which may be in a natural, dyed, raw, roasted, or salted state, or in any combination thereof. However, nuts of obviously dissimilar forms are not to be commingled. To allow for variations in quality caused by grading and handling, a percentage of the nuts may fail to meet all of the requirements of the grade. The different grades are distinguished by an increased tolerance for defects, e.g., a lot of *No. 2* nuts will contain a higher percentage of nuts that are non-split, off-sized, damaged, or otherwise not up to grade.

GRADES

These pistachios are graded according to a very technical system whereby *penalty* points are assessed for such factors as edibility, poor appearance, or defects in workmanship. The more penalty points assessed, the lower the grade. The grade descriptions which follow are intended only as a general consumer guide. For more detailed information, please consult the source cited below.

U.S. Fancy, U.S. No. 1, and U.S. No. 2. Nuts which are free from foreign material, loose kernels, shell pieces, particles, dust, and blanks. The shells are free from non-split shells (when shells are not opened or are partially opened and will not allow an $^{18}/_{1000}$ inch thick by 1.4 inch wide gauge to slip into the opening) and from shells not split on suture. They are free from damage by adhering hull material. The are also free from light stain (when the aggregate amount of yellow to light brown or light gray discoloration is noticeably contrasting with the predominate color of the shell and affects more than ¼ of the total shell surface or, on dyed nuts, when readily noticeable) and from dark stain (when an aggregate amount of dark brown, dark gray or black discoloration affects more than ⅛ of the total shell surface, or, on dyed nuts, when readily noticeable). The kernels are well dried or very well dried when specified in connection with the grade. They are free from damage by minor mold, immature kernels, kernel spots, and other internal (kernel) defects. Free from serious damage by minor insect or vertebrate injury, insect damage, mold, rancidity, decay, and other internal defects. The nuts are of a size not less than $^{26}/_{64}$ inch in diameter as measured by a round hole screen.

Source:
Agricultural Marketing Service, USDA, 7 CFR sections 51.2540 to 51.2546 (1992), Washington: Government Printing Office.

Pistachio Nuts, Shelled

These standards are applicable to raw, roasted, or salted pistachio kernels. However, nuts of obviously dissimilar forms are not to be commingled. To allow for variations in quality caused by handling, a percentage of the nuts may fail to meet all of the requirements of the grade. The grades are distinguished by the higher percentage of defects allowed in Grades 1 and 2.

GRADES

These pistachios are graded according to a very technical system

whereby *penalty* points are assessed for such factors as edibility, poor appearance, or defects in workmanship. The more penalty points assessed, the lower the grade. The grade descriptions which follow are intended only as a general consumer guide. For more detailed information, please consult the source cited below.

U.S. Fancy, U.S. No. 1, and U.S. No. 2. Well dried (firm and crispy) or very well dried (firmer and crispier), free from foreign material (including in-shell nuts, shells, or shell fragments), and free from damage caused by minor mold, immature kernels, spotting, and other defects. Also free from serious damage caused by mold, minor insect or vertebrate injury, insect damage, rancidity, decay, and other defects. Unless otherwise specified, the kernels meet the size classification of *Whole Kernels*.

SIZES

Whole Kernels. 80 percent or more by weight shall be whole kernels and not more than 5 percent of the total sample will pass through a $^{16}/_{64}$ inch round opening.

Whole and Pieces. 40 percent or more by weight are whole kernels and not more than 15 percent of the total sample will pass through a $^{16}/_{64}$ inch round opening.

Large Pieces. Portions of kernels of which not more than 10 percent will remain on a $^{24}/_{64}$ inch round opening.

Small Pieces. Portions of kernels of which not more than 10 percent will remain on a $^{16}/_{64}$ inch round opening.

Mixed Sizes. A mixture of any combination of whole kernels or pieces. The percentage of whole kernels and/or pieces may be specified. Not more than 5 percent of the total sample will pass through a $^{5}/_{64}$ inch round opening.

Source:
Agricultural Marketing Service, USDA, 7 CFR sections 512555 to 51.2560 (1992), Washington: Government Printing Office.

Walnuts, in the Shell

These standards apply only to walnuts commonly known as English or Persian walnuts (*Juglans regia*). They do not apply to the walnuts commonly known as black walnuts (*Juglans nigra*). To allow for variations in quality caused by grading and handling, a percentage of the walnuts may fail to meet all of the requirements of the grade.

GRADES

These walnuts are graded according to a very technical system whereby penalty points are assessed for such factors as edibility, poor appearance, or defects in workmanship. The more penalty points assessed the lower the grade. The grade descriptions which follow are intended only as a general consumer guide. For more detail please consult the source cited below.

U.S. No. 1. Walnuts in shells which are dry, practically clean, bright, and free from splits (walnuts with the seam opened completely around the nut), injury by discoloration, and damage caused by broken shells, perforated shells, adhering hulls, or other means. The kernels are well dried (firm and crisp, not leathery or pliable) and free from decay, dark discoloration (a color darker than amber), and rancidity; they are also free from damage caused by mold, shriveling, insects, or other means. At least 70 percent, by count, of the walnuts have kernels which are not darker than light amber and which are free from grade defects.

U.S. No. 2. Walnuts in shells which are dry, practically clean, free from splits, and free from damage caused by broken shells, perforated shells, adhering hulls, discoloration, or other means. The kernels are well dried and free from decay, dark discoloration, and rancidity; they are also free from damage caused by mold, shriveling, insects, or other means. At least 60 percent, by count, of the walnuts have kernels which are not darker than light amber, and which are free from grade defects.

U.S. No. 3. Walnuts in shells which are dry, fairly clean, free from splits, free from damage caused by broken shells, and free from serious damage caused by discoloration, perforated shells, adhering hulls, or other means. The kernels are well dried and free from decay, dark discoloration, and rancidity; they are also free from damage caused by mold, shriveling, insects or other means. There is no requirement in this grade for the percentage of walnuts having kernels which are light amber or light.

Unclassified. Walnuts in the shell which have not been classified in accordance with any of the foregoing grades. The term *unclassified* is not a grade within the meaning of these standards but is provided as a designation to show that no grade has been applied to the lot.

SIZES

Mammoth. Not over 12 percent, by count, pass through a round opening $^{96}\!/_{64}$ inches in diameter.

Jumbo. Not over 12 percent, by count, pass through a round opening $^{80}\!/_{64}$ inches in diameter.

Large. Not over 12 percent, by count, pass through a round opening $^{77}\!/_{64}$ inches in diameter. For walnuts of the *Eureka* variety, the limiting dimension for diameter shall be $^{76}\!/_{64}$ inches.

Medium. At least 88 percent, by count, pass through a round opening $^{77}\!/_{64}$ inches in diameter and of which not over 12 percent, by count, pass through a round opening $^{73}\!/_{64}$ inches in diameter.

Standard. Not over 12 percent, by count, pass through a round opening $^{73}\!/_{64}$ inches in diameter.

Baby. At least 88 percent, by count, pass through a round opening $^{74}\!/_{64}$ inches in diameter and of which not over 10 percent, by count, pass through a round opening $^{60}\!/_{64}$ inch in diameter.

Minimum Diameter. In lieu of one of the foregoing classifications, size of walnuts may be specified in terms of minimum diameter, or minimum and maximum diameter.

Source:
Agricultural Marketing Service, USDA, 7 CFR sections 51.2945 to 51.2966 (1992), Washington: Government Printing Office.

Walnuts, Shelled

These standards apply only to walnuts commonly known as English or Persian walnuts (*Juglans regia*). They do not apply to the walnuts commonly known as black walnuts (*Juglans nigra*).

GRADES

These walnuts are graded according to a very technical system whereby *penalty* points are assessed for such factors as edibility, poor appearance, or defects in workmanship. The more penalty points assessed, the lower the grade. The grade descriptions which follow are intended only as a general consumer guide. For more detailed information, please consult the source cited below.

U.S. No. 1. Portions of walnut kernels which are well dried (the portion of kernel is firm and crisp, not pliable or leathery), clean, and free from shell, foreign material, insect injury, decay, and rancidity; they are also free from damage caused by shriveling, mold, discoloration of the meat, or other means. The color of any lot may be Extra Light, Light, Light Amber, or Amber.

U.S. Commercial. Portions of walnut kernels which meet the requirements of *U.S. No. 1* grade, except for increased tolerances for defects such as shriveling, mold, and discoloration. The color of the walnuts in this grade is not darker than Amber classification, and color need not be specified.

Unclassified. Portions of walnut kernels which have not been classified in accordance with either of the foregoing grades. The term unclassified is not a grade within the meaning of these standards but is provided as a designation to show that no grade has been applied to the lot.

SIZES

Halves. Lot consists of 85 percent or more, by weight, half kernels, and the remainder is three-fourths half kernels.

Pieces and Halves. Lot consists of 20 percent or more, by weight, half kernels, and the remainder is portions of kernels that cannot pass through a sieve with 2 inch round openings.

Pieces. Lot consists of portions of kernels that cannot pass through a sieve with $^{24}\!/_{64}$ inch round openings.

Small Pieces. Lot consists of portions of kernels that pass through a sieve with $^{24}\!/_{64}$ inch round openings but that cannot pass through a sieve with $^{8}\!/_{64}$ inch round openings.

Source:
Agricultural Marketing Service, USDA, 7 CFR sections 51.2275 to 51.2296 (1992), Washington: Government Printing Office.

Seafood

Catfish, Freshwater

The U.S. Standards for Grades apply to catfish that are either farmraised or taken from rivers and lakes. These standards apply to the common commercial species and hybrids which include channel catfish (*Ictalurus punctatus*), white catfish (*Ictalurus catus*), blue catfish (*Ictalurus furcatus*), and flathead catfish (*Pylodictis olivaris*).

GRADES

The grade is determined by evaluating the fresh product in the fresh and cooked states or the frozen product in the frozen, thawed, and cooked states. Grade determination is based primarily on flavor and odor and on physical defects. A product receives an evaluation of *good flavor and odor* (minimum requirement for a *Grade A* product) or *reasonably good flavor and odor* (minimum requirement for a *Grade B* and a *Grade C* product). Each sample unit is then examined for physical defects including dehydration, overall condition, discoloration, uniformity, skinning cuts, etc. The grade descriptions which follow are intended only as a general consumer guide. For more detailed information, please consult the source cited below.

U.S. Grade A. A fresh or frozen product that possesses good flavor and odor. The product has the normal, pleasant flavor and odor characteristics of the species and is free from off-odors and off-flavors of any kind. The cooked fish flesh is tender, firm, and moist without excess water. The fish may have slight dehydration.

U.S. Grade B. A fresh or frozen product that possesses reasonably good flavor and odor. The product may be somewhat lacking in good flavor and odor characteristics of the species, but it is free from objectionable off-odors and off-flavors of any kind. The cooked fish flesh may be noticeably dry, tough, mushy, rubbery, watery, or stringy, or may have moderate dehydration.

U.S. Grade C. A fresh or frozen product that possesses reasonably good flavor and odor. The product may be somewhat lacking in good flavor and odor characteristics of the species, but it is free from objectionable off-odors and off-flavors of any kind. The cooked fish flesh may be markedly dry, tough, mushy, rubbery, watery, or stringy, or have excessive dehydration.

TYPES

Fresh. Fresh products are packaged in accordance with good commercial practices and maintained at temperatures necessary for the preservation of the product.

Frozen. Frozen products are frozen to 0 degrees F at their center and maintained at temperatures of 0 degrees F or less.

STYLES

Skin On or Skinless. The skin is left on the fish (*skin on*), or has been removed (*skinless*).

Headed and Gutted. The head and internal organs of the fish have been removed.

Headed and Dressed. The fish has been headed and gutted and the fins are usually removed. This style of fish may be presented with or without the dorsal spine or the collar bone.

Whole Fillets. Practically boneless pieces of fish that are cut parallel to the entire length of the backbone, with the belly flaps included and with or without the black membrane of the fish.

Trimmed Fillets. Whole fillets without belly flaps.

Fillet Strips. Strips of fillets that weigh not less than ¾ ounce.

Steaks. Units of fish not less than 1½ ounces in weight which are sawn or cut approximately perpendicular to the backbone. The number of tail sections that may be included in a package must not exceed the number of fish cuts per package. (One tail per fish per package.)

Nuggets. Pieces of belly flaps with or without the black membrane and weighing not less than ¾ ounce.

Bone-In. A fillet cut with bones. (The product must be clearly labeled on the principal display panel that the product contains bones.)

Source:
National Marine Fisheries Service, NOAA, Commerce Department, "United States Standards for Grades of North American Freshwater Catfish and Products Made Therefrom," 50 part 267 (1991), Washington: Government Printing Office.

Caviar

Caviar. The unqualified term *caviar* should be applied only to specially prepared sturgeon fish eggs. This type of caviar is also called *sturgeon caviar.*

_____ **Caviar.** As in *Whitefish Caviar,* a type of caviar prepared from the eggs of fish other than the sturgeon. This product may be colored with a color additive if the label bears a prominent declaration of the presence of the artificial color.

Source:
Food and Drug Administration, *Compliance Policy Guides,* Guide 7109.01, 10/30/89, Washington: National Technical Information Service.

Crabmeat

Deviled Crabs, Crab Cakes, Crab Burger. A product that is labeled *crab* should not contain any other kind of seafood. Fish flakes or other non-crab seafoods may be used with crabmeat in deviled, cakes, cocktails, and other products, provided that the presence of the non-crab ingredients is properly revealed as a part of the product's name, e.g., *Deviled Crabs with Fish Flakes.* When the fish ingredient predominates, it appears before the word *crab* in the name.

Crabmeat. Products labeled as *crabmeat,* from domestic sources without qualification, are generally accepted to have been derived from the blue crab. Crabmeat may also be labeled with certain common and usual names as in *King Crabmeat, Kegani (Korean) Crabmeat,* and *Snow Crabmeat.*

Source:
Food and Drug Administration, *Compliance Policy Guides,* Guide 7108.03, 10/01/80, Washington: National Technical Information Service.

Fish, Whole or Dressed

These grades apply to whole or dressed fish, whether fresh or frozen, of any species suitable for use as human food and pro-

cessed and maintained in accordance with good manufacturing practices.

PRODUCT FORMS

Fresh
Frozen Solid Packs; Glazed or Unglazed
Frozen Individually; Glazed or Unglazed

STYLES

Whole
Dressed; Eviscerated
Head On or Headless
With or Without Fins
Skin On, Scaled or Unscaled; Semi-skinned (Epidermis Removed) or Skinless

GRADES

This product is graded according to a very technical system whereby *penalty* points are assessed for such factors as edibility, poor appearance, or defects in workmanship. The more penalty points assessed, the lower the grade. The grade descriptions which follow are intended only as a general consumer guide. For more detailed information, please consult the source cited below.

U.S. Grade A. Possess reasonably good flavor and odor. May have slight defects in the appearance of the flesh, eyes, gills, and skin, and a slight amount of discoloration. The skin may be slightly dehydrated and can be readily removed by scraping with a blunt instrument. There is only a slight degree of improper cleaning of the belly cavity and improper heading. Improper heading refers to the presence of pieces of gills, gill cover, pectoral fins, or collarbone after the fish have been headed. No ragged cuts should be evident after heading. All viscera, kidney, spawn, and blood should be removed. The texture of the cooked fish is fairly firm, only slightly tough or rubbery, does not form a fibrous mass in the mouth, and is moist but not mushy.

U.S. Grade B. Possesses reasonably good flavor and odor. May have moderate defects in the appearance of the flesh and moderate discoloration over 10 percent and up to 50 percent of the total area. There may be moderate dehydration affecting less than 3 percent of the area, and requiring a knife or other sharp instrument to remove. There may be a moderate degree of improper heading and cleaning of the body cavity. The texture of the cooked fish may be moderately tough or rubbery or have a noticeable tendency to form a fibrous mass in the mouth. It may be moist but not mushy.

Substandard. Does not possess reasonably good flavor and odor. May have excessive surface defects that are noticeable and seriously objectionable. May be excessively discolored in an area involving 50 percent or more of the total area. May have excessive dehydration affecting more than 3 percent of the area and requiring a knife or other sharp instrument to remove. May have an excessive degree of improper heading and cleaning of the body cavity that is conspicuously noticeable and seriously affects the appearance, desirability, and eating quality of the fish. The cooked fish may be excessively tough or rubbery, have a marked tendency to form a fibrous mass in the mouth, or is very dry or very mushy.

Source:

National Marine Fisheries Service, NOAA, Commerce Department, "United States Standards for Grades of Whole or Dressed Fish," 50 part 261 (1991), Washington: Government Printing Office.

Fish Fillets

These grades apply to fresh or frozen fillets of fish of any species that are suitable for use as human food.

TYPES

Fresh

Frozen Individually (Individually Quick Frozen [IQF]); Glazed or Unglazed

STYLES

Single.

Skin On; Skin On Scaled; Skin On White Side Only (Applies Only To Flatfish)

Skin Off (Skinless)

Butterfly

BONE CLASSIFICATIONS

Practically Boneless Fillet

Bone-in (fillet cut, with bones)

GRADES

This product is graded according to a very technical system whereby *penalty* points are assessed for such factors as edibility, poor appearance, or defects in workmanship. The more penalty points assessed, the lower the grade. The grade descriptions which follow are intended only as a general consumer guide. For more detailed information, please consult the source cited below.

U.S. Grade A. Possesses good flavor and odor characteristic of the species. There may be slight dehydration affecting more than 5 percent of the surface area which can be readily removed by scraping with a blunt instrument. There may be a slight degree of defects in workmanship. The texture of the cooked fish is fairly firm, does not form a fibrous mass in the mouth, and is moist but not mushy.

U.S. Grade B. Possesses reasonably good flavor and odor characteristic of the species. There may be moderate dehydration or a moderate degree of defects in workmanship. The texture of the cooked fish may be moderately tough or rubbery, or may have noticeable tendency to form a fibrous mass in the mouth, or may be moist but not mushy.

U.S. Grade C. Possesses minimal acceptable flavor and odor characteristic of the species with no objectionable off-flavors

or off-odors. There may be excessive dehydration or defects in workmanship. The texture of the cooked fish may be excessively tough or rubbery, it may have a tendency to form a fibrous mass in the mouth, or may be very dry or very mushy.

Substandard. Fails to meet the limits for physical defects for *U.S. Grade C* quality.

Source:

National Marine Fisheries Service, NOAA, Commerce Department, "United States Standards for Grades of Fish Fillets," 50 CFR part 263 (1991), Washington: Government Printing Office.

Grade Marks

The approved grade mark or identification may be used on containers, labels, or otherwise indicated for any processed fish product that has been packed under inspection and has been certified by an inspector as meeting the requirements of the grade, quality, or classification.

GRADE MARKS

The grade marks approved for use are similar in form and design to any of the 5 examples below:

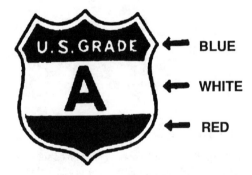

Figure 1. Shield using red, white, and blue background or other colors appropriate for the label.

Figure 2. Shield with plain background.

411

U.S.   GRADE   A

Figure 3.

U.S. GRADE

B

Figure. 4.

U.S. GRADE

C

Figure. 5.

INSPECTION MARKS

The approved inspection marks may be used on containers, labels, or otherwise indicated for any processed product that has been packed under inspection and has been certified by an inspector as meeting the requirements of such quality or grade classification. The inspection marks approved for use are similar in form and design to the three examples below.

Statement enclosed within a circle.

PACKED UNDER
FEDERAL
INSPECTION

U.S.DEPARTMENT
OF COMMERCE

Statement without the use of the circle.

PACKED BY

- -
- -

UNDER FEDERAL INSPECTION
U.S. DEPT. OF COMMERCE

Statement without the use of the circle.

COMBINED MARKS

Grade and inspection marks may be combined into a consolidated grade and inspection mark for use on processed products that have been packed under inspection.

Fish products which have not been packed under inspection cannot be identified by approved grade or inspection marks, but such products may be inspected on a lot inspection basis and identified by an authorized representative of the Commerce Department by stamping the shipping cases and inspection certificates covering the lot with marks similar to the one below.

Source:
National Marine Fisheries Service, NOAA, Commerce Department, "Inspection and Certification of Establishments and Fishery Products for Human Consumption," 50 CFR part 260 (1991), Washington: Government Printing Office.

Halibut, Frozen Steaks

Frozen halibut steaks are clean, wholesome units of frozen raw fish flesh with normally associated skin and bone and are two ounces or more in weight. Each steak has two parallel surfaces and is derived from whole or subdivided halibut slices of uniform thickness which result from sawing or cutting perpendicular to the axial length, or backbone, of a whole halibut. The steaks are prepared from either frozen or unfrozen halibut. They are processed and frozen in accordance with good commercial practices and are maintained at temperatures necessary for the preservation of the product.

STYLES

Style I (Random Weight Pack). The individual steaks are of random weight and neither the weight not the range of weights are specified.

Style II (Uniform Weight or Portion Pack). All steaks in the package or in the lot are of a specified weight or range of weights.

GRADES

Halibut is graded by a point system on the following factors: dehydration of the surface area, uniformity of thickness, uniformity of weight, defects in product preparation, discoloration of the meat, and texture. The grade descriptions which follow are intended only as a general consumer guide. For more detailed information, please consult the source cited below.

U.S. Grade A. Possesses good flavor and odor which is free from rancidity and from off-flavors and off-odors of any kind.

U.S. Grade B. The fish flesh may be somewhat lacking in the good flavor and odor characteristic of halibut, is reasonably free of rancidity, and is free from objectionable off-flavors and off-odors.

Substandard. The flavor fails to meet the requirements of *U.S. Grade B.*

Source:
National Marine Fisheries Service, Commerce Department, "United States Standards for Grades of Whole or Dressed Fish," 50 CFR part 261 (1991), Washington: Government Printing Office.

Kapchunka Fish

A ready-to-eat, salt-cured, air-dried, whole, uneviscerated fish (usually white fish), which may or may not be smoked. This type of product is an ethnic food sold under various names, including *Kapchunka, Rybetz,* and *Rostov.* These fish products are cured by layering whole, uneviscerated, raw fish and salt in approximately a one-to-one ratio in a tank under refrigeration for a minimum of 25 days. After curing, the fish are removed from the accumulated brine, rinsed, and hung at ambient temperatures to air dry for 3 to 7 days. When the drying is complete, the fish are packed in cardboard boxes and stored under refrigeration until distribution and sale. Unfortunately, since 1981, there have been three out-

breaks of botulism due to consumption of this food. Accordingly, the Food and Drug Administration considers this product to be a potentially life-threatening acute health hazard because of the possible presence of *C. botulinum* toxin. The curing processes employed commercially do not reliably ensure the production of a product free of *botulinum* toxin, as evidenced by repeated incidents of illness and deaths over the last several years.

Source:
Food and Drug Administration, *Compliance Policy Guides,* Guide 7108.17, Reissued 10/27/88, Washington: National Technical Information Service.

Kipper

Kipper. A fish which has been split through the back from tail to head, eviscerated, lightly salted, and lightly smoked; e.g., *kippered herring.*

Kipper, Unsplit. A fish which has been headed and eviscerated (but not split), lightly salted, and lightly smoked; e.g., *kippered herring, unsplit.*

Source:
Food and Drug Administration, *Compliance Policy Guides,* Guide 7102.03, Revised 10/30/89, Washington: National Technical Information Service.

Lobster

Lobster. When used unqualifiedly the term lobster is understood in the United States to mean only the North Atlantic lobster of the species *Homarus americanus.*

European Lobster. Used only for the species *Homarus vulgaris.*

Norwegian Lobster or Deep-Sea Lobster. Used for the species *Nephrops norwegicus. Deep-Sea Lobster* is the preferred name in the United States.

Spiny Lobster or Rock Lobster or Marine Crayfish. Used for the following species: *Panulirus ornatus, Panulirus argus, Panulirus rissonii, Jasus lalundi.*

Slipper Lobster. Used for the species *Ibacus ciliatus* and *Theus orientalis.*

Longotino. Used for the following species: *Pleuroncodes monodon* and *Cervimumda joni.* The name *Rock Lobster-Like Tail Meat* is no longer used.

Crayfish or Crawfish. Understood to mean the freshwater crayfishes (Family *Astacidae*).

Source:
Food and Drug Administration, *Compliance Policy Guides,* Guide 7108.23, 01/01/80, Washington: National Technical Information Service.

Oysters

Shell Oysters. Live oysters of any of the species *Ostrea virginica, Ostrea gigas,* or *Ostrea lurida,* in the shell, which, after removal from their beds, have not been floated or otherwise held under conditions which result in the addition of water.

Extra Large Oysters. Oysters of the species *Ostrea virginica* that are of such size that one gallon contains not more than 160 oysters and a quart of the smallest oysters selected from the gallon contains not more than 44 oysters.

Large Oysters. Oysters of the species *Ostrea virginica* that are of such a size that one gallon contains more than 160 oysters but not more than 210 oysters. A quart of the smallest oysters selected from the gallon contains not more than 58 oysters, and a quart of the largest oysters selected from the gallon contains not more than 36 oysters.

Medium Oysters. Oysters of the species *Ostrea virginica* that are of such a size that one gallon contains more than 210 oysters, but not more than 300 oysters. A quart of the smallest oysters selected from the gallon contains not more than 83 oysters, and a quart of the largest oysters contains more than 46 oysters.

Small Oysters. Oysters of the species *Ostrea virginica* that are of such a size that one gallon contains more than 300 oysters, but not more than 500 oysters. A quart of the smallest oysters selected from the gallon contains not more than 138 oysters, and a quart of the largest oysters contains more than 68 oysters.

Very Small Oysters. Oysters of the species *Ostrea virginica* and are of such size that one gallon contains more than 500 oysters, and a quart of the largest oysters selected form the gallon contains more than 112 oysters.

Olympia Oysters. Oysters of the species *Ostrea lurida*.

Large Pacific Oysters. Oysters of the species *Ostrea gigas* that are of such a size that one gallon contains not more than 64 oysters, and the largest oyster in the container is not more than twice the weight of the smallest oyster.

Medium Pacific Oysters. Oysters of the species *Ostrea gigas* that are of such size that one gallon contains more than 64 oysters and not more than 96 oysters, and the largest oyster in the gallon is not more than twice the weight of the smallest.

Small Pacific Oysters. Oysters of the species *Ostrea gigas* that are of such size that one gallon contains more than 96 oysters and not more than 144 oysters, and the largest oyster in the container is not more than twice the weight of the smallest oyster.

Extra Small Pacific Oyster. Oysters of the species *Ostrea gigas* that are of such size that one gallon contains more than 144 oysters, and the largest oyster in the container is not more than twice the weight of the smallest oyster.

Source:
Food and Drug Administration, "Fish and Shellfish," 21 CFR part 161 (1991) Washington: Government Printing Office.

Salmon, Canned Pacific

Salmon packed in hermetically sealed containers and so processed by heat as to prevent spoilage and soften bones. The species of fish called salmon are:

Oncorhynchus tshawytscha Chinook, king, spring

Oncorhynchus nerka Blueback, red, sockeye
Oncorhynchus kisutch Coho, Cohoe, medium, red, silver
Oncorhynchus gorbuscha Pink
Oncorhynchus keta Chum, keta
Oncorhynchus masou Masou, cherry

Regular. Consists of sections or steaks which are cut transversely from the fish and filled vertically into the can. In preparation, segments of skin or large backbone may be removed.

Skinless and Backbone Removed. Consists of the regular form of canned salmon from which the skin and vertebrae have been removed.

Minced Salmon. Salmon which has been minced or ground.

Salmon Tips or Tidbits. Small pieces of salmon.

No Salt Added. Salmon to which no salt has been added.

Source:
Food and Drug Administration, "Fish and Shellfish," 21 CFR part 161 (1991), Washington: Government Printing Office.

Salmon Steaks, Frozen

Frozen salmon steaks are clean, wholesome units of frozen raw fish flesh with normally associated skin and bone and are 2.5 ounces or more in weight.

STYLES

Style I (Random Weight Pack). The individual steaks are of random weight, and neither the individual steak weight nor the range of weights is specified. The steaks in the lot represent the random distribution cut from the head to tail of a whole, dressed salmon.

Style II (Random Weight Combination Pack). The individual steaks are of random weight, and neither the individual steak weight nor range of weights is specified.

Style III (Uniform Weight or Portion Pack). All steaks in the package or in the lot are of a specified weight or range of weights.

GRADES

Salmon steaks are graded according to a very technical system whereby *penalty* points are assessed for such factors as edibility, poor appearance, or defects in workmanship. The more penalty points assessed, the lower the grade. The grade descriptions which follow are intended only as a general consumer guide. For more detailed information, please consult the source cited below.

U.S. Grade A. Possesses good flavor and odor. The thickness of individually frozen salmon steaks are not less than ½ inch and not greater than 1½ inches. They are only slightly affected by workmanship defects including: blood spots, bruises, cleaning, cutting, fins, foreign material, collar bone, girdle, loose skin, pugh marks, sawdust, and scales. There may be slight discoloration and slight nonuniformity of color.

U.S. Grade B. Possesses at least reasonably good flavor and odor. May have moderate defects in workmanship and an undesirable increase in toughness and/or dryness, fibrousness, and watery nature of salmon examined in the cooked state.

Substandard. Fails to meet the requirements of *U.S. Grade B.*

Source:
National Marine Fisheries Service, NOAA, Commerce Department, "United States Standards for Grades of Whole or Dressed Fish," 50 CFR part 261 (1991), Washington: Government Printing Office.

Shrimp

These grades apply to clean, wholesome shrimp of the regular processed commercial species that are fresh or frozen, raw or cooked.

TYPES

Fresh

Frozen Individually (Individually Quick Frozen [IQF]); Glazed or Unglazed

Frozen Solid Pack; Glazed or Unglazed

STYLES

Parboiled. Heated for a period of time such that the surface of the product reaches a temperature adequate to coagulate the protein.

Cooked. Heated for a period of time such that the thermal center of the shrimp reaches a temperature adequate to coagulate the protein.

PRODUCT FORMS

Heads On. Head, shell, tail fins on.

Headless. Only head removed; shell, tail fins on.

Peeled, Round, Tail Off. All shell and tail fins removed with segments unsplit, and vein not removed.

Peeled, Round, Tail On. All shell removed, except last shell segment and tail fins, with segment unslit and vein not removed.

Peeled and Deveined, Round, Tail Off. All shell and tail fins removed with segments shallowly slit to last segment, and vein removed to last segment.

Peeled and Deveined, Round, Tail On. All shell removed, except last shell segment and tail fins, with segments shallowly slit to last segment, and vein removed to last segment.

Peeled and Deveined, Fantail or Butterfly Tail Off. All shell and tail fin removed with segments deeply slit to last segment, and vein removed to last segment.

Peeled and Deveined, Fantail or Butterfly, Tail On. All shell removed, except last segment, and vein removed to last segment.

Peeled and Deveined, Fantail or Butterfly, Tail On. All shell removed, except last shell segment and tail fins, with segments deeply slit to last segment, and vein removed to last segment.

Peeled and Deveined, Western. All shell removed, except last shell segment and tail fins, with segments split completely to last segment, and vein removed to last segment.

Shell on Pieces. Head removed, shell and tail fins when existing not removed.

Peeled and Deveined, Round Pieces. All shell removed with segments shallowly slit, except last segment when existing; vein removed, except last segment when existing.

Peeled and Deveined Butterfly Pieces. All shell removed with segments deeply slit, except last segment when existing; vein removed, except last segment when existing.

Peeled Undeveined Pieces. All shell removed.

GRADES

Shrimp is graded according to a very technical system whereby *penalty* points are assessed for such factors as edibility, poor appearance, or defects in workmanship. The more penalty points assessed, the lower the grade. The grade descriptions which follow are intended only as a general consumer guide. For more detailed information, please consult the source cited below.

U.S. Grade A. Possesses good flavor and odor characteristics of the species. Has the normal, pleasant flavor and odor characteristics of freshly caught shrimp that is free from off-flavors and odors of any kind. May have a scarcely noticeable desiccation of the shrimp flesh that will not affect the desirability and/or eating quality of the shrimp. The texture of the cooked shrimp is firm, slightly resilient but not tough, moist but not mushy.

U.S. Grade B. Possesses reasonably good flavor and odor characteristics of the species. The product may be somewhat lacking in good flavor and odor characteristics of freshly caught shrimp but is free from objectionable off-flavors and off-odors of any kind. The flesh may have moderate dehydration that does not seriously affect the desirability and/or eating quality of the shrimp. The texture of the cooked shrimp may be moderately tough, moist, but not mushy.

U.S. Grade C. Possesses minimum acceptable flavor and odor characteristics of the species.

Substandard. Possesses minimum acceptable flavor and odor characteristics of the species but exceeds the tolerance level for physical defects for *U.S. Grade C.*

Ungraded. Shrimp which do not possess minimum flavor and odor characteristics of the species will not be graded.

Source:
Food and Drug Administration, "United States Standards for Grades of Crustacean Shellfish Products," 50 CFR part 265 (1991), Washington: Government Printing Office.

Shrimp, Canned Wet Pack

Veined. Shrimp with readily visible dark vein (dorsal tract, back vein, or sand vein).

Deveined. Shrimp containing not less than 95 percent by weight of shrimp prepared by removing the dark vein from the first five segments by deliberate cutting action.

Broken. Shrimp that consists of less than four segments.

Prawns. The word *prawns* may appear on the label in parentheses immediately after the word *shrimp* or *shrimps* if the shrimp are of large or extra large size.

Cleaned or "Contains No Dark Veins." Deveined shrimp containing not less than 95 percent by weight of shrimp prepared by removing the dark vein from the first five segments by deliberate cutting action.

SIZES

Size designations and counts of shrimp in canned shrimp.

	Number of Blanched Shrimp per Ounce Size	
Name	Non-Deveined	Deveined
Colossal	Less than 2.5	Less than 2.7
Jumbo	Less than 3.5	Less than 3.8
Large	3.5 to 5.0 inclusive	3.8 to 5.4 inclusive
Medium	More than 5.0 but not more than 9.0	More than 5.4 but not more than 9.8
Small	More than 9.0 but not more than 17	More than 9.8 but not more than 18.4
Tiny	More than 17	More than 18.4

Source:

Food and Drug Administration, "United States Standards for Grades of Crustacean Shellfish Products," 50 CFR part 265 (1991), Washington: Government Printing Office.

Shrimp, Frozen Raw Breaded

Shrimp prepared by coating shrimp with batter and breading ingredients. The food is frozen.

Butterfly, Tail Off. Prepared by splitting the shrimp. Tail fins and all shell segments are removed.

Composite Units. Each unit consists of two or more whole shrimp or pieces of shrimp, or both, formed and pressed into composite units prior to coating. Tail fins and all shell segments are removed. Large composite units, prior to coating, may be cut into smaller units.

Fantail or Butterfly. Prepared by splitting the shrimp. The shrimp are peeled, except that tail fins remain attached, and the shell segment immediately adjacent to the tail fins may be left attached.

Lightly Breaded. Contains not less than 65 percent of shrimp material.

Pieces. Each unit consists of a piece or a part of a shrimp. Tail fins and all shell segments are removed.

Round, Tail Off. Round shrimp, not split. Tail fins and all shell segments are removed.

Round or Round Shrimp, Not Slit. The shrimp are peeled, except that tail fins remain attached, and the shell segment immediately adjacent to the tail fins may be left attached.

Shrimp. The tail portion of shrimp.

Source:
Food and Drug Administration, "Fish and Shellfish," 21 CFR part 161 (1991), Washington: Government Printing Office.

Tuna, Canned

Solid or Solid Pack. Consists of loins free from any surface tissue discolored by diffused hemolyzed blood, cut in transverse segments to which no free fragments are added.

Chunk, Chunks, Chunk Style. Consists of a mixture of pieces of tuna in which the original muscle structure is retained. The pieces may vary in size, but not less than 50 percent of the weight of the pressed contents of a container is retained on a 1.2 inch mesh screen.

Flakes or Flake. Consists of a mixture of pieces of tuna in which more than 50 percent of the weight of the pressed contents of the container will pass through a 1.2 inch mesh screen, but in which the muscular structure of the flesh is retained.

Grated. Consists of a mixture of particles of tuna that have been reduced to uniform size, that will pass through a 1.2 inch mesh screen, and in which the particles are discrete and do not comprise a paste.

White. Lighter than light tuna.

Light. Lighter than dark tuna.

Dark. Includes all dark tuna.

Blended. This color designation may be applied only to tuna flakes consisting of a mixture of tuna flakes of which not less than 20 percent by weight meet the color standard for either white tuna or light tuna, and the remainder of which fall within the color standard for dark tuna.

Tanno. When solid pack tuna in packed in olive oil, the designation *Tanno* may appear on the label.

Smoked. The tuna are smoked.

Packed in _____. When the packing medium is vegetable oil or olive oil, the label bears the name of the packing medium.

Source:
Food and Drug Administration, "Fish and Shellfish," 21 CFR part 161 (1991), Washington: Government Printing Office.

Vegetables

Anise, Sweet

SweetAnise os often sold as *fennel*. It is graded according to a technical system whereby penalty points are assessed for such factors as edibility, poor appearance, or defects in workmanship. The more penalty points assessed the lower the grade. The grade descriptions below are intended only as a general consumer guide.

U.S. No. 1. Stalks of sweet anise which are firm (not soft or wilted) and tender (crisp and succulent). Not more than one coarse outer branch is left on each side on the bulb to protect the tender inside portion, and the portion of the root remaining is not more than ½ inch in length. Tops may be either full length or cut back to not less than 10 inches. The bulbs are of a light greenish to white color. They are free from decay and from damage caused by growth cracks, pithy branches, wilting, freezing, seed stems, dirt, discoloration, disease, insects, or mechanical or other means. Unless otherwise specified, the minimum diameter of each bulb is not less than 2 inches.

Unclassified. Stalks of sweet anise which have not been classified in accordance with the foregoing grade. The term *unclassified* is not a grade within the meaning of these standards but is provided as a designation to show that no grade has been applied to the lot.

Source:
Agricultural Marketing Service, USDA, 7 CFR sections 51.2900 to 51.2908 (1992), Washington: Government Printing Office.

Artichokes, Globe

Artichoke. The unqualified term *artichoke* is used as the name for the flower buds of the globe artichoke (*Cynara scolymus*).

Jerusalem Artichoke. The common name for the tuber *Heliathus tuberosus*. It belongs to the sunflower family and is widely cultivated for its tuber, which is used as a vegetable directly, in pickles and relishes, and as a source of insulin used in the manufacture of fructose.

GRADES

This product is graded according to a technical system whereby penalty points are assessed for such factors as edibility, poor appearance, or defects in workmanship. The more penalty points assessed the lower the grade. The grade descriptions which follow are intended only as a general consumer guide. For more detailed information, please consult the source cited below.

U.S. No. 1. The artichokes are properly trimmed. The stem is smoothly cut and not excessively long. The artichokes are not excessively long and pointed. They are not overdeveloped and do not have a brownish color. The scales are not tough, leathery, and stringy, and the flowers in the centers of the buds have not turned dark pink or purple and have not become fuzzy. The buds are reasonably firm and not more than slightly spread. They are free from decay and are not damaged by any other cause.

U.S. No. 2. Artichokes which are not overdeveloped, not badly spread, and free from decay. Not seriously damaged (any damage that seriously detracts from the eating quality or appearance). Fairly uniform in size. Have an increased tolerance for defects over U.S. No. 1.

Source:
Agricultural Marketing Service, USDA, 7 CFR sections 51.3785 to 51.3796 (1992), Washington: Government Printing Office.
Food and Drug Administration, *Compliance Policy Guides*, Guide 7114.01, Revised 12/08/88, Washington: National Technical Information Service.

Asparagus

GRADES

This product is graded according to a very technical system whereby penalty points are assessed for such factors as edibility, poor appearance, or defects in workmanship. The more penalty points assessed the lower the grade. The grade descriptions which follow are intended only as a general consumer guide. For more detailed information, please consult the source cited below.

U.S. No. 1. Stalks of asparagus which are fairly straight, fresh (not limp or flabby), and well trimmed (at least two-thirds of the butt of the stalk is smoothly trimmed, not stringy or frayed, in a plane approximately parallel to the bottom of the container). They are free from decay and free from damage caused by spreading or broken tips, dirt, disease, insects, or other means. Unless otherwise specified, the diameter of each stalk is not less than ½ inch, and not less than two-thirds of the stalk length is of a green color.

U.S. No. 2. Stalks of asparagus which are not badly misshapen, fresh, and fairly well trimmed (at least one-third of the butt of the stalk is smoothly trimmed in a plane approximately parallel to the bottom of the container, and the butt is not badly stringy or frayed). They are free from decay and free from serious damage caused by spreading or broken tips, dirt, disease, insects or other means. Unless otherwise specified, the diameter of each stalk is not less than 5/16 inch, and not less than one-half of the stalk length is of a green color. Has a higher tolerance for defects than U.S. No. 1.

Unclassified. Stalks of asparagus which have not been classified in accordance with any of the foregoing grades. The term *unclassified* is not a grade within the meaning of these standards but is provided as a designation to show that no grade has been applied to the lot.

SIZE

Very Small. Less than 5/16 in.
Small. 5/16 to 8/16 in.
Medium. 8/16 to 11/16 in.
Large. 11/16 to 14/16 in.
Very Large. 14/16 in. and up

Source:
Agricultural Marketing Service, USDA, 7 CFR sections 51.3720 to 51.3734 (1992), Washington: Government Printing Office.

Asparagus, Canned

Canned asparagus is the canned product prepared from clean, sound, succulent shoots of the asparagus plant.

STYLES

Spears (Stalks). May be peeled or unpeeled. Consists of the head

and adjoining portion of the shoot that is 3¾ inches or more in length.
Tips. Consists of the head and adjoining portion of the shoot that is less than 3¾ inches but not less than 2¾ inches in length.
Points. Consists of the head and adjoining portion of the shoot that is less than 2¾ inches in length.
Cut Spears (Cut Stalks). Consists of shoots cut transversely into pieces. The recommended minimum percent, by count, of heads in cut spears is given in the accompanying table.

Length of units	Percent by count
1¼ inches or less	15
Over 1¼ inches	20

Bottom Cuts or Cuts-Tips Removed. Consists of portions of shoots with heads removed that are cut transversely into pieces.
Mixed. Consists of two or more of the foregoing styles.

GRADES

U.S. Grade A or U.S. Fancy. The quality of canned asparagus that possesses a good flavor and character, a clear liquor, a good color, and that is practically free from defects.
U.S. Grade C or U.S. Standard. The quality of canned asparagus that possesses a fairly good character and flavor, a fairly clear liquor, a fairly good color, and that is fairly free from defects.
Substandard. The quality of canned asparagus that fails to meet the requirements of U.S. Grade C or U.S. Standard.

TYPES

Green (All Green). Canned asparagus which are typical green, light green, or yellowish green in color.
Green Tipped. Canned asparagus spears, tips, and points, of which one-half or more of the unit measured from the tip end is green, light green, or yellowish green in color.
Green Tipped and White. Consists of (1) spears, tips, and points of canned asparagus which are typical white or yellowish white in color, and may have green, light green, or yellowish green heads, and the green color may extend to not more than one-half of the length of the stalk measured from the tip end; and (2) green tipped and white spears, tips, and points, when cut into units, may consist of a mixture of typical white, yellowish white, green, light green, or yellowish green units.
White. Canned asparagus which are typical white or yellowish white in color.

SIZE

The size (diameter) of asparagus spears, tips, and points in canned asparagus is determined by measuring the largest diameter across the base at right angles to the longitudinal axis of the unit. Units compressed in processing should be restored to their approximate original contour before sizing. Asparagus spears longer than 5 inches are measured at a point 5 inches from the top of the spear.

Units 5 inches in length and less are measured at the base or largest cut end of the unit. Canned asparagus spears, tips, and points are considered as meeting a designated size when not more than 20 percent of the units are of the next size smaller or larger.

Designation	Diameter (16ths of inch)
Small	Approximately $^6/_{16}$
Medium	$^6/_{16}$ to $^8/_{16}$
Large	$^8/_{16}$ to $^{10}/_{16}$
Extra large or mammoth	$^{10}/_{16}$ to $^{13}/_{16}$
Colossal	$^{13}/_{16}$ to $^{16}/_{16}$
Giant	$^{16}/_{16}$ and over,
Blend of sizes	A mixture of 2 or more of the foregoing sizes.

Sources:

Agricultural Marketing Service, USDA, 7 CFR sections 52.2541 to 52.2558 (1991), Washington: Government Printing Office.
Food and Drug Administration, "Certain Other Canned Vegetables," 21 CFR 155.200 (1991), Washington: Government Printing Office.

Asparagus, Green for Processing

GRADES

This product is graded according to a very technical system whereby penalty points are assessed for such factors as edibility, poor appearance, or defects in workmanship. The more penalty points assessed the lower the grade. The grade descriptions which follow are intended only as a general consumer guide. For more detailed information, please consult the source cited below.

U.S. No. 1. Fresh, fairly well formed, and free from decay and broken tips. Also free from damage cause by doubles, spreading tips, knife cuts, broken butts, hail, freezing, dirt, disease, beetles, etc. Not less than ¼ inch in diameter and 7½ inches in length. Unless otherwise specified, the spear has a green color extending at least 4½ inches below the tip.

U.S. No. 2. Fresh, free from decay, and free from damage caused by dirt. Free from serious damage caused by disease, beetles or other insects, or mechanical or other means. Unless otherwise specified, each spear is not more than 7½ inches in length and has a green color extending at least 3 inches below the tip.

Source:
Agricultural Marketing Service, USDA, 7 CFR sections 51.4075 to 51.40851 (1992), Washington: Government Printing Office.

Avocados

GRADES

Avocados are graded according to a technical system whereby penalty points are assessed for such factors as edibility, poor appearance, or defects in workmanship. The more penalty points assessed the lower the grade. The grade descriptions which follow are intended only as a general consumer guide. For more detailed information, please consult the source cited below.

U.S. No. 1. Mature but not overripe avocados of similar varietal characteristics. They are well formed, clean, well trimmed, and have a color characteristic of the variety. The stem, when present, is cut off fairly smoothly at a point not more than ¼ inch beyond the shoulder of the avocado. They are free from decay, anthracnose, and freezing injury. Also free from damage caused by bruises, cuts or other skin breaks, pulled stems, russeting or similar discoloration, scars, scab, sunburn, sunscald, sprayburn, cercospora spot, other disease, insects, or mechanical or other means.

U.S. Combination. A combination of U.S. No. 1 and U.S. No. 2 avocados. At least 60 percent meet the requirements of U.S. No. 1.

U.S. No. 2. Avocados of similar varietal characteristics which are mature but not overripe. The avocado may be slightly abnormal in shape but not to the extent that the appearance is seriously affected. They are clean, fairly well colored (shows a shade of color which is fairly characteristic of the variety), and well trimmed. They are free from decay and freezing injury and are free from serious damage cause by anthracnose, bruises, cuts or other skin breaks, pulled stems, russeting or similar discoloration, scars, scab, sunburn, sunscald, sprayburn, cercospora spot, other disease, insects, or mechanical or other means.

U.S. No. 3. Avocados of similar varietal characteristics which are mature but not overripe. They are not badly misshapen and are free from decay and from serious damage caused by anthracnose. They are also free from very serious damage caused by freezing injury, bruises, cuts or other skin breaks, pulled stems, russeting or similar discoloration, scars, scab, sunburn, sunscald, sprayburn, cercospora spot, other disease, insects, dirt, or mechanical or other means.

Unclassified. Avocados which have not been classified in accordance with any of the foregoing grades. The term *unclassified* is not a grade within the meaning of these standards, but is provided as a designation to show that no grade has been applied to the lot.

Source:
Agricultural Marketing Service, USDA, 7 CFR sections 51.3050 to 51.3069 (1992), Washington: Government Printing Office.

Beans, Baked (Canned)

Canned baked beans is the product prepared from dry, mature beans used for canning, but not including soybeans. (Ingredients permissible under the provisions of the Federal Food, Drug, and Cosmetic Act may be used.) Baked beans are prepared by washing, soaking, and baking by the application of dry heat in open or loosely covered containers in a closed oven at atmospheric pressure. Cooking continues for sufficient time to produce the desired texture and flavor. It is packed in hermetically sealed containers and sufficiently processed by heat to assure preservation.

TYPES

White Beans
Red kidney beans
Yelloweye Beans (including soldier beans)
Other Colors or Types Suitable for Baking (except soybeans)

STYLES

In Brown Sugar, Molasses, or New England Sauce. Packed with nutritive carbohydrate sweetening ingredient(s) and any other safe and suitable ingredient(s).

In Tomato Sauce. Packed with tomato pulp or a similar tomato product and any other safe and suitable ingredient(s).

GRADES

Canned baked beans are graded according to a technical system whereby penalty points are assessed for such factors as edibility, poor appearance, or defects in workmanship. The more penalty points assessed the lower the grade. The grade descriptions which follow are intended only as a general consumer guide. For more detailed information, please consult the source cited below.

U.S. Grade A. The product has practically similar varietal characteristics. The consistency is such that the product forms a well-rounded mound when emptied from the container. The sauce is of such quantity and character that it clings to the beans with not more than a reasonable separation from the mound. The product is practically free from defects such as loose skin, broken, mashed, and blemished beans, or any other defects that may affect appearance or eating quality. The baked beans have a good, typical texture that may be slightly soft or slightly firm. The skins are tender. The product has a good baked bean flavor and odor which is characteristic of the variety of bean and style of pack with all flavor components in proper balance. The product is free from objectionable flavors and objectionable odors, and it has a uniform color typical of the baked variety and style of pack.

U.S. Grade B. Possesses reasonably similar varietal characteristics. The consistency is such that the product forms a mound that may tend to take the shape of the container with little leveling or that may level itself substantially with a fairly large amount of sauce separation from the beans. The product is reasonably free from defects. It has a reasonably good, typical texture that may be firm or soft but not hard or mushy. The skins may be slightly tough. The product has a reasonably good baked bean flavor and odor and is free from objectionable flavors and objectionable odors. The baked beans have a reasonably uniform color typical of the baked variety and style of pack.

Substandard. Fails to meet the requirements of U.S. Grade B.

Source:
Agricultural Marketing Service, USDA, 7 CFR sections 52.6461 to 52.6473 (1991), Washington: Government Printing Office.

Beans, Frozen

Frozen green beans and frozen wax beans, hereinafter called frozen beans, are prepared from the clean, sound, succulent pods of the bean plant. The pods are stemmed, washed, blanched, sorted, and properly drained.

STYLES

Whole. Whole pods of any length.
Cut. Pods that are cut transversely into pieces less than 2¾ inch but not less than ¾ inch in length.
Short Cut. Pods that are cut transversely into pieces less than ¾ inch in length.
Minced. A mixture of two or more of the following styles of frozen beans: whole, cut, or short cut.
Sliced Lengthwise. Pods that are sliced lengthwise. Also known as *French Style, French Sliced Julienne,* or *Shoestring.*

TYPES

Round Type. Having a width not greater than 1½ times the thickness of the beans.
Romano or Italian Type. Having a width greater than 1½ times the thickness of the beans.

KINDS OF PACK

Regular. Processed in such a manner that the brightness is not affected by the process.
Multi-Blanch. Brightness is affected by the process.
Special Pack. The frozen bean pack intentionally contains beans of two or more varietal characteristics (such as a mixture of green and wax beans).

GRADES

Frozen beans are graded according to a technical system whereby penalty points are assessed for such factors as edibility, poor appearance, or defects in workmanship. The more penalty points assessed the lower the grade. The grade descriptions which follow are intended only as a general consumer guide. For more detailed information, please consult the source cited below.

U.S. Grade A. Have similar varietal characteristics and a good flavor and odor. They have a good overall brightness as a mass that is not affected by dullness. For the style of *Sliced Lengthwise,* they are practically free from small pieces. They have an appearance or eating quality that is not materially affected by sloughing.

U.S. Grade B. Have similar varietal characteristics and a good flavor and odor. They have a reasonably good overall brightness as a mass, but may be slightly dull. They are reasonably free from small pieces for the style *Sliced Lengthwise.* Have an appearance or eating quality that is not seriously affected by sloughing.

U.S. Grade C. Have similar varietal characteristics and a fairly good flavor and odor. They have a reasonably good overall brightness as a mass, but may be dull and off-color.

Substandard. The quality of frozen beans that fails to meet the requirements of U.S. Grade C.

Source:
Agricultural Marketing Service, USDA, 7 CFR sections 52.2331 to 52.2334 (1991), Washington: Government Printing Office.

Beet Greens

This entry is applicable to beet greens consisting of either plants (with or without attached roots) or cut leaves, but is not applicable to a mixture of plants and cut leaves in the same container. It applies only to the common red-rooted table varieties of beets (*Beta vulgaris*), but not to mangel wurzel varieties primarily grown for stock feed or to sugar beets (*Beta vulgaris saccharifera*).

GRADES

Beet greens are graded according to a technical system whereby penalty points are assessed for such factors as edibility, poor appearance, or defects in workmanship. The more penalty points assessed the lower the grade. The grade descriptions which follow are intended only as a general consumer guide. For more detailed information, please consult the source cited below.

U.S. No. 1. Beet greens of similar varietal characteristics which are fresh and not more than slightly wilted. They are fairly clean and fairly tender (not tough or excessively fibrous). The length of leaf stem or petiole is not more than the length of the leaf blade. The overall length of the leaf blade, including blade and petiole, is not more than 11 inches. They are free from decay, weeds, grass, other kinds of leaves, and other foreign material. Also free from damage caused by discoloration, freezing, disease, insects, or mechanical or other means. In the case of beet greens with roots attached, the roots are free from damage by any cause, and the maximum diameter of the root is not larger than ⅝ inch. The leaf blades of beet greens are not longer than 6½ inches.

Unclassified. Beet greens which have not been classified in accordance with the foregoing grade. The term *unclassified* is not a grade within the meaning of these standards but is provided as a designation to show that no grade has been applied to the lot.

Source:
Agricultural Marketing Service, USDA, 7 CFR sections 51.2860 to 51.2872 (1992), Washington: Government Printing Office.

Beets

This entry is applicable to the common red-rooted table varieties of beets (*Beta vulgaris*). It is not applicable to mangel wurzel varieties, which are primarily grown for stock feed, or to sugar beets.

STYLES

Bunched Beets. Beets which are tied in bunches. The tops are full length or removed to not less than 6 inches.

Beets with Short-Trimmed Tops. Unless otherwise specified, beets showing leaf stems ranging to not more than 4 inches in length.

Topped Beets. Beets with tops removed to not more than ½ inch in length.

GRADES

Beets are graded according to a technical system whereby penalty points are assessed for such factors as edibility, poor appearance, or defects in workmanship. The more penalty points assessed the lower the grade. The grade descriptions which follow are intended only as a general consumer guide. For more detailed information, please consult the source cited below.

U.S. No. 1. Beets of similar varietal characteristics. The roots are well-trimmed, firm, fairly smooth, fairly well shaped, and fairly clean. They are free from soft rot and from damage caused by cuts, freezing, growth cracks, disease, rodents, insects, or mechanical or other means. Bunched beets or beets with short trimmed tops have tops which are fresh, free from decay, and free from damage caused by discoloration freezing, disease, insects, or mechanical or other means. Unless otherwise specified, the diameter of each beet is not less than 1½ inches.

U.S. No. 2. Beets of similar varietal characteristics. The roots are well trimmed, firm, not excessively rough, and not seriously misshapen. They are free from soft rot and from serious damage caused by cuts, dirt, freezing, growth cracks, disease, rodents, insects, or mechanical or other means. Bunched beets or beets with short-trimmed tops have tops which are fresh, free from decay, and free from damage caused by discoloration, freezing, disease, insects, or mechanical or other means. Unless otherwise specified, the diameter of each beet is less than 1½ inches.

Unclassified. Beets which have not been classified in accordance with either of the foregoing grades. The term *unclassified* is not a grade, but is provided as a designation to show that no grade has been applied to the lot.

Source:
Agricultural Marketing Service, USDA, "United States Standards for Beets," 7 CFR sections 51.375 to 51.394 (1992), Washington: Government Printing Office.

Beets, Canned

STYLES

Whole. Retain the approximate original conformation of the whole beet.

Slices or Sliced Beets. Slices of beets, irrespective of whether such slices are corrugated, fluted, wavy, or scalloped.

Quarters or Quartered. The whole beet is cut into four approximately equal quarters.

Dice or Diced. The beets are chopped into uniform cubes.

Julienne, French Style, or Shoestring. Strips of beets.

Cut. Beets which are not uniform in size or shape.

GRADES

Canned beets are graded according to a technical system whereby penalty points are assessed for such factors as edibility, poor appearance, or defects in workmanship. The more penalty points assessed the lower the grade. The grade descriptions which follow are intended only as a general consumer guide. For more detailed information, please consult the source cited below.

U.S. Grade A or U.S. Fancy. Possess similar varietal characteristics and a normal flavor and odor free from objectionable flavor and odors of any kind. The color is uniform, bright, and typical of canned beets. The product is practically free from beets blemished by brown or black internal or external discoloration or damaged by mechanical injury, pathological injury, insect injury, or other means. The beets are tender, not fibrous, and possess a uniform character. The beets are practically uniform in size and shape within the following guidelines:

Whole Beets. Not more than 2¼ inches in diameter.

Quartered Beets. Prepared from beets not more than 2½ inches in diameter.

Sliced Beets. Each slice is not more than ⁵⁄₁₆ inch in thickness and not more than 3½ inches in diameter.

Diced Beets. Have edges measuring not more than ⅜ inch.

Julienne, French Style, or Shoestring. Have sections measuring not more than ³⁄₁₆ inch.

Cut. The individual units weigh not less than ¼ ounce or more than 2 ounces each.

U.S. Grade C or U.S. Standard. Possess similar varietal characteristics, a normal flavor and odor, and a fairly good color which may be variable or slightly dull. The beets are fairly free from defects. They are fairly tender but not tough or hard. They may possess a few stringy or coarse fibers. The beets are uniform in size and shape within the following guidelines:

Whole Beets. Not more than 2½ inches in diameter.

Quartered Beets. Prepared from beets not more than 3½ inches in diameter.

Sliced Beets. Each slice is not more than ⅜ inch in thickness and not more than 3½ inches in diameter.

Diced Beets. Have edges measuring not more than ½ inch.

Julienne, French Style, or Shoestring. Have sections measuring not more than ³⁄₁₆ inch.

Cut. The individual units weigh not less than ⅛ ounce or more than 3 ounces each.

Substandard. Fails to meet the requirements of U.S. Grade C.

Source:
Agricultural Marketing Service, USDA, 7 CFR section 52.521 (1991), Washington: Government Printing Office.

Broccoli

GRADES

Italian Sprouting Broccoli, the complete common name for the green vegetable usually known simply as *broccoli,* is graded according to a technical system whereby penalty points are assessed for such factors as edibility, poor appearance, or defects in workmanship. The more penalty points assessed the lower the grade. The grade descriptions which follow are intended only as a general consumer guide. For more detailed information, please consult the source cited below.

U.S. Grade A. All coarse, damaged, and discolored leaves and leaves extending more than 1½ inches above the top of the head have been removed, and cross cuts on butts and lengthwise cuts on split stalks are smooth. The stem and external portion of the head has a light green or darker shade of green color except that a purplish color is allowed on the external portion of the head. The clusters are fairly compact. The broccoli is not flabby or more than slightly wilted. The broccoli is succulent, and the stems are not fibrous, tough, or stringy. They are clean and free from decay. Also free from damage caused by discoloration, freezing, hollow stem or pithiness, scars, disease, insects, or mechanical or other means. In packaging, broccoli stalks on the shown face are reasonably representative in size and quality of the contents of the container. The length of the stalks are not more than 6 inches or less than 3 inches, and the diameter of the stem is not less than ¼ inch.

U.S. Grade B. Stalks or parts of stalks of broccoli which meet the requirements of U.S. Grade A except for compactness of bud clusters and increased tolerances for other defects due to natural or mechanical means.

Off-Grade. Italian sprouting broccoli which fails to meet the requirements of either of the foregoing grades.

DEFINITIONS

Stalk. A portion of the broccoli plant including the stem, bud clusters, and leaves.

Source:
Agricultural Marketing Service, USDA, 7 CFR sections 51.400 to 51.412 (1992), Washington: Government Printing Office.

Broccoli, Bunched

GRADES

Bunched broccoli is graded according to a technical system whereby penalty points are assessed for such factors as edibility, poor appearance, or defects in workmanship. The more penalty points assessed the lower the grade. The grade descriptions which follow are intended only as a general consumer guide. For more detailed information, please consult the source cited below.

U.S. Fancy. Each bunch is free from decay and from damage caused by over-maturity, discoloration of bud clusters or leaves, freezing, wilting, dirt, foreign material, disease, insects, or mechanical or other means. The bud clusters in each bunch are generally compact. The individual buds in the bud cluster are small and tightly crowded together. The bud clusters on the stalk are generally close together, feel fairly firm, and moderately resistant to pressure. Each bunch is neatly and fairly evenly cut off at the base and closely trimmed (only 5 percent is stems and leaves longer than the length of the bunch). The diameter of each stalk is not less than 2½ inches. The length of each stalk is not less than 6 inches or more than 8½ inches.

U.S. No. 1. Each bunch is free from decay and from damage caused by over-maturity, discoloration of bud clusters or leaves, freezing, wilting, dirt, foreign material, disease, insects, or mechanical or other means. The bud clusters in each bunch are generally fairly compact. Each bunch is neatly and fairly evenly cut off at the base and is well trimmed, fairly well trimmed, or leafy. There are no requirements for diameter, but diameter may be specified for any lot. Unless otherwise specified, the length of each stalk is not less than 5 inches or more than 9 inches.

U.S. No. 2. Each bunch is free from decay and from damage caused by over-maturity and insects. It is free from serious damage caused by discoloration of bud clusters or leaves, freezing, wilting, dirt or other foreign material, disease, or mechanical or other means. Each bunch is fairly well trimmed (unless otherwise specified as closely trimmed, or well trimmed, or leafy). There are no requirements for diameter or length, but size may be specified for any lot in connection with the grade.

Unclassified. Broccoli which has not been classified in accordance with any of the foregoing grades. The term *unclassified* is not a grade but is provided as a designation to show that no grade has been applied to the lot.

SIZE

Diameter. The terms *heads* and *shoots* may be used to designate size of stalks. If heads and shoots are mixed, the percentage of heads may be specified. The minimum or maximum diameter may be specified for the lot as a whole or for a certain percentage of the lot. For example: 2 inches minimum, or 50 percent 3¼ inches or larger, or 75 percent 2½ inches or larger.

Length. The minimum or maximum length may be specified in connection with U.S. No. 1 or U.S. No. 2 grades: for example, 7 inches minimum length, or 6½ to 8½ inches long.

Source:
Agricultural Marketing Service, USDA, 7 CFR sections 51.3555 to 51.3573 (1992), Washington: Government Printing Office.

Brussels Sprouts

GRADES

Brussels sprouts are graded according to a technical system whereby penalty points are assessed for such factors as edibility, poor appearance, or defects in workmanship. The more penalty points assessed the lower the grade. The grade descriptions which follow are intended only as a general consumer guide. For more detailed information, please consult the source cited below.

U.S. No. 1. Brussels sprouts which have a characteristic light green or a darker shade of green color. They are firm, have reasonable solidity, and are fairly compact. However, they may yield slightly to moderate pressure. They are not withered or burst. They are free from soft decay and seed stems (seed stalks showing or where the formation of seed stalks has plainly begun). They are also free from damage caused by discoloration, dirt or other foreign material, freezing, disease, insects, or mechanical or other means. Unless otherwise specified, the diameter of each Brussels sprout is not less than 1 inch, and the length is not more than 2¾ inches.

U.S. No. 2. Brussels sprouts which are not lighter than yellowish-green. They are not soft or puffy, and each is of reasonable weight for its size. However, they may have considerable open spaces between the leaves in the lower portion of the head. They are not withered or burst. They are free from soft decay, seed stems, and damage caused by insects. They are free from serious damage caused by discoloration, dirt or other foreign material, freezing, disease, or mechanical or other means. Unless otherwise specified, the diameter of each Brussels sprout is not less than 1 inch, and the length is not more than 2¾ inches.

Unclassified. Brussels sprouts which have not been classified in accordance with the foregoing grades. The term *unclassified* is not a grade within the meaning of these standards but is provided as a designation to show that not grade has been applied to the lot.

Source:
Agricultural Marketing Service, USDA, 7 CFR sections 51.2250 to 51.2262 (1992), Washington: Government Printing Office.

Brussels Sprouts, Frozen

Frozen Brussels sprouts are prepared from the clean, sound, succulent heads of the Brussels sprouts plant (*Brassica oleracea gemmifera*) by trimming, washing, blanching, and properly draining.

GRADES

Frozen Brussels sprouts are graded according to a technical system whereby penalty points are assessed for such factors as edibility, poor appearance, or defects in workmanship. The more penalty points assessed the lower the grade. The grade descriptions which follow are intended only as a general consumer guide. For more detailed information, please consult the source cited below.

U.S. Grade A. The Brussels sprouts have similar varietal characteristics and a normal flavor and odor. The color has a good overall brightness. The Brussels sprouts are free from grit or silt that affect the appearance or eating quality, although they may have loose leaves and loose small pieces that may slightly affect the appearance or eating quality.

U.S. Grade B. Have similar varietal characteristics, a normal flavor and odor, and a reasonably good overall brightness. They are free from grit or silt that affect the appearance or eating quality, although they may have loose leaves and loose small pieces that may materially affect the appearance or eating quality.

U.S. Grade C. Have similar varietal characteristics, a normal flavor and odor, and a fairly good overall brightness. They have no more than a slight trace of grit or silt, although they may have loose leaves and loose small pieces that may seriously affect the appearance or eating quality.

Substandard. Fails to meet the requirements of U.S. Grade C.

Source:
Agricultural Marketing Service, USDA, 7 CFR section 52.651 (1991), Washington: Government Printing Office.

Cabbage

GRADES

Cabbage is graded according to a technical system whereby penalty points are assessed for such factors as edibility, poor appearance, or defects in workmanship. The more penalty points assessed the lower the grade. The grade descriptions which follow are intended only as a general consumer guide. For more detailed information, please consult the source cited below.

U.S. No. 1. Heads of cabbage of one variety or similar varietal characteristics. They are of reasonable solidity and are not withered, puffy, or burst. Puffy means that the heads are very light in weight in comparison to size or have excessive air spaces in the central portion. They normally feel firm at time of harvesting but often soften quickly. They are free from soft rot, seed stems, and damage caused by discoloration, freezing, disease, insects, or mechanical or other means. The stems are cut so that they do not extend more than ½ inch beyond the point of attachment of the outermost leaves. Unless otherwise specified, each head is well trimmed with the head not having more than four wrapper leaves.

U.S. Commercial. Heads of cabbage which meet the requirements for U.S. No. 1 grade except for an increased tolerance for defects and except that the heads are only reasonably firm. Unless otherwise specified, each head is well trimmed.

Unclassified. Cabbage which has not been classified in accordance with the foregoing grades. The term *unclassified* is not a grade within the meaning of these standards but is provided as a designation to show that no definite grade has been applied to the lot.

SIZE

The minimum size or minimum and maximum sizes may be specified in connection with the grades as *U.S. No. 1, 1 pound*

minimum, or *U.S. No. 1, 2 to 4 pounds,* or any lot may be classified as *Small, Medium, Large, Small to Medium,* or *Medium to Large* in accordance with the facts.

Type	Small	Medium	Large
Pointed	Under 1½	1½ to	Over 3
Danish and domestic	Under 2	2 to 5	Over 5

Source:
Agricultural Marketing Service, USDA, 7 CFR sections 51.450 to 51.464 (1992), Washington: Government Printing Office.

Carrots, Bunched

GRADES

Bunched carrots are graded according to a technical system whereby penalty points are assessed for such factors as edibility, poor appearance, or defects in workmanship. The more penalty points assessed the lower the grade. The grade descriptions which follow are intended only as a general consumer guide. For more detailed information, please consult the source cited below.

U.S. No. 1. Carrots of similar varietal characteristics. The roots are not soft, flabby, or shriveled. They are fairly clean and have an orange, orange red, or orange scarlet color, but not a pale orange or distinct yellow color. They are not rough, ridged, or covered with secondary rootlets. They are not forked or misshapen. They are free from soft rot and from damage caused by freezing, growth cracks, sunburn, pithiness, woodiness, internal discoloration, oil spray, dry rot, other disease, insects, or mechanical or other means. Bunches have tops which are fresh, not badly wilted, and free from decay. Also free from damage caused by freezing, seed stems, yellowing or other discoloration, disease, insects, or mechanical or other means. Unless otherwise specified, the bunches have full tops and the length of the tops is not more than 20 inches. Unless otherwise specified, the diameter of each carrot is not less than ¾ inch.

U.S. Commercial. Carrots which meet the requirements of U.S. No. 1 except for an increased tolerance for defects of the roots.

Unclassified. Carrots which have not been classified in accordance with either of the foregoing grades. The term *unclassified* is not a grade within the meaning of these standards, but is provided as a designation to show that no grade has been applied to the lot.

Standard Bunches. Generally, each bunch of carrots including tops, weighs not less than 1 pound and contains at least 4 carrots.

CARROTS, WITH SHORT TRIMMED TOPS

These grades (U.S. Grade No. 1 and U.S. Commercial) are the same as for bunched carrots except that the leaf stems are cut back to not more than 4 inches in length.

U.S. CONSUMER STANDARDS

U.S. consumer standards represent an alternate set of voluntary standards designed more for the benefit of the consumer than for the growers and distributors. Consumer standards are not as frequently used as those written for the members of the industry.

Bunched Carrots. Untopped carrots which are tied in bunches.

Carrots with Short-Trimmed Tops. Carrots which have attached leaf stems ranging up to 4 inches in length.

Topped. Carrots which have practically all of the tops clipped off.

Grades. Carrots are graded according to a technical system whereby penalty points are assessed for such factors as edibility, poor appearance, or defects in workmanship. The more penalty points assessed the lower the grade. The grade descriptions which follow are intended only as a general consumer guide. For more detailed information, please consult the source cited below.

> *U.S. Grade A.* Carrots of similar varietal characteristics. The roots are firm, clean, fairly well colored, fairly smooth, and well formed. They are free from soft rot and from damage caused by freezing, growth cracks, sunburn, pithiness, woodiness, internal discoloration, oil spray, dry rot, other disease, insects, or mechanical or other means. Bunched carrots or carrots with short-trimmed tops have tops or leaf stems, respectively, which are fresh, free from decay, and free from damage caused by freezing, seed stems, yellowing or other discoloration, disease, insects, or mechanical or other means. Tops of bunched carrots may be full length or clipped back but are not less than 12 inches or more than 20 inches in length. Each bunch weighs not less than one pound, including the tops, and contains at least 4 carrots. Topped carrots are free from secondary new top growth and are well trimmed. When packaged, all styles of carrots on the shown face are reasonably representative in size and quality of the contents of the container. Unless otherwise specified, the diameter of each carrot is not less than ¾ inch or more than 1½ inches, and the length is not less than 5 inches.

> *U.S. Grade B.* Meet the requirements of U.S. Grade A except for an increased tolerance for defects of the roots.

Standard Sizing. Carrots in packages of 2 pounds or less may be certified as *Standard Sizing,* provided the variation in diameter of the carrots is not more than ⅜ inch and the variation in length is not more than 2½ inches. Not more than 20 percent of the packages in any lot may contain carrots which fail to meet the requirements for Standard Sizing.

Source:
Agricultural Marketing Service, USDA, 7 CFR sections 51.495 to 51.513 and 51.2455 to 51.2498 (1992), Washington: Government Printing Office.

Carrots, Canned

Canned carrots are prepared from the clean, sound root of the carrot plant (*Daucus carota*).

STYLES

Whole or Whole Carrots. Canned carrots consisting of whole carrots that retain the approximate original conformation of the whole carrot.

Slices or Sliced. Produced by slicing whole carrots transversely to the longitudinal axis.

Quarters. Produced by cutting whole carrots longitudinally into four equal units.

Diced. Produced by cutting whole carrots into cubes having edges, other than the rounded outer edges, measuring approximately ½ inch or less.

Julienne, French Style, or Shoestring. Strips of carrots.

Cut. Do not conform to any of the foregoing styles.

GRADES

Canned carrots are graded according to a technical system whereby penalty points are assessed for such factors as edibility, poor appearance, or defects in workmanship. The more penalty points assessed the lower the grade. The grade descriptions which follow are intended only as a general consumer guide. For more detailed information, please consult the source cited below.

U.S. Grade A or U.S. Fancy. Possess similar varietal characteristics and a normal flavor and odor. The canned carrots possess an orange-yellow color, and the presence of green units may only slightly affect the appearance or eating quality. They are practically free from defects such as unpeeled units, units blemished or seriously blemished by brown or black internal or external discoloration, sunburn or green colored units, pathological injury, insect injury, and units blemished or seriously blemished by other means. The carrots are tender and firm but not fibrous; they possess a practically uniform texture. They are practically uniform in size and shape, with the size of the individual whole carrots not more than 1¾ inches in diameter. Quartered carrots are prepared from carrots not more than 2½ inches in diameter. Sliced carrots are ⅜ inch in thickness when measured at the thickest portion, with the diameter of each slice not more than 2½ inches. Diced carrots are practically uniform in size and shape, with edges measuring approximately ½ inch or less. Julienne style have cross sections measuring approximately 3⁄16 inch. Cut units weigh not less than ¼ ounce.

U.S. Grade C or U.S. Standard. Possess similar varietal characteristics and a normal flavor and odor. The color may be slightly dull but not off-color, and the presence of green units does not materially affect the appearance or eating quality. They are fairly free from defects. The carrots are fairly tender, may be variable in texture, but are not soft or mushy, tough or hard. There may be present a few units which possess a coarse or fibrous texture. They are fairly uniform in size and shape, with the size of individual whole carrots not more than 2¼ inches in diameter. Quartered carrots are prepared from carrots not more than 2½ inches in diameter. Sliced carrots are ⅜ inch in thickness when measured at the thickest portion, with the diameter of each slice not more than 2½ inches. Diced carrots are practically uniform in size and shape, with edges measuring approximately ½ inch or less. Julienne style have cross sections measuring approximately ³⁄₁₆ inch. Cut units weigh not less than ¼ ounce.

Substandard. Fails to meet the requirements of U.S. Grade C or U.S. Standard.

Source:
Agricultural Marketing Service, USDA, 7 CFR sections 52.671 to 51.686 (1992), Washington: Government Printing Office.

Carrots, Frozen

Frozen carrots are prepared from the fresh root of the carrot plant (*Daucus carota*) by washing, sorting, peeling, trimming, and blanching. They are frozen in accordance with good commercial practice and maintained at temperatures necessary for the preservation of the product.

STYLES

Whole. Retain the approximate conformation of a whole carrot.

Halves. Cut longitudinally into two units.

Quarters. Cut longitudinally into four equal units.

Slices. Sliced transversely to the longitudinal axis.

Diced. Cube-shaped units.

Double-Diced. Rectangular shapes which resemble the equivalent of two cube-shaped units.

Strips. Longitudinally cut strips and includes such forms as French style (or shoestring).

Chips. Small-sized units (such as less than one-half cube) and variously shaped pieces or slivers in which the longest-edge dimension approximates not more than ½ inch.

Cut. Cut units which do not conform to any of the foregoing styles.

GRADES

Frozen carrots are graded according to a technical system whereby penalty points are assessed for such factors as edibility, poor appearance, or defects in workmanship. The more penalty points assessed the lower the grade. The grade descriptions which follow are intended only as a general consumer guide. For more detailed information, please consult the source cited below.

U.S. Grade A or U.S. Fancy. Possess similar varietal characteristics and a good flavor and odor characteristic of frozen carrots that are free from objectionable flavors and odors of any kind (as evaluated after thawing and after cooking). They possess an orange-yellow color that is bright and typical of frozen carrots; the presence of green, white, or orange-brown units does not more than slightly affect the appearance or eating quality. They are practically uniform in size and shape and practically free from defects such as units damaged by mechanical injury, unpeeled units, and units blemished or seriously blemished by brown or black internal or external discoloration, sunburn, green or white coloring, pathological injury, or insect injury. The carrots are tender, not fibrous or mushy, and possess a practically uniform texture.

U.S. Grade B or U.S. Extra Standard. Possess similar varietal

characteristics and a normal flavor and odor. They have the typical color of frozen carrots; the color may be slightly dull but not off-color; and the presence of green, white, or orange-brown units does not materially affect the appearance or eating quality of the product. They are reasonably uniform in size and shape for the applicable style and reasonably free from defects. The carrots are reasonably tender and may be variable in texture, but they are not tough, hard, or mushy. There may be present a few units which possess a coarse, fibrous, or mushy texture.

Substandard. Fails to meet the requirements of U.S. Grade B.

Source:
Agricultural Marketing Service, USDA, 7 CFR sections 52.671 to 52.686 (1991), Washington: Government Printing Office.

Cauliflower

Cauliflower is the fresh flowerhead of the cauliflower plant (*Brassica oleracea botrytis*).

GRADES

Cauliflower is graded according to a technical system whereby penalty points are assessed for such factors as edibility, poor appearance, or defects in workmanship. The more penalty points assessed the lower the grade. The grade descriptions which follow are intended only as a general consumer guide. For more detailed information, please consult the source cited below.

U.S. No. 1. Consists of clean heads of cauliflower. The flower clusters are closely united, and the curd is solid. The color is white, creamy white, or cream; the size is not less than 4 inches in diameter. The jacket leaves are of normal color and are not wilted. The butts are smoothly trimmed, and jacket leaves do not exceed the number and length necessary for protection against bruising and do not extend above the crown of the curd. No jacket leaves are required on heads which are individually wrapped or packed with cushions, partitions, or other protective means. The jacket leaves are not caked or badly smeared with dirt or other foreign matter. The product is free from any soft or mushy breakdown of the curd, butt, or leaves. Also free from damage caused by bruising, cuts, discoloration, enlarged bracts, fuzziness, hollow stem, insects, mold, riciness, wilting, and other means. Free from serious damage by any cause.

U.S. Commercial. Consists of heads of cauliflower which meet the requirements for the U.S. No. 1 grade except there is an increased tolerances for defects.

Unclassified. Cauliflower which has not been classified in accordance with either of the foregoing grades. The term *unclassified* is not a grade within the meaning of these standards but is provided as a designation to show that no grade has been applied to the lot.

Source:
Agricultural Marketing Service, USDA, 7 CFR sections 51.540 to 51.556 (1992), Washington: Government Printing Office.

Cauliflower, Frozen

Frozen cauliflower is prepared from the fresh flower heads of the cauliflower plant (*Brassica oleracea botrytis*) by trimming, washing, and blanching and is frozen and maintained at temperatures necessary for preservation of the product.

GRADES

Frozen cauliflower is graded according to a technical system whereby penalty points are assessed for such factors as edibility, poor appearance, or defects in workmanship. The more penalty points assessed the lower the grade. The grade descriptions which follow are intended only as a general consumer guide. For more detailed information, please consult the source cited below.

U.S. Grade A or U.S. Fancy. The cauliflower in this grade possesses similar varietal characteristics. The product after cooking has a good, characteristic, normal flavor and odor and is free from objectionable flavors and odors of any kind. The buds or buttons possess a characteristic white to light cream color over the tops. The color may be slightly variable and the product may possess a characteristic green color or bluish tint on the branches. The product is practically free from defects, contains no seriously damaged clusters, and not more than a total of 15 percent may be poorly trimmed clusters or damaged clusters. The character is such that not less than 80 percent of the cauliflower are firm and complete clusters of buds or buttons. The remainder of the clusters may be reasonably firm and reasonably compact or may be slightly soft, slightly ricey, or slightly fuzzy.

U.S. Grade B or U.S. Extra Standard. The cauliflower in this grade possesses similar varietal characteristics. After cooking, the cauliflower may be lacking in good flavor and odor but is free from objectionable flavors and odors of any kind. The buds or buttons may possess a variable characteristic color ranging from white or light to dull white or dark cream over the tops. May possess a characteristic green color or bluish tint on the branches and greenish yellow to light green modified leaves or bracts. The buds or buttons may possess a color darker than dark cream, but not seriously darkened. The color disappears upon cooking to the extent that the appearance of the product is no more than slightly affected. The product is reasonably free from defects, and the character is such that not less than 60 percent of the cauliflower are at least reasonably firm and compact clusters of buds or buttons. The remainder of the clusters may be soft, ricey, or fuzzy, but not more than 10 percent may be mushy.

Substandard. Fails to meet the requirements of U.S. Grade B or U.S. Extra Standard.

Source:
Agricultural Marketing Service, USDA, 7 CFR sections 52.721 to 52.729 (1991), Washington: Government Printing Office.

Celery

GRADES

Celery is graded according to a technical system whereby penalty points are assessed for such factors as edibility, poor appearance, or defects in workmanship. The more penalty points assessed the lower the grade. The grade descriptions which follow are intended only as a general consumer guide. For more detailed information, please consult the source cited below.

U.S. Extra No. 1. Consists of stalks of celery of similar varietal characteristics and which are well developed, well formed, clean, and compact. Not more than two relatively thin, short, spindly, or coarse and fibrous outer branches remain on the stalk. The main root has been cut off so as not to extend more than 1 inch below the point of attachment of the lowest outer branch. Secondary rootlets are not of such number or length as to materially affect the appearance of the stalk. The appearance is not materially affected by the presence of discolored

Well formed lower limit "bowing" for U.S. Extra No. 1.

Fairly well formed lower limit bowing U.S. No.1

Well formed lower limit "twisting" U.S. Extra No. 1

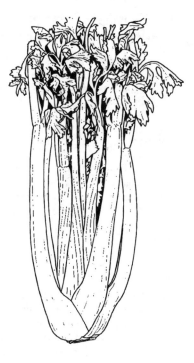

Well formed lower limit combination "bowing & twisting" U.S. Extra No. 1

Fairly well formed lower limit "twisting" U.S. No. 1

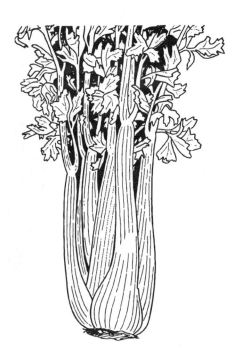

Well developed lower limit width & thickness of midribs U.S. Extra No. 1

Fairly well developed lower limit width & thickness of midribs U.S. No. 1

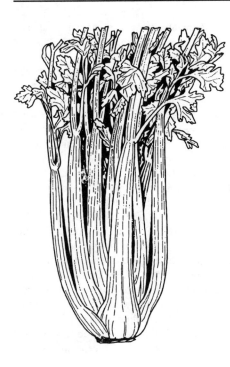

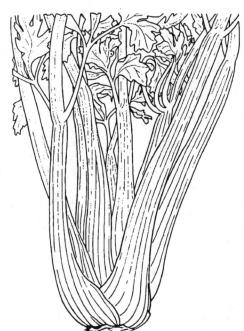

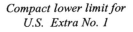

*Compact lower limit for
U.S. Extra No. 1*

*Fairly compact lower limit
for U.S. No. 1*

*Well trimmed. Maximum extent
appearance may be affected by removal
of leaves or portions of leaves. U.S.
Extra No. 1 and U.S. No. 1*

leaves or by excessive removal of leaves. The stalks are free from black heart, brown stem, soft rot, or doubles and are free from damage caused by freezing, growth cracks, horizontal cracks, pithy branches, seed stems, suckers, wilting, blight, other disease, insects, or mechanical or other means. The stalks are green, unless specified as fairly well blanched or mixed blanch. The average midrib length of the outer whorl of branches is not less than 7 inches. Unless otherwise specified, stalks are of such length as to extend from one side, end, or bottom of the container to within 1½ inches of the corresponding opposite side, end, or top of the container.

U.S. No. 1. Consists of stalks of celery of similar varietal characteristics and which are fairly well developed, fairly well formed, well trimmed, fairly compact, and free from black heart and soft rot. Also free from damage caused by freezing, growth cracks, horizontal cracks, pithy branches, seed stems, suckers, dirt doubles, wilting, blight, other disease, insects, or mechanical or other means. Stalks are green; and, unless otherwise specified, the average midrib length of the outer whorl of branches is not less than 6 inches.

U.S. No. 2. Consists of stalks of celery of similar varietal characteristics and which are reasonably well developed, reasonably well formed, fairly well trimmed, and free from black heart and soft rot. Also free from serious damage caused by freezing, growth cracks, horizontal cracks, pithy branches, seed stems, dirt, doubles, wilting, blight, other disease, insects, or mechanical or other means. Stalks are green; and, unless otherwise specified, the average midrib length of the outer whorl of branches is not less than 4 inches.

Unclassified. Stalks of celery which have not been classified in accordance with any of the foregoing grades. The term *unclassified* is not a grade within the meaning of these standards but is provided as a designation to show that no grade has been applied to the lot.

Source:
Agricultural Marketing Service, USDA, 7 CFR sections 51.560 to 51.588 (1992), Washington: Government Printing Office.

Celery, Canned

TYPES OF PACK

Canned Salad Celery (acidified)
Canned Cooked Celery

STYLES

Diced. Stalks that have been cut into approximately cube-shaped units.

Sliced or Cut. Stalks that are cut transversely into units approximately ¾ inch or less in length. Sliced may be one of the following sub-styles:

> *Straight Cut.* Stalks that are cut at approximately right angles to the length of the stalk.
>
> *Bias Cut.* Celery stalks that are cut at approximately 45 degree angle to the length of the stalk.

Chopped. Randomly chopped into units of varying sizes and shapes.

GRADES

Canned celery is graded according to a technical system whereby penalty points are assessed for such factors as edibility, poor appearance, or defects in workmanship. The more penalty points assessed the lower the grade. The grade descriptions which follow are intended only as a general consumer guide. For more detailed information, please consult the source cited below.

U.S. Grade A. Has a good characteristic bright appearance. The celery is uniform in texture and is practically free from coarse, stringy, or tough units. The celery is crisp and firm. It is pliable and tender, but not soft. The color is uniform in the range between green to white, and the flavor is free from objectionable flavor and odor of any kind.

U.S. Grade B. The celery has a reasonably good characteristic bright appearance. It lacks uniformity in texture and is reasonably free from coarse, stringy, or tough units. The celery lacks crispness and firmness. It lacks pliability and tenderness and may be soft, but not mushy. The color lacks uniformity in the range between green to white.

Substandard. Fails to meet the requirements for U.S. Grade B.

Source:
Agricultural Marketing Service, USDA, 7 CFR sections 52.6571 to 52.6582 (1991), Washington: Government Printing Office.

Celery, Stalks

GRADES

Celery stalks are graded according to a technical system whereby penalty points are assessed for such factors as edibility, poor appearance, or defects in workmanship. The more penalty points assessed the lower the grade. The grade descriptions which follow are intended only as a general consumer guide. For more detailed information, please consult the source cited below.

U.S. Grade AA. Stalks of celery of similar varietal characteristics and which are well developed and have good heart formation. The outside coarse and damaged branches have been removed, and the root or roots have been neatly trimmed to a reasonable length for the size of the stalk. They are clean, fairly compact, and free from black heart, brown stem, decay (except dry type crater rot), and doubles. Also free from damage caused by crater rot, wilting, cutworms, freezing, suckers, growth cracks, hollow crown, pithy branches, seed stems, rust, cracked stem,

other diseases, insects, or mechanical or other means. The average midrib length of the outer whorl of branches on stalks in this grade is not less than 7 inches.

U.S. Grade A. Consists of stalks of celery of similar varietal characteristics and which are fairly well developed and have fairly good heart formation. They are clean, well trimmed, and not badly spread. They are free from black heart, decay (except dry type crater rot), and doubles. Also free from damage caused by crater rot, brown stem, wilting, cutworms, freezing, suckers, growth cracks, hollow crown, pithy branches, seed stems, rust, cracked stem, other diseases, insects, or mechanical or other means. The average midrib length of the outer whorl of branches on stalks in this grade is not less than 5 inches.

U.S. Grade B. Consists of stalks of celery of similar varietal characteristics and which are fairly well developed. They are clean, well trimmed, and free from black heart, decay (except dry type crater rot), and doubles. Also free from serious damage caused by crater rot, brown stem, wilting, cutworms, freezing, suckers, growth cracks, hollow crown, pithy branches, seed stems, rust, cracked stem, other diseases, insects, or mechanical or other means. The average midrib length of the outer whorl of branches on stalks in this grade is not less than 4 inches.

BLANCHING

There are no requirements in the grades as to blanching. However, celery stalks may be classed as *green* when they have a medium to dark green appearance, *fairly well blanched* when the midrib portions of the branches on the stalks are generally of a light greenish to creamy white color, or *well blanched* when the midrib portions of the branches on the stalks are generally of a creamy white color. Not more than 5 percent of the stalks in any lot may fail to meet the requirements of any of the above classes.

Source:
Agricultural Marketing Service, USDA, 7 CFR sections 51.595 to 51.613 (1992), Washington: Government Printing Office.

Collard Greens or Broccoli Greens

These standards are applicable to collard greens, broccoli greens, or mixtures of the two which may consist of leaves, parts of leaves, plants, or mixtures of leaves and plants.

GRADES

U.S. No. 1. Collard greens or broccoli greens of similar varietal characteristics. They are not more than slightly wilted and are not tough or excessively fibrous. The appearance of the greens is not materially affected by the presence of dirt, dust, or other foreign material. The main stem does not extend more than 1 inch below the point of attachment of the first leaf. The greens have a characteristic color for the variety or type. They are free from decay and from damage caused by coarse stalks and seed stems, discoloration, freezing, foreign material, disease, insects, or mechanical or other means.

Unclassified. Collard greens or broccoli greens which have not been classified in accordance with the foregoing grade. The term *unclassified* is not a grade within the meaning of these standards but is provided as a designation to show that no definite grade has been applied to the lot.

Source:
Agricultural Marketing Service, USDA, 7 CFR sections 51.520 to 51.531 (1992), Washington: Government Printing Office.

Corn, Canned Cream Style

Canned, cream style corn is the canned product properly prepared from the clean, sound, succulent kernels of sweet corn.

GRADES

Canned, cream style corn is graded according to a technical system whereby penalty points are assessed for such factors as edibility, poor appearance, or defects in workmanship. The more penalty points assessed the lower the grade. The grade descriptions which follow are intended only as a general consumer guide. For more detailed information, please consult the source cited below.

U.S. Grade A or U.S. Fancy. Possesses similar varietal characteristics. The cut kernels are tender and possess a practically uniform color typical of tender sweet corn. The product is bright and practically free from off-variety kernels. The cream style corn, after stirring and emptying from the container to a dry flat surface, possesses a heavy cream-like consistency with not more than a slight appearance of curdling and forms a slightly mounded mass; at the end of two minutes after emptying, there is practically no separation of free liquor. The kernels are in the milk, early cream, or middle cream stage of maturity and have a tender texture. The corn has a very good characteristic flavor and odor typical of tender canned sweet corn.

U.S. Grade B or U.S. Extra Standard. The quality of canned, cream style corn that possesses similar varietal characteristics. The corn is reasonably tender and has a reasonably uniform color which may lack brightness but not to the extent that the appearance is materially affected. It is reasonably free from off-variety kernels. The cream style corn, after stirring and emptying from the container to a dry flat surface, has a reasonably good creamy consistency (with not more than a moderate appearance of curdling) and may flow just enough to level off to a nearly uniform depth or may be moderately stiff and moderately mounded; at the end of two minutes, there may be a slight separation of free liquor. The kernels are in the middle cream stage to late cream stage of maturity and have a reasonably tender texture. They are reasonably free from defects and possesses a good flavor.

U.S. Grade C or U.S. Standard. The kernels possess a fairly

uniform color that may be dull, but not to the extent that the appearance is seriously affected, and is fairly free from off-variety kernels. The consistency, after stirring and emptying the corn on a dry flat surface, may be thin (but not excessively thin), or thick but not excessively dry, pasty, or crumbly, or moderately but not excessively curdled. At the end of two minutes after emptying on the dry flat surface, there may be a moderate but not excessive separation of free liquor. The kernels are in the early dough or dough stage of maturity and may be firm, but not hard or tough.

Substandard. Fails to meet the requirements of U.S. Grade C or U.S. Standard and may or may not meet the minimum standards of quality.

Source:
Agricultural Marketing Service, USDA, 7 CFR sections 52.851 to 52.863 (1991), Washington: Government Printing Office.

Corn, Canned Whole Kernel or Whole Grain

Canned, whole kernel (or whole grain) corn is the canned product properly prepared from the clean, sound, succulent kernels of sweet corn. The product is considered *Vacuum Pack* or *Vacuum Packed* when the liquid in the container is not more than 20 percent of the net weight and when the container is closed under conditions creating a high vacuum.

COLOR

White
Golden or Yellow

GRADES

Canned, whole kernel corn is graded according to a technical system whereby penalty points are assessed for such factors as edibility, poor appearance, or defects in workmanship. The more penalty points assessed the lower the grade. The grade descriptions which follow are intended only as a general consumer guide. For more detailed information, please consult the source cited below.

U.S. Grade A or U.S. Fancy. The kernels possess a practically uniform color typical of tender sweet corn. The product is bright and practically free from off-variety kernels. The kernels are in the milk or early cream stage of maturity and have a tender texture. The product, including added seasoning ingredients, has a very good characteristic flavor and odor typical of tender canned sweet corn. The appearance of the product is not more than slightly affected by the presence of ragged cut kernels, torn kernels, irregular cut kernels, and kernels with attached cob tissue.

U.S. Grade B or U.S. Extra Standard. The kernels possess a reasonably uniform, typical color that may lack brightness, but not to the extent that the appearance is materially affected. It is reasonably free from off-variety kernels. The kernels are in the cream stage of maturity and have a reasonably tender texture. The product, including added seasoning ingredients, has a good characteristic flavor and odor typical of reasonably tender canned sweet corn. The appearance of the product is not materially affected by the presence of ragged cut kernels, torn kernels, irregular cut kernels, and kernels with attached cob tissue.

U.S. Grade C or U.S. Standard. The kernels possess a fairly uniform, typical color that may be dull, but not to the extent that the appearance is seriously affected. It is fairly free from off-variety kernels. The kernels are in the early dough or dough stage and may be firm, but not hard or tough. The product may be lacking in good flavor and odor but is free from objectionable flavors and odors of any kind. The appearance of the product is not seriously affected by the presence of ragged cut kernels, torn kernels, irregular cut kernels, and kernels with attached cob tissue.

Substandard. Canned, whole kernel (or whole grain) corn that fails to meet the requirements of U.S. Grade C or U.S. Standard and may or may not meet the minimum standards of quality for canned whole kernel (or whole grain) corn.

Source:
Agricultural Marketing Service, USDA, 7 CFR sections 52.881 to 52.894 (1991), Washington: Government Printing Office.
Food and Drug Administration, "Canned Corn," 21 CFR 155.130 (1991), Washington: Government Printing Office.

Corn, Frozen Whole Kernel or Whole Grain

Frozen, whole kernel (or whole grain) corn is the frozen product prepared from fresh, clean, sound, succulent kernels of sweet corn of either the white or golden (or yellow) varieties by removing the husk and silk and by sorting, trimming, washing, and blanching the corn before or after removal from the cob. The whole kernel (or whole grain) corn is frozen in accordance with good commercial practice and maintained at temperatures necessary for the preservation of the product.

COLOR

Golden or Yellow
White

GRADES

Frozen, whole kernel corn is graded according to a technical system whereby penalty points are assessed for such factors as edibility, poor appearance, or defects in workmanship. The more penalty points assessed the lower the grade. The grade descriptions which follow are intended only as a general consumer guide. For more detailed information, please consult the source cited below.

U.S. Grade A or U.S. Fancy. The quality of frozen, whole kernel (or whole grain) corn that possesses similar varietal characteristics and, after cooking, has a good characteristic normal flavor and odor. It is free from objectionable flavors and objectionable odors of any kind. The kernels possess a practically uniform color typical of tender sweet corn. The product is bright and is practically free from off-variety kernels. The kernels are in the milk or early cream stage of maturity and have a tender texture. The product is practically free from pieces of cob, husk, silk, other harmless extraneous vegetable matter, pulled kernels, ragged kernels, crushed kernels, loose skins, and damaged or seriously damaged kernels.

U.S. Grade B or U.S. Extra Standard. The quality of frozen, whole kernel (or whole grain) corn that possesses similar varietal characteristics, a good flavor and odor, is reasonably tender, possesses a reasonably good color, and is reasonably free from defects.

U.S. Grade C or U.S. Standard. The quality of frozen, whole kernel (or whole grain) corn that possesses similar varietal characteristics. The product, after cooking, may be lacking in good flavor and odor but is free from objectionable flavors and odors of any kind. The kernels possess a fairly uniform color typical of fairly tender sweet corn. The product may be dull, but not to the extent that the appearance is seriously affected; it is fairly free from off-variety kernels. The kernels are in the early dough or dough stage and have a fairly tender texture. Possesses a fairly good color and is fairly free from defects.

Substandard. The quality of frozen, whole kernel (or whole grain) corn that fails to meet the requirements of U.S. Grade C or U.S. Standard.

Source:
Agricultural Marketing Service, USDA, 7 CFR sections (1991), Washington: Government Printing Office.

Corn, Green

GRADES

Green corn is graded according to a technical system whereby penalty points are assessed for such factors as edibility, poor appearance, or defects in workmanship. The more penalty points assessed the lower the grade. The grade descriptions which follow are intended only as a general consumer guide. For more detailed information, please consult the source cited below.

U.S. Fancy. Consists of ears of green corn of similar varietal characteristics and which are practically free from loose husks. The shank is not more than 6 inches in length and does not extend more than 1 inch beyond the point of attachment of the outside husk. The ears are fairly straight and are not stunted. They are free from smut decay, worms, or insect injury. Also free from injury caused by rust, discoloration, birds, disease, or mechanical or other means. Cobs are fairly well filled with plump and milky kernels and well covered with fresh husks. The length of each cob is not less than 6 inches, and the ears are not clipped.

U.S. No. 1. Consists of ears of green corn of similar varietal characteristics and which are well trimmed, well developed, and free from smut and decay. Also free from injury caused by rust and from damage caused by discoloration, birds, worms, other insects, other disease, or mechanical or other means. Cobs are fairly well filled with plump and milky kernels and fairly well covered with fresh husks. Each ear may be clipped (neatly cut off at approximately a right angle to the longitudinal axis), but each clipped ear is properly clipped. Unless otherwise specified, the length of each cob, clipped or unclipped, is not less than 5 inches.

U.S. No. 2. Consists of ears of green corn of similar varietal characteristics and which are fairly well trimmed and fairly well developed. They are free from smut and decay and free from serious damage caused by birds, worms, other insects, other disease, or mechanical or other means. Cobs are not poorly filled. Kernels are plump and milky and fairly well covered with fresh husks. Each ear may be clipped, but each clipped ear should be properly clipped. Unless otherwise specified, the length of each cob, clipped or unclipped, is not less than 4 inches.

Unclassified. Consists of ears of green corn which have not been classified in accordance with any of the foregoing grades. The term *unclassified* is not a grade within the meaning of these standards but is provided as a designation to show that no grade has been applied to the lot.

Source:
Agricultural Marketing Service, USDA, 7 CFR sections 51.835 to 51.857 (1992), Washington: Government Printing Office.

Corn, Sweet for Processing

GRADES

Sweet corn for processing is graded according to a technical system whereby penalty points are assessed for such factors as edibility, poor appearance, or defects in workmanship. The more penalty points assessed the lower the grade. The grade descriptions which follow are intended only as a general consumer guide. For more detailed information, please consult the source cited below.

U.S. No. 1. Ears of sweet corn of similar color characteristics and which are fresh and free from damage by freezing, cross pollination, denting, worms, birds, fermentation, smut, other disease, or other means. Kernels on each ear have developed beyond the blister stage but have not reached the hard stage of maturity.

U.S. No. 2. Ears of sweet corn of similar color characteristics and which are fresh and free from damage by freezing, fermentation, smut, or other disease. They are also free from serious damage by cross pollination, denting, worms, birds, or other means. Kernels on each ear have developed beyond the blister stage but have not reached the hard stage of maturity. Unless otherwise specified, each ear is not less than an average of 3 inches of the cob covered with kernels.

Culls. Cars of sweet corn which fail to meet the requirements of U.S. No. 2 grade.

MATURITY CLASSIFICATIONS

In addition to the grade classification, a lot of sweet corn may be classified for general overall maturity in terms of one of the following maturity classifications:

A-1. Includes ears in the milk stage or younger. More than half are in the very tender early milk stage, and none of the remainder are bordering on the cream stage.

A-2. Includes ears in the milk stage or younger with not more than 5 percent bordering on the cream stage.

A-3. Includes ears in the milk stage with more than 5 percent bordering on the cream stage.

A-B. Includes ears generally in the milk stage with 1 to 10 percent in the cream stage.

B. Includes ears mostly in the milk stage with more than 10 percent in the cream stage.

B-C. Includes ears generally in either the milk or the cream stage with 1 to 10 per stage.

C. Includes ears more than 10 percent of which are in the dough stage.

Blister Stage. The kernels are not sufficiently mature for processing. They are small, underdeveloped, have very tender pericarps, and contain watery or cloudy liquid which runs freely when released.

Milk Stage. The kernels are moderately to well filled out, have tender pericarps which break with light pressure from the thumb nail, and contain a milky or thin creamy liquid which spreads or runs moderately when released.

Cream Stage. The kernels have attained full size, have fairly tender pericarps which break with moderate pressure from the thumb nail, and contain a thick creamy substance which spreads or runs very little when released.

Dough Stage. The kernels have attained full size, have tough pericarps which require heavy pressure from the thumb nail to break, and contain a soft doughy substance which does not spread or run when released.

Hard Stage. The kernels have very tough pericarps, and contain a heavy, sticky, doughy substance. Ears in this stage are overmature for any processing purpose.

Source:
Agricultural Marketing Service, USDA, 7 CFR sections 51.3365 to 51.3379 (1992), Washington: Government Printing Office.

Corn on the Cob, Frozen

Frozen corn on the cob is the product which is prepared from sound, properly matured, fresh, sweet corn ears by removing husk and silk and by sorting, trimming, and washing to assure a clean and wholesome product. The ears are blanched, then frozen and stored at temperatures necessary for the preservation of the product.

STYLES

Trimmed. Ears trimmed at both ends to remove tip and stalk ends and/or cut to specific lengths.

Natural. Ears trimmed at the stalk end only to remove all or most of the stalk.

LENGTHS

Regular. Ears which are predominantly over 3½ inches in length.

Short. Ears which are predominantly 3½ inches or less in length.

COLOR

Golden or Yellow

White

GRADES

Corn on the cob is graded according to a technical system whereby penalty points are assessed for such factors as edibility, poor appearance, or defects in workmanship. The more penalty points assessed the lower the grade. The grade descriptions which follow are intended only as a general consumer guide. For more detailed information, please consult the source cited below.

U.S. Grade A or U.S. Fancy. The product has a good, characteristic, normal flavor and odor and is free from objectionable flavors and odors of any kind. The corn has a typical, bright color, and the ears are well filled with kernels. None of the ears are materially affected by missing or underdeveloped kernels. The kernels are in the milk or early cream stage of maturity, and the pericarp is reasonably tender. They are practically free from defects such as broken and blemished kernels, poorly trimmed ears, attached stalk, husk, and readily noticeable silk.

U.S. Grade B or U.S. Extra Standard. The product may be lacking in good flavor and odor but is free from objectionable flavors and odors of any kind. The color may be slightly dull but is not of abnormal color. The ears are reasonably well filled with kernels, and the appearance of the ears is not seriously affected by missing or underdeveloped kernels. The kernels are in the cream stage or better stage of maturity, and the pericarp is fairly tender. They are at least reasonably free from defects.

Substandard. Fails to meet the requirements of U. S. Grade B.

STAGES

Blister Stage. The kernel contents are either thin and watery, slightly cloudy, or translucent. The pericarp is generally very pale in color. An ear is considered to be in the blister stage if more than one-fifth of the kernels are in the blister stage.

Milk Stage. The kernel contents are opaque and viscous. Light pressure is required to remove contents.

Early Cream Stage. The kernel contents are slightly creamy and viscous. Reasonably firm pressure is required to remove contents which show only slight separation of clear liquid.

Cream Stage. The kernel contents are creamy and thick. Firm pressure is required to remove contents which show no free liquid.

Dough or Over-Mature Stage. The kernel contents are semisolid or hard and require considerable pressure to remove contents which appears starchy or dough-like.

Source:
Agricultural Marketing Service, USDA, 7 CFR sections 52.931 to 52.946 (1991), Washington: Government Printing Office.

Corn on the Cob, Husked

GRADES

Husked corn on the cob is graded according to a technical system whereby penalty points are assessed for such factors as edibility, poor appearance, or defects in workmanship. The more penalty points assessed the lower the grade. The grade descriptions which follow are intended only as a general consumer guide. For more detailed information, please consult the source cited below.

U.S. Grade A. Consists of husked ears or portions of ears of corn on the cob of similar varietal characteristics. The ears are practically free from husks and silk, and the shank does not extend more than ½ inch from the base of the cob. The ears are not stunted and are clean, free from decay and insect injury, and free from damage. Cobs are well filled with tender, plump, and milky kernels. The rows of kernels show fairly uniform development, and the appearance of the unit is not materially affected by poorly developed rows. The kernels break with only moderate pressure from the thumbnail. Each ear may be clipped (neatly cut off at approximately a right angle to the longitudinal axis) at one or both ends, but the length of each unit is not less than 3 inches. Each clipped ear is properly clipped.

U.S. Grade B. Consists of husked ears or portions of ears of corn on the cob which meet the requirements of U.S. Grade A except for an increased tolerance for defects.

Off-Grade. Husked ears or portions of ears of corn on the cob which fail to meet the requirements of the foregoing grades.

Source:
Agricultural Marketing Service, (Consumer Standards) USDA, 7 CFR sections 51.810 to 51.822 (1992), Washington: Government Printing Office.

Cucumbers

GRADES

Cucumbers are graded according to a technical system whereby penalty points are assessed for such factors as edibility, poor appearance, or defects in workmanship. The more penalty points assessed the lower the grade. The grade descriptions which follow are intended only as a general consumer guide. For more detailed information, please consult the source cited below.

U.S. Fancy. Cucumbers which are well colored, well formed, and not overgrown. They are fresh, firm, and free from decay, sunscald, and injury caused by scars. Also free from damage caused by yellowing, sunburn, dirt or other foreign material, freezing, mosaic or other disease, insects, cuts, bruises, or mechanical or other means. The maximum diameter of each cucumber is not more than 2⅜ inches, and the length of each cucumber is not less than 6 inches.

U.S. Extra No. 1. A combination of U.S. Fancy and U.S. No. 1 cucumbers. At least 50 percent of the cucumbers in the lot meet the requirements of the U.S. Fancy grade, and the remainder meet the requirements of the U.S. No. 1 grade. The maximum diameter of each cucumber is not more than 2⅜ inches, and the length of each cucumber is not less than 6 inches.

U.S. No. 1. Cucumbers which are fairly well colored, fairly well formed, and not overgrown. They are fresh, firm, and free from decay, sunscald, and damage caused by scars, yellowing, sunburn, dirt or other foreign materials, freezing, mosaic or other disease, insects, cuts, bruises, or mechanical or other means. Unless otherwise specified, the maximum diameter of each cucumber is not more than 2⅜ inches, and the length of each cucumber is not less than 6 inches.

U.S. No. 1 Small. Cucumbers which meet all requirements for the U.S. No. 1 grade except for size. The diameter of each cucumber is not less than 1½ inches or more than 2 inches. There are no requirements for length.

U.S. No. 1 Large. Cucumbers which meet all requirements for the U.S. No. 1 grade except for size. The minimum diameter of each cucumber is not less than 2¼ inches; and, unless otherwise specified, the length of each cucumber is not less than 6 inches. There are no maximum diameter and length requirements.

U.S. No. 2. Cucumbers which are moderately colored, not badly deformed, and not overgrown. They are fresh, firm, free from decay, and free from damage caused by freezing, sunscald, and cuts. They are free from serious damage caused by scars, yellowing, sunburn, dirt or other foreign material, mosaic or other disease, insects, bruises, or mechanical or other means. Unless otherwise specified, the maximum diameter of each cucumber is not more than 2⅜ inches, and the length of each cucumber is not less than 5 inches

Unclassified. Cucumbers which have not been classified in accordance with any of the foregoing grades. The term *unclassified* is not a grade within the meaning of these standards but is provided as a designation to show that no grade has been applied to the lot.

Source:
Agricultural Marketing Service, USDA, 7 CFR sections 51.2220 to 51.2239 (1992), Washington: Government Printing Office.

Dandelion Greens

GRADES

Dandelion greens are graded according to a technical system

whereby penalty points are assessed for such factors as edibility, poor appearance, or defects in workmanship. The more penalty points assessed the lower the grade. The grade descriptions which follow are intended only as a general consumer guide. For more detailed information, please consult the source cited below.

U.S. No. 1. Dandelion greens of similar varietal characteristics and which are fresh and not more than slightly wilted. They are fairly tender, are not tough or excessively fibrous, and are free of mud, dirt, etc. They are well trimmed (cut at the crown of the root or cut so that the roots do not extend more than approximately 1½ inches below the crown). Also free from decay and free from damage caused by seed stems, discoloration, freezing, foreign material, disease, insects, or mechanical or other means.

Unclassified. Dandelion greens which have not been classified in accordance with the foregoing grade. The term *unclassified* is not a grade within the meaning of these standards but is provided as a designation to show that no definite grade has been applied to the lot.

Source:
Agricultural Marketing Service, USDA, 7 CFR sections 51.2585 to 51.2596 (1992), Washington: Government Printing Office.

Eggplant

GRADES

Eggplant is graded according to a technical system whereby penalty points are assessed for such factors as edibility, poor appearance, or defects in workmanship. The more penalty points assessed the lower the grade. The grade descriptions which follow are intended only as a general consumer guide. For more detailed information, please consult the source cited below.

U.S. Fancy. Eggplants of similar varietal characteristics and which have a uniformly good color over practically the entire surface. They are not flabby, soft, or shriveled. They are clean and well shaped. The eggplant has the normal shape (the shape may be slightly irregular, provided the appearance of the eggplant is not more than slightly affected). They are free from decay and worm holes and from injury caused by scars, freezing, disease, insects, or mechanical or other means.

U.S. No. 1. Eggplants of similar varietal characteristics and which may have streaks of green color that do not materially affect appearance. They are firm, clean, and fairly well shaped (may be slightly abnormal in shape but not unpleasingly so). They are free from decay and worm holes and free from damage caused by scars, freezing, disease, insects, or mechanical or other means.

U.S. No. 2. Eggplants which are firm, free from decay, and free from serious damage caused by freezing, disease, insects, or mechanical or other means that seriously affect the appearance, the edibility, or the shipping quality of the eggplant.

Unclassified. Eggplants which have not been classified in accordance with any of the foregoing grades. The term *unclassified* is not a grade within the meaning of these standards but is provided as a designation to show that no grade has been applied to the lot.

Source:
Agricultural Marketing Service, USDA, 7 CFR sections 51.2190 to 51.2207 (1992), Washington: Government Printing Office.

Figs, Dried

Dried figs are the fruit of the fig tree (*Ficus carica*) from which the greater portion of moisture has been removed. The dried figs are prepared from clean, sound fruit and are sorted and thoroughly cleaned to assure a clean, sound, wholesome product. The figs may or may not be sulfured or otherwise bleached.

COLOR TYPES

White figs or White Type Figs. White to dark brown in color, includes such varieties as Adriatic, Calimyrna, and Kadota.

Black Figs or Black Type Figs. Black or dark purple in color, as in the Mission varieties.

DRIED FIGS

Style I. Whole.

Style I (a). Whole dried figs packed without special arrangement in a container.

Style I (b). Whole dried figs which are changed from their original dried form by purposely flattening and shaping and are placed in a definite arrangement in a container. The dried figs may or may not be split slightly across the eye but are not split to the extent that the seed cavity is materially exposed.

Style I (c). Whole dried figs which are changed from their original dried form by purposely flattening and shaping and are placed in a staggered-layer arrangement in a container. The figs are split across the base to the extent that the seed cavity may be materially exposed.

Style II, Sliced (or Sliced Figs). Dried whole figs that have been cut into slices not less than ¼ inch in thickness, and such slices are not recut showing more than two cut surfaces.

SIZES

Adriatic or Kadota

No. 1 (Jumbo Size). 1⁹⁄₁₆ inches or larger in width.

No. 2 (Extra Fancy Size). 1¹⁵⁄₁₆ inches to, but not including, 1⁹⁄₁₆ inches in width.

No. 3 (Fancy Size). 1³⁄₁₆ inches to, but not including, 1¹⁵⁄₁₆ inches in width.

No. 4 (Extra Choice Size). 1¹⁄₁₆ inches to, but not including, 1³⁄₁₆ inches in width.

No. 5 (Choice Size). ¹⁵⁄₁₆ inch to, but not including, 1¹⁄₁₆ inches in width.

No. 6 (Standard Size). Less than ¹⁵⁄₁₆ inch in width.

Calimyrna

No. 1 (Jumbo Size). 1⁹⁄₁₆ inches or larger in width.

No. 2 (Extra Fancy Size). 1⁶⁄₁₆ inches to, but not including, 1⁹⁄₁₆ inches in width.

No. 3 (Fancy Size). 1³⁄₁₆ inches to, but not including, 1⁶⁄₁₆ inches in width.

No. 4 (Extra Choice Size). 1¹⁄₁₆ inches to, but not including, 1³⁄₁₆ inches in width.

No. 5 (Choice Size). ¹⁵⁄₁₆ inch to, but not including, 1¹⁄₁₆ inches in width.

No. 6 (Standard Size). Less than ¹⁵⁄₁₆ inch in width.

Black Mission

No. 1 (Jumbo Size). 1¹⁵⁄₁₆ inches or larger in width.

No. 2 (Extra Fancy Size). 1³⁄₁₆ inches to, but not including, 1⁵⁄₁₆ inches in width.

No. 3 (Fancy Size). 1¹⁄₁₆ inches to, but not including, 1³⁄₁₆ inches in width.

No. 4 (Extra Choice Size). ¹⁵⁄₁₆ inch to, but not including, 1¹⁄₁₆ inches in width.

No. 5 (Choice Size). ¹³⁄₁₆ inch to, but not including, ¹⁵⁄₁₆ inch in width.

No. 6 (Standard Size). Less than ¹³⁄₁₆ inch in width.

GRADES

Dried figs are graded according to a technical system whereby penalty points are assessed for such factors as edibility, poor appearance, or defects in workmanship. The more penalty points assessed the lower the grade. The grade descriptions which follow are intended only as a general consumer guide. For more detailed information, please consult the source cited below.

U.S. Grade A or U.S. Fancy. The figs are of one variety or similar varieties. They are well-ripened. The interior shows very good sugary tissue development that is syrupy and gum-like in consistency and texture. The figs are practically uniform in size with a uniform, typical color. They have a clean and distinct dried fig flavor and odor free from any flavors or odors such as scorching or caramelization and free from other slight abnormal flavors or odors.

U.S. Grade B or U.S. Choice. The figs are of one variety or similar varieties. They are reasonably well-ripened. The interior shows good sugary tissue development that is gummy but slightly fibrous in consistency and texture, *or* one third or less of the interior of the fig may be entirely lacking in sugary tissue, if the remainder of the interior of the fig is syrupy and gum-like in consistency and texture. They are reasonably uniform in size and possess a reasonably uniform typical color. They have a clean and distinct dried fig flavor and odor which may possess very slight flavors or odors characteristic of slight scorching or slight caramelization. May possess other very slight abnormal flavors or odors.

U.S. Grade C or U.S. Standard. The figs are of one variety or of similar varieties. They are fairly well-ripened. The sugary tissue in the interior of the fig is gummy and fibrous in consistency and texture, *or* one-third or less of the interior of the fig may be entirely lacking in sugary tissue, if the remainder of the interior of the fig is gummy but slightly fibrous in consistency and texture, *or* more than one-third (but less than one-half) of the interior of the fig may be entirely lacking in sugary tissue, if the remainder of the interior of the fig is syrupy and gum-like in consistency and texture. They are fairly uniform in size and have a fairly uniform typical color. They have a clean and distinct dried fig flavor and odor which may possess slight flavors or odors characteristic of scorching or caramelization. They may not possess any flavor in amounts resulting in objectionable or off-flavors.

Source:
Agricultural Marketing Service, USDA, 7 CFR sections 52.1021 to 52.1032 (1992), Washington: Government Printing Office.

French Fried Potatoes, Frozen

Frozen French fried potatoes are prepared from mature, sound, white or Irish potatoes (*Solanum tuberosum*). The potatoes are washed, sorted, and trimmed as necessary to assure a clean and wholesome product. The potatoes may or may not be cut into pieces. The potatoes are processed in accordance with good commercial practice which includes deep frying or blanching in a suitable fat or oil and which may include the addition of any ingredient permissible under the Federal Food, Drug, and Cosmetic Act. The prepared product is frozen and stored at temperatures necessary for its preservation.

FRY COLOR TYPE

The term fry color refers to the color change which occurs solely because of the frying process. Potato units may be designated as to fry color in accordance with USDA color standards for frozen French fried potatoes:

Extra Light
Light
Medium Light
Medium
Dark

TYPES

Retail Type. Intended for household consumption.
Institutional Type. Intended for the hotel, restaurant, or other large feeding establishment trade.

STYLES

Straight Cut. Smooth cut surfaces.
Crinkle Cut. Corrugated cut surfaces.
Strips. This style consists of elongated pieces of potato with practically parallel sides and of any cross-sectional shape.
Shoestring. Strips, either straight cut or crinkle cut, with a cross-sectional area predominantly less than that of a square measuring ⅜ by ⅜ inch.
Slices. This style consists of pieces of potato with two practically parallel sides and which otherwise conform generally to the shape of the potato.
Dices. Cut into approximate cubes.

Rissole. Whole or nearly whole potatoes.

LENGTH

The length designations apply to strip styles only.
Extra Long. Eighty percent or more are 2 inches or longer in length, and 30 percent or more are 3 inches or longer in length.
Long. Seventy percent or more are 2 inches or longer in length, and 15 percent or more are 3 inches or longer in length.
Medium. Fifty percent or more are 2 inches or longer in length.
Short. Less than 50 percent are 2 inches or longer in length.

GRADES

Frozen French fried potatoes are graded according to a technical system whereby penalty points are assessed for such factors as edibility, poor appearance, or defects in workmanship. The more penalty points assessed the lower the grade. The grade descriptions which follow are intended only as a general consumer guide. For more detailed information, please consult the source cited below.

U.S. Grade A or U.S. Fancy. Have the good characteristic flavor and odor of properly prepared French fried potatoes free from rancidity and bitterness. They have the bright, characteristic color of properly prepared frozen French fried potatoes. They are practically uniform in size and symmetry and practically free from defects. The external surfaces of the units are moderately crisp, show no noticeable separation from the inner portion, and are not excessively oily. The interior portions are well cooked, tender, and practically free from sogginess, (shoestring style strips and dices may be moderately crisp throughout).

U.S. Grade B or U.S. Extra Standard. Have a reasonably good flavor and a characteristic frozen French fry potato color which may be dull but not off-color. They are reasonably uniform in size and symmetry, reasonably free from defects, and possess a reasonably good texture. The external surfaces of the units may be slightly hard or slightly tough, show no more than a moderate separation from the interior portion, and are not excessively oily. The interior portions are well cooked, reasonably tender, and reasonably free from sogginess.

Substandard. Fail to meet the requirements of U.S. Grade B.

Source:
Agricultural Marketing Service, USDA, 7 CFR sections 52.2391 to 52.2404 (1991), Washington: Government Printing Office.

Hominy, Canned

Canned hominy is the canned product prepared from clean, sound field corn, either white or golden (yellow), by removal of the pericarp, precooking or other processing, soaking, and sorting. The product is packed in a liquid packing medium or in a gelled packing medium, in accordance with good commercial practice, and is sufficiently processed by heat to assure preservation in hermetically sealed containers. *Vacuum pack* means packed in not more than 20 percent, by weight, of liquid packing medium and the container is closed under conditions creating a high vacuum.

COLOR

White

Golden or Yellow

STYLES

Style I Whole. Prepared from whole kernels of white or yellow field corn and packed in a liquid packing medium.

Style II Grits. Prepared from coarse kernel particles of white or yellow field corn from which the pericarp and germ have been removed and packed in a liquid packing medium. Vacuum pack canned hominy grits means packed in not more than 20 percent, by weight, of liquid packing medium and the container is closed under conditions creating a high vacuum.

Style III Grits, Gelled Pack. Prepared from coarse kernel particles of white or yellow field corn from which the pericarp and germ have been removed and packed in a gelled packing medium.

GRADES

Canned hominy is graded according to a technical system whereby penalty points are assessed for such factors as edibility, poor appearance, or defects in workmanship. The more penalty points assessed the lower the grade. The grade descriptions which follow are intended only as a general consumer guide. For more detailed information, please consult the source cited below.

U.S. Grade A or U.S. Fancy. Possesses similar varietal characteristics and a normal flavor. The kernels possess a practically uniform, bright color typical of white or golden (yellow) hominy. The product contains not more than 2 percent of off-variety kernels. The product is practically free from harmless extraneous material such as pieces of cob, hulls, and loose germs. The kernels or pieces of kernels may be reasonably firm and tender and reasonably free from hard kernels and from excessively soft kernels or pieces of kernels. The liquor is light in color, may be slightly cloudy or slightly opaque, and may be slightly viscous, but it is reasonably free from starchy globules and sediment.

U.S. Grade C or U.S. Standard. Possesses similar varietal characteristics and a normal flavor. The kernels or pieces of kernels may possess a fairly uniform, typical color and may be slightly dull. The product contains not more than 3 percent of off-variety kernels or pieces of kernels. It is fairly free from defects and possesses a fairly good character. The kernels or pieces of kernels may be fairly firm and tender and fairly free from hard kernels and from excessively soft kernels or pieces of kernels. It has a fairly good liquor which may be definitely cloudy or opaque and viscous but not gelled. It is fairly free from starchy globules and sediment.

Substandard. Fails to meet the requirements of U.S. Grade C.

Source:

Agricultural Marketing Service, USDA, 7 CFR sections 52.3281 to 52.3295 (1991), Washington: Government Printing Office.

Kale

GRADES

Kale is graded according to a technical system whereby penalty points are assessed for such factors as edibility, poor appearance, or defects in workmanship. The more penalty points assessed the lower the grade. The grade descriptions which follow are intended only as a general consumer guide. For more detailed information, please consult the source cited below.

U.S. No. 1. Plants of kale which have the same general character of growth and color. The butt is trimmed off to not more than ¾ inch from the point of attachment of the outer leaves. Yellow, discolored, dried, or otherwise damaged leaves which materially affect the appearance of the plant have been removed. The plants are free from decay and from damage caused by yellow or discolored leaves, seed stems, wilting, bud burn, freezing, dirt, disease, insects, or mechanical or other means.

U.S. Commercial. Plants of kale which meet the requirements of U.S. No. 1 except that bronze or slightly yellowish color affecting only the edges of the leaves is permitted, provided these edges are not dried.

Unclassified. Kale which have not been classified in accordance with either of the foregoing grades. The term *unclassified* is not a grade within the meaning of these standards but is provided as a designation to show that no grade has been applied to the lot.

Source:

Agricultural Marketing Service, USDA, 7 CFR sections 51.3930 to 51.3937 (1992), Washington: Government Printing Office.

Leafy Greens, Canned

Canned leafy greens (other than spinach) is the product properly prepared from the succulent leaves of any one of the plants listed below and packed with the addition of water in hermetically sealed containers and sufficiently processed by heat to prevent spoilage. The products may be acidified and/or seasoned with one or more of the acidifying or seasoning ingredients permitted under the Federal Food, Drug, and Cosmetic Act.

TYPES

Collards.

Kale.

Mustard Greens.

Turnip Greens.

Mixed Leafy Greens. Consists of a substantial mixture of any two of the above types.

Poke Salad. Consists of leaves and adjoining stem of the pokeberry plant (*Phytolocca americana*).

STYLES

Whole. Whole leaf and adjoining portion of stem.

Cut or Sliced. Leaves and adjoining portion of stem cut predominantly into large ¾ inch pieces approximately or into approximate strips.

Chopped. Leaves and adjoining portions of the stem cut into small pieces less than approximately ¾ inch.

GRADES

Canned leafy greens are graded according to a technical system whereby penalty points are assessed for such factors as edibility, poor appearance, or defects in workmanship. The more penalty points assessed the lower the grade. The grade descriptions which follow are intended only as a general consumer guide. For more detailed information, please consult the source cited below.

U.S. Grade A or U.S. Fancy. Has a good flavor and odor characteristic of the type and has an attractive appearance and eating quality.

U.S. Grade B or U.S. Extra Standard. Has a good flavor and odor characteristic of the type and has a reasonably attractive appearance and eating quality. The product may be affected by some discoloration or may have a mushy texture, a tough texture, coarse or fibrous stems, ragged cutting, or shredded leaves and stems.

Substandard. Fails to meet the requirements for U.S. Grade B.

Source:

Agricultural Marketing Service, USDA, 7 CFR sections 52.6081 to 52.6094 (1991), Washington: Government Printing Office.

Lettuce

GRADES

Lettuce is graded according to a technical system whereby penalty points are assessed for such factors as edibility, poor appearance, or defects in workmanship. The more penalty points assessed the lower the grade. The grade descriptions which follow are intended only as a general consumer guide. For more detailed information, please consult the source cited below.

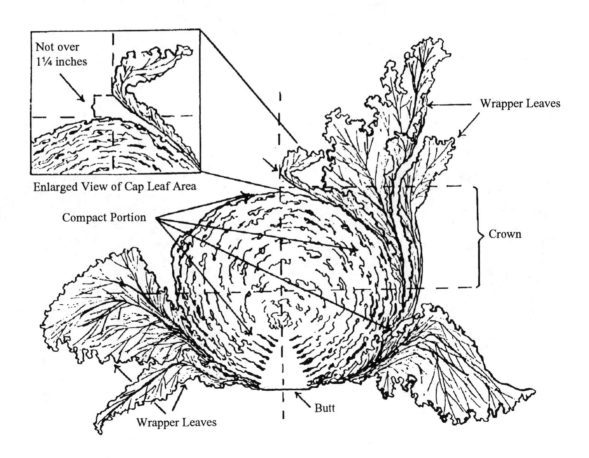

Lettuce Terminology (Iceberg Type)

U.S. Fancy. Consists of lettuce of similar varietal characteristics. The head as a whole has normal succulence. The wrapper leaves and the outermost head leaves are not more than slightly wilted. One-half or more of the exterior surface of the head, exclusive of the wrapper leaves, has at least a light green color. The head is not soft, split, or broken open. It is free from decay, russet spotting, and doubles (two heads on the same stem). Also free from injury caused by tipburn, downy mildew, field freezing, and discoloration. The butt is trimmed off closely below the point of attachment of the outer leaves, unless specified as closely trimmed. The wrapper leaves do not exceed 7 in number; on a head of iceberg-type lettuce, the wrapper leaves do not exceed 3 in number.

U.S. No. 1. Has similar varietal characteristics and is fresh, green, not soft, and not burst. It is free from decay and doubles and is not damaged by any other cause. Each head is fairly well trimmed, unless specified as closely trimmed. Has a greater tolerance for defects.

U.S. No. 2. Has similar varietal characteristics and is not burst. It is free from decay and is not seriously damaged by any other cause. Unless otherwise specified, each head is reasonably trimmed. The butt is trimmed off closely below the point of attachment of the outer leaves; on a head of iceberg-type lettuce, the wrapper leaves do not exceed 12 in number.

Source:
Agricultural Marketing Service, USDA, 7 CFR sections 51.2510 to 51.2534 (1992), Washington: Government Printing Office.

Lettuce, Greenhouse Leaf

GRADES

Greenhouse leaf lettuce is graded according to a technical system whereby penalty points are assessed for such factors as edibility, poor appearance, or defects in workmanship. The more penalty points assessed the lower the grade. The grade descriptions which follow are intended only as a general consumer guide. For more detailed information, please consult the source cited below.

U.S. Fancy. Plants of leaf lettuce of similar varietal characteristics. They are well grown and not stunted or poorly developed. They are well trimmed. The stem is trimmed off to within ¾ inch of the point of attachment of the first whorl of leaves, and leaves which are more than slightly bleached or discolored have been removed. They are free from decay and from injury caused by coarse stems, bleached or discolored leaves, sprayburn, dirt, wilting, freezing, disease, insects, or other means.

U.S. No. 1. Plants of leaf lettuce of similar varietal characteristics which are well grown and fairly well trimmed. The stem is trimmed off to within ¾ inch of the point of attachment of the first whorl of leaves, and leaves which are materially bleached or discolored have been removed. They are free from decay and from damage caused by coarse stems, bleached or discolored leaves, sprayburn, dirt, wilting, freezing, disease, in-

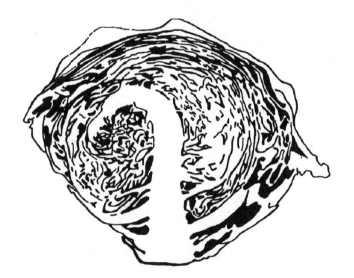
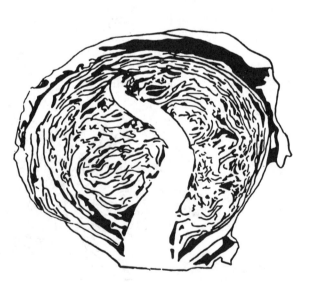

Maximum extent to which head may be affected by seedstem in U.S. No. 1 grade

sects, or other means.

Unclassified. Plants of leaf lettuce which have not been classified in accordance with any of the foregoing grades. The term *unclassified* is not a grade within the meaning of these standards but is provided as a designation to show that no grade has been applied to the lot.

Source:
Agricultural Marketing Service, USDA, 7 CFR sections 51.3455 to 51.3466 (1992), Washington: Government Printing Office.

Lettuce, Romaine

GRADES

Romaine lettuce is graded according to a technical system whereby penalty points are assessed for such factors as edibility, poor appearance, or defects in workmanship. The more penalty points assessed the lower the grade. The grade descriptions which follow are intended only as a general consumer guide. For more detailed information, please consult the source cited below.

U.S. No. 1. Fresh romaine plants of similar varietal characteristics. The plant has normal succulence, but the outermost leaves may be slightly wilted. It is well developed and well trimmed. The stem is trimmed off close to the point of attachment of the outer leaves. It is free from decay and from damage caused by seed stems, broken, bruised or discolored leaves, tipburn, wilting, foreign material, freezing, dirt, disease, insects, or mechanical or other means.

Unclassified. Romaine plants which have not been classified in accordance with the foregoing grade. The term *unclassified* is not a grade within the meaning of these standards but is provided as a designation to show that no grade has been applied to the lot.

Source:
Agricultural Marketing Service, USDA, 7 CFR sections 51.3295 to 51.3310 (1992), Washington: Government Printing Office.

Lima Beans

GRADES

Lima beans are graded according to a technical system whereby penalty points are assessed for such factors as edibility, poor appearance, or defects in workmanship. The more penalty points assessed the lower the grade. The grade descriptions which follow are intended only as a general consumer guide. For more detailed information, please consult the source cited below.

U.S. No. 1. Lima beans of similar varietal characteristics. More than one-half of each pod is filled with fairly well and/or well developed beans, but no pod has less than two fairly well and/or well developed beans. The beans are not excessively small or badly misshapen (badly constricted, crooked, curled, twisted,

or otherwise badly malformed). They are fresh and not more than slightly wilted and flabby. They do not have pods that are becoming yellow and dry. The beans do not show a tinge of green color on the cotyledons after removing the outer skin. They are not hard, starchy, and brittle. They are free from soft decay, sprouted beans, and worm holes. They are also free from damage caused by dirt, russeting, scars, leaves or other foreign matter, freezing, hail, disease, insects, or mechanical or other means.

U.S. Combination. A combination of U.S. No. 1 and U.S. No. 2 lima beans. At least 75 percent meet the requirements of U.S. No. 1 grade.

U.S. No. 2. Pods of lima beans of similar varietal characteristics. Not less than one-third of each pod is filled with fairly well and/or well developed beans. They are fairly fresh, are not over-mature, and are free from soft decay. They are also free from serious damage caused by dirt, russeting scars, leaves or other foreign matter freezing, hail, disease, insects, or mechanical or other means. Has an increase tolerance for defects.

Unclassified. Pods of lima beans which have not been classified in accordance with any of the foregoing grades. The term *unclassified* is not a grade within the meaning of these standards but is provided as a designation to show that no grade has been applied to the lot.

Source:
Agricultural Marketing Service, USDA, 7 CFR sections 51.3805 to 51.3818 (1992), Washington: Government Printing Office.

Lima Beans, Canned

Seeds shelled from the pod of the lima bean plant.

TYPES

Thin-Seeded. Such as Henderson Bush and Thorogreen varieties.
Thick-Seeded Baby Potato. Such as Baby Potato, Baby Fordhook, and Evergreen varieties.
Thick-Seeded. Such as Fordhook variety.

GRADES

Canned lima beans are graded according to a technical system whereby penalty points are assessed for such factors as edibility, poor appearance, or defects in workmanship. The more penalty points assessed the lower the grade. The grade descriptions which follow are intended only as a general consumer guide. For more detailed information, please consult the source cited below.

U.S. Grade A or U.S. Fancy. Possess similar varietal characteristics and a normal flavor and odor. Has a bright color which is predominately green, although there may be a small percentage of light or white beans (between 1 and 10 percent). The beans are practically free from defects such as loose skins, loose cotyledons, broken beans, sprouted beans, and discolored or blemished beans. The product has a practically clear liquor that may be slightly cloudy, and not more than a small amount of sediment is present. The beans are young and tender.

U.S. Grade B or U.S. Extra Standard. Possess similar varietal characteristics and a normal flavor and odor. The color of over 50 percent of the beans is green with the remainder lighter in color, provided that not more than 25 percent are white. The beans are reasonably free from defects. The liquor may be somewhat cloudy and may contain a considerable amount of sediment. The beans are reasonably young and tender.

U.S. Grade C or U.S. Standard. Possess similar varietal characteristics and a normal flavor and odor. The color of less than 50 percent of the beans is green, and all may be white. The beans are fairly free from defects and have a fairly clear liquor that may be dull in color but not to the extent that the appearance is seriously affected. The liquor may be rather viscous, cream-like, or starchy. The beans are fairly mature and possess a fairly tender texture. They may be either firm and mealy (but not hard) or soft (but not mushy).

Substandard. Fails to meet the requirements of U.S. Grade C or U.S. Standard.

Source:
Agricultural Marketing Service, USDA, 7 CFR sections 52.471 to 52.484 (1992), Washington: Government Printing Office.
Food and Drug Administration, 21 CFR 155.200 (1991), Washington: Government Printing Office.

Lima Beans, Frozen

Frozen lima beans is the frozen product prepared from the clean, sound, succulent seed of the lima bean plant without soaking. The beans are shelled, washed, blanched, and properly drained. They are then frozen in accordance with good commercial practice and maintained at temperatures necessary for the preservation of the product.

TYPES

Thin-Seeded. Such as Henderson Bush and Thorogreen varieties.

Thick-Seeded Baby Potato. Such as Baby Potato, Baby Fordhook, and Evergreen.

Thick-Seeded. Such as Fordhook variety.

GRADES

Frozen lima beans are graded according to a technical system whereby penalty points are assessed for such factors as edibility, poor appearance, or defects in workmanship. The more penalty points assessed the lower the grade. The grade descriptions which follow are intended only as a general consumer guide. For more detailed information, please consult the source cited below.

U.S. Grade A or U.S. Fancy. Possess similar varietal characteristics and a good normal flavor and odor. The beans are free from objectionable flavors and objectionable odors of any kind. The beans are tender and possess a good, bright, typical color. They are practically free from defects such as harmless

extraneous vegetable material, pieces of beans, shriveled beans, sprouted beans, light discoloration, and beans that are blemished.

U.S. Grade B or U.S. Extra Standard. Possess similar varietal characteristics and a good flavor. They are reasonably tender and possess a reasonably good color. They are reasonably free from defects.

U.S. Grade C or U.S. Standard. Possess similar varietal characteristics and a fairly good flavor which may be lacking in good flavor and odor but is free from objectionable flavors and objectionable odors of any kind. They are fairly tender, possess a fairly good color, and are fairly free from defects.

Substandard. Fails to meet the requirements of U.S. Grade C or U.S. Standard.

Source:
Agricultural Marketing Service, USDA, 7 CFR section 52.501 (1991), Washington: Government Printing Office.

Lima Beans, Frozen Speckled Butter

Frozen, speckled butter (lima) beans is the frozen product prepared from the clean, sound, freshly vined (but not seed-dry) seed of the speckled butter (lima) bean plant (*Phaseolus limensis*). The skins of the seed are pigmented, and the external colors range from variegated speckling of green, pink, red, and/or lavender to purple. The product is prepared by shelling the pods and by washing, blanching, and properly draining the seeds which may have been sorted and blended or otherwise prepared in accordance with good commercial practice. The beans are frozen in accordance with good commercial practice and maintained at temperatures necessary for the preservation of the product.

GRADES

Frozen, speckled butter lima beans are graded according to a technical system whereby penalty points are assessed for such factors as edibility, poor appearance, or defects in workmanship. The more penalty points assessed the lower the grade. The grade descriptions which follow are intended only as a general consumer guide. For more detailed information, please consult the source cited below.

U.S. Grade A or U.S. Fancy. Before and after cooking, the beans have a good, characteristic flavor and odor that are free from objectionable flavors and odors of any kind. The overall color is bright and typical. Not less than 15 percent of the beans possess at least a slight tinge of green in the cotyledons, and not more than 20 percent possess a light tan to tan color. No more than 4 beans per 10 ounces are light brown to brown or a pronounced mottled brown. The beans are practically free from such defects as pieces of beans, shriveled beans, sprouted beans, beans that are blemished or seriously blemished, and other defects that affect the appearance or edibility of the product. The beans are reasonably tender and are practically uniform in texture and tenderness.

U.S. Grade B or U.S. Extra Standard. The product may be slightly lacking in good flavor but is free from objectionable flavors and objectionable odors of any kind. The overall color may be slightly dull. The beans may possess a light tan to tan color. No more than 8 beans per 10 ounces are light brown to brown or a pronounced mottled brown. The beans are reasonably free from defects. They are fairly tender and may be variable in texture and tenderness. The cotyledons may be mealy but are not hard.

Substandard. Fails to meet the requirements of U.S. Grade B.

Source:
Agricultural Marketing Service, USDA, 7 CFR sections 52.5241 to 52.5250 (1991), Washington: Government Printing Office.

Mixed Vegetables, Frozen

Frozen mixed vegetables consist of three or more succulent vegetables properly prepared and properly blanched. The product may contain vegetables (such as small pieces of sweet red peppers or sweet green peppers) added as garnish. It is frozen and maintained at temperatures necessary for the preservation of the product.

Frozen mixed vegetables, other than small pieces of vegetables added as garnish, consist of the following kinds and styles of vegetables as basic vegetables:

Green or Wax Beans. Cut styles predominantly of ½ inch to 1½ inch cuts.

Lima Beans. Any single varietal type.

Carrots. Diced style, predominantly of ⅜ inch to ½ inch cubes.

Sweet Corn. Golden (or yellow) in whole kernel style.

Peas. Early type or sweet type.

Frozen mixed vegetables consist of three, four, or five basic vegetables in the following proportions:

Three Vegetables. A mixture of three basic vegetables in which any one vegetable is not more than 40 percent by weight of all the frozen mixed vegetables.

Four Vegetables. A mixture of four basic vegetables in which none of the vegetables is less than 8 percent by weight nor more than 35 percent by weight of all the frozen mixed vegetables.

Five Vegetables. A mixture of five basic vegetables in which none of the vegetables is less than 8 percent by weight nor more than 30 percent by weight of all the frozen mixed vegetables.

GRADES

Frozen mixed vegetables are graded according to a technical system whereby penalty points are assessed for such factors as edibility, poor appearance, or defects in workmanship. The more penalty points assessed the lower the grade. The grade descriptions which follow are intended only as a general consumer guide. For more detailed information, please consult the source cited below.

U.S. Grade A or U.S. Fancy. Possess similar varietal characteristics and a good color that is bright and characteristic of young or tender vegetables that have been properly prepared and processed. Any pieces of vegetable material used for garnish are reasonably bright. Lima beans, if present, possess a bright color that is typical for the varietal type. The product is practically free from defects such as damaged units, and any other defects which detract from the appearance or edibility of the product. After cooking, the combined vegetables are tender and possess a good flavor and odor free from objectionable flavors and odors of any kind.

U.S. Grade B or U.S. Extra Standard. Each basic vegetable possesses similar varietal characteristics. All vegetables possess a reasonably bright color characteristic of young and tender mixed vegetables. Pieces of vegetable material used for garnish may be only fairly bright but not off-color. Lima beans, if present, possess a reasonably bright typical color. The product is reasonably free from defects, and the combined vegetables after cooking are reasonably tender and practically free from tough fibers. The product possess a good flavor and odor.

U.S. Grade C or U.S. Standard. Each basic vegetable possesses similar varietal characteristics and a fairly good color. The vegetables are fairly free from defects and, after cooking, are fairly tender and reasonably free from tough fibers. They may be lacking in good flavor and odor but are free from objectionable flavors.

Substandard. Fail to meet the requirements of U.S. Grade C or U.S. Standard.

Source:
Agricultural Marketing Service, USDA, 7 CFR sections 52.2131 to 52.2161 (1991), Washington: Government Printing Office.

Mushrooms

GRADES

Mushrooms are graded according to a technical system whereby penalty points are assessed for such factors as edibility, poor appearance, or defects in workmanship. The more penalty points assessed the lower the grade. The grade descriptions which follow are intended only as a general consumer guide. For more detailed information, please consult the source cited below.

U.S. No. 1. Mushrooms of similar varietal characteristics and which are mature and at least fairly well shaped. The mushroom cap is not flattened, scalloped, indented, or otherwise deformed to an extent which materially detracts from the appearance or marketing quality. It is well trimmed, and the cap is expanded to the extent that the protective covering or *veils* joining the margin of the cap to the stem have broken and exposed the gills or underside of the cap. Also free from disease, spots, insect injury, decay, and damage by any cause. Size is specified in terms of diameter and, unless otherwise specified, meets the requirements of one of the following size classifications:

Small to Medium. Up to 1⅝ inches in diameter.

Large. Over 1⅝ inches in diameter.

U.S. No. 2. The requirements for this grade are the same as for U.S. No. 1 except for a greater tolerance for open veils and a larger tolerance for defects.

Unclassified. Mushrooms which have not been classified in accordance with either of the foregoing grades. The term *unclassified* is not a grade within the meaning of these standards but is provided as a designation to show that no grade has been applied to the lot.

Source:

Agricultural Marketing Service, USDA, 7 CFR sections 51.3385 to 51.3397 (1992), Washington: Government Printing Office.

Mushrooms, Canned

Canned mushrooms is the product prepared from sound, succulent, fresh mushrooms by proper trimming, washing, and sorting. They are packed with the addition of water in hermetically sealed containers and sufficiently processed by heat to assure preservation of the product. Salt, monosodium glutamate, or both may be added in a quantity sufficient to season the product. Ascorbic acid (Vitamin C) may be added in a quantity not to exceed 37.5 milligrams for each ounce of drained weight of mushrooms.

COLOR TYPES

White or Cream
Brown

STYLES

Whole. Consists of the caps and attached stems. The stems are more than ⅛ inch in length when measured from the under side of the cap to the cut end of the stem.

Buttons. Consists of the caps and attached stems. The stems are cut transversely below the veil. In 85 percent or more (by count) of the units, the attached stem, when measured from the under side of the cap to the cut end of the stem, does not exceed ⅛ inch in length; in the remaining units, none of the attached stems may be more than ¼ inch in length.

Sliced. Consists of units which have been sliced from whole mushrooms. In 80 percent or more (by weight) of all the units, the direction of the slice is approximately parallel to the longitudinal axis of the stem; not more than 5 percent (by weight) of all the units may be detached portions of stems.

Random Sliced Whole. Consists of units which have been sliced from whole mushrooms in a random manner. The direction of the slice may materially deviate from approximately parallel to the longitudinal axis of the stem; not more than 15 percent (by weight) of all the units may be detached portions of stem.

Sliced Buttons. Consists of units which have been sliced from button mushrooms so that in 90 percent or more (by weight) of all the units the direction of the slice is approximately parallel to the longitudinal axis of the stem.

Stems and Pieces or Pieces and Stems. Consists of units which do not conform to any of the foregoing styles and are predominantly broken or cut portions of the caps and stems. May contain units of any of the foregoing styles.

SIZES

Sizes of canned mushrooms in the styles of whole and buttons:

No. 0 (Midget). Will pass through a round opening ½ inch in diameter.

No. 1 (Tiny). Will pass through a round opening ⅝ in diameter but will not pass through a round opening ½ inch in diameter.

No. 2 (Small). Will pass through a round opening ⅞ inch in diameter but will not pass through a round opening ⅝ inch in diameter.

No. 3 (Medium). Will pass through a round opening 1⅛ inches in diameter but will not pass through a round opening ⅞ inch in diameter.

No. 4 (Large). Will pass through a round opening 1⅝ inches in diameter but will not pass through a round opening 1⅛ inches in diameter.

No. 5 (Extra Large). Those too large to pass through a round opening 1⅝ inches in diameter.

GRADES

Canned mushrooms are graded according to a technical system whereby penalty points are assessed for such factors as edibility, poor appearance, or defects in workmanship. The more penalty points assessed the lower the grade. The grade descriptions which follow are intended only as a general consumer guide. For more detailed information, please consult the source cited below.

U.S. Grade A or U.S. Fancy. Possess similar varietal characteristics and a normal flavor and odor. They possess a practically uniform and bright color.

White or Cream. The color of the surface of the caps is not darker than medium cream. The color may possess a slight tannish cast. The color of the gills of the sliced units is not darker than light tannish gray.

Brown. The color of the surface of the caps is not darker than light brown. The color may possess a slight grayish cast. The color of the gills of the sliced units is not darker than medium brownish gray.

They are practically uniform in size and shape, except for the style of stems and pieces, and are practically free from defects. They possess a good character; the units are firm and tender and practically free from fibrous or rubbery units.

U.S. Grade B or U.S. Extra Standard. Possess similar varietal characteristics and a normal flavor and odor. Possess a fairly good color that may be dull but not so as to seriously affect the appearance of the product.

White or Cream. The color of the surface of the individual caps may be dark cream and may possess a gray or brown cast; the color of the gills of sliced units is not darker than tannish gray.

Brown. The color of the surface of the individual caps may be medium brown in color and may possess a grayish cast; the color of the gills of sliced units may be dark brownish gray.

They are fairly uniform in size and shape, except for the style of stems and pieces, and are fairly free from defects. They possess a fairly good character; the units are reasonably tender, although they may be slightly soft, and are reasonably free from fibrous or rubbery units.

Substandard. The quality of canned mushrooms that fail to meet the requirements of U.S. Grade B.

Source:
Agricultural Marketing Service, USDA, 7 CFR sections 52.1481 to 52.1495 (1991), Washington: Government Printing Office.
Food and Drug Administration, 21 CFR 155.201 (1991), Washington: Government Printing Office.

Mustard Greens and Turnip Greens

These standards are applicable to either mustard greens or turnip greens consisting of either plants (crown or root attached), or cut leaves. They are not applicable to mixtures of plants and cut leaves or mixtures of mustard greens and turnip greens in the same container.

Mustard greens and turnip greens are graded according to a technical system whereby penalty points are assessed for such factors as edibility, poor appearance, or defects in workmanship. The more penalty points assessed the lower the grade. The grade descriptions which follow are intended only as a general consumer guide. For more detailed information, please consult the source cited below.

U.S. No. 1. Mustard greens or turnip greens of one type. No mixture of types are permitted which materially affects the appearance of the lot. The leaves are not more than slightly wilted. The greens are not old, tough, or excessively fibrous. The appearance of the mustard or turnip greens is not materially affected by the presence of mud, dirt, or other foreign material. They are free from decay and from damage caused by seed stems, discoloration, freezing, foreign material, disease, insects, or mechanical or other means. In the case of turnip greens with roots attached, the roots are not soft, flabby, or shriveled. They are free from damage by any cause. Unless otherwise specified, the maximum diameter of the root is 1½ inches.

Unclassified. Mustard greens or turnip greens which have not been classified in accordance with the foregoing grade. The term *unclassified* is not a grade within the meaning of these standards but is provided as a designation to show that no definite grade has been applied to the lot.

Source:
Agricultural Marketing Service, USDA, 7 CFR section 51.1030 to 51.1042 (1992), Washington: Government Printing Office.

Okra

Okra is graded according to a technical system whereby penalty points are assessed for such factors as edibility, poor appearance, or defects in workmanship. The more penalty points assessed the lower the grade. The grade descriptions which follow are intended only as a general consumer guide. For more detailed information, please consult the source cited below.

U.S. No. 1. Pods of okra of similar varietal characteristics and which are fresh, tender, not badly misshapen, free from decay, and free from damage caused by dirt or other foreign matter, disease, insects, or mechanical or other means.

Unclassified. Pods of okra which have not been classified in accordance with the foregoing grade. The term *unclassified* is not a grade within the meaning of these standards but is provided as a designation to show that no grade has been applied to the lot.

Source:
Agricultural Marketing Service, USDA, 7 CFR sections 51.3945 to 51.3948 (1992), Washington: Government Printing Office.

Okra, Canned

Canned okra is the product prepared from clean, sound, succulent, immature pods of either the green or white varieties of the okra plant. They are properly trimmed and sorted, may or may not have undergone partial fermentation, and are washed, packed, and processed in accordance with good commercial practice.

TYPES

Type I. Partially fermented in a salt brine before processing.
Type II. Not been fermented before processing.

STYLES

Whole. Whole pods with stems removed and with or without the caps removed.
Whole Salad. Whole pods with stems attached. The stems are at least ½ inch but do not exceed 1 inch in length.
Cut. With the caps and stems removed and which have been cut transversely into pieces.

GRADES

Canned okra is graded according to a technical system whereby penalty points are assessed for such factors as edibility, poor appearance, or defects in workmanship. The more penalty points assessed the lower the grade. The grade descriptions which follow are intended only as a general consumer guide. For more detailed information, please consult the source cited below.

U.S. Grade A or U.S. Fancy. Possesses similar varietal characteristics and a normal flavor. The outer surfaces of the okra pods possess a practically uniform color typical for the type and variety of young, tender, properly prepared, and properly processed canned okra. In 90 percent of the most uniform pods, the length of the longest unit is not more than twice the length of the shortest, and the overall length does not exceed

3½ inches. The product is practically free from extraneous vegetable matter, small pieces, poorly trimmed units, misshapen pods, and damaged units. The units are tender and practically free from any fibrous material which is objectionable upon eating. The seeds are in the early stages of development

U.S. Grade C or U.S. Standard. Possesses similar varietal characteristics and a normal flavor. Has a fairly good and uniform color and is fairly uniform in size so that in the whole styles, in 90 percent of the pods, the length of the longest unit is not more than three times the length of the shortest. The product is fairly free from defects. It may be fairly tender, and the seeds may have passed the early stages of development

Substandard. Fails to meet the requirements of U.S. Grade C or U.S. Standard.

Source:

Agricultural Marketing Service, USDA, 7 CFR sections 52.3331 to 52.3344 (1991), Washington: Government Printing Office.

Food and Drug Administration, 21 CFR 155.200 (1991), Washington: Government Printing Office.

Okra, Frozen

Frozen okra is the product prepared from the clean, sound, succulent, and edible fresh pods of the okra plant (*Hibiscus esculentus*) of the green variety. The product is properly prepared and properly processed and is then frozen and stored at temperatures necessary for preservation.

STYLES

Whole Okra. Trimmed whole pods of any length and which may possess an edible portion of the cap. The length of a whole pod is determined by measuring from the outermost point of the tip end of the pod to the outermost point of the stem end of the pod, exclusive of any inedible stem portion which may be present.

Cut Okra. Trimmed whole pods which may possess an edible portion of cap and which have been cut transversely into pieces of approximate uniform length. The length of a unit of cut okra is determined by measuring the longitudinal axis of the unit.

GRADES

Frozen okra is graded according to a technical system whereby penalty points are assessed for such factors as edibility, poor appearance, or defects in workmanship. The more penalty points assessed the lower the grade. The grade descriptions which follow are intended only as a general consumer guide. For more detailed information, please consult the source cited below.

U.S. Grade A or U.S. Fancy. Possesses similar varietal characteristics in all styles. Has a good flavor and odor. The color is bright, practically uniform, and typical of for young, tender okra. No more than 10 percent possess a slightly dull color,

possess a slight yellowish-green to brownish-green cast, or vary materially from the overall general, uniform color. None possess a noticeable yellow or brown color or are off-color. The okra is practically free from defects, and the units are fleshy and tender. The seeds are in the early stages of maturity. Not more than 2 whole pods or 4 cut units (as applicable) per sample possess tough fibers.

U.S. Grade B or U.S. Extra Standard. Possesses similar varietal characteristics in the whole style but may or may not possess similar varietal characteristics in the cut style. Has a normal flavor and odor. The color may be slightly dull but is typical for reasonably young, tender okra. No more than 20 percent of the units in the sample unit may possess a color that is typical of less than reasonably young, tender okra. The okra is fairly free from defects and has a reasonably good character. The units may have lost their fleshy texture to a considerable extent. The seeds may have passed the early stages of maturity. Not more than 4 whole pods or 8 cut units per sample possess tough fibers.

Substandard. Fails to meet the requirements of U.S. Grade B.

Source:

Agricultural Marketing Service, USDA, 7 CFR sections 52.1511 to 52.1518 (1991), Washington: Government Printing Office.

Onions, Bermuda-Granex-Grano Type

GRADES

Bermuda-Granex-Grano type onions are graded according to a technical system whereby penalty points are assessed for such factors as edibility, poor appearance, or defects in workmanship. The more penalty points assessed the lower the grade. The grade descriptions which follow are intended only as a general consumer guide. For more detailed information, please consult the source cited below.

U.S. No. 1. Onions of similar varietal characteristics and which are mature and fairly well shaped. They are not appreciably three, four-, or five-sided, thick necked, or badly pinched. They are free from decay, wet sunscald, doubles, and bottlenecks (abnormally thick necks with only fairly well developed bulbs). Also free from damage caused by seed stems, splits, moisture, roots, dry sunscald, sunburn, sprouting, staining, dirt or other foreign material, disease, insects, or mechanical or other means.

U.S. Combination. A combination of U.S. No. 1 and U.S. No. 2 onions. At least 50 percent of the onions in each lot meet the requirements of U.S. No. 1 grade.

U.S. No. 2. Onions of similar varietal characteristics and which are not soft or spongy and which are free from decay, sunscald, and bottlenecks. Also free from damage that seriously affects appearance, edibility, or shipping quality.

Unclassified. Onions which have not been classified in accordance with any of the foregoing grades. The term *unclassified* is not a grade but is provided as a designation to show that no grade has been applied to the lot.

SIZE

Unless otherwise specified, onions should not be less than 1½ inches in diameter, with 60 percent or more 2 inches or larger in diameter.

Small. From 1 to 2¼ inches in diameter.

Repacker or Prepacker. From 1¾ to 3 inches in diameter, with 60 percent or more 2 inches or larger in diameter.

Medium. From 2 to 3½ inches in diameter.

Large or Jumbo. 3 inches or larger in diameter.

Source:
Agricultural Marketing Service, USDA, 7 CFR sections 51.3195 to 51.3208 (1992), Washington: Government Printing Office.

Onions, Canned

Canned onions is the canned product consisting of whole onions that are properly prepared from clean, sound, succulent onion bulbs. The product is packed in accordance with good commercial practice and is sufficiently processed by heat to assure preservation of the product in hermetically sealed containers.

SIZES

Tiny
Small
Medium

GRADES

Canned onions are graded according to a technical system whereby penalty points are assessed for such factors as edibility, poor appearance, or defects in workmanship. The more penalty points assessed the lower the grade. The grade descriptions which follow are intended only as a general consumer guide. For more detailed information, please consult the source cited below.

U.S. Grade A or U.S. Fancy. Possess similar varietal characteristics and a normal flavor. Has a reasonably bright color which may include typical greenish areas on the surface of the bulbs. They are practically uniform in size and shape and practically free from defects like extraneous vegetable material. Also free from onion bulbs that are blemished or seriously blemished or affected by mechanical damage, loose scales, or detached centers. The onions are reasonably firm and tender, and not more than 10 percent are soft or spongy.

U.S. Grade C or U.S. Standard. Possess similar varietal characteristics and a normal flavor. They have a characteristic color which may include typical greenish areas on the surface of the bulbs. The product is not materially affected by oxidation, dull grayish-white casts, watery-white casts, or other discoloration. They are fairly uniform in size and shape and fairly free

from defects. The onions are fairly firm and tender, and not more than 20 percent are soft or spongy.

Substandard. Fail to meet the requirements of U.S. Grade C or U.S. Standard.

Source:
Agricultural Marketing Service, USDA, 7 CFR sections 52.2041 to 52.3053 (1991), Washington: Government Printing Office.

Onions, Common Green

GRADES

Common green onions are graded according to a technical system whereby penalty points are assessed for such factors as edibility, poor appearance, or defects in workmanship. The more penalty points assessed the lower the grade. The grade descriptions which follow are intended only as a general consumer guide. For more detailed information, please consult the source cited below.

U.S. No. 1. Green onions which are not more than slightly curved, angular, crooked, lopsided, or otherwise slightly misshapen. They are firm, young, and tender. The appearance of the onion is not materially injured by dirt. They are free from decay and from damage caused by seed stems, roots, foreign material, disease, insects, or mechanical or other means. The bulb is not broken above the point of root attachment and is practically free from dead, discolored, or slick outer skins. Fresh, clean, loose skins which do not materially affect the appearance of the individual onion or the bunch are permitted. The tops are fresh, not withered or badly wilted. They have a normal green color characteristic of healthy plants. A slight discoloration of the extreme tips and slight scarring caused by thrips are not objectionable. They are free from damage caused by broken or bruised leaves or by clipping. When all the tops of the onions have been evenly clipped back in accordance with good commercial practice, they are specified as *Clipped Tops* in connection with the grade. The overall length is not more than 24 inches nor less than 8 inches, and the onions are not less than ¼ inch or more than 1 inch in diameter.

U.S. No. 2. Green onions which are not badly misshapen, and which are fairly firm and fairly young. They are not tough, stringy, or advanced to the stage where the neck is flabby. They are fairly clean, free from decay, and free from serious damage caused by seed stems, roots, foreign material, disease, insects, mechanical, or other means. The bulbs are not broken above the point of root attachment and are reasonably free from dead, discolored, or slick outer skins. Fresh, fairly clean, loose skins which do not seriously affect the appearance of the individual onion or the bunch are permitted. The tops are fresh and of fairly good green color. The tops are pale, yellowish green, or otherwise slightly discolored. They are free from serious damage caused by broken or bruised leaves or by clipping. When all the tops of the onions have been evenly clipped back in accordance with good commercial practice, they are specified as *Clipped Tops* in connection with the grade. Unless otherwise specified, the overall length (roots excepted) of the onions is not less than 8 inches, and the onions is not less than ¼ inch or more than 1½ inches in diameter.

Unclassified. Onions which are not graded in conformity with either of the foregoing grades. The term *unclassified* is not a grade within the meaning of these standards but is provided as a designation to show that no definite grade has been applied to the lot.

SIZES

The following terms and definitions are provided for describing the diameters of any lot:

Small. Less than ½ inch.

Medium. ½ to 1 inch, inclusive.

Large. Over 1 inch.

Source:
Agricultural Marketing Service, USDA, 7 CFR sections 51.1055 to 51.1071 (1992), Washington: Government Printing Office.

Onions (Other Than Bermuda-Granex-Grano and Creole Types)

GRADES

Onions are graded according to a technical system whereby penalty points are assessed for such factors as edibility, poor appearance, or defects in workmanship. The more penalty points assessed the lower the grade. The grade descriptions which follow are intended only as a general consumer guide. For more detailed information, please consult the source cited below.

U.S. No. 1. Onions of similar varietal characteristics and which are mature, fairly firm, and fairly well shaped. They are free from sunscald and from doubles (onions that have developed more than one bulb joined only at the base). Also free from bottlenecks (onions with abnormally thick necks with only fairly well developed bulbs) and scallions (thick necks and relatively small and poorly developed bulbs). Free from damage caused by seed stems, splits, tops, roots, dry sunscald, sunburn, sprouts, freezing, peeling, cracked fleshy scales, watery scales, dirt or staining, foreign matter, disease, insects, or other means. Unless otherwise specified the diameter is not less than 1½ inches. Yellow, brown, or red onions have 40 percent or more and white onions have 30 percent or more of the onions in any lot 2 inches or larger in diameter.

U.S. No. 1 Boilers. Onions which meet all the requirements for the U.S. No. 1 grade except for size. The diameter of onions of this grade is not less than 1 inch nor more than 1⅞ inches.

U.S. No. 1 Picklers. Onions which meet all the requirements for the U.S. No. 1 grade except for size. The maximum diameter of onions of this grade is not more than 1 inch.

U.S. Commercial. Onions of similar varietal characteristics and which are mature. They are not soft, spongy, or badly misshapen. They are free from decay, wet sunscald, doubles, bottlenecks, and scallions. Also free from damage caused by seed stems, tops, roots, dry sunscald, sunburn, sprouts, freezing, cracked fleshy scales, watery scales, disease, insects, or other means. They are free from serious damage caused by staining, dirt, or other foreign matter. The diameter is not less than 1½ inches.

U.S. No. 2. Onions of one type. They are mature, but not soft or spongy. They are free from decay, wet sunscald, and scallions. They are also free from serious damage caused by seed stems, dry sunscald, sprouts, freezing, watery scales, disease, insects, or other means. The diameter is not less than 1½ inches. This grade has a higher tolerance for defects. Accordingly, a higher percentage of onions may be off-size or contain minor defects.

Unclassified. Onions which have not been classified in accordance with any of the foregoing grades. The term *unclassified* is not a grade within the meaning of these standards but is provided as a designation to show that no grade has been applied to the lot.

SIZES

Small. From 1 to 2¼ inches in diameter.

Medium. From 2 to 3¼ inches in diameter. For onions grown in Minnesota, Iowa, and states east of the Mississippi River, medium is 1½ to 3¼ inches in diameter

Large or Jumbo. 3 inches or larger in diameter.

Source:
Agricultural Marketing Service, USDA, 7 CFR sections 51.2830 to 51.2854 (1992), Washington: Government Printing Office.

Parsnips

GRADES

Parsnips are graded according to a technical system whereby penalty points are assessed for such factors as edibility, poor appearance, or defects in workmanship. The more penalty points assessed the lower the grade. The grade descriptions which follow are intended only as a general consumer guide. For more detailed information, please consult the source cited below.

U.S. Grade A. Firm parsnips of similar varietal characteristics. The root is not soft, flabby, or shriveled. They are clean, and the tops are cut back to not more than 1 inch in length. Roots may be clipped if they are neatly cut off. The root is not forked or misshapen, rough, ridged, or covered with secondary rootlets. They are free from soft rot and from damage caused by freezing, growth cracks, discoloration, pithiness, woodiness, sunburn, oil spray, dry rot, other disease, insects, or mechanical or other means. Parsnips on the shown face are reasonably representative in size and quality of the contents of the container. Unless otherwise specified, the diameter of each parsnip is not less than 1 inch and not more than 2¼ inches.

U.S. Grade B. Parsnips of similar varietal characteristics and which are firm, clean, well trimmed, and not badly deformed. The root is not so forked or badly misshapen as to seriously affect the appearance. They are not more than slightly rough and are free from soft rot and from damage caused by freezing, growth cracks, discoloration, pithiness, woodiness, sunburn, oil spray, dry rot, other disease, insects, or mechanical or other means. Parsnips on the shown face should be reasonably representative in size and quality of the contents of the container. Unless otherwise specified, the diameter of each parsnip is not less than 1 inch and not more than 2¼ inches. This grade has a higher tolerance for parsnips that are off-size, affected by soft rot, or damaged.

Off-Grade. Parsnips which fail to meet the requirements of the foregoing grades.

Source:
Agricultural Marketing Service, USDA, (Consumer Standards) 7 CFR sections 51.2310 to 51.2322 (1992), Washington: Government Printing Office.

Peas

GRADES

Fresh peas are graded according to a technical system whereby penalty points are assessed for such factors as edibility, poor appearance, or defects in workmanship. The more penalty points assessed the lower the grade. The grade descriptions which follow are intended only as a general consumer guide. For more detailed information, please consult the source cited below.

U.S. No. 1. Pods of peas of similar varietal characteristics and which are not over-mature or excessively small. They are not crooked, badly twisted, or water-soaked. More than two-thirds of the pod contains peas which are at least fairly well developed. They are fresh, firm, free from decay, and free from damage caused by black calyxes, freezing, splitting, hail, dirt, leaves, other foreign matter, mildew, other diseases, insects, or mechanical or other means. The peas are at least fairly tender.

U.S. No. 1 Green Calyxes. Peas that meet the requirements of U.S. No. 1 grade. An average of three-fourths or more of the pods in any lot, but not less than one-half of the pods in each container, have calyxes which are of a fairly good green color.

U.S. Fancy. Pods of peas which are well filled and which have an average of not less than one-half of the pods in each container with calyxes which are of a fairly good green color. The peas meet the requirements of U.S. No. 1 grade in all other respects.

Unclassified. Peas which have not been classified in accordance with the foregoing grades. The term *unclassified* is not a grade within the meaning of these standards but is provided as a designation to show that no definite grade has been applied to the lot.

Source:
Agricultural Marketing Service, USDA, 7 CFR sections 51.1375 to 51.1387 (1992), Washington: Government Printing Office.

Peas, Canned

Canned peas is the canned product prepared from clean, sound, shelled, succulent peas.

TYPES

Early Peas. Alaska or other smooth skin varieties.
Sweet Peas. Sweet, wrinkled varieties.

GRADES

Canned peas are graded according to a technical system whereby penalty points are assessed for such factors as edibility, poor appearance, or defects in workmanship. The more penalty points assessed the lower the grade. The grade descriptions which follow are intended only as a general consumer guide. For more detailed information, please consult the source cited below.

U.S. Grade A or U.S. Fancy. Possess similar varietal characteristics and a good, characteristic, normal flavor and odor free from objectionable flavors and objectionable odors of any kind. The color of the liquor is typical, but may possess a slight cloudiness or slight tint of green. Not more than a slight quantity of suspended material or sediments may be present, and the liquor is not viscous. The peas possess a bright color typical of tender peas. The product is reasonably free from peas that materially detract from the overall color appearance (includes peas commonly referred to as blond or cream colored peas). It is practically free from defects such as pieces of peas, minor discoloration, and spotted or otherwise discolored peas.

U.S. Grade B or U.S. Extra Standard. Possess similar varietal characteristics. Has a good flavor and a reasonably good liquor that may be cloudy but not off-color. Not more than a moderate quantity of suspended material or sediment is present, and the liquor is not more than slightly viscous. The peas are reasonably bright and reasonably free from peas that materially detract from the overall color appearance (includes peas commonly referred to as blond or cream colored peas). Reasonably free from defects and reasonably tender.

U.S. Grade C or U.S. Standard. Possess a fairly good flavor that may be lacking in good, characteristic, normal flavor and odor but is free from objectionable flavors and objectionable odors of any kind. Possess a fairly good liquor that may be very cloudy. It may possess a pronounced accumulation of sediment, may be dull but not off-color, and may be viscous. Possess a fairly good color. The appearance of the product is fairly free from peas that materially detract from the overall color appearance (includes peas commonly referred to as blond or cream colored peas).

Substandard. Fail to meet the requirements of U.S. Grade C or U.S. Standard.

SIZES OF PEAS

The size of a pea is determined on the basis of the diameter of the circular opening(s) through which the pea will pass or will not pass without force or pressure. The size designations applicable to peas in canned peas are as follows:

Size	Will not pass through—	Will pass through—
Size 1		9⁄32
Size 2	9⁄32	10⁄32
Size 3	10⁄32	11⁄32
Size 4	11⁄32	12⁄32
Size 5	12⁄32	13⁄32
Size 6	13⁄32	14⁄32
Size 7	14⁄32	

Source:

Agricultural Marketing Service, USDA, 7 CFR sections 52.2281 to 52.2294 (1991), Washington: Government Printing Office.
Food and Drug Administration, 21 CFR 155.200 (1991), Washington: Government Printing Office.

Peas, Field (Canned)

STYLES

Canned. Canned field peas or canned black-eyed peas.

Snap or Snaps. A piece or pieces of immature unshelled pods.

Canned Peas without Snaps. Peas which do not contain immature unshelled pods or pieces thereof.

Canned Peas with Snaps. Canned peas which contain pieces of immature unshelled pods.

Unit. An individual field pea or black-eyed pea or a piece of immature unshelled pod of either.

GRADES

Canned field peas are graded according to a technical system whereby penalty points are assessed for such factors as edibility, poor appearance, or defects in workmanship. The more penalty points assessed the lower the grade. The grade descriptions which follow are intended only as a general consumer guide. For more detailed information, please consult the source cited below.

U.S. Grade A or U.S. Fancy. The quality of canned peas that possess similar varietal characteristics and a normal flavor and odor. They are tender and in a fairly early stage of maturity. They are practically free from extraneous vegetable matter, loose skins, pieces of skins, loose cotyledons, pieces of cotyledons, mashed or broken units, and units blemished by pathological or insect injury. They possess a fairly uniform color typical of fairly young field peas or black-eye peas of similar varietal characteristics.

U.S. Grade C or U.S. Standard. The quality of canned peas that possess similar varietal characteristics and that are fairly tender. They may be mealy, but not hard, and are fairly free from defects. They possess a normal flavor and odor and have a color that may be variable and typical of nearly mature field peas or black-eye peas of similar varietal characteristics.

Source:

Agricultural Marketing Service, USDA, 7 CFR sections 52.1641 to 52.1651 (1991), Washington: Government Printing Office.

Peas, Frozen

Frozen peas is the frozen product prepared from the clean, sound, succulent seed of the common garden pea (*Pisum sativum*) by shelling, washing, blanching, sorting, and proper draining. The peas are frozen in accordance with good commercial practice and maintained at temperatures necessary for the preservation of the product.

GRADES

Frozen peas are graded according to a technical system whereby penalty points are assessed for such factors as edibility, poor appearance, or defects in workmanship. The more penalty points assessed the lower the grade. The grade descriptions which follow are intended only as a general consumer guide. For more detailed information, please consult the source cited below.

U.S. Grade A or U.S. Fancy. Possess similar varietal characteristics and a good flavor. They have a good, bright, practically uniform, green color that is typical for the variety. Off-color peas do not more than slightly affect the overall color appearance, and not more than one-half of 1 percent are blond, cream colored, or seriously detract from the overall color appearance. They are practically free from defects such as harmless vegetable material, pieces of peas, and blemished peas. They are tender and in such a state of maturity that not more than 10 percent will sink in a solution containing 13 percent, by weight, of salt. After cooking, the frozen peas are very tender upon eating.

U.S. Grade B or U.S. Extra Standard. Possess similar varietal characteristics and a fairly good flavor. They possess a reasonably good color, and not more than 1½ percent are blond, cream colored, or seriously detract from the overall color appearance. They are reasonably free from defects and are reasonably tender. Not more than 12 percent will sink in a 15 percent salt solution.

U.S. Grade C or U.S. Standard. Possess similar varietal characteristics and a fairly good flavor. They have a fairly good color, and not more than 2 percent, by count, of all the peas are blond, cream colored, or seriously detract from the overall color appearance. They are fairly free from defects and are fairly tender. Not more than 16 percent will sink in a 16 percent salt solution.

Substandard. Fails to meet the requirements of U.S. Grade C.

Source:
Agricultural Marketing Service, USDA, 7 CFR sections 52.3511 to 52.3520 (1991), Washington: Government Printing Office.

Peas, Frozen Field and Black-eyed

Frozen field peas and frozen black-eyed peas is the frozen product prepared from clean, sound, fresh, seed of proper maturity of the field pea plant (*Vigna sinensis*). The peas are shelled, sorted, washed, blanched, and properly drained. They are then frozen and maintained at temperatures necessary for preservation. Frozen peas may contain succulent, unshelled pods (snaps) of the field pea plant as an optional garnishing ingredient.

TYPES

SINGLE TYPE

Frozen peas that have distinct similarities of color and shape for the type are not considered mixed. Single types include, but are not limited to, the following:

Black-Eyed Peas. Similar varietal types, such as purple hull peas, that have a light-colored skin, a definite eye (contrasting color around the hilum), and are bean shaped.

Crowder Peas. Various groups, such as Brown Crowder, that are nearly round in shape and have blunt or square ends.

Cream Peas. Various groups, including White Acre, that have a solid cream-colored skin and are generally bean shaped.

Field Peas. Any varietal group or type of the field pea plant that has similar color and shape characteristics. Includes black-eyed peas, crowder peas, and cream peas.

MIXED TYPE

Frozen peas that are a mixture of two or more distinct single varietal groups or are not distinguishable as a single varietal group are considered mixed type.

GRADES

Frozen field and black-eyed peas are graded according to a technical system whereby penalty points are assessed for such factors as edibility, poor appearance, or defects in workmanship. The more penalty points assessed the lower the grade. The grade descriptions which follow are intended only as a general consumer guide. For more detailed information, please consult the source cited below.

U.S. Grade A. Has a bright, overall appearance and, after cooking, has a good, characteristically normal flavor and odor free from objectionable flavors and objectionable odors of any kind. Is practically free from grit. The units are tender and in a reasonably young stage of maturity. They are practically uniform in texture and tenderness. Weight of broken peas does not exceed 0.25 ounce for White Acre peas and 0.25 ounce for all other types.

U.S. Grade B. Has an overall appearance that may be dull but is not off-color. After cooking, may be lacking in good flavor but is free from objectionable flavors and objectionable odors of any kind. Is practically free from grit. The units are reasonably tender and in a fairly young stage of maturity. They may be variable in texture and tenderness; the cotyledons may be mealy or firm, but are not hard. Weight of broken peas does not exceed 0.5 ounce for White Acre peas and 1 ounce for all other types.

Substandard. Fail to meet the requirements for U.S. Grade B.

Source:
Agricultural Marketing Service, USDA, 7 CFR sections 52.1661 to 52.1674 (1991), Washington: Government Printing Office.

Peas, Southern

The standards contained in this part apply only to the seed pods of plants of the species *Vigna sinensis*, generally known as *southern peas, cowpeas,* or *field peas.* Well recognized general types are *black-eyed, crowders, creams,* and *purple hulls,* each of which includes many varieties.

GRADES

Southern peas are graded according to a technical system whereby penalty points are assessed for such factors as edibility, poor appearance, or defects in workmanship. The more penalty points assessed the lower the grade. The grade descriptions which follow are intended only as a general consumer guide. For more detailed information, please consult the source cited below.

U.S. No. 1. Pods of southern peas of similar varietal characteristics and which are fairly well formed. They are not curved or crooked, and at least ⅔ of the length of the pod is filled with peas which are at least fairly well developed. They are not over-mature (shows definite drying or shriveling) or excessively young (the pod has not developed any peas suitable for shelling). They are free from decay and worm holes and from damage caused by stems, leaves, trash, stings, insect injury, scars, discoloration, wilting, dirt or other adhering foreign material, disease, or mechanical or other means. Unless otherwise specified, each pod is not less than 5 inches in length.

U.S. Commercial. Pods of southern peas which meet the requirements of U.S. No. 1 grade, except that they are free from serious damage caused by stems, leaves, and trash. There is no requirement for minimum length. Also, there is a higher tolerance for defects.

Unclassified. Peas which have not been classified in accordance with either of the foregoing grades. The term *unclassified* is not a grade but is provided as a designation to show that not grade has been applied to the lot.

Source:
Agricultural Marketing Service, USDA, 7 CFR sections 51.2670 to 51.2682 (1992), Washington: Government Printing Office.

Peas and Carrots, Canned

Canned peas and carrots is the product which has been properly prepared from clean, sound, succulent garden peas and clean, sound carrots. The peas and carrots are packed in a suitable packing medium with or without the addition of salt, sugar, or other ingredient(s) permissible under the Federal Food, Drug, and Cosmetic Act. They are sufficiently processed by heat to assure preservation of the product in hermetically sealed containers.

STYLES

Peas. Sweet type peas make up 50 percent of the product.

Carrots. Not less than 25 percent are carrots of one of the following styles:

Sliced. Parallel slices which may be corrugated, fluted, wavy, scalloped, or crinkle cut.

Diced. Approximate cube-shaped.

Double-Diced. Approximate rectangular shaped.

Strips. Three-eighth inch in width strips of various lengths.

GRADES

Canned peas and carrots are graded according to a technical system whereby penalty points are assessed for such factors as edibility, poor appearance, or defects in workmanship. The more penalty points assessed the lower the grade. The grade descriptions which follow are intended only as a general consumer guide. For more detailed information, please consult the source cited below.

U.S. Grade A or U.S. Fancy. The overall color is at least reasonably bright and is not more than slightly affected by variations in color. The carrots are a typical orange-yellow color, and the presence of green, white, or orange-brown units does not more than slightly affect the appearance or eating quality. The color of the peas is typical of at least reasonably young and tender peas with practically no blond or cream colored peas. The product is practically free from defects which detract from appearance or edibility. The carrots are tender, not fibrous, and have a practically uniform texture. The product and each of the vegetables has a good, characteristic, normal flavor and odor.

U.S. Grade B or U.S. Extra Standard. The product possesses an overall color which may be slightly dull but is not off-color. The color of each of the vegetables may be variable but not to the extent that the appearance of the product is seriously affected. The presence of green, white, or orange-brown units does not seriously affect the appearance of the carrots. The color of the peas is typical of fairly young and tender peas. The product is reasonably free from defects. The carrots are at least reasonably tender, may be variable in texture, but are not tough, hard, or mushy; not more than 5 percent possess coarse, fibrous material. The skins of not more than 5 percent may be ruptured to a width of 1/16 inch or more. The product may be lacking in good flavor and odor but is free from objectionable flavors and odors of any kind.

Substandard. Fails to meet the requirements of U.S. Grade B.

Source:
Agricultural Marketing Service, USDA, 7 CFR sections 52.6201 to 52.6214 (1991), Washington: Government Printing Office.

Peas and Carrots, Frozen

Frozen peas and carrots is the product prepared from the fresh, clean, sound, immature seed of the common garden pea (*Pisum sativum*) and the fresh, clean, sound roots of the carrot plant (*Daucus carota sativa*). The peas are prepared by shelling, washing, sorting, and blanching. The carrots are prepared by washing, sorting, trimming, peeling, cutting into approximate cubes, and blanching. The prepared ingredients are properly drained and mixed, are frozen in accordance with good commercial practice, and are maintained at temperatures necessary for the preservation of the product.

KINDS, TYPES, STYLES, AND PROPORTIONS

Peas. Not less than 50 percent of early type or sweet type peas.

Carrots. Not less than 25 percent of diced style carrots, predominantly 1/4 inch to 3/8 inch cubes.

GRADES

Frozen peas and carrots are graded according to a technical system whereby penalty points are assessed for such factors as edibility, poor appearance, or defects in workmanship. The more penalty points assessed the lower the grade. The grade descriptions which follow are intended only as a general consumer guide. For more detailed information, please consult the source cited below.

U.S. Grade A or U.S. Fancy. Each vegetable possesses similar varietal characteristics. The vegetables possess a good color that is bright and typical of young and tender peas and tender diced carrots. The appearance of the product is not more than slightly affected by variations in the color of the carrots and of the peas. The product is practically free from defects such as leaves, stems, pods, and predominantly spherical or cylindrical harmless material from other plants. The peas are reasonably tender, and the carrots are tender (not fibrous) and possess a practically uniform texture. They have a good, characteristic, normal flavor and odor free from objectionable flavors and odors of any kind.

U.S. Grade B or U.S. Extra Standard. Each vegetable possesses similar varietal characteristics. The vegetables possess a reasonably good color and are reasonably free from defects. They possess a reasonably good character. May be lacking in good flavor and odor but is free from objectionable flavors and odors of any kind.

U.S. Grade C or U.S. Standard. Each vegetable possesses similar varietal characteristics. The vegetables possess a fairly good color which may be dull but not off-color. The color of each ingredient may be variable, but not to the extent that the appearance of the product is seriously affected. They are fairly free from defects and possess a fairly good character. The peas in U.S. Grade C or U.S. Standard are at least fairly tender, and the carrots are at least reasonably tender.

Substandard. Fail to meet the requirements of U.S. Grade C or U.S. Standard.

Source:

Agricultural Marketing Service, USDA, 7 CFR sections 52.2501 to 52.2510 (1991), Washington: Government Printing Office.

Peppers, Sweet

GRADES

Sweet peppers are graded according to a technical system whereby penalty points are assessed for such factors as edibility, poor appearance, or defects in workmanship. The more penalty points assessed the lower the grade. The grade descriptions which follow are intended only as a general consumer guide. For more detailed information, please consult the source cited below.

U.S. Fancy. Mature, green, sweet peppers of similar varietal characteristics. They are not soft, shriveled, limp, or pliable; they may yield to slight pressure. They are well shaped and not more than slightly curved. They are free from sunscald, freezing injury, and decay. They are also free from injury caused by scars, hail, sunburn, disease, insects, or mechanical or other means. The diameter of each pepper is not less than 3 inches, and the length is not less than 3½ inches. Any lot of peppers which meets all the requirements of this grade, except those relating to green color, may be designated as U.S. Fancy with the characteristic color specified in connection with this grade, provided that at least 90 percent of the peppers show any amount of the specified characteristic color.

U.S. Fancy Mixed Color. Peppers that fail to meet the color requirements of either U.S. Fancy or U.S. Fancy (color specified), but they meet all of the other requirements of U.S. Fancy.

U.S. No. 1. Mature, green, sweet peppers of similar varietal characteristics and which are firm and fairly well shaped. They may be more than slightly indented or curved, but they are not of the type commonly known as *buttom*. They are not decidedly crooked, constricted, or deformed. They are free from sunscald and decay and from damage caused by freezing injury, hail, scars, sunburn, disease, insects, or mechanical or other means. Unless otherwise specified, the diameter of each pepper is not less than 2½ inches, and the length of each pepper is not less than 2½ inches. Any lot of peppers which meets all the requirements of this grade, except those relating to green color, may be designated as U.S. No. 1 with the characteristic color specified in connection with this grade, provided that at least 90 percent of the peppers show any amount of the specified characteristic color.

U.S. No. 1 Mixed Color. Peppers that fail to meet the color requirements of either U.S. No. 1 or U.S. No. 1 (color specified), but they meet all of the other requirements of U.S. No. 1.

U.S. No. 2. Mature, green, sweet peppers of similar varietal characteristics and which are firm, not seriously misshapen, and free from sunscald and decay. Also free from serious damage caused by freezing injury, hail, scars, sunburn, disease, insects, or mechanical or other means. Any lot of peppers which meets all the requirements of this grade, except those relating to green color, may be designated as U.S. No. 2 with the characteristic color specified in connection with this grade, provided that at least 90 percent of the peppers show any amount of the specified characteristic color.

U.S. No. 2 Mixed Color. Peppers that fail to meet the color requirements of either U.S. No. 2 or U.S. No. 2 (color specified), but they meet all of the other requirements of U.S. No. 2.

Unclassified. Sweet peppers which have not been classified in accordance with any of the foregoing grades. The term *unclassified* is not a grade within the meaning of these standards but is provided as a designation to show that no grade has been applied to the lot.

Source:

Agricultural Marketing Service, USDA, 7 CFR sections 51.3270 to 51.3286 (1992), Washington: Government Printing Office.

Peppers, Sweet (Frozen)

Frozen sweet peppers is the frozen product prepared from fresh, clean, sound, firm pods of the common commercial varieties of sweet peppers. They are properly prepared, may or may not be blanched, and are then frozen in accordance with good commercial practice and maintained at temperatures necessary for the preservation of the product.

TYPES

Type I. Green.

Type II. Red.

Type III. Mixed (green and red).

STYLES

Whole Stemmed. Pepper pods with stem and core removed.

Whole Unstemmed. Unpeeled pepper pods with stems trimmed to not more than ½ inch in length.

Halved. Stemmed, unpeeled, pepper pods cut approximately in half from stem to blossom end.

Sliced. Whole stemmed, unpeeled pepper pods or pieces of pepper pods which have been cut into strips.

Diced. Whole stemmed, unpeeled pepper pods or pieces of pepper pods which have been cut into approximate square pieces measuring ½ inch or less.

GRADES

Sweet frozen peppers are graded according to a technical system whereby penalty points are assessed for such factors as edibility, poor appearance, or defects in workmanship. The more penalty points assessed the lower the grade. The grade descriptions which follow are intended only as a general consumer guide. For more detailed information, please consult the source cited below.

U.S. Grade A or U.S. Fancy. Possess similar varietal characteristics and a normal flavor free from objectionable flavor and odors of any kind. They have a good, characteristic, bright color. The peppers are practically uniform in size and symmetry and practically free from such defects as grit, sand, silt, seeds, undeveloped seeds, core and stem material, trimmings, and damaged or seriously damaged units. The units are firm, full fleshed, and tender.

U.S. Grade B or U.S. Extra Standard. Possess similar varietal characteristics and a normal flavor. They have a reasonably good, bright, characteristic color. The peppers are reasonably uniform in size and symmetry and reasonably free from defects. The units are reasonably full fleshed and may lack firmness but are not soft or mushy.

Substandard. Fails to meet the requirements of U.S. Grade B or U.S. Extra Standard.

Source:
Agricultural Marketing Service, USDA, 7 CFR sections 52.3001 to 52.3011 (1991), Washington: Government Printing Office.

Pimientos, Canned

Canned pimientos means the canned product properly prepared from clean, sound, succulent pods of the pimiento plant (*Capsicum annuum*).

For the purposes of these grade standards, pimientos are a group of sweet peppers of the pimiento-type or Spanish pepper. This group includes Pimiento, Perfection, Truheart, and similar varieties. Pimiento fruit pods are smooth, typically conical or heart-shaped, pointed at the blossom end, thick walled, red to reddish-yellow color, and possess a mild and sweet distinct pimiento flavor.

The finished product is prepared from peeled pods and may contain acidifying and firming agents and any other ingredient permissible under the provisions of the Federal Food, Drug, and Cosmetic Act.

TYPES OF PACK

Regular Pack. The drained weight is not less than 66 percent of the water capacity of the container.
Heavy Pack. Little free liquid and drained weight is not less than 90 percent of the water capacity of the container.

STYLES

Whole. Retain the approximate conformation of a whole pod pimiento.
Halves. Cut longitudinally into two approximately equal parts.
Pieces. Cut or broken into units with at least 1 square inch area each and may include less than 50 percent, by weight, of whole pods.
Whole and Pieces. A combination of whole and pieces of pimien-

tos and containing not less than 50 percent, by weight, of whole pimientos.
Slices. Sliced into strips.
Diced. Cut into approximately square pieces.
Chopped. Cut or broken into units of less than 1 square inch area each.

GRADES

Canned pimientos are graded according to a technical system whereby penalty points are assessed for such factors as edibility, poor appearance, or defects in workmanship. The more penalty points assessed the lower the grade. The grade descriptions which follow are intended only as a general consumer guide. For more detailed information, please consult the source cited below.

U.S. Grade A or U.S. Fancy. Possess similar varietal characteristics and a normal flavor. The overall color is bright, practically uniform, and typical of canned pimientos. The pimientos are practically uniform in size and practically free from grit, sand, silt, seeds, core and stem material, peel, units blemished internally or externally by brown or black discoloration, and insect injury. The character is firm, full fleshed, and tender without apparent disintegration. Possess a practically uniform texture.

U.S. Grade C or U.S. Standard. Possess similar varietal characteristics and a normal flavor. Has an overall color that may be variable and slightly dull; none of the units may be green or of a greenish cast or off-color. They are fairly uniform in size and shape and fairly free from defects. The units may be somewhat lacking in firmness and fleshiness and may show some evidence of disintegration, but they are not soft, mushy, or tough.

Substandard. Fails to meet the requirements of U.S. Grade C.

Source:
Agricultural Marketing Service, USDA, 7 CFR sections 52.2681 to 52.2695 (1991), Washington: Government Printing Office.
Food and Drug Administration, 21 CFR 155.200 (1991), Washington: Government Printing Office.

Potatoes

GRADES

Potatoes are graded according to a technical system whereby penalty points are assessed for such factors as edibility, poor appearance, or defects in workmanship. The more penalty points assessed the lower the grade. The grade descriptions which follow are intended only as a general consumer guide. For more detailed information, please consult the source cited below.

U.S. Grade A Small; U.S. Grade A Medium; U.S. Grade A Medium to Large; U.S. Grade A Large. Potatoes of each of these grades are of one variety or similar varietal characteristics. They are fairly well shaped and fairly clean. They are free from freezing injury, black heart, late blight, soft rot, or wet breakdown. Also free from damage caused by sunburn, second growth, growth cracks, air cracks, hollowheart, internal discoloration,

SIZE RANGE REQUIREMENTS FOR U.S. GRADES A & B POTATOES

Size	Round or intermediate shaped varieties		Long varieties		Tolerance for size (%)	
	Min. dia.	Max. dia.	Min. dia. or wt.	Max. dia. or wt.	Undersize	Oversize
Small	1½	2¼	1½ in.	4	3	15
Medium	2¼	3	4 oz	10	5	15
Medium to large	2¼	4	4 oz.	16	5	15
Large	3	4	10 oz.	16	5	15

cuts, shriveling, sprouting, scab, dry rot, rhizoctonia, diseases, wireworm, insects, or other means. Potatoes of these grades should be mature. Potatoes which are not mature and the outer skin loosens or *feathers* readily under the usual handling practices need not meet the maturity requirement if they are firm and are designated as *Early* (for example, *U.S. Grade A Medium-Early*). Potatoes on the shown face should be reasonably representative in size and quality of the contents of the containers.

U.S. Grade B Small; U.S. Grade B Medium; U.S. Grade B Medium to Large; U.S. Grade B Large. Potatoes of each of these grades meet the requirements for their U.S. Grade A counterparts except for the increased tolerance for defects specified below.

Source:
Agricultural Marketing Service, (Consumer Standards) USDA, 7 CFR sections 51.1575 to 51.1587 (1992), Washington: Government Printing Office.

Potatoes, White (Canned)

STYLES

Whole. Peeled white potatoes that retain the approximate original conformation of the whole potato.

Slices or Sliced. Peeled, whole white potatoes cut into slices of substantially uniform thickness.

Dice or Diced. Peeled, whole white potatoes cut into slices of substantially uniform thickness.

Shoestring, French Style, or Julienne. Peeled, whole white potatoes cut into rectangular units having length measurements which are three or more times the width measurements.

Pieces. Peeled, whole white potatoes of random size and/or shape, or potatoes that have been cut into approximate quarters or wedge-shaped units.

Combination. Any combination of two or more of the foregoing styles constitutes a style and is considered as a mixture of the individual styles that comprise the combination.

SIZES

Based on a 20-ounce sample unit.

Size 1 (Tiny). At least 80 percent are not more than 0.98 inch in diameter, and 20 percent may have a diameter of more than 0.98 inch but not more than 1.49 inches.

Size 2 (Small). At least 80 percent have a diameter of more than 0.98 inch but not more than 1.49 inches. 10 percent may have a diameter of 0.98 or less, and 10 percent may have a diameter of more than 1.49 inches but not more than 2 inches.

Size 3 (Medium). At least 80 percent have a diameter of more than 1.49 inch, but not more than 2 inches. 10 percent may have a diameter of more than 0.98 inches, but not more than 1.49 inches. 10 percent may have a diameter of more than 2 inches.

Size 4 (Large). At least 90 percent have a diameter of more than 2 inches. 10 percent may have a diameter of more than 1.49 inches, but not more than 2 inches.

GRADES

Canned white potatoes are graded according to a technical system whereby penalty points are assessed for such factors as edibility, poor appearance, or defects in workmanship. The more penalty points assessed the lower the grade. The grade descriptions which follow are intended only as a general consumer guide. For more detailed information, please consult the source cited below.

U.S. Grade A. The potatoes are firm and tender and have a fine and even grain. There may be sloughing to a degree, but it does not more than slightly affect the appearance of the product. The product has a distinctive flavor and odor which is characteristic of properly prepared and processed canned white potatoes. They are free from objectionable flavors or odors and are practically free from damaged or blemished units.

U.S. Grade B. The potatoes are reasonably tender and may be variable in texture, ranging from somewhat soft to firm, but are not tough, hard, or mushy. There may be a moderate amount of sloughing. May be lacking in good flavor and odor but are free from objectionable flavors or odors. Possess a reasonably good color, although the units individually or collectively may be variable in color, dull, slightly oxidized, or otherwise discolored (but not to the extent that the appearance of the product is seriously affected). Any defects present do not materially affect the appearance or edibility of the product.

Substandard. The quality of canned white potatoes that fails to meet the requirements for U.S. Grade B.

Source:
Agricultural Marketing Service, USDA, 7 CFR sections 52.1811 to 52.1821 (1991), Washington: Government Printing Office.
Food and Drug Administration, 21 CFR 155.200 (1991), Washington: Government Printing Office.

Potatoes, Hash Brown (Frozen)

Frozen hash brown potatoes are prepared from mature, sound, white or Irish potatoes (*Solanum tuberosum*) that are washed, peeled, sorted, and trimmed to assure a clean and wholesome product. The potatoes so prepared are blanched (may or may not be fried) and are shredded or diced or chopped. They are frozen and stored at temperatures necessary for their preservation.

STYLES

Shredded. Cut into thin strips with cross-sectional dimensions from 1 mm by 2 mm to 4 mm by 6 mm and formed into a solid mass before freezing.

Diced. Cut into cube shaped units from 6 mm to 15 mm on an edge and loose frozen.

Chopped. Random cut into pieces less than 32 mm in their greatest dimension and loose frozen.

GRADES

Frozen hash brown potatoes are graded according to a technical system whereby penalty points are assessed for such factors as edibility, poor appearance, or defects in workmanship. The more penalty points assessed the lower the grade. The grade descriptions which follow are intended only as a general consumer guide. For more detailed information, please consult the source cited below.

U.S. Grade A. Hash brown potatoes have the characteristic flavor and odor of properly prepared potatoes. The flavor is free from bitterness, pronounced scorched or caramelized flavors, and off-flavors and off-odors of any kind. As a mass before heating, the potatoes have a bright, uniform white to light cream color which is not more than slightly affected by yellowish, greenish, grayish, or otherwise discolored units. After heating, the cooked surface has a fairly uniform brown color. The hash brown potatoes are practically free from crushed units, discolored eyes, and discoloration which affect their appearance or edibility. The potatoes are firm and tender and are not more than slightly affected by units which are hard, mushy, pasty, soggy, dry, or oil soaked.

U.S. Grade B. The hash brown potatoes have a normal flavor and odor. The potatoes, as a mass before heating, have a reasonably bright, uniform white to cream color which is not seriously affected by yellowish, greenish, grayish, or otherwise discolored units. After heating, the cooked surface may brown only slightly or unevenly, but is not charred. The hash brown potatoes are reasonably firm and tender, are reasonably free from defects, and are not seriously affected by units which are hard, mushy, pasty, soggy, dry, or oil soaked.

Substandard. Fails to meet the requirements of U.S. Grade B.

Source:
Agricultural Marketing Service, USDA, 7 CFR sections 52.6401 to 52.6410 (1991), Washington: Government Printing Office.

Potatoes, Peeled

Peeled potatoes are clean, sound, fresh tubers of the potato plant prepared by washing, peeling, trimming, and sorting, and by proper treatment, to prevent discoloration, by any means permissible under the provisions of the Federal Food, Drug, and Cosmetic Act. The product is properly packed in suitable containers and securely closed to maintain the product in a sanitary condition.

STYLES

Whole. Retain the approximate original conformation of the whole potato.

Whole and Cut. Consisting of not less than 50 percent, by weight, of whole potatoes and the remainder cut into pieces.

Cut and Whole. Consisting of less than 50 percent, by weight, of whole potatoes, and the remainder cut into pieces.

Sliced. Consisting of potato slices of practically uniform thickness with parallel surfaces.

Diced. Consisting of cubed potatoes.

French Style or Shoestring. Consisting of strips of potatoes.

Cut. Cut into pieces which do not conform to the foregoing styles.

GRADES

Peeled potatoes are graded according to a technical system whereby penalty points are assessed for such factors as edibility, poor appearance, or defects in workmanship. The more penalty points assessed the lower the grade. The grade descriptions which follow are intended only as a general consumer guide. For more detailed information, please consult the source cited below.

U.S. Grade A. Possess similar varietal characteristics and a normal flavor and odor. They have a good color that is practically uniform and free from oxidation. When cooked until tender, the potatoes show no appreciable discoloration. They are practically free from defects such as peel, blemished units, and mechanical damage. They possess a good, fairly firm texture and are practically free from tough outer surfaces. They are practically uniform in size.

Whole. Not less than 1½ inches in diameter. At least 40 percent of long varieties are 4¾ ounces in weight or larger, and 60 percent of round or intermediate varieties are 2⅛ inches or more in diameter.

Whole and Cut Potatoes. The whole potatoes are not less than 1½ inches in diameter, and the largest unit is not more than five times the weight of the smallest unit.

Cut and Whole Potatoes. The whole potatoes are not less than 1½ inches in diameter, and the largest unit is not more than five times the weight of the smallest unit.

Sliced Potatoes. In 90 percent of the slices of the most uniform diameter, the diameter of the largest slice is not more than twice the diameter of the smallest slice and is not less than 1½ inches.

Diced Potatoes. The units are practically uniform in size. The aggregate weight of the units which are smaller than one-half of the predominant size of the cubes and of all large and irregular units does not exceed 20 percent of the weight of all the units.

French Style or Shoestring. The strips of potatoes are practically uniform in size. The aggregate weight of all the strips less than 1 inch in length and strips of substantially smaller cross section than the predominant size of strips does not exceed 15 percent of the weight of all the strips.

Cut. The largest unit is not more than five times the weight of the smallest unit and not more than 25 percent, by weight, of individual units weigh less than ½ ounce each.

U.S. Grade B. Possess similar varietal characteristics and a normal flavor and odor. They have a reasonably good color. The units, individually or collectively, may be variable, dull, slightly oxidized, or otherwise discolored, but not to the extent that the appearance is materially affected. When cooked until tender, the potatoes show no material discoloration as a result of cooking. Are reasonably free from defects and possess a reasonably good texture that may be slightly flabby. They are reasonably free from tough outer surfaces. They are reasonably uniform in size.

Whole. The potatoes may vary considerably in size and are not less than 1½ inches in diameter.

Whole and Cut Potatoes. The units may vary considerably in size. The largest unit is not more than six times the weight of the smallest unit.

Cut and Whole Potatoes. The units may vary considerably in size. The largest unit is not more than six times the weight of the smallest unit.

Sliced Potatoes. In 90 percent of the slices of the most uniform diameter, the diameter of the largest slice is not more than three times the diameter of the smallest slice, and the smallest slice is not less than 1½ inches in diameter.

Diced Potatoes. The units are reasonably uniform in size. The aggregate weight of the units which are smaller than one-half of the predominant size of the cubes and of all large and irregular units does not exceed 30 percent of the weight of all the units.

French Style or Shoestring. The strips of potatoes are reasonably uniform in size. The aggregate weight of all strips less than 1 inch in length and strips of substantially smaller cross section than the predominant size of strips does not exceed 25 percent of the weight of all the strips.

Cut. The units may vary considerably in size, and not more than 50 percent, by weight, of individual units weigh less than ½ ounce each.

Substandard. Fail to meet the requirements of U.S. Grade B.

Source:
Agricultural Marketing Service, USDA, 7 CFR sections 52.2421 to 52.2432 (1991), Washington: Government Printing Office.

Pork and Beans, Canned

Canned pork and beans (canned dried white beans with pork) is the product prepared from dry mature white beans of the species *Phaseolus vulgans,* with pork or pork fat, and with a packing medium or sauce consisting of water, tomato products, and any other safe and suitable ingredients. The product is prepared by washing, soaking, blanching, or other processing. It is packed in hermetically sealed containers and sufficiently processed by heat to assure preservation.

TYPES

Pea Beans or Navy Beans.
Small White Beans.
Flat Small White Beans.
Great Northern Beans.
Other Types of White Beans (except White Lima Beans).

GRADES

Caned pork and beans are graded according to a technical system whereby penalty points are assessed for such factors as edibility, poor appearance, or defects in workmanship. The more penalty points assessed the lower the grade. The grade descriptions which follow are intended only as a general consumer guide. For more detailed information, please consult the source cited below.

U.S. Grade A. Practically similar varietal characteristics. The sauce is smooth and is neither grainy nor lumpy. The product is practically free from matting. When emptied on a flat surface, it forms a slightly mounded mass of beans and sauce with not more than a slight separation of liquid. The product is practically free from such defects as loose skin, broken beans, mashed beans, blemished beans, or any other defects that may affect appearance or eating quality. The beans have a good, typical texture that may be slightly granular or slightly firm. The skins are tender. The product has a good, characteristic flavor and odor and is free from objectionable flavors and objectionable odors of any kind. The flavor of the sauce is rich, distinct, and characteristic of the ingredients. The beans have a color that is bright, typical, and reasonably uniform. The sauce is reasonably bright and has the distinguishing color characteristics of the addition of tomato products.

U.S. Grade B. The beans have reasonably similar varietal characteristics. The sauce is reasonably smooth and may be slightly grainy or slightly lumpy. The product may have a thick consistency but is reasonably free from matting. When emptied on a flat surface, it may have practically no separation of liquid or may have a thin consistency with separation of liquid, but it should not be watery. It is reasonably free from defects. The beans may be firm or soft, and the presence of hard and mushy beans does not materially affect the eating quality. The skins may be slightly tough, and the beans may be granular or mealy. The product may be lacking in good flavor and odor, but it is free from objectionable flavors and odors of any kind. The flavor of the sauce may be weak. The beans have a color that is fairly uniform and may be slightly dull, but not off-color. The sauce may be lacking in the distinguishing color characteristics of the addition of tomato products.

Substandard. Fails to meet the requirements of U.S. Grade B.

Source:
Agricultural Marketing Service, USDA, 7 CFR sections 52.6441 to 52.6451 (1991), Washington: Government Printing Office.

Pumpkin and Squash, Canned

Canned pumpkin and canned squash is the canned product prepared from clean, sound, properly matured, golden-fleshed, firm-shelled, sweet varieties of either pumpkins or squashes. The pumpkins and squash are washed, stemmed, cut, steamed, and reduced to a pulp. The product is properly sieved and finished in accordance with good commercial practice and is then sufficiently processed by heat to assure preservation of the product in hermetically sealed containers.

GRADES

Canned pumpkin and squash are graded according to a technical system whereby penalty points are assessed for such factors as edibility, poor appearance, or defects in workmanship. The more penalty points assessed the lower the grade. The grade descriptions which follow are intended only as a general consumer guide. For more detailed information, please consult the source cited below.

U.S. Grade A or U.S. Fancy. Possesses a practically uniform, bright color typical of canned pumpkin or canned squash prepared from well-matured pumpkin or squash. Possesses a good consistency. After emptying the contents onto a dry-flat surface, the product retains the approximate shape of the container or holds a high mound formation; and, at the end of two minutes, the highest point of the mound is not less than 60 percent of the height of the container. The canned pumpkin or canned squash particles are evenly divided. The product is fine grained and smooth, but not pasty. The pumpkin or squash particles are not hard. The product is practically free from defects such as sand, grit, silt, pieces of seed, fiber, and coarse, dark, or off-colored particles.

U.S. Grade C or U.S. Standard. Possesses a color typical of fairly well-matured pumpkin or squash. May possess a slight tinge of gray or tan color and may be variable or slightly dull, but not to the extent that the appearance or eating quality is materially affected. After emptying the contents onto a dry-flat surface, the product may flow just enough to level off to a nearly uniform depth or may be moderately mounded; and, at the end of two minutes, not more than 30 cubic centimeters of free liquor separates for each 30 ounces of net contents. The canned pumpkin or canned squash particles are evenly divided. The product may be slightly coarse and slightly pasty, but not decidedly pasty. The pumpkin or squash particles are not hard. The product is fairly free from defects and possesses a normal flavor.

Substandard. Fails to meet the requirements of U.S. Grade C or U.S. Standard.

Source:
Agricultural Marketing Service, USDA, 7 CFR sections 52.2741 to 52.2751 (1991), Washington: Government Printing Office.

Radishes

TYPES

Topped Radishes. The tops are clipped back to not more than three-eighths inch in length.
Bunched Radishes. Have full length tops which are tied in bunches.

SIZE

Small. Less than ¾ inch in diameter.
Medium. Less than ¾ to 1 inch in diameter.
Large. Over 1 to 1¼ inches in diameter.
Very Large. Over 1¼ inches in diameter.

GRADES

Radishes are graded according to a technical system whereby penalty points are assessed for such factors as edibility, poor appearance, or defects in workmanship. The more penalty points assessed the lower the grade. The grade descriptions which follow are intended only as a general consumer guide. For more detailed information, please consult the source cited below.

U.S. No. 1. Radishes of similar varietal characteristics. The roots are clean, well formed, smooth, firm, and tender. They are not stringy or woody. They are free from decay and from damage caused by freezing, growth cracks, air cracks, cuts, pithiness, disease, insects, or other means. Bunched radishes have tops which are fresh, free from decay, and free from damage caused by freezing, seed stems, yellowing or other discoloration, disease, insects, or other means. Unless otherwise specified, the diameter of each root is not less than ⅝ inch.

U.S. Commercial. Radishes which meet the requirements for the U.S. No. 1 grade except for the increased tolerances for defects.

Source:
Agricultural Marketing Service, USDA, 7 CFR sections 51.2395 to 51.2413 (1992), Washington: Government Printing Office.

Rhubarb, Field Grown

GRADES

Field grown rhubarb is graded according to a technical system whereby penalty points are assessed for such factors as edibility, poor appearance, or defects in workmanship. The more penalty points assessed the lower the grade. The grade descriptions which follow are intended only as a general consumer guide. For more detailed information, please consult the source cited below.

U.S. Fancy. Stalks of rhubarb of similar varietal characteristics and which are very well colored. The pink or red color predominates on three-fourths or more of the length of the stalk. They are fresh (not limp or wilted) and tender. The are straight, have not more than a slight concave curvature of the face, and are not more than slightly twisted along the longitudinal axis of the stalk. They are clean and well trimmed. The top has been neatly knife-trimmed so that not more than 2 inches of the midribs and thin leaf tissue remains. Most of the basal husk has been removed. The stalks do not have an open texture with air spaces in the central portion. They are free from decay and from damage caused by scars, freezing, disease, insects, or mechanical or other means. The diameter of each stalk is not less than 1 inch, and the length not less than 10 inches.

U.S. No. 1. Stalks of rhubarb of similar varietal characteristics and which are well colored. A pink or red color predominates on one-half or more of the length of the stalk. They are fresh, tender, straight, clean, well trimmed, and not pithy. They are free from decay and from damage caused by scars, freezing, disease, insects, or mechanical or other means. Unless otherwise specified, the diameter of each stalk is not less than ¾ inch, and the length not less than 10 inches.

U.S. No. 2. Stalks of rhubarb of similar varietal characteristics and which are fairly well colored. A pink or red color predominates on one-fourth or more of the stalk. The stalk is not badly twisted or crooked. They are clean, well trimmed, and not pithy. They are free from decay and from serious damage caused by scars, freezing, disease, insects, or mechanical or other means. Unless otherwise specified, the diameter of each stalk is not less than ½ inch, and the length not less than 8 inches.

Unclassified. Rhubarb which has not been classified in accordance with any of the foregoing grades. The term *unclassified* is not a grade within the meaning of these standards but is provided as a designation to show that no grade has been applied to the lot.

Source:
Agricultural Marketing Service, USDA, 7 CFR sections 51.3665 to 51.3683 (1992), Washington: Government Printing Office.

Shallots, Bunched

SIZE

Small. Less than ⅜ inch.
Medium. ⅜ to ¾ inch, inclusive.
Large. Over ¾ inch.

GRADES

Bunched shallots are graded according to a technical system

whereby penalty points are assessed for such factors as edibility, poor appearance, or defects in workmanship. The more penalty points assessed the lower the grade. The grade descriptions which follow are intended only as a general consumer guide. For more detailed information, please consult the source cited below.

U.S. No. 1. Shallots of similar varietal characteristics. They are fairly well formed, not more than slightly curved, crooked, or misshapen, and do not show more than slight bulb formation. The edible portion of the shallot is not soft. They are young and tender. They are well trimmed and separated so that not more than two are attached together. They are fairly clean and free from decay. Also free from damage caused by seed stems, foreign material, disease, insects, or mechanical or other means. The tops are fresh (not withered or badly wilted). They have a good green color, although a slight discoloration of the extreme tips is not objectionable. They are free from damage caused by broken or bruised leaves. Unless otherwise specified, the overall length (roots excepted) of the shallots should not exceed 22 inches, and the shallots should be not less than ¼ of an inch or more than ¾ of an inch in diameter.

U.S. No. 2. Shallots which are not badly misshapen. They are fairly firm with the edible portion not more than slightly soft. They are fairly young and tender (not tough, stringy, or advanced to the stage where the neck is flabby). They are fairly well trimmed and are separated so that not more than three are attached together. They are fairly clean and free from decay. Also free from serious damage caused by seed stems, foreign material, disease, insects, mechanical, or other means. The tops are fresh and of fairly good green color (the tops are pale or yellowish green or otherwise slightly discolored). They are free from serious damage caused by broken or bruised leaves. Unless otherwise specified, the minimum size of the shallots is not less than ¼ of an inch in diameter.

Unclassified. Shallots which are not graded in conformity with either of the foregoing grades. The term *unclassified* is not a grade but is provided as a designation to show that no definite grade as been applied to the lot.

Source:
Agricultural Marketing Service, USDA, 7 CFR sections 51.1630 to 51.1650 (1992), Washington: Government Printing Office.

Snap Beans

These standards can be applied to all beans used in their entirety, as opposed to shelled beans, and includes types such as snap, pole, and wax beans. These standards do not apply to types such as fava, lima, pinto, or calico beans.

GRADES

Snap beans are graded according to a technical system whereby penalty points are assessed for such factors as edibility, poor appearance, or defects in workmanship. The more penalty points assessed the lower the grade. The grade descriptions which follow are intended only as a general consumer guide. For more detailed information, please consult the source cited below.

U.S. Fancy. Beans of similar varietal characteristics and which are of reasonable and fairly uniform size. They are not excessively short for the variety and have not been prematurely picked. They are well formed, bright, clean, fresh, young, tender, and firm (not wilted or flabby). They are free from soft rot and from damage caused by leaves, leaf stems, other foreign matter, hail, disease, insects, or mechanical or other means.

U.S. No. 1. Beans of similar varietal characteristics and which are of reasonable size. They are fairly well formed and are not badly crooked, curled, twisted, or otherwise badly misshapen for the variety. They are fairly bright, fresh, fairly young and tender, and firm. The beans are free from soft rot and from damage caused by dirt, leaves, leaf stems, other foreign matter, hail disease, insects, or mechanical or other means. Has an increased tolerance for defects.

U.S. No. 2. Beans of similar varietal characteristics and which are fairly fresh, firm, and not over-mature. They are free from soft rot and from serious damage caused by dirt, leaves, leaf stems, other foreign matter, hail, disease, insects, or mechanical or other means. Has an increase tolerance for defects.

Source:
Agricultural Marketing Service, USDA, 7 CFR sections 51.3829 to 51.3843 (1992), Washington: Government Printing Office.

Spinach, Bunched

These standards are applicable to spinach of the goosefoot (*Chenopodiaceae*) family, which is bunched and packed separately in containers as either leaves or plants.

GRADES

Bunched spinach is graded according to a technical system whereby penalty points are assessed for such factors as edibility, poor appearance, or defects in workmanship. The more penalty points assessed the lower the grade. The grade descriptions which follow are intended only as a general consumer guide. For more detailed information, please consult the source cited below.

U.S. No. 1. Bunched spinach of similar varietal characteristics. They are well grown and are not stunted or poorly developed. They are fairly clean and well trimmed. For plants, the roots are no longer than 1 inch below the common point of attachment of the leaf stems. For leaves, not more than 15 percent of the leaves in the bunch have leaf stems longer than the length of the attached leaf. They are not more than slightly wilted. They are free from decay and from damage caused by coarse stalks, seed stems, flower buds, discoloration, wilting, foreign material, insects, freezing, and mechanical or other means.

U.S. No. 2. Bunched spinach of similar varietal characteristics. They are well grown, reasonably clean, and fairly well trimmed. For plants, the roots are no longer than 1 inch below the common point of attachment of the leaf stems. For leaves, not

more than 15 percent of the leaves in the bunch have leaf stems longer than one and one-half times the length of the attached leaf. They are fresh and free from decay. Also free from serious damage by coarse stalks, seed stems, flower buds, discoloration, wilting, foreign material, insects, freezing, and mechanical or other means.

Source:
Agricultural Marketing Service, USDA, 7 CFR sections 51.2891 to 51.2896 (1992), Washington: Government Printing Office.

Spinach, Canned

Canned spinach is the product properly prepared from the succulent leaves of the spinach plant and packed with the addition of water in hermetically sealed containers. It is sufficiently processed by heat to prevent spoilage. Citric acid or a vinegar may be added in a quantity not more than sufficient to permit effective processing by heat without discoloration or other impairment of the product. One or more optional seasoning ingredients may be added.

STYLES

Whole Leaf. Consists substantially of the leaf and adjoining portion of the stem.

Cut Leaf or Sliced. Consists of the leaf and adjoining portion of stem that has been cut predominantly into large pieces approximating ¾ inch or more in the longest dimension or cut predominantly into approximate strips.

Chopped. Consists of the leaf and adjoining portion of stem that has been cut predominantly into small pieces less than approximately ¾ inch in the longest dimension.

GRADES

Canned spinach is graded according to a technical system whereby penalty points are assessed for such factors as edibility, poor appearance, or defects in workmanship. The more penalty points assessed the lower the grade. The grade descriptions which follow are intended only as a general consumer guide. For more detailed information, please consult the source cited below.

U.S. Grade A or U.S. Fancy. Canned spinach that has a good flavor and odor and is attractive in appearance and eating quality. It is not adversely affected due to a mushy texture, disintegration, ragged cutting, shredded leaves, shredded stems, or portions of stems.

U.S. Grade B or U.S. Extra Standard. Canned spinach that has a good flavor and odor and is reasonably attractive in appearance and eating quality.

Substandard. Canned spinach that fails to meet the requirements for U.S. Grade B or U.S. Extra Standard.

Sources:
Agricultural Marketing Service, USDA, 7 CFR sections 52.1901 to 52.1914

(1991), Washington: Government Printing Office.
Food and Drug Administration, 21 CFR 155.200 (1991), Washington: Government Printing Office.

Spinach, Plants

GRADES

Spinach plants are graded according to a technical system whereby penalty points are assessed for such factors as edibility, poor appearance, or defects in workmanship. The more penalty points assessed the lower the grade. The grade descriptions which follow are intended only as a general consumer guide. For more detailed information, please consult the source cited below.

U.S. No. 1. Spinach plants of similar varietal characteristics and which are well grown and not stunted or poorly developed. They are not more than slightly wilted and are fairly clean. They are well trimmed and cut at the crown of the root, or they are cut so that the root is not longer than 1 inch. They are free from decay and from damage caused by coarse stalks, seed stems, discoloration, foreign material, second growth, freezing, disease, insects, or mechanical or other means.

U.S. Commercial. Spinach plants which meet all the requirements for U.S. No. 1 grade except that the spinach plants need only be free from damage by dirt and except for an increase in tolerances.

Unclassified. Spinach plants which have not been classified in accordance with either of the foregoing grades. The term *unclassified* is not a grade within the meaning of these standards but is provided as a designation to show that no grade has been applied to the lot.

Source:
Agricultural Marketing Service, USDA, 7 CFR sections 51.2880 to 51.2890 (1992), Washington: Government Printing Office.

Squash, Cooked (Frozen)

Frozen cooked squash is the clean, sound, properly matured product made from varieties of fall or late type squash which have been properly prepared by washing, cutting, cleaning, steaming, reducing to a pulp, and removing seed and fiber. The product is then frozen in accordance with good commercial practice and maintained at temperatures necessary for the preservation of the product.

GRADES

Cooked frozen squash is graded according to a technical system whereby penalty points are assessed for such factors as edibility, poor appearance, or defects in workmanship. The more penalty points assessed the lower the grade. The grade descriptions which follow are intended only as a general consumer guide. For more

detailed information, please consult the source cited below.

U.S. Grade A or U.S. Fancy. The warmed, mixed squash, after emptying from a container to a dry, flat surface, forms a well-mounded mass; at the end of two minutes, there is not more than a slight separation of free liquor. The warmed, mixed squash possesses a practically uniform, bright, typical color and is free from discoloration due to oxidation or other causes. It possesses an even texture and is granular, but not lumpy, pasty, or salvy. The squash particles are not hard. After heating, the squash possesses a good flavor and odor free from objectionable flavors and odors of any kind. The product is practically free from defects such as sand, grit, silt, pieces of seed, fiber, and dark or off-colored particles.

U.S. Grade B or U.S. Extra Standard. The consistency of the warmed, mixed squash is such that after emptying from the container to a dry, flat surface, it may be reasonably stiff, but not excessively stiff, and forms a moderately mounded mass. At the end of two minutes, there may be a moderate, but not excessive, separation of free liquor. The color may be variable or slightly dull but is not off-color. The warmed, mixed squash has an even texture, may lack granular characteristics, and may be slightly pasty or slightly salvy but not decidedly pasty or salvy. The squash particles are not hard. Possesses a fairly good flavor and odor which, after heating, may be lacking in good flavor and odor, but it is free from objectionable flavors and odors. It is reasonably free from defects.

Substandard. Fails to meet the requirements of U.S. Grade B or U.S. Extra Standard.

Source:
Agricultural Marketing Service, USDA, 7 CFR sections 52.1941 to 52.1950 (1991), Washington: Government Printing Office.

Squash, Summer

These standards apply only to squash which are picked in the immature stages of development and eaten without the removal of seeds and seed cavity tissue. Squash commonly used in this manner are yellow crookneck, yellow straightneck, white scallop (patty pan, cymling), zucchini, cocozelle, etc., each including one or more varieties. Because of the size differences between varieties and the difference in size preference in various markets, there are no size requirements in the grades.

GRADES

Summer squash is graded according to a technical system whereby penalty points are assessed for such factors as edibility, poor appearance, or defects in workmanship. The more penalty points assessed the lower the grade. The grade descriptions which follow are intended only as a general consumer guide. For more detailed information, please consult the source cited below.

U.S. No. 1. Squash of one variety or similar varietal characteristics, with stems or portions of stems attached. It is fairly young and has a fairly tender skin, fairly tender undeveloped seeds, and firm, moist seed cavity tissue. It is not so badly twisted, grooved, or otherwise misshapen as to damage the appearance of the squash. It is firm and free from decay and breakdown. Also free from damage caused by discoloration, cuts, bruises, scars, freezing, dirt or other foreign material, disease, insects, or mechanical or other means.

U.S. No. 2. Squash of one variety or similar varietal characteristics and which are not old and tough. They are firm, free from decay and breakdown, and free from damage caused by freezing. They are also free from serious damage caused by discoloration, cuts, bruises, scars, dirt or other foreign material, disease, insects, or mechanical or other means. Has an increased tolerance for defects.

Unclassified. Squash which has not been classified in accordance with any of the foregoing grades. The term *unclassified* is not a grade within the meaning of these standards but is provided as a designation to show that no grade has been applied to the lot.

Source:
Agricultural Marketing Service, USDA, 7 CFR sections 51.4050 to 51.4062 (1992), Washington: Government Printing Office.

Squash, Summer (Canned)

Canned squash (summer type) is the canned product prepared from clean, sound, succulent, immature summer type squash which has been washed, properly trimmed, and sorted. The product is packed in accordance with good commercial practice and is sufficiently processed by heat to assure preservation of the product in hermetically sealed containers.

STYLES

Whole. Whole squash with stems removed.
Sliced Crosswise. Cut at right angle to the longitudinal axis into slices of approximately uniform thickness with parallel surfaces.
Diced. Cut into fairly uniform diced units.
Cut. Cut into units which are not uniform in size or shape.

GRADES

Canned summer type squash is graded according to a technical system whereby penalty points are assessed for such factors as edibility, poor appearance, or defects in workmanship. The more penalty points assessed the lower the grade. The grade descriptions which follow are intended only as a general consumer guide. For more detailed information, please consult the source cited below.

U.S. Grade A or U.S. Fancy. Possesses similar varietal characteristics and a normal flavor. Has a good color which is bright and typical of properly processed young and tender squash. The squash is fairly free from defects such as harmless extraneous vegetable material, sand, grit, or silt, poorly cut units, units

damaged by mechanical injury, and units damaged by discoloration, scars, insect, injury, or other means. The character of the squash is such that the units are practically intact and are fleshy and tender. The seeds are in the immature stage.

U.S. Grade C or U.S. Standard. Possesses similar varietal characteristics and a normal flavor. The color is typical of fairly young and tender squash. The product is practically free from defects and possesses a fairly good character such that the units may show slight disintegration, may have lost to a considerable extent their fleshy texture, and may be fairly tender. The seeds may have passed the immature stage of maturity, but are not hard.

Substandard. Fails to meet the requirements of U.S. Grade C or U.S. Standard.

Source:
Agricultural Marketing Service, USDA, 7 CFR sections 52.3581 to 52.3592 (1991), Washington: Government Printing Office.

Squash, Summer (Frozen)

Frozen summer type squash is prepared from the fresh, sound, immature fruit of the squash (summer type) plant. The squash is properly prepared and blanched and is then frozen in accordance with good commercial practice and maintained at temperatures necessary for the preservation of the product.

STYLES

Sliced
Cut

GRADES

Frozen summer type squash is graded according to a technical system whereby penalty points are assessed for such factors as edibility, poor appearance, or defects in workmanship. The more penalty points assessed the lower the grade. The grade descriptions which follow are intended only as a general consumer guide. For more detailed information, please consult the source cited below.

U.S. Grade A or U.S. Fancy. Frozen squash that possesses similar varietal characteristics. After cooking, it has a good, characteristic, normal flavor and odor and is free from objectionable flavors and odors of any kind. It possesses a good color that is bright and typical of young and tender squash. The units are practically intact and are fleshy and tender. The seeds are in the immature stage. The product is practically free from harmless extraneous vegetable material, sand, grit, silt, poorly cut units, units damaged by mechanical injury, and units damaged by discoloration, scars, insect injury, or any other means.

U.S. Grade B or U.S. Extra Standard. Frozen squash that possesses similar varietal characteristics. After cooking, it may be lacking in good flavor and odor, but it is free from objectionable flavors and odors of any kind. It possesses a reasonably good color that is typical of reasonably young and tender squash. The units may show slight disintegration, may have lost (to a considerable extent) their fleshy texture, and may be reasonably tender. The seeds may have passed the immature stage of maturity. The product is reasonably free from defects.

Substandard. Fails to meet the requirements of U.S. Grade B or U.S. Extra Standard.

Source:
Agricultural Marketing Service, USDA, 7 CFR sections 52.1961 to 52.1979 (1991), Washington: Government Printing Office.

Squash and Pumpkins, Fall and Winter Types

These grade standards apply to squash and pumpkin, both of the cucurbit family (*Cucurbita pepo, C. moshata, C. maxima, C. mixsta*), having a hard shell and mature seeds.

GRADES

Fall and winter type squash and pumpkins are graded according to a technical system whereby penalty points are assessed for such factors as edibility, poor appearance, or defects in workmanship. The more penalty points assessed the lower the grade. The grade descriptions which follow are intended only as a general consumer guide. For more detailed information, please consult the source cited below.

U.S. No. 1. Squash or pumpkin which are of similar varietal characteristics. They are well matured and not broken or cracked. They are free from soft rot or wet breakdown. Also free from damage caused by scars, dry rot, freezing, dirt, disease, insects, and mechanical or other means.

U.S. No. 2. Squash or pumpkin of similar varietal characteristics, fairly well matured (the outer skin is not tender), and not broken or cracked. Free from soft rot or wet breakdown. Free from serious damage caused by scars, dry rot, freezing, dirt, disease, insects, and mechanical or other means.

Source:
Agricultural Marketing Service, USDA, 7 CFR sections 51.4030 to 51.4035 (1992), Washington: Government Printing Office.

Squash Labeled as Pumpkin

Certain varieties of firm-shelled, golden-fleshed, sweet squash are often labeled as *pumpkin* or *canned pumpkin*. Pumpkin and squash are sometimes mixed intentionally to obtain the consistency most acceptable to users. Also, the labeling of squash seeds as *pumpkin seed* is sometimes done when the squash seeds are practically indistinguishable from pumpkin seeds, or when the squash seeds are mixed with the seeds of the pie or field pumpkin.

Source:
Food and Drug Administration, *Compliance Policy Guides*, Guide 7114.22 and 7114.25, Reissued 12/08/88, Washington: National Technical Information Service.

Succotash, Canned

Canned succotash is composed of cream style or whole grain corn and lima beans or snap beans, with or without tomatoes. It may be packed with the addition of water and with or without the addition of sugar or salt. It is sufficiently processed by heat to assure preservation of the product in hermetically sealed containers.

GRADES

Canned succotash is graded according to a technical system whereby penalty points are assessed for such factors as edibility, poor appearance, or defects in workmanship. The more penalty points assessed the lower the grade. The grade descriptions which follow are intended only as a general consumer guide. For more detailed information, please consult the source cited below.

U.S. Grade A or U.S. Fancy. Consists of cream style or whole grain sweet corn and lima or snap beans which meet the requirements of U.S. Grade A or U.S. Fancy for the respective canned or frozen commodities. If tomatoes are an ingredient, they must meet the requirements of U.S. Grade A canned tomatoes for color and absence of defects.

U.S. Grade B or U.S. Extra Standard. Consists of cream style or whole grain sweet corn and lima or snap beans which meet the requirements of U.S. Grade B or U.S. Extra Standard for the respective canned or frozen commodities. If tomatoes are an ingredient, they must meet the requirements of U.S. Grade B canned tomatoes for color and absence of defects.

U.S. Grade C or U.S. Standard. Consists of cream style or whole grain sweet corn and lima or snap beans which meet the requirements of U.S. Grade C or U.S. Standard for the respective canned or frozen commodities. If tomatoes are an ingredient, they must meet the requirements of U.S. Grade C canned tomatoes for color and absence of defects.

Grade D or Substandard. Fails to meet the requirements of U.S. Grade C or U.S. Standard.

Source:
Agricultural Marketing Service, USDA, 7 CFR sections 52.6001 to 52.6007 (1991), Washington: Government Printing Office.

Succotash, Frozen

Frozen succotash is the frozen product prepared from fresh, clean, sound, succulent kernels of sweet corn, the immature seed of varieties of lima beans and vegetable soybeans, or fresh immature pods of green beans and wax beans. The ingredients are mixed and properly drained and then frozen in accordance with good commercial practice and maintained at temperatures necessary for the preservation of the product. When soybeans, green beans, or wax beans are used, the product is designated as frozen soybean succotash or frozen green bean (or wax bean) succotash, as the case may be.

GRADES

Frozen succotash is graded according to a technical system whereby penalty points are assessed for such factors as edibility, poor appearance, or defects in workmanship. The more penalty points assessed the lower the grade. The grade descriptions which follow are intended only as a general consumer guide. For more detailed information, please consult the source cited below.

U.S. Grade A or U S. Fancy. Possesses similar varietal characteristics. After cooking, it has a good, characteristic normal flavor and odor and is free from objectionable flavors and odors of any kind. It is tender and possesses a color typical of young and tender vegetables that have been properly prepared and properly processed. The frozen, whole kernel (or whole grain) corn is practically free from off-colored kernels and from defects such as pieces of pod, leaves, stems, pieces of cob, husk, other similar vegetable matter, damaged units, and any other defects.

U.S. Grade B or U.S. Extra Standard. Possesses similar varietal characteristics. After cooking, it may be lacking in good flavor and odor, but it is free from objectionable flavors and odors of any kind. It is reasonably tender and possess a color typical of reasonably young and tender vegetables. The frozen, whole kernel (or whole grain) corn is reasonably free from off-colored kernels and is reasonably free from defects.

U.S. Grade C or U.S. Standard. Possesses similar varietal characteristics, a fairly good flavor and odor, and is fairly tender. Possesses a color that may be dull but not to the extent that the appearance is materially affected. The whole kernel (or whole grain) corn in the frozen succotash is fairly free from off-variety kernels and is fairly free from defects.

Substandard. Fails to meet the requirements of U.S. Grade C or U.S. Standard.

Source:
Agricultural Marketing Service, USDA, 7 CFR sections 52.2011 to 52.2022 (1991), Washington: Government Printing Office.

Sweet Potatoes

GRADES

Sweet potatoes are graded according to a technical system whereby penalty points are assessed for such factors as edibility, poor appearance, or defects in workmanship. The more penalty points assessed the lower the grade. The grade descriptions which follow

are intended only as a general consumer guide. For more detailed information, please consult the source cited below.

U.S. Extra No. 1. Sweet potatoes of similar varietal characteristics and which are firm and not more than slightly flabby or shriveled. They are smooth and free from veining. They are fairly clean and are not so curved, crooked, constricted, or otherwise misshapen as to detract form the appearance. They are free from freezing, injury, internal breakdown, black rot, other decay, or wet breakdown. Also free from damage caused by secondary rootlets, sprouts, cuts, bruises, scars, growth cracks, scurf, pox (soil rot), other diseases, wireworms, weevils, other insects, or other means. The length is not less than 3 inches or more than 9 inches. Maximum weight is not more than 18 ounces. Maximum diameter is not more than 3¼ inches. Minimum diameter, unless otherwise specified, is not less than 1¾ inches.

U.S. No. 1. Sweet potatoes of one type which are firm, fairly smooth, fairly clean, and fairly well shaped. They are free from freezing injury, internal breakdown, black rot, other decay, or wet breakdown. They are also free from damage caused by secondary rootlets, sprouts, cuts, bruises, scars, growth cracks, scurf, wireworms, weevils, other insects, or other means. The maximum diameter is not more than 3½ inches. Maximum weight is not more than 20 ounces. Length, unless otherwise specified, is not less than 3 inches or more than 9 inches. Minimum diameter, unless otherwise specified, is not less than 1¾ inches.

U.S. Commercial. Sweet potatoes which meet all the requirements of the U.S. No. 1 grade except that an increased tolerance for defects is allowed.

U.S. No. 2. Sweet potatoes of one type which are firm and which are free from freezing, injury, internal breakdown, black rot, other decay, or wet breakdown. They are free from serious damage caused by dirt or other foreign materials, cuts, bruises, scars, growth cracks, pox (soil rot), other diseases, wireworms, weevils, other insects, or other means. Unless otherwise specified, the minimum diameter is not less than 1½ inches, and the maximum weight not more than 36 ounces.

Unclassified. Sweet potatoes which have not been classified in accordance with any of the foregoing grades. The term *unclassified* is not a grade within the meaning of these standards but is provided as a designation to show that no grade has been applied to the lot.

Source:
Agricultural Marketing Service, USDA, 7 CFR sections 51.1600 to 51.1617 (1992), Washington: Government Printing Office.

Sweet Potatoes, Canned

COLOR TYPES

Golden
Yellow
Mixed (golden and yellow)

STYLES

Whole. Have the appearance of being essentially whole or almost whole.

Halves or Halved. Cut longitudinally into approximate halves.

Sections. Cut transversely into approximately cylindrical units 2 inches or more in length, and the diameter of the unit cannot be more than approximately ⅓ of the length.

Pieces, Cuts, or Cut. Have been randomly cut into portions of varying sizes and shapes.

Mashed. Wholly comminuted or pureed.

Whole and Pieces. A combination of whole and pieces with not less than 50 percent of the drained weight being whole sweet potatoes.

Mixed. Any combination of two or more of the foregoing styles excluding mashed style.

TYPES OF PACK

Regular Pack. Packed in a liquid packing medium. Applies to all styles, except mashed style.

Vacuum Pack. Packed under conditions creating a high vacuum in the container.

Solid Pack. Packed in the absence of a packing medium. Applies to mashed style only.

GRADES

Canned sweet potatoes are graded according to a technical system whereby penalty points are assessed for such factors as edibility, poor appearance, or defects in workmanship. The more penalty points assessed the lower the grade. The grade descriptions which follow are intended only as a general consumer guide. For more detailed information, please consult the source cited below.

U.S. Grade A. In regular pack and vacuum pack, the sweet potato units have a uniformly smooth texture, are practically free from internal tough or coarse fibers, and may be slightly variable in tenderness but hold their apparent original conformation. In solid-pack, the mass has a smooth texture and is practically free from tough or coarse fibers. The sweet potato mass is sufficiently firm to approximate the general shape of the container with some settling permitted. It is not dry and may show no more than a slight separation of free liquid after two minutes. The sweet potatoes have a distinctive flavor and odor characteristic of properly processed sweet potatoes (including the packing medium) and are free from objectionable flavors or odors.

U.S. Grade B. In regular pack and vacuum pack, the sweet potato units have a reasonably uniform, smooth texture, are substantially free from internal tough or coarse fibers, may be variable in tenderness, and may be firm to soft but hold their apparent original conformation. In solid-pack, the mass has a reasonably smooth texture which may be slightly grainy; it is substantially free from tough or coarse fibers. The sweet potato mass is sufficiently soft so as not to approximate the general shape of the container, but it is not free flowing. It may

be noticeably dry, but not hard or rubbery. There may be moderate separation of free liquid after two minutes. The processed sweet potatoes (including the packing medium) may be lacking in good flavor and odor, but they are free from objectionable flavors or objectionable odors.

Substandard. Fails to meet the requirements for U.S. Grade B.

Sources:
Agricultural Marketing Service, USDA, 7 CFR sections 52.2041 to 52.2054 (1991), Washington: Government Printing Office.
Food and Drug Administration, 21 CFR 155.201 (1991), Washington: Government Printing Office.

Sweet Potatoes, Frozen

Frozen sweet potatoes is the product prepared from the clean, sound root of sweet potatoes (*Ipomoea batatas*) by washing, sorting, trimming, draining, and peeling. The product may or may not be cooked, may be prepared with the addition of suitable seasoning ingredient(s), sweetening ingredient(s), antioxidant(s), edible oil(s), spices, or other suitable additives. Such ingredients may or may not be admixed with the sweet potatoes, or they may be contained separately from the sweet potato ingredient. When the sweet potatoes are cooked or partially cooked and are packed with a high density syrup and/or sugar to produce a candied effect, the sweet potatoes may be considered *candied sweet potatoes*. In lieu of peeling, the product may be prepared as unpeeled sweet potatoes in baked or stuffed form, with or without the addition of edible fat or oil to the peel. Stuffed form consists of cooked potatoes where the flesh has been removed from the peel, has been comminuted or crushed, and has been replaced in the peel or a preformed shell. The product is frozen in accordance with good commercial practice and maintained at temperatures necessary for the preservation of the product.

COLORS

Golden

Yellow

Mixed (golden and yellow)

STYLES

Whole. Peeled.

Baked. Unpeeled.

Stuffed. In peel or preformed shell.

Sliced. Peeled units, cut longitudinally and/or crosswise.

French-Cut. Peeled units cut into strips which may have flat or corrugated surfaces.

Diced. Peeled units cut into cube-shape units.

Cut or Chunks. Peeled units of irregular sizes and shapes.

Mashed or Soufflé. Peeled, cooked, and wholly comminuted or crushed sweet potatoes which may be molded or formed into pre-determined size and shape.

Mixed or Combination. A combination of two or more styles.

GRADES

Frozen sweet potatoes are graded according to a technical system whereby penalty points are assessed for such factors as edibility, poor appearance, or defects in workmanship. The more penalty points assessed the lower the grade. The grade descriptions which follow are intended only as a general consumer guide. For more detailed information, please consult the source cited below.

U.S. Grade A or U.S. Fancy. Possess similar varietal characteristics. The flavor of the product before and after cooking is characteristic of properly prepared sweet potatoes and is free from objectionable flavors and odors of any kind. The color is a reasonably bright, characteristic color (either yellow or golden, but not mixed). The sweet potatoes are practically uniform in size. They are practically free from such defects as particles of peel, broken skins, rootlets, fibrous ends, discolored areas, corky areas, and from other defects that detract from the appearance or edibility of the product. The flesh of whole baked potatoes is not soggy or dry and is practically free from tough or coarse internal fibers. For whole stuffed, halves stuffed, and mashed styles, the texture and consistency of the mass or stuffing are free from lumps and tough or coarse fibers. All other styles possess a uniformly smooth texture, are practically free from tough or coarse fibers, and may be firm to soft, but hold their apparent original conformation and size without material disintegration.

U.S. Grade B or U.S. Extra Standard. May possess similar or mixed varietal color characteristics and have a normal flavor and odor. The color is yellow, golden, or mixed and may vary among the units and may be no more than slightly dull. The potatoes are reasonably uniform in size and free from defects. The flesh of whole baked style is not excessively dry and is reasonably free from tough or coarse internal fibers. For whole stuffed, halves stuffed, and mashed styles, the texture and consistency of the mass or stuffing may be coarse and stiff but practically free from lumps, and not more than a few tough or coarse fibers may be present. For all other styles, the units possess a reasonably uniform smooth texture, are reasonably free from tough or coarse fibers, and 75 percent or more, by weight, of the units hold their apparent original conformation and size without material disintegration.

Substandard. Fails to meet the requirements of U.S. Grade B or U.S. Extra Standard.

Source:

Agricultural Marketing Service, USDA, 7 CFR sections 52.5001 to 52.5012 (1991), Washington: Government Printing Office.

Tomatoes, Fresh

GRADES

Tomatoes are graded according to a technical system whereby penalty points are assessed for such factors as edibility, poor appearance, or defects in workmanship. The more penalty points assessed the lower the grade. The grade descriptions which follow

Lower limit for U.S. No. 1

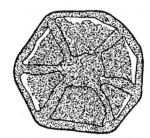

Lower limit for U.S. No. 2

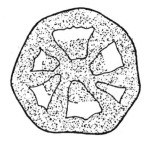

Lower limit for U.S. No. 3

Puffiness. *The proportion of open space permitted is dependent upon the thickness of walls. Tomatoes with thicker walls than those in the above illustrations may have proportionately greater amounts of open space. Tomatoes with thinner walls than illustrated shall have proportionately lesser amounts of open space.*

are intended only as a general consumer guide. For more detailed information, please consult the source cited below. To allow for variations in quality caused by grading and handling, a percentage of the tomatoes may fail to meet all of the requirements of the grade.

U.S. No. 1. Mature tomatoes of similar varietal characteristics. They have reached the stage of development which will insure a proper completion of the ripening process, and the contents of two or more seed cavities have developed a jelly-like consistency. The seeds are well developed. They are not

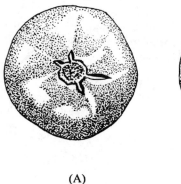

(A)   (B)

Growth Cracks. (A) Maximum aggregate length of radial growth cracks permitted on 2 ½ inch tomato in U.S. No. 1 grade. (B) Concentric growth cracks which affect appearance to same extent as maximum aggregate length of radial growth cracis permitted in U.S. No. 1 grade.

overripe or soft and will yield readily to slight pressure. They are practically free from dirt. They are well developed and show normal growth (those which are ridged and peaked at the stem end, contain dry tissue, and usually contain open spaces below the level of the stem scar are not considered well developed). They are not more than moderately kidney-shaped, lopsided, elongated, angular, or otherwise moderately deformed. They are not conspicuously ridged or rough. The tomatoes are free from decay, freezing injury, and sunscald and are not damaged by any other cause.

U.S. Combination. A combination of U.S. No. 1 and U.S. No. 2 tomatoes. At least 60 percent by count, meet the requirements of U.S. No. 1 grade.

U.S. No. 2. Tomatoes with similar varietal characteristics. They are mature (not overripe or soft), clean, and well developed. They are reasonably well formed and not decidedly kidney-shaped, lopsided, elongated, angular, or otherwise decidedly deformed. They are not more than slightly rough and are not decidedly ridged or grooved. They are free from decay, freezing injury, and sunscald. They are not seriously damaged by other causes such as cuts and broken skins. This grade has a higher tolerance for defective or damaged tomatoes than U.S. No. 1.

U.S. No. 3. Tomatoes which have similar varietal characteristics and are mature (not overripe or soft), and clean. They are well developed but may be misshapen or decidedly kidney-shaped, lopsided, elongated, angular, or otherwise decidedly deformed. They are free from decay and freezing injury and are not seriously damaged by sunscald. The tomatoes are not very seriously damaged by any other causes (such as fresh or healed cuts and broken skins extending through the tomato wall). This grade has a higher tolerance for defective or damaged tomatoes than U.S. No. 2.

SIZE

| Size designation | Diameter in inches | |
	Minimum	Maximum
Small	2⁴/32	2⁹/32
Medium	2⁸/32	2¹⁷/32
Large	2¹⁶/32	2²⁵/32
Extra Large	2²⁴/32	

Source:

Agricultural Marketing Service, USDA, 7 CFR sections 51.1855 to 1867 (1992), Washington: Government Printing Office.

Tomatoes, Canned

STYLES

Whole. Peeled or unpeeled whole or almost whole.

Sliced. Peeled or unpeeled and cut into units of approximately uniform thickness.

Halves. Peeled or unpeeled and cut into two approximately equal halves.

Wedges. Peeled or unpeeled and cut into approximate quarters or wedge-shaped sectors.

Diced. Peeled or unpeeled and cut into approximate cube-shaped units.

TYPE OF PACK

Regular. Packed in solution of tomato juice, tomato puree, or tomato paste.

GRADES

Canned tomatoes are graded according to a technical system whereby penalty points are assessed for such factors as edibility, poor appearance, or defects in workmanship. The more penalty points assessed the lower the grade. The grade descriptions which follow are intended only as a general consumer guide. For more detailed information, please consult the source cited below.

U.S. Grade A. The color of at least 90 percent are USDA Tomato Red. A very small portion (less than 5 percent) may be less red or yellow but none may be vivid green. The product has good character. For whole, halves, wedges, or sliced tomatoes, not more than 15 percent, by count, are excessively soft or mushy. In diced tomatoes, not more than 15 percent, by weight, are excessively soft or mushy.

U.S. Grade B. The color of at least 50 percent of the tomatoes is USDA Tomato Red. A larger portion (less than 10 percent) may be less red or yellow but none may be vivid green. Has reasonably good character. In whole, halves, wedges, or sliced tomatoes, not more than 25 percent, by count, are excessively soft or mushy. In diced tomatoes, not more than 25 percent, by weight, are excessively soft or mushy.

U.S. Grade C. Meets the FDA requirements for strength and redness of color. Has a fairly good character. In whole, halves, wedges, or sliced tomatoes, more than 25 percent, by count, are excessively soft or mushy. In diced tomatoes, more than 25 percent, by weight, are excessively soft or mushy.

Substandard. Fails the requirements for U.S. Grade C.

Source:
Agricultural Marketing Service, USDA, 7 CFR sections 52.5161 to 52.5171 (1991), Washington: Government Printing Office.
Food and Drug Administration, 21 CFR 155.201 (1991), Washington: Government Printing Office.

Tomatoes, Fresh (Consumer Standards)

GRADES

These standards apply only to field grown tomatoes, not to those grown in greenhouses. Fresh tomatoes are graded according to a technical system whereby penalty points are assessed for such factors as edibility, poor appearance, or defects in workmanship. The more penalty points assessed the lower the grade. The grade descriptions which follow are intended only as a general consumer guide. For more detailed information, please consult the source cited below. To allow for variations in quality caused by grading and handling, a percentage of the tomatoes may fail to meet all of the requirements of the grade.

U.S. Grade A. Tomatoes of similar varietal characteristics and which are mature and are at least turning, but are not overripe or soft. They are well developed, at least fairly well formed, and fairly smooth. They are free from soft rot, freezing injury, and damage caused by dirt, bruises, cuts, shriveling, sunscald, sunburn, puffiness, cat faces, growth cracks, scars, dry rot, other diseases, insects, hail, or mechanical or other means. Tomatoes on the shown face are reasonably representative in size and quality of the contents of the container.

U.S. Grade B. Tomatoes of similar varietal characteristics and which are mature and are at least turning, but are not overripe, soft, or badly misshapen. They are free from soft rot, freezing injury, and serious damage caused by dirt, bruises, cuts, shriveling, sunscald, sunburn, puffiness, cat faces, growth cracks, scars, dry rot, other diseases, insects, hail, or mechanical or other means. Tomatoes on the shown face are reasonably representative in size and quality of the contents of the container.

Off Grade. Tomatoes which fail to meet the requirements of either of the foregoing grades.

MATURITY CLASSIFICATIONS

Tomatoes which are characteristically red when ripe, but are not overripe or soft, may be classified for maturity as follows:

Turning. At least some part of the surface of the tomato, but less than one-half of the surface in the aggregate, is covered with pink color.

Pink. The tomato shows from one-half to three-fourths of the surface in the aggregate covered with pink or red color.

Hard Ripe. The tomato shows three-fourths or more of the surface in the aggregate covered with pink or red color.

Firm Ripe. The tomato shows three-fourths or more of the surface in the aggregate covered with red color characteristic of reasonably well-ripened tomatoes.

SIZES

Small. Under 3 oz.
Medium. 3 to 6 oz.
Large. Over 6 to 10 oz.
Very Large. Over 10 oz.

The tomatoes may also be classed in terms of combinations of the above sizes, as *Small to Medium, Medium to Large, Small to Very Large,* etc., in accordance with the facts.

Source:
Agricultural Marketing Service, USDA, 7 CFR sections 51.1900 to 51.1913 (1992), Washington: Government Printing Office.

Tomatoes, Greenhouse

GRADES

Greenhouse tomatoes are graded according to a technical system whereby penalty points are assessed for such factors as edibility, poor appearance, or defects in workmanship. The more penalty points assessed the lower the grade. The grade descriptions which follow are intended only as a general consumer guide. For more detailed information, please consult the source cited below.

U.S. No. 1. Tomatoes of similar varietal characteristics (bright red varieties cannot be mixed with varieties having a purplish tinge). The contents of two or more seed cavities have developed a jelly-like consistency, and the seeds are well developed. External color shows at least a definite break from green to tannish-yellow, pink, or red color on not less than 10 percent of the surface. They are not overripe or soft. They are fairly well formed and not more than slightly kidney-shaped, lopsided, elongated, angular, or otherwise slightly deformed. They are free from decay, sunscald, and freezing injury. They are also free from damage caused by bruises, cuts, shriveling, puffiness, cat faces, growth cracks, scars, disease, insects, or other means.

U.S. No. 2. Tomatoes of similar varietal characteristics and which are mature, but not overripe or soft. They are clean, reasonably well formed, and not more than moderately kidney shaped, lopsided, elongated, angular, or otherwise moderately deformed. They are free from decay, sunscald, and freezing injury. They are also free from serious damage which detracts from appearance, edibility, or marketing quality.

Unclassified. Tomatoes which have not been classified in accordance with any of the foregoing grades. The term *unclassified* is not a grade within the meaning of these standards but is provided as a designation to show that no grade applied to the lot.

SIZE

Small. Under 3½ inches.
Medium. 3½ to 9 ounces.
Large. Over 9 ounces.

Source:
Agricultural Marketing Service, USDA, 7 CFR sections 51.3345 to 51.3360 (1992), Washington: Government Printing Office.

Turnip Greens, with Turnips (Frozen)

Frozen turnip greens with turnips is the product prepared from the clean, sound, succulent leaves and the clean, sound, succulent roots of the turnip plant (*Brassica rapa*) by washing, sorting, trimming, blanching, and proper draining. It is then frozen in accordance with good commercial practice and maintained at temperatures necessary for the preservation of the product.

STYLES

Style I, Whole Leaf. Consists of the leaf with adjacent portions of the stem mixed together with a single form of the turnip root ingredient.
Style II, Sliced. Consists of leaves with adjacent portions of the stem which have been sliced into reasonably uniform strips mixed together with a single form of the turnip root ingredient.
Style III, Cut or Chopped. Consists of leaves with adjacent portions of the stem which have been cut or chopped into small pieces mixed together with a single form of the turnip root ingredient.

COLOR

White
Yellow

GRADES

This product is graded according to a technical system whereby penalty points are assessed for such factors as edibility, poor appearance, or defects in workmanship. The more penalty points assessed the lower the grade. The grade descriptions which follow are intended only as a general consumer guide. For more detailed information, please consult the source cited below.

U.S. Grade A or U.S. Fancy. The turnip ingredient is fairly uniform in size, and each ingredient possesses similar varietal characteristics. After cooking, it has a good, normal flavor and odor and is free from objectionable flavors and odors of any kind. The leafy ingredient possesses a bright, practically uniform green color that is typical of young, tender turnip greens. The turnip ingredient possesses a practically uniform, bright, characteristic color for the variety of young, tender turnips. The product is practically free from defects such as sand, grit, silt, harmless weeds, grass, and from damaged leaf and turnip ingredient. The leafy ingredient is tender and practically free from coarse or tough leaves and stems. The turnip ingredient possesses a tender texture and is practically free from fibrous or pithy units.

U.S. Grade B or U. S. Extra Standard. Each ingredient possesses similar varietal characteristics. After cooking, it may be lacking in good flavor and odor, but it is free from objectionable flavors and odors. It has a reasonably good, bright, and typical color. It is reasonably free from defects. The leafy ingredient is reasonably tender and free from coarse or tough leaves and stems. The turnip ingredient possesses a reasonably tender texture and is reasonably free from fibrous or pithy units.

Substandard. Fails to meet the requirements of U.S. Grade B or U.S. Extra Standard.

Source:
Agricultural Marketing Service, USDA, 7 CFR sections 52.3731 to 52.3743 (1991), Washington: Government Printing Office.

Turnips or Rutabagas

STYLES

Bunched Turnips. Turnips which are tied in bunches. The tops are full length or removed to not less than 6 inches.
Turnips with Short-Trimmed Tops. Unless otherwise specified, turnips showing leaf stems ranging to no more than 4 inches in length.
Topped Turnips or Rutabagas. Tops removed to not more than ¾ inch in length.

GRADES

This product is graded according to a technical system whereby penalty points are assessed for such factors as edibility, poor appearance, or defects in workmanship. The more penalty points assessed the lower the grade. The grade descriptions which follow are intended only as a general consumer guide. For more detailed information, please consult the source cited below. To allow for variations in quality caused by grading and handling, a percentage of the turnips or rutabagas may fail to meet all of the requirements of the grade.

U.S. No. 1. Turnips or rutabagas of similar varietal characteristics. The roots are well trimmed. Unattractive secondary rootlets have been removed, and any objectionably long or coarse tail-like part of the root has been cut off. The root is not soft, flabby, or shriveled; it is fairly smooth (not rough or ridged). It is fairly well shaped, fairly clean, and free from soft rot. It is also free from damage caused by cuts, discoloration, freezing, growth cracks, pithiness, woodiness, watercore, dry rot, other disease, insects, rodents, or mechanical other means. Bunched turnips or turnips with short-trimmed tops have tops which are fresh and are free from decay and damage caused by discoloration, freezing, disease, insects, or mechanical or other means. Unless otherwise specified, the diameter of each turnip or rutabaga is not less than 1¾ inches.

U.S. No. 2. Turnips or rutabagas of similar varietal characteristics. The roots are well trimmed and firm. They are not excessively rough or seriously misshapen. They are free from soft rot and from serious damage caused by cuts, dirt, discoloration, freezing, growth cracks, pithiness, woodiness, watercore, dry rot, disease, insects, rodents, or mechanical or other means. Bunched turnips or turnips with short-trimmed tops have tops which are fresh and are free from decay and damage caused by

discoloration, freezing, disease, insects, or mechanical or other means. Unless otherwise specified, the diameter of each turnip or rutabaga is not less than 1¾ inches.

Unclassified. Turnips or rutabagas which have not been classified in accordance with either of the foregoing grades. The term *unclassified* is not a grade within the meaning of these standards, but is provide as a designation to show that no grade has been applied to the lot.

Source:

Agricultural Marketing Service, USDA, 7 CFR sections 51.2610 to 51.2630 (1992), Washington: Government Printing Office.

Miscellaneous Foods

Bouillon

Bouillon. The stock made from meat, usually chicken or beef.

Chicken Bouillon Cube or Beef Bouillon Cube. Made from evaporated bouillon with sufficient chicken or beef extractives present to give definite characteristics, especially flavor, of the designated source. When dissolved in water according to directions, the resulting product is bouillon.

Chicken-Flavored Bouillon Cube or Beef-Flavored Bouillon Cube. Contains hydrolyzed plant protein with sufficient chicken and beef extractives to give definite flavor.

Vegetable Protein Bouillon Cube. The food contains no meat or meat extractives.

Granulated. If the food is in granular form, the word *granulated* may be used in the name of the food in lieu of the word cube, e.g., *Chicken Bouillon-Granulated* or *Granulated Beef-Flavored Bouillon.*

Source:
Food and Drug Administration, *Compliance Policy Guides*, Guide 7116.03, revised 09/01/87, Washington: National Technical Information Service.

Bread, Rolls, and Buns

Bread, white bread, rolls, white rolls, buns, and white buns are the foods produced by baking mixed yeast-leavened dough.

Eggs. When the food contains not less than 2.56 percent by weight of whole egg solids, the name of the food may be called *egg bread, egg rolls,* or *egg buns,* as applicable, accompanied by the statement *Contains_____ medium-sized egg(s) per pound*— the blank to be filled in with the number which represents the whole egg content of the food expressed to the nearest one-fifth egg. When the label bears any representation, other than in the ingredient listing, of the presence of egg (e.g., the word *egg* or any phonetic equivalent spelling of the word egg, or a picture of an egg), the food shall contain not less than 2.56 percent of whole egg solids.

Enriched Bread, Rolls, and Buns. Contains in each pound 1.8 milligrams of thiamine, 1.1 milligrams of riboflavin, 15 milligrams of niacin, and 12.5 milligrams of iron. May contain added calcium. May also contain wheat germ or partly defatted wheat germ, but the total quantity is not to be more than 5 percent of the flour ingredient. Enriched flour may be used, in whole or in part, instead of flour.

Milk Bread, Rolls, and Buns. The only moistening ingredient permitted in the preparation of the dough is milk or, as an alternative, a combination of dairy products in such a proportion that the weight of the nonfat milk solids is not more than 2.3 times and not less than 1.2 times the weight of the milkfat, with or without water. It is in a quantity that provides not less than 8.2 parts milk solids for each 100 parts by weight of flour. No buttermilk, buttermilk product, cheese whey, cheese whey product, or milk protein is used. The name of the food is *milk bread, milk rolls, milk buns,* as applicable.

Raisin Bread, Rolls, and Buns. Not less than 50 parts by weight of seeded or seedless raisins are used for each 100 parts by weight of flour used. Water extract of raisin may be used, but not to replace raisins. The name of the food is *raisin bread, raisin rolls,* or *raisin buns,* as applicable. When the food contains not less than 2.56 percent by weight of whole egg solids, the name of the food may be *raisin and egg bread, raisin and egg rolls,* or *raisin and egg buns.*

Whole Wheat Bread. The dough is made from the optional ingredient whole wheat flour, bromated whole wheat flour, or a combination of these. The name of the food is *whole wheat bread, graham bread, entire wheat bread, whole wheat rolls, graham rolls, entire wheat rolls, whole wheat buns, graham buns, or entire wheat buns,* as applicable.

Honey Bread. When the word *honey* is used to describe bread, buns, or other bakery products, the product should contain enough honey to give it a characteristic honey flavor. The U.S. Food and Drug Administration believes that at least 8 percent honey (based on weight of flour) should be used in a bread labeled as honey bread. The use of less honey is not prohibited, but in this case, *honey* should not be featured in the labeling.

Source:
Food and Drug Administration, *Compliance Policy Guides*, Guide 7102.03, reissued 03/08/88, Washington: National Technical Information Service.

Cacao Nibs

Cracked cocoa is the food prepared by heating and cracking dried or cured and cleaned cacao beans and removing the shell. Cacao nibs or the cacao beans from which they are prepared may be processed by heating with one or more of the following optional alkali ingredients: bicarbonate, carbonate or hydroxide of sodium, ammonium or potassium, or carbonate or oxide of magnesium.

When cacao nibs are processed with any optional alkali ingredient, the label bears the statement *Processed with alkali;* but in lieu of the word *alkali,* the specific common name of the alkali ingredient may be used.

Candied Citron

Candied Citron. This term is only applied to the candied peel of the fruit of the citron tree, a citrus fruit similar to the lemon but larger and possessing a thick rind.

Candied Citron Melon. The candied rind of the citrus melon.

American Citron or Candied Domestic Citron. Used to describe the American product of the citrus fruit *citron.*

Source:
Food and Drug Administration, *Compliance Policy Guides*, Guide 7105.09, reissued 10/01/88, Washington: National Technical Information Service.

Chili Sauce

Chili sauce is prepared from mature tomatoes of the red or reddish varieties. These tomatoes are peeled and then chopped or crushed. Alternatively, all (or a portion) of the tomatoes may be chopped, crushed, or macerated and the peelings screened out so that at least a substantial portion of the seed remains in the product. To this mixture are added salt, spices, vinegar, and nutritive sweetening ingredients. Vegetable flavoring ingredients, such as chopped onion, chopped green or red pepper, chopped green tomatoes, chopped celery, and sweet pickle relish, may also be added, but only in quantities that do not materially alter the tomato appearance of the product. The chili sauce is packed in hermetically sealed containers and is sufficiently processed by heat, before or after sealing, to assure its preservation.

GRADES

Chili sauce is graded according to a very technical system whereby penalty points are assessed for such factors as edibility, poor appearance, or defects in workmanship. The more penalty points assessed the lower the grade. The grade descriptions which follow are intended only as a general consumer guide. For more detail please consult the source cited below.

U.S. Grade A or U.S. Fancy. Possesses a good color, consistency, and character. It is practically free from such defects as dark specks or scale-like particles, discolored seeds, tomato peel, etc. It has a good flavor and its color is bright. The color of the tomato ingredient is predominant and characteristic of well ripened tomatoes. The added seasoning ingredients do not materially detract from the appearance of the product. The chili sauce is heavy bodied and when emptied from the container to a flat surface forms a moderately molded mass and shows not more than a slight separation of free liquid at the edges of the mass. The product does not have a finely comminuted appearance, and the onion, celery, pickle relish, and other similar ingredients are tender, reasonably firm, or crisp in texture. The chili sauce has a good distinct flavor free from scorching or any other objectionable flavor.

U.S. Grade C or U.S. Standard. Possesses a fairly good color, consistency, and character. It is fairly free from defects and possesses a fairly good flavor. The color of the chili sauce may be slightly dull but not off-color. The added seasoning ingredients do not seriously detract from the appearance of the product. When emptied from the container to a flat surface, the sauce may tend to level itself, or may show a moderate separation of free liquid at the edges of the mass, but is not excessively stiff or excessively liquid. The sauce may be finely comminuted, and the other vegetable ingredients may be only fairly tender. The sauce may be lacking in good characteristic flavor, but is free from objectionable or off flavors of any kind.

Substandard. Fails to meet the requirements of *U.S. Grade C* or *U.S. Standard.*

Source:
Agricultural Marketing Service, USDA, 7 CFR sections 52.2191 to 52.2202 (1991), Washington: Government Printing Office.

Chocolate

Chocolate liquor, chocolate, baking chocolate, bitter chocolate, cooking chocolate, chocolate coating, or bitter chocolate coating are the solid or semi-solid foods prepared by finely grinding cacao nibs. To such ground cacao nibs, cacao fat or cocoa or both may be added in quantities needed to adjust the cacao fat content of the finished chocolate liquor. Chocolate liquor may be spiced, flavored, or otherwise seasoned with one or more of the following optional ingredients:

Ground Spice. When the food is seasoned with a spice ingredient, the label bears the statement *Spiced, Spice added, With added spice, Spiced with ____,* or *With added ____,* the blank being filled in with the specific common name of the spice used.

Ground Vanilla Beans. *A*ny natural food flavoring oil, oleoresin, or extract. When the food is flavored with these ingredients, the label bears the statement *Flavored, Flavoring added, With added flavoring,* or *Flavored with ____, ____ added,* or *With added ____,* the blank being filled in with the specific common name of the flavoring used.

Vanillin, Ethyl Vanillin, or Other Artificial Food Flavoring. When the food is flavored with these ingredients, the label bears the statement *Artificially flavored, Artificial flavoring added, With artificial flavoring, Artificially flavored with ____,* or *With ____, an artificial flavoring,* the blank being filled in with the specific common name of the artificial flavoring used.

Butter, Milk Fat, Dried Malted Cereal Extract, Ground Coffee, Ground Nut Meats. When the food is seasoned with these ingredients, the label bears the statement *Seasoned with ____,* the blank being filled in with the specific common name of the substance used as seasoning.

Salt

TYPES

Breakfast cocoa. Prepared by pulverizing the residual material remaining after part of the cacao fat has been removed from ground cacao nibs. It may be spiced, flavored, or otherwise seasoned with one or more of the following optional ingredients:

Ground spice
Ground vanilla beans
Vanillin, ethyl vanillin, or other artificial food flavoring
Salt

Cocoa. Contains less than 22 percent but not less than 10 percent of cacao fat.

Low-Fat Cocoa. Contains less than 10 percent of cacao fat.

Milk Chocolate. Sweet milk chocolate, milk chocolate coating, sweet milk chocolate coating. The solid or semi-solid food prepared from chocolate liquor (with or without the addition of cacao fat) and one or more of the following optional dairy ingredients: milk; concentrated, evaporated, sweetened condensed, or dried skim or whole milk; butter; milk fat; or cream. The finished milk chocolate contains not less than 3.66 percent by weight of milk fat; not less than 12 percent by weight of milk solids; and not less than 10 percent by weight of chocolate liquor.

Buttermilk Chocolate. The dairy ingredients used are limited to sweet cream buttermilk, concentrated sweet cream buttermilk, dried sweet cream buttermilk, or any two of these. The finished buttermilk chocolate contains less than 3.66 percent by weight of milk fat; and, instead of milk solids, it contains

not less than 12 percent by weight of sweet cream buttermilk solids.

Skim Milk Chocolate. Skim milk chocolate, sweet skim milk chocolate, skim milk chocolate coating, sweet skim milk chocolate coating. The dairy ingredients used are limited to concentrated, evaporated, sweetened condensed skim milk, nonfat dry milk, skim milk, and any two or more of these. The finished skim milk chocolate contains less than 3.66 percent by weight of milk fat; and, instead of milk solids, it contains not less than 12 percent by weight of skim milk solids.

CHOCOLATE FLAVORED

Chocolate Flavored or Natural Chocolate Flavored. Used on the labeling of any nonstandardized food in which the consumer could reasonably expect a chocolate ingredient but which contains cocoa as the sole source of chocolate flavoring.

Sources:
Food and Drug Administration, *Compliance Policy Guides*, Guide 7105.15, 5/13/88, Washington: National Technical Information Service.
Food and Drug Administration, "Cacao Products," 21 CFR Part 163 (1991), Washington: Government Printing Office.

Fruit Jellies

Jellies are made from a mixture of one or a permitted combination of the fruit juice ingredients below. The mixture is concentrated with or without heat. The volatile flavoring materials or essence from the mixture may be captured during concentration, separately concentrated, and added back to the mixture, together with any concentrated essence accompanying any optional fruit ingredient.

Artificially Sweetened. Sweetened with saccharin, sodium saccharin, calcium saccharin, or any combination of two or more of these.

TYPES

Type I, Standardized. Prepared from a single variety of fruit juice ingredient.

Type II, Standardized. Prepared from a mixture of two or more varieties of fruit juice ingredients.

Type III, Nonstandardized. Prepared from a single variety of fruit or nonfruit juice ingredient.

Type IV, Nonstandardized. Prepared from a mixture of two or more varieties of fruit and/or nonfruit juice ingredient(s).

KINDS

Apple
Apricot
Blackberry (other than Dewberry)
Black raspberry
Boysenberry
Cherry

Crabapple
Cranberry
Damson, Damson Plum
Dewberry (other than Boysenberry, Loganberry, and Young
-berry)
Fig
Gooseberry
Grape
Grapefruit
Greengage, Greengage Plum
Guava
Loganberry
Orange
Peach
Pineapple
Plum (other than Damson, Greengage, and Prune)
Pomegranate
Prickly Pear
Quince
Raspberry, Red Raspberry
Red Currant, Currant (other than Black Currant)
Strawberry
Youngberry

GRADES

Fruit jellies are graded according to a very technical system whereby penalty points are assessed for such factors as edibility, poor appearance, or defects in workmanship. The more penalty points assessed the lower the grade. The grade descriptions which follow are intended only as a general consumer guide. For more detail please consult the source cited below.

U.S. Grade A. The jelly has a tender to slightly firm texture and retains a compact shape without excessive syneresis (weeping). The color is characteristic of the juice ingredient(s), and the jelly has a sparkling luster or may be not more than slightly cloudy. The jelly is free from dullness of color and defects. It has a distinct and normal flavor characteristic of the fruit or nonfruit ingredient(s) after preserving and is free from any caramelized flavor or any objectionable flavors.

U.S. Grade B. The jelly may lack firmness, but it is not syrupy. It may be more than slightly firm but is not tough or rubbery. The color is characteristic of the juice ingredient(s), and the jelly may be more than slightly cloudy and may have a slight dullness of color. The product has a reasonably good flavor that is characteristic of the fruit or nonfruit ingredient(s) after preserving. It may have a slightly caramelized flavor but is free from any bitter flavor or other objectionable flavor or off-flavor of any kind.

Substandard. Fails to meet the requirements of *U.S. Grade B.*

Sources:
Agricultural Marketing Service, USDA, 7 CFR sections 52.1081 to 52.1091 (1991), Washington: Government Printing Office.
Food and Drug Administration, "Fruit Jelly," 21 CFR 150.140 to 150.141 (1991), Washington: Government Printing Office.

Fruit Preserves or Jams

TYPES

Type I. Fruit preserves (or jams) that are prepared from a single fruit (except apple) listed in Group I or Group II.
Type II. Fruit preserves (or jams) that are prepared from more than a single fruit listed in Group I and Group II.

Group I

Any one singly or in combination with not more than four of the following:
Blackberry (other than Dewberry)
Black Raspberry
Blueberry
Boysenberry
Cherry
Crabapple
Dewberry (other than Boysenberry, Loganberry and Youngberry)
Elderberry
Grape
Grapefruit
Huckleberry
Loganberry
Orange
Pineapple
Raspberry
Red Raspberry
Rhubarb
Strawberry
Tangerine
Tomato

Group II

Any one singly or in combination with not more than four of the following fruits and fruits in Group I:
Apple (Type II Preserves only)
Apricot
Cranberry
Currant (other than Black Currant)
Damson
Damson Plum
Fig
Gooseberry
Greengage
Greengage Plum
Guava
Nectarine
Peach (Clingstone and Freestone)
Pear
Plum (other than Greengage Plum and Damson Plum)
Quince
Red Currant

GRADES

Fruit preserves and jams are graded according to a very technical system whereby penalty points are assessed for such factors as edibility, poor appearance, or defects in workmanship. The more penalty points assessed the lower the grade. The grade descriptions which follow are intended only as a general consumer guide. For more detail please consult the source cited below.

U.S. Grade A or U.S. Grade A for Manufacturing. The fruit or fruit particles are dispersed uniformly throughout the product. The product has a tender gel or may have no more than a very slight tendency to flow, except that a slightly less viscous consistency may be present when the fruit is chiefly in the form of whole or almost whole units. The color is bright, practically uniform throughout, and characteristic of the variety or varieties of the fruit ingredients. The product is free from dullness of color due to any cause (including oxidation or improper processing or improper cooling). The product possesses a good and distinct flavor characteristic of the applicable kind of fruit ingredient. The product is practically free from defects such as caps, leaves, stems, seeds, pits, peel, and from blemished units, underdeveloped units, or otherwise damaged units. It is also free from any defects not specifically mentioned that affect the appearance or edibility of the product.

U.S. Grade B or U.S. Choice. The fruit or fruit particles are dispersed reasonably uniformly throughout the product. The product may be firm but is not rubbery or may be noticeably viscous but is not excessively thin. The color is reasonably bright and uniform throughout and characteristic of the variety or varieties of the fruit ingredients. The color may be slightly dull but may not be off-color due to oxidation or improper processing or improper cooling or other causes. The product possesses a flavor reasonably characteristic of the kind of fruit ingredients. It may possess a slightly caramelized flavor but is free from any bitter flavor or other objectionable flavor or off-flavor of any kind.

Substandard. Fails to meet the standards of *U.S. Grade B* or *U.S. Choice.*

Source:
Food and Drug Administration, HHS, "Fruit Butters, Jellies, Preserves, and Related Products," 21 CFR Part 150 (1991), Washington: Government Printing Office.

Garlic

To allow for variations in quality caused by grading and handling, a percentage of the garlic may fail to meet all of the requirements of the grade.

GRADES

Garlic is graded according to a very technical system whereby penalty points are assessed for such factors as edibility, poor appearance, or defects in workmanship. The more penalty points

assessed the lower the grade. The grade descriptions which follow are intended only as a general consumer guide. For more detail please consult the source cited below.

U.S. No. 1. Garlic of similar varietal characteristics (white and red garlic shall not be mixed) which is mature and well cured. The cloves are not spreading but fit closely together for practically the entire length of the individual cloves. The cloves are well filled and fairly plump. The cloves are free from mold, decay, and shattered cloves, and from damage caused by dirt or staining, sunburn, sunscald, cuts, sprouts, tops, roots, disease, insects, or mechanical or other means. Each bulb is fairly well enclosed in its outer sheath. Unless otherwise specified, the minimum diameter of each bulb is not less than 1½ inches.

Unclassified. Garlic which has not been classified in accordance with the foregoing grade. The term unclassified is not a grade but is provided as a designation to show that no definite grade has been applied to the lot.

Source:
Agricultural Marketing Service, USDA, 7 CFR sections 51.3880 to 51.3888 (1992), Washington: Government Printing Office.

Hollandaise Sauce

An emulsion of butter, egg yolk, acidifying ingredients (such as lemon juice or vinegar), and seasoning (such as salt and pepper). Traditionally, hollandaise sauce has been made with butter, but in recent years there has been substantial change in consumer use and acceptance of margarine as an alternative to butter. When margarine is used, its presence is declared on the hollandaise sauce label in the list of ingredients.

Source:
Food and Drug Administration, *Compliance Policy Guides*, Guide 7109.11, 10/01/80, Washington: National Technical Information Service.

Honey

Honey is separated from the comb by centrifugal force, gravity, straining, or by other means.

TYPES

Liquid. Honey that is free from visible crystals.

Crystallized. Honey that is solidly granulated or crystallized, irrespective of whether candied, fondant, creamed, or spread types of crystallized honey.

Partially Crystallized. Honey that is a mixture of liquid honey and crystallized honey.

STYLES

Filtered. Honey that has been filtered to the extent that all or most of the fine particles, pollen grains, air bubbles, or other materials normally found in suspension, have been removed.

Strained. Honey that has been strained to the extent that most of the particles, including comb, propolis, or other defects normally found in honey have been removed. Grains of pollen, small air bubbles, and very fine particles would not normally be removed.

COLOR DESIGNATIONS

Honey color is determined (after adjusting for cloudiness) by means of the color standard approved by Unites States Department of Agriculture (USDA) as measured on the Pfund scale, a standard used by the honey industry.

Water White. Water white or lighter.

Extra White. Darker than water white, but not darker than extra white.

White. Darker than extra white, but not darker than white.

Extra Light Amber. Darker than white, but not darker than extra light amber.

Light Amber. Darker than extra light amber, but not darker than light amber.

Dark Amber. Darker than amber.

GRADES

Honey is graded in the filtered style according to a very technical system whereby penalty points are assessed for such factors as edibility, poor appearance, or defects in workmanship. The more penalty points assessed the lower the grade. The grade descriptions which follow are intended only as a general consumer guide. For more detail please consult the source cited below.

Filtered Style

U.S. Grade A. Practically free from defects that affect appearance or edibility. Good aroma, free from caramelization, smoke, fermentation, and chemicals. Clear: may contain air bubbles that do not affect appearance and may contain a trace of pollen grains or other finely divided particles in suspension.

U.S. Grade B. Reasonably free from defects. Those present do not materially affect appearance or edibility. Reasonably good flavor and aroma, practically free from caramelization, and free from smoke, fermentation, and chemicals. Reasonably clear: may contain air bubbles, pollen grains, or other finely divided particles in suspension.

U.S. Grade C. Fairly free from defects, and those present do not seriously affect appearance or edibility. Fairly good flavor and aroma, reasonably free from caramelization, and free from smoke, fermentation, and chemicals. Fairly clear: may contain air bubbles, pollen grains, or other finely divided particles in suspension.

Source:
Agricultural Marketing Service, USDA, 7 CFR sections 52.1391 to 52.1405 (1991), Washington: Government Printing Office.

Horseradish Roots

To allow for variations in quality caused by grading and handling, a percentage of the horseradish roots may fail to meet all of the requirements of the grade.

GRADES

This product is graded according to a very technical system whereby penalty points are assessed for such factors as edibility, poor appearance, or defects in workmanship. The more penalty points assessed the lower the grade. The grade descriptions which follow are intended only as a general consumer guide. For more detail please consult the source cited below.

U.S. Fancy. Horseradish roots which are firm, and not appreciably soft, flabby, wilted, or withered. All secondary roots which are less than ⅝ inch in diameter at the point of attachment to the main root are trimmed to not more than 1 inch, and the tops are trimmed to not more than ½ inch. The root is not forked or branched. It may be slightly curved or crooked, but it should not diverge more than 45 degrees from the course of a straight root. The root is fairly smooth, not bark-like or pitted. It is free from decay and hollow heart and from damage caused by dirt, sunburn, cuts, cracks, internal discoloration, mold, freezing, insects, mechanical or other means. Each root should have good head formation. The root should be not less than 8 inches in length when the diameter is 1½ inches or more. If the length is greater than 8 inches, the diameter may be 1/16 inch less for each additional half inch in length. However, no root should be less than 1¼ inches in diameter.

U.S. No. 1. Horseradish roots which are firm and well trimmed. The root may be moderately curved or crooked but shall not diverge more than 90 degrees from the course of a straight root. It is not excessively rough and is free from decay, hollow heart, and damage caused by dirt, sunburn, cuts, cracks, internal discoloration, mold, freezing, insects, etc. Each root should have fairly good head formation. The roots should be not less than 6 inches in length when the diameter is 1¼ inches or more. However, if the length is greater than 6 inches, the diameter may be 1/16 inch less for each additional ½ inch of length, but no root shall be less than 1 inch in diameter.

U.S. No. 2. Horseradish roots which are firm, well trimmed, free from decay and hollow heart, and free from serious damage caused by dirt, sunburn, cuts, cracks, internal discoloration, mold, freezing, insects, mechanical or other means. The roots should be not less than 4 inches in length and not less than ½ inch in diameter.

Source:
Agricultural Marketing Service, USDA, 7 CFR sections 51.3900 to 51.3918 (1992), Washington: Government Printing Office.

Iodized Salt

Iodized Salt or *Iodized Table Salt* is salt for human food use to which iodide has been added in the form of cuprous iodide or potassium iodide. The statement *This salt supplies iodide, a necessary nutrient* also appears on the packaging. Salt or table salt for human food use to which iodide has not been added bears the statement, *This salt does not supply iodide, a necessary nutrient.* Salt, table salt, iodized salt, or iodized table salt to which anticaking agents have been added may bear a label statement describing the characteristics imparted by the agent(s), e.g., *free flowing.* Individual serving-sized packages containing less than ½ ounce and packages containing more than 2½ pounds of salt are exempt from these labeling requirements.

Source:
Food and Drug Administration, "Salt and Iodized Salt," 21 CFR 100.155 (1991), Washington: Government Printing Office.

Macaroni Products

Macaroni products are prepared by drying formed units of dough made from any combination of semolina, durum flour, or farina flour, water, and with or without any of the following optional ingredients: (1) between 0.5 and 2.0 percent egg white, or frozen or dried egg white; (2) between 0.5 and 1 percent disodium phosphate; (3) onions, celery, garlic, or bay leaf; (4) salt; (5) not more than 13 percent gum gluten; or (6) more than 2 percent concentrated glyceryl monostearate (containing not less than 90 percent monoester).

Macaroni. Tube-shaped and between 0.11 and 0.27 inch in diameter.

Spaghetti. Tube-shaped or cord-shaped (not tubular) and between 0.06 and 0.11 inch in diameter.

Vermicelli. Cord-shaped (not tubular) and not more than 0.06 inch in diameter.

Disodium Phosphate. When disodium phosphate is used, the label shall bear the statement *Disodium phosphate added for quick cooking.*

Seasoning. When seasoning is used, the label bears the statement *Seasoned with ____,* the blank being filled in with the common name of the ingredient or, in the case of bay leaves, the statement *Spiced, Spice added,* or *Spiced with bay leaves.*

Glyceryl Monostearate. When glyceryl monostearate is used, the label bears the statement *Glyceryl monostearate added* or the statement *With added glyceryl monostearate.*

Enriched Macaroni Products with Fortified Protein. Contains between 4 and 5 milligrams of thiamine, not less than 1.7 milligrams and not more than 2.2 milligrams of riboflavin, not less than 27 milligrams and not more than 34 milligrams of niacin or niacinamide, and not less than 13 milligrams and not more than 16.5 milligrams of iron (Fe). May also contain vitamin D in such quantity that each pound of the finished food contains not less than 250 United States Pharmacoepia (USP) units and not more than 1,000 USP units of vitamin D. May also contain calcium in such quantity that each pound of the finished food contains not less than 500 milligram and not more than 625 milligram of calcium (Ca).

Fortified Protein. The protein content is not less than 20 percent by weight. The protein quality is not less than 95 percent that of casein. The total solids content is not less than 87 percent by weight. The name of any food covered by this section is *Enriched Wheat ____ Macaroni Product with Fortified Protein,* the blank being filled in with appropriate word(s) such as *Soy* to show the source of any flours or meals used that were made from nonwheat cereals or from oilseeds. When any other ingredient is added in such proportion as to contribute 10 percent or more of the quantity of protein contained in the finished food, the name includes the statement *Made with ____,* the blank being filled with the name of each such ingredient, e.g., *Made with nonfat milk.*

MILK MACARONI PRODUCTS

Milk is used as the sole moistening ingredient in preparing the dough; or, in lieu of milk, one or more of the following milk ingredients is used: dried milk, a mixture of butter with skim milk, concentrated skim milk, evaporated skim milk, or nonfat dry milk (dried skim milk). The name of each food is *Milk Macaroni Product;* or, alternatively, the name is *Milk Macaroni, Milk Spaghetti,* or *Milk Vermicelli,* as the case may be.

NONFAT MILK MACARONI PRODUCTS

In preparing the dough, nonfat dry milk or concentrated skim milk is used in an amount such that the finished macaroni product contains not less than 12 percent and not more than 25 percent of milk solids-not-fat. Carrageenan or salts of carrageenan may be used in a quantity not in excess of 0.833 percent by weight of the milk solids-not-fat used.

Carrageenan. When the ingredient carrageenan (a colloid used to aid in suspension of one ingredient in another) or the salt of carrageenan is used, the label shall bear the statement *Carrageenan added* or *Salts of carrageenan added* or the statement *With added carrageenan* or *With added salts of carrageenan.*

ENRICHED NONFAT MILK MACARONI PRODUCTS

Each such food contains in each pound not less than 4 milligrams and not more than 5 milligrams of thiamine, not less than 1.7 milligrams and not more than 2.2 milligrams of riboflavin, not less than 27 milligrams and not more than 34 milligrams of niacin or niacinamide, and not less than 13 milligrams and not more than 16.5 milligrams of iron (Fe). These substances may be added through direct addition, wholly or in part, through the use of dried yeast, dried torula yeast, partly defatted wheat germ, enriched farina, or enriched flour. They may be added in a harmless carrier used only in the quantity necessary to effect an intimate and uniform distribution of the substance in the finished macaroni product. Iron may be added only in a form that is harmless and assimilable. The names for the foods described by this section are *Enriched macaroni product made with nonfat milk;* or, alternatively, *Enriched macaroni made with nonfat milk, Enriched spaghetti made with nonfat milk,* or *Enriched vermicelli made with nonfat milk,* as the case may be.

VEGETABLE MACARONI PRODUCTS

Tomato (of any red variety), artichoke, beet, carrot, parsley, or spinach is added to the dough in such quantity that the solids are not less than 3 percent of the finished product. The vegetable used may be fresh, canned, dried, or in the form of puree or paste. The name of each food is ___ *macaroni product,* the blank being filled in with the name of the vegetable; or, alternatively, the name is ___ *macaroni,* ___ *spaghetti,* or ___ *vermicelli,* as the case may be.

Source:
Food and Drug Administration, "Macaroni and Noodle Products," 21 CFR Part 139 (1991), Washington: Government Printing Office.

Maple Syrup

Maple syrup is derived by concentration and heat treatment of the sap of the maple tree (*Acer*) or by a solution of water and maple sugar (*maple concrete*). It contains not less than 66 percent by weight of soluble solids derived solely from the sap of the maple tree. The concentration may be adjusted with added water. It may contain one or more of the following optional ingredients:
Salt
Chemical preservatives
Defoaming agents
The label should contain the names of all optional ingredients used. The solids content of the finished maple syrup should be not less than 66 percent by weight. It is recommended that each container be filled with syrup as full as practicable and that the product occupy not less than 90 percent of the volume of the container.

GRADES

Maple syrup is graded according to a very technical system whereby penalty points are assessed for such factors as edibility, poor appearance, or defects in workmanship. The more penalty points assessed the lower the grade. The grade descriptions which follow are intended only as a general consumer guide. For more detail please consult the source cited below.

U.S. Grade A. The syrup color is bright and typical of maple syrup prepared from sound, properly gathered sap. In addition, it meets the following United States Department of Agriculture (USDA) spectral requirements:
U.S. Grade A Light Amber
U.S. Grade A Medium Amber
U.S. Grade A Dark Amber
The syrup has a good maple flavor characteristic of the color. It is clean, practically clear, practically free from damage, and free from serious damage.
U.S. Grade B for Reprocessing. Federal inspection certificates limit U.S. Grade B maple syrup to a quality suitable for reprocessing only; it is considered unsuitable for consumer labeling.

Substandard. Fails to meet the requirements for *U.S. Grade B for Reprocessing.*

Sources:
Agricultural Marketing Service, USDA, 7 CFR sections 52.5961 to 52.5967 (1991), Washington: Government Printing Office.
Food and Drug Administration, "Maple Sirup," 21 CFR 168.140 (1991), Washington: Government Printing Office.

Molasses, Sugarcane

Sugarcane molasses is the clean, sound, liquid product obtained by evaporating the juice of sugarcane and removing all or any part of the commercially crystallizable sugar.

GRADES

Molasses is graded according to a very technical system whereby penalty points are assessed for such factors as edibility, poor appearance, or defects in workmanship. The more penalty points assessed the lower the grade. The grade descriptions which follow are intended only as a general consumer guide. For more detail please consult the source cited below.

U.S. Grade A or U.S. Fancy. Possesses a good flavor. Meets United States Department of Agriculture (USDA) requirements for sugar, ash, and sulfites. Possesses a good color that is bright and typical. It is practically free from defects, meaning that the appearance and edibility of the product are not affected by the presence of harmless extraneous material which may be in suspension or deposited as sediment in the container.
U.S. Grade B or U.S. Choice. Possesses a reasonably good flavor. Meets the United States Department of Agriculture (USDA) requirements for sugar, ash, and sulfites. Possesses a reasonably bright color and is reasonably free from defects.
U.S. Grade C or U.S. Standard. Possesses a fairly good flavor. Meets Unites States Department of Agriculture (USDA) requirements for sugar, ash, and sulfites. Possesses a fairly good color and is fairly free from defects
Substandard. Fails to meet the requirements of *U.S. Grade C.*

Source:
Agricultural Marketing Service, USDA, 7 CFR sections 52.3651 to 52.3670 (1991), Washington: Government Printing Office.

Mustard, Prepared

Prepared Mustard. A paste composed of a mixture of ground mustard seed and/or mustard flour and/or mustard cake, with salt, vinegar, and with or without sugar and/or dextrose, spices, or other condiments. In the fat-, salt-, and sugar-free solids, it contains not more than 24 percent of carbohydrates, not more than 12 percent of crude fiber, and not less than 5.6 percent of nitrogen.

Mustard Seed. The seed of *Brassica hirta* (white mustard), *B. nigra* (black mustard), *B. juncea*, or varieties or closely related species. *Brassica hirta* (white mustard) contains no appreciable amount of volatile oil.

Brassica Nigra (Black Mustard). *B. nigra* and *B. juncea* yield 0.6 percent of volatile mustard oil (calculated as allylisothiocyanate). The varieties and species closely related to the types of *B. nigra* and *B. juncea* yield not less than 0.6 percent of volatile mustard oil, similar in character and composition to the volatile oils yielded by *B. nigra* and *B. juncea*.

Ground Mustard Seed or Mustard Meal. Unbolted, ground mustard seed which conforms to the appropriate standards for mustard seed.

Mustard Cake. Ground mustard seed, or mustard meal, from which a portion of the fixed oil has been removed.

Mustard Flour, Ground Mustard or Mustard. The powder made from mustard seed with the hulls largely removed and with or without the removal of a portion of the fixed oil.

Source:
Food and Drug Administration, *Compliance Policy Guides*, Guide 7109.15, 10/01/80, Washington: National Technical Information Service.

Olive Oil

Olive oil is the edible oil obtained from the fruit of the olive tree (*Olea europaea*). The oil is clarified, has a specific gravity of 0.910 to 0.915 at 25° C; has an iodine number (Hanus) of 79 to 90; has a refractive index of 1.4668 to 1.4683 at 25° C; and is packed in containers suitable for preservation of the product.

GRADES

Olive oil is graded according to a very technical system whereby penalty points are assessed for such factors as edibility, poor appearance, or defects in workmanship. The more penalty points assessed the lower the grade. The grade descriptions which follow are intended only as a general consumer guide. For more detail please consult the source cited below.

U.S. Grade A or U.S. Fancy. Possesses the typical greenish to light yellow color of olive oil. Has a free fatty acid content (calculated as oleic) of not more than 1.4 percent. It is entirely free from sediment and no water or other liquid immiscible with the olive oil is present. It has a typical olive oil odor free from strong green olive odors, from musty, moldy, butyric, zapatera odors, or any other off-odors. It has a typical olive oil flavor free from strong green olive flavors, from musty, moldy, butyric, zapatera, rancid, or any other off-flavors.

U.S. Grade B or U.S. Choice. Possesses the typical greenish to light yellow color of olive oil. It possesses a free fatty acid content, calculated as oleic, of not more than 2.5 percent. It is reasonably free from sediment and no water or other liquid immiscible with the olive oil is present. It possesses reasonably good typical odor and flavor and is reasonably free from off-flavors.

U.S. Grade C or U.S. Standard. Possesses the typical greenish to light yellow color of olive oil. It has a free fatty acid content, calculated as oleic, of not more than 3.0 percent. It is fairly free from defects, has a fairly good typical odor and flavor, and is fairly free from off-flavors of any kind.

U.S. Grade D or Substandard. The quality of olive oil that fails to meet the requirements of *U.S. Grade C* or *U.S. Standard*.

COMMON NAMES

Extra Virgin Olive Oil. Olive oil derived only from the pressing of olives which does not require any refining. It is simply filtered. It has a distinctive taste and odor, a fruity flavor that varies in intensity from strong to subtle, and a maximum acidity of not more than 1 percent.

Virgin Olive Oil. Like extra virgin olive oil, virgin olive oil is also derived only from the pressing of olives and does not require any refining. It is simply filtered. It has a mild taste and odor, a strong fruity flavor that varies in intensity, and a maximum acidity of not more than 2 percent.

Olive Oil. Usually described as *pure* or *100 percent pure*. A blend of refined olive oil and extra virgin or virgin olive oil. Pressed olive oil that does not meet the standards for extra virgin or virgin olive oil is refined to neutralize the acidity. Because the refined oil is neutral, it must be blended with virgin olive oil to enhance the flavor.

Olive Pomace Oil. A blend of refined olive pomace oil and virgin olive oil. Pomace is the crushed olive material that remains after pressing. Olive oil is extracted with the use of solvents from this pomace. After refining, the oil is blended with virgin olive oil to produce olive pomace oil which has all the nutritional benefits of olive oil.

Sources:
Agricultural Marketing Service, USDA, 7 CFR sections (1991), Washington: Government Printing Office.
Product Literature, American Olive Oil Association, Matawan, NJ, 1992.

Olives, Canned

Canned ripe olives are prepared from properly matured olives which have first been treated to remove the characteristic bitterness. They are packed in a solution of sodium chloride, with or without spices, processed by heat and packed in hermetically sealed containers. Canned olives which are not oxidized in processing and which possess the tan to light bronze color of olives of advanced maturity are commonly referred to as *tree-ripened* or *home-cured* and are not covered in this entry.

TYPES

Ripe Type. Treated and oxidized in processing to produce a typical dark brown to black color.

Green-Ripe. These have not been oxidized in processing; these

Olives, Canned *Consumers' Guide to Product Grades and Terms*

olives range in color from yellow-green, green-yellow, or other greenish casts, and may be mottled.

STYLES

Whole. Have not been pitted.
Pitted. Pits have been removed.
Halved. Pitted olives in which each olive is cut lengthwise into two equal parts.
Segmented. Pitted olives in which each olive is cut lengthwise into three or more equal parts.
Sliced. Parallel slices of fairly uniform thickness prepared from pitted olives.
Chopped. Random-size cut pieces or cut bits prepared from pitted olives.
Broken Pitted. Large pieces that may have been broken in pitting but have not been sliced or cut.

SIZE DESIGNATIONS

Small. Approximately 16-17 millimeters in diameter.

Medium. 17-19 millimeters in diameter.
Large. 19-20 millimeters in diameter.
Extra Large. 10-22 millimeters in diameter.
Jumbo. 22-24 millimeters in diameter.
Colossal. 24-26 millimeters in diameter.
Super Colossal. 26 millimeters in diameter and over.

GRADES

Canned olives are graded according to a very technical system whereby penalty points are assessed for such factors as edibility, poor appearance, or defects in workmanship. The more penalty points assessed the lower the grade. The grade descriptions which follow are intended only as a general consumer guide. For more detail please consult the source cited below.

U.S. Grade A. Has a good flavor. Ripe type olives have a practically uniform black or dark brown color while green-ripe type olives have a normal yellow-green, green-yellow, or other greenish cast and may have a typical mottled appearance. No off-color dark brown, dark purple, or black olives are present.

SIZE DESIGNATIONS FOR CANNED WHOLE AND PITTED RIPE OLIVES

Designation	Count Per Pound	Illustration	Approximate Diameter Range Illustrated (mm)
Small	28-140		16-17
Medium	106-121		17-19
Large	91-105		19-20
Extra Large	65-88		20-22
Jumbo	51-60		22-24
Colossal	41-50		24-26
Super Colossal	40 or less		26 and over

The olives are practically free from defects such as harmless extraneous vegetable material, blemishes, wrinkles, mutilated olives, and other defects which affect the appearance or edibility of the product. The olives have a fleshy texture. Not less than 95 percent are uniform in texture and are tender but not soft. The remaining 5 percent may be soft, but not excessively soft.

U.S. Grade B. Has a good flavor. Ripe type olives have a reasonably uniform black, dark brown, or reddish-brown color while green-ripe type olives have a normal color. The olives are reasonably free from defects and have a fleshy texture, but not less than 90 percent are uniform in texture and are tender but not soft. The 10 percent may be soft but not more than 5 percent may be excessively soft.

U.S. Grade C. The flavor may be slightly lacking in distinctly characteristic flavor, but the olives are free from objectionable flavors of any kind. Ripe type olives have a fairly uniform black, dark brown, or reddish-brown color while green-ripe type olives are normal in color but may vary markedly for the type; no more than 10 percent, by count, of off-color olives may be present. They are fairly free from defects and generally have a fleshy texture characteristic, and not less than 80 percent are practically uniform in texture and are tender but not soft. The remaining 20 percent may be soft, but not more than 10 percent may be excessively soft.

Substandard. Fails to meet the applicable requirements for *U.S. Grade C.*

Source:
Agricultural Marketing Service, USDA, 7 CFR sections 52.3751 to 52.3764 (1991), Washington: Government Printing Office.

Olives, Green

Green olives are completely fermented and cured fruit of the olive tree (*Olea europaea*) which have been prepared from a firm fruit of suitable maturity and variety that have been properly treated to partially remove the characteristic bitterness. The cured olives and the brine packing media have a pH of not more than 4.00 and a sodium chloride content of not less than 6.00 percent. Not more than a trace of reducing sugars may be present. Suitable garnishes, spices, seasoning ingredients, or any other ingredient(s) permitted under the Federal Food, Drug, and Cosmetic Act may be added.

TYPES OF PACK

Thrown Pack. Packaged without regard to placement or arrangement within the package.

Placed or Stick. Packaged in such a manner as to indicate that the individual olives have been carefully positioned in a definite pattern.

STYLES

Whole or Plain. Have not been pitted.
Pitted. Pits have been removed.

Stuffed. Have pimiento, onion, almond, celery, or any other suitable ingredient stuffed into the pit cavity.
Halved. Pitted green olives cut lengthwise into two equal parts.
Sliced. Cut into parallel slices of fairly uniform thickness.
Chopped, Minced, or Relish-Type. Small random-sized cut pieces or cut bits.
Broken, Pitted, or Salad Pack. Pitted olives (broken or stuffed) that have not been cut or sliced.

SIZES

Subpetite, Petite. Approximately 181 to 220 olives per pound.
Petite or Midget. 141 to 180 olives per pound.
Small, Select, Standard. 128 to 140 olives per pound.
Medium. 106 to 127 olives per pound.
Large. 91 to 105 olives per pound.
Extra Large. 76 to 90 olives per pound.
Mammoth. 65 to 75 olives per pound.
Giant. 53 to 64 olives per pound.
Jumbo. 42 to 52 olives per pound.
Colossal. 33 to 41 olives per pound.
Super Colossal. 32 or fewer olives per pound.
Mixed Sizes.

GRADES

Green olives graded according to a very technical system whereby penalty points are assessed for such factors as edibility, poor appearance, or defects in workmanship. The more penalty points assessed the lower the grade. The grade descriptions which follow are intended only as a general consumer guide. For more detail please consult the source cited below.

U S. Grade A or U.S. Fancy. Have normal flavor and odor and a good, uniform, bright yellow-green to green exterior color that is characteristic of the variety. The olives are uniform in size and practically free of defects, blemishes, wrinkles, mutilated olives, internal gas pockets, and any other defects which affect the appearance or edibility of the product. The olives have a uniform tender texture that is characteristic of the variety and that is firm, crisp, and fleshy. The olives are practically free of slip skins.

U.S. Grade B or U.S. Choice. Have similar varietal characteristics and normal flavor and odor. The color is a reasonably uniform yellow-green to green exterior color. The olives are reasonably uniform in size and reasonably free of defects. They have a reasonably uniform tender texture that is characteristic of the variety. There may be a moderate variation in the firmness, crispness, and fleshiness. The olives are reasonably free of slip skins.

U.S. Grade C or U.S. Standard. Have similar varietal characteristics, a normal flavor and odor, a fairly good color, are fairly uniform in size and fairly free of defects. The olives have a fairly good texture that is typical of the variety. They may vary from fairly firm and crisp to fairly hard and tough. The olives are fairly free of slip skins.

Substandard. Fails to meet the applicable requirements of *U.S. Grade C.*

Source:
Agricultural Marketing Service, USDA, 7 CFR sections 52.5441 to 52.5458 (1991), Washington: Government Printing Office.

Orange Marmalade

Orange marmalade is the semi-solid or gel-like product prepared from orange fruit ingredients together with one or more sweetening ingredients and may contain suitable food acids, food pectins, lemon juice, or lemon peel. The ingredients are concentrated by cooking to such a point that the soluble solids of the finished marmalade are not less than 65 percent.

KINDS

Sweet Orange Marmalade. Consists principally of such varieties as Navel and Valencia or other commercial dessert varieties of oranges other than tangerines. Prepared from not less than 30 parts by weight of orange fruit ingredient to 70 parts by weight of sweetening ingredient.

Bitter Orange Marmalade. Consists principally of the Seville or sour type of oranges other than tangerines. Prepared from not less than 25 parts by weight of orange fruit ingredient to 75 parts by weight of sweetening ingredient.

Sweet and Bitter Orange Marmalade. Consists of a blend of sweet oranges and bitter oranges other than tangerines. Prepared from not less than 30 parts by weight of orange fruit ingredient to 70 parts by weight of sweetening ingredient.

STYLES

Sliced. The peel in the orange marmalade is in thin strips.

Chopped. The peel in the orange marmalade is in small pieces (such as irregular shapes and dice-like shapes).

TYPES

Type I, Clear. The peel is suspended in a translucent semi-solid or gel-like mass.

Type II, Natural. The peel is suspended in a cloudy or opaque semi-solid or gel-like mass.

GRADES

Orange marmalade is graded according to a very technical system whereby penalty points are assessed for such factors as edibility, poor appearance, or defects in workmanship. The more penalty points assessed the lower the grade. The grade descriptions which follow are intended only as a general consumer guide. For more detail please consult the source cited below.

U.S. Grade A or U.S. Fancy. Possesses a uniform, bright color characteristic of properly prepared and processed orange marmalade. It is nearly free from green-colored peel and dullness of color due to oxidation or improper processing or improper cooling. Practically free from defects. There may be present on an average for each 16 ounces net weight not more than 1 seed or portion of seed and not more than 6 pieces of blemished peel. In a single container, the appearance and eating quality of the product is not materially affected by the presence of seeds, portions of seeds, blemished peel, objectionable material, harmless extraneous material, or any other defects. Possesses a good and distinct flavor and aroma characteristic of properly processed orange marmalade. The flavor is neither excessively tart nor excessively sweet. The product is free from caramelized or objectionable flavor and odors of any kind. It has a firm but tender gel and may possess no more than a very slight tendency to flow. It contains a substantial, but not excessive, amount of peel. The peel is evenly distributed and tender. In sliced style, the thin strips of peel are predominantly of strips approximating ¹⁄₃₂ inch to ¹⁄₁₆ inch in width. In chopped style, the small pieces of peel are reasonably uniform in size.

U.S. Grade B or U.S. Choice. Reasonably good color which is practically free from green-colored peel but may be slightly dull, but not off-color. Reasonably good consistency and character. It may be definitely firm but is neither excessively gummy nor excessively rubbery. The product may be viscous but is not excessively thin. The peel is fairly evenly distributed and is reasonably tender. In sliced style, the thin strips of peel are predominantly of strips approximating no more than ¹⁄₈ inch in width. In chopped style, the small pieces of peel are fairly uniform in size. There may be present on an average for each 16 ounces net weight not more than a total of 2 seeds or portions of seeds and not more than 10 pieces of blemished peel. In a single container, the appearance and eating quality of the product is not seriously affected by the presence of seeds, portions of seeds, blemished peel, objectionable material, harmless extraneous material, or any other defects. Possesses a reasonably good flavor and odor that may be excessively tart or sweet. It may possess a slightly caramelized flavor but is free from objectionable flavor and objectionable odor of any kind.

U.S. Grade D or Substandard. Fails to meet the requirements of *U.S. Grade B* or *U.S. Choice*.

Source:
Agricultural Marketing Service, USDA, 7 CFR section 52.1451 (1991), Washington: Government Printing Office.

Orgeat Syrup

Orgeat or Orzata Syrup. The food prepared essentially from sugar (sucrose) syrup and milk of almonds.

Imitation Orgeat or Orzatya Syrup. Syrups flavored with oil of bitter almonds and in which gum benzoin or a similar substance has been added to produce the turbidity characteristic of milk of almonds.

Source:
Food and Drug Administration, *Compliance Policy Guides*, Guide 7105.06, Reissued 01/01/80, Washington: National Technical Information Service.

Parsley

These standards do not apply to parsley tops marketed with a part of the root attached.

GRADES

Parsley is graded according to a very technical system whereby penalty points are assessed for such factors as edibility, poor appearance, or defects in workmanship. The more penalty points assessed the lower the grade. The grade descriptions which follow are intended only as a general consumer guide. For more detail please consult the source cited below.

U.S. No. 1. Parsley of similar varietal characteristics and of good green color. It is free from decay and from damage caused by seedstems, yellow or discolored leaves, wilting, freezing, dirt, disease, insects, etc. In order to allow for variations incident to proper grading and handling, not more than 5 percent, by weight, of the parsley in any lot may be below the requirements of this grade, including not more than 0.5 percent which is affected by decay.

Unclassified. Parsley which has not been classified in accordance with the foregoing grade. The term *unclassified* is not a grade within the meaning of these standards but is provided as a designation to show that no grade has been applied to the lot.

Source:
Agricultural Marketing Service, USDA, 7 CFR sections 51.4000 to 51.4004 (1992), Washington: Government Printing Office.

Pickles

Pickles describe the products prepared entirely or predominantly from cucumbers (*Cucumis sativus*). Clean, sound ingredients are used which may or may not have been previously subjected to fermentation and curing in a salt brine (solution of sodium chloride, NaCl). The prepared pickles are packed in a vinegar solution, to which may be added salt and other vegetable(s), nutritive sweetener(s), seasoning(s), flavoring(s), and spice(s). The product is packed in suitable containers and heat treated or otherwise processed to assure preservation.

STYLES

Whole. The cucumber ingredient is whole.

Sliced Crosswise or Crosscut. Cut into slices transversely to the longitudinal axis. The cut surfaces may have flat-parallel or corrugated-parallel (waffle cut) surfaces.

Sliced Lengthwise. Cut longitudinally into halves, quarters, or other triangular shapes, or otherwise into units with parallel surfaces with or without ends removed.

Cut. Cut or broken into units which may or may not be uniform in size or shape.

Relish. Finely cut or finely chopped pickles.

TYPES

Dill Pickles (Natural or Genuine). Cured in salt brine with dill herb.

Dill Pickles (Processed). Cured pickles packed in a vinegar solution with dill flavoring(s).

Sour Pickles. Cured pickles packed in a vinegar solution.

Sweet Pickles and Mild Sweet Pickles. Cured pickles packed in a vinegar solution with suitable nutritive sweetening ingredient(s).

Sour Mixed Pickles. Cured pickles packed in a vinegar solution. The pickles may be of any style or combination of styles other than relish. Sour mixed pickles contain onions and cauliflower and other ingredients.

Sweet Mixed Pickles and Mild Sweet Mixed Pickles. Cured pickles packed in a vinegar solution with suitable nutritive sweetening ingredient(s). The pickles may be of any style or combination of styles other than relish. Such pickles contain onions and cauliflower and other ingredients.

Sour Mustard Pickles or Sour Chow-Chow Pickles. Cured pickles of the same styles and ingredients as sour mixed pickles except that instead of a liquid solution they are packed in a prepared mustard sauce of proper consistency.

Sweet Mustard Pickles or Sweet Chow-Chow Pickles. Cured pickles of the same styles and ingredients as sweet mixed pickles except that instead of a liquid solution they are packed in a sweetened prepared mustard sauce of proper consistency.

TYPES OF PACK

Cured Type. Cured by natural fermentation in a salt brine solution (NaCl) which may contain dill herb or other flavorings. The pickle ingredient may be partially desalted and then processed or preserved in a vinegar solution with other ingredients.

Sour Pickle Relish. Consists of cured, finely cut, or finely chopped cucumber pickles packed in a vinegar solution. Sour pickle relish may contain other finely cut or chopped vegetable ingredients.

Sweet Pickle Relish and Mild Sweet Pickle Relish. Consists of cured, finely cut, or finely chopped cucumbers packed in a vinegar solution with suitable nutritive sweetening ingredient(s). Sweet pickle relish may contain other finely cut or chopped vegetable ingredients.

Fresh-Pack Type. Pickles of fresh-pack type are prepared from uncured, unfermented cucumbers and are packed in a vinegar solution with other ingredients of various compositions to give the characteristics of the particular type of pickle. They are sufficiently processed by heat to assure preservation of the product in hermetically sealed containers.

Fresh-Pack Dill Pickles. Packed in a vinegar solution with dill flavoring(s).

Fresh-Pack Sweetened Dill Pickles. Packed in a vinegar solution with nutritive sweetening ingredient(s) and dill flavoring(s).

Fresh-Pack Sweetened Dill Relish. Consists of finely cut or finely chopped cucumbers packed in a vinegar solution with suitable nutritive sweetening ingredient(s) and dill flavoring(s). The relish may contain other finely cut or finely chopped vegetable ingredients.

Fresh-Pack Sweet Pickles and Fresh-pack Mild Sweet Pickles.

Fresh-pack sweet pickles and fresh-pack mild sweet pickles are packed in a vinegar solution with nutritive sweetening ingredient(s).

Fresh-Pack Sweet Relish and Fresh-pack Mild Sweet Relish. Fresh-pack sweet relish and fresh-pack mild sweet relish consist of finely cut or finely chopped cucumbers packed in a vinegar solution with suitable nutritive sweetening ingredient(s). The relish may contain other finely cut or finely chopped vegetable ingredients.

Fresh-Pack Dietetic Pickles. Fresh-pack dietetic pickles may be prepared in any style with or without the addition of sweetening ingredient(s), salt (sodium chloride, NaCl), and other suitable ingredient(s).

SIZES

Count per gallon, diameters in inches.

Midget. Approximately 270 or more pickles per gallon and ¾ inch or less in diameter.

Small Gherkin. 135 to 269 per gallon and up to $1^{15}/_{16}$ inches.

Large Gherkin. 65 to 134 per gallon and up to $1^{1}/_{16}$ inches.

Small. 40 to 64 per gallon and between $1^{1}/_{16}$ and $1^{3}/_{8}$ inches.

Medium. 26 to 39 per gallon and between $1^{3}/_{8}$ and $1^{1}/_{2}$ inches.

Large. 18 to 25 per gallon and between $1^{1}/_{2}$ and $1^{3}/_{4}$ inches.

Extra Large. 12 to 17 per gallon and between $1^{3}/_{4}$ to $2^{1}/_{8}$ inches.

GRADES

Pickles are graded according to a very technical system whereby penalty points are assessed for such factors as edibility, poor appearance, or defects in workmanship. The more penalty points assessed the lower the grade. The grade descriptions which follow are intended only as a general consumer guide. For more detail please consult the source cited below.

U.S. Grade A or U.S. Fancy. The cucumbers possess similar varietal characteristics and good distinctive flavor for the type. The typical skin color of the cucumbers ranges from a translucent light green to dark green and is practically free from bleached areas. The product is free of ripe cucumbers or other off-color vegetable ingredients. For fresh-pack type, the typical skin color of the cucumber ingredient ranges from an opaque yellow-green to green. The units within a single style may vary moderately in size but not to the extent that the overall appearance of the product is materially affected. It is practically free from defects such as grit, attached stems, misshapen pickles, discoloration, or mechanical damage which affect its appearance or edibility. The cucumbers and other vegetable ingredient(s) are firm and crisp and are practically free from large objectionable seeds, detached seeds, and tough skins. For cured types, there may be not more than 5 percent cucumbers, by count, that are shriveled, soft, or slippery (very slight shriveling is permitted in sweet pickles) or 5 percent with hollow centers, or 10 percent, by count, of whole, sliced, or cut cucumbers with chalky white areas. For fresh-pack type there may be not more than 10 percent cucumbers, by count, that are shriveled, soft, or flabby, and 15 percent, by count, of whole cucumbers with hollow centers.

U.S. Grade B or U.S. Extra Standard. The cucumbers possess similar varietal characteristics and reasonably good flavor. Flavor may be somewhat lacking, but it is free from objectionable flavors and odors. For color-cured type, the typical skin color of the cucumber ingredient ranges from light green to dark green and is reasonably free from bleached areas. The pickles are free from ripe cucumbers or other off-color vegetable ingredients. In fresh-pack type, the typical skin color of the cucumber ingredient ranges from yellow-green to green. In pickle relish, all of the pickle ingredients possess a good, fairly uniform color typical of the respective ingredient. May or may not be at least reasonably uniform in size, meaning that the cucumbers may vary considerably in size and may fail to meet in some respects the criteria for variation in diameter, length, or weight, but not to the extent that the overall appearance of the product is seriously affected. Reasonably free from defects and are reasonably firm and crisp. Pickles are reasonably free from cucumbers with large, objectionable seeds, detached seeds, and tough skins. For cured type, there may be not more than 10 percent cucumbers, by count, that are markedly shriveled, soft, or slippery; 10 percent, by count, of whole cucumbers with hollow centers; and 20 percent, by count, of whole, sliced, or cut cucumbers with chalky white areas. For fresh-pack type, there may be not more than 15 percent cucumbers, by count, that are markedly shriveled, soft, or flabby, and 25 percent, by count, of whole cucumbers with hollow centers.

Source:
Agricultural Marketing Service, USDA, 7 CFR sections 52.1681 to 52.1702 (1991), Washington: Government Printing Office.

Pimiento, Minced

A pimiento (or pimento) product made from minced pimientos that are bonded and pressed into sheets and cut in the form of pimiento strips ordinarily used for stuffing olives. Olives stuffed with such a product should bear the name *olives stuffed with minced pimientos* or an equally descriptive designation.

Source:
Food and Drug Administration, *Compliance Policy Guides*, Guide 7110.20, 10/01/80, Washington: National Technical Information Service.

Radishes

To allow for variations in quality caused by grading and handling, a percentage of the radishes may fail to meet all of the requirements of the grade.

TYPES

Topped Radishes. The tops are clipped back to not more than ⅜ inch in length.

Bunched Radishes. Have full length tops which are tied in bunches.

SIZE

Small. Less than ¾ inch in diameter.
Medium. Less than ¾ to 1 inch in diameter.
Large. Over 1 to 1¼ inches in diameter.
Very Large. Over 1¼ inches in diameter.

GRADES

Radishes are graded according to a very technical system whereby penalty points are assessed for such factors as edibility, poor appearance, or defects in workmanship. The more penalty points assessed the lower the grade. The grade descriptions which follow are intended only as a general consumer guide. For more detail please consult the source cited below.

U.S. No. 1. Radishes of similar varietal characteristics, the roots of which are clean, well formed, smooth, firm, tender (not stringy or woody), free from decay, and free from damage caused by freezing, growth cracks or air cracks, cuts, pithiness, disease, insects, or other means. Bunched radishes have tops which are fresh and free from decay and free from damage caused by freezing, seedstems, yellowing or other discoloration, disease, insects, or other means. Unless otherwise specified, the diameter of each root shall be not less than ⅝ inch.

U.S. Commercial. Radishes which meet the requirements for the *U.S. No. 1* grade except there is an increased tolerances for defects.

Source:
Agricultural Marketing Service, USDA, 7 CFR sections 51.2395 to 51.2413 (1992), Washington: Government Printing Office.

Refiners' Syrup

Refiners' syrup is a liquid product obtained from the refining of cane or beet sugar. The total soluble nonsugar solids content of refiners' syrup exceeds 6 percent of the total soluble solids. All of the syrup constituents have been subjected to the processes of clarification and decolorization, or equivalent purification, and it may be partially or wholly inverted.

GRADES

Refiners' syrup is graded according to a very technical system whereby penalty points are assessed for such factors as edibility, poor appearance, or defects in workmanship. The more penalty points assessed the lower the grade. The grade descriptions which follow are intended only as a general consumer guide. For more detail please consult the source cited below.

U.S. Fancy or U.S. Grade A. Possesses a flavor characteristic of refiners' syrup of fancy quality with no sediment. It is free of foreign matter and has a ratio of total sugars (sucrose plus reducing sugars) to solids of not less than 92 percent.

U.S. Choice or U.S. Grade B. Possesses a flavor characteristic of refiners' syrup of choice quality. It contains no sediment and is free of foreign matter. It has a ratio of total sugars (sucrose plus reducing sugars) to solids of not less than 86 percent.

U.S. Extra Standard or U.S. Grade C. Possesses a flavor characteristic of refiners' syrup of standard quality. It contains no excess of sediment and is practically free of foreign matter. It has a ratio of total sugars (sucrose plus reducing sugars) to solids of not less than 78 percent.

U.S. Standard or U.S. Grade D. Possesses a flavor characteristic of refiners' syrup of standard quality. It contains no excess of sediment and is practically free of foreign matter. It has a ratio of total sugars (sucrose plus reducing sugars) to solids of not less than 70 percent.

U.S. Substandard or U.S. Grade E. Fails to meet the specifications for *U.S. Standard* Refiners' Syrup.

Source:
Agricultural Marketing Service, USDA, 7 CFR sections 52.6401 to 52.6064 (1991), Washington: Government Printing Office.

Sauerkraut, Canned (or Packaged)

Canned (or packaged) sauerkraut (canned kraut) is prepared from clean, sound, well matured heads of the cabbage plant (*Brassica oleracea capitata*) which have been properly trimmed and cut. Salt is added, and the cabbage is cured by natural fermentation. The product may or may not be packed with pickled peppers, pimientos, tomatoes, or other flavoring ingredients which give the product specific flavor characteristics. The product may be (a) canned in hermetically sealed containers and processed sufficiently with heat to assure preservation, or (b) packaged in sealed containers and preserved with or without the addition of benzoate of soda or any other ingredient permissible under the provisions of the Federal Food, Drug, and Cosmetic Act or applicable state laws or regulations.

STYLES

Shredded. Prepared from cabbage cut into shreds.
Chopped. Prepared from cabbage chopped into small pieces.

GRADES

Sauerkraut is graded according to a very technical system whereby penalty points are assessed for such factors as edibility, poor appearance, or defects in workmanship. The more penalty points assessed the lower the grade. The grade descriptions which follow are intended only as a general consumer guide. For more detail please consult the source cited below.

U.S. Grade A or U.S. Fancy. Possesses a bright, uniform, white to light cream appearance characteristic of properly prepared and processed canned kraut. The shreds are uniform in thickness and the presence of pieces markedly smaller or larger than the predominant size of pieces does not more than slightly affect the appearance of the product. It is practically free from such defects as coarse pieces of leaves, large and coarse pieces of core material, and blemished, spotted, or otherwise dark or discolored shreds or pieces. The kraut is crisp and firm and easy to cut. It has a good characteristic kraut flavor which is free from off-flavors and off-odors of any kind.

U.S. Grade B or U.S. Extra Standard. Possesses a reasonably bright, uniform, cream to light straw general appearance. It is reasonably uniform in thickness and reasonably free from defects. The kraut is reasonably crisp, firm, and possesses a reasonably good characteristic kraut flavor which is free from off-flavors and off-odors of any kind.

U.S. Grade C or U.S. Standard. Possesses a dark straw, slightly green, or yellowish general appearance and may be dull or slightly variable, but not off-color. There may be very short or very fine pieces or large and irregular pieces which do not seriously affect the appearance of the product. Fairly free from defects, the kraut may lack crispness, may be soft or slightly tough, but is not excessively tough or excessively soft or mushy. Possesses a fairly good kraut flavor which is free from objectionable flavors and odors which may seriously affect the eating quality of the product.

Substandard. Fails to meet the requirements of *U.S. Grade C* or *U.S. Standard.*

Source:
Agricultural Marketing Service, USDA, 7 CFR sections 52.2951 to 52.2966 (1991), Washington: Government Printing Office.

Sauerkraut, Bulk or Barreled

Bulk or barreled sauerkraut, hereinafter referred to as sauerkraut or bulk sauerkraut, is a product with a characteristic acid flavor. It is obtained by the full fermentation, chiefly lactic, of properly prepared and shredded cabbage in the presence of not less than 2 percent or more than 3 percent of salt. It contains, upon completion of the fermentation, not less than 1.5 percent of acid (expressed as lactic acid).

GRADES

This product is graded according to a very technical system whereby penalty points are assessed for such factors as edibility, poor appearance, or defects in workmanship. The more penalty points assessed the lower the grade. The grade descriptions which follow are intended only as a general consumer guide. For more detail please consult the source cited below.

U.S. Grade A (First Quality). Is a color approximating, or is lighter than, Olive Buff (according to Ridgway's Color Standards and Nomenclature), with the shreds uniformly cut to approximately 1/32 inch in thickness. The product is practically free from defects and blemishes; is of fine, crisp texture; and possesses a normal, well developed, sauerkraut flavor.

U.S. Grade C (Second Quality). May have a variable straw color, but not darker than Dark Olive Buff. The shreds may lack uniformity of thickness. The product is reasonably free from defects and blemishes; is of reasonably fine, crisp texture; and

possesses a normal sauerkraut flavor.

Substandard. Fails to meet the requirements of the foregoing grades.

Source:
Agricultural Marketing Service, USDA, 7 CFR section 52.3451 (1991), Washington: Government Printing Office.

Sirup, or Syrup

Honey, Honey Drips. If honey is represented as the characterizing flavor in table syrup, the total quantity of honey should be not less than 10 percent by weight of the finished syrup.

Open Kettle, Country, Country Made, Home Made, or Farm. When these terms are used on the labels of syrups, the syrups should have been produced in the manner indicated by the term. For example, a syrup labeled as *Open Kettle* should have been made in an open kettle.

Source:
Food and Drug Administration, *Compliance Policy Guides*, Guide 7105.08, Reissued 10/01/80, Washington: National Technical Information Service.

Starch

The term *starch,* when used alone, is considered the common or usual name for starch made from corn; alternatively, the name *cornstarch* may be used. Starches from other sources are designated by a term that indicates the source of the starch, for example, *potato starch, wheat starch,* or *tapioca starch. Modified food starch* contains an additive.

Source:
Food and Drug Administration, *Compliance Policy Guides*, Guide 7104.01, 01/01/80, Washington: National Technical Information Service.

Sugar

The word *sugar* in the list of ingredients for a food means sucrose, i.e., sugar from sugar cane or sugar beets. Other nutritive sweeteners should be declared by their common or usual names, e.g., fructose, dextrose, honey, high fructose corn syrup, etc. Sugar is refined by separating the sugar that is stored in the cane stalk or beet root from the rest of the plant material. For sugar cane, this is accomplished by (a) grinding the cane to extract the juice; (b) boiling the juice until the syrup thickens and crystallizes; (c) spinning the crystals in a centrifuge to produce raw sugar; (d) shipping the raw sugar to a refinery where it is (e) washed and filtered to remove impurities and color; and (f) crystallized, dried, and packaged. Beet sugar processing is accomplished in one continuous process without the raw sugar stage. The sugar beets are washed, sliced and soaked in hot water to remove the juice. The sugar-laden juice is purified, filtered, concentrated and dried in a series of steps similar to sugar cane processing.

RAW SUGAR

This term is generally applied to sugar as it leaves the sugar factory mill for further refinement in sugar refineries. In general, raw sugar is unsuitable for food because it contains impurities which are removed in the refining process.

BARLEY SUGAR

The term *barley sugar* is loosely applied. When sugar is heated to 160 degrees C, it melts without losing weight and, on cooling, congeals to a transparent, amorphous, yellowish mass. This mass becomes gradually opaque on the surface from the formation of minute crystals. The resulting product is sometimes referred to as barley sugar. Also, when rock candy is heated to 185 degrees C, it melts into a viscid liquid which, when suddenly cooled, forms a transparent mass. This mass is also called *barley sugar*.

TYPES

Brown Sugar. Brown sugar consists of sugar crystals contained in a molasses syrup with natural flavor and color components. Many sugar refiners produce brown sugar by preparing and boiling a special syrup containing these components until brown sugar crystals form. In the final processing, the crystals are spun dry in a centrifuge; some of the syrup remains, giving the sugar its characteristic brown color. Other refiners produce brown sugar by blending a special molasses syrup with white sugar crystals.

Turbinado Sugar. Raw sugar that has been partially refined by washing in a centrifuge under sanitary conditions. Surface molasses is removed in the washing process. In total sugar content, turbinado is closer to refined sugar than to raw sugar. It can be purchased in many health food stores and some supermarkets.

Confectioners Sugar (Powdered Sugar). Granulated sugar, finely ground to a smooth powder and sifted. About 3 percent cornstarch is added to prevent caking.

Granulated Sugar. Essentially, pure crystalline sucrose. Standard granulated sugar products sold by both beet and cane refiners will contain at least 99.8 percent sucrose. These products are processed to a variety of crystal-size distributions to meet the requirements of the various applications: coarse, sanding, X-fine, fruit, bakers special, powdered sugar 6X, powdered sugar 10X.

Superfine or Ultrafine Sugar. A very fine-grained sugar. Refined granulated sugar is used for normal baking, canning, and table use, while super-fine granulated sugar is ideal for extra fine-textured cakes and meringues, sweetening fruits, and iced drinks.

Blended Sugar. In some locales, dextrose, a corn-derived sweetener, is added to granulated cane or beet sugar to create a white granulated blend that may be less expensive than traditional sugar. Dextrose is about 70 percent as sweet as sugar and is

more hydroscopic (water attracting). Because of these characteristics, blends may not perform exactly as sugar in certain recipes.

High-Fructose Corn Syrup. Corn syrups are manufactured by treating corn starch with acids or enzymes. Standard corn syrups, used by the food industry as well as the consumer, contain dextrose and other saccharides. High-fructose corn syrup (HFCS) is made by treating dextrose with enzymes. The result (HFCS) is a liquid mixture of dextrose and fructose that is used by food manufacturers in soft drinks, canned fruits, jams, and other food applications.

Light and Dark Brown Sugar. Dark brown sugar has more color and a stronger molasses flavor than light brown sugar. The choice of one or the other is a matter of personal preference. Lighter types are generally used in baking, making butterscotch, condiments, and glazes for ham. The dark brown sugar, with its rich flavor, is desirable for gingerbread, mincemeat, baked beans, plum pudding, and other full-flavored foods.

Sources:
Consumer Fact Sheet, Washington: The Sugar Association, 1992.
Food and Drug Administration, *Compliance Policy Guides*, Guides 7105.05 and 7105.07, Reissued 01/01/80, Washington: National Technical Information Service.

Sugarcane Syrup

Sugarcane syrup is the clean, sound, liquid product obtained by evaporating the juice of sugarcane without the removal of any of the soluble solids or by dissolving sugarcane concrete in water.

TYPES

Sulfured. Made by the sulfitation process and contains not more than 100 parts per million of sulfur dioxide.

Unsulfured. Not made by the sulfitation process.

GRADES

Sugarcane syrup is graded according to a very technical system whereby penalty points are assessed for such factors as edibility, poor appearance, or defects in workmanship. The more penalty points assessed the lower the grade. The grade descriptions which follow are intended only as a general consumer guide. For more detail please consult the source cited below.

U.S. Grade A or U.S. Fancy. Possesses a good color that is bright and typical of syrup properly prepared and processed from sound, well matured sugarcane. Has a good, characteristic flavor for the type of sugarcane syrup and is free from objectionable flavors, including those caused by scorching or fermentation or by the presence of any foreign or disagreeable flavor or odor. It is practically free from defects like harmless extraneous material, such as particles of fiber, carbon, or earthly material which may be in suspension or deposited as sediment in the container. It is practically clear, meaning that the sugarcane syrup may contain not more than a trace of finely divided particles of suspended material which does not affect the appearance or edibility of the product.

U.S. Grade B or U.S. Choice. Possesses a reasonably bright color. Has a reasonably good flavor and is free from objectionable flavors, including, but not limited to, those caused by scorching or fermentation or by the presence of any foreign or disagreeable flavor or odor. It is reasonably free from defects and reasonably clear. The sugarcane syrup may contain finely divided particles of suspended material but it does not materially affect the appearance or edibility of the product.

U.S. Grade C or U.S. Standard. Possesses a fairly good color and flavor. Is fairly free from defects and is fairly clear, meaning that the appearance or edibility of the sugarcane syrup may be materially but not seriously affected by the presence of finely divided particles of suspended material.

Substandard. Fails to meet the requirements of *U.S. Grade C* or *U.S. Standard.*

Source:
Agricultural Marketing Service, USDA, 7 CFR sections 52.3101 to 52.3120 (1991), Washington: Government Printing Office.

Tobacco Products

Chewing Tobacco. Any leaf tobacco that is not intended to be smoked.

Smokeless Tobacco. Any snuff or chewing tobacco.

Pipe Tobacco. Any tobacco which, because of its appearance, type, packaging, or labeling, is suitable for use and is likely to be offered to, or purchased by, consumers as tobacco to be smoked in a pipe.

Snuff. Any finely cut, ground, or powdered tobacco that is not intended to be smoked.

Tax Class C. An alternate designation for chewing tobacco.

Tax Class M. An alternate designation for snuff.

Tax Class L. An alternate designation for pipe tobacco.

Tobacco Products. Cigars, cigarettes, smokeless tobacco, and pipe tobacco. The term does not include smoking tobacco that is not suitable for use or is not likely to be offered to, or purchased by, consumers as tobacco to be smoked in a pipe.

In Bond. The status of tobacco products and cigarette papers and tubes which come within the coverage of a bond securing the payment of internal revenue taxes.

CIGARS

50th. A box of 20 cigars. Equal to ⅟₅₀ of a thousand. Other standard counts include 20th, 40th, and 100th.

10 Top. A box of 50 cigars consisting of 5 rows of 10 cigars each.

13 Top. A box of 50 cigars packed in four rows: 3 rows of 13 with the bottom row consisting of 11 cigars and a spacer.

5 Top. A box of 25 cigars consisting a 5 rows of 5 cigars each.

8-9-8. A box of 25 cigars packed with a row of 8 cigars on top and bottom and with a row of 9 in the middle.

BTX, Stay Fresh, Fresh-loc, etc. Refers to the type of cellophane

in which the cigar is wrapped to keep it fresh.

Cetro. A cigar approximately 7 inches long.

Churchill. Similar to a Cetro but with a larger diameter.

Cigar. Any roll of tobacco wrapped in leaf tobacco or in any substance containing tobacco (other than any roll of tobacco which is a cigarette)

Class A. Large cigars with a wholesale price or sale price of not more than $33.00 per thousand.

Class B. Large cigars with a wholesale price or sale price of more than $33.00 per thousand but not more than $51.00 per thousand.

Class C. Large cigars with a wholesale price or sale price of more than $51.00 per thousand but not more than $66.00 per thousand.

Class D. Large cigars with a wholesale price or sale price of more than $66.00 per thousand but not more than $105.00 per thousand.

Class E. Large cigars with a wholesale price or sale price of more than $105.00 per thousand but not more than $120.00 per thousand.

Class F. Large cigars with a wholesale price or sale price of more than $120.00 per thousand but not more than $154.00 per thousand.

Class G. Large cigars with a wholesale price or sale price of more than $154.00 per thousand but not more than $235.294 per thousand.

Class H. Large cigars with a wholesale price or sale price of more than $235.294 per thousand.

Corona. A cigar approximately 5½ inches long.

Double Corona. The same length as a Corona but with a larger diameter.

Filler. The tobacco in the body of the cigar.

Fire Cured. Method of curing light green claro wrapper by exposure to extreme heat.

Homogenized Tobacco Leaf or Homogenized Tobacco (H.T.L.). Tobacco that has been processed into a single sheet by the addition of an emulsifier. Homogenized tobacco is required for use in high speed cigar machines.

Hand Packed or Envuilto a mano. Cigars placed in the box by hand.

Hand Rolled. A machine made cigar that had the wrapper applied by hand.

Large Cigars. Cigars weighing more than three pounds per thousand.

Long Filler. Filler made from large tobacco leaves. Burns slower than cigars made from short filler.

Longsdale or Palma. A cigar approximately 6 inches long.

Mild, Very Mild, Extra Mild. Generic advertising terms used by manufacturers to distinguish their products.

No. 1. A cigar approximately 6½ inches long.

Panetela Larga. A thin-sized cigar approximately 7 inches long.

Panetela. A cigar approximately 6 inches long.

Petit Corona. A cigar approximately 5 inches long.

Short Filler. Filler made from small pieces of tobacco. Burns faster than cigars made of long filler. Cigars with short filler have a hotter, harsher taste.

Small Cigars. Cigars weighing not more than three pounds per thousand.

T.P. Stands for Tobacco Products. Every tobacco factory has its own number and the number is stamped on the back of the cigar box. Cigars imported into the United States may not have a number stamped on the box.

Wrapper. The tobacco used to wrap the filler. May be of a different variety, quality, and color.

CIGARETTES

Cigarette Paper. Paper, or any other material except tobacco, prepared for use as a cigarette wrapper. Also refers to taxable books or sets of cigarette papers, i.e., books or sets of cigarette papers containing more than 25 papers each.

Cigarette Tubes. Cigarette paper made into a hollow cylinder for use in making cigarettes.

Cigarette. Any roll of tobacco wrapped in paper or in any substance not containing tobacco and any roll of tobacco wrapped in any substance containing tobacco which, because of its appearance, the type of tobacco used in the filler, or its packaging and labeling, is likely to be offered to, or purchased by, consumers as a cigarette.

Class A. The taxing class for small cigarettes.

Class B. The taxing class for large cigarettes.

Large Cigarettes. Cigarettes weighting more than three pounds per thousand.

Small Cigarettes. Cigarettes weighing not more than three pounds per thousand.

Sources:
Bureau of Alcohol, Tobacco, and Firearms, US Department of the Treasury, 27 CFR Sections 270.1 to 270.313, 1991, Washington: Government Printing Office.
Rothman, Lew, *Lew Rothman's Cigar Almanac,* first edition, Belleville, NJ: Education Systems and Publications, 1980.

Tomato Catsup

GRADES

Tomato catsup is graded according to a very technical system whereby penalty points are assessed for such factors as edibility, poor appearance, or defects in workmanship. The more penalty points assessed the lower the grade. The grade descriptions which follow are intended only as a general consumer guide. For more detail please consult the source cited below.

U.S. Grade A or U.S. Fancy. Possesses a good color typical of tomato catsup made from well-ripened red tomatoes. Shows no discoloration in the neck of the bottle. Possesses a good consistency such that the tomato catsup shows not more than a slight separation of free liquid when poured on a flat grading tray. It is not excessively stiff and flows not more than 9 centimeters in 30 seconds at 20 degrees C. It is practically free from defects such as dark specks or scale-like particles, seeds, particles of seed, tomato peel, core material, or other similar substances. It possesses a good and distinct flavor that is characteristic of good quality ingredients. The flavor is free from scorching or any objectionable flavor of any kind. It

possesses a good finish with a total solids content of not less than 33 percent, by weight.

U.S. Grade B or U.S. Extra Standard. Possesses a good color and consistency. It is practically free from defects, possesses a good flavor, a good finish, and has a total solids content of not less than 29 percent, by weight

U.S. Grade C or U.S. Standard. Possesses a fairly good color and has a fairly good consistency. It may show a noticeable, but not excessive, separation of free liquid when poured on a flat grading tray. It is not excessively stiff and flows not more than 14 centimeters in 30 seconds at 20 degrees C. It is fairly free from defects and possesses a good finish. It has a fairly good flavor characteristic of the ingredients; there may be slight traces of undesirable flavors such as scorched, bitter, or astringent, but it is free from objectionable or off-flavor of any kind. It has a total solids content of not less than 25 percent, by weight

Substandard. Fails to meet the requirements of *U.S. Grade C* or *U.S. Standard.*

Source:
Agricultural Marketing Service, USDA, 7 CFR sections 52.2001 to 52.2112 (1991), Washington: Government Printing Office.

Tomato Paste

The standards in this entry cover canned tomato paste processed by heat to assure preservation in hermetically sealed containers as well as tomato paste which may be preserved by other means.

NATURAL TOMATO SOLUBLE SOLIDS

Extra Heavy. 39.3 percent or more natural tomato soluble solids.

Heavy. 32 percent or more, but less than 39.3 percent.

Medium. 28 percent or more but less than 32 percent.

Light. 24 percent or more, but less than 28 percent.

TEXTURE

Texture is the degree of fineness or coarseness of the product. Texture is classified when the product is diluted with water to between 8 percent and 9 percent, inclusive, of natural tomato soluble solids.

Fine. Has a smooth, uniform finish.

Coarse. Has a coarse, slightly granular finish.

GRADES

U.S. Grade A or U.S. Fancy. Has a good flavor and odor characteristic of ripe, good quality tomatoes. The flavor and odor is no more than slightly affected by stems, sepals, leaves, crushed seeds, cores, and by immature, soured, or overripe tomatoes. Also free from the effects of unsatisfactory preparation, processing, or storage or from any other factor not specifically mentioned. The flavor may be influenced by any optional ingredient which may have been added. It has a good bright, typical, red tomato paste color. Is practically free from defects such as dark specks or scale-like particles, seeds or objectionable particles of seeds, objectionable tomato peel, harmless extraneous material, or any other similar substances.

U.S. Grade C or U.S. Standard. Has at least a fairly good flavor and odor which may be affected by stems, sepals, leaves, crushed seeds, cores; by immature, soured, or overripe tomatoes; from the effects of unsatisfactory preparation, processing, or storage; or from any other factor not specifically mentioned. Has a typical red tomato paste color which may be slightly dull or may have a slightly brownish cast. It is fairly free from defects.

Substandard. Fails to meet the requirements of *U.S. Grade C.*

Source:
Agricultural Marketing Service, USDA, 7 CFR sections 52.5041 to 52.5051 (1991), Washington: Government Printing Office.

Tomato Puree

Tomato puree contains not less than 8 percent, but less than 24 percent of natural tomato soluble solids.

NATURAL TOMATO SOLUBLE SOLIDS

Extra Heavy Concentration. 15 percent or more, but less than 24 percent.

Heavy Concentration. 11.3 percent or more, but less than 15 percent.

Medium Concentration. 10.2 percent or more, but less than 11.3 percent.

Light Concentration. 8 percent or more, but less than 10.2 percent.

TYPES OF TEXTURE

Fine. A smooth uniform finish.
Coarse. A coarse slightly granular finish.

GRADES

U.S. Grade A. Has a distinct tomato puree flavor characteristic of ripe, good quality tomatoes and inclusive of salt which may be added. The flavor and odor may be no more than slightly affected by such factors as stems, sepals, leaves, crushed seeds, cores, immature, soured, or overripe tomatoes. Also free from the effects of unsatisfactory preparation, processing, or storage. It is practically free from defects such as dark specks or scale-like particles, seeds or objectionable particles of seeds, objectionable tomato peel, harmless extraneous material, or any other similar substances.

U.S. Grade C. Has a fairly good flavor and odor which may be affected, but not to a serious degree, stems, sepals, leaves, crushed seeds, cores, and immature, soured, or overripe tomatoes. Also free from the effects of unsatisfactory preparation, processing, or storage. Has at least a fairly good color which may be slightly dull or have a slight yellow, yellow-

orange, or brownish cast. Is at least fairly free from defects.
Substandard. Fails to meet the requirements of *U.S. Grade C.*

Sources:
Agricultural Marketing Service, USDA, 7 CFR sections 52.5081 to 52.5091 (1991), Washington: Government Printing Office.
Food and Drug Administration, "Tomato Concentrates," 21 CFR 155.192 (1991), Washington: Government Printing Office.

Tomato Sauce

Tomato sauce is the concentrated product prepared from the liquid extracted of mature, sound, whole tomatoes; the sound residue from preparing such tomatoes for canning; or the residue from partial extraction of juice. To this is added salt and spices and to which may be added one or more nutritive sweetening ingredients: vinegar or vinegars, onion, garlic, or other vegetable flavoring ingredients. The refractive index of the tomato sauce at 20 degrees C is not less than 1.3461.

GRADES

Tomato sauce is graded according to a very technical system whereby penalty points are assessed for such factors as edibility, poor appearance, or defects in workmanship. The more penalty points assessed the lower the grade. The grade descriptions which follow are intended only as a general consumer guide. For more detail please consult the source cited below.

U.S. Grade A or U.S. Fancy. Possesses a good color. Has a good consistency so that the tomato sauce shows not more than a slight separation of free liquid when poured on a flat grading tray, but is not excessively stiff. It is practically free from defects; any defects present, such as particles of seed, tomato peel, core material, or other similar substances, do not more than slightly affect the appearance or eating quality of the product. It possesses a good flavor characteristic of good quality ingredients. The flavor is free from scorching or any objectionable flavor of any kind. It has a good finish.

U.S. Grade C or U.S. Standard. Possesses a fairly good color. The consistency is such that the tomato sauce may show a noticeable, but not excessive, separation of free liquid when poured on a flat grading tray; it is not excessively stiff. It is fairly free from defects and any defects present may be noticeable but are not so large, so numerous, or of such contrasting color as to seriously affect the appearance or eating quality of the product. It possesses a fairly good flavor in which there may be slight traces of undesirable flavor, such as scorched, bitter, or astringent, but is free from objectionable or off-flavors of any kind. Possesses a good finish.

Substandard. Fails to meet the requirements of *U.S. Grade C* or *U.S. Standard.*

TERMINOLOGY

Tomato Sauce. Typically consists of a spiced tomato product concentrated to contain not less than 8.37 percent of salt-free tomato solids. It may be made by adding spices to tomato puree.

Spanish Style or Tomato Hot Sauce. Contains added peppers (sweet peppers or hot peppers). It contains a minimum of 8.37 percent of salt-free tomato solids.

Sources:
Agricultural Marketing Service, USDA, 7 CFR sections 52.2371 to 52.2381 (1991), Washington: Government Printing Office.
Food and Drug Administration, *Compliance Policy Guides*, Guide 7109.21, 10/01/80, Washington: National Technical Information Service.

Turnips

To allow for variations in quality caused by grading and handling, a percentage of the turnips may fail to meet all of the requirements of the grade.

TYPES

Bunched Turnips. Turnips with full length tops which are tied in bunches.

Bunched Turnips with Clipped Tops. Turnips with tops which are clipped back to not less than 6 inches in length and are tied in bunches.

Topped Turnips. Turnips with the tops removed to not more than ¾ inch in length.

GRADES

Turnips are graded according to a very technical system whereby penalty points are assessed for such factors as edibility, poor appearance, or defects in workmanship. The more penalty points assessed the lower the grade. The grade descriptions which follow are intended only as a general consumer guide. For more detail please consult the source cited below.

U.S. Grade A. Turnips of similar varietal characteristics. The roots are clean, firm, smooth, well formed, well trimmed, free from soft rot, and free from damage caused by cuts, discoloration, freezing, growth cracks, oil spray, pithiness, woodiness, watercore, dry rot, other disease, insects, or mechanical or other means. Bunched turnips or bunched turnips with clipped tops have tops which are fresh (the tops are of a normal green color and not badly wilted) and free from freezing, seedstems, yellowing or other discoloration, disease, insects, or mechanical or other means. In packaging, turnips on the shown face must be reasonably representative in size and quality of the contents of the container. Unless otherwise specified, the diameter of each turnip root must be not less than 1¾ inches nor more than 2¾ inches.

U.S. Grade B. Turnips of similar varietal characteristics. The roots are clean, firm, fairly smooth, fairly well formed, well trimmed, free from soft rot, free from damage caused by cuts, discoloration, freezing, growth cracks, oil spray, pithiness, woodiness, watercore, dry rot, other disease, insects, or mechanical or other means. Bunched turnips or bunched turnips with clipped tops have tops which are fresh, free from decay, and free from damage caused by freezing, seedstems, yellowing or other discoloration, disease, insects, or mechanical or other means. In packaging, turnips on the shown face must be reasonably representative in size and quality of the contents of the container. Unless otherwise specified, the diameter of each turnip root shall be not less than 1¾ inches nor more than 2¾ inches. This grade has a higher tolerance for defects.

Off Grade. Turnips which fail to meet the requirements of either of the foregoing grades.

Source:
Agricultural Marketing Service, USDA, 7 CFR sections 51.2425 to 51.1442 (1992), Washington: Government Printing Office.

Vinegar

Natural vinegars as they come from the generators normally contain in excess of 4 grams of acetic acid per 100 cubic centimeters. When vinegar is diluted with water, the label should bear a statement such as *diluted with water to ____ percent acid strength,* with the blank filled with the actual percent of acetic acid, which should not be less than 4 percent.

Vinegar, Cider Vinegar, Apple Vinegar. Made by the alcoholic and subsequent acetous fermentations of the juice of apples.

Wine Vinegar, Grape Vinegar. Made by the alcoholic and subsequent acetous fermentations of the juice of grapes.

Malt Vinegar. Made by the alcoholic and subsequent acetous fermentations, without distillation, of an infusion of barley malt or cereals whose starch has been converted by malt.

Sugar Vinegar. Made by the alcoholic and subsequent acetous fermentations of sugar syrup, molasses, or refiners' syrup.

Glucose Vinegar. Made by the alcoholic and subsequent acetous fermentations of a solution of glucose.

Spirit Vinegar, Distilled Vinegar, Grain Vinegar. Made by the acetous fermentation of dilute distilled alcohol.

Vinegar, Made from a Mixture of Spirit Vinegar and Cider Vinegar. This product should be labeled as a blend of the products with the product names in order of predominance. This labeling is applicable to a similar product made by acetous fermentations of a mixture of alcohol and cider stock.

Vinegar Made from Dried Apples, Apple Cores, or Apple Peels. Should be labeled as *vinegar made from ____,* where the blank is filled in with the name of the apple product(s) used as the source of fermentable material.

Source:
Food and Drug Administration, *Compliance Policy Guides*, Guide 7109.22, 04/01/83, Washington: National Technical Information Service.

Appendix

(Standards Organizations)

This *Appendix* contains a listing of U.S. standards issuing organizations that may be of interest to consumers.

ABRASIVE ENGINEERING SOCIETY
108 Elliott Drive
Butler, PA 16001-1118

ABRASIVE GRAIN ASSOCIATION
30200 Detroit Road
Cleveland, OH 44145-1967

ACCREDITED GEMOLOGISTS ASSOCIATION
915 Lootens
San Rafael, CA 94901

ACCREDITING BUREAU OF HEALTH EDUCATION SCHOOLS
Oak Manor Offices
29089 US 20 West
Elkhart, IN 46514

ACOUSTICAL SOCIETY OF AMERICA
500 Sunnyside Boulevard
Woodberry, NY 11797

ADAPSO
1300 North 17th Street
Suite 300
Arlington, VA 22209

ADHESIVE AND SEALANT COUNCIL
1627 K Street, NW
Suite 1000
Washington, DC 20006

ADHESIVES MANUFACTURERS ASSOCIATION
111 East Wacker Drive
Chicago, IL 60601

ADVANCED TELEVISION SYSTEMS COMMITTEE
1776 K Street, NW
Suite 300
Washington, DC 20007

ADVISORY COMMISSION ON TEXTBOOK SPECIFICATION
111 Prospect Street
Suite 405
Stamford, CT 06901

AERONAUTICAL RADIO, INC.
2551 Riva Road
Annapolis, MD 21401

AEROSPACE INDUSTRIES ASSOCIATION OF AMERICA
1250 I Street, NW
Washington, DC 20005

AGRICULTURE COUNCIL OF AMERICA
1250 I Street, NW
Suite 601
Washington, DC 20005

AIR AND WASTE MANAGEMENT ASSOCIATION
P.O. Box 2861
Pittsburgh, PA 15230

AIR CONDITIONING AND REFRIGERATION INSTITUTE
1501 Wilson Boulevard
6th Floor
Arlington, VA 22209

AIR CONDITIONING CONTRACTORS OF AMERICA
1513 16th Street, NW
Washington, DC 20036

AIR DISTRIBUTION INSTITUTE
4415 West Harrison Street
Suite 242-C
Hillside, IL 60162

AIR MOVEMENT AND CONTROL ASSOCIATION
30 West University Drive
Arlington Heights, IL 60004

AIRCRAFT LOCKNUT MANUFACTURERS ASSOCIATION
2017 Walnut Street
Philadelphia, PA 19103

AIRCRAFT OWNERS AND PILOTS ASSOCIATION
421 Aviation Way
Frederick, MD 21701

ALL-AMERICA ROSE SELECTIONS
221 North LaSalle Street
Suite 3900
Chicago, IL 60601

ALLIED UNDERWEAR ASSOCIATION
100 East 42nd Street
New York, NY 10017

AMERICAN TURPENTINE FARMERS ASSOCIATION COOPERATIVE
P.O. Box 430
Valdosta, GA 31603

AMERICAN ACADEMY OF PEDIATRICS
141 NW Point Boulevard
Elk Grove Village, IL 60009

AMERICAN ALLIANCE FOR HEALTH, PHYSICAL EDUCATION, RECREATION, AND DANCE
1900 Association Drive
Reston, VA 22091

AMERICAN ARCHITECTURAL MANUFACTUR-ERS ASSOCIATION
2700 River Road
Suite 118
Des Plaines, IL 60018

AMERICAN ASSOCIATION OF ADVERTISING AGENCIES
666 Third Avenue
New York, NY 10017

AMERICAN ASSOCIATION OF CEREAL CHEMISTS
3440 Pilot Knob Road
St. Paul, MN 55121

AMERICAN ASSOCIATION OF GRAIN INSPECTION AND WEIGHING AGENCIES
1629 K Street, NW
Suite 1100
Washington, DC 20006

AMERICAN ASSOCIATION OF TEXTILE CHEMISTS
P.O. Box 12215
Research Triangle Park, NC 27709

AMERICAN ASSOCIATION OF BLOOD BANKS
1117 North 19th Street
Suite 600
Arlington, VA 22209

AMERICAN ASSOCIATION OF POISON CONTROL CENTERS
Children's Hospital
4800 Sand Point Way, NE
Seattle, WA 98105

AMERICAN BEEFALO WORLD REGISTRY
116 Executive Park
Louisville, KY 40207

AMERICAN BEEKEEPING FEDERATION
P.O. 1038
Jesup, GA 31545

AMERICAN BOAT AND YACHT COUNCIL
405 Headquarters Drive, Suite 3
P.O. Box 747
Millersville, MD 21108

AMERICAN BOWLING CONGRESS
Equipment Specification Department
5301 South 76th Street
Greendale, WI 53129

AMERICAN BRUSH MANUFACTURERS ASSOCIATION
1900 Arch Street
Philadelphia, PA 19103

AMERICAN BUTTER INSTITUTE
888 16th Street, NW
Washington, DC 20006

AMERICAN CANOE MANUFACTURERS UNION
439 East 51st Street
New York, NY 10022

AMERICAN CHEESE SOCIETY
34 Downing Street
New York, NY10014

AMERICAN CONCRETE PAVEMENT ASSOCIATION
3800 North Wilke Road
Suite 490
Arlington Heights, IL 60004

AMERICAN CUSTOM GUNMAKERS GUILD
P.O. Box 812
Burlington, IA 52601-0812

AMERICAN CUTLERY MANUFACTURERS ASSOCIATION
1101 14th Street, NW
Suite 1100
Washington, DC 20005

AMERICAN DAIRY PRODUCTS INSTITUTE
130 North Franklin Street
Chicago, IL 60606

AMERICAN DEHYDRATED ONION AND GARLIC ASSOCIATION
1 Maritime Plaza
Suite 23
San Francisco, CA 94111

AMERICAN DIAMOND INDUSTRY ASSOCIATION
71 West 47th Street
Suite 705
New York, NY 10036

AMERICAN EGG BOARD
1460 Renaissance Drive
Suite 301
Park Ridge, IL 60068

AMERICAN FIBER MANUFACTURERS ASSOCIATION, INC.
1150 17th Street, NW
Washington, DC 20036

AMERICAN FINE CHINA GUILD
133 Franklin Corner Road
Lawrenceville, NJ 08648

AMERICAN FISHING TACKLE MANUFACTURERS ASSOCIATION
1250 Grove Avenue
Suite 300
Barrington, IL 60010

AMERICAN FROZEN FOOD INSTITUTE
1764 Old Meadow Lane
Suite 350
McLean, VA 22102

AMERICAN FUR INDUSTRY
363 7th Avenue
7th Floor
New York, NY 10001

AMERICAN FURNITURE MANUFACTURERS ASSOCIATION
P.O. Box HP-7
223 Wrenn Street
High Point, NC 27261

AMERICAN GALVANIZERS ASSOCIATION
1101 Connecticut Avenue, NW
Suite 700
Washington, DC 20036

AMERICAN GAS ASSOCIATION
AGA Laboratories
Cleveland, OH 44131

AMERICAN GEM SOCIETY
5901 West Third Street
Los Angeles, CA 90036

AMERICAN GREENHOUSE VEGETABLE GROWERS
31 North Market Street
Elysburg, PA 17824

AMERICAN HARDBOARD ASSOCIATION
520 North Hicks Road
Palatine, IL 60067

AMERICAN HOME ECONOMICS ASSOCIATION
1555 King Street
Alexandria, VA 22314

AMERICAN LADDER INSTITUTE
c/o Smith, Bucklin, and Associates
111 East Wacker Drive, Suite 600
Chicago, IL 60601

AMERICAN LIGHTING ASSOCIATION
435 North Michigan Avenue
Suite 1717
Chicago, IL 60611

AMERICAN LUMBER STANDARDS COMMITTEE
P.O. Box 210
Germantown, MD 20875

AMERICAN MUSHROOM INSTITUTE
907 East Baltimore Pike
Elysburg, PA 17824

AMERICAN OPTOMETRIC ASSOCIATION
243 North Lindbergh Boulevard
St. Louis, MO 63141

AMERICAN PAPER INSTITUTE
260 Madison Avenue
New York, NY 10016

AMERICAN PETROLEUM INSTITUTE
1220 L Street, NW
Washington, DC 20005

AMERICAN PEWTER GUILD
c/o Fischer Pewter Headquaters
440 Southlake Boulevard
Richmond, VA 23236

AMERICAN PLYWOOD ASSOCIATION
P.O. Box 11700
Tacoma, WA 98411

AMERICAN PRINTED FABRICS COUNCIL
45 West 36th Street
3rd Floor
New York, NY 10018

AMERICAN RETREADERS ASSOCIATION
P.O. Box 17203
Louisville, KY 40217

AMERICAN SEAFOOD RETAILERS
P.O. Box 1500
Cos Cob, CT 22209

AMERICAN SEED TRADE ASSOCIATION
Executive Building, Suite 964
1030 15th Street, NW
Washington, DC 20005

AMERICAN SOCIETY OF BREWING CHEMISTS
3340 Pilot Knob Road
St. Paul, MN 55121

AMERICAN SOD PRODUCERS ASSOCIATION
1855-A Hicks Road
Rolling Meadows, IL 60008

AMERICAN SOYBEAN ASSOCIATION
P.O. Box 27300
Street Louis, MO 63141

AMERICAN SPEECH, LANGUAGE, AND HEARING ASSOCIATION
10801 Rockville Pike
Rockville, MD 10852

AMERICAN SPICE TRADE ASSOCIATION
580 Sylvan Avenue
P.O. Box 1267
Englewood Cliffs, NJ 07632

AMERICAN TENNIS INDUSTRY FEDERATION
200 Castlewood Drive
North Palm Beach, FL 33408

AMERICAN TEXTILE MANUFACTURERS INSTITUTE
1801 K Street, Northwest
Suite 900
Washington, DC 20006

AMERICAN TRUCK DEALERS
8400 Westpark Drive
McLean, VA 22102

AMERICAN WATCHMAKERS INSTITUTE
3700 Harrison Avenue
Cincinnati, OH 45211

AMERICAN WATER WORKS ASSOCIATION
6666 West Quincy Avenue
Denver, CO 80235

AMERICAN WINE SOCIETY
3006 Latta Road
Rochester, NY 14612

AMERICAN WIRE PRODUCERS ASSOCIATION
1101 Connecticut Avenue, NW
Suite 700
Washington, DC 20036

AMERICAN WOOD-PRESERVERS ASSOCIATION
P.O. Box 849
Stevensville, MD 21666

AMERICAN YARN SPINNERS ASSOCIATION
2500 Lowell Road
P.O. Box 99
Gastonia, NC 28053

APRICOT PRODUCERS OF CALIFORNIA
1064 Woodland Avenue
Suite E
Modesto, CA 95351

ARCHERY MANUFACTURERS ORGANIZATION
200 Castlewood Drive
North Palm Beach, FL 33408

ART AND CRAFT MATERIALS INSTITUTE, INC.
715 Boylston Street
Boston, MA 02116

**ASBESTOS INFORMATION ASSOCIATION/
NORTH AMERICA**
1745 Jefferson Davis Highway
Crystal Square 4, Suite 509
Arlington, VA 22202

**ASPHALT ROOFING MANUFACTURERS
ASSOCIATION**
6288 Montrose Road
Rockville, MD 20852

**ASSOCIATION GLASS AND POTTERY
MANUFACTURERS**
2800 East Military Road
Zanesville, OH 43701

**ASSOCIATION OF WALL AND CEILING
INDUSTRIES INTERNATIONAL**
1600 Cameroon Street
Alexandria, VA 22314

**ASSOCIATION OF AMERICAN PLANT FOOD
CONTROL OFFICIALS**
c/o University of Kentucky
Lexington, KY 40546

ASSOCIATION OF AMERICAN PUBLISHERS
220 East 23rd Street
New York, NY 10010

TEXAS DEPARTMENT OF HEALTH
1100 West 49th Street
Austin, TX 78756

**ASSOCIATION OF HOME APPLIANCE
MANUFACTURERS**
20 North Wacker Drive
Chicago, IL 60606

**ASSOCIATION OF OFFICIAL SEED CERTIFYING
AGENCIES**
3709 Hillsborough Street
Raleigh, NC 27607

ASSOCIATION OF SMOKED FISH PRODUCTS
5 Hayward Street
Quincy, MA 02171

**AUTOMATIC IDENTIFICATION
MANUFACTURERS**
1326 Freeport Road
Pittsburgh, PA 15238

AUTOMOTIVE INFORMATION COUNCIL
13505 Dulles Technology Drive
Herndon, VA 22071-3415

BARBECUE INDUSTRY ASSOCIATION
710 East Ogden Avenue
Suite 113
Naperville, IL 60563

BATTERY COUNCIL INTERNATIONAL
111 East Wacker Drive
Chicago, IL 60601

BEER INSTITUTE
1226 I Street, NW
Suite 825
Washington, DC 20005

BEVERAGE NETWORK
4437 Concord
Skokie, IL 60076

BICYCLE INSTITUTE
1818 R Street, NW
Washington, DC 20009

BILLIARD CONGRESS OF AMERICA
1901 Broadway Street
Suite 310
Iowa City, IA 52240

BOOK MANUFACTURERS INSTITUTE
111 Prospect Street
Suite 405
Stanford, CT 06901

BRICK INSTITUTE OF AMERICA
11490 Commerce Park Drive
Suite 300
Reston, VA 22091

BUILDING STONE INSTITUTE
420 Lexington Ave
New York, NY 10170

**BUSINESS AND INSTITUTIONAL FURNITURE
MANUFACTURERS ASSOCIATION**
2235 Burton, SE
Grand Rapids, MI 49506

CALIFORNIA AVOCADO COMMISSION
1251 East Dyer Road
No. 200
Santa Ana, CA 92705

CALIFORNIA DRY BEAN ADVISORY BOARD
531-D North Alta Avenue
Dinuba, CA 93618

497

CALIFORNIA FIG ADVISORY BOARD
P.O. Box 709
Fresno, CA 93712

CALIFORNIA GRAPE AND TREE FRUIT LEAGUE
1540 East Shaw Avenue
Suite 120
Fresno, CA 93710

CALIFORNIA ICEBERG LETTUCE COMMISSION
P.O. Box 3354
Monterey, CA 93942

CALIFORNIA PRUNE BOARD
103 World Trade Center
San Francisco, CA 94111-4293

CALIFORNIA RAISIN ADVISORY BOARD
P.O. Box 231
Fresno, CA 93708

CAN MANUFACTURERS INSTITUTE
1625 Massachusetts Avenue, NW
Washington, DC 20036

CAR AUDIO SPECIALISTS ASSOCIATION
2101 L Street, NW
Suite 800
Washington, DC 20037

CARPET AND RUG INSTITUTE
Box 2048
Dalton, GA 30720

CARPET CUSHION COUNCIL
P.O. Box 546
Riverside, CT 06878

CASKET MANUFACTURERS ASSOCIATION OF AMERICA
708 Church Street
Evanston, IL 60201

CAST IRON SOIL PIPE INSTITUTE
5959 Shallowford Road
Suite 419
Chattanooga, TN 37421

CEDAR SHAKE AND SHINGLE BUREAU
525 116th Avenue, NE
Suite 275
Bellevue, WA 98004

CELLULOSE INDUSTRY STANDARDS PROGRAM
1315 Talbott Tower
Dayton, OH 45402

CENTER FOR HAZARDOUS MATERIALS RESEARCH
320 William Pitt Way
University of Pittsburgh Applied Research Center
Pittsburgh, PA 15238

CERTIFIED COLOR MANUFACTURERS ASSOCIATION
1620 I Street, NW
Suite 925
Washington, DC 20006

CHAIN LINK MANUFACTURERS INSTITUTE
1776 Massachusetts Avenue, NW
Suite 500
Washington, DC 20036

CHAMPAGNE NEWS AND INFORMATION BUREAU
355 Lexington Avenue
New York, NY 10017

CHEMICAL SPECIALTIES MANUFACTURERS ASSOCIATION
1913 I Street, NW
Washington, DC 20006

CHOCOLATE MANUFACTURERS ASSOCIATION
7900 Westpark Drive
Suite A-320
McLean, VA 22102

CIDER ASSOCIATION OF NORTH AMERICA
North Branch Cider Mill
P.O. Box 13
North Branch, NY 12766

CLOCK MANUFACTURERS AND MARKETING ASSOCIATION
710 East Agden Avenue
Suite 113
Naperville, IL 60563

COFFEE DEVELOPMENT GROUP
1400 I Street, NW
Suite 650
Washington, DC 20005

COGNAC INFORMATION BUREAU
11 East 47th Street
New York, NY 10017

COLOR ASSOCIATION OF THE UNITED STATES
409 West 44th Street
New York, NY 10036

COMPUTER SOFTWARE AND SERVICES INDUSTRY ASSOCIATION (ADAPSO)
1300 North 17th Street
Suite 300
Alexandria, VA 22209

CONSUMER FEDERATION OF AMERICA
1424 16th Street, NW
Washington, DC 20036

CONTACT LENS SOCIETY OF AMERICA
11735 Bowman Green Drive
Reston, VA 22090

CONTRACT STATIONERS FORUM
c/o National Office Products Association
301 North Fairfax Street
Alexandria, VA 22314

COOKWARE MANUFACTURERS ASSOCIATION
P.O. Box 1177
Lake Geneva, WI 53147

COPYING PRODUCTS AND INKED RIBBON ASSOCIATION
P.O. Box 518
Hyannis, MA 02601

CORDAGE INSTITUTE
42 North Street
Hingham, MA 02043

COSMETIC, TOILETRY, AND FRAGRANCE ASSOCIATION
1100 Vermont Avenue, NW
Suite 800
Washington, DC 20005

COUNCIL ON ALTERNATE FUELS
1225 I Street, NW
Suite 320
Washington, DC 20005

COUNCIL ON PLASTICS AND PACKAGING IN THE ENVIRONMENT
1275 K Street, NW
Suite 900
Washington, DC 20005

CRAFTED WITH PRIDE IN THE USA COUNCIL
1045 Avenue of the Americas
New York, NY 10018

CULTURED MARBLE INSTITUTE
435 North Michigan Avenue
Suite 1717
Chicago, IL 60611

DFA OF CALIFORNIA
303 Brokaw Road
P.O. Box 270A
Santa Clara, CA 95052

DIAMOND WALNUT GROWERS
1050 South Diamond Street
P.O. Box 1727
Stockton, CA 05201

DISTILLED SPIRITS COUNCIL OF THE U.S.
1250 I Street, NW
Washington, DC 20005

DIVING EQUIPMENT MANUFACTURERS ASSOCIATION
P.O. Box 217
Tustin, CA 92681

DOOR AND HARDWARE INSTITUTE
7711 Old Springhouse Road
McLean, VA 22102

ELASTIC FABRIC MANUFACTURERS COUNCIL OF THE TEXTILE ASSOCIATION
230 Congress Street
Boston, MA 02110

FEATHER AND DOWN ASSOCIATION
8 Wildwood Circle
Larchmont, NY 10538

FILTER MANUFACTURERS COUNCIL
300 Sylvan Avenue
P.O. Box 1638
Englewood Cliffs, NJ 07632

FLORIDA DEPARTMENT OF CITRUS
P.O. Box 148
Lakeland, FL 33802

FLORIDA MANGO FORUM
20900 Southwest 376th Street
Homestead, FL 33034

FLORIDA TOMATO EXCHANGE
P.O. Box 140635
Orlando, FL 32814

FOOTWEAR INDUSTRIES OF AMERICA
1420 K Street, NW
Suite 600
Washington, DC 20005

FRAGRANCE FOUNDATION
142 East 30th Street
New York, NY 10016

FRESH GARLIC ASSOCIATION
c/o Caryl Saunders Association
P.O. Box 2410
Sausalito, CA 94966-2410

FRICTION MATERIALS STANDARDS INSTITUTE
588 Monroe Turnpike
Monroe, CT 06468

GAS APPLIANCE MANUFACTURERS
1901 North Moore Street
Suite 1100
Arlington, VA 22209

GEMOLOGICAL INSTITUTE OF AMERICA
1660 Stewart Street
Santa Monica, CA 90406

GLASS PACKAGING INSTITUTE
1801 K Street, NW
Suite 1105-L
Washington, DC 20006

GLASS TEMPERING ASSOCIATION
White Lakes Professional Building
3310 Harrison Street
Topeka, KS 66611

GOLD INSTITUTE/SILVER INSTITUTE
1112 16th Street, NW
Suite 240
Washington, DC 20036

GUMMED INDUSTRIES ASSOCIATION
Five Darrow Center
P.O. Box 92
Greenlawn, NY 11740

HACK AND BAND SAW MANUFACTURERS ASSOCIATION OF AMERICA
1230 Keith Building
Cleveland, OH 44115

HAND TOOLS INSTITUTE
25 North Broadway
Tarrytown, NY 10591

HARDWOOD PLYWOOD MANUFACTURERS ASSOCIATION
1825 Michael Faraday Drive
Box 2789
Reston, VA 22090

HAZARDOUS WASTE FEDERATION
c/o Department 3220
Division 3314
P.O. Box 5800
Albuquerque, NM 87185

HEARING INDUSTRIES ASSOCIATION
1255 23rd Street, NW
Suite 850
Washington, DC 20037

HOBBY INDUSTRY ASSOCIATION
319 East 54th Street
Lemwood Park, NJ 07407

ICE SKATING INSTITUTE OF AMERICA
355 West Dundee Road
Buffalo Grove, IL 60089

IDAHO POTATO COMMISSION
P.O. Box 1068
Boise, ID 83701

INFANT FORMULA COUNCIL
5775 Peachtree-Dunwoody Road
Suite 500-G
Atlanta, GA 30342

INSTITUTE FOR PERSONAL COMPUTING
P.O. Box 558250
Miami, FL 33255

INSULATED CABLE ENGINEERS ASSOCIATION
P.O. Box 440
South Yarmouth, MA 02664

INSULATED STEEL DOOR SYSTEMS INSTITUTE
30200 Detroit Road
Cleveland, OH 44145

INTERNATIONAL WILD RICE ASSOCIATION
7200 Sawtelle Avenue
Yuba City, CA 95993

INTERNATIONAL FENCE INDUSTRY ASSOCIATION
5300 Memorial Drive
Suite 116
Stone Mountain, GA 30083

INTERNATIONAL APPLE INSTITUTE
6707 Old Dominion Drive
Suite 320
McLean, VA 22101

INTERNATIONAL ASSOCIATION OF PLUMBING AND MECHANICAL OFFICIALS
20001 Walnut Drive South
Walnut, CA 91789

INTERNATIONAL BANANA ASSOCIATION
1101 Vermont Avenue, NW
Suite 306
Washington, DC 20005

INTERNATIONAL BOTTLED WATER ASSOCIATION
113 North Henry Street
Alexandria, VA 22314

INTERNATIONAL FABRICARE INSTITUTE
12251 Tech Road
Silver Spring, MD 20904

INTERNATIONAL FOOD SERVICE MANUFACTURERS
321 North Clark Street
Suite 2900
Chicago, IL 60610

INTERNATIONAL JELLY AND PRESERVE ASSOCIATION
5775 Peachtree-Dunwoody Road
Suite 500-G
Atlanta, GA 30342

INTERNATIONAL PUMPKIN ASSOCIATION
2155 Union Street
San Fransico, CA 94123

INTERNATIONAL SILK ASSOCIATION
c/o Gerlit Co., Inc.
1359 Broadway
New York, NY 10018

INTERNATIONAL SLEEP PRODUCTS ASSOCIATION
333 Commerce Street
Alexandria, VA 22314

INTERNATIONAL STAPLE, NAIL, AND TOOL ASSOCIATION
435 North Michigan Avenue
Suite 1717
Chicago, IL 60611

INTERNATIONAL TAPE/DISC ASSOCIATION
505 Eighth Avenue
Floor 12A
New York, NY 10018

INTERNATIONAL TIRE ASSOCIATION (ITA)
P.O. Box 1067
Farmington, CT 06034

JUVENILE PRODUCERS MANUFACTURERS ASSOCIATION
P.O. Box 955
Marlton, NJ 08059

KIWIFRUIT GROWERS OF CALIFORNIA
7300 Lincolnshire Drive
Suite 200
Sacramento, CA 95823

KOSHER WINE INSTITUTE
175 5th Avenue
New York, NY 10010

LEAFY GREENS COUNCIL
Box 76067
St. Paul, MN 55175

LEMON ADMINISTRATIVE COMMITTEE
25129 The Old Road
Suite 304
Newhall, CA 91381

LIBRARY BINDING INSTITUTE
8013 Centre Park Drive
Austin, TX 78754

LIGHT AIRCRAFT MANUFACTURERS ASSOCIATION
22 Deer Oaks Center
Pleasanton, CA 94566

MAPLE FLOORING MANUFACTURERS ASSOCIATION
60 Revere Drive
Northbrook, IL 60062

MARBLE INSTITUTE OF AMERICA
33505 State Street
Farmington, MI 48024

MARKING DEVICE ASSOCIATION
435 North Michigan Avenue
Suite 1717
Chicago, IL 60611

METAL LADDER MANUFACTURERS ASSOCIATION
P.O. Box 580
Osgood Road
Greenville, PA 16125

MANUFACTURERING JEWELERS AND SILVERSMITHS OF AMERICA
100 India Street
Providence, RI 02903

MINERAL INSULATION MANUFACTURERS ASSOCIATION
1420 King Street
Suite 410
Alexandria, VA 22314

MODEL RAILROAD INDUSTRY ASSOCIATION
P.O. Box 28129
Denver, CO 80228

MOTOR VEHICLE MANUFACTURERS ASSOCIATION OF THE USA
7430 2nd Avenue
Suite 300
Detroit, MI 48202

NATIONAL ART MATERIALS TRADE ASSOCIATION
178 Lakeview Avenue
Clifton, NJ 07011

NATIONAL ASSOCIATION OF CHAIN MANUFACTURERS
20 North Wacker Drive
Suite 3318
Chicago, IL 60606

NATIONAL ASSOCIATION OF CHEWING GUM MANUFACTURERS
2 Greentree Centre
Marlton, NJ 08053

NATIONAL ASSOCIATION OF GARAGE DOOR MANUFACTURERS
655 Irving Park at Lake Shore Drive
Suite 201 Park Place
Chicago, IL 60613

NATIONAL ASSOCIATION OF HOSIERY MANUFACTURERS
447 South Share Amity Road
Charlotte, NC 28211

NATIONAL ASSOCIATION OF JEWELRY APPRAISERS
4210 North Brown Avenue
Scottsdale, AZ 85251

NATIONAL ASSOCIATION OF PHARMACEUTICAL MANUFACTURERS
747 3rd Avenue
New York, NY 10017

NATIONAL ASSOCIATION OF PHOTOGRAPHIC MANUFACTURERS
550 Mamaroneck Avenue
Harrison, NY 10528

NATIONAL ASSOCIATION OF SCISSORS AND SHEARS MANUFACTURERS
c/o Acme United Corp.
Fairfield, CT 06430

NATIONAL ASSOCIATION OF FRUITS, FLAVORS, AND SYRUPS
5 Ravine Drive
P.O. Box 776
Matawan, NJ 07747

NATIONAL ASSOCIATION OF MARGARINE MANUFACTURERS
1101 15th Street, NW
Suite 202
Washington, DC 20005

NATIONAL ASSOCIATION OF MIRROR DESIGNERS
9005 Congressional Center
Potomac, MD 20854

NATIONAL AUTOMOTIVE PARTS ASSOCIATION
2999 Circle 75 Parkways
Atlanta, GA 30339

NATIONAL CABLE TELEVISION INSTITUTE
P.O. Box 27277
Denver, CO 80227

NATIONAL CANDLE ASSOCIATION
1850 New York Avenue, NW
Suite 615
Washington, DC 20005

NATIONAL CLAY POT MANAFACTURERS ASSOCIATION
P.O. Box 485
Jackson, MO 63755

NATIONAL COFFEE ASSOCIATION OF THE USA
110 Wall Street
New York, NY 10005

NATIONAL CONFECTIONERS ASSOCIATION OF THE USA
7900 Westpark Drive
Suite A-320
McLean, VA 22102

NATIONAL COTTON COUNCIL OF AMERICA
1918 North Parkway
Memphis, TN 38112

NATIONAL ELECTRICAL MANUFACTURERS ASSOCIATION
2101 L Street, NW
Washington, DC 20037

NATIONAL FIRE SPRINKLER ASSOCIATION, INC.
P.O. Box 100
Patterson, NY 12563

NATIONAL FOOD PROCESSORS ASSOCIATION
1401 New York Avenue, NW
Suite 400
Washington, DC 20005

NATIONAL FOREST PRODUCTS ASSOCIATION
1250 Connecticut Avenue, NW
Washington, DC 20036

NATIONAL INSTITUTE OF INFANT SERVICES
Diaper Service Accreditation Council
2017 Walnut Street
Philadelphia, PA 19103

NATIONAL INSTITUTE OF OILSEED PRODUCTS
2600 Garden Road
Suite 208
Monterey, CA 93940

NATIONAL JUICE PRODUCTS ASSOCIATION
P.O. Box 1531
Tampa, FL 33601

NATIONAL KEROSENE HEATER ASSOCIATION
3310 West End Avenue
5th Floor
Nashville, TN 37203

NATIONAL KNITWEAR AND SPORTSWEAR ASSOCIATION
386 Park Avenue South
New York, NY 10016

NATIONAL KOSHER FOOD TRADE ASSOCIATION
21 West 38th Street
New York, NY 10018

NATIONAL LIVESTOCK AND MEAT BOARD
444 North Michigan Avenue
Chicago, IL 60611

NATIONAL LUBRICATING GREASE INSTITUTE
4635 Wyandotte Street
Kansas City, MO 63112

NATIONAL MODEL RAILROAD ASSOCIATION
4121 Cromwell Road
Chattanooga, TN 37421

NATIONAL OAK FLOORING MANUFACTURERS ASSOCIATION
22 North Front Street
660 Falls Building
P.O. Box 3009
Memphis, TN 38103

NATIONAL OILSEED PROCESSORS ASSOCIATION
1255 23rd Street, NW
Washington, DC 20037

NATIONAL ONION ASSOCIATION
1 Greeley National Plaza
Suite 510
Greeley, CO 80631

NATIONAL OPERATING COMMITTEE FOR STANDARDS IN ATHLETIC EQUIPMENT
11724 Plaza Circle
Kansas City, MO 64153

NATIONAL PARTICLEBOARD ASSOCIATION
18928 Premier Center
Gaithersburg, MD 20879

NATIONAL PASTA ASSOCIATION
2101 Wilson Boulevard
No. 920
Arlington, VA 22201

NATIONAL POTATO PROMOTION BOARD
1385 South Colorado Boulevard.
Suite 512
Denver, CO 80222

NATIONAL PROPANE GAS ASSOCIATION
1600 Eisenhower Lane
Lisle, IL 60532

NATIONAL RETAIL MERCHANTS ASSOCIATION
100 West 31st Street
New York, NY 10001

NATIONAL RIFLE ASSOCIATION OF AMERICA
1600 Rhode Island Avenue, NW
Washington, DC 20036

NATIONAL TILE AND ROOFING MANUFACTURERS ASSOCIATION
3127 Los Feliz Blvd.
Los Angeles, CA 90039

NATIONAL ROOFING CONTRACTORS ASSOCIATION
6250 River Road
Suite 8030
Rosemont, IL 60018

NATIONAL SAFETY COUNCIL
444 North Michigan Avenue
Chicago, IL 60611

NATIONAL SASH AND DOOR JOBBERS ASSOCIATION
2400 East Devon Avenue
Suite 314
Des Plaines, IL 60018

NATIONAL SCHOOL SUPPLY EQUIPMENT ASSOCIATION
8300 Colesville Road
No. 250
Silver Spring, MD 20910-3243

NATIONAL SOFT DRINK ASSOCIATION
1101 16th Street, NW
Washington, DC 20036

NATIONAL SPA AND POOL INSTITUTE
2111 Eisenhower Avenue
Alexandria, VA 22314

NATIONAL TABLETOP ASSOCIATION
355 Lexington Avenue
17th Floor
New York, NY 10017

NATIONAL TERRAZZO AND MOSAIC ASSOCIATION
3166 Des Plaines Avenue
Suite 24
Des Plaines, IL 60018

NATIONAL TIRE DEALERS AND RETREADERS ASSOCIATION
1250 I Street, NW
Suite 400
Washington, DC 20005

NATIONAL VAN CONVERSION ASSOCIATION
2 West Main Street
Suite 2
Greenfield, IN 46140

NATIONAL WATER WELL ASSOCIATION
6375 Riverside Drive
Dublin, OH 43017

NATIONAL WATERBED RETAILERS ASSOCIATION
36 South Main Street
No. 1806
Chicago, IL 60603

NATIONAL WHEEL AND RIM ASSOCIATION
5121 Bowden Road
Suite 303
Jacksonville, FL 32216

NATIONAL WOOD FLOORING ASSOCIATION
11046 Manchester Road
St. Louis, MO 63122

NATIONAL WOOD WINDOW AND DOOR ASSOCIATION
1400 East Touhy Avenue
Des Plaines, IL 60018

NATIONAL WOODEN PALLET AND CONTAINER ASSOCIATION
1625 Massachusetts Avenue, NW
Suite 200
Washington, DC 20036

NATIONAL ASSOCIATION OF WRITING INSTRUMENTS
5024-R Campbell Boulevard
Baltimore, MD 21236

NONPRESCRIPTION DRUG MANUFACTURERS ASSOCIATION
1150 Connecticut Avenue, NW
Washington, DC 20036

NORTH AMERICAN MAPLE SYRUP COUNCIL
Route 2, P.O. Box 326
Hortonville, WI 54944

NORTH AMERICAN STRAWBERRY GROWERS ASSOCIATION
P.O. Box 20268
Columbus, OH 43220

NORTHEASTERN LUMBER MANUFACTURERS ASSOCIATION
272 Tuttle Road
P.O. Box 87A
Cumberland Center, ME 04021

NORTHERN TEXTILE ASSOCIATION
230 Congress Street
Boston, MA 02110

OLIVE OIL ASSOCIATION
5 Ravine Drive
P.O. Box 776
Matawan, NJ 07747

OPTICAL LABORATORIES ASSOCIATION
Technical Services Department
P.O. Box 2000
Merrifield, VA 22116-2000

OPTICAL MANUFACTURERS ASSOCIATION
6055A Arlington Boulevard
Falls Church, VA 22044

ORGANIC FOOD ALLIANCE
2111 Wilson Boulevard
Suite 531
Arlington, VA 22201

ORGANIC FOOD PRODUCTION ASSOCIATION OF NORTH AMERICA
P.O. Box 1078
Greenfield, MA 01301

ORIENTAL RUG RETAILERS OF AMERICA
1600 Wilson Boulevard
Suite 905
Arlington, VA 22209

PAINTING AND DECORATING CONTRACTORS OF AMERICA
3913 Old Lee Highway
Suite 33B
Fairfax, VA 22030

PAPERBOARD PACKAGING COUNCIL
1101 Vermont Avenue, NW
Suite 411
Washington, DC 20005

PHARMACEUTICAL MANUFACTURERS ASSOCIATION
1100 15th Street, NW
Washington, DC 20005

PHOTO MARKETING ASSOCIATION INTERNATIONAL
3000 Picture Pl.
Jackson, MI 49201

PHOTOGRAPHIC SOCIETY OF AMERICA
3000 United Founders Boulevard
Suite 103
Oklahoma City, OK 73112

PIN, CLIP, AND FASTENER SERVICES
179 Allyn Street
Suite 304
Hartford, CT 06103

PINEAPPLE GROWERS ASSOCIATION OF HAWAII
P.O. Box 3380
Honolulu, HI 96801

PORCELAIN ENAMEL INSTITUTE
1101 Connecticut Avenue, NW
Suite 700
Washington, DC 20036

PORTABLE POWER EQUIPMENT MANUFACTURERS ASSOCIATION
4720 Montgomery Lane
Suite 812
Bethesda, MD 20814

POTATO ASSOCIATION OF AMERICA
Route 1
P.O. Box 115
Hancock, WI 54943

POWER TOOL INSTITUTE
P.O. Box 818
Yachats, OR 60613-3198

PRESSURE SENSITIVE TAPE COUNCIL
104 Wilmot
Suite 201
Deerfield, IL 60015

PRIMARY GLASS MANUFACTURERS COUNCIL
White Lakes Professional Building
3310 Harrison
Topeka, KS 66611

RECORDING INDUSTRY ASSOCIATION OF AMERICA
1020 19th Street, NW
Suite 200
Washington, DC 20036

RECREATION VEHICLE INDUSTRY ASSOCIATION
1896 Preston White Drive
Reston, VA 22090

REDWOOD INSPECTION SERVICE
405 Enfrente Drive
Suite 200
Novato, CA 94949

REFRACTORIES INSTITUTE
301 Fifth Avenue
Suite 326
Pittsburgh, PA 15222

RESILIENT FLOOR COVERING INSTITUTE
966 Hungerford Drive
Suite 128
Rockville, MD 20850

RICE COUNCIL FOR MARKET DEVELOPMENT
P.O. Box 740123
Houston, TX 77274

ROOF COATINGS MANUFACTURERS ASSOCIATION
60 Revere Drive
Suite 500
Northbrook, IL 60062

SAFETY GLAZING CERTIFICATION COUNCIL
Industrial Park 3933
Route 11, P.O. Box 2040
Cortland, NY 13045-0950

SALT INSTITUTE
700 North Fairfax
Fairfax Plaza, Suite 600
Alexandria, VA 22314-2040

SCALE MANUFACTURERS ASSOCIATION
932 Hungerford Drive, No. 36
Rockville, MD 20850

SCREEN MANUFACTURERS ASSOCIATION
655 Irving Park at Lake Shore Drive
Suite 201, Park Place
Chicago, IL 60613

SEALANT WATERPROOFING AND RESTORATION INSTITUTE
3101 Broadway
Suite 585
Kansas City, MO 64111

SHEET METAL AND AIR CONDITIONING CONTRACTORS
P.O. Box 70
Merrifield, VA 22116

SHELVING MANUFACTURERS ASSOCIATION
8720 Red Oak Boulevard
Suite 201
Charlotte, NC 28217

SNELL MEMORIAL FOUNDATION
P.O. Box 493
St. James, NY 11780

SOAP AND DETERGENT ASSOCIATION
475 Park Avenue, South
New York, NY 10016

SOCIETY OF AMERICAN FLORISTS
1601 Duke Street
Alexandria, VA 22314

SOCIETY OF AMERICAN SILVERSMITHS
P.O. Box 2599
Cranston, RI 02910

SOUTHERN CYPRESS MANUFACTURERS ASSOCIATION
2831 Airways Boulevard
Suite 205
Memphis, TN 38132

SOUTHERN FOREST PRODUCTS ASSOCIATION
P.O. Box 52468
New Orleans, LA 70152

SOUTHERN PINE INSPECTION BUREAU
4709 Scenic Highway
Pensacola, FL 32504

SPECIALTY VEHICLES INSTITUTE
2 Jenner Street
Suite 150
Irvine, CA 92718

SPONGE AND CHAMOIS INSTITUTE
511 Harwood Building
Scarsdale, NY 10583

SPORTING ARMS AND AMMUNITION MANUFACTURERS INSTITUTE
555 Danbury Road
Wilton, CT 06897

SPORTING GOODS MANUFACTURERS ASSOCIATION
200 Castlewood Drive
North Palm Beach, FL 33408

SPORTS CAR CLUB OF AMERICA
9033 East Easter Place
Englewood, CO 80112

STEEL DOOR INSTITUTE
30200 Detroit Road
Cleveland, OH 44145-1967

STEEL WINDOW INSTITUTE
1230 Keith Building
Cleveland, OH 44115

STUCCO MANUFACTURERS ASSOCIATION
507 Evergreen
Pacific Grove, CA 93950

SUGAR ASSOCIATION
1101 15th Street
Suite 600
Washington, DC 20005

SUMP AND SEWAGE PUMP MANUFACTURERS ASSOCIATION
P.O. Box 298
Winnetka, IL 60093

SUNGLASS ASSOCIATION OF AMERICA
71 East Avenue
Norwalk, CT 06851

SUNTANNING ASSOCIATION FOR EDUCATION
337 West Patrick Street
Suite 201
Frederricki, MD 21701

TEA COUNCIL OF THE USA
230 Park Avenue
New York, NY 10169

TECHNICAL ASSOCIATION OF THE PULP AND PAPER INDUSTRY (TAPPI)
Technology Park/Atlanta
P.O. Box 105113
Atlanta, GA 30348

TELECOMMUNICATIONS INDUSTRY FORUM
5430 Grosvenor Lane
Suite 200
Bethesda, MD 20814

THE FERTILIZER INSTITUTE
501 Second Avenue, NE
Washington, DC 20002

TILE COUNCIL OF AMERICA
P.O. Box 326
Princeton, NJ 08542

TIRE AND RIM ASSOCIATION
175 Montrose West Avenue
Copely, OH 44321

TIRE INDUSTRY SAFETY COUNCIL
National Press Building
Suite 844
Washington, DC 20045

TIRE RETREAD INFORMATION BUREAU
26555 Carmel Ranch Boulevard.
Suite 3
Carmel, CA 93923

TOBACCO INSTITUTE
1875 I Street, NW
Suite 800
Washington, DC 20006

TOBACCO MERCHANTS ASSOCIATION OF U.S.A.
P.O. Box 8019
Princeton, NJ 08543

TOY MANUFACTURERS OF AMERICA
200 Fifth Avenue
New York, NY 10010

TRAILER HITCH MANUFACTURERS ASSOCIATION
1050 Connecticut Avenue, NW
Suite 500
Washington, DC 20036

UNDERWRITERS LABORATORIES, INC.
333 Pfingsten Road
Northbrook, IL 60062

UNIFORM CODE COUNCIL
8163 Old Yankee
Suite J
Dayton, OH 45458

UNITED FRESH FRUIT AND VEGETABLE ASSOCIATION
727 North Washington Street
Alexandria, VA 22314

UNITED SKI INDUSTRIES ASSOCIATION
20 Maple Street
P.O. Box 2883
Springfield, MA 01101

UNITED STATES CUTTING TOOL INSTITUTE
1230 Keith Building
Cleveland, OH 44115-2180

UNITED STATES GOLF ASSOCIATION
Golf House
P.O. Box 708
Far Hills, NJ 07931-0708

U.S. HIDE, SKIN, AND LEATHER ASSOCIATION
1700 North Moore Street
Suite 1600
Arlington, VA 22209

VACUUM CLEANER MANUFACTURERS ASSOCIATION
P.O. Box 2642
North Canton, OH 44720

VANILLA INFORMATION BUREAU
928 Broadway
New York, NY 10010

VINEGAR INSTITUTE
5775 Peachtree-Dunwoody Road
Suite 500-G
Atlanta, GA 30342

VINYL SIDING INSTITUTE
355 Lexington Avenue
4th Floor
New York, NY 10017

WALLCOVERING MANUFACTURERS ASSOCIATION
355 Lexington Avenue
17th Floor
New York, NY 10017

WATER SKI INDUSTRY ASSOCIATION
200 Castlewood Drive
North Palm Beach, FL 33408

WATERBED MANUFACTURERS ASSOCIATION
5757 West Century Boulevard
Suite 512
Los Angeles, CA 90045

WEST COAST LUMBER INSPECTION BUREAU
P.O. Box 23145
Portland, OR 97223

WESTERN WOOD PRODUCTS ASSOCIATION
Yeon Building
522 Southwest Fifth Avenue
Portland, OR 97204-2122

WHEAT QUALITY COUNCIL
404 Humboldt
Suite G
Manhattan, KS 66502

WINE AND SPIRITS GUILD OF AMERICA
1766 Dupont Avenue South
Minneapolis, MN 55403

WOOD MOULDING AND MILLWORK PRODUCERS
P.O. Box 25278
1730 Southwest Skyline
Portland, OR 97225

WOODWORK INSTITUTE OF CALIFORNIA
P.O. Box 11428
1833 Broadway
Fresno, CA 93773

WRITING INSTRUMENT MANUFACTURERS ASSOCIATION
2 Greentree Centre
Suite 225
P.O. Box 955
Marlton, NJ 08053

Index

Symbols

A

anodized 134
  cookware 133
Always, gemstones 156
Alzheimer's Disease 133
AM (Amplitude Modulation) 81, 94, 101
Amandine 394
Amber 154
  pecans 406
Ambergris, fragrances 119
Ambient Temperature, tires 65
American Association of Textile Chemists and Color-
  ists 205
American Citron 472
American Dental Association 115
American National Standards Institute 3
American Pima Cotton 206
American Single Roll, wallcoverings 144
American Society for Testing and Materials 3
American Sod Producers Association 264
American Softwood Lumber Standard 243
American Upland Cotton 205
Amertrine 154
Amethyst 154
Ammonia
  fertilizers 262
  warning labels 27
Ammoniacal 259
Ammoniacal Copper Arsenate
  wood preservative 237
Ammoniacal Copper Zinc Arsenate
  wood preservative 237
Ammonium Chloride, warning labels 27
Ammonium Nitrate, warning labels 27
Ammonium Sulfate, warning labels 28
Ample, apparel 217
Amplifier 81, 101
Amplitude Separation 81
Amusement Ride 191
AMV Automobiles 56
Amyl Acetate, warning labels 28
Analgesic
  liniment 120
  medication 120
Analog 81, 98, 150, 166
Analog Recording 81
Analog to Digital Converter 79
Analysis 259
Anaphylactic Shock, alergens 120
Anaphylaxis, alergens 120
Anatomic 215
Anchored Beads, tires 65
Andouille Pork 380
Anesthetic Medication 120
Angle 171
Angora 217
Anidex, textile labeling 211
Aniline Finish on Leather 215
Anise, sweet 417

Anklets 207
ANL (Automatic Noise Limiter) 94
Annealed Glass 176
Anniversary Clock 150
Announce Only 99
Announcement, paper 194
Annual 259
Annual Bluegrass 259, 264
Annual Fuel Utilization Efficiency Percentage 139
Annual Rings 229
Anodized Aluminum Cookware 134
Anodizing 163
ANSI Paper Speed (formally ASAP), photographic
  film 195
ANSI 3
Antacid 120
Antenna 79, 81, 94, 101
Anti-Caking Agents 274
Anti-lock Braking System ABS 56
Anti-Ozonant, tires 65
Anti-Static 79, 81
Antiarthritic 120
Antibacterial 120
Antibiotic 120
Antidiarrheal 120
Antiemetic 120
Antiflatulent 120
Antifungal 120
Antihistamine 120
Antimagnetic Watches 166
Antimicrobial Soap 120
Antioxidants 274
  in foods 267
  tires 65
Antiperspirant 120
Antipyretic 120
  medication 122
Antique Firearm 189
Antiquing 163
Antireflective Coatings, eyeglasses 118
Antiseptic
  alcohol 115
  clothing finish 204
  medicines 120
Antiskid, tires 65
Antiskid Depth, tires 65
Antispasmodic 120
Antistatic, clothing finish 204
Antitussive 120
Antron Nylon 217
APA Performance Rated Panels 233
APA Rated
  sheathing 234, 235
  siding 235
  Sturd-I-Floor 235
APA Registered Plywood 234
APA Sanded & Touch-Sanded Plywood 236
APC (Automatic Phase Control) 102

C

G

N

P

terminology 178
PAL 105, 110
Palm Fiber 131
Pancetta 375
Panetela Cigar 488
Panetela Larga Cigar 488
Panicle 261
Panty/Pantyhose 208
  definition 208
Papain 375
Paper 193
  craft 21
  Ecologo qualifications 21
  fine 21
  Green Seal environmental standards 25
  newsprint 21
  recycled grades 48
  recycling 47
Paper Products
  envrionmental standards 25
Paper Towels
  Green Seal environmental standards 25
Para-Dichlorobenzene, warning labels 39
PARA 233
Paraffin-Dipped, monteray jack cheese 301
Paraformaldehyde, warning labels 39
Parallax Focus (Focusing) 86
Parallel Venation 261
Parallel 93
Parasite 261
Parboiled Shrimp 415
Parental Lock/Channel Block 105
Park Trailer 63
Parma Ham, Prosciutto Di Parma 364
Parsley, grades 483
Parsnips, consumer standards 448
PART 233
Partially Crystallized Honey 475
Partially Defatted
  beef fatty tissue 356
  cooked beef or pork fatty tissue 375
Partially Hydrogenated 274
Particleboard
  formaldehyde in 25
  grade nomenclature 253
  labeling 253
  production methods 253
Parvemargarine 273
Passive AF, cameras 187
Passive Packaging, foods 141
Passive System, car alram 56
Passive 97
Pastelles 375
Pastellillos 375
Pasteurized
  milk 306
  orange juice 289
Pasties 375

Pastitsio 375
Pastrami
  beef, cooked beef cured with spices 375
  turkey 375
Pasture Sod 265
PAT 233
Pate De Foie 375
Pathogen 261
Patina 163, 166
Patties (Jamaican Style) 375
Paua Shells 165
Paupiette 375
Pause 100
Pave 163
Paving, brick 172
Paws, chicken 375
Pay Load 70
PCM, electronics 98
PCs (See Consumer Electronics/Computers)
Pea Beans, canned pork and beans 457
Peaking Circuit 110
Peanut Butter
  grades 403
  styles 404
  textures 403
  types 404
Peanuts
  cleaned Virginia type 404
  in mixed nuts 403
  shelled runner type 404
  shelled Spanish type 405
  shelled Virginia type 405
Pearl Grain 165
Pearls
  cultured 164
  grading 164
  terminology 165
  types 164
Pears
  for canning 340
  summer and fall 339
  winter 339
Peas
  canned 452
    sizes 450
    types 449
  canned field 450
    grades 450
    styles 450
  frozen 452
    grades 450
  frozen field and black-eye 451
    grades 451
    types 451
  frozen mixed vegetables 443
  grades 449
  outhern
    grades 451

SDG 233
SE, motor oil 58
SE-Tenant, Postage Stamps 196
Sea Grass 131
Sea Island
  cotton 205
Seal of Acceptance
  dental products 115
Seal of Recognition
  dental products 116
Seals
  appliance certifications 133
Seals of Approval
  green report definition 12
Seamless 164
  steel doors 175
  stockings 210
Search 101, 111
Seasonal Energy Efficiency Ratio 127, 139
Seasoned
  redwood 240
Seasoning 231
  of macaroni products 477
Seat, Rim 74
SECAM 106
Second & Better Grade
  unfinished flooring 226
Second Audio Program (SAP) 106
Second Grade
  unfinished flooring 226
  unfinished pecan flooring 227
Second Grade Red
  unfinished pecan flooring 227
Second-Hand 131
  fur 207
Secondary and Micro Plant Nutrients 257
Seconds
  carpets 132
  cherries, sulfured 322
  hardwood 228
  stockings 210
Section, tires 71
Section Height, tires 71
Sections
  canned sweet potatoes 465
Sedge 261
Seed 261
Seed Bed 261
Seed Coat 261
Seed Count 259, 262
Seed Cultured Pearls 165
Seedpod 262
SEER, Seasonal Energy Efficiency Ratio 139
  air conditioners 127
Segmented
  canned olives 480
SEL 233
Select

beef 352
bullock grades 354
fence boards 240
hardwood 228
redwood 240
steer, heifer, and cow 354
western softwood 249
Select Heart
  redwood 240
Select Merchantable
  western softwood 250
Select Plain Sawn
  unfinished oak flooring 226
Select Quarter Sawn
  unfinished oak flooring 226
Select Structural
  western softwood 248
Select Tight Knot
  wood siding 242
Selective Herbicide 262
Selectivity 84, 97
Selenous Acid
  warning labels 41
Self Cleaning
  tire treads 71
Self-Drinking, tea 292
Self-Medication 123
Self-Polishing-Type
  floor polish 142
Self-Timer 86
Self-Vulcanization 215
Self-Winding Watch 166
Sell Date
  on foods 268
Seltzer Waters 293
Selvage, Postage Stamps 196
Semi-Boarded
  garments 219
Semi-Skinned (epidermis removed)
  fish 410
Semipostal, Postage Stamps 196
Sencha, tea 291
Sensitivity (of radar detector) 97
Sensitivity 84, 87, 106, 111
  to drugs 123
Sensitizer 26
  strong 26
Separation 84
Separation, tires 71
Sequestrants 275
Serdelowa
  sausage 391
Serial 93
Serial Number
  tires 71
Serkelki
  sausage 391
Serrated 262

T

Tramp, tires 73
Transaxle 57
Transducer 85
Transfer Case 57
Transistor 85, 106
Translocate 262
Translucency
    of dinnerware 135
Transmission 57
Transmitter 85, 101, 106, 111
Transpiration 262
Transportable
    cellular phone 87
Trap Focus, Cameras 187
Travel Trailer 63
Tread, tires 73
Tread Depth, tires 73
Tread Design, tires 73
Tread Life, tires 73
Tread Radius, tires 73
Tread Separation, tires 73
Tread Wear Indicators 73
Tread Width, tires 73
Treadwear 64
Treated
    plywood 236
Treated Lumber
    trade names 238
Treated With
    creosote solutions 236
    creosote-petroleum 236
    radiation, foods 270
Tree-Ripened
    olives 479
Treosulphan
    carcinogen 8
Trephah 273
Trichinae Treated
    bacon 351
Trichinae Treatment
    sausage 392
Trichloroethane
    ozone depleting 46
    warning labels 43
Trichloroethylene
    warning labels 43
Trichloroisocyanuric Acid
    warning labels 44
Tricks Mode 111
Triethylenetetramine
    warning labels 44
Trilobal Nylon 217
Trilobal Yarn 209, 220
Trim 239
Trimmed Fillets
    freshwater catfish 409
Trimmings
    ham 364

Triple Chimes 151
Trisodium Phosphate
    warning labels 44
Trivial
    environmental claims 13
    source of calories 271
    source of sodium 271
Tropic Cure Pork Products 378
Troy Ounce 163, 166
Truck Camper 63
True Tone 101
Truffles 378
Tsavorite 154
TSS
    tampons 126
Tube (Inner) 73
Tube Growth, tires 73
Tube Socks 210
Tubeless Liner, tires 73
Tubular Bell Chime 151
Tubular Tire 185
Tufsyn (R), tires 73
Tulip
    endangered species 229
Tuna
    canned 416
Tuner 85, 106
Tung Oil
    warning labels 44
Tuning Eye 85, 106
Tuning System 106
Turbinado 378
    sugar 487
Turbo 90
Turbo Lag 59
Turbocharger 59
Turf 262
Turfgrass Sod
    grades 264
Turgidity 262
Turkey
    Braunschweiger sausage 392
    hickory smoked 385
    meatballs 379
Turkey Chops 385
Turkey Ham 395
Turkey Loaf, Cured, Chopped, Canned 385
Turkey Salisbury Steak 385
Turning
    fresh tomatoes (consumer standards) 468
Turning Radius 73
Turnip Greens 445
    canned leafy greens 438
    frozen with turnips
    color 469
    grades 469
    styles 469
Turnips

U

V

X

X
  cognac 285
X Band 97
X-rays 47
XO
  cognac 285
XGA monitors 92
XTAL 107
Xylene
  warning labels 44

Y

Y/C Connections 87, 112
Yankee Pot Roast 378
Yarn
  definition 220
  made in USA 214
  raw 219
  spun 219
  textured 219
  wrapped 220
  yarn count 220
Yearling
Mutton
  grades 365
Yearling Turkey 382
Yearling 378
Yeast Infection
  medication 123
Yellow
  canned sweet potatoes 464
  frozen sweet potatoes 465

frozen turnip greens with turnips 469
  stained cotton 206
Yelloweye beans 420
Yin-Chen, tea 291
Ying-Mei, tea 291
Yogurt 310
Young Guinea 382
Young Hyson, tea 291
Young Lamb
  choice grade 367
  good grade 367
  prime grade 367
Young Turkey 382
Yunnan, tea 290

Z

Zero
  calories 271
  sodium 271
  sugars 271
Zinc
  in batteries 19
Zinc and Magnesium Silico Fluorides
  warning labels 45
Zinc Chloride
  warning labels 44, 45
Zinc Sulfate
  warning labels 45
Zinthane
  in golf balls 190
Zircon 154
Zoom Lens 80, 87
  cameras 187
Zoom Ratio 87
Zoysia 262